PLUNKETT'S E-COMMERCE & INTERNET BUSINESS ALMANAC 2019

The only comprehensive guide to the e-commerce and Internet industry

Jack W. Plunkett

Published by:
Plunkett Research®, Ltd., Houston, Texas
www.plunkettresearch.com

PLUNKETT'S E-COMMERCE & INTERNET BUSINESS ALMANAC 2019

Editor and Publisher:
Jack W. Plunkett

Executive Editor and Database Manager:
Martha Burgher Plunkett

Senior Editor and Researchers:
Isaac Snider
Shuang Zhou

Editors, Researchers and Assistants:
Michael Cappelli
Annie Paynter
Anoosh Saidi
Jorden Smith
Gina Sprenkel

Information Technology Manager:
Rebeca Tijiboy

Special Thanks to:
eMarketer
Nielsen Online
Pew Internet & American Life Project
U.S. Census Bureau, Economics and Statistics
Administration
U.S. Federal Communications Commission (FCC)

Plunkett Research®, Ltd.
P. O. Drawer 541737, Houston, Texas 77254 USA
Phone: 713.932.0000   Fax: 713.932.7080
www.plunkettresearch.com

Plunkett Research®, Ltd.
P. O. Drawer 541737
Houston, Texas 77254-1737
Phone: 713.932.0000, Fax: 713.932.7080 www.plunkettresearch.com

ISBN13 # 978-1-62831-485-4 (eBook Edition # 978-1-62831-808-1)

Limited Warranty and Terms of Use:

PLUNKETT'S E-COMMERCE & INTERNET BUSINESS ALMANAC 2019

CONTENTS

Continued on next page

INTRODUCTION

PLUNKETT'S E-COMMERCE & INTERNET BUSINESS ALMANAC is designed as a general source for researchers of all types.

The data and areas of interest covered are intentionally broad, ranging from the various types of businesses involved in e-commerce and the internet, to technologies and access providers, to an in-depth look at the major firms (which we call "THE E-COMMERCE 500") within the many sectors that make up the e-commerce and internet industry, including technology, services, retailing, telecommunications and much more.

This reference book is designed to be a general source for researchers. It is especially intended to assist with market research, strategic planning, employment searches, contact or prospect list creation and financial research, and as a data resource for executives and students of all types.

PLUNKETT'S E-COMMERCE & INTERNET BUSINESS ALMANAC takes a rounded approach for the general reader. This book presents a complete overview of the e-commerce and internet field (see "How To Use This Book"). For example, the impact of the internet upon retail sales is discussed in exacting detail, along with easy-to-use tables on all facets of the internet in general, from the types of services involved to names and descriptions of the

divisions and affiliates of the major firms within this industry.

THE E-COMMERCE 500 is our unique grouping of the biggest, most successful corporations in all segments of the e-commerce and internet industry. Tens of thousands of pieces of information, gathered from a wide variety of sources, have been researched and are presented in a unique form that can be easily understood. This section includes thorough indexes to THE E-COMMERCE 500, by geography, industry, sales, brand names, subsidiary names and many other topics. (See Chapter 4.)

Especially helpful is the way in which PLUNKETT'S E-COMMERCE & INTERNET BUSINESS ALMANAC enables readers who have no business background to readily compare the financial records and growth plans of e-commerce companies and major industry groups. You'll see the mid-term financial record of each firm, along with the impact of earnings, sales and strategic plans on each company's potential to fuel growth, to serve new markets and to provide investment and employment opportunities.

No other source provides this book's easy-to-understand comparisons of growth, expenditures, technologies, corporations and many other items of great importance to people of all types who may be studying this, one of the fastest growing industries in the world today.

By scanning the data groups and the unique indexes, you can find the best information to fit your personal research needs. The major companies in e-commerce and internet fields are profiled and then ranked using several different groups of specific criteria. Which firms are the biggest employers? Which companies earn the most profits? These things and much more are easy to find.

In addition to individual company profiles, an overview of internet technology and its trends is provided. This book's job is to help you sort through easy-to-understand summaries of today's trends in a quick and effective manner.

Whatever your purpose for researching the e-commerce and internet field, you'll find this book to be a valuable guide. Nonetheless, as is true with all resources, this volume has limitations that the reader should be aware of:

- Financial data and other corporate information can change quickly. A book of this type can be no more current than the data that was available as of the time of editing. Consequently, the financial picture, management and ownership of the firm(s) you are studying may have changed since the date of this book. For example, this almanac includes the most up-to-date sales figures and profits available to the editors as of early 2019. That means that we have typically used corporate financial data as of mid-2018.

- Corporate mergers, acquisitions and downsizing are occurring at a very rapid rate. Such events may have created significant change, subsequent to the publishing of this book, within a company you are studying.

- Some of the companies in THE E-COMMERCE 500 are so large in scope and in variety of business endeavors conducted within a parent organization, that we have been unable to completely list all subsidiaries, affiliations, divisions and activities within a firm's corporate structure.

- This volume is intended to be a general guide to a vast industry. That means that researchers should look to this book for an overview and, when

conducting in-depth research, should contact the specific corporations or industry associations in question for the very latest changes and data. Where possible, we have listed contact names, toll-free telephone numbers and internet site addresses for the companies, government agencies and industry associations involved so that the reader may get further details without unnecessary delay.

- Tables of industry data and statistics used in this book include the latest numbers available at the time of printing, generally through mid-2018. In a few cases, the only complete data available was for earlier years.

- We have used exhaustive efforts to locate and fairly present accurate and complete data. However, when using this book or any other source for business and industry information, the reader should use caution and diligence by conducting further research where it seems appropriate. We wish you success in your endeavors, and we trust that your experience with this book will be both satisfactory and productive.

Jack W. Plunkett
Houston, Texas
February 2019

HOW TO USE THIS BOOK

The two primary sections of this book are devoted first to the e-commerce and internet business as a whole and then to the "Individual Data Listings" for THE E-COMMERCE 500. If time permits, you should begin your research in the front chapters of this book. Also, you will find lengthy indexes in Chapter 4 and in the back of the book.

📹 Video Tip

For our brief video introduction to the e-commerce and internet business, see
www.plunkettresearch.com/video/ecommerce.

THE E-COMMERCE & INTERNET BUSINESS

Chapter 1: Major Trends Affecting the E-Commerce & Internet Business. This chapter presents an encapsulated view of the major trends that are creating rapid changes in the e-commerce and internet business today.

Chapter 2: E-Commerce & Internet Business Statistics. This chapter presents in-depth statistics ranging from an industry overview to the globalization of markets and much more.

Chapter 3: Important E-Commerce & Internet Business Contacts – Addresses, Telephone Numbers and Internet Sites.
This chapter covers contacts for important government agencies, e-commerce and internet organizations and trade groups. Included are numerous important internet sites.

THE E-COMMERCE 500

Chapter 4: THE E-COMMERCE 500: Who They Are and How They Were Chosen. The companies compared in this book were carefully selected from the e-commerce and internet business, largely in the United States. A number of the firms are based outside the U.S. as well. For a complete description, see THE E-COMMERCE 500 indexes in this chapter.

Individual Data Listings:

Look at one of the companies in THE E-COMMERCE 500's Individual Data Listings. You'll find the following information fields:

Company Name:

The company profiles are in alphabetical order by company name. If you don't find the company you are seeking, it may be a subsidiary or division of one of the firms covered in this book. Try looking it up in the Index by Subsidiaries, Brand Names and Selected Affiliations in the back of the book.

Industry Code:

Industry Group Code: An NAIC code used to group companies within like segments.

Types of Business:

A listing of the primary types of business specialties conducted by the firm.

Brands/Divisions/Affiliations:

Major brand names, operating divisions or subsidiaries of the firm, as well as major corporate affiliations—such as another firm that owns a significant portion of the company's stock. A complete Index by Subsidiaries, Brand Names and Selected Affiliations is in the back of the book.

Contacts:

The names and titles up to 27 top officers of the company are listed, including human resources contacts.

Growth Plans/ Special Features:

Listed here are observations regarding the firm's strategy, hiring plans, plans for growth and product development, along with general information regarding a company's business and prospects.

Financial Data:

Revenue (2018 or the latest fiscal year available to the editors, plus up to five previous years): This figure represents consolidated worldwide sales from all operations. These numbers may be estimates.

R&D Expense (2018 or the latest fiscal year available to the editors, plus up to five previous years): This figure represents expenses associated with the research and development of a company's goods or services. These numbers may be estimates.

Operating Income (2018 or the latest fiscal year available to the editors, plus up to five previous years): This figure represents the amount of profit realized from annual operations after deducting operating expenses including costs of goods sold, wages and depreciation. These numbers may be estimates.

Operating Margin % (2018 or the latest fiscal year available to the editors, plus up to five previous years): This figure is a ratio derived by dividing operating income by net revenues. It is a measurement of a firm's pricing strategy and operating efficiency. These numbers may be estimates.

SGA Expense (2018 or the latest fiscal year available to the editors, plus up to five previous years): This figure represents the sum of selling, general and administrative expenses of a company, including costs such as warranty, advertising, interest, personnel, utilities, office space rent, etc. These numbers may be estimates.

Net Income (2018 or the latest fiscal year available to the editors, plus up to five previous years): This figure represents consolidated, after-tax net profit from all operations. These numbers may be estimates.

Operating Cash Flow (2018 or the latest fiscal year available to the editors, plus up to five previous years): This figure is a measure of the amount of cash generated by a firm's normal business operations. It is calculated as net income before depreciation and after income taxes, adjusted for working capital. It is a prime indicator of a company's ability to generate enough cash to pay its bills. These numbers may be estimates.

Capital Expenditure (2018 or the latest fiscal year available to the editors, plus up to five previous years): This figure represents funds used for investment in or improvement of physical assets such as offices, equipment or factories and the purchase or creation of new facilities and/or equipment. These numbers may be estimates.

EBITDA (2018 or the latest fiscal year available to the editors, plus up to five previous years): This figure is an acronym for earnings before interest, taxes, depreciation and amortization. It represents a company's financial performance calculated as revenue minus expenses (excluding taxes, depreciation and interest), and is a prime indicator of profitability. These numbers may be estimates.

Return on Assets % (2018 or the latest fiscal year available to the editors, plus up to five previous years): This figure is an indicator of the profitability of a company relative to its total assets. It is calculated by dividing annual net earnings by total assets. These numbers may be estimates.

Return on Equity % (2018 or the latest fiscal year available to the editors, plus up to five previous years): This figure is a measurement of net income as a percentage of shareholders' equity. It is also called the rate of return on the ownership interest. It is a vital indicator of the quality of a company's operations. These numbers may be estimates.

Debt to Equity (2018 or the latest fiscal year available to the editors, plus up to five previous years): A ratio of the company's long-term debt to its shareholders' equity. This is an indicator of the overall financial leverage of the firm. These numbers may be estimates.

Address:

The firm's full headquarters address, the headquarters telephone, plus toll-free and fax numbers where available. Also provided is the internet address.

Stock Ticker, Exchange: When available, the unique stock market symbol used to identify this firm's common stock for trading and tracking purposes is indicated. Where appropriate, this field may contain "private" or "subsidiary" rather than a ticker symbol. If the firm is a publicly-held company headquartered outside of the U.S., its international ticker and exchange are given.

Total Number of Employees: The approximate total number of employees, worldwide, as of the end of 2018 (or the latest data available to the editors).

Parent Company: If the firm is a subsidiary, its parent company is listed.

Salaries/Bonuses:

(The following descriptions generally apply to U.S. employers only.)

Highest Executive Salary: The highest executive salary paid, typically a 2018 amount (or the latest year available to the editors) and typically paid to the Chief Executive Officer.

Highest Executive Bonus: The apparent bonus, if any, paid to the above person.

Second Highest Executive Salary: The next-highest executive salary paid, typically a 2018 amount (or the latest year available to the editors) and typically paid to the President or Chief Operating Officer.

Second Highest Executive Bonus: The apparent bonus, if any, paid to the above person.

Other Thoughts:

Estimated Female Officers or Directors: It is difficult to obtain this information on an exact basis, and employers generally do not disclose the data in a public way. However, we have indicated what our best efforts reveal to be the apparent number of women who either are in the posts of corporate officers or sit on the board of directors. There is a wide variance from company to company.

Hot Spot for Advancement for Women/Minorities: A "Y" in appropriate fields indicates "Yes." These are firms that appear either to have posted a substantial number of women and/or minorities to high posts or that appear to have a good record of going out of their way to recruit, train, promote and retain women or minorities. (See the Index of Hot Spots For Women and Minorities in the back of the book.) This information may change frequently and can be difficult to obtain and verify. Consequently, the reader should use caution and conduct further investigation where appropriate.

Glossary: A short list of e-commerce and internet business terms.

Chapter 1

MAJOR TRENDS AFFECTING THE E-COMMERCE & INTERNET BUSINESS

1)   Introduction to the E-Commerce & Internet Business

📹 Video Tip

For our brief video introduction to the e-commerce and internet business, see www.plunkettresearch.com/video/ecommerce.

The global internet audience continues to grow steadily, with the worldwide base of broadband internet users (including fixed and wireless) standing in excess of 4.3 billion as 2019 began. This vast base of high speed internet users encourages businesses to innovate in order to offer an ever-evolving array of online services. Sectors that are growing very rapidly online include the sale of entertainment products, travel, apparel and consumer electronics. Even groceries have moved into the fast lane, as online grocery and household product sales are growing quickly thanks to a growing list of same-day delivery options. The most powerful trends on the internet include access via wireless devices, the migration of entertainment, including TV programming, to the web and cloud-based software-as-a-service.

Today, consumers are more focused than ever on finding the best prices while shopping in the most convenient or satisfying manner. Consequently, e-commerce firms that offer high value at consistently low prices are well-positioned to prosper. The standout winner in e-commerce continues to be Amazon, where sales have soared thanks to aggressive pricing, free shipping for its "Prime" members and an ever-growing variety of merchandise categories. Amazon's revenues soared from $34.2 billion in 2010 to $233 billion in 2018. The firm's sales outside of North America are booming as well, despite the fact that it has major foreign competitors, particularly from companies based in China.

Analysts at eMarketer reported American e-commerce sales in 2018 of an estimated $526.1 billion (up significantly from $454.9 billion in 2017). This figure includes online retail product sales, travel sales and digital downloads, but not online gambling. Global internet e-commerce sales exceeded $2.84 trillion in 2018, according to eMarketer, and could top $3.45 trillion in 2019. China is posting phenomenal growth in e-commerce, up by 29.1% in 2018, according to analysts at eMarketer, to a total of $1,462.4 billion.

Online travel booking continues to enjoy strong growth, in a broad sector that includes car rental, hotel bookings, transportation and tourist attraction sales. The success of new accommodation sharing sites like Airbnb and vacation home rental sites like HomeAway is boosting this trend.

China's e-commerce leaders remain much smaller than rival Amazon.com
Estimated revenues 2018, billions of US$:

Amazon	$233 bil.
Tencent	$44 bil.
Alibaba	$40 bil.

Online and mobile advertising during 2018 in the U.S. collectively reached $125.8 billion, according to eMarketer, taking 55% of the total advertising market. Online advertising is surpassing TV advertising in America. Online leader Google's recent results are a good indicator of the strong growth in online advertising. The firm saw revenues soar in fiscal 2018, to $136.8 billion.

Growth in broadband subscriptions worldwide continues at a strong pace. The number of American homes and businesses with broadband access capabilities topped 111.3 million by the end of 2018, according to Plunkett Research estimates, thanks in part to modest monthly fees at internet service providers. This number does not include mobile broadband subscriptions, estimated at another 322.4 million.

A significant evolution is taking place in the world of business, as more and more telecommunications services move to the Internet. VOIP (internet-based telephone calls via Voice over Internet Protocol) continues to grow in popularity. Meanwhile, the concept of "unified communications" threatens to completely revolutionize business by combining all communications into one screen on the desktop, including phone, fax, e-mail, instant messaging, voice mail and teleconferencing. Voice communications will be digitized and archived, just as e-mail is today. A user's communications tools will move seamlessly from the desktop to the mobile device.

Convergence: The internet is about saving time (and therefore often saving money), as well as broadening available choices while eliminating physical and geographical boundaries. The full potential of the internet has barely been tapped. New methods of taking advantage of online efficiencies are becoming widely accepted, as access to high-speed internet connections becomes commonplace. The long-awaited phenomenon of "convergence" of entertainment, computing and communications arrived around 2004 when enough consumers had subscriptions to fast broadband to create a true mass market worthy of the immense investments required to launch products of broad appeal, such as downloads of movies via Netflix. The smartphone revolution accelerated this trend. Now, the latest televisions come equipped with built-in internet connections. This is creating radical changes in the way TV viewers obtain their movies and TV programming. For example, subscribers to Netflix, Hulu or Amazon Prime are able to stream downloaded movies directly to their internet-connected TV sets.

A Brief History of the Online Sector: The e-commerce and internet sector has evolved rapidly, going through several distinct stages since its beginnings in the 1970s:

The Internet Is Born: First, there were the early days, when the internet was seen by many as a realm for techies only, one that would produce few, if any, commercial enterprises. Initially designed in 1973, the internet was a series of communication protocols written by Vinton Cerf as part of a project sponsored by the U.S. Department of Defense's Defense Advanced Research Projects Agency (DARPA). The first demonstration of a three-network internet protocol-based connection occurred in November 1977. Eventually, a well-enabled internet was rolled out in 1983, primarily as a failsafe method of defense communications and as a means for researchers at various universities to communicate.

The Web Is Created: Next, the World Wide Web and the coding language of HTML were conceived in 1989 and implemented between 1990 and 1993 by Tim Berners-Lee, enabling a never-ending hyperlinked cyber world where sharing unlimited data became user-friendly thanks to the magic of linked pages.

The Boom Ensues: Starting in 1993 and 1994, entrepreneurs and financiers realized that hyperlinked, electronically posted data could be commercialized with vast, global potential. A dramatic revolution in retailing, publishing and entertainment was visualized, one in which consumers and business people alike would eagerly pay for the convenience of online shopping, trading and viewing of published data. An economic boom ensued, the likes of which hadn't been seen since the beginnings of earlier technological breakthroughs: electricity, the railroad, the telephone, the automobile and the passenger-carrying airliner.

Thousands of hopeful new businesses were launched. Capitalization for these new internet-

enabled companies ranged from cash-strapped ventures launched in garages with Visa card credit lines, to companies like WebVan that received vast sums from professionally managed venture capital firms only to fail miserably. Roughly 6,000 new firms of significant size raised a cumulative total of more than $100 billion in venture capital in the boom period (1994-2000). About 450 of these companies sold their stock to the public via IPOs (initial public offerings). Stock markets soared and instant billionaires were made, although many of those stocks later plummeted. Venture funds that cashed out early reaped phenomenal gains, and financiers easily found additional investors for new venture capital pools. Companies with little or no sales and profits, led by the success of Netscape's IPO, found eager buyers for their newly issued stocks. The NASDAQ index of stocks rose to 5,000 by early in the year 2000, and the Chairman of the Federal Reserve warned of "exuberant optimism." Some said this boom couldn't last—others said it was the beginning of a "new economy" that would last forever.

The Bust: In mid-2000, the internet industry entered a bleak and dreary phase after the NASDAQ collapsed in March, bringing the entire sector to its knees. By October 10, 2002, the NASDAQ was down to 1,108 from a high of 5,132 in March 2000. Hundreds of thousands of people lost their jobs. Stock portfolio values plummeted. Thousands of firms closed their doors, filed bankruptcy, downsized or were scooped up at bargain prices by competitors. Sellers of hardware, software, consulting and telecommunications services suffered mightily. Entrepreneurs found it nearly impossible to raise funds to launch or sustain their businesses. The dream of a "new economy" became a nightmare for some—profits still matter; business cycles still happen.

The Reality Phase: By early 2003, this sector's dark clouds were abating, and a "reality phase" was taking shape. Well-conceived, internet-based businesses were proving their value. Consumers had become devoted fans of buying over the internet. Businesses of all types were finding that the internet creates true operating efficiencies and drives profitability. For example, while most of the airline industry suffered terribly in recent years, value-based discount airlines Southwest and JetBlue enjoyed superior financial performance, in no small part because of their use of e-commerce to efficiently book reservations and sell tickets online. "Efficiency" is the most important factor in the e-commerce and internet sector's newfound success. Consumers find the internet to be a terrific way to efficiently expend their shopping and banking efforts. Travelers find the internet to be an efficient way to book hotels rooms, flights and rental cars. Consumers of all types use eBay to look for bargains, autotrader.com to look for cars at great prices and iTunes to download music. Corporate procurement managers find the internet to be the most efficient way to purchase needed goods and inventory. Hundreds of millions of people worldwide find e-mail, instant messaging and VOIP telephony to be the most efficient ways to communicate.

Low Costs Fuel the Steady Global Growth Phase: Today, access to fast internet, both wired and wireless, is available at bargain prices in a vast footprint across the globe. Even in relatively undeveloped nations, both consumers and businesses have grown to rely on the internet for everyday needs. Inexpensive devices and wireless networks continue to proliferate in much of the world. Mobile computing is accelerating at blazing speed thanks to moderately-priced smartphones and service plans, offering fast internet access and very advanced features.

Meanwhile, the cost of developing and maintaining web sites has plummeted, opening the door to millions of self-funded entrepreneurs, and making it easier for venture capital firms to fund startups using low amounts of cash. Trends such as open software and cloud computing, along with modular software development tools, have made it easier, faster and cheaper to start sophisticated web sites.

2) Bricks, Clicks and Catalogs Create Synergies While Online Sales Growth Surges

Analysts at eMarketer estimated worldwide e-commerce sales of $2.842 trillion in 2018, up from $2.304 trillion in 2017 and $1.845 trillion in 2016. These sales figures include online retail sales, digital downloads, sales of tickets to events and travel. Global online sales have been supported by very strong results at Amazon.com, largely due to its competitive pricing, expansion of merchandise categories, free shipping for members of its "Prime" service and convenience of use.

Global internet users reached 4.388 billion in early 2019 according to a study by Hootsuite and We Are Social. Several factors will encourage consumers to do more of their shopping online, including the difficulty of getting to and parking at retail stores, the fact that consumers feel pressed for time, the widespread adoption of high-speed internet access, and the fact that the lowest prices can often be found online.

Online shopping often goes hand-in-hand with in-store shopping, or at least in-store browsing. A large number of shoppers browse web sites to gain information, later visiting a physical store to make a purchase. The reverse is also often true—many store owners worry that shoppers look at merchandise in their stores and then go home to look for the best possible prices at online sites. Some shoppers add the items that they are considering to their shopping carts on Amazon.com, but don't click the purchase button. Then they go to retail stores, smartphones in hand, and compare prices and features in the stores to their Amazon lists. If the merchandise looks good in person and Amazon's price is better, then they may decide to purchase via Amazon, especially if they belong to the Amazon Prime service that provides free shipping. Best Buy successfully countered this practice by matching the prices of online competitors, and emphasizing customers' ability to see and touch the merchandise in-store, speak to experts in-person and take merchandise home immediately. In addition, Best Buy emphasizes the availability of its experienced service people to install consumer electronics in the home.

Many of the most successful retail firms of all types will be those that take full advantage of the personal touch of traditional, store-based retailing and combine it with the growing popularity of catalog and internet-based retailing.

Best Online Practices for Retailers:
- Seamless integration of store, catalog and internet-based offerings to consumers, providing choices of 1) place and method of purchase, 2) method of pickup or shipment and 3) place or method of returns, repairs and additional services as needed.
- Communication of a seamless brand identity and level of service throughout catalogs, retail stores and web sites.

For good examples of companies that are evolving toward such "seamless" strategies, study Costco, Wal-Mart, REI, The Gap, Staples, Saks and Pottery Barn. At Pottery Barn, customers find enhanced flexibility and customer service thanks to the opportunity to shop via the web, Pottery Barn catalogs or Pottery Barn stores. Pottery Barn stores hand out copies of catalogs—which feature the web address of Potterybarn.com, as well as phone ordering options. The point is to create loyalty-inducing convenience for customers, giving them options for purchasing when, where and how they please.

Staff members at Men's Wearhouse are using smartphones to interact with online customers through messaging and video chat, creating an interactive, multi-channel experience for shoppers. Store personnel can send photos of clothing and accessories, field questions and make suggestions, and are paid commissions for the online orders that they facilitate. Men's Wearhouse (which is owned by Tailored Brands, Inc.) is using an app developed by Hero (www.usehero.com) that connects online shoppers with instore employees. In-store staff can wave their smartphones over merchandise tags to generate web links for their online customers, for purchase. They can also set up in-store appointments.

Hudson Bay Co.'s Saks department store chain opened a new store in lower Manhattan that hopes to incorporate the online shopping experience in-store. The slightly smaller store, called Saks Downtown, focuses on women's clothing, shoes and accessories. It has more than 1,000 pairs of shoes and 800 pairs of sunglasses on display and is designed with a circular traffic pattern to mimic the seemingly endless supply of items available online. More importantly, staff are carefully trained to use the Saks.com web site to connect with customers, answer their questions, make style suggestions and invite them to come into the store. Nordstrom is experimenting with very small stores that stock no inventory while allowing customers to try on samples, with purchases to be delivered to their homes. These new stores also feature a high level of personal service.

Wal-Mart offers "Pick Up Today," a program in which registered Wal-Mart shoppers order items online and then pick them up at their local store the same day. Best Buy has similar services, as do Bloomingdale's and Macy's.

These shop online—but pickup in the store strategies were born because retailers were fighting a practice called "showrooming," in which shoppers browse for merchandise in stores but buy on rival retailers' web sites, especially Amazon.com. Amazon not only has a vast selection of items and free shipping for Prime members, its prices are also highly competitive.

One thing in favor of brick and mortar stores is their ability to accept payments in cash. A sizeable number of Americans remain wary of online security and the possibility of identity theft, and they refuse to purchase items online via credit cards, even though they may comparison shop for prices. Also, there are a large number of consumers who are called "underbanked," that is, who are without bank accounts or credit cards. Wal-Mart offers customers the ability to order items online and then pick them up in stores using cash for payment.

Department stores are making a major shift in operations to support online orders. In yet another effort to compete with Amazon.com's success, Macy's converted many of its stores to include expanded storerooms with cutting-edge technology to track inventory and generate shipping labels. Excess store inventory is shifted to highlighted positions on the company's web site, and merchandise that has sold out at the online distribution center may be found in stores, thereby remaining on the web site for sale and delivery by UPS. Online orders are being filled by stores closest to consumers, increasing efficiency and lowering costs.

Macy's is taking the technology a step further in select stores, where it is displaying merchandise with only one item of each style (instead of cramming the racks with every size available). Shoppers can look at the sample, and then use an app on their cell phones to let staff know what size and style they want to try on. Staff members collect the items from stockrooms and send them to fitting rooms via special hatches. Customers are alerted as to which fitting room is theirs via their phones. The practice allows Macy's to display more styles and avoid a cumbersome tangle of vast numbers of coat hangers.

Some brick and mortar retailers are opting to make selected merchandise available for online purchase only. Shoppers can browse samples in the stores and then place orders on their phones or at instore computer stations.

At the same time, a growing number of formerly online-only businesses are opening brick and mortar stores. Examples include women's clothing site Boston Proper (a subsidiary of Chico's FAS), Rent the Runway, a dress and accessories rental site, and online eyeglass retailer Warby Parker. Likewise, Bonobos (a clothing retailer now owned by Wal-Mart) has samples in showroom stores but no inventory on-hand. Bonobos has opened these "Guideshops" in dozens of major cities across the U.S.

Brick and mortar stores are teaming up with e-tailers to provide store-within-a-store locations. In select Kohl's store in the U.S., Amazon operates small departments where smart home products such as Alexa and Amazon Echo can be experienced, and in-home installations scheduled. Kohls also accepts Amazon returns, even using its own shipping infrastructure to send merchandise back to competing stores. In a short list of U.S. Walgreens stores, online subscription beauty product company Birchbox has kiosks where customers can create their own boxes of sample-sized cosmetics. Drugstore rival CVS is working to install on-demand Glamsquad beauty technicians in four of its stores, offering $40 blowouts and $30 makeup applications.

As more and more people embrace online shopping, brick and mortar retailers must evolve to offer more convenience and speed. Shoppers are spending less time in stores as they prefer browsing on web sites and social media such as Facebook, Pinterest and Instagram. Chico's FAS reported that customers who once spent two hours in their stores now spend 45 minutes. Prices must transparently match those of competitors, or there may be no sale.

SPOTLIGHT: Instant Smartphone Buying

A number of companies are implementing technology that allows shoppers to instantly purchase merchandise using their cellphones. ShopThis!, a partnership between MasterCard and Condé Nast, offers digital-edition magazine readers the ability to tap a shopping cart icon to buy items described in articles or featured in advertisements. Peapod, an online grocer that serves areas on the U.S. Northeast and Midwest, has a feature on its mobile app that affords users the ability to scan bar codes on grocery items at home or anywhere, automatically placing the item in the app's shopping cart, ready for purchase. Another company, Paydiant, is working on technology that will allow TV watchers to scan quick response (QR) codes with their phones directly from their TV sets to buy desired items. For the three days from Wednesday through Black Friday in 2018 (the day after Thanksgiving and historically the busiest U.S. shopping day of the year), analysts at Adobe Systems, Inc. estimated that online sales grew 26.4% over 2017 to reach $6 billion.

Cyber Monday (the Monday following Thanksgiving) in 2018 saw a record-breaking $7.9 billion in sales. Smartphone sales accounted for 54% of retail site visits on Cyber Monday and 28% of purchases.

---

3) Amazon Continues to Boost Its Market Share

The standout winner in e-commerce of late is Amazon, where global sales have soared thanks to aggressive discount pricing and an ever-growing variety of merchandise categories. The gross value of merchandise sold through the company's "Marketplace" partners is nearly equal to Amazon's own sales. (Amazon records only the service fees it charges these Marketplace retailers, not the full price of the merchandise sold.) Amazon has become a market leader in vital merchandise categories including apparel and such consumer goods as health and beauty products.

Amazon's phenomenal growth is a result of excellent corporate strategy plus its competitive pricing and convenience. Shoppers don't have to drive to a store, thereby saving on gasoline as well as time. Amazon has also diversified to an amazing extent, offering everything from jewelry to appliances to groceries to industrial and scientific supplies. Shipping can be expedited through the Amazon Prime program which, for a modest annual fee, offers unlimited free two-day shipping, the option to upgrade to one-day shipping for a few dollars and no minimum order size. According to estimates from Consumer Intelligence Research Partners, Amazon had 90 million Prime members in the U.S. alone as of late 2017, and those customers spend on average about $1,300 per year, compared to only $700 for non-Prime customers. Amazon Prime Now offers two-hour delivery for groceries and other household items in many major U.S. cities.

Also, Amazon has been placing banks of lockers in retailers such as grocery, convenience and drug stores in urban areas. Amazon packages can be placed in these special lockers, so that customers can later pick up packages themselves, using access codes sent by email, instead of trying to be at home to meet delivery by UPS, FedEx or the U.S. Postal Service. Deutsche Post DHL has offered a free locker service in Germany for years.

In late 2017, Amazon introduced a home access system called Amazon Key. The $249.99 door-lock and security camera allows access for delivery by couriers, controlled by a smartphone app. Amazon is also working with apartment house owners to install locker storage units called Hub by Amazon that accept deliveries from all couriers, not just those with shipments from Amazon. Apartment residents receive email or text notices of package arrival, including a code for access to the assigned storage locker.

In 2017, the Amazon acquired specialty super market firm Whole Foods Market, Inc. for $13.7 billion. This is an extension of Amazon's rapidly expanding grocery sales strategy. The company also offers AmazonFresh, a grocery delivery service for

Prime members in select U.S. cities for an additional monthly membership fee.

4) Retailers Offer Expedited Delivery to Compete with Amazon

Other retailers are attempting to challenge Amazon's commanding market share by offering their own version of Amazon Prime and/or same day delivery. A number of retailers including Lord & Taylor, Staples, Kate Spade New York, GNC and Brooks Brothers utilize ShopRunner, a cooperative shipping service. Like Prime, users pay an annual membership fee for free two-day shipping, free returns and no minimum order size.

As for same-day delivery, a handful of retailers are offering the service, despite its challenges. Wal-Mart, for example, has a pickup grocery concept in which customers pickup online orders at drive-through kiosks and implementing Shipping Pass, an unlimited shipping program similar to Amazon Prime. Wal-Mart recently started relying on dozens of its Supercenters as distribution centers for online orders. Collectively, they handle more than one-fifth of the merchandise purchased on Walmart.com. About one-half of the firm's online orders are picked up in or delivered from stores. Restoration Hardware Holdings, Inc.'s Lands' End and Barnes and Noble offer a similar two-day delivery program, also named Shipping Pass. Luxury fashion site Net-a-Porter offers Premier, a same-day delivery service for customers in New York and select locations in New Jersey. eBay subsidiary Shutl is a package-delivery system based in the UK that uses vans and bikes to deliver purchases. U.S. grocery store chain Kroger has been working with electric vehicle startup Nuro, Inc. to develop driverless delivery vehicles.

Meanwhile, Wal-Mart acquired Jet.com, an e-commerce retailer of general merchandise for $3.3 billion in 2016. Wal-Mart also purchased men's clothing company Bonobos in 2017 for $310 million, largely due to the clothier's focus on online sales. In addition, the giant retailer spent $166 million on e-commerce startups such as ModCloth and Shoebuy.com. Wal-Mart expected its fiscal 2019 e-commerce revenues to grow by 40%. Wal-Mart customers who shop online and in stores generally spend twice as much as those who shop in-store only.

In China, e-commerce leaders such as JD.com and Yihaodian have been aggressively expanding their delivery networks and options, including same-day delivery in major cities. Yihaodian was originally owned by Wal-Mart but was sold to JD.com in 2016.

5) Package Delivery by Drone

The next big step in the use of drones may be package delivery. Could the future for Amazon and other retailers eventually include deliveries by unmanned aerial drones? Amazon has been testing the concept using drones with a range of 10 miles and a payload of under five pounds (appropriate for about 90% of Amazon's deliveries). Google, the U.S. Postal Service and Airbus SE have also developed and tested units for deliveries. U.S. drone delivery would be dependent upon cost, technologies, safety concerns, consumer acceptance and shifts in FAA rules regarding unmanned flight. Initial FAA proposed rules for commercial use of drones were issued in February 2015 and expanded with Part 107 in 2016, but they make package delivery unfeasible for the time being as operators must stay within sight of the drones.

However, in 2018, the FAA launched its UAS Integration Pilot Program, which partners government agencies in select U.S. cities with private sector firms to accelerate the adoption and use of drones for deliveries. Specifically, the program will explore the problems of universal traffic management, security procedures, hacking and general commercial use.

In 2016, China's number two e-commerce company JD.com began using drones to deliver packages to remote rural villages. As of early 2018, the firm had drones that could fly up to 62 mph carrying packages of up to 66 pounds. JD.com is currently testing heavy-duty drones that can carry up to one ton or more, and is investing $150 million with the help of the Shaanxi province government. In the UK, Amazon made its first drone delivery in December 2016. Zipline (www.flyzipline.com), a startup headed by former Google, SpaceX, Boeing and NASA veterans, starting delivery of medical supplies by drone to very remote areas in Rwanda in 2016. Drone delivery is also a reality in Reykjavik, Iceland since 2018 when food delivery company Aha signed a deal with Flytrex (www.flytrex.com) of Israel.

Delivery drones require more complex designs than those used to gather video footage or sense changes in temperature or pressure. For example, Google's Project Wing delivery drones have wings capable of switching to upright mode in order to hover while recipients take deliveries. Another Project Wing model has fixed wings combined with vertical-axis rotors similar to those used on quadcopters. As of mid-2018, Project Wing was conducting daily experimental flights.

6)   Wi-Fi Enables Wireless Traffic Growth

While cellular phone companies are investing billions of dollars in technologies to give their subscribers enhanced services such and 4G mobile internet, Wi-Fi is more vital than ever for wireless access. As the number of cellular device subscriptions for smartphones, tablets and aircards has soared, so has the demand placed upon cellular networks. Wi-Fi acts as a vital relief valve. Wireless device owners increasingly want to access immense files, such as Netflix movies on demand. If the world's rapidly increasing wireless data traffic relied solely on cellular networks, the system would be under severe stress. However, since wireless device owners frequently have access to Wi-Fi as an alternative for a large portion of the day, they can switch to Wi-Fi from cellular as needed, reducing their total cellular subscription costs and dramatically reducing the load placed on cellular networks. The role played by Wi-Fi will remain vitally important, even as ultrafast 5G cellular networks are rolled out. At the same time, Wi-Fi will become even more important to the world's technology users as connected devices proliferate in the rapidly growing Internet of Things (IoT).

Experts at Cisco, with their Cisco Visual Networking Index, estimate that by 2022, the global number of internet-connected mobile devices will reach 3.6 per capita (nearly 28.5 billion devices). Smartphones will represent about 44% of these devices and connections. Cisco also estimated that, during 2015 for the first time ever, more than 50% of mobile traffic was offloaded to Wi-Fi rather than remaining on cellular networks.

Wi-Fi routers have very high theoretical data transfer speeds, but actual speeds rely on local internet connections. On the fixed end, each Wi-Fi network is tied into an internet router. This means that the actual download speed enjoyed by the Wi-Fi user is limited to the speed of the internet service connected to the router. If a user has a local internet connection with a 50 meg download speed via a cable modem, then the local Wi-Fi system will also be limited to 50 meg.

Wi-Fi networks are easy and inexpensive to set up. The signal utilizes public domain, unlicensed radio spectrum. They are frequently found in homes and offices, as well as such high-traffic areas as coffee shops, fast food restaurants, airports, hotels, bookstores, shopping malls and other public places. For example, Starbucks coffee shops offer Wi-Fi connections. Select McDonald's restaurants offer Wi-Fi, and hotels provide Wi-Fi to guests. AT&T,

Inc. now operates more than 125,000 hotspots around the globe.

Smartphones users are generally eager to take advantage of available Wi-Fi, as it reduces their total cellular network usage and therefore their cellphone bills. One of the most aggressive builders of Wi-Fi networks is Boingo (www.boingo.com). Charging a modest monthly fee for unlimited connect time, the firm has developed a system of thousands of such networks worldwide. Boingo has over 1 million locations around the world for its wireless connection service. The firm's locations include airports, hotels, restaurants and other places, such as convention centers.

Wi-Fi is now advancing through enhanced technologies. Recent enhancements include MU-MIMO (multi-user, multiple-input, multiple-output), which allows a Wi-Fi device to handle data requests from multiple sources at once. Another recent technology known as OFDMA (orthogonal frequency-division multiple access) can split a Wi-Fi channel into many data pipes simultaneously. Kumu Networks, Inc., a startup based in Santa Clara, California (kumunetworks.com), has developed "full duplex" technology that enables Wi-Fi to transmit and receive simultaneously, effectively doubling the speed and capability of the network.

7)   Global Internet Market Tops 4.2 Billion Users/Ultrafast Broadband Expands, both Fixed and Wireless

By the end of 2018, fixed broadband connections in the U.S. totaled 111 million homes and businesses by wireline (DSL), direct fiber, satellite or cable, up from 102.2 million in 2015, according to Plunkett Research estimates. Fueling this growth has been intense price competition between cable and DSL providers. The internet is now reaching a vast U.S. market.

In addition, there were more than 322 million wireless internet subscriptions in America as of the end of 2018. The majority of American cellphones are now smartphones. Big improvements in the devices, such as the latest iPhones and Android-based units, along with enhanced high-speed access via 4G networks, are fueling this growth. In addition, most major e-commerce, news and entertainment sites have carefully designed their web pages to perform reasonably well on the "third screen," that is, cellphones (with TV being the first screen and desktop or laptop computers being the second screen). Globally, the International the number of internet users was more than 4.2 billion as of mid-

2018, (including wireless), according to Plunkett Research estimates.

Internet access speeds continue to increase dramatically. Google launched its "Google Fiber" ultra-high-speed internet service in Kansas City, Kansas in 2012, and soon expanded into Austin, Texas; Provo, Utah; and Atlanta, Georgia. This system allows homes and businesses to have 1 gigabit per second access, roughly 100 to 200 times the speed of typical DSL or mobile broadband. More than 1,000 U.S. towns and cities applied for the service when it was first announced, but Google is gauging the results of this initial effort before making any decisions about rolling it out.

AT&T initially launched a similar 1 gigabit service in competition with Google in the Austin area called AT&T FIBER. The firm offers this fast service in dozens of cities across the U.S.

What will widespread use of fast internet access mean to consumers? The opportunities for new or enhanced products and services are endless, and the amount of entertainment, news, commerce and personal services designed to take advantage of broadband will continue to grow rapidly. For example, education support and classes via broadband is rapidly growing into a major industry.

Broadband in the home is essential for everyday activities ranging from children's homework to shopping to managing financial accounts. Online entertainment and information options, already vast, will grow daily. Some online services are becoming indispensable, and always-on is the new accepted standard. The quality of streaming video and audio is becoming clear and reliable, making music and movie downloads extremely fast, and allowing internet telephone users to see their parties on the other end as if they were in the same room. Compression and caching techniques are evolving, and distribution and storage costs are expected to plummet. Consumers are accepting pay-per-view or pay-per-use service offerings because of their convenience and moderate cost. A very significant portion of today's radio, television and movie entertainment is migrating to the web.

8) Fiber-to-the-Home (FTTH) Gains Traction

The major telephone firms are looking for ways to increase revenues through enhanced services while retaining their customer bases. One such way is through the delivery of ultra-high-speed internet access, combined with enhanced entertainment and telephone options, often by installing true fiber-to-the-home (FTTH) networks.

Under traditional telephone and internet service, homes are served by copper wires, which are limited to relatively slow service. However, old-fashioned copper networks are not up to the demands of today's always-on internet consumers. Fiber-optic cable might be used in trunk lines to connect regions and cities to each other at the switch and network level, but speed drops significantly once the service hits local copper lines.

Things are much more advanced in major markets today. In an AT&T project, fiber is being brought into special hubs in existing neighborhoods. From those hubs, fast services are delivered into the home with advanced technologies on short, final runs of copper wire.

FTTH, in contrast, delivers fiber-optic cable all the way from the network to the local switch directly into the living room—with this system, internet delivery speeds and the types of entertainment and data delivered can be astounding. Google's "Google Fiber" service offers extremely fast download speeds of 1,000 Mbps (one gigabit), roughly 50 to 100 times faster than typical DSL or cable service. By 2018, Google offered the service in cities including Atlanta, Georgia; Austin, Texas; Charlotte, North Carolina; Kansas City, Missouri; Kansas City, Kansas; Nashville, Tennessee; and Provo Utah, among others. This puts tremendous competitive pressure on other internet access companies. It also makes consumers wonder why they have been paying high monthly rates for slow service for many years. In response, AT&T has begun providing 1,000 Mbps service in several major cities. The long-term result is going to be much better, faster internet access in major U.S. cities, at a reasonable cost.

Verizon has completed a multi-year FTTH program that makes it the U.S. leader in FTTH. Verizon's FTTH (called FiOS) offers exceptional speeds, with 500 Mbps download speed now available in some areas.

The Fiber-to-the-Home Council (www.ftthcouncil.org) tracks FTTH trends. In many cases, FTTH has been provided by local government or by subdivision developers who are determined to provide leading-edge connectivity as a value-added feature to new homes.

FTTH technologies, though expensive, may save the Bells from being trampled by the cable companies. Fiber-optic networks can give consumers extremely fast internet connections. Such ultra-high-speeds will also allow consumers to download movies in seconds and make videoconferencing a meaningful reality for businesses. (Additional fiber terms used in the industry include FTTP for Fiber-to-the-premises and FTTO for fiber-to-the-office.)

FTTH has been widely adopted in South Korea, Hong Kong, Japan, the United Arab Emirates and Taiwan, according to the FTTH Councils of Asia-Pacific, Europe and North America.

9)   Cloud Computing and Software as a Service (SaaS) Point the Way to the Future

There is a now-unstoppable trend toward downplaying the role of packaged software that is installed on the desktop, relying more on internet-based applications. This trend is called Software as a Service (SaaS). In fact, Sun Microsystem's famous positioning line of long standing, "The network is the computer," pretty well sums up this movement, a thought that "uses the internet as the computing platform of the future." Microsoft, Google, IBM, Oracle and other leading firms are quickly enhancing their own suites of internet-based applications.

Meanwhile, cloud computing is the use of remote servers owned and operated by third-party service providers to store and access data, as opposed to servers owned by the user. Service firms that offer cloud services for a fee run clusters of computers networked together, often based on open standards. Such cloud networks can consist of thousands of computers. Cloud services enable a client company to immediately increase computing capability without any investment in physical infrastructure. (The word "cloud" is also broadly used to describe any data or application that runs via the internet.) The concept of cloud is also increasingly linked with software as a service.

Gartner expected IT spending on cloud services to grow to $214 billion in 2019, up 17.5% from 2018. The transition rate is expected to even out to 2% per year as cloud adoption becomes mainstream, and the firm believes that as much as $1 trillion in IT spending will move to the cloud between 2018 and 2021.

Amazon.com was one of the earliest companies to offer cloud services, and it remains a leader in this field. Since it must operate immense server capacity anyway, Amazon decided in early 2006 to offer cloud computing services on those servers to outside parties. Amazon Web Services (AWS) have been extremely popular. Using AWS requires no long-term contract or up-front investment. Charges are reasonable and usage-based (a few cents per gigabyte per month in the U.S.). Remote servers, remote storage and the Amazon SimpleDB database are among the most popular offerings. AWS generated $17.46 billion in revenues for Amazon during 2017 (with fourth quarter performance up 45% over the previous quarter). In 2018, AWS revenue continued to rise, up 45.7% in the third quarter alone to reach $6.68 billion. Microsoft's Azure cloud services revenues grew at a sizzling pace during 2017 and into 2018.

Amazon, Microsoft and Google are investing vast sums to build new data centers for cloud services. For 2017, IBM reported total cloud revenues up 24% to $17 billion. By the third quarter of 2018, cloud revenue represented 20% of total IBM revenue. However, this intense competition is driving some firms to the sidelines, as evidenced by HP's late-2015 announcement that it would stop offering public cloud services.

Software that is sold and operates only via the cloud is a growing trend. Adobe Systems, Inc., for example, a maker of extremely popular design software, is selling its biggest software products as online services only available by subscription to Adobe Creative Cloud.

The result of these efforts has become a wide variety of software that is accessed only via the internet instead of the desktop. Some software can be accessed for free, but many rich software applications are rented to the user by subscription or by fees based on the amount of time used. The growing use of smartphones is accelerating this trend. Also, the sharing of data, whether for business collaboration (such as Microsoft's Office 365 and Salesforce's customer management solution) or simply for fun (such as Facebook), has simplified dramatically thanks to the cloud. Business models and profit streams are being altered as a result.

A major goal of publishing software in the cloud is for the user to be able to eliminate much of the money and staff effort that an organization typically invests in building, managing and updating software in the traditional manner on a computer network. At the same time, the cloud enables software providers to build steady streams of renewable subscription revenues. Salesforce, a customer relationship management (CRM) software leader, has achieved great success by selling internet-based (SaaS) access to its tools. NetSuite is another major provider of internet-based applications. Its offering for businesses includes CRM, enterprise resource planning (ERP), accounting, e-commerce and much more, all on a subscription basis. Among the advantages of SaaS are no software to purchase and no software to install or maintain.

10) China Is the World's Largest E-commerce Market and Continues to Boom

China is posting phenomenal growth in e-commerce. For 2018, eMarketer expected $1.46 trillion in Chinese online sales, up from $1.132 trillion in 2017. The company forecasted $1.989 trillion in Chinese e-commerce sales in 2019. This growth is due to widely available internet access, a growing middle class, the development of Chinese e-commerce businesses such as Alibaba.com and Tencent, sophisticated payment technologies and aggressive development of fast product delivery services.

Alibaba.com, owner of a wide variety of online platforms and services, had 699 million active users in early 2019. Its flagship web site is Taobao, which is similar to eBay. It offers an enormous array of merchandise but relies on third parties for fulfillment, delivery and logistics as well as other services. A newer Alibaba site, Tmall, is a marketplace for luxury brands of clothing, food and electronics. Tmall is perfectly positioned to serve China's growing middle class.

China's Singles' Day, an e-commerce holiday and the world's largest internet shopping event, brought in a record $30.8 billion in sales for Alibaba alone, in November 2018, compared to the previous record of $25.4 billion in 2017. A notable difference between Chinese and U.S. online buyers is that in China, shoppers often buy from digital marketplaces rather than traditional brick and mortar retailers' web sites. These marketplaces, including Alibaba, are megasites similar to eBay or Amazon Marketplace.

Alibaba has competitors, including JD.com and Yihaodian. JD.com offers same-day delivery services in 40 cities (Alibaba offers it through its Cainiao logistics arm), while Yihaodian became 100% owned by Wal-Mart as of mid-2015. With Wal-Mart's backing, Yihaodian has grown to have hundreds of distribution centers.

Many western companies are enjoying reasonable levels of success in doing business in China. Although the establishment of a Chinese-licensed business unit and the opening of an account in a Chinese bank are still difficult and time consuming requirements, there are some initiatives that are making the effort easier. Alibaba created Tmall Global in 2014, an international marketplace in which foreign companies can sell to Chinese

customers without creating Chinese subsidiaries or setting up bank accounts. Ant Financial, an Alibaba spinoff, takes care of transaction processing with the firms' home-country banks, while shipping and handling are overseen by delivery firm Cainiao. Another Tmall Global plus is that it has worked with the Chinese government to create bonded warehouses in several cities that are free from standard import duties in some cases, and taxed at a lower rate than wholesale purchases.

Internet Research Tip: The Internet in China

For the latest information on internet usage and web sites in China, visit the China Internet Network Information Center, www.cnnic.net.cn. The group publishes extremely useful research and survey results, and its web site is available in English as well as the Chinese language.

---

11) India Is the New E-Commerce Battle Ground

Of India's 1.4 million people, roughly 800 million live in rural areas with little if any access to traditional retailers. With the recent rollout of 4G wireless service in much of the country, those millions of shoppers are front and center for marketing efforts by the world's e-tailers. This market poses unique challenges, since many of these potential customers don't have credit cards or delivery addresses and are new to online shopping. Some don't have smartphones. However, eMarketer estimated that e-commerce revenue in India could multiply from the 2018 level of $33 billion to reach $72 billion by 2022.

Amazon bet heavily on the explosive growth potential in India, where it began operations in 2014. To win over customers, Amazon enabled motorbike delivery centers around the country, with riders who understand confusing streets and arcane addresses and offers customers the ability to pay in cash when items are delivered.

The company redesigned its shopping app in India. It offers tips in Hindi on how to find products (after humans translated descriptions of about 35,000 items, machine learning is now doing the Hindi translation, with more languages to follow), no email address is required to establish an account (just a phone number) and customers can pay by cash on delivery or using the Amazon Pay digital wallet (no credit cards or bank accounts required).

Amazon is attempting to overcome the fact that many poorly-educated rural consumers do not know how to type, don't understand how to conduct an effective online search, and often are unable to read. Amazon works with more than 14,000 small, local stores that it refers to as Easy Stores, with well-trained storeowners available to assist new consumers in online buying. The store owners provide online shopping expertise that many consumers still lack, accept the payments and allow the consumers to pick up the packages at the stores upon arrival.

U.S.-based retail giant Wal-Mart acquired India's Flipkart in 2018. Flipkart is India's largest e-commerce firm. The site offers guaranteed same-day delivery in India's largest cities.

While U.S.-based firms Wal-Mart and Amazon were making massive investments in Indian e-commerce in an effort to dominate massive market share, the Indian government stepped in to make their strategies much more difficult. Government leaders noted how China had encouraged the growth of highly innovative local e-commerce firms (including Alibaba and JD.com) by making it difficult for foreign-owned companies to participate in the market. Effective February 1, 2019, foreign-owned firms are prohibited from entering into exclusive agreements for the online sale of other companies' products. The new rules also cracked down on practices whereby e-commerce firms were shifting merchandise distribution to networks of wholesale distributors that they controlled, thereby circumventing rules intended to control growth of foreign companies. (Rules prohibited foreign firms selling multiple brands from holding their own inventory or shipping merchandise directly to consumers.) India hopes to protect the interests of local storeowners in this manner, while fostering the growth of its own domestic online platforms.

The long-term effect on Wal-Mart's Flipkart and Amazon remains to be seen. Meanwhile, domestic investment and innovation is growing. Giant India-based conglomerate Tata Group launched its own e-commerce platform in February 2016 called Tata CLiQ. Another major Indian firm, Reliance Industries (which spent $35 billion to create India's first all 4G wireless network in 2018), announced its own e-commerce platform called Jio. Delivery will continue to be one of the biggest competitive battles in India's rapidly growing e-commerce sector.

12) Social Media Generates Billions of Dollars in Global Online and Mobile Ad Revenues

With more than 3 billion social media users worldwide, global ad spending on such platforms is soaring. Facebook (www.facebook.com) continues to be the dominant site among social media worldwide. As of the end of 2018, the company had 2.27 billion monthly active users in general, and 1.49 billion daily active users. Facebook is building targeted advertising revenues based on likes and dislikes established in users' profiles, to the extent that it is now one of the largest generators of online advertising revenue. Advertisers want to be where potential customers are, and Facebook reported in late 2017 that its average user spends 20 minutes each day on Facebook and its Instagram and Messenger platforms (not counting its WhatsApp).

Facebook Connect allows members to log onto other sites such as CitySearch.com or Yelp.com using their Facebook identification to tie activities on those sites back to their personal Facebook pages. A CitySearch restaurant review, for example, appears as part of a Facebook posting.

In a similar vein, Facebook launched Open Stream API, which allows developers to export the site's news feeds to any other site. Facebook users can access their friends' news feeds from any number of other sites without having to login to Facebook. Facebook also has enabled developers to tap into its Messenger platform, which means that users won't have to exit Messenger in order to access a favorite app that is Messenger-enabled.

Advertisers have the ability to track customers who are directed to their sites from Facebook, as well as specify goals such as increasing "Likes" or converting more clicks to sales. Advertisers also have control of where ads appear on Facebook, either in users' newsfeeds or in a column of ads on the right side of the site's pages. In addition, advertisers can use the site's Custom Audience tool to specify potential customer attributes (gender, interests, location, etc.) and the Lookalike Audiences tool to find potential customers who are similar to existing customers.

Google failed to gain traction with its initial social media platform called Buzz. Google tried again with a social networking effort called Google+, but after suffering a number of data leaks, announced plans to shut down the network in April 2019.

LinkedIn is designed to help users network for business opportunities, and to help job seekers and recruiters connect. The site was launched in 2003, and by late 2018, it had exceeded 600 million registered users, 70% of whom are from outside the U.S. LinkedIn has revolutionized the employee recruiting industry single-handed, as each user's home page's functions well as an online resume. Recruiters constantly comb the users' information in order to identify people with certain qualifications, using sophisticated online tools provided by LinkedIn on a monthly subscription basis. In 2016, LinkedIn was acquired by Microsoft for about $26 billion. Microsoft is focusing on adding services and features to its cloud-based businesses, and sees LinkedIn as a logical extension of Microsoft's services for business customers.

On the video front, YouTube (www.youtube.com), part of Google since 2006, has long been a free-of-charge site for sharing video uploaded by YouTube members. The company earns very significant revenues through the sale of online ads. In addition, it intends to be a major provider of premium online content for paid subscribers. The site has social media elements, since members connect to create video groups that share similar interests. Videos can be uploaded by their creators as available for public viewing, or as private videos with limited access.

In order to add to its videos contributed by amateur users and professionals or corporations who want to build video audiences, YouTube has partnered with major content providers such as CBS, Sony Music Group, the BBC, NBA, Warner Music Group, The Sundance Channel and Universal Music Group. YouTube is truly global in scope. In an effort to encourage international users, YouTube has established local sites in dozens of nations.

Twitter is working to attract advertisers with tools such as Amplify, which allows Twitter to sell ads in conjunction with television and other media companies. Using Amplify, networks post brief video replays of just-aired programming sponsored by advertisers. A&E Networks, BBC America and ESPN were early partners with Amplify. Many TV ads and some programs feature Twitter hashtags to promote discussions.

Twitter and Facebook face stiff competition from newer social outlets including Pinterest, Snapchat and Tumblr. Snapchat users share photos and videos taken on their smartphones. Snapchat offers Discover, a service that links content from a broad array of sources such as ESPN, the Food Network, CNN, National Geographic, Yahoo! News and Warner Music Group. Users swipe their mobile screens from left to right to change images, and up and down to view full video or news articles posted by the content sources, which include advertising.

Pinterest is an extremely social site that enables users to create online bulletin boards ("pinboards") of photos, videos, ideas, dreams and comments. Each image posted is called a "pin."

In China, a social media app called Weixin/WeChat has largely taken the place of Facebook and Twitter (both of which are officially banned in China). Google sites, including YouTube, as well as Instagram, are also banned. The Weixin/WeChat app features games, chat and social media in one package. Weixin is owned by Tencent, a Chinese internet firm known for its online games and the QQ instant messenger service. Tencent markets Weixin outside China, particularly in Southeast Asia, Europe and Latin America under the brand WeChat.

Online and mobile sites face losses in ad revenue when users install ad blocker software, a practice that is growing quickly.

13) Overview of the Social Media Industry

Since most social media accounts and activities are free-of-charge, the challenge for social media firms has been to monetize their vast user bases. By September 2018, Facebook had roughly 2.27 billion monthly users (the majority are on mobile devices) and LinkedIn counted more than 600 million, while Twitter had more than 335 million. LinkedIn, for example, has quite successful in generating revenues. It not only sells advertising, but also sells subscriptions to account upgrades for users who are interested in deeper services. Since LinkedIn, largely aimed at business professionals and job seekers, is a popular way for salespeople to initiate conversations with potential customers, and for corporate recruiters and human resources managers to seek new hires, the site has had significant success in generating recurring revenues. In 2016, LinkedIn was acquired by Microsoft for about $26 billion.

Facebook has rapidly become one of the most successful of all the world's advertising platforms. Both Facebook and LinkedIn have made it extremely easy for small to mid-size businesses to design and initiate their own ads on social media, where these advertisers have the option of carefully targeting their ads to select groups of users by interest, occupation, education, geography or habits. At the same time, these sites have broad appeal to major national advertisers.

While Twitter has not been as successful as Facebook and LinkedIn in generating revenue growth, it has nonetheless carved out a unique position in global communications. Many celebrities and politicians tweet daily—perhaps several times a day. For example, the tweeting activity of 2016's U.S. presidential primary campaigns was notorious, and avidly read by millions of Americans daily. Elsewhere some organizations are finding Twitter to be the most effective way to instantly communicate with their customers. Some airlines, for example, encourage passengers to tweet their comments, questions and concerns to airline representatives in order to obtain immediate answers. Jun, a small city in Spain, has been closely watched due to its great success in using Twitter as a means of communicating with, and serving, its population of 3,500. The city's various departments tweet out their plans and projects, and in many cases, residents may use tweets to request services or report problems, as a fast, simple alternative to filling out paper forms. The tiny police force receives daily tweets about local problems that may need attention, such as bad drivers, domestic violence or suspicious behavior. These tweets reach the city's police instantly. The practice has been described as making police assistants out of all residents.

A newer service of great interest is Pinterest, a virtual pin board on which users post photos, recipes, notes, lists or anything else pertaining to hobbies, projects and other interests. Pinterest has firm plans for building advertising revenues.

While the social media pioneers were largely U.S.-based, and the audiences of leading sites like Facebook are global, many nations can boast of their own local social media success stories. This is particularly important in China, where the government limits access to many of the outside world's most popular sites such as YouTube and Facebook. Additional popular Chinese services include 51.com, Weixin/WeChat and Kaixin0001.com. Moreover, Ushi.cn is a Chinese service targeted at the LinkedIn-type of professional user.

14) Digital Advertising Soars, Has Larger Market Share of U.S. Advertising Than TV

Both the online audience and the level of sophistication in online advertising continue to increase dramatically. Advertisers large and small have made the internet a significant part of their advertising strategies. eMarketer projected $125.8

billion in U.S. digital ad spending in 2019, up from $83.0 billion in U.S. digital ad spending for 2017 (including mobile platforms). Digital advertising accounted for about 55% of the total market during 2019.

Online advertising includes paid search, display ads, video ads and other categories. To take advantage of the growing base of online consumers, as well as the increases in connection and computing speeds, advertisers have developed rich media techniques such as very catchy ads and video content.

The digital advertising market has expanded to include social media such as Facebook and LinkedIn, where advertising has been growing at a fast clip. Advertisers, including national firms, are taking social media very seriously. Consumers are spending a significant amount of each day on Facebook and similar pages, and these sites offer tremendous tools that enable advertisers to reach specific, niche markets. Sophisticated tracking technology that is now commonplace on the internet allows advertisers to see how online ads are performing in real-time. Meanwhile, Amazon.com has become one of the most successful online advertising platforms, generating billions of dollars yearly in fees for display ads on its shopping sites.

Advertising Via Paid Search Results: Search engines such as Google provide targeted search result placement, also known as "paid search results," in the form of prominent links to a client's site. Ads on Google's search results pages appear near the "natural" search results. What is vital about these ads is that they are generated by the key words a user enters in his or her search. Advertisers pay search engines to have their links appear whenever certain words or collections of words are part of a search. For example, a paid search result for a light fixture company might appear whenever "lighting" or "lamp" is entered as part of a search. Advertisers pay for each user click on their ads. Google and other search engine sites generally sell keyword placements to the highest bidders.

Another popular online method is "pay-per-click" advertising. For example, Google's extremely successful AdSense program enables an advertiser to upload a text- or image-based ad into Google's system. Google's sophisticated technology places the ads on third-party sites that contain content related to the advertisement inserted there. Every time a consumer clicks on the ad, he or she is taken to the advertiser's own web site, which results in a small pay-per-click fee being charged to the advertiser.

This fee is shared between Google and the owner of the third-party site where the click originated.

Yet another method of online advertising is "textual" or "in-text." Advertisers pay for certain words in news or general interest articles to by hyperlinked on third-party sites. When users click the underlined word, a related ad pops up, complete with a link to the advertiser's web site. Online advertising company Vibrant Media, Inc., (www.vibrantmedia.com) for example, offers in-text ad products that can include text, flash media and video.

SPOTLIGHT: Nielsen and Partners Track Mobile Video Viewing

In partnership with Facebook, Google and other sites, Nielsen is tracking video viewers on smartphones, tablets and laptops. Video player manufacturers now include code that send pings to Nielsen servers with information about the device used to watch a video. Nielsen's servers communicate with Facebook about those device addresses, and the social media site matches the addresses with member information. Facebook sends Nielsen data such as age and sex of the associated viewers. Experian, another partner, adds buying patter information related to those viewers. Nielsen sells this information to advertisers, enabling these advertisers to best tailor their ads to reach specific audiences on specific devices.

Behavioral Targeting: A concept sometimes called "behavioral targeting" uses technology to analyze an individual internet user's tastes, habits, interests and concerns. A primary method of such targeting has long been the placement of cookies on users' computers. Cookies track a user's actions, such as web sites visited, and relay data on these actions to marketing analysis databases. (Cookies are also used to enable a web site to recognize a user when he or she returns to a web page.) Over a period of time, a pattern of web site visits will show a user's unique interests, enabling targeting of ads. Data may also be gathered every time a user clicks on an ad.

An enhancement to this idea is technology that tracks all page visits of all internet subscribers within a given geographical area. This site visit history can be analyzed at the individual level, enabling an internet service provider to offer highly-targeted ads based on a subscriber's internet use history and apparent interests. Acxiom Corp. (www.acxiom.com) is a major player in targeted online ads, maintaining a database of households

with information taken from a wide variety of sources, including public real estate and motor vehicle records, warranty cards that customers complete and return to manufacturers and travel histories.

Google uses extremely sophisticated technology to gauge the interests of online consumers and to place relevant ads in their view. Google's effort to target ads in this manner vastly improves its ability to deliver relevant ads to consumers and serve advertisers' interests, all while increasing Google's ability to generate revenues.

Another practice is "retargeting," which displays ads for items that were viewed on an advertiser's web site but were not yet purchased. For example, a user might browse for dog beds on a pet-related site. When that user moves to an unrelated site, perhaps a news site, an ad showing the very dog beds previously viewed appears on the news page.

To some extent, internet companies make it possible for consumers to opt-out of these practices, when consumers are willing to take the time to manage their user profiles. In addition, web browser options and security settings within Apple, Microsoft and other popular software enable consumers, who are willing to take the time and trouble, to restrict the use of cookies and other tracking technology.

The EU has enacted a "General Data Protection Regulation (GDPR)" that requires websites to alert consumers to the use of cookies. Many other aspects of a site's use of consumer information are also tightly controlled by GDPR, with companies of all types required to take significant steps to protect consumers' privacy and data security.

Google, Yahoo!, AOL, Time Warner and NBCUniversal agreed to place a Do Not Track option on their sites which limit how data compiled by tracking consumer behavior is used. Another threat to online advertising is ad-blocking software. For example, AdBlock Plus is a banner, pop-up and video ad blocker used by a large number of consumers.

15) Programmatic Ad Buying Dominates the Digital Media Market

Technology experts have devised automated systems in which advertisers specify the type of ad, types of page locations and price they are willing to pay for an ad. The ads are then placed by a third party (an "exchange") into vacant slots that match the advertiser's criteria. The practice, which is also referred to as programmatic buying, utilizes a set of complicated algorithms running during the milliseconds it takes for a web page to load.

Omnicom Group reports that it can bid for up to 10 million online ads every second. The practice already places ads on smartphones, tablets and desktops, but will exponentially grow as televisions and billboards increasingly become connected to the internet.

Sophisticated online ad management systems make it relatively simple for advertisers, agencies and web site owners to track ad space inventories and advertising campaigns. This ability for advertisers and their agencies to tightly control their advertising spending creates new cost-effectiveness, and is a powerful boost to overall online ad spending.

16) Online Travel Agencies (OTAs) Continue Strong Growth in Bookings/Hotels Fight to Keep Control of the Customer

One of the biggest single changes in the travel industry has been the exceptionally rapid rise of online travel agencies, also known as OTAs. Around the globe, vast numbers of business and leisure travelers alike rely on the internet as their primary means of gaining travel information, reserving hotels or booking air tickets. According to eMarketer, digital travel sales in America during 2018 (including sales made on mobile devices) were expected to reach $198.15 billion, up from $189.62 billion in 2017 and $180.59 billion in 2016. Sales for 2019 were expected to reach $206.08 billion.

Expedia, Travelocity, Orbitz, Hotwire and Booking Holdings, Inc. (formerly Priceline Group and owner of Booking.com) are among the largest firms offering online travel booking services in North America. In Europe, major online travel booking firms include EasyGroup (a holding company that owns and operates a number of travel and entertainment brands including easyCar, easyHotel and easyJet), Lastminute.com (a subsidiary of Travelocity Europe Limited) and eBookers. The numbers involved are massive. Booking.com offers over 28.3 million listings in 228 countries and territories.

Other important players include China's Ctrip.com and eLong, UK-based Opodo and India's MakeMyTrip. Meanwhile, Airbnb began allowing hotels to list on its site in 2018, charging the hotels a 3% booking fee (compared to the 12%-25% fee hotels are charged by booking sites such as Expedia and Priceline). Hotels list on Airbnb through third-party distribution networks such as SiteMinder.

In September 2015, Expedia completed its $1.3 billion acquisition of Orbitz. Expedia already owned

several sites, including hotels.com and Travelocity. From a U.S. travel market perspective, there will now be only two significant corporate OTA groups: Expedia and Priceline. Together, these corporate enterprises will control about 95% of the American OTA market. The two giants, Priceline and Expedia, each now have massive existing customer bases. They have enormous marketing budgets that can be used to battle competitors that might emerge. Both have extremely powerful, deeply experienced digital marketing and technology teams that may be able to out-produce and out-compete the strategies of emerging firms. They each own several respected, dominant booking brands. The firms also have reached the point of massive scale whereby they have significant clout with suppliers, and they have the potential to make their loyalty programs even more compelling and competitive due to scale.

Meanwhile, an extremely popular travel reviews and information site, TripAdvisor, has evolved into an online booking site. It is in a good position to compete head-on with Priceline and Expedia. There are even more changes in store with the online travel booking business thanks to recent entries by Google and Amazon.

SPOTLIGHT: Hotel Booking on Google, A Slam-Dunk for the Online Search Giant

Google has invested heavily in travel-related technologies and assets as well, including the Frommer's brand of travel guides and the widely used ITA airline reservation system. Now, it has launched a hotel booking service. This strategy offers multiple advantages in addition to a new commission-based revenue stream for the search engine company.

From the consumer's point-of-view, reserving a room on Google offers greater ease of booking on mobile devices, as there is no hand-off to second or third-party sites. It also means fewer screens and pages to deal with, ease of comparing hotel locations and prices and instant payment for Google Wallet users. It offers speed and convenience similar to Amazon's One-Click purchase button.

From Google's point-of-view, this new business will increase user engagement and site traffic. Users must sign in to their Google accounts to complete bookings (and therefore must establish a user account if he/she doesn't have one). This new business will also drive users to establish Google Wallet accounts and to add hotel reviews.

Google already owns substantial travel information assets, and this move into hotels is likely only a small first step into extremely promising travel industry territory. Google could easily establish travel loyalty rewards as well. Google has more opportunity in this market since Amazon shut down its hotel booking site, Amazon Destinations, in late 2015.

Consumers like the OTAs because they offer a wide choice of hotel brands, prices and locations in one view. Some sites operate as "metasearch" engines, enabling the consumer to link directly to a hotel's site for booking. The largest, however, operate as true online booking agencies.

Hotels typically pay from 12% to as much as 25% commission for these bookings. In addition to the fees, OTAs are causing serious alarm at hotel chains, which fear they are losing control of the loyalty of and relationship with their customers. This is due to several strategies employed by the OTAs, including continual addition of new travel planning features to their web sites and apps, as well as extremely popular loyalty points programs of their own. Hotels.com, for example, offers a free hotel night, with no restrictions, after booking 10 nights total. This is a much simpler, easier-to-use program than those offered by most chains.

Major hotel chains and airlines have invested immense sums in their own, branded internet sites. These travel providers benefit because the use of their own online booking systems eliminates fees to middlemen and wages to human reservation agents. Encouraging travelers to book through the hotel and airline companies' own sites also gives the firms control over marketing and branding, and enables them to promote loyalty programs. Consumers benefit because they have seamless access to travel information, frequent flyer accounts and other perks. A major consideration is access to loyalty points. Hotel chains are also offering discounts through their loyalty programs. For example, Choice Hotels International offers a "member rate" of up to 10% off at some of its properties.

Most, if not all, chains have adopted aggressive online tactics and are denying awards points to customers who book their rooms through third-party sites. In addition, chains are offering "best price guarantees." For example, if a guest sees a better price at an OTA but books through the hotel chain, the hotel will give the guest another 25% off. Hotels are also boosting their digital offerings for loyalty program members who book directly with the hotels.

These include smartphone apps that enable instant check-in, fast check-out, smartphone-based electronic room keys, digital concierge services and smartphone-based scheduling of hotel services and room service orders.

In most cases, hotels and OTAs have rate parity agreements in their contracts. This means that hotels may not be able to offer lower prices than those provided to the OTAs. However, the hotel chains may offer special prices to select groups of guests, such as loyalty plan members. This means that competitive advantage has to be created in some other manner, like loyalty programs, or special free perks for guests. In this regard, it's vital for hotel chains to take advantage of assets that they control. For example, Hyatt is among chains enabling direct booking guests to look at a floor plan and choose the actual room that they will stay in. Other hotels are including free meals or drinks for certain guests.

Traditional travel agencies have endured vast changes in recent years, including the growing trend among corporate travelers to use online booking services. Some travel agents have successfully repositioned themselves as "consultants," charging hourly fees for their expertise. Others specialize in providing unique knowledge about travel to out-of-the-way places such as Cambodia, French Polynesia or Africa.

The largest national travel agencies run sophisticated web sites of their own. They act as outsourced travel departments for their major corporate clients and arrange discounts for clients who purchase massive amounts of travel. For example, Carlson Wagonlit is a leading global business travel agency, with offices in more than 150 nations. Many large travel agencies that focus on leisure travelers buy hotel and aircraft space at wholesale and then create highly profitable tour packages to popular tourist destinations such as Cancun, Jamaica and Orlando.

17) Apple's iTunes Set the Standard in the Music Industry, but Digital Sales Slow

The sale of legal, downloadable music via the internet and smartphones has grown into an immense business, but it is facing daunting competition from internet-based music services like Pandora and Spotify, as well as from satellite-based radio service SiriusXM. Nielsen reported that combined sales of recorded CDs and music downloads sold in the U.S. declined from 116.1 million units during 2015 to 100.3 million in 2016 and 81.9 million units in 2017 (with digital sales accounting for 43.7% in 2016). As of mid-2018, consumption was up year over year by 18.4%. On a global scale, total recorded music sales rose slightly, from $15.0 billion in 2015 to $17.3 billion in 2017, according to the International Federation of the Phonographic Industry (IFPI). Profit margins for record companies, once a healthy 15% to 20% during the 1980s, have fallen dramatically, although they are benefitting from the receipt of royalties from services like Pandora.

A big step forward for the music industry came in the form of the groundbreaking iTunes Music Store, a digital service provided by Apple Computer, Inc. This global service offers single track and album files for download from major music companies. The music-playing capabilities of the wildly popular iPhone added to the power of Apple's entertainment empire.

iTunes, Apple's online music store, set the standard for ease of use and broad selections of music. The music companies benefit, receiving about $0.65 in gross revenue per $0.99 retail-priced song. More importantly, the advent of iTunes was a watershed for the industry, enabling it for the first time to significantly limit music file piracy in a manner that is extremely popular with consumers.

However, as internet-based music subscription services become more popular, iTunes music sales are slowing. Apple acquired Beats, which included Beats Audio hardware and the streaming service Beats Music for $3 billion. The acquisition fueled the launch of the Apple Music subscription service, a streaming app. Apple Music is a direct attempt to compete with subscription sites such as Pandora and Spotify.

18) Pandora and Spotify Lead in Streaming Music Via Internet Radio but Face Challenge from Apple Music/SiriusXM Tops 33 Million Subscribers

More and more people are shifting to streaming music services, accessed via online subscriptions or ad-supported plans. This is hurting recorded music sales, as consumers who subscribe to Pandora and similar services see little need to buy their own copies of their favorite songs. However, music publishers offset this revenue loss by licensing music to Pandora, Spotify and similar subscription services. In fact, streaming music over the internet means that more people are accessing more music than ever before.

BuzzAngle Music reported, for the U.S. market, 534.6 billion audio streams for all of 2018, up 41.8% from 2017's 376.9 billion. By the fourth quarter of 2018, 85% of all audio streams were subscription-based, up 50% from 2017. Physical album sales fell 15.3% from 2017 to 2018. The Recording Industry Association of America reported that industry revenue rose 10% during the first six months of 2018 to $4.6 billion, largely due to strong growth at subscription services like Spotify and Apple Music. Industry analysts estimate that subscription access results in roughly 70% of subscriber fees being paid to the music companies.

Streaming Music: A number of services offer ad-supported free streaming music services including Spotify, Pandora, Amazon Prime Music, Google Play music, and the recently launched Apple Music. Most also offer premium subscription access for a few dollars per month that is ad free.

Pandora's web-based platform allows its 68.8 million active users to build unique virtual radio stations based on their personal music preferences. Pandora allows up to 100 personalized stations to be created per account. The firm's technology is based in part on the Music Genome Project, which analyzes and catalogues thousands of songs from multiple genres to create a comprehensive database that breaks down songs by 480 individual musical attributes. In February 2019, Pandora was acquired by SiriusXM Holdings, Inc., the satellite radio service provider, for $3.5 billion, potentially creating one of the largest audio entertainment companies in the world.

Pandora offers free accounts, which are ad-supported but restrict the ability to skip songs, as well as premium subscriptions through Pandora One, which give listeners the ability to skip an unlimited amount of songs, has no limit on monthly listening hours, delivers higher quality audio and removes advertisements. The firm branched out into mobile listening by releasing software for internet-enabled smartphones and tablets. It has also established partnerships with consumer electronics manufacturers, including Panasonic, Pioneer, Samsung and Sony, to integrate its software into new devices, as well as automakers like Honda, Ford, Lexus and Mercedes to include its software pre-installed on certain new model vehicles.

Competitor Spotify, Ltd. also offers a wide range of listening options. Spotify is a web-based subscription music service offering streaming music to registered users in Sweden, Norway, Finland, the Netherlands, the U.K., France, Spain and the U.S., with roughly 100 million listeners to the free service, plus more than 83 million paying subscribers by mid-2018. The firm's library of music is accessed via its proprietary Spotify streaming music player program, which users can download and install on a variety of platforms, offering them access to Spotify's entire music library and the ability to listen to chosen tracks at any time and in any order.

Spotify users can create personalized playlists and have the option to share these playlists with other Spotify users who can then edit the playlists and make their own updates, enabling a collaborative approach to online, peer-to-peer music sharing. The company offers two main access tiers. Spotify Free, allows free access to the online music library and is supported through advertisements, while the fee-based subscription service, Spotify Premium, offer a variety of upgraded features and does not include advertising. Subscribers to Spotify Premium can access Spotify on a variety of mobile platforms, including the iPhone, the iPod Touch, Android-based phones and Windows Mobile-based phones. Spotify also connects users to a range of music sellers, providing links to online music stores where customers can purchase albums and individual songs for download. Additionally, it introduced Spotify Platform, which allows third-party developers to create music-based apps.

Apple Music has been attempting to catch up with pioneers Spotify and Pandora. Paid subscribers are charged a modest fee per month for ad-free service. In addition to on-demand streaming service, Apple Music offers a 24-hour global internet radio station and a portal in which artists connect with listeners.

A major competitor is Tencent Music Entertainment Group, founded in 2016 in China. The firm's apps include QQ Music, Kugou and Kuwo, and have more than 700 million active users and 120 million paying subscribers. Parent Tencent Holdings Limited acquired China Music Corporation in 2016 to strengthen its music offerings, and subsequently changed China Music's name to Tencent Music Entertainment Group. In mid-2018, Sony/ATV Music Publishing acquired an equity stake in Tencent Music, and in October 2018, the firm filed for an initial public offering (IPO) of around $2 billion in the U.S.

Satellite Radio: While Spotify and Pandora have gained tremendous audiences in internet radio, they have not benefited financially as much as the world leader in delivering radio via satellite: SiriusXM.

Sirius XM Holdings, Inc., operating as Sirius XM Radio, is a U.S.-based satellite radio provider. (It also owns an interest in a related company Canada, where broadcasts are made in French and English.) It offers hundreds of channels to its more than 33.6 million subscribers, consisting of dozens of channels of commercial-free music; as well as popular channels of sports, news and talk that may include advertising in some cases, traffic and weather; and Latino channels.

The company's primary source of revenue is subscription fees, with most of its customers subscribing to Sirius on an annual basis. Sirius radios for the car, truck, home, RV, boat, office and store are distributed through automakers and retail locations nationwide as well as online through SiriusXM.com. Sirius also has agreements with every major automaker to offer its radios as factory or dealer-installed options in their vehicles. In addition, satellite radio services are offered to customers of certain rental car companies.

Sirius Internet Radio is an internet-only version of the firm's service that delivers a simulcast of select music and non-music channels. Additional services provided by the firm include Travel Link, a collection of data services that provides users with information on weather, fuel prices, movie listing and sports scores and scheduling; and both real-time weather and traffic services. The fact that voice-activated personal assistants, such as Amazon Echo and Google Home, can take verbal commands to find play music (by artist, genre or specific title), will add to the subscription music trend.

19) Overview of the Mobile Apps Industry

Mobile apps (short for "applications"), including those for magazines, information services such as health site WebMD, games, newspapers, catalogs and ebooks, to name but a few of the tens of thousands of uses, didn't really exist before the introduction of the iconic iPhone smartphone (although online "widgets," which offer similar features, had been around for quite some time). The Apple iTunes App Store launched in July 2008 with only about 500 apps available. By the third quarter of 2018, Apple had more than 2 million apps for sale or downloadable free of charge. Apple reports that its App Store sales grew from $38 billion in total revenues for 2017 to $46.6 billion in 2018.

The vast majority of apps are downloadable free-of-charge, as they are offered to consumers to enable them to more quickly access internet-based stores and services via mobile devices. You might think of this as app-based advertising. For example, airlines such as United Airlines and Singapore Airlines offer free apps that make it easier to make purchases from the airlines. Apps sold for a fee generate only modest revenues per average app, with roughly 500 downloads daily per average app. App fees tend to be in the $3.00 range. Paid apps usually are free of advertisements.

Meanwhile, vast numbers of apps are also available for the Android mobile phone operating system (the world's leading smartphone platform), as well as for Windows phones and other devices. Android is the mobile operating system developed by Google, and it is the most popular operating system in the mobile world.

App developers that want their products to be in broad distribution are forced to develop at least three versions, one each for Apple, Windows and Android. There are other operating systems to consider as well. Over the mid-term, wide adoption of an advanced internet markup language known as HTML5 will make it easier to develop apps that will run on any device, and may eliminate the need for multiple app editions. Mobile internet browsers have become much more complex, making them capable of running advanced programs directly on the smartphone rather than in the cloud.

On all platforms, the most popular apps include games such as *Angry Birds;* tools such as Google Maps; and entertainment- and media-related apps, such as those for Pandora internet-based radio. At the same time, apps provide tools for business people, travelers, students, hobbyists, wine drinkers, people who like to cook, job seekers, children, sports fans, shoppers, car enthusiasts and myriad other special interest niches.

The number of apps on the market has become so massive that consumers are less likely to be willing to sort through app stores to find useful tools. Instead, to a growing extent, they rely on recommendations from friends, emails from trusted sources and magazine reviews in order to find new apps to download. Many smartphone users have downloaded a large number of apps, but only use a few of them on a regular basis.

Since the development of apps requires extensive programming and creative services, the app industry encompasses revenues and fees far beyond app store revenues. For example, corporate spending on app development has been soaring. Also, a large number of software companies have achieved success in selling app development tools and platforms to software coders. A study published in January 2016 called *Unleashing Innovation and Growth* by the Progressive Policy Institute estimated that mobile

apps had spawned 1.66 million current U.S. jobs, including jobs that could be described as direct, indirect and spillover employment. Apple stated in 2017 that the ecosystem involved in its iOS apps has also created 1.2 million jobs in Europe and 1.4 million jobs in China.

20) Cable and Satellite TV Struggle with Cord-Cutting/Cheaper Streaming Options Proliferate, Including Netflix

Cord-Cutting: In the race for media consumers, cable companies and satellite firms are losing subscribers, as viewers increasingly turn to the internet for video programming, a practice that is being to as "cord cutting." There are millions of "Zero-TV" households, in which video watchers see content on devices other than traditional TV, according to Nielsen. In particular, people aged 25 or younger often do not own televisions, but watch programs solely on devices such as smartphones and tablets. More than 10 million U.S. homes have cut the cord or skipped over pay-TV distributors since 2010 according to MoffettNathanson LLC.

A significant challenge facing cable and satellite companies is programming costs. Historically, they increased their subscription fees year after year in order to boost profits while covering increased costs. Some programming is extremely expensive to produce, especially sports programming (due to immense licensing fees paid to the sports leagues), and the cable and satellite firms have been passing those higher costs on to their customers.

Cable and satellite firms, along with telecom companies, are fighting back with innovations such as Comcast's xfinitytv.com, which includes the ability for subscribers to watch recent episodes online, on-demand. AT&T U-Verse has a web site similar to Comcast's xfinitytv.com, as well as an app that acts as a remote control and a digital video recorder. In addition, it can download programming onto mobile devices for later viewing. DirecTV's remote-control app streams live TV programming and enables wireless devices to act as remote controls for TV viewing. DISH Network offers an automatic ad-skipping feature called AutoHop.

Competition from Netflix: Netflix.com is the largest movie and TV show rental site in the world, with more than 130 million subscribers in over 190 countries. For a monthly subscription fee, users can enjoy streaming an unlimited number of movies. Netflix's business model initially was based on mailing DVD copies of movies to its subscribers. This was a costly business, involving multiple warehouses and massive postage and handling expenses. Eventually, however, the firm invested in state of the art technology to enable it to focus on streaming via the internet. While Netflix still supported DVD subscribers as of 2019, this is not where its future lies.

Playback of a Netflix streaming movie starts a few seconds after download begins. Subscribers instantly watch movies and TV episodes streamed over the internet to PCs, Macs, game consoles, tablets, smartphones and TVs. Among the devices streaming from Netflix are Microsoft's Xbox 360, Nintendo's Wii and Sony's PS3 consoles; an array of Blu-ray disc players, internet-connected TVs, home theater systems, digital video recorders and internet video players; Apple's iPhone, iPad and iPod touch, as well as Apple TV and Google TV.

The Netflix streaming content library includes media acquired through deals with corporations such as: ABC, Nickelodeon, Disney, Twentieth Century Fox, Paramount, Miramax, Lionsgate, MGM and CBS, among others. Additionally, through its Netflix Originals division, the company produces content available exclusively on Netflix, which continues to rack up growing numbers of Emmy nominations. The company spent between $12 billion and $13 billion on content in 2018. An estimated $10 billion of that amount was for the production of its own unique films (far exceeding production budgets of any television company or film studio on non-sports content). Netflix produced 82 feature films in 2018 while Warner Brothers produced 23 and Disney 10.

Netflix's efforts to shift to streaming video not only is cost effective, it is also positioning the company to take on cable channels such as HBO and Showtime. Operating on a business model dramatically different from those of cable TV channels, Netflix has become a true web-based entertainment platform, highly competitive with traditional cable networks and systems.

Development of Lower-Cost Subscriptions and Online Video Streaming Platforms: In an effort to attract consumers who are not willing to pay for traditional cable and satellite subscriptions, many companies are offering stripped-down packages with limited programing. Some of these services are cable- or satellite-based, but many are delivered only via the internet. These services are offered by top cable, satellite and media firms including: CBS, DIRECTV, Hulu, Netflix, DISH and HBO. The competition is already intense, and others may jump into the fray. Watch for business models and offerings to evolve, as providers attempt to establish

market share and attain profitability on these platforms.

Comcast's Digital Economy Service, a cable-based offering, includes only local broadcast channels and a limited selection of cable channels. Time Warner Cable offers a basic package that offers up to 200 digital channels and 100 HD channels, with on demand programs at no extra cost. Satellite provider DirecTV offers its own version, calling it a family package.

In early 2015, DISH Network introduced Sling TV, a moderately priced streaming internet-based service targeting young, mobile-intense viewers who refuse to subscribe to cable TV. Sling TV offers up to 180 of the most popular cable networks including ESPN, the Disney Channel, the Food Network, HGTV, TNT, TBS and CNN (but broadcast networks ABC, CBS, NBC and Fox are not included). Users select from basic Sling Orange or Sling Blue packages, which offer about 30 channels each (for about $25 per month), or can opt for a combination of the two ($40 per month). In addition, viewers can buy ad-on channels at modest cost. Vital differences from cable TV subscriptions include no long-term contract, a vastly lower monthly fee (in exchange for a much smaller selection of channels), no credit check and no need for additional hardware.

CBS All Access is a streaming service that offers subscribers limited commercial or commercial free access to its programming, and is available in more than 90% of the U.S. CBS holds back certain key content from other streaming providers.

Meanwhile, AT&T, after its $50 billion acquisition of satellite provider DirecTV in 2015, launched DirecTV Now. It offers streaming bundles of live channels and on-demand content at lower prices than its full DirecTV service. In addition to DirecTV, AT&T planned to launch an additional streaming service in late 2019, which will feature content from its June 2018 acquisition of Time Warner.

Sony's launch of its cloud-based TV service, called PlayStation Vue, is another competitor. Sony is relying on its base of millions of PlayStation video game users to help grow this new service. Vue includes content from CBS, Fox, Viacom and NBCUniversal. Vue offers a package of live TV channels, TV episodes on-demand and DVR capabilities with content streamed from existing internet connections. Users are not asked to sign a long-term contract.

Apple's iTunes offers films and TV shows from most major U.S. studios. Feature length films can download quickly if the customer has very high-speed broadband access, and may be purchased or rented online.

Amazon Instant Video offers its Prime premium service with the ability to watch a vast selection of titles instantly. In April 2014, Amazon entered the TV hardware arena with the launch of Fire, an inexpensive device for streaming video and games. The company has expanded Amazon Prime Video services to more than 200 countries and territories, and offered live NFL Thursday Night Football games in the U.S. Amazon's budget for production of unique content was estimated at $5 billion for 2018, and it is likely to continue to escalate its production spending in an effort to compete with Netflix.

Streaming one hour of a standard movie via Netflix can use 1 gigabit of bandwidth at standard settings. However, Netflix offers a reduced bandwidth setting that can reduce this by 70% to 300 megabits. High definition movies can require up to 3 gigabits of bandwidth per hour. These requirements create both headaches and revenue opportunities for internet service providers of all types, from cable to DSL to smartphone service. Simply put, downloading or streaming a movie uses up vast amounts of bandwidth and places great strain on internet providers' infrastructure, whether wired or wireless.

Disney launched an ESPN streaming service in 2018 called ESPN+ and planned another family-friendly service for 2019. This is the first time the entertainment empire will sell TV content directly to consumers instead of going through cable or satellite companies. In its first six months, ESPN+ signed up more than 1 million paying subscribers. Apple also planned to spend $1 billion per year to produce TV programming by 2018, and its budget is likely to grow quickly.

In November 2017, Philo was launched. The $16 per month service offers 43 channels, including AMC, A&E, Comedy Central, Food Network and TLC, and is backed by five companies that supply the programming: Discovery Communications, Inc., Viacom, Inc., Scripps Networks Interactive, A+E Networks and AMC Networks, Inc.

21) Quality of Care and Health Care Outcomes Data Are Available Online, Creating a New Level of Transparency

From the earliest days of the internet, one of the most popular activities online has been searching for information about illness, disease, pharmaceuticals and their side effects, as well as information related to care and diagnosis, such as options for surgery. Now, online activity about health care has risen to a massive level. With rapidly rising health care costs and concerns about the quality of care received for the dollar spent, many patients, employers and insurance providers are using online databases for information regarding doctors and hospitals—call it comparison shopping for health care. For example, there are growing numbers of web sites that track data on hospitals, such as the U.S. Department of Health and Human Services' web site, Hospital Compare (www.medicare.gov/hospitalcompare/search.html). Hospital Compare uses data from Medicare and Medicaid to track performance at thousands of facilities across the U.S. Also, many insurers make hospital data available to members on their web sites.

These databases typically enable an insurer or patient to compare specific hospitals to the national average on statistics such as mortality rates. For example, the Hospital Compare site compares each hospital in Houston, Texas to the Texas state average and to the national average. Data includes many items concerning patient experiences and satisfaction, surgical outcomes, readmission, hospital-related infections, and time spent waiting for care in emergency rooms. Also, average costs for various types of procedures are now available online on web sites that are attempting to earn profits from such services, although the quality of the data may vary.

The Medicare claims database is a digital record of the bills Medicare pays. It is used by federal investigators to sniff out fraud and for analysis by researchers and consultants for cost and utilization studies. Medicare has begun making some data about payments to individual physicians available. The database covers millions of caregivers and beneficiaries, but it is prohibited by law from disclosing patients' names.

Internet Research Tip:
Top web sites for health care information include:
National Cancer Institute, www.cancer.gov
Centers for Disease Control and Prevention (CDC), www.cdc.gov
FamilyDoctor.org, www.familydoctor.org
Health Finder, www.healthfinder.gov , a service of the U.S. Dept. of Health & Human Services
KidsHealth, www.kidshealth.org
Mayo Clinic, www.mayoclinic.org
NIH National Institute on Aging, www.nia.nih.gov/health
Medscape, www.medscape.com

Elsewhere, corporations in various segments of the health industry may publish interesting cost and outcomes information. For example, health diagnostics and monitoring devices firm Alere, formerly Inverness Medical Innovations, Inc., provides an online database giving the exact CPT procedure code and Medicare reimbursement rate for hundreds of procedures such as cholesterol tests at www.codemap.com/alere. The data is sorted geographically as well as by type of care.

Data on individual doctors is becoming available online, at such web sites as www.drscore.com and www.findadoc.com. The quality of the data from such sites may vary, and one should use caution. Nonetheless, the information is intriguing. Findadoc, for example, enables the user to look up doctors by location and specialty, and then view their hospital affiliations, languages spoken and patient ratings for such qualities as bedside manner and wait time.

Quantum Health (www.quantum-health.com), a Columbus, Ohio health care coordinator, offers comparative health care data to its corporate clients, plus a laundry list of services that help employees covered by company insurance navigate the often confusing health care system and get the most out of their health benefits. Quantum Health services include informing patients of what questions they should ask their physicians about their conditions, assistance in finding specialists, advice on medical tests that should or should not be taken and education on disease management and prevention. Quantum reports that its employer clients have enjoyed reduced spending on workers' health care, thanks to reductions in waste and unnecessary care, better results from disease management and a 25% reduction in health benefits-related workload. Two of its most impressive statistics are a 22% reduction in readmissions and a 4% reduction in emergency room usage.

The Affordable Care Act of 2010 (ACA) includes a provision that hospitals and doctors that score poorly on patient surveys can be denied Medicare reimbursement fees. Surveys such as those from Press Ganey, Gallup and National Research Corp., on which patients score health care providers on care experiences (based on patient surveys) including waiting times, pain relief and bedside manner, are becoming powerful arbiters in how patients are treated.

22) Online Banking Grows on Smartphones/The Internet and ATMs Replace Branches and Tellers

Banks have learned that combining the convenience of online banking with a chain of branch locations and ATMs allows them to fill the entire range of many customers' needs. This is similar to the trend among major retailers of combining e-commerce and physical storefronts, thereby creating synergies between bricks and clicks. Virtually all banks now have web sites where customers can monitor the status of their accounts, including checking, savings, investments and loans; make money-transfers to pay bills; and apply for services online. For the most part, online banking has been an enormous success.

In the wake of the 2008-09 financial crisis, banks were under pressure to cut costs. Many did so by closing branch locations. Thousands of U.S. branch locations have closed. Online banking, in combination with ATMs, goes a long way to fill the gap left by fewer brick and mortar bank locations. The end result is greater operating efficiency for banks. Nonetheless, online banking presents a long list of costs and challenges, including security and hacking issues.

A number of financial firms are targeting America's massive Generation Y as a growth sector for new customers (referring to 85+ million people born between 1982 and 2002). Strategies include updated financial sites that offer services such as bill paying, fund transfers, multiple accounts management and investment options. Mint.com, a site from Intuit, Inc., is quickly becoming one of the most popular financial tools in the internet. It offers account management and investment tracking.

Another formerly online-only bank, GoBank, targets young 20-somethings in the U.S. who prefer to perform some banking tasks (such as checking balances) on their smartphones. Fees are minimal, and there are no minimum balance requirements. GoBank is owned by Green Dot Corporation, which also owns Green Dot Bank where assets deposited by GoBank users are held. In 2014, Green Dot partnered with Wal-Mart to launch GoBank checking accounts. Other online-only banks, including Simple and Moven, are actually banking service providers that depend on brick and mortar banks such as Bancorp Bank and CBW Bank to hold assets and provide additional banking functions.

E*Trade Financial, a major online stock broker, entered the online and electronic banking field in a big way. It owns a nationwide system of ATMs under the E*Trade brand and has a rapidly growing base of online bank deposits.

Companies that offer a network of ATMs and physical branches, as well as online services, find the combination to be extremely effective. It costs a modest amount to service a customer who primarily relies on online services to manage accounts and relies on ATMs to get cash. The extremely rapid growth of broadband internet access in U.S. homes and businesses, along with the now-massive number of people accessing the internet via smartphones, encouraged banks to fill their internet sites with robust features. Brick and mortar branches still offer a few services that online banks cannot, such as cashier's checks and safe deposit boxes, and a large percentage of customers want to know they can walk into a branch for assistance when needed. Bank of America has opened a small number of employee-free branches, where customers can use ATMs and converse with remote tellers via video phones.

Bank of America offers SafePass, a 6-digit, one-time passcode sent as a text message to customers' smartphones which can then be used to authorize fund transfers, administer the online payment system and receive higher transfer limits. Major security software providers include RSA, the security division of EMC Corporation (www.rsa.com/en-us), Symantec (www.symantec.com) and Entrust (www.entrust.com).

Biometrics are becoming more common with regard to smartphone security. Customers by the millions at Wells Fargo, Bank of America and JP Morgan Chase use fingerprints to log into their bank

accounts via smartphone. Retinal scans are also in use at Wells Fargo for corporate accounts. In addition, Citigroup uses voice recognition to verify its credit card customers.

In 2018, banks including HSBC and OCBC Bank of Singapore instituted facial recognition technology for corporate customers to speed log-in times and increase security (see www.nec.com/en/global/solutions/safety/face_recognition/index.html for more about facial recognition technology). By September 2019, the EU will require multi-factor identification for online payments greater than €30 (about $35), which may include biometric data in addition to a password and/or a digital device such as a USB token.

As for the future, many analysts expect tools known as chatbots to quickly grow in use for mobile and online banking. Chatbots are computer programs that simulate conversation with customers via ATM screens and smartphones. Already in use to answer simple questions about recent transactions and spending limits, chatbots will likely become full-scale automated financial assistants capable of making payments and tracking budgets.

SPOTLIGHT: Bank Cafes, Non-Traditional Branch Banks

A new twist on brick and mortar bank branches are new cafes that offer gourmet coffee, free Wi-Fi and staff that help customers use the bank's web site and answer questions about the bank's services. There are no tellers and customers may perform banking tasks themselves online via laptop or smartphone. Capital One Financial opened its first such a café in Boston and then rolled out the concept. It describes its on-site employees as "ambassadors" rather than tellers. Bank of America, J.P. Morgan Chase & Co. and PNC Financial Services Group are also trying to cut the number of tellers and alternatively have "relationship bankers" who assist customers in using cutting edge ATMs or in completing banking tasks on smartphones.

---

23) Insurance Direct Selling and E-Commerce Grow

The roles of insurance intermediaries and agents, along with the overall structure of the insurance market, are changing dramatically as a result of e-commerce influences. Insurance sites on the internet enable consumers to generate a large number of competing insurance quotes within seconds. Because the tasks of providing information and writing transactions have typically been the primary functions of insurance agents, electronic markets that can perform these tasks more efficiently and with fewer costs threaten to displace agents. The future role of the insurance agent may evolve toward value-added customer service and consultation. This is similar to the evolution of the role of travel agents since the booming popularity of booking travel reservations via the internet. The extremely rapid adoption of smartphones on a global basis means that firms that deal with consumer lines such as auto insurance must adopt mobile strategies in order to gain new customers and satisfy the service needs of existing account.

Thanks to extremely successful direct sales efforts by firms like GEICO and Progressive, direct sales in the U.S. personal auto insurance market are booming. Direct marketing is also taking over in nations other than the U.S., with a signification portion of all new car insurance policies in the UK, for example, sold through direct marketing. Independent agencies will continue to lose market share as technology and direct sales gain in use.

Independent agents face tough and growing competition from internet-based sales. At the same time, underwriters utilizing captive agency systems have found growth opportunities by increasing e-commerce efforts or acquiring independent agencies and integrating them into their captive systems. The internet is an extremely effective way for underwriter web sites to generate leads for captive agencies.

Moreover, thanks to the growing success of internet sites that enable consumers to shop for the best life insurance prices, direct selling is playing a growing role in the life sector as well. A study published in 2016 found that 74% of U.S. insurance consumers used the internet to obtain insurance information or ask for quotes. Nonetheless, only 25% were found to make the final purchase online, with the rest preferring to deal with agents in person or via the telephone. The internet is playing a big role in the homeowner's market as well. For example, Liberty Mutual, GEICO and State Farm make it extremely fast and convenient for consumers to get homeowner's quotes online.

Thanks in part to the rising popularity of e-commerce, many insurance underwriters are now utilizing both direct sales and sales through agents in their business models. For example, the Progressive Corporation, an underwriter of automobile insurance, makes buying insurance online or over the phone extremely user-friendly. At the same time, it offers its auto insurance policies through about 30,000 independent agents, one of the largest agent networks in the U.S. Log onto www.progressive.com and you can get an instant quote on a policy for an automobile, motorcycle, boat or recreational vehicle, in addition to homeowner's and renter's insurance. Customers can also use the Progressive web site to file a claim or make a payment. Its easy-to-use web site (which includes pages in Spanish) is part of Progressive's overall strategy to utilize a high level of service, advanced technologies and direct sales to offer a competitive combination of coverage, service and pricing. Meanwhile, Progressive also uses the internet to promote business for its independent agents. With the www.progressiveagent.com/home.aspx web site, Progressive encourages consumers to use the internet to locate an agent.

Insurers selling over the internet may enjoy a substantial cost advantage over the course of a customer's lifetime, relative to non-internet-based insurers. This is due to reduced sales costs, lower customer service expenses and more advanced information-gathering capacities. Consequently, e-commerce has prompted many insurers to upgrade and integrate their information systems.

As of the beginning of 2018, Plunkett Research estimated that broadband connections at homes and businesses in the U.S. totaled more than 381.3 million (including mobile, residential and office subscriptions). In order to remain competitive, insurance firms are forced to attempt to capitalize on the vast size of the online consumer market.

The increased value of online connections results in decreased transaction costs. Products such as travel, credit or burial insurance have relatively high fixed costs and low value, but nonetheless have significant transaction costs when sold via traditional methods. Consequently, customers purchasing these products generally pay a high price per dollar of coverage. The internet can automate the sales and underwriting process for such insurance products. This means that prices can be lowered and more insurance can be sold by reducing transaction costs. Increased access through e-commerce is also influencing some consumers to purchase broader, high-value insurance products, such as liability umbrellas. Meanwhile, the security of insurance customers' data online is an important consideration, since large amounts of highly personal information are at stake.

Banks are becoming increasingly competitive in insurance sales, partly because they are adopting direct marketing methods. Large numbers of bank holding companies have acquired or established insurance agency subsidiaries. While these subsidiaries may operate using traditional agents, many of them use substantial direct marketing as well. For example, if you are a Bank of America customer, you are likely to receive life insurance offers in your monthly bank statements. This generates insurance leads for Bank of America at nominal cost.

Major Insurance-Comparing and Selling Sites on the Internet

Insure.com
www.insure.com provides instant insurance quotes from the most diverse array of insurers offered by any one source. The site works with over 200 insurance companies in all 50 states.

Insurance.com
www.insurance.com is an online insurance agency that offers all types of insurance with emphasis on auto coverage (it also owns another comparison insurance shopping site, www.4insurance.com).

CoverHound
Coverhound.com is a San Francisco-based firm that compares options from insurers including Progressive, esurance and Safeco, and links users directly with the selected company for policy purchase.

PolicyGenius
www.policygenius.com sells a variety of insurance products from top insurers such as AIG, MetLife, Prudential and Embrace Pet Insurance.

---

24) The Internet of Things (IoT) and M2M to Boom, Enhanced by Artificial Intelligence (AI)

The phrase "Internet of Things" or "IoT" is becoming increasingly widespread. It refers to a wireless communications strategy known as M2M or machine-to-machine. M2M can be as simple as a refrigerator that lets a smartphone app know when you are running low on milk (via Wi-Fi). In industry, M2M can create a vast, exceedingly complex network of wireless sensors monitoring all of the devices in a massive factory.

Massive investments in research, development and the application of new technologies is occurring in this field. For example, in 2017, computer giant Dell Technologies announced it would invest $1 billion over three years in the development of state-of-the-art hardware and software to help connect devices to the internet.

A Wireless Sensor Network (WSN) consists of a grouping of remote sensors that transmit data wirelessly to a receiver that is collecting information into a database. Special controls may alert the network's manager to changes in the environment, traffic or hazardous conditions within the vicinity of the sensors. Long-term collection of data from remote sensors can be used to establish patterns and make predictions, as well as to manage surveillance in real time. Another term that is coming into wide use is M2M2P or machine-to-machine-to-people. The "to-people" part refers to the fact that consumers, workers and professionals will increasingly be actively involved in the gathering of data, its analysis and its usage. For example, M2M2P systems that automatically collect data from patients' bedsides; analyze, chart and store that data; and make the data available to doctors or nurses so that they may take any necessary actions are becoming increasingly powerful. Such systems, part of the growing trend of electronic health records (EHR), can also include bedside comments spoken into tablet computers by physicians that are transcribed automatically by voice recognition software and then stored into EHR.

The long-term trend of miniaturization is playing a vital role in M2M. Intel and other firms are working on convergence of MEMS (microelectromechanical systems—tiny devices or switches that can measure changes such as acceleration or vibration), RFID (wireless radio frequency identification devices) and sometimes tiny computer processors (microprocessors embedded with software). In a small but powerful package, such remote sensors can monitor and transmit the stress level or metal fatigue in a highway bridge or an aircraft wing, or monitor manufacturing processes and product quality in a factory. In our age of growing focus on environmental quality, they can be designed to analyze surrounding air for chemicals, pollutants or particles, using lab on a chip technology that already largely exists. Some observers have referred to these wireless sensors as "smart dust," expecting vast quantities of them to be scattered about the Earth as the sensors become smaller and less expensive over the near future. Energy efficiency is going to benefit greatly, particularly in newly-built offices and factories. An important use of advanced sensors will be to monitor and control energy efficiency on a room-by-room, or even square meter-by-square meter, basis in large buildings.

In an almost infinite variety of possible, efficiency-enhancing applications, artificial intelligence (AI) software can use data gathered from smart dust to forecast needed changes, and robotics or microswitches can then act upon that data, making adjustments in processes automatically. For example, such a system of sensors and controls could make adjustments to the amount of an ingredient being added to the assembly line in a paint factory or food processing plant; increase fresh air flow to a factory room; or adjust air conditioning output in one room while leaving a nearby hallway as is. The ability to monitor conditions such as these 24/7, and provide instant analysis and reporting to engineers, means that potential problems can be deterred, manufacturing defects can be avoided, and energy efficiency can be enhanced dramatically. Virtually all industry sectors and processes will benefit.

Look for data sensors in homes to proliferate over the near- to mid-term. In the insurance business, live data emanating from sensors in homes could lead to more intelligent policies. Monitoring data via smartphone could be a significant opportunity for companies in the senior care, child care and pet care sectors.

Internet Research Tip: Cisco Global Cloud Index:

Network equipment maker Cisco has posted a "Cisco Global Cloud Index" online, which provides a massive amount of data regarding the growth of the total market in data gathering, connections and transfer.

https://www.cisco.com/c/en/us/solutions/collateral/service-provider/global-cloud-index-gci/white-paper-c11-738085.html

In addition, Cisco posts a highly informative Internet of Things page at www.cisco.com/web/solutions/trends/iot/overview.html which includes a two-minute IoT video.

The growth potential of M2M is enormous, and many facets of industry and society will benefit. However, it is difficult at this stage to estimate just how big the market may become. According to IHS, about 26.66 billion devices were connected to the internet as of early 2019, with about 30.73 billion devices to be connected by 2020.

Meanwhile, French technology firm SigFox offers a simple, inexpensive wireless network, designed specifically for M2M needs. The network transmits data at a rate of 100 bits per second, which is slower by a factor of 1,000 than most smartphone networks, but does so cheaply while it fills simple transmission needs such as those from many wireless sensors (such as Whistle, a clip-on collar sensor that tracks dog activity levels). Base stations use a wireless chip that costs only $1 to $2, and customers pay modest service charges per year per device. As of early 2019, SigFox had deployed its technology in about 60 countries covering 1 billion people.

Intel and other firms have developed methods that enable such remote sensors to bypass the need for internal batteries. Instead, they can run on "power harvesting circuits" that are able to reap power from nearby television signals, FM radio signals, Wi-Fi networks or RFID readers.

Memory chips used in sensors are much smaller than those in smartphones and laptops, opening a major opportunity for manufacturers such as Adesto Technologies. The firm makes chips that store between 32 kilobits and one megabit of data, making them a good fit for small monitors such as fitness data tracking wristbands. Future applications might include location-based beacons in retail stores that alert nearby customers to selected items by cellphone. Smoke detectors with small memory chips could sense battery life, while blood transfusion bags could track their locations, ages and content viabilities.

IBM is investing $3 billion between 2015 and 2019 in alliance with the Weather Company (which owns The Weather Channel). IBM plans to use data regarding weather conditions to empower businesses in insurance, energy, retail and logistics to make better decisions. Working with the Weather Company, it has access to the Weather Channel's 700,000 forecasts per second.

In 2017, the Federal Communications Commission (FCC) completed a spectrum auction of licenses to transmit in the 600-megahertz band, a low-frequency bandwidth that enables relatively small amounts of data to be transmitted across long distances and penetrate objects like buildings, metal doors and concrete walls, obstacles that can make traditional cell reception difficult if not impossible. Wireless are setting up and maintaining a host of devices (everything from smoke detectors to flood sensors to security systems and thermostat controls) with constant access to clear, secure signals. Consumers are using their smartphones to turn on their air conditioners, check door locks or cut the water supply if the washing machine overflows, regardless of where they happen to be at the time.

Internet Research Tip: Internet of Things (IoT) Networks:

For more information on wireless network systems and remote sensors, see:

Analog Devices,
   www.analog.com/en/applications/technology/sm
   artmesh-pavilion-
   home.html%20.analog.com/en/applications/techn
   ology/smartmesh-pavilion-home.html%20

C3 IoT, Inc., https://c3.ai/industries/

Moog, Inc., www.moog.com

25) Manhattan's FreshDirect Sets the Pace in Grocery Sales Over the Internet/Amazon Competes in Groceries

The Holy Grail of e-commerce is to convince grocery shoppers to order over the internet. Online grocery selling is such an appealing target because of the sheer size of the retail grocery market. However, creating a viable online grocery business has proved to be a daunting challenge. Food retailing, with its highly perishable inventory, is a low-profit-margin enterprise—one in which consumers tend to make multiple trips to the market each month to select and purchase first-hand. Estimates of the size of the online groceries market vary to some extent. Analysts at Cowen Group expect online grocery spending to grow from about $33 billion in 2016 to $70 billion by 2021.

The most closely-watched online grocer in the industry today is FreshDirect LLC, a unique business launched in 2001. FreshDirect is an online retail grocery business serving customers in New York City and the surrounding areas. It offers fresh food and grocery items, including fruits and vegetables, meat, seafood, deli items, cheese, dairy, coffee, tea, bakery goods, pasta and frozen food as well as kosher, gluten free, local and organic produce, health and beauty items and wine. It also provides catering services and a full line of ready-to-heat meals prepared by its on-staff chefs. FreshDirect owns and operates a 300,000-square-foot state-of-the-art processing facility, which enables the company to process and ship fresh meats, produce and dairy products quickly and efficiently. The company is also sometimes able to offer lower prices than traditional retail grocers, due to the lack of the need to operate expensive retail stores. Products may be delivered in the mornings if the order is placed by 7 p.m. the previous day and in the evenings if placed by 11 p.m. Deliveries are made from 6:30 a.m.-11:00 p.m. seven days a week. Faster delivery is available

through a service called Foodkick. Customers can also pick up their orders at the distribution facility. The firm served select counties in New York, New Jersey, Connecticut, Pennsylvania and Delaware. FreshDirect customers have the ability to shop by lifestyle, by clicking on gluten-free, kosher, organic or other groups. Satisfaction is 100% guaranteed.

Peapod, an aggressive home grocery delivery service that has been in business since 1989, has built a base of online shoppers slowly but surely. Peapod had a presence in 24 major cities and suburban areas as of early 2019, including cities in Massachusetts, Virginia, Maryland, Wisconsin, Washington, D.C., Connecticut, New York, Rhode Island, Illinois, Indiana and New Jersey. Peapod entered the New York City market for the first time in 2011, where it must compete directly against FreshDirect. Peapod spent $94 million building a warehouse in Jersey City, New Jersey in 2014. Customers order online via Peapod.com and, for a fee, receive home delivery of their groceries, which are packed at warehouses near participating supermarkets. Despite its lengthy history and wealth of experience, Peapod struggled financially at first. It was acquired in 2001 by one of the world's largest supermarket chains, European-based Royal Ahold, through its Ahold USA unit.

Amazon.com joined the online grocery market in mid-2006. Amazon started by offering only non-perishable items via its normal website. However, it soon began a special service in select regions, where it accepts online orders and makes deliveries of fresh produce, dairy, meats and fish. In late 2014, Amazon launched Prime Now, which delivers groceries and consumer goods in as little as one to two hours. Amazon has been aggressively rolling out warehouses in major cities all over the U.S. to serve its growing Prime Now business. In late 2016, Amazon opened its first brick and mortar grocery store called Amazon Go in Seattle, Washington. The 1,800 square-foot store offers prepared foods and grocery staples, and requires shoppers to scan a smartphone app linked to an Amazon account upon arrival. The app maintains a virtual cart of the items selected by the shopper, and charges the related account accordingly when the shopper leaves the store, without any interaction with a human cashier. Initially open only to Amazon employees for testing, the company opened the store to the public in 2017. Later stores may offer curbside pickup service.

In 2017, the firm acquired specialty super market firm Whole Foods Market, Inc. for $13.7 billion, sending shockwaves through the grocery industry. This is an extension of Amazon's grocery strategy, which is to become a top-five U.S. grocery retailer by 2025. Reaching this goal would generate more than $30 billion in annual food and beverage spending on Amazon.com and its other web sites.

Wal-Mart offers Walmart Grocery, a pickup and delivery service in which online orders can be picked up at store drive-through lanes, often on the same day. The firm also offers same day delivery in select U.S. markets, and planned to offer it in more than 1,000 stores. In 2018, the retail giant began testing grocery delivery using Spark Delivery, with plans to offer the service in 100 U.S. cities in 2019. Online grocery shopping is rapidly becoming commonplace at major supermarket chains, with consumers' options ranging from ordering online and picking up curbside, to delivery to the home. For example, the massive grocery firm Kroger offers a click and collect service called ClickList in stores nationwide, including many of its subsidiary brands such as Fred Meyer and Smith's.

Another twist on grocery shopping online is Instacart, a San Francisco-based startup that models online shopping, somewhat on the same business model as Uber. Customers use an app to enter a list of groceries and other items they want and nearby shoppers pick up the items and deliver them using their own cars, bikes or other transportation. Shoppers are independent contractors. This work may be attractive to people like students or stay-at-home parents who want to control their own schedules while making extra money. Instacart charges a delivery fee and marks up store prices about 20% for each item delivered. In November 2017, Instacart and Albertsons Companies announced an agreement in which Instacart will provide the grocer with on-demand, same day delivery service. In December 2017, Target Corporation announced its $550 million acquisition of grocery delivery startup Shipt.

Online grocery shoppers tend to be busy professionals, time-challenged parents of small children or people who largely stay at home because of a lack of mobility. They tend to be better educated and make larger average purchases than walk-in store customers. They also tend to be very loyal, because they are seeking a timesaving convenience. Watch for steady growth in online grocery sales, driven largely by marketing initiatives at existing supermarket firms rather than startups.

Grocery delivery in China has become commonplace. Dozens of startup companies, including Quick Bee, New Dada and Dianwoda, employ couriers on electric motorbikes who pick up orders from supermarkets, convenience stores and independent shops for quick delivery. The firms charge for each delivery (starting at about five yuan or 72 cents U.S. per package) and receive commissions from retailers. Retail giants Alibaba Group Holding and JD.com are investing heavily in these startups. Alibaba invested nearly 1 billion yuan ($150 million) in Dianwoda in 2016, and New Dada is 40% owned by JD.com.

26) Designers and Manufacturers Bypass the Middleman with Direct-to-Consumer Online Business Models

Digital marketing, the power of e-commerce and today's simple access to global manufacturers have combined to launch another interesting trend: companies that claim to source their merchandise at the same manufacturers used by well-known brands, and then sell, via their web sites only, high quality items direct to consumers are modest prices. The intent is to bypass middlemen and retail stores, and thus offer very high value.

New apparel companies are among the leaders in this field. One of the better known companies with this business model is Everlane, www.everlane.com, which states, "We spend months finding the best factories around the world—the very same ones that produce your favorite designer labels." Online apparel firms with similar business models include JustFab, ShoeDazzle and BirchBox. In fact, the list has gotten very long.

Such companies must offer excellent service, reasonable prices and cost-free returns, in addition to a compelling merchandise line, in order to competitive. Even when they do so, there is reason to question whether or not they can compete successfully against companies such as Ralph Lauren that have massive supply chains, unbeatable design and marketing teams and immense buying power. If apparel manufacturers that rely on traditional marketing feel threatened by online-only, off-brand upstarts, it would be simple enough for them to launch their own businesses based on this business model, using a different brand name in order to avoid sales channel conflicts.

Meanwhile, brands and logos owned by companies like Ralph Lauren are extremely powerful in the minds of consumers and are exceptionally difficult for smaller firms to compete against. There is also the "wait for name brands to go on sale" mentality that is now standard in consumer behavior. That is, department stores and specialty clothing retailers have essentially trained consumers to expect their favorite apparel brands to be on sale. If you see something new that you like in stores today at full retail price, you know that it will almost undoubtedly be marked down by 25% to 40% soon. At the end of the season it may be marked down by as much as 70%.

Nonetheless, there are some niche markets where the direct to consumer model may make a lot of sense. Eyeglasses are a standout in this regard. Once a consumer's eye exam is completed and a prescription written, glasses can be made virtually anywhere. Traditionally, however, consumers have ordered their eyeglasses (in particular, expensive designer frames) in expensive retail store fronts that operate at high overhead. Consumers can try out various styles of frames in these stores, and turn over their prescription to a sales clerk so that glasses can be custom ordered. However, the actual manufacturing of lenses, and their assembly into frames, will be done elsewhere.

This is where a successful new company called Warby Parker comes in. Its founder saw opportunity in this multi-step supply chain and notoriously high prices. At www.warbyparker.com, customers can select from basic frame styles, upload their prescriptions and order attractive glasses for around $100 to $300, which is a comparative bargain. While Warby Parker has built a considerable following with its online business model, its strategy includes both bricks and clicks, as it is opening a growing number of retail showrooms in major cities in the U.S. (Of course, there has long been a modestly-priced alternative in the eyeglasses market: companies that operate hundreds of storefronts that offer both eye exams and frame selections. After the exam and sale, the eyeglasses are manufactured in a lab owned by the same firm that owns and operates the stores. This vertical integration can offer relatively low prices at high volume, but may not appeal to fashion conscious consumers.)

Large numbers of direct-to-consumer businesses are springing up offering everything from custom shirts to bed linens to shoes. Deal Décor sells furniture under this model. Crane and Canopy has gotten good press coverage of its business model, which is very similar to that of Everlane. This firm, at www.craneandcanopy.com, sells sheets, duvet covers and other bed linens that it claims are from the same factories, with the same quality textiles, as those offered by designer labels. Here again, the price is lower than standard retail prices found in stores, at least until such stores put their goods on sale.

The business of shipping goods directly from manufacturers in China to consumers around the world is booming. Chinese retailer LightInTheBox offers more than 700,000 items, from wedding dresses to table linens to iPhone chargers to faucets, at competitive prices that are free of middleman markups. Costs are kept down further by LightInTheBox's proximity to its suppliers, so that its inventory is kept low. The company does business in 27 languages, so it employs part-time workers from around the world who connect with customers via phone and email.

27) Fashion Rental Grows Thanks to Online Apparel Pioneer Rent the Runway

Growing numbers of women are expanding their wardrobes, at least temporarily, by renting clothes and accessories. Users may rent selected items for several days at a fraction of the items' retail prices, or subscribe to a monthly service which likely includes several items per shipment.

Rent the Runway, an online site that rents dresses, jewelry and accessories, makes luxury affordable to its 6 million members. The site offers 65,000 dresses (many from top designers such as Badgley Mischka, Herve Leger and Vera Wang) and 25,000 pieces of jewelry which members rent for a few days and return in prepaid and addressed Mylar UPS envelopes. The company's research found that on average, an American woman purchases 64 new pieces of clothing per year, of which about 50% are worn only once. The company's warehouse operations are housed in a 160,000-square-foot facility. In addition to packing and shipping, the facility has been carefully designed to incorporate dry-cleaning and sterilization of returned apparel, making Rent the Runway the largest dry-cleaning operation, in one building, in the U.S.

Starting in 2017, Rent the Runway varied its offerings from one-time, one--item rentals to monthly subscriptions, including RTR Unlimited which allows the rental of unlimited numbers of pieces on rotation with no return dates. The company reports that most people wear only 20% of their closets. This indicates that a continual stream of rented attire may have great appeal to certain consumers.

Meanwhile, retailer Ann Taylor launched its Infinite Style rental service in 2017. The online monthly subscription service allows members to receive three items per shipment, and up to three shipments per month, with the next shipment sent when the previous three items are returned. The company pays for shipping.

There are a number of fashion rental web sites, each with a particular focus. For example, Gwynnie Bee offers plus-size subscribers access to clothing in U.S. sizes 10-32, while Style Lend offers subscribers designer clothing from members' closets, generally in sizes 0, 2 or 4. The Mr. Collection offers men's clothing to monthly subscribers.

Top Fashion Rental Companies:
Gwynnie Bee, closet.gwynniebee.com
Le Tote, www.letote.com
Rent the Runway, www.renttherunway.com
Style Lend, www.stylelend.com
The Ms. Collection, www.themscollection.com
The Mr. Collection, www.themrcollection.com

---

28) Light-Weight Satellites and Solar-Powered Drones Used for Internet Access and Whole Earth Imaging

A company called Planet Labs, Inc., which builds small satellites for Earth observation, has raised significant investor financing. It operates under the brand "Planet," and utilizes commonly available electronics components to manufacture and launch satellites at breakthrough prices. In early 2017, it announced that it had acquired Google's own satellite business unit, known as Terra Bella, in exchange for stock in Planet. This gives Planet an excellent base of very high-resolution imaging satellites to complement the medium resolution satellites that have been Planet's main focus. Planet planned an early 2017 launch of 88 satellites to add to its existing base of 60. Earlier, Planet had picked up five satellites with its acquisition of RapidEye.

Meanwhile, Facebook has been working on a cooperative called Internet.org with Samsung, Nokia, Qualcomm and Ericsson in an effort to cut costs of broadband via smartphones. The hope is to lower the costs for a unit of wireless access to 1% of 2012 levels by 2022. (That is, the organization thinks that current access costs are about 100 times too expensive to be useful to remote, extremely low-income people who currently are not online.) This is an extremely ambitious goal. Cuts might be made by improving network and smartphone software efficiency. For example, Facebook is developing strategies to reduce the average amount of data used by its Android mobile app from 12 megabytes per day to 1 megabyte.

ViaSat, Inc. provides broadband access for passengers on JetBlue Airways and Qantas Airways using advanced technology installed on a small number of large, extra-powerful satellites. The company is working on ViaSat-3, its most powerful spacecraft to date, to increase its coverage area based on shifting demand. The craft is planned for launch into orbit by mid-2019 with service beginning in 2020.

Facebook has been investigating solar-powered drones, as well as satellites and lasers that might deliver internet access to the underserved billions (Facebook hit a snag in early 2016 when Indian regulators banned free mobile data programs that favor certain internet services over others).

The end goal of all of these ideas is to boost global internet usage, which would mean billions of new potential users for Google and Facebook. Google began the effort in 2012 by offering users in some developing countries free access to Gmail and simple searches through partnerships with cellphone carriers.

Another concept, low-orbit satellites are being pushed by O3b and other firms because they offer much faster internet speeds than traditional satellites. This is due to the fact that data is transmitted over a much shorter distance. Google is an investor in O3b.

Cruise ships are perfect customers for fast internet access via low-orbit satellites. RCL (Royal Caribbean Lines), one of the world's largest cruise lines, is working with O3b to offer its passengers the ultimate in floating connectivity. (Users report that speed is definitely higher than on other cruise ships, but still subject to the fluctuations that satellite services is known for.) RCL claims that it offers more bandwidth than every other cruise ship in the world combined. Guests are encouraged to Tweet, Skype, Stream movies (using accounts with DIRECTV, Netflix or Hulu), connect with friends or play Xbox Live with gamers worldwide. Its newest ships even offer live, global gaming rooms.

OneWeb, a startup headquartered in Florida, plans to launch as many as 900 small satellites at lower orbits than those traditionally employed by communications satellites. It plans to target airlines and military customers in addition to disaster relief and emergency services.

SpaceX, a rocket manufacturer backed by PayPal founder and Tesla automotive executive Elon Musk, wants to fly more complex satellites. While flying at the same low altitude as those proposed by OneWeb, SpaceX's unit would offer faster data transmission speeds over long distances than that offered by land-based cable connections. In addition to basic internet access to rural areas, SpaceX could serve the needs of businesses with time-sensitive demands such as financial traders.

SPOTLIGHT: OneWeb and Low-Orbit Satellites

Private space launch firms and advanced technologies that enable the manufacture of very small, very inexpensive satellites will soon enable much less expensive internet access and data communications in many parts of the world.

OneWeb Ltd. has designed an advanced, low-earth-orbit satellite constellation to provide global coverage, particularly to parts of the earth that currently lack reliable or affordable internet access. Its constellation will eventually consist of as many as 900 satellites.

OneWeb's satellites are designed to orbit relatively close to the earth, allowing for better internet access speeds, while they interlock with each other electronically to create coverage over the entire planet. Small, low-cost user terminals will communicate with the satellite network and provide wireless internet access. These terminals will provide connectivity with no change in latency (speed) during satellite handovers in order to ensure continuous quality of voice, gaming and web surfing experience.

Compared to traditional satellites, OneWeb units have fewer components, and are lighter in weight, easier to manufacture and cheaper to launch. The satellites contain on-board propulsion and state-of-the-art positioning GPS sensors that ground-track their placements within meters. The on-board propulsion systems are capable of performing maneuvers to steer clear of space debris. When an OneWeb satellite nears the end of its service life, it will de-orbit automatically. The initial phase of the constellation launch is slated to begin by early 2019. Investors in the firm include Qualcomm, Virgin Group, Airbus Group SE and Coca-Cola.

Space launch rocket services have been contracted to Arianespace SA and Virgin Galactic. OneWeb broke ground on its $85 million high-volume satellite manufacturing plant in Exploration Park, Florida during 2017.

---

29) "Sharing Economy" Gains Market Share in Travel with Online Sites Like Airbnb, HomeAway and Many Global Competitors

One of the most remarkable growth stories in e-commerce has been the advent of new ways to book non-traditional accommodations for travelers. This "sharing economy" (also known as collaborative consumption) affords consumers the ability to rent or borrow everything from hotel rooms to cars to private homes. Revenue from U.S. private accommodations was expected to reach $36.6 billion in 2018, according to a Phocuswright report.

An early leader was VRBO, which stands for Vacation Rental by Owner, a site that allows property owners, especially owners of second homes and resort condos, to advertise their properties online to people seeking vacation accommodations. VRBO was acquired by startup HomeAway, Inc., a firm that originated when venture capital firm Austin Ventures agreed to back entrepreneur Brian Sharples in this promising business sector. The staff of Austin, Texas-based HomeAway includes many executives who were formerly at Austin-based online information company Hoovers.com. HomeAway also owns Travelmob, a sharing-economy accommodations site focused on Asia. HomeAway was acquired by Expedia in 2015 for $3.9 billion.

Booking.com, a major presence in online hotel room booking and a subsidiary of Priceline, has is also offering shared-space and vacation property listings on its site.

The biggest disruptor to the hotel industry is San Francisco-based Airbnb, Inc., founded in 2008. Airbnb.com members who are willing to let travelers stay in their homes can post their information, including pricing and accommodation details. The accommodations range from a bedroom in an occupied house or apartment to a luxury apartment or condo reserved entirely for the guest. In turn, travelers may search in a given market for members who are willing to accommodate them. Airbnb is utilized in more than 81,000 cities in 191 countries. Since its founding, the company has expanded to list more than 5 million accommodations. Members are encouraged to write reviews describing the positive and/or negative aspects of their stays. These reviews are partially encouraged so that renters and travelers may view profiles and feedback before staying in homes or letting others stay in their homes, thereby reducing the risk of danger or other negative situations. The Airbnb network is also connected to Facebook, allowing members to search the social networking platform for additional information regarding certain hosts and guests. Airbnb charges room owners a 3% host fee and an additional fee of 6% to 12% per guest. The average commission is about 12% of total revenues. The typical guest stays longer, on average, than a guest in a traditional hotel.

Airbnb expanded to offer local-led activities in cities around the world in 2016. Activities are varied and may include bike rides, walking tours or fishing trips, to name a few, and are typically provided by Airbnb hosts. In 2018, the company launched Airbnb Plus, a luxury service that matches higher-paying guests with quality-inspected home or apartment rentals.

Airbnb is establishing new standards for hosts with regard to cleanliness, communication and cancellations, and offers a mobile app to facilitate communication between hosts and guests. Hosts are encouraged to earn badges for "business travel ready" listings that offer such amenities as Wi-Fi and hairdryers. In growing numbers of cities, hosts are now required to purchase short-term rental licenses and collect and remit municipal taxes.

Literally hundreds of competitors and imitators have sprung up around the world. Some are focused on particular locales, travelers or types of accommodations. For example, OneFineStay.com (which was acquired by AccorHotels for $170 million in 2016) is focused on renting a curated collection of better homes and condos in major cities, including New York, Paris, Los Angeles and London as well as resort destinations in the Caribbean, Hawaii and Central America, among others.

Despite their wide popularity, room- and home-sharing sites face multiple challenges. Fraud has been a problem, with unscrupulous site members collecting fees for rentals of properties that they claim to own, but are in fact owned by others. Guest safety is a serious issue. There have been accidents, dog bites, even a guest locked into his room by a host seeking sexual favors. At most sites, there are no room inspections and no way to enforce room standards. Guest room rentals may not be covered under a homeowner's insurance policy. Likewise, such rentals may not be allowed under homeowner's association rules and municipal law. Last, but not least, the market may become saturated, with only a limited number of properties available to add to inventory.

Nonetheless, the traditional hotel industry sees room-sharing as a significant competitive threat that is already taking market share. The long-term result may be hotel chains creating their own branded sharing sites, listing both their own hotel properties and rooms or condos owned by others. Hotels may build hybrid properties as well, with apartment towers for room sharing next door to traditional hotel properties. The hotels could run the apartments to high standards, and could build oversized pools, spas and other common area facilities to be shared with guests from the apartments next door.

30) Digital Assistants Include Amazon's Echo and Google's Home/Alexa and Similar Software Power Third-Party Developers

Apple, Google, Amazon and Microsoft are competing to offer the best voice-activated systems that can do anything from reporting the time and weather, to playing music on request, to performing web searches, to telling jokes, to making purchases from internet sites. These platforms utilize the latest in artificial intelligence in order to become more useful over time. Apple's Siri is available on iPhones, iPads, Apple Watches and through an app in some vehicles. Google Now is an app available on a variety of mobile devices as is Microsoft's Cortana app. Amazon's Alexa web app is installed on a gadget called Amazon Echo that sits on a countertop, desk or shelf. Alexa software can be installed on other devices as well. RBC Capital Markets predicts 128 million households will be using Alexa by 2020. Google offers a similar device called Google Home. All of these apps and platforms are voice-activated, and use connections to other apps and systems to find information such as directions, time, date, weather and trivia, or make purchases, which are reported audibly (users can choose their device's voice gender and language). The next step for these handy assistants is the ability to connect with apps relating to climate control, lighting and/or security enabling users to simply say, for example, "Set home temperature to 72 degrees," or "Activate alarm system," and have the action performed, even from remote locations.

Importantly, most systems are open to third-party developers. For example, Amazon has opened "Lex" to developers, which is the artificial intelligence engine behind the Alexa and Echo platforms. Lex is tied into Amazon's AWS cloud computing system. Software and product developers can incorporate Lex, enabling voice-activated or click-activated responsiveness (often in the form of specific task-oriented icons or apps known as "bots"). This gives these developers instant access to extremely powerful cloud computing, artificial intelligence and voice-activation in one easy-to-launch package. Amazon charges a modest fee per thousand uses or data accesses. This ease-of-use has spurred a tidal wave of new product development worldwide, with the potential to revolutionize the manner in which consumers interface with their digital devices and the internet.

Top Voice-Activated Technology Platforms and their Unique Advantages:

Alexa: Owned by Amazon. Connects to Amazon AWS Cloud services, making it easy to embed Alexa software in third-party products.

Siri: Owned by Apple. Siri, already familiar to hundreds of millions of iPhone users worldwide, has evolved into a very sophisticated digital assistant.

Cortana: Owned by Microsoft. Microsoft had deep partnerships and experience with third-party corporate software and technology firms, making this an easy platform for others to embed.

Google Assistant: Owned by Google. Assistant capitalizes on Google's constantly evolving expertise in search and artificial intelligence.

Source: Plunkett Research, Ltd.

---

31) Embedded LTE Wi-Fi and Onboard Apps Incorporated by Auto Makers in New Car Infotainment Systems

Advanced information systems in automobiles, such as the Ford Sync system, utilize Wi-Fi to receive their initial software customization at the factory. For example, Wi-Fi may be used at the plant to load one type of emergency response package for cars intended for sale in the U.S., and another for cars that will be sold in other nations. Now, Tesla and other makers use Wi-Fi to install software updates to their vehicles.

As a next step, several car makers, including Ford, GM, Chrysler and Volkswagen are turning their vehicles into Wi-Fi hotspots, so that passengers can use their laptops, tablet computers and other devices on the road.

As advanced wireless broadband systems, such as LTE, are ultrafast, such systems can offer passengers access to conduct business, watch videos, listen to music of their choice and send emails. The GENIVI Alliance (www.genivi.org) has been formed by several auto industry leaders in order to create an open standard for "In-Vehicle Infotainment" or IVI. Members include GM, BMW, Volvo, Honda, Nissan and parts maker Visteon.

One way to enable onboard internet hotspots is to create a system whereby an owner's smartphone becomes a single internet connection for all passengers and all of their devices. However, auto makers are now embedding independent wireless

receivers into their cars—systems that require their own wireless service contracts. GM is offering embedded 4G broadband provided by AT&T for onboard Wi-Fi. (GM's popular OnStar telematics system has long featured built-in wireless communications for directions and emergency phone calls.)

Meanwhile, car makers are rushing to develop sophisticated smartphone apps and onboard apps that enable owners to customize and communicate with their cars. Ford's AppLink service is available on most Ford models, including the Mustang, Fusion Hybrid, Focus, F-150 pickup and the E-Series van. Ford's SYNC already offers real-time traffic information, turn-by-turn directions and personalized sports and weather reports, in addition to hands-free operation of cellphones and sound systems.

Under new developments in AppLink, car owners will be able to download entertainment of their choice to SYNC for listening while they drive. The wildly popular Pandora music service was among the first offerings. But this is just the beginning of the services apps will bring to onboard SYNC infotainment systems. Owners will be able to download travel and time management apps, such as systems that will alert them to changes in the status of flights while in route to the airport. Voice-activated apps may even enable drivers to update their social media such as Facebook or Twitter.

Meanwhile, Ford wants apps to enable owners to better manage their cars remotely. Such apps will include systems to diagnose car performance and maintenance. SYNC Destination enables owners to enter a destination into a smartphone at their convenience, and then beam it to the car for turn-by-turn guidance later. A car maker's ability to offer the maximum synchronization with a consumer's smartphone in a safe and entertaining manner is rapidly becoming one of the most hotly contested fields in the automobile market.

Toyota, GM, Tesla and Mercedes-Benz, among others, are also jumping on the app access wagon in varying degrees. At Tesla, for example, new models sport 17-inch video monitors in the dashboard with USB plugs for internet access. At GM, the touch screen measures eight inches and can be activated by voice, touch or controls mounted on the steering wheel. Mercedes has developed an app called DriveStyle, and BMW offers an app program called ConnectedDrive.

Google's Android Auto as well as Apple's CarPlay stream phone data through a car's USB port to a monitor set into the dashboard. Proponents say the displays keep drivers from looking down at their smartphones or dashboards. Detractors are concerned that the displays are simply more distractions from the road.

An advanced system is installed in the new BMW 7-series sedan which includes the ability for the car to park itself when a driver exits the vehicle and presses a button on a remote control. The 7-series also has a color heads-up display that projects information on the windshield with 75% more display area than previous models, and the infotainment center offers its own app store. In addition, the vehicle has gesture control, allowing drivers to accept or reject phone calls and adjust sound system volume by waving their hands.

Apple has agreements with a number of auto manufacturers including Audi, BMW, GM, Honda and Toyota to install its Siri voice command service in new vehicles. The service utilizes "eyes free" buttons that engage Siri so that the driver can request information from the internet on everything from weather to navigation to nearby restaurant reviews.

The use of digital assistants such as Amazon's Alexa is expanding into vehicles. BMW announced in late 2016 that its "Connected" services would enable Alexa users to lock car doors or check tire pressures remotely. Ford is also integrating Alexa into its Fusion and Escape models. While driving, users can receive alerts regarding shopping lists and nearby stores that offer the necessary items. Mercedes-Benz offers a similar feature called In Car Office, which integrates Microsoft Exchange calendars into vehicles.

Samsung Electronics, with its subsidiary Harman International Industries (which Samsung acquired in 2016 for $2 billion), is working on a fully digital vehicle cockpit design featuring a bank of screens stretching from one side of the car to the other. Drivers will be able to adjust controls in the vehicle or use smart apps to command changes via digital assistants at home or at the office. Passengers will be able to watch streaming video or surf the internet. Samsung hopes to have the system installed in vehicles by the 2021-2022 model year.

There is some concern that connectivity opens the door for hackers who might take control of crucial systems such as braking, steering or engine startup and shutdown. Hackers also might be able to unlock doors and drive off using cellular, Bluetooth or other wireless connections. Manufacturers are working on ways to secure automotive computer systems. Toyota, for example, programs its onboard

computers to recognize outside commands and reject them.

32) Subscription Fashion Services Grow, Including Stitch Fix

Stitch Fix (www.stitchfix.com) is an online apparel shopping service. Customers complete a Style Profile of sizes and style and price preferences, and then a personal stylist selects and ships five pieces of clothing for shipment. Customers try on the items at home, buying and keeping the things they like and shipping the rest back at no charge. These custom selections are shipped to each customer on a regular basis. Similar services include Trunk Club, owned by Nordstrom (www.trunkclub.com), and Amazon's new Prime Wardrobe service.

Fashion rental site Rent the Runway offers wardrobe subscription services called RTR Update and RTR Unlimited that allow subscribers to rent four pieces of clothing per month or unlimited pieces on rotation. Retailer Ann Taylor also offers a subscription service, Infinite Style, that has no time limits and offers unlimited exchanges.

33) Amazon Becomes One of the World's Leading Sellers of Apparel and Shoes

Amazon.com is attempting to dominate online fashion shopping in the same way it has revolutionized other retail categories including books, electronics and groceries. It first jumped into the fashion pool with the acquisition of Shopbop in 2006, followed by the purchase of online footwear site Zappos in 2009 and discount luxury clothing and accessories site MyHabit in 2011. Starting in 2013, Amazon began taking on high fashion, working out deals with designers such as Michael Kors, Calvin Klein, Catherine Malandrino and Vivienne Westwood. In 2016, Amazon launched seven in-house fashion lines, including Lark & Ro women's clothing, Franklin Tailored men's suits and accessories and Scout + Ro children's clothing.

The company invested heavily in improving selection and photography of the items for better presentation. Amazon's Prime Wardrobe service lets customers subscribe to a service that ships apparel on a regular basis. Members can try on the clothing, keep what they like, and return the rest with no shipping charges.

Well Fargo & Co. forecasted that Amazon would surpass T.J. Maxx (owned by TJX Cos.) and Macy's, Inc. to become the second-largest seller of apparel and footwear in the U.S. in 2017. By 2021, analysts at Cowen forecast that Amazon's share of the U.S.

apparel market will reach 16%. Analysts at Nomura estimated that Amazon may control $45 to $85 billion of the global retail apparel market by 2020.

The giant online retailer was granted a patent in 2017 for on-demand apparel panel cutting and manufacturing, making Amazon part of the "click, buy and make" movement. In addition, the firm has developed a technology system utilizing a camera and scanning software to automatically take customers' measurements and upload them to Amazon accounts. The system is powered by Amazon's Alexa tabletop personal assistant.

Amazon has also invested heavily in tools and content that can help online customers make better choices while they shop. For example, it operates a massive photography studio where models try on apparel and shoes. This studio makes hundreds of thousands of apparel and shoe photos yearly for use on the Amazon websites. They also may make notes about how the items fit. Amazon also posts comments from customers about how items fit. For example, items may be rated as fits as expected, too small, somewhat small, somewhat large or too large. This not only drives customer satisfaction and confidence, it also reduces return shipping costs.

Chapter 2

E-COMMERCE & INTERNET BUSINESS STATISTICS

Contents:

E-Commerce & Internet Business Statistics and Market Size Overview

Worldwide E-Commerce & Internet Market	Amount	Units	Year	Source
Total Retail Sales, Worldwide[1]	23,882	Bil. US$	2018	eMarketer
Previous Year Total Retail Sales, Worldwide[1]	22,588	Bil. US$	2017	eMarketer
Retail E-Commerce Sales, Worldwide [2]	2,842	Bil. US$	2018	eMarketer
Previous Year Retail E-Commerce Sales, Worldwide[2]	2,304	Bil. US$	2017	eMarketer
Digital Buyers Penetration, Worldwide[2]	47.3	%	2018	eMarketer
Digital Advertising Spending (including Online & Mobile), Worldwide	273.3	Bil. US$	2018	eMarketer
Digital Ad Spending as a Percent of All Ad Spending, Worldwide	43.5	%	2018	eMarketer
Percentage of Individuals Using the Internet, Worldwide	51.2	%	2018	ITU
Percentage of Households with Internet Access, Worldwide	57.8	%	2018	ITU
Fixed (wired)-Broadband Subscriptions, Worldwide	14.1	Per 100 Inhabitants	2018	ITU
Active Mobile-broadband Subscriptions	69.3	Per 100 inhabitants	2018	ITU
Mobile Cellular Subscriptions, Worldwide	107	Per 100 inhabitants	2018	ITU

U.S. E-Commerce & Internet Market	Amount	Units	Year	Source
Total Retail Sales, U.S.[1]	5,343	Bil. US$	2018	PRE
Previous Year Total Retail Sales, U.S.[1]	5,074	Bil. US$	2017	Census
Retail E-Commerce Sales, U.S.[3]	526.1	Bil. US$	2018	eMarketer
Previous Year Retail E-Commerce Sales, U.S.[3]	454.9	Bil. US$	2017	eMarketer
Digital Advertising Spending, U.S. (including Online & Mobile)	125.8	Bil. US$	2019	eMarketer
Digital Ad Spending as a Percent of All Ad Spending, U.S.	55.0	%	2019	eMarketer
Internet Users, U.S.[4]	284.0	Million	2019	eMarketer
Percent of U.S. Adults Who Use the Internet	89	%	2018	PEW
High Speed Internet Subscribers, U.S., Fixed, Home & Business	111.3	Million	Dec-18	PRE
High Speed Internet Subscribers, U.S., Wireless, incl. Smartphone	322.4	Million	Dec-18	PRE
Home Broadband Adoption, U.S.	65	%	Jan-18	PEW

[1] Including food services.

[2] Includes travel, digital downloads and event tickets purchased via any digital channel. Excludes gambling.

[3] Includes travel, digital downloads and event tickets purchased via any digital channel. Excludes gambling, event tickets.

[4] Includes individuals of any age who use the internet from any location via any device at least once per month.

ITU = International Telecommunication Union   PEW = Pew Internet & American Life Project
Census = U.S. Census Bureau   PRE = Plunkett Research Estimate

Estimated Quarterly U.S. Retail Sales, Total & E-Commerce:
1st Quarter 2009-3rd Quarter 2018

*(In Millions of US$; Not Seasonally Adjusted, Holiday & Trading-Day Differences;
Does Not Include Food Services)*

Quarter	Retail Sales in US$ Mil.		E-commerce as a % of Total Retail Sales	% Change Over Same Quarter Previous Year	
	Total	E-commerce[*]		Total Sales	E-commerce
2009 Q1	828,531	32,284	3.9	-12.8	-5.8
2009 Q2	905,572	32,924	3.6	-11.9	-3.9
2009 Q3	911,423	34,494	3.8	-8.8	3.0
2009 Q4	966,945	45,805	4.7	1.0	15.7
2010 Q1	875,915	37,059	4.2	5.7	14.8
2010 Q2	960,943	38,467	4.0	6.1	16.8
2010 Q3	950,872	40,075	4.2	4.3	16.2
2010 Q4	1,030,318	54,320	5.3	6.6	18.6
2011 Q1	943,598	44,158	4.7	7.7	19.2
2011 Q2	1,034,613	45,294	4.4	7.7	17.7
2011 Q3	1,027,247	45,979	4.5	8.0	14.7
2011 Q4	1,097,494	64,133	5.8	6.5	18.1
2012 Q1	1,015,512	51,403	5.1	7.6	16.4
2012 Q2	1,078,406	52,183	4.8	4.2	15.2
2012 Q3	1,067,088	53,436	5.0	3.9	16.2
2012 Q4	1,141,223	73,235	6.4	4.0	14.2
2013 Q1	1,040,436	57,898	5.6	2.5	12.6
2013 Q2	1,121,936	59,637	5.3	4.0	14.3
2013 Q3	1,117,586	60,624	5.4	4.7	13.5
2013 Q4	1,178,492	82,558	7.0	3.3	12.7
2014 Q1	1,061,162	65,593	6.2	2.0	13.3
2014 Q2	1,177,460	68,772	5.8	4.9	15.3
2014 Q3	1,170,088	70,103	6.0	4.7	15.6
2014 Q4	1,230,730	93,970	7.6	4.4	13.8
2015 Q1	1,084,227	74,695	6.9	2.2	13.9
2015 Q2	1,194,236	78,357	6.6	1.4	13.9
2015 Q3	1,193,089	80,159	6.7	2.0	14.3
2015 Q4	1,254,441	106,953	8.5	1.9	13.8
2016 Q1	1,121,354	85,361	7.6	3.4	14.3
2016 Q2	1,219,462	90,166	7.4	2.1	15.1
2016 Q3	1,218,452	91,898	7.5	2.1	14.6
2016 Q4	1,297,066	121,686	9.4	3.4	13.8
2017 Q1	1,161,416	97,511	8.4	3.6	14.2
2017 Q2	1,273,412	104,407	8.2	4.4	15.8
2017 Q3	1,270,345	106,241	8.4	4.3	15.6
2017 Q4	1,368,553	141,719	10.4	5.5	16.5
2018 Q1	1,225,399	113,244	9.2	5.5	16.1
2018 Q2	1,341,878	120,479	9.0	5.4	15.4
2018 Q3[P]	1,332,071	121,460	9.1	4.9	14.3

[P] Preliminary Estimate.
[*] E-commerce sales are sales of goods and services over the Internet, an extranet, Electronic Data Interchange (EDI) or other online system. Payment may or may not be made online.
Source: U.S. Census Bureau
Plunkett Research, ® Ltd.
www.plunkettresearch.com

E-Commerce Related Services Quarterly Revenue, U.S.: 2017-2018

(In Millions of US$)

NAICS Code[1]	Kind of business	2018		2017		% of Total[2]
		2Q*	1Q	4Q	3Q	
5112	Software publishers	67,528	64,376	64,854	57,722	100.0
	Government	5,056	4,751	4,769	4,882	7.5
	Business	43,684	41,149	40,310	36,586	64.7
	Households consumers & individuals	18,788	18,476	19,775	16,254	27.8
5171	Wired telecommunications carriers	82,492	81,810	83,320	82,619	100.0
	Government	2,715	2,732	2,669	2,729	3.3
	Business	25,631	25,705	26,004	25,435	31.1
	Households consumers & individuals	54,146	53,373	54,647	54,455	65.6
5172	Wireless telecommunications carriers (except satellite)	66,599	65,699	69,814	65,398	100.0
	Government	1,531	1,497	1,506	1,379	2.3
	Business	23,150	22,709	23,994	22,402	34.8
	Households consumers & individuals	41,918	41,493	44,314	41,617	62.9
518	Data processing, hosting & related services	46,371	43,721	44,251	40,977	100.0
	Government	S	S	S	S	S
	Business	S	S	40,657	37,596	S
	Households consumers & individuals	1,054	1,104	S	S	2.3
519	Other information services (including Internet publishing & broadcasting & web search portals)	51,871	48,463	52,839	45,987	100.0
	Government	S	S	S	S	S
	Business	S	S	S	S	S
	Households consumers & individuals	S	S	S	S	S
5415	Computer systems design & related services	100,261	95,283	97,025	95,877	100.0
	Government	28,112	S	S	S	28.0
	Business	S	67,834	67,691	S	S
	Households consumers & individuals	828	S	S	S	0.8

Notes: Estimates are not adjusted for seasonal variation or for price changes and are based on data from the Quarterly Services Survey. For additional information see www.census.gov/services.

S = Estimate does not meet publication standards because of high sampling variability (coefficient of variation is greater than 30%) or poor response quality (total quantity response rate is less than 50%). Unpublished estimates derived from this table by subtraction are subject to these same limitations and should not be attributed to the U.S. Census Bureau.

D = Estimate in table is withheld to avoid disclosing data of individual companies.

[1] For a full description of the NAICS codes used in this table, see www.census.gov/eos/www/naics/.

[2] Percentages for class of customer using 2nd quarter 2018 numbers.

* Preliminary estimate.

Source: U.S. Census Bureau
Plunkett Research, ® Ltd.
www.plunkettresearch.com

U.S. Retail Trade Sales, Total & E-commerce: 2015-2018

(In Millions of US$; Latest Year Available)

NAICS Code	Kind of Business	2018		2017		2016		2015	
		Total*	E-comm.*	Total	E-comm.	Total	E-comm.	Total	E-comm.
	Total Retail Trade	**5,342,633**	**486,180**	**5,073,726**	**449,878**	**4,856,334**	**389,111**	**4,725,993**	**340,164**
441	Motor vehicles & parts dealers	920,389	NA	892,924	NA	1,144,419	32,016	1,094,112	31,154
442	Furniture & home furnishings stores	87,225	NA	83,645	NA	111,468	1,076	106,570	985
443	Electronics & appliance stores	69,116	NA	67,386	NA	98,780	2,186	103,658	2,209
444	Building materials & garden equipment & supplies stores	296,391	NA	285,316	NA	349,285	2,251	331,611	1,921
445	Food & beverage stores	550,560	NA	530,663	NA	700,816	2,463	685,381	1,932
446	Health & personal care stores	254,248	NA	244,947	NA	326,879	D	315,244	D
447	Gasoline Stations	388,529	NA	338,028	NA	418,700	D	444,027	D
448	Clothing & clothing accessories stores	190,136	NA	181,073	NA	259,617	7,843	255,798	6,731
451	Sporting goods, hobby, book & music stores	57,653	NA	59,779	NA	86,596	2,219	85,701	2,059
452	General merchandise stores	509,152	NA	492,067	NA	676,554	318	674,889	202
453	Miscellaneous store retailers	99,380	NA	95,358	NA	122,467	3,723	119,350	3,470
454	Nonstore retailers	481,007	NA	436,388	NA	560,753	334,197	509,652	288,699
4541	Electronic shopping & mail order houses	621,354	441,161	545,047	381532.9*	487,782	332,681	433,987	287,333

Notes: Estimates are not adjusted for price changes and include data for businesses with or without paid employees.

D = Denotes an estimate withheld to avoid disclosing data of individual companies; data are included in higher-level totals.

NA = Not Available

*Plunkett Research Estimate

Source: U.S. Census Bureau
Plunkett Research, ® Ltd.
www.plunkettresearch.com

Total & E-commerce Sales for Electronic Shopping & Mail-Order Houses, by Merchandise Line, U.S.: 2015-2018

(In Millions of US$; Latest Year Available)

Merchandise Lines[1]	2018		2017		2016		2015	
	Total*	E-comm.*	Total	E-comm.*	Total	E-comm.	Total	E-comm.
Total Electronic Shopping & Mail-Order Houses (NAICS 4541)	**621,354**	**441,161**	**545,047**	**381,533**	**487,782**	**332,681**	**433,987**	**287,333**
Books & magazines	NA	NA	NA	NA	14,732	13,100	13,966	12,233
Clothing & clothing accessories (includes footwear)	NA	NA	NA	NA	68,281	59,135	61,876	52,258
Computer hardware	NA	NA	NA	NA	23,595	18,686	22,275	15,302
Computer software	NA	NA	NA	NA	11,834	10,550	9,299	8,292
Drugs, health aids & beauty aids	NA	NA	NA	NA	129,459	29,692	116,187	24,226
Electronics & appliances	NA	NA	NA	NA	43,993	39,433	38,514	34,316
Food, beer & wine	NA	NA	NA	NA	11,371	9,129	9,285	7,062
Furniture & home furnishings	NA	NA	NA	NA	44,077	39,510	37,110	32,728
Jewelry					9,192	6,882	9,053	6,542
Audio and video recordings (includes purchased downloads)	NA	NA	NA	NA	9,558	8,665	8,665	7,780
Office equipment & supplies	NA	NA	NA	NA	10,688	9,069	9,265	9,070
Sporting Goods	NA	NA	NA	NA	15,730	13,389	13,697	11,737
Toys, hobby goods & games	NA	NA	NA	NA	17,439	14,332	15,486	12,482
Other merchandise[2]	NA	NA	NA	NA	64,703	51,512	57,005	44,524
Nonmerchandise receipts[3]	NA	NA	NA	NA	13,130	9,597	12,304	8,781

Notes: Estimates are not adjusted for price changes.

[1] Estimates include data for businesses with or without paid employees and are grouped according to merchandise categories used in the Annual Retail Trade Survey.

[2] Includes other merchandise such as collectibles, souvenirs, auto parts and accessories, hardware, lawn and garden equipment and supplies, and jewelry.

[3] Includes nonmerchandise receipts such as auction commissions, customer training, customer support, advertising, and shipping and handling.

*Plunkett Research Estimate

NA = Not Available

Source: U.S. Census Bureau

Plunkett Research, ® Ltd.

www.plunkettresearch.com

Internet Publishing & Broadcasting & Web Search Portals: Estimated Revenue & Expenses, U.S.: 2013-2018

(In Millions of US$; Latest Year Available)

NAICS Code 51913	2018*	2017	2016	2015	2014	2013
Total Operating Revenue	**194,690**	**170,781**	**148,039**	**125,868**	**109,414**	**96,951**
Publishing & broadcasting of content on the Internet		42,806	37,948	33,763	34,079	30,765
Licensing of rights to use intellectual property		4,317	4,125	3,590	4,133	3,782
Online advertising space		105,190	90,288	75,266	54,670	49,805
All other operating revenue		18,468	15,678	13,249	16,532	12,599
Total Operating Expenses	**155,752**	**136,426**	**117,929**	**109,619**	**94,306**	**76,765**

Notes: Estimates are based on data from the 2017 Service Annual Survey and administrative data. Dollar volume estimates are published in millions of dollars; consequently, results may not be additive.

* Plunkett Research Estimate.

Source: U.S. Census Bureau

Plunkett Research, ® Ltd.

www.plunkettresearch.com

Internet Access Technologies Compared

(In Millions of Bits per Second - Mbps)

Type of Access	Maximum Data Rate (In Mbps)	Characteristics
Dialup		
Dialup	.0288, .0336, .056	Analog modems that require dialup connection. Slowest method of Internet access.
ISDN	.064, .128	Integrated Services Digital Network. Digital access that requires dialup connection.
Wired Broadband		
ADSL	1.5 - 24 Downstream .5 - 3.5 Upstream	Asymmetrical Digital Subscriber Line. Highest speeds are on ADSL2+ (ULL).
SDSL	2.3	Symmetric Digital Subscriber Line. Downstream and upstream data transfer rates are similar. Ideal for businesses because of synchronous speed and high-speed router capabilities.
VDSL	24 - 100 Downstream 2.3 - 16 Upstream	Very High bit-Rate DSL.
Cable Modem	4 - 2,000 Downstream .384 - 50 Upstream	2 Gigabyte (2 GB) speeds are possible with DOCSIS 3.1 technology.
FTTH	15 to 1,000 Downstream 5 to 1,000 Upstream	Fiber to the Home (Home, Node, Premises, etc). Google Fiber is a leading provider. Google is developing 10 Gigabyte (10 GB) technologies.
T1/DS1	1.544	Ideal for businesses with high bandwidth requirements.
T3/DS3	44.736	Equivalent to 30 T1 circuits.
E1 (Europe)	2.048	European version of T1.
E3 (Europe)	34.368	European version of T3.
OC3	155.52	High-speed access. Uses optical fiber technology.
OC12	622.08	Offers higher speed access than OC3. Uses optical fiber technology.
OC48	2,488.32	Offers one of the fastest data rates. Uses optical fiber technology. Extremely expensive to setup and maintain.
OC768	39,813.12	Network line used by AT&T, Cisco and others.
Wireless Broadband		
802.15.3 (UWB)	100 - 2,000	UWB stands for ultrawideband. It is useful for high-speed, short distance data transfer.
802.11 (Wi-Fi)	11 - 250	Typical home and business wireless networks. Higher-speed standards may be referred to as Wi-Fi Direct or MIMO.
802.15 Bluetooth	3 to 25	Bluetooth offers high speed data transfer. Newer versions work over longer distances (up to 200 ft.) than early models.
802.16 (WiMAX)	15 - 375	Enables long-distance data transfers, but not in widespread use.
Satellite	3 - 100	Limited upstream speeds. Low-Earth Orbit satellites may offer faster speeds.
CDMA2000 EV-DO	up to 14.7	EV-DO Rev. A is 3.1 Mbps, Rev. B is 14.7 Mbps
HSPA	14.4	Popular 3G cellular
HSPA+	42 - 168	Advanced cellular, Release 8 is 42 Mbps, Release 9 is 84 Mbps and Release 10 is 168 Mbps.
LTE (3G-4G)	36 to 326	"Long Term Evolution" technology for cellular networks.
LTE Advanced (4G -5G)	100-1,000 Download up to 500 Upload	An upgraded version of LTE that is classified by the ITU as 4G. Sometimes called an IMT-Advanced technology.
5G	10,000	5G NR (2017-18) provides upgrades to existing 4G networks as a modest speed upgrade. 5G 15 was the first standalone specification (2017-19).

Note: 1 Mbps = 1,000 Kbps; 1,000 Mbps = 1 Gigabyte (1 GB)

Number of Business & Residential High Speed Internet Lines, U.S.: 2013-2018

(In Thousands)

Types of Technology	Dec-13	Dec-14	Dec-15	Dec-16	Dec-17*	Dec-18*
ADSL	30,690	29,533	28,134	26,527	24,614	22,839
SDSL	108	72	60	42	34	27
Other Wireline[1]	772	773	694	655	649	643
Cable Modem	54,009	55,785	59,706	63,325	66,007	68,803
FTTP[2]	7,745	9,077	10,498	12,053	13,960	16,169
Satellite	1,849	2,006	2,071	1,864	1,637	1,438
Fixed Wireless	858	999	1,054	1,238	1,293	1,351
Total Fixed	**96,032**	**98,245**	**102,216**	**105,704**	**108,194**	**111,270**
Mobile Wireless (Smartphone)	197,365	239,957	273,679	299,256	310,595	322,364
Total Lines	**293,397**	**338,202**	**375,895**	**404,960**	**418,790**	**433,634**

Notes: High-speed lines are connections to end-user locations that deliver services at speeds exceeding 200 kbps in at least one direction. Advanced services lines, which are a subset of high-speed lines, are connections that deliver services at speeds exceeding 200 kbps in both directions. Line counts presented in this report are not adjusted for the number of persons at a single end-user location who have access to, or who use, the Internet-access services that are delivered over the high-speed connection to that location.

[1] Power Line and Other are summarized with Other Wireline to maintain firm confidentiality.

[2] Fiber to the premises.

* Plunkett Research Estimate.

Source: U.S. Federal Communications Bureau (FCC)
Plunkett Research, ® Ltd.
www.plunkettresearch.com

Home Broadband Adoption
Demographics, U.S.: January 2018

Demographic Group	Have Broadband at Home
All Adult Americans	65%
Sex	
Male	66%
Female	64%
Age	
18-29	67%
30-49	70%
50-64	68%
65+	50%
Race/Ethnicity	
White	72%
Black	57%
Hispanic	47%
Annual Household Income	
< $30K	45%
$30K-$50K	67%
$50K-$75K	79%
>$75K	87%
Education Attainment	
Less Than High School Graduate	24%
High School Graduate	56%
Some College	68%
College Graduate	85%
Community Type	
Rural	58%
Urban	67%
Suburban	70%

Source: Pew Research Center Surveys.
Plunkett Research, ® Ltd.
www.plunkettresearch.com

Smartphone Adoption Demographics, U.S.: January 2018

Demographic Group	Have a Smartphone
All Adult Americans	77%
Sex	
Women	75%
Men	78%
Age	
18-29	94%
30-49	89%
50-64	73%
65 and older	46%
Race/Ethnicity	
White	77%
Black	75%
Hispanic	77%
Annual Household Income	
< $30,000	67%
$30,000-$49,999	82%
$50,000-$74,999	83%
$75,000+	93%
Education Attainment	
Less than High School Graduate	57%
High School Graduate	69%
Some College	80%
College Graduate	91%
Community Type	
Urban	83%
Suburban	78%
Rural	65%

Source: Pew Research Center Surveys.

Plunkett Research, ® Ltd.

www.plunkettresearch.com

Internet Users by Demographic Group, U.S.: 2018

Demographic Group	Use Internet
All Adult Americans	89%
Sex	
Male	89%
Female	88%
Age	
18-29	98%
30-49	97%
50-64	87%
65 and older	66%
Race/Ethnicity	
White, Non-Hispanic	89%
Black, Non-Hispanic	87%
Hispanic	88%
Annual Household Income	
< $30,000	81%
$30,000-$49,999	93%
$50,000-$74,999	97%
$75,000+	98%
Education Attainment	
Less than High School Graduate	65%
High School Graduate	84%
Some College	93%
College Graduate	97%
Community Type	
Urban	92%
Suburban	90%
Rural	78%

Source: Pew Internet & American Life Project

Plunkett Research, ® Ltd.

www.plunkettresearch.com

Amazon.com, Inc. Annual Sales & Income: 2012-2018

(In Millions of US$)

Region/Product Line	2018	2017	2016	2015	2014	2013	2012
Net Sales	232,887	177,866	135,987	107,006	88,988	74,452	61,093
North America	141,366	106,110	79,785	63,708	55,469	44,517	34,813
Media	NA	NA	13,580	12,483	11,567	10,809	9,189
Electronics & other general merchandise	NA	NA	64,887	50,401	38,517	29,985	23,273
Other[1]	NA	NA	1,318	824	5,385	3,723	2,351
International	65,866	54,297	43,983	35,418	33,510	29,934	26,280
Media	NA	NA	10,631	10,026	10,938	10,907	10,753
Electronics & other general merchandise	NA	NA	33,107	25,196	22,369	18,817	15,355
Other[1]	NA	NA	245	196	212	211	172
Net Income (Loss)	10,073	3,033	2,371	596	(241)	274	(39)

[1] Includes non-retail activities, such as Amazon Web Services (AWS), which are included in the North America segment, and advertising services and co-branded credit card agreements, which are included in both segments.

NA = Not Available

Source: Amazon.com, Inc.
Plunkett Research, ® Ltd.
www.plunkettresearch.com

eBay Annual Statistics: 2012-2017

(Annual, 2012-2017)	2017	2016	2015	2014	2013	2012
Consolidated Net Revenues (In Millions of US$)	9,567	8,979	8,592	8,790	16,047	14,072
Consolidated Net Income/Loss (In Millions of US$)	-1,016	7,266	1,725	46	2,856	2,609
Active Buyers* (In Millions)	170.0	167.0	162.0	154.0	142.6	122.7

* All buyers who successfully closed a transaction on our Marketplace and StubHub platforms within the previous 12-month period. Buyers may register more than once, and as a result, may have more than one account.

Source: eBay

Plunkett Research, ® Ltd.

www.plunkettresearch.com

Employment in E-commerce & Internet-related Fields, U.S.: 1999-2018

(In Thousands of Employed Workers)

Year	Software Publishers (5112)	Data Processing, Hosting & Related Services (518)	Internet Publishing & Broadcasting & Web Search Portals (51913)	Electronic Shopping & Mail-order Houses (45411)	Business to Business Electronic Markets (42511)
1999	235.0	307.1	78.1	238.5	93.7
2000	260.6	315.7	110.8	258.4	94.2
2001	268.9	316.8	100.4	242.1	90.3
2002	253.3	303.9	76.3	225.6	80.9
2003	238.9	280.0	67.2	220.3	68.3
2004	235.9	267.1	66.1	230.5	61.5
2005	237.9	262.5	67.2	241.9	57.7
2006	244.0	263.2	69.1	243.2	56.6
2007	255.3	267.8	72.9	250.0	54.1
2008	263.6	260.3	80.6	254.9	50.3
2009	257.7	248.5	83.3	247.2	44.4
2010	260.9	243.0	92.0	249.8	40.9
2011	271.4	245.8	109.6	264.8	38.0
2012	287.1	254.9	125.2	281.3	36.9
2013	299.6	269.6	142.3	301.4	36.2
2014	315.5	279.5	163.3	327.7	35.3
2015	334.4	296.2	184.3	346.0	34.5
2016	358.8	303.9	203.5	368.8	33.9
2017	381.2	318.0	223.8	392.1	32.6
2018*	407.9	329.9	244.5	398.7	31.5

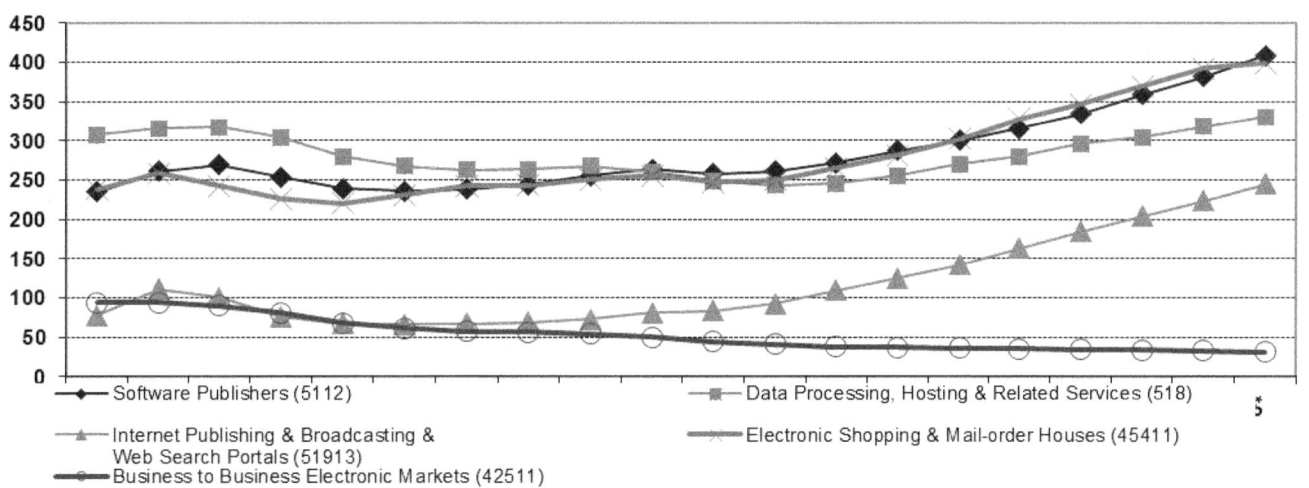

Source: U.S. Bureau of Labor Statistics

Plunkett Research, Ltd.

www.plunkettresearch.com

Chapter 3

IMPORTANT E-COMMERCE & INTERNET BUSINESS CONTACTS

Addresses, Telephone Numbers and Internet Sites

Contents:

1) Advertising Resources
2) Advertising/Marketing Associations
3) Apps Industry Associations
4) Audience & Circulation Research
5) Broadcasting, Cable, Radio & TV Associations
6) Careers-Computers/Technology
7) Careers-First Time Jobs/New Grads
8) Careers-General Job Listings
9) Careers-Job Reference Tools
10) Computer & Electronics Industry Associations
11) Computer & Electronics Industry Resources
12) Consulting Industry Associations
13) Corporate Information Resources
14) E-Commerce Education & Training
15) Economic Data & Research
16) Electronic Health Records/Continuity of Care Records
17) Electronic Publishing Associations
18) Engineering, Research & Scientific Associations
19) Entertainment & Amusement Associations-General
20) Entertainment and Video Statistics in Europe
21) Financial Technology Associations, FinTech
22) Games Industry Associations
23) Industry Research/Market Research
24) Internet & Online Business Resources
25) Internet Industry Associations
26) Internet Industry Resources
27) Internet Usage Statistics
28) Logistics & Supply Chain Associations
29) MBA Resources
30) Outsourcing Industry Resources
31) Participatory Sensing Resources
32) Payment, E-Commerce and Data Interchange Technology
33) Printers & Publishers Associations
34) Privacy & Consumer Matters
35) Research & Development, Laboratories
36) Science & Technology Resources
37) Software Industry Associations
38) Software Industry Resources
39) Stocks & Financial Markets Data
40) Technology Law Associations
41) Technology Transfer Associations
42) Telecommunications Industry Associations
43) Telecommunications Resources
44) Trade Associations-General
45) Trade Associations-Global
46) U.S. Government Agencies
47) Wireless & Cellular Industry Associations

1) Advertising Resources

Interactive Advertising Bureau (IAB)
116 E. 27th St., Fl. 7
New York, NY 10016 US
Phone: 212-380-4700
E-mail Address: *randall@iab.net*
Web Address: www.iab.net

The Interactive Advertising Bureau (IAB) is dedicated to helping online, email, wireless and interactive advertisers increase their revenues. The organization publishes numerous research reports and articles regarding the Internet advertising industry.

Web Marketing Today
125 S. Park St., Ste.430
Traverse City, MI 49684 USA
Phone: 231-946-0606
Web Address: webmarketingtoday.com
Web Marketing Today is a free weekly online magazine covering the e-commerce industry. It publishes tutorials, articles, podcasts and webinars for smaller and local businesses.

2) Advertising/Marketing Associations

4A's (American Association of Advertising Agencies)
1065 Ave. of the Americas, Fl. 16
New York, NY 10018 USA
Phone: 212-682-2500
Web Address: www.aaaa.org
The 4A's (American Association of Advertising Agencies) is the national trade association representing the advertising agency industry in the U.S.

American Institute of Graphic Arts (AIGA)
233 Broadway, Fl. 17
New York, NY 10279 USA
Phone: 212-807-1990
Web Address: www.aiga.org
The American Institute of Graphic Arts (AIGA) strives to further excellence in communication design, both as a strategic tool for business and as a cultural force.

American Marketing Association (AMA)
130 E. Randolph St., Fl. 22
Chicago, IL 60601 USA
Phone: 312-542-9000
Fax: 312-542-9001
Toll Free: 800-262-1150
Web Address: www.ama.org
The American Marketing Association (AMA) serves marketing professionals in both business and education and serves all levels of marketing practitioners, educators and students.

Art Directors Club, Inc. (ADC)
106 W. 29th St.

New York, NY 10001 USA
Phone: 212-643-1440
Fax: 212-643-4266
E-mail Address: info@adcglobal.org
Web Address: www.adcglobal.org
The Art Directors Club (ADC) is an international not-for-profit organization of creative leaders in advertising, graphic design, interactive media, broadcast design, typography, packaging, environmental design, photography, illustration and related disciplines.

Association for the Advancement of Relationship Marketing (AARM)
Phone: 416-561-6841
E-mail Address: administration@aarm.org
Web Address: www.aarm.org
The Association for the Advancement of Relationship Marketing (AARM) is an association of professionals in relationship marketing, especially in direct and interactive marketing.

eMarketing Association (eMA)
40 Blue Ridge Dr.
Charlestown, RI 02813 USA
Fax: 408-884-2461
Toll Free: 800-496-2950
E-mail Address: admin@emarketingassociation.com
Web Address: www.emarketingassociation.com
eMarketing Association (eMA) is the largest international association of electronic marketing professionals, with members in over 40 countries worldwide. The organization provides a forum to exchange knowledge and ideas and to make professional contacts.

International Advertising Association (IAA)
747 Third Ave., Fl. 2
New York, NY 10017 USA
Phone: 646-722-2612
Fax: 646-722-2501
E-mail Address: iaa@iaaglobal.org
Web Address: www.iaaglobal.org
The International Advertising Association (IAA) is a strategic partnership that champions the common interests of disciplines across the full spectrum of the marketing communications industry.

NEMOA (National Etailing & Mailing Organization of America)
P.O. Box 658
Scarborough, ME 04070 USA
Phone: 207-885-0090

Fax: 207-885-0097
E-mail Address: terri@nemoa.org
Web Address: www.nemoa.org
NEMOA offers direct marketing merchants of all
sizes, and the vendors that service them, an
affordable network to share knowledge, learn about
industry trends and connect with peers and experts in
a non-selling environment.

Search Engine Marketing Association (SEMPO)
401 Edgewater Pl., Ste. 600
Wakefield, MA 01880 USA
Phone: 781-876-8866
E-mail Address: info@sempo.org
Web Address: www.sempo.org
Search Engine Marketing Association (SEMPO), is a
global nonprofit organization serving the search
engine marketing industry and marketing
professionals engaged in it. SEMPO was founded in
2002.

3)   Apps Industry Associations

Association for Competitive Technology (ACT)
1401 K St. NW, Ste. 502
Washington, DC 20005 USA
Phone: 202-331-2130
Fax: 202-331-2139
Web Address: www.actonline.org
The Association for Competitive Technology (ACT)
is an international advocacy and education
organization representing more than 5,000 small and
mid-size app developers and information technology
firms. It has offices in Washington, DC and in
Brussels, Belgium.

4)   Audience & Circulation Research

Media Rating Council (MRC)
420 Lexington Ave., Ste. 343
New York, NY 10170 USA
Phone: 212-972-0300
Fax: 212-972-2786
E-mail Address: staff@mediaratingcouncil.org
Web Address: www.mediaratingcouncil.org
The Media Rating Council (MRC) is a nonprofit
regulatory agency that promotes valid, accurate
audience measurement services for the media
industry.

5)   Broadcasting, Cable, Radio & TV Associations

**National Cable and Telecommunications
Association (NCTA)**
25 Massachusetts Ave. NW, Ste. 100
Washington, DC 20001-1413 USA
Phone: 202-222-2300
Fax: 202-222-2514
E-mail Address: info@ncta.com
Web Address: www.ncta.com
The National Cable and Telecommunications
Association (NCTA) is the principal trade association
of the cable television industry in the United States. It
represents cable operators as well as over 200 cable
program networks that produce TV shows.

6)   Careers-Computers/Technology

ComputerJobs.com, Inc.
1995 N. Park Pl., Ste. 375
Atlanta, GA 30339 USA
Toll Free: 800-850-0045
Web Address: www.computerjobs.com
ComputerJobs.com, Inc. is an employment web site
that offers users a links to computer-related job
opportunities organized by skill and market.

Dice.com
12150 Meredith Dr.
Urbandale, IA 50323 USA
Phone: 515-280-1144
Fax: 515-280-1452
Toll Free: 888-321-3423
E-mail Address: techsupport@dice.com
Web Address: www.dice.com
Dice.com provides free employment services for IT
jobs. The site includes advanced job searches by
geographic location and category, availability
announcements and resume postings, as well as
employer profiles, a recruiter's page and career links.
It is maintained by Dice Holdings, Inc., a publicly
traded company.

**Institute for Electrical and Electronics Engineers
(IEEE) Job Site**
445 Hoes Ln.
Piscataway, NJ 08855-1331 USA
Phone: 732-981-0060
Toll Free: 800-678-4333
E-mail Address: candidatejobsite@ieee.org
Web Address: careers.ieee.org

The Institute for Electrical and Electronics Engineers (IEEE) Job Site provides a host of employment services for technical professionals, employers and recruiters. The site offers job listings by geographic area, a resume bank and links to employment services.

Pencom Systems, Inc.
152 Remsen St.
Brooklyn, NY 11201 USA
Phone: 718-923-1111
Fax: 718-923-6065
E-mail Address: tom@pencom.com
Web Address: www.pencom.com
Pencom Systems, Inc., an open system recruiting company, hosts a career web site geared toward high-technology and scientific professionals, featuring an interactive salary survey, career advisor, job listings and technology resources. Its focus is the financial services industry within the New York City area.

7)   Careers-First Time Jobs/New Grads

Alumni-Network Recruitment Corporation
Alumni-Network Recruitment Corporation
Oakville, ON Canada
Phone: 905-465-2547
E-mail Address: karen@alumni-network.com
Web Address: www.alumni-network.com
Alumni-Network Recruitment Corporation is a professional search and recruiting firm, specializing in ERP, E-Commerce and Engineering.

CollegeGrad.com, Inc.
950 Tower Ln., Fl. 6
Foster City, CA 94404 USA
E-mail Address: info@quinstreet.com
Web Address: www.collegegrad.com
CollegeGrad.com, Inc. offers in-depth resources for college students and recent grads seeking entry-level jobs.

MonsterCollege
444 N. Michigan Ave., Ste. 600
Chicago, IL 60611 USA
E-mail Address: info@college.monster.com
Web Address: www.college.monster.com
MonsterCollege provides information about internships and entry-level jobs, as well as career advice and resume tips, to recent college graduates.

National Association of Colleges and Employers (NACE)
62 Highland Ave.
Bethlehem, PA 18017-9085 USA
Phone: 610-868-1421
E-mail Address: customer_service@naceweb.org
Web Address: www.naceweb.org
The National Association of Colleges and Employers (NACE) is a premier U.S. organization representing college placement offices and corporate recruiters who focus on hiring new grads.

8)   Careers-General Job Listings

CareerBuilder, Inc.
200 N La Salle St., Ste. 1100
Chicago, IL 60601 USA
Phone: 773-527-3600
Fax: 773-353-2452
Toll Free: 800-891-8880
Web Address: www.careerbuilder.com
CareerBuilder, Inc. focuses on the needs of companies and also provides a database of job openings. The site has over 1 million jobs posted by 300,000 employers, and receives an average 23 million unique visitors monthly. The company also operates online career centers for 140 newspapers and 9,000 online partners. Resumes are sent directly to the company, and applicants can set up a special e-mail account for job-seeking purposes. CareerBuilder is primarily a joint venture between three newspaper giants: The McClatchy Company, Gannett Co., Inc. and Tribune Company.

CareerOneStop
Toll Free: 877-872-5627
E-mail Address: info@careeronestop.org
Web Address: www.careeronestop.org
CareerOneStop is operated by the employment commissions of various state agencies. It contains job listings in both the private and government sectors, as well as a wide variety of useful career resources and workforce information. CareerOneStop is sponsored by the U.S. Department of Labor.

LaborMarketInfo (LMI)
Employment Development Dept.
P.O. Box 826880, MIC 57
Sacramento, CA 94280-0001 USA
Phone: 916-262-2162
Fax: 916-262-2352
Web Address: www.labormarketinfo.edd.ca.gov

LaborMarketInfo (LMI) provides job seekers and employers a wide range of resources, namely the ability to find, access and use labor market information and services. It provides statistics for employment demographics on both a local and regional level, as well as career searching tools for California residents. The web site is sponsored by California's Employment Development Office.

Recruiters Online Network

E-mail Address: rossi.tony@comcast.net
Web Address: www.recruitersonline.com
The Recruiters Online Network provides job postings from thousands of recruiters, Careers Online Magazine, a resume database, as well as other career resources.

USAJOBS

USAJOBS Program Office
1900 E St. NW, Ste. 6500
Washington, DC 20415-0001 USA
Phone: 818-934-6600
Web Address: www.usajobs.gov
USAJOBS, a program of the U.S. Office of Personnel Management, is the official job site for the U.S. Federal Government. It provides a comprehensive list of U.S. government jobs, allowing users to search for employment by location; agency; type of work; or by senior executive positions. It also has special employment sections for individuals with disabilities, veterans and recent college graduates; an information center, offering resume and interview tips and other information; and allows users to create a profile and post a resume.

9) Careers-Job Reference Tools

Vault.com, Inc.

132 W. 31st St., Fl. 17
New York, NY 10001 USA
Fax: 212-366-6117
Toll Free: 800-535-2074
E-mail Address: customerservice@vault.com
Web Address: www.vault.com
Vault.com, Inc. is a comprehensive career web site for employers and employees, with job postings and valuable information on a wide variety of industries. Its features and content are largely geared toward MBA degree holders.

10) Computer & Electronics Industry Associations

Asian-Oceanian Computing Industry Organization (ASOCIO)

No. 15 Jalan 16/11
c/o PIKOM, Phileo Damansara, 1106 &1107
Petaling Jaya, Selangor 46350 Malaysia
Phone: 60-3-7955-2922
Fax: 60-3-7966-2933
E-mail Address: razib@asocio.org
Web Address: www.asocio.org
The Asian-Oceanian Computing Industry Organization's (ASOCIO) objective is to promote the development of the computing industry in the region.

China Electronics Chamber of Commerce (CECC)

No. 15 Bldg., Cuiwei Zhongli
Haidian District
Beijing, 100036 China
Phone: 86-10-6825-6762
Fax: 86-10-6825-6764
E-mail Address: ceccinfo@126.com
Web Address: www.cecc.org.cn
China Electronics Chamber of Commerce (CECC), which is led by the Ministry of Information Industry, is the national professional organization for telecommunications and mobile electronics. The group circulates industry information and mediates between its members and the government.

Communications and Information Network Association of Japan (CIAJ)

2-2-12 Hamamatsucho, Minato-ku
Fl. 3, JEI Hamamatsucho Bldg.
Tokyo, 105-0013 Japan
Phone: 81-3-5403-9363
Fax: 81-3-5463-9360
E-mail Address: webmaster@ciaj.or.jp
Web Address: www.ciaj.or.jp/en/
Communications and Information Network Association of Japan (CIAJ) works to help the development of the communication and information network industry in Japan through the promotion of info-communication technologies.

Computer & Communications Industry Association (CCIA)

900 17th St. NW, Ste. 1100
Washington, DC 20006 USA
Phone: 202-783-0070
Fax: 202-783-0534

Web Address: www.ccianet.org
The Computer & Communications Industry
Association (CCIA) is a non-profit membership
organization for companies and senior executives
representing the computer, Internet, information
technology (IT) and telecommunications industries.

Computer Technology Industry Association (CompTIA)
3500 Lacey Rd., Ste. 100
Downers Grove, IL 60515 USA
Phone: 630-678-8300
Toll Free: 866-835-8020
Web Address: www.comptia.org
The Computer Technology Industry Association
(CompTIA) is the leading association representing
the international technology community. Its goal is to
provide a unified voice, global advocacy and
leadership, and to advance industry growth through
standards, professional competence, education and
business solutions.

Electronic Industries Association of India (ELCINA)
422 Okhla Industrial Estate
ELCINA House
New Delhi, Delhi 110020 India
Phone: 91-11-2692-4597
Fax: 91-11-2692-3440
E-mail Address: info@elcina.com
Web Address: www.elcina.com
The Electronic Industries Association of India
(ELCINA) is an organization for the promotion of
electronic hardware manufacturing through active
representation and advice to the Indian government.

Electronics and Computer Software Export Promotion Council (ESC)
Opp. Asiad Village
Fl. 3, PHD House
New Delhi, Delhi 110016 India
Phone: 91-11-2696-5103
Fax: 91-11-2685-3412
E-mail Address: info@escindia.com
Web Address: www.escindia.in
The Electronics and Computer Software Export
Promotion Council (ESC) represents the info-
communication technology industry through
electronics and IT trade facilitation.

Information Technology Association of Canada (ITAC)
5090 Explorer Dr., Ste. 801

Mississauga, ON L4W 4T9 Canada
Phone: 905-602-8345
Fax: 905-602-8346
E-mail Address: dwhite@itac.ca
Web Address: www.itac.ca
The Information Technology Association of Canada
(ITAC) represents the IT, software, computer and
telecommunications industries in Canada.

Information Technology Industry Council (ITI)
1101 K St. NW, Ste. 610
Washington, DC 20005 USA
Phone: 202-737-8888
Fax: 202-638-4922
E-mail Address: info@itic.org
Web Address: www.itic.org
The Information Technology Industry Council (ITI)
is a premier group of the nation's leading high-tech
companies and widely recognized as one of the tech
industry's most effective lobbying organization in
Washington, in various foreign capitals and the
World Trade Organization (WTO).

Information Technology Management Association (ITMA)
Robinson Rd.
P.O. Box 3297
Singapore, 905297 Singapore
Phone: 65-8171-4456
Fax: 65-6410-8008
E-mail Address: secretariat@itma.org.sg
Web Address: www.itma.org.sg
Information Technology Management Association
(ITMA) represents professionals working in the field
of IT management in Singapore.

Korea Association of Information and Telecommunications (KAIT)
NO. 1678-2, 2nd Fl. Dong-Ah Villat 2 Town
Seocho-dong, Seocho-gu
Seoul, 137-070 Korea
Phone: 82-2-580-0582
E-mail Address: webmaster@kait.or.kr
Web Address: www.kait.or.kr/eng
The Korea Association of Information and
Telecommunications (KAIT) was created to develop
and promote the InfoTech, computer, consumer
electronics, wireless, software and
telecommunications sectors in Korea.

Manufacturers' Association for Information Technology (MAIT)
4/2, Siri Institutional Area, August Kranti Marg

Fl. 4, PHD House, Ramakrishna Dalmia Wing
New Delhi, Delhi 110-016 India
Phone: 91-11-2685-5487
Fax: 91-11-2685-1321
E-mail Address: contact@mait.com
Web Address: www.mait.com
The Manufacturers' Association for Information
Technology (MAIT) is an organization that focuses
on the promotion of the hardware, training,
design/R&D and the associated services sectors of
the Indian IT industry.

Singapore Computer Society

53/53A Neil Rd.
Singapore, 088891 Singapore
Phone: 65-6226-2567
Fax: 65-6226-2569
E-mail Address: scs.secretariat@scs.org.sg
Web Address: www.scs.org.sg
The Singapore Computer Society is a membership
society for infocomm professionals in Singapore.

World Information Technology and Services Alliance (WITSA)

8300 Boone Blvd., Ste. 450
Vienna, VA 220182 USA
Phone: 571-633-0620
Fax: 703-893-1269
E-mail Address: info@witsa.org
Web Address: www.witsa.org
The World Information Technology and Services
Alliance (WITSA) is a consortium of over 70
information technology (IT) industry associations
from economies around the world. WITSA members
represent over 90% of the world IT market. Founded
in 1978 and originally known as the World
Computing Services Industry Association, WITSA is
an advocate in international public policy issues
affecting the creation of a robust global information
infrastructure.

11) Computer & Electronics Industry Resources

Centre for Development of Advanced Computing (C-DAC)

Pune University Campus
Ganesh Khind
Pune, 411 007 India
Phone: 91-20-2570-4100
Fax: 91-20-2569-4004
Web Address: www.cdac.in

The Centre for Development of Advanced
Computing (C-DAC) is a research and development
institution created for the design, development and
deployment information technology solutions for
economic and human advancement. C-DAC is a
branch of India's Department of Information
Technology (DIT), Ministry of Communications &
Information Technology (MCIT).

Computer Professionals for Social Responsibility (CPSR)

P.O. Box 20046
Stanford, CA 94309-0046 USA
Phone: 650-989-1294
E-mail Address: cpsr@cpsr.org
Web Address: www.cpsr.org
Computer Professionals for Social Responsibility
(CPSR) is a global organization promoting the
responsible use of computer technology. CPSR is a
public interest alliance of computer scientists and
others concerned about the impact of computer
technology on society.

Department of Electronics and Information Technology (India)

Electronics Niketan
6 CGO Complex, Lodhi Rd.
New Delhi, 110003 India
Phone: 91-11-2430-1851
E-mail Address: webmaster@deity.gov.in
Web Address: deity.gov.in
The Department of Electronics and Information
Technology, a part of the Ministry of
Communications & Information Technology (MIT)
of the Government of India, is charged with
promoting the information technology and
communications industries.

EETimes

Web Address: www.eetimes.com
The EETimes is an online magazine devoted to
electronic engineers in the semiconductor, systems
and software design fields.

Information Technology and Innovation Foundation (ITIF)

1101 K St. NW, Ste. 610
Washington, DC 20005 USA
Phone: 202-449-1351
E-mail Address: mail@itif.org
Web Address: www.itif.org
Information Technology and Innovation Foundation
(ITIF) is a non-partisan research and educational

institute (a think tank) with a mission to formulate and promote public policies to advance technological innovation and productivity internationally, in Washington, and in the States. Recognizing the vital role of technology in ensuring American prosperity, ITIF focuses on innovation, productivity, and digital economy issues.

12) Consulting Industry Associations

Institute of Certified E-Commerce Consultants (ICECC)
Web Address: www.icecc.com
The Institute of Certified E-Commerce Consultants (ICECC) is a global association for the accreditation of e-commerce professionals.

TechServe Alliance
1420 King St., Ste. 610
Alexandria, VA 22314 USA
Phone: 703-838-2050
Web Address: www.techservealliance.org
The TechServe Alliance, is an association that aims to advance excellence and ethics within the IT & engineering staffing and solutions industry. Its membership offers collaborative networking and knowledge sharing, updated operational and market trends and commitment to fair business practices and ethical code of conducts.

13) Corporate Information Resources

bizjournals.com
120 W. Morehead St., Ste. 400
Charlotte, NC 28202 USA
Toll Free: 866-853-3661
E-mail Address: gmurchison@bizjournals.com
Web Address: www.bizjournals.com
Bizjournals.com is the online media division of American City Business Journals, the publisher of dozens of leading city business journals nationwide. It provides access to research into the latest news regarding companies both small and large. The organization maintains 42 websites and 64 print publications and sponsors over 700 annual industry events.

Business Wire
101 California St., Fl. 20
San Francisco, CA 94111 USA
Phone: 415-986-4422
Fax: 415-788-5335

Toll Free: 800-227-0845
E-mail Address: info@businesswire.com
Web Address: www.businesswire.com
Business Wire offers news releases, industry- and company-specific news, top headlines, conference calls, IPOs on the Internet, media services and access to tradeshownews.com and BW Connect On-line through its informative and continuously updated web site.

Edgar Online, Inc.
11200 Rockville Pike, Ste. 310
Rockville, MD 20852 USA
Phone: 301-287-0300
Fax: 301-287-0390
Toll Free: 888-870-2316
Web Address: www.edgar-online.com
Edgar Online, Inc. is a gateway and search tool for viewing corporate documents, such as annual reports on Form 10-K, filed with the U.S. Securities and Exchange Commission.

PR Newswire Association LLC
350 Hudson St., Ste. 300
New York, NY 10014-4504 USA
Fax: 800-793-9313
Toll Free: 800-776-8090
E-mail Address: MediaInquiries@prnewswire.com
Web Address: www.prnewswire.com
PR Newswire Association LLC provides comprehensive communications services for public relations and investor relations professionals, ranging from information distribution and market intelligence to the creation of online multimedia content and investor relations web sites. Users can also view recent corporate press releases from companies across the globe. The Association is owned by United Business Media plc.

Silicon Investor
E-mail Address: si.admin@siliconinvestor.com
Web Address: www.siliconinvestor.com
Silicon Investor is focused on providing information about technology companies. Its web site serves as a financial discussion forum and offers quotes, profiles and charts.

14) E-Commerce Education & Training

eLab
Owen Graduate School of Management
Vanderbilt University, 401 21st Ave. S.
Nashville, TN 37203 USA

Phone: 615-322-7217
Fax: 615-343-7177
E-mail Address: elab@owen.vanderbilt.edu
Web Address: elab.vanderbilt.edu
eLab, located at the Sloan Center for Internet
Retailing at Vanderbilt University, was chartered to
perform cutting-edge e-commerce research, often in
cooperation with private enterprise.

15) Economic Data & Research

Centre for European Economic Research (The, ZEW)
L 7, 1
Mannheim, 68161 Germany
Phone: 49-621-1235-01
Fax: 49-621-1235-224
E-mail Address: empfang@zew.de
Web Address: www.zew.de/en
Zentrum fur Europaische Wirtschaftsforschung, The
Centre for European Economic Research (ZEW),
distinguishes itself in the analysis of internationally
comparative data in a European context and in the
creation of databases that serve as a basis for
scientific research. The institute maintains a special
library relevant to economic research and provides
external parties with selected data for the purpose of
scientific research. ZEW also offers public events
and seminars concentrating on banking, business and
other economic-political topics.

Economic and Social Research Council (ESRC)
Polaris House
North Star Ave.
Swindon, SN2 1UJ UK
Phone: 44-01793 413000
E-mail Address: esrcenquiries@esrc.ac.uk
Web Address: www.esrc.ac.uk
The Economic and Social Research Council (ESRC)
funds research and training in social and economic
issues. It is an independent organization, established
by Royal Charter. Current research areas include the
global economy; social diversity; environment and
energy; human behavior; and health and well-being.

Eurostat
5 Rue Alphonse Weicker
Joseph Bech Bldg.
Luxembourg, L-2721 Luxembourg
Phone: 352-4301-1
E-mail Address: eurostat-pressoffice@ec.europa.eu
Web Address: ec.europa.eu/eurostat

Eurostat is the European Union's service that
publishes a wide variety of comprehensive statistics
on European industries, populations, trade,
agriculture, technology, environment and other
matters.

Federal Statistical Office of Germany
Gustav-Stresemann-Ring 11
Wiesbaden, D-65189 Germany
Phone: 49-611-75-2405
Fax: 49-611-72-4000
Web Address: www.destatis.de
Federal Statistical Office of Germany publishes a
wide variety of nation and regional economic data of
interest to anyone who is studying Germany, one of
the world's leading economies. Data available
includes population, consumer prices, labor markets,
health care, industries and output.

India Brand Equity Foundation (IBEF)
Fl. 20, Jawahar Vyapar Bhawan
Tolstoy Marg
New Deli, 110001 India
Phone: 91-11-43845500
Fax: 91-11-23701235
E-mail Address: info.brandindia@ibef.org
Web Address: www.ibef.org
India Brand Equity Foundation (IBEF) is a public-
private partnership between the Ministry of
Commerce and Industry, the Government of India
and the Confederation of Indian Industry. The
foundation's primary objective is to build positive
economic perceptions of India globally. It aims to
effectively present the India business perspective and
leverage business partnerships in a globalizing
marketplace.

National Bureau of Statistics (China)
57, Yuetan Nanjie, Sanlihe
Xicheng District
Beijing, 100826 China
Fax: 86-10-6878-2000
E-mail Address: info@gj.stats.cn
Web Address: www.stats.gov.cn/english
The National Bureau of Statistics (China) provides
statistics and economic data regarding China's
economy and society.

Organization for Economic Co-operation and Development (OECD)
2 rue Andre Pascal
Cedex 16
Paris, 75775 France

Phone: 33-1-45-24-82-00
Fax: 33-1-45-24-85-00
E-mail Address: webmaster@oecd.org
Web Address: www.oecd.org
The Organization for Economic Co-operation and
Development (OECD) publishes detailed economic,
government, population, social and trade statistics on
a country-by-country basis for over 30 nations
representing the world's largest economies. Sectors
covered range from industry, labor, technology and
patents, to health care, environment and
globalization.

**Statistics Bureau, Director-General for Policy
Planning (Japan)**
19-1 Wakamatsu-cho
Shinjuku-ku
Tokyo, 162-8668 Japan
Phone: 81-3-5273-2020
E-mail Address: toukeisoudan@soumu.go.jp
Web Address: www.stat.go.jp/english
The Statistics Bureau, Director-General for Policy
Planning (Japan) and Statistical Research and
Training Institute, a part of the Japanese Ministry of
Internal Affairs and Communications, plays the
central role of producing and disseminating basic
official statistics and coordinating statistical work
under the Statistics Act and other legislation.

Statistics Canada
150 Tunney's Pasture Driveway
Ottawa, ON K1A 0T6 Canada
Phone: 514-283-8300
Fax: 514-283-9350
Toll Free: 800-263-1136
E-mail Address: STATCAN.infostats-
infostats.STATCAN@canada.ca
Web Address: www.statcan.gc.ca
Statistics Canada provides a complete portal to
Canadian economic data and statistics. Its conducts
Canada's official census every five years, as well as
hundreds of surveys covering numerous aspects of
Canadian life.

16) Electronic Health Records/Continuity of Care Records

**American Health Information Management
Association (AHIMA)**
233 N. Michigan Ave., Fl. 21
Chicago, IL 60601-5809 USA
Phone: 312-233-1100
Fax: 312-233-1090

Toll Free: 800-335-5535
Web Address: www.ahima.org
The American Health Information Management
Association (AHIMA) is a professional association
that consists health information management
professionals who work throughout the health care
industry.

17) Electronic Publishing Associations

International Digital Publishing Forum (IDPF)
113 Cherry St., Ste. 70-719
Seattle, WA 98104 USA
Phone: 206-451-7250
E-mail Address: membership@idpf.org
Web Address: www.idpf.org
The International Digital Publishing Forum (IDPF) is
a trade and standards organization dedicated to the
development and promotion of electronic publishing,
including electronic newspapers, books and other
types of media. Members include software
developers, authors and publishers of many types.
The organization developed the ePub (electronic
publication) open standard for the publication of
eBooks.

18) Engineering, Research & Scientific Associations

**American Society for Engineering Education
(ASEE)**
1818 North St. NW, Ste. 600
Washington, DC 20036-2479 USA
Phone: 202-331-3500
Fax: 202-265-8504
E-mail Address: board@asee.org
Web Address: www.asee.org
The American Society for Engineering Education
(ASEE) is nonprofit organization dedicated to
promoting and improving engineering and
technology education.

IEEE Communications Society (ComSoc)
3 Park Ave., Fl. 17
New York, NY 10016 USA
Phone: 212-705-8900
Fax: 212-705-8999
Web Address: www.comsoc.org
The IEEE Communications Society (ComSoc) is
composed of industry professionals with a common
interest in advancing communications technologies.

Institute of Electrical and Electronics Engineers (IEEE)

3 Park Ave., Fl. 17
New York, NY 10016-5997 USA
Phone: 212-419-7900
Fax: 212-752-4929
Toll Free: 800-678-4333
E-mail Address: society-info@ieee.org
Web Address: www.ieee.org
The Institute of Electrical and Electronics Engineers (IEEE) is a nonprofit, technical professional association of more than 430,000 individual members in approximately 160 countries. The IEEE sets global technical standards and acts as an authority in technical areas ranging from computer engineering, biomedical technology and telecommunications, to electric power, aerospace and consumer electronics.

Optical Society of America (OSA)

2010 Massachusetts Ave. NW
Washington, DC 20036-1023 USA
Phone: 202-223-8130
Fax: 202-223-1096
E-mail Address: info@osa.org
Web Address: www.osa.org
The Optical Society of America (OSA) is an interdisciplinary society offering synergy between all components of the optics industry, from basic research to commercial applications such as fiber-optic networks. It has a membership group of over 16,000 individuals from over 100 countries. Members include scientists, engineers, educators, technicians and business leaders.

Society of Cable Telecommunications Engineers (SCTE)

140 Philips Rd.
Exton, PA 19341-1318 USA
Fax: 610-884-7237
Toll Free: 800-542-5040
E-mail Address: scte@scte.org
Web Address: www.scte.org
The Society of Cable Telecommunications Engineers (SCTE) is a nonprofit professional association dedicated to advancing the careers and serving the industry of telecommunications professionals by providing technical training, certification and information resources.

19) Entertainment & Amusement Associations-General

Airline Passenger Experience Association (APEX)

355 Lexington Ave., Fl. 15
New York, NY 10017-6603 USA
Phone: 212-297-2177
Fax: 212-370-9047
E-mail Address: info@apex.aero
Web Address: apex.aero
The Airline Passenger Experience Association (APEX), formerly the World Airline Entertainment Association (WAEA), is a worldwide network representing airlines, airline suppliers and related companies committed to excellence in inflight entertainment (IFE), communications and services.

20) Entertainment and Video Statistics in Europe

European Audiovisual Observatory

76 Allee de la Robertsau
Strasbourg, 67000 France
Phone: 33-0-3-9021-6000
Fax: 33-0-3-9021-6019
Web Address: www.obs.coe.int
The European Audiovisual Observatory is part of the Council of Europe in Strasbourg, France. It is a public service organization. The Observatory was created in 1992 in order to collect and distribute information about the audiovisual industries in Europe. The group publishes statistics and research on film, broadcasting (including TV and radio), video, satellite, cable and DVD markets. The Observatory provides information on the various audiovisual markets in Europe and their financing. It also analyses and reports on the legal issues affecting the different sectors of the audiovisual industry.

21) Financial Technology Associations, FinTech

Electronic Transactions Association

1620 L St. NW, Ste. 1020
Washington, DC 20036 USA
Phone: 202-828-2635
Fax: 202-828-2639
Toll Free: 800-695-5509
Web Address: www.electran.org
The Electronic Transactions Association is the leading trade association for the payments industry, representing 550 companies worldwide involved in

electronic transaction processing products and services. The purpose of ETA is to influence, monitor and shape the payments industry by providing leadership through education, advocacy and the exchange of information. ETA's membership spans the breadth of the payments industry to include independent sales organizations (ISOs), payments networks, financial institutions, transaction processors, mobile payments products and services, payments technologies, and software providers (ISV) and hardware suppliers.

Innovate Finance
One Canada Square
Canary Wharf
London, E14 5AB UK
Web Address: new.innovatefinance.com
Innovate Finance is an independent not-for-profit membership association representing the UK's global FinTech community. Founded in 2014 with the support of the City of London and Canary Wharf Group, Innovate Finance aims to accelerate the UK's leading position in the global financial services sector by directly supporting the next era of technology-led financial services innovators, from start-ups to institutions.

22) Games Industry Associations

Entertainment Software Association (ESA)
575 7th St. NW, Ste. 300
Washington, DC 20004 USA
Phone: 202-223-2400
E-mail Address: esa@theesa.com
Web Address: www.theesa.com
The Entertainment Software Association (ESA) is a U.S. trade association for companies that publish video and computer games for consoles, personal computers and the Internet. The ESA owns the E3 Media & Business Summit, a major invitation-only annual trade show for the video game industry.

Game Manufacturers Association (GAMA)
240 N. Fifth St., Ste. 340
Columbus, OH 43215 USA
Phone: 614-255-4500
Fax: 614-255-4499
E-mail Address: ed@gama.org
Web Address: www.gama.org
The Game Manufacturers Association (GAMA) is an international non-profit trade association serving the hobby games industry. It hosts two annual events, the GAMA Trade Show and Origins Game Fair, and

publishes a quarterly information newsletter, GAMATimes.

Hong Kong Digital Entertainment Industry Support Centre
78 Tat Chee Ave.
HKPC Building
Kowloon, Hong Kong Hong Kong
Phone: 852-2788-5678
Fax: 852-2788-5900
E-mail Address: hkpcenq@hkpc.org
Web Address: www.hkpc.org/en/industry-support-services/support-centres/hong-kong-software-industry-information-centre
The Hong Kong Digital Entertainment Industry Support Centre comprises three major sectors in Hong Kong, namely entertainment software, computer animation and digital effects in the production of videos and films. The center supports the development of professionals in the field of animation, design and programming, as well as promotes traditional industries through business development, marketing and branding.

International Game Developers Association (IGDA)
19 Mantua Rd.
Mt. Royal, NJ 08061 USA
Phone: 856-423-2990
Web Address: www.igda.org
The International Game Developers Association (IGDA) represents members involved in the video game production industry. The firm aims to promote professional development within the gaming industry and advocates for issues that affect the game developer community, including anti-censorship issues.

23) Industry Research/Market Research

ClickZ
Phone: 44-208-0806-489
E-mail Address: info@clickz.com
Web Address: www.clickz.com
ClickZ, is an online publication that offers news, information and e-commerce statistics.

Forrester Research
60 Acorn Park Dr.
Cambridge, MA 02140 USA
Phone: 617-613-5730
Toll Free: 866-367-7378
E-mail Address: press@forrester.com

Web Address: www.forrester.com
Forrester Research is a publicly traded company that
identifies and analyzes emerging trends in technology
and their impact on business. Among the firm's
specialties are the financial services, retail, health
care, entertainment, automotive and information
technology industries.

Gartner, Inc.
56 Top Gallant Rd.
Stamford, CT 06902 USA
Phone: 203-964-0096
E-mail Address: info@gartner.com
Web Address: www.gartner.com
Gartner, Inc. is a publicly traded IT company that
provides competitive intelligence and strategic
consulting and advisory services to numerous clients
worldwide.

Kantar Retail
24-28 Bloomsbury Way
London, WC1A 2PX SE1 2QY UK
Phone: 44-207-450-2627
Web Address: www.kantarretail.com
Kantar Retail, formed by the amalgamation of
Cannondale Associates, Glendinning Management
Consultants, Management Ventures Inc. and Retail
Forward, is a consulting business that provides in-
depth market research on retail. This firm's web site
contains press releases with forecasts and statistics
regarding retail activity and trends.

MarketResearch.com
11200 Rockville Pike, Ste. 504
Rockville, MD 20852 USA
Phone: 240-747-3093
Fax: 240-747-3004
Toll Free: 800-298-5699
E-mail Address:
customerservice@marketresearch.com
Web Address: www.marketresearch.com
MarketResearch.com is a leading broker for
professional market research and industry analysis.
Users are able to search the company's database of
research publications including data on global
industries, companies, products and trends.

Plunkett Research, Ltd.
P.O. Drawer 541737
Houston, TX 77254-1737 USA
Phone: 713-932-0000
Fax: 713-932-7080

E-mail Address:
customersupport@plunkettresearch.com
Web Address: www.plunkettresearch.com
Plunkett Research, Ltd. is a leading provider of
market research, industry trends analysis and
business statistics. Since 1985, it has served clients
worldwide, including corporations, universities,
libraries, consultants and government agencies. At
the firm's web site, visitors can view product
information and pricing and access a large amount of
basic market information on industries such as
financial services, InfoTech, e-commerce, health care
and biotech.

24) Internet & Online Business Resources

E-Commerce Guide
950 Tower Ln., 6th Fl.
Foster City, CA 94404 USA
E-mail Address: info@quinstreet.com
Web Address: www.ecommerce-guide.com
E-Commerce Guide, a QuinStreet, Inc. company,
provides news, trends, products and solutions guides.

E-Commerce Times News Network (ECT)
16133 Ventura Blvd., Ste. 700
Encino, CA 91436 USA
Phone: 818-461-9700
Fax: 818-461-9710
Toll Free: 877-238-5500
E-mail Address: contact@ectnews.com
Web Address: www.ecommercetimes.com
The E-Commerce Times News Network (ECT)
provides news and information about e-commerce.

InternetNews.com
950 Tower Ln., Fl. 6
Foster City, CA 94404 USA
E-mail Address: info@quinstreet.com
Web Address: www.internetnews.com
InternetNews.com offers real-time business news
specifically designed for Internet technology
managers. News categories include hardware,
software, mobility, content, networking and search.

25) Internet Industry Associations

Asia & Pacific Internet Association (APIA)
P.O. Box 12600
Kuala Lumpur, 50784 Malaysia
E-mail Address: apia-sec@apia.org
Web Address: www.apia.org

Asia & Pacific Internet Association (APIA) is a nonprofit trade association whose aim is to promote the business interests of the Internet-related service industry in the Asia Pacific region. The site contains a list of organizations, standards, regional Internet registries and related Asia Pacific organizations.

China Internet Network Information Center
4, S. 4th St., Zhongguancun
Fl. 1, Bldg. 1, Software Park
Beijing, 100190 China
Phone: 86-10-58813000
Fax: 86-10-58812666
E-mail Address: service@cnnic.cn
Web Address: www.cnnic.cn
The China Internet Network Information Center compiles Internet information and databases regarding the Internet community and facilitates the development and application of Internet resources and relevant technologies in China.

Cooperative Association for Internet Data Analysis (CAIDA)
9500 Gilman Dr.
Mail Stop 0505
La Jolla, CA 92093-0505 USA
Phone: 858-534-5000
E-mail Address: info@caida.org
Web Address: www.caida.org
The Cooperative Association for Internet Data Analysis (CAIDA), representing organizations from the government, commercial and research sectors, works to promote an atmosphere of greater cohesion in the engineering and maintenance of the Internet. CAIDA is located at the San Diego Supercomputer Center (SDSC) on the campus of the University of California, San Diego (UCSD).

Federation of Internet Service Providers of the Americas (FISPA)
c/o Jim Hollis
8200 Raintree Ln., Ste. 100
Charlotte, NC 28277 USA
Phone: 704-844-2540
Fax: 704-844-2728
Toll Free: 877-919-4521
Web Address: www.fispa.org
The Federation of Internet Service Providers of the Americas (FISPA) encourages discussion, education and collective buying power for organizations involved in providing Internet access, web hosting, web design and other Internet products and services.

International Academy of Digital Arts and Sciences (IADAS)
22 W. 21st St., Fl. 7
New York, NY 10010 USA
Phone: 212-675-4890
E-mail Address: dmdavies@iadas.net
Web Address: www.iadas.net
The International Academy of Digital Arts and Sciences (IADAS) is dedicated to the progress of new media worldwide. It runs The Webby Awards, honoring web sites for technological and creative achievements, as well as The Lovie Awards, honoring individuals involved in managing, designing, marketing online web sites, advertising, mobile apps and social content for European market.

Internet and Mobile Association of India (IAMAI)
406 Ready Money Terr.
167 Dr. Annie Besant Rd.
Mumbai, 400 018 India
E-mail Address: gaurav@iamai.in
Web Address: www.iamai.in
The Internet & Mobile Association of India (IAMAI) is an industry organization representing the interests of India's online and mobile value-added services industry.

Internet Association
Phone: 202-803-5783
Web Address: https://internetassociation.org
The Internet Association is a trade association that exclusively represents leading global internet companies on matters of public policy. It offers posts, reports and resources relating to election advertising, patents, net neutrality, trade, privacy, data security, sharing economy and global internet governance.

Internet Law & Policy Forum (ILPF)
2440 Western Ave., Ste. 709
Seattle, WA 98121 USA
Phone: 206-727-0700
Fax: 206-374-2263
E-mail Address: admin@ilpf.org
Web Address: www.ilpf.org
The Internet Law & Policy Forum (ILPF) is dedicated to the global development of the Internet through legal and public policy initiatives. It is an international nonprofit organization whose member companies develop and deploy the Internet in every aspect of business today.

Internet Society (ISOC)
1775 Wiehle Ave., Ste. 201

Reston, VA 20190-5108 USA
Phone: 703-439-2120
Fax: 703-326-9881
E-mail Address: isoc@isoc.org
Web Address: www.isoc.org
The Internet Society (ISOC) is a nonprofit organization that provides leadership in public policy issues that influence the future of the Internet. The organization is the home of groups that maintain infrastructure standards for the Internet, such as the Internet Engineering Task Force (IETF) and the Internet Architecture Board (IAB).

Internet Systems Consortium, Inc. (ISC)

950 Charter St.
Redwood City, CA 94063 USA
Phone: 650-423-1300
Fax: 650-423-1355
E-mail Address: info@isc.org
Web Address: www.isc.org
The Internet Systems Consortium, Inc. (ISC) is a nonprofit organization with extensive expertise in the development, management, maintenance and implementation of Internet technologies.

NetCoalition

400 N. Capitol St. NW, Ste. 585
Washington, DC 20001 USA
Phone: 202-347-8099
Web Address: www.netcoalition.com
NetCoalition serves as a leading discussion forum for exchanging ideas about the Internet.

Organization for the Advancement of Structured Information Standards (OASIS)

25 Corporate Dr., Ste. 103
Burlington, MA 01803-4238 USA
Phone: 781-425-5073
Fax: 781-425-5072
E-mail Address: info@oasis-open.org
Web Address: www.oasis-open.org
The Organization for the Advancement of Structured Information Standards (OASIS) is a consortium which drives the development and adoption of e-business standards. It produces Web services standards, along with standards for security, e-business, and standardization efforts in the public sector and for application-specific markets. Founded in 1993, OASIS has more than 5,000 participants representing over 600 organizations and individual members in 100 countries.

Right Click, Inc. (The)

P.O. Box 175
Clemmons, NC 27012 USA
Phone: 336-774-1411
E-mail Address: info@therightclickinc.com
Web Address: www.therightclickinc.com
The Right Click, Inc., formerly CyberSkills, provides training and courseware materials for technology and business applications.

US Internet Service Provider Association (US ISPA)

700 12th St. NW, Ste. 700E
Washington, DC 20005 USA
Phone: 202-904-2351
E-mail Address: kdean@usispa.org
Web Address: www.usispa.org
US Internet Service Provider Association (US ISPA) is a leading provider of technical, business, policy and regulatory support to ISPs (Internet service providers).

World Wide Web Consortium (W3C)

32 Vassar St., Bldg. 32-G515
Cambridge, MA 02139 USA
Phone: 617-253-2613
Fax: 617-258-5999
E-mail Address: susan@w3.org
Web Address: www.w3.org
The World Wide Web Consortium (W3C) develops technologies and standards to enhance the performance and utility of the World Wide Web. The W3C is hosted by three different organizations: the European Research Consortium for Informatics and Mathematics (ERICM) handles inquiries about the W3C in the EMEA region; Keio University handles W3C's Japanese and Korean correspondence; and the Computer Science & Artificial Intelligence Lab (CSAIL) at MIT handles all other countries, include Australia and the U.S.

26) Internet Industry Resources

American Registry for Internet Numbers (ARIN)

3635 Concorde Pkwy., Ste. 200
Chantilly, VA 20151-1125 USA
Phone: 703-227-9840
Fax: 703-263-0417
E-mail Address: info@arin.net
Web Address: www.arin.net
The American Registry for Internet Numbers (ARIN) is a nonprofit organization that administers and registers Internet protocol (IP) numbers. The

organization also develops policies and offers educational outreach services.

Berkman Center for Internet & Society
23 Everett St., Fl. 2
Cambridge, MA 02138 USA
Phone: 617-495-7547
Fax: 617-495-7641
E-mail Address: cyber@law.harvard.edu
Web Address: cyber.law.harvard.edu
The Berkman Center for Internet & Society, housed at Harvard University's law school, focuses on the exploration of the development and inner-workings of laws pertaining to the Internet. The center offers Internet courses, conferences, advising and advocacy.

CommerceNet
955A Alma St.
Palo Alto, CA 94301 USA
Phone: 650-289-4040
Fax: 650-289-4041
E-mail Address: info@commerce.net
Web Address: www.commerce.net
CommerceNet, an entrepreneurial research institute, is also an industry consortium for companies using, promoting and building electronic commerce solutions on the Internet.

Computer Emergency Response Team (CERT)
4500 5th Ave.
Pittsburgh, PA 15213-2612 USA
Phone: 412-268-7090
Fax: 412-268-6989
E-mail Address: cert@cert.org
Web Address: www.cert.org
The Computer Emergency Response Team (CERT) is part of the Software Engineering Institute (SEI), a federally funded research and development center at Carnegie Mellon University in Pittsburgh, Pennsylvania. CERT develops and promotes systems management practices to resist Internet security incidents.

Congressional Internet Caucus Advisory Committee (ICAC)
1401 K St. NW, Ste. 200
Washington, DC 20008 USA
Phone: 202-638-4370
E-mail Address: tlordan@netcaucus.org
Web Address: www.netcaucus.org
The Congressional Internet Caucus Advisory Committee (ICAC) works to educate the public, as well as a bipartisan group from the U.S. House and Senate about Internet-related policy issues.

InformationWeek
303 Second St., S. Tower, Fl. 9, Ste. 900
San Francisco, CA 94107-1243 USA
Phone: 415-947-6000
Web Address: www.informationweek.com
InformationWeek is an online community comprising of a diverse range of IT professionals who offer insights and share their experiences with technologies, products and technology trends. It mainly consists of nine technology and vertical communities: strategic CIO, software, cloud, big data, mobile, government, security, healthcare and infrastructure.

Internet Assigned Numbers Authority (IANA)
12025 Waterfront Dr., Ste. 300
Los Angeles, CA 90094 USA
Phone: 310-301-5800
Fax: 310-823-8649
E-mail Address: iana@iana.org
Web Address: www.iana.org
The Internet Assigned Numbers Authority (IANA) serves as the central coordinator for the assignment of parameter values for Internet protocols. IANA is operated by the Internet Corporation for Assigned Names and Numbers (ICANN).

Internet Education Foundation
1634 I St. NW, Ste. 1100
Washington, DC 20006 USA
Phone: 202-638-4370
Fax: 202-637-0968
E-mail Address: tlordan@neted.org
Web Address: www.neted.org
The Internet Education Foundation is a nonprofit organization dedicated to educating the public and policymakers about the potential of the global Internet to promote democracy, communications and commerce.

InterNIC
Web Address: www.internic.net
InterNIC provides public information regarding Internet domain name registration services.

National Informatics Centre (NIC)
Lodhi Rd.
A-Block, CGO Complex
New Delhi, Delhi 110 003 India
Phone: 91-11-24305000

E-mail Address: wim@nic.in
Web Address: www.nic.in
The National Informatics Centre (NIC), under the
Department of Information Technology of the
Government of India, provides support to India's
governmental agencies through the applications of
information technology and technological activities.

OASIS UDDI
E-mail Address: communications@oasis-open.org
Web Address: uddi.xml.org
The web site of OASIS UDDI, an international
technology consortium, provides information about
UDDI, the Universal Description, Discovery and
Integration protocol, a critical component of web
services. The web site is structured as a community
forum hosted by OASIS.

27) Internet Usage Statistics

ClickZ Network
55 Broad St., Fl. 22
New York, NY 10004 USA
Phone: 646-736-1842
Fax: 212-732-3857
Toll Free: 800-955-2719
Web Address: www.clickz.com
The ClickZ Network is a resource for interactive
marketing news, information, commentary, advice
and opinions. The web site seeks to provide valuable
tools for marketers.

comScore, Inc.
11950 Democracy Dr., Ste. 600
Reston, VA 20190 USA
Phone: 703-438-2000
Fax: 703-438-2051
Toll Free: 866-276-6972
Web Address: www.comscore.com
comScore, Inc. provides excellent data on consumer
behavior and audiences, particularly in terms of how
consumers access and use online sites and digital data
and entertainment. They are global leaders in Internet
usage data.

eMarketer
11 Times Square
New York, NY 10036 USA
Toll Free: 800-405-0844
Web Address: www.emarketer.com
eMarketer is a comprehensive, objective and easy-to-
use resource for any person or business interested in
online marketing and emerging media. The firm

offers news articles, market projections and analytical
commentaries.

Nielsen
85 Broad St.
New York, NY 10004 USA
Toll Free: 800-864-1224
Web Address: www.nielsen.com
Nielsen offers detailed, real-time Internet, retail and
media research and analysis.

Pew Internet & American Life Project
1615 L St. NW, Ste. 800
Washington, DC 20036 USA
Phone: 202-419-4300
Fax: 202-419-4349
E-mail Address: info@pewinternet.org
Web Address: www.pewinternet.org
The Pew Internet & American Life Project, an
initiative of the Pew Research Center, produces
reports that explore the impact of the Internet on
families, communities, work and home, daily life,
education, health care and civic and political life.

28) Logistics & Supply Chain Associations

Reverse Logistics Association (RLT)
2300 Lakeview Pkwy., Ste. 700
Alpharetta, GA 30009 USA
Phone: 801-331-8949
Fax: 801-206-0090
E-mail Address: info@RLA.org
Web Address: www.reverselogisticstrends.com
The Reverse Logistics Association (RLT) provides
news and information for third party service
providers involved in the management and movement
of goods that are returned for replacement, repair,
refurbishment or recycling.

29) MBA Resources

MBA Depot
Web Address: www.mbadepot.com
MBA Depot is an online community and information
portal for MBAs, potential MBA program applicants
and business professionals.

30) Outsourcing Industry Resources

CIO Outsourcing Center
492 Old Connecticut Path
P.O. Box 9208

Framingham, MA 01701-9208 USA
Phone: 508-872-0080
E-mail Address: rhein@cio.com
Web Address: www.cio.com/topic/3195/Outsourcing
CIO Outsourcing Center, a feature on CIO.com, provides data for chief information officers about technology outsourcing. CIO.com and the Outsourcing Center are products of CXO Media Inc., which is itself a division of International Data Group.

31) Participatory Sensing Resources

Center for Embedded Networked Sensing (CENS) at UCLA
UCLA 3563 Boelter Hall
Los Angeles, CA 90095-1596 USA
Phone: 310-206-2476
Fax: 310-206-3053
E-mail Address: xuanmai@cens.ucla.edu
Web Address: research.cens.ucla.edu
The Center for Embedded Networked Sensing (CENS) at UCLA is a research department focused on developing wireless sensing systems applicable to scientific and societal issues. The center maintains a multidisciplinary approach, with faculty and students from such diverse fields as Computer Science, Electrical Engineering, Civil and Environmental Engineering, Biology, Statistics, Education, Urban Planning and Theater, Film, and Television.

32) Payment, E-Commerce and Data Interchange Technology

Center for Research in Electronic Commerce
McCombs School of Business
CBA 6.426, 2100 Speedway, Stop B6500
Austin, TX 78712-1170 USA
Phone: 512-471-7962
Fax: 512-471-3034
E-mail Address: abw@uts.cc.utexas.edu
Web Address: cism.mccombs.utexas.edu/
The Center for Research in Electronic Commerce at the University of Texas is a leading research institution in generating critical knowledge and understanding in the fields of information systems and management, electronic commerce and the digital economy.

Data Interchange Standards Association (DISA)
8300 Greensboro Dr., Ste. 800
McLean, VA 22102 USA
Phone: 703-970-4480

Fax: 703-970-4488
E-mail Address: info@disa.org
Web Address: http://www.disa.org/about.cfm
The Data Interchange Standards Association (DISA) is a leading nonprofit organization that supports the development and use of electronic business interchange standards in e-commerce.

Global Business Dialogue on e-Society (GBDe)
Phone: 301-523-0891
E-mail Address: gbde@wcore.com
Web Address: www.gbd-e.org
The Global Business Dialogue on e-Society (GBDe) is a company-led response to the need for strengthened international coordination with regard to worldwide electronic commerce. Its committees include members like Hitachi, Cisco, NEC and NTT Docomo.

RosettaNet
7877 Washington Village Dr., Ste. 300
Dayton, OH 45459 USA
Phone: 937-435-3870
E-mail Address: info@gs1us.org
Web Address: www.rosettanet.org
RosettaNet, a subsidiary of GS1 US, is a nonprofit organization whose mission is to develop e-business process standards that serve as a frame of reference for global trading networks. The organization's standards provide a common language for companies within the global supply chain.

33) Printers & Publishers Associations

MPA-The Association of Magazine Media
810 7th Ave., Fl. 24
New York, NY 10019 USA
Phone: 212-872-3700
E-mail Address: mpa@magazine.org
Web Address: www.magazine.org
MPA-The Association of Magazine Media (formerly the Magazine Publishers of America, Inc.) is the industry association for consumer magazines in all formats, including printed, mobile and online.

34) Privacy & Consumer Matters

Better Business Bureau Online (BBBO)
3033 Wilson Blvd., Ste. 600
Arlington, VA 22201 USA
Phone: 703-276-0100
Web Address: www.bbb.org/online/

The Better Business Bureau Online (BBBO) is the online version of the Better Business Bureau, an organization that attempts to foster high standards of customer service and online privacy.

Electronic Frontier Foundation (EFF)
815 Eddy St.
San Francisco, CA 94109 USA
Phone: 415-436-9333
Fax: 415-436-9993
E-mail Address: info@eff.org
Web Address: www.eff.org
The Electronic Frontier Foundation (EFF) is a nonprofit, non-partisan organization that strives to protect user privacy and free speech online, fight illegal surveillance, support freedom-enhancing technologies and advocate for users and innovators. It advances its mission through impact litigation, policy analysis, grassroots activism and technology development.

Electronic Privacy Information Center (EPIC)
1718 Connecticut Ave. NW, Ste. 200
Washington, DC 20009 USA
Phone: 202-483-1140
Fax: 202-483-1248
E-mail Address: info@epic.org
Web Address: www.epic.org
The Electronic Privacy Information Center (EPIC) is public interest research center, established to focus public attention on emerging civil liberties issues and to protect privacy, the First Amendment and constitutional values.

Federal Trade Commission-Privacy and Security
600 Pennsylvania Ave. NW
Washington, DC 20580 USA
Phone: 202-326-2222
Web Address: business.ftc.gov/privacy-and-security
Federal Trade Commission-Privacy and Security is responsible for many aspects of business-to-consumer and business-to-business trade and regulation.

Get Safe Online
Clifton House
Four Elms Rd.
Cardiff, CF24 1LE UK
E-mail Address: info@getsafeonline.org
Web Address: www.getsafeonline.org
Get Safe Online is a joint initiative between the U.K. government, law enforcement, leading businesses and the public sector. Its aim is to provide computer users

and small businesses with free, independent, user-friendly advice that will allow them to use the internet confidently, safely and securely. It provides videos and online advice about such subjects as identify theft, computer security and safe purchasing practices for products, services and travel.

National Fraud Information Center (NFIC)
1701 K St. NW, Ste. 1200
c/o National Consumers League
Washington, DC 20006 USA
Phone: 202-835-3323
Fax: 202-835-0747
Toll Free: 800-876-7060
E-mail Address: info@nclnet.org
Web Address: www.fraud.org
The National Fraud Information Center (NFIC) covers all types of fraud and provides information about reporting fraud, as well as posting fraud alerts.

Privacy International
62 Britton St.
London, EC1M 5UY UK
Phone: 44-20-3422-4321
E-mail Address: info@privacy.org
Web Address: www.privacyinternational.org
Privacy International is a government and business watchdog, alerting individuals to wiretapping and national security activities, medical privacy infringement, police information systems and the use of ID cards, video surveillance and data matching.

Privacy Times
P.O. Box 302
Cabin John, MD 20818 USA
Phone: 301-229-7002
Fax: 301-229-8011
E-mail Address: evan@privacytimes.com
Web Address: www.privacytimes.com
Privacy Times is a publication targeting attorneys and professionals wishing to follow legislation and developments in the information privacy arena, including the Freedom of Information Act, direct marketing, Caller ID and credit reports.

TRUSTe
835 Market St.
Ste. 800, Box 137
San Francisco, CA 94103-1905 USA
Phone: 415-520-3490
Fax: 415-520-3420
Toll Free: 888-878-7830
E-mail Address: eleanor@truste.com

Web Address: www.truste.com
TRUSTe formed an alliance with all major portal
sites to launch the Privacy Partnership campaign, a
consumer education program designed to raise the
awareness of Internet privacy issues. The
organization works to meet the needs of business web
sites while protecting user privacy.

35) Research & Development, Laboratories

Electronics and Telecommunications Research Institute (ETRI)
218 Gajeongno
Yuseong-gu
Daejeon, 34129 Korea
Phone: 82-42-860-6114
E-mail Address: k21human@etri.re.kr
Web Address: www.etri.re.kr
Established in 1976, the Electronics and
Telecommunications Research Institute (ETRI) is a
nonprofit government-funded research organization
that promotes technological excellence. The research
institute has successfully developed information
technologies such as TDX-Exchange, High Density
Semiconductor Microchips, Mini-Super Computer
(TiCOM), and Digital Mobile Telecommunication
System (CDMA). ETRI's focus is on information
technologies, robotics, telecommunications, digital
broadcasting and future technology strategies.

Institute for Telecommunication Sciences (ITS)
325 Broadway
Boulder, CO 80305-3337 USA
Phone: 303-497-3571
E-mail Address: info@its.bldrdoc.gov
Web Address: www.its.bldrdoc.gov
The Institute for Telecommunication Sciences (ITS)
is the research and engineering branch of the
National Telecommunications and Information
Administration (NTIA), a division of the U.S.
Department of Commerce (DOC). Its research
activities are focused on advanced
telecommunications and information infrastructure
development.

36) Science & Technology Resources

Technology Review
1 Main St., Fl. 13
Cambridge, MA 02142 USA
Phone: 617-475-8000

Fax: 617-475-8000
Web Address: www.technologyreview.com
Technology Review, an MIT enterprise, publishes
tech industry news, covers innovation and writes in-
depth articles about research, development and
cutting-edge technologies.

37) Software Industry Associations

Apache Software Foundation
1901 Munsey Dr.
Forest Hill, MD 21050-2747 USA
Fax: 919-573-9199
E-mail Address: apache@apache.org
Web Address: www.apache.org
Apache Software Foundation is one of the largest
open software successes. Apache is used by about
two-thirds of all web sites worldwide. Its software
manages the interaction between a web site and the
viewer's browser.

Business Software Alliance (BSA)
20 F St. NW, Ste. 800
Washington, DC 20001 USA
Phone: 202-872-5500
Fax: 202-872-5501
E-mail Address: info@bsa.org
Web Address: www.bsa.org
The Business Software Alliance (BSA) is a leading
global software industry association. BSA educates
consumers regarding software management,
copyright protection, cyber security, trade, e-
commerce and other Internet-related issues.

Colorado Technology Association
1245 Champa St.
Denver, CO 80202 USA
Phone: 303-592-4070
E-mail Address:
membership@coloradotechnology.org
Web Address: www.coloradotechnology.org/
The Colorado Technology Association, formerly the
Colorado Software & Internet Association, promotes
the technology industry in Colorado through
networking and organization.

European Software Institute (ESI)
Parque Tecnologico de Bizkaia
Edificio 202
Zamudio, Bizkaia E-48170 Spain
Phone: 34-946-430-850
Fax: 34-901-706-009
Web Address: www.esi.es

The European Software Institute (ESI) is a nonprofit foundation launched as an initiative of the European Commission, with the support of leading European companies working in the information technology field.

Information Systems Security Association (ISSA)
12100 Sunset Hills Rd., Ste. 130
Reston, VA 20190 USA
Phone: 703-234-4077
Fax: 703-435-4390
Toll Free: 866-349-5818
E-mail Address: mdelacruz@issa.org
Web Address: www.issa.org
The Information Systems Security Association (ISSA) is an international nonprofit organization of information security professionals. It offers educational forums, publishes resources and networking opportunities to its members.

Korea Software Industry Association (KOSA)
Donghwa Bldg. 3F
206 Hakdong-ro, Gangnam-gu
Seoul, Korea
Phone: 82-2-2188-6900
Fax: 82-2-2188-6901
E-mail Address: choicy@sw.or.kr
Web Address: www.sw.or.kr
The Korea Software Industry Association (KOSA) is Korea's nonprofit trade organization representing more than 1,200 member companies in the software industry.

Linux Foundation (The)
1 Letterman Dr.
Building D, Ste. D4700
San Francisco, CA 94129 USA
Phone: 415-723-9709
Fax: 415-723-9709
E-mail Address: info@linuxfoundation.org
Web Address: www.linuxfoundation.org
The Linux Foundation, founded in 2007 by the merger of Open Source Development Labs (OSDL) and the Free Standards Group, is a nonprofit organization that standardizes, protects and promotes the work of Linux creator Linus Torvalds. It provides necessary services and resources to make and keep open source software competitive with closed platforms. The foundation is supported by a global consortium of global open source IT industry leaders, with facilities in the U.S. and Japan.

New Mexico Technology Council (NMTC)
317 Commercial St., NE
Albuquerque, NM 87102 USA
Phone: 505-227-1086
E-mail Address: nyika@nmtechcouncil.org
Web Address: www.nmtechcouncil.org
The New Mexico Technology Council (NMTC) represents the interests of the software industry in New Mexico. Its members include businesses, tech professionals and organizations who work to promote technology industry in New Mexico.

Singapore Infocomm Technology Federation (SiTF)
79 Ayer Rajah Crescent, Ste. 02-03/04/05
Singapore, 139955 Singapore
Phone: 65-6325-9700
Fax: 65-6325-4993
E-mail Address: info@sitf.org.sg
Web Address: sitf.org.sg
Singapore Infocomm Technology Federation (SiTF) is an infocom industry association that has four chapters: Cloud Computing Chapter, Digital Media Wireless Chapter, Security and Governance Chapter and Singapore Enterprise Chapter.

Software & Information Industry Association (SIIA)
1090 Vermont Ave. NW, Fl. 6
Washington, DC 20005-4095 USA
Phone: 202-289-7442
Fax: 202-289-7097
Web Address: www.siia.net
The Software & Information Industry Association (SIIA) is a principal trade association for the software and digital content industry.

Software Association of Oregon (SAO)
123 NE, Third Ave., Ste. 210
Portland, OR 97232 USA
Phone: 503-228-5401
Web Address: www.techoregon.org
The Technology Association of Oregon, formerly Software Association of Oregon (SAO) promotes the growth of technology industry by offering opportunities, such as networking, professional and business development programs, advocacy, industry promotions and talent development.

Washington Technology Industry Association
2200 Alaskan Way, Ste. 390
Seattle, WA 98121 USA
Phone: 206-448-3033

E-mail Address: info@washingtontechnology.org
Web Address: www.washingtontechnology.org
The Washington Technology Industry Association
promotes and helps coordinate the software industry
in the state of Washington.

38) Software Industry Resources

Software Engineering Institute (SEI)-Carnegie Mellon
4500 5th Ave.
Pittsburgh, PA 15213-2612 USA
Phone: 412-268-5800
Fax: 412-268-5758
Toll Free: 888-201-4479
E-mail Address: info@sei.cmu.edu
Web Address: www.sei.cmu.edu
The Software Engineering Institute (SEI) is a
federally funded research and development center at
Carnegie Mellon University, sponsored by the U.S.
Department of Defense through the Office of the
Under Secretary of Defense for Acquisition,
Technology, and Logistics [OUSD (AT&L)]. The
SEI's core purpose is to help users make measured
improvements in their software engineering
capabilities.

39) Stocks & Financial Markets Data

SiliconValley.com
Phone: 408-920-5615
E-mail Address: svfeedback@mercurynews.com
Web Address: www.siliconvalley.com
SiliconValley.com, run by San Jose Mercury News
and owned by MediaNews Group, offers a summary
of current financial news and information regarding
the field of technology.

40) Technology Law Associations

International Technology Law Association (ITechLaw)
401 Edgewater Pl., Ste. 600
Wakefield, MA 01880 USA
Phone: 781-876-8877
Fax: 781-224-1239
E-mail Address: office@itechlaw.org
Web Address: www.itechlaw.org
The International Technology Law Association
(ITechLaw) offers information concerning Internet
and converging technology law. It represents lawyers
in the field of technology law.

41) Technology Transfer Associations

Licensing Executives Society (USA and Canada), Inc.
11130 Sunrise Valley Dr., Ste. 350
Reston, VA 20191 USA
Phone: 703-234-4058
Fax: 703-435-4390
E-mail Address: info@les.org
Web Address: www.lesusacanada.org
Licensing Executives Society (USA and Canada),
Inc., established in 1965, is a professional association
composed of about 3,000 members who work in
fields related to the development, use, transfer,
manufacture and marketing of intellectual property.
Members include executives, lawyers, licensing
consultants, engineers, academic researchers,
scientists and government officials. The society is
part of the larger Licensing Executives Society
International, Inc. (same headquarters address), with
a worldwide membership of some 12,000 members
from approximately 80 countries.

42) Telecommunications Industry Associations

Asia-Pacific Telecommunity (APT)
Chaengwattana Rd., 12/49 Soi 5
Bangkok, 10210 Thailand
Phone: 66-2-573-0044
Fax: 66-2-573-7479
E-mail Address: aptmail@apt.int
Web Address: www.aptsec.org
The Asia-Pacific Telecommunity (APT) is an
organization of governments, telecom service
providers, manufacturers of communication
equipment, research & development organizations
and other stakeholders active in the field of
communication and information technology. APT
serves as the focal organization for communication
and information technology in the Asia-Pacific
region.

CompTel
900 17th St. NW, Ste. 400
Washington, DC 20006 USA
Phone: 202-296-6650
E-mail Address: gnorris@comptel.org
Web Address: www.comptel.org
CompTel is a trade organization representing voice,
data and video communications service providers and
their supplier partners. Members are supported

through education, networking, policy advocacy and trade shows.

DigitalEurope
Rue de la Science 14
Brussels, 1040 Belgium
Phone: 32-2-609-5310
Fax: 32-2-609-5339
E-mail Address: info@digitaleurope.org
Web Address: www.digitaleurope.org
DigitalEurope is dedicated to improving the business environment for the European information and communications technology and consumer electronics sector. Its members include 57 leading corporations and 37 national trade associations from across Europe.

European Telecommunications Standards Institute (ETSI)
ETSI Secretariat
650, route des Lucioles
Sophia-Antipolis Cedex, 06921 France
Phone: 33-4-92-94-42-00
Fax: 33-4-93-65-47-16
E-mail Address: info@etsi.org
Web Address: www.etsi.org
The European Telecommunications Standards Institute (ETSI) is a non-profit organization whose mission is to produce the telecommunications standards to be implemented throughout Europe.

International Federation for Information Processing (IFIP)
Hofstrasse 3
Laxenburg, A-2361 Austria
Phone: 43-2236-73616
Fax: 43-2236-73616-9
E-mail Address: ifip@ifip.org
Web Address: www.ifip.org
The International Federation for Information Processing (IFIP) is a multinational, apolitical organization in information & communications technologies and sciences recognized by the United Nations and other world bodies. It represents information technology societies from 56 countries or regions, with over 500,000 members in total.

International Multimedia Telecommunications Consortium (IMTC)
Bishop Ranch 6, 2400 Camino Ramon, Ste. 375
San Ramon, CA 94583 USA
Phone: 925-275-6600
Fax: 925-275-6691

Web Address: www.imtc.org
The International Multimedia Telecommunications Consortium (IMTC) is a non-profit corporation that promotes interoperable multimedia conferencing and telecommunications solutions based on international standards.

International Telecommunications Union (ITU)
Place des Nations
Geneva 20, 1211 Switzerland
Phone: 41-22-730-5111
Fax: 41-22-733-7256
E-mail Address: itumail@itu.int
Web Address: www.itu.int
The International Telecommunications Union (ITU) is an international organization for the standardization of the radio and telecommunications industry. It is an agency of the United Nations (UN).

Pacific Telecommunications Council (PTC)
914 Coolidge St.
Honolulu, HI 96826-3085 USA
Phone: 808-941-3789
Fax: 808-944-4874
E-mail Address: info@ptc.org
Web Address: www.ptc.org
The Pacific Telecommunications Council (PTC), through its member network, promotes the development and use of telecommunications and information and communications technologies to enhance the lives of people living in the Pacific hemisphere.

Telecommunications Industry Association (TIA)
1320 N. Courthouse Rd., Ste. 200
Arlington, VA 22201 USA
Phone: 703-907-7700
Fax: 703-907-7727
E-mail Address: smontgomery@tiaonline.org
Web Address: www.tiaonline.org
The Telecommunications Industry Association (TIA) is a leading trade association in the information, communications and entertainment technology industry. TIA focuses on market development, trade promotion, trade shows, domestic and international advocacy, standards development and enabling e-business.

TeleManagement Forum (TM Forum)
240 Headquarters Plz., E. Twr., 10th Fl.
Morristown, NJ 07960-6628 USA
Phone: 973-944-5100
Fax: 973-944-5110

E-mail Address: info@tmforum.org
Web Address: www.tmforum.org
The TeleManagement Forum (TM Forum) is a
nonprofit global organization that provides
leadership, strategic guidance and practical solutions
to improve the management and operation of
information and communications services.

Voice On the Net (VON) Coalition, Inc.
2300 N St. NW
Pillsbury Winthrop Shaw Pittman LLP
Washington, DC 20037 USA
Phone: 202-663-8215
E-mail Address: glenn.richards@pillsburylaw.com
Web Address: www.von.org
Voice On the Net (VON) Coalition, Inc. is an
organization is an advocate for the IP telephony
industry. The VON Coalition supports that the IP
industry should remain free of governmental
regulations. It also serves to educate consumers and
the media on Internet communications technologies.

43) Telecommunications Resources

Department of Telecommunication (Gov. of India)
19 Teen Murti, Marg
New Delhi, 1 India
Phone: 91-11-2373-9191
Fax: 91-11-2372-3330
E-mail Address: secy-dot@nic.in
Web Address: www.dot.gov.in
The Government of India's Department of
Telecommunication web site provides information,
directories, guidelines, news and information related
to the telecom, Internet, Wi-Fi and wireless
communication industries. It is a branch of India's
Ministry of Communications & Information
Technology.

International Communications Project (The)
Unit 2, Marine Action
Birdhill Industrial Estate
Birdhill, Co Tipperary Ireland
Phone: 353-86-108-3932
Fax: 353-61-749-801
E-mail Address: robert.alcock@intercomms.net
Web Address: www.intercomms.net
The International Communications Project
(InterComms) is an authoritative policy, strategy and
reference publication for the international
telecommunications industry.

44) Trade Associations-General

BUSINESSEUROPE
168 Ave. de Cortenbergh 168
Brussels, 1000 Belgium
Phone: 32-2-237-65-11
Fax: 32-2-231-14-45
E-mail Address: main@businesseurope.eu
Web Address: www.businesseurope.eu
BUSINESSEUROPE is a major European trade
federation that operates in a manner similar to a
chamber of commerce. Its members are the central
national business federations of the 34 countries
throughout Europe from which they come.
Companies cannot become direct members of
BUSINESSEUROPE, though there is a support group
which offers the opportunity for firms to encourage
BUSINESSEUROPE objectives in various ways.

45) Trade Associations-Global

World Trade Organization (WTO)
Centre William Rappard
Rue de Lausanne 154
Geneva 21, CH-1211 Switzerland
Phone: 41-22-739-51-11
Fax: 41-22-731-42-06
E-mail Address: enquiries@wto.og
Web Address: www.wto.org
The World Trade Organization (WTO) is a global
organization dealing with the rules of trade between
nations. To become a member, nations must agree to
abide by certain guidelines. Membership increases a
nation's ability to import and export efficiently.

46) U.S. Government Agencies

Bureau of Economic Analysis (BEA)
4600 Silver Hill Rd.
Washington, DC 20233 USA
Phone: 301-278-9004
E-mail Address: customerservice@bea.gov
Web Address: www.bea.gov
The Bureau of Economic Analysis (BEA), an agency
of the U.S. Department of Commerce, is the nation's
economic accountant, preparing estimates that
illuminate key national, international and regional
aspects of the U.S. economy.

Bureau of Labor Statistics (BLS)
2 Massachusetts Ave. NE
Washington, DC 20212-0001 USA

Phone: 202-691-5200
Fax: 202-691-7890
Toll Free: 800-877-8339
E-mail Address: blsdata_staff@bls.gov
Web Address: stats.bls.gov
The Bureau of Labor Statistics (BLS) is the principal
fact-finding agency for the Federal Government in
the field of labor economics and statistics. It is an
independent national statistical agency that collects,
processes, analyzes and disseminates statistical data
to the American public, U.S. Congress, other federal
agencies, state and local governments, business and
labor. The BLS also serves as a statistical resource to
the Department of Labor.

FCC-VoIP Division
445 12th St. SW
Washington, DC 20554 USA
Fax: 866-418-0232
Toll Free: 888-225-5322
E-mail Address: FOIA@fcc.gov
Web Address: www.fcc.gov/voip
The FCC-VoIP Division is dedicated to the
promotion and regulation of the VoIP (Voice over
Internet Protocol) industry. It operates as part of the
Federal Communications Commission (FCC). VoIP
allows users to call from their computer (or adapters)
over the Internet to regular telephone numbers.

Federal Communications Commission (FCC)
445 12th St. SW
Washington, DC 20554 USA
Fax: 866-418-0232
Toll Free: 888-225-5322
E-mail Address: PRA@fcc.gov
Web Address: www.fcc.gov
The Federal Communications Commission (FCC) is
an independent U.S. government agency established
by the Communications Act of 1934 responsible for
regulating interstate and international
communications by radio, television, wire, satellite
and cable.

Federal Communications Commission (FCC)-
Wireless Telecommunications Bureau
445 12th St. SW
Washington, DC 20554 USA
Phone: 202-418-0600
Fax: 202-418-0787
Toll Free: 888-225-5322
E-mail Address: PRA@fcc.gov
Web Address: www.fcc.gov/wireless-
telecommunications#block-menu-block-4

The Federal Communications Commission (FCC)-
Wireless Telecommunications Bureau handles nearly
all FCC domestic wireless telecommunications
programs and policies, including cellular and
smarftphones, pagers and two-way radios. The
bureau also regulates the use of radio spectrum for
businesses, aircraft/ship operators and individuals.

National Telecommunications and Information
Administration (NTIA)
1401 Constitution Ave. NW
Herbert C. Hoover Bldg.
Washington, DC 20230 USA
Phone: 202-482-2000
Web Address: www.ntia.doc.gov
The National Telecommunications and Information
Administration (NTIA), an agency of the U.S.
Department of Commerce, is the Executive Branch's
principal voice on domestic and international
telecommunications and information technology
issues.

Office of Technology and Electronic Commerce
(OTEC)
1401 Constitution Ave. NW
International Trade Administration
Washington, DC 20230 USA
E-mail Address: OTEC@mail.doc.gov
Web Address:
web.ita.doc.gov/ITI/itiHome.nsf/(HotNews)/HotNew
s
The Office of Technology and Electronic Commerce
(OTEC) supports the growth and competitiveness of
the U.S. telecommunications industry in the area of
foreign trade. It focuses on electronic commerce,
information technology and telecommunications.
OTEC is a division of the International Trade
Administration (ITA) of the U.S. Department of
Commerce (DOC).

U.S. Census Bureau
4600 Silver Hill Rd.
Washington, DC 20233-8800 USA
Phone: 301-763-4636
Toll Free: 800-923-8282
E-mail Address: pio@census.gov
Web Address: www.census.gov
The U.S. Census Bureau is the official collector of
data about the people and economy of the U.S.
Founded in 1790, it provides official social,
demographic and economic information. In addition
to the Population & Housing Census, which it

conducts every 10 years, the U.S. Census Bureau numerous other surveys annually.

U.S. Department of Commerce (DOC)
1401 Constitution Ave. NW
Washington, DC 20230 USA
Phone: 202-482-2000
E-mail Address: TheSec@doc.gov
Web Address: www.commerce.gov
The U.S. Department of Commerce (DOC) regulates trade and provides valuable economic analysis of the economy.

U.S. Department of Labor (DOL)
200 Constitution Ave. NW
Washington, DC 20210 USA
Phone: 202-693-4676
Toll Free: 866-487-2365
Web Address: www.dol.gov
The U.S. Department of Labor (DOL) is the government agency responsible for labor regulations.

U.S. Patent and Trademark Office (PTO)
600 Dulany St.
Madison Bldg.
Alexandria, VA 22314 USA
Phone: 571-272-1000
Toll Free: 800-786-9199
E-mail Address: usptoinfo@uspto.gov
Web Address: www.uspto.gov
The U.S. Patent and Trademark Office (PTO) administers patent and trademark laws for the U.S. and enables registration of patents and trademarks.

U.S. Securities and Exchange Commission (SEC)
100 F St. NE
Washington, DC 20549 USA
Phone: 202-942-8088
Toll Free: 800-732-0330
E-mail Address: help@sec.gov
Web Address: www.sec.gov
The U.S. Securities and Exchange Commission (SEC) is a nonpartisan, quasi-judicial regulatory agency responsible for administering federal securities laws. These laws are designed to protect investors in securities markets and ensure that they have access to disclosure of all material information concerning publicly traded securities. Visitors to the web site can access the EDGAR database of corporate financial and business information.

47) Wireless & Cellular Industry Associations

Broadband Wireless Association (BWA)
Phone: 44-7765-250610
E-mail Address: helen.duncan@quadritech.co.uk
Web Address: www.broadband-wireless.org
The Broadband Wireless Association (BWA) provides representation, news and information for the European broadband wireless industry.

Industrial Internet Consortium
109 Highland Ave.
Needham, MA 02492 USA
Phone: 781-444-0404
E-mail Address: info@iiconsortium.org
Web Address: www.iiconsortium.org
The Industrial Internet Consortium was founded in 2014 to further development, adoption and wide-spread use of interconnected machines, intelligent analytics and people at work. Through an independently-run consortium of technology innovators, industrial companies, academia and government, the goal of the IIC is to accelerate the development and availability of intelligent industrial automation for the public good.

Li-Fi Consortium
E-mail Address: info@lificonsortium.org
Web Address: www.lificonsortium.org
The Li-Fi Consortium is a membership group founded to set standards and promote utilization of next-generation optical wireless networks, which are sometimes referred to as Li-Fi. Li-Fi is somewhat like Wi-Fi, except that it utilizes light as a means to transmit data.

Open Mobile Alliance (OMA)
4330 La Jolla Village Dr., Ste. 110
San Diego, CA 92122 USA
Phone: 858-623-0742
Fax: 858-623-0743
E-mail Address: erose@omaorg.org
Web Address: www.openmobilealliance.org
The Open Mobile Alliance (OMA) facilitates global user adoption of mobile data services by specifying market driven mobile service enablers that ensure service interoperability across devices, geographies, service providers, operators and networks, while allowing businesses to compete through innovation and differentiation.

Wi-Fi Alliance
10900-B Stonelake Blvd., Ste. 126
Austin, TX 78759 USA
Phone: 512-498-9434
Fax: 512-498-9435
Web Address: www.wi-fi.org
The Wi-Fi Alliance is a non-profit group that
promotes wireless interoperability via Wi-Fi (802.11
standards). It also provides consumers with current
information about Wi-Fi systems. The alliance
currently includes over 350 member organizations.

WiMAX Forum
9009 SE Adams St., Ste. 2259
Clackamas, OR 97015 USA
Phone: 858-605-0978
Fax: 858-461-6041
Web Address: www.wimaxforum.org
The WiMAX Forum supports the implementation
and standardization of long-range wireless Internet
connections. It is a non-profit organization dedicated
to the promotion and certification of interoperability
and compatibility of broadband wireless products.

Wireless Communications Alliance (WCA)
1510 Page Mill Rd.
Palo Alto, CA 94304-1125 USA
E-mail Address: promote@wca.org
Web Address: www.wca.org
The Wireless Communications Alliance (WCA) is a
non-profit business association for companies and
organizations working with wireless technologies. It
promotes networking, education and the exchange of
information amongst its members.

**Wireless Communications Association
International (WCAI)**
1333 H St. NW, Ste. 700 W
Washington, DC 20005-4754 USA
Phone: 202-452-7823
Web Address: www.wcai.com
The Wireless Communications Association
International (WCAI) is a nonprofit trade association
representing the wireless broadband industry.

Chapter 4

THE E-COMMERCE 500: WHO THEY ARE AND HOW THEY WERE CHOSEN

Includes Indexes by Company Name, Industry & Location

The companies chosen to be listed in PLUNKETT'S E-COMMERCE & INTERNET BUSINESS ALMANAC comprise a unique list. THE E-COMMERCE 500 were chosen specifically for their dominance in the many facets of the e-commerce and internet business in which they operate. Complete information about each firm can be found in the "Individual Profiles," beginning at the end of this chapter. These profiles are in alphabetical order by company name.

THE E-COMMERCE 500 companies are from all parts of the United States, Canada, Europe, Asia/Pacific and beyond. THE E-COMMERCE 500 includes companies that are deeply involved in the technologies, services and trends that keep the entire industry forging ahead.

Simply stated, THE E-COMMERCE 500 contains the largest, most successful, fastest growing firms in e-commerce and related industries in the world. To be included in our list, the firms had to meet the following criteria:

1) Generally, these are corporations based in the U.S., however, the headquarters of many firms are located in other nations.

2) Prominence, or a significant presence, in e-commerce, e-commerce-based services, equipment and supporting fields. (See the following Industry Codes section for a complete list of types of businesses that are covered).

3) The companies in THE E-COMMERCE 500 do not have to be exclusively in the e-commerce field.

4) Financial data and vital statistics must have been available to the editors of this book, either directly from the company being written about or from outside sources deemed reliable and accurate by the editors. A small number of companies that we would like to have included are not listed because of a lack of sufficient, objective data.

INDEX OF COMPANIES WITHIN INDUSTRY GROUPS

The industry codes shown below are based on the 2012 NAIC code system (NAIC is used by many analysts as a replacement for older SIC codes because NAIC is more specific to today's industry sectors, see www.census.gov/NAICS). Companies are given a primary NAIC code, reflecting the main line of business of each firm.

Industry Group/Company	Industry Code	2017 Sales	2017 Profits
Advertising, Public Relations and Marketing Services			
Digitas	541800	622,000,000	
mktg inc	541800	155,000,000	
Student Advantage LLC	541800		
Advertising/Marketing - Online			
AKQA Inc	541810E	731,000,000	
AppNexus Inc	541810E	2,200,000,000	
CDK Global Inc	541810E	2,220,199,936	295,600,000
Critical Mass Inc	541810E		
Cyber Communications Inc	541810E	815,000,000	
Groupon Inc	541810E	2,843,877,120	14,040,000
InMobi Pte Ltd	541810E	280,000,000	-12,700,000
LivingSocial Inc	541810E	160,000,000	
Macquarium Inc	541810E		
MoreVisibility.com Inc	541810E		
MXM	541810E		
Onstream Media Corporation	541810E	14,500,000	
Performics Inc	541810E		
Quotient Technology Inc	541810E	322,115,008	-15,077,000
Rakuten Affiliate Network	541810E		
Return Path Inc	541810E	90,000,000	
VerticalResponse Inc	541810E		
Vibrant Media Inc	541810E		
Xaxis	541810E	860,000,000	
YesMail.com Inc	541810E		
Automobile (Car) and Light Truck Dealers (Used)			
Carvana Co	441120	858,870,016	-62,841,000
Automobile (Car) Reservations (e.g. Uber), Ticket Offices, Time Share and Vacation Club Rentals and Specialty Reservation Services			
Amadeus IT Group SA	561599	5,527,748,608	1,142,411,136
Didi Chuxing Technology Co Ltd (DiDi)	561599	2,000,000,000	
Lyft Inc	561599	1,050,000,000	-620,000,000
Uber Inc	561599	7,700,000,000	-4,500,000,000
Cable TV Programming, Cable Networks and Subscription Video			
Hulu LLC	515210	2,870,000,000	
Netflix Inc	515210	11,692,712,960	558,929,024
Walt Disney Company (The)	515210	55,137,001,472	8,979,999,744
Computer and Data Systems Design, Consulting and Integration Services			
Accenture plc	541512	36,765,478,912	3,445,148,928
Atos SE	541512	14,365,060,096	679,932,544
IBM Technology Services & Cloud Platforms	541512	34,934,000,000	4,344,000,000

Industry Group/Company	Industry Code	2017 Sales	2017 Profits
Infosys Limited	541512	10,208,000,000	2,140,000,000
Perficient Inc	541512	485,260,992	18,581,000
Sapient Corporation	541512	1,681,000,000	
Sopra Steria Group SA	541512	4,551,880,000	205,314,000
Tata Consultancy Services Limited (TCS)	541512	18,094,166,016	4,032,327,168
Wipro Limited	541512	7,829,330,944	1,207,610,112
Computer Manufacturing, Including PCs, Laptops, Mainframes and Tablets			
Dell Technologies Inc	334111	61,642,000,000	-1,672,000,000
Computer Networking & Related Equipment Manufacturing			
Arista Networks Inc	334210A	1,646,185,984	423,200,992
Cisco Systems Inc	334210A	48,005,001,216	9,608,999,936
Juniper Networks Inc	334210A	5,027,200,000	306,200,000
Computer Programming and Custom Software Development and Consulting			
Lionbridge Technologies Inc	541511	595,000,000	
Squarespace Inc	541511	420,000,000	
Computer Software, Accounting, Banking & Financial			
Adaptive Insights Inc	511210Q	81,791,000	-44,720,000
Apttus Corporation	511210Q	185,000,000	
Ariba Inc	511210Q	650,000,000	
Avalara Inc	511210Q	213,159,008	-64,126,000
BlackLine Inc	511210Q	177,031,008	-38,061,000
Bottomline Technologies Inc	511210Q	349,412,000	-33,137,000
Coupa Software Inc	511210Q	133,775,000	-37,607,000
DocuSign Inc	511210Q	381,459,008	-115,412,000
Expensify Inc	511210Q		
Gusto	511210Q		
Intuit Inc	511210Q	5,176,999,936	971,000,000
Namely Inc	511210Q	35,000,000	
Sage Intacct Inc	511210Q	70,000,000	
Workday Inc	511210Q	1,569,406,976	-408,278,016
Computer Software, Business Management & ERP			
Alteryx Inc	511210H	131,607,000	-17,499,000
Anaplan Inc	511210H	120,499,000	-40,194,000
Apptio Inc	511210H	188,519,008	-25,621,000
Asana Inc	511210H		
BMC Software Inc	511210H	2,500,000,000	
CA Technologies	511210H	4,036,000,000	775,000,000
Greenhouse Software Inc	511210H		
iCIMS Inc	511210H	150,000,000	
Intralinks Inc	511210H	321,000,000	
Oracle NetSuite	511210H	871,000,000	
RealPage Inc	511210H	670,963,008	377,000
SAP SE	511210H	26,723,469,312	4,576,934,912
ServiceMax Inc	511210H	70,000,000	
Sisense Inc	511210H		
Smartsheet Inc	511210H	66,964,000	-15,184,000

Industry Group/Company	Industry Code	2017 Sales	2017 Profits
SMS Assist LLC	511210H		
Symphony Technology Group	511210H	2,800,000,000	
TIBCO Software Inc	511210H	1,100,000,000	
Workfront Inc	511210H		
Yardi Systems Inc	511210H		
Zoho Corporation Private Limited	511210H	270,678,000	43,968,200
Computer Software, Content & Document Management			
Box Inc	511210L	398,604,992	-151,787,008
EasyAsk Inc	511210L		
Open Text Corporation	511210L	2,291,056,896	1,025,659,008
Computer Software, Data Base & File Management			
Domo Inc	511210J	74,540,000	-183,120,000
Embarcadero Technologies Inc	511210J	160,000,000	
MongoDB Inc	511210J	101,385,000	-86,681,000
Oracle Corporation	511210J	37,728,002,048	9,335,000,064
Qualtrics LLC	511210J	141,000,000	
Segment.io Inc	511210J		
Sumo Logic Inc	511210J		
Teradata Corporation	511210J	2,156,000,000	-67,000,000
Computer Software, E-Commerce, Web Analytics & Applications Management			
Acquia Inc	511210M	175,000,000	
AppDirect Inc	511210M		
AppDynamics Inc	511210M	185,000,000	
BigCommerce Holdings Inc	511210M		
BroadVision Inc	511210M	6,357,000	-9,899,000
Digital River Inc	511210M	420,000,000	
Computer Software, E-Commerce, Web Analytics & Applications Management			
Dynatrace LLC	511210m	512,000,000	
Computer Software, E-Commerce, Web Analytics & Applications Management			
Fastly Inc	511210M		
iCrossing Inc	511210M		
Computer Software, E-Commerce, Web Analytics & Applications Management			
Infor	511210m	2,855,800,000	-186,800,000
Computer Software, E-Commerce, Web Analytics & Applications Management			
Kibo Software Inc	511210M		
Mixpanel Inc	511210M	100,000,000	
Sea Limited	511210M	414,190,016	-560,484,992
Turbonomic Inc	511210M		
Ushahidi Inc	511210M	3,520,014	362,907
Computer Software, Educational & Training			
Blackboard Inc	511210P	690,000,000	
Computer Software, Electronic Games, Apps & Entertainment			
DeNA Co Ltd	511210G	1,333,908,480	285,934,240
Electronic Arts Inc (EA)	511210G	4,845,000,192	967,000,000

Industry Group/Company	Industry Code	2017 Sales	2017 Profits
Linden Research Inc (Linden Lab)	511210G	70,000,000	
Optimizely Inc	511210G		
Zynga Inc	511210G	861,390,016	26,639,000
Computer Software, Healthcare & Biotechnology			
ABILITY Network Inc	511210D		
Epocrates Inc	511210D	140,000,000	
Flatiron Health Inc	511210D		
MedeAnalytics Inc	511210D		
PointClickCare	511210D	159,319,000	
Computer Software, Multimedia, Graphics & Publishing			
Adobe Systems Inc	511210F	7,301,505,024	1,693,954,048
Campaign Monitor	511210F		
Extreme Reach Inc	511210F		
Hootsuite Media Inc	511210F		
Lithium Technologies LLC	511210F		
MediaPlatform Inc	511210F		
Piksel Inc	511210F	60,727,400	
RealNetworks Inc	511210F	78,718,000	-16,305,000
SendGrid Inc	511210F	111,888,000	-6,253,000
Sprinklr Inc	511210F	110,250,000	
Computer Software, Network Management, System Testing, & Storage			
F5 Networks Inc	511210B	2,090,040,960	420,760,992
NetScout Systems Inc	511210B	1,162,112,000	33,291,000
Nutanix Inc	511210B	766,868,992	-458,011,008
Radware Ltd	511210B	211,368,992	-7,493,000
ServiceNow Inc	511210B	1,933,026,048	-149,130,000
Veeam Software Inc	511210B		
Computer Software, Operating Systems, Languages & Development Tools			
Datadog Inc	511210I		
MapR Technologies Inc	511210I		
Microsoft Corporation	511210I	89,950,003,200	21,204,000,768
MuleSoft LLC	511210I	296,456,000	-79,980,000
Progress Software Corporation	511210I	397,572,000	37,417,000
Red Hat Inc	511210I	2,411,802,880	253,703,008
Rogue Wave Software Inc	511210I		
Computer Software, Product Lifecycle, Engineering, Design & CAD			
InVisionApp Inc	511210N		
Procore Technologies Inc	511210N	60,000,000	
Computer Software, Sales & Customer Relationship Management			
Determine Inc	511210K	27,463,000	-9,452,000
ForeSee Results Inc	511210K	81,000,000	
Gainsight Inc	511210K		
InsideSales.com Inc	511210K		
Lightspeed POS Inc	511210K		
LivePerson Inc	511210K	218,876,000	-18,191,000

Industry Group/Company	Industry Code	2017 Sales	2017 Profits
LiveRamp Holdings Inc	511210K	880,246,976	4,108,000
Medallia Inc	511210K	137,812,500	
NewVoiceMedia	511210K	40,377,500	-26,106,100
SalesForce.com Inc	511210K	8,391,984,128	179,632,000
Shopify Inc	511210K	673,304,000	-39,995,000
SugarCRM	511210K	300,000,000	
Support.com Inc	511210K	60,121,000	-1,526,000
Talkdesk Inc	511210K		
US Interactive Inc	511210K		
WalkMe Inc	511210K		
Computer Software, Security & Anti-Virus			
AlienVault Inc	511210E		
Axway Inc	511210E	359,119,000	48,513,500
Carbon Black Inc	511210E	162,014,000	-55,827,000
Check Point Software Technologies Ltd	511210E	1,854,658,048	802,923,008
Cloudflare Inc	511210E	100,000,000	
Cylance Inc	511210E	100,000,000	
Duo Security Inc	511210E	100,000,000	
Entrust Datacard Corporation	511210E	150,000,000	
ForeScout Technologies Inc	511210E	220,871,008	-91,205,000
Illumio	511210E		
LifeLock Inc	511210E	681,000,000	
Lookout Inc	511210E		
McAfee LLC	511210E	2,681,000,000	
Netskope Inc	511210E		
OneSpan Inc	511210E	193,291,008	-22,399,000
Symantec Corporation	511210E	4,019,000,064	-106,000,000
Trend Micro Inc	511210E	1,311,688,064	226,452,192
Veracode Inc	511210E		
VeriSign Inc	511210E	1,165,095,040	457,248,000
WatchGuard Technologies Inc	511210E		
Zscaler Inc	511210E	125,717,000	-35,460,000
Computer Software, Supply Chain & Logistics			
BluJay Solutions Ltd	511210A	115,000,000	
JAGGAER	511210A	122,000,000	
JDA Software Group Inc	511210A	935,000,000	
Manhattan Associates Inc	511210A	594,598,976	116,481,000
Steel Connect Inc	511210A	436,620,000	-25,827,000
Computer Software, Telecom, Communications & VOIP			
BlueJeans Network Inc	511210C		
Fuze Inc	511210C		
Intercom Inc	511210C		
PagerDuty Inc	511210C		
Skype Technologies Sarl	511210C		
Slack Technologies Inc	511210C	160,000,000	
Twilio Inc	511210C	399,020,000	-63,708,000
WhatsApp Inc	511210C		
Yello Mobile Inc	511210C	378,000,000	
Zoom Video Communications Inc	511210C		

Industry Group/Company	Industry Code	2017 Sales	2017 Profits
Consulting Services, Marketing			
comScore Inc	541613	403,548,992	-281,392,992
Onvia Inc	541613	25,000,000	
Credit Card Processing, Online Payment Processing, EFT, ACH and Clearinghouses			
Adyen BV	522320	1,100,000,000	
Authorize.Net Holdings Inc	522320		
CyberSource Corporation	522320	377,000,000	
Elavon Inc	522320	1,600,000,000	
First Data Corporation	522320	12,051,999,744	1,464,999,936
Fiserv Inc	522320	5,696,000,000	1,246,000,000
Global Payments Inc	522320	3,975,162,880	468,424,992
Klarna Inc	522320	550,718,000	42,054,900
PayPal Holdings Inc	522320	13,093,999,616	1,795,000,064
Stripe Inc	522320	1,500,000,000	
Total System Services Inc (TSYS)	522320	4,927,965,184	586,185,024
VeriFone Systems Inc (Verifone)	522320	1,870,976,000	-173,828,992
Zuora Inc	522320	115,000,000	
Data Processing, Business Process Outsourcing (BPO) and Internet Content Hosting Services			
Aegis Limited	518210	122,000,000	
Automatic Data Processing Inc (ADP)	518210	12,379,799,552	1,733,400,064
Cyxtera Technologies Inc	518210	1,365,000,000	
GoDaddy Inc	518210	2,231,899,904	136,400,000
Health Catalyst	518210	70,000,000	
NeuStar Inc	518210	1,270,339,392	
Register.com Inc	518210		
Switch Inc	518210	378,275,000	-15,208,000
Tucows Inc	518210	329,420,736	22,326,594
Web.com Group Inc	518210	749,260,992	53,629,000
Electronic Auctions			
eBay Inc	454112	9,566,999,552	-1,016,000,000
Financial Data Publishing - Print & Online			
Bloomberg LP	511120A	9,658,000,000	
FactSet Research Systems Inc	511120A	1,221,179,008	258,259,008
Thomson Reuters Corporation	511120A	11,333,000,192	1,395,000,064
Flower, Nursery Stock and Florists' Supplies Wholesale Distribution			
FTD Companies Inc	424930	1,084,028,032	-234,040,992
Greeting Card Publishers			
American Greetings Corporation LLC	511191	1,900,000,000	
Hallmark Cards Inc	511191	3,912,000,000	
Insurance Agencies, Risk Management Consultants and Insurance Brokers			
EHealth Inc	524210	172,355,008	-25,412,000
Life Quotes Inc	524210		
Internet Search Engines, Online Publishing, Sharing, Gig and Consumer Services, Online Radio, TV and Entertainment Sites and Social Media			
Alibaba Group Holding Limited	519130	23,034,593,280	6,356,333,568

Industry Group/Company	Industry Code	2017 Sales	2017 Profits
Alphabet Inc (Google)	519130	110,854,995,968	12,661,999,616
Ancestry.com LLC	519130	1,000,000,000	
ANGI Homeservices Inc	519130	736,385,984	-103,118,000
App Annie Limited	519130		
Autohome Inc	519130	903,811,776	291,309,824
Automattic Inc	519130		
AutoWeb Inc	519130	142,124,992	-64,964,000
Baidu Inc	519130	12,342,856,704	2,663,474,688
Bankrate LLC	519130	445,000,000	
Blucora Inc	519130	509,556,992	27,039,000
Brightcove Inc	519130	155,912,992	-19,519,000
BuzzFeed Inc	519130	280,000,000	
Cars.com Inc	519130	626,262,016	224,443,008
CBS Interactive Inc	519130		
CoStar Group Inc	519130	965,230,016	122,695,000
Cox Automotive Inc	519130	7,410,000,000	
Crackle Inc (dba SonyCrackle)	519130		
Craigslist Inc	519130	380,000,000	
Digg Inc	519130		
Dotdash	519130	210,000,000	
Dropbox Inc	519130	1,106,800,000	-111,700,000
eHarmony Inc	519130	360,000,000	
E-machitown Co Ltd	519130	120,000,000	
Evernote Corporation	519130	230,000,000	
Everyday Health Inc	519130	266,000,000	
Facebook Inc	519130	40,653,000,704	15,934,000,128
GitHub Inc	519130	182,500,000	
Gree Inc	519130	606,346,496	112,384,976
Hoover's Inc	519130		
IAC/InterActiveCorp	519130	3,307,238,912	304,924,000
Indiegogo Inc	519130		
Instagram	519130	3,500,000,000	
Internet Brands Inc	519130	175,000,000	
Kakao Corporation	519130	1,846,900,000	119,449,000
Kickstarter PBC	519130		
LaShou Group Inc	519130		
Leaf Group Ltd	519130	128,990,000	-31,133,000
LinkedIn Corporation	519130	3,859,000,000	
LiveWorld Inc	519130		
LookSmart Group Inc	519130	5,000,000	
Mail.Ru Group Limited	519130	897,354,000	39,557,500
MailChimp (The Rocket Science Group LLC)	519130	588,000,000	
Major League Baseball Advanced Media LP (MLBAM)	519130	110,000,000	
MapQuest.com Inc	519130		
Marchex Inc	519130	90,291,000	-6,087,000
MarketWatch Inc	519130		
Match Group Inc	519130	1,330,660,992	350,148,000
Meituan Dianping	519130	5,026,630,000	-2,753,069,568
mixi Inc	519130	1,921,573,504	555,311,296

Industry Group/Company	Industry Code	2017 Sales	2017 Profits
Move Inc (Realtor.com)	519130	280,000,000	
MyHeritage Ltd	519130	133,000,000	18,100,000
Myspace LLC	519130		
Naver Corporation	519130	4,161,894,656	687,541,888
NaviSite Inc	519130		
NetEase Inc	519130	7,873,851,392	1,558,402,560
NeuLion Inc	519130	95,570,000	-31,315,000
NIC Inc	519130	336,508,000	51,614,000
OfferUp Inc	519130		
OpenTable Inc	519130	331,000,000	
Photobucket Inc	519130		
Ping An Healthcare and Technology Co Ltd	519130	286,825,000	93,970,600
Pinterest Inc	519130	470,000,000	
ProQuest LLC	519130	572,000,000	
REA Group Ltd	519130	470,262,752	144,374,704
Renren Inc	519130	202,102,000	-110,427,000
Rocket Internet SE	519130	44,034,700	-7,156,040
Roofoods Limited (Deliveroo)	519130	373,899,000	-247,601,000
Salon Media Group Inc	519130	4,570,000	-9,570,000
Seek Limited	519130	726,126,272	238,352,144
Shutterfly Inc	519130	1,190,201,984	30,085,000
SINA Corporation	519130	1,583,884,032	156,568,992
Snap Inc (Snapchat)	519130	824,948,992	-3,445,065,984
Sogou Inc	519130	908,356,992	82,200,000
Sohu.com Inc	519130	1,860,962,048	-554,526,016
SVMK Inc (SurveyMonkey)	519130	218,772,992	-24,010,000
Tencent Holdings Ltd	519130	34,602,901,504	10,407,358,464
TheStreet Inc	519130	62,469,392	2,626,837
Thumbtack Inc	519130		
TrueCar Inc	519130	323,148,992	-32,849,000
Twitter Inc	519130	2,443,299,072	-108,063,000
Verizon Media Group	519130	2,050,000,000	
Vimeo LLC	519130	81,100,000	
WebMD Health Corp	519130	740,298,321	
Whitepages Inc	519130		
Wikimedia Foundation	519130	91,242,418	22,105,660
XO Group Inc	519130	160,556,000	5,534,000
Yandex NV	519130	1,365,890,688	127,448,656
Yelp Inc	519130	846,812,992	152,858,000
Youku Tudou Inc	519130	1,050,000,000	
YouTube LLC	519130	6,250,000,000	
Zillow Inc	519130	1,076,793,984	-94,420,000
ZipRecruiter Inc	519130		
Local Messengers and Food Delivery			
Delivery Hero SE	492210	651,638,000	
GrubHub Inc	492210	683,067,008	98,983,000
Instacart	492210	815,000,000	

Industry Group/Company	Industry Code	2017 Sales	2017 Profits
Market Research, Business Intelligence and Opinion Polling			
Forrester Research Inc	541910	337,672,992	15,140,000
Gartner Inc	541910	3,311,493,888	3,279,000
Mortgage Brokers and Loan Brokers			
E-LOAN Inc	522310		
Newspaper Publishing			
Dow Jones & Company Inc	511110	2,950,000,000	
New York Times Company (The)	511110	1,675,639,040	4,296,000
News Corporation	511110	8,138,999,808	-738,000,000
Online Sales, B2C Ecommerce			
1-800 Contacts Inc	454111	431,000,000	
1-800-Flowers.Com Inc	454111	1,193,624,960	44,041,000
3 Suisses	454111	2,800,000,000	
AbeBooks Inc	454111		
AG Interactive Inc	454111	60,000,000	
Alibris Inc	454111	140,000,000	
Amazon.com Inc	454111	177,865,998,336	3,032,999,936
ASOS plc	454111	2,429,278,720	80,950,696
Audible Inc	454111		
B2W-Companhia Global Do Varejo	454111	1,896,294,912	-109,570,976
BackCountry.com	454111		
Blue Nile Inc	454111	500,000,000	
Bluefly Inc	454111	110,000,000	
Bonobos Inc	454111	140,000,000	
Boohoo.com PLC	454111	372,089,056	30,887,554
Brandless Inc	454111		
Build.com Inc	454111	807,600,000	
Chewy Inc (Chewy.com)	454111	2,000,000,000	
Coupang	454111	2,490,000,000	-598,178,000
Deem Inc	454111		
eMusic.com Inc	454111		
Etsy Inc	454111	441,231,008	81,800,000
Eventbrite Inc	454111	201,596,992	-38,547,000
Everlane	454111	133,000,000	
Fab.com	454111		
Fanatics Inc	454111	2,415,000,000	
Fandango Inc	454111		
Farfetch Ltd	454111	385,966,016	-112,275,000
Flipkart Internet Private Limited	454111	3,336,940,000	-318,164,000
FreshDirect LLC	454111	615,000,000	
Freshly Inc	454111		
Houzz Inc	454111	350,000,000	
Jasper Infotech Pvt Ltd	454111	166,708,000	-715,984,000
JD.com Inc	454111	52,732,719,104	-22,159,042
Jet.com Inc	454111		
MercadoLibre Inc	454111	1,398,094,976	13,780,000
MovieTickets.com Inc	454111		
Newegg Inc	454111	2,810,000,000	

Industry Group/Company	Industry Code	2017 Sales	2017 Profits
Ocado Group plc	454111	1,974,850,000	1,349,120
Overstock.com Inc	454111	1,744,755,968	-109,878,000
Ozon.ru	454111	374,591,000	
Peapod LLC	454111	680,000,000	
Poshmark Inc	454111		
PSI Capital Inc	454111		
Qurate Retail Inc	454111	10,380,999,680	1,208,000,000
Rakuten Commerce LLC	454111		
Rakuten Inc	454111	8,760,704,000	1,025,758,784
Reformation (The, LYMI Inc)	454111	100,000,000	
Rent the Runway	454111	128,000,000	
Revolve Group Inc	454111	399,597,000	5,000,000
Shopping.com Ltd	454111		
Snapdeal	454111	198,956,000	-715,984,000
Stamps.com Inc	454111	468,708,992	150,603,008
Stitch Fix Inc	454111	977,139,008	-594,000
Suning.com Co Ltd	454111	28,855,700,000	1,457,620,000
Teespring Inc	454111	150,000,000	
ThinkGeek Inc	454111	166,000,000	
VANCL	454111		
Vente-Privee	454111	3,588,000,000	
Vipshop Holdings Limited	454111	10,611,447,808	283,747,168
VitaCost.com Inc	454111	432,000,000	
Wayfair LLC	454111	4,720,894,976	-244,614,000
Wish.com	454111		
YOOX Net-A-Porter Group SpA (YNAP)	454111	2,366,848,768	21,020,520
Zalando SE	454111	4,000,000,000	
Zappos.com Inc	454111	2,810,000,000	
Zulily LLC	454111	1,500,000,000	
Optical Goods Stores			
Warby Parker	446130	315,000,000	
Outsourced Computer Facilities Management and Operations Services			
IBM Global Services	541513	16,348,000,000	1,401,000,000
International Business Machines Corporation (IBM)	541513	79,138,996,224	5,752,999,936
Personal Care Products; Cosmetics and Makeup; Fragrances and Perfumes; and Hair Care Products Manufacturing			
Honest Company Inc (The)	325620	330,000,000	
Professional Training, Management Development and Corporate Employee Training			
HealthStream Inc	611430	247,662,000	10,004,000
Radio Networks, Including Commercial Networks Supporting Radio Broadcasting, and Public Radio Networks			
Pandora Media Inc	515111	1,466,812,032	-518,395,008
Spotify Technology SA	515111	4,658,950,656	-1,406,798,208
Tencent Music Entertainment Group	515111	1,598,142,976	192,982,208
Radio, Television and Other Electronics Stores			
Frys Electronics Inc	443142	2,320,000,000	

Industry Group/Company	Industry Code	2017 Sales	2017 Profits
Recruiting & Job Services Online			
CareerBuilder Inc	561311A	733,000,000	
Ladders (The)	561311A		
Monster Worldwide Inc	561311A	660,000,000	
Satellite Telecommunications			
OneWeb Ltd	517410		
Planet Labs Inc	517410		
Securities Brokerage, Discount Brokers and Online Stock Brokers			
Boursorama	523120	255,000,000	
Charles Schwab Corporation (The)	523120	8,439,000,064	2,353,999,872
E*Trade Financial Corporation	523120	2,366,000,128	614,000,000
TD Ameritrade Holding Corporation	523120	3,604,999,936	872,000,000
TradeStation Group Inc	523120	155,000,000	
Telecommunications, Telephone and Network Equipment Manufacturing, including PBX, Routers, Switches and Handsets Manufacturing			
ADTRAN Inc	334210	666,899,968	23,840,000
Avaya Holdings Corp	334210	3,272,000,000	-182,000,000
Ciena Corporation	334210	2,801,687,040	1,261,953,024
ECI Telecom Ltd	334210	380,000,000	
Harmonic Inc	334210	358,246,016	-82,955,000
Huawei Technologies Co Ltd	334210	92,080,000,000	
Oclaro Inc	334210	600,968,000	127,859,000
Tellabs Inc	334210	1,391,000,000	
UTStarcom Inc	334210	120,000,000	
Westell Technologies Inc	334210	62,965,000	-15,941,000
Telephone, Internet Access, Broadband, Data Networks, Server Facilities and Telecommunications Services Industry			
Akamai Technologies Inc	517110	2,502,995,968	218,320,992
Altice USA Inc	517110	9,326,570,496	1,520,030,976
Amazon Web Services Inc (AWS)	517110	17,460,000,000	4,330,000,000
AT&T Inc	517110	160,545,996,800	29,450,000,384
Boingo Wireless Inc	517110	204,368,992	-19,366,000
CenturyLink Inc	517110	17,656,000,512	1,388,999,936
Charter Communications Inc	517110	41,580,998,656	9,895,000,064
ChinaCache International Holdings Ltd	517110	124,080,280	-53,726,624
Cincinnati Bell Inc	517110	1,288,499,968	35,100,000
Cogent Communications Group Inc	517110	485,175,008	5,876,000
Comcast Corporation	517110	84,525,998,080	22,713,999,360
CoreSite Realty Corporation	517110	481,820,992	74,855,000
Cox Communications Inc	517110	11,550,000,000	
DigitalOcean Inc	517110	135,000,000	
DirecTV LLC (DIRECTV)	517110	35,584,900,000	4,305,000,000
EarthLink	517110	1,100,000,000	
Equinix Inc	517110	4,368,428,032	232,982,000
Frontier Communications Corporation	517110	9,127,999,488	-1,804,000,000
HC2 Holdings Inc	517110	1,563,069,952	-46,911,000

Industry Group/Company	Industry Code	2017 Sales	2017 Profits
Internap Corporation	517110	280,718,016	-45,343,000
Internet Initiative Japan Inc	517110	1,463,611,776	29,371,754
j2 Global Inc	517110	1,117,837,952	139,424,992
Level 3 Parent LLC	517110		
Liberty Global plc	517110	3,590,000,128	-778,099,968
Net2Phone Inc	517110		
Rackspace Hosting Inc	517110	2,200,000,000	
Rogers Communications Inc	517110	10,492,773,376	1,269,400,832
Shaw Communications Inc	517110	3,621,984,000	631,361,856
SoftBank Group Corp	517110	82,563,481,600	13,230,074,880
Telecomunicaciones de Puerto Rico Inc	517110	800,000,000	
Telephone and Data Systems Inc (TDS)	517110	5,043,999,744	153,000,000
United Internet AG	517110	4,761,114,624	736,206,080
United Online Inc	517110	191,000,000	
Verizon Communications Inc	517110	126,034,001,920	30,101,000,192
Vonage Holdings Corp	517110	1,002,286,016	-33,933,000
WebEx Communications Inc	517110		
Windstream Holdings Inc	517110	5,852,899,840	-2,116,600,064
XO Communications LLC	517110	1,600,000,000	
Television Broadcasting			
TEGNA Inc	515120	1,903,026,048	273,744,000
Travel Agencies			
Airbnb Inc	561510	2,570,000,000	93,000,000
Booking Holdings Inc	561510	11,400,000,000	
Ctrip.com International Ltd	561510	3,897,430,016	311,742,176
Expedia Inc	561510	10,059,843,584	377,964,000
HomeAway Inc	561510	856,000,000	
Hotels.com LP	561510		
Hotwire Inc	561510		
KAYAK	561510	435,000,000	
LastMinute.com (LMnext UK Ltd)	561510	37,274,300	2,594,920
lastminute.com NV (lm holding)	561510	294,835,264	-7,347,246
MakeMyTrip Limited	561510	447,616,000	-110,168,000
Orbitz Worldwide Inc	561510	800,000,000	
Sabre Corporation	561510	3,598,483,968	242,531,008
Sabre Travel Network	561510	2,550,470,000	848,336,000
Travelocity.com LP	561510		
Travelport Worldwide Limited	561510	2,447,279,104	142,463,008
Travelzoo Inc	561510	106,524,000	3,530,000
TripAdvisor Inc	561510	1,556,000,000	-19,000,000
trivago NV	561510	1,179,412,864	-14,217,205
Tujia Online Information Technology (Beijing) Co Ltd	561510		
Wireless Communications and Radio and TV Broadcasting Equipment Manufacturing, including Cellphones (Handsets)			
Apple Inc	334220	229,233,999,872	48,350,998,528
Wireless Telecommunications Carriers (except Satellite)			
America Movil SAB de CV	517210	52,112,195,584	1,495,876,992
China Mobile Limited	517210	107,772,264,448	16,631,834,624

Industry Group/Company	Industry Code	2017 Sales	2017 Profits
Jio (Reliance Jio Infocomm Limited)	517210	17,797,100	-5,235,450
KDDI Corporation	517210	44,043,657,216	5,070,662,656
Mobile TeleSystems PJSC	517210	6,432,134,656	813,864,832
NTT DOCOMO Inc	517210	42,525,155,328	6,052,779,008
SK Telecom Co Ltd	517210	15,585,536,000	2,312,768,512
Sprint Corporation	517210	33,347,000,320	-1,206,000,000
Telenor ASA	517210	14,522,840,064	1,394,929,280
T-Mobile International AG	517210	35,500,000,000	
T-Mobile US Inc	517210	40,604,000,256	4,536,000,000
Veon Ltd	517210	9,473,999,872	-483,000,000
Verio Inc	517210		
Vodafone Group plc	517210	54,256,844,800	-7,172,961,792

ALPHABETICAL INDEX

Cylance Inc
Cyxtera Technologies Inc
Datadog Inc
Deem Inc
Delivery Hero SE
Dell Technologies Inc
DeNA Co Ltd
Determine Inc
Didi Chuxing Technology Co Ltd (DiDi)
Digg Inc
Digital River Inc
DigitalOcean Inc
Digitas
DirecTV LLC (DIRECTV)
DocuSign Inc
Domo Inc
Dotdash
Dow Jones & Company Inc
Dropbox Inc
Duo Security Inc
Dynatrace LLC
E*Trade Financial Corporation
EarthLink
EasyAsk Inc
eBay Inc
ECI Telecom Ltd
eHarmony Inc
EHealth Inc
Elavon Inc
Electronic Arts Inc (EA)
E-LOAN Inc
E-machitown Co Ltd
Embarcadero Technologies Inc
eMusic.com Inc
Entrust Datacard Corporation
Epocrates Inc
Equinix Inc
Etsy Inc
Eventbrite Inc
Everlane
Evernote Corporation
Everyday Health Inc
Expedia Inc
Expensify Inc
Extreme Reach Inc
F5 Networks Inc
Fab.com
Facebook Inc
FactSet Research Systems Inc
Fanatics Inc
Fandango Inc
Farfetch Ltd
Fastly Inc
First Data Corporation
Fiserv Inc
Flatiron Health Inc
Flipkart Internet Private Limited
ForeScout Technologies Inc

ForeSee Results Inc
Forrester Research Inc
FreshDirect LLC
Freshly Inc
Frontier Communications Corporation
Frys Electronics Inc
FTD Companies Inc
Fuze Inc
Gainsight Inc
Gartner Inc
GitHub Inc
Global Payments Inc
GoDaddy Inc
Gree Inc
Greenhouse Software Inc
Groupon Inc
GrubHub Inc
Gusto
Hallmark Cards Inc
Harmonic Inc
HC2 Holdings Inc
Health Catalyst
HealthStream Inc
HomeAway Inc
Honest Company Inc (The)
Hootsuite Media Inc
Hoover's Inc
Hotels.com LP
Hotwire Inc
Houzz Inc
Huawei Technologies Co Ltd
Hulu LLC
IAC/InterActiveCorp
IBM Global Services
IBM Technology Services & Cloud Platforms
iCIMS Inc
iCrossing Inc
Illumio
Indiegogo Inc
Infor
Infosys Limited
InMobi Pte Ltd
InsideSales.com Inc
Instacart
Instagram
Intercom Inc
Internap Corporation
International Business Machines Corporation (IBM)
Internet Brands Inc
Internet Initiative Japan Inc
Intralinks Inc
Intuit Inc
InVisionApp Inc
j2 Global Inc
JAGGAER
Jasper Infotech Pvt Ltd
JD.com Inc
JDA Software Group Inc

Jet.com Inc
Jio (Reliance Jio Infocomm Limited)
Juniper Networks Inc
Kakao Corporation
KAYAK
KDDI Corporation
Kibo Software Inc
Kickstarter PBC
Klarna Inc
Ladders (The)
LaShou Group Inc
LastMinute.com (LMnext UK Ltd)
lastminute.com NV (lm holding)
Leaf Group Ltd
Level 3 Parent LLC
Liberty Global plc
Life Quotes Inc
LifeLock Inc
Lightspeed POS Inc
Linden Research Inc (Linden Lab)
LinkedIn Corporation
Lionbridge Technologies Inc
Lithium Technologies LLC
LivePerson Inc
LiveRamp Holdings Inc
LiveWorld Inc
LivingSocial Inc
Lookout Inc
LookSmart Group Inc
Lyft Inc
Macquarium Inc
Mail.Ru Group Limited
MailChimp (The Rocket Science Group LLC)
Major League Baseball Advanced Media LP (MLBAM)
MakeMyTrip Limited
Manhattan Associates Inc
MapQuest.com Inc
MapR Technologies Inc
Marchex Inc
MarketWatch Inc
Match Group Inc
McAfee LLC
Medallia Inc
MedeAnalytics Inc
MediaPlatform Inc
Meituan Dianping
MercadoLibre Inc
Microsoft Corporation
mixi Inc
Mixpanel Inc
mktg inc
Mobile TeleSystems PJSC
MongoDB Inc
Monster Worldwide Inc
MoreVisibility.com Inc
Move Inc (Realtor.com)
MovieTickets.com Inc
MuleSoft LLC

MXM
MyHeritage Ltd
Myspace LLC
Namely Inc
Naver Corporation
NaviSite Inc
Net2Phone Inc
NetEase Inc
Netflix Inc
NetScout Systems Inc
Netskope Inc
NeuLion Inc
NeuStar Inc
New York Times Company (The)
Newegg Inc
News Corporation
NewVoiceMedia
NIC Inc
NTT DOCOMO Inc
Nutanix Inc
Ocado Group plc
Oclaro Inc
OfferUp Inc
OneSpan Inc
OneWeb Ltd
Onstream Media Corporation
Onvia Inc
Open Text Corporation
OpenTable Inc
Optimizely Inc
Oracle Corporation
Oracle NetSuite
Orbitz Worldwide Inc
Overstock.com Inc
Ozon.ru
PagerDuty Inc
Pandora Media Inc
PayPal Holdings Inc
Peapod LLC
Perficient Inc
Performics Inc
Photobucket Inc
Piksel Inc
Ping An Healthcare and Technology Co Ltd
Pinterest Inc
Planet Labs Inc
PointClickCare
Poshmark Inc
Procore Technologies Inc
Progress Software Corporation
ProQuest LLC
PSI Capital Inc
Qualtrics LLC
Quotient Technology Inc
Qurate Retail Inc
Rackspace Hosting Inc
Radware Ltd
Rakuten Affiliate Network

Rakuten Commerce LLC
Rakuten Inc
REA Group Ltd
RealNetworks Inc
RealPage Inc
Red Hat Inc
Reformation (The, LYMI Inc)
Register.com Inc
Renren Inc
Rent the Runway
Return Path Inc
Revolve Group Inc
Rocket Internet SE
Rogers Communications Inc
Rogue Wave Software Inc
Roofoods Limited (Deliveroo)
Sabre Corporation
Sabre Travel Network
Sage Intacct Inc
SalesForce.com Inc
Salon Media Group Inc
SAP SE
Sapient Corporation
Sea Limited
Seek Limited
Segment.io Inc
SendGrid Inc
ServiceMax Inc
ServiceNow Inc
Shaw Communications Inc
Shopify Inc
Shopping.com Ltd
Shutterfly Inc
SINA Corporation
Sisense Inc
SK Telecom Co Ltd
Skype Technologies Sarl
Slack Technologies Inc
Smartsheet Inc
SMS Assist LLC
Snap Inc (Snapchat)
Snapdeal
SoftBank Group Corp
Sogou Inc
Sohu.com Inc
Sopra Steria Group SA
Spotify Technology SA
Sprinklr Inc
Sprint Corporation
Squarespace Inc
Stamps.com Inc
Steel Connect Inc
Stitch Fix Inc
Stripe Inc
Student Advantage LLC
SugarCRM
Sumo Logic Inc
Suning.com Co Ltd

Support.com Inc
SVMK Inc (SurveyMonkey)
Switch Inc
Symantec Corporation
Symphony Technology Group
Talkdesk Inc
Tata Consultancy Services Limited (TCS)
TD Ameritrade Holding Corporation
Teespring Inc
TEGNA Inc
Telecomunicaciones de Puerto Rico Inc
Telenor ASA
Telephone and Data Systems Inc (TDS)
Tellabs Inc
Tencent Holdings Ltd
Tencent Music Entertainment Group
Teradata Corporation
TheStreet Inc
ThinkGeek Inc
Thomson Reuters Corporation
Thumbtack Inc
TIBCO Software Inc
T-Mobile International AG
T-Mobile US Inc
Total System Services Inc (TSYS)
TradeStation Group Inc
Travelocity.com LP
Travelport Worldwide Limited
Travelzoo Inc
Trend Micro Inc
TripAdvisor Inc
trivago NV
TrueCar Inc
Tucows Inc
Tujia Online Information Technology (Beijing) Co Ltd
Turbonomic Inc
Twilio Inc
Twitter Inc
Uber Inc
United Internet AG
United Online Inc
US Interactive Inc
Ushahidi Inc
UTStarcom Inc
VANCL
Veeam Software Inc
Vente-Privee
Veon Ltd
Veracode Inc
VeriFone Systems Inc (Verifone)
Verio Inc
VeriSign Inc
Verizon Communications Inc
Verizon Media Group
VerticalResponse Inc
Vibrant Media Inc
Vimeo LLC
Vipshop Holdings Limited

VitaCost.com Inc
Vodafone Group plc
Vonage Holdings Corp
WalkMe Inc
Walt Disney Company (The)
Warby Parker
WatchGuard Technologies Inc
Wayfair LLC
Web.com Group Inc
WebEx Communications Inc
WebMD Health Corp
Westell Technologies Inc
WhatsApp Inc
Whitepages Inc
Wikimedia Foundation
Windstream Holdings Inc
Wipro Limited
Wish.com
Workday Inc
Workfront Inc
Xaxis
XO Communications LLC
XO Group Inc
Yandex NV
Yardi Systems Inc
Yello Mobile Inc
Yelp Inc
YesMail.com Inc
YOOX Net-A-Porter Group SpA (YNAP)
Youku Tudou Inc
YouTube LLC
Zalando SE
Zappos.com Inc
Zillow Inc
ZipRecruiter Inc
Zoho Corporation Private Limited
Zoom Video Communications Inc
Zscaler Inc
Zulily LLC
Zuora Inc
Zynga Inc

INDEX OF HEADQUARTERS LOCATION BY U.S. STATE

To help you locate the firms geographically, the city and state of the headquarters of each company are in the following index.

ALABAMA
ADTRAN Inc:Huntsville

ARIZONA
Axway Inc:Phoenix
Carvana Co:Tempe
GoDaddy Inc:Scottsdale
JDA Software Group Inc:Scottsdale
LifeLock Inc:Tempe

ARKANSAS
Windstream Holdings Inc:Little Rock

CALIFORNIA
Adaptive Insights Inc:Palo Alto
Adobe Systems Inc:San Jose
Airbnb Inc:San Francisco
AKQA Inc:San Francisco
Alibris Inc:Emeryville
AlienVault Inc:San Mateo
Alphabet Inc (Google):Mountain View
Alteryx Inc:Irvine
Anaplan Inc:San Francisco
App Annie Limited:San Francisco
AppDirect Inc:San Francisco
AppDynamics Inc:San Francisco
Apple Inc:Cupertino
Apttus Corporation:San Mateo
Ariba Inc:Sunnyvale
Arista Networks Inc:Santa Clara
Asana Inc:San Francisco
Automattic Inc:San Francisco
AutoWeb Inc:Irvine
Avaya Holdings Corp:Santa Clara
BlackLine Inc:Woodland Hills
BlueJeans Network Inc:Mountain View
Boingo Wireless Inc:Los Angeles
Box Inc:Redwood City
Brandless Inc:San Francisco
BroadVision Inc:Redwood City
Build.com Inc:Chico
Campaign Monitor:San Francisco
CBS Interactive Inc:San Francisco
Charles Schwab Corporation (The):San Francisco
Cisco Systems Inc:San Jose
Cloudflare Inc:San Francisco
Coupa Software Inc:San Mateo
Crackle Inc (dba SonyCrackle):Culver City
Craigslist Inc:San Francisco

CyberSource Corporation:Mountain View
Cylance Inc:Irvine
Deem Inc:San Francisco
DirecTV LLC (DIRECTV):El Segundo
DocuSign Inc:San Francisco
Dropbox Inc:San Francisco
eBay Inc:San Jose
eHarmony Inc:Santa Monica
EHealth Inc:Mountain View
Electronic Arts Inc (EA):Redwood City
Epocrates Inc:San Mateo
Equinix Inc:Redwood City
Eventbrite Inc:San Francisco
Everlane:San Francisco
Evernote Corporation:Redwood City
Expensify Inc:San Francisco
Facebook Inc:Menlo Park
Fandango Inc:Los Angeles
Fastly Inc:San Francisco
ForeScout Technologies Inc:San Jose
Frys Electronics Inc:San Jose
Gainsight Inc:Redwood City
GitHub Inc:San Francisco
Gusto:San Francisco
Harmonic Inc:San Jose
Honest Company Inc (The):Santa Monica
Hotwire Inc:San Francisco
Houzz Inc:Palo Alto
Hulu LLC:Santa Monica
Illumio:Sunnyvale
Indiegogo Inc:San Francisco
Instacart:San Francisco
Instagram:Menlo Park
Intercom Inc:San Francisco
Internet Brands Inc:El Segundo
Intuit Inc:Mountain View
j2 Global Inc:Los Angeles
Juniper Networks Inc:Sunnyvale
Leaf Group Ltd:Santa Monica
Linden Research Inc (Linden Lab):San Francisco
LinkedIn Corporation:Mountain View
Lithium Technologies LLC:San Francisco
LiveRamp Holdings Inc:San Francisco
LiveWorld Inc:San Jose
Lookout Inc:San Francisco
Lyft Inc:San Francisco
MapR Technologies Inc; San Jose
MarketWatch Inc; San Francisco
McAfee LLC; Santa Clara
Medallia Inc; Palo Alto
MediaPlatform Inc; Beverly Hills
Mixpanel Inc; San Francisco
Move Inc (Realtor.com); San Jose
MuleSoft LLC; San Francisco
Myspace LLC; Beverly Hills
Netflix Inc; Los Gatos
Netskope Inc; Los Altos
Newegg Inc; City of Industry

Nutanix Inc; San Jose
Oclaro Inc; San Jose
OpenTable Inc; San Francisco
Optimizely Inc; San Francisco
Oracle Corporation; Redwood City
Oracle NetSuite; San Mateo
PagerDuty Inc; San Francisco
Pandora Media Inc; Oakland
PayPal Holdings Inc; San Jose
Pinterest Inc; San Francisco
Planet Labs Inc; San Francisco
Poshmark Inc; Redwood City
Procore Technologies Inc; Carpinteria
PSI Capital Inc; Santa Monica
Quotient Technology Inc; Mountain View
Rakuten Commerce LLC; Aliso Viejo
Reformation (The, LYMI Inc); Los Angeles
Revolve Group Inc; Cerritos
Sage Intacct Inc; San Jose
SalesForce.com Inc; San Francisco
Salon Media Group Inc; San Francisco
Segment.io Inc; San Francisco
ServiceMax Inc; San Ramon
ServiceNow Inc; Santa Clara
Shopping.com Ltd; San Jose
Shutterfly Inc; Redwood City
Slack Technologies Inc; San Francisco
Snap Inc (Snapchat); Venice
Stamps.com Inc; El Segundo
Stitch Fix Inc; San Francisco
Stripe Inc; San Francisco
SugarCRM; Cupertino
Sumo Logic Inc; Redwood City
Support.com Inc; Sunnyvale
SVMK Inc (SurveyMonkey); San Mateo
Symantec Corporation; Mountain View
Symphony Technology Group; Palo Alto
Talkdesk Inc; San Francisco
Teespring Inc; San Francisco
Thumbtack Inc; San Francisco
TIBCO Software Inc; Palo Alto
TrueCar Inc; Santa Monica
Twilio Inc; San Francisco
Twitter Inc; San Francisco
Uber Inc; San Francisco
United Online Inc; Woodland Hills
US Interactive Inc; Santa Clara
VeriFone Systems Inc (Verifone); San Jose
VerticalResponse Inc; San Francisco
WalkMe Inc; San Francisco
Walt Disney Company (The); Burbank
WebEx Communications Inc; San Jose
WhatsApp Inc; Mountain View
Wikimedia Foundation; San Francisco
Wish.com; San Francisco
Workday Inc; Pleasanton
Yardi Systems Inc; Santa Barbara
Yelp Inc; San Francisco

YouTube LLC; San Bruno
ZipRecruiter Inc; Santa Monica
Zoom Video Communications Inc; San Jose
Zscaler Inc; San Jose
Zuora Inc; San Mateo
Zynga Inc; San Francisco

COLORADO

CoreSite Realty Corporation; Denver
Level 3 Parent LLC; Broomfield
MapQuest.com Inc; Denver
Photobucket Inc; Denver
Qurate Retail Inc; Englewood
Rogue Wave Software Inc; Louisville
SendGrid Inc; Denver

CONNECTICUT

Booking Holdings Inc; Norwalk
Charter Communications Inc; Stamford
FactSet Research Systems Inc; Norwalk
Frontier Communications Corporation; Norwalk
Gartner Inc; Stamford
KAYAK; Stamford

DISTRICT OF COLUMBIA

Blackboard Inc; Washington
Cogent Communications Group Inc; Washington
LivingSocial Inc; Washington

FLORIDA

Chewy Inc (Chewy.com); Dania Beach
Cyxtera Technologies Inc; Coral Gables
Fanatics Inc; Jacksonville
MoreVisibility.com Inc; Boca Raton
MovieTickets.com Inc; Boca Raton
Onstream Media Corporation; Pompano Beach
TradeStation Group Inc; Plantation
Ushahidi Inc; Orlando
VitaCost.com Inc; Boca Raton
Web.com Group Inc; Jacksonville

GEORGIA

Cox Automotive Inc; Atlanta
Cox Communications Inc; Atlanta
EarthLink; Atlanta
Elavon Inc; Atlanta
Global Payments Inc; Atlanta
Macquarium Inc; Atlanta
MailChimp (The Rocket Science Group LLC); Atlanta
Manhattan Associates Inc; Atlanta
Total System Services Inc (TSYS); Columbus

ILLINOIS

CareerBuilder Inc; Chicago
Cars.com Inc; Chicago
CDK Global Inc; Hoffman Estates
FTD Companies Inc; Downers Grove

Groupon Inc; Chicago
GrubHub Inc; Chicago
Life Quotes Inc; Darien
OneSpan Inc; Chicago
Orbitz Worldwide Inc; Chicago
Peapod LLC; Chicago
Performics Inc; Chicago
SMS Assist LLC; Chicago
Telephone and Data Systems Inc (TDS); Chicago
Tellabs Inc; Naperville
Westell Technologies Inc; Aurora
YesMail.com Inc; Chicago

INDIANA

Determine Inc; Carmel

KANSAS

NIC Inc; Olathe
Sprint Corporation; Overland Park

LOUISIANA

CenturyLink Inc; Monroe

MARYLAND

Ciena Corporation; Hanover

MASSACHUSETTS

Acquia Inc; Boston
Akamai Technologies Inc; Cambridge
Brightcove Inc; Cambridge
Carbon Black Inc; Waltham
Digitas; Boston
Dynatrace LLC; Waltham
EasyAsk Inc; Burlington
Extreme Reach Inc; Needham
Forrester Research Inc; Cambridge
Fuze Inc; Boston
Lionbridge Technologies Inc; Waltham
Monster Worldwide Inc; Weston
NaviSite Inc; Andover
NetScout Systems Inc; Westford
Progress Software Corporation; Bedford
Sapient Corporation; Boston
Steel Connect Inc; Waltham
TripAdvisor Inc; Needham
Turbonomic Inc; Boston
Veracode Inc; Burlington
Wayfair LLC; Boston

MICHIGAN

Duo Security Inc; Ann Arbor
ForeSee Results Inc; Ann Arbor
ProQuest LLC; Ann Arbor

MINNESOTA

ABILITY Network Inc; Minneapolis
Digital River Inc; Minnetonka

Entrust Datacard Corporation; Shakopee

MISSOURI
Hallmark Cards Inc; Kansas City
Perficient Inc; Saint Louis

NEBRASKA
TD Ameritrade Holding Corporation; Omaha

NEVADA
LookSmart Group Inc; Henderson
Switch Inc; Las Vegas
Zappos.com Inc; Las Vegas

NEW HAMPSHIRE
Bottomline Technologies Inc; Portsmouth

NEW JERSEY
Audible Inc; Newark
Automatic Data Processing Inc (ADP); Roseland
Hoover's Inc; Short Hills
iCIMS Inc; Holmdel
Jet.com Inc; Hoboken
Net2Phone Inc; Newark
Vonage Holdings Corp; Holmdel

NEW YORK
1-800-Flowers.Com Inc; Carle Place
Altice USA Inc; Bethpage
ANGI Homeservices Inc; New York
AppNexus Inc; New York
Bankrate LLC; New York
Bloomberg LP; New York
Bluefly Inc; New York
Bonobos Inc; New York
BuzzFeed Inc; New York
CA Technologies; New York
Datadog Inc; New York
Digg Inc; Brooklyn
DigitalOcean Inc; New York
Dotdash; New York
Dow Jones & Company Inc; New York
E*Trade Financial Corporation; New York
E-LOAN Inc; New York
eMusic.com Inc; New York
Etsy Inc; Brooklyn
Everyday Health Inc; New York
Fab.com; New York
First Data Corporation; New York
Flatiron Health Inc; New York
FreshDirect LLC; Long Island City
Freshly Inc; New York
Greenhouse Software Inc; New York
IAC/InterActiveCorp; New York
IBM Global Services; Armonk
IBM Technology Services & Cloud Platforms; Armonk
iCrossing Inc; New York

Infor; New York
International Business Machines Corporation (IBM); Armonk
Intralinks Inc; New York
InVisionApp Inc; New York
Kickstarter PBC; New York
Ladders (The); New York
LivePerson Inc; New York
Major League Baseball Advanced Media LP (MLBAM); New York
mktg inc; New York
MongoDB Inc; New York
MXM; New York
Namely Inc; New York
NeuLion Inc; Plainview
New York Times Company (The); New York
News Corporation; New York
Rakuten Affiliate Network; New York
Register.com Inc; New York
Rent the Runway; New York
Return Path Inc; New York
Sisense Inc; New York
Sprinklr Inc; New York
Squarespace Inc; New York
Student Advantage LLC; Ithaca
TheStreet Inc; New York
Thomson Reuters Corporation; New York
Travelzoo Inc; New York
Verizon Communications Inc; New York
Verizon Media Group; New York
Vibrant Media Inc; New York
Vimeo LLC; New York
Warby Parker; New York
WebMD Health Corp; New York
Xaxis; New York
XO Group Inc; New York

NORTH CAROLINA
JAGGAER; Morrisville
Red Hat Inc; Raleigh

OHIO
AG Interactive Inc; Cleveland
American Greetings Corporation LLC; Cleveland
Cincinnati Bell Inc; Cincinnati
Teradata Corporation; Dayton

PENNSYLVANIA
Comcast Corporation; Philadelphia

TENNESSEE
HealthStream Inc; Nashville

TEXAS
AT&T Inc; Dallas
BigCommerce Holdings Inc; Austin
Blucora Inc; Irving

BMC Software Inc; Houston
Dell Technologies Inc; Round Rock
Embarcadero Technologies Inc; Austin
HomeAway Inc; Austin
Hotels.com LP; Dallas
Kibo Software Inc; Dallas
Match Group Inc; Dallas
MedeAnalytics Inc; Richardson
Rackspace Hosting Inc; San Antonio
RealPage Inc; Richardson
Sabre Corporation; Southlake
Sabre Travel Network; Southlake
Travelocity.com LP; Dallas

UTAH

1-800 Contacts Inc; Orem
Ancestry.com LLC; Lehi
Authorize.Net Holdings Inc; American Fork
BackCountry.com; Salt Lake City
Domo Inc; American Fork
Health Catalyst; Salt Lake City
InsideSales.com Inc; Provo
Overstock.com Inc; Midvale
Qualtrics LLC; Provo
Verio Inc; Orem
Workfront Inc; Lehi

VIRGINIA

comScore Inc; Reston
HC2 Holdings Inc; Herndon
Internap Corporation; Renton
NeuStar Inc; Sterling
OneWeb Ltd; Arlington
TEGNA Inc; McLean
ThinkGeek Inc; Fairfax
VeriSign Inc; Reston
XO Communications LLC; Herndon

WASHINGTON

Amazon Web Services Inc (AWS); Seattle
Amazon.com Inc; Seattle
Apptio Inc; Bellevue
Avalara Inc; Seattle
Blue Nile Inc; Seattle
CoStar Group Inc; Northwest
Expedia Inc; Bellevue
F5 Networks Inc; Seattle
Marchex Inc; Seattle
Microsoft Corporation; Redmond
OfferUp Inc; Seattle
Onvia Inc; Seattle
RealNetworks Inc; Seattle
Smartsheet Inc; Bellevue
T-Mobile US Inc; Bellevue
WatchGuard Technologies Inc; Seattle
Whitepages Inc; Seattle
Zillow Inc; Seattle
Zulily LLC; Seattle

WISCONSIN

Fiserv Inc; Brookfield

INDEX OF NON-U.S. HEADQUARTERS LOCATION BY COUNTRY

ARGENTINA
MercadoLibre Inc; Buenos Aires

AUSTRALIA
REA Group Ltd; Richmond
Seek Limited; Melbourne

BRAZIL
B2W-Companhia Global Do Varejo; Rio de Janeiro

CANADA
AbeBooks Inc; Victoria
Critical Mass Inc; Calgary
Hootsuite Media Inc; Vancouver
Lightspeed POS Inc; Montreal
Open Text Corporation; Waterloo
PointClickCare; Mississauga
Rogers Communications Inc; Toronto
Shaw Communications Inc; Calgary
Shopify Inc; Ottawa
Tucows Inc; Toronto

CHINA
Alibaba Group Holding Limited; Hangzhou
Autohome Inc; Beijing
Baidu Inc; Beijing
ChinaCache International Holdings Ltd; Beijing
Ctrip.com International Ltd; Shanghai
Didi Chuxing Technology Co Ltd (DiDi); Hangzhou
Huawei Technologies Co Ltd; Shenzhen
JD.com Inc; Daxing Distr., Beijing
LaShou Group Inc; Beijing
Meituan Dianping; Beijing
NetEase Inc; Haidian Dist., Beijing
Ping An Healthcare and Technology Co Ltd; Shanghai
Renren Inc; Beijing
SINA Corporation; Shanghai
Sogou Inc; Beijing
Sohu.com Inc; Beijing
Suning.com Co Ltd; Nanjing
Tencent Holdings Ltd; Shenzhen
Tencent Music Entertainment Group; Shenzhen
Tujia Online Information Technology (Beijing) Co Ltd; Beijing
VANCL; Beijing
Vipshop Holdings Limited; Guangzhou
Youku Tudou Inc; Beijing

FRANCE
3 Suisses; Villeneuve d'Ascq
Atos SE; Bezons Cedex
Boursorama; Boulogne-Billancourt
Sopra Steria Group SA; Paris
Vente-Privee; Paris

GERMANY
Delivery Hero SE; Berlin
Rocket Internet SE; Berlin
SAP SE; Walldorf
T-Mobile International AG; Bellevue
trivago NV; Dusseldorf
United Internet AG; Montabaur
Zalando SE; Berlin

HONG KONG
China Mobile Limited; Hong Kong
UTStarcom Inc; Hong Kong

INDIA
Aegis Limited; Mumbai
Flipkart Internet Private Limited; Koramangala, Bengaluru
Infosys Limited; Bangalore
InMobi Pte Ltd; Bangalore
Jasper Infotech Pvt Ltd; New Delhi
Jio (Reliance Jio Infocomm Limited); Mumbai
MakeMyTrip Limited; Gurgaon
Snapdeal; New Delhi
Tata Consultancy Services Limited (TCS); Mumbai
Wipro Limited; Bangalore
Zoho Corporation Private Limited; Vallancherry Village

IRELAND
Accenture plc; Dublin

ISRAEL
Check Point Software Technologies Ltd; Tel Aviv
ECI Telecom Ltd; Petah Tikva
MyHeritage Ltd; Or Yehuda
Radware Ltd; Tel Aviv

ITALY
YOOX Net-A-Porter Group SpA (YNAP); Milan

JAPAN
Cyber Communications Inc; Tokyo
DeNA Co Ltd; Tokyo
E-machitown Co Ltd; Tokyo
Gree Inc; Tokyo
Internet Initiative Japan Inc; Tokyo
KDDI Corporation; Tokyo
mixi Inc; Tokyo
NTT DOCOMO Inc; Tokyo
Rakuten Inc; Tokyo
SoftBank Group Corp; Tokyo
Trend Micro Inc; Tokyo

KOREA
Coupang; Seoul
Kakao Corporation; Jeju-si Jeju-do

Naver Corporation; Bundang-gu
SK Telecom Co Ltd; Seoul
Yello Mobile Inc; Seoul

LUXEMBOURG
Skype Technologies Sarl; Luxembourg
Spotify Technology SA; Luxembourg City

MEXICO
America Movil SAB de CV; Delegacion Miguel Hidalgo

NORWAY
Telenor ASA; Fornebu

PUERTO RICO
Telecomunicaciones de Puerto Rico Inc; Guaynabo

RUSSIA
Mail.Ru Group Limited; Moscow
Mobile TeleSystems PJSC; Moscow
Ozon.ru; Moscow
Yandex NV; Moscow

SINGAPORE
Sea Limited; Singapore

SPAIN
Amadeus IT Group SA; Madrid

SWEDEN
Klarna Inc; Stockholm

SWITZERLAND
Veeam Software Inc; Baar

THE NETHERLANDS
Adyen BV; Amsterdam
lastminute.com NV (lm holding); Amsterdam
Veon Ltd; Amsterdam

UNITED KINGDOM
ASOS plc; London
BluJay Solutions Ltd; Manchester
Boohoo.com PLC; Manchester
Farfetch Ltd; London
LastMinute.com (LMnext UK Ltd); Amsterdam
Liberty Global plc; London
NewVoiceMedia; Basingstoke
Ocado Group plc; Hatfield
Piksel Inc; York
Roofoods Limited (Deliveroo); London
Travelport Worldwide Limited; Berkshire
Vodafone Group plc; Newbury

Individual Profiles
On Each Of
THE E-COMMERCE 500

1-800 Contacts Inc

www.1800contacts.com

NAIC Code: 454111

TYPES OF BUSINESS:
Direct Selling-Contact Lenses & Supplies
Contact Lens Manufacturing
Optical Retail Referral
Online Sales
Contact Lens Accessories

BRANDS/DIVISIONS/AFFILIATES:
AEA Investors LP
Thomas H Lee Partners LP
1-800-CONTACTS
1800Contacts.com
Glasses.com

CONTACTS: Note: Officers with more than one job title may be intentionally listed here more than once.
Brian W. Bethers, CEO
John F. Nichols, VP-Trade Rel.

GROWTH PLANS/SPECIAL FEATURES:
1-800 Contacts, Inc. is a provider of prescription contact lenses by mail. The firm sells most popular brands of contact lenses, including Acuvue, Avaira, Biofinity, Biomedics, DAILIES, PureVision, SofLens and more. The company's central distribution facility has an inventory of more than 15 million contacts. 1-800 Contacts offers customer service 24 hours a day, seven days a week, filling orders by phone at 1-800-CONTACTS and through the internet at 1800Contacts.com. Orders can also be placed by mail or fax. Order services include email shipping confirmation, online order tracking and email correspondence. The firm also sells contact lens accessories, such as contact lens solution and plastic cases. Glasses.com offers frames and lenses for glasses in much the same way as 1800contacts.com, offering a wide variety of frames for affordable prices. 1-800 Contacts is majority-owned by AEA Investors, LP, with Thomas H. Lee Partners owning a minority stake.

The company offers its employees a 401(k) plan; medical, dental and vision coverage; flexible spending accounts for health care and dependent care expenses; life and disability coverage; an employee assistance program; prescription drug plans; tuition reimbursement; an onsite fitness center; and a grill/cafeteria with subsidized meals at its headquarters.

FINANCIAL DATA: Note: Data for latest year may not have been available at press time.

In U.S. $	2018	2017	2016	2015	2014	2013
Revenue	450,000,000	431,000,000	430,000,000	425,000,000	410,000,000	400,000,000
R&D Expense						
Operating Income						
Operating Margin %						
SGA Expense						
Net Income						
Operating Cash Flow						
Capital Expenditure						
EBITDA						
Return on Assets %						
Return on Equity %						
Debt to Equity						

CONTACT INFORMATION:
Phone: 801-924-9900   Fax: 801-924-9923
Toll-Free: 800-266-8228
Address: 51 West Center St., Orem, UT 84057 United States

STOCK TICKER/OTHER:
Stock Ticker: Private   Exchange:
Employees: 1,101   Fiscal Year Ends: 12/31
Parent Company: AEA Investors LP

SALARIES/BONUSES:
Top Exec. Salary: $ Bonus: $
Second Exec. Salary: $ Bonus: $

OTHER THOUGHTS:
Estimated Female Officers or Directors:
Hot Spot for Advancement for Women/Minorities:

1-800-Flowers.Com Inc

www.1800flowers.com

NAIC Code: 454111

TYPES OF BUSINESS:

Direct Selling-Flowers
Online & Catalog Sales
Wine Distribution
Gardening Accessories
Gourmet Foods
Gifts
Retail Stores

BRANDS/DIVISIONS/AFFILIATES:

BloomNet
Fruit Bouquet
Cheryl's & Co
Popcorn Factory (The)
Harry & David
Cushman's
Moose Munch
Napco

CONTACTS: Note: Officers with more than one job title may be intentionally listed here more than once.

Christopher McCann, CEO
William Shea, CFO
James Mccann, Chairman of the Board
Arnie Leap, Chief Information Officer
Michael Manley, General Counsel
Thomas Hartnett, President, Divisional
Mark Nance, President, Subsidiary
Gerard Gallagher, Senior VP, Divisional

GROWTH PLANS/SPECIAL FEATURES:

1-800-FLOWERS.COM, Inc. sells and delivers floral arrangements, plants, gift baskets, popcorn, gourmet food, wine, confections, balloons and stuffed animals. Customers can purchase the company's products through its toll-free numbers and websites. It operates in three business categories: consumer floral, gourmet food and gift baskets and the BloomNet wire service segment. The consumer floral business category consists of fresh cut flowers and floral and fruit arrangements under the banners Fruit Bouquet, delivering fruit arrangements through FruitBouquets.com and flower delivery through the fresh from the farm program. This division also offers the Goodsey gifting line. The gourmet food and gift baskets category includes the Cheryl's & Co. and Mrs. Beasley's brands, delivering baked goods; and The Popcorn Factory. Additionally, 1-800-Baskets.com sells gourmet gift baskets made by DesignPac. Specialty premium gifts and gourmet food products under the Harry & David, Wolferman's and Cushman's and Moose Munch brands are also sold under this segment. The BloomNet wireservice segment includes house clearing services, which settles orders between sending and receiving florists; advertising; communications, which enables BloomNet florists to send and receive orders and correspond with other members using Bloomlink, a proprietary electronic communication system; web hosting and point of sale (POS); and wholesale products, which allows florists to purchase branded and non-branded floral supplies for the fulfillment of 1-800-Flowers.com brand orders. A majority of 1-800-FLOWERS orders are fulfilled by BloomNet members, which include independent and company-owned florists, with the remainder filled by third- party vendors. The BloomNet segment also operates BloomNet Technologies and Napco. The company offers same-day and next day delivery in addition to international delivery services through independent wire services and partnerships.

The company offers its employees a 401(k) plan, a profit sharing plan and health coverage.

FINANCIAL DATA: Note: Data for latest year may not have been available at press time.

In U.S. $	2018	2017	2016	2015	2014	2013
Revenue	1,151,921,000	1,193,625,000	1,173,024,000	1,121,506,000	756,345,000	735,497,000
R&D Expense				34,745,000	22,518,000	21,700,000
Operating Income	41,048,000	46,359,000	43,282,000	37,617,000	23,706,000	25,786,000
Operating Margin %		14.19%	3.68%	3.35%	3.13%	3.50%
SGA Expense	376,250,000	401,643,000	402,558,000	385,709,000	249,601,000	238,908,000
Net Income	40,791,000	44,041,000	36,875,000	20,287,000	15,372,000	12,321,000
Operating Cash Flow	58,341,000	61,010,000	57,673,000	125,733,000	42,539,000	34,645,000
Capital Expenditure	33,306,000	33,653,000	33,938,000	32,572,000	22,985,000	20,044,000
EBITDA	73,517,000	79,735,000	75,666,000	66,741,000	43,554,000	44,584,000
Return on Assets %		8.31%	7.31%	5.27%	5.93%	4.78%
Return on Equity %		16.77%	16.35%	10.35%	8.72%	7.44%
Debt to Equity		0.35	0.40	0.56		

CONTACT INFORMATION:

Phone: 516 237-6000   Fax:
Toll-Free:
Address: One Old Country Rd., Carle Place, NY 11514 United States

STOCK TICKER/OTHER:

Stock Ticker: FLWS
Employees: 4,633
Parent Company:

Exchange: NAS
Fiscal Year Ends: 06/30

SALARIES/BONUSES:

Top Exec. Salary: $975,000   Bonus: $
Second Exec. Salary: $775,000   Bonus: $

OTHER THOUGHTS:

Estimated Female Officers or Directors: 1
Hot Spot for Advancement for Women/Minorities:

3 Suisses

NAIC Code: 454111

TYPES OF BUSINESS:

Fashion Apparel
Online Retail

BRANDS/DIVISIONS/AFFILIATES:

Otto GmbH

GROWTH PLANS/SPECIAL FEATURES:

3 Suisses is a designer and online retailer of high fashion apparel for men, women and children based in France. Apparel includes dresses, swimwear, blouses, shirts, sweaters, coats, pants, skirts, jackets, athleticwear, sleepwear and outerwear. Related items include shoes, jewelry, bags, scarves, belts, hats, gloves and sunglasses. Additionally, the company offers household and leisure products. Its key demographic is women between the ages of 35 and 45. Customers can place orders by phone, online or through its catalog. The company is 51%-owned by Otto GmbH. In June 2018, it was announced that the Belgian branch of 3 Suisses had declared bankruptcy.

CONTACTS: Note: Officers with more than one job title may be intentionally listed here more than once.

Marc Opelt, Chmn. Otto Management Board
Diego du Monceau, Chmn.-3 Suisses Int'l Group
Denis Terrien, CEO-3 Suisses Int'l Group

FINANCIAL DATA: Note: Data for latest year may not have been available at press time.

In U.S. $	2018	2017	2016	2015	2014	2013
Revenue		2,800,000,000	2,720,000,000	2,678,008,325	2,225,000,000	2,200,000,000
R&D Expense						
Operating Income						
Operating Margin %						
SGA Expense						
Net Income						
Operating Cash Flow						
Capital Expenditure						
EBITDA						
Return on Assets %						
Return on Equity %						
Debt to Equity						

CONTACT INFORMATION:

Phone: 0-892-621-500   Fax:
Toll-Free:
Address: 243-245 rue Jean Jaures, Villeneuve d'Ascq, 59650 France

STOCK TICKER/OTHER:

Stock Ticker: Subsidiary   Exchange:
Employees: 2,500   Fiscal Year Ends: 12/31
Parent Company: Otto GmbH

SALARIES/BONUSES:

Top Exec. Salary: $ Bonus: $
Second Exec. Salary: $ Bonus: $

OTHER THOUGHTS:

Estimated Female Officers or Directors: 1
Hot Spot for Advancement for Women/Minorities:

AbeBooks Inc

www.abebooks.com

NAIC Code: 454111

TYPES OF BUSINESS:

Online Book Sales
Book Inventory & Order Management

BRANDS/DIVISIONS/AFFILIATES:

Amazon.com Inc
Abebooks.com
Abebooks.co.uk
AbeBooks.de
AbeBooks.fr
IberLibros.com
ZVAB.com
BookFinder.com

CONTACTS: *Note: Officers with more than one job title may be intentionally listed here more than once.*

Arkady Vitrouk, CEO
Hannes Blum, Pres.
Richard Davies, Mgr.-Public Rel. & Publicity

GROWTH PLANS/SPECIAL FEATURES:

AbeBooks, Inc., a subsidiary of Amazon.com, Inc., is one of the world's largest online marketers of new, used, out-of-print and rare books. Its website features millions of books offered through independent book dealers, who pay a membership fee of $25 to $300 per month to sell their books through the firm's portal. The fee depends on how many books they sell. Aside from its English language websites (Abebooks.com and Abebooks.co.uk), the company maintains AbeBooks.de for German language shoppers, AbeBooks.fr for French shoppers, AbeBooks.it for Italian shoppers and IberLibros.com for Spanish language books. Affiliated companies include ZVAB.com, a global marketplace for rare German books, offering more than 35 million used, antiquarian and out-of-print books; BookFinder.com, a price comparison shopping service dedicated to books; and FillZ, a book inventory and order management company that helps booksellers offer books through multiple online marketplaces. AbeBooks' blog, Reading Copy, is a daily source of company and book-related news.

FINANCIAL DATA: *Note: Data for latest year may not have been available at press time.*

In U.S. $	2018	2017	2016	2015	2014	2013
Revenue						
R&D Expense						
Operating Income						
Operating Margin %						
SGA Expense						
Net Income						
Operating Cash Flow						
Capital Expenditure						
EBITDA						
Return on Assets %						
Return on Equity %						
Debt to Equity						

CONTACT INFORMATION:

Phone: 250-412-3258   Fax: 250-475-6014
Toll-Free:
Address: 655 Tyee Rd., Ste. 500, Victoria, BC V9A 6X5 Canada

STOCK TICKER/OTHER:

Stock Ticker: Subsidiary   Exchange:
Employees: 135   Fiscal Year Ends: 12/31
Parent Company: Amazon.com Inc

SALARIES/BONUSES:

Top Exec. Salary: $ Bonus: $
Second Exec. Salary: $ Bonus: $

OTHER THOUGHTS:

Estimated Female Officers or Directors:
Hot Spot for Advancement for Women/Minorities:

ABILITY Network Inc

abilitynetwork.com

NAIC Code: 511210D

TYPES OF BUSINESS:

Computer Software, Healthcare & Biotechnology

BRANDS/DIVISIONS/AFFILIATES:

Inovalon Holdings Inc

CONTACTS: *Note: Officers with more than one job title may be intentionally listed here more than once.*

Jamison Rice, Managing Dir.
Ken Ernsting, COO
Bud Meadows, Chief Revenue Officer

GROWTH PLANS/SPECIAL FEATURES:

ABILITY Network, Inc. provides web-based healthcare technology. Thousands of payers and providers utilize ABILITY to simplify administrative and clinical processes. Other providers and partners include hospice, home health, hospital, physician/clinical practices, skilled nursing, specialty, clearinghouses, revenue cycle management firms and software vendors. ABILITY's products include analytics and reporting, billing management, claims management, electronic audits/appeals management, Medicare analytics, Medicare performance benchmarking, Medicare eligibility verification, all-payer claims and remittance, all-payer revenue cycle management, all-payer eligibility verification, patient statements, workforce management, as well as direct data entry and fiscal intermediary standard system connection (DDE/FISS). In April 2018, ABILITY Network was acquired by Inovalon Holdings, Inc., a leading technology company providing advanced, cloud-based platforms.

ABILITY offers its employees medical, dental, vision, life, AD&D and disability insurance; 401(k); paid time off and holidays; and employee assistance, referral and tuition reimbursement programs.

FINANCIAL DATA: *Note: Data for latest year may not have been available at press time.*

In U.S. $	2018	2017	2016	2015	2014	2013
Revenue						
R&D Expense						
Operating Income						
Operating Margin %						
SGA Expense						
Net Income						
Operating Cash Flow						
Capital Expenditure						
EBITDA						
Return on Assets %						
Return on Equity %						
Debt to Equity						

CONTACT INFORMATION:

Phone: 612-460-4327   Fax: 612-460-4343
Toll-Free: 877-340-5610
Address: 100 N. 6th St., Ste. 900A, Minneapolis, MN 55403 United States

STOCK TICKER/OTHER:

Stock Ticker: Subsidiary   Exchange:
Employees: 550   Fiscal Year Ends:
Parent Company: Inovalon Holdings Inc

SALARIES/BONUSES:

Top Exec. Salary: $ Bonus: $
Second Exec. Salary: $ Bonus: $

OTHER THOUGHTS:

Estimated Female Officers or Directors:
Hot Spot for Advancement for Women/Minorities:

Accenture plc

www.accenture.com

NAIC Code: 541512

TYPES OF BUSINESS:

IT Consulting
Computer Operations Outsourcing
Supply Chain Management
Technology Research
Software Development
Human Resources Consulting
Management Consulting
Research & Development

BRANDS/DIVISIONS/AFFILIATES:

accenturestrategy
accentureconsulting
accenturedigital
accenturetechnology
accentureoperations

CONTACTS: Note: Officers with more than one job title may be intentionally listed here more than once.

Pierre Nanterme, CEO
Jo Deblaere, COO
David P. Rowland, CFO
Amy Fuller, CMO
Ellyn J. Shook, Chief Human Resources Officer
Paul R. Daugherty, Chief Technology Officer & Innovation
Martin I. Cole, Group CEO-Tech.
Sander vant Noordende, Group CEO-Prod.
Richard Lumb, Group CEO-Financial Services
Stephen J Rohleder, Group CEO-Health & Public Service
Michael J Salvino, Group CEO-Business Process Outsourcing
Julie Spellman Sweet, General Counsel
David C. Thomlinson, Chief Oper. & Geographic Strategy Officer
Shawn Collinson, Chief Strategy Officer
Michael R. Sutcliff, Group CEO-Accenture Digital
Robert E. Sell, Group CEO-Comm., Media & Tech.
Mark A. Knickrehm, Group CEO-Accenture Strategy
Gianfranco Casati, Group CEO-Growth Markets
Adrian Lajtha, Chief Leadership Officer
Jean-Marc Ollagnier, Group CEO-Resources
Pierre Nanterme, Chmn.

GROWTH PLANS/SPECIAL FEATURES:

Accenture plc is a leading provider of technology, management consulting and business process services. The firm serves clients in more than 120 countries across over 40 industries, including three-quarters of the Global Fortune 500. It has 6,000 patents and patent pending applications in 44 countries. Accenture's products include: accenturestrategy, which combines its expertise in business with technology and operations strategy; accentureconsulting, which transforms businesses via industry expertise and data insights; accenturedigital, which helps clients provide better customer experiences via digital intelligence and connections; accenturetechnology, which powers businesses with cutting-edge solutions using both established as well as emerging/innovative technologies; and accentureoperations, which delivers outcomes through infrastructure, security, cloud and business process services. Accenture's products and solutions serve industries such as automotive, communications, media, high tech, natural resources, travel, banking, capital markets, consumer goods, industrial equipment, public service, energy, insurance, retail, health, life sciences, software/platforms, utilities and many more. In December 2018, Accenture agreed to acquire NYC-based Adaptly, a digital media services company that enables leading brands to manage data-driven campaigns across prominent digital advertising channels and platforms.

Accenture offers its employees medical, dental, long-term disability, life and AD&D coverage; legal coverage; profit sharing; 401(k); and adoption assistance.

FINANCIAL DATA: Note: Data for latest year may not have been available at press time.

In U.S. $	2018	2017	2016	2015	2014	2013
Revenue	41,603,430,000	36,765,480,000	34,797,660,000	32,914,420,000	31,874,680,000	30,394,280,000
R&D Expense						
Operating Income	5,841,041,000	4,632,609,000	4,810,445,000	4,435,869,000	4,282,497,000	4,066,638,000
Operating Margin %		12.60%	13.82%	13.47%	13.43%	13.37%
SGA Expense	6,601,872,000	6,397,883,000	5,466,982,000	5,373,370,000	5,401,969,000	5,317,537,000
Net Income	4,059,907,000	3,445,149,000	4,111,892,000	3,053,581,000	2,941,498,000	3,281,878,000
Operating Cash Flow	6,026,691,000	4,973,039,000	4,575,115,000	4,092,137,000	3,486,085,000	3,303,128,000
Capital Expenditure	619,187,000	515,919,000	496,566,000	395,017,000	321,870,000	369,593,000
EBITDA	6,754,408,000	5,433,366,000	6,348,882,000	5,071,031,000	4,936,065,000	4,946,357,000
Return on Assets %		15.91%	21.15%	16.87%	16.90%	19.57%
Return on Equity %		41.74%	60.07%	51.46%	55.02%	72.08%
Debt to Equity						

CONTACT INFORMATION:

Phone: 353-1-646-2000   Fax:
Toll-Free:
Address: 1 Grand Canal Sq., Dublin, 2 Ireland

STOCK TICKER/OTHER:

Stock Ticker: ACN   Exchange: NYS
Employees: 469,000   Fiscal Year Ends: 08/31
Parent Company:

SALARIES/BONUSES:

Top Exec. Salary: $1,136,125   Bonus: $
Second Exec. Salary: Bonus: $
$1,136,125

OTHER THOUGHTS:

Estimated Female Officers or Directors: 6
Hot Spot for Advancement for Women/Minorities: Y

Sales, profits and employees may be estimates. Financial information, benefits and other data can change quickly and may vary from those stated here.

Acquia Inc

www.acquia.com

NAIC Code: 511210M

TYPES OF BUSINESS:

Computer Software, E-Commerce & Web Analytics
Software
Cloud

BRANDS/DIVISIONS/AFFILIATES:

Acquia
Acquia Cloud
Acquia Lift
Drupal
Acquia Lightning

CONTACTS: *Note: Officers with more than one job title may be intentionally listed here more than once.*

Mike Sullivan, CEO
Stephen Reny, COO
Chris Andersen, CFO
Lynne Capozzi, CMO
Heather Hartford, Chief People Officer
Jairo Romero, Chief Revenue Officer
Dries Buytaert, Chmn.

GROWTH PLANS/SPECIAL FEATURES:

Acquia, Inc. provides a cloud platform for building, delivering and optimizing digital experiences. Global organizations use the platform to create a single foundation source for delivering enhanced customer experience. The Acquia platform enables organizations to engage in and analyze customer experiences, and easily deploy and manage them at scale in order to drive transformation business results. The firm's Acquia Cloud product enables customers to build and manage digital experiences; Acquia Lift personalizes the customer journey, merging content and data from any source; Drupal is a web content management solution that helps organizations create and deliver personalized content and digital experiences across web, mobile and social channels; and Acquia Lightning is a Drupal 8 starter kit for building and authoring digital experiences quickly and easily. Services offered by Acquia include global customer support, consultancy and advisory, as well as training and certification. Primary industries that use Acquia products include government, high tech, consumer brands, media/entertainment, life sciences, non-profit, higher education, healthcare and financial services. Customers of the firm have included SABMiller, BBC, Cisco, Stanford University and the Australian Government. In December 2018, Acquia expanded its Asia-Pacific presence to Japan by opening a new regional office in Tokyo.

FINANCIAL DATA: *Note: Data for latest year may not have been available at press time.*

In U.S. $	2018	2017	2016	2015	2014	2013
Revenue	200,000,000	175,000,000	150,000,000	128,000,000	100,000,000	68,000,000
R&D Expense						
Operating Income						
Operating Margin %						
SGA Expense						
Net Income						
Operating Cash Flow						
Capital Expenditure						
EBITDA						
Return on Assets %						
Return on Equity %						
Debt to Equity						

CONTACT INFORMATION:

Phone: 617-588-9600   Fax:
Toll-Free: 888-922-7842
Address: 53 State St., 10/Fl, Boston, MA 02109 United States

STOCK TICKER/OTHER:

Stock Ticker: Private   Exchange:
Employees: 900   Fiscal Year Ends: 12/31
Parent Company:

SALARIES/BONUSES:

Top Exec. Salary: $ Bonus: $
Second Exec. Salary: $ Bonus: $

OTHER THOUGHTS:

Estimated Female Officers or Directors:
Hot Spot for Advancement for Women/Minorities:

Adaptive Insights Inc

www.adaptiveinsights.com

NAIC Code: 511210Q

TYPES OF BUSINESS:

Computer Software, Accounting, Banking & Financial Software

BRANDS/DIVISIONS/AFFILIATES:

Adaptive Suite
Adaptive Planning
Adaptive Reporting
Adaptive Discovery
Adaptive Consolidation
Adaptive Technology Foundation
Workday Inc

CONTACTS: Note: Officers with more than one job title may be intentionally listed here more than once.

Tom Bogan, CEO
Fred Gewant, Chief Revenue Officer
Connie DeWitt, CMO
Amy Reichanadter, Chief People Officer
Scott LaFramboise, VP-Global Sales
Robert S. Hull, Chmn.

GROWTH PLANS/SPECIAL FEATURES:

Adaptive Insights, Inc. provides cloud-based corporate performance management (CPM) and business intelligence (BI) software. Adaptive Insights' software-as-a-service (SaaS) delivery model offers fast deployments, ease of use, limited need for IT support, automatic upgrades and lower costs. No new hardware, software or IT support is required with Adaptive Insight's software, instead, just a browser and an internet connection are needed. With automatic upgrades, all users immediately get access to new features. Adaptive Insights' products include the Adaptive Suite, Adaptive Planning, Adaptive Reporting, Adaptive Discovery, Adaptive Consolidation, Adaptive Technology Foundation and Licensing. Its products include workforce management, revenue management, expense management, capital management, profitability analysis and balance sheet and cash flow monitoring. Industries served by the firm include software/technology, healthcare, business services, nonprofit, higher education, manufacturing, retail, financial services, insurance and energy/utilities. The firm is headquartered in California, USA, with additional global headquarters in London, U.K.; Sydney, Australia; and Tokyo, Japan. Offices are located worldwide, including the U.S., Australia, India and Mexico. It has a presence in more than 50 countries. In August 2018, Adaptive Insights was acquired by Workday, Inc., a leader in enterprise cloud applications for finance and human resource.

The company offers its employees health benefits, paid time off and other perks, each of which vary depending on location.

FINANCIAL DATA: Note: Data for latest year may not have been available at press time.

In U.S. $	2018	2017	2016	2015	2014	2013
Revenue	106,508,000	81,791,000	61,706,000			
R&D Expense						
Operating Income						
Operating Margin %						
SGA Expense						
Net Income	-42,673,000	-44,720,000	-59,138,000			
Operating Cash Flow						
Capital Expenditure						
EBITDA						
Return on Assets %						
Return on Equity %						
Debt to Equity						

CONTACT INFORMATION:

Phone: 650-528-7500   Fax: 650-528-7501
Toll-Free: 800-303-6346
Address: 3350 W. BayshoreRd., Ste. 200, Palo Alto, CA 94303 United States

STOCK TICKER/OTHER:

Stock Ticker: Subsidiary   Exchange:
Employees: 498   Fiscal Year Ends: 01/31
Parent Company: Workday Inc

SALARIES/BONUSES:

Top Exec. Salary: $ Bonus: $
Second Exec. Salary: $ Bonus: $

OTHER THOUGHTS:

Estimated Female Officers or Directors:
Hot Spot for Advancement for Women/Minorities:

Adobe Systems Inc

www.adobe.com

NAIC Code: 511210F

TYPES OF BUSINESS:

Computer Software, Multimedia, Graphics & Publishing
Document Management Software
Photo Editing & Management Software
Graphic Design Software

BRANDS/DIVISIONS/AFFILIATES:

Adobe Experience Cloud
Adobe LiveCycle
Adobe Connect
Marketo Inc

CONTACTS: Note: Officers with more than one job title may be intentionally listed here more than once.

Shantanu Narayen, CEO
John Murphy, CFO
Mark Garfield, Chief Accounting Officer
Ann Lewnes, Chief Marketing Officer
Abhay Parasnis, Chief Technology Officer
John Warnock, Co-Founder
Charles Geschke, Director
Matthew Thompson, Executive VP, Divisional
Donna Morris, Executive VP, Divisional
Scott Belsky, Executive VP, Divisional
Bryan Lamkin, Executive VP
Bradley Rencher, Executive VP
Michael Dillon, General Counsel

GROWTH PLANS/SPECIAL FEATURES:

Adobe Systems, Inc. is one of the largest software companies in the world. The company operates in three segments, namely digital media, digital experience and publishing, with a current focus on investing in digital media and digital experience, its two strategic growth areas. Digital media provides products, services and solutions that enable individuals, teams and enterprises to create, publish and promote their content anywhere. Its customers include content creators, web designers, app developers and digital media professional, as well as management in marketing departments and agencies, companies and publishers. Customers also include workers who create, collaborate and distribute documents. The digital experience segment provides solutions and services for creating, managing, executing, measuring and optimizing digital marketing and advertising campaigns across multiple channels. Its customers include marketers, advertisers, agencies, publishers, merchandisers, web analysts, marketing executives, information management executives, product development executives and sales and support executives. This division processes more than 180 trillion data transactions in a given year with its analytics products, which provides customers with a data platform that can be used to gain insight and optimize digital experiences through the Adobe Experience Cloud. By combining the creativity of the digital media business and the science of the digital experience offerings, Adobe helps customers more efficiently and effectively make, manage, measure and monetize their content across all channels. Last, the publishing segment contains legacy products and services that address diverse market opportunities such as eLearning solutions, technical document publishing, web application development and high-end printing. This division offers Adobe LiveCycle, an enterprise document and forms platform; and Adobe Connect, a web conferencing platform. In October 2018, Adobe acquired Marketo, Inc., a revenue performance management company, for $4.75 billion, its largest transaction to date.

Adobe offers employees comprehensive benefits.

FINANCIAL DATA: Note: Data for latest year may not have been available at press time.

In U.S. $	2018	2017	2016	2015	2014	2013
Revenue		7,301,505,000	5,854,430,000	4,795,511,000	4,147,065,000	4,055,240,000
R&D Expense		1,224,059,000	975,987,000	862,730,000	844,353,000	826,631,000
Operating Income		2,168,095,000	1,492,094,000	904,654,000	432,568,000	449,220,000
Operating Margin %		29.69%	25.48%	18.86%	10.43%	11.07%
SGA Expense		2,822,298,000	2,487,907,000	2,215,161,000	2,195,640,000	2,140,578,000
Net Income		1,693,954,000	1,168,782,000	629,551,000	268,395,000	289,985,000
Operating Cash Flow		2,912,853,000	2,199,728,000	1,469,502,000	1,287,482,000	1,151,686,000
Capital Expenditure		178,122,000	203,805,000	184,936,000	148,332,000	188,358,000
EBITDA		2,538,040,000	1,837,115,000	1,277,438,000	734,698,000	744,876,000
Return on Assets %		12.43%	9.56%	5.59%	2.53%	2.84%
Return on Equity %		21.32%	16.20%	9.13%	3.97%	4.33%
Debt to Equity		0.22	0.25	0.27	0.13	0.22

CONTACT INFORMATION:

Phone: 408 536-6000   Fax: 408 536-6799
Toll-Free: 800-833-6687
Address: 345 Park Ave., San Jose, CA 95110 United States

STOCK TICKER/OTHER:

Stock Ticker: ADBE   Exchange: NAS
Employees: 15,706   Fiscal Year Ends: 11/30
Parent Company:

SALARIES/BONUSES:

Top Exec. Salary: $1,000,000   Bonus: $
Second Exec. Salary: Bonus: $
$720,192

OTHER THOUGHTS:

Estimated Female Officers or Directors: 5
Hot Spot for Advancement for Women/Minorities: Y

ADTRAN Inc

NAIC Code: 334210

www.adtran.com

TYPES OF BUSINESS:
Carrier Networks
Dedicated Enterprise Networks

BRANDS/DIVISIONS/AFFILIATES:
ADTRAN Mosaic Software-Defined Access
ADTRAN ProServices
ProStart
ProCare
ProCloud

CONTACTS: Note: Officers with more than one job title may be intentionally listed here more than once.

Thomas Stanton, CEO
Roger Shannon, CFO
Roy Nichols, Director Emeritus
James Wilson, Senior VP, Divisional
Kevin Heering, Senior VP, Divisional
Eduard Scheiterer, Senior VP, Divisional
Charles Marsh, Senior VP, Divisional
Michael Foliano, Senior VP, Divisional

GROWTH PLANS/SPECIAL FEATURES:

ADTRAN, Inc. designs, manufactures, markets and services network access applications for communications networks for use across IP, asynchronous transfer mode and time division multiplexed architectures. The company's products are used to enable voice, data, video and internet communications across copper, fiber and wireless networks; to deploy new broadband networks; and to upgrade slower, established networks. ADTRAN operates in two segments: network solutions and services & support. Network solutions products and services provide solutions supporting fiber- and copper-based infrastructures and a growing number of wireless and coax-based solutions, lowering the overall cost to deploy advanced services across a wide range of applications. Complementing these solutions is the ADTRAN Mosaic Software-Defined Access (SD-Access) architecture, which combines modern Web-scale technologies with open source platforms to facilitate rapid innovation in multi-technology, multi-vendor environments. The Mosaic cloud platform and Mosaic OS, combined with programmable network elements, provide operators with a highly agile, open-services architecture. The services & support segment enables the customers of the firm to more quickly and cost-effectively expand their networks, the firm provide a full-range of network implementation, maintenance and managed services. Solutions include ADTRAN ProServices, a comprehensive and flexible service program designed to offer complete networking lifecycle support. The ProServices portfolio consists of three service offerings: ProStart, ProCare and ProCloud.

The firm offers employees medical, dental and vision insurance; life and disability insurance; flexible spending accounts; an employee assistance program; onsite medical services; a 401(k) plan; education assistance; and a computer purchase plan.

FINANCIAL DATA: Note: Data for latest year may not have been available at press time.

In U.S. $	2018	2017	2016	2015	2014	2013
Revenue		666,900,000	636,781,000	600,064,000	630,007,000	641,744,000
R&D Expense		130,434,000	124,804,000	129,876,000	132,258,000	131,055,000
Operating Income		37,737,000	34,735,000	13,479,000	47,111,000	48,465,000
Operating Margin %		5.65%	5.45%	2.24%	7.47%	7.55%
SGA Expense		135,489,000	131,805,000	123,542,000	131,958,000	129,366,000
Net Income		23,840,000	35,229,000	18,646,000	44,620,000	45,794,000
Operating Cash Flow		-42,379,000	42,000,000	18,547,000	55,837,000	59,764,000
Capital Expenditure		14,720,000	21,441,000	11,753,000	11,256,000	8,173,000
EBITDA		60,935,000	61,874,000	40,549,000	75,428,000	77,808,000
Return on Assets %		3.56%	5.41%	2.71%	5.83%	5.46%
Return on Equity %		4.87%	7.34%	3.62%	7.73%	7.06%
Debt to Equity		0.05	0.05	0.05	0.05	0.07

CONTACT INFORMATION:
Phone: 256 963-8000   Fax: 256 963-8004
Toll-Free: 800-923-8726
Address: 901 Explorer Blvd., Huntsville, AL 35806 United States

STOCK TICKER/OTHER:
Stock Ticker: ADTN
Employees: 2,033
Parent Company:

Exchange: NAS
Fiscal Year Ends: 12/31

SALARIES/BONUSES:
Top Exec. Salary: $637,364   Bonus: $
Second Exec. Salary: $372,300   Bonus: $

OTHER THOUGHTS:
Estimated Female Officers or Directors:
Hot Spot for Advancement for Women/Minorities:

Adyen BV

NAIC Code: 522320

TYPES OF BUSINESS:

Payment Processing-Intermediary

BRANDS/DIVISIONS/AFFILIATES:

CONTACTS: *Note: Officers with more than one job title may be intentionally listed here more than once.*

Piero Overmars, Chmn.

GROWTH PLANS/SPECIAL FEATURES:

Adyen BV is a global multichannel payments company. The firm's technology enables companies to accept payments worldwide from all sales channels via connection to a single and scalable payment platform. Adyen builds all of its systems from the ground up, with an infrastructure that meets the highest standards of security and stability. Businesses can accept e-commerce payments on Adyen's payment platform through ready-to-use payment pages (HPP), a direct application programming interface (API), or via a client-side encryption solution (EE). Adyen also helps businesses create streamlined shopping that is simple, convenient and customized for each consumer. Payment services include online payments, mobile payments and internet-based point-of-sale payment solutions. Next generation solutions for payment and acquiring include full purchasing capabilities by linking merchants to acquirers all over the world via one contract and one technical interface. Adyen can route transactions from anywhere in the world, day or night, supporting more than 250 specific payment methods, including bitcoin and WeChat Pay, and all valid currencies. The company enables easy and flexible integrations with Apple Pay, as well as in-app and in-store Android Pay. Industries served include retail, digital, airlines, gaming, hospitality and ticketing. Based in the Netherlands, the firm has global offices, including Sweden, the U.S., the U.K., France, Germany, Belgium, Singapore, Brazil, Spain, China, Australia, Mexico and Italy.

FINANCIAL DATA: *Note: Data for latest year may not have been available at press time.*

In U.S. $	2018	2017	2016	2015	2014	2013
Revenue		1,100,000,000	727,000,000	365,000,000	175,000,000	
R&D Expense						
Operating Income						
Operating Margin %						
SGA Expense						
Net Income						
Operating Cash Flow						
Capital Expenditure						
EBITDA						
Return on Assets %						
Return on Equity %						
Debt to Equity						

CONTACT INFORMATION:

Phone: 31-20-240-1660   Fax:
Toll-Free:
Address: Simon Carmiggeltstraat 6-50, Amsterdam,   1011 DJ
Netherlands

STOCK TICKER/OTHER:

Stock Ticker: Private
Employees: 500
Parent Company:

Exchange:
Fiscal Year Ends: 12/31

SALARIES/BONUSES:

Top Exec. Salary: $ Bonus: $
Second Exec. Salary: $ Bonus: $

OTHER THOUGHTS:

Estimated Female Officers or Directors:
Hot Spot for Advancement for Women/Minorities:

Aegis Limited

www.aegisglobal.com

NAIC Code: 518210

TYPES OF BUSINESS:

Business Process Outsourcing
Customer Management Services

BRANDS/DIVISIONS/AFFILIATES:

STARTEK Inc
AegisLISAn

CONTACTS: Note: Officers with more than one job title may be intentionally listed here more than once.

Lance Rosenzweif, Global CEO
Joseph Duryea, Global Chief Revenue Officer
Ramesh Kamath, CFO
S.M. Gupta, Global Chief People Officer
Neeti Khaitan, Chief Relationship Officer, North America
Wayne White, Global CIO
V Nandakumar, CEO-Eng. Bus.
Sandeep Gulati, Exec. VP
Sudhir Agarwal, Pres., Mergers & Acquisitions & Strategy
Subir Ghosh, Pres., Aegis Global Academy
Peter Bloom, Pres., Global Equality & Customer Experience
S.K. Jha, Managing Dir.
Fernando Padron, Sr. VP
Aparup Sengupta, Chmn.
Christopher Luxford, Pres., Australia & New Zealand

GROWTH PLANS/SPECIAL FEATURES:

Aegis Limited provides business process outsourcing (BPO) services. Aegis solutions are categorized into three groups: outsourcing, technology and social business. Aegis' multi-channel outsourcing services include customer lifecycle management, as well as shared services such as data management, finance/accounting services and human resource outsourcing services. The technology group provides seamless solutions including business analytics, automation solutions and web integration solutions. The social business group is comprised of AegisLISAn, the company's product that is built on the framework of technology, analytics, execution and domain intelligence. AegisLISAn's basic technology is web-based and hosted on shared cloud in order to provide ease of deployment and fast turnaround. Its premium technology automates at scale. Analytics provide actionable insights for a brand's customer perception, competitive position, campaign effectiveness and industry trends. Execution is comprised of the management of end-user engagements with resources and specialists specifically trained in social media. This process helps define the best social media practices to offer customers and consumers across all channels. Domain intelligence provides in-depth domain comprehension and competitive benchmarks for designing and building a result-driven social media road map. In July 2018, Aegis, a portfolio company of Capital Square Partners (CSP), was acquired by STARTEK, Inc. Under the terms of the agreement, STARTEK will issue CSP 20.6 million shares of its common stock in exchange for all the outstanding common stock of Aegis.

FINANCIAL DATA: Note: Data for latest year may not have been available at press time.

In U.S. $	2018	2017	2016	2015	2014	2013
Revenue		122,000,000	120,000,000	110,000,000	100,000,000	
R&D Expense						
Operating Income						
Operating Margin %						
SGA Expense						
Net Income						
Operating Cash Flow						
Capital Expenditure						
EBITDA						
Return on Assets %						
Return on Equity %						
Debt to Equity						

CONTACT INFORMATION:

Phone: 91-22-6733-5000 Fax: 91-22-2495-4490
Toll-Free: 877-892-3447
Address: Essar Techno Park, LBS Marg, Off BKC, Kurla (W), Mumbai, Maharashtra 40070 India

STOCK TICKER/OTHER:

Stock Ticker: Subsidiary
Employees: 40,000
Parent Company: STARTEK Inc

Exchange:
Fiscal Year Ends: 12/31

SALARIES/BONUSES:

Top Exec. Salary: $ Bonus: $
Second Exec. Salary: $ Bonus: $

OTHER THOUGHTS:

Estimated Female Officers or Directors: 1
Hot Spot for Advancement for Women/Minorities:

AG Interactive Inc

www.americangreetings.com

NAIC Code: 454111

TYPES OF BUSINESS:

Online Greeting Cards
Wallpapers & Screensavers
Online Invitations
Avatars
Emoticons, Winks & Expressions
Instant Messaging Desktop Backgrounds
Mobile Wallpapers
Reminders

BRANDS/DIVISIONS/AFFILIATES:

American Greetings Corporation LLC
AmericanGreetings.com
BlueMoutain.com
Cardstore.com

CONTACTS: Note: Officers with more than one job title may be intentionally listed here more than once.

John W. Beeder, CEO
Gregory M. Steinberg, CFO
Christine M. Kaprosy, Chief Commercial Officer
Christopher W. Haffke, Chief Human Resources Officer
Kathy McConaughy, Chief Creative Officer
Ned Newhouse, Sr. VP-Advertising

GROWTH PLANS/SPECIAL FEATURES:

AG Interactive, Inc. (AGI) offers online greetings, photo sharing and customized printing services and other personalized digital content through a network of websites including AmericanGreetings.com, BlueMountain.com and Cardstore.com. AGI is a subsidiary of American Greetings Corporation, LLC. Customers may purchase single items or an annual subscription that allows unlimited use of the company's e-card and photo customizing services. Besides subscription fees, AGI generates sales from advertising. The firm's paid customer subscriptions number nearly 4 million. Users can choose among several different products and services, including typical online messages, personalized cards designed to be printed on printers and customized gifts with their digital photos rendered on coffee mugs, t-shirts and other items. In addition to e-cards and gifts, AGI's products include online avatars, active backgrounds for instant messaging desktops, screensavers and wallpapers, mobile wallpapers, an online reminders service and online invitations. Its services are produced in more than 20 languages for distribution in nearly 80 countries worldwide.

FINANCIAL DATA: Note: Data for latest year may not have been available at press time.

In U.S. $	2018	2017	2016	2015	2014	2013
Revenue	65,000,000	60,000,000	56,483,000	58,995,000	61,084,000	64,440,000
R&D Expense						
Operating Income						
Operating Margin %						
SGA Expense						
Net Income			19,126,000	21,668,000	15,550,900	16,574,000
Operating Cash Flow						
Capital Expenditure						
EBITDA						
Return on Assets %						
Return on Equity %						
Debt to Equity						

CONTACT INFORMATION:

Phone: 216-889-5000   Fax: 216-889-5371
Toll-Free: 800-711-4474
Address: 1 American Rd., Cleveland, OH 44144 United States

STOCK TICKER/OTHER:

Stock Ticker: Subsidiary   Exchange:
Employees: 650   Fiscal Year Ends: 02/28
Parent Company: American Greetings Corporation LLC

SALARIES/BONUSES:

Top Exec. Salary: $ Bonus: $
Second Exec. Salary: $ Bonus: $

OTHER THOUGHTS:

Estimated Female Officers or Directors: 3
Hot Spot for Advancement for Women/Minorities: Y

Airbnb Inc

NAIC Code: 561510

www.airbnb.com

TYPES OF BUSINESS:

Online Homestay Reservations
Room Rental Reservations
Tour Booking Online
Restaurant Reservations
Luxury Accommodations Booking

BRANDS/DIVISIONS/AFFILIATES:

Airbnb.com
Airbnb for Business
Airbnb Experiences
Beyond by Airbnb
Airbnb Plus
Airbnb Citizen

CONTACTS: *Note: Officers with more than one job title may be intentionally listed here more than once.*

Brian Chesky, CEO
Belinda Johnson, COO
Dave Stephenson, CFO
Joe Gebbia, Chief Product Officer
Aristotle Balogh, CTO

GROWTH PLANS/SPECIAL FEATURES:

Airbnb, Inc., founded in 2008, operates an online booking site for travelers and those who offer guest accommodation space. Through Airbnb.com, members who are willing to let travelers stay in their homes, guest houses, hotels, resort properties and other accommodations can post their information, including pricing, photos and amenities. In turn, travelers may search within a market for places to stay. Airbnb offers nearly 5 million listings spanning over 191 countries and 81,000 cities. Members are encouraged to write reviews describing the positive or negative aspects of their stays. These reviews are partially encouraged so that renters and travelers may view profiles and feedback before committing to a guest stay. The company offers booking of tours, restaurant reservations and events in addition to lodging options. Airbnb Experiences, the tour and event booking offering, offers more than 15,000 experiences run in more than 1,000 markets around the world. Beyond by Airbnb offers luxury trips and Airbnb Plus offers luxury accommodations. Airbnb for Business allows employees and employers to book business travel for co-workers. Airbnb also runs Airbnb Citizen, a platform for Airbnb to offer advice and stories to those who rent through Airbnb. Airbnb charges room owners a 3% host fee and an additional guest service fee that ranges between 0% to 20%, and is calculated using a variety of factors. The firm sets standards for cleanliness, communication and cancellations and offers a mobile app to facilitate guest/host communication. The firm has a goal of achieving $10 billion in yearly revenues by 2020, and a goal of serving 1 billion guests yearly by 2028.

About 41% of employees are women.

FINANCIAL DATA: *Note: Data for latest year may not have been available at press time.*

In U.S. $	2018	2017	2016	2015	2014	2013
Revenue	3,800,000,000	2,570,000,000	1,624,000,000	908,000,000	515,000,000	264,000,000
R&D Expense						
Operating Income						
Operating Margin %						
SGA Expense						
Net Income		93,000,000				
Operating Cash Flow						
Capital Expenditure						
EBITDA						
Return on Assets %						
Return on Equity %						
Debt to Equity						

CONTACT INFORMATION:

Phone: 415-728-0000   Fax:
Toll-Free:
Address: 888 Brannan St., Fl. 4, San Francisco, CA 94107 United States

STOCK TICKER/OTHER:

Stock Ticker: Private   Exchange:
Employees: 4,227   Fiscal Year Ends: 12/31
Parent Company:

SALARIES/BONUSES:

Top Exec. Salary: $ Bonus: $
Second Exec. Salary: $ Bonus: $

OTHER THOUGHTS:

Estimated Female Officers or Directors:
Hot Spot for Advancement for Women/Minorities: Y

Akamai Technologies Inc

www.akamai.com

NAIC Code: 517110

TYPES OF BUSINESS:

Online Information Service-Streaming Content
e-Business Software
Web Analytics
Online Content Distribution Support Services

BRANDS/DIVISIONS/AFFILIATES:

Akamai Intelligent Platform

CONTACTS: *Note: Officers with more than one job title may be intentionally listed here more than once.*

F. Leighton, CEO
James Benson, CFO
Frederic Salerno, Director
Robert Blumofe, Executive VP, Divisional
Adam Karon, Executive VP
James Gemmell, Executive VP
Aaron Ahola, General Counsel
William Wheaton, Other Executive Officer
Rick Mcconnell, President

GROWTH PLANS/SPECIAL FEATURES:

Akamai Technologies, Inc., a software and internet content company, provides enterprise e-business infrastructure services that enable its clients to deliver web content and applications at increased speeds and with improved reliability. Akamai's cloud-based distribution network is one of the largest in the world. The Akamai Intelligent Platform is a cloud-based platform for securely distributing and accelerating web content, enterprise applications and video. It resides on more than 200,000 servers deployed in over 1,700 networks and 130 countries worldwide. The proprietary software continually maps the internet to create a comprehensive knowledge of network conditions, provide instant device-level detection and optimization, and identify, absorb and block security threats. Akamai's massively-distributed platform provides businesses with significant advantage in terms of performance, reliability, cost and the ability to withstand attacks. Customers are primarily from the web and mobile performance, cloud security and media delivery industries.

Akamai offers its employees medical, dental and vision coverage; short- and long-term disability; parental leave; an employee assistance program; a 401(k); life and AD&D insurance; and an employee stock purchase plan.

FINANCIAL DATA: *Note: Data for latest year may not have been available at press time.*

In U.S. $	2018	2017	2016	2015	2014	2013
Revenue		2,502,996,000	2,340,049,000	2,197,448,000	1,963,874,000	1,577,922,000
R&D Expense		222,434,000	167,628,000	148,591,000	125,286,000	93,879,000
Operating Income		394,476,000	470,923,000	468,673,000	494,619,000	417,653,000
Operating Margin %		15.76%	20.12%	21.32%	25.18%	26.46%
SGA Expense		900,087,000	798,840,000	771,218,000	659,687,000	506,290,000
Net Income		218,321,000	316,132,000	321,406,000	333,948,000	293,487,000
Operating Cash Flow		800,983,000	866,298,000	764,151,000	658,070,000	563,908,000
Capital Expenditure		414,778,000	316,289,000	444,983,000	318,627,000	260,073,000
EBITDA		707,274,000	812,386,000	772,868,000	741,114,000	602,084,000
Return on Assets %		4.86%	7.38%	7.84%	9.59%	10.56%
Return on Equity %		6.68%	9.96%	10.59%	11.98%	11.79%
Debt to Equity		0.20	0.19	0.20	0.20	

CONTACT INFORMATION:

Phone: 617 444-3000   Fax:
Toll-Free: 877-425-2624
Address: 150 Broadway, Cambridge, MA 02142 United States

SALARIES/BONUSES:

Top Exec. Salary: $545,000   Bonus: $
Second Exec. Salary: Bonus: $
$472,500

STOCK TICKER/OTHER:

Stock Ticker: AKAM   Exchange: NAS
Employees: 6,490   Fiscal Year Ends: 12/31
Parent Company:

OTHER THOUGHTS:

Estimated Female Officers or Directors: 4
Hot Spot for Advancement for Women/Minorities: Y

AKQA Inc

www.akqa.com

NAIC Code: 541810E

TYPES OF BUSINESS:
Online Marketing
E-Mail Marketing
Web Site Design
Web Site Hosting

BRANDS/DIVISIONS/AFFILIATES:
WPP plc

CONTACTS: Note: Officers with more than one job title may be intentionally listed here more than once.
Ajaz Ahmed Zaidi, CEO
Lester M. Peintuck, CFO
Sam Kelly, Dir.-Bus. Dev. & Mktg.
Stuart Sproule, Managing Dir.

GROWTH PLANS/SPECIAL FEATURES:
AKQA, Inc. is an agency specializing in creating digital services and products. The company creates websites, conducts e-mail marketing campaigns and produces online interactive advertising. Additionally, the firm offers website hosting services. AKQA's digital innovation and service is recognized worldwide for its design and delivery of iconic digital products. Its social media team provides a sustained, integrated, managed and measurable ecosystem that is guided by its clients' commercial requirements and new opportunities, across multiple channels and platforms. AKQA's data science team delivers solutions to complex and challenging client requirements, offering advanced algorithm, analytic, software and technological expertise. The company's engineering approach delivers digital ecosystems that improve performance and is motivated by engineering frictionless solutions. Clients have included Rolls-Royce, Nike, Google, Tidal x Usher, Starbucks, Jordan and Verizon. Among the company's most notable achievements is the design of Microsoft's X-Box 360 console interface. AKQA has offices worldwide, and operates as a subsidiary of WPP plc.

FINANCIAL DATA: Note: Data for latest year may not have been available at press time.

In U.S. $	2018	2017	2016	2015	2014	2013
Revenue	760,000,000	731,000,000	715,000,000	675,595,898	624,738,838	557,117,349
R&D Expense						
Operating Income						
Operating Margin %						
SGA Expense						
Net Income						
Operating Cash Flow						
Capital Expenditure						
EBITDA						
Return on Assets %						
Return on Equity %						
Debt to Equity						

CONTACT INFORMATION:
Phone: 415-645-9400   Fax: 415-645-9420
Toll-Free:
Address: 360 Third St., Fl. 5, San Francisco, CA 94107 United States

STOCK TICKER/OTHER:
Stock Ticker: Subsidiary   Exchange:
Employees: 2,000   Fiscal Year Ends: 12/31
Parent Company: WPP plc

SALARIES/BONUSES:
Top Exec. Salary: $ Bonus: $
Second Exec. Salary: $ Bonus: $

OTHER THOUGHTS:
Estimated Female Officers or Directors:
Hot Spot for Advancement for Women/Minorities:

Alibaba Group Holding Limited www.alibabagroup.com/en/global/home

NAIC Code: 519130

TYPES OF BUSINESS:

Internet Publishing and Broadcasting and Web Search Portals

BRANDS/DIVISIONS/AFFILIATES:

Taobao Marketplace (Taobao.com)
Tmall.com
AliExpress.com
Alibaba.com
1688.com
Alimama.com
Alibaba Cloud Computing Ltd
Cainiao Network

CONTACTS: Note: Officers with more than one job title may be intentionally listed here more than once.

Daniel Yong Zhang, CEO
J. Michael Evans, Pres.
Maggie Wu, CFO
Chris Pen-hung Tung, CMO
Judy Tong, Chief People Officer
Jeff Zhang, CTO
Polo Shao, Group Sec.
Zeng Ming, Chief Strategy Officer
Joe Tsai, Vice-Chmn.
Lucy Peng, CEO-Small & Micro Financial Svcs. Group
Leo Jiang, Sr. VP
Zhang Yu, VP
Jack Yun Ma, Chmn.

GROWTH PLANS/SPECIAL FEATURES:

Alibaba Group Holding Limited (AGH) is a Chinese holding company that controls a family of internet-based businesses. The online businesses are engaged in such practices as online payment, consumer e-commerce, cloud computing, online travel and providing business-to-business (B2B) marketplaces. AGH's businesses include: Taobao Marketplace (Taobao.com), a Chinese consumer-to-consumer marketplace with hundreds of millions of product listings; Tmall.com, a business-to-consumer marketplace with over 100,000 international and domestic Chinese brands; AliExpress (AliExpress.com), a global retail marketplace; Alibaba.com, a global wholesale trade that serves millions of buyers and suppliers; 1688.com, a wholesale marketplace; Alimama (Alimama.com), a marketing technology platform; Alibaba Cloud Computing Ltd. (Aliyun.com), which develops highly scalable platforms for cloud computing and data management; Ant Financial Services Group, which serves small and micro enterprises as well as consumers; and Cainiao Network is a logistics data platform operator serving China's online and mobile commerce sector.

FINANCIAL DATA: Note: Data for latest year may not have been available at press time.

In U.S. $	2018	2017	2016	2015	2014	2013
Revenue	36,422,990,000	23,034,590,000	14,720,060,000	11,090,510,000	7,641,280,000	5,023,504,000
R&D Expense	3,311,551,000	2,482,863,000	2,006,666,000	1,551,134,000	741,220,500	546,200,800
Operating Income	10,240,430,000	6,993,786,000	4,360,001,000	3,440,061,000	3,669,864,000	1,646,607,000
Operating Margin %		30.36%	29.22%	30.58%	47.54%	41.75%
SGA Expense	6,336,686,000	4,155,521,000	2,985,257,000	2,374,147,000	1,275,342,000	946,282,300
Net Income	9,327,910,000	6,356,334,000	10,400,080,000	3,530,876,000	3,393,198,000	1,241,723,000
Operating Cash Flow	18,217,030,000	11,690,410,000	8,271,748,000	5,998,603,000	3,839,123,000	2,106,795,000
Capital Expenditure	4,342,245,000	2,553,594,000	1,578,350,000	1,121,363,000	695,085,200	364,279,400
EBITDA	18,336,080,000	11,205,190,000	13,115,080,000	5,747,406,000	4,460,858,000	1,836,533,000
Return on Assets %		10.02%	23.05%	13.16%	26.32%	15.14%
Return on Equity %		17.61%	39.43%	27.63%	157.44%	53.41%
Debt to Equity		0.27	0.24	0.34	1.04	

CONTACT INFORMATION:

Phone: 86-571-8502-2088   Fax: 86-571-8526-9066
Toll-Free:
Address: 969 W. Wen Yi Rd., Yu Hang Dist., Hangzhou, Zhejiang 311121 China

STOCK TICKER/OTHER:

Stock Ticker: BABA   Exchange: NYS
Employees: 66,421   Fiscal Year Ends:
Parent Company:

SALARIES/BONUSES:

Top Exec. Salary: $ Bonus: $
Second Exec. Salary: $ Bonus: $

OTHER THOUGHTS:

Estimated Female Officers or Directors: 4
Hot Spot for Advancement for Women/Minorities: Y

Alibris Inc

NAIC Code: 454111

www.alibris.com

TYPES OF BUSINESS:

Online Bookseller-Rare & Used
Business-to-Business Services
Rare Manuscripts & Prints
Online Retailer-DVDs & CDs

BRANDS/DIVISIONS/AFFILIATES:

Oak Hill Capital Partnes
AM Holding Inc
Alibris UK

CONTACTS: Note: Officers with more than one job title may be intentionally listed here more than once.

Tommaso Trionfi, CEO

GROWTH PLANS/SPECIAL FEATURES:

Alibris, Inc. provides an online marketplace for independent sellers of new, used and hard-to-find books, music, video games and movies. The company is owned by AM Holding, Inc., itself a subsidiary of Oak Hill Capital Partners. The firm provides bookstores, online booksellers, libraries and consumers in the U.S. and the U.K. with out-of-print, used, foreign-language and rare and collectible materials. The Alibris website contains a database of millions of books and textbooks, manuscripts, movies, music and e-books from thousands of sellers worldwide. If a product is not currently being sold in the marketplace, customers can submit a Book Fetch request, and the company will email them when the product is available. Students also have the option to rent textbooks for up to 90% off the purchase price. In addition, the company offers the Alibris for Library Service, which offers libraries one-stop search and acquisition solutions as well as acceptance of purchase orders, free search services, want list matching and consolidated shipping services. The firm has partnerships with a number of major retail companies, including Amazon.com, Barnes & Noble, Chapters/Indigo (Canada) and Waterstone's (UK). The program allows anyone to sell their new and used books, used textbooks, DVDs and CDs and video games, as well as rare and out-of-print books across Alibris's network of sales channels. Alibris operates in Europe through Alibris U.K.

FINANCIAL DATA: Note: Data for latest year may not have been available at press time.

In U.S. $	2018	2017	2016	2015	2014	2013
Revenue		140,000,000	135,000,000	130,000,000	120,000,000	100,000,000
R&D Expense						
Operating Income						
Operating Margin %						
SGA Expense						
Net Income						
Operating Cash Flow						
Capital Expenditure						
EBITDA						
Return on Assets %						
Return on Equity %						
Debt to Equity						

CONTACT INFORMATION:

Phone: 510-500-0856 Fax:
Toll-Free:
Address: 1250 45th St., Ste. 100, Emeryville, CA 94608 United States

STOCK TICKER/OTHER:

Stock Ticker: Private Exchange:
Employees: 120 Fiscal Year Ends: 12/31
Parent Company: Oak Hill Capital Partners

SALARIES/BONUSES:

Top Exec. Salary: $ Bonus: $
Second Exec. Salary: $ Bonus: $

OTHER THOUGHTS:

Estimated Female Officers or Directors:
Hot Spot for Advancement for Women/Minorities: Y

Sales, profits and employees may be estimates. Financial information, benefits and other data can change quickly and may vary from those stated here.

AlienVault Inc

www.alienvault.com

NAIC Code: 511210E

TYPES OF BUSINESS:

Computer Software, Security & Anti-Virus

BRANDS/DIVISIONS/AFFILIATES:

Open Threat Exchange
Unified Security Management
USM Anywhere
Open Source Security Information Management
AT&T Inc

CONTACTS: *Note: Officers with more than one job title may be intentionally listed here more than once.*

Barmak Meftah, CEO
Marcu Bragg, COO
Andy Johnson, CFO
Shanel Vandergriff, Sr. VP-Mktg.
Roger Thornton, CTO

GROWTH PLANS/SPECIAL FEATURES:

AlienVault, Inc., is a developer of commercial and open source solutions to manage cyber-attacks. The firm's open source product is the Open Threat Exchange (OTX). The OTX is the world's largest crowd-sourced computer-security platform with over 100,000 participants in 140 countries, who contribute over 19 million threat indicators daily. OTX delivers community-generated threat data, enables collaborative research and automates the process of updating security infrastructure with threat data from any source. The platform enables anyone in the security community to actively discuss, research, validate and share the latest threat data, trends and techniques, strengthening their own defenses while helping others do the same. The paid security products of AlienVault includes Unified Security Management (USM), a unified threat detection and compliance management solution that is both easy-to-use and affordable. The USM platform provides five security capabilities in a single console: discovers assets, locates all assets on a network before a bad actor does; assesses vulnerability, identifies systems on a network vulnerable to exploitation; detects intrusions, finds malicious traffic on a network; monitors behavior, identifies suspicious behavior and potentially compromised systems; and manages security information and events (SIEM), which correlates and analyzes security and event data from across the network. USM Anywhere is a software-as-a-service (SaaS) security monitoring platform designed to centralize threat detection, incident response and compliance management of cloud, hybrid cloud and on-premises environments from a cloud-based console. In addition to OTX and USM, AlienVault also runs the Open Source Security Information Management (OSSIM) project. OSSIM leverages the power of the OTX by allowing users to both contribute and receive real-time information about malicious hosts. The project provides a feature-rich open source SIEM complete with event collection, normalization and correlation. In August 2018, AT&T, Inc., to create a cybersecurity solutions business division, acquired AlienVault.

FINANCIAL DATA: *Note: Data for latest year may not have been available at press time.*

In U.S. $	2018	2017	2016	2015	2014	2013
Revenue						
R&D Expense						
Operating Income						
Operating Margin %						
SGA Expense						
Net Income						
Operating Cash Flow						
Capital Expenditure						
EBITDA						
Return on Assets %						
Return on Equity %						
Debt to Equity						

CONTACT INFORMATION:

Phone: 650-713-3333   Fax: 650-212-7637
Toll-Free:
Address: 1100 Park Place, Ste. 300, San Mateo, CA 94402 United States

STOCK TICKER/OTHER:

Stock Ticker: Private   Exchange:
Employees: 278   Fiscal Year Ends:
Parent Company: AT&T Inc

SALARIES/BONUSES:

Top Exec. Salary: $ Bonus: $
Second Exec. Salary: $ Bonus: $

OTHER THOUGHTS:

Estimated Female Officers or Directors:
Hot Spot for Advancement for Women/Minorities:

Alphabet Inc (Google)

NAIC Code: 519130

www.google.com

TYPES OF BUSINESS:

Search Engine-Internet
Paid Search Listing Advertising Services
Online Software and Productivity Tools
Online Video and Photo Services
Travel Booking
Analytical Tools
Venture Capital
Online Maps

BRANDS/DIVISIONS/AFFILIATES:

Google LLC
Search
Android
Maps
Chrome
YouTube
GooglePlay
Gmail

CONTACTS: *Note: Officers with more than one job title may be intentionally listed here more than once.*

Sundar Pichai, CEO, Subsidiary
Diane Greene, CEO, Subsidiary
Larry Page, CEO
Ruth Porat, CFO
John Hennessy, Chairman of the Board
Sergey Brin, Director
David Drummond, Other Executive Officer
James Campbell, Vice President

GROWTH PLANS/SPECIAL FEATURES:

Alphabet, Inc. owns a collection of businesses, the largest of which is Google, LLC, an information company offering a leading online search and advertising platform. Alphabet states that its primary job is to make the internet available to as many people as possible, and does this by tailoring hardware and software experiences that suit the needs of emerging markets, mainly through Android and Chrome. Google's core products include Search, Android, Maps, Chrome, YouTube, GooglePlay and Gmail, each of which have more than 1 billion monthly active users. Within Google, Alphabet's investments in machine learning are what enable the firm to continually innovate and build Google products, making them smarter and more useful over time. Machine learning also dramatically improves the energy efficiency of the company's data centers. Alphabet's other businesses include Access, Calico, CapitalG, GV, Nest, Verily, Waymo and X, all of which are not primarily engaged in the company's main internet offerings. Across these businesses, machine learning has the capability of doing things like helping self-driving cars better detect and respond to others on the road, or aiding clinicians in detecting diabetic retinopathy. Therefore, these firms utilize technology to try and solve big problems across many industries. They are early-stage businesses with the goal to become thriving ones in the medium- to long-term.

Employee perks at the main campus include on-site wellness, fitness, massage and health care facilities; along with free cafes, snacks and micro-kitchens. Other benefits for qualified employees include generous savings plans, training programs and flexible schedules.

FINANCIAL DATA: *Note: Data for latest year may not have been available at press time.*

In U.S. $	2018	2017	2016	2015	2014	2013
Revenue		110,855,000,000	90,272,000,000	74,989,000,000	66,001,000,000	59,825,000,000
R&D Expense		16,625,000,000	13,948,000,000	12,282,000,000	9,831,999,000	7,952,000,000
Operating Income		28,882,000,000	23,716,000,000	19,360,000,000	16,496,000,000	13,966,000,000
Operating Margin %		26.05%	26.27%	25.81%	24.99%	23.34%
SGA Expense		19,765,000,000	17,470,000,000	15,183,000,000	13,982,000,000	12,049,000,000
Net Income		12,662,000,000	19,478,000,000	16,348,000,000	14,444,000,000	12,920,000,000
Operating Cash Flow		37,091,000,000	36,036,000,000	26,024,000,000	22,376,000,000	18,659,000,000
Capital Expenditure		13,471,000,000	11,198,000,000	10,151,000,000	15,847,000,000	8,806,000,000
EBITDA		34,217,000,000	30,418,000,000	24,818,000,000	22,339,000,000	18,518,000,000
Return on Assets %		6.94%	12.36%	11.36%	11.93%	12.62%
Return on Equity %		8.68%	15.01%	14.07%	15.06%	16.24%
Debt to Equity		0.02	0.02	0.01	0.03	0.02

CONTACT INFORMATION:

Phone: 650 253-0000   Fax: 650 253-0001
Toll-Free:
Address: 1600 Amphitheatre Pkwy., Mountain View, CA 94043 United States

STOCK TICKER/OTHER:

Stock Ticker: GOOG   Exchange: NAS
Employees: 85,080   Fiscal Year Ends: 12/31
Parent Company:

SALARIES/BONUSES:

Top Exec. Salary: $1,250,000   Bonus: $
Second Exec. Salary: Bonus: $
$650,000

OTHER THOUGHTS:

Estimated Female Officers or Directors: 3
Hot Spot for Advancement for Women/Minorities: Y

Alteryx Inc

NAIC Code: 511210H

www.alteryx.com

TYPES OF BUSINESS:
Computer Software, Business Management & ERP

BRANDS/DIVISIONS/AFFILIATES:
Alteryx Analytics
Alteryx Designer
Alteryx Server
Alteryx Connect
Alteryx Promote
Alteryx Analytics Gallery
Alteryz ANZ

CONTACTS: Note: Officers with more than one job title may be intentionally listed here more than once.
Dean Stoecker, CEO
Kevin Rubin, CFO
Seth Greenberg, Chief Marketing Officer
Derek Knudsen, Chief Technology Officer
Olivia Adams, Co-Founder
Christopher Lal, General Counsel
Langley Eide, Other Executive Officer
Robert Jones, Other Executive Officer
Jay Bourland, Senior VP, Divisional

GROWTH PLANS/SPECIAL FEATURES:
Alteryx, Inc. provides data blending and advanced analytics software solutions. The company's products enable business analysts the ability to easily prep, blend and analyze business data through a repeatable workflow. From there, they deploy and share analytics at scale within mere hours (not weeks) for deeper insights. The Alteryx Analytics platform connects to and cleanses data from data warehouses, cloud applications, spreadsheets and other sources. The data is retrieved to perform analytics (predictive, statistical and spatial) using the same intuitive user interface, without writing any code. The Alteryx Designer delivers a repeatable workflow for self-service data analytics. The Alteryx Server is a scalable platform for deploying and sharing analytics. Alteryx Connect is a collaborative data exploration platform that combines data cataloging with human insight, and enables analysts to quickly and easily find, manage, understand and collaborate on the information that resides in their organization. Alteryx Promote is a data science model production system that provides end-to-end data science system for developing, deploying and managing predictive models and real-time decision application programming interfaces (APIs). The Alteryx Analytics Gallery is a cloud-based analytics platform that enables organizations to obtain the value of big data quickly. Headquartered in California, the firm has additional offices in Colorado, Illinois and Texas, as well as internationally in the U.K., Australia, Denmark, Germany, Czech Republic, Singapore and Canada. In February 2018, Alteryx expanded its reach in Australia by acquiring Alteryx ANZ, a master distributor.

FINANCIAL DATA: Note: Data for latest year may not have been available at press time.

In U.S. $	2018	2017	2016	2015	2014	2013
Revenue		131,607,000	85,790,000	53,821,000	37,984,000	
R&D Expense		29,342,000	17,481,000	11,103,000	7,787,000	
Operating Income		-18,199,000	-23,022,000	-21,086,000	-20,212,000	
Operating Margin %		-13.82%	-26.83%	-39.17%	-53.21%	
SGA Expense		98,661,000	75,305,000	53,283,000	41,876,000	
Net Income		-17,499,000	-24,258,000	-21,450,000	-20,329,000	
Operating Cash Flow		18,943,000	-6,031,000	-8,035,000	-3,428,000	
Capital Expenditure		3,669,000	4,307,000	2,714,000	531,000	
EBITDA		-14,242,000	-21,345,000	-20,327,000	-19,867,000	
Return on Assets %		-9.67%	-29.44%	-24.76%		
Return on Equity %		-22.25%				
Debt to Equity						

CONTACT INFORMATION:
Phone: 888-836-4274 Fax: 714-516-2410
Toll-Free:
Address: 3345 Michelson Dr., Ste. 400, Irvine, CA 92612 United States

STOCK TICKER/OTHER:
Stock Ticker: AYX
Employees: 424
Parent Company:

Exchange: NYS
Fiscal Year Ends:

SALARIES/BONUSES:
Top Exec. Salary: $375,000 Bonus: $
Second Exec. Salary: $320,833 Bonus: $

OTHER THOUGHTS:
Estimated Female Officers or Directors:
Hot Spot for Advancement for Women/Minorities:

Altice USA Inc

www.alticeusa.com/

NAIC Code: 517110

TYPES OF BUSINESS:

Cable Television Service
Professional Sports Teams
Television Programming
Communications Services
Movie Theatres
Voice Over Internet Protocol
High-Speed Internet

BRANDS/DIVISIONS/AFFILIATES:

Altice NV
Suddenlink Communications
Optimum
Lightpath
Altice Media Solutions
News 12 Networks
Altice Business
a4 Media & Data Solutions LLC

CONTACTS: Note: Officers with more than one job title may be intentionally listed here more than once.

Dexter Goei, Chairman of the Board
Abdelhakim Boubazine, Co- President
Charles Stewart, Director
David Connolly, Executive VP
Lisa Rosenblum, Vice Chairman

GROWTH PLANS/SPECIAL FEATURES:

Altice USA, a subsidiary of Altice NV, is a leading media and telecommunications firm, offering telecommunication and digital voice, TV and high-speed internet services. The company serves more than 4.9 million customers across 21 states. The company is composed of several brands: Suddenlink Communications, Optimum, Lightpath, Altice Media Solutions, News 12 Networks and a4. Suddenlink provides digital cable television, voice services and high-speed internet to business and residential customers in the western, Midwestern and southern states. Optimum provides services in the New York tristate area, which include high-speed internet, digital cable services and voice services, as well as Optimum WiFi, its branded service that offers some of the fastest speeds in the nation. Lightpath, also marketed as Altice Business, develops customized, commercial telecommunications services and solutions for both medium and large-sized businesses, including schools and hospitals in the New York tristate area. Altice Media Solutions is the advertising and sales division of Altice USA and is driven by advanced technologies and exclusive census-level data of audiences. Its offerings include targeted advertising on digital, cable TV and other platforms to Fortune 500 brands, local businesses and programmers. News 12 Networks provide 24- hour, regional news programming services with seven individual news channels and five traffic and weather channels servicing to New Jersey, Connecticut, Long Island, Westchester, the Bronx, Hudson Valley and Brooklyn. A4 Media & Data Solutions, LLC provides data-driven, audience-based advertising solutions to the media industry, including AMS, programmers and multichannel video programming distributors. Total Audience Data, its flagship portfolio of products, consists of advanced analytics tools providing granular measurement of consumer groups, accurate hyper-local ratings and other insights into target audience behavior not available through traditional sample-based measurement services.

FINANCIAL DATA: Note: Data for latest year may not have been available at press time.

In U.S. $	2018	2017	2016	2015	2014	2013
Revenue		9,326,570,000	6,017,212,000			
R&D Expense						
Operating Income		1,017,785,000	700,061,000			
Operating Margin %		10.91%	11.63%			
SGA Expense						
Net Income		1,520,031,000	-832,030,000			
Operating Cash Flow		2,001,743,000	1,184,455,000			
Capital Expenditure		993,071,000	625,647,000			
EBITDA		3,202,258,000	2,065,702,000			
Return on Assets %		4.26%	-2.28%			
Return on Equity %		40.40%	-40.99%			
Debt to Equity		3.88	10.72			

CONTACT INFORMATION:

Phone: 516 803-2300   Fax: 516 803-2273
Toll-Free:
Address: 1111 Stewart Ave., Bethpage, NY 11714 United States

STOCK TICKER/OTHER:

Stock Ticker: ATUS
Employees: 16,000
Parent Company: Altice NV

Exchange: NYS
Fiscal Year Ends: 12/31

SALARIES/BONUSES:

Top Exec. Salary: $ Bonus: $
Second Exec. Salary: $ Bonus: $

OTHER THOUGHTS:

Estimated Female Officers or Directors: 4
Hot Spot for Advancement for Women/Minorities: Y

Amadeus IT Group SA

NAIC Code: 561599

www.amadeus.com

TYPES OF BUSINESS:

Reservation Services
Online Travel Services
Corporate Travel Software-Hosted

BRANDS/DIVISIONS/AFFILIATES:

Amadeus Altea Suite
Altea Reservation
Altea Inventory
Altea Departure Control
Altea eCommerce
Amadeus.net
CheckMyTrip.com
Amadeus IT Holding SA

CONTACTS: *Note: Officers with more than one job title may be intentionally listed here more than once.*

Luis Maroto, CEO
Wolfgang Krips, Exec. VP-Oper.
Ana de Pro, CFO
Sabine Hansen Peck, Sr. VP- Human Resources
Herve Couturier, Exec. VP-R&D
Denis Lacroix, VP-Product Dev. & Sales
Tomas Lopez Fernebrand, General Counsel
Eberhard Haag, Exec. VP-Global Oper.
Alex Luzarraga, VP-Corp. Strategy
Denis Lacroix, VP-e-commerce Platforms
Francisco Perez-Lozao Ruter, Sr. VP-New Bus.
Julia Sattel, VP-Airline IT
Claude Giafferri, VP
Petra Euler, Managing Dir.- Amadeus Germany
Jose Antonio Tazon Gargia, Chmn.
David Brett, Pres., Amadeus Asia Pacific
Holger Taubmann, Sr. VP-Dist.

GROWTH PLANS/SPECIAL FEATURES:

Amadeus IT Group SA operates one of the largest travel reservation and ticketing systems in the world. The company operates in two segments: distribution and IT solutions. The distribution segment provides travel distribution services in Europe, the Middle East, Africa, the Asia Pacific region and South and Central America. Its service distribution network includes access to airlines, car rental companies, hotels, ferry & cruise lines, tour operators, rail operators and travel insurance companies. The IT solutions segment features the Amadeus Altea Suite, a customer management suite that focuses on inventory management, departure control and sales and reservations. It consists of three modules: Altea Reservation, which enables customers to manage bookings, fare prices and ticketing through a single interface; Altea Inventory, which permits airlines to create and manage schedules, seat capacity and associated fares; and Altea Departure Control, which covers flight departure aspects, including check-in, boarding passes and gate control. In addition, the firm offers Altea eCommerce, a suite of solutions that seeks to improve airline e-commerce sales and support processes. Amadeus also operates Amadeus.net, a travel planning tool used to help customers find flights, hotels and car rentals, and CheckMyTrip.com, a service that allows people to check the status of their itineraries. The company operates as a subsidiary of Amadeus IT Holding SA.

FINANCIAL DATA: *Note: Data for latest year may not have been available at press time.*

In U.S. $	2018	2017	2016	2015	2014	2013
Revenue		5,527,749,000	5,095,115,000	4,456,989,000	3,893,114,000	3,535,452,000
R&D Expense						
Operating Income		1,507,267,000	1,380,940,000	1,199,475,000	1,088,606,000	1,011,536,000
Operating Margin %		27.26%	27.10%	26.91%	27.96%	28.61%
SGA Expense						
Net Income		1,142,411,000	940,333,600	779,078,000	719,343,200	640,914,500
Operating Cash Flow		1,773,591,000	1,700,688,000	1,450,017,000	1,237,709,000	1,165,539,000
Capital Expenditure		697,247,900	677,883,100	626,610,700	486,991,400	468,378,400
EBITDA		2,104,957,000	1,943,774,000	1,687,519,000	1,497,905,000	1,359,104,000
Return on Assets %		12.81%	11.17%	10.38%	10.89%	10.63%
Return on Equity %		37.33%	32.97%	33.25%	34.32%	33.42%
Debt to Equity		0.66	0.52	0.56	0.83	0.77

CONTACT INFORMATION:

Phone: 34 915820100   Fax: 34 915820188
Toll-Free:
Address: Salvador de Madariaga 1, Madrid, 28027 Spain

STOCK TICKER/OTHER:

Stock Ticker: AMADF   Exchange: PINX
Employees: 13,881   Fiscal Year Ends: 12/31
Parent Company:

SALARIES/BONUSES:

Top Exec. Salary: $ Bonus: $
Second Exec. Salary: $ Bonus: $

OTHER THOUGHTS:

Estimated Female Officers or Directors: 4
Hot Spot for Advancement for Women/Minorities: Y

Amazon Web Services Inc (AWS)

www.aws.amazon.com

NAIC Code: 517110

TYPES OF BUSINESS:

Cloud Computing Services
Software
Cloud

BRANDS/DIVISIONS/AFFILIATES:

Amazon.com Inc
AWS Free Tier
Amazon EC2

CONTACTS: Note: Officers with more than one job title may be intentionally listed here more than once.

Andrew Jassy, CEO

GROWTH PLANS/SPECIAL FEATURES:

Amazon Web Services, Inc. (AWS) is a business unit within Amazon.com, Inc. that offers a suite of cloud-computing services. Cloud computing is the on-demand delivery of compute power, database storage, applications and other IT resources through a cloud services platform via the internet with pay-as-you-go pricing. These services operate from strategically located offices worldwide, including North America, South America, Europe, and Asia Pacific. AWS also offers free software products that run on the AWS Free Tier, if qualified. The free software products can be used on an Amazon EC2 tx.micro instance for up to 750 hours per month and pay no additional charges for the Amazon EC2 instance (during the 12 months). EC2 refers to Amazon's elastic compute cloud. AWS' many products are divided into 23 groups: analytics, application integration, audio reality/virtual reality, cost management, blockchain, business applications, compute, customer engagement, database, desktop and app streaming, developer tools, game tech, Internet of Things, machine learning, management & governance, media services, migration and transfer, mobile, networking and content delivery, robotics, satellite, security/identity/compliance, and storage.

FINANCIAL DATA: Note: Data for latest year may not have been available at press time.

In U.S. $	2018	2017	2016	2015	2014	2013
Revenue		17,460,000,000	12,219,000,000	7,880,000,000	4,644,000,000	3,108,000,000
R&D Expense						
Operating Income						
Operating Margin %						
SGA Expense						
Net Income		4,330,000,000	3,108,000,000	1,507,000,000	926,000,000	580,000,000
Operating Cash Flow						
Capital Expenditure						
EBITDA						
Return on Assets %						
Return on Equity %						
Debt to Equity						

CONTACT INFORMATION:

Phone: 206-266-4064   Fax: 206-266-7010
Toll-Free:
Address: 1200 12th Ave. S., Ste. 1200, Seattle, WA 98144 United States

STOCK TICKER/OTHER:

Stock Ticker: Subsidiary   Exchange:
Employees: Fiscal Year Ends: 12/31
Parent Company: Amazon.com Inc

SALARIES/BONUSES:

Top Exec. Salary: $ Bonus: $
Second Exec. Salary: $ Bonus: $

OTHER THOUGHTS:

Estimated Female Officers or Directors:
Hot Spot for Advancement for Women/Minorities:

Amazon.com Inc

www.amazon.com

NAIC Code: 454111

TYPES OF BUSINESS:

Online Retailing and Related Services
Robotics
Cloud Computing Services
Logistics Services
Retail Supermarkets & Grocery Delivery
Online Household Goods Retail
Online Auto & Industrial Retail
E-Commerce Support & Hosting

BRANDS/DIVISIONS/AFFILIATES:

Amazon Web Services (AWS)
Amazon Marketplace
Amazon Prime
Echo
Whole Foods Market
Amazon Go

CONTACTS: Note: Officers with more than one job title may be intentionally listed here more than once.

Andrew Jassy, CEO, Divisional
Jeffrey Wilke, CEO, Divisional
Jeffrey Bezos, CEO
Brian Olsavsky, CFO
Shelley Reynolds, Chief Accounting Officer
David Zapolsky, General Counsel
Jeffrey Blackburn, Senior VP, Divisional

GROWTH PLANS/SPECIAL FEATURES:

Amazon.com, Inc. is an internet consumer-shopping site that offers millions of new, used, refurbished and collectible items in categories such as books, movies, music and games, electronics and computers, home and garden, toys, children's goods, grocery, apparel and jewelry, health and beauty, sports, outdoors, digital downloads, tools and auto and industrial. The company, which serves more than 50 million members, operates in three segments: North America (which generates about 60% of annual revenue), international (33%) and Amazon Web Services (AWS) (7%), which offers computing, storage, database and other service offerings globally for start-ups, enterprises, government agencies and academic institutions. The Amazon Marketplace and Merchants programs allow third parties to integrate their products on Amazon websites and provide related fulfillment and advertising services to third-party merchants; allow customers to shop for products owned by third parties using Amazon's features and technologies; and enable customers to complete transactions that include multiple sellers in a single checkout process. Amazon Prime memberships afford members a host of perks including free two-day shipping, streaming music and video, delivery from participating restaurants and much more. The company also sells proprietary electronic devices, including eReaders, tablets, TVs and phones; as well as the Echo personal digital assistant. The firm serves authors and independent publishers with Kindle Direct Publishing, an online platform that lets independent authors and publishers choose a 70% royalty option and make their books available in the Kindle Store. Subsidiary Whole Foods Market is a supermarket chain featuring foods without artificial preservatives, colors, flavors, sweeteners and hydrogenated fats, with stores throughout the U.S and internationally. During 2018, Amazon opened Amazon Go stores, the first in Seattle, which uses cameras and sensors to detect items that a shopper purchases. The firm plans to open as many as 3,000 Amazon Go locations throughout the U.S. by 2021.

FINANCIAL DATA: Note: Data for latest year may not have been available at press time.

In U.S. $	2018	2017	2016	2015	2014	2013
Revenue		177,866,000,000	135,987,000,000	107,006,000,000	88,988,000,000	74,452,000,000
R&D Expense		22,620,000,000	16,085,000,000	12,540,000,000	9,275,000,000	6,565,000,000
Operating Income		4,106,000,000	4,186,000,000	2,233,000,000	178,000,000	745,000,000
Operating Margin %		2.30%	3.07%	2.08%	.20%	1.00%
SGA Expense		13,743,000,000	9,665,000,000	7,001,000,000	5,884,000,000	4,262,000,000
Net Income		3,033,000,000	2,371,000,000	596,000,000	-241,000,000	274,000,000
Operating Cash Flow		18,434,000,000	16,443,000,000	11,920,000,000	6,842,000,000	5,475,000,000
Capital Expenditure		11,955,000,000	6,737,000,000	4,589,000,000	4,893,000,000	3,444,000,000
EBITDA		16,132,000,000	12,492,000,000	8,308,000,000	4,845,000,000	3,900,000,000
Return on Assets %		2.82%	3.18%	.99%	- .50%	.75%
Return on Equity %		12.90%	14.51%	4.94%	-2.35%	3.05%
Debt to Equity		1.36	0.78	1.05	1.16	0.53

CONTACT INFORMATION:

Phone: 206 266-1000　　　Fax:
Toll-Free:
Address: 410 Terry Ave. N., Seattle, WA 98109 United States

STOCK TICKER/OTHER:

Stock Ticker: AMZN
Employees: 613,300
Parent Company:

Exchange: NAS
Fiscal Year Ends: 12/31

SALARIES/BONUSES:

Top Exec. Salary: $175,000　　　Bonus: $
Second Exec. Salary:　　　Bonus: $
$175,000

OTHER THOUGHTS:

Estimated Female Officers or Directors: 3
Hot Spot for Advancement for Women/Minorities: Y

America Movil SAB de CV

www.americamovil.com

NAIC Code: 517210

TYPES OF BUSINESS:
Cell Phone Service
Wireless Internet
Local & Long Distance
Satellite & Cable TV

BRANDS/DIVISIONS/AFFILIATES:
Telmex
Telcel
Claro
Telefonos de Mexico SAB de CV
Telefonos del Norests SA de CV

CONTACTS: Note: Officers with more than one job title may be intentionally listed here more than once.
Daniel Hajj Aboumrad, CEO
Patrick Slim Domit, Vice-Chmn.
Alejandro Cantu Jimenez, General Counsel
Salvador Cortes Gomez, COO-Mexico
Fernando Ocampo Carapia, CFO-Mexico
Juan Antonio Aguilar, CEO-Central America
Enrique Luna Roshard, CFO-Central America
Juan Carlos Archila Cabal, CEO-Colombia
Fernando Gonzalez Apango, CFO-Colombia
Carlos Slim Domit, Chmn.

GROWTH PLANS/SPECIAL FEATURES:
America Movil SAB de CV is a holding company that, through numerous subsidiaries, provides wireless communications services in Mexico, Latin America, Central America, the U.S. and Europe. In total, the firm serves more than 362 million mobile customers, including 279 million wireless subscribers, 33 million landlines, 28.6 million broadband accesses and 21.5 million PayTV units across 25 countries. Formed in September 2000, America Movil transformed from a long-distance company based in Mexico to a worldwide wireless enterprise under the direction of Mexican billionaire Carlos Slim Helu. The company offers services through several regional subsidiaries and joint ventures in Mexico, Brazil, the Southern Cone region (which includes Argentina, Chile, Paraguay and Uruguay), Colombia, Panama, the Andean Region, Central America, the Caribbean and the U.S. In Latin America, America Movil operates under the following brands: Telmex, Telcel and Claro, and under the A1 brand in Central and Eastern Europe. In March 2018, the company announced plans to separate subsidiaries Telefonos de Mexico SAB de CV and Telefonos del Norests SA de CV into stand-alone entities, separating the firm's wholesale operations (through the separated companies) from its regulated fixed services (which would remain with America Movil).

FINANCIAL DATA: Note: Data for latest year may not have been available at press time.

In U.S. $	2018	2017	2016	2015	2014	2013
Revenue		52,112,200,000	49,754,520,000	45,612,830,000	43,268,730,000	40,097,990,000
R&D Expense						
Operating Income		5,108,179,000	5,591,079,000	7,215,398,000	7,985,628,000	7,868,487,000
Operating Margin %		9.80%	11.23%	15.81%	18.45%	19.62%
SGA Expense		12,274,450,000	11,635,140,000	10,381,530,000	9,471,458,000	8,527,867,000
Net Income		1,495,877,000	441,196,000	1,788,098,000	2,353,866,000	3,806,523,000
Operating Cash Flow		11,108,290,000	12,027,750,000	8,351,500,000	12,273,230,000	9,578,887,000
Capital Expenditure		6,974,097,000	7,907,567,000	7,731,528,000	7,426,099,000	6,210,347,000
EBITDA		12,481,700,000	10,354,980,000	10,688,940,000	11,755,590,000	11,622,340,000
Return on Assets %		1.95%	.61%	2.72%	4.00%	7.35%
Return on Equity %		14.55%	5.38%	23.63%	23.86%	29.60%
Debt to Equity		3.32	2.99	5.01	2.96	2.29

CONTACT INFORMATION:
Phone: 52-55-2581-4449   Fax: 52-55-2581-4422
Toll-Free:
Address: Lago Zurich 245, Plaza Carso, Delegacion Miguel Hidalgo, 11529 Mexico

STOCK TICKER/OTHER:
Stock Ticker: AMX
Employees: 190,000
Parent Company:

Exchange: NYS
Fiscal Year Ends: 12/31

SALARIES/BONUSES:
Top Exec. Salary: $ Bonus: $
Second Exec. Salary: $ Bonus: $

OTHER THOUGHTS:
Estimated Female Officers or Directors: 2
Hot Spot for Advancement for Women/Minorities:

American Greetings Corporation LLC   www.americangreetings.com

NAIC Code: 511191

TYPES OF BUSINESS:

Greeting Cards
Gift Wrap
Party Supplies
Stationery
Digital Media
Online Greetings Cards

BRANDS/DIVISIONS/AFFILIATES:

Clayton Dubilier & Rice LLC
AmericanGreetings.com
justWink.com
BlueMountain.com
CardStore.com
Recycled Paper Greetings
Papyrus
DesignWare

CONTACTS: *Note: Officers with more than one job title may be intentionally listed here more than once.*

John W. Beeder, CEO
John W. Beeder, Pres.
Gregory M. Steinberg, CFO
Thomas H. Johnston, Sr. VP-Creative & Merch.
Christopher W. Haffke, General Counsel
Robert D. Tyler, Corp. Controller
Erwin Weiss, Sr. VP
Jeffrey Weiss, Co-CEO
Gregory Steinberg, Treas.
Morry Weiss, Chmn.

GROWTH PLANS/SPECIAL FEATURES:

American Greetings Corporation LLC designs, manufactures and sells everyday and seasonal greeting cards and other social expression products. The firm's products are sold across the U.S., as well as in countries all over the world, including Canada, the U.K., Australia and New Zealand. The company markets its products through AG Interactive, Inc. (AGI), a subsidiary that focuses on digital media marketing. American Greetings' major domestic greeting card brands are Recycled Paper Greetings, Papyrus, Carlton Cards, Just For You, Tender Thoughts, American Greetings and Gibson. Besides greeting cards, the firm's product lines also include Plus Mark gift wrap, stationery, DesignWare party goods and AGI in-store display fixtures. AGI also provides ringtones, avatars, emoticons and other digital content products. American Greetings operates through the following internet sites: AmericanGreetings.com, justWink.com, BlueMountain.com and CardStore.com. These sites offer services including email greetings, personalized printable greeting cards, photo sharing and design/verse content services for use in CD-ROM software products. American Greetings' largest customers include mass merchandisers, national supermarket chains and major drug stores. During 2018, after a 100+-year history of being majority-owned by the Sapirstein, Stone and Weiss family line, American Greetings became 60%-owned by private equity company Clayton, Dubilier & Rice LLC, with the Weiss family retaining a 40% share.

American Greetings employee discounts and other company perks, which vary per location.

FINANCIAL DATA: *Note: Data for latest year may not have been available at press time.*

In U.S. $	2018	2017	2016	2015	2014	2013
Revenue	2,000,000,000	1,900,000,000	1,889,994,000	1,986,352,000	1,941,809,000	1,868,739,000
R&D Expense						
Operating Income						
Operating Margin %						
SGA Expense						
Net Income			129,842,000	65,107,000	50,522,000	49,918,000
Operating Cash Flow						
Capital Expenditure						
EBITDA						
Return on Assets %						
Return on Equity %						
Debt to Equity						

CONTACT INFORMATION:

Phone: 216 252-7300   Fax: 216 255-6777
Toll-Free:
Address: 1 American Rd., Cleveland, OH 44144 United States

SALARIES/BONUSES:

Top Exec. Salary: $ Bonus: $
Second Exec. Salary: $ Bonus: $

STOCK TICKER/OTHER:

Stock Ticker: Joint Venture   Exchange:
Employees: 27,000   Fiscal Year Ends: 02/28
Parent Company: Clayton Dubilier & Rice LLC

OTHER THOUGHTS:

Estimated Female Officers or Directors:
Hot Spot for Advancement for Women/Minorities: Y

Anaplan Inc

www.anaplan.com

NAIC Code: 511210H

TYPES OF BUSINESS:
Computer Software, Business Management & ERP
Software

BRANDS/DIVISIONS/AFFILIATES:

GROWTH PLANS/SPECIAL FEATURES:
Anaplan, Inc. develops cloud-based enterprise planning and modeling solutions for companies worldwide. The Anaplan platform plans and manages performance via smart technology, enabling connection, versatility, foresight, scale and self-service. It enables business users to easily build sophisticated apps without coding. It accelerates planning speed and precision by connecting solutions across the entire business model. Anaplan's solutions primarily serve finance, sales, supply chain, workforce, marketing and IT businesses. Based in California, the firm has 21 global offices, and more than 950 customers, including some of the largest companies in the world.

CONTACTS: Note: Officers with more than one job title may be intentionally listed here more than once.
Frank Calderoni, CEO
Anup Signh, CFO
Maria Pergolino, CMO
Marilyn Miller, Chief People Officer

FINANCIAL DATA: Note: Data for latest year may not have been available at press time.

In U.S. $	2018	2017	2016	2015	2014	2013
Revenue	168,347,000	120,499,000	71,525,000			
R&D Expense	30,908,000	23,868,000	19,288,000			
Operating Income	-45,919,000	-38,935,000	-52,859,000			
Operating Margin %						
SGA Expense	131,373,000	96,159,000	74,592,000			
Net Income	-47,554,000	-40,194,000	-54,227,000			
Operating Cash Flow	-14,501,000	-26,161,000	-52,804,000			
Capital Expenditure	15,366,000	4,971,000	6,988,000			
EBITDA	-38,520,000	-34,611,000	-50,271,000			
Return on Assets %						
Return on Equity %						
Debt to Equity						

CONTACT INFORMATION:
Phone: 415-742-8199   Fax: 415-202-6481
Toll-Free:
Address: 625 2nd St., Ste. 101, San Francisco, CA 94107 United States

STOCK TICKER/OTHER:
Stock Ticker: PLAN   Exchange: NYS
Employees: 1,102   Fiscal Year Ends: 01/31
Parent Company:

SALARIES/BONUSES:
Top Exec. Salary: $ Bonus: $
Second Exec. Salary: $ Bonus: $

OTHER THOUGHTS:
Estimated Female Officers or Directors:
Hot Spot for Advancement for Women/Minorities:

Ancestry.com LLC

www.ancestry.com

NAIC Code: 519130

TYPES OF BUSINESS:

Internet-Based Genealogy Database
Social Networking Website

BRANDS/DIVISIONS/AFFILIATES:

Permira Holdings Limited
GIC Private Limited
Silver Lake
AncestryDNA
AncestryProGenealogists
Archives.com
Find A Grave
Fold3

CONTACTS: *Note: Officers with more than one job title may be intentionally listed here more than once.*

Margo Georgiadis, CEO
Howard Hochhauser, COO
Tim Sullivan, Pres.
Nat Natarajan, CTO
Evan Wittenberg, Exec. VP-People
Sriram Thiagarajan, CIO
Eric Shoup, Exec. VP-Prod.
William Stern, General Counsel
Ken Chahine, Sr. VP
Olivier Van Calster, Sr. VP-Int'l

GROWTH PLANS/SPECIAL FEATURES:

Ancestry.com, LLC creates, updates and maintains an online family history resource that provides access to digitized historical records on a subscription basis. Ancestry.com is an online community of approximately 3 million paying subscribers (as of late-2018), which combines access to more than 10 billion digitized historical records, such as U.S. Federal Censuses, immigration records and military records reaching back to the Revolutionary War. AncestryDNA offers a fee-based, mail-in saliva sample DNA test designed to help customers learn more about their genetic origins; AncestryProGenealogists comprises a team of expert researchers and genealogists to help conduct research, trace family trees and help clients connect with their past; Archives.com, is a site for anyone who wants to begin discovering heritage roots; Find A Grave is a free resource for finding grave sites of famous people, friends and family; RootsWeb is a free online community for sharing family history information at RootsWeb.Ancestry.com; Newspapers.com comprises an historical digital archive of over 8,000 newspapers dating to the 1700s; Ancestry Institution is a family history resource of more than 10,000 archives, ancestry libraries, schools and other institutions; Fold3 offers global military records, including stories, photos and personal documents, of men and women who have served; and Ancestry Academy offers video instruction from family history and genealogy experts. Based in Utah, the company maintains offices in both the U.S. and internationally. Permira Holdings Limited, GIC Private Limited and Silver Lake hold equity interests in Ancestry.com, LLC.

The firm offers employees health, vision, dental, life and disability insurance; bonuses; and retirement plans.

FINANCIAL DATA: *Note: Data for latest year may not have been available at press time.*

In U.S. $	2018	2017	2016	2015	2014	2013
Revenue	1,050,000,000	1,000,000,000	850,000,000	683,105,000	619,544,000	540,391,000
R&D Expense						
Operating Income						
Operating Margin %						
SGA Expense						
Net Income			300,000,000	29,418,000	-18,728,000	-79,700,000
Operating Cash Flow						
Capital Expenditure						
EBITDA						
Return on Assets %						
Return on Equity %						
Debt to Equity						

CONTACT INFORMATION:

Phone: 801 705-7000   Fax: 901 705-7001
Toll-Free: 800-262-3787
Address: 1300 W. Traverse Parkway, Lehi, UT 84043 United States

STOCK TICKER/OTHER:

Stock Ticker: Private   Exchange:
Employees: 1,600   Fiscal Year Ends: 12/31
Parent Company:

SALARIES/BONUSES:

Top Exec. Salary: $ Bonus: $
Second Exec. Salary: $ Bonus: $

OTHER THOUGHTS:

Estimated Female Officers or Directors:
Hot Spot for Advancement for Women/Minorities:

ANGI Homeservices Inc

www.angihomeservices.com

NAIC Code: 519130

TYPES OF BUSINESS:
Online Business Reviews
Consumer Information and Help

BRANDS/DIVISIONS/AFFILIATES:
IAC/InterActiveCorp
Angie's List
HomeAdvisor
CraftJack
HomeStars
Instapro
mHelpDesk
MyBuilder

CONTACTS: Note: Officers with more than one job title may be intentionally listed here more than once.
Jeffrey Kip, CEO, Divisional
Glenn Schiffman, CFO
Joseph Levin, Chairman of the Board
Michael Schwerdtman, Chief Accounting Officer
Allison Lowrie, Chief Marketing Officer
William Ridenour, Chief Technology Officer
Angela Hicks Bowman, Co-Founder
Christopher Terrill, Director
Brandon Ridenour, Other Executive Officer
Craig Smith, President

GROWTH PLANS/SPECIAL FEATURES:
ANGI Homeservices, Inc. (formerly Angie's List, Inc.) provides a marketplace for home services from 10 brands across eight countries. The firm's brands include: Angie's List, an online review platform from which members can research, hire, rate and review local providers in more than 700 service categories; HomeAdvisor, where homeowners can find pre-screened local service professionals, view average project costs, read verified ratings and reviews and instantly book home improvement, maintenance and repair appointments online; CraftJack, a third-party lead generation service that connects home service professionals with homeowners looking to complete home projects; HomeStars, which connects homeowners with reputable home renovators, repairmen and retailers throughout Canada; Instapro, which connects homeowners with service professionals for home renovation projects in Italy; mHelpDesk, a software solution and app designed to automate home service and repair businesses, including estimates, invoices, managing employees, scheduling and accessing customer information on-the-go; MyBuilder, from which U.K.-based homeowners can discover vetted tradesmen, read the tradesman's entire work history and read verified reviews from previous clients; MyHammer, from which consumers located in Germany, Austria or the U.K. can search for and find local craftsmen; Travaux, a France-based service that connects homeowners with home service professionals concerning construction, renovation and/or development; Werkspot, on which consumers post service requests to which qualified professionals respond with proposals, and the consumer chooses the professional based on proposals and user reviews; and mHelpDesk, a software solution and app designed to automate home service and repair business. In October 2018, ANGI acquired Handy, an on-demand platform and gig marketplace connecting people and household service provider.

FINANCIAL DATA: Note: Data for latest year may not have been available at press time.

In U.S. $	2018	2017	2016	2015	2014	2013
Revenue		736,386,000	323,329,000	344,125,000	315,011,000	245,642,000
R&D Expense		47,907,000	55,990,000	36,661,000	34,039,000	26,197,000
Operating Income		-147,871,000	-3,094,000	13,258,000	-10,362,000	-31,081,000
Operating Margin %		-20.08%	-.95%	3.85%	-3.28%	-12.65%
SGA Expense		764,473,000	230,140,000	238,132,000	238,574,000	210,454,000
Net Income		-103,118,000	-7,857,000	10,243,000	-12,074,000	-32,989,000
Operating Cash Flow		41,823,000	1,635,000	26,691,000	4,629,000	8,906,000
Capital Expenditure		26,837,000	18,796,000	34,766,000	37,841,000	8,871,000
EBITDA		-108,093,000	10,054,000	19,660,000	-4,786,000	-27,012,000
Return on Assets %		-12.69%	-4.72%	6.21%	-9.28%	-32.68%
Return on Equity %		-20.66%	-741.57%			
Debt to Equity		0.26	12.47			

CONTACT INFORMATION:
Phone: 212/314/7230 Fax:
Toll-Free:
Address: 555 W. 18th St., New York, NY 10011 United States

STOCK TICKER/OTHER:
Stock Ticker: ANGI Exchange: NAS
Employees: 1,567 Fiscal Year Ends: 12/31
Parent Company:

SALARIES/BONUSES:
Top Exec. Salary: $600,000 Bonus: $2,500,000
Second Exec. Salary: $446,923 Bonus: $300,000

OTHER THOUGHTS:
Estimated Female Officers or Directors: 2
Hot Spot for Advancement for Women/Minorities:

Sales, profits and employees may be estimates. Financial information, benefits and other data can change quickly and may vary from those stated here.

App Annie Limited

www.appannie.com

NAIC Code: 519130

TYPES OF BUSINESS:

Internet Publishing and Broadcasting and Web Search Portals
Software

BRANDS/DIVISIONS/AFFILIATES:

App Annie Connect
Market Data Intelligence

CONTACTS: *Note: Officers with more than one job title may be intentionally listed here more than once.*

Ted Krantz, CEO
Bertrand Schmitt, Chief Strategist
Susan Kim, CFO
Danielle Levitas, Exec. VP-Global Mktg. & Market Insights
Natasha Kehimkar, Chief People Officer
Aaron Mahimainathan, Chief Product Officer

GROWTH PLANS/SPECIAL FEATURES:

App Annie Limited provides cloud-based app analytics services and market intelligence for the purpose of growing business. The company's App Annie Connect offering analyzes and tracks the performance of the user's app store, its advertising and in-app usage data, for free. App store platforms include iOS, tvOS, Google, Amazon and Windows. The analytics data can be accessed anytime from any device. This product enables users to spot opportunities to grow their audience, improve time spent in the app and to maximize revenue. App Annie's Market Data Intelligence product provides detailed app download, revenue, demographic and usage estimates for every major mobile app. It offers help in understanding user engagement through metrics such as active users, market penetration, duration and frequency of use. Market Data Intelligence, for a fee, lets users explore the app's user base by age and gender, and analyze cross-app usage patterns in order to enhance product development and marketing efforts. Market Data Intelligence also helps users to identify keywords that would optimize their app store presence and uncover when and where competitors are running user acquisition campaigns. It offers users access to estimates for millions of competitor apps in an effort to discover which store, country, category or device is driving success. App Annie is a resource for anyone and any business competing in the app economy, including investors, marketers, sales, operators or property managers. Based in California, USA, the company has 15 global offices.

App Annie offers its employees medical, dental and vision coverage; 401(k); and paid vacations and holidays.

FINANCIAL DATA: *Note: Data for latest year may not have been available at press time.*

In U.S. $	2018	2017	2016	2015	2014	2013
Revenue						
R&D Expense						
Operating Income						
Operating Margin %						
SGA Expense						
Net Income						
Operating Cash Flow						
Capital Expenditure						
EBITDA						
Return on Assets %						
Return on Equity %						
Debt to Equity						

CONTACT INFORMATION:

Phone: 415-638-6840   Fax:
Toll-Free:
Address: 23 Geary St., Ste 400/800, San Francisco, CA 94108 United States

STOCK TICKER/OTHER:

Stock Ticker: Private   Exchange:
Employees: 450   Fiscal Year Ends:
Parent Company:

SALARIES/BONUSES:

Top Exec. Salary: $ Bonus: $
Second Exec. Salary: $ Bonus: $

OTHER THOUGHTS:

Estimated Female Officers or Directors:
Hot Spot for Advancement for Women/Minorities:

AppDirect Inc

www.appdirect.com

NAIC Code: 511210M

TYPES OF BUSINESS:

Cloud Applications Management Tools

BRANDS/DIVISIONS/AFFILIATES:

AppMarket
AppBilling
AppDistribution
AppReserller
AppDevices
AppInsights
AppWise
AppHelp

CONTACTS: *Note: Officers with more than one job title may be intentionally listed here more than once.*

Daniel Saks, Co-CEO
Michael DiFilippo, CFO
Joshua Schnoll, VP-Mktg.
Anna Meyer, VP-People
Andy Sen, CTO
Nicolas Desmarais, Chmn.

GROWTH PLANS/SPECIAL FEATURES:

AppDirect, Inc. provides a platform for selling, distributing and managing cloud-based products and services. This platform enables organizations of all sizes the capability of getting to market quickly. The firm's products are divided into two groups: cloud monetization and cloud management. The cloud monetization group comprises: AppMarket, offering cloud marketplace and management solutions; AppBilling, a billing and payment manager; AppDistribution, a cloud distribution service; AppReseller, offering reseller management solutions; and AppDevices, a connected device and vehicle management solution. The cloud management group comprises: AppIdentity, offering identity and access management; AppInsights, offering data analytics and visualization; AppWise, offering an intelligent workspace; and AppHelp, offering support solutions. After the sale, the cloud management suite enables enhanced customer engagement and retention by providing a seamless experience across all offerings. The company's products and solutions serve the telecommunications, internet service provider, software, enterprise electronic, industrial manufacturing, managed service provider, automotive original equipment manufacturer and financial services industries. Headquartered in California, USA, AppDirect has additional offices throughout the U.S., Canada, Germany, India, Australia, the U.K. and Argentina.

FINANCIAL DATA: *Note: Data for latest year may not have been available at press time.*

In U.S. $	2018	2017	2016	2015	2014	2013
Revenue						
R&D Expense						
Operating Income						
Operating Margin %						
SGA Expense						
Net Income						
Operating Cash Flow						
Capital Expenditure						
EBITDA						
Return on Assets %						
Return on Equity %						
Debt to Equity						

CONTACT INFORMATION:

Phone: 415-852-3919   Fax: 415-874-3001
Toll-Free:
Address: 650 California St., 25/Fl, San Francisco, CA 94108 United States

STOCK TICKER/OTHER:

Stock Ticker: Private   Exchange:
Employees: 650   Fiscal Year Ends:
Parent Company:

SALARIES/BONUSES:

Top Exec. Salary: $ Bonus: $
Second Exec. Salary: $ Bonus: $

OTHER THOUGHTS:

Estimated Female Officers or Directors:
Hot Spot for Advancement for Women/Minorities:

AppDynamics Inc

NAIC Code: 511210M

www.appdynamics.com

TYPES OF BUSINESS:

Application Performance Management Software
Performance Monitoring
Data Analytics

BRANDS/DIVISIONS/AFFILIATES:

Cisco Systems Inc
App iQ
Enterprise iQ
Map iQ
Baseline iQ
Diagnostic iQ
Business iQ

CONTACTS: *Note: Officers with more than one job title may be intentionally listed here more than once.*

David Wadhwani, CEO
Dan Wright, COO
Andrew Savitz, CMO
Bhaskar Sunkara, CTO
Bhaskar Sunkara, VP-Prod. Mgmt.
Ed Rowe, Sr. VP-Eng.
Joe Sexton, Pres., Worldwide Field Oper.
Stuart Horne, VP-Bus. Dev.
Hatim Shafique, VP-Customer Success & Oper.

GROWTH PLANS/SPECIAL FEATURES:

AppDynamics is an application performance management (APM) company, offering performance solutions to smart device application (app) developers to ensure apps perform quickly and efficiently. The firm's APM services include DevOps, monitoring business, performance analytics, microservices, IT operations, cloud migration and scaling, continuous delivery and cloud monitoring. AppDynamics' performance monitoring platform is a unified monitoring architecture for apps or for enterprises as a whole. The App iQ and Enterprise iQ platforms include the Map iQ, Baseline iQ, Diagnostic iQ and Business iQ solutions for multi-cloud environments. These solutions provide innovative features to monitor every aspect of the app and/or business enterprise. End-user monitoring solutions track every business transaction, whether via tap, swipe or click, each real user performance is tracked and monitored via the same dashboard. End-user monitoring modules include browser real-user monitoring, mobile real-user monitoring and browser synthetic monitoring. Customers span retail, technology, financial services sectors and more, and include Carhartt, Okta and Nasdaq. Based in San Francisco, California, the company has offices located in Texas, the U.K., France, Germany, Australia, Singapore and India. During 2017, AppDynamics was acquired by Cisco Systems, Inc., an American multinational technology conglomerate based in California.

FINANCIAL DATA: *Note: Data for latest year may not have been available at press time.*

In U.S. $	2018	2017	2016	2015	2014	2013
Revenue	194,250,000	185,000,000	150,592,000	81,865,000	23,600,000	
R&D Expense						
Operating Income						
Operating Margin %						
SGA Expense						
Net Income			-134,059,000	-94,247,000	-68,338,000	
Operating Cash Flow						
Capital Expenditure						
EBITDA						
Return on Assets %						
Return on Equity %						
Debt to Equity						

CONTACT INFORMATION:

Phone: 415-442-8400   Fax: 415-442-8499
Toll-Free:
Address: 303 2nd St., N. Tower, 8/Fl, San Francisco, CA 94107 United States

STOCK TICKER/OTHER:

Stock Ticker: Subsidiary   Exchange:
Employees: 1,000   Fiscal Year Ends:
Parent Company: Cisco Systems Inc

SALARIES/BONUSES:

Top Exec. Salary: $ Bonus: $
Second Exec. Salary: $ Bonus: $

OTHER THOUGHTS:

Estimated Female Officers or Directors:
Hot Spot for Advancement for Women/Minorities:

Apple Inc

www.apple.com

NAIC Code: 334220

TYPES OF BUSINESS:

Electronics Design and Manufacturing
Software
Computers and Tablets
Retail Stores
Smartphones
Online Music Store
Apps Store
Home Entertainment Software & Systems

BRANDS/DIVISIONS/AFFILIATES:

iPhone
iPad
Apple Watch
Apple TV
iOS
watchOS
HomePod
AirPods

CONTACTS: Note: Officers with more than one job title may be intentionally listed here more than once.

Timothy Cook, CEO
Luca Maestri, CFO
Arthur Levinson, Chairman of the Board
Chris Kondo, Chief Accounting Officer
Jeffery Williams, COO
Katherine Adams, General Counsel
Eduardo Cue, Senior VP, Divisional
Daniel Riccio, Senior VP, Divisional
Johny Srouji, Senior VP, Divisional
Craig Federighi, Senior VP, Divisional
Philip Schiller, Senior VP, Divisional
Angela Ahrendts, Senior VP, Divisional

GROWTH PLANS/SPECIAL FEATURES:

Apple, Inc. designs, manufactures and markets personal computers, portable digital music players and mobile communication devices and sells a variety of related software, services, peripherals and networking applications. The company's products and services include iPhone, iPad, Mac, Apple Watch, Apple TV; a portfolio of consumer and professional software applications; iOS, macOS, watchOS and tvOS operating systems; iCloud, Apple Pay and a variety of accessory, service and support offerings. iPhone is the company's line of smartphones based on its iOS operating system. iCloud stores music, photos, contacts, calendars, mail, documents and more, keeping them up-to-date and available across multiple iOS devices, Mac and Windows personal computers and Apple TV. Other products include apple-branded and third-party accessories; the HomePod wireless speaker; AirPods wireless headphone; and iPod touch, a flash memory-based digital music and medial player that works with the iTunes store, App Store, iBooks store and Apple Music (collectively referred to as digital content and services) for purchasing and playing digital content and apps. The firm has more than 500 brick and mortar stores in 24 countries, but also sells its products worldwide through online stores and direct sales force, as well as through third-party cellular network carriers, wholesalers, retailers and value-added resellers. During 2018, Apple agreed acquired Texture, a digital magazine subscription service by Next Issue Media, LLC, which gives users unlimited access to their favorite titles for a monthly subscription fee. That December, Apple announced a major expansion of its operations in Austin, including a $1 billion new campus, with plans to establish new sites in Seattle, San Diego and Culver City. Apple added 6,000 jobs in America in 2018, with plans to create 20,000 jobs in the U.S. by 2023.

Apple offers employees comprehensive health benefits, retirement plans and various employee assistance programs.

FINANCIAL DATA: Note: Data for latest year may not have been available at press time.

In U.S. $	2018	2017	2016	2015	2014	2013
Revenue	265,595,000,000	229,234,000,000	215,639,000,000	233,715,000,000	182,795,000,000	170,910,000,000
R&D Expense	14,236,000,000	11,581,000,000	10,045,000,000	8,067,000,000	6,041,000,000	4,475,000,000
Operating Income	70,898,000,000	61,344,000,000	60,024,000,000	71,230,000,000	52,503,000,000	48,999,000,000
Operating Margin %		26.76%	27.83%	30.47%	28.72%	28.66%
SGA Expense	16,705,000,000	15,261,000,000	14,194,000,000	14,329,000,000	11,993,000,000	10,830,000,000
Net Income	59,531,000,000	48,351,000,000	45,687,000,000	53,394,000,000	39,510,000,000	37,037,000,000
Operating Cash Flow	77,434,000,000	63,598,000,000	65,824,000,000	81,266,000,000	59,713,000,000	53,666,000,000
Capital Expenditure	13,313,000,000	12,795,000,000	13,548,000,000	11,488,000,000	9,813,000,000	9,076,000,000
EBITDA	87,046,000,000	76,569,000,000	73,333,000,000	84,505,000,000	61,813,000,000	57,048,000,000
Return on Assets %		13.87%	14.92%	20.44%	18.00%	19.33%
Return on Equity %		36.86%	36.90%	46.24%	33.61%	30.63%
Debt to Equity		0.72	0.58	0.44	0.25	0.13

CONTACT INFORMATION:

Phone: 408 996-1010   Fax: 408 974-2483
Toll-Free: 800-692-7753
Address: One Apple Park Way, Cupertino, CA 95014 United States

STOCK TICKER/OTHER:

Stock Ticker: AAPL   Exchange: NAS
Employees: 132,000   Fiscal Year Ends: 09/30
Parent Company:

SALARIES/BONUSES:

Top Exec. Salary: $3,000,000   Bonus: $
Second Exec. Salary: Bonus: $
$1,019,231

OTHER THOUGHTS:

Estimated Female Officers or Directors:
Hot Spot for Advancement for Women/Minorities:

AppNexus Inc

www.appnexus.com

NAIC Code: 541810E

TYPES OF BUSINESS:

Online Marketing Services
Advertising

BRANDS/DIVISIONS/AFFILIATES:

AT&T Inc
Xandr
AppNexus Publisher

CONTACTS: *Note: Officers with more than one job title may be intentionally listed here more than once.*

Brian O'Kelley, CEO
Michael Rubenstein, Pres.
Jonathan Hsu, CFO
Catherine Williams, Chief Data & Marketplace Offr.
Nithya Das, Chief People Officer
Ben John, CTO
Ryan Christensen, COO

GROWTH PLANS/SPECIAL FEATURES:

AppNexus, Inc. is a technology company that creates, supplies and supports marketplaces for internet advertising. Its open and unified ad tech platform enables customers to more effectively buy and sell media, allowing them to innovate, differentiate and transform their businesses. The platform enables clients to build a trading desk to include data-driven insights, providing a way to access and buy inventory at scale without writing a single line of code. It teaches clients how to use the platform to improve performance, access advanced analytics and build proprietary tools to differentiate themselves from competition. AppNexus also enables clients to build a custom exchange that delivers broad access to both brand-focused and direct response demand, powerful yield management tools and full publisher ad serving capabilities. Clients can learn to maximize their inventory's value with AppNexus' real-time bidding and custom exchange offering. Its AppNexus Publisher products offers publishers a single digital ad delivery platform built to maximize revenue across all demand sources. AppNexus builds its cloud infrastructure specifically for the ad tech industry, allowing clients to do the same for their technology stack and performance increase. Customers include Wayfair, Scibids, Fandom, Light Reaction, Greenhouse Group, Microsoft and more. AppNexus is headquartered in New York City, and has more than 25 offices worldwide, including Mexico, Canada, Brazil, Netherlands, France, Germany, Italy, Sweden, Switzerland, Spain, the U.K., Australia, Singapore and Japan. During 2018, AppNexus was acquired by AT&T, Inc.'s Xandr division acquired.

FINANCIAL DATA: *Note: Data for latest year may not have been available at press time.*

In U.S. $	2018	2017	2016	2015	2014	2013
Revenue		2,200,000,000	2,100,000,000	2,050,000,000	2,000,000,000	
R&D Expense						
Operating Income						
Operating Margin %						
SGA Expense						
Net Income						
Operating Cash Flow						
Capital Expenditure						
EBITDA						
Return on Assets %						
Return on Equity %						
Debt to Equity						

CONTACT INFORMATION:

Phone: 646-825-6460　　Fax: 646-825-6465
Toll-Free:
Address: 28 W. 23rd St., 4/Fl, New York, NY 10010 United States

STOCK TICKER/OTHER:

Stock Ticker: Subsidiary　　　　　Exchange:
Employees: 975　　　　　　　　　Fiscal Year Ends:
Parent Company: AT&T Inc

SALARIES/BONUSES:

Top Exec. Salary: $　　　　Bonus: $
Second Exec. Salary: $　　　Bonus: $

OTHER THOUGHTS:

Estimated Female Officers or Directors:
Hot Spot for Advancement for Women/Minorities:

Sales, profits and employees may be estimates. Financial information, benefits and other data can change quickly and may vary from those stated here.

Apptio Inc

NAIC Code: 511210H

TYPES OF BUSINESS:
Computer Software, Business Management & ERP

BRANDS/DIVISIONS/AFFILIATES:
Vista Equity Partners

GROWTH PLANS/SPECIAL FEATURES:
Apptio, Inc. builds advanced data and analytics applications for technology business management (TBM). The company helps information technology (IT) leaders make informed decisions as they plan, analyze and optimize technology investments in pursuit of digital transformation. Apptio's software uses machine learning to translate technology costs and utilization across on-premises systems, vendors, projects, agile and cloud systems into a holistic, business-centric view. Companies of all sizes and geographies use Apptio, including half of the Fortune 100. In January 2019, Apptio was taken private by Vista Equity Partners, and delisted from being publicly traded.

CONTACTS: Note: Officers with more than one job title may be intentionally listed here more than once.
Sachin Gupta, CEO
Kurt Shintaffer, CFO
John Morrow, Executive VP, Divisional
Lawrence Blasko, Other Executive Officer

FINANCIAL DATA: Note: Data for latest year may not have been available at press time.

In U.S. $	2018	2017	2016	2015	2014	2013
Revenue		188,519,008	160,568,992	129,251,000	106,615,000	
R&D Expense						
Operating Income						
Operating Margin %						
SGA Expense						
Net Income		-25,621,000	-31,553,000	-41,007,000	-32,872,000	
Operating Cash Flow						
Capital Expenditure						
EBITDA						
Return on Assets %						
Return on Equity %						
Debt to Equity						

CONTACT INFORMATION:
Phone: 866-470-0320   Fax:
Toll-Free:
Address: 11100 NE 8th St., Ste. 600, Bellevue, WA 98004 United States

STOCK TICKER/OTHER:
Stock Ticker: Private   Exchange:
Employees: 731   Fiscal Year Ends:
Parent Company: Vista Equity Partners

SALARIES/BONUSES:
Top Exec. Salary: $ Bonus: $
Second Exec. Salary: $ Bonus: $

OTHER THOUGHTS:
Estimated Female Officers or Directors:
Hot Spot for Advancement for Women/Minorities:

Apttus Corporation

NAIC Code: 511210Q

apttus.com

TYPES OF BUSINESS:

Computer Software, Accounting, Banking & Financial
Software

BRANDS/DIVISIONS/AFFILIATES:

Thoma Bravo
Apttus Omni
Max
X-Author

CONTACTS: Note: Officers with more than one job title may be intentionally listed here more than once.

Frank Holland, CEO
Raj Verma, Chief Revenue Officer
Gregg Hampton, CFO
Ben Allen, CMO
Colleen Carr, Chief People Officer
Praniti Lakhwara, CIO
David Murphy, Chmn.

GROWTH PLANS/SPECIAL FEATURES:

Apttus Corporation provides cloud-based quote-to-cash software. The Apttus Omni powers all of the firm's quote-to-cash products, including configure-price-quote, contract management, buy-side contract management, e-commerce and revenue management. The company combines these applications with behavioral applications via promotions, sales compensation and rebates. All Apttus applications can be further enhanced with machine learning to recommend relevant, intelligent actions. It offers conversational and intuitive user interfaces. Apttus Omni's end-to-end applied artificial intelligence revenue process, Max, eliminates manual tasks, keeps all stakeholders informed, collapses cycle times, lowers selling costs and provides a comprehensive revenue view of the customer that is actionable in real time. Apttus' X-Author solution increases adoption of these tools across the organization by allowing Microsoft Word and Excel to function as user interfaces. X-Author can also be used to improve the adoption of customer relations management systems such as Salesforce and Microsoft Dynamics 365. The firm has more than 600 customers and 1 million users worldwide. Industries served by the firm include communications, financial services, healthcare, high tech, life sciences, manufacturing and media/entertainment. Apttus is based in California, USA, with additional offices in the U.S., the U.K., Europe, Middle East, India, Japan and Australia. In October 2018, Thoma Bravo, a private equity investment firm, became the majority investor in Apttus. Financial details of the transaction were not disclosed.

The company offers its employees healthcare plans, paid time off, fitness programs and other perks.

FINANCIAL DATA: Note: Data for latest year may not have been available at press time.

In U.S. $	2018	2017	2016	2015	2014	2013
Revenue	190,000,000	185,000,000	150,000,000	91,000,000	70,000,000	50,000,000
R&D Expense						
Operating Income						
Operating Margin %						
SGA Expense						
Net Income						
Operating Cash Flow						
Capital Expenditure						
EBITDA						
Return on Assets %						
Return on Equity %						
Debt to Equity						

CONTACT INFORMATION:

Phone: 650-445-7700   Fax:
Toll-Free:
Address: 1400 Fashion Island Blvd., Ste. 100, San Mateo, CA 94404
United States

STOCK TICKER/OTHER:

Stock Ticker: Private   Exchange:
Employees: 1,300   Fiscal Year Ends:
Parent Company: Thoma Bravo

SALARIES/BONUSES:

Top Exec. Salary: $ Bonus: $
Second Exec. Salary: $ Bonus: $

OTHER THOUGHTS:

Estimated Female Officers or Directors:
Hot Spot for Advancement for Women/Minorities:

Ariba Inc

NAIC Code: 511210Q

www.ariba.com

TYPES OF BUSINESS:

Computer Software, Accounting, Banking & Financial
Procurement & Logistics Solutions
Business Process Software
Consulting Services

BRANDS/DIVISIONS/AFFILIATES:

SAP SE
SAP Ariba
Ariba Network

CONTACTS: Note: Officers with more than one job title may be intentionally listed here more than once.

Barry Padgett, Pres.
James Lee, COO
Nicholas Zagorski, CFO
Tifenn Dano Kwan, CMO
Alejandra Franco, Dir.-Human Resources
Marcell Vollmer, Chief Digital Officer
Matthew Zack, Sr. VP-Corp. Dev.
Charles Jackson, Exec. VP
Michael J. Arenth, Sr. VP-Global Customer Mgmt.

GROWTH PLANS/SPECIAL FEATURES:

Ariba, Inc. provides cloud procurement solutions for buyers and suppliers. The firm is a subsidiary of SAP SE, and is therefore branded under the SAP Ariba label. The company's cloud-based Ariba Network is a business network where customers can collaborate with any company, anytime, anywhere. There are about 2 million businesses to discover and collaborate with on the Ariba Network, covering 190 countries worldwide. This collaborative business community provides potential buying or selling opportunities. Annually, approximately $2.3 trillion in business commerce transact and 34 million sales leads are created. Solutions offered by the firm include supplier management, strategic sourcing, supply chain, procurement, financial supply chain, platform solutions, integration solutions and services for buyers. SAP Ariba is open to all systems and all types of goods and services. It offers an end-to-end automated system that removes complexity and allows buyers and suppliers to manage everything from contracts to payments all in one place. Ariba's website offers resources, demos and explanations about its network, solutions and capabilities. The firm is headquartered in California, USA.

FINANCIAL DATA: Note: Data for latest year may not have been available at press time.

In U.S. $	2018	2017	2016	2015	2014	2013
Revenue		650,000,000	640,000,000	630,000,000	615,000,000	600,000,000
R&D Expense						
Operating Income						
Operating Margin %						
SGA Expense						
Net Income						
Operating Cash Flow						
Capital Expenditure						
EBITDA						
Return on Assets %						
Return on Equity %						
Debt to Equity						

CONTACT INFORMATION:

Phone: 650-390-1000   Fax: 650-390-1100
Toll-Free:
Address: 910 Hermosa Ct., Sunnyvale, CA 94089 United States

STOCK TICKER/OTHER:

Stock Ticker: Subsidiary
Employees: 2,432
Parent Company: SAP SE

Exchange:
Fiscal Year Ends: 09/30

SALARIES/BONUSES:

Top Exec. Salary: $ Bonus: $
Second Exec. Salary: $ Bonus: $

OTHER THOUGHTS:

Estimated Female Officers or Directors:
Hot Spot for Advancement for Women/Minorities:

Arista Networks Inc

www.aristanetworks.com

NAIC Code: 334210A

TYPES OF BUSINESS:

Cloud Computing Routers

GROWTH PLANS/SPECIAL FEATURES:

Arista Networks, Inc. supplies cloud networking solutions for large data center and high-performance computing environments. These solutions help meet the needs of large-scale internet companies, cloud service providers and next-generation data centers. Arista's cloud networking solutions consist of its extensible operating systems (EOS), a set of network applications and its 10/25/40/50/100/400 Gigabit Ethernet switches. EOS+ is a software platform for network programmability and automation, allowing customers to take advantage of pre-built and custom EOS applications, as well as integration with a wide range of technology partner solutions. CloudVision is a network-wide offering for workload orchestration and workflow automation. Arista's Macro-Segmentation Services is enabled via Arista CloudVision, and extends the concept of fine-grained inter-hypervisor security to cloud networks by enabling dynamic security and services of physical to virtual workloads. Arista cEOS is a containerized packaging of EOS software and its agents for easy deployment in cloud infrastructure. Arista has delivered its cloud networking solutions to more than 4,900 end customers worldwide, in over 80 countries. Its end customers span a range of industries and include large internet companies, service providers, financial services organizations, government agencies, media and entertainment companies and others. Products are sold through a direct sales force and channel partners.

BRANDS/DIVISIONS/AFFILIATES:

EOS+
CloudVision
Arista cEOS

CONTACTS: *Note: Officers with more than one job title may be intentionally listed here more than once.*

Jayshree Ullal, CEO
Andy Bechtolsheim, Chairman of the Board
Kenneth Duda, Chief Technology Officer
Marc Taxay, General Counsel
Anshul Sadana, Other Executive Officer
John McCool, Other Executive Officer
Ita Brennan, Senior VP

FINANCIAL DATA: *Note: Data for latest year may not have been available at press time.*

In U.S. $	2018	2017	2016	2015	2014	2013
Revenue		1,646,186,000	1,129,167,000	837,591,000	584,106,000	361,224,000
R&D Expense		349,594,000	273,581,000	209,448,000	148,909,000	98,587,000
Operating Income		470,272,000	243,409,000	149,308,000	125,513,000	66,148,000
Operating Margin %		28.56%	21.55%	17.82%	21.48%	18.31%
SGA Expense		241,903,000	206,126,000	184,804,000	117,669,000	73,803,000
Net Income		423,201,000	184,189,000	121,102,000	86,850,000	42,460,000
Operating Cash Flow		631,627,000	131,440,000	200,533,000	114,516,000	34,648,000
Capital Expenditure		15,279,000	21,419,000	19,989,000	13,134,000	20,316,000
EBITDA		498,180,000	265,110,000	162,832,000	137,809,000	70,438,000
Return on Assets %		20.16%	12.66%	12.08%	11.72%	14.52%
Return on Equity %		30.50%	19.30%	17.72%	21.96%	100.30%
Debt to Equity		0.02	0.03	0.05	0.07	0.60

CONTACT INFORMATION:

Phone: 408-547-5500   Fax: 408-538-8920
Toll-Free: 866-547-5502
Address: 5453 Great America Pkwy., Santa Clara, CA 95054 United States

STOCK TICKER/OTHER:

Stock Ticker: ANET   Exchange: NYS
Employees: 1,500   Fiscal Year Ends:
Parent Company:

SALARIES/BONUSES:

Top Exec. Salary: $275,000   Bonus: $150,000
Second Exec. Salary: $300,000   Bonus: $120,000

OTHER THOUGHTS:

Estimated Female Officers or Directors: 1
Hot Spot for Advancement for Women/Minorities:

Asana Inc

asana.com

NAIC Code: 511210H

TYPES OF BUSINESS:

Computer Software, Business Management & ERP Software

BRANDS/DIVISIONS/AFFILIATES:

CONTACTS: Note: Officers with more than one job title may be intentionally listed here more than once.

Dustin Moskovitz, CEO
Justin Rosenstein, Co-Founder
Tim Wan, Head-Finance
Dave King, Head-Mktg.
Anna Binder, Head-People

GROWTH PLANS/SPECIAL FEATURES:

Asana, Inc. develops online task management software solutions that allow teams to assign tasks and deadlines, and to track progress. Via tasks, projects, conversations and dashboards, Asana enables teams to move work from start to finish. On the dashboards, progress for any project is easily visible to everyone working on the project, without having to schedule a status meeting or sending an email. All tasks are listed on a calendar for a clear view of when work is due and when it is complete. Files are easily accessible, as well as any attachments that go along with them. Team conversations through chat-like features help teams brainstorm for more and/or better ideas, allowing everyone to add their input. Inboxes are configurable, sending team updates only to the persons involved instead of being flooded with unnecessary messages. With Asana Premium, custom fields can be utilized for data tracking; private projects can be created for sensitive work; searches can be customized; unlimited projects may be added to the dashboard; and projects can have more than 15 team members. Asana integrates with Dropbox, Slack, Chrome, OKTA, GitHub and Google Drive. Pricing includes a free basic version for up to 15 team members, with basic dashboards and search, and unlimited tasks, projects and conversations; while premium ($9.99/month, billed annually) offers unlimited members and dashboards, advanced search and reporting, custom fields, task dependencies, private teams and projects, admin controls, customer success webinars, priority support and more; business ($19.99/month, billed annually) offers everything in Premium, as well as portfolios, the ability to lock custom fields, resource management and an onboarding plan built with Asana's Customer Success team; and enterprise (contact Asana for a quote) includes everything in business as well as advanced administration controls, dedicated customer success manager, and strict control over data and security.

FINANCIAL DATA: Note: Data for latest year may not have been available at press time.

In U.S. $	2018	2017	2016	2015	2014	2013
Revenue						
R&D Expense						
Operating Income						
Operating Margin %						
SGA Expense						
Net Income						
Operating Cash Flow						
Capital Expenditure						
EBITDA						
Return on Assets %						
Return on Equity %						
Debt to Equity						

CONTACT INFORMATION:

Phone: 415-525-3888 Fax:
Toll-Free:
Address: 1550 Bryant St., Ste. 800, San Francisco, CA 94103 United States

STOCK TICKER/OTHER:

Stock Ticker: Private Exchange:
Employees: 215 Fiscal Year Ends:
Parent Company:

SALARIES/BONUSES:

Top Exec. Salary: $ Bonus: $
Second Exec. Salary: $ Bonus: $

OTHER THOUGHTS:

Estimated Female Officers or Directors:
Hot Spot for Advancement for Women/Minorities:

Sales, profits and employees may be estimates. Financial information, benefits and other data can change quickly and may vary from those stated here.

ASOS plc
NAIC Code: 454111

TYPES OF BUSINESS:
Online Apparel Sales
eCommerce
Online Fashion Marketplace

BRANDS/DIVISIONS/AFFILIATES:
ASOS White
ASOS Black
ASOS Maternity
ASOS Swim
ASOS Curve
ASOS Tall
Green Room (The)

CONTACTS: Note: Officers with more than one job title may be intentionally listed here more than once.
Nick Beighton, CEO
Nick Beighton, Corp. Sec.
Adam Crozier, Chmn.
Jon Kamaluddin, Dir.-Intl

GROWTH PLANS/SPECIAL FEATURES:
ASOS plc is a U.K.-based online retailer of fashion and beauty products. The company's inventory is comprised of about 80,000 products, including womenswear, menswear, footwear, accessories, jewelry and beauty items. With over 18.4 million active customers worldwide, the firm's website targets the twenty-something-year-old demographic and attracts millions of visitors a month. More than 63 million total orders were placed during 2018, a 27% increase from the previous year. The company's store websites, based in the U.K., U.S. and Australia, provide customized shopping through localized pricing, currency rates, sizing and language options. ASOS sells its own label and other world-renowned brands at asos.com. ASOS' own private labels include ASOS White, ASOS Black, ASOS Maternity, ASOS Swim, ASOS Curve, ASOS Tall and The Green Room. Its non-proprietary offerings include over 850 brands, such as New Look, Pull & Bear, Jack Wills and The Kooples. The company also generates revenue from ASOS Marketplace, an online site that allows individuals to list, buy and sell new and pre-owned fashion and apparel. This site offers a basic membership, which has no monthly charge and requires a 10% commission fee on all sales; and a boutique, which requires a flat monthly rate and a 20% commission fee. International sales account for more than 60% of the firm's business. Customers can purchase an ASOS Premier membership, which offers unlimited next day delivery service, free return collection and a complimentary ASOS magazine.

FINANCIAL DATA: Note: Data for latest year may not have been available at press time.

In U.S. $	2018	2017	2016	2015	2014	2013
Revenue	3,052,763,000	2,429,279,000	1,824,737,000	1,453,309,000	1,231,903,000	971,655,900
R&D Expense						
Operating Income	128,687,600	100,525,400	79,561,530	51,728,880	55,056,580	68,770,210
Operating Margin %		4.13%	2.91%	4.10%	4.78%	7.07%
SGA Expense	1,433,623,000	1,109,694,000	832,491,400	674,174,100	557,449,700	434,589,100
Net Income	104,061,400	80,950,700	30,814,310	46,557,380	46,663,470	51,687,210
Operating Cash Flow	118,584,600	184,254,400	165,058,600	117,518,700	86,708,180	93,675,490
Capital Expenditure	268,993,700	203,955,300	100,020,200	63,644,170	78,774,750	39,563,550
EBITDA	198,019,800	153,945,200	119,594,900	89,244,040	78,701,500	86,156,300
Return on Assets %		8.60%	4.32%	8.59%	10.68%	13.12%
Return on Equity %		26.29%	11.14%	17.11%	20.92%	25.61%
Debt to Equity						

CONTACT INFORMATION:
Phone: 44 2077561000   Fax: 44 2077561001
Toll-Free:
Address: Hampstead Rd., Greater London House, London, NW1 7FB United Kingdom

STOCK TICKER/OTHER:
Stock Ticker: ASOMF   Exchange: PINX
Employees: 3,579   Fiscal Year Ends: 08/31
Parent Company:

SALARIES/BONUSES:
Top Exec. Salary: $713,528   Bonus: $
Second Exec. Salary: Bonus: $
$294,672

OTHER THOUGHTS:
Estimated Female Officers or Directors: 3
Hot Spot for Advancement for Women/Minorities: Y

AT&T Inc

NAIC Code: 517110

www.att.com

TYPES OF BUSINESS:

Local Telephone Service
Wireless Telecommunications
Long-Distance Telephone Service
Corporate Telecom, Backbone & Wholesale Services
Internet Access
Entertainment & Television via Internet
Satellite TV
VOIP

BRANDS/DIVISIONS/AFFILIATES:

Home Box Office Inc (HBO)
Turner Broadcasting System Inc
Warner Bros Entertainment Inc
FiberTower Corp
Time Warner Inc

CONTACTS: *Note: Officers with more than one job title may be intentionally listed here more than once.*

Brian Lesser, CEO, Divisional
John Stankey, CEO, Divisional
John Donovan, CEO, Subsidiary
Lori Lee, CEO, Subsidiary
Randall Stephenson, CEO
John Stephens, CFO
David McAtee, General Counsel
David Huntley, Other Executive Officer
Robert Quinn, Senior Executive VP, Divisional
William Blase, Senior Executive VP, Divisional

GROWTH PLANS/SPECIAL FEATURES:

AT&T, Inc. is one of the world's largest providers of diversified telecommunications services. The company and its subsidiaries offers communications, digital entertainment services and products to consumers in the U.S., Mexico and Latin America, as well as to businesses and other providers of telecommunications services worldwide. AT&T also owns and operates three regional sports networks. Services and products include wireless communications, data/broadband and internet services, digital video services, local and long-distance telephone services, telecommunications equipment, managed networking and wholesale services. The company operates through four business segments: communication, generating revenues greater than $150 billion in 2017; media business, $31 billion; international, $8 billion; and advertising & analytics business. The communications segment provides mobile, broadband, video and other communications services to over 100 million U.S.-based consumers and nearly 3.5 million companies, ranging from the smallest business to nearly all the Fortune 1000, with highly secure, smart solutions. The media business segment consists of the operations of Home Box Office, Inc. (HBO); Turner Broadcasting System, Inc. (Turner); and Warner Bros Entertainment, Inc. Together these firms create premium content, operate one of the largest TV and film studios and own a vast library of entertainment. The international business provides mobile service in Mexico to consumers and businesses, plus pay-tv services across 11 countries in South America and the Caribbean. The advertising & analytics business segment provides marketers with advanced solutions using valuable customer insights from AT&T's TV, mobile and broadband services, combined with extensive ad inventory from Turner and AT&T's pay-tv services. In February 2018, the firm acquired FiberTower Corp., giving it millimeter wave spectrum. That June, it acquired media company Time Warner, Inc. In August of the same year, AT&T, to create a cybersecurity solutions business division, acquired AlienVault, Inc., a developer of commercial and open source solutions to manage cyber-attacks.

FINANCIAL DATA: *Note: Data for latest year may not have been available at press time.*

In U.S. $	2018	2017	2016	2015	2014	2013
Revenue		160,546,000,000	163,786,000,000	146,801,000,000	132,447,000,000	128,752,000,000
R&D Expense						
Operating Income		23,863,000,000	24,708,000,000	24,785,000,000	13,866,000,000	30,479,000,000
Operating Margin %		14.86%	15.08%	16.88%	10.46%	23.67%
SGA Expense		34,917,000,000	36,347,000,000	32,954,000,000	39,697,000,000	28,414,000,000
Net Income		29,450,000,000	12,976,000,000	13,345,000,000	6,224,000,000	18,249,000,000
Operating Cash Flow		39,151,000,000	39,344,000,000	35,880,000,000	31,338,000,000	34,796,000,000
Capital Expenditure		20,647,000,000	21,516,000,000	19,218,000,000	21,199,000,000	20,944,000,000
EBITDA		45,826,000,000	50,569,000,000	46,828,000,000	31,846,000,000	50,112,000,000
Return on Assets %		6.94%	3.21%	3.83%	2.18%	6.63%
Return on Equity %		22.31%	10.55%	12.76%	7.01%	19.90%
Debt to Equity		0.89	0.92	0.96	0.88	0.76

CONTACT INFORMATION:

Phone: 210 821-4105   Fax:
Toll-Free:
Address: 208 S. Akard St., Dallas, TX 75202 United States

STOCK TICKER/OTHER:

Stock Ticker: T
Employees: 273,210
Parent Company:

Exchange: NYS
Fiscal Year Ends: 12/31

SALARIES/BONUSES:

Top Exec. Salary: $1,800,000   Bonus: $
Second Exec. Salary: $1,035,833   Bonus: $

OTHER THOUGHTS:

Estimated Female Officers or Directors: 4
Hot Spot for Advancement for Women/Minorities: Y

Sales, profits and employees may be estimates. Financial information, benefits and other data can change quickly and may vary from those stated here.

Atos SE

atos.net/en/

NAIC Code: 541512

TYPES OF BUSINESS:

IT Consulting
Business Process Outsourcing
Payment Solutions
e-Commerce Consulting
Supply Chain Management
Customer Relationship Management
Product Lifecycle Management
Web Design

BRANDS/DIVISIONS/AFFILIATES:

Atos
Atos Worldgrid
Unify
Worldline
Convergence Creators Holding GmbH
Syntel Inc

CONTACTS: *Note: Officers with more than one job title may be intentionally listed here more than once.*

Thierry Breton, CEO
Eric Grall, Pres.
Elie Girard, CFO
Marc Meyer, Head-Communications
Philippe Mareine, Head-Human Resources
Robert Goegele, Head-Mfg., Retail & Svcs
Philippe Mareine, Gen. Sec.
Charles Dehelly, Sr. Exec. VP-Global Oper.
Marc Meyer, Head-Talent & Comm.
Michel-Alain Proch, Head-Finance
Francis Meston, Head-System Integration
Eric Grall, Head-Managed Svcs.
Ingo Juraske, Head-Public Sector, Health Care & Transport
Jeremy Hore, Head-Siemens Account
Gilles Grapinet, Sr. Exec. VP-Global Functions

GROWTH PLANS/SPECIAL FEATURES:

Atos SE is a leading European digital services firm. The company's products cover artificial intelligence (AI), cyber security, convergence creation, data center applications, transformation, defense/mission critical, enterprise servers, high-performance computing, quantum learning machine and integrated systems. The firm comprises four brands: Atos, Atos Worldgrid, Unify and Worldline. The Atos brand is the primary brand of the group, and offers digital services products and solutions. The other brand's offerings are based on Atos digital services. Atos Worldgrid delivers integration projects and real time smart energy solutions to energy and utilities companies across the power, water, oil and gas value chains. Unify provides collaboration solutions for unified communication and real time capabilities, enhancing social collaboration, digital transformation and business performance for its clients. Worldline serves the payments and transactional services industry. Solutions offered by these brands include application transformation/management, business acceleration, canopy-orchestrated hybrid cloud, data insight, digital transformation, digital workplace, automation, robotics, cyber security, digital customer experience, payments, e-transactions and more. Atos employs people in 73 countries, serving a global client base. During 2018, Atos acquired Siemens' subsidiary, Convergence Creators Holding GmbH, a global multi-industry digital transformation solutions provider; and acquired Syntel, Inc., a U.S.-based provider of integrated IT and knowledge process services.

Atos offers employees share purchase plans, competitive base pay, eLearning programs, performance rewards and insurance plans.

FINANCIAL DATA: *Note: Data for latest year may not have been available at press time.*

In U.S. $	2018	2017	2016	2015	2014	2013
Revenue						
R&D Expense						
Operating Income						
Operating Margin %						
SGA Expense						
Net Income						
Operating Cash Flow						
Capital Expenditure						
EBITDA						
Return on Assets %						
Return on Equity %						
Debt to Equity						

CONTACT INFORMATION:

Phone: 33 173260000   Fax:
Toll-Free:
Address: River Ouest 80, Quai Voltaire, Bezons Cedex, 95877 France

SALARIES/BONUSES:

Top Exec. Salary: $ Bonus: $
Second Exec. Salary: $ Bonus: $

STOCK TICKER/OTHER:

Stock Ticker: AEXAF   Exchange: PINX
Employees: 101,000   Fiscal Year Ends: 12/31
Parent Company:

OTHER THOUGHTS:

Estimated Female Officers or Directors: 5
Hot Spot for Advancement for Women/Minorities: Y

Sales, profits and employees may be estimates. Financial information, benefits and other data can change quickly and may vary from those stated here.

Audible Inc

NAIC Code: 454111

TYPES OF BUSINESS:

Audio Books-Online Sales
Audio Programming Software
Time-Shifted Radio Programming
Digital Audio Players
Educational Audio Materials

BRANDS/DIVISIONS/AFFILIATES:

Amazon.com Inc
Audible.com
AudibleListener

CONTACTS: *Note: Officers with more than one job title may be intentionally listed here more than once.*

Donald R. Katz, CEO
Anthony Nash, CFO
Guy A. Story, Jr., Chief Scientist
Guy A. Story Jr., CTO
Beth Anderson, Exec. VP
Foy C. Sperring, Jr., Exec. VP-Customer Experience

GROWTH PLANS/SPECIAL FEATURES:

Audible, Inc., a subsidiary of Amazon.com, Inc., provides internet-delivered premium spoken audio content for playback on personal computers and mobile devices. The company offers a variety of software systems and audio programming software designed to download, store and play between 2 and 24 hours of content from its online store, Audible.com. Audible sells a wide array of audio content, including educational materials, humor, periodicals, fiction, nonfiction and time-shifted radio programming comprised of 150,000 different programs and 2,700 content providers. For an annual membership fee, the company's AudibleListener membership plans provide up to one free audiobook per month, two Audible originals, a 30% discount on additional purchases, exposure to periodic sales and member-only free content offerings. It also has partnerships with leading audiobook, magazine and newspaper publishers as well as broadcasters, business information providers and educational and cultural institutions. Audible.com features daily selected audio content from The Wall Street Journal and The New York Times, both available on a subscription basis. Other publications offered include Fast Company, Forbes, Harvard Business Review and Scientific American. In addition, the site offers a large collection of audiobook bestsellers and classics by authors such as Stephen King, James Patterson, William Shakespeare and Jane Austen as well as speeches, lectures and on-demand radio programs. Around 425,000 titles are available for purchase on its U.S., U.K., German, Australian and French websites.

The firm offers employees health insurance, a 401(k) savings plan and a stock ownership program.

FINANCIAL DATA: *Note: Data for latest year may not have been available at press time.*

In U.S. $	2018	2017	2016	2015	2014	2013
Revenue						
R&D Expense						
Operating Income						
Operating Margin %						
SGA Expense						
Net Income						
Operating Cash Flow						
Capital Expenditure						
EBITDA						
Return on Assets %						
Return on Equity %						
Debt to Equity						

CONTACT INFORMATION:

Phone: 973-820-0400   Fax:
Toll-Free: 888-283-5051
Address: 1 Washington Park, Fl. 16, Newark, NJ 07102 United States

STOCK TICKER/OTHER:

Stock Ticker: Subsidiary   Exchange:
Employees: 172   Fiscal Year Ends: 12/31
Parent Company: Amazon.com Inc

SALARIES/BONUSES:

Top Exec. Salary: $ Bonus: $
Second Exec. Salary: $ Bonus: $

OTHER THOUGHTS:

Estimated Female Officers or Directors: 1
Hot Spot for Advancement for Women/Minorities: Y

Authorize.Net Holdings Inc

www.authorize.net

NAIC Code: 522320

TYPES OF BUSINESS:

Software-Payment Processing & Antifraud
Transaction Products & Services
Billing Schedule Products

BRANDS/DIVISIONS/AFFILIATES:

Visa Inc
CyberSource Corporation
Authorize.net Payment Gateway
Advanced Fraud Detection Suite

CONTACTS: *Note: Officers with more than one job title may be intentionally listed here more than once.*

Roy D. Banks, Pres.
David Schwartz, Global Mktg.
Eugene J. DiDonato, VP

GROWTH PLANS/SPECIAL FEATURES:

Authorize.Net Holdings, Inc. is a payment processing services company. It provides merchants with payment processing services that enable the authorization, settlement and management of credit card and electronic check transactions in both card-present and card-not-present markets via websites, retail stores, mail order/telephone order call centers and mobile devices. The firm's primary product is the Authorize.Net Payment Gateway, which, in addition to credit card processing, offers a number of standard-related services, including card code verification, which validates customer information using the three-or-four digit security code on a credit card; address verification service (AVS), for billing address checking; virtual terminal, which allows merchants to manually enter transactions through a web browser; verified merchant seal, which allows customers to authenticate merchant sites; and virtual point of sale, which allows merchants to process transactions via a computer and credit card reader. The company also provides merchant reporting services. Value-added services include e-check acceptance; automated recurring billing, which allows merchants to create a recurring billing schedule for good or service purchases; and the Advanced Fraud Detection Suite, a set of transaction filters and Internet Protocol (IP) address tools for the identification, management and prevention of fraudulent transactions. Authorize.Net provides its payment processing products primarily through a network of reseller partners, including independent sales organizations, merchant service providers and financial institutions. The firm operates as a subsidiary of CyberSource Corporation, which is itself a subsidiary of Visa, Inc.

Parent company CyberSource offers employees health and life insurance, retirement savings plans and vacation time.

FINANCIAL DATA: *Note: Data for latest year may not have been available at press time.*

In U.S. $	2018	2017	2016	2015	2014	2013
Revenue						
R&D Expense						
Operating Income						
Operating Margin %						
SGA Expense						
Net Income						
Operating Cash Flow						
Capital Expenditure						
EBITDA						
Return on Assets %						
Return on Equity %						
Debt to Equity						

CONTACT INFORMATION:

Phone: 801-492-6450   Fax: 801-492-6489
Toll-Free: 877-447-3938
Address: 808 E. Utah Valley Dr., American Fork, UT 84003 United States

STOCK TICKER/OTHER:

Stock Ticker: Subsidiary   Exchange:
Employees: 200   Fiscal Year Ends: 12/31
Parent Company: Visa Inc

SALARIES/BONUSES:

Top Exec. Salary: $ Bonus: $
Second Exec. Salary: $ Bonus: $

OTHER THOUGHTS:

Estimated Female Officers or Directors:
Hot Spot for Advancement for Women/Minorities:

Autohome Inc

www.autohome.com.cn

NAIC Code: 519130

TYPES OF BUSINESS:

Automobile Information for Consumers
Online Portal

BRANDS/DIVISIONS/AFFILIATES:

Autohome Mall
autohome.com.cn
che168.com

CONTACTS: *Note: Officers with more than one job title may be intentionally listed here more than once.*

Min Lu, CEO

GROWTH PLANS/SPECIAL FEATURES:

Autohome, Inc. operates an online marketplace for automobile consumers, auto dealers and auto makers in China. The firm's two websites, autohome.com.cn and che168.com, are accessible through PCs and mobile devices. Autohome's media services are provided to approximately 100 automakers operating in China. The company also provides subscription services to dealers, allowing them to market their inventory and services through Autohome's websites and mobile apps, extending the reach of their physical showrooms to internet users. Autohome's online transaction platform, Autohome Mall, is a one-stop platform for users to review automotive-related information, purchase coupons offered by automakers or dealers for discounts and make purchases to complete transactions. The platform provides direct vehicle sales and commission-based services as it facilitates transactions. The company plans to invest in developing and expanding auto finance strategies in order to quickly respond to the needs of consumers.

FINANCIAL DATA: *Note: Data for latest year may not have been available at press time.*

In U.S. $	2018	2017	2016	2015	2014	2013
Revenue		903,811,800	867,637,100	504,136,900	310,423,200	177,052,900
R&D Expense		127,894,100	83,153,210	39,863,780	23,052,350	11,883,250
Operating Income		297,369,100	167,858,000	174,616,400	131,599,800	80,759,120
Operating Margin %		32.90%	19.34%	34.63%	42.39%	45.61%
SGA Expense		280,809,500	268,331,600	192,274,700	100,249,000	47,700,800
Net Income		291,309,800	178,707,100	144,176,200	108,960,700	66,388,500
Operating Cash Flow		359,915,900	236,628,200	212,752,100	148,992,600	86,433,470
Capital Expenditure		15,648,440	12,929,080	12,976,230	6,232,772	6,764,274
EBITDA		310,298,400	178,017,100	182,851,500	143,004,500	87,419,490
Return on Assets %		18.45%	14.51%	15.46%	17.03%	15.48%
Return on Equity %		27.97%	21.90%	23.26%	25.47%	24.19%
Debt to Equity						

CONTACT INFORMATION:

Phone: 86 1059857001 Fax:
Toll-Free:
Address: 10/Fl. Tower B, 3 Dan Ling St., Beijing, 100080 China

STOCK TICKER/OTHER:

Stock Ticker: ATHM   Exchange: NYS
Employees: 3,752   Fiscal Year Ends: 12/31
Parent Company:

SALARIES/BONUSES:

Top Exec. Salary: $ Bonus: $
Second Exec. Salary: $ Bonus: $

OTHER THOUGHTS:

Estimated Female Officers or Directors:
Hot Spot for Advancement for Women/Minorities:

Automatic Data Processing Inc (ADP)

NAIC Code: 518210

TYPES OF BUSINESS:

Data Processing Services
Business Outsourcing Solutions
Information Services
Payroll Processing

BRANDS/DIVISIONS/AFFILIATES:

ADP TotalSource
RUN Powered by ADP
ADP Vantage HCM
ADP GlobalView HCM
ADP Workforce Now

CONTACTS: *Note: Officers with more than one job title may be intentionally listed here more than once.*

Carlos Rodriguez, CEO
Michael Eberhard, Treasurer
Jan Siegmund, CFO
Brock Albinson, Chief Accounting Officer
John Jones, Director
Michael Bonarti, General Counsel
Dermot OBrien, Other Executive Officer
Sreeni Kutam, Other Executive Officer
Don McGuire, President, Divisional
Thomas Perrotti, President, Divisional
John Ayala, President, Divisional
Douglas Politi, President, Divisional
Deborah Dyson, President, Divisional
Maria Black, President, Divisional
Stuart Sackman, Vice President, Divisional
Donald Weinstein, Vice President, Divisional

GROWTH PLANS/SPECIAL FEATURES:

Automatic Data Processing, Inc. (ADP) is one of the world's largest providers of cloud-based human capital management (HCM) solutions to employers, as well as business outsourcing services, analytics and compliance expertise. The company serves approximately 740,000 clients in more than 110 countries. ADP operates in two segments: employer services and professional employer organization (PEO) services. The employer services segment offers a comprehensive range of business outsourcing and HCM solutions including payroll services, benefits administration, talent management, human resource management, time and attendance management, insurance services, retirement services and compliance services. Integrated HCM solutions include RUN Powered by ADP, a software platform for managing small business payroll, HR management and tax compliance administration; ADP Vantage HCM, a solution for multinational corporations; ADP Workforce Now, a flexible HCM solution for mid-sized and large businesses; and ADP GlobalView HCM, a solution for mid-sized and large businesses to standardize their HCM strategies. The PEO services segment, which operates as ADP TotalSource, provides small and medium sized businesses with comprehensive employment administration outsourcing solutions (through a co-employment relationship) including employee recruitment, payroll, payroll tax filing, human resources guidance, 401(k) plan administration, benefits administration, compliance services, health and workers' compensation coverage and other supplemental benefits for employees. ADP TotalSource has approximately 12,000 clients in all 50 states; the businesses it serves have a combined total of 530,000 worksite employees.

Employee benefits in the U.S. include medical, dental and vision insurance; health care and dependent care flexible spending accounts; life, AD&D and disability coverage; a pension and 401(k) plan; a stock purchase and stock option plan; auto & home insurance programs; tuition reimbursement; and a scholarship program.

FINANCIAL DATA: *Note: Data for latest year may not have been available at press time.*

In U.S. $	2018	2017	2016	2015	2014	2013
Revenue	13,325,800,000	12,379,800,000	11,667,800,000	10,938,500,000	12,206,500,000	11,310,100,000
R&D Expense						
Operating Income	2,511,700,000	2,326,800,000	2,190,500,000	2,014,000,000	2,222,700,000	2,039,900,000
Operating Margin %		18.79%	18.77%	18.41%	18.20%	18.03%
SGA Expense	2,971,500,000	2,783,200,000	2,637,000,000	2,496,900,000	2,762,400,000	2,620,600,000
Net Income	1,620,800,000	1,733,400,000	1,492,500,000	1,452,500,000	1,515,900,000	1,405,800,000
Operating Cash Flow	2,515,200,000	2,125,900,000	1,859,900,000	1,905,600,000	1,821,400,000	1,577,200,000
Capital Expenditure	470,800,000	470,600,000	386,000,000	335,500,000	367,700,000	282,900,000
EBITDA	2,651,400,000	2,927,200,000	2,579,500,000	2,355,100,000	2,616,900,000	2,410,400,000
Return on Assets %		4.28%	3.88%	4.45%	4.71%	4.45%
Return on Equity %		40.98%	32.13%	25.30%	23.57%	22.85%
Debt to Equity		0.50	0.44			

CONTACT INFORMATION:

Phone: 973 974-5000   Fax: 973 974-5390
Toll-Free: 800-225-5237
Address: 1 ADP Blvd., Roseland, NJ 07068 United States

STOCK TICKER/OTHER:

Stock Ticker: ADP   Exchange: NAS
Employees: 57,000   Fiscal Year Ends: 06/30
Parent Company:

SALARIES/BONUSES:

Top Exec. Salary: $1,055,000   Bonus: $
Second Exec. Salary: Bonus: $
$693,600

OTHER THOUGHTS:

Estimated Female Officers or Directors: 1
Hot Spot for Advancement for Women/Minorities: Y

Automattic Inc

automattic.com

NAIC Code: 519130

TYPES OF BUSINESS:
Internet Publishing and Broadcasting and Web Search Portals

BRANDS/DIVISIONS/AFFILIATES:
WordPress.com
WooCommerce
Simplenote
Longreads
VaultPress
Akismet
Gravatar
Crowdsignal

CONTACTS: *Note: Officers with more than one job title may be intentionally listed here more than once.*
Matt Mullenweg, CEO

GROWTH PLANS/SPECIAL FEATURES:
Automattic, Inc. builds and operates websites worldwide. The company's sites include, but are not limited to, WordPress.com, for blogging or as a website; WooCommerce, an e-commerce site; Jetpack, a plugin for sites and includes stats, backups, speed and power; Simplenote, which synchronizes notes across devices; Longreads, for storytelling; VaultPress, providing automatic backups and scanning for website security purposes; Akismet, which filters spam; Gravatar, which syncs a picture across all of a user's profiles; Crowdsignal, which collects readers' opinions; Cloudup, which beams links, files, photos and more to the cloud for storage and sharing; and Simperium, for moving data across apps via one API (application program interface). Automattic also serves nonprofit and open source projects in the U.S. and internationally. The company is headquartered in San Francisco, California, USA, but has employees across 60 countries.

Automatic offers its employees an open vacation policy; company-sponsored life insurance; open maternity/paternity leave; and country-specific health, dental, vision insurance, as well as retirement plans and other perks.

FINANCIAL DATA: *Note: Data for latest year may not have been available at press time.*

In U.S. $	2018	2017	2016	2015	2014	2013
Revenue						
R&D Expense						
Operating Income						
Operating Margin %						
SGA Expense						
Net Income						
Operating Cash Flow						
Capital Expenditure						
EBITDA						
Return on Assets %						
Return on Equity %						
Debt to Equity						

CONTACT INFORMATION:
Phone: 877-273-3049   Fax: 415-840-0710
Toll-Free:
Address: 60 29th St., Ste. 343, San Francisco, CA 94110 United States

STOCK TICKER/OTHER:
Stock Ticker: Private   Exchange:
Employees: 835   Fiscal Year Ends:
Parent Company:

SALARIES/BONUSES:
Top Exec. Salary: $ Bonus: $
Second Exec. Salary: $ Bonus: $

OTHER THOUGHTS:
Estimated Female Officers or Directors:
Hot Spot for Advancement for Women/Minorities:

Sales, profits and employees may be estimates. Financial information, benefits and other data can change quickly and may vary from those stated here.

AutoWeb Inc

NAIC Code: 519130

www.autoweb.com

TYPES OF BUSINESS:

Automotive Media & Marketing Services
Online Car Sales Support

BRANDS/DIVISIONS/AFFILIATES:

Autobytel Inc
Autobytel.com
MyGarage
iControl
WebLeads+

CONTACTS: Note: Officers with more than one job title may be intentionally listed here more than once.

Jared Rowe, CEO
Joseph Hannan, CFO
Michael Fuchs, Chairman of the Board
Glenn Fuller, Chief Administrative Officer
Tim Branham, Chief Technology Officer
Wesley Ozima, Controller
Taren Peng, Senior VP, Divisional

GROWTH PLANS/SPECIAL FEATURES:

AutoWeb Inc, formerly Autobytel, Inc., a digital marketing company for the automotive industry that assists automotive retail dealers and automotive manufacturers market and sell new and used vehicles to consumers by utilizing its digital sales enhancing products and services. The company owns and operates a network of websites both for consumers and dealers. The flagship website, Autobytel.com, provides consumers with information and tools to assist consumers with vehicle purchase decisions, dealer enquiries for buying or leasing vehicles, vehicle financing and other automotive needs. Customers can choose from a variety of colors, accessories and methods of payment and then have the site search all retail dealerships within a given radius from the user's home for a vehicle that matches the selected specifications. MyGarage, found on Autobytel.com, has tools to calculate repair cost, diagnose problems, and car care advice among other features. Other products and services for dealers and manufacturers include iControl, WebLeads+, customer relationship management (CRM) products, customer loyalty programs and retention marketing programs.In October 2017, Autobytel changed its name to AutoWeb and its ticker symbol from ABTL to AUTO.

FINANCIAL DATA: Note: Data for latest year may not have been available at press time.

In U.S. $	2018	2017	2016	2015	2014	2013
Revenue		142,125,000	156,684,000	133,226,000	106,278,000	78,361,000
R&D Expense		12,567,000	13,986,000	11,740,000	8,014,000	7,303,000
Operating Income		-1,000,000	6,078,000	7,649,000	5,999,000	2,527,000
Operating Margin %		- .70%	3.87%	5.74%	5.64%	3.22%
SGA Expense		26,425,000	32,781,000	29,145,000	25,942,000	19,166,000
Net Income		-64,964,000	3,871,000	4,646,000	3,411,000	38,144,000
Operating Cash Flow		11,488,000	18,242,000	12,200,000	7,890,000	4,332,000
Capital Expenditure		10,399,000	2,148,000	2,719,000	1,124,000	686,000
EBITDA		6,653,000	13,381,000	11,670,000	8,226,000	4,402,000
Return on Assets %		-50.32%	2.42%	3.59%	3.53%	59.15%
Return on Equity %		-69.56%	3.39%	5.23%	5.08%	84.20%
Debt to Equity		0.13	0.13	0.20	0.18	0.14

CONTACT INFORMATION:

Phone: 949-225-4500   Fax:
Toll-Free:
Address: 18872 MacArthur Blvd., Ste. 200, Irvine, CA 92612 United States

STOCK TICKER/OTHER:

Stock Ticker: AUTO
Employees: 254
Parent Company:

Exchange: NAS
Fiscal Year Ends: 12/31

SALARIES/BONUSES:

Top Exec. Salary: $550,000   Bonus: $
Second Exec. Salary: $385,000   Bonus: $

OTHER THOUGHTS:

Estimated Female Officers or Directors: 1
Hot Spot for Advancement for Women/Minorities:

Avalara Inc

www.avalara.com

NAIC Code: 511210Q

TYPES OF BUSINESS:

Computer Software, Accounting, Banking & Financial
Tax Software

BRANDS/DIVISIONS/AFFILIATES:

CONTACTS: Note: Officers with more than one job title may be intentionally listed here more than once.

Scott McFarlane, CEO
William Ingram, CFO
Jared Vogt, Director
Alesia Pinney, Executive VP
Pascal Dooren, Executive VP

GROWTH PLANS/SPECIAL FEATURES:

Avalara, Inc. provides a cloud-based software platform for businesses of all sizes to manage transactional taxes. The firm's automated compliance solutions can be utilized across all types of transactional tax, including sales and use tax, value-added tax (VAT), lodging tax, excise tax and communications tax. Avalara's tax solutions comprise tax calculations, returns and filings, tax document management and professional services. The company's software integrates with more than 500 formats, including ShopifyPlus, Oracle, Microsoft Dynamics, Intuit QuickBooks, Salesforce and SAP. For businesses selling internationally, Avalara's VAT can help; enter details about VAT transactions into VAT Expert and it will show how they should be taxed. VAT solutions include automation, services, cross-border transactions, Brazil and India compliance and more. Headquartered in Washington, the firm has domestic offices in North Carolina, California, Colorado, Wisconsin and Texas, as well as internationally in Belgium, Brazil, India and the U.K. During 2018, Avalara began trading on the New York Stock Exchange under ticker symbol: AVLR, and nearly doubled its shares on its first day of trading.

FINANCIAL DATA: Note: Data for latest year may not have been available at press time.

In U.S. $	2018	2017	2016	2015	2014	2013
Revenue		213,159,000	167,426,000	123,158,000		
R&D Expense		41,264,000	32,848,000	29,787,000		
Operating Income		-54,162,000	-54,293,000	-79,743,000		
Operating Margin %		-25.40%	-32.42%	-64.74%		
SGA Expense		168,080,000	140,358,000	132,369,000		
Net Income		-64,126,000	-57,888,000	-77,764,000		
Operating Cash Flow		-3,541,000	-21,696,000	-47,008,000		
Capital Expenditure		13,955,000	6,660,000	7,912,000		
EBITDA		-51,901,000	-44,522,000	-71,495,000		
Return on Assets %		-35.49%	-31.71%			
Return on Equity %						
Debt to Equity						

CONTACT INFORMATION:

Phone: 877-780-4848   Fax: 206-780-5011
Toll-Free:
Address: 255 S. King St., Ste. 1800, Seattle, WA 98104 United States

STOCK TICKER/OTHER:

Stock Ticker: AVLR   Exchange: NYS
Employees: 1,495   Fiscal Year Ends: 12/31
Parent Company:

SALARIES/BONUSES:

Top Exec. Salary: $410,000   Bonus: $
Second Exec. Salary: $330,000   Bonus: $

OTHER THOUGHTS:

Estimated Female Officers or Directors:
Hot Spot for Advancement for Women/Minorities:

Avaya Holdings Corp

www.avaya.com

NAIC Code: 334210

TYPES OF BUSINESS:

Telecommunications Systems
Telecommunications Software
Consulting Services
Networking Systems & Software
Network Maintenance, Management & Security Services
Systems Planning & Integration
Unified Communications Systems

BRANDS/DIVISIONS/AFFILIATES:

Silver Lake Partners
TPC Capital

CONTACTS: *Note: Officers with more than one job title may be intentionally listed here more than once.*

James Chirico, CEO
William Watkins, Chairman of the Board
Luino DellOsso, Chief Accounting Officer
Shefali Shah, Chief Administrative Officer
William Rowe, General Manager, Divisional
Nicholas Nikolopoulos, Senior VP, Divisional
Laurent Philonenko, Senior VP, Divisional
Jaroslaw Glembocki, Senior VP, Divisional
Patrick OMalley, Senior VP

GROWTH PLANS/SPECIAL FEATURES:

Avaya Holdings Corp. operates as a holding company which, through its subsidiary Avaya Inc, is a leading global provider of unified communications solutions, customer experience management and cloud services. The company's unified communications solutions include conferencing and infrastructure solutions that support real-time engagement by integrating voice, video, data, messaging, conferencing, mobility and more. Its customer experience management solution is designed with a discipline of treating customer relationships as assets in order to transform them into loyal customers via persistent conversation and consistent experience via context. This product offers an omnichannel assisted experience, an omnichannel automated experience and actionable insights. Avaya's cloud services include a subscription-based hosted service in the cloud for high-performance video conferencing, voice over internet protocol (IP), unified communications and remote collaboration. The firm's cloud solutions for partners and service providers enable them to deliver cloud services for every size enterprise, including unified communications, contact center applications and video. The solutions can integrate with other applications by using open standards, APIs and other capabilities. They can be customized for BYOD and deliver standards-based endpoint support. Its multi-tenant capabilities enable partners to optimize their infrastructure for the entire customer base. Partners include channel partners, technology partners, consultants and more. Avaya is owned by private equity firms Silver Lake Partners and TPG Capital. In November 2017, Avaya obtained U.S. Bankruptcy Court approval for its reorganization plan.

FINANCIAL DATA: *Note: Data for latest year may not have been available at press time.*

In U.S. $	2018	2017	2016	2015	2014	2013
Revenue		3,272,000,000	3,702,000,000	4,081,000,000	4,371,000,000	4,708,000,000
R&D Expense		229,000,000	275,000,000	338,000,000	379,000,000	445,000,000
Operating Income		284,000,000	331,000,000	434,000,000	362,000,000	367,000,000
Operating Margin %		8.67%	8.94%	10.63%	8.28%	7.79%
SGA Expense		1,282,000,000	1,413,000,000	1,432,000,000	1,531,000,000	1,521,000,000
Net Income		-182,000,000	-730,000,000	-168,000,000	-253,000,000	-376,000,000
Operating Cash Flow		291,000,000	113,000,000	215,000,000	39,000,000	151,000,000
Capital Expenditure		59,000,000	96,000,000	124,000,000	135,000,000	124,000,000
EBITDA		374,000,000	126,000,000	725,000,000	629,000,000	500,000,000
Return on Assets %		-5.52%	-12.18%	-3.04%	-4.00%	-5.29%
Return on Equity %						
Debt to Equity						

CONTACT INFORMATION:

Phone: 908-953-6000   Fax:
Toll-Free: 866-462-8292
Address: 4655 Great American Pkwy., Santa Clara, CA 95054 United States

STOCK TICKER/OTHER:

Stock Ticker: AVYA   Exchange: NYS
Employees: 15,953   Fiscal Year Ends: 09/30
Parent Company:

SALARIES/BONUSES:

Top Exec. Salary: $ Bonus: $
Second Exec. Salary: $ Bonus: $

OTHER THOUGHTS:

Estimated Female Officers or Directors: 1
Hot Spot for Advancement for Women/Minorities:

Axway Inc

NAIC Code: 511210E

www.axway.com

TYPES OF BUSINESS:

Computer Software, Security & Anti-Virus
E-Mail, Firewall & Anti-Spam Software
Secure File Transfer Software
Professional Services
Security Software
Business Processing Management
Tracking Software

BRANDS/DIVISIONS/AFFILIATES:

Sopra Steria Group SA
Axway AMPLIFY

CONTACTS: Note: Officers with more than one job title may be intentionally listed here more than once.

Patrick Donovan, CEO
Scott Hausman, Exec. VP-Strategy & Corp. Dev.
Joel Depernet, Exec. VP-Solution, Prod. & Eng.
Roland Royer, Chief Customer Officer
Vince Padua, Chief Technology & Innovation Officer
Rohit Khanna, Sr. VP-Consulting & Professional Svcs.
Pierre Pasquier, Chmn.

GROWTH PLANS/SPECIAL FEATURES:

Axway, Inc. is a leading provider of multi-enterprise solutions, serving more than 11,000 enterprises in 100 countries. Its Axway AMPLIFY platform unifies a business' employees, suppliers, partners and developers in order to create a powerful customer experience network that meets consumer demands. The platform's capabilities include analytics, application program interface (API) lifecycle management, app development, community management and integration. For IT and architects, Axway's product offers big data integration, cloud integration, identity federation, identity validation, mobility and Internet of Things (IoT). For developers, it offers cross-platform application, development, API development and DevOps. Businesses and industries served by the firm include automotive, banking/financial services, healthcare, life sciences, manufacturing, consumer packaged goods, retail, U.S. federal government and many more. Axway offers various types of support, including downloads, documentation, contact support, how-to videos, webinars, training courses, resource library, cloud consulting, API management consulting and managed file transfer consulting.

FINANCIAL DATA: Note: Data for latest year may not have been available at press time.

In U.S. $	2018	2017	2016	2015	2014	2013
Revenue	377,074,950	359,119,000	338,395,324	319,110,596	287,239,556	315,000,000
R&D Expense						
Operating Income						
Operating Margin %						
SGA Expense						
Net Income		48,513,500	35,400,461	31,291,524	29,316,122	35,595,000
Operating Cash Flow						
Capital Expenditure						
EBITDA						
Return on Assets %						
Return on Equity %						
Debt to Equity						

CONTACT INFORMATION:

Phone: 480-627-1800   Fax: 480-627-1801
Toll-Free: 877-564-7700
Address: 6811 E. Mayo Blvd., Ste. 400, Phoenix, AZ 85054 United States

STOCK TICKER/OTHER:

Stock Ticker: AXW
Employees: 1,900
Parent Company:

Exchange: Amsterdam
Fiscal Year Ends: 12/31

SALARIES/BONUSES:

Top Exec. Salary: $ Bonus: $
Second Exec. Salary: $ Bonus: $

OTHER THOUGHTS:

Estimated Female Officers or Directors:
Hot Spot for Advancement for Women/Minorities:

B2W-Companhia Global Do Varejo

ri.b2w.digital/en

NAIC Code: 454111

TYPES OF BUSINESS:

Online Retailing
Online Ticket & Travel Sales
Consumer Financing

BRANDS/DIVISIONS/AFFILIATES:

Americanas.com
Submarino
Submarino Finance
Shoptime
SouBarato
Submarino Viagens
Cartao Submarino

CONTACTS: Note: Officers with more than one job title may be intentionally listed here more than once.

Marcio Cruz Meirelles, CEO
Carlos Eduardo Rosalba Padilha, COO
Fabio da Silva Abrate, CFO
Cruz Marcio Meirelles, Chief Commercial Officer
Fabio da Silva Abrate, Investor Rel. Officer
Timotheo Jose Barros, Co-COO
Carlos Eduardo Rosalba Padilha, Co-COO
Carlos Henreique de Lucca Strong Gatto, Co-COO
Jean Pierre Lessa, Co-COO
Santos Ferriera, Co-COO

GROWTH PLANS/SPECIAL FEATURES:

B2W-Companhia Global Do Varejo is one of the largest e-commerce retailers in Latin America. Based in Brazil, the firm operates through a portfolio of online brands, including Americanas.com, Submarino, Submarino Finance, Shoptime and SouBarato. Americanas.com offers items in more than 1 million products, including electronics, CDs, DVDs, computers/IT, home appliances, books, games, toys, stationery, fragrances and wines. Items can be purchased through the website, by telephone or at the more than 900 kiosks in brick-and-mortar stores. Americanas.com also operates delivery services, travel services, mobile app and a business to business service. Submarino sells books, CDs, DVDs, electronics, computers/IT, videogames and online services. Submarino also operates business-to-business services. Submarino Finance operates the Cartao Submarino Mastercard, which offers special advantages on the Submarino site, such as exclusive discounts and installment payment options, differentiated credit limits and digital finance, which offers cards and financial products for Americanas.com, Shoptime and Sou Barato. Shoptime is Brazil's first home shopping channel and operates through internet, telesales and catalogues. Viewers can tune in to Shoptime via satellite or cable TV channels, as well as make purchases through Shoptime.com.br website and from the company's catalog. The segment offers four private label brands: Casa and Conforto, Fun Kitchen, La Cuisine and Life Zone. SouBarato operates through soubarato.com.br and markets new and repackaged products, which are otherwise in perfect condition at prices below the market average. The product offerings include watches, perfumes, electronics, smart phones, computers and other merchandise. Products can be discounted as much as 70%.

FINANCIAL DATA: Note: Data for latest year may not have been available at press time.

In U.S. $	2018	2017	2016	2015	2014	2013
Revenue		1,896,295,000	2,290,568,000	2,400,410,000	2,120,805,000	1,621,395,000
R&D Expense						
Operating Income		66,003,840	96,156,960	59,390,960	97,637,620	72,693,140
Operating Margin %		3.48%	4.19%	4.57%	4.60%	4.48%
SGA Expense		237,764,400	258,173,200	295,353,200	348,935,300	268,078,900
Net Income		-109,571,000	-129,386,700	-111,417,500	-43,490,980	-42,492,080
Operating Cash Flow		-117,815,800	-209,274,800	-68,488,190	-194,868,000	74,161,810
Capital Expenditure		101,179,700	122,466,800	192,081,400	216,383,800	190,174,700
EBITDA		167,221,100	44,218,000	57,608,050	39,290,830	34,370,590
Return on Assets %		-3.59%	-4.81%	-4.75%	-2.29%	-2.79%
Return on Equity %		-11.78%	-16.80%	-14.46%	-8.35%	-17.74%
Debt to Equity		1.19	1.21	1.34	0.43	3.70

CONTACT INFORMATION:

Phone: 55 22066000   Fax: 55 22066898
Toll-Free:
Address: 60 Rua Coelho e Castro, Rio de Janeiro, RJ 20081902 Brazil

STOCK TICKER/OTHER:

Stock Ticker: BCGVY   Exchange: GREY
Employees: Fiscal Year Ends: 12/31
Parent Company:

SALARIES/BONUSES:

Top Exec. Salary: $ Bonus: $
Second Exec. Salary: $ Bonus: $

OTHER THOUGHTS:

Estimated Female Officers or Directors: 1
Hot Spot for Advancement for Women/Minorities:

BackCountry.com

NAIC Code: 454111

TYPES OF BUSINESS:

Sporting Goods-Online Retail
Outdoor Sports Equipment
Athletic Apparel
Ski Equipment

BRANDS/DIVISIONS/AFFILIATES:

TSG Consumer Partners LLC
bergfreunde.de
motorsport.com
Competitive Cyclist
Steep & Cheap

CONTACTS: Note: Officers with more than one job title may be intentionally listed here more than once.

Jonathan Nielsen, CEO
Pete Labore, COO
Josh Burke, CFO
Diana Seung, Exec. VP-Merchandising
Thomas Jeon, Exec. VP-People
Peter Eischeid, Exec. VP-Tech. and Product
Jonathan Nielson, Exec. VP-Prod.
Brendan Quirk, Exec. VP-Customer Experience

GROWTH PLANS/SPECIAL FEATURES:

BackCountry.com, owned by the private equity firm TSG Consumer Partners, LLC, is an online retailer of outdoor gear. The company was founded by Jim Holland, a two-time Olympian and six-time national champion Nordic ski jumper, and John Bresee, former editor of Powder Magazine. BackCountry offers a wide selection of goods for outdoor activities, including men's, women's and children's clothing, shoes, skis and skiing accessories, snowboards and snowboard accessories, hiking and camping gear, trail running products, snowshoeing products, technical climbing gear, kayaks and kayak accessories and outdoor travel products (backpacks, car racks, etc.). The company's selection of goods encompasses over 1,000 brands, including The North Face, Oakley, Patagonia, Marmot, Oakley, Rossignol, K2 and more. BackCountry has been expanding since its inception and has fostered spin-off eCommerce storefronts, each focused on a specific niche of the outdoor sporting market. These internet stores include bergfreunde.de, a premier source for high-end outdoor gear and clothing in Europe; competitivecyclist.com, a source for pro-caliber cycling gear and clothing; motosport.com for motorcycle enthusiast; and steapandcheap.com, a showroom of limited-time, limited quantity deals. The company processes orders and ships from a 200,000-square-foot distribution center in Salt Lake City, Utah and a 320,000-square-foot distribution center in Christiansburg, Virginia. The firm also maintains offices in Portland, Oregon, the motosport.com headquarters; Costa Rica, BackCountry's first international office; and Germany, the headquarters of bergfreunde.de.

The firm offers employees medical, dental and vision insurance; life and AD&D insurance; flexible spending accounts; a 401(k) plan; an employee assistance program; employee discounts; and discounted ski passes at various world-class resorts in the Park City/Salt Lake area.

FINANCIAL DATA: Note: Data for latest year may not have been available at press time.

In U.S. $	2018	2017	2016	2015	2014	2013
Revenue						
R&D Expense						
Operating Income						
Operating Margin %						
SGA Expense						
Net Income						
Operating Cash Flow						
Capital Expenditure						
EBITDA						
Return on Assets %						
Return on Equity %						
Debt to Equity						

CONTACT INFORMATION:

Phone: 800-409-4502   Fax: 801-973-4552
Toll-Free: 800-409-4502
Address: 2607 S. 3200 W., Salt Lake City, UT 84119 United States

SALARIES/BONUSES:

Top Exec. Salary: $ Bonus: $
Second Exec. Salary: $ Bonus: $

STOCK TICKER/OTHER:

Stock Ticker: Private   Exchange:
Employees: 1,200   Fiscal Year Ends: 12/31
Parent Company: TSG Consumer Partners LLC

OTHER THOUGHTS:

Estimated Female Officers or Directors: 1
Hot Spot for Advancement for Women/Minorities:

Baidu Inc

NAIC Code: 519130

www.baidu.com

TYPES OF BUSINESS:
Online Search Portals
Online Advertising Services
Social Networking
Entertainment
News
Online Payment Services

BRANDS/DIVISIONS/AFFILIATES:
iQiyi
Baidu Nuomi
Baidu Deliveries
Baidu Maps
Baidu Connect
Baidu Wallet
PPStream Inc
Baidu Cloud

CONTACTS: *Note: Officers with more than one job title may be intentionally listed here more than once.*
Robin Li, CEO
Yaqin Zhang, Pres.
Herman Yu, CFO
Jing Wang, VP-Eng.
Victor Liang, VP-Legal Affairs
Hailong Xiang, VP-Commercial Oper.
Guang Zhu, VP-Public Rel.
Robin Li, Chmn.

GROWTH PLANS/SPECIAL FEATURES:
Baidu, Inc. is a leading Chinese language search engine. The firm provides a way for people to find what they are looking for, and also offers a platform for businesses to reach potential customers. Baidu operates in three segments: search services, transaction services and iQiyi. Search services are keyword-based marketing services targeted at and triggered by internet users' search queries, which primarily include Baidu's pay-for-performance (P4P) services and other online marketing services. Transaction services include Baidu Nuomi, Baidu Takeout Delivery, Baidu Maps, Baidu Connect, Baidu Wallet and Baidu Cloud. These services and applications/websites provide merchants with a turn-key solution to easily participate in Baidu's online marketing and transaction services without high startup costs or the need for infrastructure investment. Baidu Nuomi offers services and products that enable or facilitate users to conduct online and offline transactions such as entertainment, including film, transportation ticketing and tourism; dining; hotel reservation; health information and products; and beauty information and products. Baidu Deliveries is an online platform on which users can place food delivery orders with restaurants. Baidu Maps integrates map data from third-party suppliers and web information, providing users with services relating to locations, routes and local merchants on their personal computers (PCs) or mobile devices. Baidu Connect provides leads for merchants via other Baidu products such as search and maps. Baidu Wallet provides online and mobile payment services. Baidu Cloud allows user to upload files to a cloud server. Last, iQiyi is an online subscription video platform with a content library that includes licensed movies, television series, cartoons, variety shows and other programs. This platform is comprised of PPStream, Inc., a sub-brand of iQiyi. In April 2018, the firm spun-off its financial services unit, Du Xiaoman Financial, with the $1.9 billion help of a group of investors led by TPG.

FINANCIAL DATA: *Note: Data for latest year may not have been available at press time.*

In U.S. $	2018	2017	2016	2015	2014	2013
Revenue		12,342,860,000	10,267,550,000	9,661,005,000	7,138,933,000	4,649,026,000
R&D Expense		1,881,504,000	1,477,311,000	1,480,951,000	1,015,989,000	597,696,400
Operating Income		2,283,623,000	1,462,514,000	1,698,644,000	1,863,423,000	1,628,810,000
Operating Margin %		18.50%	14.24%	17.58%	26.10%	35.03%
SGA Expense		1,910,611,000	2,193,329,000	2,485,247,000	1,510,987,000	752,941,100
Net Income		2,663,475,000	1,692,927,000	4,899,386,000	1,919,208,000	1,530,900,000
Operating Cash Flow		4,785,260,000	3,239,408,000	2,826,685,000	2,610,524,000	2,007,389,000
Capital Expenditure		2,030,388,000	1,529,561,000	1,131,472,000	930,740,500	535,720,300
EBITDA		5,042,278,000	3,492,065,000	6,521,362,000	2,776,180,000	2,224,402,000
Return on Assets %		8.43%	7.05%	27.20%	15.45%	18.03%
Return on Equity %		17.62%	13.48%	51.09%	29.32%	32.62%
Debt to Equity		0.31	0.37	0.42	0.45	0.44

CONTACT INFORMATION:
Phone: 86 1059928888   Fax: 86 1059920000
Toll-Free:
Address: No. 10 Shangdi, 10th St., Beijing, 100085 China

STOCK TICKER/OTHER:
Stock Ticker: BIDU
Employees: 42,000
Parent Company:

Exchange: NAS
Fiscal Year Ends: 12/31

SALARIES/BONUSES:
Top Exec. Salary: $ Bonus: $
Second Exec. Salary: $ Bonus: $

OTHER THOUGHTS:
Estimated Female Officers or Directors: 1
Hot Spot for Advancement for Women/Minorities:

Sales, profits and employees may be estimates. Financial information, benefits and other data can change quickly and may vary from those stated here.

Bankrate LLC

NAIC Code: 519130

www.bankrate.com

TYPES OF BUSINESS:

Portal-Financial Services
Financial Information
Banking Information
eCommerce

BRANDS/DIVISIONS/AFFILIATES:

Red Ventures
Bankrate.com
CreditCards.com
Caring.com
Quizzle.com
Bankrate.com/uk/

CONTACTS: *Note: Officers with more than one job title may be intentionally listed here more than once.*

Kenneth Esterow, CEO
Christopher Speltz, CEO, Subsidiary
Peter Morse, Director
James Gilmartin, General Counsel

GROWTH PLANS/SPECIAL FEATURES:

Bankrate, LLC is an internet-based consumer banking and personal finance network. The company is a leading publisher, aggregator and distributor of personal finance content on the internet. Its flagship website, Bankrate.com, is an aggregator of information on over 300 financial products and fees, including mortgages, credit cards, automobile loans, money market accounts, certificates of deposit, checking and ATM fees, home equity loans and online banking fees. It regularly aggregates data from thousands of financial institutions in all 50 U.S. states. Besides Bankrate.com, the firm's other flagship sites include CreditCards.com, which provides consumer inquiries to credit card issuers and principally record sales after the credit card issuers approve the consumer's credit application; and Caring.com, which provides caregiving content concerning senior living communities in the U.S., as well as advice from family advisors and online tools and directories. In addition, Quizzle.com provides tools, services and content which includes credit monitoring, identity theft protection, debt management, credit reports/credit scores, budget planning and credit management techniques. In November 2017, Bankrate was taken private by Red Ventures, a leading digital consumer choice platform, for approximately $1.4 billion. Bankrate subsequently ceased from being publicly traded. In early-2018, Bankrate expanded into the U.K. with an office based in London, and offering the Bankrate.com/uk/ website.

FINANCIAL DATA: *Note: Data for latest year may not have been available at press time.*

In U.S. $	2018	2017	2016	2015	2014	2013
Revenue	467,250,000	445,000,000	434,160,992	370,534,016	544,942,976	457,432,000
R&D Expense						
Operating Income						
Operating Margin %						
SGA Expense						
Net Income			-34,134,000	-13,346,000	5,172,000	-10,002,000
Operating Cash Flow						
Capital Expenditure						
EBITDA						
Return on Assets %						
Return on Equity %						
Debt to Equity						

CONTACT INFORMATION:

Phone: 917-368-8600   Fax:
Toll-Free: 855-733-0700
Address: 477 Madison Ave., Ste. 430, New York, NY 10022 United States

STOCK TICKER/OTHER:

Stock Ticker: Private   Exchange:
Employees: 600   Fiscal Year Ends: 12/31
Parent Company: Red Ventures

SALARIES/BONUSES:

Top Exec. Salary: $ Bonus: $
Second Exec. Salary: $ Bonus: $

OTHER THOUGHTS:

Estimated Female Officers or Directors:
Hot Spot for Advancement for Women/Minorities:

BigCommerce Holdings Inc

www.bigcommerce.com

NAIC Code: 511210M

TYPES OF BUSINESS:

Computer Software, E-Commerce & Web Analytics
e-Commerce

BRANDS/DIVISIONS/AFFILIATES:

BigCommerce Pty Ltd

CONTACTS: *Note: Officers with more than one job title may be intentionally listed here more than once.*

Brent Bellm, CEO
Robert Alvarez, COO
Alexandra Shapiro, CMO
Sherri Manning, Sr. VP-People & Culture
Brian Dhatt, CTO

GROWTH PLANS/SPECIAL FEATURES:

BigCommerce Holdings, Inc., operating through BigCommerce Pty Ltd., provides an e-commerce platform that powers thousands of online stores in over 150 countries. The company's software products include the e-commerce website builder, website design shop, host security, analytics, payment acceptance, and handles shipping and order fulfillment. These features help drive business and convert visitors. BigCommerce also enables its clients to connect their online store with Square, a mobile point-of-sale solution used by more than 2.2 million sellers. This feature lets users sell merchandise both online and off. BigCommerce users can also sell to millions on marketplaces such as eBay, Amazon and more, as well as on social media websites. BigCommerce's flexible platform comprises advanced native features like faceted search, and also offers hundreds of single-click integrations with industry-leading software in order to expand client stores. Its open application program interface (API) architecture allows users to build new functions and integrations. BigCommerce serves businesses of all sizes, whether small or enterprise. Clients of the firm include Toyota, Travelpro, Gibsun, Spinning, Kodak, Ben & Jerry's, Paul Mitchell, Camelbak and many more. Prices range from $29.95 per month for the standard plan, to $249.95 per month for the pro plan, and enterprises are given a tailored quote. BigCommerce is headquartered in Austin, Texas, with additional offices in San Francisco, California and Sydney, Australia. In January 2018, BigCommerce and Handshake formed a partnership to bring a suite of enhanced business-to-business (B2B) capabilities to BigCommerce customers worldwide. In June of the same year, the firm announced the opening of its first ever European office in London.

FINANCIAL DATA: *Note: Data for latest year may not have been available at press time.*

In U.S. $	2018	2017	2016	2015	2014	2013
Revenue						
R&D Expense						
Operating Income						
Operating Margin %						
SGA Expense						
Net Income						
Operating Cash Flow						
Capital Expenditure						
EBITDA						
Return on Assets %						
Return on Equity %						
Debt to Equity						

CONTACT INFORMATION:

Phone: 512-758-7588   Fax:
Toll-Free: 888-699-8911
Address: 11305 Four Points Dr., Bldg. 2, Fl. 3, Austin, TX 78726 United States

STOCK TICKER/OTHER:

Stock Ticker: Private   Exchange:
Employees: 460   Fiscal Year Ends: 12/31
Parent Company:

SALARIES/BONUSES:

Top Exec. Salary: $ Bonus: $
Second Exec. Salary: $ Bonus: $

OTHER THOUGHTS:

Estimated Female Officers or Directors:
Hot Spot for Advancement for Women/Minorities:

Blackboard Inc

www.blackboard.com

NAIC Code: 511210P

TYPES OF BUSINESS:

Online Educational Software
e-Learning Software
Content Management Software

BRANDS/DIVISIONS/AFFILIATES:

Providence Equity Partners LLC
Blackboard Mass Notifications
Teacher Communication
Mobile Learning
Blackboard Ally
Blackboard Collaborate
Blackboard Open LMS
Blackboard Open Content

CONTACTS: Note: Officers with more than one job title may be intentionally listed here more than once.

William Ballhaus, CEO
Rick Essex, CFO
Denise Haselhorst, Chief People Officer
Mark Strassman, Sr. VP-Prod. Mgmt.
Gary Lang, Sr. VP-Prod. Dev.
David Marr, Sr. VP-Blackboard Transact
Katie Blot, Sr. VP-Education Svcs.
Maurice Heiblum, Sr. VP-Higher Education, Corp. & Gov't. Markets
Mark Belles, Sr. VP-K-12
William Ballhaus, Chmn.
Matthew Small, Sr. VP-Int'l

GROWTH PLANS/SPECIAL FEATURES:

Blackboard, Inc. is a provider of enterprise software applications and related services to the education industry. Its product line consists of various software applications that serve the K-12 education group or the higher education, business and government group. The K-12 platform comprises a portfolio of software, services and integrations needed for teaching, learning and community engagement. Its products include Blackboard Classroom, Blackboard Web Community Manager, Blackboard Mobile Communications app, Blackboard Mass Notifications app, Teacher Communication, Blackboard Social Media Manager, Blackboard Collaborate, Blackboard Open Content, Blackboard Learn, Blackboard Personalized Learning and Mobile Learning. The higher education, business and government platform works to improve every aspect of the education experience, from universities to professional training. Payment solutions are offered, as well as registration and reporting, accessibility and conferencing. Government divisions include local, state, federal and military; and business markets include healthcare, financial services and extended enterprises. These platforms are fully online environments. This group's products include Blackboard Ally, Blackboard App, Blackboard Collaborate, Blackboard Instructor, Blackboard Intelligence, Blackboard Learn, Blackboard Connect, Mobile Learning, Blackboard Open LMS, Blackboard Transact and Blackboard Open Content. Headquartered in Washington, D.C., USA, the firm has worldwide offices in the Asia-Pacific, Europe, Middle East, Africa, Latin America, Caribbean and North America. Blackboard is privately-owned by Providence Equity Partners, LLC.

The firm offers employees medical, dental, vision and life insurance; disability coverage; and employee discounts.

FINANCIAL DATA: Note: Data for latest year may not have been available at press time.

In U.S. $	2018	2017	2016	2015	2014	2013
Revenue		690,000,000	700,000,000	685,000,000	650,000,000	638,000,000
R&D Expense						
Operating Income						
Operating Margin %						
SGA Expense						
Net Income						
Operating Cash Flow						
Capital Expenditure						
EBITDA						
Return on Assets %						
Return on Equity %						
Debt to Equity						

CONTACT INFORMATION:

Phone: 202-463-4860   Fax: 202-463-4863
Toll-Free: 800-424-9299
Address: 650 Massachusetts Ave. NW, 6/Fl., Washington, DC 20001-3796 United States

STOCK TICKER/OTHER:

Stock Ticker: Private   Exchange:
Employees: 2,700   Fiscal Year Ends: 12/31
Parent Company: Providence Equity Partners LLC

SALARIES/BONUSES:

Top Exec. Salary: $ Bonus: $
Second Exec. Salary: $ Bonus: $

OTHER THOUGHTS:

Estimated Female Officers or Directors: 2
Hot Spot for Advancement for Women/Minorities:

Sales, profits and employees may be estimates. Financial information, benefits and other data can change quickly and may vary from those stated here.

BlackLine Inc

www.blackline.com

NAIC Code: 511210Q

TYPES OF BUSINESS:

Computer Software, Accounting, Banking & Financial

BRANDS/DIVISIONS/AFFILIATES:

GROWTH PLANS/SPECIAL FEATURES:

BlackLine, Inc. provides financial controls and automation solutions that enable continuous accounting, both in the U.S. and internationally. These solutions help businesses manage their quarterly financial reports. BlackLine's software solutions allow customers to address various aspects of the financial closing process, including account reconciliations, variance analysis of account balances, journal entry capabilities and a range of data matching capabilities. The company serves customers of all sizes, across every industry because it was built from the cloud up. Primary industries that utilize BlackLine solutions include banking, credit union, biotechnology, pharmaceutical, communications, consumer goods, financial services, food and beverage, healthcare, hospitality, insurance, manufacturing, oil and gas, retail and technology.

The company offers its employees medical, dental and vision benefits; and fitness health offerings.

CONTACTS: Note: Officers with more than one job title may be intentionally listed here more than once.

Mark Partin, CFO
Patrick Villanova, Chief Accounting Officer
Karole Morgan-Prager, Chief Administrative Officer
Marc Huffman, COO
Therese Tucker, Director
John Brennan, Director
Mario Spanicciati, Director
Mark Woodhams, Senior VP, Divisional

FINANCIAL DATA: Note: Data for latest year may not have been available at press time.

In U.S. $	2018	2017	2016	2015	2014	2013
Revenue		177,031,000	123,123,000	83,607,000	51,677,000	
R&D Expense		23,874,000	21,125,000	18,216,000	9,705,000	
Operating Income		-35,060,000	-33,934,000	-34,812,000	-18,179,000	
Operating Margin %		-19.80%	-27.56%	-41.63%	-35.17%	
SGA Expense		146,731,000	105,721,000	77,474,000	43,553,000	
Net Income		-38,061,000	-39,159,000	-24,734,000	-16,752,000	
Operating Cash Flow		6,424,000	-4,808,000	1,006,000	8,943,000	
Capital Expenditure		8,626,000	4,994,000	12,367,000	2,866,000	
EBITDA		-17,510,000	-16,510,000	-20,073,000	-4,724,000	
Return on Assets %		-8.83%	-11.07%	-8.64%	-5.86%	
Return on Equity %		-12.98%	-17.11%	-14.12%	-9.10%	
Debt to Equity				0.17	0.13	

CONTACT INFORMATION:

Phone: 818-223-9008   Fax:
Toll-Free:
Address: 21300 Victory Blvd., 12/Fl, Woodland Hills, CA 91367 United States

STOCK TICKER/OTHER:

Stock Ticker: BL   Exchange: NAS
Employees: 597   Fiscal Year Ends:
Parent Company:

SALARIES/BONUSES:

Top Exec. Salary: $375,000   Bonus: $
Second Exec. Salary: Bonus: $
$350,833

OTHER THOUGHTS:

Estimated Female Officers or Directors:
Hot Spot for Advancement for Women/Minorities:

Bloomberg LP

www.bloomberg.com

NAIC Code: 511120A

TYPES OF BUSINESS:

Financial Data and News Publishing
Magazine Publishing
Management Software
Multimedia Presentation Services
Broadcast Television
Radio Broadcasting
Electronic Exchange Systems
Economic Data

BRANDS/DIVISIONS/AFFILIATES:

Bloomberg Businessweek
Bloomberg Terminal
Bloomberg Tradebook
Bloomberg Vault
Bloomberg Government
Bloomberg New Energy Finance Limited
Bloomberg BNA
Bloomberg Intelligence

CONTACTS: Note: Officers with more than one job title may be intentionally listed here more than once.

John Eastright, CEO
Daniel M. Fine, COO
Daniel L. Doctoroff, Pres.
Mike McCarty, CFO
Steve Crossman, VP, Sales
Christina Correira, Chief HR Officer
Rich Thompson, CTO
Jason Schechter, Chief Communications Officer
Matthew Winkler, Editor-in-Chief, Bloomberg News
Thomas Secunda, Vice Chmn.
Gregory C. McCaffery, Chmn.

GROWTH PLANS/SPECIAL FEATURES:

Bloomberg LP is an information services, news and media company, serving the financial services industry, government offices and agencies, corporations and news organizations. The company operates in six segments: communications, financial products, enterprise products, industry products, media and media services. Communications provides press announcements involving Bloomberg through its worldwide press contact centers, including the Americas, Europe/Middle East/Africa and Asia Pacific. Bloomberg's QuickTake franchise offers Q&A-style explainers to help readers quickly navigate breaking news and understand a story's fundamentals as news develops. Financial products is comprised of the Bloomberg Terminal, a platform for financial professionals who need real-time data, news and analytics to make fast and informed decisions; and the Bloomberg Tradebook, a global agency broker that provides anonymous direct market access and algorithmic trading to more than 125 global liquidity venues across 43 countries. This division also includes Bloomberg Briefs, Bloomberg Indexes, Bloomberg SEF (swap execution facility) and Bloomberg Institute. Enterprise provides solutions such as enterprise data, distribution and information; and trading solutions that address workflow with front-end portfolio, inventory, sales and trading, as well as middle and back office operations solutions for buy-side and sell-side firms. This division's Bloomberg Vault is a secure, managed service for information governance, data analytics and trade reconstruction across the enterprise. Industry products include Bloomberg Government, a web-based information service for professionals who interact with the federal government; Bloomberg Law/BNA and Bloomberg Big Law for legal, tax and regulatory professionals; and Bloomberg New Energy Finance Limited for decision-makers in the energy system. Media delivers business and political news through Bloomberg Business, Bloomberg Politics, Bloomberg View, Bloomberg Television, Bloomberg Radio, Bloomberg Mobile Apps and news bureaus. Media Services includes advertising, Bloomberg Content Service and Bloomberg Live Conferences.

The New York City headquarters features television and radio studios, open work areas (including open executive offices), dramatically modern architecture and an infinite variety of employee snacks.

FINANCIAL DATA: Note: Data for latest year may not have been available at press time.

In U.S. $	2018	2017	2016	2015	2014	2013
Revenue	10,000,000,000	9,658,000,000	9,400,000,000	9,184,000,000	9,000,000,000	8,275,000,000
R&D Expense						
Operating Income						
Operating Margin %						
SGA Expense						
Net Income						
Operating Cash Flow						
Capital Expenditure						
EBITDA						
Return on Assets %						
Return on Equity %						
Debt to Equity						

CONTACT INFORMATION:

Phone: 212-318-2000   Fax: 917-369-5000
Toll-Free:
Address: 731 Lexington Ave., New York, NY 10022 United States

STOCK TICKER/OTHER:

Stock Ticker: Private   Exchange:
Employees: 19,000   Fiscal Year Ends: 12/31
Parent Company:

SALARIES/BONUSES:

Top Exec. Salary: $ Bonus: $
Second Exec. Salary: $ Bonus: $

OTHER THOUGHTS:

Estimated Female Officers or Directors: 8
Hot Spot for Advancement for Women/Minorities: Y

Sales, profits and employees may be estimates. Financial information, benefits and other data can change quickly and may vary from those stated here.

Blucora Inc

NAIC Code: 519130

www.blucora.com

TYPES OF BUSINESS:

Internet Search Engines
Federal Tax Preparation Software

BRANDS/DIVISIONS/AFFILIATES:

HD Vest Inc
TaxAct Inc

CONTACTS: *Note: Officers with more than one job title may be intentionally listed here more than once.*

Robert Oros, CEO, Subsidiary
Davinder Athwal, CFO
William Atwell, Chairman of the Board
John Palmer, Chief Accounting Officer
Mathieu Stevenson, Chief Marketing Officer
John Clendening, Director
Todd Mackay, Executive VP
Tran Taylor, Other Executive Officer
Ann Bruder, Other Executive Officer
Mike Hogan, President, Divisional
Curtis Campbell, President, Subsidiary

GROWTH PLANS/SPECIAL FEATURES:

Blucora, Inc. provides technology-enabled financial solutions to consumers, small business owners and tax professionals. The company operates through two business segments: wealth management and tax preparation. Wealth management distributes products and services through financial advisors who affiliate with subsidiary HD Vest, Inc.'s subsidiaries as independent contractors. HD Vest provides financial advisors with an integrated platform of brokerage, investment advisory and insurance services to assist in making each financial advisor a financial service center for his/her clients. The tax preparation segment provides digital do-it-yourself tax preparation solutions for consumers, small business owners and tax professionals through subsidiary TaxAct, Inc., which generates revenue primarily through its online service at www.TaxAct.com. Services are given through three offerings: free, which helps file federal and state simple returns; a plus offering, the basic offerings plus additional tools to maximize credits and deductions; and a premium offering, which contains all the plus offerings in addition to tools for self-employed individuals.

The firm offers employees medical, dental and vision insurance; health club subsidies; and a 401(k) plan.

FINANCIAL DATA: *Note: Data for latest year may not have been available at press time.*

In U.S. $	2018	2017	2016	2015	2014	2013
Revenue		509,557,000	455,911,000	117,708,000	580,720,000	573,980,000
R&D Expense		19,614,000	17,780,000	5,107,000	20,670,000	11,682,000
Operating Income		51,138,000	40,987,000	-4,807,000	54,376,000	74,449,000
Operating Margin %		10.03%	8.99%	-4.08%	9.36%	12.97%
SGA Expense		155,466,000	136,756,000	89,417,000	157,244,000	128,529,000
Net Income		27,039,000	-65,158,000	-40,074,000	-35,547,000	24,399,000
Operating Cash Flow		72,846,000	85,262,000	30,449,000	55,734,000	95,056,000
Capital Expenditure		5,039,000	3,812,000	1,512,000	5,213,000	4,747,000
EBITDA		64,783,000	68,448,000	14,285,000	24,670,000	82,554,000
Return on Assets %		2.67%	-5.61%	-3.68%	-3.84%	3.12%
Return on Equity %		5.64%	-14.82%	-8.51%	-7.15%	5.24%
Debt to Equity		0.62	0.98	1.16	0.56	0.22

CONTACT INFORMATION:

Phone: 972-870-6000   Fax:
Toll-Free:
Address: 6333 State Hwy. 161, Irving, TX 75038 United States

STOCK TICKER/OTHER:

Stock Ticker: BCOR   Exchange: NAS
Employees: 476   Fiscal Year Ends: 12/31
Parent Company:

SALARIES/BONUSES:

Top Exec. Salary: $549,039   Bonus: $
Second Exec. Salary: Bonus: $193,326
$316,346

OTHER THOUGHTS:

Estimated Female Officers or Directors: 3
Hot Spot for Advancement for Women/Minorities: Y

Blue Nile Inc

NAIC Code: 454111

TYPES OF BUSINESS:

Jewelry, Online Retail

BRANDS/DIVISIONS/AFFILIATES:

Bain Capital LP
Bow Street LLC
Blue Nile LLC
Blue Nile Worldwide Inc
Blue Nile (Shanghai) Trading Co Ltd
Blue Nile Jewellery Ltd
bluenile.com
bluenile.co.uk

CONTACTS: *Note: Officers with more than one job title may be intentionally listed here more than once.*

Jason T. Goldberger, CEO
Jon Sainsbury, Chief Revenue Officer
Derek Mullens, VP-Human Resources
Steven Gire, VP-Tech.
Lauren Neiswender, General Counsel
Jon Sainsbury, Other Executive Officer

GROWTH PLANS/SPECIAL FEATURES:

Blue Nile, Inc. is a U.S.-based internet retailer of jewelry. The firm offers a broad selection of diamonds and other fine jewelry through its bluenile.com, bluenile.co.uk and bluenile.ca websites. The firm offers prices 20% to 40% less than traditional jewelers. These sites feature interactive search functionality; the ability to purchase products in 23 currencies, with a 1.5% discount if a customer pays with a bank wire; detailed product information; over 150,000 independently certified diamonds; and over 1,000 styles of jewelry, including rings, wedding bands, necklaces, charms, earrings and bracelets. In addition to loose diamonds and settings, the company offers gold, platinum and silver jewelry with pearls, emeralds, rubies and sapphires. Customers can create their own jewelry by selecting a diamond and a favorite ring, pendant or earring design. Over half of the firm's revenue is derived from engagement jewelry sales. Blue Nile has developed an online cost structure and a unique supply solution that eliminates traditional layers of diamond wholesalers and brokers, which allows the company to purchase most of its products at lower prices by avoiding mark-ups imposed by those intermediaries. This in turn allows the company to offer its products to the consumer at reduced prices. Blue Nile ships its products to over 40 countries. The firm also offers the Blue Nile Credit Card, with benefits including convenient payment options, no annual fee, special offers and online management; free returns; and jewelry insurance. The firm's subsidiaries are Blue Nile, LLC, which serves customers in the U.S., Canada and Asia-Pacific; Blue Nile Worldwide, Inc., which serves customers in Europe; Blue Nile (Shanghai) Trading Co., Ltd., which serves customers in China; and Blue Nile Jewellery, Ltd., which operates a customer service and fulfillment center in Dublin, Ireland. The firm is owned by Bain Capital, LP.

FINANCIAL DATA: *Note: Data for latest year may not have been available at press time.*

In U.S. $	2018	2017	2016	2015	2014	2013
Revenue	525,000,000	500,000,000	475,000,000	480,056,992	473,516,000	450,008,000
R&D Expense						
Operating Income						
Operating Margin %						
SGA Expense						
Net Income				10,534,000	9,731,000	10,875,000
Operating Cash Flow						
Capital Expenditure						
EBITDA						
Return on Assets %						
Return on Equity %						
Debt to Equity						

CONTACT INFORMATION:

Phone: 206 336-6700   Fax: 206 336-6750
Toll-Free: 800-242-2728
Address: 411 First Avenue S., Ste. 700, Seattle, WA 98104 United States

STOCK TICKER/OTHER:

Stock Ticker: Private
Employees: 352
Parent Company: Bain Capital LP

Exchange:
Fiscal Year Ends: 01/31

SALARIES/BONUSES:

Top Exec. Salary: $ Bonus: $
Second Exec. Salary: $ Bonus: $

OTHER THOUGHTS:

Estimated Female Officers or Directors: 4
Hot Spot for Advancement for Women/Minorities: Y

Bluefly Inc

NAIC Code: 454111

www.bluefly.com

TYPES OF BUSINESS:

Online Apparel Retailer
Apparel & Accessories
Discount Fashions

BRANDS/DIVISIONS/AFFILIATES:

Clearlake Capital Group LP
Bluefly.com
#blueflypopup
Belle & Clive
EyeFly

CONTACTS: *Note: Officers with more than one job title may be intentionally listed here more than once.*

Neel Grover, CEO
Scott A. Erdman, Sr. VP-Merch.

GROWTH PLANS/SPECIAL FEATURES:

Bluefly, Inc. is a U.S. internet retailer that sells designer apparel, fashion accessories and home products through its Bluefly.com website. The company sells over 3,000 brands and more than 100,000 different types of items at discounts of up to 75% off retail prices. The firm acquires end-of-season and excess inventory of high-end designer fashion products. Bluefly uses a third-party warehouse and fulfillment center in Ohio to ship its orders; the majority of these orders are shipped within 24 hours of placement even during the holiday season. The company markets to existing customers through emails that highlight new promotions and products. Bluefly attracts new customers through print and television advertisements as well as through marketing campaigns with Facebook and YouTube. The company has a pop-up shop in New York City, which can be followed on social media for updates concerning store events, under #blueflypopup. Belle & Clive is a members-only portal that offers limited-time sales events on brand name clothing products. EyeFly is an online eyewear company. Bluefly is owned by Clearlake Capital Group, LP.

FINANCIAL DATA: *Note: Data for latest year may not have been available at press time.*

In U.S. $	2018	2017	2016	2015	2014	2013
Revenue		110,000,000	106,000,000	105,000,000	97,500,000	95,000,000
R&D Expense						
Operating Income						
Operating Margin %						
SGA Expense						
Net Income						
Operating Cash Flow						
Capital Expenditure						
EBITDA						
Return on Assets %						
Return on Equity %						
Debt to Equity						

CONTACT INFORMATION:

Phone: 212 944-8000   Fax: 212 354-3400
Toll-Free: 877-258-3359
Address: 42 W. 39th St., New York, NY 10018 United States

STOCK TICKER/OTHER:

Stock Ticker: Private   Exchange:
Employees: 83   Fiscal Year Ends: 12/31
Parent Company: Clearlake Capital Group LP

SALARIES/BONUSES:

Top Exec. Salary: $ Bonus: $
Second Exec. Salary: $ Bonus: $

OTHER THOUGHTS:

Estimated Female Officers or Directors: 1
Hot Spot for Advancement for Women/Minorities: Y

Sales, profits and employees may be estimates. Financial information, benefits and other data can change quickly and may vary from those stated here.

BlueJeans Network Inc

bluejeans.com

NAIC Code: 511210C

TYPES OF BUSINESS:

Computer Software, Telecom, Communications & VOIP

BRANDS/DIVISIONS/AFFILIATES:

BlueJeans Meetings
BlueJeans Events
BlueJeans Rooms

CONTACTS: *Note: Officers with more than one job title may be intentionally listed here more than once.*

Quentin Gallivan, CEO
Robert Park, CFO
Rosanne Saccone, CMO
Debbie Murray, Chief People Officer
Alagu Periyannan, CTO
Krish Ramakrishnan, Chmn.

GROWTH PLANS/SPECIAL FEATURES:

BlueJeans Network, Inc. provides a cloud-based video service to enable people to connect with each other anytime, anywhere and from any device. The firm believes that every phone call should be a video call, and has designed technology to make that happen. The BlueJeans name represents the company's versatile, hard-working, functional business attitude and mindset. Likewise, it is the fabric that ties together all video conferencing needs. The BlueJeans platform seamlessly delivers interactive, two-way video that is secure and ready to scale. Companies can build stronger workplace culture with easy-to-use, face-to-face video meetings. BlueJeans Meetings enables enterprise-grade video calls, all in high definition (HD) Dolby audio. For employees, this product features one-click scheduling, screen sharing, collaboration, user-friendly integrations and cloud recording and streaming. For IT, it features room system compatibility, command center analytics, verified security, 24/7/365 support options and pre-deployment planning and onboarding. BlueJeans Events connects every employee for an interactive event, including town hall meetings, all-hands events and webinars. It merges the best of live video conferencing, content sharing and live streaming capabilities into a single, easy-to-use service. BlueJeans Rooms offers one-touch conferencing for any room throughout the workplace. Headquartered in Silicon Valley, California, the firm has additional offices in California, as well as internationally in the U.K., Australia and India.

FINANCIAL DATA: *Note: Data for latest year may not have been available at press time.*

In U.S. $	2018	2017	2016	2015	2014	2013
Revenue						
R&D Expense						
Operating Income						
Operating Margin %						
SGA Expense						
Net Income						
Operating Cash Flow						
Capital Expenditure						
EBITDA						
Return on Assets %						
Return on Equity %						
Debt to Equity						

CONTACT INFORMATION:

Phone: 408-550-2828   Fax: 408-550-2829
Toll-Free: 800-403-9256
Address: 516 Clyde Ave., Mountain View, CA 94043 United States

STOCK TICKER/OTHER:

Stock Ticker: Private   Exchange:
Employees: 500   Fiscal Year Ends:
Parent Company:

SALARIES/BONUSES:

Top Exec. Salary: $ Bonus: $
Second Exec. Salary: $ Bonus: $

OTHER THOUGHTS:

Estimated Female Officers or Directors:
Hot Spot for Advancement for Women/Minorities:

BluJay Solutions Ltd

www.blujaysolutions.com

NAIC Code: 511210A

TYPES OF BUSINESS:

Computer Software, Supply Chain & Logistics
e-Commerce Software
Shipping Management Software
Trade Software

BRANDS/DIVISIONS/AFFILIATES:

Global Trade Network
BluDex
Control Tower
MessageBroker
MobileSTAR
Kewill Systems plc
CSF Solutions
Grosvenor Systems

CONTACTS: *Note: Officers with more than one job title may be intentionally listed here more than once.*

Douglas Braun, CEO
Timothy Hinson, COO
Tonya Miller, Group Financial Controller
Patrick Maley, CMO
Joy Meier, Exec. VP-Human Resources
Benny Melumad, CTO
Lee Muise, Sr. VP-Prod. Dev.
Robin Martin, Sr. VP-Professional Svcs.
James J. (Jay) Waldron, Sr. VP-Americas
Jan-Paul Boos, Sr. VP-EMEA
Guhan Periasamy, Sr. VP-Asia Pacific & Japan
Biju S. Nair, Exec. VP

GROWTH PLANS/SPECIAL FEATURES:

BluJay Solutions Ltd. develops and offers supply chain software and services to retail, manufacturing and distribution industries in the U.K. and internationally. The company's solutions are categorized into six Global Trade Network (GTN) groups: transportation GTN, compliance GTN, network GTN, warehouse GTN, commerce GTN and LaaS GTN. Transportation GTN offers transportation management solutions for shippers, logistic service providers and forwarders; yard management solutions; fleet management solutions; and freight rate indexing with BluDex. Compliance GTN offers customs management and compliance solutions. Network GTN offers: Control Tower, which synchronizes the supply chain in real-time; MessageBroker, which enables swift connection and integration with all partners; MobileSTAR, a mobile GTN for BluJay customers; connection with BluJay's carrier network; and actionable intelligence capabilities for running a continuously-improving supply chain. Warehouse GTN offers warehouse and yard management solutions. Commerce GTN enables instant access to new suppliers and products through its commerce solution for retailers and e-Commerce companies. Last, LaaS GTN provides a Logistics-as-a-Service transportation management solution. The firm has over 7,500 customers in more than 100 countries. In 2018, BluJay acquired CSF Solutions, a German customers solutions provider, in April; Grosvenor Systems, a U.K. customers solutions provider, in August; and Era Systems, an Italian customs solutions provider, in October.

FINANCIAL DATA: *Note: Data for latest year may not have been available at press time.*

In U.S. $	2018	2017	2016	2015	2014	2013
Revenue		115,000,000	115,000,000	112,000,000	107,000,000	100,000,000
R&D Expense						
Operating Income						
Operating Margin %						
SGA Expense						
Net Income						
Operating Cash Flow						
Capital Expenditure						
EBITDA						
Return on Assets %						
Return on Equity %						
Debt to Equity						

CONTACT INFORMATION:

Phone: 44-161-905-4600   Fax: 44-161-905-4611
Toll-Free:
Address: 1/Fl., 4M Bldg., Malaga Ave., Manchester Airport, Manchester, M90 3RR United Kingdom

STOCK TICKER/OTHER:

Stock Ticker: Private   Exchange:
Employees: 600   Fiscal Year Ends: 03/31
Parent Company:

SALARIES/BONUSES:

Top Exec. Salary: $ Bonus: $
Second Exec. Salary: $ Bonus: $

OTHER THOUGHTS:

Estimated Female Officers or Directors: 2
Hot Spot for Advancement for Women/Minorities: Y

BMC Software Inc

www.bmc.com

NAIC Code: 511210H

TYPES OF BUSINESS:

Computer Software, Mainframe Related
Systems Management Software
e-Business Software
Consulting & Training Services

BRANDS/DIVISIONS/AFFILIATES:

KKR & Co LP

CONTACTS: Note: Officers with more than one job title may be intentionally listed here more than once.

Peter Leav, CEO
Steve Solcher, CFO
Dan Streetman, Exec. VP-Global Mktg. & Sales
Hollie Castro, Sr. VP-Admin.
Patrick K. Tagtow, General Counsel
Steve Goddard, Sr. VP-Bus. Oper.
Ken Berryman, Sr. VP-Strategy & Corp. Dev.
Ann Duhon, Mgr.-Comm.
Derrick Vializ, VP-Investor Rel.
T. Cory Bleuer, Chief Acct. Officer
Patrick K. Tagtow, Chief Compliance Officer
Paul Avenant, Sr. VP-Solutions

GROWTH PLANS/SPECIAL FEATURES:

BMC Software, Inc. is a software vendor company that provides system management, service management and automation solutions primarily for large companies. Its software products span mainframe systems, IT service management, cloud management, IT operations, workload automation and IT automation. BMC's solutions are grouped into six categories: multi-cloud management, security and compliance, artificial intelligence and machine learning, automation and DevOps, IT optimization and service management. Multi-cloud management solutions include multi-cloud cost control, asset visibility, cloud performance management, automation across clouds, cloud security, cloud migration and services management across clouds. Security and compliance solutions include building a SecOps strategy, ensuring GDPR compliance, remediating vulnerabilities and managing policies and compliance. AI & machine learning solutions include cognitive service management, AI application to IT, big data insights, and acceleration via self-managing mainframe. Automation and DevOps solutions include automating workloads, file transfers, application deployment and data centers. IT optimization solutions cover IT infrastructure, cloud spend, applications performance, mainframe costs and database performance. Last, service management solutions offer transformation, modernization, IT asset visibility and digital workplace enhancement. During 2018, BMC was acquired by KKR & Co. LP; and BMC agreed to acquire assets of CorreLog, Inc., a provider of real-time security management to mainframe customers.

FINANCIAL DATA: Note: Data for latest year may not have been available at press time.

In U.S. $	2018	2017	2016	2015	2014	2013
Revenue		2,500,000,000	2,300,000,000	2,250,000,000	2,205,000,000	2,201,000,000
R&D Expense						
Operating Income						
Operating Margin %						
SGA Expense						
Net Income						
Operating Cash Flow						
Capital Expenditure						
EBITDA						
Return on Assets %						
Return on Equity %						
Debt to Equity						

CONTACT INFORMATION:

Phone: 713 918-8800   Fax: 713 918-8000
Toll-Free: 800-841-2031
Address: 2101 Citywest Blvd., Houston, TX 77042 United States

STOCK TICKER/OTHER:

Stock Ticker: Subsidiary   Exchange:
Employees: 6,000   Fiscal Year Ends: 03/31
Parent Company: KKR & Co LP

SALARIES/BONUSES:

Top Exec. Salary: $ Bonus: $
Second Exec. Salary: $ Bonus: $

OTHER THOUGHTS:

Estimated Female Officers or Directors: 2
Hot Spot for Advancement for Women/Minorities: Y

Boingo Wireless Inc

www.boingo.com

NAIC Code: 517110

TYPES OF BUSINESS:

Wi-Fi Internet Access
Software Development
Wireless Internet Service Provider
Mobile Advertising Services

BRANDS/DIVISIONS/AFFILIATES:

Boingo
Boingo Wi-Finder
Don't just go Boingo
Boingo Broadband
Cloud 9 Media
Concourse Communications
AWG-WIFI
Elauwit Networks LLC

CONTACTS: *Note: Officers with more than one job title may be intentionally listed here more than once.*

David Hagan, CEO
Peter Hovenier, CFO
Dawn Callahan, Chief Marketing Officer
Derek Peterson, Chief Technology Officer
Tom Tracey, Senior VP, Divisional

GROWTH PLANS/SPECIAL FEATURES:

Boingo Wireless, Inc. offers high-speed wireless internet roaming access across a network of over 1.2 million commercial Wi-Fi hotspots in more than 100 countries, including hotels, airports and other public spaces. The firm also operates Wi-Fi and internet protocol television (IPTV) networks at 62 U.S. Army, Air Force and Marines bases worldwide. Boingo operates 38 distributed antenna system (DAS) networks containing approximately 23,500 DAS nodes, making it one of the largest indoor DAS providers in the world. Revenue is generated from the firm's wireless networks, including its DAS and wholesale Wi-Fi offerings; wholesale revenue is generated from telecom operators that pay build-out fees and recurring access fees so that their cellular customers may use Boingo's DAS or small cell networks; military revenue is obtained when military personnel purchase broadband and IPTV services on military bases; usage-based Wi-Fi network access and software licensing fees are generated from enterprise customers; and advertising revenue is generated from advertisers seeking to reach consumers via sponsored Wi-Fi access. Registered trademarks include Boingo, Boingo Wi-Finder, Don't just go. Boingo., Boingo Broadband, Cloud 9 Media, Concourse Communications and AWG-WIFI, among others. In August 2018, Boingo Wireless, agreed to acquire Elauwit Networks, LLC, a leading provider of high-speed Wi-Fi and technology solutions to the student and multifamily housing market, for total cash consideration of $28.0 million.

The company offers employees medical, dental and vision coverage; domestic partner benefits; a 401(k) plan; a profit sharing plan; life and AD&D insurance; disability benefits; flexible spending accounts; and phone, transportation and education reimbursement.

FINANCIAL DATA: *Note: Data for latest year may not have been available at press time.*

In U.S. $	2018	2017	2016	2015	2014	2013
Revenue		204,369,000	159,344,000	139,626,000	119,297,000	106,746,000
R&D Expense		26,754,000	22,126,000	19,147,000	14,879,000	11,432,000
Operating Income		-20,701,000	-26,097,000	-21,631,000	-18,026,000	-1,894,000
Operating Margin %		-10.12%	-16.37%	-15.49%	-15.11%	-1.77%
SGA Expense		56,501,000	48,448,000	42,009,000	33,842,000	29,311,000
Net Income		-19,366,000	-27,331,000	-22,292,000	-19,521,000	-3,793,000
Operating Cash Flow		97,728,000	115,205,000	98,575,000	21,207,000	20,671,000
Capital Expenditure		73,308,000	107,271,000	103,116,000	70,945,000	29,540,000
EBITDA		51,894,000	26,553,000	20,238,000	13,136,000	19,296,000
Return on Assets %		-5.06%	-7.57%	-7.95%	-8.97%	-1.81%
Return on Equity %		-19.79%	-26.14%	-18.75%	-14.66%	-2.67%
Debt to Equity		0.06	0.20	0.17	0.02	

CONTACT INFORMATION:

Phone: 310 586-5180   Fax: 310 586-4060
Toll-Free: 800-880-4117
Address: 10960 Wilshire Blvd., Ste. 800, Los Angeles, CA 90024 United States

STOCK TICKER/OTHER:

Stock Ticker: WIFI   Exchange: NAS
Employees: 315   Fiscal Year Ends: 12/31
Parent Company:

SALARIES/BONUSES:

Top Exec. Salary: $530,000   Bonus: $
Second Exec. Salary: $348,000   Bonus: $

OTHER THOUGHTS:

Estimated Female Officers or Directors: 1
Hot Spot for Advancement for Women/Minorities:

Sales, profits and employees may be estimates. Financial information, benefits and other data can change quickly and may vary from those stated here.

Bonobos Inc

bonobos.com

NAIC Code: 454111

TYPES OF BUSINESS:

Men's Apparel Online
Small, Showroom Retail Stores

BRANDS/DIVISIONS/AFFILIATES:

Wal-Mart Stores Inc (Walmart)
Bonobos.com
Jet.com

CONTACTS: *Note: Officers with more than one job title may be intentionally listed here more than once.*

Andy Dunn, CEO

GROWTH PLANS/SPECIAL FEATURES:

Bonobos, Inc. is an eCommerce apparel company that designs and sells men's clothing. The firm's signature line of curved wastebanded pants aims to conform to the natural shape of a man's waist, with a unique cut and medium rise. Bonobos set out to build the best online shopping experience, and claims to be the largest clothing brand ever built on the web in the U.S. What sets the company apart from other online retail sites is that shipping is entirely free, whether receiving a package or returning it. Returns and exchanges are simple. Apparel options include bottoms, tops, tailored clothing, outerwear, golf attire, accessories (ties, belts, scarves and cashmere hats) and shoes. Bonobos also has more than 30 guideshop locations in which it suggests that customers schedule a fitting ahead of time. A guide walks customers through the entire Bonobos catalog, helps them find the perfect fit from all available options and places orders, which are shipped directly to the customer's home or office. Guideshop has nearly 70 locations throughout the U.S. The firm offers both digital and physical gift cards. During 2017, the firm was acquired by Wal-Mart Stores, Inc. The brand is not sold in Wal-Mart stores, but is sold on eCommerce websites Bonobos.com and Jet.com.

FINANCIAL DATA: *Note: Data for latest year may not have been available at press time.*

In U.S. $	2018	2017	2016	2015	2014	2013
Revenue		140,000,000	100,000,000	76,000,000	50,000,000	
R&D Expense						
Operating Income						
Operating Margin %						
SGA Expense						
Net Income						
Operating Cash Flow						
Capital Expenditure						
EBITDA						
Return on Assets %						
Return on Equity %						
Debt to Equity						

CONTACT INFORMATION:

Phone: 877-294-7737   Fax:
Toll-Free:
Address: 45 W. 25th St., 5/Fl, New York, NY 10010 United States

STOCK TICKER/OTHER:

Stock Ticker: Subsidiary   Exchange:
Employees: 325   Fiscal Year Ends:
Parent Company: Wal-Mart Stores Inc (Walmart)

SALARIES/BONUSES:

Top Exec. Salary: $ Bonus: $
Second Exec. Salary: $ Bonus: $

OTHER THOUGHTS:

Estimated Female Officers or Directors:
Hot Spot for Advancement for Women/Minorities:

Boohoo.com PLC

NAIC Code: 454111

www.boohoo.com

TYPES OF BUSINESS:

Electronic Shopping

BRANDS/DIVISIONS/AFFILIATES:

boohoo
boohooMAN
PrettyLittleThing
Nasty Gal

GROWTH PLANS/SPECIAL FEATURES:

Boohoo.com PLC is an online fashion retail group. The company's brands include boohoo, boohooMAN, PrettyLittleThing and Nasty Gal, all of which design, source, market and sell clothing, shoes, accessories and beauty products targeted toward 16-to-30-year-old consumers. PrettyLittleThing originated as an accessories-only website and now focuses on affordable, forward-thinking fashion. Nasty Gal is a distinctive brand for fashion-forward, free-thinking young women. Boohoo.com's products are designed and sourced primarily in the U.K., and also distributed globally from a central U.K. warehouse. The group sells products to customers in nearly every country in the world, with its strongest presence in the U.K., the U.S., Europe and Australia. Up to 100 new pieces appear on the boohoo.com website every day, as well as a new collection every week.

CONTACTS: Note: Officers with more than one job title may be intentionally listed here more than once.

Mahmud Kamani, Co-CEO
Carol Kane, Co-CEO
Neil Catto, CFO
Lucy Clough, Group HR Director

FINANCIAL DATA: Note: Data for latest year may not have been available at press time.

In U.S. $	2018	2017	2016	2015	2014	2013
Revenue	732,218,600	372,089,100	246,759,400	176,615,200	138,653,000	84,969,180
R&D Expense						
Operating Income	53,705,300	38,275,410	19,001,310	14,942,410	13,665,640	4,149,828
Operating Margin %	7.33	10.28%	7.70%	7.56%	9.85%	4.88%
SGA Expense	327,566,200	170,972,700	125,349,800	92,459,340	68,926,800	42,151,190
Net Income	39,972,720	30,887,550	15,707,720	10,614,520	10,642,300	3,245,605
Operating Cash Flow	87,156,500	37,243,640	22,044,860	15,357,900	7,424,480	7,079,713
Capital Expenditure	58,577,490	38,738,890	17,189,080	10,312,690	5,855,981	5,868,610
EBITDA	68,747,470	44,293,040	22,863,200	17,470,700	14,902,000	4,867,145
Return on Assets %	12.26%	16.33%	12.70%	14.74%	36.25%	14.32%
Return on Equity %	21.06%	28.78%	17.79%	22.07%	145.63%	141.75%
Debt to Equity	0.03	0.09			0.24	1.39

CONTACT INFORMATION:

Phone: 44 - 1612332050   Fax:
Toll-Free:
Address: 49/51 Dale St., Manchester, M1 2HF United Kingdom

STOCK TICKER/OTHER:

Stock Ticker: BHOOY
Employees: 2,118
Parent Company:

Exchange: PINX
Fiscal Year Ends: 02/28

SALARIES/BONUSES:

Top Exec. Salary: $363,078   Bonus: $726,157
Second Exec. Salary: $363,078   Bonus: $726,157

OTHER THOUGHTS:

Estimated Female Officers or Directors:
Hot Spot for Advancement for Women/Minorities:

Sales, profits and employees may be estimates. Financial information, benefits and other data can change quickly and may vary from those stated here.

Booking Holdings Inc

www.priceline.com

NAIC Code: 561510

TYPES OF BUSINESS:

Online Retail-Travel Services
Auction-Based Travel Sales
Online Financial Services
Commission-Based Travel Bookings (Travel Agency Model)

BRANDS/DIVISIONS/AFFILIATES:

Priceline.com
Booking.com
Name Your Own Price
Priceline Group Inc
RentalCars.com
OpenTable
KAYAK
FareHarbor

CONTACTS: *Note: Officers with more than one job title may be intentionally listed here more than once.*

Glenn Fogel, CEO
Daniel Finnegan, CFO
David Goulden, Exec. VP
Glenn Fogel, Director
Peter Millones, Executive VP
Jeffrey Boyd, Chmn.

GROWTH PLANS/SPECIAL FEATURES:

Booking Holdings, Inc., formerly Priceline Group, Inc., is a leading online travel company that offers a broad range of travel services, including airline tickets, hotel rooms, car rentals, vacation packages, cruises and destination services primarily through its proprietary Priceline.com, KAYAK.com, Booking.com, Agoda.com, RentalCars.com and OpenTable.com websites. Within the U.S., the firm offers customers the ability to purchase travel services in a traditional, price-disclosed manner or the opportunity to use the Name Your Own Price service, which allows customers to make offers on travel goods and services at discounted prices. To make an offer, a customer specifies the origin and destination of the trip, the dates on which the customer wishes to depart and return, the price the customer is willing to pay and the customer's valid credit card to guarantee the offer. The company enables customers to make hotel reservations on a worldwide basis, primarily under the Booking.com and Agoda.com brands internationally, and primarily under the Priceline.com brand in the U.S. These operations offer consumers an array of accommodations such as hotels, bed and breakfasts, hostels, apartments, vacation rentals and other properties. Through subsidiary RentalCars.com, the company offers retail price-disclosed rental car reservations through approximately 49,000 locations. OpenTable is the company's brand for booking online restaurant reservations, and primarily operates in the U.S. Its international business represents approximately 88% of the company's gross bookings and contributes more than 94% of Priceline's consolidated operating income. Subsidiary KAYAK Software Corporation provides a price comparison service allowing consumers to search and compare prices for travel services. In April 2018, Booking Holdings acquired FareHarbor, a local activities and experiences booking software provider. In December, the firm acquired HotelsCombined, a hotel metasearch site. HotelsCombined will be added to KAYAK's portfolio of brands.

Employee benefits include medical, life, AD&D, disability and dental coverage; 401(k) with company match; tuition reimbursement; an employee assistance plan; flexible spending accounts; and travel agent discount benefits.

FINANCIAL DATA: *Note: Data for latest year may not have been available at press time.*

In U.S. $	2018	2017	2016	2015	2014	2013
Revenue		11,400,000,000	10,743,006,208	9,223,987,200	8,441,971,200	6,793,306,112
R&D Expense						
Operating Income						
Operating Margin %						
SGA Expense						
Net Income			2,134,987,008	2,551,360,000	2,421,753,088	1,892,663,040
Operating Cash Flow						
Capital Expenditure						
EBITDA						
Return on Assets %						
Return on Equity %						
Debt to Equity						

CONTACT INFORMATION:

Phone: 203-2998000 Fax:
Toll-Free:
Address: 800 Connecticut Ave., Norwalk, CT 06854 United States

STOCK TICKER/OTHER:

Stock Ticker: PCLN Exchange: NAS
Employees: 18,500 Fiscal Year Ends:
Parent Company:

SALARIES/BONUSES:

Top Exec. Salary: $ Bonus: $
Second Exec. Salary: $ Bonus: $

OTHER THOUGHTS:

Estimated Female Officers or Directors: 1
Hot Spot for Advancement for Women/Minorities: Y

Sales, profits and employees may be estimates. Financial information, benefits and other data can change quickly and may vary from those stated here.

Bottomline Technologies Inc

www.bottomline.com

NAIC Code: 511210Q

TYPES OF BUSINESS:

Software-Electronic Banking
Online Billing, Payment & Invoicing Software
Software-as-a-Service (SaaS)

BRANDS/DIVISIONS/AFFILIATES:

Paymode-X

CONTACTS: *Note: Officers with more than one job title may be intentionally listed here more than once.*

Robert Eberle, CEO
Richard Booth, CFO
Joseph Mullen, Chairman of the Board
John Mason, Chief Information Officer
Christine Nurnberger, Chief Marketing Officer
Eric Morgan, Controller
David Sweet, Executive VP, Divisional
Andrew Mintzer, Executive VP, Divisional
John Kelly, General Manager, Divisional
Jessica Moran, General Manager, Divisional
Norman Deluca, Managing Director, Divisional
Nigel Savory, Managing Director, Geographical
Paul Fannon, Other Corporate Officer
Brian McLaughlin, Other Executive Officer
Stephanie Lucey, Other Executive Officer

GROWTH PLANS/SPECIAL FEATURES:

Bottomline Technologies, Inc. provides cloud-based digital banking, fraud prevention, and payment and invoice services to corporations, financial institutions and banks around the world. Its services are used to streamline, automate and manage processes and transactions involving global payments, invoice approval, collections, cash management, risk mitigation, reporting and document archiving. The firm offers software as a service (SaaS) solutions, as well as software designed to run on-site at the customer's location. Bottomline's product Paymode-X, enables businesses to automate the almost entirely paper-based processes central to purchasing requisition and invoice management as well as to facilitate the ultimate payment. Legal spend management solutions offer claims litigation vendor management, legal eBilling for property and casualty (P&C) claims, legal bill review for P&C claims, legal eBilling and review for self-insured and TPAs (third-party administrators), and independent adjuster for eBilling claims and review. Cyber fraud and risk management solutions include anti-money laundering, compliance monitoring and management, enterprise case management. Digital banking solutions include banking and payments, customer acquisition, cyber fraud and risk management for banks, business banking growth, banking financial messaging and Paymode-X for banks. Financial document automation solutions include accounts payable invoice processing, collaborative document processing and archive and form creation/delivery. Healthcare solutions include patient registration, electronic signature, mobile document and payments. Financial messaging solutions include data format transformation, market data management, messaging analytics, messaging compliance, multi-network financial messaging and more.

The firm offers employees medical and dental insurance, a 401(k) plan, an employee stock purchase plan, tuition reimbursement, health club membership reimbursement, life insurance, disability coverage and discount home and auto insurance.

FINANCIAL DATA: *Note: Data for latest year may not have been available at press time.*

In U.S. $	2018	2017	2016	2015	2014	2013
Revenue	394,096,000	349,412,000	343,274,000	330,889,000	300,585,000	254,774,000
R&D Expense	57,310,000	53,002,000	47,355,000	47,185,000	39,725,000	32,974,000
Operating Income	5,831,000	-13,659,000	-3,551,000	-763,000	-2,478,000	-6,936,000
Operating Margin %		-3.90%	-1.03%	-.23%	-.82%	-2.72%
SGA Expense	135,749,000	123,997,000	123,392,000	114,643,000	106,428,000	89,901,000
Net Income	9,328,000	-33,137,000	-19,648,000	-34,680,000	-19,104,000	-14,395,000
Operating Cash Flow	76,028,000	60,975,000	67,157,000	62,700,000	52,221,000	41,576,000
Capital Expenditure	21,376,000	28,173,000	27,717,000	23,297,000	12,652,000	10,106,000
EBITDA	54,365,000	22,559,000	39,143,000	39,339,000	31,692,000	15,667,000
Return on Assets %		-5.21%	-2.92%	-4.99%	-2.97%	-2.94%
Return on Equity %		-11.90%	-6.10%	-9.42%	-5.13%	-4.29%
Debt to Equity		0.58	0.45		0.38	0.38

CONTACT INFORMATION:

Phone: 603 436-0700   Fax: 603 436-0300
Toll-Free: 800-243-2528
Address: 325 Corporate Dr., Portsmouth, NH 03801 United States

STOCK TICKER/OTHER:

Stock Ticker: EPAY   Exchange: NAS
Employees: 1,700   Fiscal Year Ends: 06/30
Parent Company:

SALARIES/BONUSES:

Top Exec. Salary: $384,167   Bonus: $239,000
Second Exec. Salary: Bonus: $200,000
$282,083

OTHER THOUGHTS:

Estimated Female Officers or Directors: 2
Hot Spot for Advancement for Women/Minorities:

Sales, profits and employees may be estimates. Financial information, benefits and other data can change quickly and may vary from those stated here.

Boursorama

NAIC Code: 523120

groupe.boursorama.fr

TYPES OF BUSINESS:

Online Brokerage Services
Financial Information
Online Banking
Insurance
Wealth Management

BRANDS/DIVISIONS/AFFILIATES:

Societe Generale Group
Boursorama Banque
Boursorama.com
Boursorama Vie

CONTACTS: Note: Officers with more than one job title may be intentionally listed here more than once.

Benoit Grisoni, Deputy Gen. Mgr.
Nicole Viviand, Dir.-Operations
Jean-Philippe Lavenir, CFO
Xavier Prin, Dir.-Mktg.
Isabelle Pla, Dir.-Human Resources
Bertrand Le Bras, Dir.-Information Systems
Diane-Charlotte Kermorgant, Head-Press Rel.
Diane-Charlotte Kermorgant, Head-Investor Rel.
Ralf Oetting, Managing Dir.-Onvista AG Germany
Xavier Prin, Portal Dir.
Benoit Grisoni, Managing Dir.-Boursorama Banque
Patrick Sommelet, Deputy CEO
Philippe Aymerich, Chmn.
Alberto Navarro, Managing Dir.-Selftrade Bank, Spain

GROWTH PLANS/SPECIAL FEATURES:

Boursorama, a subsidiary of the Societe Generale Group, is a leading European online financial and insurance services provider which operates through Boursorama Banque. The company has four main areas of activity: online banking, online brokerage, internet portal and online insurance. The online banking division has more than 1,500,000 customers, providing more than 15 services areas free of charge. Boursorama Banque offers account banking, mortgage lending and other money-related services all online. The online brokerage division provides access to major exchanges with rates tailored to the investor's profile. Its products include equities, options, futures, warrants, turbos, certificates, bonds and trackers. The internet portal division comprises the boursorama.com website, which obtains more than 30 million monthly visits and over 290 million page views per month within an average year. The website disseminates market and economic news and offers general information, as well as video content and discussion forums. Last, Boursorama's 100% online insurance division offers life insurance products through its Boursorama Vie policy portfolio.

FINANCIAL DATA: Note: Data for latest year may not have been available at press time.

In U.S. $	2018	2017	2016	2015	2014	2013
Revenue	270,000,000	255,000,000	251,000,000	250,000,000	263,553,220	235,655,590
R&D Expense						
Operating Income						
Operating Margin %						
SGA Expense						
Net Income						
Operating Cash Flow						
Capital Expenditure						
EBITDA						
Return on Assets %						
Return on Equity %						
Debt to Equity						

CONTACT INFORMATION:

Phone: 33-1-46-09-50-00   Fax:
Toll-Free:
Address: 18 Quai du Point du Jour, Boulogne-Billancourt, 92659 France

STOCK TICKER/OTHER:

Stock Ticker: Subsidiary   Exchange:
Employees: 810   Fiscal Year Ends: 12/31
Parent Company: Societe Generale Group

SALARIES/BONUSES:

Top Exec. Salary: $ Bonus: $
Second Exec. Salary: $ Bonus: $

OTHER THOUGHTS:

Estimated Female Officers or Directors: 5
Hot Spot for Advancement for Women/Minorities: Y

Box Inc
NAIC Code: 511210L

www.box.com

TYPES OF BUSINESS:
Application Software

BRANDS/DIVISIONS/AFFILIATES:
Box Solution (The)

CONTACTS: *Note: Officers with more than one job title may be intentionally listed here more than once.*
Aaron Levie, CEO
Dylan Smith, CFO
Jeff Mannie, Chief Accounting Officer
Stephanie Carullo, COO
David Leeb, General Counsel
Peter McGoff, Other Executive Officer

GROWTH PLANS/SPECIAL FEATURES:
Box, Inc. is a cloud platform company that enables organizations to securely manage their content from anywhere. Box's platform, The Box Solution, allows users to collaborate on content both internally and externally, build workflows to power mission-critical processes and deploy compliance and security features valuable to most industries. Its platform works across multiple file formats, application environments, operating systems and devices. The Box Solution features modern cloud architecture, mobility, user-focused interfacing, enterprise-grade security, administrative controls, administrative controls, tracking and reporting for deep visibility, data governance strategies, automation and workflow management, custom and third-party application development, automation and workflow management, custom application development, easy integration with other cloud-based applications and is industry-specific. The firm's user base includes more than 52 million registered users and over 83,000 paying organizations. Its solution is offered in 23 languages. In 2018, 60% of the company's orders for subscription services were from enterprise customers with at least 1,000 employees. Also in 2018 the firm collaborated with IBM, with IBM Cloud powering the first implementation of Box Zones in the U.K. Customers can now choose to store their data in Germany, Ireland, Japan, Singapore, Australia and Canada.

Employees of the firm receive benefits including medical, dental and vision coverage; subsidized gym membership; transportation discounts; and free lunches.

FINANCIAL DATA: *Note: Data for latest year may not have been available at press time.*

In U.S. $	2018	2017	2016	2015	2014	2013
Revenue	506,142,000	398,605,000	302,704,000	216,440,000	124,192,000	58,797,000
R&D Expense	136,791,000	115,928,000	102,500,000	66,402,000	45,967,000	28,996,000
Operating Income	-154,021,000	-150,655,000	-201,003,000	-166,656,000	-158,780,000	-109,129,000
Operating Margin %	-30.43	-37.79%	-66.40%	-76.99%	-127.85%	-185.60%
SGA Expense	388,124,000	321,202,000	314,107,000	269,421,000	211,031,000	124,650,000
Net Income	-154,960,000	-151,787,000	-202,948,000	-168,227,000	-168,557,000	-112,563,000
Operating Cash Flow	61,822,000	-1,218,000	-66,321,000	-84,900,000	-91,769,000	-81,751,000
Capital Expenditure	11,822,000	14,956,000	73,210,000	38,883,000	32,185,000	19,561,000
EBITDA	-113,909,000	-110,501,000	-160,609,000	-137,637,000	-140,913,000	-100,513,000
Return on Assets %	-29.59%	-30.62%	-40.99%	-49.99%	-78.33%	-57.60%
Return on Equity %	-345.50%	-142.76%	-99.96%			
Debt to Equity	4.47	0.82	0.34	0.15		

CONTACT INFORMATION:
Phone: 877-729-4269   Fax:
Toll-Free: 877-729-4269
Address: 900 Jefferson Ave., Redwood City, CA 94063 United States

STOCK TICKER/OTHER:
Stock Ticker: BOX   Exchange: NYS
Employees: 1,495   Fiscal Year Ends: 01/31
Parent Company:

SALARIES/BONUSES:
Top Exec. Salary: $333,333   Bonus: $
Second Exec. Salary: Bonus: $
$332,500

OTHER THOUGHTS:
Estimated Female Officers or Directors: 2
Hot Spot for Advancement for Women/Minorities:

Brandless Inc

brandless.com

NAIC Code: 454111

TYPES OF BUSINESS:

Electronic Shopping
Online Grocery Shopping
Online Beauty Supplies

BRANDS/DIVISIONS/AFFILIATES:

B.More
Brandless
BrandTax
BrandTax Free
Delovery
Life Liberty & The Pursuit of Fairly Priced Every

CONTACTS: Note: Officers with more than one job title may be intentionally listed here more than once.

Tina Sharkey, CEO

GROWTH PLANS/SPECIAL FEATURES:

Brandless, Inc. is a 2017 eCommerce startup that manufactures and sells food, beauty, personal care, household and stationery products. The company currently offers more than 300 products, which are made under high standards of safety, quality and social ethics such as Global Food Safety or Good Manufacturing Practices. Each product sells for $3. Food items include bars, candy, chips, pretzels, cookies, crackers, chips, fruit snacks, vegetable snacks, jerky, popcorn, puffs, seeds, nuts and trail mix. These food items are entirely-non-genetically-modified-organism (non-GMO) and over half are certified organic. Beauty and personal care items include beauty tools, grooming tools, skin care, lip treatments, body wash, shaving creams/lotions, cotton balls/rounds/swabs, oral care, hair care, hand soap, lotions, nail care, tampons/pads/liners, bath tissue, facial tissue, vitamins and supplements. These products do not include ingredients such as parabens, polypropylene, phthalates and sulfates, among hundreds of others. Feminine hygiene products are made from hypoallergenic certified organic cotton, free of chlorine, rayon, fragrance or dyes. Household products include cleaning supplies, dishwashing supplies, soap, bath/facial tissue, food/storage wraps, tableware, disposable tableware, kitchen linens and kitchen gadgets/knives/utensils. Household cleaners are non-toxic. Stationery products include writing supplies, notebooks, journals, stationery, gift bags and party supplies. These paper products are either made with bamboo and sugarcane fiber or are Forest Stewardship Council certified. Brandless' B.More membership program is $36 per year, and includes free shipping on all Brandless orders. Trademarks owned by the company include Brandless, BrandTax, BrandTax Free, B.More, Delovery and Life, Liberty & The Pursuit of Fairly Priced Everything.

FINANCIAL DATA: Note: Data for latest year may not have been available at press time.

In U.S. $	2018	2017	2016	2015	2014	2013
Revenue						
R&D Expense						
Operating Income						
Operating Margin %						
SGA Expense						
Net Income						
Operating Cash Flow						
Capital Expenditure						
EBITDA						
Return on Assets %						
Return on Equity %						
Debt to Equity						

CONTACT INFORMATION:

Phone: 415-237-6640   Fax:
Toll-Free:
Address: 800 Market St., 8/Fl, San Francisco, CA 94102 United States

STOCK TICKER/OTHER:

Stock Ticker: Private   Exchange:
Employees: Fiscal Year Ends:
Parent Company:

SALARIES/BONUSES:

Top Exec. Salary: $ Bonus: $
Second Exec. Salary: $ Bonus: $

OTHER THOUGHTS:

Estimated Female Officers or Directors:
Hot Spot for Advancement for Women/Minorities:

Sales, profits and employees may be estimates. Financial information, benefits and other data can change quickly and may vary from those stated here.

Brightcove Inc

www.brightcove.com

NAIC Code: 519130

TYPES OF BUSINESS:

Internet TV Broadcasting

BRANDS/DIVISIONS/AFFILIATES:

Brightcove Video Cloud
Brightcove Zencoder
Brightcove SSAI
Brightcove Player
Brightcove OTT Flow
Brightcove Video Marketing Suite
Brightcove Enterprise Video Suite

CONTACTS: *Note: Officers with more than one job title may be intentionally listed here more than once.*

Hugh Ray, CEO
Robert Noreck, CFO
Gary Haroian, Director
David Plotkin, Other Executive Officer

GROWTH PLANS/SPECIAL FEATURES:

Brightcove, Inc. is an internet television company that enables emerging media companies and independent producers to launch commercial broadband channels. The firm allows content owners to create, distribute and monetize internet TV channels through its Brightcove Video Cloud. This platform charges content publishers a usage fee, but it does allow them to keep all ad revenues. The Video Cloud platform features: advanced adaptive transcoding, which means it must only be uploaded to a computer once; content management; customized viewing; live and on-demand video delivery and streaming; mobile device (including iPhone and iPad) compatibility; and comprehensive audience analytics and reporting. Other products include the Brightcove Zencoder, a cloud-based video encoding service; Brightcove SSAI, a cloud-based ad insertion and video stitching service that addresses the limitations of traditional online video ad insertion technology; Brightcove Player, a cloud-based service for creating and managing video player experiences; Brightcove OTT Flow, a service for media companies and content owners to rapidly deploy high-quality, direct-to-consumer, live and on-demand video services across platforms; Brightcove Video Marketing Suite, a comprehensive suite of video technologies designed to address the needs of marketers to drive awareness, engagement and conversion; and Brightcove Enterprise Video Suite, an enterprise-class platform for internal communications, employee training, live streaming, marketing and ecommerce videos. The Brightcove professional services division provides consulting, strategy, design and development services in conjunction with cloud platform. Its service is currently used by more than 4,168 professional media customers in over 70 countries, ranging from media and technology enterprises to financial services firms and government, educational and nonprofit entities. The firm has offices in the U.S., the U.K., Australia, Spain, France, Singapore, Japan, South Korea and the UAE.

FINANCIAL DATA: *Note: Data for latest year may not have been available at press time.*

In U.S. $	2018	2017	2016	2015	2014	2013
Revenue		155,913,000	150,266,000	134,706,000	125,017,000	109,895,000
R&D Expense		31,850,000	30,171,000	29,302,000	28,252,000	21,052,000
Operating Income		-19,696,000	-8,957,000	-6,730,000	-12,118,000	-7,425,000
Operating Margin %		-12.63%	-5.96%	-4.99%	-9.69%	-6.75%
SGA Expense		79,141,000	73,205,000	65,657,000	65,150,000	59,478,000
Net Income		-19,519,000	-9,986,000	-7,580,000	-16,893,000	-10,262,000
Operating Cash Flow		-6,441,000	11,077,000	9,081,000	1,485,000	7,318,000
Capital Expenditure		4,112,000	5,494,000	2,846,000	4,552,000	3,915,000
EBITDA		-11,866,000	-1,717,000	1,594,000	-7,950,000	-4,163,000
Return on Assets %		-14.78%	-7.56%	-5.93%	-14.64%	-10.25%
Return on Equity %		-26.93%	-12.77%	-9.54%	-23.93%	-16.68%
Debt to Equity						

CONTACT INFORMATION:

Phone: 617-500-4947   Fax: 617-261-4830
Toll-Free: 888-882-1880
Address: 290 Congress St., 4/Fl, Cambridge, MA 02210 United States

STOCK TICKER/OTHER:

Stock Ticker: BCOV   Exchange: NAS
Employees: 490   Fiscal Year Ends: 12/31
Parent Company:

SALARIES/BONUSES:

Top Exec. Salary: $381,250   Bonus: $
Second Exec. Salary: Bonus: $21,166
$300,000

OTHER THOUGHTS:

Estimated Female Officers or Directors: 1
Hot Spot for Advancement for Women/Minorities: Y

BroadVision Inc

www.broadvision.com

NAIC Code: 511210M

TYPES OF BUSINESS:

Software-Web Site Tools
Human Resources Management Software
Content Management Software
Consulting & Support Services

BRANDS/DIVISIONS/AFFILIATES:

BroadVision OnDemand Ltd
Business Agility Suite
Commerce Agility Suite
QuickSilver
Clearvale
Clear
Vmoso

CONTACTS: *Note: Officers with more than one job title may be intentionally listed here more than once.*

Pehong Chen, CEO

GROWTH PLANS/SPECIAL FEATURES:

BroadVision, Inc. develops, markets and supports personalized e-business solutions. The firm provides a single high-performance framework on which customers can integrate personalization applications and toolsets, and create e-commerce and portal solutions as well as enterprise social networks. The company's software offers secure transaction processing, multi-platform availability, multilingual and multicurrency support, personalization and high scalability and configurability. The company offers several solutions, including its Business Agility Suite, Commerce Agility Suite, QuickSilver, Clearvale, Clear and Vmoso. Business Agility Suite allows web managers to personalize web page content. It also supports collaboration both inside and outside the enterprise. The Commerce Agility Suite is intended for transacting business on the web and enables lead generation, sales execution, customer support and business-to-business (B2B) and business-to-consumer channel management through a single solution. QuickSilver facilitates the publication of large and complex documents through its multiple format support, which includes HTML, PDF and Postscript formats. Clearvale is an enterprise social network solution that allows customers to publicize, personalize, and socialize their communications and collaborations from any location. Clear is a human resources (HR) management system developed to facilitate collaboration by members of a customer's organization in each phase of the HR management lifecycle. The company's international business unit, BroadVision OnDemand Ltd., headquartered in Beijing, China, is the developer of the Clear solution. Last, Vmoso is a cloud application for conducting virtual enterprise communication, mobile workgroup collaboration and social business engagement. It unifies five workplace activities in one platform: email, instant messaging, content sharing, workflow and social networking.

The firm offers its employees medical, dental, vision, life and workers' compensation insurance; flexible spending plans; an employee assistance program; a 401(k) savings plan; and an employee stock purchase plan.

FINANCIAL DATA: *Note: Data for latest year may not have been available at press time.*

In U.S. $	2018	2017	2016	2015	2014	2013
Revenue		6,357,000	7,940,000	9,442,000	13,585,000	15,599,000
R&D Expense		6,563,000	6,901,000	7,219,000	7,311,000	7,067,000
Operating Income		-10,763,000	-9,954,000	-9,660,000	-7,397,000	-5,777,000
Operating Margin %		-169.30%	-125.36%	-102.30%	-54.44%	-37.03%
SGA Expense		7,409,000	7,669,000	8,390,000	9,116,000	9,468,000
Net Income		-9,899,000	-9,485,000	-11,437,000	-9,481,000	-5,422,000
Operating Cash Flow		-9,625,000	-9,607,000	-8,201,000	-9,978,000	-6,292,000
Capital Expenditure		7,000	14,000	16,000	24,000	70,000
EBITDA		-10,731,000	-9,913,000	-9,583,000	-7,279,000	-5,643,000
Return on Assets %		-58.27%	-34.99%	-30.89%	-20.29%	-9.90%
Return on Equity %		-81.90%	-44.77%	-37.42%	-23.99%	-11.90%
Debt to Equity						

CONTACT INFORMATION:

Phone: 650 331-1000   Fax: 650 364-3425
Toll-Free: 866-246-4887
Address: 1700 Seaport Blvd., Ste 210, Redwood City, CA 94063 United States

STOCK TICKER/OTHER:

Stock Ticker: BVSN   Exchange: NAS
Employees: 145   Fiscal Year Ends: 12/31
Parent Company:

SALARIES/BONUSES:

Top Exec. Salary: $350,000   Bonus: $
Second Exec. Salary: $200,000   Bonus: $9,500

OTHER THOUGHTS:

Estimated Female Officers or Directors:
Hot Spot for Advancement for Women/Minorities:

Build.com Inc

NAIC Code: 454111

TYPES OF BUSINESS:

Electronic Shopping
Online Hardware Store

BRANDS/DIVISIONS/AFFILIATES:

Ferguson plc
Build.com Rewards

CONTACTS: Note: Officers with more than one job title may be intentionally listed here more than once.

Chris Friedland, CEO
Danielle Mohn, CMO

GROWTH PLANS/SPECIAL FEATURES:

Build.com, Inc. is an online and mobile home improvement retailer offering over 1 million home improvement products. The firm's website offers products in a variety of categories, including bathroom, which features faucets, sinks, bathtubs, bathroom hardware and accessories; kitchen, which includes kitchen appliances, garbage disposals, kitchen sinks and faucet and cabinet hardware; lighting, which includes chandeliers, pendant lighting, ceiling lights and outdoor lighting; fans, including indoor and outdoor ceiling fans, air circulators and related accessories; hardware, including door knobs, deadbolts, door levers and door entry sets; decors, including area rugs, decorative mirrors, clocks, home accents and decorative pillows; appliances, including dishwashers, refrigeration, range hoods and laundry; heating & air, including stoves and fireplaces, chimney pipes, thermostats and tankless water heaters; outdoor, which includes patio furniture, barbecue grills, firepits and outdoor kitchens; and flooring, which includes wood, laminate, cork and bamboo flooring and tile. In addition, the company offers smart home products, such as hubs and controllers, security solutions, smart locks and smart lighting among others. Build.com partners with over 575 vendors to offer end-to-end solutions to its customers. Through its website, customers can explorer do-it-yourself (DIY) project ideas, seek help and lookup contact information for professional contractors. The firm offers coupons and customers can enroll in the Build.com Rewards program for additional savings and premium deals. Build.com operates as a subsidiary of Ferguson plc (formerly Wolseley plc).

FINANCIAL DATA: Note: Data for latest year may not have been available at press time.

In U.S. $	2018	2017	2016	2015	2014	2013
Revenue		807,600,000	615,000,000	525,000,000	441,000,000	
R&D Expense						
Operating Income						
Operating Margin %						
SGA Expense						
Net Income						
Operating Cash Flow						
Capital Expenditure						
EBITDA						
Return on Assets %						
Return on Equity %						
Debt to Equity						

CONTACT INFORMATION:

Phone: Fax:
Toll-Free: 800-375-3403
Address: 402 Otterson Dr., Ste. 100, Chico, CA 95928 United States

STOCK TICKER/OTHER:

Stock Ticker: Subsidiary   Exchange:
Employees: 613   Fiscal Year Ends:
Parent Company: Ferguson plc

SALARIES/BONUSES:

Top Exec. Salary: $ Bonus: $
Second Exec. Salary: $ Bonus: $

OTHER THOUGHTS:

Estimated Female Officers or Directors:
Hot Spot for Advancement for Women/Minorities:

BuzzFeed Inc

NAIC Code: 519130

www.buzzfeed.com

TYPES OF BUSINESS:

Internet Publishing and Broadcasting and Web Search Portals

BRANDS/DIVISIONS/AFFILIATES:

GROWTH PLANS/SPECIAL FEATURES:

BuzzFeed, Inc. is a global, cross-platform network offering social news and entertainment. The firm covers a variety of topics including breaking news, politics, quizzes, videos, animals, business, entertainment and do-it-yourself articles across the web to its global audience. BuzzFeed uses analytical technology to detect what is trending on the web and to connect people in real-time with content of the moment. The company generates its advertising revenue through native advertising that matches the content of its articles. BuzzFeed is a venture-backed tech company headquartered in New York, with global offices in London, Paris, Berlin, Madrid, Sydney, Mumbai, Tokyo, Sao Paulo, Mexico City and Toronto. It has an entertainment studio in Los Angeles.

CONTACTS: Note: Officers with more than one job title may be intentionally listed here more than once.

Jonah Peretti, CEO
Greg Coleman, Pres.
Eric W. Muhlheim, CFO
Carole Robinson, Chief Communications Officer
Lenke Taylor, Chief People Officer
Ken Lerer, Chmn.

FINANCIAL DATA: Note: Data for latest year may not have been available at press time.

In U.S. $	2018	2017	2016	2015	2014	2013
Revenue		280,000,000	235,000,000	170,000,000	120,000,000	
R&D Expense						
Operating Income						
Operating Margin %						
SGA Expense						
Net Income						
Operating Cash Flow						
Capital Expenditure						
EBITDA						
Return on Assets %						
Return on Equity %						
Debt to Equity						

CONTACT INFORMATION:

Phone: 212-431-7464   Fax: 412-431-7461
Toll-Free:
Address: 111 E. 18th Street, 13/Fl, New York, NY 10003 United States

STOCK TICKER/OTHER:

Stock Ticker: Private   Exchange:
Employees: 700   Fiscal Year Ends:
Parent Company:

SALARIES/BONUSES:

Top Exec. Salary: $ Bonus: $
Second Exec. Salary: $ Bonus: $

OTHER THOUGHTS:

Estimated Female Officers or Directors:
Hot Spot for Advancement for Women/Minorities:

CA Technologies

www.ca.com

NAIC Code: 511210H

TYPES OF BUSINESS:

Computer Software, Business Management & ERP
Enterprise Management Software
Security Software
Storage Software
Application Development Software
Business Intelligence Software
Application Life Cycle Management
Consulting Services

BRANDS/DIVISIONS/AFFILIATES:

Broadcom Inc

GROWTH PLANS/SPECIAL FEATURES:

CA Technologies designs, markets and licenses enterprise IT management software, which allows businesses to run and manage critical aspects of their IT operations and data center managers and programmers to automate their daily functions. CA Technologies' solutions cover advanced analytics, agile management, artificial intelligence for IT operations (AIOps), API management (application programming interfaces), automation, cloud, continuous delivery, continuous testing, DevOps, mainframe, microservices, security and service management. Services and support by the firm include consulting, implementing, managing, upgrading, DevOps, agility, product downloads, log-in portal support and various types of technical and maintenance support. In late-2018, CA Technologies was acquired by Broadcom, Inc.

CONTACTS:
Note: Officers with more than one job title may be intentionally listed here more than once.

Hock E. Tan, CEO-Broadcom
Kieran McGrath, CFO
Paul Pronsati, Executive VP, Divisional
Jacob Lamm, Executive VP, Divisional
Ava Hahn, Executive VP
Ayman Sayed, President

FINANCIAL DATA:
Note: Data for latest year may not have been available at press time.

In U.S. $	2018	2017	2016	2015	2014	2013
Revenue	4,235,000,064	4,036,000,000	4,024,999,936	4,262,000,128	4,514,999,808	4,642,999,808
R&D Expense						
Operating Income						
Operating Margin %						
SGA Expense						
Net Income	476,000,000	775,000,000	783,000,000	846,000,000	914,000,000	955,000,000
Operating Cash Flow						
Capital Expenditure						
EBITDA						
Return on Assets %						
Return on Equity %						
Debt to Equity						

CONTACT INFORMATION:

Phone: 800 225-5224   Fax: 631 342-6800
Toll-Free: 800-225-5224
Address: 520 Madison Ave., New York, NY 10022 United States

STOCK TICKER/OTHER:

Stock Ticker: Subsidiary
Employees: 11,800
Parent Company: Broadcom Inc

Exchange:
Fiscal Year Ends: 03/31

SALARIES/BONUSES:

Top Exec. Salary: $ Bonus: $
Second Exec. Salary: $ Bonus: $

OTHER THOUGHTS:

Estimated Female Officers or Directors: 4
Hot Spot for Advancement for Women/Minorities: Y

Campaign Monitor

NAIC Code: 511210F

www.campaignmonitor.com

TYPES OF BUSINESS:
Computer Software, Multimedia, Graphics & Publishing

BRANDS/DIVISIONS/AFFILIATES:
Emma
Delivra

CONTACTS: *Note: Officers with more than one job title may be intentionally listed here more than once.*
Wellford Dillard, CEO
Ash Fagura, COO
Ethan Zoubek, Chief Revenue Officer
Shane Phair, CMO
Sharon Strauss, Chief People Officer
Shai Haim, CTO

GROWTH PLANS/SPECIAL FEATURES:
Campaign Monitor provides email marketing, automation and online surveys to help small- and medium-sized businesses grow. The company's technology solves complex problems having to do with online marketing delivery. Its products and feature tools provide everything needed to run attractive marketing campaigns, including a drag-and-drop builder, visual designer, creative marketing strategies and real-time performance metrics and analytics. With Campaign Monitor's application programming interface (API), customers can connect all their core business apps to meet their email marketing and automation needs. Price ranges depend on the amount of people the campaign will be sent to and begin at $9 per month for 2,500 emails and up to $149 per month for unlimited emails. Quotes are given for campaigns of more than 50,000 people. Customers served include agencies, retail, non-profit, entertainment, publishing, technology and hospitality. More than 250,000 companies worldwide use Campaign Monitor to run email marketing campaigns, including HuffPost, Chandon, Rip Curl, Topshop, Vice Media and Virgin. The firm has offices in San Francisco, California; New York, New York; London, England; and Sydney, Australia. In June 2018, Campaign Monitor merged with Emma and Delivra to launch the new Campaign Monitor Brand, creating the industry's most comprehensive email marketing solution

FINANCIAL DATA: *Note: Data for latest year may not have been available at press time.*

In U.S. $	2018	2017	2016	2015	2014	2013
Revenue						
R&D Expense						
Operating Income						
Operating Margin %						
SGA Expense						
Net Income						
Operating Cash Flow						
Capital Expenditure						
EBITDA						
Return on Assets %						
Return on Equity %						
Debt to Equity						

CONTACT INFORMATION:
Phone: Fax:
Toll-Free: 888-533-8098
Address: 631 Howard Street, Ste. 500, San Francisco, CA 94105 United States

STOCK TICKER/OTHER:
Stock Ticker: Private   Exchange:
Employees: 250   Fiscal Year Ends:
Parent Company:

SALARIES/BONUSES:
Top Exec. Salary: $ Bonus: $
Second Exec. Salary: $ Bonus: $

OTHER THOUGHTS:
Estimated Female Officers or Directors:
Hot Spot for Advancement for Women/Minorities:

Carbon Black Inc

www.carbonblack.com

NAIC Code: 511210E

TYPES OF BUSINESS:

Computer Software, Security & Anti-Virus

BRANDS/DIVISIONS/AFFILIATES:

Cb Predictive Security Cloud
Cb Defense
Cb Defense for Vmware
Cb Response
Cb Protection

CONTACTS: Note: Officers with more than one job title may be intentionally listed here more than once.

Mark Sullivan, Assistant Secretary
Patrick Morley, CEO
Michael Viscuso, Chief Technology Officer
Thomas Hansen, COO
Ryan Polk, Senior VP

GROWTH PLANS/SPECIAL FEATURES:

Carbon Black, Inc. is a security solutions company. Its next-generation endpoint security enables organizations to disrupt advanced attacks. Carbon Black's products include: Cb Predictive Security Cloud, Cb Defense, Db Defense for VMware, Cb Response and Cb Protection. Cb Predictive Security Cloud is a consolidated endpoint security platform that delivers innovative security services through the cloud. It applies big data analytics across all endpoints to make predictions about, and provide protection from, current, future and unknown attacks. CB Defense is a next-generation antivirus plus endpoint detection and response (EDR) in one cloud-delivered platform. Its stops commodity malware, advanced malware, non-malware attacks and ransomware. Cb Defense for VMware is an integrated solution with VMware AppDefense that provides threat detection and in-depth application behavior insight to stop attacks in-progress and accelerate response. Cb Response is a high-scalable, real-time EDR with visibility for top security operations centers and incident response teams. Cb Protection locks down servers and critical systems with 100% efficacy; its stopped 100% of attacks in NSS Labs' Advanced Endpoint Protection test. In addition, Cb Protection enables: continuous compliance for key frameworks including PCI-DSS, HIPAA, SOX, FISMA and NERC; the monitoring of critical activity and the enforcement of configurations for assessing risk and maintaining system integrity; and the security of end-of-life systems with change-control and whitelisting policies. Industries that utilize Carbon Black products include finance, local and federal governments, healthcare, manufacturing, oil/gas/utilities, retail and hospitality. Carbon Black is headquartered in Waltham, Massachusetts, with additional U.S. offices located in Boston, Colorado California and Texas as well as internationally in the U.K., Singapore, Japan and Australia. In September 2018, the firm opened its newest office in Boulder, Colorado.

FINANCIAL DATA: Note: Data for latest year may not have been available at press time.

In U.S. $	2018	2017	2016	2015	2014	2013
Revenue		162,014,000	116,239,000	70,594,000		
R&D Expense		52,047,000	36,493,000	24,042,000		
Operating Income		-55,198,000	-45,579,000	-36,582,000		
Operating Margin %		-34.06%	-39.21%	-51.82%		
SGA Expense		129,527,000	104,286,000	69,821,000		
Net Income		-55,827,000	-44,554,000	-38,652,000		
Operating Cash Flow		-7,678,000	-33,088,000	-4,097,000		
Capital Expenditure		6,067,000	6,187,000	9,558,000		
EBITDA		-48,519,000	-38,133,000	-34,508,000		
Return on Assets %		-21.69%	-17.53%			
Return on Equity %						
Debt to Equity						

CONTACT INFORMATION:

Phone: 617-393-7400   Fax: 617-393-7499
Toll-Free:
Address: 1100 Winter Street, Waltham, MA 02451 United States

STOCK TICKER/OTHER:

Stock Ticker: CBLK   Exchange: NAS
Employees: 932   Fiscal Year Ends: 12/31
Parent Company:

SALARIES/BONUSES:

Top Exec. Salary: $ Bonus: $
Second Exec. Salary: $ Bonus: $

OTHER THOUGHTS:

Estimated Female Officers or Directors:
Hot Spot for Advancement for Women/Minorities:

CareerBuilder Inc

www.careerbuilder.com

NAIC Code: 561311A

TYPES OF BUSINESS:

Portal-Career Support
Career Services
Online Recruiting
Resume Writing

BRANDS/DIVISIONS/AFFILIATES:

CareerBuilder.com
Apollo Global Management LLC

CONTACTS: Note: Officers with more than one job title may be intentionally listed here more than once.

Irina Novoselsky, CEO
Matt Ferguson, Exec. Chmn.
Brett Rasmussen, Pres., North America
Dan Fuji, CFO
Amy Heidersbach, CMO
Michelle Armer, Chief People Officer
Anthony Dupree, CIO
Hope Gurion, Chief Prod. Officer
Alex Green, General Counsel
Hunter Arnold, Pres., Asia Pacific
Tony Roy, Pres., EMEA

GROWTH PLANS/SPECIAL FEATURES:

CareerBuilder, Inc. is a global, end-to-end human capital solutions company. The firm is a leading provider of targeted interactive recruiting on the internet via CareerBuilder.com (its flagship site), as well as dozens of affiliated career sites. The company's products and services include recruitment advertising solutions, resume database search solutions, job distribution technology solutions, applicant tracking systems and candidate engagement software. CareerBuilder also offers background check and screening software, as well as supply and demand data that helps to inform an organization's overall strategy. The company serves hundreds of thousands of employers; serves five specialized markets, spanning the U.S., Europe, Canada and Asia; and powers more than 1,000 partner's career sites, including more than 130 newspapers and leading portals. The firm's mission is to empower employment. CareerBuilder is majority-owned by funds managed by affiliates of Apollo Global Management, LCC.

CareerBuilder offers its employees medical, dental and vision insurance; flexible spending accounts; short- and long-term disability coverage; life insurance; a 401(k) plan; tuition reimbursement; and an employee assistance program.

FINANCIAL DATA: Note: Data for latest year may not have been available at press time.

In U.S. $	2018	2017	2016	2015	2014	2013
Revenue		733,000,000	714,000,000			
R&D Expense						
Operating Income						
Operating Margin %						
SGA Expense						
Net Income						
Operating Cash Flow						
Capital Expenditure						
EBITDA						
Return on Assets %						
Return on Equity %						
Debt to Equity						

CONTACT INFORMATION:

Phone: 773-527-3600   Fax: 773-399-6313
Toll-Free: 800-638-4212
Address: 200 N. LaSalle St., Ste. 1100, Chicago, IL 60601 United States

STOCK TICKER/OTHER:

Stock Ticker: Joint Venture   Exchange:
Employees: 3,300   Fiscal Year Ends: 12/31
Parent Company:

SALARIES/BONUSES:

Top Exec. Salary: $ Bonus: $
Second Exec. Salary: $ Bonus: $

OTHER THOUGHTS:

Estimated Female Officers or Directors: 2
Hot Spot for Advancement for Women/Minorities: Y

Cars.com Inc   www.cars.com

NAIC Code: 519130

TYPES OF BUSINESS:

Internet Publishing and Broadcasting and Web Search Portals
Cars for Sale Web Site

BRANDS/DIVISIONS/AFFILIATES:

Cars.com
Auto.com
DealerRater.com
NewCars.com
PickupTrucks.com

CONTACTS: Note: Officers with more than one job title may be intentionally listed here more than once.

Becky Sheehan, CFO
Thomas Vetter, Director
Scott Forbes, Director
John Clavadetscher, Other Executive Officer
James Rogers, Other Executive Officer

GROWTH PLANS/SPECIAL FEATURES:

Cars.com, Inc. in an online research destination for car shoppers. The company averaged 33 million monthly visits to its sites in 2017, 59% of which were from a mobile device. The firm offers a suite of unique products and services targeting the automotive needs of its buyer and seller customers. Cars.com's flagship service is its digital automotive marketplace search engine that empowers car buyers to make informed purchasing decisions and helps sellers to engage with a substantial portion of their target customer base. This online automotive marketplace service connects buyers and sellers across five distinct websites: Cars.com, Auto.com, DealerRater.com, NewCars.com and PickupTrucks.com. While Cars.com, Auto.com, NewCar.com and PickupTrucks.com are all automotive classified sites, DealerRater.com is a site where consumers can write reviews on their car buying experiences with car dealerships and potential car buyers can use these reviews to research car dealerships with whom to do business. During 2018, Cars.com acquired Dealer Inspire, a firm that builds technology for dealerships, making the car-buying process faster and more efficient.

FINANCIAL DATA: Note: Data for latest year may not have been available at press time.

In U.S. $	2018	2017	2016	2015	2014	2013
Revenue		626,262,000	633,106,000	596,510,000		418,204,000
R&D Expense						
Operating Income		143,204,000	185,179,000	164,459,000		85,115,000
Operating Margin %		22.86%	29.24%	27.57%		20.35%
SGA Expense		328,878,000	243,234,000	242,703,000		226,539,000
Net Income		224,443,000	176,370,000	157,838,000		104,690,000
Operating Cash Flow		185,929,000	199,153,000	190,055,000		117,743,000
Capital Expenditure		32,774,000	9,701,000	9,108,000		10,678,000
EBITDA		231,843,000	268,285,000	245,277,000		94,375,000
Return on Assets %		8.87%	3.91%	6.38%		
Return on Equity %		10.95%	4.15%	6.84%		
Debt to Equity		0.33				

CONTACT INFORMATION:

Phone: 312-601-5000   Fax:
Toll-Free: 888-780-1286
Address: 300 S. Riverside Plaza, Ste. 1000, Chicago, IL 60606 United States

STOCK TICKER/OTHER:

Stock Ticker: CARS   Exchange: NYS
Employees: 1,275   Fiscal Year Ends: 12/31
Parent Company:

SALARIES/BONUSES:

Top Exec. Salary: $516,667   Bonus: $320,411
Second Exec. Salary: $479,486   Bonus: $250,000

OTHER THOUGHTS:

Estimated Female Officers or Directors:
Hot Spot for Advancement for Women/Minorities:

Sales, profits and employees may be estimates. Financial information, benefits and other data can change quickly and may vary from those stated here.

Carvana Co
NAIC Code: 441120

www.carvana.com

TYPES OF BUSINESS:
Used Car Dealers
eCommerce Used Cars

BRANDS/DIVISIONS/AFFILIATES:

CONTACTS: *Note: Officers with more than one job title may be intentionally listed here more than once.*
Ernie Garcia, CEO
Mark Jenkins, CFO
Benjamin Huston, Co-Founder
Ryan Keeton, Co-Founder
John Mckeon, Controller
Daniel Gill, Other Executive Officer
Paul Breaux, Vice President

GROWTH PLANS/SPECIAL FEATURES:
Carvana Co. operates an eCommerce platform for purchasing used cars. Consumers can research and identify a vehicle, inspect it using Carvana's proprietary 360-degree vehicle imaging technology, obtain financing and warranty coverage, purchase the vehicle and schedule delivery or pickup all from a computer or mobile device. The firm's transaction technologies and online platform enable customers to secure financing, complete the purchase and schedule delivery in as little as 10 minutes. Carvana's proprietary algorithms optimize its pool of over 9,500 vehicles, inspect and recondition the vehicles through a 150-point inspection process and manage a logistics network for delivering purchased cars directly to customers as soon as the following day. Customers in certain markets have the option to pick up their purchased vehicle at one of Carvana's proprietary vending machines. The firm's in-house distribution network serves more than 40 metropolitan markets. Car-owners can get an appraisal online, and either trade-in their vehicles in the form of a down payment or receive a check for selling the car to Carvana. Depending on the location, Carvana will either go to the car-owner's residence for a final trade-in/purchase inspection, or the vehicle can be dropped off at a vending machine. Every car sold comes with a seven-day money back guarantee. Vehicles offered include sport utility vehicles (SUVs), sedans, trucks, hatchbacks, six-cylinders, four-cylinders, all-wheel drives, four-wheel drives and more. Makes include Acura, Alfa Romeo, Audi, BMW, Buick, Cadillac, Chevrolet, Chrysler, Dodge, FIAT, Ford, Genesis, GMC, Honda, Hummer, Hyundai, Infiniti, Jaguar, Jeep, Kia, Land Rover, Lexus, Lincoln, Maserati, Mazda, Mercedes-Benz, MINI, Mitsubishi, Nissan, Porsche, Ram, Scion, Smart, Subaru, Tesla, Toyota, Volkswagen and Volvo. Most cars are no more than 10 years old.

Carvana offers its employees with health premiums and Carvana auto discounts.

FINANCIAL DATA: *Note: Data for latest year may not have been available at press time.*

In U.S. $	2018	2017	2016	2015	2014	2013
Revenue		858,870,000	365,148,000	130,392,000	41,679,000	
R&D Expense						
Operating Income		-155,309,000	-89,479,000	-35,332,000	-15,108,000	
Operating Margin %		-18.08%	-24.50%	-27.09%	-36.24%	
SGA Expense		223,400,000		36,678,000		
Net Income		-62,841,000	-93,112,000	-36,780,000	-15,238,000	
Operating Cash Flow		-199,924,000	-240,225,000	-53,508,000	-30,161,000	
Capital Expenditure		78,490,000	39,539,000	13,950,000	3,768,000	
EBITDA		-145,089,000	-84,867,000	-32,568,000	-13,425,000	
Return on Assets %		-4.08%	4.51%	-2.94%		
Return on Equity %						
Debt to Equity		1.69				

CONTACT INFORMATION:
Phone: 602-852-6604   Fax:
Toll-Free:
Address: 1930 W. Rio Salado Pkwy, Tempe, AZ 85821 United States

STOCK TICKER/OTHER:
Stock Ticker: CVNA   Exchange: NYS
Employees: 1,067   Fiscal Year Ends: 12/31
Parent Company:

SALARIES/BONUSES:
Top Exec. Salary: $400,000   Bonus: $
Second Exec. Salary: $350,000 Bonus: $

OTHER THOUGHTS:
Estimated Female Officers or Directors:
Hot Spot for Advancement for Women/Minorities:

CBS Interactive Inc

www.cbsinteractive.com

NAIC Code: 519130

TYPES OF BUSINESS:

Online Content
Web Site Management
Music Downloads
Entertainment News
Recipes

BRANDS/DIVISIONS/AFFILIATES:

CBS Corporation
CBS All Access
CBSN
GameSpot
CBS.com
CBSNews.com
CBSSports.com
CNET

CONTACTS: *Note: Officers with more than one job title may be intentionally listed here more than once.*

Jim Lanzone, CEO
Jim Lanzone, Pres.
Renee Budig, CFO
Steve Comstock, CIO
Rosabel Tao, Sr. VP-Comm.
David Rice, Sr. VP-CBS Interactive Games
Jason Kint, Sr. VP-Interactive

GROWTH PLANS/SPECIAL FEATURES:

CBS Interactive, Inc. handles the online content operations of its parent company, CBS Corporation. The firm delivers information and entertainment in the fields of technology, entertainment, sports, news, music and gaming. CBS Interactive's properties include the websites, apps and streaming services of the CBS Television Network, such as the CBS All Access digital subscription, video-on-demand and live streaming service; the 24/7 digital news network, CBSN; and CBS Sports' digital brands and properties, including GameSpot, an online sport destination for gamers, offering previews, reviews and information on video, digital and computer games. Websites and apps include, but are not limited to: CBS.com, an online television network; CBSNews.com, providing online worldwide news anytime; and CBSSports.com, providing the full spectrum of sports, from prep to pro, across all digital screens. CBS Interactive's additional sites include: CNET, which offers product reviews, technology news and downloads; TV.com, a television fan site offering forums, episode reviews and program ratings; Chowhound, enabling food enthusiasts to discover recipes and resources for cooking and eating food; Comic Vine, an online comic database featuring comic reviews, news, videos and forums; and last.fm, an online platform featuring music.

CBS Interactive offers its employees medical, dental and vision plans; wellness programs; an employee assistance program; life insurance; wellness programs; flexible spending accounts; and a 401(k) plan.

FINANCIAL DATA: *Note: Data for latest year may not have been available at press time.*

In U.S. $	2018	2017	2016	2015	2014	2013
Revenue						
R&D Expense						
Operating Income						
Operating Margin %						
SGA Expense						
Net Income						
Operating Cash Flow						
Capital Expenditure						
EBITDA						
Return on Assets %						
Return on Equity %						
Debt to Equity						

CONTACT INFORMATION:

Phone: 415-344-2000   Fax:
Toll-Free:
Address: 235 2nd St., San Francisco, CA 94105 United States

STOCK TICKER/OTHER:

Stock Ticker: Subsidiary   Exchange:
Employees: 2,080   Fiscal Year Ends:
Parent Company: CBS Corporation

SALARIES/BONUSES:

Top Exec. Salary: $ Bonus: $
Second Exec. Salary: $ Bonus: $

OTHER THOUGHTS:

Estimated Female Officers or Directors: 2
Hot Spot for Advancement for Women/Minorities: Y

CDK Global Inc

NAIC Code: 541810E

www.cdkglobal.com

TYPES OF BUSINESS:
Advertising-Automotive Dealerships & Manufacturers
Web-Based Software & CRM Tools
Training & Consulting Services
Media Services
Automotive Data Collection & Reporting
e-Commerce Services

BRANDS/DIVISIONS/AFFILIATES:
Progressus Media
ELEAD1ONE

CONTACTS: Note: Officers with more than one job title may be intentionally listed here more than once.
Brian Krzanich, CEO
Joseph Tautges, CFO
Leslie Brun, Chairman of the Board
Jennifer Williams, Chief Accounting Officer
Dean Crutchfield, Chief Information Officer
Rajiv Amar, Chief Technology Officer
Scott Mathews, Executive VP, Divisional
Lee Brunz, Executive VP
Ronald Frey, Executive VP
Amy Byrne, Executive VP
Neil Packham, President, Divisional
Daniel Flynn, President, Geographical

GROWTH PLANS/SPECIAL FEATURES:
CDK Global, Inc. provides integrated information technology and digital marketing solutions to the automotive retail and related industries. The firm operates through two business segments: CDK North America and CDK International. CDK North America comprises two divisions: retail solutions and advertising. The retail solutions division provides technology-based solutions such as automotive website platforms that help automotive retailers, original equipment manufacturers (OEMs) and other industry participants manage the acquisition, sale, financing, insuring, parts supply, repair and maintenance of vehicles in North America. These solutions help customers streamline operations, better target and serve customers and enhance the financial performance of their retail operations. This division also provides solutions to retailers and manufacturers of heavy trucks, construction equipment, agricultural equipment, motorcycles, boats and other marine and recreational vehicles. The advertising division provides advertising solutions such as management of digital advertising spend, for OEMs and automotive retailers. These solutions provide a coordinated offering across multiple marketing channels to help achieve customer marketing and sales objectives and coordinate execution between OEMs and their retailer networks. The CDK International segment provides technology-based solutions similar to the retail solutions division, but to approximately 100 countries outside the U.S. and Canada. Customers of this segment include automotive retail dealers and OEMs across Europe, the Middle East, Asia, Africa and Latin America. During 2018, CDK acquired: Progressus Media, a provider of mobile advertising solutions; and ELEAD1ONE, a customer relationship management software solutions provider.

The firm offers employees medical, dental and vision insurance; tuition reimbursement; relocation assistance; and a 401(k) plan.

FINANCIAL DATA: Note: Data for latest year may not have been available at press time.

In U.S. $	2018	2017	2016	2015	2014	2013
Revenue	2,273,200,000	2,220,200,000	2,114,600,000	2,063,500,000	1,973,600,000	1,839,200,000
R&D Expense						
Operating Income	615,400,000	507,600,000	422,700,000	359,200,000	352,700,000	313,700,000
Operating Margin %		22.86%	19.98%	17.40%	17.87%	17.05%
SGA Expense	475,800,000	477,700,000	448,500,000	431,100,000	419,400,000	422,900,000
Net Income	380,800,000	295,600,000	239,300,000	178,400,000	226,900,000	199,400,000
Operating Cash Flow	461,600,000	431,000,000	320,100,000	267,900,000	258,300,000	263,300,000
Capital Expenditure	87,100,000	94,200,000	64,300,000	63,900,000	64,500,000	47,700,000
EBITDA	687,000,000	562,800,000	473,300,000	405,200,000	412,500,000	378,900,000
Return on Assets %		11.26%	9.80%	6.98%	9.05%	8.37%
Return on Equity %		206.71%	42.35%	13.93%	13.64%	13.30%
Debt to Equity			3.30	1.26		

CONTACT INFORMATION:
Phone: 847-397-1700   Fax: 206-269-6350
Toll-Free: 800-909-8244
Address: 1950 Hassell Rd., Hoffman Estates, IL 60169 United States

STOCK TICKER/OTHER:
Stock Ticker: CDK
Employees: 8,900
Parent Company:

Exchange: NAS
Fiscal Year Ends: 06/30

SALARIES/BONUSES:
Top Exec. Salary: $595,833   Bonus: $400,000
Second Exec. Salary: $925,000   Bonus: $

OTHER THOUGHTS:
Estimated Female Officers or Directors: 1
Hot Spot for Advancement for Women/Minorities:

Sales, profits and employees may be estimates. Financial information, benefits and other data can change quickly and may vary from those stated here.

CenturyLink Inc

www.centurylink.com

NAIC Code: 517110

TYPES OF BUSINESS:

Local Telephone Service
Long-Distance Services
Internet Service Provider
Business Information Services
Fiber Network Services
Satellite TV
IPTV

BRANDS/DIVISIONS/AFFILIATES:

CONTACTS: *Note: Officers with more than one job title may be intentionally listed here more than once.*

Indraneel Dev, CFO
Harvey Perry, Chairman of the Board
Eric Mortensen, Chief Accounting Officer
Stacey Goff, Chief Administrative Officer
W. Hanks, Director
Scott Trezise, Executive VP, Divisional
Jeffrey Storey, President

GROWTH PLANS/SPECIAL FEATURES:

CenturyLink, Inc. is an international facilities-based communications company primarily engaged in providing an integrated array of services to business and residential customers. The firm's communications services include local and long-distance voice, virtual private network (VPN) data network, private line, Ethernet, information technology, wavelength, broadband, managed services, professional and other services. These services are provided in connection with selling equipment, network security and various other ancillary services. CenturyLink comprises approximately 450,000 route miles of fiber optic cable globally, and its terrestrial and subsea fiber optic long-haul network spans North America, Europe and Latin America, connecting to metropolitan fiber network that it operates. The company operates in more than 60 countries, with the majority being in the U.S. For businesses, CenturyLink provides products and services to small, medium and enterprise firms, as well as wholesale and government customers. For residential consumers, CenturyLink primarily provides broadband, local and long-distance voice, video and other ancillary services. More than 60% of the firm's annual revenue is derived from business customers, approximately 30% from residential consumers and the remainder from non-segment services. During 2018, CenturyLink sold certain former Level 3 metro network assets in the Albuquerque, New Mexico area to Unite Private Networks.

Employee benefits include medical, dental, prescription and vision coverage; an employee assistance program; retirement plans and a 401(k); flexible spending accounts; life and AD&D insurance; short-and long-term disability; and career development programs.

FINANCIAL DATA: *Note: Data for latest year may not have been available at press time.*

In U.S. $	2018	2017	2016	2015	2014	2013
Revenue		17,656,000,000	17,470,000,000	17,900,000,000	18,031,000,000	18,095,000,000
R&D Expense						
Operating Income		2,009,000,000	2,331,000,000	2,605,000,000	2,410,000,000	2,545,000,000
Operating Margin %		11.37%	13.34%	14.55%	13.36%	14.06%
SGA Expense		3,508,000,000	3,449,000,000	3,328,000,000	3,347,000,000	3,502,000,000
Net Income		1,389,000,000	626,000,000	878,000,000	772,000,000	-239,000,000
Operating Cash Flow		3,878,000,000	4,608,000,000	5,152,000,000	5,188,000,000	5,559,000,000
Capital Expenditure		3,106,000,000	2,981,000,000	2,872,000,000	3,047,000,000	3,048,000,000
EBITDA		5,957,000,000	6,254,000,000	6,817,000,000	6,849,000,000	6,063,000,000
Return on Assets %		2.26%	1.32%	1.79%	1.51%	-.45%
Return on Equity %		7.53%	4.55%	6.03%	4.79%	-1.31%
Debt to Equity		1.58	1.35	1.33	1.33	1.17

CONTACT INFORMATION:

Phone: 318 388-9000   Fax: 318 789-8656
Toll-Free:
Address: 100 CenturyLink Dr., Monroe, LA 71203 United States

STOCK TICKER/OTHER:

Stock Ticker: CTL   Exchange: NYS
Employees: 40,000   Fiscal Year Ends: 12/31
Parent Company:

SALARIES/BONUSES:

Top Exec. Salary: $248,219   Bonus: $3,732,517
Second Exec. Salary: Bonus: $1,500,000
$1,250,000

OTHER THOUGHTS:

Estimated Female Officers or Directors: 5
Hot Spot for Advancement for Women/Minorities: Y

Charles Schwab Corporation (The)

www.schwab.com

NAIC Code: 523120

TYPES OF BUSINESS:

Stock Brokerage-Retail, Online & Discount
Investment Services
Financial Services
Mutual Funds
Wealth Management
Financial Information
Banking
Online Trading Platform

BRANDS/DIVISIONS/AFFILIATES:

Charles Schwab & Co Inc
Charles Schwab Bank
Charles Schwab Investment Management Inc

CONTACTS: Note: Officers with more than one job title may be intentionally listed here more than once.

Joseph Martinetto, CEO, Subsidiary
Marie Chandoha, CEO, Subsidiary
Walter Bettinger, CEO
Peter Crawford, CFO
Charles Schwab, Chairman of the Board
Bernard Clark, Executive VP, Divisional
Nigel Murtagh, Executive VP, Divisional
Terri Kallsen, Executive VP, Divisional
David Garfield, Executive VP
Jonathan Craig, Senior Executive VP

GROWTH PLANS/SPECIAL FEATURES:

The Charles Schwab Corporation (CSC) engages in securities brokerage, banking, money management and related financial advisory services. The company manages $3.36 trillion in client brokerage accounts, 10.8 million active brokerage accounts, 1.6 million corporate retirement plan participants and 1.2 million banking accounts through its primary subsidiary, Charles Schwab & Co., Inc. (Schwab). Schwab is a securities broker-dealer with more than 345 domestic branch offices in 46 states, as well as a branch in each of the Commonwealth of Puerto Rico and London, England. It serves clients in Hong Kong through CSC subsidiaries Charles Schwab Bank, a federal savings bank located in Reno, Nevada; and Charles Schwab Investment Management, Inc., an investment advisor for the company's proprietary mutual and exchange-traded funds. CSC provides its financial services and products such as brokerage, banking, trust, advice and mutual/exchange trade funds to individuals and institutional clients through two segments: investor services and advisor services. Investor services provides retail brokerage and banking services to individual investors, retirement plan services and corporate brokerage services. Advisor services provides custodial, trading and support services to independent investment advisors (IAs), and retirement business services to independent retirement plan advisors and record keepers whose plan assets are held at Schwab Bank. In May 2018, Charles Schwab announced it was opening two Digital Accelerator hubs in Austin and San Francisco. Digital Accelerator hubs are designed to house hundreds of current and new employees focused on digital solutions.

The firm offers employees medical, dental, life, AD&D and vision insurance; health and dependent care flexible spending accounts; disability coverage; a 401(k) plan; a legal services plan; an employee discount program; an employee stock purchase plan; discounts on company products; and an employee assistance program.

FINANCIAL DATA: Note: Data for latest year may not have been available at press time.

In U.S. $	2018	2017	2016	2015	2014	2013
Revenue		8,439,000,000	7,473,000,000	6,369,000,000	6,054,000,000	5,434,000,000
R&D Expense						
Operating Income						
Operating Margin %						
SGA Expense		3,236,000,000	2,968,000,000	2,723,000,000	2,652,000,000	2,504,000,000
Net Income		2,354,000,000	1,889,000,000	1,447,000,000	1,321,000,000	1,071,000,000
Operating Cash Flow		1,263,000,000	2,662,000,000	1,246,000,000	2,348,000,000	1,656,000,000
Capital Expenditure		400,000,000	346,000,000	266,000,000	400,000,000	249,000,000
EBITDA						
Return on Assets %		.93%	.85%	.80%	.84%	.72%
Return on Equity %		14.84%	13.65%	11.92%	12.33%	11.07%
Debt to Equity		0.30	0.21	0.24	0.17	0.20

CONTACT INFORMATION:

Phone: 415 667-7000   Fax: 415 627-8894
Toll-Free: 800-648-5300
Address: 211 Main St., San Francisco, CA 94105 United States

STOCK TICKER/OTHER:

Stock Ticker: SCHW   Exchange: NYS
Employees: 16,200   Fiscal Year Ends: 12/31
Parent Company:

SALARIES/BONUSES:

Top Exec. Salary: $1,133,333   Bonus: $
Second Exec. Salary: $625,000   Bonus: $

OTHER THOUGHTS:

Estimated Female Officers or Directors: 6
Hot Spot for Advancement for Women/Minorities: Y

Sales, profits and employees may be estimates. Financial information, benefits and other data can change quickly and may vary from those stated here.

Charter Communications Inc

www.charter.com

NAIC Code: 517110

TYPES OF BUSINESS:

Cable TV Service
Internet Access
Advanced Broadband Cable Services
Telephony Services
Voice Over Internet Protocol

BRANDS/DIVISIONS/AFFILIATES:

Spectrum
Spectrum TV
Spectrum Internet
Spectrum Voice
Spectrum Business
Spectrum Enterprise Solutions
Spectrum Community Solutions
Spectrum Reach

CONTACTS: *Note: Officers with more than one job title may be intentionally listed here more than once.*

Thomas Rutledge, CEO
Michael Baird, Executive VP, Divisional
Christopher Winfrey, CFO
Kevin Howard, Chief Accounting Officer
Jonathan Hargis, Chief Marketing Officer
John Bickham, COO
John Malone, Director Emeritus
Kathleen Mayo, Executive VP, Divisional
Thomas Adams, Executive VP, Divisional
James Blackley, Executive VP, Divisional
Scott Weber, Executive VP, Divisional
Tom Montemagno, Executive VP, Divisional
Catherine Bohigian, Executive VP, Divisional
James Nuzzo, Executive VP, Divisional
Richard DiGeronimo, Executive VP, Divisional

GROWTH PLANS/SPECIAL FEATURES:

Charter Communications, Inc. operates broadband communications businesses in the U.S., offering traditional cable video programming, high-speed internet access and voice service as well as advanced broadband services. The company serves more than 27 million residential and business customers. In addition, Charter sells video and online advertising inventory to local, regional and national advertising customers, as well as fiber-delivered communications and managed information technology (IT) solutions to larger enterprise customers. The firm owns and operates regional sports networks and local sports, news and lifestyle channels; and sells security and home management services to the residential marketplace. Charter's products and services include subscription-based video services, including video on demand (VOD), high definition (HD) television, and digital video recorder (DVR), internet services and voice services. Video, internet and voice services are offered to residential and commercial customers on a subscription basis, sold as bundled or individually. The firm sells its products and services under the Spectrum brand name, including Spectrum TV, Spectrum Internet, Spectrum Voice, Spectrum Business, Spectrum Enterprise Solutions, Spectrum Community Solutions, Spectrum Reach and Spectrum Guide.

Employee benefits include medical, dental and vision coverage; a 401(k); flexible spending accounts; health savings accounts; life and AD&D insurance; short- and long-term disability; adoption reimbursement; tuition reimbursement; and employee discounts.

FINANCIAL DATA: *Note: Data for latest year may not have been available at press time.*

In U.S. $	2018	2017	2016	2015	2014	2013
Revenue		41,581,000,000	29,003,000,000	9,754,000,000	9,108,000,000	8,155,000,000
R&D Expense						
Operating Income		4,453,000,000	4,340,000,000	1,203,000,000	1,033,000,000	956,000,000
Operating Margin %		10.70%	22.64%	21.73%	21.02%	11.72%
SGA Expense		1,000,000	899,000,000			
Net Income		9,895,000,000	3,522,000,000	-271,000,000	-183,000,000	-169,000,000
Operating Cash Flow		11,954,000,000	8,041,000,000	2,359,000,000	2,359,000,000	2,158,000,000
Capital Expenditure		7,870,000,000	33,532,000,000	1,812,000,000	2,177,000,000	2,425,000,000
EBITDA		15,041,000,000	11,247,000,000	3,328,000,000	3,135,000,000	2,810,000,000
Return on Assets %		6.69%	3.73%	-.84%	-.87%	-1.02%
Return on Equity %		24.98%	17.56%	-542.00%	-123.23%	-112.66%
Debt to Equity		1.74	1.48		143.99	93.91

CONTACT INFORMATION:

Phone: 203-905-7801   Fax:
Toll-Free:
Address: 400 Atlantic St., Stamford, CT 06901 United States

STOCK TICKER/OTHER:

Stock Ticker: CHTR
Employees: 94,800
Parent Company:

Exchange: NAS
Fiscal Year Ends: 12/31

SALARIES/BONUSES:

Top Exec. Salary: $2,000,000   Bonus: $
Second Exec. Salary: $1,500,000   Bonus: $

OTHER THOUGHTS:

Estimated Female Officers or Directors: 1
Hot Spot for Advancement for Women/Minorities:

Check Point Software Technologies Ltd

www.checkpoint.com

NAIC Code: 511210E

TYPES OF BUSINESS:

Computer Software, Security & Anti-Virus
Firewall Software
VPN Software
Support Services

BRANDS/DIVISIONS/AFFILIATES:

Check Point Infinity
SandBlast Zero-Day Protection
SandBlast Mobile
Check Point Capsule
Dome9

CONTACTS: Note: Officers with more than one job title may be intentionally listed here more than once.

Gil Shwed, CEO
Amnon Bar-Lev, Pres.
Tal Payne, CFO
Dorit Dor, VP-Prod.
Marius Nacht, Chmn.

GROWTH PLANS/SPECIAL FEATURES:

Check Point Software Technologies, Ltd. develops, markets and supports a range of network security, data security and management software and combined hardware/software products. The company offers its more than 100,000 business customers an extensive portfolio of network and gateway security solutions, data and endpoint security solutions and management solutions. Its products operate under a unified security architecture, Check Point Infinity, a consolidated security across networks, cloud and mobile. Other products include: next-generation threat prevention solutions, such as SandBlast Zero-Day Protection, threat prevention appliances and software, threat intelligence, web security and DDoS protection; mobile security, such as SandBlast Mobile and Check Point Capsule; endpoint security; next-generation firewalls for public and private cloud, data centers and small/medium/enterprise businesses; and security management, including policy management, workflow and orchestration, integration threat management and smart appliances. Industries served by the company include retail/point of sale, financial, automated teller machines, critical infrastructure, public/private cloud, government and federal institutions, healthcare, service providers as well as governance, risk and compliance (GRC). Check Point currently holds 73 U.S. patents, more than 36 U.S. patents pending, and additional patents issued and patent applications pending worldwide. In October 2018, the firm acquired Dome9 of Tel Aviv, Israel to enhance its fully consolidated Infinity architecture and its Cloud Security offering with advanced active policy enforcement and mulit-cloud protection capabilities.

FINANCIAL DATA: Note: Data for latest year may not have been available at press time.

In U.S. $	2018	2017	2016	2015	2014	2013
Revenue		1,854,658,000	1,741,301,000	1,629,838,000	1,495,816,000	1,394,105,000
R&D Expense		192,386,000	178,372,000	149,279,000	133,300,000	121,764,000
Operating Income		923,917,000	852,270,000	839,717,000	801,054,000	760,905,000
Operating Margin %		49.81%	48.94%	51.52%	53.55%	54.58%
SGA Expense		525,392,000	508,656,000	451,785,000	384,921,000	348,802,000
Net Income		802,923,000	724,847,000	685,866,000	659,571,000	652,800,000
Operating Cash Flow		1,109,608,000	946,237,000	946,731,000	785,882,000	811,286,000
Capital Expenditure		28,784,000	24,050,000	17,348,000	12,736,000	9,563,000
EBITDA		1,009,722,000	936,766,000	920,799,000	876,279,000	846,781,000
Return on Assets %		15.03%	14.09%	13.69%	13.41%	13.83%
Return on Equity %		22.64%	20.64%	19.13%	18.22%	18.78%
Debt to Equity						

CONTACT INFORMATION:

Phone: 972 37534555   Fax: 972 35759256
Toll-Free: 800-429-4391
Address: 5 Ha'Solelim St,, Tel Aviv, 6789705 Israel

SALARIES/BONUSES:

Top Exec. Salary: $ 436   Bonus: $
Second Exec. Salary: $ 433   Bonus: $

STOCK TICKER/OTHER:

Stock Ticker: CHKP   Exchange: NAS
Employees: 1,967   Fiscal Year Ends: 12/31
Parent Company:

OTHER THOUGHTS:

Estimated Female Officers or Directors: 3
Hot Spot for Advancement for Women/Minorities: Y

Chewy Inc (Chewy.com)

www.chewy.com

NAIC Code: 454111

TYPES OF BUSINESS:

Electronic Shopping
Pet and Pet Supplies Stores

BRANDS/DIVISIONS/AFFILIATES:

PetSmart Inc
Chewy.com
Chewy.com Rescue and Shelter Network

CONTACTS: *Note: Officers with more than one job title may be intentionally listed here more than once.*

J.K. Symancyk, CEO-PetSmart, Inc.

GROWTH PLANS/SPECIAL FEATURES:

Chewy, Inc., commonly referred to as Chewy.com, is an online retailer of pet food and other pet related products. The firm is a subsidiary of PetSmart, Inc. With items from over 1,000 brands in stock and ready to ship, Chewy offers pet foods and pet products for dogs; cats; fish; birds; small pets such as rabbits, hamsters, gerbils, guinea pigs and chinchillas; reptiles; and horses. Headquartered in Dania Beach, Florida, with fulfillment centers in Nevada, Pennsylvania and Indiana, the firm offers same day shipping on all orders placed before 4 pm and a freshness guarantee combined with a 365-day hassle-free return policy. Customer service agents make up approximately one sixth of the firm's total employees, teams of which are available 24/7/365, and are trained in pet care in order to be better able to address customer questions, concerns and needs. In addition to its online pet food and pet products business, Chewy also operates the Chewy.com Rescue and Shelter Network. This network is free to all registered nonprofit organizations specializing in assisting the needs of pets and grants these organizations access to programs providing donations and fundraising opportunities. A portion of each purchase made on Chewy.com is donated to the organizations within the network.

FINANCIAL DATA: *Note: Data for latest year may not have been available at press time.*

In U.S. $	2018	2017	2016	2015	2014	2013
Revenue		2,000,000,000	880,000,000			
R&D Expense						
Operating Income						
Operating Margin %						
SGA Expense						
Net Income						
Operating Cash Flow						
Capital Expenditure						
EBITDA						
Return on Assets %						
Return on Equity %						
Debt to Equity						

CONTACT INFORMATION:

Phone: 954-793-4144 Fax:
Toll-Free: 800-672-4399
Address: 1855 Griffin Rd., Dania Beach, FL 33004 United States

STOCK TICKER/OTHER:

Stock Ticker: Subsidiary Exchange:
Employees: 3,700 Fiscal Year Ends:
Parent Company: PetSmart Inc

SALARIES/BONUSES:

Top Exec. Salary: $ Bonus: $
Second Exec. Salary: $ Bonus: $

OTHER THOUGHTS:

Estimated Female Officers or Directors:
Hot Spot for Advancement for Women/Minorities:

China Mobile Limited

www.chinamobileltd.com

NAIC Code: 517210

TYPES OF BUSINESS:
Mobile Phone Service
Wireless Music Service
News & Information Service
Instant Messaging Service
Data Services

BRANDS/DIVISIONS/AFFILIATES:
China Mobile Communications Group Co Ltd
SPD Bank

CONTACTS: *Note: Officers with more than one job title may be intentionally listed here more than once.*
Li Yue, CEO
Xue Taohai, CFO
Huang Wnelin, VP
Sha Yuejia, VP
Liu Aili, VP
Xi Guohua, Chmn.

GROWTH PLANS/SPECIAL FEATURES:
China Mobile Limited (CML) is a leading provider of mobile telecommunications services in Mainland China. CML is one of the largest wireless communications providers in the world in terms of total subscribers, with approximately 899 million customers. The firm is a publicly-traded subsidiary of China Mobile Communications Group Co., Ltd., owning a majority 72.72%. CML provides wireless products and services in all 31 Chinese provinces, regions and municipalities, including Hong Kong, through more than 40 wholly-owned subsidiaries. The company offers voice services comprising local calls, domestic long-distance calls, international long-distance calls, intra-provincial roaming, inter-provincial roaming and international roaming, as well as providing voice value-added services such as caller identity display, caller restrictions, call waiting, call forwarding, call holding, voice mail, conference calls and more. The company also offers: SMS (short message services) and other data services; and MMS (multimedia message services), which allows users to combine and deliver several types of messages, including graphics, sounds, text, and motion pictures over wireless networks. In addition, CML provides high-speed internet through wireless local area networks (WLAN) throughout Mainland China. The company's 4G business is based on the TDD mode long-term evolution (LTE) technology and has over 650 million subscribers (by then end of 2017). The firm owns minority interests in SPD Bank.

FINANCIAL DATA: *Note: Data for latest year may not have been available at press time.*

In U.S. $	2018	2017	2016	2015	2014	2013
Revenue		107,772,300,000	103,101,500,000	97,267,550,000	93,354,490,000	91,714,140,000
R&D Expense		5,532,739,000				
Operating Income		19,853,590,000	18,794,660,000	16,830,350,000	18,455,270,000	20,812,680,000
Operating Margin %		18.42%	18.22%	17.30%	19.76%	22.69%
SGA Expense		27,999,890,000	26,546,840,000	22,469,470,000	18,910,220,000	20,505,310,000
Net Income		16,631,830,000	15,825,850,000	15,796,450,000	15,904,150,000	17,710,700,000
Operating Cash Flow		35,731,400,000	36,922,910,000	34,214,170,000	30,711,530,000	32,743,670,000
Capital Expenditure		28,269,560,000	27,763,390,000	25,309,630,000	25,007,500,000	20,432,830,000
EBITDA		43,528,110,000	41,293,100,000	41,000,280,000	37,775,180,000	38,432,280,000
Return on Assets %		7.51%	7.37%	7.96%	8.87%	10.96%
Return on Equity %		11.63%	11.46%	12.23%	13.28%	16.09%
Debt to Equity						

CONTACT INFORMATION:
Phone: 85 231218888   Fax: 85 225119092
Toll-Free:
Address: 99 Queen's Rd. Central, The Center, 60/Fl, Hong Kong, Hong Kong

STOCK TICKER/OTHER:
Stock Ticker: CHL   Exchange: NYS
Employees: 465,000   Fiscal Year Ends: 12/31
Parent Company: China Mobile Communications Group Co Ltd

SALARIES/BONUSES:
Top Exec. Salary: $497,700   Bonus: $
Second Exec. Salary: $91,599   Bonus: $

OTHER THOUGHTS:
Estimated Female Officers or Directors: 1
Hot Spot for Advancement for Women/Minorities: Y

ChinaCache International Holdings Ltd www.chinacache.com

NAIC Code: 517110

TYPES OF BUSINESS:

Internet Content Delivery (Third-Party Networks)
Managed Internet Data Services
Analysis Services

BRANDS/DIVISIONS/AFFILIATES:

ChinaChache Xin Run Technology (Beijing) Co Ltd

CONTACTS: Note: Officers with more than one job title may be intentionally listed here more than once.

Song Wang, CEO
Ken Zhang, Pres.
Song Wang, Chmn.

GROWTH PLANS/SPECIAL FEATURES:

ChinaCache International Holdings Ltd. is a China-based IT services provider. IT services include content delivery network (CDN), data center management, internet exchange center operations and cloud hosting. ChinaCache assists foreign companies to enter the China market, and guides them through its complex internet landscape for establishing businesses, applying for internet content provider (ICP)/Bei'An, improving website speed and other purposes. The firm is a leading CDN service provider in China, with hundreds of employees located worldwide. More than 30,000 servers and 8.2 billion pages are served by ChinaCache every day. The company's CDN, datacenter and internet exchange services have been integrated into a 3-tier internet ecosystem. ChinaCache's solutions also serve the gaming, media, entertainment, travel, education/academic and eCommerce sectors. In April 2018, ChinaCache terminated its agreement to sell 79% of ChinaCache Xin Run Technology (Beijing) Co. Ltd. to investors.

FINANCIAL DATA: Note: Data for latest year may not have been available at press time.

In U.S. $	2018	2017	2016	2015	2014	2013
Revenue		124,080,300	153,430,300	197,003,000	201,463,100	160,562,800
R&D Expense		11,897,370	15,138,480	15,006,330	16,937,750	14,947,240
Operating Income		-36,746,660	-70,762,030	-19,338,240	-2,545,299	-4,980,862
Operating Margin %		-29.61%	-46.11%	-9.81%	-1.26%	-3.10%
SGA Expense		29,761,030	50,881,230	46,301,030	39,563,680	40,480,560
Net Income		-53,726,620	-132,944,800	-12,907,830	-995,619	-4,981,590
Operating Cash Flow		-14,414,140	-27,241,640	112,132,900	40,806,560	17,673,590
Capital Expenditure		12,943,050	8,620,745	13,123,370	36,857,560	20,317,560
EBITDA		-40,944,970	-107,593,100	8,647,815	13,871,140	4,718,022
Return on Assets %		-21.82%	-41.56%	-4.07%	-.47%	-3.31%
Return on Equity %			-315.52%	-11.39%	-.91%	-5.20%
Debt to Equity				0.15	0.03	

CONTACT INFORMATION:

Phone: 86 106408-4466   Fax: 86 106408-5888
Toll-Free: 866-998-3399
Address: No. 7 Jiuxianqiao North Rd., Chaoyang Dist., A, Bldg 3, Beijing, 100015 China

STOCK TICKER/OTHER:

Stock Ticker: CCIH   Exchange: NAS
Employees: 1,196   Fiscal Year Ends: 12/31
Parent Company:

SALARIES/BONUSES:

Top Exec. Salary: $ Bonus: $
Second Exec. Salary: $ Bonus: $

OTHER THOUGHTS:

Estimated Female Officers or Directors: 4
Hot Spot for Advancement for Women/Minorities: Y

Ciena Corporation

www.ciena.com

NAIC Code: 334210

TYPES OF BUSINESS:

Communications Networking Equipment
Software & Support Services
Consulting Services
Switching Platforms
Packet Interworking Products
Access Products
Network & Service Management Tools

BRANDS/DIVISIONS/AFFILIATES:

8700 Packetwave

CONTACTS: Note: Officers with more than one job title may be intentionally listed here more than once.

Gary Smith, CEO
James Moylan, CFO
Patrick Nettles, Chairman of the Board
Andrew Petrik, Chief Accounting Officer
Stephen Alexander, Chief Technology Officer
David Rothenstein, General Counsel
James Frodsham, Other Executive Officer
Scott McFeely, Senior VP, Divisional
Jason Phipps, Senior VP, Divisional
Rick Hamilton, Senior VP, Divisional

GROWTH PLANS/SPECIAL FEATURES:

Ciena Corporation provides communications networking equipment, software and services that support the transport, switching, aggregation and management of voice, video and data traffic. Its product portfolio includes a range of communications networking equipment and software that is utilized from the core of communications networks, from metropolitan network infrastructures to the network edge, where end users gain access to communications services. Products are offered in three major categories: converged packet optical, packet networking and optical transport. Ciena's converged packet optical portfolio includes networking solutions optimized for the convergence of coherent optical transport, OTN (optical transport network) switching and packet switching. This portfolio also includes products that provide packet switching capability to allocate network capacity efficiently and enable rapid service delivery. Packet Networking products allow customers to deliver new, revenue-generating services to customers and enterprise end users. These products have applications from the edge of metro and core networks where they aggregate traffic, to the access tiers of networks where they can be deployed to support wireless backhaul infrastructures and to deliver business data services. This segment's 8700 Packetwave is a multi-terabit packet switching platform for high-density metro networks and inter-data center wide area networks. Optical transport products include stand-alone WDM (wavelength division multiplexing) and SONET/SDH-based (synchronous optical networking/synchronous digital hierarchy) optical transport solutions that add capacity to core, regional and metro networks, as well as enable cost-effective and efficient transport voice, video and data traffic at high transmission speeds. In 2018, Ciena agreed to acquire Packet Design, LLC, a provider of network performance management software focused on Layer 3 network optimization, topology and route analytics, and DonRiver, a global software and services company.

Ciena offers medical, dental and vision insurance; short- and long-term disability; flexible spending accounts; stock options; 401(k); as well as employee and educational assistance.

FINANCIAL DATA: Note: Data for latest year may not have been available at press time.

In U.S. $	2018	2017	2016	2015	2014	2013
Revenue	3,094,286,000	2,801,687,000	2,600,573,000	2,445,669,000	2,288,289,000	2,082,546,000
R&D Expense	491,564,000	475,329,000	451,794,000	414,201,000	401,180,000	383,408,000
Operating Income	253,196,000	238,655,000	165,715,000	134,613,000	46,053,000	5,394,000
Operating Margin %		8.51%	6.37%	5.50%	2.01%	.25%
SGA Expense	554,193,000	498,773,000	482,559,000	457,238,000	455,149,000	426,602,000
Net Income	-344,690,000	1,261,953,000	72,584,000	11,667,000	-40,637,000	-85,431,000
Operating Cash Flow	229,261,000	234,882,000	289,520,000	262,112,000	89,816,000	44,678,000
Capital Expenditure	67,616,000	94,600,000	107,185,000	62,109,000	48,216,000	43,814,000
EBITDA	314,050,000	334,880,000	285,066,000	210,710,000	133,209,000	90,858,000
Return on Assets %		36.93%	2.60%	.48%	-2.09%	-4.63%
Return on Equity %		86.95%	10.46%	4.23%		
Debt to Equity		0.30	1.37	2.07		

CONTACT INFORMATION:

Phone: 410 694-5700   Fax: 410 694-5750
Toll-Free: 800-921-1144
Address: 7035 Ridge Rd., Hanover, MD 21076 United States

STOCK TICKER/OTHER:

Stock Ticker: CIEN   Exchange: NYS
Employees: 5,555   Fiscal Year Ends: 10/31
Parent Company:

SALARIES/BONUSES:

Top Exec. Salary: $420,000   Bonus: $615,000
Second Exec. Salary: $900,000   Bonus: $

OTHER THOUGHTS:

Estimated Female Officers or Directors: 2
Hot Spot for Advancement for Women/Minorities:

Sales, profits and employees may be estimates. Financial information, benefits and other data can change quickly and may vary from those stated here.

Cincinnati Bell Inc

www.cincinnatibell.com

NAIC Code: 517110

TYPES OF BUSINESS:

Local Telephone Service
Wireless Local Phone Service
Long-Distance Service
Data Services
Internet Access
Digital Services
Payphone Services
IT Consulting

BRANDS/DIVISIONS/AFFILIATES:

Cincinnati Bell Telephone Company LLC
Cincinnati Bell Extended Territories LLC
CBTS Technology Solutions LLC
Hawaiian Telecom Holdco Inc

CONTACTS: Note: Officers with more than one job title may be intentionally listed here more than once.

Andrew Kaiser, CFO
Phillip Cox, Chairman of the Board
Thomas Simpson, COO
Leigh Fox, Director
Christi Cornette, Other Executive Officer
Joshua Duckworth, Vice President, Divisional
Shannon Mullen, Vice President
Christopher Wilson, Vice President

GROWTH PLANS/SPECIAL FEATURES:

Cincinnati Bell, Inc. provides integrated communications and information technology (IT) solutions to residential and business customers. The company operates through two business segments: entertainment and communications and IT services and hardware. The entertainment and communications segment provides high-speed data, video and voice solutions over an expanding fiber network, as well as a copper network. Subsidiary Cincinnati Bell Telephone Company, LLC, is the incumbent local exchange carrier for a geography that covers about 25 miles around Cincinnati, and includes parts of northern Kentucky and southeastern Indiana. This segment also provides voice and data services in Dayton and Mason, Ohio, through Cincinnati Bell Extended Territories, LLC, a subsidiary of Cincinnati Bell Telephone. Long distance and voice-over-internet-protocol (VoIP) services are provided primarily through CBTS Technology Solutions LLC, a subsidiary of the company, and operate within the entertainment and communications segment. The IT services and hardware segment sells and services end-to-end communications and IT systems and solutions. These systems and solutions include professional services such as consulting and staff augmentation; unified communications, including voice monitoring and managed IP telephony; cloud services, including virtual data centers, storage and backup; monitoring and management, including network monitoring and management and security; and the licensing of IT hardware and software. In July 2018, Cincinnati Bell completed an acquisition of Hawaiian Telecom Holdco, Inc., an integrated communications provider serving Hawaii and is the state's fiber-centric technology leader.

FINANCIAL DATA: Note: Data for latest year may not have been available at press time.

In U.S. $	2018	2017	2016	2015	2014	2013
Revenue		1,288,500,000	1,185,800,000	1,167,800,000	1,278,200,000	1,256,900,000
R&D Expense						
Operating Income		89,300,000	106,000,000	135,100,000	120,600,000	179,300,000
Operating Margin %		6.93%	8.93%	11.56%	9.43%	14.26%
SGA Expense		240,900,000	218,700,000	220,500,000	227,500,000	265,000,000
Net Income		35,100,000	102,100,000	353,700,000	75,600,000	-54,700,000
Operating Cash Flow		203,400,000	173,200,000	110,900,000	175,200,000	78,800,000
Capital Expenditure		210,500,000	286,400,000	283,600,000	182,300,000	196,900,000
EBITDA		344,200,000	420,800,000	723,900,000	512,700,000	294,400,000
Return on Assets %		1.33%	6.12%	20.97%	3.32%	-2.61%
Return on Equity %						
Debt to Equity						

CONTACT INFORMATION:

Phone: 513 397-9900   Fax: 513 784-1613
Toll-Free: 800-345-6301
Address: 221 E. Fourth St., Cincinnati, OH 45202 United States

STOCK TICKER/OTHER:

Stock Ticker: CBB   Exchange: NYS
Employees: 3,400   Fiscal Year Ends: 12/31
Parent Company:

SALARIES/BONUSES:

Top Exec. Salary: $775,913   Bonus: $
Second Exec. Salary: $422,950   Bonus: $

OTHER THOUGHTS:

Estimated Female Officers or Directors:
Hot Spot for Advancement for Women/Minorities: Y

Cisco Systems Inc

www.cisco.com

NAIC Code: 334210A

TYPES OF BUSINESS:

Computer Networking Equipment
Routers & Switches
Real-Time Conferencing Technology
Server Virtualization Software
Data Storage Products
Security Products
Teleconference Systems and Technology
Unified Communications Systems

BRANDS/DIVISIONS/AFFILIATES:

Jasper
AppDynamics Inc
MindMeld
Stealthwatch Cloud
BroadSoft
Accompany
Duo Security

CONTACTS: *Note: Officers with more than one job title may be intentionally listed here more than once.*

Charles Robbins, CEO
Prat Bhatt, Chief Accounting Officer
Geraldine Elliott, Chief Marketing Officer
Kelly Kramer, Executive VP
David Goeckeler, Executive VP
Maria Martinez, Executive VP
Mark Chandler, Executive VP
Irving Tan, Senior VP, Divisional

GROWTH PLANS/SPECIAL FEATURES:

Cisco Systems, Inc. designs and sells a broad range of technologies that power the internet. The company's products and services are grouped into the categories of infrastructure platforms, applications and security. Infrastructure platforms consist of Cisco's core networking technologies of switching, routing, data center products, and wireless that are designed to work together to deliver networking capabilities and transport and/or store data. These technologies consist of both hardware and software that help customers build networks, automate, orchestrate, integrate and digitize data. The applications category primarily consists of software-related offerings that utilize the core networking and data center platforms to provide their function. These offerings encompass hardware- and software-based solutions, including licenses and software-as-a-service (SaaS). Applications include collaboration products/solutions such as unified communications, telepresence and conferencing; and the Internet of Things (IoT) and analytics software from Jasper and AppDynamics. Cisco's Jasper control center platform enables enterprises to automate the lifecycle of connected devices, including tools designed to automatically and remotely onboard, manage and monetize their IoT devices. Subsidiary AppDynamics, Inc. is an application intelligence software company, whose products enable companies to improve application and business performance. Subsidiary MindMeld is an AI company with a platform that enables customers to build intelligent and human-like conversational interfaces for any application or device. Last, the security category includes Cisco's unified threat management products, advanced threat security products and web security products, all of which are designed to provide a highly secure environment for customers. Its Stealthwatch Cloud offering offers behavioral threat detection for infrastructure-as-a-service and platform-as-a-service environments. During 2018, Cisco acquired BroadSoft, Accompany and Duo Security; sold its service provider video software solutions business to Permira Funds; and announced its intent to purchase silicon photonics leader, Luxtera, Inc.

FINANCIAL DATA: *Note: Data for latest year may not have been available at press time.*

In U.S. $	2018	2017	2016	2015	2014	2013
Revenue	49,329,000,000	48,005,000,000	49,247,000,000	49,161,000,000	47,142,000,000	48,607,000,000
R&D Expense	6,332,000,000	6,059,000,000	6,296,000,000	6,207,000,000	6,294,000,000	5,942,000,000
Operating Income	12,667,000,000	12,729,000,000	12,928,000,000	11,254,000,000	9,763,000,000	11,301,000,000
Operating Margin %		26.51%	26.25%	22.89%	20.70%	23.24%
SGA Expense	11,386,000,000	11,177,000,000	11,433,000,000	11,861,000,000	11,437,000,000	11,802,000,000
Net Income	110,000,000	9,609,000,000	10,739,000,000	8,981,000,000	7,853,000,000	9,983,000,000
Operating Cash Flow	13,666,000,000	13,876,000,000	13,570,000,000	12,552,000,000	12,332,000,000	12,894,000,000
Capital Expenditure	834,000,000	964,000,000	1,146,000,000	1,227,000,000	1,275,000,000	1,160,000,000
EBITDA	16,174,000,000	15,434,000,000	15,746,000,000	14,209,000,000	12,711,000,000	14,161,000,000
Return on Assets %		7.64%	9.13%	8.21%	7.61%	10.34%
Return on Equity %		14.81%	17.42%	15.43%	13.56%	18.08%
Debt to Equity		0.38	0.38	0.35	0.36	0.21

CONTACT INFORMATION:

Phone: 408 526-4000   Fax: 408 526-4100
Toll-Free: 800-553-6387
Address: 170 W. Tasman Dr., San Jose, CA 95134 United States

STOCK TICKER/OTHER:

Stock Ticker: CSCO   Exchange: NAS
Employees: 74,200   Fiscal Year Ends: 07/31
Parent Company:

SALARIES/BONUSES:

Top Exec. Salary: $194,712   Bonus: $6,500,000
Second Exec. Salary: $187,500   Bonus: $6,000,000

OTHER THOUGHTS:

Estimated Female Officers or Directors: 10
Hot Spot for Advancement for Women/Minorities: Y

Sales, profits and employees may be estimates. Financial information, benefits and other data can change quickly and may vary from those stated here.

Cloudflare Inc

NAIC Code: 511210E

www.cloudflare.com

TYPES OF BUSINESS:

Computer Software, Security & Anti-Virus
Web Content Delivery

BRANDS/DIVISIONS/AFFILIATES:

Anycast
Cloudflare Load Balancing
Argo Smart Routing
Cloudflare Stream

CONTACTS: *Note: Officers with more than one job title may be intentionally listed here more than once.*

Matthew Prince, CEO
Lee Holloway, Lead Engineer
Michelle Zatlyn, Head-User Experience

GROWTH PLANS/SPECIAL FEATURES:

Cloudflare, Inc. is a web performance and security firm, helping companies deliver content safely and quickly. The company routes all a website's traffic through its globally-distributed network, weeding out attackers from harming the website. Performance products include CDN (content delivery network), DNS (domain name system), web optimizers, Chinese network performance, load balancing and smart routing. The CDN consists of specially-designed hardware and software platforms located in 155 data centers worldwide (21 in China). Using its proprietary technology Anycast, Cloudflare routes visitors to the nearest center, reducing hops and lowering latency. The DNS is powered by the same network as the CDN, Cloudflare uses its DNS infrastructure to ensure a faster and more secure DNS process. Optimizers ensure that every web page renders as fast and efficiently as possible from any device. Users can choose any combination of web content optimization features. Cloudflare partners with Baidu, a Chinese web-search service, to deliver its products to China. Cloudflare Load Balancing addresses latency and access issues by providing local and global load balancing services and system health checks. Argo Smart Routing reduces internet latency on average by 36% and reduces timeouts by 42% and uses the same network of data centers as the CDN. Security products use proprietary software which detects new attacks by mitigating DDoS attacks, alerting the system to known threats, failed browser integrity checks, active security stops, blocks by IP address rules and blocks by country rules. Analytics provide in depth data on website traffic, which helps to monitor threats including crawlers and bots. Last, Cloudflare offers Cloudflare Stream, a video streaming and delivery service using Cloudflare's global Anycast network to quickly deliver video, reduce startup times and reduce buffering. Using Cloudflare's network reduces the bandwidth needed to successfully stream and upload video.

FINANCIAL DATA: *Note: Data for latest year may not have been available at press time.*

In U.S. $	2018	2017	2016	2015	2014	2013
Revenue		100,000,000	80,000,000	78,000,000	45,000,000	10,000,000
R&D Expense						
Operating Income						
Operating Margin %						
SGA Expense						
Net Income						
Operating Cash Flow						
Capital Expenditure						
EBITDA						
Return on Assets %						
Return on Equity %						
Debt to Equity						

CONTACT INFORMATION:

Phone: 650-319-8930   Fax: 650-230-7173
Toll-Free:
Address: 665 3rd St. Ste. 207, San Francisco, CA 94107 United States

STOCK TICKER/OTHER:

Stock Ticker: Private   Exchange:
Employees: 311   Fiscal Year Ends:
Parent Company:

SALARIES/BONUSES:

Top Exec. Salary: $ Bonus: $
Second Exec. Salary: $ Bonus: $

OTHER THOUGHTS:

Estimated Female Officers or Directors: 1
Hot Spot for Advancement for Women/Minorities:

Cogent Communications Group Inc

www.cogentco.com

NAIC Code: 517110

TYPES OF BUSINESS:

Facilities-Based Internet Service Provider
VoIP Service

BRANDS/DIVISIONS/AFFILIATES:

CONTACTS: Note: Officers with more than one job title may be intentionally listed here more than once.

Robert Beury, Assistant Secretary
David Schaeffer, CEO
Thaddeus Weed, CFO
R. Kummer, Chief Technology Officer
James Bubeck, Other Executive Officer
Bryant Banks, Vice President, Divisional
Henry Kilmer, Vice President, Divisional
Timothy ONeill, Vice President, Divisional

GROWTH PLANS/SPECIAL FEATURES:

Cogent Communications Group, Inc. is a facilities-based provider of low-cost, high-speed internet access and internet protocol (IP) communications services. The firm's network is specifically designed and optimized to transmit data using IP. Cogent delivers its services primarily to small- and medium-sized businesses, communications service providers and other bandwidth-intensive organizations in North America, Europe and Asia. The company offers on-net internet access at speeds ranging from 100 megabits per second to 100 gigabits per second. This on-net service is offered via Cogent's own facilities, which run all the way to its customers' premises. Corporate customers are located in multi-tenant office buildings and in Cogent's data centers and typically include law firms, financial services firms, advertising and marketing firms and other professional services businesses. Bandwidth-intensive customers include universities, other internet service providers, telephone companies, cable television companies, web hosting companies, content delivery networks and commercial content and application service providers. Cogent delivers its internet, ethernet and colocation services to over 78,000 enterprise and net-centric customers. The firm serves more than 200 markets in 43 countries across its facilities-based, all-optical IP network.

FINANCIAL DATA: Note: Data for latest year may not have been available at press time.

In U.S. $	2018	2017	2016	2015	2014	2013
Revenue		485,175,000	446,900,000	404,234,000	380,003,000	347,979,000
R&D Expense						
Operating Income		72,056,000	56,890,000	46,094,000	42,950,000	46,154,000
Operating Margin %		14.85%	12.72%	11.40%	11.30%	13.26%
SGA Expense		127,915,000	120,709,000	113,103,000	107,679,000	87,242,000
Net Income		5,876,000	14,929,000	4,896,000	797,000	56,689,000
Operating Cash Flow		111,702,000	107,967,000	83,809,000	73,046,000	81,851,000
Capital Expenditure		45,801,000	45,234,000	35,582,000	60,032,000	49,031,000
EBITDA		155,511,000	140,298,000	124,519,000	123,917,000	113,142,000
Return on Assets %		.81%	2.13%	.68%	.10%	8.32%
Return on Equity %				13.69%	.57%	32.09%
Debt to Equity					7.11	2.05

CONTACT INFORMATION:

Phone: 202 295-4200   Fax:
Toll-Free: 877-875-4432
Address: 2450 N St. NW, Washington, DC 20037 United States

STOCK TICKER/OTHER:

Stock Ticker: CCOI
Employees: 897
Parent Company:

Exchange: NAS
Fiscal Year Ends: 12/31

SALARIES/BONUSES:

Top Exec. Salary: $303,919   Bonus: $
Second Exec. Salary: $299,453   Bonus: $

OTHER THOUGHTS:

Estimated Female Officers or Directors:
Hot Spot for Advancement for Women/Minorities:

Comcast Corporation

corporate.comcast.com

NAIC Code: 517110

TYPES OF BUSINESS:

Cable Television
VoIP Service
Cable Network Programming
High-Speed Internet Service
Video-on-Demand
Advertising Services
Interactive Program Schedules
Wireless Services

BRANDS/DIVISIONS/AFFILIATES:

XFINITY
NBC Universal
Telemundo
Sky plc
Comcast Spectator
Philadelphia Flyers
Wells Fargo Center
Amblin Partners

CONTACTS: *Note: Officers with more than one job title may be intentionally listed here more than once.*

Stephen Burke, CEO, Subsidiary
Dave Watson, CEO, Subsidiary
Brian Roberts, CEO
Michael Cavanagh, CFO
Daniel Murdock, Chief Accounting Officer
Joseph Collins, Director Emeritus
Judith Rodin, Director Emeritus
Arthur Block, Executive VP
David Cohen, Senior Executive VP

GROWTH PLANS/SPECIAL FEATURES:

Comcast Corporation provides information, entertainment and communications products and services. Comcast operates through five segments: cable communications, cable networks, broadcast television, filmed entertainment and theme parks. The cable communications segment maintains the firm's video, high-speed internet and voice servicing operations, serving residential customers under the XFINITY brand. This division also sells advertising, as well as video, high-speed internet, voice and other services to small- and medium-sized businesses. The cable networks segment includes the firm's national cable networks, its regional sports and news networks, its international cable networks and its cable television production operations. The broadcast television segment consists primarily of the company's NBC and Telemundo broadcast networks, its 11 NBC- and 17 Telemundo-owned local broadcast television stations and its broadcast television production operations. Filmed entertainment is comprised of the studio operations of Universal Pictures, which produces, acquires, markets and distributes filmed entertainment worldwide. Theme parks is comprised of the Universal theme parks in Orlando, Florida; Hollywood, California; and Osaka, Japan. Additionally, subsidiary Comcast Spectator owns the Philadelphia Flyers and the Wells Fargo Center in Philadelphia, Pennsylvania, and operates arena management-related businesses. In October 2018, Comcast acquired control of UK/EU media and telecommunications giant Sky plc at a value of $38.8 billion. In December 2018, Comcast announced that, in conjunction with Amazon, its customers will be able to watch Amazon Prime Video on Comcast's Xfinity X1 at no additional cost.

FINANCIAL DATA: *Note: Data for latest year may not have been available at press time.*

In U.S. $	2018	2017	2016	2015	2014	2013
Revenue		84,526,000,000	80,403,000,000	74,510,000,000	68,775,000,000	64,657,000,000
R&D Expense						
Operating Income		17,987,000,000	16,859,000,000	15,998,000,000	14,904,000,000	13,563,000,000
Operating Margin %		21.27%	20.96%	21.47%	21.67%	20.97%
SGA Expense		31,330,000,000	29,523,000,000	27,282,000,000	24,940,000,000	23,553,000,000
Net Income		22,714,000,000	8,695,000,000	8,163,000,000	8,380,000,000	6,816,000,000
Operating Cash Flow		21,403,000,000	19,240,000,000	18,778,000,000	16,945,000,000	14,160,000,000
Capital Expenditure		11,297,000,000	10,821,000,000	9,869,000,000	8,542,000,000	7,605,000,000
EBITDA		28,675,000,000	26,853,000,000	24,754,000,000	23,101,000,000	29,809,000,000
Return on Assets %		12.36%	5.01%	5.00%	5.26%	4.21%
Return on Equity %		37.06%	16.37%	15.55%	16.20%	13.62%
Debt to Equity		0.86	1.03	0.93	0.83	0.87

CONTACT INFORMATION:

Phone: 215 286-1700   Fax:
Toll-Free: 800-266-2278
Address: One Comcast Center, Philadelphia, PA 19103 United States

STOCK TICKER/OTHER:

Stock Ticker: CMCSA
Employees: 166,000
Parent Company:

Exchange: NAS
Fiscal Year Ends: 12/31

SALARIES/BONUSES:

Top Exec. Salary: $3,103,566   Bonus: $
Second Exec. Salary: $2,881,100   Bonus: $

OTHER THOUGHTS:

Estimated Female Officers or Directors: 16
Hot Spot for Advancement for Women/Minorities: Y

comScore Inc

NAIC Code: 541613

TYPES OF BUSINESS:

Marketing Consulting Services

BRANDS/DIVISIONS/AFFILIATES:

Campaign Essentials

CONTACTS: Note: Officers with more than one job title may be intentionally listed here more than once.

Gregory Fink, CFO
Joseph Rostock, Chief Information Officer
Bryan Wiener, Director
Brent Rosenthal, Director
William Livek, Director
Carol Dibattiste, General Counsel
Christopher Wilson, Other Executive Officer
Daniel Hess, Other Executive Officer
Sarah Hofstetter, President

GROWTH PLANS/SPECIAL FEATURES:

comScore, Inc. is a leading cross-platform measurement company. The firm measures audiences, brands and consumer behavior at massive scale. Built on precision and innovation, comScore's data footprint combines proprietary digital, TV and movie intelligence with vast demographic details to quantify consumers' multiscreen behavior. More than 1.9 trillion global interactions are captured by the firm monthly. This approach helps media companies monetize their complete audiences and allows marketers to reach audiences more effectively. Industries the company serves include agencies, consumer packaged goods, education, energy, financial services, government, health care, investment research, manufacturing, media, pharmaceutical, professional services, retail, technology, telecommunications and travel. comScore's Campaign Essentials (vCE) software features sophisticated ad fraud protection, expanded reported capabilities, technology innovation and recent industry certifications. vCE is a multi-platform advertising measurement offering. The company has more than 3,200 clients and a global footprint in more than 70 countries.

FINANCIAL DATA: Note: Data for latest year may not have been available at press time.

In U.S. $	2018	2017	2016	2015	2014	2013
Revenue		403,549,000	399,460,000	270,803,000	329,151,000	286,860,000
R&D Expense		89,023,000	86,975,000	52,718,000	60,364,000	41,025,000
Operating Income		-202,460,000	-162,936,000	-71,264,000	-2,358,000	1,519,000
Operating Margin %		-50.16%	-40.78%	-26.31%	-.71%	.52%
SGA Expense		288,558,000	270,445,000	168,837,000	166,448,000	146,396,000
Net Income		-281,393,000	-117,173,000	-78,222,000	-9,903,000	-2,333,000
Operating Cash Flow		-56,405,000	-55,912,000	59,357,000	49,497,000	44,574,000
Capital Expenditure		10,182,000	7,106,000	4,325,000	7,649,000	4,597,000
EBITDA		-144,298,000	-105,601,000	-40,061,000	22,855,000	26,253,000
Return on Assets %		-26.25%	-10.45%		-2.76%	-.66%
Return on Equity %		-36.04%	-12.94%		-5.29%	-1.18%
Debt to Equity					0.07	0.06

CONTACT INFORMATION:

Phone: 703 438-2000   Fax: 703 438-2051
Toll-Free:
Address: 11950 Democracy Road, Reston, VA 20190 United States

STOCK TICKER/OTHER:

Stock Ticker: SCOR   Exchange: NAS
Employees: 1,292   Fiscal Year Ends: 12/31
Parent Company:

SALARIES/BONUSES:

Top Exec. Salary: $355,590   Bonus: $2,008,000
Second Exec. Salary: Bonus: $444,000
$443,700

OTHER THOUGHTS:

Estimated Female Officers or Directors: 1
Hot Spot for Advancement for Women/Minorities:

Sales, profits and employees may be estimates. Financial information, benefits and other data can change quickly and may vary from those stated here.

CoreSite Realty Corporation

NAIC Code: 517110

TYPES OF BUSINESS:

Data Center Operation
Colocation Services
Peering Services

BRANDS/DIVISIONS/AFFILIATES:

CONTACTS: *Note: Officers with more than one job title may be intentionally listed here more than once.*

Jeffrey Finnin, CFO
Robert Stuckey, Chairman of the Board
Mark Jones, Chief Accounting Officer
Derek McCandless, General Counsel
Paul Szurek, President
Juan Font, Senior VP, Divisional
Steven Smith, Senior VP, Divisional
Brian Warren, Senior VP, Divisional
Dominic Tobin, Senior VP, Divisional

GROWTH PLANS/SPECIAL FEATURES:

CoreSite Realty Corporation is a real estate investment trust (REIT) that owns, operates, constructs and manages data centers and provides data center solutions. Data centers are highly specialized and secure buildings that house networking, storage and communications technology infrastructure, including servers, storage devices, switches, routers and fiber optic transmission equipment. These buildings are designed to provide the power, cooling and network connectivity necessary to efficiently operate mission-critical equipment. Through the data centers, CoreSite assists more than 1,200 clients, which are grouped into the following industry verticals: enterprise, which includes digital content, multimedia, systems integrators, managed service providers, as well as financial, healthcare, education, government, manufacturing and professional services; cloud and IT service providers; and networks and mobility, which includes domestic and international telecommunications carriers, internet service providers and content delivery networks (CDNs). CoreSite's 20 data centers are located in Boston, Chicago, Denver, Los Angeles, Miami, New York, Virginia, Washington, D.C. and Silicon Valley.

FINANCIAL DATA: *Note: Data for latest year may not have been available at press time.*

In U.S. $	2018	2017	2016	2015	2014	2013
Revenue		481,821,000	400,352,000	333,292,000	272,420,000	234,833,000
R&D Expense						
Operating Income		124,988,000	94,743,000	64,457,000	46,208,000	34,949,000
Operating Margin %		25.90%	23.63%	19.32%	16.93%	14.76%
SGA Expense		79,849,000	75,495,000	71,184,000	62,793,000	61,381,000
Net Income		74,855,000	58,709,000	34,706,000	22,765,000	18,841,000
Operating Cash Flow		209,356,000	170,525,000	142,573,000	99,516,000	97,723,000
Capital Expenditure		7,850,000	5,878,000	7,736,000	5,893,000	7,128,000
EBITDA		252,387,000	201,971,000	158,582,000	124,226,000	98,748,000
Return on Assets %		4.19%	3.85%	2.35%	1.37%	1.12%
Return on Equity %		20.80%	16.20%	10.36%	6.78%	4.76%
Debt to Equity		3.34	2.15	1.29	1.53	1.06

CONTACT INFORMATION:

Phone: 866-777-2673   Fax:
Toll-Free:
Address: 1001 17th St., Ste. 500, Denver, CO 80202 United States

STOCK TICKER/OTHER:

Stock Ticker: COR   Exchange: NYS
Employees: 422   Fiscal Year Ends: 12/31
Parent Company:

SALARIES/BONUSES:

Top Exec. Salary: $580,000   Bonus: $
Second Exec. Salary: Bonus: $
$413,269

OTHER THOUGHTS:

Estimated Female Officers or Directors:
Hot Spot for Advancement for Women/Minorities:

CoStar Group Inc

www.costar.com

NAIC Code: 519130

TYPES OF BUSINESS:

Online Commercial Real Estate Information

BRANDS/DIVISIONS/AFFILIATES:

CoStar
LoopNet
Apartments.com
BizBuySell
LandsofAmerica
CoStar Property
Cozy Services Ltd
Realla

CONTACTS: Note: Officers with more than one job title may be intentionally listed here more than once.

Andrew Florance, CEO
Scott Wheeler, CFO
Michael Klein, Chairman of the Board
Frank Simuro, Chief Technology Officer
Frank Carchedi, Executive VP, Divisional
Matthew Linnington, Executive VP, Divisional
Giles Newman, Managing Director, Geographical
Frederick Saint, President, Subsidiary
Cameron Stewart, President, Subsidiary
Jonathan Coleman, Secretary
Lisa Ruggles, Senior VP, Divisional
Donna Tanenbaum, Vice President, Divisional

GROWTH PLANS/SPECIAL FEATURES:

CoStar Group, Inc. provides information, analytics and online marketplaces to the commercial real estate industry in the U.S. and the U.K. The firm provides industry professionals and consumers of commercial real estate and apartments ways to explore and complete transactions. The company's five flagship brands include CoStar, LoopNet, Apartments.com, BizBuySell and LandsofAmerica. Subscription-based information services comprise the CoStar suite, which is sold as a platform consisting of CoStar Property, CoStar COMPS, CoStar Tenant, CoStar Investment Analysis, CoStar Real Estate Manager, CoStar Private Sale Network, CoStar Portfolio Strategy, CoStar Brokerage Applications, CoStar Mobile, CoStar Lease, CoStar Risk and CoStar Advertising. LoopNet is an online marketplace that enables commercial property owners, landlords and real estate agents working on their behalf to list properties for sale or for lease, and to submit detailed information about property listings. Apartments.com comprises a network of apartment marketing sites, including ApartmentFinder.com and ApartmentHomeLiving.com. This network of subscription-based services offers renters a searchable database of apartment listings and provides professional property management companies and landlords with an advertising destination. BizBuySell and BizQuest.com are leading online marketplaces for operating businesses for sale. Business sellers pay a fee to list their operating businesses for sale, and interested buyers can search the respective sites' listings for free. These sites also allow interested business buyers to search hundreds of franchise opportunities, and franchisors can list their availabilities in the directory on a cost-per-lead basis. LandsofAmerica and LandAndFarm are online marketplaces for rural land for sale. Sellers pay a fee to list their land for sale, and interested buyers can search the listings for free. During 2018, CoStar Group acquired Cozy Services Ltd., a provider of online rental solutions; and U.K. commercial property marketplace, Realla.

The firm offers employees medical, dental, vision, life and disability insurance; 401(k); and various employee assistance programs.

FINANCIAL DATA: Note: Data for latest year may not have been available at press time.

In U.S. $	2018	2017	2016	2015	2014	2013
Revenue		965,230,000	837,630,000	711,764,000	575,936,000	440,943,000
R&D Expense		88,850,000	76,400,000	65,760,000	55,426,000	46,757,000
Operating Income		173,816,000	144,905,000	39,386,000	109,310,000	69,337,000
Operating Margin %		18.00%	17.29%	1.60%	14.04%	12.28%
SGA Expense		464,490,000	419,780,000	417,733,000	254,221,000	195,664,000
Net Income		122,695,000	85,071,000	-3,465,000	44,869,000	29,734,000
Operating Cash Flow		234,703,000	195,944,000	131,245,000	143,909,000	108,298,000
Capital Expenditure		24,499,000	18,766,000	35,061,000	27,444,000	19,042,000
EBITDA		237,715,000	216,843,000	90,524,000	151,766,000	94,538,000
Return on Assets %		4.85%	3.98%	-.16%	2.68%	2.45%
Return on Equity %		5.69%	5.32%	-.22%	3.67%	3.39%
Debt to Equity			0.18	0.21	0.24	0.13

CONTACT INFORMATION:

Phone: 202-346-6500   Fax: 202 346-6370
Toll-Free: 800-204-5960
Address: 1331 L Street NW, Northwest, WA 20005 United States

STOCK TICKER/OTHER:

Stock Ticker: CSGP   Exchange: NAS
Employees: 3,064   Fiscal Year Ends: 12/31
Parent Company:

SALARIES/BONUSES:

Top Exec. Salary: $742,039   Bonus: $
Second Exec. Salary: Bonus: $
$464,318

OTHER THOUGHTS:

Estimated Female Officers or Directors:
Hot Spot for Advancement for Women/Minorities: Y

Sales, profits and employees may be estimates. Financial information, benefits and other data can change quickly and may vary from those stated here.

Coupa Software Inc

coupa.com

NAIC Code: 511210Q

TYPES OF BUSINESS:

Computer Software, Accounting, Banking & Financial

BRANDS/DIVISIONS/AFFILIATES:

Unified Spend Suite
Hiperos
Aquiire
DCR Workforce

CONTACTS: *Note: Officers with more than one job title may be intentionally listed here more than once.*

Robert Bernshteyn, CEO
Todd Ford, CFO
Chandar Pattabhiram, CMO
Ray Martinelli, Exec. VP-Human Resources
David Williams, VP-IT

GROWTH PLANS/SPECIAL FEATURES:

Coupa Software, Inc. is a U.S. maker of cloud-based software that helps companies manage spending. The company's solutions include maximizing profitability, supplier success, financial compliance, scaling for growth, accounts payable automation, mobile productivity, global operations, multi-enterprise resource planning integration, spend visibility, mergers/acquisitions integration and data cleansing. These solutions are for emerging, small, mid-size and Fortune 500 businesses. Coupa Software's Unified Spend Suite includes procurement, invoicing, expenses, sourcing, inventory, contract lifecycle management, budgeting, analytics, open business networking, supplier information management, storefront and more. Industries primarily served by Coupa Software include education, financial services, food and beverage, healthcare, pharmaceutical, high-tech, manufacturing, oil and gas, public sector and retail. During 2018, the firm acquired Hiperos, a third-party risk management provider; Aquiire, a real-time supplier of catalog search solutions; and DCR Workforce, offering contingent workforce management, related services and procurement.

Coupa Software offers employees a variety of health insurance options, 401(k), paid time off and more.

FINANCIAL DATA: *Note: Data for latest year may not have been available at press time.*

In U.S. $	2018	2017	2016	2015	2014	2013
Revenue	186,780,000	133,775,000	83,678,000	50,845,000		
R&D Expense						
Operating Income						
Operating Margin %						
SGA Expense						
Net Income	-43,805,000	-37,607,000	-46,156,000	-27,300,000		
Operating Cash Flow						
Capital Expenditure						
EBITDA						
Return on Assets %						
Return on Equity %						
Debt to Equity						

CONTACT INFORMATION:

Phone: 650-931-3200   Fax:
Toll-Free:
Address: 1855 S. Grant St., San Mateo, CA 94402 United States

STOCK TICKER/OTHER:

Stock Ticker: COUP
Employees: 833
Parent Company:

Exchange:
Fiscal Year Ends: 01/31

SALARIES/BONUSES:

Top Exec. Salary: $ Bonus: $
Second Exec. Salary: $ Bonus: $

OTHER THOUGHTS:

Estimated Female Officers or Directors:
Hot Spot for Advancement for Women/Minorities:

Coupang

NAIC Code: 454111

www.coupang.com

TYPES OF BUSINESS:

Electronic Shopping
E-commerce

BRANDS/DIVISIONS/AFFILIATES:

GROWTH PLANS/SPECIAL FEATURES:

Coupang provides an eCommerce platform similar to Amazon.com. The site partners with merchants and sells a wide variety of merchandise, including baby goods, fashion, beauty products, consumables, home goods, home decorations, books, toys, sporting goods and electronic devices. It also sells tickets for travel and cultural events. Coupang offers same-day delivery, and its merchandise can be accessed via web or mobile app. Headquartered in South Korea, the firm has offices in Beijing, Los Angeles, Seattle, Silicon Valley and Shanghai.

CONTACTS: Note: Officers with more than one job title may be intentionally listed here more than once.

Bom Suk Kim, CEO

FINANCIAL DATA: Note: Data for latest year may not have been available at press time.

In U.S. $	2018	2017	2016	2015	2014	2013
Revenue		2,490,000,000	1,700,000,000	964,212,000	310,000,000	40,000,000
R&D Expense						
Operating Income						
Operating Margin %						
SGA Expense						
Net Income		-598,178,000	-464,912,000	-465,224,000		
Operating Cash Flow						
Capital Expenditure						
EBITDA						
Return on Assets %						
Return on Equity %						
Debt to Equity						

CONTACT INFORMATION:

Phone: 8202-1577-7011   Fax: 8202-3441-7011
Toll-Free:
Address: 70B, 24/Fl, Doosan-ro, Geumcheon-gu, Seoul, 02121 South Korea

STOCK TICKER/OTHER:

Stock Ticker: Private   Exchange:
Employees: 10,000   Fiscal Year Ends:
Parent Company:

SALARIES/BONUSES:

Top Exec. Salary: $ Bonus: $
Second Exec. Salary: $ Bonus: $

OTHER THOUGHTS:

Estimated Female Officers or Directors:
Hot Spot for Advancement for Women/Minorities:

Cox Automotive Inc

NAIC Code: 519130

www.coxautoinc.com

TYPES OF BUSINESS:
Internet Search Portals

BRANDS/DIVISIONS/AFFILIATES:
Cox Enterprises Inc
VinSolutions
Dealer-Auction.com
Ready Logistics
Kelley Blue Book
NextGear Capital
Autotrader
Xtime

CONTACTS: *Note: Officers with more than one job title may be intentionally listed here more than once.*
Sandy Schwartz, Pres.
Mark O'Neil, COO
Mark F. Bowser, CFO
John Kovac, CMO
Janet Barnard, Chief People Officer
Bryan Landerman, Exec. VP-IT

GROWTH PLANS/SPECIAL FEATURES:
Cox Automotive, Inc. provides automotive resources and tools for consumers, dealers and manufacturers for the purpose of maximizing value at every step of the car buying and selling process. These sources and tools include leading brands and solutions such as VinSolutions, an automotive software solution that integrates systems and tools to deliver a single view of the customer across the dealership process, for maintaining customer relationship management; Dealer-Auction.com, an online trade-only auction of vehicles direct from franchise dealers; Ready Logistics, offering end-to-end logistics services and solutions for shippers and transporters by connecting auctions, dealers, commercial and consumer clients nationwide; Kelley Blue Book, a provider of new and used vehicle information; and NextGear Capital, a provider of lending products, including lines of credit, for dealers to purchase new and used inventory at over 1,000 auto and specialty auctions and other inventory sources throughout the U.S., Canada, the U.K. and Ireland. Other brands and solutions include Autotrader, AutoStreets, Bitauto, CarsGuide, Dealer.com, Dealer Solutions, Dealertrack, HomeNet, Jingzhengu, Mahindra First Choice, Manheim, Modix, Molicar, Motors.co.uk, Movex, RMS Automotive, vAuto and Xtime. Cox Automotive, a wholly-owned subsidiary of Cox Enterprises, Inc., partners with more than 40,000 dealers, uniting more than 20 brands in order to provide its vehicle buying/selling services on a global scale. In August 2018, Cox Automotive announced plans to create a mobility solutions business division to deliver advanced fleet management solutions and support consumer mobility.

FINANCIAL DATA: *Note: Data for latest year may not have been available at press time.*

In U.S. $	2018	2017	2016	2015	2014	2013
Revenue		7,410,000,000	7,300,000,000	7,100,000,000	6,600,000,000	6,200,000,000
R&D Expense						
Operating Income						
Operating Margin %						
SGA Expense						
Net Income						
Operating Cash Flow						
Capital Expenditure						
EBITDA						
Return on Assets %						
Return on Equity %						
Debt to Equity						

CONTACT INFORMATION:
Phone: Fax:
Toll-Free: 855-449-0010
Address: 3003 Summit Blvd., Ste. 200, Atlanta, GA 30319 United States

STOCK TICKER/OTHER:
Stock Ticker: Subsidiary   Exchange:
Employees: 33,000   Fiscal Year Ends: 12/31
Parent Company: Cox Enterprises Inc

SALARIES/BONUSES:
Top Exec. Salary: $ Bonus: $
Second Exec. Salary: $ Bonus: $

OTHER THOUGHTS:
Estimated Female Officers or Directors:
Hot Spot for Advancement for Women/Minorities:

Cox Communications Inc

NAIC Code: 517110

www.cox.com/residential/home.cox

TYPES OF BUSINESS:

Cable TV Service and Internet Access
Digital Cable TV Service
Cable-Based Internet Access
Local & Long-Distance Phone Service
Commercial Telecommunications Services
Data & Video Transport Services

BRANDS/DIVISIONS/AFFILIATES:

Cox Enterprises Inc
Cox Business Services
Managed IP PBX
Cox Media
Kudzu.com

CONTACTS: Note: Officers with more than one job title may be intentionally listed here more than once.

Patrick J. Esser, Pres.
Jill Campbell, COO
Mark Bowser, CFO
Mark Greatrex, CMO
Kevin Hart, CTO
Len Barlik, Exec. VP-Prod. Mgmt. & Dev.
Asheesh Saksena, Chief Strategy Officer
Joseph J. Rooney, Sr. VP-Social Media, Advertising & Brand Mktg.
William (Bill) J. Fitzsimmons, Chief Acct. Officer
Philip G. Meeks, Sr. VP-Cox Bus.
Jennifer W. Hightower, Sr. VP-Law & Policy
David Pugliese, Sr. VP-Product Mktg.
Mark A. Kaish, Sr. VP-Tech. Oper.
George Richter, VP-Supply Chain Mgmt.

GROWTH PLANS/SPECIAL FEATURES:

Cox Communications, Inc., owned by Cox Enterprises, Inc., is a broadband communications and entertainment company, serving millions of customers throughout the U.S. Cox offers advanced digital video, high speed internet, and local and long-distance telephone services over its own nationwide IP network in 18 states. Cox Business Services provides data, video and voice solutions to small and regional businesses such as schools and universities, government organizations and financial institutions. The firm's Managed IP PBX service provides small business customers that have limited internal information technology departments with telecommunication systems that are monitored and managed around the clock by Cox Business. Cox Media offers national and local cable advertising in traditional spot and new media formats, along with promotional opportunities and production services. The company also maintains Kudzu.com, an online directory that aggregates user reviews and ratings on local businesses, merchants and service providers.

FINANCIAL DATA: Note: Data for latest year may not have been available at press time.

In U.S. $	2018	2017	2016	2015	2014	2013
Revenue	12,000,000,000	11,550,000,000	11,000,000,000	10,650,000,000	10,400,000,000	9,900,000,000
R&D Expense						
Operating Income						
Operating Margin %						
SGA Expense						
Net Income						
Operating Cash Flow						
Capital Expenditure						
EBITDA						
Return on Assets %						
Return on Equity %						
Debt to Equity						

CONTACT INFORMATION:

Phone: 404-843-5000   Fax: 404-843-5939
Toll-Free: 888-566-7751
Address: 1400 Lake Hearn Dr., Atlanta, GA 30319 United States

STOCK TICKER/OTHER:

Stock Ticker: Subsidiary   Exchange:
Employees: 23,000   Fiscal Year Ends: 12/31
Parent Company: Cox Enterprises Inc

SALARIES/BONUSES:

Top Exec. Salary: $ Bonus: $
Second Exec. Salary: $ Bonus: $

OTHER THOUGHTS:

Estimated Female Officers or Directors: 3
Hot Spot for Advancement for Women/Minorities: Y

Crackle Inc (dba SonyCrackle)

www.sonycrackle.com

NAIC Code: 519130

TYPES OF BUSINESS:

Internet Streaming Movies & Television Shows
Original Content
Advertising

BRANDS/DIVISIONS/AFFILIATES:

Sony Pictures Entertainment Inc
Sony Crackle
Always On

CONTACTS: *Note: Officers with more than one job title may be intentionally listed here more than once.*

David Samuel, Co-Pres.
Joshua M. Felser, Co-Pres.
Aviv Eyal, CTO
Eric Berger, Sr. VP-Digital Networks

GROWTH PLANS/SPECIAL FEATURES:

Crackle, Inc., doing business as Sony Crackle, is the multi-platform, online video entertainment subsidiary of Sony Pictures Entertainment, Inc.. The company distributes full-length digital content and original short-form series from Sony Pictures' library of television series and feature films through a streaming network that includes Sony devices, IPTV, leading social networks and viral web and app distribution. The firm maintains distribution partnerships with content providers for cable TV, set-top boxes, mobile phones, PCs, video game consoles and virtual worlds, including Aniplex, FOX Digital, Lionsgate Entertainment, Metro-Goldwyn-Mayer, Red Bull, Universal Studios, The Walt Disney Company, Miramax and many more. Digital content plays on its proprietary media player, the Sony Crackle, allowing partners to easily integrate the content into their online channels. Content includes: movies, films originally produced by Sony Pictures, Sony Pictures Classics, Columbia TriStar or Screen Gems; television, which offers content from Sony Pictures Television; minisodes, which are current and archived TV episodes that have been edited down to five minutes or less; and Sony Crackle originals, which are content from TV shows produced in-house before digital, TV and DVD distribution. Sony Crackle's Always On personalized feature automatically plays the user's favorites, and also allows them to search and stream on Roku, PlayStation, Xbox, Apple TV, iPhone, Android and more. The company's target audience is men from 18-34 years of age. Sony Crackle is available in 21 countries and English, Spanish and Portugese

FINANCIAL DATA: *Note: Data for latest year may not have been available at press time.*

In U.S. $	2018	2017	2016	2015	2014	2013
Revenue						
R&D Expense						
Operating Income						
Operating Margin %						
SGA Expense						
Net Income						
Operating Cash Flow						
Capital Expenditure						
EBITDA						
Return on Assets %						
Return on Equity %						
Debt to Equity						

CONTACT INFORMATION:

Phone: 415-877-4800   Fax: 415-331-5501
Toll-Free:
Address: 10202 West Washington Blvd, Ste. 2141, Culver City, CA 90232 United States

SALARIES/BONUSES:

Top Exec. Salary: $ Bonus: $
Second Exec. Salary: $ Bonus: $

STOCK TICKER/OTHER:

Stock Ticker: Subsidiary   Exchange:
Employees: 100   Fiscal Year Ends: 12/31
Parent Company: Sony Pictures Entertainment Inc

OTHER THOUGHTS:

Estimated Female Officers or Directors:
Hot Spot for Advancement for Women/Minorities:

Craigslist Inc

www.craigslist.org

NAIC Code: 519130

TYPES OF BUSINESS:

Online Classified Ads Platform
User Forum

BRANDS/DIVISIONS/AFFILIATES:

Craigslist.org
Craigslist Charitable Fund

CONTACTS: *Note: Officers with more than one job title may be intentionally listed here more than once.*

Jim Buckmaster, CEO
Craig Newmark, Chmn.

GROWTH PLANS/SPECIAL FEATURES:

Craigslist, Inc. operates Craigslist.org, an online community offering local classifieds and forums. Craigslist currently has over 700 local sites in 70 countries, allowing users in those cities to post listings for everything from classified and personal ads to jobs, housing, goods, services, local activities and advice. In addition to English, the site is available in Catalan, Danish, Dutch, Filipino, French, German, Italian, Norwegian, Portuguese, Spanish, Swedish and Turkish. The site averages more than 80 million classified ads each month, 1 million new job postings and 50 billion page-views monthly and has nearly 60 million unique visitors per month in the U.S. alone. More than 200 million people use Craigslist to post their views on 100 different discussion forums. Although Craigslist is a commercial enterprise, it retains its original .org URL in order to emphasis its mission as a sort of community service and to reflect its non-corporate culture. The company relies almost entirely on word-of-mouth advertising and has resisted the efforts of advertisers to purchase space on the site, meaning that users may navigate the site without seeing banner ads or other advertisements. Through its Craigslist Charitable Fund, the company continues to create grants for 501(c)3 nonprofit organizations. Craigslist has released many open source projects including for download.

Craigslist offers its employees health and dental insurance, a 3-1 match on charitable donations, a monthly transportation stipend, a monthly technology stipend for tech staff and a 401(k) matching program.

FINANCIAL DATA: *Note: Data for latest year may not have been available at press time.*

In U.S. $	2018	2017	2016	2015	2014	2013
Revenue		380,000,000	365,000,000	348,000,000	335,000,000	167,500,000
R&D Expense						
Operating Income						
Operating Margin %						
SGA Expense						
Net Income						
Operating Cash Flow						
Capital Expenditure						
EBITDA						
Return on Assets %						
Return on Equity %						
Debt to Equity						

CONTACT INFORMATION:

Phone: 415-566-6394   Fax: 415-504-6394
Toll-Free:
Address: 1381 9th Ave., San Francisco, CA 94122 United States

STOCK TICKER/OTHER:

Stock Ticker: Private   Exchange:
Employees: 55   Fiscal Year Ends:
Parent Company:

SALARIES/BONUSES:

Top Exec. Salary: $ Bonus: $
Second Exec. Salary: $ Bonus: $

OTHER THOUGHTS:

Estimated Female Officers or Directors: 4
Hot Spot for Advancement for Women/Minorities: Y

Critical Mass Inc
NAIC Code: 541810E

www.criticalmass.com

TYPES OF BUSINESS:
Online Advertising & Marketing
Web Development Services
Brand Development Services
e-Commerce Services

BRANDS/DIVISIONS/AFFILIATES:
Omnicom Group Inc

CONTACTS: *Note: Officers with more than one job title may be intentionally listed here more than once.*
Dianne Wilkins, CEO
John McLaughlin, COO
Chris Gokiert, Pres.
Lee Tamkee, CFO
Conor Brady, Chief Creative Officer
Scott Ross, Exec. Tech. Dir.
Jaime Escobar, Dir.-Oper.
Diane Heun, VP-Bus. Dev.
Katy Zack, Dir.-Comm.
Darren Delichte, Sr. VP
Matt Di Paolo, Sr. VP
Amanda Levy, Sr. VP
Shaina Boone, Sr. VP-Mktg. Science
Chris Gokiert, Pres.
Jaime Escobar, Gen. Mgr.-Latin America

GROWTH PLANS/SPECIAL FEATURES:
Critical Mass, Inc. is a digital marketing company. It offers web design services as well as helping clients introduce new products, drive sales, reduce customer support costs, build loyalty and increase use of online channels. Services include creating marketing strategies through its insight and planning unit; e-marketing, including e-mail campaign management; experience design, which helps clients develop brands and brand presence; technology support, including e-commerce and application development; and social media, which connects people in order to engage and activate them. The firm also offers associated web design services, including producing computer graphics and animation. Through its services, the company aids clients in improving marketing efforts in online environments, reengineering websites, standardizing brand presence, moving customers to online channels and personalizing a customer's electronic experience. Besides its Calgary headquarters, the company has primary offices in Calgary, Chicago, Cupertino, Hong Kong, London, Los Angeles, Nashville, New York, San Jose, Sao Paulo, Tokyo and Toronto. Critical Mass operates as a subsidiary of Omnicom Group, Inc.

FINANCIAL DATA: *Note: Data for latest year may not have been available at press time.*

In U.S. $	2018	2017	2016	2015	2014	2013
Revenue						
R&D Expense						
Operating Income						
Operating Margin %						
SGA Expense						
Net Income						
Operating Cash Flow						
Capital Expenditure						
EBITDA						
Return on Assets %						
Return on Equity %						
Debt to Equity						

CONTACT INFORMATION:
Phone: 403-262-3006   Fax: 403-262-7185
Toll-Free:
Address: 1011 9th Ave. SE, Ste. 300, Calgary, AB T2G 0H7 Canada

STOCK TICKER/OTHER:
Stock Ticker: Subsidiary   Exchange:
Employees: 950   Fiscal Year Ends: 12/31
Parent Company: Omnicom Group Inc

SALARIES/BONUSES:
Top Exec. Salary: $ Bonus: $
Second Exec. Salary: $ Bonus: $

OTHER THOUGHTS:
Estimated Female Officers or Directors: 6
Hot Spot for Advancement for Women/Minorities: Y

Ctrip.com International Ltd

NAIC Code: 561510

www.ctrip.com

TYPES OF BUSINESS:

Online Hotel & Flight Booking
Travel Agencies

BRANDS/DIVISIONS/AFFILIATES:

Ctrip.com
C-Travel International Limited
Ctrip.com (Hong Kong) Limited
Ctrip Computer Technology (Shanghai) Co Ltd
Ctrip Travel Information Technology (Shanghai) Co
Ctrip Travel Network Technology (Shanghai) Co Ltd
Ctrip Information Technology (Nantong) Co Ltd

CONTACTS: Note: Officers with more than one job title may be intentionally listed here more than once.

Jane Ji Sun, CEO

GROWTH PLANS/SPECIAL FEATURES:

Ctrip.com International, Ltd. is a travel service provider of accommodation reservation, transportation ticketing, packaged tours and corporate travel management in China. Customers can access the company's aggregated information and make bookings online in Chinese at Ctrip.com, as well as in local languages at sites for customers who speak English, German, French, Spanish, Russian, Korean and Japanese. Ctrip.com is designed more for independent travel than for group excursions, although services are offered for these as well. The company sells air tickets as an agent for all major domestic Chinese airlines and has supply relationships with more than 1.3 million hotels in China and abroad. Ctrip.com engages in various marketing campaigns, including onsite promotions; cross marketing with Chinese domestic airlines, telecommunications service providers and banks; online marketing; traditional advertising; and customer awards programs. In addition to its branch offices in major cities throughout China, the firm maintains a network of ticketing and third-party agency offices in more than 70 cities in China. Approximately 45% of total annual revenues is derived from transportation ticketing, with accommodation reservation deriving 35%, packaged tours 11%, corporate travel 3% and other products and services the remaining percent. Ctrip.com is a holding company incorporated in the Cayman Islands and conducts all business through its subsidiaries and affiliates, some of which include C-Travel International Limited; Ctrip.com (Hong Kong) Limited; Ctrip Computer Technology (Shanghai) Co., Ltd.; Ctrip Travel Information Technology (Shanghai) Co., Ltd.; Ctrip Travel Network Technology (Shanghai) Co., Ltd.; Ctrip Information Technology (Nantong) Co., Ltd; ezTravel Co. Ltd.; and HKWOT (BVI) Limited.

FINANCIAL DATA: Note: Data for latest year may not have been available at press time.

In U.S. $	2018	2017	2016	2015	2014	2013
Revenue		3,897,430,000	2,798,452,000	1,586,001,000	1,069,249,000	783,971,300
R&D Expense		1,054,633,000	1,118,805,000	479,791,200	337,842,400	181,298,400
Operating Income		425,866,400	-228,271,800	55,455,890	-21,946,580	122,024,400
Operating Margin %		10.92%	-8.15%	3.49%	-2.05%	15.56%
SGA Expense		1,736,078,000	1,219,564,000	607,820,100	447,637,300	278,822,600
Net Income		311,742,200	-208,220,400	364,957,000	35,327,640	145,292,600
Operating Cash Flow		1,028,782,000	767,378,000	443,715,000	285,049,500	356,977,400
Capital Expenditure		71,922,350	100,281,200	95,782,840	698,240,000	94,856,030
EBITDA		826,065,700	-45,021,380	527,427,000	69,845,270	192,498,100
Return on Assets %		1.39%	-1.08%	3.34%	.93%	6.14%
Return on Equity %		2.74%	-2.46%	9.27%	2.68%	13.29%
Debt to Equity		0.34	0.48	0.41	0.84	0.66

CONTACT INFORMATION:

Phone: 86 2134064880   Fax: 86 2152510000
Toll-Free:
Address: 968 Jin Zhong Rd., Shanghai, Shanghai 200335 China

STOCK TICKER/OTHER:

Stock Ticker: CTRP   Exchange: NAS
Employees: 37,000   Fiscal Year Ends: 12/31
Parent Company:

SALARIES/BONUSES:

Top Exec. Salary: $ Bonus: $
Second Exec. Salary: $ Bonus: $

OTHER THOUGHTS:

Estimated Female Officers or Directors:
Hot Spot for Advancement for Women/Minorities: Y

Cyber Communications Inc

www.cci.co.jp

NAIC Code: 541810E

TYPES OF BUSINESS:

Internet Advertising
Marketing Support
Travel Agencies
Software Development
Insert Advertising
RSS Feed Advertising

BRANDS/DIVISIONS/AFFILIATES:

Dentsu Inc

GROWTH PLANS/SPECIAL FEATURES:

Cyber Communications, Inc. (CCI), based in Japan, is an internet advertising company focused on buying, marketing and selling internet advertising space as well as providing advertising delivery technology and support services. The company is a wholly-owned subsidiary of the Japanese advertising agency Dentsu, Inc. and serves over 500 advertising agencies. As an advertising media representative, the firm acts as a marketing company, linking internet media and advertising agencies with advertisers and purchasing and selling advertising space. Its specialties include smart device marketing, solution services, social media marketing and ad platforms. Other services include advertising effectiveness analysis, creative production services and cross-media and technology. CCI has branch offices in Osaka, Nagoya and Fukuoka, Japan. In November 2018, the firm and Voyage Group, Inc. announced their pending merger and business name change to Carta Holdings Co., Ltd., to take place in early 2019.

CONTACTS: *Note: Officers with more than one job title may be intentionally listed here more than once.*

Akio Niizawa, Managing Dir.
Akio Niizawa, Pres.
Chiaki Kobayashi, Chief Tech. Strategy Officer

FINANCIAL DATA: *Note: Data for latest year may not have been available at press time.*

In U.S. $	2018	2017	2016	2015	2014	2013
Revenue		815,000,000	800,000,000	750,000,000	725,000,000	732,000,000
R&D Expense						
Operating Income						
Operating Margin %						
SGA Expense						
Net Income						
Operating Cash Flow						
Capital Expenditure						
EBITDA						
Return on Assets %						
Return on Equity %						
Debt to Equity						

CONTACT INFORMATION:

Phone: 81-3-5425-6111   Fax: 81-3-5425-6110
Toll-Free:
Address: 1-13-1 Tsukiji, Chuo-ku, Tokyo, 104-0045 Japan

STOCK TICKER/OTHER:

Stock Ticker: Subsidiary
Employees: 946
Parent Company: Dentsu Inc

Exchange:
Fiscal Year Ends: 03/31

SALARIES/BONUSES:

Top Exec. Salary: $ Bonus: $
Second Exec. Salary: $ Bonus: $

OTHER THOUGHTS:

Estimated Female Officers or Directors: 2
Hot Spot for Advancement for Women/Minorities:

CyberSource Corporation

www.cybersource.com

NAIC Code: 522320

TYPES OF BUSINESS:

E-Commerce Processing Services & Systems
Risk Management Solutions
Credit Card Processing
Tax Calculation
Fraud Screening
Compliance Services
Consulting Services

BRANDS/DIVISIONS/AFFILIATES:

Visa Inc

CONTACTS: *Note: Officers with more than one job title may be intentionally listed here more than once.*

Andre Machicao, Sr. VP
Michael Walsh, Pres.
Neil Buckley, VP-Prod. Dev.
David J. Kim, General Counsel
John McDonnell, VP-Bus. Dev.
Carolyn Brackett, VP-Channels & Alliances
David A. Glaser, VP-Professional Svcs.
Trish Martin, VP-Customer Support
John Bodine, VP-Sales & Mktg.

GROWTH PLANS/SPECIAL FEATURES:

CyberSource Corporation, a subsidiary of Visa, Inc., provides secure electronic payment and risk management services to organizations that sell products and services over the internet. The company's payment systems allow eCommerce merchants to accept a range of online payment options, including credit cards, electronic checks and global payment options. CyberSource's payment management platform helps companies optimize business results by actively managing every aspect of its payment operations, from payment acceptance and processing to order screening, fraud management and enterprise payment security. Payment processing solutions include cross-channel payments, gateway and processing connections, payment cards, online and mobile digital payments, direct debit and bank transfers, reconciliation reports, payer authentication, global tax calculation, recurring billing and account updater. Fraud management solutions include managed risk services, payer authentication, account takeover protection, loyalty fraud management, fraud alert, delivery address verification and export compliance. Payment security solutions include secure acceptance via web and mobile channels, as well as payment tokenization. CyberSource's solutions serve merchants of all sizes, operating in the most varied geographies and industry verticals. Its partner program is available to technology providers, system integrators, financial institutions and payment solution providers. More than 400,000 businesses worldwide use CyberSource solutions. The firm is based in California, with offices throughout Asia, Europe, Latin America, the Middle East, Africa and the U.S.

Offered through parent company Visa, employee benefits include medical, dental and vision coverage; short- and long-term disability; life insurance; a 401(k) plan; flexible spending accounts; educational assistance; a cafeteria plan; and an onsite fitness center.

FINANCIAL DATA: *Note: Data for latest year may not have been available at press time.*

In U.S. $	2018	2017	2016	2015	2014	2013
Revenue		377,000,000	340,000,000	330,000,000	305,000,000	285,000,000
R&D Expense						
Operating Income						
Operating Margin %						
SGA Expense						
Net Income						
Operating Cash Flow						
Capital Expenditure						
EBITDA						
Return on Assets %						
Return on Equity %						
Debt to Equity						

CONTACT INFORMATION:

Phone: 650-432-7350   Fax: 650-625-9145
Toll-Free: 800-530-9095
Address: 1295 Charleston Rd., Mountain View, CA 94043 United States

STOCK TICKER/OTHER:

Stock Ticker: Subsidiary   Exchange:
Employees: 654   Fiscal Year Ends: 12/31
Parent Company: VISA Inc

SALARIES/BONUSES:

Top Exec. Salary: $ Bonus: $
Second Exec. Salary: $ Bonus: $

OTHER THOUGHTS:

Estimated Female Officers or Directors: 2
Hot Spot for Advancement for Women/Minorities: Y

Sales, profits and employees may be estimates. Financial information, benefits and other data can change quickly and may vary from those stated here.

Cylance Inc

www.cylance.com

NAIC Code: 511210E

TYPES OF BUSINESS:

Computer Software, Security & Anti-Virus
Security
Software

BRANDS/DIVISIONS/AFFILIATES:

CylancePROTECT
CylanceThreatZERO
CylanceOPTICS
Cylance Smart Antivirus

CONTACTS: *Note: Officers with more than one job title may be intentionally listed here more than once.*

Stuart McClure, CEO
Daniel Doimo, Pres.
Brian Robins, CFO
Vina Leite, Chief People Officer
Kumud Kalia, CIO

GROWTH PLANS/SPECIAL FEATURES:

Cylance, Inc. develops and provides antivirus and endpoint protection and prevention software solutions. Its CylancePROTECT antivirus and application control solution is designed for fixed-function devices, and leverages artificial intelligence to detect and prevent malware from executing on endpoints in real-time. CylanceThreatZERO is a next-generation protection offering, going further than detecting approximately 40% of malware, but all of it. After configuration and deployment of the product, Cylance ensures the environment contains zero threats, and educates customer's teams and employees on security best practices, current malware trends and deployment strategies. CylanceOPTICS is a detection and response solution. Cylance Smart Antivirus is the firm's antivirus software. Cylance Smart Antivirus comes as a subscription and can be bought for one device for $29 for a year or $49 for two years; five devices for $69 for one year or $109 for two years; and 10 devices for $99 for one year or $149 for two years. Cylance products and services are offered for businesses and the home, as well as for the education, energy, critical infrastructure, finance, healthcare, retail and federal government sectors. In November 2018, the firm agreed to be acquired by BlackBerry Ltd. for $1.4 billion. The transaction was expected to close in the first quarter of 2019.

FINANCIAL DATA: *Note: Data for latest year may not have been available at press time.*

In U.S. $	2018	2017	2016	2015	2014	2013
Revenue		100,000,000	36,000,000			
R&D Expense						
Operating Income						
Operating Margin %						
SGA Expense						
Net Income						
Operating Cash Flow						
Capital Expenditure						
EBITDA						
Return on Assets %						
Return on Equity %						
Debt to Equity						

CONTACT INFORMATION:

Phone: Fax:
Toll-Free: 888-997-6795
Address: 400 Spectrum Center Dr., Ste. 900, Irvine, CA 92618 United States

STOCK TICKER/OTHER:

Stock Ticker: Private   Exchange:
Employees: 600   Fiscal Year Ends:
Parent Company:

SALARIES/BONUSES:

Top Exec. Salary: $ Bonus: $
Second Exec. Salary: $ Bonus: $

OTHER THOUGHTS:

Estimated Female Officers or Directors:
Hot Spot for Advancement for Women/Minorities:

Cyxtera Technologies Inc

www.cyxtera.com

NAIC Code: 518210

TYPES OF BUSINESS:

Hosting & Collocation Services
Virtual Private Networks
Managed Hosting Services
Networking Services
Government-Related IT Services

BRANDS/DIVISIONS/AFFILIATES:

CenturyLink Inc
AppGate SDP
AppGate Insight
Brainspace 6.1
DMARC Compass
Immunity Inc

CONTACTS: Note: Officers with more than one job title may be intentionally listed here more than once.

Manuel D. Medina, CEO
Nelson Fonseca, COO
Rene A. Rodriguez, CFO
Simon West, CMO
Frank Barnett, Chief Human Resources Officer
Leo Casusol, CIO
Andrew Higginbotham, Sr. VP-Cloud & Tech.
Pete Bazil, General Counsel
Pete Bazil, Chief Commercial Officer
Marc Capri, Sr. VP-Global Advanced Svcs.
Mark Smith, Managing Dir.-Asia

GROWTH PLANS/SPECIAL FEATURES:

Cyxtera Technologies, Inc., a subsidiary of CenturyLink, Inc., provides a secure platform for connecting and protecting dedicated infrastructure, private clouds and public clouds. For enterprises, government agencies and service providers, Cyxtera offers secure IT infrastructure capabilities paired with agile, dynamic software-defined security. The company's AppGate SDP (software-defined perimeter) is a network security model that dynamically creates one-to-one network connections between users and the resources they access. It grants access based on individual user and environmental factors. AppGate for the public cloud allows enterprises to implement a global, highly-available secure access system in any hybrid environment with greater control and improved economics. It dynamically creates a secure, encrypted network segment of one that is tailored for each user session. AppGate Insight is a software-defined segmentation for hybrid IT infrastructure, grouping virtual assets for micro-segmentation purposes. It automatically and continuously discovers all assets in the virtual fabric, allowing the grouping of the assets into logical zones and visualizes asset relationships and the traffic flows between them for improved analytics. Other solutions by Cyxtera include threat analytics services; Brainspace 6.1, which conducts digital investigations; and DMARC Compass email fraud protection. Headquartered in Florida, Cyxtera serves more than 3,500 customers. In June 2018, the firm completed its acquisition of Immunity, Inc., a leader in offense-oriented cyber security techniques and technologies.

FINANCIAL DATA: Note: Data for latest year may not have been available at press time.

In U.S. $	2018	2017	2016	2015	2014	2013
Revenue		1,365,000,000	1,350,000,000	1,355,035,500	1,365,000,000	1,376,000,000
R&D Expense						
Operating Income						
Operating Margin %						
SGA Expense						
Net Income						
Operating Cash Flow						
Capital Expenditure						
EBITDA						
Return on Assets %						
Return on Equity %						
Debt to Equity						

CONTACT INFORMATION:

Phone: 305-537-9500   Fax:
Toll-Free: 855-699-8372
Address: BAC Colonnade Office Twr., 2333 Ponce De Leon Blvd., Ste. 900, Coral Gables, FL 33134 United States

STOCK TICKER/OTHER:

Stock Ticker: Subsidiary   Exchange:
Employees: 1,100   Fiscal Year Ends: 12/31
Parent Company: CenturyLink Inc

SALARIES/BONUSES:

Top Exec. Salary: $ Bonus: $
Second Exec. Salary: $ Bonus: $

OTHER THOUGHTS:

Estimated Female Officers or Directors: 1
Hot Spot for Advancement for Women/Minorities:

Datadog Inc

www.datadoghq.com

NAIC Code: 511210I

TYPES OF BUSINESS:

Computer Software, Operating Systems, Languages & Development Tools Software

BRANDS/DIVISIONS/AFFILIATES:

CONTACTS: *Note: Officers with more than one job title may be intentionally listed here more than once.*

Olivier Pomel, CEO
David Obstler, CFO
Alex Rosemblat, VP-Mktg.
Alexis Le-Quoc, CTO

GROWTH PLANS/SPECIAL FEATURES:

Datadog, Inc. provides a software-as-a-service (SaaS) monitoring platform for cloud applications to enterprises. With turn-key integrations, Datadog seamlessly aggregates metrics and events across the full DevOps stack, including SaaS and cloud providers, automation tools, monitoring and instrumentation, source control and bug tracking, as well as databases and common server components. All the integrations listed on the firm's website (more than 250 of them) are supported by Datadog. These include, but are not limited to, Amazon, Apache, Microsoft Azure, bitbucket, Cassandra, Docker, Elastic, Google Cloud, HipChat, Java, MySquare, NGiNX, Pagerduty and Slack. These capabilities enable DevOps teams to work collaboratively in order to avoid downtime, resolve performance issues and ensure that development and deployment cycles finish on time. Customers can build real-time interactive dashboards with Datadog, which is comprised of all high-resolution metrics and events for manipulation and graphing. They can search and correlate metrics and events, share, obtain alerts on critical issues, and instrument apps, including writing new integrations. Datadog's interactive Notebooks offering provides an interactive environment that helps DevOps teams explore application performance data, create reproducible postmortems, build runbooks and document infrastructure. Customers of the firm include 21st Century Fox, AT&T, DreamWorks, Sonos, Samsung, Whole Foods Market, T-Mobile, ActiVision, WeWork, Ferrari, Cargill and many more. Based in New York, Datadog has domestic offices throughout the U.S., as well as international offices in France, Germany, Ireland, Spain, Italy, Sweden, Australia and Japan.

The company offers its employees medical insurance, open paid time off, commuter benefits, 401(k), catered lunches and other perks.

FINANCIAL DATA: *Note: Data for latest year may not have been available at press time.*

In U.S. $	2018	2017	2016	2015	2014	2013
Revenue						
R&D Expense						
Operating Income						
Operating Margin %						
SGA Expense						
Net Income						
Operating Cash Flow						
Capital Expenditure						
EBITDA						
Return on Assets %						
Return on Equity %						
Debt to Equity						

CONTACT INFORMATION:

Phone: Fax:
Toll-Free: 866-329-4466
Address: 620 8th Ave., 45/Fl, New York, NY 10018 United States

STOCK TICKER/OTHER:

Stock Ticker: Private   Exchange:
Employees: 600   Fiscal Year Ends:
Parent Company:

SALARIES/BONUSES:

Top Exec. Salary: $ Bonus: $
Second Exec. Salary: $ Bonus: $

OTHER THOUGHTS:

Estimated Female Officers or Directors:
Hot Spot for Advancement for Women/Minorities:

Deem Inc

www.deem.com

NAIC Code: 454111

TYPES OF BUSINESS:
Online Business Services and Travel Marketplace
Expense Management Tools
Marketing Tools

BRANDS/DIVISIONS/AFFILIATES:
Deem Work Fource
Deem Emerging
Deem Open Expense

CONTACTS: *Note: Officers with more than one job title may be intentionally listed here more than once.*
John F. Rizzo, CEO
Bret McGinnis, VP
David Shiba, Sr. VP
Tahnee Perry, VP-Mktg.
Peg Wynn, Dir.-Human Resources
Neil Markey, Sr. VP-CIO
Gabriel Sandoval, Chief Legal Officer
Andrew McGraw, Sr. VP-Bus. Travel
Wade Jones, Gen. Mgr.-Deem Offers

GROWTH PLANS/SPECIAL FEATURES:
Deem, Inc. is a commerce-as-a-service network with applications for every kind of business, providing end-to-end customer acquisition and engagement experience for business to consumer (B2C) and business to business (B2B) companies. Deem provides an integrated cloud suite of spend and expense management applications that enable companies of all sizes to purchase virtually any product or service in the context of corporate policy, employee roles and negotiated discounts resulting in savings on every transaction. The Deem Work Fource is a suite of travel booking and management tools that combines design, machine learning and customization to provide the business travel ecosystem with a seamless platform, from shopping and booking to applying policy and managing costs. It features free 24-hour check-in on Southwest Airlines, automatic calendar integration, guided training and help for booking/managing trips, a problem-solving Deem Facebook messenger platform, a Google search engine and more. Deem Emerging is a self-service travel platform for managing business travel and expense. Last, Deem Open Expense enables users to integrate Deem travel data to any expense platform. Deem travel booking transactions flow automatically into the linked expense platform, providing a seamless user experience. Open integration allows for the application of all policy requirements and system settings. Deem serves more than 50,000 corporate customers worldwide, speaking more than 15 languages.

FINANCIAL DATA: *Note: Data for latest year may not have been available at press time.*

In U.S. $	2018	2017	2016	2015	2014	2013
Revenue						
R&D Expense						
Operating Income						
Operating Margin %						
SGA Expense						
Net Income						
Operating Cash Flow						
Capital Expenditure						
EBITDA						
Return on Assets %						
Return on Equity %						
Debt to Equity						

CONTACT INFORMATION:
Phone: 415-590-8300   Fax: 415-590-8301
Toll-Free:
Address: 642 Harrison St., San Francisco, CA 94107 United States

STOCK TICKER/OTHER:
Stock Ticker: Private   Exchange:
Employees: 250   Fiscal Year Ends:
Parent Company:

SALARIES/BONUSES:
Top Exec. Salary: $ Bonus: $
Second Exec. Salary: $ Bonus: $

OTHER THOUGHTS:
Estimated Female Officers or Directors:
Hot Spot for Advancement for Women/Minorities:

Delivery Hero SE

www.deliveryhero.com

NAIC Code: 492210

TYPES OF BUSINESS:

Online Restaurant Pick-Up and Delivery

BRANDS/DIVISIONS/AFFILIATES:

GROWTH PLANS/SPECIAL FEATURES:

Delivery Hero SE is an online food and beverage ordering service. The company is based in Berlin, and operates internationally in more than 40 countries across the Americas, Asia-Pacific, Europe and the Middle East/Africa. Delivery Hero's network comprises nearly 30 brands, via business-to-consumer (B2C) and business-to-business (B2B) strategies. Restaurant partners allow users to find restaurants in their area through Delivery Hero's online and mobile applications. Searches are usually filtered by cuisine or menus, and provide hours of operation information as well as reviews. Payments for orders and delivery can then be made by credit card, PayPal or with cash on delivery. During 2018, Delivery Hero changed its legal form from a German stock corporation (AG) to a European stock corporation (SE/Societas Europaea). That December, it agreed to sell its German food delivery businesses Lieferheld, Pizza.de and foodora to Takeaway.com in exchange for cash and an equity stake in Takeaway.com NV.

CONTACTS: Note: Officers with more than one job title may be intentionally listed here more than once.

Niklas Ostberg, CEO

FINANCIAL DATA: Note: Data for latest year may not have been available at press time.

In U.S. $	2018	2017	2016	2015	2014	2013
Revenue		651,638,000	312,907,000	181,362,000	120,215,000	57,351,900
R&D Expense						
Operating Income						
Operating Margin %						
SGA Expense						
Net Income						
Operating Cash Flow						
Capital Expenditure						
EBITDA						
Return on Assets %						
Return on Equity %						
Debt to Equity						

CONTACT INFORMATION:

Phone: 49-30-54-4459100   Fax:

Toll-Free:

Address: Oranienburger St. 70, Berlin, 10117 Germany

STOCK TICKER/OTHER:

Stock Ticker: DHER   Exchange:

Employees: 10,778   Fiscal Year Ends: 06/30

Parent Company:

SALARIES/BONUSES:

Top Exec. Salary: $ Bonus: $

Second Exec. Salary: $ Bonus: $

OTHER THOUGHTS:

Estimated Female Officers or Directors:

Hot Spot for Advancement for Women/Minorities:

Dell Technologies Inc

www.delltechnologies.com/en-us/index.htm

NAIC Code: 334111

TYPES OF BUSINESS:

Computer Manufacturing
Direct Sales
Technical & Support Services
Online Music Service
Web Hosting Services
Printers & Accessories
Personal Music Players
Storage Devices

BRANDS/DIVISIONS/AFFILIATES:

Dell
Dell EMC
Pivotal
RSA
Secureworks
VirtuStream
Vmware

CONTACTS: Note: Officers with more than one job title may be intentionally listed here more than once.

Michael Dell, CEO
Thomas Sweet, CFO
Maya McReynolds, Chief Accounting Officer
Jeremy Burton, Chief Marketing Officer
Richard Rothberg, General Counsel
Karen Quintos, Other Executive Officer
Rory Read, Other Executive Officer
Steven Price, Other Executive Officer
Marius Haas, Other Executive Officer
William Scannell, President, Divisional
Howard Elias, President, Divisional
Jeffrey Clarke, Vice Chairman, Divisional

GROWTH PLANS/SPECIAL FEATURES:

Dell Technologies, Inc. is a multinational information technology corporation. The firm provides transformational devices, processes and services in order to modernize data centers, drive progress and help clients thrive within the digital era. Dell organizes its products and services into the following business units: Client Solutions Group (CSG), Infrastructure Solutions Group (ISG) and VMware. Offerings by CSG include branded hardware, such as personal computers (PCs), notebooks, and branded peripherals, such as monitors and projectors, as well as third-party software and peripherals. CSG hardware and services also provide the architecture to enable the Internet of Things and connected ecosystems to securely and efficiently capture massive amounts of data for analytics and actionable insights for commercial customers. CSG also offers attached software, peripherals, and services, including support and deployment, configuration, and extended warranty services. Services and products offered by the ISG includes traditional storage solutions as well as next-generation storage solutions of Dell EMC; high-performance rack, blade, tower, and hyperscale servers; and networking products that help business customers transform and modernize their infrastructure, mobilize and enrich end-user experiences, and accelerate business applications and processes. ISG also includes the cloud software and infrastructure-as-a-service solutions of Virtustream. The VMware reportable segment reflects the operations of VMware, Inc. within Dell Technologies. VMware provides compute, cloud, mobility, networking and security infrastructure software to businesses that provides a flexible digital foundation for the applications that empower businesses to serve their customers globally. Brands by Dell Technologies include Dell, Dell EMC, Pivotal, RSA, Secureworks, VirtuStream and VMware.

Dell offers employees medical, dental, vision, life, disability, auto and home insurance; 401(k); and discounts and various assistance programs.

FINANCIAL DATA: Note: Data for latest year may not have been available at press time.

In U.S. $	2018	2017	2016	2015	2014	2013
Revenue	78,660,000,000	61,642,000,000	61,000,000,000	54,142,001,152	58,100,000,000	56,939,999,232
R&D Expense						
Operating Income						
Operating Margin %						
SGA Expense						
Net Income	-3,728,000,000	-1,672,000,000	-1,104,000,000	-1,220,999,936		2,372,000,000
Operating Cash Flow						
Capital Expenditure						
EBITDA						
Return on Assets %						
Return on Equity %						
Debt to Equity						

CONTACT INFORMATION:

Phone: 512 338-4400   Fax: 512 283-6161
Toll-Free: 800-289-3355
Address: One Dell Way, Round Rock, TX 78682 United States

STOCK TICKER/OTHER:

Stock Ticker: DVMT
Employees: 145,000
Parent Company:

Exchange: NYS
Fiscal Year Ends: 01/31

SALARIES/BONUSES:

Top Exec. Salary: $ Bonus: $
Second Exec. Salary: $ Bonus: $

OTHER THOUGHTS:

Estimated Female Officers or Directors: 1
Hot Spot for Advancement for Women/Minorities: Y

Sales, profits and employees may be estimates. Financial information, benefits and other data can change quickly and may vary from those stated here.

DeNA Co Ltd

NAIC Code: 511210G

www.dena.jp

TYPES OF BUSINESS:

Computer Software, Electronic Games, Apps & Entertainment
Social Networking
Online Payment Service
Online Travel Service
Online Auctions
Apps

BRANDS/DIVISIONS/AFFILIATES:

AI Business
Mobage
MOV
MYCOD
SHOWROOM
Everystar
Mobaoku
Yokohama DeNA Baystars

CONTACTS: *Note: Officers with more than one job title may be intentionally listed here more than once.*

Isao Moriyasu, CEO
Shintaro Asako, CFO
Tomoko Namba, Chmn.

GROWTH PLANS/SPECIAL FEATURES:

DeNA Co., Ltd. develops and operates a range of mobile and online services organized into nine categories. The artificial intelligence (AI) category includes: AI Business, which develops and operates a range of AI-technology-based services in DeNA's games, eCommerce, entertainment content distribution, sports, healthcare and automotive businesses; and AI R&D, which works with businesses to create AI-based services together. Games includes: mobile games, which are free-to-play via mobile apps and browser; Mobage, an entertainment platform in Japan that hosts free-to-play games, novels and other content; Yahoo! Mobage, offering social games for PC browsers; and AndApp, which enables users to play mobile game apps on PC browsers under the same user account. Automotive includes: MOV, a taxi dispatch app; Anyca, a peer-to-peer carsharing app; EasyRide, a robo-vehicle mobility service; and Robot Shuttle, a driverless, shared transportation service. Healthcare includes: MYCOD, a direct-to-consumer genetic testing service; KenCoM, a health insurance management platform; and Aruite Otoku, a walking app for improved health. Social live streaming includes: SHOWROOM, a virtual stage for watching artists perform live while interacting with them in real-time; and Pococha, a social live streaming community where users can tune in or broadcast their own live stream. Entertainment includes: Everystar, a Japanese mobile site for user-generated novels; Manga Box, a weekly manga magazine app; MyAnimeList, an anime website; and Hacka Doll, a news aggregation app. eCommerce & others includes: Mobaoku, a fashion auction site; Paygent, providing payment collection services to businesses; and Shumee-to Club, a social networking website for hobbyists. Sports includes: Yokohama DeNA Baystars, featuring a Japanese professional baseball league; Yokohama DeNA Running Club, featuring a long-distance track and field team; and Kawasaki Brave Thunder, a basketball team. Last, new business includes: Strategic Investment Office, which pursues strategic investments for DeNA.

FINANCIAL DATA: *Note: Data for latest year may not have been available at press time.*

In U.S. $	2018	2017	2016	2015	2014	2013
Revenue	1,292,947,000	1,333,908,000	1,333,009,000	1,321,043,000	1,681,814,000	1,878,033,000
R&D Expense						
Operating Income	255,120,200	215,002,600	183,808,200	229,695,400	493,442,000	712,748,600
Operating Margin %	19.73	17.90%	15.30%	18.58%	29.58%	37.92%
SGA Expense	590,985,900	572,684,700	575,959,100	550,070,500	629,832,600	640,722,400
Net Income	213,166,000	285,934,200	105,047,900	138,672,400	293,679,500	422,798,000
Operating Cash Flow	349,436,000	210,392,500	247,727,400	258,719,200	260,286,800	484,119,900
Capital Expenditure	170,646,000	138,922,900	126,280,100	150,313,500	136,223,600	98,610,490
EBITDA	395,323,100	350,122,400	307,834,300	365,343,900	585,652,300	792,965,200
Return on Assets %	7.14%	11.14%	4.78%	7.19%	16.14%	26.25%
Return on Equity %	9.32%	14.71%	6.53%	10.04%	24.36%	42.62%
Debt to Equity						

CONTACT INFORMATION:

Phone: 81 353041701   Fax:
Toll-Free:
Address: 2-21-1 Shibuya, Shibuya-ku, Tokyo, 150-8510 Japan

STOCK TICKER/OTHER:

Stock Ticker: DNACF
Employees: 3,522
Parent Company:

Exchange: PINX
Fiscal Year Ends: 03/31

SALARIES/BONUSES:

Top Exec. Salary: $ Bonus: $
Second Exec. Salary: $ Bonus: $

OTHER THOUGHTS:

Estimated Female Officers or Directors: 1
Hot Spot for Advancement for Women/Minorities:

Determine Inc

www.determine.com

NAIC Code: 511210K

TYPES OF BUSINESS:

Contract Lifecycle Management Software
Interactive Sales Software
Professional & Technical Services
Sales Execution Software
Pricing Management

BRANDS/DIVISIONS/AFFILIATES:

CONTACTS: *Note: Officers with more than one job title may be intentionally listed here more than once.*

Patrick Stakenas, CEO
John Nolan, CFO
Alan Howe, Director

GROWTH PLANS/SPECIAL FEATURES:

Determine, Inc. is a global provider of software-as-a-service (SaaS) source to pay and enterprise contract lifecycle management (ECLM) solutions. The company's technologies allow customers to manage the full scope of source to pay and ECLM using Determine's cloud platform. This platform gives procurement, finance and legal professionals the ability to deliver insights through analysis of their supplier relationships and contractual requirements. The cloud platform data enables businesses to discover unseen supplier and spend data, help make informed decisions, drive new revenue, improve workflow efficiencies and mitigate risk. Determine's source to pay software includes strategic sourcing, supplier management, contract management and procure-to-pay applications. ECLM solutions include supplier management sourcing, contract management procurement, invoice management, financial management and business applications analytics. Services offered by the company include implementation, training and adoption, as well as customer support. Determine sells its cloud solutions primarily through its direct sales force, along with strategic and original equipment manufacturers.

Employment benefits include medical, dental, vision, life, AD&D and disability coverage; flexible spending accounts; an employee stock purchase plan; 401(k) plans; paid holidays; ping-pong breaks; and discount gym memberships.

FINANCIAL DATA: *Note: Data for latest year may not have been available at press time.*

In U.S. $	2018	2017	2016	2015	2014	2013
Revenue	28,119,000	27,463,000	26,760,000	20,877,000	15,789,000	17,559,000
R&D Expense						
Operating Income						
Operating Margin %						
SGA Expense						
Net Income	-9,948,000	-9,452,000	-14,021,000	-13,746,000	-8,179,000	-4,749,000
Operating Cash Flow						
Capital Expenditure						
EBITDA						
Return on Assets %						
Return on Equity %						
Debt to Equity						

CONTACT INFORMATION:

Phone: 650-532-1500   Fax:
Toll-Free: 877-806-1932
Address: 615 West Carmel Dr., Ste. 100, Carmel, IN 46032 United States

STOCK TICKER/OTHER:

Stock Ticker: DTRM   Exchange: NAS
Employees: 148   Fiscal Year Ends: 03/31
Parent Company:

SALARIES/BONUSES:

Top Exec. Salary: $ Bonus: $
Second Exec. Salary: $ Bonus: $

OTHER THOUGHTS:

Estimated Female Officers or Directors: 2
Hot Spot for Advancement for Women/Minorities:

Didi Chuxing Technology Co Ltd (DiDi)

www.xiaojukeji.com/en/index.html
NAIC Code: 561599

TYPES OF BUSINESS:
Car Ride Dispatch Service, Mobile App-Based
Ride Sharing Service
Private Luxury Car Service
Designated Driving Service
Car Leasing
Car Maintenance

BRANDS/DIVISIONS/AFFILIATES:
DiDi Taxi
DiDi Express
DiDi Premier
DiDi Luxe
DiDi Bus
DiDi Designated Driving
DiDi Enterprise Solutions
DiDi Bike Sharing

CONTACTS: Note: Officers with more than one job title may be intentionally listed here more than once.
Cheng Wei, CEO
Jean Liu, Pres.
Bo Zhang, CTO

GROWTH PLANS/SPECIAL FEATURES:
Didi Chuxing is the largest mobile ride-sharing platform in China. The company offers a full range of app-based transportation options for 550 million users, including DiDi Taxi, DiDi Express, DiDi Premier, DiDi Luxe, DiDi Bus, DiDi Designated Driving, DiDi Enterprise Solutions, DiDi Bike Sharing, E-bike Sharing, Car Sharing and food delivery. DiDi partners with Grab, Lyft, Ola, Uber, 99, Taxify and Careem in a global ride-hailing network that reaches over 80% of the world's population across over 1,000 cities. Currently, DiDi provides ride-hailing services in Brazil under the 99 brand, operates DiDi-branded mobility services in Mexico and Australia, and provides taxi-hailing service in Japan through a joint venture.

FINANCIAL DATA: Note: Data for latest year may not have been available at press time.

In U.S. $	2018	2017	2016	2015	2014	2013
Revenue	3,770,000,000	2,000,000,000	1,000,000,000			
R&D Expense						
Operating Income						
Operating Margin %						
SGA Expense						
Net Income						
Operating Cash Flow						
Capital Expenditure						
EBITDA						
Return on Assets %						
Return on Equity %						
Debt to Equity						

CONTACT INFORMATION:
Phone: 86 40 0766 6998   Fax:
Toll-Free:
Address: No. 447 Wen San Road, Hangzhou, 310013 China

STOCK TICKER/OTHER:
Stock Ticker: Private
Employees: 15,000
Parent Company:

Exchange:
Fiscal Year Ends:

SALARIES/BONUSES:
Top Exec. Salary: $ Bonus: $
Second Exec. Salary: $ Bonus: $

OTHER THOUGHTS:
Estimated Female Officers or Directors:
Hot Spot for Advancement for Women/Minorities:

Digg Inc

NAIC Code: 519130

www.digg.com

TYPES OF BUSINESS:

Online Media Aggregator
News and Internet Story Sharing
Advertising Services

BRANDS/DIVISIONS/AFFILIATES:

BuySellAds.com Inc
Daily Digg (The)

GROWTH PLANS/SPECIAL FEATURES:

Digg, Inc. operates a community website that allows users to share items found elsewhere on the internet. The site's content is generated by individuals submitting links and small descriptor blurbs for pieces of media they find interesting. Other users can then vote up (or down) the submissions to rate their popularity. Featured content ranges from news stories to images, videos, websites and blogs. Each submission includes an area for community comments for people to contribute their views. Items also can be re-shared through certain social media networks, such as Facebook, Tumblr and Twitter. Digg is available on the web via iOS or Android devices. Digg updates known as The Daily Digg are available via email. In April 2018, Digg was acquired by BuySellAds.com, Inc. from Betaworks Studio, LLC

CONTACTS: Note: Officers with more than one job title may be intentionally listed here more than once.

Gary Liu, CEO
Kevin Barnett, Dir.-Front End Dev.
John Borthwick, CEO-betaworks
Andrew McLaughlin, Chmn.

FINANCIAL DATA: Note: Data for latest year may not have been available at press time.

In U.S. $	2018	2017	2016	2015	2014	2013
Revenue						
R&D Expense						
Operating Income						
Operating Margin %						
SGA Expense						
Net Income						
Operating Cash Flow						
Capital Expenditure						
EBITDA						
Return on Assets %						
Return on Equity %						
Debt to Equity						

CONTACT INFORMATION:

Phone: 415-355-3000   Fax:
Toll-Free:
Address: 109 S. 5th St., Brooklyn, NY 11249 United States

STOCK TICKER/OTHER:

Stock Ticker: Subsidiary   Exchange:
Employees: 25   Fiscal Year Ends:
Parent Company: BuySellAds.com Inc

SALARIES/BONUSES:

Top Exec. Salary: $ Bonus: $
Second Exec. Salary: $ Bonus: $

OTHER THOUGHTS:

Estimated Female Officers or Directors: 2
Hot Spot for Advancement for Women/Minorities:

Digital River Inc

NAIC Code: 511210M

TYPES OF BUSINESS:

E-Commerce Software
E-Commerce Outsourcing
Digital Software Delivery
Web Development
Marketing & Merchandising Services
Fraud Screening
Transaction Processing

BRANDS/DIVISIONS/AFFILIATES:

Commerce Cloud

CONTACTS: *Note: Officers with more than one job title may be intentionally listed here more than once.*

Adam Coyle, CEO
Kathy Tompt, Chief of Staff
Matthew Reck, CFO
James Gagliardi, Chief Product Officer
KT Schmidt, Chief Administrative Officer
Ryan Douglas, CIO
Kevin Crudden, General Counsel

GROWTH PLANS/SPECIAL FEATURES:

Digital River, Inc. provides end-to-end e-commerce, payments and marketing solutions to diverse companies throughout the U.S., Europe, Asia Pacific and South America. The firm's offerings are categorized into: Commerce Cloud, monetization and billing and global services. Digital River's Commerce Cloud is a software-as-a-service (SaaS) commerce scaled for worldwide expansion, and is an agile, always-on system for speed to global markets. It is equipped with self-service tools so clients can control, merchandise and sell products seamlessly online. Commerce Cloud enables business transactions from virtually anywhere, with over 190 bank connections worldwide, in 26 languages and 108 currencies. Digital River's network of warehouses and logistics partners equips clients with inventory tools to manage pre-orders, back orders, split shipments, reporting and more. The company's platform handles every type of monetization for a global economy, including subscription revenue optimization via fixed, tiered and pro-rated pricing plans as well as a range of billing plans. Digital River also offers shoppers free trials of its products before subscribing, which lowers the barrier to entry and attracts dedicated consumers. Its microtransaction and wallet module enables clients to sell across multiple economies, payment methods and devices. Last, global services include risk management, with Digital River taking on the transactional liabilities and financial risks of the client's global commerce. The company has 18 legal entities in key regions with teams of local experts to navigate the rules and relationships of various markets, including Asian credit card regulations, denied persons screening in Europe, compliance in South America and more. This division also offers full service tax management via tools that validate addresses, sequence invoices and registration numbers, inform about international trade regulations and more. These features make calculating, collecting, reporting and remitting tax information much easier for Digital River clients.

Digital River offers its employees comprehensive benefits.

FINANCIAL DATA: *Note: Data for latest year may not have been available at press time.*

In U.S. $	2018	2017	2016	2015	2014	2013
Revenue	450,000,000	420,000,000	401,500,000	381,000,000	376,500,000	389,679,008
R&D Expense						
Operating Income						
Operating Margin %						
SGA Expense						
Net Income						
Operating Cash Flow						
Capital Expenditure						
EBITDA						
Return on Assets %						
Return on Equity %						
Debt to Equity						

CONTACT INFORMATION:

Phone: 952 253-1234   Fax: 952 646-5604
Toll-Free:
Address: 1038 Bren Rd. W., Minnetonka, MN 55343 United States

STOCK TICKER/OTHER:

Stock Ticker: Private   Exchange:
Employees: 1,317   Fiscal Year Ends: 12/31
Parent Company:

SALARIES/BONUSES:

Top Exec. Salary: $ Bonus: $
Second Exec. Salary: $ Bonus: $

OTHER THOUGHTS:

Estimated Female Officers or Directors: 3
Hot Spot for Advancement for Women/Minorities: Y

DigitalOcean Inc

NAIC Code: 517110

www.digitalocean.com

TYPES OF BUSINESS:
Web Hosting Services

BRANDS/DIVISIONS/AFFILIATES:
Droplet

CONTACTS: *Note: Officers with more than one job title may be intentionally listed here more than once.*

Mark Templeton, CEO
Karl Alomar, COO
Steve Senneff, CFO
Tom Berger, VP-Mktg.
Matt Hoffman, VP-Human Resources
Shiven Ramji, VP-Product

GROWTH PLANS/SPECIAL FEATURES:

DigitalOcean, Inc. is a New York-based cloud hosting service provider. The firm provides cloud infrastructure for developers to build websites and applications upon. There are more than 1 million developer users of DigitalOcean's cloud hosting service who take advantage of its 12 data centers located throughout the world, in nearly 200 countries. The company's products include: Droplet, a solid-state drive (SSD) cloud server that deploys in seconds; block storage, with volumes up to 16 terabytes (TB) and the ability to attach multiple volumes to a Droplet; spaces, to store, serve, backup and archive media, web content, images and static files; managed Kubernetes, which is designed for simple and cost-effective container orchestration; load balancing, for scaling applications and improving availability, security and performance across the entire infrastructure; and app deployment, featuring pre-built apps that can be deployed with a single click. DigitalOcean offers a variety of monthly memberships ranging from the $5 a month plan with 1 gigabyte of memory, to a high-volume plan costing $960 a month with 192 gigabytes of memory. In addition, block storage, spaces, backups, snapshots and networking prices are offered in various formats, including only pay what you use, monthly options, percentage of computing, per load balancer and free cloud firewalls. Tools and services offered by the company include monitoring and alerts, cloud firewalls, team accounts, command line interface (CLI), API, pre-built open source apps, 99.99% service level agreement (SLA), domain name system (DNS), worldwide availability and 24/7 technical support.

DigitalOcean offers its employees comprehensive health benefits, commuter benefits, 401(k) and education support.

FINANCIAL DATA: *Note: Data for latest year may not have been available at press time.*

In U.S. $	2018	2017	2016	2015	2014	2013
Revenue		135,000,000	118,000,000	77,000,000	37,000,000	
R&D Expense						
Operating Income						
Operating Margin %						
SGA Expense						
Net Income						
Operating Cash Flow						
Capital Expenditure						
EBITDA						
Return on Assets %						
Return on Equity %						
Debt to Equity						

CONTACT INFORMATION:
Phone: 347-903-7918   Fax:
Toll-Free:
Address: 101 Ave. of Americas, 10/Fl, New York, NY 10013 United States

STOCK TICKER/OTHER:
Stock Ticker: Private   Exchange:
Employees: 400   Fiscal Year Ends:
Parent Company:

SALARIES/BONUSES:
Top Exec. Salary: $ Bonus: $
Second Exec. Salary: $ Bonus: $

OTHER THOUGHTS:
Estimated Female Officers or Directors:
Hot Spot for Advancement for Women/Minorities:

Digitas

NAIC Code: 541800

TYPES OF BUSINESS:

Database Marketing Services
Strategic Consulting Services
Customer Relationship Management
Online Advertising & Marketing Services
E-Commerce Platforms, Web Design & Development

BRANDS/DIVISIONS/AFFILIATES:

Publicis Groupe SA
Marketing Cloud

CONTACTS: *Note: Officers with more than one job title may be intentionally listed here more than once.*

Michael Kahn, Global Pres.
Peter Miller, Global CFO
Jill Kelly, Chief Mktg. & Communications Officer
Erin Quill Keough, Chief Talent Officer
Jill Kelly, Exec. VP-Corp. Comm.
Tony Weisman, CEO-North America
Lincoln Bjorkman, Chief Creative Officer-North America
Vincent Digonnet, Pres., Asia Pacific
Sav Evangelous, Exec. Creative Dir.-Int'l
Stephan Beringer, Pres.

GROWTH PLANS/SPECIAL FEATURES:

Digitas is a leading marketing and technology agency. The firm specializes in creating marketing engines that drive customer acquisition, cross-selling, loyalty, affinity and customer care operations across digital and direct media for its Fortune 500 clientele. Its marketing channels include direct mail, websites, online advertising, e-mail, print advertising, mobile applications, television commercials and events and promotions. Digitas's Marketing Cloud is a suite of processes and tools specially created to help clients engage audiences on a global scale, across multiple platforms in real time. The company designs and builds web portals from scratch, provides affiliate marketing, designs brand content, engages and measures user experience, creates mobile applications, embeds its social media expertise into its technology and products, manages/hosts websites, provides analytics services, provides search engine optimization, sets up pay-per-click marketing strategies, provides user research solutions and more. Headquartered in Massachusetts, the firm has additional U.S. offices as well as many international offices located across Latin America, Europe, Asia Pacific, the Middle East and Africa. Digitas operates as a subsidiary of Publicis Groupe SA. In March 2018, the firm announced that it was changing its name back to Digitas from DigitasLBi.

Digitas offers employees health, dental and vision insurance; vacation days; flex days; paid holidays; and a 401(k) plan.

FINANCIAL DATA: *Note: Data for latest year may not have been available at press time.*

In U.S. $	2018	2017	2016	2015	2014	2013
Revenue		622,000,000	615,000,000	590,000,000	589,000,000	575,000,000
R&D Expense						
Operating Income						
Operating Margin %						
SGA Expense						
Net Income						
Operating Cash Flow						
Capital Expenditure						
EBITDA						
Return on Assets %						
Return on Equity %						
Debt to Equity						

CONTACT INFORMATION:

Phone: 617-867-1000   Fax:
Toll-Free:
Address: 33 Arch St., Boston, MA 02110 United States

STOCK TICKER/OTHER:

Stock Ticker: Subsidiary   Exchange:
Employees: 1,740   Fiscal Year Ends: 12/31
Parent Company: Publicis Groupe SA

SALARIES/BONUSES:

Top Exec. Salary: $ Bonus: $
Second Exec. Salary: $ Bonus: $

OTHER THOUGHTS:

Estimated Female Officers or Directors: 6
Hot Spot for Advancement for Women/Minorities: Y

DirecTV LLC (DIRECTV)

www.directv.com

NAIC Code: 517110

TYPES OF BUSINESS:

Satellite Broadcasting
Commercial Satellite Fleet
Satellite-Based Internet Services
Digital Television

BRANDS/DIVISIONS/AFFILIATES:

AT&T Inc
DirectNOW
Genie HD DVR

CONTACTS: *Note: Officers with more than one job title may be intentionally listed here more than once.*

Michael White, CEO
Patrick Doyle, CFO
Romulo Pontual, Chief Technology Officer
Larry Hunter, Executive VP
Joseph Bosch, Executive VP
Bruce Churchill, Executive VP
Steven Adams, Senior VP
Fazal Merchant, Senior VP

GROWTH PLANS/SPECIAL FEATURES:

DirecTV, LLC (DIRECTV), a wholly-owned subsidiary of AT&T, Inc., is a leading provider of digital television entertainment throughout the U.S. and Latin America. The company manages a fleet of satellites in geostationary orbit to ensure strong coverage of the North American continent. DIRECTV's current (as of June 2018) packages include: Select, offering 155 channels for a monthly fee; Entertainment, offering 160 channels; Choice, offering 185 channels; XTRA, offering 235 channels; Ultimate, offering more than 250 channels; and Premier, offering more than 330 channels. Choice through Premier options receive the firm's NFL Sunday season package for free. DirectNOW offers streaming services of more than 60 live channels, as well as 25,000 titles on demand, with no annual contract, installation or equipment needed. DirectNOW packages start at $35 per month. DIRECTV's Genie HD DVR enables customers to seamlessly swap what they are watching from one TV to another, or from tablet to TV, anywhere in the home. Genie HD can record up to five shows at once and store up to 200 hours of HD entertainment. In addition, shows that have aired within the last 72 hours can be rewound and watched as live shows with Genie's DIRECTV 72 Hour Rewind feature. DIRECTV packages can be bundled with AT&T services, and the firm offers DIRECTV services for businesses.

Employees receive medical, dental and vision coverage; flexible spending accounts; wellness plans; employee assistance programs; and a 401(k) savings plan with a matching contribution opportunity.

FINANCIAL DATA: *Note: Data for latest year may not have been available at press time.*

In U.S. $	2018	2017	2016	2015	2014	2013
Revenue		35,584,900,000	33,703,000,000	34,000,000,000	33,260,000,000	31,754,000,000
R&D Expense						
Operating Income						
Operating Margin %						
SGA Expense						
Net Income		4,305,000,000	32,000,000	-100,000	3,102,000,000	2,995,000,000
Operating Cash Flow						
Capital Expenditure						
EBITDA						
Return on Assets %						
Return on Equity %						
Debt to Equity						

CONTACT INFORMATION:

Phone: 310-964-5000   Fax:
Toll-Free:
Address: 2260 E. Imperial Hwy., El Segundo, CA 90245 United States

STOCK TICKER/OTHER:

Stock Ticker: Subsidiary   Exchange:
Employees: 32,150   Fiscal Year Ends: 12/31
Parent Company: AT&T Inc

SALARIES/BONUSES:

Top Exec. Salary: $ Bonus: $
Second Exec. Salary: $ Bonus: $

OTHER THOUGHTS:

Estimated Female Officers or Directors: 3
Hot Spot for Advancement for Women/Minorities: Y

DocuSign Inc

NAIC Code: 511210Q

www.docusign.com

TYPES OF BUSINESS:

Online Signature Management Software

BRANDS/DIVISIONS/AFFILIATES:

Digital Transaction Management
DocuSign eSignature
DocuSign Global Trust Network (The)

CONTACTS: Note: Officers with more than one job title may be intentionally listed here more than once.

Daniel Springer, CEO
Michael Sheridan, CFO
Keith Krach, Chairman of the Board
Kirsten Wolberg, Chief Technology Officer
Scott Olrich, Co-COO
Reginald Davis, General Counsel
William Hudspith, President, Divisional

GROWTH PLANS/SPECIAL FEATURES:

DocuSign, Inc. provides a cloud-based electronic signature platform that helps organizations, businesses, enterprises and individuals of all sizes collect information, automate data workflows and sign on various devices. Its platform automates manual and paper-based processes that allow users to manage documented business transactions, including identity management, authentication, digital signature, forms/data collection, collaboration and workflow automation and storage. Docusign's Digital Transaction Management is a category of software designed to safely and securely manage document-based transactions digitally, and removes friction inherent in processes that involve people, documents and data inside and beyond the firewall. Its DocuSign eSignature application programming interface (API) enables the sending of electronic signature requests and the eSign of documents via mobile app. It also tracks documents in real-time. These electronic processes create faster, easier and secure transactions. DocuSign provides training and support services. More than 425,000 companies and over 200 million users in 188 countries utilize DocuSign. More than 64% of documents are completed within one hour on The DocuSign Global Trust Network. DocuSign offers transaction management services and is the National Association of REALTORS Official and Exclusive provider of electronic signature services under the REALTOR Benefits Program. DocuSign has domestic offices in San Francisco, Illinois, New York and Seattle, USA, with international offices in Ireland, Israel, the U.K., Australia, France, Brazil, Singapore and Japan. In September 2018, the firm completed its acquisition of SpringCM, a cloud-based document generation and contract lifecycle management software company.

FINANCIAL DATA: Note: Data for latest year may not have been available at press time.

In U.S. $	2018	2017	2016	2015	2014	2013
Revenue	518,504,000	381,459,000	250,481,000			
R&D Expense	92,428,000	89,652,000	62,255,000			
Operating Income	-51,653,000	-115,817,000	-119,304,000			
Operating Margin %	-9.96	-30.36%	-47.63%			
SGA Expense	359,456,000	305,147,000	233,675,000			
Net Income	-52,276,000	-115,412,000	-122,559,000			
Operating Cash Flow	54,979,000	-4,790,000	-67,995,000			
Capital Expenditure	18,929,000	43,330,000	28,305,000			
EBITDA	-16,798,000	-85,976,000	-105,192,000			
Return on Assets %	-9.30%	-23.62%	-25.48%			
Return on Equity %						
Debt to Equity						

CONTACT INFORMATION:

Phone: 866-219-4318   Fax:
Toll-Free:
Address: 221 Main St., Ste. 1000, San Francisco, CA 94105 United States

STOCK TICKER/OTHER:

Stock Ticker: DOCU   Exchange: NAS
Employees: 2,255   Fiscal Year Ends: 01/31
Parent Company:

SALARIES/BONUSES:

Top Exec. Salary: $360,769   Bonus: $
Second Exec. Salary: $242,308   Bonus: $

OTHER THOUGHTS:

Estimated Female Officers or Directors:
Hot Spot for Advancement for Women/Minorities:

Sales, profits and employees may be estimates. Financial information, benefits and other data can change quickly and may vary from those stated here.

Domo Inc

www.domo.com

NAIC Code: 511210J

TYPES OF BUSINESS:

Computer Software, Data Base & File Management
Software

BRANDS/DIVISIONS/AFFILIATES:

Domo Data Science Suite

CONTACTS: *Note: Officers with more than one job title may be intentionally listed here more than once.*

Joshua James, CEO
Bruce Felt, CFO
Catherine Wong, Executive VP, Divisional

GROWTH PLANS/SPECIAL FEATURES:

Domo, Inc. provides computer software, specializing in business intelligence tools and data visualization. The company's Domo software connects businesses with the data needed to improve business results, and to make smarter decisions faster. Domo runs on the business cloud, and offers more than 1,000 apps in order to quickly leverage the expertise and workflows businesses teams need to succeed. Its infrastructure enables companies to build custom apps via design tools, and use application program interfaces (APIs) to connect to proprietary data sources and systems in real-time. Domo serves executives across every role, and is scalable across business size, whether a startup of 50 or an enterprise of 50,000. Because Domo's business cloud is an open system platform, it is not constrained to one specific model or deployment methodology. The Domo Data Science Suite brings both basic and advanced data science capabilities directly into the Domo platform, making it simpler and faster to automatically deliver new insights directly to decision makers across the business. The firm's solutions serve various department roles, including business intelligence, CEO, finance, IT, marketing, operations, sales and services. Industries served include education, financial services, healthcare, high tech, hospitality, manufacturing, media/entertainment, professional services, retail/e-commerce and transportation. During 2018, Domo began trading on the Nasdaq under ticker symbol: DOMO.

FINANCIAL DATA: *Note: Data for latest year may not have been available at press time.*

In U.S. $	2018	2017	2016	2015	2014	2013
Revenue	108,524,000	74,540,000				
R&D Expense	78,261,000	76,164,000				
Operating Income	-175,781,000	-182,860,000				
Operating Margin %	-161.97	-245.31%				
SGA Expense	161,125,000	148,041,000				
Net Income	-176,562,000	-183,120,000				
Operating Cash Flow	-148,657,000	-144,144,000				
Capital Expenditure	7,596,000	11,644,000				
EBITDA	-167,650,000	-177,661,000				
Return on Assets %	-120.40%	-132.77%				
Return on Equity %						
Debt to Equity						

CONTACT INFORMATION:

Phone: 801-899-1000   Fax:
Toll-Free: 800-899-1000
Address: 772 East Utah Valley Dr., American Fork, UT 84003 United States

STOCK TICKER/OTHER:

Stock Ticker: DOMO   Exchange: NAS
Employees: 796   Fiscal Year Ends:
Parent Company:

SALARIES/BONUSES:

Top Exec. Salary: $350,000   Bonus: $450,000
Second Exec. Salary: $350,000   Bonus: $175,000

OTHER THOUGHTS:

Estimated Female Officers or Directors:
Hot Spot for Advancement for Women/Minorities:

Dotdash
NAIC Code: 519130

www.about.com

TYPES OF BUSINESS:
Online Information
Niche Online Communities
Human-Filtered Online Directories

BRANDS/DIVISIONS/AFFILIATES:
IAC/InterActiveCorp
Very Well
Spruce (The)
Lifewire
Balance (The)
Trip Savvy
ThoughtCo

CONTACTS: *Note: Officers with more than one job title may be intentionally listed here more than once.*
Neil Vogel, CEO
Alex Ellerson, COO
Tim Quinn, CFO
Sandy Pinos-Chin, Sr. Dir.-Human Resources
Nabil Ahmad, CTO
Nabil Ahmad, Sr. VP-Tech.
Tricia Han, Sr. VP-Product
Brad Simon, General Counsel
Chris Coluzzi, Sr. VP-Oper.
Igor Lebovic, Sr. VP-Growth
Alex Ellerson, Sr. VP-Content
Brian Colbert, Chief Revenue Officer

GROWTH PLANS/SPECIAL FEATURES:
Dotdash, formerly About.com, is an internet directory that operates topic-specific web guide sites that offer expert solutions to a variety of daily needs, including healthcare, technology, cooking, travel and parenting. The firm is a subsidiary of IAC/InterActiveCorp. Dotdash has more than 100 million unique visitors every month. The sites are grouped into six brand categories: Very Well, The Spruce, Lifewire, The Balance, Trip Savvy and ThoughtCo. Very Well takes a human approach to health and well-being, delivering accessible solutions and an alternative to clinical sites. Verywell.com has more than 16 million monthly unique users, with its writers comprising doctors, pharmacists, dietitians, trainers and other professionals. The Spruce is a home and food website for people looking for information on home improvements or upgrading cooking and baking skills. Thespruce.com has 3.3 million millennial users, 30 million monthly unique users and 5 million homeowners. Lifewire helps people get the most out of technology, and shows them how to fix, choose what to buy and get the best out of what they have. Lifewire.com has 10 million monthly unique visitors. The Balance is a financial site to help people gain better control of their money or career plans. It helps them earn more, spend smarter, invest well and build a more secure future at its www.thebalance.com website. The Balance has 24 million monthly unique visitors, with 57% of them being female. Trip Savvy is a travel site written by local experts to offer vacationers guidance and confidence before traveling. Tripsavvy.com has 6.3 million monthly unique visitors. Last, ThoughtCo. provides in-depth articles on many subjects, including science, history, math and religion. Thoughtco.com has 74,000 pieces of content and 13 million monthly unique visitors. Headquartered in New York, the firm has offices in Chicago and San Francisco.

FINANCIAL DATA: *Note: Data for latest year may not have been available at press time.*

In U.S. $	2018	2017	2016	2015	2014	2013
Revenue	215,000,000	210,000,000	200,588,940	185,000,000	160,000,000	150,000,000
R&D Expense						
Operating Income						
Operating Margin %						
SGA Expense						
Net Income						
Operating Cash Flow						
Capital Expenditure						
EBITDA						
Return on Assets %						
Return on Equity %						
Debt to Equity						

CONTACT INFORMATION:
Phone: 212-204-4000   Fax:
Toll-Free:
Address: 1500 Broadway, Fl. 6, New York, NY 10036 United States

STOCK TICKER/OTHER:
Stock Ticker: Subsidiary   Exchange:
Employees: Fiscal Year Ends: 12/31
Parent Company: IAC/InterActiveCorp

SALARIES/BONUSES:
Top Exec. Salary: $ Bonus: $
Second Exec. Salary: $ Bonus: $

OTHER THOUGHTS:
Estimated Female Officers or Directors: 1
Hot Spot for Advancement for Women/Minorities: Y

Dow Jones & Company Inc

www.dowjones.com

NAIC Code: 511110

TYPES OF BUSINESS:

Newspaper Publishing-Financial News
Business Publishing
Community Newspapers
Electronic & Online Publishing
Financial Indices
Financial Information Services

BRANDS/DIVISIONS/AFFILIATES:

Dow Jones Curation Services
Dow Jones Risk & Compliance
Dow Jones Newswires
WSJ Pro
Wall Street Journal (The)
Barrons
MarketWatch
News Corporation

CONTACTS: Note: Officers with more than one job title may be intentionally listed here more than once.

William Lewis, CEO
Anna Sedgley, COO
Edwin A. Finn, Jr., Pres.
Christina Van Tassell, CFO
Mark Musgrave, Chief People Officer
Ramin Beheshti, Chief Product & Technology Officer
Stephen Orban, Head-Tech.
Dean Del Vecchio, Chief Admin. Officer
Mark H. Jackson, General Counsel
Joseph Vincent, Head-Oper.
Ingrid Verschuren, Head-Data Strategy
Michael Rolnick, Head-Digital
Paula Keve, Chief Comm. Officer
Christina Komporlis, Head-Print Circulation
Daniel Hayter, Head-Institutional Sales
Georgene Huang, Head-Institutional Products
Daniel Hayter, Head-Institutional Sales, Americas
Rupert Murdoch, Chmn.
Kelly E. Leach, Managing Dir.-EMEA

GROWTH PLANS/SPECIAL FEATURES:

Dow Jones & Company, Inc., a subsidiary of News Corporation, is a global provider of business and financial news information. With millions of readers worldwide, the firm distributes information through newspapers, newswires, magazines, television, radio stations and the internet. Its products include: Dow Jones Curation Services, a curation offering providing relevant world news content grouped by subject matter according to personal business needs; Dow Jones Factiva, a global news database featuring nearly 33,000 sources; Dow Jones Risk & Compliance, a provider of third-party risk management and regulatory compliance solutions; and Dow Jones Newswires, delivering comprehensive global business insights, rolling market commentary and expert analysis. Other products include WSJ Pro, a global, industry-specific membership offering reporting, insight and data; Dow Jones Private Equity & Venture Capital, a suite of news and data on companies backed by venture capital and private equity in every region, industry and stage of development; and The Wall Street Journal, which includes coverage of U.S. and world news, politics, arts, culture, lifestyle, sports, health and more. Barron's is a source of market ideas and insights to help self-directed investors grow their portfolios; MarketWatch provides financial news and market data; Financial News provides news, analysis and commentary on wholesale financial and European securities industries across the sectors of investment banking, asset management, private equity, trading and technology and Fintech; and Dow Jones DJX unites Factiva, Risk and Compliance, Private Equity/Venture Capital and Dow Jones Newswires in one place. In addition, Dow Jones Integrated Solutions integrates premium data into client and third-party products via feeds and APIs; and Dow Jones Reprints provides transaction-based services for the licensing of Dow Jones' branded content. In March 2018, subsidiary Dow Jones Risk & Compliance acquired Cerico, a digital compliance tool company for international business.

FINANCIAL DATA: Note: Data for latest year may not have been available at press time.

In U.S. $	2018	2017	2016	2015	2014	2013
Revenue	3,000,000,000	2,950,000,000	2,810,000,000	2,650,000,000	2,500,000,000	2,350,000,000
R&D Expense						
Operating Income						
Operating Margin %						
SGA Expense						
Net Income						
Operating Cash Flow						
Capital Expenditure						
EBITDA						
Return on Assets %						
Return on Equity %						
Debt to Equity						

CONTACT INFORMATION:

Phone: 212-416-2000   Fax: 412-416-4348
Toll-Free: 800-223-2274
Address: 200 Liberty St., 1 World Financial Ctr., New York, NY 10281
United States

STOCK TICKER/OTHER:

Stock Ticker: Subsidiary
Employees: 7,100
Parent Company: News Corporation

Exchange:
Fiscal Year Ends: 12/31

SALARIES/BONUSES:

Top Exec. Salary: $ Bonus: $
Second Exec. Salary: $ Bonus: $

OTHER THOUGHTS:

Estimated Female Officers or Directors: 10
Hot Spot for Advancement for Women/Minorities: Y

Dropbox Inc
NAIC Code: 519130

www.dropbox.com

TYPES OF BUSINESS:
Online Data Storage and Sharing
Online Storage and Sharing Database

BRANDS/DIVISIONS/AFFILIATES:
Standard Dropbox
Dropbox Paper
Advanced Dropbox
Enterprise Dropbox

CONTACTS: *Note: Officers with more than one job title may be intentionally listed here more than once.*
Andrew Houston, CEO
Ajay Vashee, CFO
Arash Ferdowsi, Co-Founder
Bart Volkmer, General Counsel
Yamini Rangan, Other Executive Officer
Quentin Clark, Senior VP, Divisional
Lin-Hua Wu, Vice President, Divisional

GROWTH PLANS/SPECIAL FEATURES:
Dropbox, Inc. is an online database that allows users to store and share personal photos, documents and videos from anywhere via any device. Over 500 million users across 180 countries use Dropbox. Consumers can choose from three different subscriptions and storage plans. These plans include: Standard Dropbox, for $12.50 per user, per month, offering 3 terabytes (TB) of storage space with easy-to-use sharing and collaboration tools, 120 days of file recovery, 256-bit AES and SSL/TLS encryption, smart sync, Dropbox Paper administration tools, Office 365 integration, admin console and audit log, granular sharing permissions, user and company-managed groups, remote device wipe, require two-factor authentication, unlimited API access to security and productivity platform partners, 25,000 API calls/month for data transport partners and live chat support; Advanced Dropbox ($20 per user, per month), contains everything in Standard, but offers as much space as needed as well as sophisticated administration, audit and integration features; and Enterprise Dropbox (for large organizations and the subscription price is negotiated), offering everything in Advanced, as well as account capture, network control, enterprise mobility management and support, domain insights, integration and development support, assigned account success manager, advanced training for end users and admins and 24/7 support. Based in San Francisco, the firm has offices in Austin, Dublin, Herzliya, London, New York, Paris, Seattle, Sydney, Hamburg, Amsterdam, Washington, D.C. and Tokyo. During 2018, Dropbox began trading on the Nasdaq under ticker symbol DBX.

FINANCIAL DATA: *Note: Data for latest year may not have been available at press time.*

In U.S. $	2018	2017	2016	2015	2014	2013
Revenue		1,106,800,000	844,800,000	603,800,000		
R&D Expense		380,300,000	289,700,000	201,600,000		
Operating Income		-113,700,000	-193,500,000	-306,200,000		
Operating Margin %		-10.27%	-22.90%	-50.71%		
SGA Expense		471,300,000	358,000,000	301,000,000		
Net Income		-111,700,000	-210,200,000	-325,900,000		
Operating Cash Flow		330,300,000	252,600,000	14,800,000		
Capital Expenditure		26,100,000	123,700,000	83,300,000		
EBITDA		68,100,000	-1,900,000	-156,600,000		
Return on Assets %		-11.03%	-20.93%			
Return on Equity %						
Debt to Equity						

CONTACT INFORMATION:
Phone: 415-986-7057   Fax:
Toll-Free: 855-237-6726
Address: 333 Brannan St, San Francisco, CA 94107 United States

STOCK TICKER/OTHER:
Stock Ticker: DBX   Exchange: NAS
Employees: 1,858   Fiscal Year Ends: 12/31
Parent Company:

SALARIES/BONUSES:
Top Exec. Salary: $ Bonus: $
Second Exec. Salary: $ Bonus: $

OTHER THOUGHTS:
Estimated Female Officers or Directors: 1
Hot Spot for Advancement for Women/Minorities:

Duo Security Inc

NAIC Code: 511210E

duo.com

TYPES OF BUSINESS:
Computer Software, Security & Anti-Virus
Software
Security

BRANDS/DIVISIONS/AFFILIATES:
Cisco Systems Inc

GROWTH PLANS/SPECIAL FEATURES:
Duo Security, Inc. provides cloud-based access security for companies of all sizes. The firm protects organizations against data breaches by ensuring that only legitimate users and appropriate devices have access to sensitive data and applications anytime, anywhere. Duo Security's security product offers two-factor authentication, checks the security health of devices, blocks access when risks appear and protects every application from unauthorized access (on-premise or cloud-based). Duo Security has 500 million authentications each month and more than 14,000 paying customers. In October 2018, the firm was acquired by Cisco Systems, Inc., the worldwide technology leader, for $2.35 billion.

CONTACTS: *Note: Officers with more than one job title may be intentionally listed here more than once.*
Douglas Song, Managing Dir.
Jonathan Oberheide, CTO
Paul DiMarzo, Exec. VP-Corp. Dev.
Jim Cyb, Sr. VP-Worldwide Sales
Steve McElfresh, Sr. VP-People
Raffaele Mautone, CIO

FINANCIAL DATA: *Note: Data for latest year may not have been available at press time.*

In U.S. $	2018	2017	2016	2015	2014	2013
Revenue		100,000,000	73,000,000			
R&D Expense						
Operating Income						
Operating Margin %						
SGA Expense						
Net Income						
Operating Cash Flow						
Capital Expenditure						
EBITDA						
Return on Assets %						
Return on Equity %						
Debt to Equity						

CONTACT INFORMATION:
Phone: Fax:
Toll-Free: 866-760-4247
Address: 123 N. Ashley, Ste. 200, Ann Arbor, MI 48104 United States

STOCK TICKER/OTHER:
Stock Ticker: Subsidiary   Exchange:
Employees: 740   Fiscal Year Ends:
Parent Company: Cisco Systems Inc

SALARIES/BONUSES:
Top Exec. Salary: $ Bonus: $
Second Exec. Salary: $ Bonus: $

OTHER THOUGHTS:
Estimated Female Officers or Directors:
Hot Spot for Advancement for Women/Minorities:

Dynatrace LLC

NAIC Code: 511210m

www.dynatrace.com

TYPES OF BUSINESS:

Application Performance Management Tools
Software

BRANDS/DIVISIONS/AFFILIATES:

Digital Performance Platform

CONTACTS: *Note: Officers with more than one job title may be intentionally listed here more than once.*

John Van Siclen, CEO
Matthias Scharer, VP-Business Operations
Kevin Burns, CFO
Stephen Pace, Sr. VP-Global Sales
Denise Mitchell, VP-Human Resources
Bernd Greifeneder, CTO

GROWTH PLANS/SPECIAL FEATURES:

Dynatrace, LLC provides application performance management software. Its Digital Performance Platform makes digital performance visible and actionable primarily for business and IT industries. This all-in-one platform provides full analytic insights by monitoring every customer journey and business transaction, helping businesses make the best decisions possible. All relevant metrics, from real user behavior to application performance, including infrastructure, containers and cloud services, are tracked. Pre-configured and automatically-adjusted dashboards ensure ease of use, and installation requires no manual configuration at all. Artificial intelligence continuously auto-detects dependencies, learns application behavior, detects anomalies and proactively pinpoints root causes of issues. Dynatrace is designed for the world's largest environments and scales up to more than 100,000 hosts. Dynatrace helps clients go beyond release automation by introducing performance goals into development and test phases, not just production. Dynatrace is available as SaaS, managed or on premise, and seamlessly integrates into client IT landscapes, natively with open application program interfaces. Monitoring can begin in under five minutes after integration. Information technology can be automated by incorporating Dynatrace into the delivery pipeline, production environment and orchestration layer. The firm comprises more than 8,000 customers, including 72 of the Fortune 100. Headquartered in Massachusetts, USA, the company has locations in North America, Europe, Middle East, Africa, Asia-Pacific and Latin America.

FINANCIAL DATA: *Note: Data for latest year may not have been available at press time.*

In U.S. $	2018	2017	2016	2015	2014	2013
Revenue		512,000,000	400,000,000	376,600,000	326,900,000	55,900,000
R&D Expense						
Operating Income						
Operating Margin %						
SGA Expense						
Net Income						
Operating Cash Flow						
Capital Expenditure						
EBITDA						
Return on Assets %						
Return on Equity %						
Debt to Equity						

CONTACT INFORMATION:

Phone: 781-530-1000   Fax:
Toll-Free: 888-833-3652
Address: 1601 Trapelo Rd., Ste. 116, Waltham, MA 02451 United States

STOCK TICKER/OTHER:

Stock Ticker: Private   Exchange:
Employees: 1,700   Fiscal Year Ends:
Parent Company:

SALARIES/BONUSES:

Top Exec. Salary: $ Bonus: $
Second Exec. Salary: $ Bonus: $

OTHER THOUGHTS:

Estimated Female Officers or Directors:
Hot Spot for Advancement for Women/Minorities:

E*Trade Financial Corporation

www.etrade.com

NAIC Code: 523120

TYPES OF BUSINESS:

Stock Brokerage/Investment Management-Online
Lending
Portfolio Tracking & Records Management
Corporate Stock Plan Solutions
Venture Capital
Market Making
Financial Planning Services
Banking

BRANDS/DIVISIONS/AFFILIATES:

E*TRADE Securities LLC
Aperture LLC
OptionsHouse
E*TRADE Bank
E*TRADE Savings Bank
E*TRADE Financial Corporate Services
E*TRADE Mobile
E*TRADE.com

CONTACTS: Note: Officers with more than one job title may be intentionally listed here more than once.

Karl Roessner, CEO
Chad Turner, CFO
Rodger Lawson, Chairman of the Board
Brent Simonich, Chief Accounting Officer
Michael Pizzi, COO
Michael Curcio, Other Executive Officer
Lori Sher, Secretary

GROWTH PLANS/SPECIAL FEATURES:

E*TRADE Financial Corporation is a financial services company primarily serving individual retail investors and corporate clients under the E*TRADE Financial brand. The company also provides investor-focused banking products, mainly sweep deposits, to retail investors. E*TRADE operates directly as well as through numerous subsidiaries, many of which are overseen by governmental and self-regulatory organizations. Its investment choices include stocks, futures, options, exchange-traded funds (ETFs), mutual funds and bonds. The firm's most significant subsidiaries include: E*TRADE Securities, LLC, a registered broker-dealer that clears and settles securities transactions for customers; Aperture, LLC (which does business as OptionsHouse), a registered broker-dealer that provides brokerage products and services primarily to active traders through its derivatives platform; E*TRADE Bank, along with its subsidiary E*TRADE Savings Bank, which are federally-chartered savings banks that provide Federal Deposit Insurance Corporation (FDIC) insurance on qualifying amounts of customer deposits and other banking and cash management capabilities; E*TRADE Financial Corporate Services, a provider of software and services for managing equity compensation plans to corporate customers; and E*TRADE Capital Management LLC, a registered investment adviser which provides investment advisory services for E*TRADE's customers. The company's E*TRADE Mobile and desktop platforms allow customers to securely trade, monitor, pay bills and transfer funds between accounts via iPhone, iPad, Android phones, tablets and desktop computers. E*TRADE.com provides tools, guidance, actionable ideas, research and education for the handling of finances. In November 2018, E*TRADE announced it had acquired approximately 1 million Capital One Financial Corporation retail brokerage accounts at a price of $109 million.

The firm offers its employees benefits including flexible spending accounts; pharmacy benefits; life insurance; medical, dental and vision insurance; tuition assistance; an employee assistance program; and paid vacation.

FINANCIAL DATA: Note: Data for latest year may not have been available at press time.

In U.S. $	2018	2017	2016	2015	2014	2013
Revenue		2,366,000,000	1,941,000,000	1,363,000,000	1,701,000,000	1,609,337,000
R&D Expense						
Operating Income						
Operating Margin %						
SGA Expense		988,000,000	849,000,000	816,000,000	776,000,000	767,658,000
Net Income		614,000,000	552,000,000	268,000,000	293,000,000	86,012,000
Operating Cash Flow		1,121,000,000	1,625,000,000	832,000,000	701,000,000	1,117,082,000
Capital Expenditure		102,000,000	75,000,000	70,000,000	87,000,000	46,608,000
EBITDA						
Return on Assets %		1.04%	1.16%	.58%	.63%	.18%
Return on Equity %		9.71%	9.45%	4.79%	5.72%	1.76%
Debt to Equity		0.15	0.16	0.17	0.49	0.63

CONTACT INFORMATION:

Phone: 646 521-4300   Fax:
Toll-Free: 800-387-2331
Address: 1271 Avenue of the Americas, Fl. 14, New York, NY 10020
United States

STOCK TICKER/OTHER:

Stock Ticker: ETFC   Exchange: NAS
Employees: 3,600   Fiscal Year Ends: 12/31
Parent Company:

SALARIES/BONUSES:

Top Exec. Salary: $850,000   Bonus: $
Second Exec. Salary: Bonus: $
$850,000

OTHER THOUGHTS:

Estimated Female Officers or Directors: 3
Hot Spot for Advancement for Women/Minorities: Y

EarthLink

NAIC Code: 517110

TYPES OF BUSINESS:

Internet Service Provider (ISP)
Web Hosting Services
Voice Services
Managed IT & Data Hosting
Value-Added Services

BRANDS/DIVISIONS/AFFILIATES:

Windstream Holdings Inc

GROWTH PLANS/SPECIAL FEATURES:

EarthLink, the consumer division of Windstream Holdings, Inc., is a leading next-generation internet service provider. With access available across the U.S., the firm offers fast and reliable connectivity, customer support and customizable features. Internet access offerings include dial-up, high-speed digital subscriber line (DSL), free-standing DSL hyperlink internet, and a hyperlink and Apple TV option. Website tools and services include site design, domain and email hosting and solutions for businesses. Software and tools include security, WiFi privacy and access solutions.

CONTACTS: *Note: Officers with more than one job title may be intentionally listed here more than once.*

Tony Thomas, CEO
Julie Shimer, Chairman of the Board
Bradley Ferguson, Executive VP, Divisional
Louis Alterman, Executive VP
Samuel Desimone, Executive VP
John Dobbins, Executive VP
Gerard Brossard, Executive VP
Rick Froehlich, Executive VP
Valerie Benjamin, Senior VP, Divisional
R. Thurston, Vice President
Alan L. Wells, Chmn.-Windstream Holdings, Inc.

FINANCIAL DATA: *Note: Data for latest year may not have been available at press time.*

In U.S. $	2018	2017	2016	2015	2014	2013
Revenue		1,100,000,000	1,099,800,000	1,097,251,968	1,176,894,976	1,240,605,952
R&D Expense						
Operating Income						
Operating Margin %						
SGA Expense						
Net Income			7,680,000	-43,210,000	-72,752,000	-538,827,008
Operating Cash Flow						
Capital Expenditure						
EBITDA						
Return on Assets %						
Return on Equity %						
Debt to Equity						

CONTACT INFORMATION:

Phone: 404 815-0770   Fax:
Toll-Free: 800-327-8454
Address: 1439 Peachtree St., Atlanta, GA 30309 United States

STOCK TICKER/OTHER:

Stock Ticker: Subsidiary
Employees: 2,138
Parent Company: Windstream Holdings Inc

Exchange:
Fiscal Year Ends: 12/31

SALARIES/BONUSES:

Top Exec. Salary: $ Bonus: $
Second Exec. Salary: $ Bonus: $

OTHER THOUGHTS:

Estimated Female Officers or Directors: 5
Hot Spot for Advancement for Women/Minorities: Y

EasyAsk Inc

www.easyask.com

NAIC Code: 511210L

TYPES OF BUSINESS:

Software-Search & Information Retrieval
E-Commerce Software

BRANDS/DIVISIONS/AFFILIATES:

EasyAsk for eCommerce
eCommerce Mobile
EasyAsk Business
Quiri

CONTACTS: *Note: Officers with more than one job title may be intentionally listed here more than once.*

Craig Bassin, CEO
Richard Wood, VP-Dev.
Evan Bobotas, VP-Sales & Bus. Dev.
Richard Wood, VP-Dev.
John Morrell, VP-Prod. Mktg.

GROWTH PLANS/SPECIAL FEATURES:

EasyAsk, Inc. is a natural language search and information retrieval solutions company that provides single-point access to content for eCommerce and business intelligence. The company's natural language technology applies advanced linguistic understanding to break down content and produce better answers to search engine queries. The technology also interprets the intent of the question so customers can use their own vocabularies and still get useful results without being dependent on typical search engine text-matching. Quiri is a natural language query for analytics and applications with a natural language interface. EasyAsk for eCommerce is marketed towards retail merchandisers and offers websites search features such as full spectrum search, search within context, results grouping with relevant attributes, intelligent category search, search display control and search to landing page. The firm's eCommerce Mobile edition is a mobile web application platform that offers customized e-commerce searches for customers utilizing mobile online services. The EasyAsk Business edition accelerates and simplifies information, helping improve business operations. This program is aimed at business managers, executives, analysts and professional staff. The company has customers in businesses worldwide, including retail, financial services, healthcare, pharmaceutical, government and manufacturing. EasyAsk also offers a voice responsive mobile solution that allows professionals to interact with customer relationship management (CRM) data.

FINANCIAL DATA: *Note: Data for latest year may not have been available at press time.*

In U.S. $	2018	2017	2016	2015	2014	2013
Revenue						
R&D Expense						
Operating Income						
Operating Margin %						
SGA Expense						
Net Income						
Operating Cash Flow						
Capital Expenditure						
EBITDA						
Return on Assets %						
Return on Equity %						
Debt to Equity						

CONTACT INFORMATION:

Phone: 781-402-5635   Fax: 781-280-7380
Toll-Free: 800-425-8200
Address: 200 Summit Dr., South Tower, 3/Fl., Burlington, MA 01803 United States

STOCK TICKER/OTHER:

Stock Ticker: Private   Exchange:
Employees: 20   Fiscal Year Ends: 12/31
Parent Company:

SALARIES/BONUSES:

Top Exec. Salary: $ Bonus: $
Second Exec. Salary: $ Bonus: $

OTHER THOUGHTS:

Estimated Female Officers or Directors:
Hot Spot for Advancement for Women/Minorities:

eBay Inc

NAIC Code: 454112

www.ebay.com

TYPES OF BUSINESS:

Online Retail-Auctions
Online Payment Processing
Memorabilia & Collectibles
E-Commerce Services

BRANDS/DIVISIONS/AFFILIATES:

StubHub
www.ebay.com
www.stubhub.com
Mobile.de
Kijijiji
Gumtree
Marktplaats
eBay Kleinanzeigen

CONTACTS: *Note: Officers with more than one job title may be intentionally listed here more than once.*

Devin Wenig, CEO
Scott Schenkel, CFO
Thomas Tierney, Chairman of the Board
Brian Doerger, Chief Accounting Officer
Marie Huber, General Counsel
Kristin Yetto, Other Executive Officer
Raymond Pittman, Other Executive Officer
Stephen Fisher, Senior VP, Divisional
Wendy Jones, Senior VP, Divisional
Jae Lee, Senior VP, Geographical
Scott Cutler, Senior VP, Geographical
Jooman Park, Senior VP, Geographical

GROWTH PLANS/SPECIAL FEATURES:

EBay, Inc. is a global commerce leader, connecting millions of buyers and sellers worldwide. The company's technologies and services power its marketplace, StubHub and classifieds platforms, which organize a way for sellers around the world to offer their inventory for sale, and buyers to find and buy virtually anytime and anywhere. The marketplace platforms of eBay include its online website www.ebay.com, localized counterparts and eBay mobile applications. StubHub platforms include the firm's online ticket platform located at www.stubhub.com and the StubHub mobile application. These platforms provide fans with a safe, convenient place to purchase tickets to games, concerts and theater shows, as well as an easy way to sell tickets. The firm's classifieds platforms include a collection of brands such as Mobile.de, Kijiji, Gumtree, Marktplaats, eBay Kleinanzeigen and others. These platforms provide online classifieds around the world, helping people to find what they are looking for in their local communities. In May 2018, eBay notified Flipkart and Walmart that it intended to sell its holdings in Flipkart, which would represent gross proceeds of approximately $1.1 billion and end its current strategic relationship with Flipkart.

Employees of eBay are offered health insurance, wellness programs, financial advising and counseling, among other services.

FINANCIAL DATA: *Note: Data for latest year may not have been available at press time.*

In U.S. $	2018	2017	2016	2015	2014	2013
Revenue		9,567,000,000	8,979,000,000	8,592,000,000	17,902,000,000	16,047,000,000
R&D Expense		1,224,000,000	1,114,000,000	923,000,000	2,000,000,000	1,768,000,000
Operating Income		2,265,000,000	2,325,000,000	2,197,000,000	3,514,000,000	3,371,000,000
Operating Margin %		23.67%	25.89%	25.57%	19.62%	21.00%
SGA Expense		3,546,000,000	3,268,000,000	3,389,000,000	5,430,000,000	4,763,000,000
Net Income		-1,016,000,000	7,266,000,000	1,725,000,000	46,000,000	2,856,000,000
Operating Cash Flow		3,146,000,000	2,826,000,000	4,033,000,000	5,677,000,000	4,995,000,000
Capital Expenditure		666,000,000	626,000,000	668,000,000	1,271,000,000	1,250,000,000
EBITDA		3,244,000,000	4,558,000,000	3,237,000,000	5,144,000,000	4,966,000,000
Return on Assets %		-4.07%	34.90%	5.48%	.10%	7.27%
Return on Equity %		-10.92%	84.90%	13.02%	.21%	12.83%
Debt to Equity		1.14	0.71	1.03	0.34	0.17

CONTACT INFORMATION:

Phone: 408 376-7400   Fax: 408 558-7401
Toll-Free: 800-322-9266
Address: 2065 Hamilton Ave., San Jose, CA 95125 United States

STOCK TICKER/OTHER:

Stock Ticker: EBAY   Exchange: NAS
Employees: 12,600   Fiscal Year Ends: 12/31
Parent Company:

SALARIES/BONUSES:

Top Exec. Salary: $521,385   Bonus: $500,000
Second Exec. Salary: Bonus: $
$1,000,000

OTHER THOUGHTS:

Estimated Female Officers or Directors: 1
Hot Spot for Advancement for Women/Minorities: Y

ECI Telecom Ltd

www.ecitele.com

NAIC Code: 334210

TYPES OF BUSINESS:

Digital Communications Equipment Manufacturing
Optical Networking Equipment
Broadband Access Equipment
Data Encryption Services

BRANDS/DIVISIONS/AFFILIATES:

Swarth Group (The)
Ashmore Group plc
Elastic Services Platform
Apollo OPT
Neptune
Mercury NFV
Muse

CONTACTS: Note: Officers with more than one job title may be intentionally listed here more than once.

Darryl Edwards, CEO
Giora Bitan, CFO
Fernando Valdivielso, VP- Global Sales & Mktg.
Adi Bildner, VP-Global Human Resources
Tali Rosenwaks, Head-R&D
Hayim Porat, CTO
Tali Rosenwaks, Head-Eng.
Arnie Taragin, General Counsel
Hezi Basok, Exec. VP-Global Bus. Oper.
Eran Dariel, Gen. Mgr.-Portfolio Bus.
Eran Talmon, Head-Global Svcs. Div.
Shaul Shani, Chmn.

GROWTH PLANS/SPECIAL FEATURES:

ECI Telecom Ltd., based in Israel, delivers elastic network solutions to service providers, utilities and data center/cloud providers worldwide. The company's elastic network solutions ensure open, future-proof and secure communications. ECI's products include the following: the Elastic Services Platform, which simplifies service delivery and lifecycle management, and offers network assurance, optimization and automation; Apollo OPT, a family of optical transport and switching platforms that work seamlessly to provide scalable, high-density and energy-efficient solutions from access to core; Neptune, a family of elastic multiprotocol label switching products; Mercury NFV solutions (network functions virtualization), providing end-users with low-latency experiences, deploying NFV at the mobile edge, the customer premises and in the network as an edge cloud; and Muse, a modular suite of applications that enables ECI customers to create and turn up new services rapidly, and to ensure the network is optimized. ECI also offers cyber security solutions and provides management, insights and professional services. Industries served by ECI products, solutions and services include service providers, critical industries and data center interconnect service providers. ECI has offices located in the Americas, Europe, Africa and Asia. The firm is privately-owned by The Swarth Group and the Ashmore Group plc.

FINANCIAL DATA: Note: Data for latest year may not have been available at press time.

In U.S. $	2018	2017	2016	2015	2014	2013
Revenue		380,000,000	785,000,000	774,000,000	750,000,000	700,000,000
R&D Expense						
Operating Income						
Operating Margin %						
SGA Expense						
Net Income						
Operating Cash Flow						
Capital Expenditure						
EBITDA						
Return on Assets %						
Return on Equity %						
Debt to Equity						

CONTACT INFORMATION:

Phone: 972-3-926-6555   Fax: 972-3-926-6500
Toll-Free:
Address: 30 Hasivim St., Petah Tikva, 49517 Israel

STOCK TICKER/OTHER:

Stock Ticker: Private   Exchange:
Employees: 1,706   Fiscal Year Ends: 12/31
Parent Company: Swarth Group (The)

SALARIES/BONUSES:

Top Exec. Salary: $ Bonus: $
Second Exec. Salary: $ Bonus: $

OTHER THOUGHTS:

Estimated Female Officers or Directors: 1
Hot Spot for Advancement for Women/Minorities:

eHarmony Inc

www.eharmony.com

NAIC Code: 519130

TYPES OF BUSINESS:

Online Dating Services

BRANDS/DIVISIONS/AFFILIATES:

Compatibility Matching System
Two Of You Together (The)
eHarmony.com
Compatible Partners
eHarmony Labs

CONTACTS: *Note: Officers with more than one job title may be intentionally listed here more than once.*

Grant Langston, CEO
Erin O'malia Gehan, Sr. VP-Mktg.
Ashley Chisholm, VP-Human Resources
Prateek Jain, Sr. VP-IT
Ron Sarian, VP
David Chen, VP-Corp. Dev.
Jaime Rupert, Dir.-Corp. Comm.
David Chen, VP-Finance
Steve Carter, VP-Matching
Grant Langston, VP-Customer Experience
Dan Erickson, Dir.-Special Projects

GROWTH PLANS/SPECIAL FEATURES:

eHarmony, Inc. operates eHarmony.com, a subscription-based online dating portal. The firm uses a patented compatibility algorithm, the Compatibility Matching System, to match users with what the company feels are ideal relationship partners. Potential users answer a questionnaire to create an introductory profile before qualifying as members. These questions also form the basis of the user's profile, which is used in the algorithm to determine a compatibility score with other subscribers. Popular demographic categories include Christian singles, Jewish singles, Black singles, Hispanic singles, Asian singles, 30s singles and senior singles. eHarmony's The Two Of You Together feature displays matches that score at advanced levels of compatibility in order to reveal to the user the reason he/she is considered compatible with the match. In addition to eHarmony.com, the firm operates Compatible Partners, a site for gay and lesbian users; eHarmony Labs, a relationship research facility; and advice sites for dating and relationship advice. Outside of the U.S., service is available internationally in Canada, Australia and the U.K. eHarmony's membership pool comprises singles living in all 50 U.S. states, and more than 200 countries worldwide.

eHarmony offers its employees medical, dental and vision insurance; life and AD&D insurance; paid maternity/paternity/adoption leave; short- and long-term disability; flex spending accounts; travel assistance; and a 401(k) retirement plan.

FINANCIAL DATA: *Note: Data for latest year may not have been available at press time.*

In U.S. $	2018	2017	2016	2015	2014	2013
Revenue		360,000,000	350,000,000	330,000,000	310,000,000	390,000,000
R&D Expense						
Operating Income						
Operating Margin %						
SGA Expense						
Net Income						
Operating Cash Flow						
Capital Expenditure						
EBITDA						
Return on Assets %						
Return on Equity %						
Debt to Equity						

CONTACT INFORMATION:

Phone: 626-795-4814   Fax: 626-585-4040
Toll-Free:
Address: 2401 Colorado Ave., Ste. A200, Santa Monica, CA 90404
United States

STOCK TICKER/OTHER:

Stock Ticker: Private
Employees: 220
Parent Company:

Exchange:
Fiscal Year Ends:

SALARIES/BONUSES:

Top Exec. Salary: $ Bonus: $
Second Exec. Salary: $ Bonus: $

OTHER THOUGHTS:

Estimated Female Officers or Directors: 2
Hot Spot for Advancement for Women/Minorities: Y

EHealth Inc

NAIC Code: 524210

www.ehealthinsurance.com

TYPES OF BUSINESS:

Health Insurance Brokerage-Online
Health Insurance
Student Health Insurance
Short-term Health Insurance
Health Savings Accounts
Dental Insurance
Term Life Insurance
Dental Discount Cards

BRANDS/DIVISIONS/AFFILIATES:

eHealthInsurance Services Inc
eHealth.com
eHealthInsurance.com
eHealthMedicare.com
Medicare.com
GoMedigap.com
PlanPrescriber.com

CONTACTS: *Note: Officers with more than one job title may be intentionally listed here more than once.*

Scott Flanders, CEO
Derek Yung, CFO
Timothy Hannan, Chief Marketing Officer
Ian Kalin, Chief Technology Officer
David Francis, COO
Ellen Tauscher, Director
Robert Hurley, President, Divisional
Jay Jennings, Senior VP, Divisional

GROWTH PLANS/SPECIAL FEATURES:

EHealth, Inc. is a leading private health insurance exchange where individuals, families and small businesses can compare health insurance products from leading insurers side-by-side and purchase and enroll in coverage online through its websites or by phone. Websites include eHealth.com, eHealthInsurance.com, eHealthMedicare.com, Medicare.com, GoMedigap.com and PlanPrescriber.com. The company, along with wholly-owned subsidiary eHealthInsurance Services, Inc., are licensed to market and sell health insurance in all 50 states and Washington, D.C. EHealth organizes and presents health insurance online in a user-friendly format, enabling its customers to choose from a variety of health insurance products. The firm generates revenue primarily from commissions it receives from health insurance carriers, generally based on a percentage of the premium its members have paid to the carrier. It also, in some instances, receives commission override payments for achieving certain sales volume thresholds. In addition to the revenue the company derives from the sale of health insurance products, it generates revenue from its online sponsorship advertising program and from licensing the use of its ecommerce technology. Products offered by eHealth include preferred provider organization (PPO), health maintenance organization (HMO), indemnity plans, short-term medical insurance, student health insurance, health savings account (HSA) eligible health insurance plans and ancillary products such as dental, vision and life insurance. Elements of its platform include online rate quoting, comprehensive plan information, plan comparison, recommendations and online application and enrollment forms. The platform also uses Electronic Processing Interchange technology to integrate its online application process with health insurance carriers' technology systems. Members are able to enroll in select plans online through subsidiary PlanPrescriber.com. Revenue derived from carriers owned by Humana, UnitedHealthcare and Aetna represent approximately 22%, 16% and 9% of eHealth's revenue, respectively.

FINANCIAL DATA: *Note: Data for latest year may not have been available at press time.*

In U.S. $	2018	2017	2016	2015	2014	2013
Revenue		172,355,000	186,960,000	189,541,000	179,677,000	179,180,000
R&D Expense		32,889,000	32,749,000	36,351,000	40,390,000	32,579,000
Operating Income		-28,873,000	-6,152,000	-1,110,000	-6,762,000	3,732,000
Operating Margin %		-16.75%	-3.29%	-.58%	-3.76%	2.08%
SGA Expense		165,026,000	156,147,000	148,969,000	140,026,000	135,994,000
Net Income		-25,412,000	-4,882,000	-4,763,000	-16,205,000	1,723,000
Operating Cash Flow		-15,541,000	4,083,000	13,696,000	1,779,000	20,947,000
Capital Expenditure		5,078,000	3,726,000	2,996,000	8,104,000	7,326,000
EBITDA		-23,532,000	-637,000	4,818,000	-1,041,000	8,412,000
Return on Assets %		-25.72%	-4.39%	-4.33%	-11.86%	.94%
Return on Equity %		-36.63%	-6.33%	-6.35%	-15.69%	1.13%
Debt to Equity						

CONTACT INFORMATION:

Phone: 650 584-2700   Fax: 650 961-2153
Toll-Free: 800-977-8860
Address: 440 E. Middlefield Rd., Mountain View, CA 94043 United States

STOCK TICKER/OTHER:

Stock Ticker: EHTH   Exchange: NAS
Employees: 944   Fiscal Year Ends: 12/31
Parent Company:

SALARIES/BONUSES:

Top Exec. Salary: $600,000   Bonus: $
Second Exec. Salary: $390,769   Bonus: $

OTHER THOUGHTS:

Estimated Female Officers or Directors: 1
Hot Spot for Advancement for Women/Minorities:

Sales, profits and employees may be estimates. Financial information, benefits and other data can change quickly and may vary from those stated here.

Elavon Inc

NAIC Code: 522320

TYPES OF BUSINESS:

Payment Processing Terminal Products
Payment Processing Software
Gift Cards
Currency Conversion
Acquisition Services

BRANDS/DIVISIONS/AFFILIATES:

US Bancorp
CenPOS

CONTACTS: *Note: Officers with more than one job title may be intentionally listed here more than once.*

Jamie Walker, CEO
Brian Mahony, Chief Strategy Officer
Simon Haslam, Pres.
Brad Herring, CFO
Thomas Phillips, CIO
Marianne Johnson, Head-Prod. & Innovation
Mindy Doster, General Counsel
Brian Mahony, Chief Strategy Officer
Guy Harris, Pres., North America
Carlos Navarro, Pres., Latin America

GROWTH PLANS/SPECIAL FEATURES:

Elavon, Inc. provides end-to-end payment processing solutions to over 1 million retailers, financial institutions, associations and government agencies in the U.S., Europe, Canada, Mexico and Brazil. Elavon products and services include credit and debit card processing, payment terminal products, software and internet products to enhance payment acceptance capabilities, gateway/value-added resellers (VAR), point-of-sale (POS) solutions, electronic check services, gift cards, dynamic currency conversion, multi-currency support and cross-border acquiring. The company serves all stages of the acquisition process, with services such as transaction processing, risk and underwriting, settlement, equipment deployment, chargeback management, reporting and customer service. Elavon markets its services through alliance partner channels, such as financial institutions, trade associations and independent sales organizations. The firm operates as a subsidiary of U.S. Bancorp, and processes more than 3 billion transactions every year. In January 2019, Elavon acquired CenPOS, a firm offering integrated payment software solutions to large enterprises within the three industry verticals of travel and entertainment, automotive and general business-to-business transactions.

FINANCIAL DATA: *Note: Data for latest year may not have been available at press time.*

In U.S. $	2018	2017	2016	2015	2014	2013
Revenue		1,600,000,000	1,592,000,000	1,547,000,000	1,511,000,000	
R&D Expense						
Operating Income						
Operating Margin %						
SGA Expense						
Net Income						
Operating Cash Flow						
Capital Expenditure						
EBITDA						
Return on Assets %						
Return on Equity %						
Debt to Equity						

CONTACT INFORMATION:

Phone: 678-731-5000   Fax:
Toll-Free:
Address: Two Concourse Pkwy., Ste. 800, Atlanta, GA 30328 United States

STOCK TICKER/OTHER:

Stock Ticker: Subsidiary
Employees: 1,400
Parent Company: US Bancorp

Exchange:
Fiscal Year Ends: 12/31

SALARIES/BONUSES:

Top Exec. Salary: $ Bonus: $
Second Exec. Salary: $ Bonus: $

OTHER THOUGHTS:

Estimated Female Officers or Directors: 5
Hot Spot for Advancement for Women/Minorities: Y

Electronic Arts Inc (EA)

www.ea.com

NAIC Code: 511210G

TYPES OF BUSINESS:

Computer Software, Electronic Games, Apps & Entertainment
Online Interactive Games
E-Commerce Sales
Mobile Games
Apps

BRANDS/DIVISIONS/AFFILIATES:

Battlefield
Mass Effect
Need for Speed
Sims vs Zombies (The)
Origin
Respawn Entertainment LLC
Titanfall

CONTACTS: Note: Officers with more than one job title may be intentionally listed here more than once.

Andrew Wilson, CEO
Blake Jorgensen, CFO
Lawrence Probst, Chairman of the Board
Kenneth Barker, Chief Accounting Officer
Christopher Bruzzo, Chief Marketing Officer
Kenneth Moss, Chief Technology Officer
Joel Linzner, Executive VP, Divisional
Matt Bilbey, Executive VP, Divisional
Matthew Bilbey, Executive VP, Divisional
Jacob Schatz, Executive VP
Laura Miele, Other Executive Officer
Patrick Soderlund, Other Executive Officer
Vijayanthimala Singh, Other Executive Officer

GROWTH PLANS/SPECIAL FEATURES:

Electronic Arts, Inc. (EA) develops, markets, publishes and distributes games, content and services that can be played by consumers on a variety of platforms. These platforms include consoles such as PlayStation and Xbox, personal computers (PCs), mobile phones and tablets. Some of the company's games are based on its wholly-owned intellectual property, including Battlefield, Mass Effect, Need for Speed, The Sims vs. Zombies; and some games leverage content that EA licenses from others, such as FIFA, Madden NFL and Star Wars. EA also publishes and distributes games developed by third parties. The company's products and services can be purchased through multiple distribution channels, including physical and online retailers, platform providers (console manufacturers, providers of free-to-download PC games and mobile carriers) and through EA's own digital distribution platform, Origin. In December 2017, the firm acquired Respawn Entertainment, LLC, a leading independent game development studio and creators of AAA shooter and action games including the critically-acclaimed Titanfall franchise

EA offers its employees health care coverage, employee assistance programs, onsite childcare, employee discount programs, business travel accident insurance, retirement savings/pension and free EA games.

FINANCIAL DATA: Note: Data for latest year may not have been available at press time.

In U.S. $	2018	2017	2016	2015	2014	2013
Revenue	5,150,000,000	4,845,000,000	4,396,000,000	4,515,000,000	3,575,000,000	3,797,000,000
R&D Expense	1,320,000,000	1,205,000,000	1,109,000,000	1,094,000,000	1,125,000,000	1,153,000,000
Operating Income	1,434,000,000	1,224,000,000	898,000,000	945,000,000	-3,000,000	84,000,000
Operating Margin %	27.84	25.26%	20.42%	20.93%	-.08%	2.21%
SGA Expense	1,110,000,000	1,112,000,000	1,028,000,000	1,033,000,000	1,090,000,000	1,142,000,000
Net Income	1,043,000,000	967,000,000	1,156,000,000	875,000,000	8,000,000	98,000,000
Operating Cash Flow	1,692,000,000	1,383,000,000	1,223,000,000	1,067,000,000	712,000,000	324,000,000
Capital Expenditure	107,000,000	123,000,000	93,000,000	95,000,000	97,000,000	106,000,000
EBITDA	1,627,000,000	1,427,000,000	1,102,000,000	1,176,000,000	264,000,000	432,000,000
Return on Assets %	12.79%	13.09%	17.51%	14.75%	.14%	1.85%
Return on Equity %	24.10%	25.93%	35.94%	32.06%	.34%	4.14%
Debt to Equity	0.21	0.24	0.29	0.01	0.23	0.24

CONTACT INFORMATION:

Phone: 650 628-1500   Fax: 650 628-1414
Toll-Free:
Address: 209 Redwood Shores Parkway, Redwood City, CA 94065
United States

STOCK TICKER/OTHER:

Stock Ticker: EA   Exchange: NAS
Employees: 9,300   Fiscal Year Ends: 03/31
Parent Company:

SALARIES/BONUSES:

Top Exec. Salary: $1,141,731   Bonus: $
Second Exec. Salary: Bonus: $
$821,539

OTHER THOUGHTS:

Estimated Female Officers or Directors: 2
Hot Spot for Advancement for Women/Minorities:

Sales, profits and employees may be estimates. Financial information, benefits and other data can change quickly and may vary from those stated here.

E-LOAN Inc

NAIC Code: 522310

www.eloan.com

TYPES OF BUSINESS:

Online Mortgage Broker
Debt Consolidation
Personal Loans

BRANDS/DIVISIONS/AFFILIATES:

Popular Inc
Banco Popular North America

GROWTH PLANS/SPECIAL FEATURES:

E-LOAN, Inc. is an online lender of personal loans. The firm is the wholly-owned subsidiary of Banco Popular North America, a New York state-chartered bank, which is itself a subsidiary of Popular, Inc. The E-LOAN website and mobile app offer tools and information for borrowers, including loan calculator, debt consolidation calculator, 24-hour loan status access, and resources about personal finance, home improvement and debt management. Personal loans of up to $35,000 can be obtained, with no origination fees, and rates starting at 5.49% annual percental rate (APR) (as of October 2018). Applying for a loan occurs online as well, and types of loans can be used for debt consolidation, medical expenses, auto expenses, credit card debt and other purposes. All loans are subject to credit approval.

CONTACTS: Note: Officers with more than one job title may be intentionally listed here more than once.

Ignacio Alvarez, CEO-Popular
Mark Lefanowicz, Pres.

FINANCIAL DATA: Note: Data for latest year may not have been available at press time.

In U.S. $	2018	2017	2016	2015	2014	2013
Revenue						
R&D Expense						
Operating Income						
Operating Margin %						
SGA Expense						
Net Income						
Operating Cash Flow						
Capital Expenditure						
EBITDA						
Return on Assets %						
Return on Equity %						
Debt to Equity						

CONTACT INFORMATION:

Phone: 847-994-5800   Fax:
Toll-Free:
Address: 85 Broad St., 10/Fl, New York, NY 10004 United States

STOCK TICKER/OTHER:

Stock Ticker: Subsidiary   Exchange:
Employees: 930   Fiscal Year Ends: 12/31
Parent Company: Popular Inc

SALARIES/BONUSES:

Top Exec. Salary: $ Bonus: $
Second Exec. Salary: $ Bonus: $

OTHER THOUGHTS:

Estimated Female Officers or Directors:
Hot Spot for Advancement for Women/Minorities:

E-machitown Co Ltd

corp.emachi.co.jp

NAIC Code: 519130

TYPES OF BUSINESS:

Internet Advertising
E-Mail Hosting
Server Hosting
Hotel Reservations

BRANDS/DIVISIONS/AFFILIATES:

Hikari Tsushin Inc
SBM Gourmet Solutions Inc
GoLuck Inc

GROWTH PLANS/SPECIAL FEATURES:

E-machitown Co., Ltd. provides media advertising services primarily to small- and medium-sized businesses. The company conducts its operations in two segments: business solutions and media advertising. The business solutions segment offers server solutions, website design and communication services for more than 100,000 business. This division enables these companies to utilize email with their own domain names. The media advertising segment provides internet advertising services and mobile web content in addition to running the company's regional information portal, e-machitown, and other accommodation sites. In addition, subsidiary SBM Gourmet Solutions, Inc. operates foodservice mobile websites; and GoLuck, Inc., provides services to amusement establishments in Japan. E-machitown operates as a subsidiary of Hikari Tsushin, Inc.

CONTACTS: *Note: Officers with more than one job title may be intentionally listed here more than once.*

Takashi Asai, Managing Dir.

FINANCIAL DATA: *Note: Data for latest year may not have been available at press time.*

In U.S. $	2018	2017	2016	2015	2014	2013
Revenue		120,000,000	115,000,000	120,000,000	115,000,000	125,000,000
R&D Expense						
Operating Income						
Operating Margin %						
SGA Expense						
Net Income						
Operating Cash Flow						
Capital Expenditure						
EBITDA						
Return on Assets %						
Return on Equity %						
Debt to Equity						

CONTACT INFORMATION:

Phone: 81-3-5954-7555   Fax: 81-3-5957-0747
Toll-Free:
Address: 1-4-10 Nishi-Ikebukuro, Toshima-ku, Tokyo, 171-0021 Japan

STOCK TICKER/OTHER:

Stock Ticker: Subsidiary   Exchange:
Employees: 305   Fiscal Year Ends: 03/31
Parent Company: Hikari Tsushin Inc

SALARIES/BONUSES:

Top Exec. Salary: $ Bonus: $
Second Exec. Salary: $ Bonus: $

OTHER THOUGHTS:

Estimated Female Officers or Directors:
Hot Spot for Advancement for Women/Minorities:

Embarcadero Technologies Inc

www.embarcadero.com

NAIC Code: 511210J

TYPES OF BUSINESS:

Software, Application & Database Management

BRANDS/DIVISIONS/AFFILIATES:

Idera Inc
RAD Studio
C++Builder
Delphi
InterBase
RAD Server

CONTACTS: *Note: Officers with more than one job title may be intentionally listed here more than once.*

Atanas Popov, Gen. Mgr.
Michael Swindell, Sr. VP-Prod. Mgmt.
Tony de la Lama, Sr. VP-Eng.
Michael Swindell, Sr. VP-Strategy
David Intersimone, VP-Developer Rel.
Steve Young, Chmn.
Nigel Brown, Gen. Mgr.-Int'l

GROWTH PLANS/SPECIAL FEATURES:

Embarcadero Technologies, Inc. is a technology company that addresses application and database lifecycle operations for corporate clients. The firm designs and develops products for information transmission across databases. These products compress time frames and increase database performance and availability, allowing companies to more efficiently build, optimize and manage their databases and applications. Products are offered in subgroups such as modeling and architecture tools, application development, database management and development, performance optimization and embedded database systems. Examples of Embarcadero software include RAD Studio, a fast way to develop cross-platform native apps with flexible cloud services and broad Internet of Things (IoT) connectivity; C++Builder, a development tool for many platforms with an enhanced clang compiler; Delphi, an object pascal IDE (integrated development environment) and component library for cross-platform native app development with flexible cloud services and broad IoT connectivity; InterBase, a high scalable, full-featured, admin-free, Unicode-enabled, SQL-standard compliant cross-platform database engine; and RAD Server, a turn-key application foundation for rapidly building and deploying services based applications. Major industry sectors served by Embarcadero include government, healthcare, financial services, food services, insurance, pharmaceuticals, education, research and technology, travel and utilities. The firm also markets products through independent distributors in various countries worldwide. Embarcadero Technologies is a subsidiary of Idera, Inc., an application and server management software provider.

FINANCIAL DATA: *Note: Data for latest year may not have been available at press time.*

In U.S. $	2018	2017	2016	2015	2014	2013
Revenue		160,000,000	150,000,000	141,000,000	130,000,000	120,000,000
R&D Expense						
Operating Income						
Operating Margin %						
SGA Expense						
Net Income						
Operating Cash Flow						
Capital Expenditure						
EBITDA						
Return on Assets %						
Return on Equity %						
Debt to Equity						

CONTACT INFORMATION:

Phone: 512-226-8080   Fax: 415-434-1721
Toll-Free:
Address: 10801 North Mopac Expressway, Bldg. 1, Ste. 100, Austin, TX 78759 United States

STOCK TICKER/OTHER:

Stock Ticker: Private   Exchange:
Employees: 222   Fiscal Year Ends: 12/31
Parent Company: Idera Inc

SALARIES/BONUSES:

Top Exec. Salary: $ Bonus: $
Second Exec. Salary: $ Bonus: $

OTHER THOUGHTS:

Estimated Female Officers or Directors: 1
Hot Spot for Advancement for Women/Minorities:

eMusic.com Inc

www.emusic.com

NAIC Code: 454111

TYPES OF BUSINESS:

Online Music-Retail
MP3 Subscription Services
Audiobook Subscription Services

BRANDS/DIVISIONS/AFFILIATES:

TriPlay Communications Ltd
eStories

CONTACTS: *Note: Officers with more than one job title may be intentionally listed here more than once.*

Tamir Koch, CEO-TriPlay
Molly Neuman, VP-Label Relations
Daniel C. Stein, Pres., JDS Capital Management, Inc.
Madeline Milne, Managing Dir.-Europe

GROWTH PLANS/SPECIAL FEATURES:

eMusic.com, Inc. is a discovery-and-download e-Commerce marketplace for people who like music. Discovery is the heart of eMusic, and believes the best discoveries are inspired by unique and personal interest. eMusic enables listeners to explore its dynamic assortment of features designed to tap into those music interests and tastes, leading them to music they will enjoy. After exploring the eMusic catalog, listeners can purchase discoveries a la carte at any time, or become an eMusic member and save 25-50%, with most tracks priced at $0.49 each. Every penny of membership goes directly toward downloading music. Member plans start at $8.99/month. Members can also change, supplement or cancel their plan whenever they'd like. Music purchases are automatically uploaded to a personal eMusic cloud account. Listeners can upload and store an unlimited number of tracks for free; use the smart playlist feature to rediscover music or build a mix for any occasion; and/or sync and play the entire collection wherever they go via iPhone and Android apps. The eMusic website features new albums and bands via staff interviews, and within the site's Editors' Picks. Users can dig further into a musician's catalog through eMusic's search engine, and also locate like-kind music types with its browse function. Personalized recommendations will be provided as well. In addition, the company has an eStories website, delivering audiobook service that comprises 120,000 audiobook titles. These titles include best-sellers spanning every genre, and new releases are added every week. Personalized search and discovery tools make it easy to find interesting stories. After a 30-day trial, members pay $11.99 per month, with the basic plan including one audiobook each month. Audiobooks can be listened to via iPhone and Android apps, and stories will automatically sync across up to 10 devices. eMusic is owned by Israeli-based TriPlay Communications Ltd.

FINANCIAL DATA: *Note: Data for latest year may not have been available at press time.*

In U.S. $	2018	2017	2016	2015	2014	2013
Revenue						
R&D Expense						
Operating Income						
Operating Margin %						
SGA Expense						
Net Income						
Operating Cash Flow						
Capital Expenditure						
EBITDA						
Return on Assets %						
Return on Equity %						
Debt to Equity						

CONTACT INFORMATION:

Phone: 212-201-9240   Fax: 212-201-9204
Toll-Free:
Address: 625 Broadway, 2/Fl., New York, NY 10012 United States

STOCK TICKER/OTHER:

Stock Ticker: Private   Exchange:
Employees: 184   Fiscal Year Ends: 12/31
Parent Company: TriPlay Communications Ltd

SALARIES/BONUSES:

Top Exec. Salary: $ Bonus: $
Second Exec. Salary: $ Bonus: $

OTHER THOUGHTS:

Estimated Female Officers or Directors: 3
Hot Spot for Advancement for Women/Minorities: Y

Entrust Datacard Corporation

www.entrust.com

NAIC Code: 511210E

TYPES OF BUSINESS:

Computer Software, Security & Anti-Virus
Digital Identification & Certificates

BRANDS/DIVISIONS/AFFILIATES:

CONTACTS: *Note: Officers with more than one job title may be intentionally listed here more than once.*

Todd Wilkinson, CEO
Jeff Smolinksi, Sr. VP-Operations
Kurt Ishaug, CFO
Phil Kasper, Sr. VP-Global Sales
Beth Klehr, Chief Human Resources Officer
Anudeep Parhar, CIO
Robert (Bob) VanKirk, Sr. VP-American Sales
Ray Wizbowski, CMO
Mark Reeves, Sr. VP-Int'l Sales

GROWTH PLANS/SPECIAL FEATURES:

Entrust Datacard Corporation is a global provider of security applications that protect and secure digital identities and information. The firm designs, produces and sells security, policy and access management software products and related services. Solutions include financial cards, passports, identification cards, authentication solutions (cloud-based, mobile, hybrid), digital certificates, border control, credential lifecycle management and transaction technologies. Entrust products are divided into 12 categories: SSL certificates, digital signing certificates, central card issuance, software, ID card printers, financial card printers, public key infrastructure (PKI), authentication, Internet of Things security, passport systems, accessories and supplies. Accessories include devices such as pin pads, magnetic strip encoders and digital signature pads. Supplies include print ribbons, overlays, laminates, tactile impression solutions, cleaning supplies, topping foils, card delivery stickers/labels and more. Entrust serves enterprise, government and consumer clients located in more than 150 countries. Headquartered in Minnesota, USA, the firm has 34 worldwide locations.

Employee benefits include medical and dental coverage, bonus plans and employee assistance.

FINANCIAL DATA: *Note: Data for latest year may not have been available at press time.*

In U.S. $	2018	2017	2016	2015	2014	2013
Revenue		150,000,000	145,000,000	140,500,000	130,000,000	112,000,000
R&D Expense						
Operating Income						
Operating Margin %						
SGA Expense						
Net Income						
Operating Cash Flow						
Capital Expenditure						
EBITDA						
Return on Assets %						
Return on Equity %						
Debt to Equity						

CONTACT INFORMATION:

Phone: 952-933-1223   Fax:
Toll-Free: 800-621-6972
Address: 1187 Park Place, Shakopee, MN 55379 United States

STOCK TICKER/OTHER:

Stock Ticker: Private   Exchange:
Employees: 370   Fiscal Year Ends: 12/31
Parent Company:

SALARIES/BONUSES:

Top Exec. Salary: $ Bonus: $
Second Exec. Salary: $ Bonus: $

OTHER THOUGHTS:

Estimated Female Officers or Directors:
Hot Spot for Advancement for Women/Minorities:

Epocrates Inc

www.epocrates.com

NAIC Code: 511210D

TYPES OF BUSINESS:
Computer Software, Healthcare & Biotechnology

BRANDS/DIVISIONS/AFFILIATES:
Athenahealth Inc
Epocrates
Epocrates Plus

CONTACTS: *Note: Officers with more than one job title may be intentionally listed here more than once.*
Heather Gervais, Sr. VP-Commercial
Anne Meneghetti, Sr. VP-Medical Info.
Abbe Don, VP-User Experience
Jeffery R. Immelt, Chmn.-Athenahealth, Inc.

GROWTH PLANS/SPECIAL FEATURES:
Epocrates, Inc. designs and develops tools and technologies for medical professionals to access data through mobile devices. The company's medical reference application offers features that display how Epocrates supports care decisions. Its drug information allows users to review drug prescribing and safety information for thousands of branded, generic and over-the-counter drugs. Drug information includes adult and pediatric dosing for FDA-approved and off-label indications; black box warnings, contraindications, adverse reactions and drug interactions; safety/monitoring, including pregnancy risk categories, location safety ratings, monitoring parameters and similar drug names; pharmacology, including metabolism, excretion, subclass and mechanism of action; and manufacturer, DEA/FDA status and approximate retail price. Epocrates products include two versions: Epocrates, which is comprised of drug information, interaction check, pill identification, formulary, athenaText and tables/graphs; and Epocrates Plus, which offers everything regular Epocrates does, as well as clinical practice guidelines, disease information, alternative medicine information, ICD-9 and CPT billing and diagnosis codes, infectious disease treatment information and laboratory test and panel information. The company provides discounts for medical schools and institutions. Epocrates is an Athenahealth, Inc. company.

Epocrates offers its employees medical, dental and vision coverage; life insurance; short- and long-term disability; a 401(k) plan; a flexible spending plan; an employee assistance program; and discount gym membership.

FINANCIAL DATA: *Note: Data for latest year may not have been available at press time.*

In U.S. $	2018	2017	2016	2015	2014	2013
Revenue		140,000,000	135,000,000	125,000,000	110,000,000	115,000,000
R&D Expense						
Operating Income						
Operating Margin %						
SGA Expense						
Net Income						
Operating Cash Flow						
Capital Expenditure						
EBITDA						
Return on Assets %						
Return on Equity %						
Debt to Equity						

CONTACT INFORMATION:
Phone: 650 227-1700   Fax:
Toll-Free:
Address: 1100 Park Pl., Ste. 300, San Mateo, CA 94403 United States

STOCK TICKER/OTHER:
Stock Ticker: Subsidiary
Employees: 320
Parent Company: Athenahealth Inc

Exchange:
Fiscal Year Ends: 12/31

SALARIES/BONUSES:
Top Exec. Salary: $ Bonus: $
Second Exec. Salary: $ Bonus: $

OTHER THOUGHTS:
Estimated Female Officers or Directors: 3
Hot Spot for Advancement for Women/Minorities: Y

Equinix Inc

NAIC Code: 517110

www.equinix.com

TYPES OF BUSINESS:

Data Networks
Internet Exchange Services

BRANDS/DIVISIONS/AFFILIATES:

Equinix
Smart Hands
Itconic
Cloudmas
Infomart Dallas
Metronode

CONTACTS: Note: Officers with more than one job title may be intentionally listed here more than once.

Charles Meyers, CEO
Keith Taylor, CFO
Peter Van Camp, Chairman of the Board
Simon Miller, Chief Accounting Officer
Michael Campbell, Other Executive Officer
Eric Schwartz, President, Geographical
Karl Strohmeyer, President, Geographical
Samuel Lee, President, Geographical

GROWTH PLANS/SPECIAL FEATURES:

Equinix, Inc. provides network neutral co-location, interconnection and managed services to more than 9,800 enterprises. The company operates data centers in 48 markets across the Americas; Europe, Middle East and Africa (EMEA); and Asia Pacific. The firm's proprietary Equinix platform incorporates International Business Exchange (IBX) data centers with unique ecosystems and a global footprint to offer customers accelerated business growth by safeguarding the client's infrastructure, housing their applications and assets closer to the user for improved overall performance and enabling the client to collaborate with numerous customers and partners. The platform includes more than 1,700 networks. The company's products and services include co-location services, such as cabinets, AC and DC power and operations space; direct connection between business partners, which allows customers to easily trade network traffic without purchasing circuits; and managed IT infrastructure services, which use the company's IBX hubs to optimize customers' infrastructure and resources. The firm's Smart Hands service provides access to IBX technical staff when a customer's own staff is unavailable. In October 2017, Equinix acquired the Zenium data center business in Istanbul for $93 million and closed the transaction for the purchase of Itconic, a leading data center, connectivity and cloud infrastructure solutions provider in Spain and Portugal, and Cloudmas, an Itconic subsidiary that is focused on supporting enterprise adoption and use of cloud services, for â‚¬215 million ($259 million). In April 2018, the firm acquired Infomart Dallas, including its operations and tenants, from ASB Real Estate Investments and completed the acquisition of Metronode, a leading data center provider in Australia.

U.S. employees receive medical, dental, vision, disability, life and AD&D insurance; parental leave; 401(k); employee stock & employee assistance plans; and a flexible spending account.

FINANCIAL DATA: Note: Data for latest year may not have been available at press time.

In U.S. $	2018	2017	2016	2015	2014	2013
Revenue		4,368,428,000	3,611,989,000	2,725,867,000	2,443,776,000	2,152,766,000
R&D Expense						
Operating Income		847,649,000	657,816,000	609,065,000	511,772,000	466,950,000
Operating Margin %		19.40%	18.21%	22.34%	20.94%	21.69%
SGA Expense		1,327,630,000	1,133,303,000	825,296,000	734,119,000	621,413,000
Net Income		232,982,000	126,800,000	187,774,000	-259,547,000	94,685,000
Operating Cash Flow		1,439,233,000	1,016,580,000	894,793,000	689,420,000	604,608,000
Capital Expenditure		1,378,725,000	1,113,365,000	868,120,000	660,203,000	572,406,000
EBITDA		1,808,010,000	1,389,222,000	1,035,633,000	836,977,000	793,542,000
Return on Assets %		1.48%	1.10%	2.06%	-3.39%	1.38%
Return on Equity %		4.15%	3.56%	7.48%	-10.97%	3.94%
Debt to Equity		1.45	1.50	2.02	2.02	1.66

CONTACT INFORMATION:

Phone: 650 598-6000   Fax: 650 513-7900
Toll-Free: 800-322-9280
Address: 1 Lagoon Dr., 4/Fl, Redwood City, CA 94065 United States

STOCK TICKER/OTHER:

Stock Ticker: EQIX   Exchange: NAS
Employees: 5,993   Fiscal Year Ends: 12/31
Parent Company:

SALARIES/BONUSES:

Top Exec. Salary: $1,084,661   Bonus: $
Second Exec. Salary: Bonus: $
$639,231

OTHER THOUGHTS:

Estimated Female Officers or Directors: 3
Hot Spot for Advancement for Women/Minorities: Y

Etsy Inc

www.etsy.com

NAIC Code: 454111

TYPES OF BUSINESS:

Online Craft Marketplace
Handmade Arts & Crafts
Crafting Supplies
Vintage Clothing & Goods

BRANDS/DIVISIONS/AFFILIATES:

Etsy.com

CONTACTS: Note: Officers with more than one job title may be intentionally listed here more than once.

Josh Silverman, CEO
Rachel Glaser, CFO
Frederick Wilson, Chairman of the Board
Michael Fisher, Chief Technology Officer
Linda Kozlowski, COO
Jill Simeone, General Counsel

GROWTH PLANS/SPECIAL FEATURES:

Etsy, Inc. operates Etsy.com, an eCommerce website specializing in unique handmade goods, clothing and other arts- and-crafts-inspired merchandise. The website, first established in 2005, is designed as an online marketplace where independent artists and crafts people can make use of the Etsy technology platform to sell their wares to the site's registered members. The site showcases more than 50 million items for sale, and is comprised of 37.1 million active buyers (as of September 2018). Approximately 2 million sellers maintain their own individual online storefronts within the overall Etsy environment, where they can post photographs and descriptions of items being sold. Etsy shoppers can use a system of product tags and keyword searches, along with several other methods, to shop throughout the whole site, or narrow their browsing to favorite sellers' products. Additional tools on the site allow users to search for wares by various product categories, to find items listed recently, to shop for items that will match a user-defined color scheme or to shop for items by the location of the seller (such as where to find locally-produced goods that can be shipped quickly to the buyer). Sellers pay a small fee to Etsy when initially listing their products, as well as a percentage of all sales made through the site. Unlike more general-purpose e-commerce sites such as eBay, Etsy enforces relatively strict guidelines regarding what can be sold through the portal, with products falling in three broad categories: handmade goods, which must be made by the seller and cannot be mass-produced; crafting supplies, such as yarn, beads or crafting tools; and vintage goods, which the company defines as items at least 20 years old. Etsy buyers and sellers are present in nearly every country in the world.

FINANCIAL DATA: Note: Data for latest year may not have been available at press time.

In U.S. $	2018	2017	2016	2015	2014	2013
Revenue		441,231,000	364,967,000	273,499,000	195,591,000	125,022,000
R&D Expense		74,616,000	55,083,000	42,694,000	36,634,000	27,548,000
Operating Income		15,058,000	17,577,000	-1,884,000	-6,251,000	733,000
Operating Margin %		3.41%	4.81%	-.68%	-3.19%	.58%
SGA Expense		200,571,000	168,979,000	135,710,000	91,575,000	48,962,000
Net Income		81,800,000	-29,901,000	-54,063,000	-15,243,000	-796,000
Operating Cash Flow		67,420,000	46,759,000	29,211,000	12,087,000	16,542,000
Capital Expenditure		13,156,000	47,750,000	20,835,000	9,584,000	17,072,000
EBITDA		70,592,000	26,853,000	-7,918,000	7,553,000	12,740,000
Return on Assets %		13.77%	-5.27%	-13.47%	-8.58%	-.74%
Return on Equity %		22.03%	-8.85%	-22.53%	-19.89%	-19.88%
Debt to Equity		0.16	0.18	0.17	0.02	

CONTACT INFORMATION:

Phone: 718-880-3660   Fax:
Toll-Free:
Address: 117 Adams St., Brooklyn, NY 11201 United States

STOCK TICKER/OTHER:

Stock Ticker: ETSY   Exchange: NAS
Employees: 1,043   Fiscal Year Ends: 12/31
Parent Company:

SALARIES/BONUSES:

Top Exec. Salary: $234,375   Bonus: $250,000
Second Exec. Salary: Bonus: $
$341,667

OTHER THOUGHTS:

Estimated Female Officers or Directors:
Hot Spot for Advancement for Women/Minorities: Y

Sales, profits and employees may be estimates. Financial information, benefits and other data can change quickly and may vary from those stated here.

Eventbrite Inc

www.eventbrite.com

NAIC Code: 454111

TYPES OF BUSINESS:

Online Event Ticket Sales
Credit Card Charge Processing

BRANDS/DIVISIONS/AFFILIATES:

Eventbrite.com
Ticketea
Picatic

CONTACTS: *Note: Officers with more than one job title may be intentionally listed here more than once.*

Julia Hartz, CEO
Randy Befumo, CFO
Kevin Hartz, Chairman of the Board
Andrew Dreskin, Director
Samantha Harnett, General Counsel
Omer Cohen, Other Executive Officer
Brian Irving, Other Executive Officer
Patrick Poels, Senior VP, Divisional

GROWTH PLANS/SPECIAL FEATURES:

Eventbrite, Inc. is an entertainment event promotion website that allows users to create event web pages, promote their events and manage event entry through Eventbrite.com. The site's pages are customizable and can be used to promote fundraisers, parties, trainings, conferences, concerts, performances, festivals, political events, sporting events, retreats, religious events and classes. The firm offers simple tools for designing event web pages that are mobile compatible and offer a variety of payment methods. The firm's promotional tools allow event planners to send personalized email invitations; promote events on LinkedIn, Facebook and Twitter through their account; and track attendees and ticket sales. On the event day, users can print out a guest list or check in attendees using the company's app to scan tickets. Attendees can print their tickets or use the Eventbrite mobile app to check in to events. Event planners can also sell tickets at the door using the firm's mobile box office app and credit card scanner for the iPad. Membership to the site is free, but the firm has different ticketing packages for those selling tickets through the site. Users looking for events to attend can search the site by type of event, price range, location and date. The firm's Neon application is a one-stop to manage orders, track sales and check attendees into an event. Its RFID technology platform streamlines entry management and reduces wait times at large events. Tickets are processed in more than 170 countries, covering approximately 3 million events and 203 million tickets in one years' time. During 2018, Eventbrite began trading on the New York Stock Exchange under ticker symbol: EB; and acquired Spanish ticketing service Ticketea; and Vancouver-based ticketing and event registration platform, Picatic.

FINANCIAL DATA: *Note: Data for latest year may not have been available at press time.*

In U.S. $	2018	2017	2016	2015	2014	2013
Revenue		201,597,000	133,499,000			
R&D Expense		30,608,000	22,723,000			
Operating Income		-33,407,000	-35,053,000			
Operating Margin %						
SGA Expense		122,729,000	90,140,000			
Net Income		-38,547,000	-40,392,000			
Operating Cash Flow		29,821,000	2,785,000			
Capital Expenditure		8,678,000	8,466,000			
EBITDA		-12,680,000	-29,109,000			
Return on Assets %						
Return on Equity %						
Debt to Equity						

CONTACT INFORMATION:

Phone: 415-692-7779   Fax: 415-520-3420
Toll-Free: 888-810-2063
Address: 155 5th St., 7/FL, San Francisco, CA 94103 United States

STOCK TICKER/OTHER:

Stock Ticker: EB
Employees: 1,016
Parent Company:

Exchange: NYS
Fiscal Year Ends:

SALARIES/BONUSES:

Top Exec. Salary: $357,500   Bonus: $
Second Exec. Salary: $335,000   Bonus: $

OTHER THOUGHTS:

Estimated Female Officers or Directors: 3
Hot Spot for Advancement for Women/Minorities: Y

Everlane

NAIC Code: 454111

www.everlane.com

TYPES OF BUSINESS:

Online Apparel Sales

BRANDS/DIVISIONS/AFFILIATES:

GROWTH PLANS/SPECIAL FEATURES:

Everlane is primarily an eCommerce shopping retailer. The company discloses the origin of all products, as well as the cost breakdown of each garment, such as labor, materials, transportation and taxes/fees. The site also provides price comparison with traditional retailers' merchandise. Everlane products include men's and women's apparel and accessories. Apparel includes sweaters, outerwear, tops, t-shirts, sweatshirts, pants, denim, shorts, skirts, dresses and undergarments; and accessories include backpacks/bags, ties, leather goods, scarves, hats, gloves and shoes. Everlane also sells stationery and gift cards. The firm's mobile app enables shoppers to browse and buy its luxury items directly from their smartphones. The app features the current weather in order to offer suggestions of what to wear. Everlane's factories are based in the Americas, Europe and Asia. Everlane brick-and-mortar stores are located in New York City and San Francisco.

CONTACTS: Note: Officers with more than one job title may be intentionally listed here more than once.

Michael Preysman, CEO

FINANCIAL DATA: Note: Data for latest year may not have been available at press time.

In U.S. $	2018	2017	2016	2015	2014	2013
Revenue		133,000,000	95,000,000	50,000,000	25,000,000	12,000,000
R&D Expense						
Operating Income						
Operating Margin %						
SGA Expense						
Net Income						
Operating Cash Flow						
Capital Expenditure						
EBITDA						
Return on Assets %						
Return on Equity %						
Debt to Equity						

CONTACT INFORMATION:

Phone: 414-834-5249   Fax:
Toll-Free:
Address: 2170 Folsom St., San Francisco, CA 94110 United States

STOCK TICKER/OTHER:

Stock Ticker: Private   Exchange:
Employees: 50   Fiscal Year Ends:
Parent Company:

SALARIES/BONUSES:

Top Exec. Salary: $ Bonus: $
Second Exec. Salary: $ Bonus: $

OTHER THOUGHTS:

Estimated Female Officers or Directors:
Hot Spot for Advancement for Women/Minorities:

Evernote Corporation

www.evernote.com

NAIC Code: 519130

TYPES OF BUSINESS:

Online Scheduling and Organizing Tool
Handwriting Recognition Software

BRANDS/DIVISIONS/AFFILIATES:

Evernote
Evernote Basic
Evernote Premium
Evernote Business
Evernote Web Clipper

CONTACTS: *Note: Officers with more than one job title may be intentionally listed here more than once.*

Chris O'Neill, CEO
Linda Kozlowski, COO
Jeff Shotts, CFO
Andrew Malcolm, Head-Mktg.
Bethany Brodsky, Head-Human Resources
Alex Pashintsev, VP-R&D
Dave Engberg, CTO
Philip Constantinou, VP-Prod.
Alice Harmon, VP-Admin.
Alex Pachikov, VP-Bus. Dev.
Leonora Teng, VP-Finance
Linda Kozlowski, Head-Int'l Mktg.
Seth Hitchings, VP-Evernote Platform
Luis Samra, Gen. Mgr.-Latin America
Troy Malone, Gen. Mgr.-Asia Pacific
Phil Libin, Chmn.
Hitoshi Hokamura, Chmn.-Evernote Japan

GROWTH PLANS/SPECIAL FEATURES:

Evernote Corporation is a software company focused on developing tools for users to create, archive and access data in the form of notes, images, reminders and voice files. On the Evernote platform, users can compile clippings from web pages, handwritten notes, photos, computer documents and voice memos into notebooks where the information can be quickly accessed later. The program also enables notebook sharing, allowing users to collaborate on various projects regardless of distance. The firm's free subscription, Evernote Basic, allows users to upload 60 megabytes (MB) per month and sync capabilities across two devices. For $7.99 per month, Evernote Premium offers 10 gigabytes (GB) per month across an unlimited number of devices. For $14.99 per month, Evernote Business offers more than 20GB per month (2GB per user with multiple users) across an unlimited number of devices and unlimited number of collaboration spaces. The Evernote program is compatible with Windows and Mac desktop operating systems as well as iOS, Android and Windows mobile operating systems. Evernote Web Clipper allows users to click and save part or all of web pages for later reference. The company's search handwriting platform can identify 28 typewritten and 11 handwritten languages, enabling users to locate hand-written notes that they have uploaded to Evernote via scan or photo. The handwriting search tool locates notes when searching a key word. Based in Redwood City, California, the firm has additional domestic offices in San Diego and Austin, as well as international offices in Beijing, New Delhi, Tokyo and Zurich.

FINANCIAL DATA: *Note: Data for latest year may not have been available at press time.*

In U.S. $	2018	2017	2016	2015	2014	2013
Revenue		230,000,000	220,000,000	220,000,000	200,000,000	180,000,000
R&D Expense						
Operating Income						
Operating Margin %						
SGA Expense						
Net Income						
Operating Cash Flow						
Capital Expenditure						
EBITDA						
Return on Assets %						
Return on Equity %						
Debt to Equity						

CONTACT INFORMATION:

Phone: 408-746-9900   Fax:
Toll-Free:
Address: 305 Walnut St., Redwood City, CA 94063 United States

STOCK TICKER/OTHER:

Stock Ticker: Private   Exchange:
Employees: 300   Fiscal Year Ends:
Parent Company:

SALARIES/BONUSES:

Top Exec. Salary: $ Bonus: $
Second Exec. Salary: $ Bonus: $

OTHER THOUGHTS:

Estimated Female Officers or Directors: 4
Hot Spot for Advancement for Women/Minorities: Y

Everyday Health Inc

www.everydayhealth.com

NAIC Code: 519130

TYPES OF BUSINESS:

Online Health Information Services

BRANDS/DIVISIONS/AFFILIATES:

J2 Global Inc

CONTACTS: *Note: Officers with more than one job title may be intentionally listed here more than once.*

Maureen Connolly, VP-Editor in Chief
Jeff Blatt, Exec. VP-Gen. Mgr.
Brian Cooper, CFO
Scott Wolf, Executive VP
Jed Savage, Executive VP
Alan Shapiro, General Counsel

GROWTH PLANS/SPECIAL FEATURES:

Everyday Health, Inc. operates a digital marketing and communications platform for health care marketers primarily in the U.S. The platform combines digital content from leading health brands with data and analytics technology to present updated, informed content for users. The content can be accessed by Everyday Health's consumers and professionals anytime, anywhere, across multiple channels, including the web, mobile devices, video and social media. The multi-brand, multi-channel content experience helps with decision making, and allows companies to engage with consumers and healthcare professionals. Its portfolio of properties consists of websites, mobile applications and social media destinations, reaching approximately 50 million consumers every month. Consumers use Everyday Health's tools to manage health and wellness needs such as weight loss, exercise, healthy pregnancy, nutrition and medical conditions. The company also provides health care professionals with news, tools and information needed to keep in touch with current industry, legislative and regulatory developments in major medical specialties. More than 700,000 practicing U.S. physicians can be reached, ranging across numerous specialty areas. Everyday Health's website offers links and access to free newsletters, a symptom checker, drug finder, calorie counter, meal planner and recipes. Everyday Health operates as a wholly-owned subsidiary of j2 Global, Inc., an American technology company based in California.

FINANCIAL DATA: *Note: Data for latest year may not have been available at press time.*

In U.S. $	2018	2017	2016	2015	2014	2013
Revenue		266,000,000	250,000,000	231,991,008	184,324,992	155,850,000
R&D Expense						
Operating Income						
Operating Margin %						
SGA Expense						
Net Income				-11,640,000	12,683,000	-18,236,000
Operating Cash Flow						
Capital Expenditure						
EBITDA						
Return on Assets %						
Return on Equity %						
Debt to Equity						

CONTACT INFORMATION:

Phone: 646-728-9500   Fax: 646-728-9501
Toll-Free:
Address: 345 Hudson St., 16/Fl, New York, NY 10014 United States

STOCK TICKER/OTHER:

Stock Ticker: Subsidiary   Exchange:
Employees: 560   Fiscal Year Ends:
Parent Company: j2 Global Inc

SALARIES/BONUSES:

Top Exec. Salary: $ Bonus: $
Second Exec. Salary: $ Bonus: $

OTHER THOUGHTS:

Estimated Female Officers or Directors: 4
Hot Spot for Advancement for Women/Minorities: Y

Expedia Inc

NAIC Code: 561510

www.expedia.com

TYPES OF BUSINESS:

Online Travel Services
Online Reservations
Corporate Travel Services
Vacation Packages
Retail Travel Services Kiosks
Destination Activities & Tours
Online Travel Information
Inventory-Based Hotel Room Offerings

BRANDS/DIVISIONS/AFFILIATES:

Expedia.com
Hotwire.com
Classic Vacations
Expedia CruiseShipCenters
trivago GmbH
Travelocity
HomeAway Inc
Orbtiz Worldwide Inc

CONTACTS: Note: Officers with more than one job title may be intentionally listed here more than once.

Mark Okerstrom, CEO
Alan Pickerill, CFO
Barry Diller, Chairman of the Board
Lance Soliday, Chief Accounting Officer
Victor Kaufman, Director
Robert Dzielak, Other Executive Officer

GROWTH PLANS/SPECIAL FEATURES:

Expedia, Inc. is an online travel service offering travel shopping and reservation services, publishing schedules, pricing and availability information for numerous airlines, lodging properties, car rental companies, cruise lines and multiple-destination service providers, including restaurants, attractions and tours. The company's travel portfolio includes more than 590,000 properties, 1.5 million live vacation rental listings in 200 countries, as well as 550 airlines. The Expedia brand web sites, for both USA (Expedia.com) and international travelers, offer a large variety of travel products and services available directly to travelers. It also operates as a merchant by directly contracting from suppliers and selling discounted products directly to the consumer. The firm owns Hotels.com, which provides a full portfolio of hotel contacts around the world, and Hotwire.com, a web site that offers travelers discount airfare. Other portfolio of brands includes: Classic Vacations, a premium vacation packaging agency; Expedia CruiseShipCenters, a network of cruise vacation retail locations; trivago GmbH, an online hotel metasearch company; Travelocity, a leading online travel brand in the United States and Canada; HomeAway, a global online marketplace for the vacation rental industry, which also includes the VRBO, VacationRentals.com and BedandBreakfast.com brands, among others; Orbitz and CheapTickets, leading U.S. travel websites, as well as ebookers, a full-service travel brand with websites in seven European countries; Egencia, a travel management service for corporate customers; Expedia Local Expert, which specializes in local tours and attractions; Expedia Affiliate Network, which powers bookings for leading airlines and hotels; and CarRentals.com, an online car rental booking company.

The company offers employees medical, life, AD&D, disability, dental and vision insurance; flexible spending accounts; onsite flu shots; a 401(k); adoption assistance; an employee assistance program; a group legal program; tuition reimbursement; travel assistance; business travel accident insurance; pet insurance; and discounts for auto and home insurance.

FINANCIAL DATA: Note: Data for latest year may not have been available at press time.

In U.S. $	2018	2017	2016	2015	2014	2013
Revenue		10,059,840,000	8,773,564,000	6,672,317,000	5,763,485,000	4,771,259,000
R&D Expense		1,386,787,000	1,235,019,000	830,244,000	686,154,000	577,820,000
Operating Income		641,876,000	552,499,000	518,437,000	543,394,000	432,532,000
Operating Margin %		6.38%	6.29%	7.76%	9.42%	9.06%
SGA Expense		5,999,205,000	5,072,207,000	3,850,412,000	3,275,241,000	2,651,142,000
Net Income		377,964,000	281,848,000	764,465,000	398,097,000	232,850,000
Operating Cash Flow		1,799,154,000	1,564,334,000	1,368,045,000	1,366,959,000	763,200,000
Capital Expenditure		710,330,000	749,348,000	787,041,000	328,387,000	308,581,000
EBITDA		1,488,020,000	1,243,950,000	1,552,502,000	908,162,000	671,526,000
Return on Assets %		2.20%	1.80%	6.23%	4.75%	3.14%
Return on Equity %		8.73%	6.26%	22.99%	20.26%	10.52%
Debt to Equity		0.82	0.76	0.65	0.97	0.58

CONTACT INFORMATION:

Phone: 425 679-7200　　　Fax: 425 564-7240
Toll-Free: 800-397-3342
Address: 333 108th Ave. NE, Bellevue, WA 98004 United States

STOCK TICKER/OTHER:

Stock Ticker: EXPE　　　　　　Exchange: NAS
Employees: 20,075　　　　　　　Fiscal Year Ends: 12/31
Parent Company:

SALARIES/BONUSES:

Top Exec. Salary: $824,039　　　Bonus: $1,250,000
Second Exec. Salary:　　　　　　Bonus: $1,000,000
$465,000

OTHER THOUGHTS:

Estimated Female Officers or Directors: 1
Hot Spot for Advancement for Women/Minorities:

Expensify Inc

www.expensify.com

NAIC Code: 511210Q

TYPES OF BUSINESS:

Computer Software, Accounting, Banking & Financial
Software

BRANDS/DIVISIONS/AFFILIATES:

SmartScan

CONTACTS: Note: Officers with more than one job title may be intentionally listed here more than once.

David Barrett, CEO

GROWTH PLANS/SPECIAL FEATURES:

Expensify, Inc. provides expense reporting software for web and mobile applications. The company's proprietary receipt-scanning feature, SmartScan, enables users to be completely paperless. Once a user SmartScans a receipt, Expensify automatically codes and reports the expense before auto-submitting it for approval. Expensify is capable of analyzing unique company policies in order to determine which expenses actually need a manager's review; the rest are approved automatically. When needed, as soon as reports are fully approved, Expensify's reimbursement system delivers money back into the employee's bank account the very next day. In addition, any changes made in an organization's Expensify account, whether it is adding new expense accounts, employees or even a new department, Expensify automatically syncs them in real-time. Expensify inbox reports point out specific areas where individuals need to look via its embedded Guided Review feature. Expensify integrates with QuickBooks and Direct Deposit, among other platforms. The company's track and submit plans are for individuals looking to store and organize their receipts, primarily freelancers, entrepreneurs, realtors and those who need to track their business expenses for Schedule C tax deductions. These plans allow users to keep their receipts in a central repository accessible by their accountant. Industries served by the firm include non-profits, professional services, restaurants and hospitality, as well as startups. Expensify reimburses millions of dollars every day and processes billions every year on a global scale. Expensify is headquartered in California, USA, as well as internationally, in the U.K. and Australia.

FINANCIAL DATA: Note: Data for latest year may not have been available at press time.

In U.S. $	2018	2017	2016	2015	2014	2013
Revenue						
R&D Expense						
Operating Income						
Operating Margin %						
SGA Expense						
Net Income						
Operating Cash Flow						
Capital Expenditure						
EBITDA						
Return on Assets %						
Return on Equity %						
Debt to Equity						

CONTACT INFORMATION:

Phone: 570-123-4567   Fax:
Toll-Free: 800-745-9064
Address: 548 Market St., Ste. 61434, San Francisco, CA 94104 United States

STOCK TICKER/OTHER:

Stock Ticker: Private   Exchange:
Employees: 101   Fiscal Year Ends:
Parent Company:

SALARIES/BONUSES:

Top Exec. Salary: $ Bonus: $
Second Exec. Salary: $ Bonus: $

OTHER THOUGHTS:

Estimated Female Officers or Directors:
Hot Spot for Advancement for Women/Minorities:

Extreme Reach Inc

extremereach.com

NAIC Code: 511210F

TYPES OF BUSINESS:

Computer Software, Multimedia, Graphics & Publishing Software

BRANDS/DIVISIONS/AFFILIATES:

Carlyle Group (The)

CONTACTS: *Note: Officers with more than one job title may be intentionally listed here more than once.*

Tim Conley, CEO
Jorge Martell, CFO
Melinda McLaughlin, CMO
Jennifer Wambold, Chief Human Resources Officer
Dan Brackett, CTO

GROWTH PLANS/SPECIAL FEATURES:

Extreme Reach, Inc. provides a cloud-based solution that unites the TV and video advertising workflow, as well as all aspects of talent and rights management in a single, easy-to-use platform. The company's technology singlehandedly manages, deploys and tracks TV and video ads across every screen. At the same time, the platform and Extreme Reach teams manage the talent and rights that go along with the ads, wherever they play. The firm serves some of the world's largest brands, agencies, production houses, TV and video media destinations, as well as the talent community. Extreme Reach's technology and expertise enables them to power related aspects of the industry, including news content delivery, TV syndication content/ad management and delivery, direct response advertising preparation and delivery, production/crew payroll and post-production services. The company is headquartered in Massachusetts, USA, with more than 15 locations throughout the U.S. as well as in Canada and the U.K. It is majority-owned by The Carlyle Group.

FINANCIAL DATA: *Note: Data for latest year may not have been available at press time.*

In U.S. $	2018	2017	2016	2015	2014	2013
Revenue						
R&D Expense						
Operating Income						
Operating Margin %						
SGA Expense						
Net Income						
Operating Cash Flow						
Capital Expenditure						
EBITDA						
Return on Assets %						
Return on Equity %						
Debt to Equity						

CONTACT INFORMATION:

Phone: 781-577-2016   Fax: 877-484-8836
Toll-Free: 877-769-9382
Address: 75 2nd Ave., Ste. 720, Needham, MA 02494 United States

STOCK TICKER/OTHER:

Stock Ticker: Private   Exchange:
Employees: 850   Fiscal Year Ends:
Parent Company: Carlyle Group (The)

SALARIES/BONUSES:

Top Exec. Salary: $ Bonus: $
Second Exec. Salary: $ Bonus: $

OTHER THOUGHTS:

Estimated Female Officers or Directors:
Hot Spot for Advancement for Women/Minorities:

F5 Networks Inc

www.f5.com

NAIC Code: 511210B

TYPES OF BUSINESS:

Computer Software, Network Management, System Testing & Storage
Internet Traffic Management Solutions
Firewall Software
File Virtualization

BRANDS/DIVISIONS/AFFILIATES:

BIG-IP
VIPRION
Silverline
iRules
iRules LX
iControl
iApps
iCall

CONTACTS: *Note: Officers with more than one job title may be intentionally listed here more than once.*

Francis Pelzer, CFO
Ryan Kearny, Chief Technology Officer
Alan Higginson, Director
Francois Locoh-Donou, Director
Steve McMillan, Executive VP, Divisional
Chad Whalen, Executive VP, Divisional
Scot Rogers, Executive VP
Ana White, Executive VP
Tom Fountain, Executive VP
Kara Sprague, General Manager, Divisional

GROWTH PLANS/SPECIAL FEATURES:

F5 Networks, Inc. provides application delivery networking products that improve the security, availability and performance of network applications. The core technology of the firm is the full-proxy, programmable, massively-scalable software platform called TMOS (Traffic Management Operating System). The TMOS platform supports a broadest array of application services, including local and global traffic management, network and application security, access management, web acceleration and several other network and application services. These services are available as software modules that can run individually or as part of an integrated solution on the high-performance, scalable, purpose-built BIG-IP appliances and chassis-based VIPRION systems; or as software-only Virtual Editions that run on major hypervisors in public and private clouds. The cloud-based Silverline software-as-a-service (SaaS) offerings allow customers to subscribe to online denial-of-service protection and application security services. The core features and functions of TMOS enable the firm's products to inspect and modify the content of IP traffic flows at network speeds and sessions between users and applications and support a broad and growing array of services. The built-in scripting language, iRules and iRules LX, enables customers and third parties to write customized rules to inspect and modify traffic. TMOS also has an open software interface called iControl, which allows the firm's products to communicate with one another and with third-party products; a set of features called iApps that speed deployment of services and give users an application-centric view of how applications are managed and delivered; and a scripting framework called iCall that lets users configure their F5 devices inline. The company sells its products and services to large enterprise customers and service providers through a variety of channels, including distributors, value-added resellers and systems integrators.

Employee benefits include medical, dental and vision coverage; flexible spending accounts; life and disability insurance; employee stock and employee assistance programs; 401(k); and tuition assistance.

FINANCIAL DATA: *Note: Data for latest year may not have been available at press time.*

In U.S. $	2018	2017	2016	2015	2014	2013
Revenue	2,161,407,000	2,090,041,000	1,995,034,000	1,919,823,000	1,732,046,000	1,481,314,000
R&D Expense	366,084,000	350,365,000	334,227,000	296,583,000	263,792,000	209,614,000
Operating Income	609,325,000	577,065,000	556,428,000	552,899,000	493,557,000	430,818,000
Operating Margin %		27.61%	27.89%	28.79%	28.49%	29.08%
SGA Expense	824,517,000	809,126,000	767,174,000	738,080,000	664,738,000	585,442,000
Net Income	453,689,000	420,761,000	365,855,000	365,014,000	311,183,000	277,314,000
Operating Cash Flow	761,068,000	740,281,000	711,535,000	684,541,000	548,992,000	499,693,000
Capital Expenditure	53,465,000	42,681,000	68,238,000	67,086,000	22,718,000	26,583,000
EBITDA	668,816,000	638,213,000	613,204,000	605,482,000	539,678,000	470,823,000
Return on Assets %		17.57%	15.84%	16.23%	14.09%	13.39%
Return on Equity %		34.85%	29.24%	27.17%	21.40%	19.33%
Debt to Equity						

CONTACT INFORMATION:

Phone: 206 272-5555   Fax: 206 272-5556
Toll-Free: 888-882-4447
Address: 401 Elliott Ave. W., Seattle, WA 98119 United States

STOCK TICKER/OTHER:

Stock Ticker: FFIV
Employees: 4,395
Parent Company:

Exchange: NAS
Fiscal Year Ends: 09/30

SALARIES/BONUSES:

Top Exec. Salary: $375,000   Bonus: $800,000
Second Exec. Salary: $540,052   Bonus: $

OTHER THOUGHTS:

Estimated Female Officers or Directors: 3
Hot Spot for Advancement for Women/Minorities: Y

Fab.com
NAIC Code: 454111

www.fab.com

TYPES OF BUSINESS:
Electronic Shopping

BRANDS/DIVISIONS/AFFILIATES:
PCH International Ltd

GROWTH PLANS/SPECIAL FEATURES:

Fab.com is a design eCommerce retailer. Through its website, the firm offers urban-inspired products in which designers express their personal sense of style. All products are said to be unique, well-designed and of high quality. Items are categorized into four departments: technology & related accessories, home accents, dining & entertaining, and fun. Currently (January 2019), the most popular items include Vibes Hi-Fi earplugs, portable personal security alarms, a leather cord wrap travel pouch, salt and pepper robots, trademarked Death Star ice products, playable art and more. Items not marked as Final Sale can be returned within 30 days of delivery for free. Fab.com operates as a subsidiary of PCH International Ltd.

CONTACTS: Note: Officers with more than one job title may be intentionally listed here more than once.

Jason Goldberg, CEO
Matt Baer, Sr. VP-Merch. Oper.
Sunil Kedar, Sr. VP-Eng.
Bhojani Ashfaq, Dir-Admin
Alex Do, VP-e-commerce
Pierre Coker, Mgr.-Finance & Accounting
Eleanor Bowley, Dir.-Buying
Kelly Bradford, Sr. Mgr.-Inventory Control
Margaret Breitton, Mgr.-Supply Chain Analytics
Lingy Chan, Dir.-Art
Rob Bongaerts, Sr. VP-Logistics Europe
Dania Barbosa, Mgr.-Sourcing

FINANCIAL DATA: Note: Data for latest year may not have been available at press time.

In U.S. $	2018	2017	2016	2015	2014	2013
Revenue						
R&D Expense						
Operating Income						
Operating Margin %						
SGA Expense						
Net Income						
Operating Cash Flow						
Capital Expenditure						
EBITDA						
Return on Assets %						
Return on Equity %						
Debt to Equity						

CONTACT INFORMATION:
Phone: 646-684-3076   Fax:
Toll-Free: 877-463-4322
Address: 95 Morton St., New York, NY 100014 United States

STOCK TICKER/OTHER:
Stock Ticker: Private
Employees: 25
Parent Company: PCH International Ltd

Exchange:
Fiscal Year Ends:

SALARIES/BONUSES:
Top Exec. Salary: $ Bonus: $
Second Exec. Salary: $ Bonus: $

OTHER THOUGHTS:
Estimated Female Officers or Directors: 5
Hot Spot for Advancement for Women/Minorities: Y

Facebook Inc

NAIC Code: 519130

investor.fb.com/

TYPES OF BUSINESS:

Social Networking
Advertising Services
Developer Tools
Online Video
3-D Headset Manufacturing
Apps

BRANDS/DIVISIONS/AFFILIATES:

Facebook Platform
Instagram
Messenger
WhatsApp Messenger
Oculus
Portal
Portal+

CONTACTS: Note: Officers with more than one job title may be intentionally listed here more than once.

Mark Zuckerberg, CEO
David Wehner, CFO
Susan Taylor, Chief Accounting Officer
Michael Schroepfer, Chief Technology Officer
Sheryl Sandberg, COO
Christopher Cox, Other Executive Officer
David Fischer, Vice President, Divisional
Colin Stretch, Vice President

GROWTH PLANS/SPECIAL FEATURES:

Facebook, Inc. owns and operates a free social networking utility for communicating online with family, friends and acquaintances. As of September 2018, the company had 2.27 billion monthly active users in general, and 1.49 billion daily active users who specifically used the company's mobile products. Some of the site's core functions and applications include individual profiles and home pages; friend lists; group pages; and photos, videos, events and other shared items. Communication is enabled through means such as in-site instant messaging, personal messages, public posts and status updates. Third-party applications (such as games, quizzes and personality tests) can also be added to users' pages to further personalize the site. For privacy, the firm gives users the ability to limit, to some extent, who can view their profile, postings and other personal information. The company's Facebook Platform is a set of development tools and application programming interfaces that enable developers to integrate with Facebook to create social apps and websites. Millions of apps and websites have been integrated as part of the platform. Facebook generates the majority of its revenues from advertising, which can be customized to reach specifically targeted audiences by accessing information users provide the company on their individual profiles. Subsidiary Instagram is a mobile phone-based photo-sharing service that makes it simple for users to upload photos to their profiles; Messenger is a mobile-to-mobile messaging application; WhatsApp Messenger is a cross-platform mobile messaging app that allows people to exchange messages on mobile devices; and Oculus, a virtual reality technology and content platform that power products and enable users to immerse and interact in connected environments. In late-2018, Facebook launched a brand of smart displays called Portal and Portal+, comprising enhanced smart speakers for Amazon's Alexa and Facebook Messenger.

Facebook offers its employees comprehensive benefits.

FINANCIAL DATA: Note: Data for latest year may not have been available at press time.

In U.S. $	2018	2017	2016	2015	2014	2013
Revenue		40,653,000,000	27,638,000,000	17,928,000,000	12,466,000,000	7,872,000,000
R&D Expense		7,754,000,000	5,919,000,000	4,816,000,000	2,666,000,000	1,415,000,000
Operating Income		20,203,000,000	12,427,000,000	6,225,000,000	4,994,000,000	2,804,000,000
Operating Margin %		49.69%	44.96%	34.72%	40.06%	35.61%
SGA Expense		7,242,000,000	5,503,000,000	4,020,000,000	2,653,000,000	1,778,000,000
Net Income		15,934,000,000	10,217,000,000	3,688,000,000	2,940,000,000	1,500,000,000
Operating Cash Flow		24,216,000,000	16,108,000,000	8,599,000,000	5,457,000,000	4,222,000,000
Capital Expenditure		6,733,000,000	4,491,000,000	2,523,000,000	1,831,000,000	1,362,000,000
EBITDA		23,625,000,000	14,870,000,000	8,162,000,000	6,176,000,000	3,821,000,000
Return on Assets %		21.29%	17.81%	8.19%	10.07%	9.03%
Return on Equity %		23.84%	19.70%	9.13%	11.34%	10.95%
Debt to Equity						0.01

CONTACT INFORMATION:

Phone: 650 543-4800   Fax:
Toll-Free:
Address: 1601 Willow Rd., Menlo Park, CA 94025 United States

STOCK TICKER/OTHER:

Stock Ticker: FB
Employees: 17,048
Parent Company:

Exchange: NAS
Fiscal Year Ends: 12/31

SALARIES/BONUSES:

Top Exec. Salary: $795,769   Bonus: $640,378
Second Exec. Salary: $711,539   Bonus: $633,317

OTHER THOUGHTS:

Estimated Female Officers or Directors: 2
Hot Spot for Advancement for Women/Minorities: Y

FactSet Research Systems Inc

www.factset.com

NAIC Code: 511120A

TYPES OF BUSINESS:
Online Financial & Economic Data
Financial Software
Consulting Services

BRANDS/DIVISIONS/AFFILIATES:
BISAM Technologies SA
Interactive Data Managed Solutions

CONTACTS: Note: Officers with more than one job title may be intentionally listed here more than once.
F. Snow, CEO
Helen Shan, CFO
Philip Hadley, Chairman of the Board
Matthew McNulty, Chief Accounting Officer
Gene Fernandez, Chief Technology Officer
Rachel Stern, Executive VP
John Wiseman, Executive VP
Robert Robie, Executive VP

GROWTH PLANS/SPECIAL FEATURES:

FactSet Research Systems, Inc. supplies financial information and analytical applications to global investors, including portfolio managers, performance analysts, risk managers, sell-side equity researchers, investment bankers and fixed income professionals. Headquartered in Norwalk, Connecticut, the company operates 63 locations in 23 countries. FactSet has more than 89,000 users and 3,500 clients in over 50 countries worldwide, with access to data from more than 220 data suppliers, 115 news sources and 85 exchanges. It combines the content of tens of thousands of companies from multiple sources (stock markets, research firms, governments and others) into a single online platform of information and analytics. The firm integrates content from premier providers such as Thomson Reuters, Standard & Poor's, Axioma, Interactive Data Corporation, Dow Jones & Company, Northfield Information Services, Barclays Capital, Intex Solutions and many more. FactSet's operations are organized into three reportable segments based on geographic operations: the U.S., Europe and Asia Pacific. The majority of fiscal revenue is derived from its U.S. clients, with Europe being next and Asia Pacific the remainder. The U.S. segment services finance professionals including financial institutions throughout the Americas, while the European and Asia Pacific segments service investment professionals located throughout Europe and Asia, respectively. The European segment is headquartered in London, England and maintains offices in France, Germany, the Netherlands, Latvia, Dubai, Bulgaria, Switzerland, Spain and Italy. The Asia Pacific segment is headquartered in Tokyo, Japan with offices in Hong Kong, Australia, the Philippines, China and India. FactSet's client retention rate is over 95%.

FactSet offers U.S. employees medical, dental, life, disability, vision, AD&D and business travel insurance; wellness programs; disability and maternity leave; counseling services; flexible spending accounts; 401(k) and employee stock purchase plans; and tuition reimbursement.

FINANCIAL DATA: Note: Data for latest year may not have been available at press time.

In U.S. $	2018	2017	2016	2015	2014	2013
Revenue	1,350,145,000	1,221,179,000	1,127,092,000	1,006,768,000	920,335,000	858,112,000
R&D Expense						
Operating Income	366,204,000	352,135,000	349,676,000	331,918,000	302,219,000	269,419,000
Operating Margin %		28.83%	31.02%	32.96%	32.83%	31.39%
SGA Expense	324,645,000	302,464,000	290,007,000	269,511,000	264,430,000	282,314,000
Net Income	267,085,000	258,259,000	338,815,000	241,051,000	211,543,000	198,637,000
Operating Cash Flow	385,668,000	320,527,000	331,140,000	306,442,000	265,023,000	269,809,000
Capital Expenditure	33,520,000	36,862,000	47,740,000	25,682,000	17,743,000	18,517,000
EBITDA	423,489,000	400,429,000	387,728,000	363,267,000	336,654,000	305,198,000
Return on Assets %		21.23%	38.59%	34.43%	31.26%	28.69%
Return on Equity %		47.95%	64.59%	46.23%	40.18%	36.31%
Debt to Equity		1.02	0.57	0.06		

CONTACT INFORMATION:
Phone: 203 810-1000   Fax: 203 810-1001
Toll-Free:
Address: 601 Merritt 7, Fl. 3, Norwalk, CT 06851 United States

STOCK TICKER/OTHER:
Stock Ticker: FDS   Exchange: NYS
Employees: 8,375   Fiscal Year Ends: 08/31
Parent Company:

SALARIES/BONUSES:
Top Exec. Salary: $445,833   Bonus: $1,150,000
Second Exec. Salary: Bonus: $725,000
$300,000

OTHER THOUGHTS:
Estimated Female Officers or Directors: 3
Hot Spot for Advancement for Women/Minorities: Y

Fanatics Inc

NAIC Code: 454111

TYPES OF BUSINESS:

Electronic Shopping of Licensed Sports Merchandise

BRANDS/DIVISIONS/AFFILIATES:

Kynetic LLC
Fanatics.com
FansEdge.com
Kitbag.com
MajesticAthletic.com
FanaticsAuthentic.com
Fanatics Japan
Fanatics Germany

CONTACTS: Note: Officers with more than one job title may be intentionally listed here more than once.

Doug Mack, CEO
Steve Davis, Pres., International
Jamie Davis, Pres.
Lauren Cooks Levitan, CFO
Robin Eletto, Chief People Officer
Matt Madrigal, CTO
Jack Boyle, Pres., Merch.
Mitch Trager, Chief Strategy Officer
Meier Raivich, VP-Branding
Gary Gertzog, Exec. VP-Bus. Affairs
Michael Rubin, Exec. Chmn.

GROWTH PLANS/SPECIAL FEATURES:

Fanatics, Inc. is an online retailer of licensed sports merchandise. Customers can purchase items via online sites through the Fanatics (Fanatics.com), FansEdge (FansEdge.com), Kitbag (Kitbag.com) and Majestic (MajesticAthletic.com) brands. The firm also offers a collection of sports collectibles and memorabilia through Fanatics Authentic (FanaticsAuthentic.com). Fanatics operates more than 300 online and offline partner stores, including the e-commerce business for all major professional sports leagues (NFL, MLB, NBA, NHL, NASCAR, MLS, PGA, Premier League); major media brands (NBC Sports, CBS Sports, FOX Sports); and more than 200 collegiate and professional team properties. In addition to e-commerce, the company's capabilities include multichannel-integrated event and team retail across all leagues and major events such as Kentucky Derby, Ryder Cup and NHL's Winder Classic. International capabilities that provide a global sports retail platform is currently growing the licensed sports merchandise business in soccer as well as across all sports worldwide. Fanatics, headquartered in Florida, is privately held by Kynetic, LLC. In January 2018, Fanatics expanded into Japan by opening a new Fanatics office and company division (Fanatics Japan) in Tokyo. In May, Fanatics expanded into Germany with the opening of an office in Germany and Fanatics Germany in Hamburg. In September, the firm launched NFLSHOP.ca, an e-commerce platform for Canadian NFL fans. Also, in September, Fanatics opened a technology innovation center in Hyderabad, India.

FINANCIAL DATA: Note: Data for latest year may not have been available at press time.

In U.S. $	2018	2017	2016	2015	2014	2013
Revenue		2,415,000,000	2,000,000,000	1,500,000,000	1,250,000,000	1,000,000,000
R&D Expense						
Operating Income						
Operating Margin %						
SGA Expense						
Net Income						
Operating Cash Flow						
Capital Expenditure						
EBITDA						
Return on Assets %						
Return on Equity %						
Debt to Equity						

CONTACT INFORMATION:

Phone: 904-421-1897   Fax:
Toll-Free: 877-833-7397
Address: 8100 Nations Way, Jacksonville, FL 32256 United States

STOCK TICKER/OTHER:

Stock Ticker: Private   Exchange:
Employees: 1,800   Fiscal Year Ends:
Parent Company: Kynetic LLC

SALARIES/BONUSES:

Top Exec. Salary: $ Bonus: $
Second Exec. Salary: $ Bonus: $

OTHER THOUGHTS:

Estimated Female Officers or Directors:
Hot Spot for Advancement for Women/Minorities:

Sales, profits and employees may be estimates. Financial information, benefits and other data can change quickly and may vary from those stated here.

Fandango Inc

www.fandango.com

NAIC Code: 454111

TYPES OF BUSINESS:

Online Movie Ticket Sales
Online Community Forums

BRANDS/DIVISIONS/AFFILIATES:

Comcast Corporation
1-800-FANDANGO
FandangoNOW

CONTACTS: *Note: Officers with more than one job title may be intentionally listed here more than once.*

Paul Yanover, Pres.
Robert Leff, Sr. VP
Kevin Shepela, Chief Commercial Officer
Katie Ibay, Head-Human Resources
Braxton Woodham, CTO
Jessica Yi, Chief Prod. Officer
Dana Henry Benson, Exec. Dir.-Comm.

GROWTH PLANS/SPECIAL FEATURES:

Fandango, Inc., provides moviegoers with advance ticket sales through partnerships with major Canadian- and U.S.-based movie exhibitors. The company sells tickets for nearly 26,000 screens across North America. In advance (even months in advance), customers can select a location and show time and purchase tickets with their credit card either through the company's website, Fandango.com, or its toll-free telephone number, 1-800-FANDANGO. Online tickets can either be printed out or picked up at the theater's Fandango access port or box office, while telephone tickets are picked up on location through either a confirmation number or credit card validation. Fandango mobile applications are available for iPad, iPhone, Android and more. Besides offering movie tickets, Fandango.com also supplies additional movie-related content, including movie trailers, celebrity interviews, actor photos and movie news, and it provides an online community where users can create and share movie reviews and rate movies and actors. FandangoNOW is a video on-demand service offering a wide selection of movies and television shows. It is integrated into the Roku experience making it easy to buy or rent movies and shows, including new releases. Fandango has more than 30 theater chain partners, including AMC Theatres, Century Theatres, Cinemark Theatres, Edwards Theatres, Regal Cinemas and United Artists Theatres. The firm also occasionally offers box office information for local independent theaters. Fandango operates as a subsidiary of Comcast Corporation.

Fandango offers its employees medical, dental, vision and prescription drug coverage; life insurance; short- and long-term disability; a 401(k) plan; free movie tickets; an onsite fitness club; and free lunches on certain days of the week.

FINANCIAL DATA: *Note: Data for latest year may not have been available at press time.*

In U.S. $	2018	2017	2016	2015	2014	2013
Revenue						
R&D Expense						
Operating Income						
Operating Margin %						
SGA Expense						
Net Income						
Operating Cash Flow						
Capital Expenditure						
EBITDA						
Return on Assets %						
Return on Equity %						
Debt to Equity						

CONTACT INFORMATION:

Phone: 310-451-7690   Fax: 310-451-7861
Toll-Free:
Address: 12200 W. Olympic Blvd., Ste. 400, Los Angeles, CA 90064
United States

STOCK TICKER/OTHER:

Stock Ticker: Subsidiary   Exchange:
Employees: 317   Fiscal Year Ends: 01/31
Parent Company: Comcast Corporation

SALARIES/BONUSES:

Top Exec. Salary: $ Bonus: $
Second Exec. Salary: $ Bonus: $

OTHER THOUGHTS:

Estimated Female Officers or Directors: 2
Hot Spot for Advancement for Women/Minorities: Y

Farfetch Ltd

www.farfetch.com

NAIC Code: 454111

TYPES OF BUSINESS:

Electronic Shopping

BRANDS/DIVISIONS/AFFILIATES:

CONTACTS: *Note: Officers with more than one job title may be intentionally listed here more than once.*

Jose Neves, CEO
Andrew Robb, COO
Elliot Jordan, CFO
John Veichmanis, CMO
Sian Keane, Chief People Officer
Cipriano Sousa, CTO

GROWTH PLANS/SPECIAL FEATURES:

Farfetch Ltd. offers a global technology platform for luxury fashion, connecting creators, curators and consumers. The firm's modular, end-to-end technology platform is a single operating system built on an API-enabled proprietary stack, providing the foundation for applications, services and data. Thus, Farfetch.com is a global luxury marketplace that enables shoppers to find a vast range of products from global brands and boutiques. As of September 2018, over 3,200 different brands were available on the marketplace, ranging from heritage brands to emerging ones. Shopping categories include womenswear, menswear, kidswear, vintage, fine watches and jewelry. The company ships to 190 countries, and its localized websites offer 12 languages as well as multilingual customer support. Same-day delivery is offered in 19 major global cities. More than 2.6 consumers and nearly 1,000 sellers are connected to the marketplace. In December 2018, Farfetch agreed to acquire sneaker and streetwear marketplace, Stadium Goods.

FINANCIAL DATA: *Note: Data for latest year may not have been available at press time.*

In U.S. $	2018	2017	2016	2015	2014	2013
Revenue		385,966,000	242,116,000	142,305,000		
R&D Expense						
Operating Income		-94,494,000	-88,680,000	-57,470,000		
Operating Margin %						
SGA Expense		288,280,000	198,661,000	126,969,000		
Net Income		-112,275,000	-81,414,000	-60,353,000		
Operating Cash Flow		-59,320,000	-47,079,000	-37,258,000		
Capital Expenditure		31,613,000	18,598,000	16,012,000		
EBITDA		-99,552,000	-72,861,000	-58,619,000		
Return on Assets %						
Return on Equity %						
Debt to Equity						

CONTACT INFORMATION:

Phone: 44-20-7549-5400 Fax:
Toll-Free:
Address: 211 Old St., The Bower, 4/Fl, London, EC1V 9NR United Kingdom

STOCK TICKER/OTHER:

Stock Ticker: FTCH
Employees: 3,009
Parent Company:

Exchange: NYS
Fiscal Year Ends: 12/31

SALARIES/BONUSES:

Top Exec. Salary: $ Bonus: $
Second Exec. Salary: $ Bonus: $

OTHER THOUGHTS:

Estimated Female Officers or Directors:
Hot Spot for Advancement for Women/Minorities:

Fastly Inc

NAIC Code: 511210M

TYPES OF BUSINESS:

Computer Software, E-Commerce & Web Analytics

BRANDS/DIVISIONS/AFFILIATES:

CONTACTS: *Note: Officers with more than one job title may be intentionally listed here more than once.*

Artur Bergman, CEO
Christopher Brown, VP-Operations

GROWTH PLANS/SPECIAL FEATURES:

Fastly, Inc. operates as a content delivery network (CDN). The company's real-time CDN gives businesses complete control over how they serve content, access to performance analytics and the ability to cache ever-changing content. Fastly is built for speed: with a capacity of several terabits per second, handling hundreds of days of video traffic per minute. The firm also protects sites and apps from web-based attacks. Its solutions are easy to deploy and scalable. Fastly's edge cloud platform is instant, agile, programmable and secure. The platform includes: Edge SDK, enabling users to harness the power of Fastly's global network to intelligently cache and deliver application logic at the edge; content delivery and image optimization; video on-demand and live streaming across multiple devices and platforms; cloud security; load balancing; and managed CDN. Industries served by the firm include digital publishing, e-commerce, online audio/video, software-as-a-service (SaaS) and travel and hospitality. Investors of the company include Amplify Partners, August Capital, Battery Ventures, Deutsche Telekom Capital Partners, Iconiq Capital, O'Reilly AlphaTech Ventures, Ridge Ventures, Sapphire Ventures, Sozo Ventures and Swisscomm Ventures. Fastly is based in San Francisco, California. In mid-2018, Fastly raised another $40 million before filing for an initial public offering, which it announced that it planned to do. This investment totaled $219 million raised over the last several years.

FINANCIAL DATA: *Note: Data for latest year may not have been available at press time.*

In U.S. $	2018	2017	2016	2015	2014	2013
Revenue						
R&D Expense						
Operating Income						
Operating Margin %						
SGA Expense						
Net Income						
Operating Cash Flow						
Capital Expenditure						
EBITDA						
Return on Assets %						
Return on Equity %						
Debt to Equity						

CONTACT INFORMATION:

Phone: 650-849-7400   Fax:
Toll-Free: 844-432-7859
Address: 651 Brannan St., Ste. 110, San Francisco, CA 94107 United States

STOCK TICKER/OTHER:

Stock Ticker: Private
Employees: 200
Parent Company:

Exchange:
Fiscal Year Ends:

SALARIES/BONUSES:

Top Exec. Salary: $ Bonus: $
Second Exec. Salary: $ Bonus: $

OTHER THOUGHTS:

Estimated Female Officers or Directors:
Hot Spot for Advancement for Women/Minorities:

First Data Corporation

www.firstdatacorp.com

NAIC Code: 522320

TYPES OF BUSINESS:

Credit Card Processing
Electronic Payment Processing
Check Verification
Prepaid Card Services
Private-Label Credit Card Services
ATMs
Terminals

BRANDS/DIVISIONS/AFFILIATES:

Clover
VisionPLUS

CONTACTS: *Note: Officers with more than one job title may be intentionally listed here more than once.*

Frank Bisignano, CEO
Guy Chiarello, Pres.
Himanshu Patel, CFO
Matthew Cagwin, Chief Accounting Officer
Thomas Higgins, Chief Administrative Officer
Christine Larsen, COO
Joseph Plumeri, Director
Adam Rosman, Executive VP
Daniel Charron, Executive VP
Andrew Gelb, Executive VP
Christopher Foskett, Executive VP
Michael Neborak, Executive VP
Gustavo Marin, Executive VP
Anthony Marino, Executive VP
Barry McCarthy, Executive VP
Ivo Distelbrink, Executive VP
Cynthia Armine-Klein, Executive VP

GROWTH PLANS/SPECIAL FEATURES:

First Data Corporation is a provider of electronic commerce and payment solutions for merchants, financial institutions and card issuers globally and has operations in more than 100 countries, serving approximately 6 million merchant locations. The company also develops, implements and manages prepaid stored-value gift card services for retailers, general use credit cards and private-label credit cards for businesses. The firm's operations are organized in three segments: global business solutions (GBS), global financial solutions (GFS) and network and security solutions (NSS). GBS provides retail point-of-sale merchant acquiring and eCommerce services, as well as next-generation offerings such as mobile payment services, webstore-in-a-box solutions, and the cloud-based Clover point-of-sale operating system, which includes a marketplace for proprietary and third-party business applications. GFS provides credit solutions for bank and non-bank issuers. These include credit and retail private-label card processing within the U.S. and international markets; and licensed financial software systems, such as First Data's VisionPLUS bank processing application, and lending solutions. This segment also provides financial institutions services such as card personalization and embossing, statement printing, client service and remittance processing. NSS provides a wide range of value-added solutions sold to GBS and GFS clients, smaller financial institutions and other enterprise clients. These solutions include electronic transfer of funds solutions, debit card processing solutions, stored value network solutions and security and fraud solutions. This division also supports digital strategies such as online and mobile banking, and mobile wallets. First Data processes more than 90 billion transactions globally, or approximately 3,000 per second. The U.S. is the company's largest market, accounting for over 10% of the U.S. gross domestic product annually.

First Data offers its employees comprehensive benefits; 401(k); flexible spending accounts; tuition reimbursement; and adoption assistance.

FINANCIAL DATA: *Note: Data for latest year may not have been available at press time.*

In U.S. $	2018	2017	2016	2015	2014	2013
Revenue		12,052,000,000	11,584,000,000	11,451,000,000	11,151,800,000	10,808,900,000
R&D Expense						
Operating Income		1,837,000,000	1,651,000,000	1,170,000,000	1,452,500,000	1,178,600,000
Operating Margin %		15.24%	14.33%	10.68%	13.02%	10.90%
SGA Expense		2,178,000,000	2,035,000,000	2,292,000,000	1,961,800,000	1,888,800,000
Net Income		1,465,000,000	420,000,000	-1,481,000,000	-457,800,000	-869,100,000
Operating Cash Flow		2,047,000,000	2,111,000,000	795,000,000	1,013,200,000	672,700,000
Capital Expenditure		518,000,000	477,000,000	602,000,000	566,500,000	378,500,000
EBITDA		2,723,000,000	2,610,000,000	1,264,000,000	2,514,300,000	2,298,700,000
Return on Assets %		3.30%	1.12%	-4.31%	-1.31%	-2.37%
Return on Equity %		67.01%	44.49%	-1370.66%		
Debt to Equity		5.68	14.86	28.04		

CONTACT INFORMATION:

Phone: 866-965-8330   Fax:
Toll-Free: 800-735-3362
Address: 225 Liberty St., 29/Fl, New York, NY 10281 United States

STOCK TICKER/OTHER:

Stock Ticker: FDC
Employees: 24,000
Parent Company: KKR & Co LP

Exchange: NYS
Fiscal Year Ends: 12/31

SALARIES/BONUSES:

Top Exec. Salary: $750,000   Bonus: $3,471,210
Second Exec. Salary: $1,320,000   Bonus: $1,287,000

OTHER THOUGHTS:

Estimated Female Officers or Directors: 1
Hot Spot for Advancement for Women/Minorities:

Sales, profits and employees may be estimates. Financial information, benefits and other data can change quickly and may vary from those stated here.

Fiserv Inc

NAIC Code: 522320

TYPES OF BUSINESS:

Financial Services
Investment Services
Online Banking
Electronic Billing & Payment
Software Applications & Investment Management Solutions

BRANDS/DIVISIONS/AFFILIATES:

Monitise plc
Dovetail Group Limited
PCLender LLC
Fiserv Forum

CONTACTS: Note: Officers with more than one job title may be intentionally listed here more than once.

Jeffery Yabuki, CEO
Kenneth Best, Chief Accounting Officer
Byron Vielehr, Chief Administrative Officer
Robert Hau, Chief Financial Officer
Glenn Renwick, Director
Kevin Schultz, President, Divisional
Devin McGranahan, President, Divisional
Lynn McCreary, Secretary

GROWTH PLANS/SPECIAL FEATURES:

Fiserv, Inc. provides integrated data processing and information management systems to more than 12,000 financial services providers, including banks, thrifts, credit unions, investment management firms, leasing and finance companies, retailers, merchants and government agencies. It operates in two primary segments: financial institution services (financial) and payments and industry products (payments). The financial segment provides banks, thrifts and credit unions with account processing services, item processing services, loan origination and servicing products, cash management and consulting services as well as other products and services that support a variety of financial transactions. The payments segment provides products and services that address a range of technology needs for the financial services industry, including internet banking, electronic bill payment, electronic funds transfer and debit processing, fraud and risk management capabilities, card and print personalization services, check imaging and investment account processing services for separately managed accounts. The company operates centers nationwide for full-service data processing, software development, item processing and check imaging, technology support and related product businesses. It operates data, development, item processing and support centers in approximately 105 cities worldwide. In late-2017, the firm acquired Monitise plc, a provider of digital banking solutions for financial institutions; Dovetail Group Limited, a provider of bank payments and liquidity management solutions; and PCLender, LLC, an internet-based mortgage software and solutions company. During 2018, Fiserv obtained the naming rights to the Fiserv Forum, home to the Milwaukee Bucks professional basketball team; and sold a 55% interest of its lending solutions business to Warburg Pincus LLC, retaining a 45% in the joint venture.

FINANCIAL DATA: Note: Data for latest year may not have been available at press time.

In U.S. $	2018	2017	2016	2015	2014	2013
Revenue		5,696,000,000	5,505,000,000	5,254,000,000	5,066,000,000	4,814,000,000
R&D Expense						
Operating Income		1,522,000,000	1,445,000,000	1,311,000,000	1,210,000,000	1,061,000,000
Operating Margin %		26.72%	26.24%	24.95%	23.88%	22.03%
SGA Expense		1,150,000,000	1,101,000,000	1,034,000,000	975,000,000	977,000,000
Net Income		1,246,000,000	930,000,000	712,000,000	754,000,000	648,000,000
Operating Cash Flow		1,483,000,000	1,431,000,000	1,346,000,000	1,307,000,000	1,039,000,000
Capital Expenditure		287,000,000	290,000,000	359,000,000	292,000,000	236,000,000
EBITDA		1,967,000,000	1,849,000,000	1,643,000,000	1,615,000,000	1,465,000,000
Return on Assets %		12.44%	9.74%	7.62%	7.99%	7.19%
Return on Equity %		47.26%	35.76%	23.91%	21.91%	18.50%
Debt to Equity		1.79	1.75	1.61	1.12	1.04

CONTACT INFORMATION:

Phone: 262 879-5000   Fax: 262 879-5275
Toll-Free: 800-872-7882
Address: 255 Fiserv Dr., Brookfield, WI 53045 United States

STOCK TICKER/OTHER:

Stock Ticker: FISV   Exchange: NAS
Employees: 23,000   Fiscal Year Ends: 12/31
Parent Company:

SALARIES/BONUSES:

Top Exec. Salary: $510,000   Bonus: $500,000
Second Exec. Salary: $840,000   Bonus: $

OTHER THOUGHTS:

Estimated Female Officers or Directors: 1
Hot Spot for Advancement for Women/Minorities:

Flatiron Health Inc

NAIC Code: 511210D

www.flatiron.com

TYPES OF BUSINESS:

Computer Software, Healthcare & Biotechnology

BRANDS/DIVISIONS/AFFILIATES:

OncoEMR
OncoAnalytics
OncoBilling
OncoTrials
OncoCloud

CONTACTS: Note: Officers with more than one job title may be intentionally listed here more than once.

Nat Turner, CEO
Zach Weinberg, Pres.
Jason Harinstein, CFO
Carol Jensen, Chief People Officer
Gil Shklarski, CTO

GROWTH PLANS/SPECIAL FEATURES:

Flatiron Health, Inc. is a healthcare technology company engaged in building data pipelines and structured databases for oncology, as well as healthcare markets. The company's goal is to make a difference in the fight against cancer; therefore, it focuses on building a disruptive software platform that connects cancer centers across the country in an effort to serve cancer patients and Flatiron customers by dramatically improving treatment and accelerating research. The firm's products include OncoEMR, an electronic health record that enables cancer care providers to manage and document the entire treatment process within one cloud-based system; OncoAnalytics, a tool that unlocks data from multiple systems, and delivers detailed clinical insights and business intelligence; OncoBilling, an integrated system for filing and managing claims with insurance companies; OncoTrials, a solution for managing oncology clinical trial programs; and a value-based oncology payment model powered by the OncoCloud suite, which is a clinically-integrated oncology care solution that saves time while also meeting complex program requirements. For life sciences industries, Flatiron's approach pairs clinical oncology experts with innovative technology to rapidly generate high-quality data directly from the electronic heath record (EHR). For academics and hospitals, it offers a better solution to unlock the value of both structure and unstructured EHR data. Currently, 2.2 million active patient records are available for research by Flatiron's solutions. In April 2018, the firm was acquired by Roche Holding AG, a world-leading healthcare and biotechnology company, for $1.9 billion.

FINANCIAL DATA: Note: Data for latest year may not have been available at press time.

In U.S. $	2018	2017	2016	2015	2014	2013
Revenue						
R&D Expense						
Operating Income						
Operating Margin %						
SGA Expense						
Net Income						
Operating Cash Flow						
Capital Expenditure						
EBITDA						
Return on Assets %						
Return on Equity %						
Debt to Equity						

CONTACT INFORMATION:

Phone: 888-662-6367   Fax:
Toll-Free:
Address: 200 5th Ave., New York, NY 10010 United States

STOCK TICKER/OTHER:

Stock Ticker: Subsidiary   Exchange:
Employees: 500   Fiscal Year Ends:
Parent Company: Roche Holding AG

SALARIES/BONUSES:

Top Exec. Salary: $ Bonus: $
Second Exec. Salary: $ Bonus: $

OTHER THOUGHTS:

Estimated Female Officers or Directors:
Hot Spot for Advancement for Women/Minorities:

Flipkart Internet Private Limited

www.flipkart.com

NAIC Code: 454111

TYPES OF BUSINESS:

Electronic Retailing
Online Apparel Sales

BRANDS/DIVISIONS/AFFILIATES:

Flipkart First
Walmart Inc.
Myntra
Jabong

CONTACTS: *Note: Officers with more than one job title may be intentionally listed here more than once.*

Binny Bansal, CEO
Amod Malviya, Sr. VP

GROWTH PLANS/SPECIAL FEATURES:

Flipkart Internet Private Limited is an e-commerce firm based in India. Flipkart began as an online book dealer in 2007, but soon expanded its product base to include a myriad of other products such as electronic goods, movies, clothing, footwear, watches, beauty and personal care, jewelry, home appliances and stationary products. The company boasts a marketplace of over 80 million products across more than 80 categories. It has more than 100 million registered users that clock millions of daily visits. In addition to regular payment options, such as credit cards and internet banking, it also offers cash on delivery. Cash on delivery (C-o-D) allows a customer to order a product online and then pay for it in cash when the item is delivered; the maximum order for a C-o-D order is a little more than $715. Flipkart offers an in-a-day guarantee and a same-day guarantee in select cities. The company also provides a paid annual subscription service, Flipkart First, in which members obtain exclusive benefits and priority service features that include free shipping for all orders, free in-a-day guarantee delivery, same-day-guarantee delivery at a 50% discount and a 60-day replacement policy. In May 2018, Flipkart announced that Walmart, Inc. would lead a group that would invest $15 billion to acquire a controlling interest of about 77% in Flipkart.

FINANCIAL DATA: *Note: Data for latest year may not have been available at press time.*

In U.S. $	2018	2017	2016	2015	2014	2013
Revenue		3,336,940,000	2,348,270,000	2,200,000,000	1,735,630,000	215,900,000
R&D Expense						
Operating Income						
Operating Margin %						
SGA Expense						
Net Income		-318,164,000	-247,210,000	-174,860,000	-5,983,236	-51,541,500
Operating Cash Flow						
Capital Expenditure						
EBITDA						
Return on Assets %						
Return on Equity %						
Debt to Equity						

CONTACT INFORMATION:

Phone: 91-80-4274-9527   Fax: 91-80-0793-1547
Toll-Free: 800-208-9898
Address: Vaishnavi Summit, 1/Fl., 7th Main, 80 Feet Rd., 3rd Block, Koramangala, Bengaluru, 560034 India

STOCK TICKER/OTHER:

Stock Ticker: Subsidiary
Employees: 33,000
Parent Company: Walmart, Inc.

Exchange:
Fiscal Year Ends: 03/31

SALARIES/BONUSES:

Top Exec. Salary: $ Bonus: $
Second Exec. Salary: $ Bonus: $

OTHER THOUGHTS:

Estimated Female Officers or Directors:
Hot Spot for Advancement for Women/Minorities:

ForeScout Technologies Inc

www.forescout.com

NAIC Code: 511210E

TYPES OF BUSINESS:

Computer Software, Security & Anti-Virus
Network Security
Cyber Security

BRANDS/DIVISIONS/AFFILIATES:

CounterACT
SecurityMatters

CONTACTS: Note: Officers with more than one job title may be intentionally listed here more than once.

Christopher Harms, CFO
Yehezkel Yeshurun, Chairman of the Board
Michael DeCesare, Director
David Dewalt, Director
Darren Milliken, General Counsel
Pedro Abreu, Other Executive Officer

GROWTH PLANS/SPECIAL FEATURES:

ForeScout Technologies, Inc. develops network security solutions that allow Global 2000 enterprises and government organizations to monitor and mitigate security exposures and cyberattacks. Its products and solutions provide the ability to see devices, including non-traditional devices, the instant clients connect to the ForeScout network. They also enable clients to control these devices and orchestrate information sharing and operation among disparate security tools in an effort to accelerate incident response. ForeScout's solutions integrate with leading network, security, mobility and IT management products to overcome security silos, automate workflows and enable significant cost savings. Its network security addresses Internet of Things (IoT), cloud computing and operational technologies (OT). More than 2,900 customers in over 80 countries improve their network security and compliance architecture with ForeScout solutions (as of mid-2018). ForeScout's CounterACT security solution identifies and evaluates network infrastructure, devices and applications the instant they connect to client networks. The firm's extended modules expand CounterACT's control capabilities by sharing contextual device data with third-party systems and by automating policy enforcement across those disparate systems. The enterprise manager provides centralized security management for global control of all CounterACT appliances deployed throughout the network; and ForeScout's control fabric architecture consists of open integration technologies that enable CounterACT and other IT solutions to exchange information and mitigate a variety of network, security and operational issues. In November 2018, ForeScout acquired SecurityMatters, which offers operational technology network protection.

ForeScout offers its employees medical, dental, vision, life and disability insurance coverage; and 401(k) matching.

FINANCIAL DATA: Note: Data for latest year may not have been available at press time.

In U.S. $	2018	2017	2016	2015	2014	2013
Revenue		220,871,000	166,841,000	125,959,000	71,113,000	
R&D Expense		47,435,000	31,490,000	17,772,000	12,302,000	
Operating Income		-87,732,000	-71,444,000	-18,078,000	-40,534,000	
Operating Margin %		-39.72%	-42.82%	-14.35%	-56.99%	
SGA Expense		202,299,000	158,546,000	93,143,000	77,469,000	
Net Income		-91,205,000	-74,774,000	-27,260,000	-43,988,000	
Operating Cash Flow		-2,735,000	-38,291,000	3,397,000	-7,840,000	
Capital Expenditure		4,517,000	22,006,000	2,757,000	1,718,000	
EBITDA		-82,075,000	-67,337,000	-22,399,000	-39,323,000	
Return on Assets %		-44.92%	-44.20%	-15.95%		
Return on Equity %						
Debt to Equity		0.28				

CONTACT INFORMATION:

Phone: 408-213-3191   Fax: 408-371-2284
Toll-Free: 866-377-8771
Address: 190 W. Tasman Dr., San Jose, CA 95134 United States

STOCK TICKER/OTHER:

Stock Ticker: FSCT   Exchange: NAS
Employees: 809   Fiscal Year Ends: 12/31
Parent Company:

SALARIES/BONUSES:

Top Exec. Salary: $410,000   Bonus: $
Second Exec. Salary: $380,000   Bonus: $

OTHER THOUGHTS:

Estimated Female Officers or Directors:
Hot Spot for Advancement for Women/Minorities:

ForeSee Results Inc

www.foreseeresults.com

NAIC Code: 511210K

TYPES OF BUSINESS:

Online Survey Software
Support Services
Survey Design & Analysis

BRANDS/DIVISIONS/AFFILIATES:

Answers Corporation
ForeSee CX Suite
CX Measurement

CONTACTS: *Note: Officers with more than one job title may be intentionally listed here more than once.*

Jay Snider, CEO
Kaj van de Loo, Chief Product Officer
Larry Freed, Pres.
Eric Head, VP-Sales
Shannon Latta, VP-Mktg. and Comm.
Mitchell Cohen, VP-Tech.
John Williams, Sr. VP-Prod. & Delivery
Dave Lewan, VP-Sales, Public Sector-West Region
Don Morrison, Sr. VP-Sales
Cia McCaffery, VP
Eric Feinberg, Sr. Dir.-Mobile Media & Entertainment

GROWTH PLANS/SPECIAL FEATURES:

ForeSee Results, Inc. specializes in customer experience analytics. The company continuously measures satisfaction with the customer experience and delivers insights on where organizations should prioritize improvements for maximum impact. ForeSee applies its technology across channels and customer touch points, including websites, contact centers, retail stores, mobile/tablet sites and apps, as well as social media initiatives. The firm's voice of customer (VOC) solutions and methodology are predictive of customer loyalty, purchase behavior, future financial success and stock prices. The ForeSee CX Suite comprises the company's architecture solution that manages all CX (customer experience) intelligence needs. The CX suite of applications include CX Measurement, feedback, replay, text analytics, case management and ratings/reviews. ForeSee's solutions serve several of industries and sectors, including retail, e-commerce, government, financial services, energy and utilities, telecommunications, consumer products, healthcare, media and entertainment, travel and hospitality. ForeSee is headquartered in Ann Arbor, Michigan, with offices in New York, Missouri, California and Ohio, USA, as well as London, U.K. and Vancouver, British Columbia. The firm operates as a subsidiary of Answers Corporation. In December 2018, ForSee signed a definitive agreement to be acquired by Verint Systems Inc., an Actionable Intelligence solutions provider that focuses on customer engagement optimization, security intelligence and fraud, risk and compliance.

FINANCIAL DATA: *Note: Data for latest year may not have been available at press time.*

In U.S. $	2018	2017	2016	2015	2014	2013
Revenue		81,000,000	75,000,000	60,000,000	56,000,000	52,000,000
R&D Expense						
Operating Income						
Operating Margin %						
SGA Expense						
Net Income						
Operating Cash Flow						
Capital Expenditure						
EBITDA						
Return on Assets %						
Return on Equity %						
Debt to Equity						

CONTACT INFORMATION:

Phone: 734-205-2600   Fax: 734-205-2601
Toll-Free: 800-621-2850
Address: 2500 Green Rd., Ste. 400, Ann Arbor, MI 48105 United States

STOCK TICKER/OTHER:

Stock Ticker: Subsidiary   Exchange:
Employees: 335   Fiscal Year Ends:
Parent Company: Answers Corporation

SALARIES/BONUSES:

Top Exec. Salary: $ Bonus: $
Second Exec. Salary: $ Bonus: $

OTHER THOUGHTS:

Estimated Female Officers or Directors: 1
Hot Spot for Advancement for Women/Minorities:

Forrester Research Inc

NAIC Code: 541910

www.forrester.com

TYPES OF BUSINESS:

Market Research
Consulting & Advisory
Workshops & Events

BRANDS/DIVISIONS/AFFILIATES:

Research
Forrester Wave (The)
Age of the Customer Research
Forrester Connect
Leadership Boards
ForecastView
FeedbackNow
Glimpzltr

CONTACTS: Note: Officers with more than one job title may be intentionally listed here more than once.

George Colony, CEO
Michael Doyle, CFO
Scott Chouinard, Chief Accounting Officer
Victor Milligan, Chief Marketing Officer
Mack Brothers, Other Executive Officer
Carrie Fanlo, Other Executive Officer
Lucia Quinn, Other Executive Officer
Kelley Hippler, Other Executive Officer
Steven Peltzman, Other Executive Officer
Ryan Darrah, Other Executive Officer

GROWTH PLANS/SPECIAL FEATURES:

Forrester Research, Inc., an independent research firm, provides research, analysis and advisory services related to technology change and its impact on evolving business models, best practices, technology investments, implementation and customer trends. Forrester's primary research product, Research, includes The Forrester Wave, which provides detailed analyses of vendors' technologies and services in addition to a library of cross-linked documents that interconnects reports, data, product rankings, best practices, evaluation tools and research archives. Age of the Customer Research addresses its clients' and prospects' opportunities and challenges in order to help transform customer experience, accelerate the organization's digital business, integrate mobility, turn business insights into actionable data and leverage privacy to drive business growth. Forrester Connect offerings are designed to help clients connect with peers as well as Forrester's products and professionals, and to coach executives to lead far-reaching change within their organizations. Its Leadership Boards are exclusive peer groups for executives and other senior leaders at large organizations worldwide. Forrester's data products and services are designed to provide fact-based customer insights to Forrester clients. This data encompasses customer experience, consumer technographics, business technographics and the ForecastView-branded ongoing data of evaluation analysis and insights. Forrester's consulting and advisory services leverage its Research, technographics and customer experience index data to assist clients with their challenges in developing and executing technology and business strategy. Forrester Research hosts multiple events in various locations worldwide, including North America, Europe and Asia throughout the year. In 2018, Forrester acquired FeedbackNow, a maker of physical buttons and monitoring software that companies deploy to measure, analyze, and improve customer experience; Glimpzlt, an artificial intelligence and machine-learning provider; and SiriusDecisions, a leading business-to-business research and advisory firm.

Forrester employees receive medical, dental and vision insurance; 401(k), stock purchase and employee assistance programs; performance bonuses; and backup childcare.

FINANCIAL DATA: Note: Data for latest year may not have been available at press time.

In U.S. $	2018	2017	2016	2015	2014	2013
Revenue		337,673,000	326,095,000	313,726,000	312,062,000	297,650,000
R&D Expense						
Operating Income		27,549,000	31,800,000	23,260,000	20,030,000	23,738,000
Operating Margin %		8.15%	9.75%	7.41%	6.41%	7.97%
SGA Expense		165,823,000	157,477,000	155,122,000	154,337,000	145,353,000
Net Income		15,140,000	17,651,000	11,996,000	10,865,000	13,024,000
Operating Cash Flow		37,493,000	41,858,000	32,466,000	28,795,000	30,713,000
Capital Expenditure		7,861,000	4,140,000	3,931,000	1,503,000	3,127,000
EBITDA		34,978,000	40,443,000	32,501,000	31,526,000	35,236,000
Return on Assets %		4.44%	5.39%	3.68%	2.95%	2.92%
Return on Equity %		10.39%	12.72%	8.92%	6.27%	5.19%
Debt to Equity						

CONTACT INFORMATION:

Phone: 617 613-5730 Fax:
Toll-Free:
Address: 60 Acorn Park Dr., Cambridge, MA 02140 United States

STOCK TICKER/OTHER:

Stock Ticker: FORR
Employees: 1,378
Parent Company:

Exchange: NAS
Fiscal Year Ends: 12/31

SALARIES/BONUSES:

Top Exec. Salary: $400,000   Bonus: $
Second Exec. Salary: $382,500   Bonus: $

OTHER THOUGHTS:

Estimated Female Officers or Directors: 3
Hot Spot for Advancement for Women/Minorities: Y

Sales, profits and employees may be estimates. Financial information, benefits and other data can change quickly and may vary from those stated here.

FreshDirect LLC

NAIC Code: 454111

TYPES OF BUSINESS:

Online Grocery Sales
Home Grocery Delivery
Catering

BRANDS/DIVISIONS/AFFILIATES:

FoodKick

CONTACTS: *Note: Officers with more than one job title may be intentionally listed here more than once.*

David McInerney, CEO
Tina Bourbeau, Exec. Chef
Amaury Garcia, Mgr.-Sortation

GROWTH PLANS/SPECIAL FEATURES:

FreshDirect, LLC is an online retail grocery business serving customers in New York City, Washington, D.C. and surrounding areas. It offers fresh food and grocery items, including fruits and vegetables, meat, seafood, deli items, cheese, dairy, coffee, tea, bakery goods, pasta and frozen food as well as kosher and gluten free foods, local and organic produce, health and beauty items and wine. It also provides catering services and a full line of ready-to-heat meals prepared by its on-staff chef. FreshDirect owns and operates a 500,000-square-foot state-of-the-art processing facility, which enables the firm to process and ship fresh meats, produce and dairy products quickly and efficiently. The company is also able to offer lower prices, on average 25% lower than traditional retail grocers, due to the lack of intermediary distribution channels. Products may be delivered in the mornings if the order is placed by 7 p.m. the previous day and in the evenings if placed by 11 p.m. Deliveries are made from 6:30 a.m.-11:00 p.m. seven days a week. Minimum order amounts for home deliveries are $30, and each order is charged a delivery fee depending on location. For offices, the minimum order amount is $50 plus a delivery fee, Monday through Friday from 8 a.m. to 4p.m. Customers can also pick up their orders at the facility. FeshDirect's mobile-first food delivery business, FoodKick, offers a curated selection of fresh food, alcohol, local goods and everyday essentials, all delivered in as little as an hour. FoodKick's service operates in Manhattan, Brooklyn and Long Island City. Offerings include a variety of local and exclusive products from partners such as Bien Cuit Bakery, Baked by Melissa, as well as RISE Coffee and Doughnut Plant.

FINANCIAL DATA: *Note: Data for latest year may not have been available at press time.*

In U.S. $	2018	2017	2016	2015	2014	2013
Revenue	645,750,000	615,000,000	555,000,000	500,000,000	450,000,000	415,000,000
R&D Expense						
Operating Income						
Operating Margin %						
SGA Expense						
Net Income						
Operating Cash Flow						
Capital Expenditure						
EBITDA						
Return on Assets %						
Return on Equity %						
Debt to Equity						

CONTACT INFORMATION:

Phone: 718-928-1000   Fax: 718-433-0648
Toll-Free:
Address: 23-30 Borden Ave., Long Island City, NY 11101 United States

STOCK TICKER/OTHER:

Stock Ticker: Private   Exchange:
Employees: 2,000   Fiscal Year Ends: 09/30
Parent Company:

SALARIES/BONUSES:

Top Exec. Salary: $ Bonus: $
Second Exec. Salary: $ Bonus: $

OTHER THOUGHTS:

Estimated Female Officers or Directors: 1
Hot Spot for Advancement for Women/Minorities:

Freshly Inc

www.freshly.com

NAIC Code: 454111

TYPES OF BUSINESS:

Meal Delivery Service
Prepared Meals
Delivered Meals

BRANDS/DIVISIONS/AFFILIATES:

CONTACTS: Note: Officers with more than one job title may be intentionally listed here more than once.

Michael Wystrach, CEO

GROWTH PLANS/SPECIAL FEATURES:

Freshly, Inc. offers an online platform from which customers can order healthy meals to be prepared by chefs and delivered to their home or business. The firm's plans include: four meals per week for about $50, including shipping; six meals per week for about $60; nine meals per week for about $90; and 12 meals per week for about $108. Menus are updated weekly, and Freshly offers dozens of lunch and dinner options to choose from. Meals are delivered ready-to-eat and are never frozen, and come with nutritional information, a full ingredient list and heating instructions. They are packaged in a refrigerated box and shipped with ice packs to be kept cold. Shipments are delivered directly to the premises and left at the door if unanswered. Delivery days are primarily Tuesday through Saturday. Freshly accommodates a variety of dietary preferences, and its entire menu is free of gluten and peanuts. Examples of meals include: Homestyle Chicken with Butternut Mac & Cheese, Penne Bolognese, Sausage Baked Penne with Sauteed Zuchini and Spinach, Chicken Tikka Masala, Slow-cooked Beef Chili, Turkey Shepherd's Pie and Southwest Veggie Bowl. Meals are made with all-natural ingredients, are high in protein and nutrient-dense vegetables.

FINANCIAL DATA: Note: Data for latest year may not have been available at press time.

In U.S. $	2018	2017	2016	2015	2014	2013
Revenue						
R&D Expense						
Operating Income						
Operating Margin %						
SGA Expense						
Net Income						
Operating Cash Flow						
Capital Expenditure						
EBITDA						
Return on Assets %						
Return on Equity %						
Debt to Equity						

CONTACT INFORMATION:

Phone: Fax:
Toll-Free: 844-373-7459
Address: 115 E. 23rd St., New York, NY 10010-4508 United States

STOCK TICKER/OTHER:

Stock Ticker: Private Exchange:
Employees: 400 Fiscal Year Ends:
Parent Company:

SALARIES/BONUSES:

Top Exec. Salary: $ Bonus: $
Second Exec. Salary: $ Bonus: $

OTHER THOUGHTS:

Estimated Female Officers or Directors:
Hot Spot for Advancement for Women/Minorities:

Frontier Communications Corporation

www.frontier.com

NAIC Code: 517110

TYPES OF BUSINESS:

Telecommunications
Internet Services
Long-Distance Phone Services
Directory Service
Access Services
Wireless Internet Services

BRANDS/DIVISIONS/AFFILIATES:

Vantage
FiOS

CONTACTS: *Note: Officers with more than one job title may be intentionally listed here more than once.*

Daniel Mccarthy, CEO
Sheldon Bruha, CFO
Pamela Reeve, Chairman of the Board
Donald Daniels, Chief Accounting Officer
Steve Gable, Chief Technology Officer
Kenneth Arndt, Executive VP, Divisional
Christopher Levendos, Executive VP, Divisional
John Maduri, Executive VP, Divisional
Kathleen Weslock, Executive VP
Mark Nielsen, Executive VP

GROWTH PLANS/SPECIAL FEATURES:

Frontier Communications Corporation provides communication services to rural, small and medium-sized towns throughout the U.S. The firm operates in 29 states as an incumbent local exchange carrier with 5.4 million customers and 3.9 million broadband subscribers. It provides local and long-distance voice, data and internet access and video services. Local services include basic telephone wireline services as well as call forwarding, conference calling, caller ID, voicemail and call waiting. Long distance services use external interexchange carrier facilities. Data and internet services offer a variety of wireline and satellite broadband services to residential, commercial and carrier customers. Residential services include broadband, dial up internet, portal and e-mail products. Commercial services include Ethernet, dedicated internet, multiprotocol label switching (MPLS), time division multiplexing (TDM) data transport services and optical transport services. These services are all supported by a 24/7 help desk and an advanced network. Access services enable other carriers to use Frontier's facilities to originate and terminate their local and long-distance voice traffic. The firm offers small and medium enterprise (SME) business customers third-party telecommunications equipment produced to fit their specific business operation needs. Frontier's video services are offered under the FiOS brand in portions of California, Texas, Florida, Indiana, Oregon and Washington, and the Vantage brand in portions of Connecticut, North Carolina, South Carolina, Minnesota, Illinois, New York, and Ohio. Satellite TV video services are offered through an agency relationship with DISH to customers in all markets.

Employees receive medical, dental and vision coverage; life insurance; tuition reimbursement; flexible spending accounts; and corporate discounts.

FINANCIAL DATA: *Note: Data for latest year may not have been available at press time.*

In U.S. $	2018	2017	2016	2015	2014	2013
Revenue		9,127,999,000	8,896,000,000	5,576,000,000	4,772,490,000	4,761,576,000
R&D Expense						
Operating Income		1,287,000,000	1,415,000,000	981,000,000	961,546,000	978,035,000
Operating Margin %		14.09%	15.90%	17.59%	20.14%	20.49%
SGA Expense		2,101,000,000	2,093,000,000	1,348,000,000	1,088,180,000	1,186,348,000
Net Income		-1,804,000,000	-373,000,000	-196,000,000	132,893,000	112,835,000
Operating Cash Flow		1,850,000,000	1,666,000,000	1,301,000,000	1,270,072,000	1,495,627,000
Capital Expenditure		1,188,000,000	1,401,000,000	863,000,000	688,096,000	634,685,000
EBITDA		531,000,000	2,939,000,000	2,072,000,000	1,997,879,000	1,999,618,000
Return on Assets %		-7.49%	-2.10%	-1.38%	.74%	.65%
Return on Equity %		-59.47%	-11.64%	-6.88%	3.44%	2.76%
Debt to Equity		7.46	3.88	2.76	2.59	1.94

CONTACT INFORMATION:

Phone: 203 614-5600   Fax: 203 614-4602
Toll-Free:
Address: 401 Merritt 7, Norwalk, CT 06851 United States

STOCK TICKER/OTHER:

Stock Ticker: FTR
Employees: 28,300
Parent Company:

Exchange: NAS
Fiscal Year Ends: 12/31

SALARIES/BONUSES:

Top Exec. Salary: $1,000,000   Bonus: $
Second Exec. Salary: $650,000   Bonus: $

OTHER THOUGHTS:

Estimated Female Officers or Directors: 7
Hot Spot for Advancement for Women/Minorities: Y

Frys Electronics Inc

www.frys.com

NAIC Code: 443142

TYPES OF BUSINESS:
Electronics, Audio & Appliance Stores
Computer & Software Products
Online Sales
Product Support Services
ISP Administrator

BRANDS/DIVISIONS/AFFILIATES:
Frys.com

CONTACTS: Note: Officers with more than one job title may be intentionally listed here more than once.
John Fry, CEO
Randy Fry, Pres.
David Fry, CFO
Kathryn J. Kolder, Exec. VP

GROWTH PLANS/SPECIAL FEATURES:
Fry's Electronics, Inc. retails electronic items through warehouse-sized electronics superstores, with each store carrying over 50,000 electronic items. The stores are located in California, Texas, Arizona, Georgia, Illinois, Indiana, Nevada, Oregon and Washington, ranging in size from 50,000 to over 180,000 square feet. While the company has grown since its inception in Silicon Valley in 1985, Fry's target customer continues to be the high-tech professional. In addition to its stores, the firm sells electronics online through Frys.com. Fry's stores offer low prices, extensive inventory and imaginatively themed concepts, with each location having its own unique theme. For example, the Palo Alto store has a Wild West theme; the Phoenix store has Aztec-themed decor; the Houston store showcases the oil industry, replete with a field of gushing oil derricks; and the Las Vegas store showcases the history of the Las Vegas Strip. Every Fry's store offers services and support for a variety of products. These products include computer hardware and software for both Microsoft and Apple operating systems; technical manuals and other books; new CDs, DVDs and Blu-ray discs; video games; audio, car audio and video equipment such as flat screen TVs; and communications equipment, such as blue tooth headsets. Other products include integrated circuits, batteries and other electronic components and accessories; appliances such as vacuums and microwaves; health and beauty products including air purifiers and electric razors; and convenience and general merchandise items. In addition to its retail arm, Fry's administers mobile and broadband ISPs and other telecom services for business clients.

FINANCIAL DATA: Note: Data for latest year may not have been available at press time.

In U.S. $	2018	2017	2016	2015	2014	2013
Revenue		2,320,000,000	2,300,000,000	2,150,000,000	2,200,000,000	2,150,000,000
R&D Expense						
Operating Income						
Operating Margin %						
SGA Expense						
Net Income						
Operating Cash Flow						
Capital Expenditure						
EBITDA						
Return on Assets %						
Return on Equity %						
Debt to Equity						

CONTACT INFORMATION:
Phone: 408-350-1484   Fax:
Toll-Free:
Address: 600 E. Brokaw Rd., San Jose, CA 95112 United States

STOCK TICKER/OTHER:
Stock Ticker: Private   Exchange:
Employees: 14,000   Fiscal Year Ends: 12/31
Parent Company:

SALARIES/BONUSES:
Top Exec. Salary: $ Bonus: $
Second Exec. Salary: $ Bonus: $

OTHER THOUGHTS:
Estimated Female Officers or Directors: 1
Hot Spot for Advancement for Women/Minorities:

FTD Companies Inc

NAIC Code: 424930

www.ftd.com

TYPES OF BUSINESS:
Flower, Nursery Stock and Florists' Supplies Wholesale Distribution

BRANDS/DIVISIONS/AFFILIATES:
FTD
Interflora

GROWTH PLANS/SPECIAL FEATURES:
FTD Companies, Inc. is a floral and gifting company. The firm provides floral, gift and related products and services to consumers, retail florists and other retail locations and companies. FTD Companies' businesses operate using the FTD and Interflora brands, supported the iconic Mercury Man logo. The firm primarily operates in the U.S., Canada, the U.K. and Ireland, with a presence in approximately 35,000 floral shops in nearly 125 countries. Other brands used by FTD Companies include ProFlowers, ProPlants, Shari's Berries, Personal Creations, RedEnvelope, Flying Flowers, Ink Cards, Postagram, Gifts.com and BloomThat. In addition to its primary offerings of floral arrangements and plants, FTD Companies also markets and sells gift items including jewelry, chocolate dip delights and other sweets, gift baskets, wine and champagne, fruit and spa products.

CONTACTS:
Note: Officers with more than one job title may be intentionally listed here more than once.

Scott Levin, CEO
Steven Barnhart, CFO
Robert Berglass, Chairman of the Board
Jeffrey Severts, Chief Marketing Officer
Simha Kumar, COO
Tom Moeller, Executive VP, Subsidiary
Rhys Hughes, President, Divisional

FINANCIAL DATA:
Note: Data for latest year may not have been available at press time.

In U.S. $	2018	2017	2016	2015	2014	2013
Revenue		1,084,028,000	1,121,999,000	1,219,753,000	640,513,000	627,343,000
R&D Expense						
Operating Income		33,792,000	15,018,000	19,813,000	37,824,000	33,832,000
Operating Margin %		3.11%	1.33%	1.62%	5.90%	5.39%
SGA Expense		362,195,000	342,289,000	370,866,000	186,311,000	175,588,000
Net Income		-234,041,000	-83,191,000	-78,826,000	22,830,000	12,502,000
Operating Cash Flow		52,817,000	76,949,000	82,325,000	47,384,000	34,203,000
Capital Expenditure		15,103,000	18,503,000	18,255,000	7,486,000	10,830,000
EBITDA		-234,466,000	6,556,000	15,157,000	60,282,000	66,492,000
Return on Assets %		-29.76%	-7.96%	-6.35%	2.22%	1.86%
Return on Equity %		-72.88%	-17.17%	-13.06%	4.66%	4.40%
Debt to Equity			0.59	0.51	0.48	0.75

CONTACT INFORMATION:
Phone: 630-719-7800   Fax:
Toll-Free:
Address: 3113 Woodcreek Dr., Downers Grove, IL 60515 United States

STOCK TICKER/OTHER:
Stock Ticker: FTD   Exchange: NAS
Employees: 1,528   Fiscal Year Ends: 12/31
Parent Company:

SALARIES/BONUSES:
Top Exec. Salary: $819,231   Bonus: $
Second Exec. Salary: $395,499   Bonus: $240,000

OTHER THOUGHTS:
Estimated Female Officers or Directors:
Hot Spot for Advancement for Women/Minorities:

Fuze Inc

www.fuze.com

NAIC Code: 511210C

TYPES OF BUSINESS:

Computer Software, Telecom, Communications & VOIP

BRANDS/DIVISIONS/AFFILIATES:

CONTACTS: *Note: Officers with more than one job title may be intentionally listed here more than once.*

Colin Doherty, CEO
Brian Day, CFO
Brian Kardon, CMO
Mary Good, Chief People Officer
Chris Conry, CIO
Steve Kokinos, Chmn.

GROWTH PLANS/SPECIAL FEATURES:

Fuze, Inc. provides a communications platform for the global enterprise, both in the U.S. and internationally. Fuze designs and sells its user platform that handles voice, video, messaging and collaboration into a single interface through a cloud architecture that is reliable, scalable and secure. Other company products include voice, a cloud-based platform that allows users to communicate over the internet using desktops, laptops or mobile devices, and lets a customer access IM, group messaging and presence in one app; HD audio and video conferencing, allowing users to organize small- or large-scale conference calls whenever and wherever the customer needs; insights, which provides analytics and bi-directional data connections through the Fuze platform; call center solutions, which provides the customer with skill-based call routing, an analytics-based workforce scheduler and analytics about customer interaction for management; and API integrations, including Google and Microsoft applications. Besides mid-to-large-sized enterprises, Fuze also serves original equipment manufacturer partners, service providers and customers that sell and deploy differentiated cloud PBX (private branch exchange) communication services. Customers of the firm have included the PGA Tour, The Associated Press, U.S. Auto Sales, TrustPilot, Sylvan Learning and AstraZeneca. Fuze is headquartered in Massachusetts, with additional offices throughout North America, the U.K., Europe and Australia. In May 2018, the firm announced it had raised $150 million in a financing round led by Summit Partners, with participation from Bessemer Venture Partners and current investors. This brought Fuze's total funding to $484.8 million.

The company offers its employees medical, dental, life and disability insurance; stock options; retirement plan; and paid holidays.

FINANCIAL DATA: *Note: Data for latest year may not have been available at press time.*

In U.S. $	2018	2017	2016	2015	2014	2013
Revenue						
R&D Expense						
Operating Income						
Operating Margin %						
SGA Expense						
Net Income						
Operating Cash Flow						
Capital Expenditure						
EBITDA						
Return on Assets %						
Return on Equity %						
Debt to Equity						

CONTACT INFORMATION:

Phone: 617-453-2052   Fax: 617-453-0170
Toll-Free: 800-890-1553
Address: 2 Copley Place, 7/Fl, Boston, MA 02116 United States

STOCK TICKER/OTHER:

Stock Ticker: Private   Exchange:
Employees: 700   Fiscal Year Ends:
Parent Company:

SALARIES/BONUSES:

Top Exec. Salary: $ Bonus: $
Second Exec. Salary: $ Bonus: $

OTHER THOUGHTS:

Estimated Female Officers or Directors:
Hot Spot for Advancement for Women/Minorities:

Gainsight Inc

NAIC Code: 511210K

www.gainsight.com

TYPES OF BUSINESS:

Computer Software, Sales & Customer Relationship Management

BRANDS/DIVISIONS/AFFILIATES:

Aptrinsic

CONTACTS: *Note: Officers with more than one job title may be intentionally listed here more than once.*

Nick Mehta, CEO
Allison Pickens, COO
Igor Beckerman, CFO
Anthony Kennada, CMO
Carol Mahoney, Chief People Officer
Karl Mosgofian, CIO
Sreedhar Peddineni, CTO

GROWTH PLANS/SPECIAL FEATURES:

Gainsight, Inc. provides enterprise software solutions that leverage the power of customer data in order to manage at-risk customers and maintain the lifetime value of beneficial ones. The company's products and solutions help businesses gain insight into: customer lifecycle, via monitoring and engagement; risk management, via big data analysis; value demonstration, by helping customers understand the value of products and services; expansion and advocacy, by locating fans and identifying the right accounts for additional sales; and cross-functional collaboration, via tracking business outcomes and streamlining operations. Gainsight's solutions include adoption management, renewal management, expansion management, advocate engagement, stakeholder alignment, risk escalation, success planning, technology and more. The firm's solutions can transform the support experience, services experiences, product success and company success. Industries served by the firm include cloud software, on-premise software, tech infrastructure and healthcare. The firm is headquartered in California, USA, with an additional office in Missouri. In late-2018, Gainsight acquired Aptrinsic, a product-led growth solution that delivers analytics and in-product engagements used to increase adoption, retention and expansion in business-to-business (B2B) companies. This acquisition strengthens Gainsight's ability to help subscription businesses maximize growth by unifying customer success and product management teams.

FINANCIAL DATA: *Note: Data for latest year may not have been available at press time.*

In U.S. $	2018	2017	2016	2015	2014	2013
Revenue						
R&D Expense						
Operating Income						
Operating Margin %						
SGA Expense						
Net Income						
Operating Cash Flow						
Capital Expenditure						
EBITDA						
Return on Assets %						
Return on Equity %						
Debt to Equity						

CONTACT INFORMATION:

Phone: Fax:
Toll-Free: 888-623-8562
Address: 1400 Bridge Pkwy, Ste. 101, Redwood City, CA 94065 United States

STOCK TICKER/OTHER:

Stock Ticker: Private   Exchange:
Employees: 385   Fiscal Year Ends:
Parent Company:

SALARIES/BONUSES:

Top Exec. Salary: $ Bonus: $
Second Exec. Salary: $ Bonus: $

OTHER THOUGHTS:

Estimated Female Officers or Directors:
Hot Spot for Advancement for Women/Minorities:

Gartner Inc

www.gartner.com

NAIC Code: 541910

TYPES OF BUSINESS:

Research-Computer Hardware & Software
Industry Research
IT Symposia & Conferences
Measurement & Advisory Services

BRANDS/DIVISIONS/AFFILIATES:

Symposium/Itxpo

CONTACTS: Note: Officers with more than one job title may be intentionally listed here more than once.

Eugene Hall, CEO
Craig Safian, CFO
Craig Safian, CFO
Michael Diliberto, Chief Information Officer
Robin Kranich, Exec. VP-Human Resources
Alwyn Dawkins, Senior VP, Divisional
Per Waern, Senior VP, Divisional
Robin Kranich, Senior VP, Divisional
Peter Sondergaard, Senior VP, Divisional
David McVeigh, Senior VP, Divisional
David Godfrey, Senior VP, Divisional
Thomas Christopher, Senior VP, Divisional
Kendall Davis, Senior VP, Divisional
Daniel Peale, Senior VP
James Smith, Chairman of the Board

GROWTH PLANS/SPECIAL FEATURES:

Gartner, Inc. is a research and advisory firm that offers independent research and analysis on IT, computer hardware, software, communications and related technology industries. With consultants in 100 countries, the firm serves more than 15,000 organizations worldwide. The company operates in four segments: research and advisory, consulting, conferences and digital markets. The research and advisory segment, the main service of the company, provides research content and advice for IT professionals, technology companies and the investment community in the form of reports and briefings, as well as peer networking services and membership programs designed specifically for Chief Information Officers (CIOs)and other senior executives. The consulting division provides customized solutions to unique client needs through on-site, day-to-day support, as well as proprietary tools for measuring and improving IT performance with a focus on coast, performance, efficiency and quality. The conferences group provides IT, supply chain, digital marketing and other business professionals the opportunity to attend various symposia, conferences and exhibitions to learn, contribute and network with their peers. Its flagship event, Symposium/ITxpo, as well as summits, focus on specific technologies and industries and offer experimental workshop-style seminars. This division also provides the latest Gartner research into applicable insight and advice at its events. Last, the company's digital markets segment gives software buyers with information to make purchasing decisions. This segment also helps software companies attract customers.

FINANCIAL DATA: Note: Data for latest year may not have been available at press time.

In U.S. $	2018	2017	2016	2015	2014	2013
Revenue		3,311,494,000	2,444,540,000	2,163,056,000	2,021,441,000	1,784,213,000
R&D Expense						
Operating Income		152,121,000	347,739,000	314,172,000	308,029,000	275,829,000
Operating Margin %		4.59%	14.22%	14.52%	15.23%	15.45%
SGA Expense		1,599,004,000	1,089,184,000	962,677,000	876,067,000	760,458,000
Net Income		3,279,000	193,582,000	175,635,000	183,766,000	182,801,000
Operating Cash Flow		254,517,000	365,632,000	345,561,000	346,779,000	315,654,000
Capital Expenditure		110,765,000	49,863,000	46,128,000	38,486,000	36,498,000
EBITDA		240,301,000	377,965,000	341,890,000	326,395,000	311,269,000
Return on Assets %		.06%	8.52%	8.61%	9.96%	10.73%
Return on Equity %		.62%		1220.91%	70.34%	54.73%
Debt to Equity		2.94	10.91		2.38	0.37

CONTACT INFORMATION:

Phone: 203 316-1111   Fax:
Toll-Free:
Address: 56 Top Gallant Rd., Stamford, CT 06902-7700 United States

STOCK TICKER/OTHER:

Stock Ticker: IT   Exchange: NYS
Employees: 8,813   Fiscal Year Ends: 12/31
Parent Company:

SALARIES/BONUSES:

Top Exec. Salary: $901,584   Bonus: $
Second Exec. Salary: Bonus: $
$503,260

OTHER THOUGHTS:

Estimated Female Officers or Directors: 3
Hot Spot for Advancement for Women/Minorities: Y

GitHub Inc

NAIC Code: 519130

TYPES OF BUSINESS:

Internet Publishing and Broadcasting and Web Search Portals

BRANDS/DIVISIONS/AFFILIATES:

Microsoft Corporation

CONTACTS: Note: Officers with more than one job title may be intentionally listed here more than once.

Nat Friedman, CEO
Mike Taylor, CFO
Paul St John, VP-Sales
Carrie Olesen, Chief Human Resources Officer
Jason Warner, Sr. VP-Technology

GROWTH PLANS/SPECIAL FEATURES:

GitHub, Inc. is a web-based version control repository (Git) and internet hosting service. The company offers all of the distributed version control and source code management functionality of Git, as well as its own features. The platform allows developers and individuals to build software for open source and private projects. GitHub supports a community of 31 million who learn, share and work together in order to build software. Once a user's code is on GitHub, they can invite others to join in with a link or an @mention. Or users can collaborate with other developers in public or invite them to join the GitHub community's unlimited private repositories. Small businesses and startups can securely develop company software on GitHub and can work together as a team in creating it. Developers will be able to champion new ideas, work together on code and track bugs on a single integrated platform. GitHub has hosted more than 100 million repositories on the platform. In October 2018, GitHub was acquired by Microsoft Corporation for $7.5 billion.

FINANCIAL DATA: Note: Data for latest year may not have been available at press time.

In U.S. $	2018	2017	2016	2015	2014	2013
Revenue		182,500,000	150,000,000	95,000,000		
R&D Expense						
Operating Income						
Operating Margin %						
SGA Expense						
Net Income						
Operating Cash Flow						
Capital Expenditure						
EBITDA						
Return on Assets %						
Return on Equity %						
Debt to Equity						

CONTACT INFORMATION:

Phone: 415-735-4488   Fax: 415-520-5597
Toll-Free:
Address: 88 Colin P Kelly Junior Street, San Francisco, CA 94107 United States

STOCK TICKER/OTHER:

Stock Ticker: Subsidiary
Employees: 800
Parent Company: Microsoft Corporation

Exchange:
Fiscal Year Ends:

SALARIES/BONUSES:

Top Exec. Salary: $ Bonus: $
Second Exec. Salary: $ Bonus: $

OTHER THOUGHTS:

Estimated Female Officers or Directors:
Hot Spot for Advancement for Women/Minorities:

Global Payments Inc

NAIC Code: 522320

www.globalpaymentsinc.com

TYPES OF BUSINESS:

Electronic Payment Processing
Credit & Debit Card Processing
Funds Transfer Services
Check Guarantee Services
Merchant Services

BRANDS/DIVISIONS/AFFILIATES:

AdvancedMD

CONTACTS: *Note: Officers with more than one job title may be intentionally listed here more than once.*

Jeffrey Sloan, CEO
Cameron Bready, CFO
David Sheffield, Chief Accounting Officer
Guido Sacchi, Chief Information Officer
William Jacobs, Director
David Green, Executive VP

GROWTH PLANS/SPECIAL FEATURES:

Global Payments, Inc. is a worldwide payment processing company. The firm enables merchants, multinational corporations, financial institutions, consumers, government agencies and other profit and nonprofit business enterprises to facilitate payments or further other economic goals. Global Payments' comprehensive offerings include, but are not limited to, authorization services, settlement and funding services, customer support and help-desk functions, chargeback resolution, terminal sales and deployment, payment security services, consolidated billing and statements, as well as online reporting. The company distributes its services through multiple channels and targets customers in many vertical industries throughout North America, Europe, the Asia-Pacific region and Brazil. The majority of merchant services revenues is generated by services priced as a percentage of transaction value or a specified fee per transaction, depending on the card type or the vertical. Global Payments' primary technology-enabled solutions include integrated payment solutions, eCommerce and omnichannel solutions and gaming solutions. Integrated payment solutions include OpenEdge in North America, Ezidebit in Asia-Pacific, education solutions in North America, and point-of-sale solutions worldwide. eCommerce and omnichannel solutions seamlessly blend payment gateway services, retail payment acceptance infrastructure and merchant acquiring capabilities to allow merchants to accept various payment methods. Gaming offers a suite of cash access solutions to the gaming market in North America. During 2018, Global Payments acquired AdvancedMD, a provider of cloud-based enterprise software solutions to physician practices; and agreed to acquire SICOM Systems, a provider of enterprise technology solutions to restaurants.

Global Payments offers employees medical, dental and vision insurance; flexible spending accounts; life insurance; disability coverage; an employee assistance program; an employee discount program; a 401(k); a stock purchase plan; and an educational assistance program.

FINANCIAL DATA: *Note: Data for latest year may not have been available at press time.*

In U.S. $	2018	2017	2016	2015	2014	2013
Revenue		3,975,163,000	2,898,150,000	2,773,718,000	2,554,236,000	2,375,923,000
R&D Expense						
Operating Income		558,868,000	424,944,000	456,597,000	405,499,000	357,213,000
Operating Margin %		14.05%	14.66%	16.46%	15.87%	15.03%
SGA Expense		1,488,258,000	1,325,567,000	1,295,014,000	1,203,512,000	1,119,860,000
Net Income		468,425,000	271,666,000	278,040,000	245,286,000	216,125,000
Operating Cash Flow		512,388,000	585,001,000	424,701,000	194,098,000	240,546,000
Capital Expenditure		181,905,000	91,591,000	92,550,000	81,411,000	98,590,000
EBITDA		1,018,681,000	618,109,000	599,051,000	541,231,000	479,354,000
Return on Assets %		3.60%	3.33%	5.66%	6.86%	7.43%
Return on Equity %		12.34%	15.50%	31.68%	22.88%	18.64%
Debt to Equity		1.20	1.59	2.21	1.37	0.77

CONTACT INFORMATION:

Phone: 770 829-8000   Fax:
Toll-Free: 800-560-2960
Address: 10 Glenlake Parkway, N. Tower, Atlanta, GA 30328 United States

STOCK TICKER/OTHER:

Stock Ticker: GPN
Employees: 4,438
Parent Company:

Exchange: NYS
Fiscal Year Ends: 05/31

SALARIES/BONUSES:

Top Exec. Salary: $1,000,000   Bonus: $
Second Exec. Salary: $620,000   Bonus: $

OTHER THOUGHTS:

Estimated Female Officers or Directors: 2
Hot Spot for Advancement for Women/Minorities: Y

GoDaddy Inc

NAIC Code: 518210

www.godaddy.com

TYPES OF BUSINESS:

Domain Name Registration
Domain Name Reselling
Research & Development, Internet Services

BRANDS/DIVISIONS/AFFILIATES:

CONTACTS: *Note: Officers with more than one job title may be intentionally listed here more than once.*

Ray Winborne, CFO
Arne Josefsberg, Chief Information Officer
Barbara Rechterman, Chief Marketing Officer
Scott Wagner, Director
Charles Robel, Director
James Carroll, Executive VP, Divisional
Nima Kelly, Executive VP
Rebecca Morrow, Other Corporate Officer
Ah Kee Low, Other Executive Officer
Steven Aldrich, Other Executive Officer
Elizabeth Rafael, Other Executive Officer

GROWTH PLANS/SPECIAL FEATURES:

GoDaddy, Inc. provides domain name registration and related services. The company has 17 million customers made up of individuals and organizations. GoDaddy operates the world's largest domain marketplace where customers can find a domain name to match their concept, with approximately 75 million domains under management. The firm is a leading technology provider to small businesses, web design professionals and individuals, offering easy-to-use cloud-based products. GoDaddy provides web site building, hosting and security tools to construct and protect each customer's online presence. Products are developed internally, and include shared web site hosting, web site hosting on virtual dedicated servers and dedicated services, managed hosting services, cloud services, cloud applications, web site builder, eCommerce solutions, search engine visibility, email accounts, office solutions via Microsoft Office 365 and email marketing solutions. GoDaddy provides localized solutions in 63 countries, with 33% of its total bookings attributable to customers outside the U.S. In July 2017, the firm announced it had signed a definatinve agreement for the sale of the PlusServer business to funds advised by BC Partners, for an enterprise value of $456 million.

The firm offers employees 100% paid medical and dental premiums, employee appreciation outings, a 401(k) plan, life and disability insurance, maternity and paternity leave, adoption assistance, subsidized lunches and employee discounts.

FINANCIAL DATA: *Note: Data for latest year may not have been available at press time.*

In U.S. $	2018	2017	2016	2015	2014	2013
Revenue		2,231,900,000	1,847,900,000	1,607,300,000	1,387,262,000	1,130,845,000
R&D Expense		355,800,000	287,800,000	270,200,000	254,440,000	207,941,000
Operating Income		66,900,000	50,100,000	-31,000,000	-61,876,000	-131,925,000
Operating Margin %		2.99%	2.71%	-1.92%	-4.46%	-11.66%
SGA Expense		827,900,000	692,100,000	643,400,000	523,557,000	440,394,000
Net Income		136,400,000	-16,500,000	-75,600,000	-143,305,000	-199,884,000
Operating Cash Flow		475,600,000	386,500,000	259,400,000	180,568,000	153,313,000
Capital Expenditure		135,200,000	62,800,000	79,300,000	67,901,000	52,089,000
EBITDA		395,600,000	195,800,000	107,400,000	91,627,000	10,519,000
Return on Assets %		2.86%	-.45%	-1.40%	-4.42%	-6.40%
Return on Equity %		26.00%	-3.33%	-11.33%	-23.43%	-21.89%
Debt to Equity		4.95	1.84	2.44	3.44	1.33

CONTACT INFORMATION:

Phone: 480-505-8800   Fax: 480-505-8844
Toll-Free:
Address: 14455 N. Hayden Rd., Ste. 219, Scottsdale, AZ 85260 United States

STOCK TICKER/OTHER:

Stock Ticker: GDDY   Exchange: NYS
Employees: 4,749   Fiscal Year Ends: 12/31
Parent Company:

SALARIES/BONUSES:

Top Exec. Salary: $1,000,000   Bonus: $
Second Exec. Salary: $750,000   Bonus: $

OTHER THOUGHTS:

Estimated Female Officers or Directors: 3
Hot Spot for Advancement for Women/Minorities: Y

Sales, profits and employees may be estimates. Financial information, benefits and other data can change quickly and may vary from those stated here.

Gree Inc

gree.jp

NAIC Code: 519130

TYPES OF BUSINESS:

Social Networking Platform
Mobile Applications

BRANDS/DIVISIONS/AFFILIATES:

Wright Flyer Studios Inc
Pokelabo Inc
Funplex Inc
ExPlay Inc
GREE Ventures Inc
GREE Advertising Inc
Glossom Inc
ADFULLY Inc

CONTACTS: *Note: Officers with more than one job title may be intentionally listed here more than once.*

Yoshikazu Tanaka, CEO
Taisei Yoshida, Sr. VP-Prod.
Masaki Fujimoto, Sr. VP-Eng.
Naoki Aoyagi, Sr. VP-Global Oper.
Kotaru Yamagishi, Exec. VP
Yuta Maeda, VP
Shozo Mizuno, VP
Naoki Aoyagi, CEO-GREE Intl

GROWTH PLANS/SPECIAL FEATURES:

Gree, Inc. is a Japanese online media and social networking company. Its social network service, GREE, provides registered members with profile creation services, online communication and information exchange with fellow members and friends. The firm operates through five business units: games, media, investment, advertising and live entertainment. Gree's portfolio of games include Seisen Cerberus, Monster Hunter Exploration and Another Eden, among others, which can be obtained through app stores as well as the internet on the GREE Platform. The company's Japan-based studio, Wright Flyer Studios, Inc., produces original mobile games for iOS and Android; and its virtual reality studio focuses on VR gaming creation. Subsidiaries within this business unit include Pokelabo, Inc.; Funplex, Inc.; and ExPlay, Inc. The media unit is engaged in an array of IT businesses, including services and media, which enrich the daily lives of its customers. Media content includes: MINE BY 3M, an online video magazine featuring women's fashion, beauty and lifestyle topics; LIMIA, an online magazine featuring home and living lifestyle content; ARINE, an online magazine for young women with the latest content on topics such as romance, fashion and beauty tips; aumo, an online magazine that focuses on making weekend outings and travel fun; and moguna, an online video recipe magazine. The investment section focuses on investments in Japan and Southeast Asia in internet business-related technology companies. This business unit is operated by GREE Ventures, Inc. Last, the advertising business operates a reward advertising business, an online video advertising business and an agency business, through which it targets the smartphone advertising market. Subsidiaries within this business unit include GREE Advertising, Inc.; Glossom, Inc.; and ADFULLY, Inc. Last, live entertainment focuses on the virtual YouTube (VTuber) market, supporting, creating, distributing and managing VTubers. VTubers are create virtual content and display it through YouTube-like media.

FINANCIAL DATA: *Note: Data for latest year may not have been available at press time.*

In U.S. $	2018	2017	2016	2015	2014	2013
Revenue	722,812,700	606,346,500	648,170,800	857,598,700	1,165,016,000	1,412,121,000
R&D Expense						
Operating Income	87,386,830	74,187,450	132,077,400	187,676,200	324,716,200	450,940,500
Operating Margin %		12.23%	20.37%	21.88%	27.87%	31.93%
SGA Expense						
Net Income	43,670,220	112,385,000	77,934,850	-95,744,280	160,906,400	208,834,200
Operating Cash Flow	84,659,770	108,081,000	69,345,500	200,226,300	319,391,900	134,387,100
Capital Expenditure	4,943,975	4,823,390	1,651,083	8,329,623	33,485,450	106,828,800
EBITDA	76,126,070	95,475,290	97,376,820	65,959,860	346,115,300	444,002,300
Return on Assets %		10.29%	7.30%	-7.69%	11.20%	13.89%
Return on Equity %		11.40%	8.50%	-9.87%	16.36%	24.76%
Debt to Equity					0.01	0.10

CONTACT INFORMATION:

Phone: 81 357709500   Fax:
Toll-Free:
Address: 6-10-1 Roppongi, Tokyo, 106-6112 Japan

STOCK TICKER/OTHER:

Stock Ticker: GREZF   Exchange: PINX
Employees: 2,568   Fiscal Year Ends:
Parent Company:

SALARIES/BONUSES:

Top Exec. Salary: $ Bonus: $
Second Exec. Salary: $ Bonus: $

OTHER THOUGHTS:

Estimated Female Officers or Directors:
Hot Spot for Advancement for Women/Minorities:

Greenhouse Software Inc

www.greenhouse.io

NAIC Code: 511210H

TYPES OF BUSINESS:

Computer Software, Business Management & ERP
Software

BRANDS/DIVISIONS/AFFILIATES:

Greenhouse Analytics

CONTACTS: *Note: Officers with more than one job title may be intentionally listed here more than once.*

Daniel Chait, CEO

GROWTH PLANS/SPECIAL FEATURES:

Greenhouse Software, Inc. provides recruiting software-as-a-service (SaaS). The company's SaaS platform enables companies to plan and outline hiring processes, get new jobs approved, accept applications online, provide various job recruitment search options, post jobs to boards and social networks, learn how to boost referrals, manage candidates and prospects, schedule interviews, create interview kits, score candidates, manage the recruitment pipeline and decide who to hire, as well as make and manage offers. Greenhouse also offers solutions for managing hiring teams, configuring notifications, control user permissions, streamline communications and create and share reports via application program interfaces (APIs). Greenhouse Analytics provides insights and recruiting performance data for those who prefer a more flexible, hands-on approach to analyzing their data. Customers of the firm include AirBnB, Evernote, Pinterest, Red Ventures, Vimeo, BuzzFeed, SurveyMonkey, DocuSign, Golden State Warriors, Lyft and J.D. Power. The company is headquartered in New York, with additional offices in San Francisco and Denver.

FINANCIAL DATA: *Note: Data for latest year may not have been available at press time.*

In U.S. $	2018	2017	2016	2015	2014	2013
Revenue						
R&D Expense						
Operating Income						
Operating Margin %						
SGA Expense						
Net Income						
Operating Cash Flow						
Capital Expenditure						
EBITDA						
Return on Assets %						
Return on Equity %						
Debt to Equity						

CONTACT INFORMATION:

Phone: 917-780-4130   Fax:
Toll-Free: 800-790-9789
Address: 18 West 18th St., 9/Fl, New York, NY 10011 United States

STOCK TICKER/OTHER:

Stock Ticker: Private
Employees: 208
Parent Company:

Exchange:
Fiscal Year Ends:

SALARIES/BONUSES:

Top Exec. Salary: $ Bonus: $
Second Exec. Salary: $ Bonus: $

OTHER THOUGHTS:

Estimated Female Officers or Directors:
Hot Spot for Advancement for Women/Minorities:

Groupon Inc

www.groupon.com

NAIC Code: 541810E

TYPES OF BUSINESS:

Online Marketing Services

BRANDS/DIVISIONS/AFFILIATES:

CONTACTS: Note: Officers with more than one job title may be intentionally listed here more than once.

Rich Williams, CEO
Michael Randolfi, CFO
Melissa Thomas, Chief Accounting Officer
Eric Lefkofsky, Co-Founder
Steve Krenzer, COO
Dane Drobny, General Counsel

GROWTH PLANS/SPECIAL FEATURES:

Groupon, Inc. is an e-Commerce retailer that connects merchants to consumers by offering goods and services, generally at a discount. Consumers access the marketplaces through Groupon's websites and mobile applications. The firm acts as a marketing agent primarily by selling vouchers (also known as Groupons) that can be redeemed for products or services with third-party merchants; and also sells merchandise inventory directly to customers. As a result, Groupon helps local merchants to attract customers and sell goods and services. The company's operations are divided into three geographical regions: North America, representing the U.S. and Canada; EMEA, representing Europe, the Middle East and Africa; and the rest of the world. Goods and services are categorized as Local Deals, Groupon Goods and Groupon Getaways (travel). Local Deals comprise multiple subcategories, including events, activities, beauty/spa, health/fitness, food, drink, home/garden and automotive. Groupon Goods offers customers the ability to find deals on merchandise across multiple product lines, including electronics, sporting goods, jewelry, toys, household items and apparel. Groupon Getaways features travel offers at both discounted and market rates, including hotels, airfare and package deals covering both domestic and international travel. Groupon earns revenue from transactions, which are either earned from direct sells or reported on a net basis as the purchase price received from the customer for the voucher less an agreed-upon portion of the purchase price paid to the merchant.

FINANCIAL DATA: Note: Data for latest year may not have been available at press time.

In U.S. $	2018	2017	2016	2015	2014	2013
Revenue		2,843,877,000	3,143,354,000	3,119,516,000	3,191,688,000	2,573,655,000
R&D Expense						
Operating Income		31,162,000	-72,216,000	-62,062,000	-13,573,000	75,743,000
Operating Margin %		1.09%	-2.29%	-1.98%	- .42%	2.94%
SGA Expense		1,302,699,000	1,429,119,000	1,447,127,000	1,562,759,000	1,425,790,000
Net Income		14,040,000	-194,587,000	20,668,000	-73,090,000	-95,393,000
Operating Cash Flow		135,079,000	117,105,000	254,870,000	288,824,000	218,432,000
Capital Expenditure		60,217,000	71,288,000	85,607,000	88,792,000	65,025,000
EBITDA		194,652,000	-32,518,000	27,655,000	97,633,000	70,831,000
Return on Assets %		.81%	-10.93%	1.02%	-3.42%	-4.68%
Return on Equity %		5.44%	-53.03%	3.35%	-9.90%	-13.08%
Debt to Equity		0.82	0.75	0.06	0.03	

CONTACT INFORMATION:

Phone: 312 676-5773   Fax:
Toll-Free: 877-788-7858
Address: 600 West Chicago Ave., Ste. 400, Chicago, IL 60654 United States

STOCK TICKER/OTHER:

Stock Ticker: GRPN
Employees: 8,323
Parent Company:

Exchange: NAS
Fiscal Year Ends: 03/31

SALARIES/BONUSES:

Top Exec. Salary: $700,000   Bonus: $
Second Exec. Salary: $482,945   Bonus: $

OTHER THOUGHTS:

Estimated Female Officers or Directors: 1
Hot Spot for Advancement for Women/Minorities:

GrubHub Inc

NAIC Code: 492210

www.grubhub.com

TYPES OF BUSINESS:

Online Restaurant Pick-Up and Delivery

BRANDS/DIVISIONS/AFFILIATES:

GrubHub
Seamless
MenuPages
Allmenus
Eat24
LevelUp
Tapingo

CONTACTS: *Note: Officers with more than one job title may be intentionally listed here more than once.*

Matthew Maloney, CEO
Adam DeWitt, CFO
Maria Belousova, Chief Technology Officer
Stanley Chia, COO
Brian Mcandrews, Director
Margo Drucker, General Counsel

GROWTH PLANS/SPECIAL FEATURES:

GrubHub, Inc. is an online and mobile food ordering company that connects diners with local takeout restaurants. Its online and mobile ordering platforms allow diners to order directly from more than 95,000 takeout restaurants in more than 1,700 U.S. cities and London. Every order is supported by the company's 24/7 customer service teams. GrubHub's portfolio of brands include GrubHub, Seamless, MenuPages, AllMenus, Eat24, LevelUp and Tapingo. GrubHub helps consumers find and order food from wherever they are via GrubHub.com. Customers type in an address and obtain the restaurants that deliver to that locale as well as a list of local pickup restaurants. Seamless allows consumers and businesses to order food for delivery or takeout at Seamless.com or by using the Seamless smartphone app. Once the order is placed, Seamless sends the order to the restaurant, a confirmation email with delivery or pickup time is sent, and either the restaurant delivers it or the consumer picks it up. More than fifty percent of GrubHub and Seamless orders are placed through mobile devices. MenuPages is a New York-based online restaurant menu guide site found at www.menupages.com, and includes international, organic and vegan menus. Allmenus.com provides menus for restaurants in select U.S. states, and includes a map as well as restaurants in nearby cities. Eat24 lets customers find and order food online from thousands of local restaurants. Eat24 is slowly being phased out and will shut down when most users have switched to GrubHub. In September 2018, Grubhub acquired LevelUp, a mobile application designed for mobile diner engagement and payment solutions. In November of that same year, GrubHub completed the acquisition of Tapingo, a leading platform for ordering food on more than 150 colleges and universities nationwide integrating mobile ordering into campus meal plans and point-of-sale systems. The deal is worth $150 million.

FINANCIAL DATA: *Note: Data for latest year may not have been available at press time.*

In U.S. $	2018	2017	2016	2015	2014	2013
Revenue		683,067,000	493,331,000	361,825,000	253,873,000	137,143,000
R&D Expense						
Operating Income		89,750,000	83,852,000	61,929,000	44,984,000	14,889,000
Operating Margin %		13.13%	16.99%	17.11%	17.71%	10.85%
SGA Expense		215,753,000	160,076,000	131,656,000	98,508,000	59,254,000
Net Income		98,983,000	49,557,000	38,077,000	24,263,000	6,747,000
Operating Cash Flow		152,740,000	97,678,000	44,755,000	72,904,000	40,819,000
Capital Expenditure		65,443,000	37,146,000	11,287,000	7,084,000	7,021,000
EBITDA		141,598,000	119,045,000	89,963,000	67,671,000	28,359,000
Return on Assets %		7.22%	4.38%	3.73%	2.74%	1.39%
Return on Equity %		9.47%	5.35%	4.62%	3.60%	1.94%
Debt to Equity		0.15				

CONTACT INFORMATION:

Phone: 877-585-7878   Fax:
Toll-Free:
Address: 111 W. Washington St., Ste. 2100, Chicago, IL 60602 United States

STOCK TICKER/OTHER:

Stock Ticker: GRUB   Exchange: NYS
Employees: 1,518   Fiscal Year Ends:
Parent Company:

SALARIES/BONUSES:

Top Exec. Salary: $651,000   Bonus: $
Second Exec. Salary: $416,000   Bonus: $

OTHER THOUGHTS:

Estimated Female Officers or Directors:
Hot Spot for Advancement for Women/Minorities:

Gusto

gusto.com

NAIC Code: 511210Q

TYPES OF BUSINESS:
Computer Software, Accounting, Banking & Financial

BRANDS/DIVISIONS/AFFILIATES:

CONTACTS: *Note: Officers with more than one job title may be intentionally listed here more than once.*
Joshua Reeves, CEO

GROWTH PLANS/SPECIAL FEATURES:

Gusto provides a cloud-based payroll, benefits and human resource solution for businesses throughout the U.S. Gusto serves more than 60,000 small business customers nationwide, and has offices in San Francisco, California as well as Denver, Colorado. The firm's platform is a single system of record that is comprised of: automated payroll, which includes tax filings, employee paystubs, W-2s and more; benefits administration tailored to each firm's needs; streamlined HR solutions, including emergency contacts, new hire documents and employee anniversaries; and 401(k) integration. Gusto offers three pricing plans: Core, which is $6 per month, per person, plus a $39-per-month base, and includes full-service payroll, employee self-service and profiles, health benefits administration, Workers' Comp administration and support; Complete, which is $12 per month, per person, plus a $39/month base, and includes everything in Core as well as employee offers and onboarding, paid time-off requests and employee directory and surveys; and Concierge, which is $12 per month, per person, plus a $149/month base, offering everything in Complete as well as certified HR pros, HR resource center and support.

Gusto offers its employees medical, dental and vision coverage; credit toward adoption or fertility treatment; parental leave; an annual free flight; an open vacation policy; and a 401(k).

FINANCIAL DATA: *Note: Data for latest year may not have been available at press time.*

In U.S. $	2018	2017	2016	2015	2014	2013
Revenue						
R&D Expense						
Operating Income						
Operating Margin %						
SGA Expense						
Net Income						
Operating Cash Flow						
Capital Expenditure						
EBITDA						
Return on Assets %						
Return on Equity %						
Debt to Equity						

CONTACT INFORMATION:
Phone: Fax:
Toll-Free: 800-936-0383
Address: 500 Third St., Ste. 405, San Francisco, CA 94107 United States

STOCK TICKER/OTHER:
Stock Ticker: Private
Employees: 300
Parent Company:

Exchange:
Fiscal Year Ends:

SALARIES/BONUSES:
Top Exec. Salary: $ Bonus: $
Second Exec. Salary: $ Bonus: $

OTHER THOUGHTS:
Estimated Female Officers or Directors:
Hot Spot for Advancement for Women/Minorities:

Hallmark Cards Inc

www.hallmark.com

NAIC Code: 511191

TYPES OF BUSINESS:

Greeting Cards Publishing
Cable Television Broadcasting
Crayons & Art Products
Television Production & Distribution
Stationery

BRANDS/DIVISIONS/AFFILIATES:

Hallmark Gold Crown
Crayola LLC
Crown Media Holdings Inc
DaySpring Cards Inc
Mary & Martha
Hallmark Business Connections
Hallmark Baby
Hallmark Marketing Corporation

CONTACTS: *Note: Officers with more than one job title may be intentionally listed here more than once.*

Donald J. Hall, Jr., CEO
David E. Hall, Pres.
Jim Shay, CFO
David E. Hall, Pres., North America Div.
Donald J. Hall, Chmn.

GROWTH PLANS/SPECIAL FEATURES:

Hallmark Cards, Inc. markets greeting cards and related products. The company operates wholesale and retail businesses for the sale of greeting and holiday cards, gifts, gift wrap, ornaments, memory-keeping products and stationery, with over 49,000 products available at any one time. The wholesale business distributes products to over 40,000 U.S. retailers and more than 100 countries, with products in approximately 30 languages. As a retailer, Hallmark distributes products in over 2,000 Hallmark Gold Crown stores, of which most are independently-owned. Its Hallmark Home division offers seasonal and holiday home collections as well as everyday items such as pillows, wall art and kitchen entertaining items. The firm also operates through several subsidiaries. Crayola, LLC produces Crayola crayons, art supplies and Silly Putty. Crown Media Holdings, Inc. operates various cable television channels, including Hallmark Channel, which is viewed by 67 million subscribers worldwide. Crown Center Redevelopment Corporation is a commercial and residential complex near Hallmark's headquarters in Kansas City, Missouri. DaySpring Cards, Inc. produces Christian greeting cards and gifts available in Christian retail stores in the U.S., and in over 60 countries. Mary & Martha is a direct sales company in which consultants sell products in the host's home or other place. Hallmark Business Connections, the firm's business-to-business (B2B) division, supplies business greeting cards and operates employee recognition programs, sales programs and corporate health and wellness programs. Hallmark Baby, a wholly-owned subsidiary of Hallmark Marketing Corporation is a digital store offering baby and children's clothing online.

The company offers its employees medical, dental and vision coverage; flexible spending plans; a 401(k) plan and profit sharing plan; child and elder care benefits; a fitness center; tuition reimbursement; and product discounts.

FINANCIAL DATA: *Note: Data for latest year may not have been available at press time.*

In U.S. $	2018	2017	2016	2015	2014	2013
Revenue	4,000,000,000	3,912,000,000	3,700,000,000	3,650,000,000	3,400,000,000	3,900,000,000
R&D Expense						
Operating Income						
Operating Margin %						
SGA Expense						
Net Income						
Operating Cash Flow						
Capital Expenditure						
EBITDA						
Return on Assets %						
Return on Equity %						
Debt to Equity						

CONTACT INFORMATION:

Phone: 816-274-5111   Fax:
Toll-Free: 800-425-5627
Address: 2501 McGee Trafficway, Kansas City, MO 64108 United States

STOCK TICKER/OTHER:

Stock Ticker: Private   Exchange:
Employees: 30,000   Fiscal Year Ends: 12/31
Parent Company:

SALARIES/BONUSES:

Top Exec. Salary: $ Bonus: $
Second Exec. Salary: $ Bonus: $

OTHER THOUGHTS:

Estimated Female Officers or Directors:
Hot Spot for Advancement for Women/Minorities:

Harmonic Inc

NAIC Code: 334210

www.harmonicinc.com

TYPES OF BUSINESS:

Networking Equipment
Video Stream Processing
Cable Edge & Access
Software

BRANDS/DIVISIONS/AFFILIATES:

CONTACTS:
Note: Officers with more than one job title may be intentionally listed here more than once.

Patrick Harshman, CEO
Sanjay Kalra, CFO
Patrick Gallagher, Chairman of the Board
Nimrod Ben-Natan, General Manager, Divisional
Tim Warren, Other Executive Officer
Neven Haltmayer, Senior VP, Divisional

GROWTH PLANS/SPECIAL FEATURES:

Harmonic, Inc. develops and sells high-performance video delivery software, products, system solutions and services. These offerings enable customers to create, prepare, store, playout and deliver a full-range of high-quality broadcast and over-the-top (OTT) video services to consumer devices, including TVs, personal computers, laptops, tablets and smartphones. Harmonic also develops and sells cable access solutions that enable cable operators to deploy high-speed internet, voice and video services to consumers' homes. The company operates its business in two segments: video and cable edge. The video business segment sells video processing and production and playout solutions worldwide to cable operators, to satellite and telecommunications pay-TV service providers, as well as to broadcast and media companies. Video-based infrastructure solutions are delivered either through shipment of Harmonic products, software licenses or as software-as-a-service (SaaS) subscriptions. The cable edge business segment sells cable access solutions and related services, including cable OS software-based converged access platform (CCAP) solutions, primarily to cable operators globally. Across these two segments, Harmonic generated approximately 48% of 2017 revenue from the Americas; 33% from Europe, the Middle East and Africa; and 19% from Asia Pacific regions.

FINANCIAL DATA:
Note: Data for latest year may not have been available at press time.

In U.S. $	2018	2017	2016	2015	2014	2013
Revenue		358,246,000	405,911,000	377,027,000	433,557,000	461,940,000
R&D Expense		95,978,000	98,401,000	87,545,000	93,061,000	99,938,000
Operating Income		-65,570,000	-52,434,000	-11,576,000	-18,810,000	-21,603,000
Operating Margin %		-18.30%	-12.91%	-3.07%	-4.33%	-4.67%
SGA Expense		136,270,000	144,381,000	120,960,000	131,322,000	134,014,000
Net Income		-82,955,000	-72,314,000	-15,661,000	-46,248,000	37,027,000
Operating Cash Flow		3,064,000	438,000	6,351,000	47,369,000	53,759,000
Capital Expenditure		11,399,000	15,107,000	14,356,000	10,065,000	14,581,000
EBITDA		-42,649,000	-18,779,000	8,167,000	18,169,000	22,367,000
Return on Assets %		-15.62%	-13.40%	-3.11%	-8.51%	5.59%
Return on Equity %		-33.92%	-24.15%	-4.47%	-10.68%	7.06%
Debt to Equity		0.56	0.43	0.29		

CONTACT INFORMATION:

Phone: 408 542-2500   Fax:
Toll-Free: 800-788-1330
Address: 4300 N. First St., San Jose, CA 95134 United States

STOCK TICKER/OTHER:

Stock Ticker: HLIT
Employees: 1,376
Parent Company:

Exchange: NAS
Fiscal Year Ends: 12/31

SALARIES/BONUSES:

Top Exec. Salary: $514,500   Bonus: $
Second Exec. Salary: $333,606   Bonus: $

OTHER THOUGHTS:

Estimated Female Officers or Directors: 1
Hot Spot for Advancement for Women/Minorities:

HC2 Holdings Inc

www.hc2.com

NAIC Code: 517110

TYPES OF BUSINESS:

International & Long-Distance Telephone Service
Internet Service Provider
Cellular Phone Service
Prepaid Calling Cards
Virtual Private Networks
Managed Hosting Services
e-Commerce Applications
Co-Location Services

BRANDS/DIVISIONS/AFFILIATES:

DBM Global Inc
Global Marine Systems Limited
American Natural Gas
Continental Insurance Group Ltd
Continental General Insurance Company
PTGi-International Carrier Services Inc
Pansend Life Sciences Ltd
Azteca America

CONTACTS: Note: Officers with more than one job title may be intentionally listed here more than once.

Philip Falcone, CEO
Michael Sena, CFO
Suzi Herbst, Chief Administrative Officer
Andrew Backman, Managing Director, Divisional
Joseph Ferraro, Other Executive Officer

GROWTH PLANS/SPECIAL FEATURES:

HC2 Holdings, Inc. is a diversified holding company that operates in six primary business segments: construction, marine services, energy, insurance, telecommunications and life sciences. These business segments are carried out through the company's subsidiaries. DBM Global, Inc. makes up the firm's construction segment, and is a fully integrated fabricator and erector of structural steel and heavy steel plate for commercial and industrial construction projects. Global Marine Systems Limited (GMSL) makes up HC2's marine services segment, offering global offshore engineering with a focus on specialist subsea services across the market sectors of telecommunications, oil & gas and offshore power. American Natural Gas (ANG) makes up the energy segment. It is a premier retailer of compressed natural gas which designs, builds, owns, operates and maintains natural gas fueling stations for transportation. Continental Insurance Group Ltd. provides a platform for HC2's run-off long-term care business, which is performed through the insurance company: Continental General Insurance Company. PTGi-International Carrier Services, Inc. provides internet-based protocol and time-division multiplexing access, and provides transport of long distance voice minutes. Last, Pansend Life Sciences Ltd. focuses on supporting health care and biotechnology product development. In 2017, the firm, through subsidiary HC2 Network, Inc., acquired Azteca America, a Spanish-language broadcast network, from affiliates of TV Azteca, S.A.B. de C.V.; through subsidiary Continental General Insurance Company, signed a definitive agreement to acquire Humana Inc.'s long-term care insurance business, KMG America Corporation; through subsidiary Global Marine Group, acquired Fugro N.V.'s trenching and cable lay services business; entered into an agreement with Mako Communications, LLC to purchase all the assets of its low power television stations; and agreed to acquire a greater 50% stake in DTV America Corp. In June 2018, HC2 completed the sale of BeneVir Biopharm, Inc. to Janssen Biotech, Inc. for $1.04 billion.

FINANCIAL DATA: Note: Data for latest year may not have been available at press time.

In U.S. $	2018	2017	2016	2015	2014	2013
Revenue		1,563,070,000	1,495,075,000	1,119,519,000	543,202,000	230,686,000
R&D Expense						
Operating Income		-72,889,000	63,651,000	1,659,000	-14,297,000	-36,353,000
Operating Margin %		-4.66%	4.25%	.14%	-2.63%	-15.75%
SGA Expense		291,575,000	152,890,000	111,957,000	81,396,000	34,692,000
Net Income		-46,911,000	-94,549,000	-35,565,000	-12,107,000	111,606,000
Operating Cash Flow		6,142,000	79,148,000	-32,561,000	32,813,000	-20,315,000
Capital Expenditure		31,925,000	29,048,000	21,324,000	5,819,000	12,577,000
EBITDA		51,916,000	26,445,000	23,333,000	-17,524,000	-856,000
Return on Assets %		-1.64%	-3.77%	-2.29%	-3.48%	57.40%
Return on Equity %		-84.64%	-152.47%	-55.40%	-27.16%	181.60%
Debt to Equity		8.10	9.69	3.95	6.68	

CONTACT INFORMATION:

Phone: 703-865-0700   Fax:
Toll-Free:
Address: 505 Huntmar Park Dr., Ste. 325, Herndon, VA 20170 United States

STOCK TICKER/OTHER:

Stock Ticker: HCHC
Employees: 2,744
Parent Company:

Exchange: NYS
Fiscal Year Ends: 12/31

SALARIES/BONUSES:

Top Exec. Salary: $300,000   Bonus: $
Second Exec. Salary: $300,000   Bonus: $

OTHER THOUGHTS:

Estimated Female Officers or Directors:
Hot Spot for Advancement for Women/Minorities:

Health Catalyst

www.healthcatalyst.com

NAIC Code: 518210

TYPES OF BUSINESS:
Data Processing, Hosting, and Related Services

BRANDS/DIVISIONS/AFFILIATES:
Adaptive Data Architecture
Medicity

CONTACTS: *Note: Officers with more than one job title may be intentionally listed here more than once.*
Dan Burton, CEO
Brent Dover, Pres.
Patrick Nelli, CFO
LInda Llewelyn, Chief People Officer
Dale Sanders, Pres.-Technology
Paul Horstmeier, COO

GROWTH PLANS/SPECIAL FEATURES:
Health Catalyst provides a comprehensive, fully-integrated suite of health care data warehousing and process improvement solutions which enable organizations to improve care. The company was formed by a group of health care veterans with data warehousing and quality improvement experience, and collaborated to revolutionize clinical process models using analytics. The firm's Adaptive Data Architecture platform utilizes a late-binding bus architecture which is agile, flexible and can be implemented in a matter of weeks. The platform helps healthcare organizations to spot trends, map out plans and implement processes, as well as organizational changes, in order to make sustainable improvements in a relatively swift and convenient manner. Examples of the unified data involved includes patient records, patient conditions, co-morbidities and even changes in scientific flow. Health Catalyst's mission-driven data warehousing, analytics and outcomes-improvement capabilities help healthcare organizations of all sizes improve clinical, financial and operational outcomes. More than 75 million patients are impacted by the company's platform. Investors of the firm include, but are not limited to, HB Ventures, CHV Capital, Sorenson Capital, Sequoia Capital, Tenaya Capital, Epic Ventures, Leavitt Group, Cougar Capital and Leerink Capital Partners. Some of the company's clients include Stanford Hospital & Clinics, AllinaHealth, Crystal Run Healthcare, John Muir Health, Kaiser Permanente Thrive, MedStar Health, Nicklaus Children's Hospital. Orlando Health, The University of Kansas Hospital, and many more. Health Catalyst is headquartered in Salt Lake City, Utah. In July 2018, Health Catalyst acquired Medicity, a leading U.S. health population management company.

FINANCIAL DATA: *Note: Data for latest year may not have been available at press time.*

In U.S. $	2018	2017	2016	2015	2014	2013
Revenue		70,000,000	66,700,000	41,000,000		
R&D Expense						
Operating Income						
Operating Margin %						
SGA Expense						
Net Income						
Operating Cash Flow						
Capital Expenditure						
EBITDA						
Return on Assets %						
Return on Equity %						
Debt to Equity						

CONTACT INFORMATION:
Phone: 801-708-6800   Fax:
Toll-Free:
Address: 3165 Millrock Dr., Ste. 400, Salt Lake City, UT 84121 United States

STOCK TICKER/OTHER:
Stock Ticker: Private
Employees: 750
Parent Company:

Exchange:
Fiscal Year Ends:

SALARIES/BONUSES:
Top Exec. Salary: $ Bonus: $
Second Exec. Salary: $ Bonus: $

OTHER THOUGHTS:
Estimated Female Officers or Directors:
Hot Spot for Advancement for Women/Minorities:

HealthStream Inc

www.healthstream.com

NAIC Code: 611430

TYPES OF BUSINESS:

Educational & Training Content
Internet-based Educational Programs

BRANDS/DIVISIONS/AFFILIATES:

Echo

CONTACTS: *Note: Officers with more than one job title may be intentionally listed here more than once.*

Gerard Hayden, CFO
Jeffrey Doster, Chief Information Officer
Jeffrey Cunningham, Chief Technology Officer
J. Pearson, COO
Robert Frist, Founder
Michael Collier, General Counsel
Michael Sousa, President, Subsidiary
Scott Roberts, Vice President, Divisional

GROWTH PLANS/SPECIAL FEATURES:

HealthStream, Inc. provides internet-based training, learning management, talent management, performance assessment, credentialing and managing simulation-based programs. The company's solutions are divided into two groups: workforce solutions and provider solutions. HealthStream's workforce solutions are primarily comprised of software-as-a-service, subscription-based products used by healthcare organizations to meet a broad range of talent management, training, certification, competency, assessment, performance appraisal and development needs. The firm's provider solutions are branded as Echo, and enable healthcare organizations to launch paperless credentialing processes, reduce provider enrollment timelines, accelerate provider onboarding processes, and drive improvement through validated provider profiles. More than 2,400 hospitals and 1,000 medical groups in the U.S. use one or more Echo products. HealthStream markets its products and services through direct sales teams based in Nashville, Tennessee (corporate headquarters), as well as in additional offices in Maryland, New York, California, Illinois and Florida. HealthStream has more than 4.7 million subscribers.

FINANCIAL DATA: *Note: Data for latest year may not have been available at press time.*

In U.S. $	2018	2017	2016	2015	2014	2013
Revenue		247,662,000	225,974,000	209,002,000	170,690,000	132,274,000
R&D Expense		27,899,000	28,897,000	24,214,000	16,463,000	11,757,000
Operating Income		9,800,000	5,567,000	13,557,000	16,375,000	14,666,000
Operating Margin %		3.95%	2.46%	6.48%	9.59%	11.08%
SGA Expense		77,680,000	72,669,000	64,848,000	52,776,000	42,394,000
Net Income		10,004,000	3,755,000	8,621,000	10,394,000	8,418,000
Operating Cash Flow		46,712,000	24,234,000	34,917,000	34,256,000	26,283,000
Capital Expenditure		17,873,000	14,806,000	15,359,000	10,202,000	8,711,000
EBITDA		36,083,000	27,774,000	30,554,000	27,306,000	22,518,000
Return on Assets %		2.47%	.96%	2.70%	4.42%	4.34%
Return on Equity %		3.41%	1.32%	3.84%	6.55%	5.97%
Debt to Equity						

CONTACT INFORMATION:

Phone: 615 301-3100   Fax: 615 301-3200
Toll-Free: 800-521-0574
Address: 209 10th Ave. S., Ste. 450, Nashville, TN 37203 United States

STOCK TICKER/OTHER:

Stock Ticker: HSTM
Employees: 1,120
Parent Company:

Exchange: NAS
Fiscal Year Ends: 12/31

SALARIES/BONUSES:

Top Exec. Salary: $319,300   Bonus: $
Second Exec. Salary: $299,536   Bonus: $

OTHER THOUGHTS:

Estimated Female Officers or Directors:
Hot Spot for Advancement for Women/Minorities:

HomeAway Inc

www.homeaway.com

NAIC Code: 561510

TYPES OF BUSINESS:

Online Vacation Property Rental Services

BRANDS/DIVISIONS/AFFILIATES:

Expedia Inc
HomeAway.com
VRBO.com
HomeAway.co.uk
HomeAway.de
Abritel.fr
HomeAway.es
BedandBreakfast.com

CONTACTS: Note: Officers with more than one job title may be intentionally listed here more than once.

John Kim, Pres.
Tren York, CFO
John J. Ostlund, CTO
Carl Shepherd, Director
Melissa Fruge, Senior VP
Barry Diller, Chmn.

GROWTH PLANS/SPECIAL FEATURES:

HomeAway, Inc., a subsidiary of Expedia, Inc., is involved in vacation rental properties. Through its website, HomeAway.com, the firm connects homeowners and property managers with travelers who prefer vacation rental homes instead of hotels. The site includes photos, detailed descriptions and lists of amenities and nearby attractions for properties located in 190 countries. HomeAway owns and operates several other online vacation rental websites, including VRBO.com and VacationRentals.com in the U.S.; HomeAway.co.uk in the U.K.; HomeAway.de in Germany; Abritel.fr and Homelidays.com in France; HomeAway.es and Toprural.com in Spain; AlugueTemporada.com.br in Brazil; Stayz.com.au and HomeAway.com.au in Australia; and Bookabach.co.nz in New Zealand. The company also owns and operates BedandBreakfast.com, an international site featuring bed-and-breakfast properties as well as the Asia Pacific short-term rental site, travelmob.com. In total, the firm lists over 2 million listings and vacation rentals. The firm's customers can purchase the HomeAway Carefree Rental Guarantee, which offers property insurance coverage. HomeAway has offices in the U.S., France, the U.K., Germany, Brazil, Switzerland, Spain and Australia.

The firm offers employees benefits including life, disability, medical, dental and vision insurance; a 401(k); vacation time; stock options; and flexible spending accounts.

FINANCIAL DATA: Note: Data for latest year may not have been available at press time.

In U.S. $	2018	2017	2016	2015	2014	2013
Revenue	900,000,000	856,000,000	689,000,000	522,800,000	446,761,984	346,488,992
R&D Expense						
Operating Income						
Operating Margin %						
SGA Expense						
Net Income			157,560,000	3,269,000	13,384,000	17,686,000
Operating Cash Flow						
Capital Expenditure						
EBITDA						
Return on Assets %						
Return on Equity %						
Debt to Equity						

CONTACT INFORMATION:

Phone: 512 684-1100   Fax:
Toll-Free: 877-228-3145
Address: 1011 W. 5th St., Ste. 300, Austin, TX 78703 United States

STOCK TICKER/OTHER:

Stock Ticker: Subsidiary   Exchange:
Employees: 1,820   Fiscal Year Ends: 12/31
Parent Company: Expedia Inc

SALARIES/BONUSES:

Top Exec. Salary: $ Bonus: $
Second Exec. Salary: $ Bonus: $

OTHER THOUGHTS:

Estimated Female Officers or Directors: 2
Hot Spot for Advancement for Women/Minorities: Y

Honest Company Inc (The)

NAIC Code: 325620

www.honest.com

TYPES OF BUSINESS:

Consumer and Personal Care Goods
Sanitary Paper Product Manufacturing, Diapers & Wipes
Infant's Formulas Manufacturing
Baby Powder and Baby Oil Manufacturing
Online Sales
Monthly Product Subscriptions

BRANDS/DIVISIONS/AFFILIATES:

Honest Beauty
honestbeauty.com

CONTACTS: *Note: Officers with more than one job title may be intentionally listed here more than once.*

Nick Vlahos, CEO
Muhammad Shazad, CFO
Janis Hoyt, Chief People Officer

GROWTH PLANS/SPECIAL FEATURES:

The Honest Company, Inc., co-founded by actress Jessica Alba, is a consumer goods company that emphasizes non-toxic household products. The firm carries more than 120 products, with its leading selling item being diapers. Products can be purchased separately or in bundles. Honest's bundled deals allow consumers to have Honest eco-friendly diapers and products delivered to their homes every month, and by doing so can save up to 40%. The Diapers & Wipes bundle is $79.95 per month. Other products include training pants, swim diapers, wipes dispensers, ointments and lotions, powders, caddies, totes and bags, bottles, nursing items, shampoos and other toiletries, cleaning items for men/women/children, formula, vitamins/supplements, as well as baby carriers, towels and baby furnishings. The Honest Company's beauty brand operates as a separate entity, with its own website (honestbeauty.com). Honest Beauty is comprised of several skin care and makeup product lines derived from botanicals that are free of parabens, phthalates, petrolatum, sulfates and other chemicals. The Honest Box is another bundle offering in which consumers can mix and match personal care, beauty, cleaning, feeding and wellness products via subscription format. Consumers can save up to 25% with the mix and match approach when compared to ordering the same items separately. In addition to its website and mobile app channels, Honest products are sold at more than 17,000 retail locations across North America. In June 2018, The Honest Company announced a $200 million minority investment from L Catterton, a global consumer-focused private equity firm. That same year, the firm announced plans to debut its Honest Beauty products in western Europe at select Douglas stores.

FINANCIAL DATA: *Note: Data for latest year may not have been available at press time.*

In U.S. $	2018	2017	2016	2015	2014	2013
Revenue		330,000,000	300,000,000	250,000,000	130,000,000	60,000,000
R&D Expense						
Operating Income						
Operating Margin %						
SGA Expense						
Net Income						
Operating Cash Flow						
Capital Expenditure						
EBITDA						
Return on Assets %						
Return on Equity %						
Debt to Equity						

CONTACT INFORMATION:

Phone: 888-862-8818   Fax:
Toll-Free: 888-862-8818
Address: 2700 Pennsylvania Ave., Ste. 1200, Santa Monica, CA 90404
United States

STOCK TICKER/OTHER:

Stock Ticker: Private   Exchange:
Employees: 275   Fiscal Year Ends:
Parent Company:

SALARIES/BONUSES:

Top Exec. Salary: $ Bonus: $
Second Exec. Salary: $ Bonus: $

OTHER THOUGHTS:

Estimated Female Officers or Directors:
Hot Spot for Advancement for Women/Minorities:

Hootsuite Media Inc

hootsuite.com

NAIC Code: 511210F

TYPES OF BUSINESS:

Computer Software, Multimedia, Graphics & Publishing

BRANDS/DIVISIONS/AFFILIATES:

CONTACTS: Note: Officers with more than one job title may be intentionally listed here more than once.

Ryan Holmes, CEO
Greg Twinney, COO
Penny Wilson, CMO
Matt Handford, Sr. VP-People

GROWTH PLANS/SPECIAL FEATURES:

Hootsuite Media, Inc. provides social media management solutions for organizations worldwide. The company's products enable companies to build on the power of social media via engagement, publishing, analytics, insights, campaigns, employee advocacy, platform management, Hootsuite extensions and tools for app creation, as well as content recommendations offered through the Hootsuite mobile app. The firm's solutions include social marketing, social selling, customer service and employee advocacy. Hootsuite has several price plans: free, a limited plan for individuals wanting to try Hootsuite, and includes three social profiles, 30 scheduled messages and one user; professional ($29/month), offering 10 social profiles/1 user, real-time analytics, unlimited scheduling and an ad spend limit of $500 per month; team ($129/month), offering 20 social profiles/3 users, customized analytic reports, unlimited scheduling, team assignments, exportable reports and an ad spend limited of $2,000 per month; business ($599/month), offering 35 social profiles/5-10 users, unlimited scheduling, analytic data exports, publishing approvals, premium app integrations, custom branded URLs, five social media certifications, 24/7 support and an ad spend of $5,000 per month; and enterprise (custom pricing), which offers a variety of enhanced customizable features and personalized training. Primary industries served by the company include financial services, healthcare, higher education and government. Hootsuite has more than 15 million users in over 175 countries. The firm is headquartered in Canada, with offices in the U.S., U.K., France, Italy, Germany, Singapore, Spain, Romania, Mexico, Australia and Romania.

FINANCIAL DATA: Note: Data for latest year may not have been available at press time.

In U.S. $	2018	2017	2016	2015	2014	2013
Revenue						
R&D Expense						
Operating Income						
Operating Margin %						
SGA Expense						
Net Income						
Operating Cash Flow						
Capital Expenditure						
EBITDA						
Return on Assets %						
Return on Equity %						
Debt to Equity						

CONTACT INFORMATION:

Phone: 604-681-4668   Fax: 604-681-4668
Toll-Free:
Address: 5 E. 8th Ave., Vancouver, BC V5T 1R6 Canada

STOCK TICKER/OTHER:

Stock Ticker: Private   Exchange:
Employees: 1,000   Fiscal Year Ends:
Parent Company:

SALARIES/BONUSES:

Top Exec. Salary: $ Bonus: $
Second Exec. Salary: $ Bonus: $

OTHER THOUGHTS:

Estimated Female Officers or Directors:
Hot Spot for Advancement for Women/Minorities:

Sales, profits and employees may be estimates. Financial information, benefits and other data can change quickly and may vary from those stated here.

Hoover's Inc

www.hoovers.com

NAIC Code: 519130

TYPES OF BUSINESS:

Online Corporate Intelligence
Reference Books
E-Commerce
Advertising Services
Sales & Marketing Lists

BRANDS/DIVISIONS/AFFILIATES:

Dun & Bradstreet Corporation (D&B)
IPO Scorecard
Hoover's Handbooks
Jobseeker Report

CONTACTS: *Note: Officers with more than one job title may be intentionally listed here more than once.*

Gary Hoover, Co-Founder
Patrick Spain, Co-Founder
Hyune Hand, Pres.

GROWTH PLANS/SPECIAL FEATURES:

Hoover's, Inc., a subsidiary of Dun & Bradstreet (D&B), is an online provider of company and industry information, designed to meet the diverse needs of business organizations, sales executives, investors and researchers of many types. Through its website, customers can access information for their professional endeavors, including financial and competitive research as well as marketing and job search activities. Hoover's core asset is its proprietary editorial content, which includes a database of more than 85 million companies and 100 million people, with coverage written and edited in-house. Hoover's also provides data on initial public offerings (through the IPO Scorecard pages), corporate news, executive biographical information, corporate financial data, Jobseeker Reports and access to items such as credit reports by D&B. While the firm's primary focus is the delivery of company intelligence via the internet, it also publishes reference books including Hoover's Handbooks. The company generates most of its revenue from the sale of annual subscriptions to its premium-level data services. Significant revenue is also generated from licensing fees, e-commerce and the sale of advertising.

FINANCIAL DATA: *Note: Data for latest year may not have been available at press time.*

In U.S. $	2018	2017	2016	2015	2014	2013
Revenue						
R&D Expense						
Operating Income						
Operating Margin %						
SGA Expense						
Net Income						
Operating Cash Flow						
Capital Expenditure						
EBITDA						
Return on Assets %						
Return on Equity %						
Debt to Equity						

CONTACT INFORMATION:

Phone: 512-374-4500   Fax: 512-374-4501
Toll-Free: 866-473-3932
Address: 103 John F Kennedy Parkway, Short Hills, NJ 07078 United States

STOCK TICKER/OTHER:

Stock Ticker: Subsidiary   Exchange:
Employees: 200   Fiscal Year Ends: 12/31
Parent Company: Dun & Bradstreet Corporation (D&B)

SALARIES/BONUSES:

Top Exec. Salary: $ Bonus: $
Second Exec. Salary: $ Bonus: $

OTHER THOUGHTS:

Estimated Female Officers or Directors:
Hot Spot for Advancement for Women/Minorities: Y

Hotels.com LP

NAIC Code: 561510

www.hotels.com

TYPES OF BUSINESS:

Online Hotel Reservations System
Online Travel Information
Lodging Options

GROWTH PLANS/SPECIAL FEATURES:

Hotels.com, LP, a subsidiary of Expedia, Inc., is a specialized provider of discount lodging reservation services for destinations around the world. Hotels.com's room supply relationships include a wide range of independent hotel operators, lodging properties, bed & breakfasts as well as hotels associated with several national chains such as Hilton, Sheraton, Radisson and Best Western. Through its website and mobile app, customers have access to hundreds of thousands of properties worldwide, with accommodations ranging from standard hotels to condos and all-inclusive resorts. The firm's booking engine allows users to quickly compare price, quality, amenities, location and availability of hotel rooms in seconds. The site also provides users with extensive virtual tours of rooms being offered as well as user reviews. Hotels.com offers various perks to its customers, including Hotels.com Rewards programs that provides customers with a one-night-free stay after every ten bookings at a partner hotel. In addition, Hotels.com offers a toll-free call center service, 800-2-Hotels, which allows customers to book accommodations over the phone as well as receive travel advice from one of the company's agents.

BRANDS/DIVISIONS/AFFILIATES:

Expedia Inc
Hotels.com Rewards
800-2-Hotels

CONTACTS: Note: Officers with more than one job title may be intentionally listed here more than once.

Scott Booker, Pres.
Stuart Silberg, CTO
Taylor Cole, Dir.-Public Rel.
Dara Khoosrowshahi, CEO-Expedia, Inc.

FINANCIAL DATA: Note: Data for latest year may not have been available at press time.

In U.S. $	2018	2017	2016	2015	2014	2013
Revenue						
R&D Expense						
Operating Income						
Operating Margin %						
SGA Expense						
Net Income						
Operating Cash Flow						
Capital Expenditure						
EBITDA						
Return on Assets %						
Return on Equity %						
Debt to Equity						

CONTACT INFORMATION:

Phone: 214-361-7311   Fax: 214-361-7299
Toll-Free: 800-246-8357
Address: 5400 LBJ Freeway, Ste. 500, Dallas, TX 75240 United States

STOCK TICKER/OTHER:

Stock Ticker: Subsidiary   Exchange:
Employees: 864   Fiscal Year Ends: 12/31
Parent Company: Expedia Inc

SALARIES/BONUSES:

Top Exec. Salary: $ Bonus: $
Second Exec. Salary: $ Bonus: $

OTHER THOUGHTS:

Estimated Female Officers or Directors: 2
Hot Spot for Advancement for Women/Minorities:

Hotwire Inc

www.hotwire.com

NAIC Code: 561510

TYPES OF BUSINESS:

Online Reservation Systems
Hotel Reservations
Car Rental Reservations
Discount Airfare
Cruise Reservations
Vacation Packages

BRANDS/DIVISIONS/AFFILIATES:

Expedia Inc
Hotwire.com
TripStarter
Trip Watcher

CONTACTS: *Note: Officers with more than one job title may be intentionally listed here more than once.*

Barbara Bates, CEO
Henrik Kjellberg, Pres.
Pierre-Etienne Chartier, VP-Oper.

GROWTH PLANS/SPECIAL FEATURES:

Hotwire, Inc., a wholly-owned subsidiary of Expedia, Inc., offers discount prices on airfare, hotel accommodations, rental cars, cruises and vacation packages through its website, Hotwire.com. The company offers discounts to customers by helping travel suppliers book unsold airline seats, hotel rooms and rental cars. The site also features the opaque purchase service, allowing customers to book travel arrangements based on hotel price, star rating and neighborhood preferences, without knowing the name of the hotel until after purchase. Hotwire offers airline tickets from domestic and international airlines. It partners with several U.S. carriers as well as international airlines. Additionally, the firm partners with a variety of hotels chains, car rental companies and technology suppliers in order to offer a wide range of options, services and solutions for consumers. Travel planning tools available through Hotwire's site include TripStarter, which helps customers plan ideal travel times to destination cities by aggregating historic airfare and hotel pricing data as well as compiling historic weather information; and Trip Watcher, which allows users to flag certain travel options and sends out price status alerts.

Hotwire offers employees health benefits; a 401(k); disability, life, medical and dental insurance; flexible spending accounts; an employee assistance program; a fitness subsidy; and discounted travel opportunities.

FINANCIAL DATA: *Note: Data for latest year may not have been available at press time.*

In U.S. $	2018	2017	2016	2015	2014	2013
Revenue						
R&D Expense						
Operating Income						
Operating Margin %						
SGA Expense						
Net Income						
Operating Cash Flow						
Capital Expenditure						
EBITDA						
Return on Assets %						
Return on Equity %						
Debt to Equity						

CONTACT INFORMATION:

Phone: 415-343-8400   Fax: 415-343-8401
Toll-Free: 866-468-9473
Address: 655 Montgomery St., Ste. 600, San Francisco, CA 94111
United States

STOCK TICKER/OTHER:

Stock Ticker: Subsidiary   Exchange:
Employees: 351   Fiscal Year Ends: 12/31
Parent Company: Expedia Inc

SALARIES/BONUSES:

Top Exec. Salary: $ Bonus: $
Second Exec. Salary: $ Bonus: $

OTHER THOUGHTS:

Estimated Female Officers or Directors:
Hot Spot for Advancement for Women/Minorities: Y

Houzz Inc

www.houzz.com

NAIC Code: 454111

TYPES OF BUSINESS:
Home Furnishings Online

BRANDS/DIVISIONS/AFFILIATES:
Houzz.com
IvyMark
Houzz Shop

CONTACTS: *Note: Officers with more than one job title may be intentionally listed here more than once.*
Adi Tatarko, CEO
Alon Cohen, Pres.
Richard Wong, CFO

GROWTH PLANS/SPECIAL FEATURES:
Houzz, Inc. is a platform for home remodeling and design. Its website, Houzz.com, lets design professionals showcase their portfolios and homeowners browse and save the photos to help them find the designs or construction professionals they are looking for. Houzz.com is a community of more than 40 million homeowners, design enthusiasts and improvement professionals across the county and around the world. Online segments include kitchen and dining, bath, bedroom, living room, kids, outdoor, exterior, home improvement, furniture, lighting, decor and more. Designers and professionals post their photos, overviews and ideas. Homeowners write reviews, ask questions and share current home improvement activities. Products can be purchased directly online and include options related to each room in the house, as well as the outdoors. Headquartered in California, USA, the firm has additional offices in the U.S., as well as in the U.K., Germany, Australia, Russia, Japan and Israel. In January 2018, Houzz launched Houzz Shop, a UK-based website that allows homeowners to purchase more than 100,000 products from over 2,500 sellers across Europe. The following February, the firm acquired IvyMark, a startup with a business engagement tool and engaged community for interior designers and home design companies.

FINANCIAL DATA: *Note: Data for latest year may not have been available at press time.*

In U.S. $	2018	2017	2016	2015	2014	2013
Revenue		350,000,000	250,000,000	125,000,000	80,000,000	40,000,000
R&D Expense						
Operating Income						
Operating Margin %						
SGA Expense						
Net Income						
Operating Cash Flow						
Capital Expenditure						
EBITDA						
Return on Assets %						
Return on Equity %						
Debt to Equity						

CONTACT INFORMATION:
Phone: 650-561-3611   Fax: 650-433-4249
Toll-Free:
Address: 310 University Ave., Ste. 2A, Palo Alto, CA 94301 United States

STOCK TICKER/OTHER:
Stock Ticker: Private
Employees: 300
Parent Company:

Exchange:
Fiscal Year Ends: 12/31

SALARIES/BONUSES:
Top Exec. Salary: $ Bonus: $
Second Exec. Salary: $ Bonus: $

OTHER THOUGHTS:
Estimated Female Officers or Directors:
Hot Spot for Advancement for Women/Minorities:

Sales, profits and employees may be estimates. Financial information, benefits and other data can change quickly and may vary from those stated here.

Huawei Technologies Co Ltd   www.huawei.com

NAIC Code: 334210

TYPES OF BUSINESS:

Telecommunications Equipment Manufacturing
Network Equipment
Software
Wireless Technology
Smartphones
5G Wireless Technology

BRANDS/DIVISIONS/AFFILIATES:

Shenzhen Huawei Investment & Holding Co
Huawei Marine Networks
Huaewi Matebook
Huawei Watch
Huawei TalkBand

CONTACTS: *Note: Officers with more than one job title may be intentionally listed here more than once.*

Ren Zhengfei, Pres.
Ding Yun (Ryan Ding), Chief Prod. & Solutions Officer
Yu Chengdong (Richard Yu), Chief Strategy Officer
Chen Lifang, Corp. Sr. VP-Public Affairs & Comm. Dept.
Guo Ping, Chmn.-Finance Committee
Zhang Ping'an (Alex Zhang), CEO-Huawei Symantec
Hu Houkun (Ken Hu), Chmn.-Huawei USA
Liang Hua, Chmn.
Wan Biao, Pres., Russia

GROWTH PLANS/SPECIAL FEATURES:

Huawei Technologies Co., Ltd., founded in 1987, is a leading global information and communications technology (ICT) solutions provider. Huawei is one of the world's leading manufacturers of smartphones. The company's ICT portfolio of end-to-end solutions in telecom and enterprise networks, devices and cloud computing are used in more than 170 countries and regions, serving more than one-third of the world's population. Huawei's consumer products include the Huawei brand of mobile smart phones, the Huawei Matebook notebook, the Huawei Watch, the Huawei TalkBand watch, ear buds, speakers, Wi-Fi connection devices and more. The company's business products include switches, routers, WLAN (wireless local area network), servers, storage, cloud computing, network energy services and more. Its carrier products include wireless network, fixed network, cloud core network, carrier software, IT infrastructure and network energy global services. Business solutions and products serve the public safety, government, railway, power grid, finance, media/entertainment and education sectors. Joint venture Huawei Marine Networks (with Global Marine Systems Limited) manufactures submarine cable. Huawei Tech, along with Seven Network Limited, manages a 4G wireless network in Australia. Huawei Technologies recently created an NB-IoT city-aware network using a one network/one platform/N-tier applications model. NB-IoT stands for NarrowBand Internet of Things, and is a low-power, wide-area network radio technology standard that enables a wide range of devices and services to be connected using cellular telecommunications bands. Huawei is one of the world's leading manufacturers of smartphones. The company invests more than $12 billion yearly in research and development, and has one of the world's largest engineering teams. It is investing very heavily in 5G wireless technologies. Huawei Technologies operates as a subsidiary of Shenzhen Huawei Investment & Holding Co., Ltd.

FINANCIAL DATA: *Note: Data for latest year may not have been available at press time.*

In U.S. $	2018	2017	2016	2015	2014	2013
Revenue		92,080,000,000	78,200,000,000	60,100,000,000	46,000,000,000	39,463,000,000
R&D Expense						
Operating Income						
Operating Margin %						
SGA Expense						
Net Income			7,000,000,000	5,700,000,000	4,300,000,000	3,468,000,000
Operating Cash Flow						
Capital Expenditure						
EBITDA						
Return on Assets %						
Return on Equity %						
Debt to Equity						

CONTACT INFORMATION:

Phone: 86-755-28780808   Fax: 86-755-28789251
Toll-Free:
Address: Section H, Bantian, Longgang District, Shenzhen, Guangdong 518129 China

STOCK TICKER/OTHER:

Stock Ticker: Subsidiary   Exchange:
Employees: 177,700   Fiscal Year Ends: 12/31
Parent Company: Shenzhen Huawei Investment & Holding Co Ltd

SALARIES/BONUSES:

Top Exec. Salary: $ Bonus: $
Second Exec. Salary: $ Bonus: $

OTHER THOUGHTS:

Estimated Female Officers or Directors: 3
Hot Spot for Advancement for Women/Minorities: Y

Hulu LLC

NAIC Code: 515210

www.hulu.com

TYPES OF BUSINESS:

Streaming Entertainment Online, Including Movies and TV Shows
Advertising

BRANDS/DIVISIONS/AFFILIATES:

Walt Disney Company (The)
21st Century Fox
Comcast
AT&T
Hulu with Live TV

CONTACTS: Note: Officers with more than one job title may be intentionally listed here more than once.

Randy Freer, CEO
Craig Erwich, Sr. VP-Operations
Elaine Paul, CFO
Kelly Campbell, CMO
Dan Phillips, Chief Technology Officer
Chadwick Ho, General Counsel
Jean-Paul Colaco, Sr. VP-Advertising

GROWTH PLANS/SPECIAL FEATURES:

Hulu, LLC provides a subscription streaming service that offers instant access to live and on-demand channels, original series and films, and a premium library of TV and movies. Hulu is primarily oriented toward television series, carrying both current and past episodes from its owners' television networks and other content partners. The service also streams anime titles from many distributors, including Funimation, TMS Entertainment, Bandai Visual and Viz Media. Hulu has more than 20 million subscribers in the U.S., with nearly 70% of viewing taking place on regular televisions via connected devices. Hulu is free for the first 30 days at startup, and then $5.99 per month for a year, then $7.99/month thereafter. This subscription service enables customers to stream on preferred devices, and have unlimited access to the Hulu streaming library with limited or no commercials. Add-ons are offered. Hulu with Live TV combines live TV offerings with Hulu's existing library of television series and films, in beta (meaning that some features or parts of the plug-in is still in testing mode and can cause issues of not used properly). The $39.99-per-month Hulu with Live TV service provides support for Xbox One, Apple TV, Chromecast, iOS and Android devices, and offers live streams of more than 50 broadcast and cable-originated channels. The Walt Disney Company, having acquired 21st Century Fox, holds 60% of Hulu; Comcast holds a 30% share; and AT&T holds the remaining 10%.

FINANCIAL DATA: Note: Data for latest year may not have been available at press time.

In U.S. $	2018	2017	2016	2015	2014	2013
Revenue		2,870,000,000	2,375,000,000	1,577,800,000	1,285,000,000	1,000,000,000
R&D Expense						
Operating Income						
Operating Margin %						
SGA Expense						
Net Income			-560,000,000	-321,000,000	-61,000,000	
Operating Cash Flow						
Capital Expenditure						
EBITDA						
Return on Assets %						
Return on Equity %						
Debt to Equity						

CONTACT INFORMATION:

Phone: 310-571-4700   Fax: 310-571-4701
Toll-Free:
Address: 2500 Broadway, 2/Fl, Santa Monica, CA 90404 United States

STOCK TICKER/OTHER:

Stock Ticker: Joint Venture   Exchange:
Employees: 725   Fiscal Year Ends: 12/31
Parent Company:

SALARIES/BONUSES:

Top Exec. Salary: $ Bonus: $
Second Exec. Salary: $ Bonus: $

OTHER THOUGHTS:

Estimated Female Officers or Directors:
Hot Spot for Advancement for Women/Minorities:

IAC/InterActiveCorp

www.iac.com

NAIC Code: 519130

TYPES OF BUSINESS:

E-Commerce, Online Advertising & Search Engines
Online Personals & Dating Services
Online Entertainment & Shopping Directories
Service Provider Listings Online

BRANDS/DIVISIONS/AFFILIATES:

Match Group Inc
ANGI Homeservices Inc
Angie's List
Vimeo
IAC Films
Apalon
SlimWare
Dotdash

CONTACTS: *Note: Officers with more than one job title may be intentionally listed here more than once.*

Barry Diller, Chairman of the Board
Joseph Levin, Director
Victor Kaufman, Director
Glenn Schiffman, Executive VP
Mark Stein, Executive VP
Gregg Winiarski, General Counsel
Michael Schwerdtman, Senior VP

GROWTH PLANS/SPECIAL FEATURES:

IAC/InterActiveCorp is a leading media and internet company organized into five segments: Match Group, ANGI Homeservices, video, applications and publishing. The Match Group consists of Match Group, Inc., which operates a dating business available in 42 languages across more than 190 countries. It offers subscription dating products via websites and mobile applications, which enable users to establish a profile and review the profiles of other users without charge. Additional features are either free or obtained by purchase. Access to premium features require a subscription. The ANGI Homeservices segment consists of ANGI Homeservices, Inc., which owns and operates HomeAdvisor, Angie's List, mHelpDesk, CraftJack and Felix, which are digital marketplaces for home services. The video segment consists of Vimeo, Electus, IAC Films and Daily Burn. Vimeo operates a global video sharing platform for creators and their audiences; Electus provides production and producer services for both unscripted and scripted television and digital content, primarily for initial sale and distribution in the U.S.; IAC Films provides production and producer services for feature films, primarily for initial sale and distribution in the U.S. and internationally; and Daily Burn is a health and fitness property that provides streaming fitness and workout videos across a variety of platforms. The applications segment consists of two divisions: consumer and partnerships. The consumers division develops and distributes downloadable desktop and mobile apps, and includes: Apalon, which houses the firm's mobile apps; and SlimWare, a community-powered software that cleans, repairs, updates, secures and optimizes computers, mobile phones and digital devices. The partnership division designs and develops browser-based search applications to be bundled and distributed with the partners' products and services. Last, the publishing segment consists of: Dotdash, Dictionary.com, The Daily Beast, Ask.com and CityGrid, which publish digital content and/or provide search services to users.

FINANCIAL DATA: *Note: Data for latest year may not have been available at press time.*

In U.S. $	2018	2017	2016	2015	2014	2013
Revenue		3,307,239,000	3,139,882,000	3,230,933,000	3,109,547,000	3,022,987,000
R&D Expense		250,879,000	197,885,000	185,766,000	160,515,000	141,330,000
Operating Income		188,466,000	242,742,000	193,644,000	378,727,000	426,203,000
Operating Margin %		5.69%	7.73%	5.99%	12.17%	14.09%
SGA Expense		2,100,478,000	1,792,423,000	1,871,205,000	1,568,047,000	1,336,601,000
Net Income		304,924,000	-41,280,000	119,472,000	414,873,000	285,784,000
Operating Cash Flow		416,690,000	292,377,000	349,405,000	424,048,000	410,961,000
Capital Expenditure		75,523,000	78,039,000	62,049,000	57,233,000	80,311,000
EBITDA		288,661,000	178,938,000	418,666,000	445,325,000	568,649,000
Return on Assets %		5.80%	-.83%	2.51%	9.75%	7.10%
Return on Equity %		14.18%	-2.24%	6.29%	22.55%	17.10%
Debt to Equity		0.81	0.84	0.96	0.54	0.64

CONTACT INFORMATION:

Phone: 212 314-7300   Fax: 212 314-7399
Toll-Free:
Address: 555 W. 18th St., New York, NY 10011 United States

SALARIES/BONUSES:

Top Exec. Salary: $1,000,000   Bonus: $4,000,000
Second Exec. Salary: $600,000   Bonus: $2,500,000

STOCK TICKER/OTHER:

Stock Ticker: IAC   Exchange: NAS
Employees: 9,100   Fiscal Year Ends: 12/31
Parent Company:

OTHER THOUGHTS:

Estimated Female Officers or Directors: 6
Hot Spot for Advancement for Women/Minorities: Y

IBM Global Services

www.ibm.com/services

NAIC Code: 541513

TYPES OF BUSINESS:

Computer Facilities Management Services
Software Applications Management
Computer Operations Outsourcing
Business and IT Consulting
Consulting
Application Management

BRANDS/DIVISIONS/AFFILIATES:

International Business Machines Corporation (IBM)

CONTACTS: *Note: Officers with more than one job title may be intentionally listed here more than once.*

Robert C. Weber, Sr. VP-Legal & Regulatory Affairs
Bob Moffat, Sr. VP-Integrated Oper.
Colleen Arnold, Sr. VP-Application Mgmt. Services
Ginni Rometty, Chmn.-IBM

GROWTH PLANS/SPECIAL FEATURES:

IBM Global Services, a segment of International Business Machines Corporation (IBM), provides software and consulting services to businesses of all sizes. IBM Global offers expert services across 18 industries, including automotive, education, electronics, retail, life sciences, government, insurance and media/telecommunications. The company primarily offers a variety of software solutions and artificial intelligence (AI) consulting services. IBM's Watson Health, IoT (Internet of Things) and certain areas of its cloud computing business fall under this segment. Watson is IBM's big bet on artificial intelligence. While the Watson supercomputing platform and its related software are providing cutting-edge solutions for virtually all industries, the largest amount of capital and manpower is invested in its efforts to serve the healthcare industry. Another major focus is in serving the financial services industry. IBM Global Services' cover applications, business process/operations, business resiliency, business strategy/design, cloud, digital workplace, network, security, technology consulting and technology support. AI services include: cognitive customer care, for improving customer experience and lowering call center operating costs with Watson AI technologies; IBM garage, for thinking, building and scaling innovations; insights, enabling the ability to read massive amounts of unstructured text in financial and legal documents, and detect billing anomalies, legal policy and more; and risk and compliance services, with the power to stay current on constantly changing regulations via AI. For developers, IBM Global offers solutions and services in regards to development, blockchain, AI, containers, analytics and Node.js.

FINANCIAL DATA: *Note: Data for latest year may not have been available at press time.*

In U.S. $	2018	2017	2016	2015	2014	2013
Revenue	16,817,000,000	16,348,000,000	16,700,000,000	17,166,000,000		
R&D Expense						
Operating Income						
Operating Margin %						
SGA Expense						
Net Income		1,401,000,000	1,732,000,000			
Operating Cash Flow						
Capital Expenditure						
EBITDA						
Return on Assets %						
Return on Equity %						
Debt to Equity						

CONTACT INFORMATION:

Phone: 914-499-1900   Fax: 914-765-7382
Toll-Free: 800-426-4968
Address: 1 New Orchard Rd., Armonk, NY 10504-1722 United States

SALARIES/BONUSES:

Top Exec. Salary: $ Bonus: $
Second Exec. Salary: $ Bonus: $

STOCK TICKER/OTHER:

Stock Ticker: Subsidiary   Exchange:
Employees: 100,000   Fiscal Year Ends: 12/31
Parent Company: International Business Machines Corporation (IBM)

OTHER THOUGHTS:

Estimated Female Officers or Directors: 1
Hot Spot for Advancement for Women/Minorities: Y

IBM Technology Services & Cloud Platforms   www.ibm.com

NAIC Code: 541512

TYPES OF BUSINESS:

Cloud Computing Services
Hybrid Cloud

BRANDS/DIVISIONS/AFFILIATES:

International Business Machines Corporation (IBM)
IBM Research
Summit
Sierra
IBM POWER9

CONTACTS: Note: Officers with more than one job title may be intentionally listed here more than once.

Ginni Rometty, Chmn.-IBM Corporate

GROWTH PLANS/SPECIAL FEATURES:

IBM Technology Services & Cloud Platforms is a major operating segment of International Business Machines Corporation (IBM). The firm provides comprehensive IT infrastructure services, creating business value for clients through integrated services that incorporate unique intellectual property within its global delivery model. By leveraging insights and experience drawn from IBM's global scale, skills and technology, with applied innovation from IBM Research, clients gain access to leading edge, high-quality services with improved productivity, flexibility, cost and outcomes. This business unit's infrastructure services delivers a portfolio of artificial intelligence (AI), cloud, project-based, outsourcing and other managed services focused on clients' enterprise IT infrastructure environments to enable digital transformation and deliver improved quality, flexibility, risk management and financial value. The portfolio includes a comprehensive set of hybrid cloud services and solutions to assist clients in building and running enterprise IT environments that utilize public and private clouds and traditional IT. Its AI and cloud platforms encompass leading edge services for developers as well as the ability to cover a wide variety of high performance workloads. These offerings integrate long-standing expertise in service management and technology with the ability to utilize the power of new technologies, including those from other IBM business segments. The portfolio is built around a key set of predictive and proactive solutions addressing systems, mobility, resiliency, networking, AI, cloud and security. IBM's Summit and Sierra supercomputers are more powerful than 1 million laptops, and are built on IBM POWER9-based services to tackle the most complex challenges. They can sift through huge data sets to help understand topics ranging from cancer cells to supernovas. The firm operates more than 45 major data centers on six continents, which support enterprise computing performance, security and data.

FINANCIAL DATA: Note: Data for latest year may not have been available at press time.

In U.S. $	2018	2017	2016	2015	2014	2013
Revenue	34,462,000,000	34,934,000,000	36,052,000,000	35,840,000,000	39,729,000,000	
R&D Expense						
Operating Income						
Operating Margin %						
SGA Expense						
Net Income		4,344,000,000	4,707,000,000			
Operating Cash Flow						
Capital Expenditure						
EBITDA						
Return on Assets %						
Return on Equity %						
Debt to Equity						

CONTACT INFORMATION:

Phone: 914-499-1900   Fax: 800-314-1092
Toll-Free: 800-426-4968
Address: 1 New Orchard Rd., Armonk, NY 10504 United States

STOCK TICKER/OTHER:

Stock Ticker: Subsidiary   Exchange:
Employees: 50,000   Fiscal Year Ends: 12/31
Parent Company: International Business Machines Corporation (IBM)

SALARIES/BONUSES:

Top Exec. Salary: $ Bonus: $
Second Exec. Salary: $ Bonus: $

OTHER THOUGHTS:

Estimated Female Officers or Directors:
Hot Spot for Advancement for Women/Minorities: Y

iCIMS Inc

NAIC Code: 511210H

www.icims.com

TYPES OF BUSINESS:

Computer Software, Business Management & ERP
Software

BRANDS/DIVISIONS/AFFILIATES:

TextRecruit
iCIMS Connect
iCIMS Recruit
iCIMS Offer
iCIMS Onboard
iCIMS UNIFi

GROWTH PLANS/SPECIAL FEATURES:

iCIMS, Inc. provides software-as-a-service (SaaS) talent acquisition solutions for businesses in the U.S. and internationally. iCIMS' recruit software allows users to easily find and screen people through its applicant tracking system. The company's solutions cover candidate marketing, high-volume recruitment, reporting, analytics, seamless integration, global recruiting, compliance, data governance and security. Its products address mobile engagement, artificial intelligence (AI) engagement, candidate relationship management, applicant tracking, offer management, employee onboarding and Platform-as-a-Service (PaaS). Products and solutions are branded as TextRecruit, iCIMS Connect, iCIMS Recruit, iCIMS Offer, iCIMS Onboard and iCIMS UNIFi. Headquartered in New Jersey, USA, the firm has an additional office in California, USA and in London, England. iCIMS supports over 4,000 contracted customers, and fills more than 4 million jobs every year.

CONTACTS: *Note: Officers with more than one job title may be intentionally listed here more than once.*

Colin Day, CEO
Ronald Kasner, Pres.
Valerie Rainey, CFO
Susan Mitale, CMO
Al Smith, VP-IT

FINANCIAL DATA: *Note: Data for latest year may not have been available at press time.*

In U.S. $	2018	2017	2016	2015	2014	2013
Revenue	200,000,000	150,000,000				
R&D Expense						
Operating Income						
Operating Margin %						
SGA Expense						
Net Income						
Operating Cash Flow						
Capital Expenditure						
EBITDA						
Return on Assets %						
Return on Equity %						
Debt to Equity						

CONTACT INFORMATION:

Phone: Fax:
Toll-Free: 800-889-4422
Address: 101 Crawfords Corner Rd., Ste. 3-100, Holmdel, NJ 07733
United States

STOCK TICKER/OTHER:

Stock Ticker: Private   Exchange:
Employees: 800   Fiscal Year Ends:
Parent Company:

SALARIES/BONUSES:

Top Exec. Salary: $ Bonus: $
Second Exec. Salary: $ Bonus: $

OTHER THOUGHTS:

Estimated Female Officers or Directors:
Hot Spot for Advancement for Women/Minorities:

iCrossing Inc

www.icrossing.com

NAIC Code: 511210M

TYPES OF BUSINESS:

Search Engine Marketing
Web Analytics Software

BRANDS/DIVISIONS/AFFILIATES:

Hearst Corporation (The)
Collaboratory (The)

CONTACTS: *Note: Officers with more than one job title may be intentionally listed here more than once.*

Mike Parker, Pres.
Mitchell Yoo, Chief Global Growth Officer
Rod Lenniger, Chief Admin. Officer
Adam Lavelle, Chief Strategy Officer
Patrick Bertermann, CEO-iCrossing Munich
Patrick Stern, Chief Creative Officer
Marlin Jackson, Exec. VP-Global Dev.
Amanda McElroy, Sr. VP-Bus. Dev.
Paul Doleman, CEO-iCrossing U.K.

GROWTH PLANS/SPECIAL FEATURES:

iCrossing, Inc., a subsidiary of The Hearst Corporation, is a search engine marketing company. The firm offers planning services, development services and a marketing platform primarily for content marketing, data analytics, digital media planning and buying, advertising campaigns, search engine optimization (SEO), brand strategy and experience design, social media marketing, search engine marketing (SEM) services, marketing to Hispanics and programmatic. Content marketing focuses on customized content production, sharing and distribution. Data analytics services include business intelligence, programmatic buying models, cross-device mobile campaign outreach and multivariate testing. Digital media planning and buying advises clients on which media to buy in order to gain maximum return-on-investment. Advertising campaigns involves multi-disciplinary approach to connect people with brands. The SEO focuses on global connectivity and visibility. Brand strategy and experience design offers full-service strategy and engagement planning. Social media marketing provides content, strategy, measurement and analysis for different social media platforms. SEM services helps create customized landing pages, content and experiences for different audiences. Marketing to Hispanics helps businesses connect with Hispanic consumers by exploring and understanding different cultural groups. Programmatic focuses on using first- and third-party data to pinpoint audiences and optimizing their experiences across different platforms. iCrossing's Collaboratory is a program dedicated to developing partnerships between brands and industry-leading platforms, publishers, start-ups and creative technologists to solve challenges, create market opportunity and build brand momentum. The firm's clients include Amazon, Bayer, Bridgestone, Blue Cross Blue Shield, the BMW Group, Church & Dwight, DIRECTV, LEGO, LG, L'Oreal, Microsoft, NBA, PepsiCo, SAP, Starwood and Toyota. Headquartered in New York, iCrossing has offices throughout the U.S., Europe, Latin America and Asia.

The company offers its employees medical, dental and vision plans; life, AD&D and disability insurances; flexible spending accounts; commuter services; and 401(k).

FINANCIAL DATA: *Note: Data for latest year may not have been available at press time.*

In U.S. $	2018	2017	2016	2015	2014	2013
Revenue						
R&D Expense						
Operating Income						
Operating Margin %						
SGA Expense						
Net Income						
Operating Cash Flow						
Capital Expenditure						
EBITDA						
Return on Assets %						
Return on Equity %						
Debt to Equity						

CONTACT INFORMATION:

Phone: 212-649-3900   Fax: 646-280-1091
Toll-Free:
Address: 300 W. 57th St., New York, NY 10019 United States

SALARIES/BONUSES:

Top Exec. Salary: $ Bonus: $
Second Exec. Salary: $ Bonus: $

STOCK TICKER/OTHER:

Stock Ticker: Subsidiary
Employees: 1,000
Parent Company: Hearst Corporation (The)

Exchange:
Fiscal Year Ends: 12/31

OTHER THOUGHTS:

Estimated Female Officers or Directors: 7
Hot Spot for Advancement for Women/Minorities: Y

Illumio
NAIC Code: 511210E

www.illumio.com

TYPES OF BUSINESS:
Computer Software, Security & Anti-Virus

BRANDS/DIVISIONS/AFFILIATES:
Illumio Adaptive Security Platform

CONTACTS: Note: Officers with more than one job title may be intentionally listed here more than once.

Andrew Rubin, CEO
Jim Yares, SVP-Global Field Operations
Remo Canessa, CFO
Wendy A. M. Yale, VP-Mktg.
Emily Couey, VP-People
P.J. Kirner, CTO

GROWTH PLANS/SPECIAL FEATURES:

Illumio is an enterprise data center and cloud computing security company. The Illumio Adaptive Security Platform (ASP) reduces cyber risk in data center and cloud environments by delivering application traffic visibility, adaptive segmentation and encryption with no dependency on the network or hypervisor. Illumio ASP is designed to continuously protect communications within and across tiers of applications, wherever they are running. The platform is decoupled from the infrastructure, and supports all modern server computing formats (Windows/Linus, virtual machines, containers) and all computing environments (data center, private and public cloud). The firm's policy compute engine (PCE) is the central brain of the Illumio ASP. The PCE discovers application topology and application flows, features rich application program interfaces (APIs) that integrate with orchestration tools and configuration management database systems and enables automatic key management for encryption. The virtual enforcement node (VEN) is a lightweight software agent that can be installed in the operating system of any server, virtual machine or container. The VEN collects telemetry (network flows, workload information) and programs the native firewall in the host. The VEN is not in the data path; it controls stateful native layer-3 and layer-4 firewalls to deliver segmentation; has no requirements for virtual chokepoints or complex traffic steering; and delivers real-time alerts of potential policy violations and tampering. Customers of the firm include Morgan Stanley, Salesforce, Workday, Oracle + NETSuite, Platronics, Creative Artists Agency, BNP Paribas and Oak Hill Advisors.

FINANCIAL DATA: Note: Data for latest year may not have been available at press time.

In U.S. $	2018	2017	2016	2015	2014	2013
Revenue						
R&D Expense						
Operating Income						
Operating Margin %						
SGA Expense						
Net Income						
Operating Cash Flow						
Capital Expenditure						
EBITDA						
Return on Assets %						
Return on Equity %						
Debt to Equity						

CONTACT INFORMATION:
Phone: 669-800-5000 Fax:
Toll-Free:
Address: 160 San Gabriel Dr., Sunnyvale, CA 94086 United States

STOCK TICKER/OTHER:
Stock Ticker: Private Exchange:
Employees: 160 Fiscal Year Ends:
Parent Company:

SALARIES/BONUSES:
Top Exec. Salary: $ Bonus: $
Second Exec. Salary: $ Bonus: $

OTHER THOUGHTS:
Estimated Female Officers or Directors:
Hot Spot for Advancement for Women/Minorities:

Indiegogo Inc

NAIC Code: 519130

TYPES OF BUSINESS:

Crowdfunding

BRANDS/DIVISIONS/AFFILIATES:

InDemand
Crowdfunding Field Guide

CONTACTS: *Note: Officers with more than one job title may be intentionally listed here more than once.*

Slava Rubin, CEO
David Mandelbrot, VP-Operations

GROWTH PLANS/SPECIAL FEATURES:

Indiegogo, Inc. offers live crowdfunding campaigns as well as an innovative product shopping and shipping online marketplace. As for funding, thousands of crowdfunding and InDemand campaigns are launched and discovered on the Indiegogo site every week. Backers are people who contribute to campaigns, whether a project is in its early stages of development or ready to be shipped as a product. Equity crowdfunding is available for those who want to invest in innovative startups and growing companies, from software to hardware, film, restaurant and more. Anyone can invest as little as $100, and no accreditation is necessary. Just as with crowdfunding, the products come straight from entrepreneurs and their teams all over the world. Marketplace orders have guaranteed shipping, and if a seller does not stick to their shipping schedule, Indiegogo will refund the purchase. Entrepreneurs download Indiegogo's Crowdfunding Field Guide to get started, then funds are raised with a crowdfunding campaign. After the campaign, money continues to be raised with InDemand, with no fundraising target and no deadline limits. Early sales are generated in the Indiegogo marketplace, from which products are sold directly to the audience. Investments can also be raised, including via securities, revenue sharing and cryptocurrency or token sales. Services offered by Indiegogo include creative; fulfillment; marketing and communications; prototyping and production; and retail, licensing and distribution. Pre-launches are free, crowdfunding has a 5% platform fee as well as third-party credit card fees, and InDemand has a 5% platform fee as well as third-party credit card fees. Last, there are two crowdfunding options: fixed, in which all contributions are returned if goal is not met; flexible, in which all contributions are kept even if campaign goal is not met.

FINANCIAL DATA: *Note: Data for latest year may not have been available at press time.*

In U.S. $	2018	2017	2016	2015	2014	2013
Revenue						
R&D Expense						
Operating Income						
Operating Margin %						
SGA Expense						
Net Income						
Operating Cash Flow						
Capital Expenditure						
EBITDA						
Return on Assets %						
Return on Equity %						
Debt to Equity						

CONTACT INFORMATION:

Phone: 866-641-4646   Fax:
Toll-Free:
Address: 965 Mission Street, 6/FL, San Francisco, CA 94103 United States

STOCK TICKER/OTHER:

Stock Ticker: Private
Employees: 85
Parent Company:

Exchange:
Fiscal Year Ends:

SALARIES/BONUSES:

Top Exec. Salary: $ Bonus: $
Second Exec. Salary: $ Bonus: $

OTHER THOUGHTS:

Estimated Female Officers or Directors:
Hot Spot for Advancement for Women/Minorities:

Infor

NAIC Code: 511210m

www.infor.com

TYPES OF BUSINESS:

Cloud Applications Management and Analytics
Software

BRANDS/DIVISIONS/AFFILIATES:

Koch Equity Development LLC
Infor CloudSuite
Infor Coleman
Birst
GT Nexus
Infor UpgradeX
Vivonet

CONTACTS: Note: Officers with more than one job title may be intentionally listed here more than once.

Charles Phillips, CEO
Pam Murphy, COO
Kevin Samuelson, CFO
Ashley Hart, CMO
Anne Benedict, Human Resources
Shahriar Rafimayeri, CIO
Soma Tomasundaram, CTO

GROWTH PLANS/SPECIAL FEATURES:

Infor is a cloud-based business applications software provider. The company builds and designs its software for specific industry needs. Infor CloudSuite offers mobile access and social technologies in order to drive analytics. The firm's other platforms include: Infor Coleman, offering artificial intelligence (AI) technologies; Birst, offering business analytics; and GT Nexus, offering network solutions. Industries include aerospace/defense, automotive, business, corporate, distribution, equipment rental, facilities management, fashion, food/beverage, human capital management, healthcare, hospitality, industrial machinery, industrial manufacturing and public sector. Infor UpgradeX is a program designed to make upgrading to the cloud fast and easy, for businesses already running Infor products on-premise. Over 68,000 organizations in 170 countries rely on Infor to help overcome market disruptions and achieve business-wide digital transformation. Koch Equity Development, LLC holds a 66.67% equity ownership stake in the company. In September 2018, Infor acquired Vivonet, which offers hospitality solutions.

Infor offers its employees health benefits and paid time-off programs.

FINANCIAL DATA: Note: Data for latest year may not have been available at press time.

In U.S. $	2018	2017	2016	2015	2014	2013
Revenue		2,855,800,000	2,691,300,000	2,428,900,000	2,761,800,000	2,718,000,000
R&D Expense						
Operating Income						
Operating Margin %						
SGA Expense						
Net Income		-186,800,000	35,200,000	19,700,000	121,700,000	-76,200,000
Operating Cash Flow						
Capital Expenditure						
EBITDA						
Return on Assets %						
Return on Equity %						
Debt to Equity						

CONTACT INFORMATION:

Phone: 646-336-1700   Fax:
Toll-Free: 866-244-5479
Address: 641 Avenue of the Americas, New York, NY 10011 United States

STOCK TICKER/OTHER:

Stock Ticker: Private   Exchange:
Employees: 15,970   Fiscal Year Ends:
Parent Company: Koch Equity Development LLC

SALARIES/BONUSES:

Top Exec. Salary: $ Bonus: $
Second Exec. Salary: $ Bonus: $

OTHER THOUGHTS:

Estimated Female Officers or Directors:
Hot Spot for Advancement for Women/Minorities:

Infosys Limited

www.infosys.com

NAIC Code: 541512

TYPES OF BUSINESS:

IT Consulting
Software Development & Services
Business Process Outsourcing

BRANDS/DIVISIONS/AFFILIATES:

Finacle
Global Delivery Model

CONTACTS: *Note: Officers with more than one job title may be intentionally listed here more than once.*

Salil S. Parekh, CEO
Kumar S. Ravi, COO
Jayesh Sanghrajka, Interim-CFO
Subrahmanyan Goparaju, Sr. VP-Infosys Labs
Sanjay Purohit, Sr. VP-Prod., Platforms & Solutions
Sanjay Jalona, Sr. VP-Mfg. & Eng. Svcs.
Nithyanandan Radhakrishnan, Sr. VP
K. Murali Krishna, Sr. VP-Computers & Comm.
N.R. Narayana Murthy, Co-Chmn.
V. Balakrishnan, Head-Infosys BPO, Fin. & India Bus. Unit
Srinath Batni, Head-Delivery Excellence
Nandita Gurjar, Sr. VP-Education & Research
Nandan Nilekani, Chmn.
Dheeshjith V.G., Sr. VP-Asia Pacific, Middle East & Africa
Chandrashekar Kakal, Sr. VP-Global Delivery

GROWTH PLANS/SPECIAL FEATURES:

Infosys Limited provides next-generation consulting, technology, engineering and outsourcing services to businesses. The company's range of customized software solutions include development, maintenance and reengineering as well as eCommerce consulting through more than 80 sales and marketing offices worldwide (as of March 2018). Business solutions include consulting and systems integration comprised of consulting, enterprise solutions, systems integration and advanced technologies; business IT services comprised of application development and maintenance; independent validation services; infrastructure management; engineering services comprised of product engineering and life cycle solutions and business process management; products, business platforms and solutions to accelerate intellectual property led innovation, including Finacle, the company's banking product, which offers solutions to address core banking, mobile banking and e-banking needs of retail, corporate and universal banks worldwide; and newer areas such as cloud computing, enterprise mobility and sustainability. Infosys' artificial intelligence (AI)-based solutions span automation, robotic process automation, blockchain, Internet of Things (IoT), autonomous vehicles and other technologies. Solutions are delivered through the company's proprietary Global Delivery Model, which divides projects into components that are executed simultaneously at client sites and at development centers in India and around the world. Approximately 60.4% of the company's fiscal 2018 revenue was derived from clients in North America, 23.7% from clients in Europe, 3.2% from clients in India, with the remainder from the rest of the world.

FINANCIAL DATA: *Note: Data for latest year may not have been available at press time.*

In U.S. $	2018	2017	2016	2015	2014	2013
Revenue	10,939,000,000	10,208,000,000	9,501,000,000	8,711,000,000	8,249,000,000	7,398,000,000
R&D Expense						
Operating Income	2,670,000,000	2,575,000,000	2,375,000,000	2,258,000,000	1,979,000,000	1,911,000,000
Operating Margin %		25.22%	24.99%	25.92%	23.99%	25.83%
SGA Expense	1,091,000,000	1,020,000,000	1,176,000,000	1,079,000,000	978,000,000	750,000,000
Net Income	2,486,000,000	2,140,000,000	2,052,000,000	2,013,000,000	1,751,000,000	1,725,000,000
Operating Cash Flow	2,257,000,000	2,099,000,000	1,862,000,000	1,756,000,000	2,003,000,000	1,738,000,000
Capital Expenditure	310,000,000	411,000,000	413,000,000	367,000,000	451,000,000	384,000,000
EBITDA	2,959,000,000	2,829,000,000	2,597,000,000	2,433,000,000	2,205,000,000	2,118,000,000
Return on Assets %		17.66%	18.66%	19.99%	19.38%	21.46%
Return on Equity %		21.44%	22.69%	24.11%	22.94%	24.80%
Debt to Equity						

CONTACT INFORMATION:

Phone: 91 8028520261   Fax: 91 8028520362
Toll-Free:
Address: Hosur Rd., Electronics City, Plot No. 44 & 97A, Bangalore, Karnataka 560 100 India

STOCK TICKER/OTHER:

Stock Ticker: INFY
Employees: 225,000
Parent Company:

Exchange: NYS
Fiscal Year Ends: 03/31

SALARIES/BONUSES:

Top Exec. Salary: $655,977   Bonus: $592,208
Second Exec. Salary: $681,855   Bonus: $522,977

OTHER THOUGHTS:

Estimated Female Officers or Directors: 2
Hot Spot for Advancement for Women/Minorities: Y

Sales, profits and employees may be estimates. Financial information, benefits and other data can change quickly and may vary from those stated here.

InMobi Pte Ltd

www.inmobi.com

NAIC Code: 541810E

TYPES OF BUSINESS:

Online Marketing Services
Advertising
Mobile

BRANDS/DIVISIONS/AFFILIATES:

InMobi Advertising Cloud
InMobi Marketing Cloud
Pinsight Media

CONTACTS: *Note: Officers with more than one job title may be intentionally listed here more than once.*

Naveen Tewari, CEO
Marc Steifman, CFO
Ravi Krishnaswamy, CTO

GROWTH PLANS/SPECIAL FEATURES:

InMobi Pte., Ltd. provides cloud-based mobile advertising services. The company's products are divided into two categories: advertising cloud and marketing cloud. The InMobi Advertising Cloud is a platform for reaching audiences, inspiring consumer action, retaining customers and growing business. Its widely-deployed SDK and Ad Mediation solutions for publishers ensure the scale and quality of audience needed to succeed in the mobile environment. The platform includes: programmatic advertising, with the ability to know exactly where ads are running, who is seeing the ads and what returns are occurring on the ad spend; and mobile video advertising, an in-app video ad format. The InMobi Marketing Cloud is a platform for uncovering insights, engaging customers and growing business. This solution enables users to design surveys, access panels and gain insights, with first-party data accessible from a single place. Customer experience can be obtained via measurements, analysis and behavior, including customer feedback from an array of channels for the purpose of increasing customer retention. InMobi's connected platforms create a unified marketing hub across the advertising and marketing clouds, for driving marketing success via insights and actions, powered by artificial intelligence (AI) at the core of these platforms. InMobi is headquartered in India, with offices strategically-located worldwide. Its investors include SoftBank, Kleiner Perkins Caufield & Byers, Sherpalo, and UC-RNT Fund. In October 2018, InMobi acquired mobile data and advertising company, Pinsight Media.

FINANCIAL DATA: *Note: Data for latest year may not have been available at press time.*

In U.S. $	2018	2017	2016	2015	2014	2013
Revenue		280,000,000	283,000,000	262,000,000	202,500,000	104,300,000
R&D Expense						
Operating Income						
Operating Margin %						
SGA Expense						
Net Income		-12,700,000	-53,000,000	-40,000,000	-44,600,000	
Operating Cash Flow						
Capital Expenditure						
EBITDA						
Return on Assets %						
Return on Equity %						
Debt to Equity						

CONTACT INFORMATION:

Phone: 91-98-8603-3649   Fax:
Toll-Free:
Address: 6-8/Fl, Block Delta, B Block, Embassy Tech. Sq., Kadubeesanahallli Village, Outer Ring Rd., Varthur Hobli, Bangalore, 560103 India

STOCK TICKER/OTHER:

Stock Ticker: Private
Employees: 800
Parent Company:

Exchange:
Fiscal Year Ends: 03/31

SALARIES/BONUSES:

Top Exec. Salary: $ Bonus: $
Second Exec. Salary: $ Bonus: $

OTHER THOUGHTS:

Estimated Female Officers or Directors:
Hot Spot for Advancement for Women/Minorities:

InsideSales.com Inc

NAIC Code: 511210K

TYPES OF BUSINESS:
Computer Software, Sales & Customer Relationship Management

BRANDS/DIVISIONS/AFFILIATES:
Sales Acceleration
Neuralytics
Predictive Playbooks
Predictive PowerDialer
Predictive Pipeline
Predictive Cloud

CONTACTS: Note: Officers with more than one job title may be intentionally listed here more than once.
Dave Elkington, CEO
Chris Harrington, COO
Alam Black, CFO
Ryan Allphin, CTO
Ken Krogue, Pres.

GROWTH PLANS/SPECIAL FEATURES:
InsideSales.com, Inc. provides a cloud-based sales acceleration platform for the creation of high-performance sales teams. The Sales Acceleration platform is fully-integrated, and delivers visibility, productivity and effectiveness so that InsideSales customers can sell more. Its solutions include sales communications, gamification, email/web tracking, predictive forecasting, opportunity scoring and lead scoring/prioritization. InsideSales customers experience revenue growth up to 30% in as little as 90 days. Sales Acceleration is built on Neuralytics, a self-learning predictive analytics engine that processes massive and complex data sets in order to produce insights and directives to drive sales. Predictive Playbooks brings the power of the platform directly to sales representatives' web browsers, allowing them to prospect, prioritize and contact leads without juggling multiple tools. It automatically syncs leads and activities to the customer relationship management (CRM) without manual data entry. NeuralView, which runs on Neuralytics, automatically identifies promising leads, opportunities and accounts. Its predictive lead scoring prescribes who is likely to convert and when to contact them. Predictive PowerDialer is an integrated system for contacting, connecting and closing more deals. It generates sales via features such as advanced list prioritization, one-click dialing, pre-recorded voice messaging email, inbound call routing and more. Predictive Pipeline blends historical data with sales judgment and predictive analysis so that customers can deliver accurate forecasts. Predictive Cloud incorporates data science and technology in a way that enables sales teams to actually sell. Based in Utah, USA, the firm has additional offices in the U.S., as well as one in the U.K. In November 2018, InsideSales.com announced a new artificial intelligence (AI)-based account management solution to help businesses grow by maximizing customer lifetime value by unlocking insights from customer data.

FINANCIAL DATA: Note: Data for latest year may not have been available at press time.

In U.S. $	2018	2017	2016	2015	2014	2013
Revenue						
R&D Expense						
Operating Income						
Operating Margin %						
SGA Expense						
Net Income						
Operating Cash Flow						
Capital Expenditure						
EBITDA						
Return on Assets %						
Return on Equity %						
Debt to Equity						

CONTACT INFORMATION:
Phone: 385-207-7252   Fax:
Toll-Free: 888-203-3761
Address: 1712 South East Bay Blvd., Ste. 100, Provo, UT 84606 United States

STOCK TICKER/OTHER:
Stock Ticker: Private
Employees: 500
Parent Company:

Exchange:
Fiscal Year Ends:

SALARIES/BONUSES:
Top Exec. Salary: $ Bonus: $
Second Exec. Salary: $ Bonus: $

OTHER THOUGHTS:
Estimated Female Officers or Directors:
Hot Spot for Advancement for Women/Minorities:

Instacart
NAIC Code: 492210

TYPES OF BUSINESS:
Grocery Delivery Services

BRANDS/DIVISIONS/AFFILIATES:
Maplebear Inc
Unata

GROWTH PLANS/SPECIAL FEATURES:
Instacart, an operating unit of Maplebear, Inc., offers an online and mobile delivery service. The firm lets customers purchase items online from various stores in the area and have them delivered to their house in as little as one hour. Unlike other online grocery shopping services that operate their own grocery distribution facilities, Instacart hires personal shoppers to hand-pick items, even grocery items, from actual stores such as H-E-B, Total Wine & More, Petco, CVS, Sur la Table and Costco, to name a few. Exclusive coupons on hundreds of items can be found on the Instacart site and mobile app. Currently, the firm services most U.S. states, as well as Toronto and Vancouver, Canada. In early 2018, Instacart acquired Toronto-based Unata, a white-label platform for grocers to offer their own grocery delivery service. Unata operates as an independent subsidiary of Instacart.

CONTACTS:
Note: Officers with more than one job title may be intentionally listed here more than once.

Apoorva Mehta, CEO
Ravi Gupta, CFO

FINANCIAL DATA:
Note: Data for latest year may not have been available at press time.

In U.S. $	2018	2017	2016	2015	2014	2013
Revenue	1,250,000,000	815,000,000	587,000,000	145,000,000	100,000,000	10,000,000
R&D Expense						
Operating Income						
Operating Margin %						
SGA Expense						
Net Income						
Operating Cash Flow						
Capital Expenditure						
EBITDA						
Return on Assets %						
Return on Equity %						
Debt to Equity						

CONTACT INFORMATION:
Phone: 206-953-2159   Fax:
Toll-Free:
Address: 420 Bryant St., San Francisco, CA 94107 United States

STOCK TICKER/OTHER:
Stock Ticker: Private   Exchange:
Employees: 300   Fiscal Year Ends:
Parent Company: Maplebear Inc

SALARIES/BONUSES:
Top Exec. Salary: $ Bonus: $
Second Exec. Salary: $ Bonus: $

OTHER THOUGHTS:
Estimated Female Officers or Directors:
Hot Spot for Advancement for Women/Minorities:

Instagram

instagram.com

NAIC Code: 519130

TYPES OF BUSINESS:

Social Media
Online Advertising
Apps

BRANDS/DIVISIONS/AFFILIATES:

Facebook Inc
Instagram Stories
IGTV

CONTACTS: *Note: Officers with more than one job title may be intentionally listed here more than once.*

Adam Mosseri, CEO

GROWTH PLANS/SPECIAL FEATURES:

Instagram is an online community of more than 800 million members who capture and share pictures and videos. The social networking service enables users to share content either publicly or privately on its platform, as well as through a variety of other social networking platforms such as Facebook, Twitter, Tumblr and Flickr. Users can also apply digital filters to their images. The maximum duration for Instagram videos is 60 seconds. Instagram Stories is a feature of the app dedicated to posting temporary moments of the day. These moments automatically disappear after a 24-hour period. Other features of the app include the saved posts feature, where users can tap the image to save it to a private archive in their profile, and a collection of customizable stickers that can be used in Instagram stories and direct messages. IGTV, a standalone vertical video application, was launched during 2018, and is primarily made for smartphones. It allows users to upload vertical videos up to 10 minutes in length or up to 60 minutes if you are verified or popular. It is available within the Instagram app and website. Instagram is owned by Facebook, Inc.

FINANCIAL DATA: *Note: Data for latest year may not have been available at press time.*

In U.S. $	2018	2017	2016	2015	2014	2013
Revenue		3,500,000,000	2,900,000,000	1,200,000,000		
R&D Expense						
Operating Income						
Operating Margin %						
SGA Expense						
Net Income						
Operating Cash Flow						
Capital Expenditure						
EBITDA						
Return on Assets %						
Return on Equity %						
Debt to Equity						

CONTACT INFORMATION:

Phone: 650-543-4800   Fax:
Toll-Free:
Address: 1 Hacker Way, Bldg. 14, 1/Fl, Menlo Park, CA 94025 United States

STOCK TICKER/OTHER:

Stock Ticker: Subsidiary   Exchange:
Employees: Fiscal Year Ends:
Parent Company: Facebook Inc

SALARIES/BONUSES:

Top Exec. Salary: $ Bonus: $
Second Exec. Salary: $ Bonus: $

OTHER THOUGHTS:

Estimated Female Officers or Directors:
Hot Spot for Advancement for Women/Minorities:

Intercom Inc

www.intercom.com

NAIC Code: 511210C

TYPES OF BUSINESS:

Computer Software, Telecom, Communications & VOIP

BRANDS/DIVISIONS/AFFILIATES:

CONTACTS: Note: Officers with more than one job title may be intentionally listed here more than once.

Eoghan McCabe, CEO
Des Traynor, Chief Strategy Officer
Ciaran Lee, CTO
John Collins, Managing Editor

GROWTH PLANS/SPECIAL FEATURES:

Intercom, Inc. provides a messaging platform for sales, marketing and customer service teams. The platform enables business teams to talk to customers via company apps, websites, across social media and email. The firm's products are grouped into three categories: acquire, offering chat with website visitors, capturing leads and continuing conversations via email, while also measuring the performance of those messages; engage, enabling targeted emails, announcements across channels, as well as push and in-app messages for onboarding and retaining customers; and customer support, providing help desk software that scales the support team via chat bot, multiple channel, self-service and automation strategies. More than 30,000 businesses use Intercom to connect with 1 billion unique people worldwide. Customers include Bitly, Tradeshift, Unity, Envoy, Copper, Keen, New Relic, Frame.io, Typeform, Moz, Droplr, BugHerd, FitBark, SalesLoft and many more. Intercom is headquartered in San Francisco, California, with an additional domestic office in Chicago, Illinois, as well as international offices in Australia, Ireland and the U.K.

Intercom offers its employees healthcare benefits, wellness programs, and an open vacation policy.

FINANCIAL DATA: Note: Data for latest year may not have been available at press time.

In U.S. $	2018	2017	2016	2015	2014	2013
Revenue						
R&D Expense						
Operating Income						
Operating Margin %						
SGA Expense						
Net Income						
Operating Cash Flow						
Capital Expenditure						
EBITDA						
Return on Assets %						
Return on Equity %						
Debt to Equity						

CONTACT INFORMATION:

Phone: 877-595-5175   Fax:
Toll-Free:
Address: 55 2nd St., 4/Fl, San Francisco, CA 94105 United States

STOCK TICKER/OTHER:

Stock Ticker: Private   Exchange:
Employees: 600   Fiscal Year Ends:
Parent Company:

SALARIES/BONUSES:

Top Exec. Salary: $ Bonus: $
Second Exec. Salary: $ Bonus: $

OTHER THOUGHTS:

Estimated Female Officers or Directors:
Hot Spot for Advancement for Women/Minorities:

Internap Corporation

www.internap.com

NAIC Code: 517110

TYPES OF BUSINESS:

Internet Access Provider
Voice-Over-Internet Protocol
Multimedia Streaming
Virtual Private Networking
Value-Added Services

BRANDS/DIVISIONS/AFFILIATES:

INAP
SingleHop LLC

CONTACTS: *Note: Officers with more than one job title may be intentionally listed here more than once.*

James Keeley, CFO
Joanna Lanni, Controller
Gary Pfeiffer, Director
Richard Diegnan, Executive VP
Corey Needles, General Manager, Divisional
Andrew Day, General Manager, Divisional
Peter Aquino, President
Mary Horne, Senior VP, Divisional
Joseph DuFresne, Vice President, Divisional
Richard Ramlall, Vice President, Divisional
John Filipowicz, Vice President

GROWTH PLANS/SPECIAL FEATURES:

Internap Corporation, branded as INAP, provides high-performance data center services including colocation, managed hosting, cloud and network services. INAP partners with clients, who range from emerging startups to Fortune 500 companies, to create secure, scalable and reliable information technology (IT) infrastructure solutions that meet their unique business requirements and needs. The company is located in 21 major metropolitan areas where data centers and customers are concentrated, including Atlanta, Boston, Chicago, Dallas, Houston, Los Angeles, Miami, New York/New Jersey, Northern Virginia, Oakland, Phoenix, Seattle and Silicon Valley, in the U.S., and also in Montreal, Amsterdam, Frankfurt, London, Hong Kong, Singapore, Sydney, Tokyo and Osaka. In addition, INAP's global network services manage connectivity through nearly 100 points-of-presence (POP) worldwide. INAP's colocation services involves providing physical space within data centers and associated services such as power, interconnection, environmental controls, monitoring and security while allowing its customers to deploy and manage their services, storage and other equipment in INAP's data centers. The firm designs the data center infrastructure, procures the capital equipment, deploys the infrastructure and is responsible for the operation and maintenance of the facility. Managed hosting services consists of leasing dedicated services as well as storage and network equipment to customers. Cloud services involve the provision of compute resources and storage services on-demand via an integrated platform. Cloud and hosting services consist of hosted infrastructure-as-a-service as a cloud platform or via managed hosting. Managed hosting provides a single tenant infrastructure environment consisting of servers, storage and network. Network services manages connectivity through INAP's POPs. In February 2018, Internap acquired SingleHop, LLC, a provider of hosted private clouds and managed hosted for $132 million.

FINANCIAL DATA: *Note: Data for latest year may not have been available at press time.*

In U.S. $	2018	2017	2016	2015	2014	2013
Revenue		280,718,000	298,297,000	318,293,000	334,959,000	283,342,000
R&D Expense						
Operating Income		11,023,000	-5,729,000	-22,943,000	-9,707,000	-6,064,000
Operating Margin %		3.92%	-1.92%	-7.20%	-2.89%	-2.14%
SGA Expense		62,728,000	70,639,000	80,666,000	81,747,000	74,559,000
Net Income		-45,343,000	-124,742,000	-48,443,000	-39,494,000	-19,830,000
Operating Cash Flow		39,165,000	46,449,000	40,208,000	53,248,000	33,683,000
Capital Expenditure		36,449,000	46,192,000	57,157,000	80,463,000	63,599,000
EBITDA		79,242,000	-16,525,000	67,948,000	66,797,000	44,166,000
Return on Assets %		-8.91%	-25.29%	-8.44%	-6.54%	-3.90%
Return on Equity %			-225.34%	-36.59%	-23.75%	-10.49%
Debt to Equity				3.19	2.32	1.85

CONTACT INFORMATION:

Phone: 404 302-9700   Fax: 404 475-0520
Toll-Free: 877-843-7627
Address: 12120 Sunset Hills Rd., Ste. 330, Renton, VA 20190 United States

STOCK TICKER/OTHER:

Stock Ticker: INAP   Exchange: NAS
Employees: 530   Fiscal Year Ends: 12/31
Parent Company:

SALARIES/BONUSES:

Top Exec. Salary: $505,000   Bonus: $
Second Exec. Salary: Bonus: $
$275,000

OTHER THOUGHTS:

Estimated Female Officers or Directors: 4
Hot Spot for Advancement for Women/Minorities: Y

International Business Machines Corporation (IBM)

www.ibm.com
NAIC Code: 541513

TYPES OF BUSINESS:

Computer Facilities and Business Process Outsourcing
Supercomputing
Business & Management Consulting
Software & Hardware
Cloud-Based Computer Services
IT Consulting & Outsourcing
Financial Services
Data Analytics and Health Care Analytics

BRANDS/DIVISIONS/AFFILIATES:

Watson

CONTACTS: *Note: Officers with more than one job title may be intentionally listed here more than once.*

Christina Montgomery, Assistant General Counsel
James Kavanaugh, CFO
Virginia Rometty, Chairman of the Board
Robert Del Bene, Chief Accounting Officer
Diane Gherson, Other Executive Officer
Martin Schroeter, Senior VP, Divisional
Kenneth Keverian, Senior VP, Divisional
John Kelly, Senior VP, Divisional
Erich Clementi, Senior VP, Divisional
Michelle Browdy, Senior VP, Divisional

GROWTH PLANS/SPECIAL FEATURES:

International Business Machines Corporation (IBM) is a global leader in computer facilities management services, business process outsourcing, supercomputing services and advanced computer hardware and software. It is one of the largest technology consulting and services businesses in the world. The firm has reorganized its primary operating segments to better reflect the dominant themes in information technologies today, such as artificial intelligence and cloud computing. IBM operates in primary segments that include: cognitive solutions (data analytics, health care analytics, supercomputing, artificial intelligence and machine learning), global business services (offering application management, consulting and business process management), technology services & cloud platforms (including technical support, infrastructure services, integration software and the operation of one of the world's most advanced cloud services systems), systems (including IBM's proprietary hardware and software), global financing, and IBM worldwide organizations. Offerings include information management software; operating systems; and Tivoli software for infrastructure management, including security and storage management. The systems units provide IBM's clients with infrastructure technologies to help meet the requirements of hybrid cloud and workloads. The global financing provides loans and leases for that assist in the marketing of IBM computer systems. For future growth, the firm has developed world-class capabilities in supercomputing (including its famous Watson computer), artificial intelligence (AI), machine learning and data analytics, particularly the analysis of massive amounts of health care data and patient outcomes information. IBM is active in over 175 countries worldwide. In October 2018, IBM agreed to acquire Red Hat, Inc., a major distributor of open-source software and technology, for $34 billion. Upon closing of the acquisition, Red Hat will join IBM's Hybrid Cloud team as a distinct unit. The transaction is expected to close in mid-2019.

IBM offers employees medical, vision, dental and disability insurance; a flexible spending account; and 401(k) and stock purchase options.

FINANCIAL DATA: *Note: Data for latest year may not have been available at press time.*

In U.S. $	2018	2017	2016	2015	2014	2013
Revenue		79,139,000,000	79,920,000,000	81,742,000,000	92,793,000,000	99,751,000,000
R&D Expense		5,787,000,000	5,751,000,000	5,247,000,000	5,437,000,000	6,226,000,000
Operating Income		11,800,000,000	13,105,000,000	15,690,000,000	18,532,000,000	19,600,000,000
Operating Margin %		14.91%	16.39%	19.19%	19.97%	19.64%
SGA Expense		19,555,000,000	20,479,000,000	19,894,000,000	22,472,000,000	22,975,000,000
Net Income		5,753,000,000	11,872,000,000	13,190,000,000	12,022,000,000	16,483,000,000
Operating Cash Flow		16,724,000,000	16,958,000,000	17,008,000,000	16,868,000,000	17,485,000,000
Capital Expenditure		3,773,000,000	4,150,000,000	4,151,000,000	4,183,000,000	4,140,000,000
EBITDA		16,556,000,000	17,341,000,000	20,268,000,000	24,962,000,000	24,604,000,000
Return on Assets %		4.73%	10.41%	11.56%	9.86%	13.43%
Return on Equity %		32.10%	73.04%	100.95%	69.37%	79.14%
Debt to Equity		2.26	1.89	2.34	2.95	1.44

CONTACT INFORMATION:

Phone: 914-499-1900   Fax: 800-314-1092
Toll-Free: 800-426-4968
Address: 1 New Orchard Rd., Armonk, NY 10504-1722 United States

SALARIES/BONUSES:

Top Exec. Salary: $1,600,000   Bonus: $
Second Exec. Salary: $830,500   Bonus: $

STOCK TICKER/OTHER:

Stock Ticker: IBM   Exchange: NYS
Employees: 398,000   Fiscal Year Ends: 12/31
Parent Company:

OTHER THOUGHTS:

Estimated Female Officers or Directors: 6
Hot Spot for Advancement for Women/Minorities: Y

Sales, profits and employees may be estimates. Financial information, benefits and other data can change quickly and may vary from those stated here.

Internet Brands Inc

www.internetbrands.com

NAIC Code: 519130

TYPES OF BUSINESS:

Auto Sales-Online
Home & Home Improvement Web Sites
Online Travel Directories
Career Web Sites
Financial Research Web Sites
Health Web Sites

BRANDS/DIVISIONS/AFFILIATES:

KKR & Co LP
CarsDirect
Medscape
www.SoberRecovery.com
AllAboutCounseling.com
Frugal Travel Guy
DentalPlans.com
WebMD Health Corp

CONTACTS: *Note: Officers with more than one job title may be intentionally listed here more than once.*

Robert N. Brisco, CEO
Lisa Morita, COO
Robert N. Brisco, Pres.
Scott A. Friedman, CFO
Chuck Hoover, CMO
Joe Rosenblum, CTO
B. Lynn Walsh, General Counsel
B. Lynn Walsh, Exec. VP-Corp. Dev.
Gregory T. Perrier, CEO

GROWTH PLANS/SPECIAL FEATURES:

Internet Brands, Inc. owns and operates eCommerce and community sites. The firm controls more than 100 websites, which attract an average of over 100 million visitors per month. These sites are grouped into five categories: automotive, health, home/travel, legal and diversified media. The automotive segment operates e-commerce automotive websites that enable consumers to research and buy cars, including CarsDirect, ChromeData, autodata, NET Driven, Auto Credit Express, The Car Connection, NewCarTestDrive.com, RacingJunk.com, Honda-tech.com, Corvette Forum, MBWorld, AudiWorld, Club Lexus, F150online, YoTaTech and Internet Brands Automotive Group. The health segment operates websites for health professionals as well as sites that connect people with health professionals. Health websites include Medscape, Demandforce, Officite, eDoctors, therapysites, Baystone Media, imatrix, sesame, Full Slate, WebMD, DentalPlans.com, Fit Day, HealthBoards, eHealth, TheGoodDrugsGuide.com, AllAboutCounseling.com, Vein, DermaNetwork, altMD, Skin Care Guide, Dentalfind.com and OnlineSurgery. Home and travel websites help people find homes and places to travel to, and include SatisFacts, doityourself, weddingbee, Apartment Ratings, inhabitat, Craftster, Fodor's Travel, Wikitravel, flyertalk, CruiseMates.com, Frugal Travel Guy, BBonline.com and My Summer Camps. Legal websites help people solve their legal problems and include martindale.com, total attorneys, ngage ICS, NOLO Law for All, Lawyers.com, AllLaw.com and AttorneyLocate.com. Diversified media websites give consumers content in categories ranging from bargain shopping to small business management. Diversified websites include Ben's Bargains, PromotionalCodes.org.uk, ultimate coupons, DVD talk, Model Mayhem, Hospital Jobs Online, Loan.com, BrokerOutpost.com and many more. Brands is owned by investment firm KKR & Co., LP. In mid-2018, Internet Brands formed a joint venture with Henry Schein, Inc. called Henry Schein One, to deliver integrated dental technology to help improve practice management, marketing and patient communication.

The firm offers employees medical, dental, vision and life insurance; short- and long-term disability; flexible spending accounts; a 401(k) plan; and an employee assistance program.

FINANCIAL DATA: *Note: Data for latest year may not have been available at press time.*

In U.S. $	2018	2017	2016	2015	2014	2013
Revenue		175,000,000	170,000,000	155,000,000	130,000,000	120,000,000
R&D Expense						
Operating Income						
Operating Margin %						
SGA Expense						
Net Income						
Operating Cash Flow						
Capital Expenditure						
EBITDA						
Return on Assets %						
Return on Equity %						
Debt to Equity						

CONTACT INFORMATION:

Phone: 310-280-4000   Fax:
Toll-Free: 800-692-2200
Address: 909 N. Sepulveda Blvd., 11/Fl, El Segundo, CA 90245 United States

STOCK TICKER/OTHER:

Stock Ticker: Private
Employees: 1,000
Parent Company: KKR & Co LP

Exchange:
Fiscal Year Ends: 12/31

SALARIES/BONUSES:

Top Exec. Salary: $ Bonus: $
Second Exec. Salary: $ Bonus: $

OTHER THOUGHTS:

Estimated Female Officers or Directors: 2
Hot Spot for Advancement for Women/Minorities: Y

Internet Initiative Japan Inc

www.iij.ad.jp

NAIC Code: 517110

TYPES OF BUSINESS:

Internet Service Provider
Web Design & Hosting
Security Services
Systems Integration
Network Equipment
IT Outsourcing & Consulting
ATM Operation

BRANDS/DIVISIONS/AFFILIATES:

Trust Networks Inc
IIJ ISDN/F
IIJ Line Management/F
Japan Travel SIM

CONTACTS: Note: Officers with more than one job title may be intentionally listed here more than once.

Koichi Suzuki, CEO
Eijiro Katsu, Pres.
Akihisa Watai, CFO
Kazuhiro Tokita, Sr. Exec. Officer
Masayoshi Tobita, Exec. Managing Officer
Junichi Shimagami, Exec. Managing Officer
Kiyoshi Ishida, Exec. Managing Officer

GROWTH PLANS/SPECIAL FEATURES:

Internet Initiative Japan, Inc. (IIJ) provides internet access and services to consumers, corporations and other internet service providers primarily throughout Japan, focusing on premium services for high-end corporate customers. The firm offers its customers internet connectivity, wide area network (WAN), systems integration and outsourcing services. IIJ's connectivity services include services for both corporate and residential usage, and include access such as asymmetric digital subscriber line (ADSL), fiber optic, worldwide interoperability for microwave access (WiMAX), 3G and long-term evolution (LTE) wireless data connection. IIJ also provides LTE SIM (subscriber identity module) cards with voice call function. For corporate customers, the firm primarily offers services such as: internet protocol (IP) and data center connectivity; IIJ mobile, broadband internet connectivity; IIJ ISDN/F, which provides internet access for integrated services digital network (ISDN) lines; mobile virtual network enabler (MVNE), for generating subscriptions; and IIJ Line Management/F services, which procures FLETS connected services. For residential customers, IIJ provides internet connectivity from its point-of-presence (POP) locations via leased lines and dial-up connections over local exchange facilities. It operates 30 primary POPs for dedicated access and one universal POP for nationwide dial-up access. The firm's WAN service is primarily marketed to its corporate customers and features a closed network service that uses dedicated lines. The company's systems integration services cover systems construction, operation and maintenance. Its outsourcing services include outsourcing relating to security, networks, servers and businesses; maintenance, monitoring and provision of network equipment; email and web servers; and unauthorized access prevention. In addition, IIJ sells prepaid SIM cards, called Japan Travel SIM, for foreign visitors, which are primarily sold in stores located in the country's train stations. Subsidiary Trust Networks, Inc. operates ATMs and their corresponding network systems.

FINANCIAL DATA: Note: Data for latest year may not have been available at press time.

In U.S. $	2018	2017	2016	2015	2014	2013
Revenue	1,633,002,000	1,463,612,000	1,304,616,000	1,141,382,000	1,059,962,000	985,534,300
R&D Expense	4,521,474	4,325,458	4,222,303	4,093,657	3,908,439	3,803,057
Operating Income	62,724,490	47,624,540	56,956,380	47,076,640	53,088,010	71,911,570
Operating Margin %	3.84	3.25%	4.36%	4.12%	5.00%	7.29%
SGA Expense	194,638,900	182,232,000	167,516,600	153,569,500	138,410,400	126,993,500
Net Income	47,389,330	29,371,750	37,458,090	30,814,790	41,205,080	49,167,540
Operating Cash Flow	123,012,800	68,340,860	111,787,500	119,771,900	81,504,890	89,406,790
Capital Expenditure	146,284,000	98,545,500	101,092,100	75,663,350	84,631,910	51,840,440
EBITDA	190,896,800	154,204,700	151,713,700	139,642,600	142,422,100	144,256,300
Return on Assets %	3.51%	2.48%	3.56%	3.12%	4.77%	6.81%
Return on Equity %	7.29%	4.81%	6.34%	5.42%	9.11%	15.08%
Debt to Equity	0.36	0.28	0.11	0.06	0.07	0.16

CONTACT INFORMATION:

Phone: 81 352056500   Fax: 81 352596311
Toll-Free:
Address: Iidabashi Grand Bloom, 2-10-2 Fujimi, Chiyoda-ku, Tokyo, 102-0071 Japan

STOCK TICKER/OTHER:

Stock Ticker: IIJI   Exchange: NAS
Employees: 3,104   Fiscal Year Ends: 03/31
Parent Company:

SALARIES/BONUSES:

Top Exec. Salary: $ Bonus: $
Second Exec. Salary: $ Bonus: $

OTHER THOUGHTS:

Estimated Female Officers or Directors:
Hot Spot for Advancement for Women/Minorities:

Intralinks Inc

www.intralinks.com

NAIC Code: 511210H

TYPES OF BUSINESS:

Software-as-a-Service Technologies

BRANDS/DIVISIONS/AFFILIATES:

SS&C Technologies Holdings Inc
Intralinks Virtual Data Room
Intralinks VIA Elite
Intralinks VIA Pro

CONTACTS: *Note: Officers with more than one job title may be intentionally listed here more than once.*

Leif O'Leary, CEO
Christopher Lafond, CFO
Michal Kimeldorfer, Executive VP, Divisional
Aditya Joshi, Executive VP, Divisional
Leif OLeary, Executive VP, Divisional
Scott Semel, Executive VP

GROWTH PLANS/SPECIAL FEATURES:

Intralinks, Inc. provides financial technology for global banking, deal-making and capital market industries. The firm pioneered the virtual data room, and its technologies enable and secure the flow of information. Intralinks facilitates strategic initiatives such as mergers and acquisitions, capital raising and investor reporting. Its solutions enhance these activities by streamlining operations, reducing risk, improving client experiences and increasing visibility. Intralinks serves nearly all of the Fortune 1000 and has executed approximately $35 trillion worth of financial transactions on its platform. Products of the company include: Intralinks Virtual Data Room, featuring web and mobile interface, 16 user roles with dynamic permission management, full-text indexing and search, question/answer workflow, and pre-configured solutions for key deal types; Intralinks VIA Elite, featuring flexible workspaces to manage large-scale users/content/business processes, dynamic permission management, custom metadata and configurable dashboards, tasking/notifications, granular user activity reporting, pre-configured solutions for key enterprise business processes and Intralinks APIs (application programming interfaces); and Intralinks VIA Pro, featuring user-defined collaborative workspaces, in-line viewing/editing/annotation, secure access from web browsers and apps, version tracking and archiving, and seamless integration on web and desktop. In September 2018, Intralinks was acquired by SS&C Technologies Holdings, Inc. from Siris Capital Group, LLC for $1.5 billion.

FINANCIAL DATA: *Note: Data for latest year may not have been available at press time.*

In U.S. $	2018	2017	2016	2015	2014	2013
Revenue		321,000,000	300,000,000	276,152,992	255,820,992	234,496,000
R&D Expense						
Operating Income						
Operating Margin %						
SGA Expense						
Net Income				-30,384,000	-26,496,000	-15,278,000
Operating Cash Flow						
Capital Expenditure						
EBITDA						
Return on Assets %						
Return on Equity %						
Debt to Equity						

CONTACT INFORMATION:

Phone: 212 543-7700   Fax: 212 543-7978
Toll-Free: 866-468-7254
Address: 150 East 42nd St., 8/Fl, New York, NY 10017 United States

STOCK TICKER/OTHER:

Stock Ticker: Subsidiary   Exchange:
Employees: 810   Fiscal Year Ends: 12/31
Parent Company: SS&C Technologies Holdings Inc

SALARIES/BONUSES:

Top Exec. Salary: $ Bonus: $
Second Exec. Salary: $ Bonus: $

OTHER THOUGHTS:

Estimated Female Officers or Directors: 1
Hot Spot for Advancement for Women/Minorities:

Intuit Inc

NAIC Code: 511210Q

www.intuit.com

TYPES OF BUSINESS:

Computer Software-Financial Management
Business Accounting Software
Consumer Finance Software
Tax Preparation Software
Online Financial Services

BRANDS/DIVISIONS/AFFILIATES:

QuickBooks Online
Mint
Turbo
Turbo Tax
Intuit Tax Freedom Project
Lacerte
ProSeries
ProConnect Tax Online

CONTACTS: *Note: Officers with more than one job title may be intentionally listed here more than once.*

Michelle Clatterbuck, CFO
Brad Smith, Chairman of the Board
Mark Flournoy, Chief Accounting Officer
H. Stansbury, Chief Technology Officer
Gregory Johnson, Executive VP
Laura Fennell, Executive VP
Scott Cook, Founder
Kerry McLean, General Counsel
Sasan Goodarzi, General Manager, Divisional
Alex Chriss, Other Executive Officer
Marianna Tessel, Other Executive Officer

GROWTH PLANS/SPECIAL FEATURES:

Intuit, Inc. is a provider of software and web-based services, specializing in financial management and tax solutions. The company has three business segments: small business, consumer and strategic partner. The small business segment targets small businesses, as well as the accounting professionals who serve them. This division's products include QuickBooks Online, which offers financial management tools; online payroll solutions; online payment solutions; an Intuit developer group, which provides tools that third-party developers need to create online and mobile applications that personalize and add value to QuickBooks; desktop payments solutions; technical support; and financial supplies. The consumer segment offers the Mint and Turbo brands of financial improvement products. Mint and Turbo help consumers understand and improve their financial lives by offering a view of their financial health. Turbo Tax solutions are designed to enable individuals to prepare and file their own federal and state personal income tax returns quickly and accurately. This division's Intuit Tax Freedom Project offers online federal and state income tax return preparation and electronic filing services at no charge to eligible taxpayers. The strategic partner segment targets professional accountants in the U.S. and Canada, who are essential to both small business success and tax preparation and filing. This division's tax offerings include Lacerte, ProSeries, ProFile and ProConnect Tax Online. During 2018, the firm acquired Exactor, Inc.; TSheets.com, LLC; and Applatix, Inc.

Intuit employees receive health, dental and life insurance; and 401(k) and employee stock purchase plans.

FINANCIAL DATA: *Note: Data for latest year may not have been available at press time.*

In U.S. $	2018	2017	2016	2015	2014	2013
Revenue	5,964,000,000	5,177,000,000	4,694,000,000	4,192,000,000	4,506,000,000	4,171,000,000
R&D Expense	1,186,000,000	998,000,000	881,000,000	798,000,000	758,000,000	685,000,000
Operating Income	1,497,000,000	1,395,000,000	1,242,000,000	886,000,000	1,314,000,000	1,233,000,000
Operating Margin %		26.94%	26.45%	21.13%	29.16%	29.56%
SGA Expense	2,298,000,000	1,973,000,000	1,807,000,000	1,771,000,000	1,746,000,000	1,641,000,000
Net Income	1,211,000,000	971,000,000	979,000,000	365,000,000	907,000,000	858,000,000
Operating Cash Flow	2,112,000,000	1,599,000,000	1,401,000,000	1,504,000,000	1,446,000,000	1,366,000,000
Capital Expenditure	124,000,000	230,000,000	522,000,000	261,000,000	201,000,000	209,000,000
EBITDA	1,776,000,000	1,634,000,000	1,476,000,000	970,000,000	1,542,000,000	1,472,000,000
Return on Assets %		23.34%	21.24%	7.17%	16.97%	16.87%
Return on Equity %		77.21%	56.05%	13.49%	27.44%	27.34%
Debt to Equity		0.32	0.42	0.21	0.16	0.14

CONTACT INFORMATION:

Phone: 650 944-6000   Fax: 650 944-3060
Toll-Free: 800-446-8848
Address: 2700 Coast Ave., Mountain View, CA 94043 United States

STOCK TICKER/OTHER:

Stock Ticker: INTU   Exchange: NAS
Employees: 8,200   Fiscal Year Ends: 07/31
Parent Company:

SALARIES/BONUSES:

Top Exec. Salary: $1,000,000   Bonus: $
Second Exec. Salary: $750,000   Bonus: $

OTHER THOUGHTS:

Estimated Female Officers or Directors: 5
Hot Spot for Advancement for Women/Minorities: Y

InVisionApp Inc

www.invisionapp.com

NAIC Code: 511210N

TYPES OF BUSINESS:

Computer Software, Product Lifecycle, Engineering, Design & CAD

BRANDS/DIVISIONS/AFFILIATES:

GROWTH PLANS/SPECIAL FEATURES:

InVisionApp, Inc. offers a web and mobile design collaboration platform. The company gives companies of all sizes the freedom to design, review and user-test products without writing a single line of code. InVision's intuitive tools for prototyping, task management and version control unifies the entire design process within one place. Features offered by the platform include design prototyping, design sharing and presentation, design feedback and commenting, real-time design meetings and whiteboarding, design organization and collaboration, project management for designers, inspection and user-testing and research. InVision is used for prototyping for websites, web apps, mobile apps, wearables and more. Over 5 million designers utilize InVision, which is free of charge.

The company offers its employees health benefits, fitness programs, salary options and the freedom to work from anywhere.

CONTACTS: *Note: Officers with more than one job title may be intentionally listed here more than once.*

Clark Valberg, CEO

FINANCIAL DATA: *Note: Data for latest year may not have been available at press time.*

In U.S. $	2018	2017	2016	2015	2014	2013
Revenue						
R&D Expense						
Operating Income						
Operating Margin %						
SGA Expense						
Net Income						
Operating Cash Flow						
Capital Expenditure						
EBITDA						
Return on Assets %						
Return on Equity %						
Debt to Equity						

CONTACT INFORMATION:

Phone: 212-209-3061   Fax: 212-371-5500
Toll-Free: 877-932-7111
Address: 41 Madison Ave., 25/Fl, New York, NY 10010 United States

STOCK TICKER/OTHER:

Stock Ticker: Private   Exchange:
Employees: 220   Fiscal Year Ends:
Parent Company:

SALARIES/BONUSES:

Top Exec. Salary: $ Bonus: $
Second Exec. Salary: $ Bonus: $

OTHER THOUGHTS:

Estimated Female Officers or Directors:
Hot Spot for Advancement for Women/Minorities:

j2 Global Inc

www.j2global.com

NAIC Code: 517110

TYPES OF BUSINESS:

Unified Messaging & Communication Services
Internet-Based Faxing
Internet Conferencing
Cloud-Based Communications Services
Customer Relationship Management Solutions

BRANDS/DIVISIONS/AFFILIATES:

MyFax
eVoice
OneBox
KeepItSafe
LiveDrive
FuseMail
ThreatTrack
Lifescript

CONTACTS: Note: Officers with more than one job title may be intentionally listed here more than once.

Vivek Shah, CEO
Richard Ressler, Chairman of the Board
Steve Dunn, Chief Accounting Officer
Jeremy Rossen, General Counsel
R. Turicchi, President

GROWTH PLANS/SPECIAL FEATURES:

jj2 Global, Inc. is a global provider of internet service. Through its cloud services division, the company provides cloud services to consumers and businesses (any size), and licenses intellectual property (IP) to third parties. This segment's cloud-based eFax and MyFax online fax services enable users to receive faxes in their email inboxes and to send faxes via the internet. eVoice and Onebox provide customers a virtual phone system with various available enhancements. KeepItSafe enables customers to securely back up data and dispose of tape or other physical systems. LiveDrive provides online backup with added file sync features for professionals and individuals. The FuseMail service provides customers email, archival and perimeter protection solutions, while Campaigner provides enhanced email marketing solutions. Campaigner also provides enhanced email marketing solutions; and the CampaignerCRM customer relationship management solution. j2's digital media division operates a portfolio of web properties providing technology, gaming and lifestyle content, and an innovative data-driven platform connecting advertisers with visitors to those properties and to visitors of third party web sites that are part of the division's advertising network. This segment consists of the web properties and business operations of Ziff Davis. The Ziff Davis portfolio of web properties, including PCMag.com, IGN.com, Speedtest.net, AskMen.com, Mashable.com, Offers.com and Everydayhealth.com, features reviews of technology, gaming and men's lifestyle products and services; news and commentary related to these vertical markets; professional networking tools for IT professionals; speed testing for internet and network connections; and online deals and discounts for consumers. In early-2018, j2 Global acquired ThreatTrack, a cloud services and security firm; and Lifescript, a digital health media firm.

FINANCIAL DATA: Note: Data for latest year may not have been available at press time.

In U.S. $	2018	2017	2016	2015	2014	2013
Revenue		1,117,838,000	874,255,000	720,815,000	599,030,000	520,801,000
R&D Expense		46,004,000	38,046,000	34,329,000	30,680,000	25,485,000
Operating Income		245,708,000	242,566,000	199,382,000	186,206,000	175,423,000
Operating Margin %		21.98%	27.74%	27.66%	31.08%	33.68%
SGA Expense		653,813,000	446,543,000	364,146,000	276,155,000	233,000,000
Net Income		139,425,000	152,439,000	133,636,000	125,327,000	107,522,000
Operating Cash Flow		264,419,000	282,387,000	229,061,000	177,231,000	193,324,000
Capital Expenditure		41,835,000	29,067,000	18,752,000	17,165,000	32,827,000
EBITDA		407,749,000	364,657,000	292,595,000	249,159,000	215,211,000
Return on Assets %		6.09%	7.79%	7.51%	8.69%	10.00%
Return on Equity %		14.22%	16.64%	15.37%	16.28%	16.52%
Debt to Equity		0.98	0.65	0.67	0.72	0.34

CONTACT INFORMATION:

Phone: 323 860-9200   Fax: 323 860-9201
Toll-Free:
Address: 6922 Hollywood Blvd., Ste. 500, Los Angeles, CA 90028 United States

STOCK TICKER/OTHER:

Stock Ticker: JCOM   Exchange: NAS
Employees: 2,426   Fiscal Year Ends: 12/31
Parent Company:

SALARIES/BONUSES:

Top Exec. Salary: $1,082,174   Bonus: $
Second Exec. Salary: $636,667   Bonus: $

OTHER THOUGHTS:

Estimated Female Officers or Directors: 2
Hot Spot for Advancement for Women/Minorities:

Sales, profits and employees may be estimates. Financial information, benefits and other data can change quickly and may vary from those stated here.

JAGGAER

www.jaggaer.com

NAIC Code: 511210A

| **TYPES OF BUSINESS:** |
| Procurement & Ordering Software |

GROWTH PLANS/SPECIAL FEATURES:

JAGGAER provides comprehensive source-to-pay solutions. These software-as-a-service (SaaS), source-to-pay solutions provide visibility, insights and recommendations to procurement leaders and suppliers. The result is a fluid supply chain driven by spend analytics, contract management and accounts payable solutions. JAGGAER's solutions are grouped into two categories: indirect and direct. Indirect solutions include accounts payable, contract management, eProcurement, inventory control, savings management, sourcing, spend analytics and supplier management. Direct solutions include bring your own data (BYOD), data intelligence, project management, quality management, supply chain management, supplier management and strategic sourcing. JAGGAER's support and services include professional services, customer support, supplier support, training, uptime report and portal solutions. Based in the U.S., the firm has additional domestic offices as well as international offices in Singapore, Germany, Mexico, Austria, Italy, France, Spain, Netherlands, the U.K., Australia, United Arab Emirates, China, Finland and Pakistan.

SciQuest offers its employees medical and dental coverage, quarterly company lunches and a 401(k).

| **BRANDS/DIVISIONS/AFFILIATES:** |
| |

CONTACTS: *Note: Officers with more than one job title may be intentionally listed here more than once.*

Robert Bonavito, CEO
Jim Bureau, Global VP
Vic Chynoweth, CFO
Zia Zahiri, CTO
Grant Collingsworth, General Counsel
Teresa Jamison, Senior VP, Divisional
Douglas Keister, Senior VP, Divisional

FINANCIAL DATA: *Note: Data for latest year may not have been available at press time.*

In U.S. $	2018	2017	2016	2015	2014	2013
Revenue		122,000,000	110,000,000	105,353,000	101,932,000	90,231,000
R&D Expense						
Operating Income						
Operating Margin %						
SGA Expense						
Net Income				1,862,000	-69,000	-4,734,000
Operating Cash Flow						
Capital Expenditure						
EBITDA						
Return on Assets %						
Return on Equity %						
Debt to Equity						

CONTACT INFORMATION:

Phone: 919 659-2100   Fax: 919 659-2199
Toll-Free: 888-638-7322
Address: 3020 Carrington Mill Blvd., Ste. 100, Morrisville, NC 27560
United States

STOCK TICKER/OTHER:

Stock Ticker: Private   Exchange:
Employees: 510   Fiscal Year Ends: 12/31
Parent Company:

SALARIES/BONUSES:

Top Exec. Salary: $ Bonus: $
Second Exec. Salary: $ Bonus: $

OTHER THOUGHTS:

Estimated Female Officers or Directors: 3
Hot Spot for Advancement for Women/Minorities: Y

Jasper Infotech Pvt Ltd

www.snapdeal.com

NAIC Code: 454111

TYPES OF BUSINESS:

Electronic Shopping

BRANDS/DIVISIONS/AFFILIATES:

Snapdeal.com

CONTACTS: *Note: Officers with more than one job title may be intentionally listed here more than once.*

Kunal Bahl, CEO
Rohit Bansal, COO
Anup Ajit Vikal, CFO
Amit Maheshwari, VP-Fashion Merch.
Amitabh Misra, VP-Eng.
Abhishek Passi, VP-Bus. Strategy
Rasika Mathur, Dir.-Corp. Comm.
Vijay Ajmera, VP-Finance
Ankit Khanna Prod Wizar, VP-Prod.
Dipakshi Khaira, Head-Customer Svcs.
Megha Ajwani, Head-Bus. Dev.
Tony Navin, VP-Bus. Dev.

GROWTH PLANS/SPECIAL FEATURES:

Jasper Infotech Pvt. Ltd., operating the Snapdeal.com website, is an online marketplace based in New Delhi, India. The firm boasts having millions of registered users and over 300,000 sellers from more than 6,000 towns and cities in India. Users view over 60 million products consisting of over 125,000 different brands in 800 shopping categories. Jasper's products are grouped into the following categories: mobile and tablets; computers, office and gaming; electronics; home and living; women's fashion; men's fashion, toys, kids and babies; daily needs, including food, household essentials, personal care and more; sports, fitness and outdoor; motors and accessories, which sells automobiles; and books, music and gift cards. In addition to these offerings, the company sells automobiles online. Jasper Infotech has online shopping apps for both Android and iOS devices that lets users shop, book flights and services, buy bus tickets and order food. The Snapdeal app has more than 40 million downloads.

FINANCIAL DATA: *Note: Data for latest year may not have been available at press time.*

In U.S. $	2018	2017	2016	2015	2014	2013
Revenue	67,024,300	166,708,000	182,655,000			
R&D Expense						
Operating Income						
Operating Margin %						
SGA Expense						
Net Income	-94,233,700	-715,984,000	-500,152,000			
Operating Cash Flow						
Capital Expenditure						
EBITDA						
Return on Assets %						
Return on Equity %						
Debt to Equity						

CONTACT INFORMATION:

Phone: 91-92126-92126   Fax:
Toll-Free:
Address: Okhla Industrial Area, Phase III, 246, 1/Fl., New Delhi, 110020 India

STOCK TICKER/OTHER:

Stock Ticker: Private
Employees: 800
Parent Company:

Exchange:
Fiscal Year Ends: 03/31

SALARIES/BONUSES:

Top Exec. Salary: $ Bonus: $
Second Exec. Salary: $ Bonus: $

OTHER THOUGHTS:

Estimated Female Officers or Directors: 4
Hot Spot for Advancement for Women/Minorities: Y

JD.com Inc

NAIC Code: 454111

ir.jd.com

TYPES OF BUSINESS:

Online Retailer

BRANDS/DIVISIONS/AFFILIATES:

JD X

CONTACTS: *Note: Officers with more than one job title may be intentionally listed here more than once.*

Richard Liu, CEO
Sidney Huang, CFO
Lei Xu, CMO
Rain Yu Long, Chief Human Resources Officer
Chen Zhang, Chief Technology Officer
Richard Liu, Chmn.

GROWTH PLANS/SPECIAL FEATURES:

JD.com, Inc. was founded in 1998, and is a leading eCommerce and retail company in China, serving over 300 million active customers with direct access to products. Through its website and mobile apps, the firm offers a wide selection of products at competitive prices. JD has more than 500 warehouses with an aggregate gross floor area of more than 124.8 million square feet, with products consisting of every major category, including electronics, apparel, home furnishings, consumer goods, fresh food, home appliances and more. JD's nationwide logistics network and data-driven delivery technologies enable the firm to provide customers with same- and next-day delivery throughout the country. It has achieved rates of over 90% on orders being delivered the same day or the next day. To accomplish these tasks and to keep up with demand, JD engages in building powerful artificial intelligence (AI) and machine learning tools that also offer insight into customer behavior and experience. Its innovative software solutions provide eCommerce and payment capabilities for its thousands of brand partners. JD has a research and development center in Silicon Valley, USA. Smart logistics research is led by the JD X division, with a focus on innovating the next generation of smart logistics in relation to automated fulfillment capabilities such as drones, autonomous delivery vehicles and automated warehouse technologies.

FINANCIAL DATA: *Note: Data for latest year may not have been available at press time.*

In U.S. $	2018	2017	2016	2015	2014	2013
Revenue		52,732,720,000	37,857,350,000	26,383,980,000	16,737,100,000	10,091,520,000
R&D Expense						
Operating Income		1,160,076	-312,162,100	-539,844,700	-844,469,900	-84,240,810
Operating Margin %			-.82%	-2.04%	-5.04%	-.83%
SGA Expense		3,752,714,000	6,049,659,000	4,073,286,000	2,790,428,000	1,080,337,000
Net Income		-22,159,040	-554,029,200	-1,364,849,000	-727,155,500	-7,262,156
Operating Cash Flow		3,612,416,000	1,275,926,000	-263,647,900	147,722,500	519,541,100
Capital Expenditure		1,652,701,000	649,119,600	771,311,600	422,358,300	188,045,700
EBITDA		768,060,200	95,876,790	-975,138,800	-479,934,200	36,622,810
Return on Assets %		-.08%	-3.10%	-12.36%	-28.00%	-11.32%
Return on Equity %		-.35%	-11.81%	-27.56%	-55.43%	-47.23%
Debt to Equity		0.20	0.32	0.09		

CONTACT INFORMATION:

Phone: 86-10 8262 5500   Fax: 86-10 8261-5208
Toll-Free:
Address: 20/Fl., Bldg. A, No. 18 Kechuang II St., Daxing Distr., Beijing, 101111 China

STOCK TICKER/OTHER:

Stock Ticker: JD
Employees: 160,000
Parent Company:

Exchange: NAS
Fiscal Year Ends:

SALARIES/BONUSES:

Top Exec. Salary: $ Bonus: $
Second Exec. Salary: $ Bonus: $

OTHER THOUGHTS:

Estimated Female Officers or Directors:
Hot Spot for Advancement for Women/Minorities:

JDA Software Group Inc

www.jda.com

NAIC Code: 511210A

TYPES OF BUSINESS:

Computer Software, Supply Chain & Logistics
Retail Industry Software
Consulting Services

BRANDS/DIVISIONS/AFFILIATES:

RedPrairie Holding Inc

CONTACTS: Note: Officers with more than one job title may be intentionally listed here more than once.

Girish Rishi, CEO
Kevin Iaquinto, CMO
Brian Boylan, Chief Human Resources Officer
David King, Exec. VP-Prod. Dev.
David Kennedy, Chief Legal Officer
David Gai, Exec. VP-Svcs.
Michael Capellas, Chmn.

GROWTH PLANS/SPECIAL FEATURES:

JDA Software Group, Inc., owned by RedPrairie Holding, Inc., is a leading provider of seamless supply chain planning and execution solutions for retailers, manufacturers, logistics providers and wholesale distributors. More than 4,000 global customers run JDA. The company offers solutions in broad categories: adaptable manufacturing & distribution solutions, profitable omni-channel retail solutions and solutions for service-based industries. Adaptable manufacturing & distribution solutions are further divided into three groups: category management, which includes assortment optimization, category knowledge base, channel clustering, floor planning, planogram generator and space planning; intelligent fulfillment, including demand, flowcasting, inventory visibility, track/trace, transportation management, warehouse labor management and warehouse management; and manufacturing planning, including agile control tower, demand planning, enterprise planning/sequencing, inventory optimization, order promising and sales/operations planning. Profitable omni-channel retail solutions are further divided into four groups: category management, including assortment optimization, category knowledge, channel clustering, floor planning, planogram generator and space planning; intelligent fulfillment, including demand, flowcasting, inventory visibility, trace/track, transportation management and warehouse management; retail planning, including allocation, assortment, demand and enterprise planning, retail lifecycle pricing and retail.me; and store operations, including enterprise stores, in-store picking, task management and workforce management. Last, solutions for service-based industries include pricing and revenue management for the hospitality, media and travel sectors. JDA services include cloud, custom solution development, customer support, education/training, implementation and performance services. The firm has more than 40 locations worldwide, with global centers in Mexico, India and Poland.

Employees of JDA are offered medical, dental and vision coverage; life insurance; and tuition reimbursement.

FINANCIAL DATA: Note: Data for latest year may not have been available at press time.

In U.S. $	2018	2017	2016	2015	2014	2013
Revenue	1,125,000,000	935,000,000	850,000,000	762,000,000	710,000,000	700,000,000
R&D Expense						
Operating Income						
Operating Margin %						
SGA Expense						
Net Income						
Operating Cash Flow						
Capital Expenditure						
EBITDA						
Return on Assets %						
Return on Equity %						
Debt to Equity						

CONTACT INFORMATION:

Phone: 480 308-3000 Fax: 480 308-3001
Toll-Free: 800-438-5301
Address: 15059 N. Scottsdale Rd., Ste. 400, Scottsdale, AZ 85254-2666
United States

STOCK TICKER/OTHER:

Stock Ticker: Private Exchange:
Employees: 4,300 Fiscal Year Ends: 12/31
Parent Company: RedPrairie Holding Inc

SALARIES/BONUSES:

Top Exec. Salary: $ Bonus: $
Second Exec. Salary: $ Bonus: $

OTHER THOUGHTS:

Estimated Female Officers or Directors: 2
Hot Spot for Advancement for Women/Minorities:

Jet.com Inc

jet.com

NAIC Code: 454111

TYPES OF BUSINESS:

Online Marketplace

BRANDS/DIVISIONS/AFFILIATES:

Wal-Mart Stores Inc

GROWTH PLANS/SPECIAL FEATURES:

Jet.com, Inc. operates an online marketplace, featuring low prices on millions of items which are sold by participating dealers. Merchandise categories include grocery, household supplies, health and beauty, electronics and computers, toys and games, home, furniture, baby, pet supplies, appliances, sports/fitness and outdoor. Shipping is free if the total of merchandise purchased is more than $35, and there is 2-day delivery on thousands of essential items. No membership is needed to purchase from Jet.com. Salt Lake City-based customer service representatives are available 24/7. Jet.com, Inc. operates as a subsidiary of Wal-Mart Stores, Inc.

CONTACTS: *Note: Officers with more than one job title may be intentionally listed here more than once.*

Marc Lore, CEO

FINANCIAL DATA: *Note: Data for latest year may not have been available at press time.*

In U.S. $	2018	2017	2016	2015	2014	2013
Revenue						
R&D Expense						
Operating Income						
Operating Margin %						
SGA Expense						
Net Income						
Operating Cash Flow						
Capital Expenditure						
EBITDA						
Return on Assets %						
Return on Equity %						
Debt to Equity						

CONTACT INFORMATION:

Phone: 844-538-2255   Fax:
Toll-Free: 855-538-4323
Address: 221 River St., Hoboken, NJ 07030 United States

STOCK TICKER/OTHER:

Stock Ticker: Subsidiary   Exchange:
Employees: 500   Fiscal Year Ends:
Parent Company: Wal-Mart Stores Inc (Walmart)

SALARIES/BONUSES:

Top Exec. Salary: $ Bonus: $
Second Exec. Salary: $ Bonus: $

OTHER THOUGHTS:

Estimated Female Officers or Directors:
Hot Spot for Advancement for Women/Minorities:

Jio (Reliance Jio Infocomm Limited)

www.jio.com

NAIC Code: 517210

TYPES OF BUSINESS:

Wireless Telecommunications Carriers (except Satellite)
LTE network

BRANDS/DIVISIONS/AFFILIATES:

Reliance Industries Limited
Jiofi
Jio
MyJio
www.jio.com

CONTACTS: *Note: Officers with more than one job title may be intentionally listed here more than once.*

Mukesh D. Ambani, Chmn.

GROWTH PLANS/SPECIAL FEATURES:

Reliance Jio Infocomm Limited (better know as simply Jio), a subsidiary of Reliance Industries Limited, is an Indian mobile network operator. The company operates a national long-term evolution (LTE) network with coverage across all telecommunication circles. Jio has built a world-class, all-IP data strong future proof network with 4G long-term evolution (LTE) technology, which utilizes voice over LTE to provide voice service on its network. The company's future-ready network can be easily upgraded to support even more data as technologies advance on to 5G, 6G and beyond. Jio provides broadband services to customers using Wi-MAX as access technology pan India. Its 4G data routers and phones are marketed under the JioFi and Jio brand names. Its MyJio app enables users to manage their Jio accounts and related devices, connect to Wi-Fi, chat, watch entertainment, listen to music, read online magazines and news, secure data, file into the cloud, make payments and connect with doctors and health test results. Devices can be purchased in-store (in the Mumbai area), as well as online at www.jio.com. Jio is a revolutionary wireless service that sells at rock bottom prices. Jio may enable even very-low-income people in India to carry a phone. Jio has the ability to offer free calls and very cheap internet access by relying on advertising and content revenues.

FINANCIAL DATA: *Note: Data for latest year may not have been available at press time.*

In U.S. $	2018	2017	2016	2015	2014	2013
Revenue		17,797,100	5,699,870	218,575	96,888	
R&D Expense						
Operating Income						
Operating Margin %						
SGA Expense						
Net Income		-5,235,450	-6,276,040	-6,190,310	-2,066,380	
Operating Cash Flow						
Capital Expenditure						
EBITDA						
Return on Assets %						
Return on Equity %						
Debt to Equity						

CONTACT INFORMATION:

Phone: 91-22-44770000   Fax:
Toll-Free:
Address: 9/Fl, Maker Chambers IV, 222, Nariman Point, Mumbai, Maharashtra 400 021 India

STOCK TICKER/OTHER:

Stock Ticker: Subsidiary   Exchange:
Employees: Fiscal Year Ends: 03/31
Parent Company: Reliance Industries Limited

SALARIES/BONUSES:

Top Exec. Salary: $ Bonus: $
Second Exec. Salary: $ Bonus: $

OTHER THOUGHTS:

Estimated Female Officers or Directors:
Hot Spot for Advancement for Women/Minorities:

Juniper Networks Inc

NAIC Code: 334210A

TYPES OF BUSINESS:

Networking Equipment
IP Networking Systems
Internet Routers
Network Security Products
Internet Software
Intrusion Prevention
Application Acceleration

BRANDS/DIVISIONS/AFFILIATES:

ACX
MX
PTX
Cloud CPE
NorthStar
EX
QFX
Junos

CONTACTS: *Note: Officers with more than one job title may be intentionally listed here more than once.*

Rami Rahim, CEO
Kenneth Miller, CFO
Scott Kriens, Chairman of the Board
Terrance Spidell, Chief Accounting Officer
Bikash Koley, Chief Technology Officer
Andy Athreya, Executive VP
Vincent Molinaro, Other Executive Officer
Brian Martin, Senior VP

GROWTH PLANS/SPECIAL FEATURES:

Juniper Networks, Inc. designs, develops and sells products and services for high-performance networks. These products help customers build highly scalable, reliable, secure and cost-effective networks for their businesses. Juniper sells its products in more than 150 countries across three geographic regions: Americas; Europe, Middle East and Africa (EMEA); and Asia Pacific. The company's offerings address high-performance network requirements for global service providers, cloud environments, enterprises, governments and research and public-sector organizations who view the network as critical to its business success. Routing products include the firm's ACX, MX and PTX, as well as its Cloud CPE end-to-end solution and NorthStar wide-area network controller. Switching products include the EX and QFX series, as well as the disaggregated version of Junos software, and the open networking switch designed to combine a cloud-optimized open compute project with the Junos operating system. Security products include the SRX series for data center gateway services, and for campus and branch gateway services; the vSRX virtual firewall; advanced malware protection; and the Sky ATP (advanced threat prevention), a cloud-based service designed to use both static and dynamic analysis with machine learning to find unknown threat signatures (zero-day attacks). Sky ATP is integrated with SRX firewalls and routers for automated enforcement. Other security products include the Cyphort software, offering security analytics for advanced threat defense. Juniper Networks owns over 3,300 issued or pending technology patents. In November 2018, Juniper announced its intent to acquire HTBASE, which has developed a unique and disruptive platform for software-defined enterprise multi-cloud.

Juniper Networks offers medical, dental, prescription and vision insurance; paid time off; and stock/savings plans.

FINANCIAL DATA: *Note: Data for latest year may not have been available at press time.*

In U.S. $	2018	2017	2016	2015	2014	2013
Revenue		5,027,200,000	4,990,100,000	4,857,800,000	4,627,100,000	4,669,100,000
R&D Expense		980,700,000	1,013,700,000	994,500,000	1,006,200,000	1,043,200,000
Operating Income		913,700,000	893,000,000	911,400,000	597,300,000	605,000,000
Operating Margin %		18.17%	17.89%	18.76%	12.90%	12.95%
SGA Expense		1,177,700,000	1,197,800,000	1,172,700,000	1,254,700,000	1,293,200,000
Net Income		306,200,000	592,700,000	633,700,000	-334,300,000	439,800,000
Operating Cash Flow		1,260,100,000	1,106,000,000	892,500,000	763,400,000	842,300,000
Capital Expenditure		151,200,000	214,700,000	210,300,000	192,900,000	243,100,000
EBITDA		1,138,600,000	1,131,800,000	1,112,000,000	166,700,000	773,800,000
Return on Assets %		3.14%	6.48%	7.44%	-3.56%	4.36%
Return on Equity %		6.35%	12.42%	13.35%	-5.47%	6.15%
Debt to Equity		0.45	0.42	0.36	0.27	0.13

CONTACT INFORMATION:

Phone: 408 745-2000   Fax: 408 745-2100
Toll-Free: 888-586-4737
Address: 1133 Innovation Way, Sunnyvale, CA 94089 United States

STOCK TICKER/OTHER:

Stock Ticker: JNPR   Exchange: NYS
Employees: 9,832   Fiscal Year Ends: 12/31
Parent Company:

SALARIES/BONUSES:

Top Exec. Salary: $1,000,000   Bonus: $
Second Exec. Salary: Bonus: $500,000
$162,879

OTHER THOUGHTS:

Estimated Female Officers or Directors: 3
Hot Spot for Advancement for Women/Minorities: Y

Kakao Corporation

www.kakaocorp.com

NAIC Code: 519130

TYPES OF BUSINESS:

Internet Portal Service
E-Mail
Video on Demand
Car Ride Dispatch Service, Mobile App-Based

BRANDS/DIVISIONS/AFFILIATES:

Daum
Daum News
KakaoTalk
Kakao Page
Emotion Cards
KakaoGame
KakaoPay
KakaoT

CONTACTS: Note: Officers with more than one job title may be intentionally listed here more than once.

Jaehyuk Lee, Head-Strategy
Hyunyoung Kim, Head-Global Mgmt.
Brian Kim, Chmn.

GROWTH PLANS/SPECIAL FEATURES:

Kakao Corporation is a global mobile lifestyle platform company, with services divided into eight categories: portal, communication, contents, commerce, game, FinTech, mobility and life and social impact. Portal services include: Daum and Daum Search, each of which are search portals; and Daum News, offering world news. Communication services include KakaoTalk, which connects people via free chats on mobile devices or desktop. This service also enables users to send up to 100 MB of various file formats, such as documents, videos, images, voice and zip; video call; voice call; open chat; search online; and create talk boards, including meeting management with alerts, schedules and voting features. Contents services comprises the Kakao Page, the firm's main webtoon, cartoon and novel platform visited by users. More than 20,000 stories are available on the Kakao Page, which is visited by over 1 million readers per day. Commerce services comprise KakaoGift, an easy gift-giving delivery service offered through KakaoTalk. Gifts are curated by occasion and also creates exclusive gifts for people who want to give special gifts. The portal offers a variety of Emotion Cards for sending to people as well. The gifts and cards are payable directly through the app. Game services include KakaoGame, which includes online/mobile app role-playing games, quizzes and more. Over 500 games are offered on Kakao Game. FinTech comprises KakaoPay, a financial platform that processes transactions such as payments, receiving bills and making monetary transfers. Mobility and life services include KakaoT, a taxi service via mobile app. Last, social impact services comprises a platform that enables users or organizations to easily create project funding campaigns or even share hurts/needs with others in an effort to offer a listening ear, understanding, help or more. Kakao's AI platform combines speech, visual, recommendation and translation technologies to create an open and scalable ecosystem.

FINANCIAL DATA: Note: Data for latest year may not have been available at press time.

In U.S. $	2018	2017	2016	2015	2014	2013
Revenue		1,846,900,000	1,365,848,000	869,392,000	763,854,989	484,577,829
R&D Expense						
Operating Income						
Operating Margin %						
SGA Expense						
Net Income		119,449,000	56,127,300	65,664,600	69,600,000	60,100,000
Operating Cash Flow						
Capital Expenditure						
EBITDA						
Return on Assets %						
Return on Equity %						
Debt to Equity						

CONTACT INFORMATION:

Phone: 82-064-795-1500   Fax: 82-2-60035401
Toll-Free:
Address: 242, Cheomdan-ro, Jeju-si Jeju-do, 690 140 South Korea

SALARIES/BONUSES:

Top Exec. Salary: $ Bonus: $
Second Exec. Salary: $ Bonus: $

STOCK TICKER/OTHER:

Stock Ticker: 35720   Exchange: Seoul
Employees: 2,446   Fiscal Year Ends: 12/31
Parent Company:

OTHER THOUGHTS:

Estimated Female Officers or Directors: 1
Hot Spot for Advancement for Women/Minorities:

Sales, profits and employees may be estimates. Financial information, benefits and other data can change quickly and may vary from those stated here.

KAYAK

www.kayak.com

NAIC Code: 561510

TYPES OF BUSINESS:

Online Travel Services

BRANDS/DIVISIONS/AFFILIATES:

KAYAK.com
KAYAK Trips
Explore
Trip Huddle
Booking Holdings Inc

CONTACTS: *Note: Officers with more than one job title may be intentionally listed here more than once.*

Daniel Stephen Hafner, CEO
Paul M. English, Pres.
Paul D. Schwenk, Sr. VP-Eng.
Keith D. Melnick, Chief Comm. Officer

GROWTH PLANS/SPECIAL FEATURES:

KAYAK operates travel planning search and aggregation sites that allow users to compile and compare data gathered from hundreds of travel sites. The company offers users comparison rates for hotels, airfare, rental cars and vacation packages. KAYAK.com's tools and features include KAYAK Trips, Explore and Trip Huddle, along with its mobile application. KAYAK Trips allows users to create, manage and share trips, and includes the capability of receiving flight status alerts in real-time. Explore is an internet feature that displays prices to various places around the world, on a map, derived from the user's existing location. Trip Huddle creates a centralized location where those in a group trip can vote on destination and travel dates, whether to rent or get a hotel and all the other important group decisions that need to be made. Prices vary depending on when flights are chosen and purchased by the consumer. Each year the company processes over 2 billion queries for travel information, and its free mobile app has been downloaded more than 40 million times. The firm is owned by Booking Holdings Inc.

FINANCIAL DATA: *Note: Data for latest year may not have been available at press time.*

In U.S. $	2018	2017	2016	2015	2014	2013
Revenue		435,000,000	421,000,000	375,000,000	360,000,000	335,000,000
R&D Expense						
Operating Income						
Operating Margin %						
SGA Expense						
Net Income				8,591,807	7,584,130	
Operating Cash Flow						
Capital Expenditure						
EBITDA						
Return on Assets %						
Return on Equity %						
Debt to Equity						

CONTACT INFORMATION:

Phone: 203 899-3100   Fax: 203-899-3125
Toll-Free:
Address: 7 Market St., Stamford, CT 06902 United States

STOCK TICKER/OTHER:

Stock Ticker: Subsidiary   Exchange:
Employees: 205   Fiscal Year Ends: 12/31
Parent Company: Priceline Group Inc (The)

SALARIES/BONUSES:

Top Exec. Salary: $ Bonus: $
Second Exec. Salary: $ Bonus: $

OTHER THOUGHTS:

Estimated Female Officers or Directors: 1
Hot Spot for Advancement for Women/Minorities: Y

KDDI Corporation

NAIC Code: 517210

www.kddi.com

TYPES OF BUSINESS:
Mobile Phone Service
Value-Added Services
Cellular Phone Sales
Local & Long-Distance Phone Service
Business Services
Internet Service
Music Downloads
Public Phones

BRANDS/DIVISIONS/AFFILIATES:
au
au Smart Value
au Smart Pass
au Smart Value
au HIKARI

CONTACTS: Note: Officers with more than one job title may be intentionally listed here more than once.
Makoto Takahashi, CEO
Makoto Takahashi, Sr. VP
Kanichiro Aritomi, Vice Chmn.
Hirofumi Morozumi, Exec. VP
Hideo Yuasa, Associate Sr. VP

GROWTH PLANS/SPECIAL FEATURES:
KDDI Corporation is a Japanese telecommunications firm with a focus on mobile services under the au brand name, which has over 22.5 million mobile subscribers in Japan. The company operates in three divisions: mobile (which accounts for the majority of revenue), fixed line and all other operations. The mobile business includes the sale of mobile phone handsets and mobile phone services. Products are marketed to both consumers and enterprises. For the consumer, there is au Smart Value and au Smart Pass. Au Smart Value offers customers a discount off their smartphone usage fees and a WiMAX router if they combine their mobile service with fixed-line communications. Au Smart Pass allows customers to pay a single flat rate in return for enhanced security and support, a point service, storage of 50 GB, unlimited app downloads and discount coupons. To businesses, the firm provides smart value for business solutions, including cloud services, au smart phone and au HIKARI business, an enterprise fiber-to-the-premises (FTTP). The fixed-line business consists of local, long-distance and international telephone services, internet services, data center services and cable TV services. The other business includes the company's call centers, content services, financial services and electricity supply services, as well as research and development activities. The company is located worldwide, including network operations centers in Tokyo, New York, Los Angeles, London, Beijing, Shanghai and Hong Kong.

FINANCIAL DATA: Note: Data for latest year may not have been available at press time.

In U.S. $	2018	2017	2016	2015	2014	2013
Revenue	46,768,120,000	44,043,660,000	41,426,750,000	25,365,040,000	24,201,890,000	22,565,360,000
R&D Expense				60,793,260	62,286,660	58,539,260
Operating Income	8,888,023,000	8,442,991,000	7,682,064,000	6,876,159,000	6,152,150,000	4,755,436,000
Operating Margin %	44.21	19.05%	18.33%	16.21%	15.30%	14.66%
SGA Expense	11,791,470,000	10,885,670,000	10,266,380,000	4,419,264,000	4,181,768,000	4,204,595,000
Net Income	5,310,626,000	5,070,663,000	4,586,533,000	3,969,381,000	2,987,144,000	2,239,806,000
Operating Cash Flow	9,845,327,000	10,769,830,000	8,204,753,000	8,925,581,000	7,162,799,000	4,859,639,000
Capital Expenditure	5,202,564,000	4,819,420,000	4,969,947,000	4,834,252,000	4,723,889,000	3,856,588,000
EBITDA	14,042,990,000	13,490,320,000	12,715,990,000	11,640,310,000	10,490,850,000	7,847,265,000
Return on Assets %	8.91%	9.05%	8.94%	8.39%	7.13%	5.97%
Return on Equity %	15.62%	15.93%	15.65%	14.92%	12.94%	11.19%
Debt to Equity	0.18	0.25	0.28	0.27	0.26	0.31

CONTACT INFORMATION:
Phone: 81 333470077   Fax:
Toll-Free:
Address: Garden Air Tower, 3-10-10, Iidabashi, Chiyoda-ku, Tokyo, 102-8460 Japan

STOCK TICKER/OTHER:
Stock Ticker: KDDIY
Employees: 38,826
Parent Company:
Exchange: PINX
Fiscal Year Ends: 03/31

SALARIES/BONUSES:
Top Exec. Salary: $ Bonus: $
Second Exec. Salary: $ Bonus: $

OTHER THOUGHTS:
Estimated Female Officers or Directors:
Hot Spot for Advancement for Women/Minorities:

Kibo Software Inc

NAIC Code: 511210M

TYPES OF BUSINESS:

E-Commerce Software
Managed Support Services
Online Marketing Services
Search Engine Optimization

BRANDS/DIVISIONS/AFFILIATES:

Vista Equity Partners
Kibo Commerce
Real-Time Individualization
Kibo Mobile Point of Commerce (mPOC)

CONTACTS: *Note: Officers with more than one job title may be intentionally listed here more than once.*

David Post, CEO
Vinesh Vis, Chief Sales Officer
Euwart Anderson, VP-Talent
Ram Venkataraman, CTO
Sam Hogin, VP-Prod. Mgmt.
James Miller, Exec. VP-Client Svcs.
George Loyer, VP-Managed Svcs.

GROWTH PLANS/SPECIAL FEATURES:

Kibo Software, Inc. operates as Kibo Commerce and provides cloud-based, omnichannel software solutions for retailers and branded manufacturers. The company's products and solutions help these customers achieve optimal performance of business-to-consumer (B2C) and business-to-business (B2B) commerce via unified consumer experiences. Kibo's unified commerce platform enables business teams to stay agile and drive connectivity by staying ahead of consumer expectations, adapting to changing market conditions, and combining marketing, operations and fulfillment systems to deliver personalized customer experiences across all channels. The firm's scalable, cloud-based eCommerce software enables business users to launch new promotions, create landing pages and publish new content. Its order management system comprises intelligent order routing and omnichannel fulfillment software solutions, which connects inventory across the entire ecosystem to customers in real-time. Kibo's Real-Time Individualization software solution features predictive, big data technology for creating one-on-one personalization across sessions, devices and touchpoints. The Kibo Mobile Point of Commerce (mPOC) combines the power of a mobile point of sale system, inventory visibility and customer data to drive in-store sales and offer enhanced customer service. Kibo is privately-owned by Vista Equity Partners.

FINANCIAL DATA: *Note: Data for latest year may not have been available at press time.*

In U.S. $	2018	2017	2016	2015	2014	2013
Revenue						
R&D Expense						
Operating Income						
Operating Margin %						
SGA Expense						
Net Income						
Operating Cash Flow						
Capital Expenditure						
EBITDA						
Return on Assets %						
Return on Equity %						
Debt to Equity						

CONTACT INFORMATION:

Phone: 877-350-3866   Fax:
Toll-Free:
Address: 717 N. Harwood St., Ste. 1900, Dallas, TX 75201 United States

STOCK TICKER/OTHER:

Stock Ticker: Private   Exchange:
Employees: 110   Fiscal Year Ends: 12/31
Parent Company: Vista Equity Partners

SALARIES/BONUSES:

Top Exec. Salary: $ Bonus: $
Second Exec. Salary: $ Bonus: $

OTHER THOUGHTS:

Estimated Female Officers or Directors: 1
Hot Spot for Advancement for Women/Minorities:

Kickstarter PBC

www.kickstarter.com

NAIC Code: 519130

TYPES OF BUSINESS:

Crowdfunding

BRANDS/DIVISIONS/AFFILIATES:

CONTACTS: Note: Officers with more than one job title may be intentionally listed here more than once.

Yancey Strickler, Head-Comm.
Charles Adler, Creative Dir.
Perry Chen, Chmn.

GROWTH PLANS/SPECIAL FEATURES:

Kickstarter PBC (Public Benefit Corporation) is a crowd funding platform for creative projects, which allows creators to receive funding directly from the public. This alternative form of funding lets audiences to engage with creators and their projects early in the process and gives creators greater freedom than traditional routes of funding. Contributors receive different incentive gifts in accordance to the level of funding they provide for projects. Incentives can include a signed copy of the finished product, acknowledgement on the finished product, an original piece related to the project, VIP access to performances, private screenings and special editions of finished products. Creators, as a part of creating their project's Kickstarter, choose what incentives will be offered. Originally begun as a venue for crowd funded independent film projects, the company has expanded to fund projects in art, comics, dance, design, fashion, food, games, music, photography, publishing, technology and theater. Film and video still represents the largest percentage of funded projects, with games following. Of the tens of thousands projects launched since the site's 2009 inception, over 14 million people have backed a project, $3.5 billion has been pledged and 137,675 projects have been successfully funded (as of January 2018). The site operates on an all-or-nothing basis. Projects must achieve their set funding goal in order to receive their proceeds. Contributors are charged for their contribution at the end of a successful project's funding cycle, with Kickstarter charging 5% of the total funds raised. Since the funds go directly to the project creators, Kickstarter is not responsible for project and incentive fulfillment.

FINANCIAL DATA: Note: Data for latest year may not have been available at press time.

In U.S. $	2018	2017	2016	2015	2014	2013
Revenue						
R&D Expense						
Operating Income						
Operating Margin %						
SGA Expense						
Net Income						
Operating Cash Flow						
Capital Expenditure						
EBITDA						
Return on Assets %						
Return on Equity %						
Debt to Equity						

CONTACT INFORMATION:

Phone: 866-749-7545   Fax:
Toll-Free:
Address: 155 Rivington St., New York, NY 10002 United States

STOCK TICKER/OTHER:

Stock Ticker: Private   Exchange:
Employees: 122   Fiscal Year Ends:
Parent Company:

SALARIES/BONUSES:

Top Exec. Salary: $ Bonus: $
Second Exec. Salary: $ Bonus: $

OTHER THOUGHTS:

Estimated Female Officers or Directors: 12
Hot Spot for Advancement for Women/Minorities: Y

Klarna Inc

NAIC Code: 522320

klarna.com

TYPES OF BUSINESS:

Consumer Lending

BRANDS/DIVISIONS/AFFILIATES:

Klarna Inc
Klarna

GROWTH PLANS/SPECIAL FEATURES:

Klarna Bank AB is a Swedish banking company under the supervision of the Swedish Financial Supervisory Authority. The firm operates Klarna, a Swedish e-payment platform that provides online payment services to e-commerce merchants. Klarna has a customer base of more than 60 million and works with over 100,000 merchants in 14 countries. The firm offers direct payments, pay after delivery options and installment plans in a smooth, single-click purchase experience that lets consumers pay when and how they want. The purpose at Klarna is to simplify buying by making buying simple and safe for consumers and selling simple and safe for merchants. Klarna's investors include Sequoia Capital, Bestseller, Permira, Visa and Atomico. Subsidiary Klarna, Inc. is based in the U.S., with offices in Ohio and New York.

CONTACTS:
Note: Officers with more than one job title may be intentionally listed here more than once.

Sebastian Siemiatkowski, CEO
Knut Frangsmyr, COO
Camilla Giesecke, CFO
David Sandstrom, CMO
Koen Koppen, CIO
Jon Kamaluddin, Chmn.

FINANCIAL DATA:
Note: Data for latest year may not have been available at press time.

In U.S. $	2018	2017	2016	2015	2014	2013
Revenue		550,718,000	438,864,250	274,488,725	256,113,600	184,665,600
R&D Expense						
Operating Income						
Operating Margin %						
SGA Expense						
Net Income		42,054,900	13,981,638	9,425,924	8,793,600	6,375,360
Operating Cash Flow						
Capital Expenditure						
EBITDA						
Return on Assets %						
Return on Equity %						
Debt to Equity						

CONTACT INFORMATION:

Phone: 46-8-120-120-10   Fax:
Toll-Free:
Address: Sveavagen 46, Stockholm, 111 34 Sweden

STOCK TICKER/OTHER:

Stock Ticker: Private   Exchange:
Employees: 1,700   Fiscal Year Ends:
Parent Company:

SALARIES/BONUSES:

Top Exec. Salary: $ Bonus: $
Second Exec. Salary: $ Bonus: $

OTHER THOUGHTS:

Estimated Female Officers or Directors: 1
Hot Spot for Advancement for Women/Minorities:

Ladders (The)

NAIC Code: 561311A

www.theladders.com

TYPES OF BUSINESS:

Online Job Postings

BRANDS/DIVISIONS/AFFILIATES:

CONTACTS: *Note: Officers with more than one job title may be intentionally listed here more than once.*

Marc Cenedella, CEO
Shankar Mishra, VP-Data Science & Analytics
Kyri Sarantakos, VP-Eng.
Tarmi Addonizio, VP-Legal Affairs

GROWTH PLANS/SPECIAL FEATURES:

The Ladders helps job-seeking professionals connect with recruiters and employers. The firm is one of the leading companies in the over $100,000 job search category, but includes all professional careers with salaries between $40,000 to $250,000, allowing access to more recruiters and employers looking to hire professionals at other stages in their careers. Ladders members have access to recruiters from over 200,000 companies, and has reviewed more than 1.5 million resumes. Ladders offers tools and services targeting professionals that are looking for new positions, to relocate or are seeking a change of industries. Free services include online features such as the ability to upload resumes, search for jobs and receive comprehensive career advice. After clients upload resumes, they are able to receive targeted job leads that match their background and career goals. The firm's team sorts through professional job postings in industries such as human resources, accounting, creative, design, education, law, marketing and finance in order to post only the top currently-available positions. In addition, Ladders' email alert system sends criteria-specific openings directly to member inboxes as the jobs become available, and members can apply within two clicks. The company offers tips from industry experts such as how to prepare for interviews, write resumes and negotiate salaries, and offers a weekly advice newsletter from the firm's CEO.

The firm offers employees medical, dental and vision insurance; short-term, long-term and life insurance; AFLAC supplemental insurance; a 401(k) plan; company athletic teams; and rewards incentive programs.

FINANCIAL DATA: *Note: Data for latest year may not have been available at press time.*

In U.S. $	2018	2017	2016	2015	2014	2013
Revenue						
R&D Expense						
Operating Income						
Operating Margin %						
SGA Expense						
Net Income						
Operating Cash Flow						
Capital Expenditure						
EBITDA						
Return on Assets %						
Return on Equity %						
Debt to Equity						

CONTACT INFORMATION:

Phone: 866-800-4640   Fax:
Toll-Free:
Address: 55 Water St., 51/Fl., New York, NY 10041 United States

STOCK TICKER/OTHER:

Stock Ticker: Private   Exchange:
Employees: 149   Fiscal Year Ends:
Parent Company:

SALARIES/BONUSES:

Top Exec. Salary: $ Bonus: $
Second Exec. Salary: $ Bonus: $

OTHER THOUGHTS:

Estimated Female Officers or Directors: 4
Hot Spot for Advancement for Women/Minorities: Y

LaShou Group Inc

NAIC Code: 519130

www.lashou.com

TYPES OF BUSINESS:

Social Networking
Location-Based Networking

GROWTH PLANS/SPECIAL FEATURES:

LaShou Group, Inc., a subsidiary of Sanpower Group Co., Ltd., operates an eCommerce platform for web-based and mobile users in China. The www.LaShou.com website offers discounts on more than 1,000 products every day in a variety of categories, including food, entertainment, health, beauty and travel. The network has nearly 50 million users and about 50,000 partner merchants.

BRANDS/DIVISIONS/AFFILIATES:

Sanpower Group Co Ltd
www.LaShou.com

CONTACTS: *Note: Officers with more than one job title may be intentionally listed here more than once.*

Leon Liang, CEO
Xiaobo Jia, Dir.

FINANCIAL DATA: *Note: Data for latest year may not have been available at press time.*

In U.S. $	2018	2017	2016	2015	2014	2013
Revenue						
R&D Expense						
Operating Income						
Operating Margin %						
SGA Expense						
Net Income						
Operating Cash Flow						
Capital Expenditure						
EBITDA						
Return on Assets %						
Return on Equity %						
Debt to Equity						

CONTACT INFORMATION:

Phone: 86 10 8444 0025   Fax: 86 10 8444 0015
Toll-Free:
Address: Wangjing Rd., No. 1, Motorola Bldg., 8/Fl, Beijing, 100028 China

STOCK TICKER/OTHER:

Stock Ticker: Subsidiary   Exchange:
Employees: 4,300   Fiscal Year Ends:
Parent Company: Sanpower Group Co Ltd

SALARIES/BONUSES:

Top Exec. Salary: $ Bonus: $
Second Exec. Salary: $ Bonus: $

OTHER THOUGHTS:

Estimated Female Officers or Directors:
Hot Spot for Advancement for Women/Minorities:

LastMinute.com (LMnext UK Ltd)

www.lastminute.com

NAIC Code: 561510

TYPES OF BUSINESS:

Online Travel Agency
Online Reservations & Ticket Sales
Vacation packages
Entertainment packages
Dining discounts/packages

BRANDS/DIVISIONS/AFFILIATES:

lastminute.com NV
LastMinute.com

CONTACTS: Note: Officers with more than one job title may be intentionally listed here more than once.

Marco Corradino, CEO
Matthew Crummack, Pres.

GROWTH PLANS/SPECIAL FEATURES:

LMnext U.K. Ltd. operates LastMinute.com, one of the U.K.'s top online travel and leisure website. The company is a wholly-owned subsidiary of lastminute.com NV. The firm offers customers last-minute opportunities for travel services, including airfare, hotel reservations, car rentals and package vacations, with thousands to choose from globally. LastMinute.com also offers tickets for entertainment events, restaurant reservations, museum admissions and other activity planning services. The company is one of the largest retailers of West End theater tickets. The firm's registered subscribers can make purchases by telephone, over the internet, mobile app and through an interactive voice recognition service from 14 days to 3 hours before departure. LastMinute.com has relationships with thousands of individual suppliers for which it serves as a third party in facilitating contracts. The company offers suppliers an alternative way to distribute excess inventory at short notice without threatening their core businesses, providing consumers with a range of products at reduced prices. The concept is based on the idea of matching supply and demand and ensuring that excess inventory is not wasted. LastMinute.com's primary markets include the U.K., France, Italy, Spain and Ireland. Services are offered in English, French, Dutch, Spanish and Italian languages.

FINANCIAL DATA: Note: Data for latest year may not have been available at press time.

In U.S. $	2018	2017	2016	2015	2014	2013
Revenue		37,274,300	35,966,400	55,522,400		
R&D Expense						
Operating Income						
Operating Margin %						
SGA Expense						
Net Income		2,594,920	-175,560	-26,134,200		
Operating Cash Flow						
Capital Expenditure						
EBITDA						
Return on Assets %						
Return on Equity %						
Debt to Equity						

CONTACT INFORMATION:

Phone: 44-20-7866-4200   Fax: 44-20-7866-4001
Toll-Free: 800-083-4000
Address: 77 Hatton Garden, Amsterdam, EC1N 8JS United Kingdom

STOCK TICKER/OTHER:

Stock Ticker: Subsidiary   Exchange:
Employees: 119   Fiscal Year Ends: 12/31
Parent Company: lastminute.com NV (lm holding)

SALARIES/BONUSES:

Top Exec. Salary: $ Bonus: $
Second Exec. Salary: $ Bonus: $

OTHER THOUGHTS:

Estimated Female Officers or Directors:
Hot Spot for Advancement for Women/Minorities:

lastminute.com NV (lm holding)

lmgroup.lastminute.com

NAIC Code: 561510

TYPES OF BUSINESS:

Online Travel Agency
Online Travel Search
Online Travel Booking

BRANDS/DIVISIONS/AFFILIATES:

lastminute.com
Volagratis
Rumbo
weg.de
Bravofly
Jetcost
Hotelscan

CONTACTS: *Note: Officers with more than one job title may be intentionally listed here more than once.*

Fabio Cannavale, CEO
Ottonel Popesco, Chmn.

GROWTH PLANS/SPECIAL FEATURES:

lastminute.com NV, also referred to as lm group, operates a portfolio of brands engaged in the industry of online travel. The firm's brands include lastminute.com, Volagratis, Rumbo, weg.de, Bravofly, Jetcost and Hotelscan. Every month the group reaches 45 million users across its websites and mobile apps, covering 17 languages and 40 countries. Users search for and book their travel and leisure experiences through the sites. Lastminute.com offers access to hotels, entertainment and spas. Volagratis is a flight search engine in Italy. Rumbo is a full-service website in Spain from which customers can search, compare and book deals on hotels, flights, packages, escapes and cruises. Weg.de offers package tours and all-inclusive deals as well as hotel accommodations, flights, cruises, rental cars and ski holidays. Bravofly offers flights and is present in more than 35 countries, with a strong brand position in France and Germany. Jetcost is a metasearch website that enables users to search for and compare flights, hotels and rental cars from a range of suppliers. It operates in 38 countries across Europe, Asia and the U.S. Last, Hotelscan is a metasearch website that enables users to search for and compare hotels, vacation rentals, bed & breakfasts and other lodging from an array of suppliers.

FINANCIAL DATA: *Note: Data for latest year may not have been available at press time.*

In U.S. $	2018	2017	2016	2015	2014	2013
Revenue		294,835,300	297,914,300	284,423,800	167,434,000	140,319,900
R&D Expense						
Operating Income		-3,974,347	14,087,350	-23,597,760	11,797,740	18,093,590
Operating Margin %		-1.34%	4.72%	-8.29%	7.04%	12.89%
SGA Expense		137,972,200	140,376,800	138,867,500	75,400,970	57,881,480
Net Income		-7,347,246	7,757,325	-20,521,030	8,322,322	14,124,940
Operating Cash Flow		11,999,360	6,983,870	-16,198,110	14,000,770	24,457,780
Capital Expenditure		14,876,750	14,427,940	18,081,060	7,460,017	6,557,844
EBITDA		9,607,235	22,890,370	-14,202,400	18,111,810	23,656,990
Return on Assets %		-1.92%	2.07%	-6.17%	3.23%	6.33%
Return on Equity %		-4.70%	4.81%	-11.84%	6.10%	16.29%
Debt to Equity						0.23

CONTACT INFORMATION:

Phone: Fax:
Toll-Free: 0800 083 4000
Address: Prins Bernhardplein 200, Amsterdam, 1097 JB Netherlands

STOCK TICKER/OTHER:

Stock Ticker: BRVFY   Exchange: GREY
Employees: 1,253   Fiscal Year Ends: 12/31
Parent Company:

SALARIES/BONUSES:

Top Exec. Salary: $ Bonus: $
Second Exec. Salary: $ Bonus: $

OTHER THOUGHTS:

Estimated Female Officers or Directors:
Hot Spot for Advancement for Women/Minorities:

Leaf Group Ltd

www.demandmedia.com

NAIC Code: 519130

TYPES OF BUSINESS:

Internet Portals
Online Video Publishing
Online Leisure Activities Information
How-to Internet Sites
Advertising Services
Domain Name Registration Services
Social Media Tools

BRANDS/DIVISIONS/AFFILIATES:

LIVESTRONG.COM
eHow
Socitey 6
Saatchi Art
Other Art Fair (The)
Deny Designs
Well+Good

CONTACTS: Note: Officers with more than one job title may be intentionally listed here more than once.

Jantoon Reigersman, CFO
James Quandt, Chairman of the Board
Wendy Voong, Chief Accounting Officer
Brian Pike, Chief Technology Officer
Sean Moriarty, Director
Dion Sanders, Executive VP, Divisional
Adam Wergeles, Executive VP, Divisional
Daniel Weinrot, Executive VP, Divisional

GROWTH PLANS/SPECIAL FEATURES:

Leaf Group Ltd. is a diversified internet company which owns and operates consumer media and marketplace businesses. The firm builds platforms across its media and marketplace properties in an effort to enable communities of creators to reach audiences in large and growing lifestyle categories, as well as to help advertisers find innovative ways to engage with their customers. Leaf Group's media brands include LIVESTRONG.COM and eHow, as well as more than 40 other media properties focused on specific categories or interests. The firm's marketplace brands include: Society 6, which provides artists with an eCommerce platform to feature and sell their original designs in the home decor and apparel categories; Saatchi Art, an online art gallery featuring a selection of original paintings, drawings, sculptures and photography; The Other Art Fair, an art fair for discovering emerging artists; and Deny Designs, which offers a collection of statement pieces for the home, created by artists, with designs printed on an assortment of premium decor products, including proprietary furniture products manufactured in-house at Deny Designs' Denver, Colorado facility. In mid-2018, Leaf Group acquired wellness site, Well+Good, enhancing its fitness and wellness category.

FINANCIAL DATA: Note: Data for latest year may not have been available at press time.

In U.S. $	2018	2017	2016	2015	2014	2013
Revenue		128,990,000	113,452,000	125,969,000	172,428,992	394,598,016
R&D Expense						
Operating Income						
Operating Margin %						
SGA Expense						
Net Income		-31,133,000	-2,011,000	-43,501,000	-267,356,992	-20,174,000
Operating Cash Flow						
Capital Expenditure						
EBITDA						
Return on Assets %						
Return on Equity %						
Debt to Equity						

CONTACT INFORMATION:

Phone: 310-656-6253   Fax:
Toll-Free:
Address: 1655 26th St., Santa Monica, CA 90404 United States

STOCK TICKER/OTHER:

Stock Ticker: LFGR   Exchange: NYS
Employees: 265   Fiscal Year Ends: 12/31
Parent Company:

SALARIES/BONUSES:

Top Exec. Salary: $ Bonus: $
Second Exec. Salary: $ Bonus: $

OTHER THOUGHTS:

Estimated Female Officers or Directors: 2
Hot Spot for Advancement for Women/Minorities: Y

Sales, profits and employees may be estimates. Financial information, benefits and other data can change quickly and may vary from those stated here.

Level 3 Parent LLC

www.level3.com

NAIC Code: 517110

TYPES OF BUSINESS:

Private Data Networks-Fiber Optic
Broadband Network Services
Managed Modem Access Services
Digital Media Capture and Distribution
High-Speed Content Upload
Server Facilities

BRANDS/DIVISIONS/AFFILIATES:

CenturyLink Inc
Level 3 Communications Inc

CONTACTS: *Note: Officers with more than one job title may be intentionally listed here more than once.*

Jeffrey Storey, CEO
Sunit Patel, CFO
Eric Mortensen, Chief Accounting Officer
James Ellis, Director
Hector Alonso, President, Divisional ·
Laurinda Pang, President, Geographical
John Ryan, Secretary

GROWTH PLANS/SPECIAL FEATURES:

Level 3 Parent LLC, formerly Level 3 Communications, Inc., is a leading provider of integrated communications services. Its primary business is the provision of communications services over its extensive broadband networks in North America, Europe and Latin America, consisting of approximately 106,000 intercity route miles. The networks supply a portfolio of services including internet protocol (IP) services (internet access, Ethernet and virtual private network services), broadband transport and colocation services to enterprises and other organization in more than 60 countries. Level 3 divides its services into two segments: Core Network Services and Wholesale Voice Services. Core Network Services consist of IP and data services, transport and fiber services, voice services, colocation and datacenter services and security services. IP and data services include Internet Services, virtual private network, content delivery network, media delivery, Vyvx broadcast service and Managed Services. Transport and fiber services include wavelengths, private lines, transoceanic services and dark fiber, as well as related professional services. Voice services offer a range of local and enterprise voice services including VoIP services and traditional circuit-switch based services. Colocation and Data Center services include data center facilities and services including cloud, hosting and application management solutions. Security services uses the firm's view of the threat landscape to enable customers to address the escalating risk of cyber-attacks. Wholesale Voice Services include voice termination and toll-free service. Wholesale long distance includes domestic and international voice termination services. The wholesale Toll Free service terminates toll free calls that are originated on the traditional telephone network. The firm is a wholly-owned subsidiary of CenturyLink, Inc.

FINANCIAL DATA: *Note: Data for latest year may not have been available at press time.*

In U.S. $	2018	2017	2016	2015	2014	2013
Revenue			8,172,000,256	8,229,000,192	6,776,999,936	6,312,999,936
R&D Expense						
Operating Income						
Operating Margin %						
SGA Expense						
Net Income			677,000,000	3,432,999,936	314,000,000	-109,000,000
Operating Cash Flow						
Capital Expenditure						
EBITDA						
Return on Assets %						
Return on Equity %						
Debt to Equity						

CONTACT INFORMATION:

Phone: 720 888-1000   Fax: 720 888-5088
Toll-Free: 877-253-8353
Address: 1025 Eldorado Blvd., Broomfield, CO 80021 United States

STOCK TICKER/OTHER:

Stock Ticker: LVLT   Exchange: NYS
Employees: 12,600   Fiscal Year Ends: 12/31
Parent Company: CenturyLink Inc

SALARIES/BONUSES:

Top Exec. Salary: $ Bonus: $
Second Exec. Salary: $ Bonus: $

OTHER THOUGHTS:

Estimated Female Officers or Directors: 2
Hot Spot for Advancement for Women/Minorities: Y

Liberty Global plc

www.libertyglobal.com

NAIC Code: 517110

TYPES OF BUSINESS:

Video, Voice & Broadband Internet Access Services
Telephony Services
VoIP Services
Mobile Telephony Services
Video on Demand Services

BRANDS/DIVISIONS/AFFILIATES:

Virgin Media
Unitymedia
Telenet
UPC
Vodafone Ziggo
ITV
All3Media
LionsGate

CONTACTS: Note: Officers with more than one job title may be intentionally listed here more than once.

Michael Fries, CEO
John Malone, Chairman of the Board
Charlie Bracken, CFO
Diederik Karsten, Exec. VP
Baptiest Coopmans, Exec. VP-IT
Bryan Hall, Executive VP
Diederik Karsten, Executive VP
Leonard Stegman, Managing Director
John Malone, Chmn.

GROWTH PLANS/SPECIAL FEATURES:

Liberty Global plc is an international provider of TV and broadband services, with operations in 10 European countries under the Virgin Media, Unitymedia, Telenet and UPC brand names. The company invests in the infrastructure and digital platforms that enable Liberty Global customers to utilize and enjoy video, internet and communications services. Liberty Global has developed market-leading products delivered through next-generation networks that connect these more than 21 million customers who subscribe to 45 million TV, broadband internet and telephone services. The firm also serves 6 million mobile subscribers and offers WiFi services across 12 million access points. In addition, Liberty Global owns 50% of VodafoneZiggo, a joint venture in the Netherlands with 4 million customers subscribing to 10 million fixed-line and 5 million mobile services. The firm has significant content investments in ITV, All3Media, ITI Neovision, Casa Systems, LionsGate, the Formula E racing series and several regional sports networks. During 2018, Liberty Global spun off Liberty Latin America into a new publicly-traded company, operating independently throughout parts of the Caribbean and South America; sold UPC Austria to T-Mobile Austria for $2.2 billion; and agreed to sell its operations in Germany, Hungary, Romania and the Czech Republic to Vodafone Group plc for approximately $22.7 billion.

FINANCIAL DATA: Note: Data for latest year may not have been available at press time.

In U.S. $	2018	2017	2016	2015	2014	2013
Revenue		3,590,000,000	2,723,800,000	1,217,300,000	1,204,600,000	1,288,800,000
R&D Expense						
Operating Income		559,200,000	481,400,000	272,200,000	248,500,000	110,200,000
Operating Margin %		15.57%	17.67%	22.36%	20.62%	8.55%
SGA Expense		688,400,000	539,200,000	193,400,000	224,000,000	225,100,000
Net Income		-778,100,000	-235,800,000	43,900,000	12,000,000	-39,100,000
Operating Cash Flow		573,900,000	468,200,000	306,500,000	289,000,000	292,200,000
Capital Expenditure		639,300,000	490,400,000	227,200,000	223,100,000	262,100,000
EBITDA		524,300,000	803,600,000	466,600,000	381,200,000	357,300,000
Return on Assets %		-5.59%	-2.70%	1.45%	.43%	
Return on Equity %		-20.52%	-10.57%	38.74%	59.40%	
Debt to Equity		1.83	1.38	11.30	102.61	

CONTACT INFORMATION:

Phone: 44-208-483-6300   Fax:
Toll-Free:
Address: Griffin House, 161 Hammersmith Rd., London, W6 8BS United Kingdom

STOCK TICKER/OTHER:

Stock Ticker: LILA
Employees: 26,700
Parent Company:

Exchange: NAS
Fiscal Year Ends: 12/31

SALARIES/BONUSES:

Top Exec. Salary: $ Bonus: $
Second Exec. Salary: $ Bonus: $

OTHER THOUGHTS:

Estimated Female Officers or Directors: 3
Hot Spot for Advancement for Women/Minorities: Y

Life Quotes Inc

www.lifequotes.com

NAIC Code: 524210

TYPES OF BUSINESS:

Online Insurance Broker
Online Price Comparison Services

BRANDS/DIVISIONS/AFFILIATES:

LifeQuotes.com
ConsumerInsuranceGuide.com

CONTACTS: *Note: Officers with more than one job title may be intentionally listed here more than once.*

Robert S. Bland, CEO
Robert Goss, Exec. VP
Michelle Zieba, VP-Sales
Margaret Thornton, Dir.-New Bus.
Robert Goss, Exec. VP

GROWTH PLANS/SPECIAL FEATURES:

Life Quotes, Inc. owns and operates an online consumer insurance information service, accessible at LifeQuotes.com and ConsumerInsuranceGuide.com, which serves self-directed insurance shoppers by providing instant quotes for various insurance products, primarily life insurance. Its proprietary and comprehensive insurance price comparison and order-entry system provides instant quotes from approximately 50 life insurance companies. When shopping for insurance, customers may specify the amount of coverage they are looking for. Besides the price quotes, the company's websites also offer reference tools and educational material to help shoppers make their final decisions. Life Quotes offers customers its quotes online, over the phone or by mail; customers can purchase insurance from the company of their choice either online or over the phone from a licensed insurance customer service staffer. In addition to life insurance products, the firm's website offers access to other types of personal insurance, including auto, homeowners, renters, long-term care, health and travel insurance, through various third-party companies. Life Quotes generates revenues from the receipt of commissions and fees paid by various sources tied directly to the volume of insurance sales or traffic it produces. In early-2018, Life Quotes announced its 350,000th policyholder.

FINANCIAL DATA: *Note: Data for latest year may not have been available at press time.*

In U.S. $	2018	2017	2016	2015	2014	2013
Revenue						
R&D Expense						
Operating Income						
Operating Margin %						
SGA Expense						
Net Income						
Operating Cash Flow						
Capital Expenditure						
EBITDA						
Return on Assets %						
Return on Equity %						
Debt to Equity						

CONTACT INFORMATION:

Phone: 630-515-0170   Fax: 630-515-0270
Toll-Free: 800-556-9393
Address: 8205 S. Cass Ave., Ste. 102, Darien, IL 60561 United States

STOCK TICKER/OTHER:

Stock Ticker: Private
Employees: 106
Parent Company:

Exchange:
Fiscal Year Ends: 12/31

SALARIES/BONUSES:

Top Exec. Salary: $ Bonus: $
Second Exec. Salary: $ Bonus: $

OTHER THOUGHTS:

Estimated Female Officers or Directors: 2
Hot Spot for Advancement for Women/Minorities:

Sales, profits and employees may be estimates. Financial information, benefits and other data can change quickly and may vary from those stated here.

LifeLock Inc

www.lifelock.com

NAIC Code: 511210E

TYPES OF BUSINESS:

Computer Software, Security & Anti-Virus

BRANDS/DIVISIONS/AFFILIATES:

Symantec Corporation
LifeLock Standard
LifeLock Advantage
LifeLock Ultimate Plus
LifeLock Wallet
ID Analytics Inc

CONTACTS: *Note: Officers with more than one job title may be intentionally listed here more than once.*

Hilary Schneider, CEO
Douglas Jeffries, Chief Administrative Officer
Roy Guthrie, Director
Sharon Segev, Executive VP
Hilary Schneider, President
Donald Beck, Senior VP, Divisional
Todd Davis, Vice Chairman
Todd Davis, Chmn.

GROWTH PLANS/SPECIAL FEATURES:

LifeLock, Inc., a subsidiary of Symantec Corporation, specializes in providing identity theft protection services. The company's individual and business plans work to prevent, detect and rectify potential cases of credit fraud. For consumers, the firm offers three primary service plans: LifeLock Standard, LifeLock Advantage and LifeLock Ultimate Plus. LifeLock Standard provides threat alerts, online access to an informational threat dashboard, stolen wallet remediation, personal information monitoring and recovery services if fraud is committed. LifeLock Advantage adds bank account activity alerts, credit scores and other protections. LifeLock Ultimate Plus supplies all services provided in the basic LifeLock plan, along with additional monitoring in public records and other databases. For enterprises, the firm provides real-time visibility into consumer behavior through its ID Score product, in order to assess the risk of identity fraud. LifeLock Wallet app offers cloud storage and places ID, insurance, loyalty and payment cards, as well as LifeLock identity theft protection, on members' smartphones. LifeLock's enterprise products help prevent clients from providing products or services to an individual misrepresenting their identity by, among other things, using another individual's social security number, name, address, phone number or date of birth. The firm offers these services through an on-demand platform under multi-year contracts with monthly transaction-based pricing. The firm's subsidiary, ID Analytics, Inc. offers consumer risk management through patented analytics.

FINANCIAL DATA: *Note: Data for latest year may not have been available at press time.*

In U.S. $	2018	2017	2016	2015	2014	2013
Revenue		681,000,000	667,500,000	587,468,992	476,016,000	369,657,984
R&D Expense						
Operating Income						
Operating Margin %						
SGA Expense						
Net Income				-51,003,000	2,495,000	52,451,000
Operating Cash Flow						
Capital Expenditure						
EBITDA						
Return on Assets %						
Return on Equity %						
Debt to Equity						

CONTACT INFORMATION:

Phone: 480 682-5100   Fax: 888 244-9823
Toll-Free: 800-543-3562
Address: 60 E. Rio Salado Parkway, Ste. 400, Tempe, AZ 85281 United States

STOCK TICKER/OTHER:

Stock Ticker: Subsidiary   Exchange:
Employees: 788   Fiscal Year Ends: 12/31
Parent Company: Symantec Corporation

SALARIES/BONUSES:

Top Exec. Salary: $ Bonus: $
Second Exec. Salary: $ Bonus: $

OTHER THOUGHTS:

Estimated Female Officers or Directors: 3
Hot Spot for Advancement for Women/Minorities: Y

Lightspeed POS Inc

NAIC Code: 511210K

TYPES OF BUSINESS:

Computer Software, Sales & Customer Relationship Management

BRANDS/DIVISIONS/AFFILIATES:

Lightspeed Loyalty

CONTACTS: *Note: Officers with more than one job title may be intentionally listed here more than once.*

Dax Dasilva, CEO
JP Chauvet, Pres.
Brandon Nussey, CFO
Chelsea Finnermore, VP-Human Resources
Bram Paperman, VP-Technology

GROWTH PLANS/SPECIAL FEATURES:

Lightspeed POS, Inc. designs and develops point of sale (POS) systems and an eCommerce platform for merchants and restaurants in Canada and internationally. For retailers, the company's solutions include inventory management, omnichannel integration, reporting and analytics, customer relationship management, mobility and cloud, integrated payments, onboarding and support. For eCommerce marketers, its solutions include inventory management, design tools, order processing, shipping, customizable checkout, marketing, search engine optimization/marketing, social media apps, reporting and international sales. For restaurants, Lightspeed solutions include inventory management, staff profile, customizable menu, hardware, tableside ordering, payments, mobility and cloud, staff management, multi-store capabilities and management, reporting, customer loyalty integrations and management, and training and support. Lightspeed has an extensive library of resources created to help entrepreneurs build profitable businesses, and comprises and wide range of topics on industry trends and best practices. Based in Canada, the firm has offices in the U.S., Belgium, the U.K., Netherlands and Australia. In December 2018, Lightspeed acquired ReUp, a digital platform that allows businesses to build a loyalty program. Lightspeed rebranded ReUp to Lightspeed Loyalty, a new platform that allows Lightspeed's customers to set up branded customer rewards, created automated marketing campaigns via mobile and email and view customer insights.

FINANCIAL DATA: *Note: Data for latest year may not have been available at press time.*

In U.S. $	2018	2017	2016	2015	2014	2013
Revenue						
R&D Expense						
Operating Income						
Operating Margin %						
SGA Expense						
Net Income						
Operating Cash Flow						
Capital Expenditure						
EBITDA						
Return on Assets %						
Return on Equity %						
Debt to Equity						

CONTACT INFORMATION:

Phone: 514-907-1801   Fax: 514-221-4499
Toll-Free: 855-300-7108
Address: 700 St. Antoine E., Ste. 300, Montreal, QC H2Y1A6 Canada

STOCK TICKER/OTHER:

Stock Ticker: Private   Exchange:
Employees: 650   Fiscal Year Ends:
Parent Company:

SALARIES/BONUSES:

Top Exec. Salary: $ Bonus: $
Second Exec. Salary: $ Bonus: $

OTHER THOUGHTS:

Estimated Female Officers or Directors:
Hot Spot for Advancement for Women/Minorities:

Linden Research Inc (Linden Lab)

lindenlab.com

NAIC Code: 511210G

TYPES OF BUSINESS:

Computer Software, Electronic Games, Apps & Entertainment Apps

BRANDS/DIVISIONS/AFFILIATES:

Linden Lab
Second Life
Blocksworld
Sansar

CONTACTS: Note: Officers with more than one job title may be intentionally listed here more than once.

Ebbe Altberg, CEO
Landon McDowel,
Aston Waldman, VP-Finance
Sheri Bryant, Head of Strategic Business Development and Marketing
Pam Beyazit, Sr. Dir-Human Resources
Jeff Petersen, CTO
Don Laabs, Sr. Dir.-Prod.
Jeff Peterson, VP-Eng.
Kelly Conway, General Counsel
Landon McDowell, VP-Oper. & Platform Eng.
John Laurence, Sr. Dir.-Prod.

GROWTH PLANS/SPECIAL FEATURES:

Linden Research, Inc. (dba Linden Lab) develops platforms that empower people to create virtual experiences. Linden Lab is the creator of Second Life, an online collaborative 3D virtual build-and-play environment that millions of users have utilized for gaming and development purposes. Second Life differs from a typical massively multiplayer online role playing game (MMORPG) in that it provides nearly unlimited interactive and creative freedom as well as providing its users with the opportunity to retain intellectual property (IP) rights over creations. Once an object has been built, its creator has the IP rights to it and can sell it to other users, called Residents. A Second Life account includes access to an avatar personalization tool, as well as building tools using geometric primitives and scripting language, adding functionality to created objects. The company's Blocksworld offering is a lighthearted build-and-play system on the iPad for both children and adults. Linden's Sansar platform was created for virtual reality (VR) experiences, and is a creative medium for making it easy for people to create, share and sell their own social VR experiences. The company is headquartered in San Francisco, California, with additional U.S. offices in Seattle, Boston, Davis and Charlottesville.

Linden Lab offers employees medical, dental and vision insurance; stock options; tuition reimbursement; and a 401(k) plan.

FINANCIAL DATA: Note: Data for latest year may not have been available at press time.

In U.S. $	2018	2017	2016	2015	2014	2013
Revenue		70,000,000	77,700,000	75,000,000	77,000,000	76,000,000
R&D Expense						
Operating Income						
Operating Margin %						
SGA Expense						
Net Income						
Operating Cash Flow						
Capital Expenditure						
EBITDA						
Return on Assets %						
Return on Equity %						
Debt to Equity						

CONTACT INFORMATION:

Phone: 415-243-9000   Fax: 415-243-9045
Toll-Free:
Address: 945 Battery St., San Francisco, CA 94111 United States

STOCK TICKER/OTHER:

Stock Ticker: Private   Exchange:
Employees: 245   Fiscal Year Ends:
Parent Company:

SALARIES/BONUSES:

Top Exec. Salary: $ Bonus: $
Second Exec. Salary: $ Bonus: $

OTHER THOUGHTS:

Estimated Female Officers or Directors: 3
Hot Spot for Advancement for Women/Minorities: Y

Sales, profits and employees may be estimates. Financial information, benefits and other data can change quickly and may vary from those stated here.

LinkedIn Corporation

NAIC Code: 519130

www.linkedin.com

TYPES OF BUSINESS:
Business-Oriented Social Networking
Advertising Services
Recruiting Tools

BRANDS/DIVISIONS/AFFILIATES:
Microsoft Corporation
LinkedIn.com
Glint

CONTACTS: *Note: Officers with more than one job title may be intentionally listed here more than once.*
Jeffrey Weiner, CEO
Reid Hoffman, Chairman of the Board
Steve Sordello, CFO
Shannon Brayton, CMO
Christina Hall, Sr. VP-Human Resources
Michael Gamson, Senior VP, Divisional
Patricia Wadors, Senior VP, Divisional
James Scott, Senior VP, Divisional
Shannon Stubo, Senior VP, Divisional
Steven Sordello, Senior VP
Michael Callahan, Senior VP

GROWTH PLANS/SPECIAL FEATURES:
LinkedIn Corporation operates an online social networking site targeting the business and professional community. On LinkedIn.com users can post profiles, connect with co-workers, post resumes and search for job openings. Other features on the site include company pages, which allows companies to showcase brands and products; and a suite of products for corporate recruitment initiatives, including sourcing and pipelining, a referral engine, career pages and recruitment ads. The site generates revenue through ad sales, user subscription fees on premium accounts and enterprise hiring software licensing fees. The company offers a range of solutions to its members, including free solutions, such as stay connected and informed, advance my career and ubiquitous access; and monetized solutions, such as talent, marketing and premium subscription. Its membership base has nearly 600 million users in over 200 countries and territories (as of December 2018), and is available in multiple languages including English, French, German, Italian, Portuguese, Spanish, Japanese, Korean, Russian, Arabic and Turkish. LinkedIn operates as a subsidiary of Microsoft Corporation. In November 2018, LinkedIn acquired Glint, a leader in employee engagement that helps people in organizations do their best work, develop their skills and improve business results.

FINANCIAL DATA: *Note: Data for latest year may not have been available at press time.*

In U.S. $	2018	2017	2016	2015	2014	2013
Revenue		3,859,000,000	3,500,000,000	2,990,910,976	2,218,767,104	1,528,545,024
R&D Expense						
Operating Income						
Operating Margin %						
SGA Expense						
Net Income				-166,144,000	-15,747,000	26,769,000
Operating Cash Flow						
Capital Expenditure						
EBITDA						
Return on Assets %						
Return on Equity %						
Debt to Equity						

CONTACT INFORMATION:
Phone: 650 687-3600   Fax:
Toll-Free:
Address: 2029 Stierlin Ct., Mountain View, CA 94043 United States

STOCK TICKER/OTHER:
Stock Ticker: Subsidiary   Exchange:
Employees: 9,372   Fiscal Year Ends: 06/30
Parent Company: Microsoft Corporation

SALARIES/BONUSES:
Top Exec. Salary: $ Bonus: $
Second Exec. Salary: $ Bonus: $

OTHER THOUGHTS:
Estimated Female Officers or Directors: 4
Hot Spot for Advancement for Women/Minorities: Y

Lionbridge Technologies Inc

www.lionbridge.com

NAIC Code: 541511

TYPES OF BUSINESS:

Software Development and Testing
Web Site Language Translation
eLearning
Interpretation Communication Services

BRANDS/DIVISIONS/AFFILIATES:

HIG Capital LLC
Freeway
GeoFluent
onDemand
Translation Workspace

CONTACTS: Note: Officers with more than one job title may be intentionally listed here more than once.

John Fennelly, CEO
Rich Tobin, COO
Clemente Cohen, CFO
Jaime Punishill, CMO
Ann Lazarus-Barnes, Sr. VP-Human Resources
Rory Cowan, Founder
Margaret Shukur, General Counsel
Richard Tobin, General Manager, Divisional
Paula Shannon, Other Executive Officer
Marc Osofsky, Senior VP, Divisional

GROWTH PLANS/SPECIAL FEATURES:

Lionbridge Technologies, Inc. is a provider of translation, marketing and multilingual communication solutions. The firm serves more than 800 enterprises worldwide. The company provides a full suite of language, testing and development outsourcing services to businesses in engineering, global marketing, machine intelligence, content and testing, translation and localization, gaming, life sciences, banking and finance and legal services. Engineering services include technical information development, customer support information development, product design and engineering, training development, graphics and multimedia creation and web and marketing content. Global marketing services include global content media, global search, multilingual SEO, global social media, global campaign operations and marketing transcreation. Machine intelligence services include linguistic staffing, linguistic and data operations and user experience testing. Content and testing services include linguistic testing and functional testing. Translation and localization services include transcreation and interpretation services. Gaming services include translation and localization, audio production, game dialogue localization, QA and functional testing, community management and global marketing services. Life sciences services include regulatory solutions, medical device solutions, clinical solutions, life sciences marketing, corporate communication and life sciences translations. Banking and finance services include financial translation services, financial writing services, financial editing and proofreading services, digital content for the financial sector, financial reporting services and regulatory compliance. Legal services include document translation services, legal localization, legal interpretation, on-site staffing, e-discovery support, document production and transcription. The firm's products include Freeway, an all-in-one localization platform; GeoFluent, over-the-phone interpretation and communication tools; OnDemand, a high-quality translation service; Translation Workspace; and connectors, connectors for CMS platforms. The firm is a subsidiary of H.I.G. Capital LLC.

Lionbridge offers employees comprehensive health benefits, savings and 401(k) plans as well as employee assistance programs.

FINANCIAL DATA: Note: Data for latest year may not have been available at press time.

In U.S. $	2018	2017	2016	2015	2014	2013
Revenue		595,000,000	587,000,000	559,984,000	490,612,000	489,196,000
R&D Expense						
Operating Income						
Operating Margin %						
SGA Expense						
Net Income				14,237,000	8,107,000	11,640,000
Operating Cash Flow						
Capital Expenditure						
EBITDA						
Return on Assets %						
Return on Equity %						
Debt to Equity						

CONTACT INFORMATION:

Phone: 866-267-0437   Fax: 781 434-6034
Toll-Free:
Address: 1050 Winter St., Ste. 2300, Waltham, MA 02451 United States

STOCK TICKER/OTHER:

Stock Ticker: Private   Exchange:
Employees: 5,500   Fiscal Year Ends: 12/31
Parent Company: HIG Capital LLC

SALARIES/BONUSES:

Top Exec. Salary: $ Bonus: $
Second Exec. Salary: $ Bonus: $

OTHER THOUGHTS:

Estimated Female Officers or Directors: 5
Hot Spot for Advancement for Women/Minorities: Y

Sales, profits and employees may be estimates. Financial information, benefits and other data can change quickly and may vary from those stated here.

Lithium Technologies LLC

www.lithium.com

NAIC Code: 511210F

TYPES OF BUSINESS:

Computer Software, Multimedia, Graphics & Publishing Software

BRANDS/DIVISIONS/AFFILIATES:

Spredfast

GROWTH PLANS/SPECIAL FEATURES:

Lithium Technologies, LLC provides a software platform to help companies connect, engage and understand their customers. Lithium's social media solutions, online community and messaging platforms easily connect customers, content and conversations wherever they are happening. The firm's software is built to meet enterprise demands, delivering a seamless digital customer experience across social networks, websites and mobile devices. Industries served by Lithium include communications, financial services, technology, retail, travel and hospitality. Based in San Francisco, California, the firm has additional offices in Texas, New York and Oregon in the U.S., as well as internationally in the U.K., France, Switzerland, Germany, India, Singapore and Australia. In late-2018, Lithium Technologies merged with Spredfast, a global social media marketing software company.

Lithium offers its employees health, dental, vision, life, disability and AD&D insurance; 401(k); paid time off; and well-being incentives.

CONTACTS: *Note: Officers with more than one job title may be intentionally listed here more than once.*

Pete Hess, CEO
Sam Monti, CFO
Katherine Calvert, CMO
Michael O'Donnell, Chief Human Resources Officer
Raju Malhotra, CTO

FINANCIAL DATA: *Note: Data for latest year may not have been available at press time.*

In U.S. $	2018	2017	2016	2015	2014	2013
Revenue						
R&D Expense						
Operating Income						
Operating Margin %						
SGA Expense						
Net Income						
Operating Cash Flow						
Capital Expenditure						
EBITDA						
Return on Assets %						
Return on Equity %						
Debt to Equity						

CONTACT INFORMATION:

Phone: 415-757-3100   Fax: 415-757-3200
Toll-Free:
Address: Pier 1, Bay 1A, San Francisco, CA 94111 United States

STOCK TICKER/OTHER:

Stock Ticker: Private   Exchange:
Employees: 400   Fiscal Year Ends:
Parent Company:

SALARIES/BONUSES:

Top Exec. Salary: $ Bonus: $
Second Exec. Salary: $ Bonus: $

OTHER THOUGHTS:

Estimated Female Officers or Directors:
Hot Spot for Advancement for Women/Minorities:

LivePerson Inc

www.liveperson.com

NAIC Code: 511210K

TYPES OF BUSINESS:

E-Commerce Software
Customer Service Software
Sales & Marketing Service Software
Live Chat Applications

BRANDS/DIVISIONS/AFFILIATES:

LiveEngage
LiveEngage for Bots
Maven

CONTACTS: Note: Officers with more than one job title may be intentionally listed here more than once.

Robert Locascio, CEO
Christopher Greiner, CFO
Alexander Spinelli, Chief Technology Officer
Daryl Carlough, Controller
Monica Greenberg, Executive VP, Divisional

GROWTH PLANS/SPECIAL FEATURES:

LivePerson, Inc. is a provider of digital engagement solutions. It offers a cloud-based platform that enables businesses to proactively connect with consumers through chat, voice and content delivery across multiple channels and screens, including websites, social media, tablets and mobile devices. LivePerson monitors and analyzes behavioral data. Annually, the firm monitors more than 2.5 billion visitor sessions per month across its customers' websites. The company is organized into two operating segments: business, which enables brands to leverage LiveEngage's intelligence engine; and consumer, which facilitates online transactions between independent service providers and individual consumers seeking information and knowledge for a fee via mobile and online messaging. LiveEngage is LivePerson's primary product. It is a cloud-based customer engagement solution that enables businesses to derive the greatest possible results from their digital assets. Through predictive intelligent targeting, LiveEngage helps brands understand their site visitors' intent and value, enabling them to connect through the most appropriate type of engagement (chat, personalized messages and offers) across all channels and devices. LiveEngage learns from every interaction, creating a feedback loop that enriches intelligence and optimizes future engagements, further enhancing business results. The company's LiveEngage for Bots is an enterprise bot management platform designed to run multiple bots at scale in the digital, marketing and care operations of large brands. More than 18,000 businesses employ LivePerson's technology, including Adobe, Citibank, HSBC, EE, IBM, L'Oreal, Orange, PNC and The Home Depot. In December 2018, LivePerson launched Maven, a conversational artificial intelligence (AI) that enables brands to replace traditional websites and 800-numbers with personalized conversations over SMS, Facebook Messenger, WhatsApp, Google RCS Business Messaging, Amazon Alexa and other messenger/voice assistant services.

FINANCIAL DATA: Note: Data for latest year may not have been available at press time.

In U.S. $	2018	2017	2016	2015	2014	2013
Revenue		218,876,000	222,779,000	239,012,000	209,931,000	177,805,000
R&D Expense		40,034,000	40,198,000	38,974,000	37,329,000	36,397,000
Operating Income		-15,232,000	-17,040,000	-7,044,000	-5,167,000	-4,474,000
Operating Margin %		-6.95%	-7.64%	-2.94%	-2.46%	-2.51%
SGA Expense		134,029,000	132,575,000	131,899,000	123,445,000	102,456,000
Net Income		-18,191,000	-25,873,000	-26,444,000	-7,348,000	-3,499,000
Operating Cash Flow		10,290,000	24,560,000	21,831,000	15,673,000	16,958,000
Capital Expenditure		17,390,000	12,344,000	12,980,000	14,040,000	8,044,000
EBITDA		1,808,000	1,644,000	13,110,000	8,994,000	6,259,000
Return on Assets %		-8.04%	-11.60%	-11.34%	-3.30%	-1.69%
Return on Equity %		-13.06%	-17.03%	-15.30%	-4.33%	-2.12%
Debt to Equity						

CONTACT INFORMATION:

Phone: 212 609-4200   Fax: 212 609-4201
Toll-Free:
Address: 475 Tenth Ave., 5/Fl, New York, NY 10018 United States

STOCK TICKER/OTHER:

Stock Ticker: LPSN   Exchange: NAS
Employees: 985   Fiscal Year Ends: 12/31
Parent Company:

SALARIES/BONUSES:

Top Exec. Salary: $552,150   Bonus: $1,000,000
Second Exec. Salary: $429,450   Bonus: $

OTHER THOUGHTS:

Estimated Female Officers or Directors: 2
Hot Spot for Advancement for Women/Minorities:

LiveRamp Holdings Inc

NAIC Code: 511210K

TYPES OF BUSINESS:

Consumer Data Management
Consumer Databases
Consulting and Analytics
Risk Mitigation Services
CDI Technology
Consumer Privacy Solutions

BRANDS/DIVISIONS/AFFILIATES:

IdentityLink
LiveRamp AbiliTec

CONTACTS: Note: Officers with more than one job title may be intentionally listed here more than once.

Scott Howe, CEO
Chris Garber, Sr. VP-Operations
Scott Howe, CEO
Warren C. Jenson, CFO
Rebecca Stone, Dir.-Mktg.
Brandon Sammut, Dir.-People & Culture
Richard Erwin, General Manager, Divisional
Dennis Self, General Manager, Divisional
James Arra, President, Divisional
Anneka Gupta, President, Divisional

GROWTH PLANS/SPECIAL FEATURES:

LiveRamp Holdings, Inc. (formerly Acxiom Corporation) provides an identity platform to brands and their partners in order to deliver innovative products and consumer experiences. The firm's IdentityLink connects people, data and devices across the digital and physical world. It powers marketplace platforms and safely connects consumers with brands and products. IdentityLink resolves people data to any of 500+ technology platforms that support targeting, personalization and measurement. The platform can resolve everything from purchase and behavioral data to campaign impressions back to a consumer for an omnichannel view. It enables publishers, data owners and platforms to have a broader array of options for connecting their data together and for obtaining new monetization opportunities. LiveRamp AbiliTec is an offline personally identifiable information (PII) resolution technology that gives platforms and the marketers they work with the ability to connect and update what they know about consumers. This resolves PII data across enterprise databases and systems so as to deliver enhanced customer experience. In October 2018, Acxiom Corporation sold its marketing solutions business to The Interpublic Group of Companies, Inc., and began operating as Acxiom, LLC. Subsequently, Acxiom changed its corporate name to LiveRamp Holdings, and focuses on its artificial intelligent identity platform. LiveRamp trades on the New York Stock Exchange under ticker symbol: RAMP.

LiveRamp offers employees health, dental and vision insurance; stock purchase plans; and paid time off.

FINANCIAL DATA: Note: Data for latest year may not have been available at press time.

In U.S. $	2018	2017	2016	2015	2014	2013
Revenue	917,406,016	880,246,976	850,088,000	1,020,059,008	1,097,544,960	1,099,358,976
R&D Expense						
Operating Income						
Operating Margin %						
SGA Expense						
Net Income	23,480,000	4,108,000	6,703,000	-11,031,000	8,863,000	57,607,000
Operating Cash Flow						
Capital Expenditure						
EBITDA						
Return on Assets %						
Return on Equity %						
Debt to Equity						

CONTACT INFORMATION:

Phone: 866-352-3267   Fax:
Toll-Free:
Address: 225 Bush St., 17/Fl., San Francisco, CA 94104 United States

STOCK TICKER/OTHER:

Stock Ticker: RAMP
Employees: 3,260
Parent Company:

Exchange: NAS
Fiscal Year Ends: 03/31

SALARIES/BONUSES:

Top Exec. Salary: $ Bonus: $
Second Exec. Salary: $ Bonus: $

OTHER THOUGHTS:

Estimated Female Officers or Directors: 4
Hot Spot for Advancement for Women/Minorities: Y

LiveWorld Inc

www.liveworld.com

NAIC Code: 519130

TYPES OF BUSINESS:

Diversified Internet Portal
Online Communities
Online Business Services
Online Marketing Services
Online Events

BRANDS/DIVISIONS/AFFILIATES:

CONTACTS: Note: Officers with more than one job title may be intentionally listed here more than once.

Peter Friedman, CEO
David Houston, CFO
Jason Kapler, VP-Mktg.
Tina Gazzano, Dir.- Human Resources
Frank Chevallier, VP-Prod. Mgmt.
Trevor Griffiths, VP-Eng.
Trevor Griffiths, VP-Oper.
Jenna Woodul, Chief Community Officer
Bruce Dembecki, VP-Moderation Svcs.
Virginie Glaenzer, VP-Mktg.
Martin Bishop, VP-Account Mgr.-Wal-Mart
Peter Friedman, Chmn.

GROWTH PLANS/SPECIAL FEATURES:

LiveWorld, Inc. is a leading provider of online customer communities and social networking and interactive services for businesses and consumers. The company offers businesses the ability to develop and expand online relationships with customers, suppliers and employees through online community software and moderation services to building their brands. LiveWorld specializes in handling the speed and scale requirements of brands to engage customers one-on-one in real-time, and deliver personalized interactions with a human touch. LiveWorld's conversation-centric engagement software comprises a single platform, which includes messaging apps, social media, web and mobile chat and short message service (SMS) all in one feed. The firm's software solutions offer real-time engagement for maximizing productivity, and allows businesses to customize features for auto-responses and chatbot engagement for dynamic customer experiences. LiveWorld's software technology includes resolutions management, comprehensive analytics and data insight. The firm develops workflows and security procedures with its customer's legal, public relations and brand guidelines in mind, and provides 24/7 global coverage with 70 language and country combinations for all social channels. For the pharmaceutical industry, LiveWorld offers adverse events management, content review and monitoring, insights and analytics strategy and community management. The firm primarily serves the adverse events management, logistics, retail, pharmaceutical, travel and consumer packaged goods sectors.

FINANCIAL DATA: Note: Data for latest year may not have been available at press time.

In U.S. $	2018	2017	2016	2015	2014	2013
Revenue				9,873,000	13,803,000	9,834,000
R&D Expense						
Operating Income						
Operating Margin %						
SGA Expense						
Net Income				-1,412,000	-378,000	812,000
Operating Cash Flow						
Capital Expenditure						
EBITDA						
Return on Assets %						
Return on Equity %						
Debt to Equity						

CONTACT INFORMATION:

Phone: 408 871-5200   Fax: 408 871-5300
Toll-Free: 800-301-9507
Address: 4340 Stevens Creek Blvd., Ste. 101, San Jose, CA 95129
United States

STOCK TICKER/OTHER:

Stock Ticker: LVWD   Exchange: PINX
Employees: 73   Fiscal Year Ends: 12/31
Parent Company:

SALARIES/BONUSES:

Top Exec. Salary: $ Bonus: $
Second Exec. Salary: $ Bonus: $

OTHER THOUGHTS:

Estimated Female Officers or Directors: 7
Hot Spot for Advancement for Women/Minorities: Y

LivingSocial Inc

www.livingsocial.com

NAIC Code: 541810E

TYPES OF BUSINESS:

Online Coupons and Discount Offers

BRANDS/DIVISIONS/AFFILIATES:

Groupon Inc
Great Deals

GROWTH PLANS/SPECIAL FEATURES:

LivingSocial, Inc. is an online coupon and discount provider that introduces its members to deals within their local area and abroad. Deals offered by the site cover a range of interests, such as local offerings and discounts on the best things to do in select cities; travel and hotel deals and packages; guided adventures; a curated selection of high-quality products; events such as sports, music or theater; and offers and services in relation to home improvement or design. The site is also a marketplace for promotion codes, digital coupons and information on sales from online brands. LivingSocial's vast network provides a platform for businesses to enhance marketing efforts. The firm's Great Deals links members to offers that are up to 85% off their regular prices, with some comprising of last-chance getaways to particular destinations. LivingSocial operates as a subsidiary of Groupon, Inc.

CONTACTS: *Note: Officers with more than one job title may be intentionally listed here more than once.*

Val Aleksenko, CIO
Jake Maas, Sr. VP-Merch. Solutions
Ryan Owens, VP-Eng.
Jim Bramson, General Counsel
Jake Maas, Sr. VP-Oper.
Doug Miller, Sr. VP-New Bus. Initiatives
Mitch Spolan, Sr. VP-National Sales
Eric Eichmann, Pres., Int'l

FINANCIAL DATA: *Note: Data for latest year may not have been available at press time.*

In U.S. $	2018	2017	2016	2015	2014	2013
Revenue		160,000,000	151,000,000	140,000,000	231,000,000	302,000,000
R&D Expense						
Operating Income						
Operating Margin %						
SGA Expense						
Net Income						
Operating Cash Flow						
Capital Expenditure						
EBITDA						
Return on Assets %						
Return on Equity %						
Debt to Equity						

CONTACT INFORMATION:

Phone: 202-695-7000   Fax:
Toll-Free: 888-808-6676
Address: 1445 New York Ave. NW, Washington, DC 20005 United States

STOCK TICKER/OTHER:

Stock Ticker: Private   Exchange:
Employees: 1,600   Fiscal Year Ends:
Parent Company: Groupon Inc

SALARIES/BONUSES:

Top Exec. Salary: $ Bonus: $
Second Exec. Salary: $ Bonus: $

OTHER THOUGHTS:

Estimated Female Officers or Directors: 3
Hot Spot for Advancement for Women/Minorities: Y

Lookout Inc

www.lookout.com

NAIC Code: 511210E

TYPES OF BUSINESS:
Computer Software, Security & Anti-Virus

BRANDS/DIVISIONS/AFFILIATES:

CONTACTS: Note: Officers with more than one job title may be intentionally listed here more than once.
Jim Dolce, CEO
Mark Nasiff, COO
Missy Ballew, Chief Human Resources Officer
Kevin Mahaffey, Chief Technology Officer

GROWTH PLANS/SPECIAL FEATURES:
Lookout, Inc. is a cybersecurity company that predicts and stops mobile attacks before harm is done to an individual or an enterprise. The company's cloud-based technology is generated by a global network of more than 100 million mobile sensors fueling a dataset of virtually all the mobile code in the world. Within this data, Lookout identifies connections that would otherwise go unseen and stop cybercriminals from attacking mobile devices. Lookout produces mobile security applications for iOS and Android devices which include a phishing/malicious website blocker, privacy advisory, photo and call history backup, device-to-device data transfer, remote locking and wiping, as well as support services. Its software also includes the ability to remotely snap a picture of the phone's environment when lost or stolen, which can help to identify the thief or location of the device. Moreover, the firm has an app that produces real-time theft alerts, including a photograph of the thief taken automatically by the device when certain actions are taken such as a mistyped phone code. Software also can include a signal flare, which automatically flags the location of a phone once the battery begins to die, so that the device user can later ping its last known location. Partners of the company include AT&T, BlackBerry, Verizon, T-Mobile, TechData, Sprint, B23, Carahsoft, Ingram, KDDI, Orange, PaRaBaL, Qualcomm and more. Its investors include Accel Partners, Andreessen Horowitz and BlackRock.

FINANCIAL DATA: Note: Data for latest year may not have been available at press time.

In U.S. $	2018	2017	2016	2015	2014	2013
Revenue						
R&D Expense						
Operating Income						
Operating Margin %						
SGA Expense						
Net Income						
Operating Cash Flow						
Capital Expenditure						
EBITDA						
Return on Assets %						
Return on Equity %						
Debt to Equity						

CONTACT INFORMATION:
Phone: 415-281-2820   Fax:
Toll-Free:
Address: 1 Front St., Ste. 2700, San Francisco, CA 94111-5386 United States

STOCK TICKER/OTHER:
Stock Ticker: Private   Exchange:
Employees: 330   Fiscal Year Ends:
Parent Company:

SALARIES/BONUSES:
Top Exec. Salary: $ Bonus: $
Second Exec. Salary: $ Bonus: $

OTHER THOUGHTS:
Estimated Female Officers or Directors:
Hot Spot for Advancement for Women/Minorities:

LookSmart Group Inc

NAIC Code: 519130

www.looksmart.com

TYPES OF BUSINESS:
Search Portal-Directory Model
Customer Analysis Software
Advertising Services
Publisher Services
Vertical Search Services
Bookmarking Services

BRANDS/DIVISIONS/AFFILIATES:
LookSmart Network
LookSmart Publisher Solutions

CONTACTS: *Note: Officers with more than one job title may be intentionally listed here more than once.*
Michael Onghai, CEO

GROWTH PLANS/SPECIAL FEATURES:
LookSmart Group, Inc., is a search advertising network and management company with over 6 billion monthly queries. Its business is focused on supporting its advertiser base through a syndicated network that specializes in pay-per-click text ads. LookSmart optimizes traffic from publishers and other networks to ultimately benefit its advertisers. LookSmart serves small businesses, brands and agencies and affiliate marketing firms. The firm has developed its own tools and processes to help identify and filter invalid traffic. These processes include automated fraud detection controls to help catch instances of unusual activity such as spiders, bots and click fraud; filtering software to help identify and remove non-converting traffic from customer's bills; and filtering software to pre-screen sites for traffic quality and click-through rate consistency. LookSmart's account managers do a thorough analysis of the client's current campaigns and identify the ones with the highest odds for success on the LookSmart Network. Once an advertising plan has been agreed upon, the firm tracks the clicks and obtains/tests data feedback; launches an initial 10-day evaluation period of the product, which is optimized continually to reach KPI (key performance indicator) goals; and then presents the initial campaign evaluation to the client, makes recommendations for ongoing spend and ramps the campaign accordingly. LookSmart Publisher Solutions can be purchased and used a la carte or as a package. Clients receive personalized service, unique analytics and transparent reporting.

FINANCIAL DATA: *Note: Data for latest year may not have been available at press time.*

In U.S. $	2018	2017	2016	2015	2014	2013
Revenue		5,000,000	6,318,000	4,548,000	4,702,000	6,679,000
R&D Expense						
Operating Income						
Operating Margin %						
SGA Expense						
Net Income			-1,051,000	-3,208,000	-6,419,000	-5,356,000
Operating Cash Flow						
Capital Expenditure						
EBITDA						
Return on Assets %						
Return on Equity %						
Debt to Equity						

CONTACT INFORMATION:
Phone: 415 348-7000   Fax:
Toll-Free:
Address: 2850 W. Horizon Ridge Pkwy., Ste. 200, Henderson, NV 89052 United States

STOCK TICKER/OTHER:
Stock Ticker: Private
Employees: 10
Parent Company:

Exchange:
Fiscal Year Ends: 12/31

SALARIES/BONUSES:
Top Exec. Salary: $ Bonus: $
Second Exec. Salary: $ Bonus: $

OTHER THOUGHTS:
Estimated Female Officers or Directors:
Hot Spot for Advancement for Women/Minorities:

Lyft Inc

www.lyft.me

NAIC Code: 561599

TYPES OF BUSINESS:
Car Ride Dispatch Service, Mobile App-Based
Bicycle Rental & Sharing Systems

BRANDS/DIVISIONS/AFFILIATES:
Blue Vision Labs
Motivate International Inc

CONTACTS: *Note: Officers with more than one job title may be intentionally listed here more than once.*
Logan Green, CEO
John Zimmer, Pres.
Brian Roberts, CFO
Amit Patel, Head-Bus. Dev.
David Estrada, VP-Gov't Rel.
Jonathan McNeill, COO

GROWTH PLANS/SPECIAL FEATURES:
Lyft, Inc. is a smartphone-based ridesharing and peer-to-peer transportation company that designs, develops and develops a mobile app that matches drivers with passengers who requires rides. Riders turn on the app and locate nearby drivers that are available on-demand. Lyft drivers can be located in small or big cities throughout North America. Riders pay automatically through the app, which is processed from the passenger's saved credit card once the ride ends. In addition, users can schedule rides up to seven days in advance. Lyft provides additional insurance policies, at no cost to the driver. The firm works with leading insurance carriers to provide various coverages including, commercial auto liability insurance up to $1 million per occurrence, contingent comprehensive and collision insurance for drivers who carry comprehensive and collision coverage on their personal auto policy, and coverage for bodily injury caused by uninsured/underinsured motorists when engaged in a ride. Drivers rate passengers after each ride. Drivers get paid for every trip on a per-minute and mile basis. Money is deposited into the driver's account each week automatically, or can be cashed out instantly with Express Pay. Drivers must be 21 years of age and own an iPhone or Android phone; must undergo a DMV check, plus a national and county background check. Vehicles need to have four external door handles and at least five total seat belts. Drivers must be a covered party on the car's in-state insurance, and have in-state license plates. All of these are confirmed through the 19-point vehicle inspection process at the DMV. Cars have Lyft age requirements as well, which vary by state. During 2018, Lyft acquired Blue Vision Labs, a London-based augmented reality startup; and bike-sharing company, Motivate International, Inc.

FINANCIAL DATA: *Note: Data for latest year may not have been available at press time.*

In U.S. $	2018	2017	2016	2015	2014	2013
Revenue	1,815,000,000	1,050,000,000	490,000,000	270,000,000	130,000,000	31,500,000
R&D Expense						
Operating Income						
Operating Margin %						
SGA Expense						
Net Income		-620,000,000	-600,000,000	-290,000,000		
Operating Cash Flow						
Capital Expenditure						
EBITDA						
Return on Assets %						
Return on Equity %						
Debt to Equity						

CONTACT INFORMATION:
Phone: 855-946-7433   Fax:
Toll-Free:
Address: 185 Berry St., Ste. 5000, San Francisco, CA 94107 United States

STOCK TICKER/OTHER:
Stock Ticker: Private   Exchange:
Employees: 500   Fiscal Year Ends:
Parent Company:

SALARIES/BONUSES:
Top Exec. Salary: $ Bonus: $
Second Exec. Salary: $ Bonus: $

OTHER THOUGHTS:
Estimated Female Officers or Directors: 2
Hot Spot for Advancement for Women/Minorities:

Macquarium Inc

www.macquarium.com

NAIC Code: 541810E

TYPES OF BUSINESS:

Consulting-Web Development
Interactive Marketing
Internet Training Systems
e-Commerce Consulting
Computer Animation

BRANDS/DIVISIONS/AFFILIATES:

GROWTH PLANS/SPECIAL FEATURES:

Macquarium, Inc. is an interactive agency and web development consulting firm. The company collaborates with clients to create e-business services designed to generate revenue, reduce costs and enhance user efficiency. Macquarium provides three primary solutions: customer experience, by formulating strategies to deliver on customer wants and needs; digital products and services, designing and building digital experiences; and digital marketing, creating emotional connections between customers and brands. The firm's specialties include customer experience strategy, user experience, service design, omnichannel strategy and design, portals and intranets, digital products and services, mobile strategy and design, product strategy and design, product design, marketing and digital marketing. The firm is based in Atlanta, and has offices in Washington D.C., Houston and San Francisco.

CONTACTS: Note: Officers with more than one job title may be intentionally listed here more than once.

Carlos Pimenta, CEO
Carlos Pimenta, Pres.
Cara Carson, CFO
Jay Cann, CTO

FINANCIAL DATA: Note: Data for latest year may not have been available at press time.

In U.S. $	2018	2017	2016	2015	2014	2013
Revenue						
R&D Expense						
Operating Income						
Operating Margin %						
SGA Expense						
Net Income						
Operating Cash Flow						
Capital Expenditure						
EBITDA						
Return on Assets %						
Return on Equity %						
Debt to Equity						

CONTACT INFORMATION:

Phone: 404-554-4000   Fax: 404-554-4001
Toll-Free:
Address: 1800 Peachtree St., Ste. 250, Atlanta, GA 30309 United States

STOCK TICKER/OTHER:

Stock Ticker: Private   Exchange:
Employees: 60   Fiscal Year Ends:
Parent Company:

SALARIES/BONUSES:

Top Exec. Salary: $ Bonus: $
Second Exec. Salary: $ Bonus: $

OTHER THOUGHTS:

Estimated Female Officers or Directors:
Hot Spot for Advancement for Women/Minorities:

Mail.Ru Group Limited

corp.mail.ru/en

NAIC Code: 519130

TYPES OF BUSINESS:

Internet Web Site Holding Company

BRANDS/DIVISIONS/AFFILIATES:

My.com
Pixonic
Delivery Club
ZakaZaka
GeekBrains
ESforce
Youla
Pandao

CONTACTS: *Note: Officers with more than one job title may be intentionally listed here more than once.*

Boris Dobrodeev, CEO
Vladimir Nikolsky, COO
Gregory Finger, Pres.
Matthew Hammond, CFO
Kirill Obukh, VP-Mktg.
Vladimir Gabrielyan, CTO
Dmitry Grishin, Chmn.
Verdi Israelian, Head-Russian Oper.

GROWTH PLANS/SPECIAL FEATURES:

Mail.Ru Group Limited is a Russian investment firm and holding company that primarily develops internet communications and entertainment services in Russia and globally. The firm's international communication brand is My.com, the largest mobile media platform in the country. It offers email services, e-commerce services, social networks services, instant messaging, games, business-to-business services, maps and media. Mail.Ru Group developed a single integrated platform that delivers its communication and entertainment internet services, including internet message strategies as well as online games, maps and navigation strategies. In addition, Mail.Ru wholly-owns Pixonic, a developer of mobile games; wholly-owns Delivery Club and ZakaZaka, each of which are online/mobile meal search and order applications; location-based and cross-border marketplaces Youla and Pandao; majority-owns GeekBrains, an educational online platform for programmers; and owns minority stakes in several internet companies in Russia, Ukraine and Israel; and runs the two largest Russian language social networking services and communication platforms, VKontakte and Odnoklassniki. In March 2018, Mail.Ru acquired ESforce, the parent of several e-sports ventures. In September, Mail.Ru joined RDIF, Alibaba Group and MegaFon to create a new social commerce joint venture in Russia, named AliExpress Russia. In December, Mail.Ru acquired 80% of United Music Agency.

FINANCIAL DATA: *Note: Data for latest year may not have been available at press time.*

In U.S. $	2018	2017	2016	2015	2014	2013
Revenue		897,354,000	702,360,000	508,439,000	506,749,216	388,142,308
R&D Expense						
Operating Income						
Operating Margin %						
SGA Expense						
Net Income		39,557,500	190,840,000	134,447,000	177,301,321	162,216,970
Operating Cash Flow						
Capital Expenditure						
EBITDA						
Return on Assets %						
Return on Equity %						
Debt to Equity						

CONTACT INFORMATION:

Phone: 44-203-178-2601   Fax:
Toll-Free:
Address: Leningradsky prospekt 39, bldg 79, Moscow, 125167 Russia

STOCK TICKER/OTHER:

Stock Ticker: MAIL
Employees: 3,046
Parent Company:

Exchange: London
Fiscal Year Ends: 12/31

SALARIES/BONUSES:

Top Exec. Salary: $ Bonus: $
Second Exec. Salary: $ Bonus: $

OTHER THOUGHTS:

Estimated Female Officers or Directors:
Hot Spot for Advancement for Women/Minorities:

MailChimp (The Rocket Science Group LLC)   mailchimp.com

NAIC Code: 519130

TYPES OF BUSINESS:

E-mail platform
Digital Marketing Tools

BRANDS/DIVISIONS/AFFILIATES:

MailChimp

CONTACTS: Note: Officers with more than one job title may be intentionally listed here more than once.

Ben Chestnut, CEO
Farrah Kennedy, COO
Rick Lynch, CFO
Tom Klein, CMO
Marti Wolf, Chief Culture Officer
Joe Uhl, VP-Operations

GROWTH PLANS/SPECIAL FEATURES:

The Rocket Science Group, LLC does business as MailChimp, an email marketing platform for people and businesses. The platform's features and integrations allow users to send marketing emails, automated messages and targeted campaigns. It also integrates with various applications and services such as Salesforce, Eventbrite, Google, Twitter, Facebook, Shopify and SurveyMonkey. Its detailed reports help provide insight for decision making purposes in order to continue to improve, learn and grow over time. MailChimp enables users to connect their store with one of its e-commerce integrations. Stores can then create targeted campaigns, automate helpful product follow-ups and send back-in-stock messages. It comprises flexible design templates for brands of any size, through its easy drag-and-drop designer. Collaboration options are also available, including multi-user accounts and comments inside the editor. MailChimp's pricing plan for new businesses is free; $10/month for growing businesses, which offers automation workflows, e-commerce-focused features and more tools than the free option; and $199/month for pro marketers, comprising improved performance and enterprise-level features for high-volume senders. The Rocket Science Group is headquartered in Atlanta, Georgia.

New hires are provided with a mentor called a Chimpanion to help them meet people from various departments and understanding the inner workings of the firm. The firm's office moto is "listen hard, change fast." Major offices are in Atlanta, Oakland and Brooklyn. A profit sharing plan is emphasized.

FINANCIAL DATA: Note: Data for latest year may not have been available at press time.

In U.S. $	2018	2017	2016	2015	2014	2013
Revenue		588,000,000	455,000,000	280,000,000		
R&D Expense						
Operating Income						
Operating Margin %						
SGA Expense						
Net Income						
Operating Cash Flow						
Capital Expenditure						
EBITDA						
Return on Assets %						
Return on Equity %						
Debt to Equity						

CONTACT INFORMATION:

Phone: 678-999-0141   Fax:
Toll-Free:
Address: 675 Ponce de Leon Ave. N.E., Ste. 5000, Atlanta, GA 30308 United States

STOCK TICKER/OTHER:

Stock Ticker: Private
Employees: 1,000
Parent Company:

Exchange:
Fiscal Year Ends:

SALARIES/BONUSES:

Top Exec. Salary: $ Bonus: $
Second Exec. Salary: $ Bonus: $

OTHER THOUGHTS:

Estimated Female Officers or Directors:
Hot Spot for Advancement for Women/Minorities:

Major League Baseball Advanced Media LP (MLBAM)
www.mlbam.com
NAIC Code: 519130

TYPES OF BUSINESS:
Online Delivery of Sporting Events
Streaming Sports Media

BRANDS/DIVISIONS/AFFILIATES:
At Bat

CONTACTS: *Note: Officers with more than one job title may be intentionally listed here more than once.*
Bob Starkey, CFO

GROWTH PLANS/SPECIAL FEATURES:
Major League Baseball Advanced Media LP (MLBAM) is a full-service solutions provider that delivers digital content through all forms of interactive media. Its capabilities are designed for web, mobile applications and connected devices while integrating live and on-demand multimedia. MLBAM's services include business & content strategy, delivering back-end infrastructure, as well as development and operational management of custom multi-platform applications; UX (user experience) & product design, providing solutions for all forms of digital presence such as websites, mobile web applications, connected devices, marketing campaigns and social media; social media & marketing, a suite of marketing solutions that are fully customizable and able to develop, integrate and manage initiatives; ticketing, which supports digital ticketing strategies such as print-at-home, mobile, season & package plans, secondary market, dynamic pricing and interactive seating; sponsorship & advertising; ecommerce & paid content, a subscription platform that supports digital products such as live and on-demand multimedia, fantasy games, gamecast applications and fan clubs with password-protected login; multimedia & live streaming, which operates and distributes live events and daily streams; mobile web & applications; and statistics & data applications, which deploys proprietary software to chronicle every pitch of every game throughout the season, in-game highlights, box scores and player stats. The firm's At Bat offering is a subscription-based application that provides live scores, statistics, pitch tracking, player cards, notifications and news via online and mobile devices.

FINANCIAL DATA: *Note: Data for latest year may not have been available at press time.*

In U.S. $	2018	2017	2016	2015	2014	2013
Revenue	130,000,000	110,000,000	900,000,000	850,000,000	800,000,000	
R&D Expense						
Operating Income						
Operating Margin %						
SGA Expense						
Net Income						
Operating Cash Flow						
Capital Expenditure						
EBITDA						
Return on Assets %						
Return on Equity %						
Debt to Equity						

CONTACT INFORMATION:
Phone: 212-485-6142   Fax: 212-485-8111
Toll-Free:
Address: 75 Ninth Ave., New York, NY 10011 United States

STOCK TICKER/OTHER:
Stock Ticker: Private   Exchange:
Employees: Fiscal Year Ends:
Parent Company:

SALARIES/BONUSES:
Top Exec. Salary: $ Bonus: $
Second Exec. Salary: $ Bonus: $

OTHER THOUGHTS:
Estimated Female Officers or Directors:
Hot Spot for Advancement for Women/Minorities:

MakeMyTrip Limited

www.makemytrip.com

NAIC Code: 561510

TYPES OF BUSINESS:

Online Travel Services

BRANDS/DIVISIONS/AFFILIATES:

MakeMyTrip (India) Private Limited
Ibibo Group Holdings (Singapore) Pte Ltd
Ibibo Group Private Limited
ITC Bangkok Co Ltd
Luxury Tours & Travel Pte Ltd
Luxury Tours (Malaysia) Sdn Bhd
MakeMyTrip Inc

CONTACTS: *Note: Officers with more than one job title may be intentionally listed here more than once.*

Deep Kalra, CEO
Mohit Kabra, CFO
Amit Somani, Chief Prod. Officer
Keyur Joshi, Chief Commercial Officer
Mohit Gupta, Chief Bus. Officer-Holidays
Deep Kalra, Chmn.
Amit Saberwal, Chief Bus. Officer-Intl Markets

GROWTH PLANS/SPECIAL FEATURES:

MakeMyTrip Limited is a leading online travel site in India. The company conducts its business primarily through Indian subsidiaries MakeMyTrip (India) Private Limited and Ibibo Group Private Limited. Ibibo is a wholly-owned subsidiary of Ibibo Group Holdings (Singapore) Pte. Ltd., which itself is wholly-owned by MakeMyTrip. The company's primary websites in India (www.makemytrip.com, www.goibibo.com and www.redbus.in) and related mobile apps enable travelers to research, plan and book a wide range of travel services and products in India as well as overseas. Services and products include air ticketing, hotels, rail tickets, bus tickets, car hire and ancillary travel requirements such as facilitating across to third-party travel insurance and visa processing. As of fiscal 2018, the firm has approximately 33.4 million active monthly users on its MakeMyTrip, goibibo and redBus mobile applications. Other subsidiaries of the company include: ITC Bangkok Co. Ltd. is based in Thailand, which operates a group of companies known as the ITC Group: Luxury Tours & Travel Pte. Ltd., based in Singapore; Luxury Tours (Malaysia) Sdn. Bhd.; and MakeMyTrip, Inc., based in the U.S. MakeMyTrip currently targets its services and travel products to leisure travelers and corporate travelers who prefer to make their own travel arrangements through the firm's online and offline sales channels.

FINANCIAL DATA: *Note: Data for latest year may not have been available at press time.*

In U.S. $	2018	2017	2016	2015	2014	2013
Revenue	675,256,000	447,616,000	336,054,000	299,662,000	255,374,600	228,822,000
R&D Expense						
Operating Income	-216,139,000	-120,174,000	-40,615,000	4,199,000	-2,079,904	-17,991,680
Operating Margin %	-32	-21.40%	-12.08%	1.40%	-.81%	-7.86%
SGA Expense	586,858,000	321,308,000	198,571,000	124,406,000	102,325,100	100,736,600
Net Income	-218,412,000	-110,168,000	-88,542,000	-18,252,000	-20,934,330	-27,592,520
Operating Cash Flow	-125,478,000	-108,457,000	-66,000,000	10,827,000	-3,957,596	13,595,900
Capital Expenditure	12,095,000	14,982,000	11,109,000	6,968,000	5,568,734	6,984,526
EBITDA	-189,889,000	-87,001,000	-75,793,000	-10,026,000	-7,359,168	-14,730,540
Return on Assets %	-13.19%	-11.32%	-25.98%	-6.63%	-9.01%	-15.12%
Return on Equity %	-14.74%	-14.86%	-75.37%	-11.44%	-15.92%	-25.08%
Debt to Equity			2.51			

CONTACT INFORMATION:

Phone: 91 1244395000   Fax:
Toll-Free: 800-102-8747
Address: 19/FI, Bldg. 5, DLF Cyber City, Gurgaon, 122002 India

STOCK TICKER/OTHER:

Stock Ticker: MMYT   Exchange: NAS
Employees: 3,426   Fiscal Year Ends: 03/31
Parent Company:

SALARIES/BONUSES:

Top Exec. Salary: $ Bonus: $
Second Exec. Salary: $ Bonus: $

OTHER THOUGHTS:

Estimated Female Officers or Directors:
Hot Spot for Advancement for Women/Minorities:

Manhattan Associates Inc

www.manh.com

NAIC Code: 511210A

TYPES OF BUSINESS:

Computer Software, Supply Chain & Logistics
Consulting & Support
RFID System Integration
Consulting Services

BRANDS/DIVISIONS/AFFILIATES:

CONTACTS: *Note: Officers with more than one job title may be intentionally listed here more than once.*

Eddie Capel, CEO
Dennis Story, CFO
John Huntz, Chairman of the Board
Linda Pinne, Chief Accounting Officer
Bruce Richards, Other Executive Officer
Robert Howell, Senior VP, Divisional

GROWTH PLANS/SPECIAL FEATURES:

Manhattan Associates, Inc. develops and provides technology-based supply chain software services. The firm's products consist of software and hardware and are used for both the managing and execution of supply chain activities. The company serves various industries, including consumer goods, food, government, high-tech/electronics, industrial/wholesale, life science, logistics service providers, retail and transportation, and specializes in demand forecasting and inventory replenishment, warehouse and labor management, performance analysis and event planning. Manhattan Associates' software solutions platform provides three major benefits: cross-functional business solutions, total cost of ownership and the power of shared components. Its software solutions modules are comprised of planning, including assortment, omni-channel, financial and item planning; inventory optimization; omni-channel central, including customer service, enterprise inventory and order management; omni-channel local, including point of sale, clienteling, store fulfillment and inventory and tablet retailing; distribution management; transportation management; supply chain convergence; and visibility. Outside of the U.S., the firm has offices in Australia, China, France, India, Japan, the Netherlands, Singapore and the U.K., as well as representatives in Mexico and reseller partnerships in Latin America, Eastern Europe, the Middle East, South Africa and Asia.

Manhattan Associates offers its employees medical, dental, vision and prescription drug coverage; flexible spending accounts; life and AD&D insurance; short- and long-term disability; a 401(k) plan; access to a credit union; discounted health club membership; and educational assistance.

FINANCIAL DATA: *Note: Data for latest year may not have been available at press time.*

In U.S. $	2018	2017	2016	2015	2014	2013
Revenue		594,599,000	604,557,000	556,371,000	492,104,000	414,518,000
R&D Expense		57,704,000	54,736,000	53,859,000	48,953,000	44,549,000
Operating Income		188,566,000	194,307,000	161,446,000	127,124,000	101,287,000
Operating Margin %		31.71%	32.14%	29.01%	25.83%	24.43%
SGA Expense		93,536,000	96,545,000	97,874,000	97,072,000	81,706,000
Net Income		116,481,000	124,234,000	103,475,000	82,000,000	67,296,000
Operating Cash Flow		164,066,000	139,346,000	120,153,000	94,162,000	89,387,000
Capital Expenditure		6,199,000	6,843,000	11,492,000	9,415,000	4,740,000
EBITDA		197,626,000	203,397,000	169,210,000	133,501,000	107,112,000
Return on Assets %		38.05%	39.12%	31.54%	26.62%	24.04%
Return on Equity %		67.65%	68.09%	54.81%	45.10%	39.22%
Debt to Equity						

CONTACT INFORMATION:

Phone: 770 955-7070   Fax: 770 995-0302
Toll-Free:
Address: 2300 Windy Ridge Pkwy., 10/Fl, Atlanta, GA 30339 United States

STOCK TICKER/OTHER:

Stock Ticker: MANH
Employees: 3,020
Parent Company:

Exchange: NAS
Fiscal Year Ends: 12/31

SALARIES/BONUSES:

Top Exec. Salary: $575,000   Bonus: $
Second Exec. Salary: $391,167   Bonus: $

OTHER THOUGHTS:

Estimated Female Officers or Directors:
Hot Spot for Advancement for Women/Minorities:

MapQuest.com Inc

www.mapquest.com

NAIC Code: 519130

TYPES OF BUSINESS:

Online Mapping Services
Driving Directions
Trip Planners
Live Traffic Reports
Advertising Services

BRANDS/DIVISIONS/AFFILIATES:

AOL Inc
MapQuest Mobile
MapQuest Enterprise Solutions
MapQuest Developers Network
MapQuest Route Planner
MapQuest Gas Prices

CONTACTS: Note: Officers with more than one job title may be intentionally listed here more than once.

James W. Thomas, VP-Admin.
James W. Thomas, Sec.
William Muenster, Sr. VP-Dev. & Prod.
James W. Thomas, Principal Acct. Officer
Michael J. Mulligan, Chmn.

GROWTH PLANS/SPECIAL FEATURES:

MapQuest.com, Inc., a subsidiary of AOL, Inc., operates a website that allows users to access interactive maps and driving directions via online, mobile app and in print. Its site reaches more than 45 million users per month. MapQuest offers additional information such as restaurant and lodging locations and city information to help with trip planning as well as computer applications for information kiosks and hotel reservation systems. The company also provides state-of-the-art mapping technology products and services for the information publishing industry as well as for the commercial, internet, telecommunications and real estate markets. The firm generates revenue through paid advertisements, including a service that pinpoints advertisers' store locations on a user's map. MapQuest Mobile, a downloadable application for iPhone and Android, allows consumers to plan trips and access the directions on their mobile devices. It utilizes the latest wireless and voice recognition technologies to provide travelers with the tools needed to continually access navigation and travel information. Mapquest Enterprise Solutions helps global brands build engaging business mapping applications with Mapquest geospatial web services. Mapquest Developers Network provides free, flexible and customizable APIs and web services to help add and enhance location content on websites. MapQuest's Route Planner optimizes routes for drivers with multiple destinations on their trips. Last, MapQuest's Gas Prices application provides maps and gas prices for nearby gas stations.

The firm offers employees medical, dental and vision insurance; health and dependent care flexible spending accounts; auto and homeowners insurance; a pre-tax commuter program; parental leave; adoption assistance; a 401(k); and tuition reimbursement.

FINANCIAL DATA: Note: Data for latest year may not have been available at press time.

In U.S. $	2018	2017	2016	2015	2014	2013
Revenue						
R&D Expense						
Operating Income						
Operating Margin %						
SGA Expense						
Net Income						
Operating Cash Flow						
Capital Expenditure						
EBITDA						
Return on Assets %						
Return on Equity %						
Debt to Equity						

CONTACT INFORMATION:

Phone: 303-486-4000   Fax: 303-486-4001
Toll-Free:
Address: 1555 Blake St., 3/Fl, Denver, CO 80202 United States

STOCK TICKER/OTHER:

Stock Ticker: Subsidiary   Exchange:
Employees: 335   Fiscal Year Ends: 12/31
Parent Company: AOL Inc

SALARIES/BONUSES:

Top Exec. Salary: $ Bonus: $
Second Exec. Salary: $ Bonus: $

OTHER THOUGHTS:

Estimated Female Officers or Directors:
Hot Spot for Advancement for Women/Minorities:

MapR Technologies Inc

www.mapr.com

NAIC Code: 511210I

TYPES OF BUSINESS:

Computer Software, Operating Systems, Languages & Development Tools Software

BRANDS/DIVISIONS/AFFILIATES:

MapR Data Platform
MapR-XD
MapR-DB
MapR-ES
MapR-Edge

CONTACTS: Note: Officers with more than one job title may be intentionally listed here more than once.

John Schroeder, CEO
Dan Atler, CFO

GROWTH PLANS/SPECIAL FEATURES:

MapR Technologies, Inc. is an enterprise software company. The firm's MapR software enable organizations to create disruptive advantage and long-term value from their data through its data platform. The MapR Data Platform delivers distributed processing, real-time analytics and enterprise-grade requirements across cloud and on-premise environments. It leverages the significant ongoing development in open source technologies such as Apache-branded Spark, Drill, Hive and Hadoop. MapR is powered by a fast, reliable, secure and open data infrastructure, reducing total cost of ownership and enabling global real-time data applications. MapR supports big data apps which serve business-critical needs that cannot afford to lose data, must run on a 24/7 basis, require immediate recovery from node and site failures, all with a small data center footprint. The data platform is 100% binary compatible with Apache's distributed file systems to ensure plug-and-play compatibility and no vendor lock-in. MapR-XD is a highly-scalable converged storage platform for high-volume enterprise storage. MapR Analytics and Machine Learning engines comprises all the tools needed to conduct real-time analytics and machine learning at scale. MapR-DB is a NoSQL database for global data-intensive applications built into the MapR Data Platform. It brings together operational applications, analytical applications, real-time streaming and other workloads to enable next-generation user experiences and business processes. MapR-ES is a global publish-subscribe event streaming system for big data. The MapR Control System is a management solution for administering the MapR Data Platform and related cluster infrastructure through an intuitive, actionable interface. MapR-Edge is a small footprint edition of the MapR Data Platform that addresses the need to capture, process and analyze Internet of Things (IoT) Edge data close to the source. The firm is headquartered in Virginia, USA, with locations in the U.S., Europe and the Asia Pacific.

FINANCIAL DATA: Note: Data for latest year may not have been available at press time.

In U.S. $	2018	2017	2016	2015	2014	2013
Revenue						
R&D Expense						
Operating Income						
Operating Margin %						
SGA Expense						
Net Income						
Operating Cash Flow						
Capital Expenditure						
EBITDA						
Return on Assets %						
Return on Equity %						
Debt to Equity						

CONTACT INFORMATION:

Phone: 408-834-7549   Fax:
Toll-Free: 855-669-6277
Address: 2833 Junction Ave., Ste. 100, San Jose, CA 95134 United States

STOCK TICKER/OTHER:

Stock Ticker: Private   Exchange:
Employees: 450   Fiscal Year Ends:
Parent Company:

SALARIES/BONUSES:

Top Exec. Salary: $ Bonus: $
Second Exec. Salary: $ Bonus: $

OTHER THOUGHTS:

Estimated Female Officers or Directors:
Hot Spot for Advancement for Women/Minorities:

Marchex Inc

NAIC Code: 519130

www.marchex.com

TYPES OF BUSINESS:

Online Marketing
Search Engine Marketing

BRANDS/DIVISIONS/AFFILIATES:

Marchex Call Marketplace
Marchex Call Analytics
Local Leads
Telmetrics
Callcap
Marchex Innovation Development Lab
Marchex Omnichannel Analytics Cloud
Marchex Audience Targeting

CONTACTS: *Note: Officers with more than one job title may be intentionally listed here more than once.*

Michael Arends, CEO
Michael Miller, Controller
Anne Devereux-Mills, Director
Russell Horowitz, Director

GROWTH PLANS/SPECIAL FEATURES:

Marchex, Inc. is an online advertising company and publisher of local content. The firm concentrates on connecting advertisers with users through mobile, online and offline channels. The firm's products include pay-per-call advertising products and the company's advertising network. The company operates in a single revenue generating segment: call-driven. Call-driven offers three primary products, Marchex Call Marketplace, a mobile advertising solution that delivers a variety of call advertising products and services to national advertisers, agencies and reseller partners; Marchex Call Analytics, which tracks calls and helps advertisers understand which marketing channels, advertisements, keywords and creative are driving calls to their business and includes Marchex Speech Analytics, Marchex Omnichannel Analytics Cloud, Marchex Site Analytics, Marchex Search Analytics, Marchex Video and Display Analytics, Marchex Social Analytics and Marchex Audience Targeting; and the Local Leads platform, a full service advertising solution for small business resellers to sell call advertising, search marketing and other lead generation products. In October 2018, Marchex launched the Marchex Innovation Development (MIND) Lab, a new research and development group to support product innovation and to help businesses engage and nurture customer relationships through voice and text. That November, Marchex acquired Telmetrics, an enterprise call and text tracking analytics company, for $13.1 million; and acquired Callcap, a call monitoring and analytics company, for $35 million.

FINANCIAL DATA: *Note: Data for latest year may not have been available at press time.*

In U.S. $	2018	2017	2016	2015	2014	2013
Revenue		90,291,000	129,547,000	143,013,000	182,644,000	152,550,000
R&D Expense		18,094,000	28,446,000	31,058,000	29,561,000	27,346,000
Operating Income		-6,361,000	-19,930,000	-1,784,000	4,894,000	-147,000
Operating Margin %		-7.04%	-15.38%	-1.24%	2.67%	-.09%
SGA Expense		29,219,000	44,061,000	34,972,000	33,174,000	30,567,000
Net Income		-6,087,000	-84,066,000	26,721,000	-19,090,000	1,817,000
Operating Cash Flow		1,692,000	-3,669,000	12,753,000	22,419,000	13,596,000
Capital Expenditure		1,577,000	1,000,000	4,158,000	3,482,000	3,195,000
EBITDA		-3,570,000	-80,709,000	3,167,000	9,081,000	9,471,000
Return on Assets %		-5.11%	-50.45%	13.83%	-11.21%	1.16%
Return on Equity %		-6.33%	-55.90%	15.53%	-13.21%	1.41%
Debt to Equity						

CONTACT INFORMATION:

Phone: 206 331-3300   Fax: 206 331-3695
Toll-Free: 800-840-1012
Address: 520 Pike St., Ste. 2000, Seattle, WA 98101 United States

STOCK TICKER/OTHER:

Stock Ticker: MCHX
Employees: 291
Parent Company:

Exchange: NAS
Fiscal Year Ends: 12/31

SALARIES/BONUSES:

Top Exec. Salary: $294,063   Bonus: $150,000
Second Exec. Salary: $92,083   Bonus: $250,000

OTHER THOUGHTS:

Estimated Female Officers or Directors: 1
Hot Spot for Advancement for Women/Minorities:

MarketWatch Inc

www.marketwatch.com

NAIC Code: 519130

TYPES OF BUSINESS:

Online Financial Information
Television & Radio Programming

BRANDS/DIVISIONS/AFFILIATES:

Dow Jones & Company Inc
Barrons.com
Financial News London
Moneyish
Mansion Global
MarketWatch Weekend
MarketWatch.com Radio Network

CONTACTS: *Note: Officers with more than one job title may be intentionally listed here more than once.*

Jim Bernard, Managing Dir.
Paul Mattison, CFO
Raju Narisetti, Managing Editor-WSJ.com

GROWTH PLANS/SPECIAL FEATURES:

MarketWatch, Inc., a wholly-owned subsidiary of Dow Jones & Company, Inc., is a financial media company providing web-based, real-time business news, financial programming and analytic tools. The firm is a member of Dow Jones Media Group, which also includes: Barrons.com, a financial information website; Financial News London, a financial newspaper and news website published in London; Moneyish, offering features, essays, videos and news about money; and Mansion Global, offering digital content about the global real estate market, featuring luxury listings for sale around the world. These free, advertising-supported websites serve the business and financial communities with timely market news and information, provided by bureaus in the U.S., Europe and Asia. In addition to business and financial news, MarketWatch sites offer in-depth commentary on trends and events, personal finance commentary and data, community features and other services designed to provide a one-stop-shop for audiences. Other features include a mutual fund center, a seasonal tax guide, market advisors and research columns. Customers have the ability to create personal user settings including portfolio trackers, news and quotes, custom views, allocation analysis, financials and charting. MarketWatch also delivers relevant financial news to user e-mail accounts, hosts investment discussion communities, offers personalized automatic alerts and provides customers with wireless capabilities. In addition, the firm sells subscription-based content for individual investors under the Hulbert Financial Digest, Retirement Weekly and ETF Trader brand names. MarketWatch produces the syndicated MarketWatch Weekend television program and provides business and financial news updates every 30 minutes on the MarketWatch.com Radio Network. MarketWatch's website has approximately 19 million visitors per month (as of October 2018).

MarketWatch offers employees health care coverage, fitness programs, a retirement savings program and tuition assistance.

FINANCIAL DATA: *Note: Data for latest year may not have been available at press time.*

In U.S. $	2018	2017	2016	2015	2014	2013
Revenue						
R&D Expense						
Operating Income						
Operating Margin %						
SGA Expense						
Net Income						
Operating Cash Flow						
Capital Expenditure						
EBITDA						
Return on Assets %						
Return on Equity %						
Debt to Equity						

CONTACT INFORMATION:

Phone: 415-439-6400   Fax: 415-439-6485
Toll-Free:
Address: 201 California St., Ste. 1300, San Francisco, CA 94111 United States

STOCK TICKER/OTHER:

Stock Ticker: Subsidiary   Exchange:
Employees: 206   Fiscal Year Ends: 12/31
Parent Company: Dow Jones & Company Inc

SALARIES/BONUSES:

Top Exec. Salary: $ Bonus: $
Second Exec. Salary: $ Bonus: $

OTHER THOUGHTS:

Estimated Female Officers or Directors:
Hot Spot for Advancement for Women/Minorities: Y

Match Group Inc

www.match.com

NAIC Code: 519130

TYPES OF BUSINESS:

Internet Dating Sites

GROWTH PLANS/SPECIAL FEATURES:

Match Group, Inc., a subsidiary of IAC/InterActiveCorp, is a global provider of dating products. The company operates a portfolio of brands, including Match, OkCupid, PlentyOfFish, Tinder, Meetic, Twoo, OurTime, LoveScout24 and Pairs, each designed to increase user's likelihood of finding a romantic connection. Its target market includes all adults in North America, Western Europe and other select countries who are not in a committed relationship and who have access to the internet. Match Group currently offers its dating products in 42 languages across more than 190 countries. Match features include the ability to both search profiles, receive algorithmic matches and the ability to attend live events, promoted by Match, with other members. OkCupid attracts users through a mathematical and question/answer approach. PlentyofFish has the ability to search profiles and receive algorithmic matches. Tinder is a mobile-only offering with location-based features. Meetic serves users in France, Spain, Italy and the Netherlands and is similar to Match. Twoo is a dating product seeded through existing social networks, with its user base being primarily concentrated in Europe, Asia and South America. OurTime serves the needs of individuals for whom commonalities around age, religion, ethnicity or circumstance are of fundamental importance when making a romantic connection. LoveScout24 provides dating products in Germany, with a strong presence in Austria and Switzerland, and is characterized by its search-based offering rather than matching products. Pairs provides dating products in Japan.

BRANDS/DIVISIONS/AFFILIATES:

IAC/InterActiveCorp
Match
OkCupid
PlentyOfFish
Tinder
Twoo
LoveScout24
Pairs

CONTACTS: *Note: Officers with more than one job title may be intentionally listed here more than once.*

Amarnath Thombre, CEO, Geographical
Amanda Ginsberg, CEO
Gary Swidler, CFO
Philip Eigenmann, Chief Accounting Officer
Joseph Levin, Director
Jared Sine, General Counsel
Sharmistha Dubey, President
Sam Yagan, Vice Chairman of the Board

FINANCIAL DATA: *Note: Data for latest year may not have been available at press time.*

In U.S. $	2018	2017	2016	2015	2014	2013
Revenue		1,330,661,000	1,222,526,000	1,020,431,000	888,268,000	803,089,000
R&D Expense		101,150,000	83,065,000	67,348,000	49,738,000	42,973,000
Operating Income		360,517,000	305,908,000	193,556,000	228,567,000	221,333,000
Operating Margin %		27.09%	25.02%	18.96%	25.73%	27.56%
SGA Expense		555,414,000	545,351,000	535,455,000	452,997,000	415,511,000
Net Income		350,148,000	171,451,000	120,383,000	147,764,000	125,003,000
Operating Cash Flow		321,091,000	234,106,000	209,082,000	173,615,000	174,797,000
Capital Expenditure		28,833,000	48,903,000	29,156,000	21,793,000	19,807,000
EBITDA		363,771,000	368,056,000	251,527,000	278,119,000	258,877,000
Return on Assets %		16.75%	8.62%	7.44%	11.36%	9.67%
Return on Equity %		70.18%	44.22%	22.32%	18.07%	14.96%
Debt to Equity		2.49	2.36	4.28	0.23	0.09

CONTACT INFORMATION:

Phone: 214-576-9352   Fax:
Toll-Free:
Address: 8750 N. Central Expressway, Ste. 1400, Dallas, TX 75231 United States

STOCK TICKER/OTHER:

Stock Ticker: MTCH   Exchange: NAS
Employees: 5,100   Fiscal Year Ends:
Parent Company: IAC/InterActiveCorp

SALARIES/BONUSES:

Top Exec. Salary: $1,000,000   Bonus: $3,000,000
Second Exec. Salary: $550,000   Bonus: $1,300,000

OTHER THOUGHTS:

Estimated Female Officers or Directors:
Hot Spot for Advancement for Women/Minorities:

McAfee LLC

NAIC Code: 511210E

www.mcafee.com

TYPES OF BUSINESS:

Computer Software, Security & Anti-Virus
Virus Protection Software
Network Management Software

BRANDS/DIVISIONS/AFFILIATES:

Thoma Bravo LLC
Intel Corporation

GROWTH PLANS/SPECIAL FEATURES:

McAfee, LLC is a cybersecurity company. The firm creates security solutions for consumer and business customers. Its solutions work with other companies' products and therefore helps businesses orchestrate cyber environments that are integrated and secure. McAfee's products enable the protection, detection and correction of threats on both sides of the spectrum: between McAfee and the business or consumer, simultaneously and collaboratively. Since McAfee products protect consumers across all connected devices, including mobile, homes and businesses can be monitored in real-time from anywhere. Moreover, McAfee works with other security players in an effort to unite against cybercriminal activities. McAfee is a joint venture between Thoma Bravo, LLC (51%) and Intel Corporation (49%).

CONTACTS: Note: Officers with more than one job title may be intentionally listed here more than once.

Christopher Young, CEO
John Giamatteo, Pres.
Michael Berry, CFO
Allison Cerra, CMO
Chatelle Lynch, Chief Human Resources Officer
Steven Grobman, CTO
Bryan Reed Barney, Exec. VP-Prod. Dev.
Ari Jaaksi, Sr. VP
Louis Riley, General Counsel
Tom Fountain, Sr. VP
Edward Hayden, Sr. VP-Finance & Acct.
Steve Redman, Exec. VP-Global Sales
Ken Levine, Sr. VP
Gert-Jan Schenk, Pres., EMEA
Barry McPherson, Exec. VP-Worldwide Delivery & Support Svcs.
Jean-Claude Broido, Pres., McAfee Japan
Barry McPherson, Exec. VP-Supply Chain & Facilities

FINANCIAL DATA: Note: Data for latest year may not have been available at press time.

In U.S. $	2018	2017	2016	2015	2014	2013
Revenue	2,815,050,000	2,681,000,000	2,450,000,000	2,375,000,000	2,216,000,000	2,190,000,000
R&D Expense						
Operating Income						
Operating Margin %						
SGA Expense						
Net Income						
Operating Cash Flow						
Capital Expenditure						
EBITDA						
Return on Assets %						
Return on Equity %						
Debt to Equity						

CONTACT INFORMATION:

Phone: 972-963-8000   Fax:
Toll-Free: 855-380-6445
Address: 2821 Mission College Blvd., Santa Clara, CA 95054 United States

STOCK TICKER/OTHER:

Stock Ticker: Joint Venture   Exchange:
Employees: 7,600   Fiscal Year Ends: 12/31
Parent Company:

SALARIES/BONUSES:

Top Exec. Salary: $ Bonus: $
Second Exec. Salary: $ Bonus: $

OTHER THOUGHTS:

Estimated Female Officers or Directors: 3
Hot Spot for Advancement for Women/Minorities: Y

Medallia Inc

NAIC Code: 511210K

www.medallia.com

TYPES OF BUSINESS:

Computer Software, Sales & Customer Relationship Management
Software
Cloud

BRANDS/DIVISIONS/AFFILIATES:

Medallia Experience Cloud

CONTACTS: *Note: Officers with more than one job title may be intentionally listed here more than once.*

Leslie Stretch, CEO
Roxanne Oulman, CFO
Sophie Chesters, CMO
Susan Lovegren, Chief People Officer
Mikael Ottosson, CTO
Borge Hald, Exec. Chmn.

GROWTH PLANS/SPECIAL FEATURES:

Medallia, Inc. provides software that improves customer experience. The firm's cloud-based software-as-a-service (SaaS) platform, the Medallia Experience Cloud, captures feedback from people no matter where they are (mobile, social, web, in-store). This data provides insight in order to solve issues, drive innovation and implement ideas that are customer-centric. Medallia's software products include capture feedback, real-time analytics, an intuitive graphical interface, native mobile apps, real-time research and testing, native text analytics, role-specific customer relations management and unified customer experience reporting. Industries served by Medallia include financial services, telecommunications, hospitality, airlines, retail, government, professional services and technology. Medallia is headquartered in California, with additional offices in New York, London, Paris, Sydney, Buenos Aires and Tel Aviv. In May 2018, Medallia opened a new office in Munich, Germany, and a production data center in Frankfurt, Germany.

FINANCIAL DATA: *Note: Data for latest year may not have been available at press time.*

In U.S. $	2018	2017	2016	2015	2014	2013
Revenue		137,812,500	131,250,000	125,000,000		
R&D Expense						
Operating Income						
Operating Margin %						
SGA Expense						
Net Income						
Operating Cash Flow						
Capital Expenditure						
EBITDA						
Return on Assets %						
Return on Equity %						
Debt to Equity						

CONTACT INFORMATION:

Phone: 650-321-3000   Fax: 650-321-3156
Toll-Free:
Address: 395 Page Mill Rd., Ste. 100, Palo Alto, CA 94306 United States

STOCK TICKER/OTHER:

Stock Ticker: Private   Exchange:
Employees: 1,000   Fiscal Year Ends:
Parent Company:

SALARIES/BONUSES:

Top Exec. Salary: $ Bonus: $
Second Exec. Salary: $ Bonus: $

OTHER THOUGHTS:

Estimated Female Officers or Directors:
Hot Spot for Advancement for Women/Minorities:

MedeAnalytics Inc

medeanalytics.com

NAIC Code: 511210D

TYPES OF BUSINESS:

Computer Software, Healthcare & Biotechnology
Software
Healthcare

BRANDS/DIVISIONS/AFFILIATES:

Thoma Bravo LLC
Bain Capital Ventures
Emergence Capital Partners

CONTACTS: Note: Officers with more than one job title may be intentionally listed here more than once.

Paul Kaiser, CEO
Neal Schwartz, COO
Jim Hagan, CFO
Kerry Martin, Sr. VP-Sales
Melissa Green Dexter, VP-Human Resources
Tyler Downs, CTO
David Weiss, Chmn.

GROWTH PLANS/SPECIAL FEATURES:

MedeAnalytics, Inc. provides cloud-based performance management software to the healthcare industry. The company's healthcare analytics solutions normalize vast amounts of complex data across multiple sources in order to produce clear, human-powered insights. For providers, the company's solutions include enterprise analytics, patient access, business office, revenue integrity, population health, performance management and provider implementation services. For payers, its solutions include health plans, state government, employers, brokers/consultants and payer implementation services. The firm's solutions are utilized by more than 1,500 clients in the U.S. and the U.K., and include hospitals, health systems, health plans, state Medicaid programs and more. MedeAnalytics' partners include The Advisory Board Company, AHIP (America's Health Insurance Plans), Healthcare Information and Management Systems Society, Health Care Compliance Association, Healthcare Financial Management Association and National Association of Healthcare Access Management. Thoma Bravo, LLC holds a majority stake in MedeAnalytics; and Bain Capital Ventures and Emergence Capital Partners hold minority shares. Based in Texas, USA, the firm has an additional domestic office in California, as well as an international office in London, U.K.

MedeAnalytics offers its employees medical, dental, vision, life and disability insurance coverage; a 401(k) and FSA plans; and paid time off.

FINANCIAL DATA: Note: Data for latest year may not have been available at press time.

In U.S. $	2018	2017	2016	2015	2014	2013
Revenue						
R&D Expense						
Operating Income						
Operating Margin %						
SGA Expense						
Net Income						
Operating Cash Flow						
Capital Expenditure						
EBITDA						
Return on Assets %						
Return on Equity %						
Debt to Equity						

CONTACT INFORMATION:

Phone: 469-916-3300   Fax: 469-916-3355
Toll-Free:
Address: 501 W. President George Bush Highway, Ste. 250, Richardson, TX 75080 United States

STOCK TICKER/OTHER:

Stock Ticker: Private   Exchange:
Employees: 369   Fiscal Year Ends:
Parent Company: Thoma Bravo LLC

SALARIES/BONUSES:

Top Exec. Salary: $ Bonus: $
Second Exec. Salary: $ Bonus: $

OTHER THOUGHTS:

Estimated Female Officers or Directors:
Hot Spot for Advancement for Women/Minorities:

MediaPlatform Inc

www.mediaplatform.com

NAIC Code: 511210F

TYPES OF BUSINESS:

Computer Software, Multimedia, Graphics & Publishing
Consulting Services

BRANDS/DIVISIONS/AFFILIATES:

WebCaster
SmartEdge
SmartPath
PrimeTime
SmartBridge
Video Business Intelligence

CONTACTS: *Note: Officers with more than one job title may be intentionally listed here more than once.*

Mike Newman, CEO
Amzi Jackson, COO
Dena Kendros, VP-Finance & Administration
Darian Germain, VP-Mktg.
Craig Myers, VP-Sales
Dena Kendros, VP-Admin.
Dena Kendros, VP-Finance
Tom Dunlap, Dir.-Client Svcs.

GROWTH PLANS/SPECIAL FEATURES:

MediaPlatform, Inc. provides webcasting software. The company's enterprise-scale mixed media software and services enable the creation, management, distribution and measurement of live and on-demand rich media presentations and training over the web. The firm partners with leading IT companies to provide seamless integration of its products into the latest media players and operating systems. MediaPlatform's enterprise private YouTube-like product allows clients to produce, manage, distribute and monitor high definition live and on-demand webcasts that feature streaming video, Microsoft PowerPoint slides, Adobe Flash animations, audio, surveys, polls and screen demos. The enterprise YouTube is available as Software-as-a-Service (SaaS) as well as an onsite installation. The firm's WebCaster platform helps organizations deliver CEO town halls and all-hands events to audiences of unlimited size. This webcasting solution enables live streaming to desktop, tablet or smartphone. SmartEdge is an enterprise content delivery network (eCDN) focused on the acceleration and optimization of HTTPs (hypertext transfer protocol) video delivery across corporate networks. This provides network-friendly delivery of secure, on-demand video and live rich media webcasts to any desktop, table or mobile device. SmartPath is a webcast distribution technology product that allows pervasive streaming and webcasting to virtually any end user. PrimeTime is an enterprise video platform for managing all of the organization's media assets. SmartBridge is a videoconferencing gateway that enables the live streaming of videoconferences to audiences of unlimited size, and provides a central repository for managing all recordings. Last, Video Business Intelligence provides deep-level insight to user experience for live streaming presentations through its engaging dashboard that organizes all the data generated during a webcast.

FINANCIAL DATA: *Note: Data for latest year may not have been available at press time.*

In U.S. $	2018	2017	2016	2015	2014	2013
Revenue						
R&D Expense						
Operating Income						
Operating Margin %						
SGA Expense						
Net Income						
Operating Cash Flow						
Capital Expenditure						
EBITDA						
Return on Assets %						
Return on Equity %						
Debt to Equity						

CONTACT INFORMATION:

Phone: 310-909-8410   Fax: 310-295-1110
Toll-Free:
Address: 8383 Wilshire Blvd., Ste. 460, Beverly Hills, CA 90211 United States

STOCK TICKER/OTHER:

Stock Ticker: Private   Exchange:
Employees: 35   Fiscal Year Ends: 12/31
Parent Company:

SALARIES/BONUSES:

Top Exec. Salary: $ Bonus: $
Second Exec. Salary: $ Bonus: $

OTHER THOUGHTS:

Estimated Female Officers or Directors: 1
Hot Spot for Advancement for Women/Minorities: Y

Meituan Dianping

www.meituan.com

NAIC Code: 519130

TYPES OF BUSINESS:

Online Reviews
Restaurant Reviews

BRANDS/DIVISIONS/AFFILIATES:

Dianping.com
Meituan.com
Mobike

GROWTH PLANS/SPECIAL FEATURES:

Meituan Dianping is a Beijing, China-based startup that offers an online-to-offline (O2O) local service platform. The web and mobile platform offers food delivery service to people's homes, provides restaurant reviews, sells groceries and movie tickets, and markets discounts to consumers who buy in groups. Dianping.com and Meituan.com each offer consumer reviews on local services, as well as group-buying, restaurant reservation, take-out service, e-coupon promotions and other online/offline services. The sites and mobile apps have more than 355 million users. Over 5 million local businesses are within the database, covering approximately 2,800 cities and counties across China (as of mid-2018). During 2018, Meituan Dianping acquired Mobike, a smart bike-sharing company, for $2.7 billion, and subsequently downsized its fleet to avoid oversupply. That September, the firm debuted on the Hong Kong stock exchange at an IPO price of HK$69 per share.

CONTACTS: Note: Officers with more than one job title may be intentionally listed here more than once.

Wang Xing, CEO
Zhang Tao, CEO-Shanghai Han Tao

FINANCIAL DATA: Note: Data for latest year may not have been available at press time.

In U.S. $	2018	2017	2016	2015	2014	2013
Revenue		4,937,781,000	1,890,247,000	584,907,700		
R&D Expense		530,720,600	344,438,900	175,231,500		
Operating Income		-649,334,300	-932,962,800	-1,232,043,000		
Operating Margin %						
SGA Expense		1,130,910,000	766,770,400	804,314,800		
Net Income		-2,753,070,000	-842,645,200	-1,530,954,000		
Operating Cash Flow		-45,145,610	-279,143,600	-582,793,700		
Capital Expenditure		108,560,600	51,756,630	52,138,670		
EBITDA		-526,455,200	-847,707,200	-1,205,646,000		
Return on Assets %						
Return on Equity %						
Debt to Equity						

CONTACT INFORMATION:

Phone: 86-215-355-9777   Fax:
Toll-Free:
Address: Tower C, Hengiiweiye Bldg., No. 4 Wangjing East Rd., Beijing, 100102 China

STOCK TICKER/OTHER:

Stock Ticker: MPNGF   Exchange: PINX
Employees: 60,000   Fiscal Year Ends: 12/31
Parent Company:

SALARIES/BONUSES:

Top Exec. Salary: $ Bonus: $
Second Exec. Salary: $ Bonus: $

OTHER THOUGHTS:

Estimated Female Officers or Directors:
Hot Spot for Advancement for Women/Minorities:

MercadoLibre Inc

www.mercadolibre.com

NAIC Code: 454111

TYPES OF BUSINESS:

Electronic Shopping
eCommerce

BRANDS/DIVISIONS/AFFILIATES:

MercadoLibre Marketplace
MercadoLibre Classifieds Service
MercadoPago
MercadoShops
MercadoEnvios
MercadoCredito

CONTACTS: *Note: Officers with more than one job title may be intentionally listed here more than once.*

Marcos Galperin, CEO
Pedro Arnt, CFO

GROWTH PLANS/SPECIAL FEATURES:

MercadoLibre, Inc. is a leading online commerce ecosystem for Latin American markets. This ecosystem comprises six integrated eCommerce services: the MercadoLibre Marketplace, the MercardoLibre Classifieds Service, the MercadoPago payments solution, the MercadoLibre advertising program, the MercadoShops online webstores solution and the MercadoEnvios shipping service. The MercadoLibre Marketplace is a fully-automated, topically-arranged online commerce service that permits both businesses and individuals to list merchandise and conduct sales and purchases online in either a fixed-price or auction-based format. The MercadoLibre Classifies Service is an online classified listing service on which users can also list and purchase motor vehicles, vessels, aircraft, real estate and services in all countries where MercadoLibre operates. MercadoPago facilitates transactions both on and off of the company's marketplace so that users can securely and promptly send payments online. In addition, MercadoCredito is based in Argentina, and designed to extend loans to specific merchants. The MercadoLibre advertising program enables businesses to promote their products and services on the internet. MercadoShops is the company's online store solution on which users can set up, manage and promote their own online store. These stores are hosted by MercadoLibre and offer integration with the other marketplace, payment and advertising services the firm offers. Users can choose from a basic, free store, or pay monthly subscriptions for enhanced functionality and value-added services on their store. Last, the MercadoEnvios shipping service offers sellers a cost-efficient way to utilize the company's distribution chain to fulfill their sales. Sellers opting into the program are able to offer a uniform and seamlessly-integrated shipping experience to their buyers at competitive prices. In addition, MercadoLibre is engaged in developing and selling enterprise software solutions to eCommerce businesses.

FINANCIAL DATA: *Note: Data for latest year may not have been available at press time.*

In U.S. $	2018	2017	2016	2015	2014	2013
Revenue		1,398,095,000	844,396,000	651,790,000	556,536,000	472,594,700
R&D Expense		127,160,000	98,479,000	76,423,000	53,599,640	40,888,140
Operating Income		144,871,000	194,773,000	155,422,000	169,966,500	153,539,100
Operating Margin %		10.36%	23.06%	23.84%	30.54%	32.48%
SGA Expense		447,569,000	243,606,000	204,951,000	173,991,800	148,090,600
Net Income		13,780,000	136,366,000	105,789,000	72,580,550	117,507,400
Operating Cash Flow		269,010,000	190,259,000	221,370,000	196,793,300	142,513,400
Capital Expenditure		74,884,000	77,370,000	64,276,000	35,282,900	114,214,400
EBITDA		121,460,000	239,955,000	194,091,000	150,402,100	177,343,900
Return on Assets %		.90%	11.50%	10.73%	9.30%	21.94%
Return on Equity %		3.65%	35.49%	30.43%	20.75%	37.10%
Debt to Equity		0.95	0.70	0.86	0.79	

CONTACT INFORMATION:

Phone: 54 1146408000 Fax:
Toll-Free:
Address: Arias 3751,7/Fl, Buenos Aires, C1430CRG Argentina

STOCK TICKER/OTHER:

Stock Ticker: MELI
Employees: 1,226
Parent Company:

Exchange: NAS
Fiscal Year Ends: 12/31

SALARIES/BONUSES:

Top Exec. Salary: $732,889 Bonus: $
Second Exec. Salary: Bonus: $
$283,068

OTHER THOUGHTS:

Estimated Female Officers or Directors:
Hot Spot for Advancement for Women/Minorities:

Microsoft Corporation

www.microsoft.com

NAIC Code: 511210I

TYPES OF BUSINESS:

Computer Software, Operating Systems, Languages & Development Tools
Enterprise Software
Game Consoles
Operating Systems
Software as a Service (SAAS)
Search Engine and Advertising
E-Mail Services
Instant Messaging

BRANDS/DIVISIONS/AFFILIATES:

Office 365
Dynamics
SQL
Windows
Visual Studio
Azure
Xbox
GitHub

CONTACTS: Note: Officers with more than one job title may be intentionally listed here more than once.

Satya Nadella, CEO
Amy Hood, CFO
John Thompson, Chairman of the Board
Frank Brod, Chief Accounting Officer
Christopher Capossela, Chief Marketing Officer
William Gates, Co-Founder
Kathleen Hogan, Executive VP, Divisional
Margaret Johnson, Executive VP, Divisional
Jean-Philippe Courtois, Executive VP
Bradford Smith, Other Executive Officer

GROWTH PLANS/SPECIAL FEATURES:

Microsoft Corporation develops, license and supports software products, services and devices. It is a technology company that builds best-in-class platforms and productivity services for a mobile-first, cloud-first world. The firm's products include operating systems; cross-device productivity applications; server applications; business solution applications; desktop and server management tools; software development tools; video games; and training and certification of computer system integrators and developers. Microsoft also designs, manufactures and sells devices such as personal computers (PCs), tablets, gaming and entertainment consoles, phones, other intelligent devices and related accessories that integrate with its cloud-based offerings. The company operates its business in two segments: productivity and business processes, which consists of products in its portfolio of productivity, communication and information services through its devices and platforms; intelligent cloud, which consists of the company's public, private and hybrid server products and cloud services; and more personal computing, which consists of products geared towards harmonizing the interests of end users, developers and IT professionals across all devices. Products offered through the productivity and business processes segment include Office 365 and Dynamics. Products offered through the intelligent cloud segment include SQL servers, Windows servers, Visual Studio, system centers and Azure, as well as enterprise and consulting services. The more personal computing segment primarily consists of Windows, including Windows OEM licensing and other non-volume licensing of the Windows operating system; Devices, including Microsoft Surface, PC accessories, and other intelligent devices; Gaming, including Xbox hardware, software and services, comprising Xbox Live transactions, subscriptions and advertising, video games and third-party video game royalties; and search advertising. In October 2018, Microsoft Corporation completed its acquisition of GitHub, Inc., a web-based version control repository (Git) and internet hosting service, for $7.5 billion.

Microsoft offers its employees health, dental and vision coverage; onsite health screenings; adoption assistance; childcare service discounts; a 401(k) plan; an employee stock purchase plan; and tuition assistance.

FINANCIAL DATA: Note: Data for latest year may not have been available at press time.

In U.S. $	2018	2017	2016	2015	2014	2013
Revenue	110,360,000,000	89,950,000,000	85,320,000,000	93,580,000,000	86,833,000,000	77,849,000,000
R&D Expense	14,726,000,000	13,037,000,000	11,988,000,000	12,046,000,000	11,381,000,000	10,411,000,000
Operating Income	35,058,000,000	22,632,000,000	21,292,000,000	28,172,000,000	27,886,000,000	26,764,000,000
Operating Margin %		25.16%	24.95%	30.10%	32.11%	34.37%
SGA Expense	22,223,000,000	20,020,000,000	19,260,000,000	20,324,000,000	20,632,000,000	20,425,000,000
Net Income	16,571,000,000	21,204,000,000	16,798,000,000	12,193,000,000	22,074,000,000	21,863,000,000
Operating Cash Flow	43,884,000,000	39,507,000,000	33,325,000,000	29,080,000,000	32,231,000,000	28,833,000,000
Capital Expenditure	11,632,000,000	8,129,000,000	8,343,000,000	5,944,000,000	5,485,000,000	4,257,000,000
EBITDA	49,468,000,000	34,149,000,000	27,616,000,000	25,245,000,000	33,629,000,000	31,236,000,000
Return on Assets %		9.75%	9.08%	6.99%	14.02%	16.58%
Return on Equity %		29.37%	22.09%	14.35%	26.16%	30.09%
Debt to Equity		1.05	0.56	0.34	0.22	0.15

CONTACT INFORMATION:

Phone: 425 882-8080   Fax: 425 936-7329
Toll-Free: 800-642-7676
Address: One Microsoft Way, Redmond, WA 98052 United States

STOCK TICKER/OTHER:

Stock Ticker: MSFT   Exchange: NAS
Employees: 131,000   Fiscal Year Ends: 06/30
Parent Company:

SALARIES/BONUSES:

Top Exec. Salary: $1,500,000   Bonus: $
Second Exec. Salary: $875,000   Bonus: $

OTHER THOUGHTS:

Estimated Female Officers or Directors: 4
Hot Spot for Advancement for Women/Minorities: Y

mixi Inc
NAIC Code: 519130

TYPES OF BUSINESS:
Social Networking & Advertising Services

BRANDS/DIVISIONS/AFFILIATES:
Hunza Inc
Diverse Inc
KUTO Inc
mixi recruitment Inc
nohana Inc
i-mercury Capital Inc
mixi America Inc
Smart Health Co Ltd

CONTACTS: *Note: Officers with more than one job title may be intentionally listed here more than once.*
Hiroyasu Kimura, Pres.

GROWTH PLANS/SPECIAL FEATURES:
Mixi, Inc. is an information technology company that provides online networking, entertainment and media services. Its business is divided into two categories: entertainment and media platform. The entertainment business comprises online gaming platforms, including: Fight League, a tag battle; Monster Strike, a hunting roll-playing game; XFLAG Store, a shopping experience game; and Marvel Tsum Tsum, a puzzle game featuring Marvel heroes. The media platform business comprises: Family Album Mitene, a family photo and video sharing app; minimo, a salon artist booking app; mixi, a social networking service; Yuzumoto, an anime character goods trading app; Find Job!, a job search website for those looking for work in the web industry; TicketCamp, a consumer-to-consumer ticket marketplace app; MQUE, an app that delivers the latest live information and concenter and event information; Pancy, a dating app that matches people based on personal data; Poiboy, a communication app for men and women; tailor, a matchmaking dating service; youbride, a leading marriage support site in Japan; VEAT, a communication app for increasing fans by uploading videos; YYC, a matchmaking site; AM, a web magazine that supports women; YUCO, a matchmaking site; ecle, a forced seating change matchmaking system; TOFUFU, a media site focused on deepening relationships for couples; SOLO, a media site for singles; Swish, a dating app; nohana, a photobook creation service for families; nohana market, an online shop for children and families; and Smart Health, a platform that supports healthy living habits via artificial intelligence (AI). Subsidiaries of the company include Hunza, Inc., operator of TicketCamp; Diverse, Inc., matchmaking services; KUTO, Inc., matchmaking/dating services; mixi recruitment, Inc., provides the FindJob! platform; nohana, Inc., a nohana photo book service; i-mercury Capital, Inc., invests, supports and executes mixi, Inc.; mixi America, Inc., which markets the firm's services in North America; and Smart Health Co., Ltd.

FINANCIAL DATA: *Note: Data for latest year may not have been available at press time.*

In U.S. $	2018	2017	2016	2015	2014	2013
Revenue	1,753,989,000	1,921,574,000	1,936,767,000	1,047,399,000	112,746,700	117,171,300
R&D Expense						
Operating Income	671,193,200	825,625,200	881,511,600	488,711,400	4,452,360	23,875,780
Operating Margin %	38.26	42.96%	45.51%	46.65%	3.94%	20.38%
SGA Expense						
Net Income	387,615,000	555,311,300	566,024,800	305,784,400	-2,105,595	15,342,090
Operating Cash Flow	463,555,600	382,847,300	640,583,300	463,054,700	2,977,516	26,306,030
Capital Expenditure	15,397,740	6,047,789	5,556,174	2,059,216	1,382,087	936,851
EBITDA	689,985,900	830,012,600	904,329,900	489,972,900	9,915,776	29,264,990
Return on Assets %	22.64%	35.00%	45.33%	50.45%	- .97%	8.32%
Return on Equity %	26.03%	44.01%	69.71%	86.76%	-1.17%	10.66%
Debt to Equity						

CONTACT INFORMATION:
Phone: 81-03-5738-5900   Fax:
Toll-Free:
Address: 1-2-20 Higashi, Shibuya-ku, 7/Fl., Tokyo, 150-001 Japan

STOCK TICKER/OTHER:
Stock Ticker: MIXIF   Exchange: PINX
Employees: 939   Fiscal Year Ends: 03/31
Parent Company:

SALARIES/BONUSES:
Top Exec. Salary: $ Bonus: $
Second Exec. Salary: $ Bonus: $

OTHER THOUGHTS:
Estimated Female Officers or Directors:
Hot Spot for Advancement for Women/Minorities:

Mixpanel Inc

mixpanel.com

NAIC Code: 511210M

TYPES OF BUSINESS:

Computer Software, E-Commerce & Web Analytics

BRANDS/DIVISIONS/AFFILIATES:

CONTACTS: *Note: Officers with more than one job title may be intentionally listed here more than once.*

Suhail Doshi, Managing Dir.
Amir Movafaghi, CEO
Matt Schmuecker, Dir.-Finance
Pierre Berlin, VP-Sales
Michelle Denman, VP-Human Resources
Jessica Wang, VP-Mktg.
Suhail Doshi, Chmn.

GROWTH PLANS/SPECIAL FEATURES:

Mixpanel, Inc. is a business analytics service and company. The firm builds advanced analytic products for mobile and web devices that help companies understand product usage, conversion rates and user retention. Mixpanel analyzes and measures billions of user actions on a monthly basis. Understanding what users are doing can be attained by installing Mixpanel's software development kit (SDK), which allows businesses to pick and choose which actions to track in their applications. SDK features include the ability to segment data for easy-to-find focus areas, to bookmark and save reports, to visualize the data in various ways and to make annotations in order to highlight significant events that have or have not yet occurred. Mixpanel has an SDK that can be installed on every major platform, and produces data that measures the actions people take in a company's application, pinpoints where and why customers are being lost, discovers who one's users are and what they do, finds out if people love the app by seeing if they return, embeds email and push notifications, and provides A/B testing to see if presented ideas are liked. Mixpanel's prices within its Engagement Plan and People Plan include a free offer for 1,000 profiles, a $999 per year offer for 50,000 profiles, and those interested in more than this can contact the company directly. A profile is associated with a person that has signed up for your application and someone you would tie data to within Mixpanel. The company's solutions serve consumer, financial services, media/entertainment and software-as-a-service (SaaS) customers. Based in San Francisco, California, the firm has additional offices in Washington, Utah and New York, as well as an international office in London, England.

FINANCIAL DATA: *Note: Data for latest year may not have been available at press time.*

In U.S. $	2018	2017	2016	2015	2014	2013
Revenue	105,000,000	100,000,000				
R&D Expense						
Operating Income						
Operating Margin %						
SGA Expense						
Net Income						
Operating Cash Flow						
Capital Expenditure						
EBITDA						
Return on Assets %						
Return on Equity %						
Debt to Equity						

CONTACT INFORMATION:

Phone: 415-688-4001   Fax:
Toll-Free:
Address: 405 Howard St., 2/Fl, San Francisco, CA 94105 United States

STOCK TICKER/OTHER:

Stock Ticker: Private   Exchange:
Employees: 300   Fiscal Year Ends:
Parent Company:

SALARIES/BONUSES:

Top Exec. Salary: $ Bonus: $
Second Exec. Salary: $ Bonus: $

OTHER THOUGHTS:

Estimated Female Officers or Directors:
Hot Spot for Advancement for Women/Minorities:

mktg inc
NAIC Code: 541800

TYPES OF BUSINESS:

Marketing Services
Experiential Marketing
Event Marketing
Interactive Marketing,
Ethnic Marketing
Radio & Television Promotional Programs
Interactive Software Development
Content Creation

BRANDS/DIVISIONS/AFFILIATES:

Dentsu Aegis Network Ltd
store.mktg.com

CONTACTS: Note: Officers with more than one job title may be intentionally listed here more than once.

Charlie Horsey, CEO
Peter Office, COO
Charles Horsey, Pres.
Bob Wilhelmy, CFO
Michelle Berg, Exec. VP-Human Resources
Matt Manning, Sr. VP-Corp. Dev.
James R. Haughton, Sr. VP
Charles Horsey, Chmn.

GROWTH PLANS/SPECIAL FEATURES:

Mktg, inc is global lifestyle marketing agency. The firm humanizes brands and connects them to people through shared passions and lifestyles through sport and entertainment marketing, live experiences, digital and social media, retail marketing, enterprise and business-to-business engagement and sponsorship marketing, which allows clients to promote their goods and services directly to consumers. The company offers these services directly to clients by a sales force operating out of U.S. offices located in Georgia, Ohio, North Carolina, Illinois, California, New York, Connecticut, as well as international offices located in Canada, the U.K., Brazil, Norway, Spain, The Netherlands, France, Denmark, Sweden, Finland, Italy, South Africa, New Zealand, Dusseldorf, Australia, India and Singapore. Clients of the firm include Smirnoff, Deichmann, Bulgari, Veltins, NFL, Gatorade, FILA, Emmi Caffe Latte, 20th Century Fox, Wells Fargo, LEGO and many more. The firm also sells clothing and lifestyle products on store.mktg.com. The firm itself operates as a subsidiary of Dentsu Aegis Network Ltd.

FINANCIAL DATA: Note: Data for latest year may not have been available at press time.

In U.S. $	2018	2017	2016	2015	2014	2013
Revenue		155,000,000	150,000,000	141,000,000	139,028,963	130,809,778
R&D Expense						
Operating Income						
Operating Margin %						
SGA Expense						
Net Income						
Operating Cash Flow						
Capital Expenditure						
EBITDA						
Return on Assets %						
Return on Equity %						
Debt to Equity						

CONTACT INFORMATION:

Phone: 212 366-3400   Fax:
Toll-Free:
Address: 32 Ave of Americas, 20/Fl, New York, NY 10013 United States

STOCK TICKER/OTHER:

Stock Ticker: Subsidiary   Exchange:
Employees: 4,750   Fiscal Year Ends: 03/31
Parent Company: Dentsu Aegis Network Ltd

SALARIES/BONUSES:

Top Exec. Salary: $ Bonus: $
Second Exec. Salary: $ Bonus: $

OTHER THOUGHTS:

Estimated Female Officers or Directors:
Hot Spot for Advancement for Women/Minorities: Y

Mobile TeleSystems PJSC

www.mtsgsm.com

NAIC Code: 517210

TYPES OF BUSINESS:

Mobile Telephone Service
Broadband Internet Services
Pay TV Services
Fixed-Line Telephone Services
Value-Added Services

BRANDS/DIVISIONS/AFFILIATES:

Mobile TeleSystems LLC
Sistema JSGC
MTS Ukraine
MTS Armenia
MTS Turkmenistan

CONTACTS: Note: Officers with more than one job title may be intentionally listed here more than once.

Alexey Kornya, CEO
Andrey Kamensky, VP-Finance, Investments and M&A
Vyacheslav Nikolaev, VP-Mktg.
Maria Golyandrina, VP-Human Resources
Andrei Ushatskiy, VP-IT
Ruslan Ibragimov, VP-Corp. & Legal Matters
Michael Hecker, VP-Strategy & Corp. Dev.
Vadim Savchenko, VP-Sales & Customer Svcs.
Konstantin Markov, Dir.
Alexey Kornya, Chmn.
Ivan Zolochevskiy, CEO
Valery Shorzhin, Dir.-Procurement Mgmt.

GROWTH PLANS/SPECIAL FEATURES:

Mobile TeleSystems PJSC (MTS) is a leading telecommunications provider in Russia and the CIS (commonwealth of independent states), providing a wide range of mobile and fixed-line voice and data services. OJSC stands for joint-stock financial corporation. The firm has a total subscriber base of 140 million. Fixed line communications services are provided in over 185 cities across Russia, covering a population of more than 53 million. Additionally, the company owns a 48.54% stake in Mobile TeleSystems LLC, a mobile operator in Belarus. MTS operates through three focus areas: data, differentiation and dividends. Data affirms the company's efforts to provide customers with the fastest, most reliable mobile and fixed-line networks in the region. This division's data network is built on 3G LTE and aims to migrate its customers from feature to smartphones. Differentiation highlights the unique products and services MTS offers to its customers, primarily its FTTB/FTTH (fiber to the building/basement and fiber to the home) solutions. This division is establishing a center for connectivity through its roll-out of GPON (Gigabit-capable passive optical networks), which will allow speeds of up to 1 Gb/s in every home or office in Moscow. Dividends confirm the company's commitment to continuous improvement in the operational efficiency of MTS and enhancement of shareholder returns. MTS Ukraine has approximately 60 million subscribers, MTS Armenia has 3 million and MTS Turkmenistan has 7 million. MTS is 50.03% owned by Sistema JSGC.

FINANCIAL DATA: Note: Data for latest year may not have been available at press time.

In U.S. $	2018	2017	2016	2015	2014	2013
Revenue		6,432,135,000	6,327,298,000	6,262,527,000	5,965,196,000	5,786,352,000
R&D Expense						
Operating Income		1,403,809,000	1,227,928,000	1,276,781,000	1,491,539,000	1,477,771,000
Operating Margin %		21.60%	19.33%	20.40%	23.09%	28.20%
SGA Expense		1,120,767,000	1,107,348,000	1,084,272,000	1,418,317,000	1,573,053,000
Net Income		813,864,800	703,959,300	718,699,500	752,580,200	1,159,455,000
Operating Cash Flow		2,100,521,000	1,896,118,000	2,092,505,000	2,316,586,000	2,314,538,000
Capital Expenditure		1,109,962,000	1,251,091,000	1,547,174,000	1,344,761,000	1,184,666,000
EBITDA		2,599,090,000	2,542,787,000	2,457,017,000	2,322,177,000	2,693,021,000
Return on Assets %		10.23%	8.09%	7.84%	9.47%	16.97%
Return on Equity %		43.21%	32.38%	30.35%	32.60%	60.79%
Debt to Equity		1.99	1.70	1.82	1.50	1.27

CONTACT INFORMATION:

Phone: 7 4952232025   Fax: 7 4959116567
Toll-Free:
Address: Vorontsovskaya 5., Bldg. 2, Russian Federation, Moscow, 109147 Russia

STOCK TICKER/OTHER:

Stock Ticker: MBT
Employees: 63,971
Parent Company: Sistema JSGC

Exchange: NYS
Fiscal Year Ends: 12/31

SALARIES/BONUSES:

Top Exec. Salary: $ Bonus: $
Second Exec. Salary: $ Bonus: $

OTHER THOUGHTS:

Estimated Female Officers or Directors: 1
Hot Spot for Advancement for Women/Minorities:

MongoDB Inc
NAIC Code: 511210J

www.mongodb.com

TYPES OF BUSINESS:
Computer Software, Data Base & File Management

BRANDS/DIVISIONS/AFFILIATES:
MongoDB Enterprise Advanced
MongoDB Stitch
MongoDB Atlas
MongoDB Mobile
MongoDB Charts
MongoDB Ops Manager
MongoDB Compass
MongoDB Connector for Apache Spark

CONTACTS: *Note: Officers with more than one job title may be intentionally listed here more than once.*
Dev Ittycheria, CEO
Michael Gordon, CFO
Meagan Eisenberg, CMO
Marjorie Toucas, VP-Worldwide Corp. Sales
Eliot Horowitz, CTO
Ron Avnur, VP-Products & Svcs.
Andrew Stephens, VP-Legal
Jeff Goldberg, VP-Global Sales Oper. & Programs
Matt Asay, VP-Mktg. & Bus. Dev.
Andrew Erlichson, VP-Education & Cloud Svcs.
Kamal Brar, VP-Asia Pacific
Paul Cross, VP-Solution Architecture
Ronnen Miller, VP-Tech. Svcs.
Kevin P. Ryan, Chmn.
Joe Morrissey, VP-EMEA

GROWTH PLANS/SPECIAL FEATURES:
MongoDB, Inc. builds the MongoDB (DB/database), the drivers that go with it, and provides related software and services. The firm's products and solutions consist of 10 offerings. MongoDB Enterprise Advanced and MongoDB Enterprise for OEM (original equipment manufacturers) is the company's commercial edition of the database and enterprise server. More than half of Fortune 100 and leading technology companies use it. MongoDB Stitch is a backend-as-a-service in the cloud. MongoDB Atlas is a hosted database service for MongoDB. The atlas makes it easy to set up, operate and scale MongoDB deployments in the cloud. MongoDB's development support solutions speed up development by four-times, provides technical support, as well as the tools and features of the MongoDB enterprise server in a package designed for development purposes. MongoDB Mobile is for modern mobile and Internet of Things (IoT) applications, enabling the storage of data from iOS/Android/IoT devices to the back-end in the cloud via a single database. MongoDB Charts provides a way to create visualizations of MongoDB data, including charts, graphs and dashboards, with the ability to share with other uses for collaboration purposes. MongoDB Ops Manager is a management application for MongoDB, which is the best way to run MongoDB within a data center or public cloud. The ops manager makes it fast and easy for clients to deploy, monitor, back up and scale MongoDB. MongoDB Compass enables clients to explore and manipulate MongoDB data for smart decision-making about indexing, document validation and more. MongoDB Connector for business intelligence (BI) stores client's enterprise data in rich, multi-dimensional documents in order to quickly build and evolve apps. Last, MongoDB Connector for Apache Spark enables clients to build new classes of real-time analytics by combining Spark with MongoDB. Offices are located throughout North America, Europe and Asia-Pacific. In late-2018, MongoDB acquired mLab.

FINANCIAL DATA: *Note: Data for latest year may not have been available at press time.*

In U.S. $	2018	2017	2016	2015	2014	2013
Revenue	154,519,000	101,385,000	65,271,000	40,788,000	65,000,000	62,000,000
R&D Expense						
Operating Income						
Operating Margin %						
SGA Expense						
Net Income	-96,359,000	-86,681,000	-73,486,000	-76,673,000		
Operating Cash Flow						
Capital Expenditure						
EBITDA						
Return on Assets %						
Return on Equity %						
Debt to Equity						

CONTACT INFORMATION:
Phone: 866-237-8815   Fax:
Toll-Free:
Address: 229 W. 43rd St., 5/Fl, New York, NY 10036 United States

STOCK TICKER/OTHER:
Stock Ticker: MDB   Exchange:
Employees: 600   Fiscal Year Ends: 01/31
Parent Company:

SALARIES/BONUSES:
Top Exec. Salary: $ Bonus: $
Second Exec. Salary: $ Bonus: $

OTHER THOUGHTS:
Estimated Female Officers or Directors: 2
Hot Spot for Advancement for Women/Minorities:

Monster Worldwide Inc

www.monster.com

NAIC Code: 561311A

TYPES OF BUSINESS:

Online Job Recruitment
Employment Advertising

BRANDS/DIVISIONS/AFFILIATES:

Monster
Monster.com
Power Resume Search
Randstad Holding NV

CONTACTS: *Note: Officers with more than one job title may be intentionally listed here more than once.*

Scott Gutz, CEO
Timothy Yates, Director
Steve DeLisle, CTO
Mark Stoever, President

GROWTH PLANS/SPECIAL FEATURES:

Monster Worldwide, Inc., parent company of Monster, is a global online employment services company, designed to bring people together to advance their careers. The firm operates in the U.S. and internationally. Through the careers segments, the company provides an online forum, Monster.com, designed to connect job seekers with employers as well as searchable jobs and career management resources. For the employer, Monster's offerings are designed to simplify the hiring process and deliver access to its community of job seekers. For job seekers, the firm's purpose is to help advance the users' careers by providing searchable job postings, a resume database, recruitment media tools and other career related content. Job seekers can search the company's job postings and post their resumes free-of-charge on each of its web sites. The firm's Power Resume Search is its proprietary semantic resume and job search database product, which leads to a 150% increase in qualified candidates and cuts recruitment time by 65%. Employers and human resources professionals pay to post jobs, search its resume database and utilize career site hosting and other ancillary services. Plans come in at $575 for one months, $750 for two months and $899 for three months. Monster is a subsidiary of the Dutch multinational human resource consulting firm, Randstad Holding NV. In early-2018, Monster sold its businesses in India, South East Asia and the Middle East to Quess Corp Limited, an Indian integrated services provider. This allows Monster to strengthen its focus on the North American and European markets.

FINANCIAL DATA: *Note: Data for latest year may not have been available at press time.*

In U.S. $	2018	2017	2016	2015	2014	2013
Revenue		660,000,000	650,000,000	666,902,976	770,012,992	807,579,008
R&D Expense						
Operating Income						
Operating Margin %						
SGA Expense						
Net Income				73,612,000	-289,288,992	-289,000
Operating Cash Flow						
Capital Expenditure						
EBITDA						
Return on Assets %						
Return on Equity %						
Debt to Equity						

CONTACT INFORMATION:

Phone: 978-461-8000   Fax: 978-461-8100
Toll-Free:
Address: 133 Boston Post Rd., Weston, MA 02493 United States

STOCK TICKER/OTHER:

Stock Ticker: Subsidiary   Exchange:
Employees: 3,700   Fiscal Year Ends: 12/31
Parent Company: Randstad Holding NV

SALARIES/BONUSES:

Top Exec. Salary: $ Bonus: $
Second Exec. Salary: $ Bonus: $

OTHER THOUGHTS:

Estimated Female Officers or Directors: 3
Hot Spot for Advancement for Women/Minorities: Y

Sales, profits and employees may be estimates. Financial information, benefits and other data can change quickly and may vary from those stated here.

MoreVisibility.com Inc

www.morevisibility.com

NAIC Code: 541810E

TYPES OF BUSINESS:

Search Engine Optimization (SEO)
Marketing Outsourcing Services

BRANDS/DIVISIONS/AFFILIATES:

Google Premier Partner
Google Marketing Platofrm Partner

CONTACTS: *Note: Officers with more than one job title may be intentionally listed here more than once.*

Dennis Pushkin, CEO
Andrew Wetzler, Pres.
Danielle Leitch, Exec. VP-Client Strategy
Khrysti Nazzaro, Dir.-Optimized Svcs.

GROWTH PLANS/SPECIAL FEATURES:

MoreVisibility.com, Inc. is a company dedicated to digital marketing strategies relating to online businesses. Emphasizing search engine optimization (SEO), the company seeks to help its customers effectively utilize an increasingly crowded and complicated online environment. Customers generally arrive at websites either through unpaid-for search engines results or from marketing agents' paid placement programs. Pay-per-click (PPC) advertising affords clients special placement in search results and requires strategic managing of a client's website and keywords to optimize results. The firm's search engine strategy often involves re-working site architecture and coding, ensuring that its clients are well positioned to be recognized by major search engines. MoreVisibility.com also provides design services, for branding and website design; development services, for the development of ecommerce, blog creation, web design and more; mobile services, for mobile strategy and mobile services; analytics; and social media services, for strategy and design. The firm also provides SEO services, which tailor site content to improve search engine ranking. The firm is a Google Premier Partner for AdWorks and a Google Marketing Platform Partner and includes certification in Google Analytics, Tag Manager, Data Studio and Optimize. For companies too busy to manage their search engine marketing, MoreVisability can serve as an outsourcer, handling all aspects of a company's search and online marketing and reporting. Company partners include Google and Bing.

FINANCIAL DATA: *Note: Data for latest year may not have been available at press time.*

In U.S. $	2018	2017	2016	2015	2014	2013
Revenue						
R&D Expense						
Operating Income						
Operating Margin %						
SGA Expense						
Net Income						
Operating Cash Flow						
Capital Expenditure						
EBITDA						
Return on Assets %						
Return on Equity %						
Debt to Equity						

CONTACT INFORMATION:

Phone: 561-620-9682   Fax: 561-620-9684
Toll-Free: 800-787-0497
Address: 975 S. Federal Hwy., 2/Fl, Boca Raton, FL 33432 United States

STOCK TICKER/OTHER:

Stock Ticker: Private   Exchange:
Employees: 45   Fiscal Year Ends:
Parent Company:

SALARIES/BONUSES:

Top Exec. Salary: $ Bonus: $
Second Exec. Salary: $ Bonus: $

OTHER THOUGHTS:

Estimated Female Officers or Directors: 2
Hot Spot for Advancement for Women/Minorities:

Move Inc (Realtor.com)

NAIC Code: 519130

www.move.com

TYPES OF BUSINESS:

Online Portal-Real Estate Data
Real Estate Software
Real Estate Publishing
Real Estate Advertising

BRANDS/DIVISIONS/AFFILIATES:

News Corporation
Realtor.com
Doorsteps
Moving.com
SeniorHousingNet
ListHub
Top Producer
Opcity

CONTACTS: *Note: Officers with more than one job title may be intentionally listed here more than once.*

Ryan O'Hara, CEO
Bryan Charap, CFO
Nate Johnson, CMO
Suhail Ansari, CTO
Raymond Picard, Executive VP, Divisional
James Caulfield, Executive VP
Errol Samuelson, President, Subsidiary

GROWTH PLANS/SPECIAL FEATURES:

Move, Inc. and its subsidiaries operate a leading network of websites for real estate search, finance, moving and home enthusiasts and provide a resource for consumers seeking information and connections needed before, during and after a move. The firm is a subsidiary of News Corporation. Move's primary network includes Realtor.com, Doorsteps, Moving.com and SeniorHousingNet. Realtor.com is a resource for home buyers and sellers, offering a comprehensive database of for-sale and for-lease properties. Doorsteps is an online tool for prospective homebuyers looking to save time and money. The tool helps users know whether it is smart to buy, how to get ready to buy and ways to make best decisions throughout the home-buying journey. Moving.com offers moving-related services, as well as tools designed to reduce the time, cost and stress associated with moving. SeniorHousingNet provides information on independent and assisted living facilities, nursing homes, retirement communities and other elderly care. The company also offers software solution products and services to help real estate professionals serve their clients and grow their businesses. These software solutions include: ListHub, a leading listing syndicator and centralized intelligence platform for the real estate industry; Top Producer, a supplier of media and technology solutions for real estate professionals, local and national advertisers and providers of home and real estate products and services; Relocation.com, is an online resource for consumers looking to move to a new home or apartment, whether it is across town, across the country or in another country; and Reesio, a document and transaction management platform that allows real estate professionals to simplify the process for home buyers and sellers by bringing the entire transaction online. In October 2018, Move, Inc. acquired Opcity, a leading real estate technology platform that uses artificial intelligence (AI) and machine learning to match potential home buyers with agents.

FINANCIAL DATA: *Note: Data for latest year may not have been available at press time.*

In U.S. $	2018	2017	2016	2015	2014	2013
Revenue		280,000,000	278,000,000	260,000,000	253,000,000	227,032,992
R&D Expense						
Operating Income						
Operating Margin %						
SGA Expense						
Net Income						
Operating Cash Flow						
Capital Expenditure						
EBITDA						
Return on Assets %						
Return on Equity %						
Debt to Equity						

CONTACT INFORMATION:

Phone: 408 558-7100   Fax:
Toll-Free:
Address: 10 Almaden Blvd., Ste. 800, San Jose, CA 95113 United States

STOCK TICKER/OTHER:

Stock Ticker: Subsidiary   Exchange:
Employees: 943   Fiscal Year Ends: 12/31
Parent Company: News Corporation

SALARIES/BONUSES:

Top Exec. Salary: $ Bonus: $
Second Exec. Salary: $ Bonus: $

OTHER THOUGHTS:

Estimated Female Officers or Directors: 5
Hot Spot for Advancement for Women/Minorities: Y

Sales, profits and employees may be estimates. Financial information, benefits and other data can change quickly and may vary from those stated here.

MovieTickets.com Inc

www.movietickets.com

NAIC Code: 454111

| TYPES OF BUSINESS: |
| Online Movie Ticket Sales |

GROWTH PLANS/SPECIAL FEATURES:

MovieTickets.com, Inc. is an online ticketing service based in the U.S. that provides customers with online access to movie tickets at theater chains all over the world. The company's connected sites enable customers to purchase movie tickets online, through mobile devices or by phone; access local show times; view movie trailers; and read reviews. MovieTickets is present in the U.S., Canada, the U.K., Ireland, Argentina, Puerto Rico, Dominican Republic and the Caribbean. The firm's partner theaters account for more than 50% of the top 100 grossing North American theaters each weekend, including Regal, Starplex, AMC, Aurora, Cineplex, IMAX and IFC Center. The company also offers retail gift cards, which can be purchased either through the website, mobile app or at many national grocery and pharmacy locations. MovieTickets.com operates as a subsidiary of Fandango, Inc.

BRANDS/DIVISIONS/AFFILIATES:

Fandango Inc

CONTACTS: Note: Officers with more than one job title may be intentionally listed here more than once.

Paul Yanover, CEO-Fandango

FINANCIAL DATA: Note: Data for latest year may not have been available at press time.

In U.S. $	2018	2017	2016	2015	2014	2013
Revenue						
R&D Expense						
Operating Income						
Operating Margin %						
SGA Expense						
Net Income						
Operating Cash Flow						
Capital Expenditure						
EBITDA						
Return on Assets %						
Return on Equity %						
Debt to Equity						

CONTACT INFORMATION:

Phone: 561-322-3200   Fax: 561-322-3222
Toll-Free:
Address: 2255 Glades Rd., Ste. 100E, Boca Raton, FL 33431 United States

STOCK TICKER/OTHER:

Stock Ticker: Subsidiary   Exchange:
Employees: 52   Fiscal Year Ends: 03/31
Parent Company: Fandango Inc

SALARIES/BONUSES:

Top Exec. Salary: $ Bonus: $
Second Exec. Salary: $ Bonus: $

OTHER THOUGHTS:

Estimated Female Officers or Directors:
Hot Spot for Advancement for Women/Minorities:

MuleSoft LLC

www.mulesoft.com

NAIC Code: 511210I

TYPES OF BUSINESS:

Computer Software, Operating Systems, Language & Development Tools

BRANDS/DIVISIONS/AFFILIATES:

Salesforce.com Inc
Anypoint Platform
Anypoint Design Center
Anypoint Management Center

CONTACTS: Note: Officers with more than one job title may be intentionally listed here more than once.

Greg Schott, CEO
Matthew Langdon, CFO
Vidya Peters, CMO
Uri Sarid, CTO

GROWTH PLANS/SPECIAL FEATURES:

MuleSoft, LLC is a software company that designs, develops and markets an integration platform for connecting applications, data sources and devices on-premise and in the cloud. This offering enables corporations to reach customers, employees and partners. The company's Anypoint Platform connects the application network, solving the most challenging connectivity issues across service-oriented architecture (SOA), software-as-a-service (SaaS) architecture and application program interfaces (APIs). Mule is the runtime engine of Anypoint Platform, combining data and application integration across legacy systems, SaaS applications and APIs with hybrid deployment options for maximum flexibility. Anypoint Design Center offers low-friction development tools that make it easy to design and test APIs, implement data and application integration flows, as well as build connectors. Anypoint Management Center is a single unified web interface used to administer all aspects of Anypoint Platform. Primary industries served by MuleSoft include financial services, government, healthcare, higher education, insurance, manufacturing, media/telecom and retail. The company's services include support, consulting, training and certification. MuleSoft is headquartered in California, with U.S. offices in Georgia, Illinois, New York and Washington, D.C., as well as internationally in the Netherlands, Argentina, Germany, Hong Kong, U.K., France, Singapore, Sweden and Australia. In May 2018, MuleSoft was acquired by Salesforce.com, Inc., and subsequently delisted from being publicly traded. MuleSoft operates as a wholly-owned subsidiary of Salesforce.

FINANCIAL DATA: Note: Data for latest year may not have been available at press time.

In U.S. $	2018	2017	2016	2015	2014	2013
Revenue		296,456,000	187,747,008	110,252,000	57,617,000	
R&D Expense						
Operating Income						
Operating Margin %						
SGA Expense						
Net Income		-79,980,000	-49,599,000	-65,439,000	-47,756,000	
Operating Cash Flow						
Capital Expenditure						
EBITDA						
Return on Assets %						
Return on Equity %						
Debt to Equity						

CONTACT INFORMATION:

Phone: 415-229-2009   Fax:
Toll-Free:
Address: 415 Mission St., San Francisco, CA 94105 United States

STOCK TICKER/OTHER:

Stock Ticker: Subsidiary   Exchange:
Employees: 841   Fiscal Year Ends:
Parent Company: Salesforce.com Inc

SALARIES/BONUSES:

Top Exec. Salary: $ Bonus: $
Second Exec. Salary: $ Bonus: $

OTHER THOUGHTS:

Estimated Female Officers or Directors:
Hot Spot for Advancement for Women/Minorities:

MXM

NAIC Code: 541810E

www.mxm.com

TYPES OF BUSINESS:

Online Advertising & Marketing
Consulting Services
Web Site Development

BRANDS/DIVISIONS/AFFILIATES:

Accenture plc
Accenture Interactive

CONTACTS: *Note: Officers with more than one job title may be intentionally listed here more than once.*

Georgine Anton, Pres.
Mark Bieschke, CTO
Brian Berri, VP-Finance
Pete Moran, Sr. VP
Theresa Martin, Exec. VP

GROWTH PLANS/SPECIAL FEATURES:

MXM is a content-powered digital marketing agency. The company designs, builds and populates content-led digital ecosystems. They are business-to-consumer (B2C), business-to-business (B2B) and across every channel and industry vertical. MXM intersects brands, consumers, content and commerce and delivers them through its digital ecosystem to provide capabilities across strategy, content, creative, analytics and technology. The strategy business model includes brand positioning, audience planning, audience segmentation, consumer journey mapping, content audits, search engine optimization (SEO) audits, content strategy and architecture, channel planning, media/distribution strategy and business/user requirement solutions. The content business model includes content gap analysis, content road map, editorial calendar, measure planning, distribution planning and SEO/SEM strategy (SEM stands for search engine marketing). The creative business model includes front-end design and visualization of the ecosystem via user-experience research/design/prototyping, websites, digital media, email, direct mail, video, print media, social platform activation, influencer programming and mobile apps. The analytics business model includes campaign planning, learning agendas, measurement planning, database design/management, testing, optimization, data visualization, and descriptive/predictive analytics by channel and across the ecosystem. Last, the technology business model involves front-to-back-end development, including responsive design websites, marketing cloud integration, content management system (CMS) integration, email management, campaign management, application architecture, database, web service development, testing, personalization implementations and metrics, reporting and analytic technology integrations. MXM is based in New York, with offices in Los Angeles, Washington DC, Dallas, Detroit and Des Moines in the U.S., as well as in India and the U.K. It is part of Accenture Interactive, which is itself a subsidiary of Accenture plc.

FINANCIAL DATA: *Note: Data for latest year may not have been available at press time.*

In U.S. $	2018	2017	2016	2015	2014	2013
Revenue						
R&D Expense						
Operating Income						
Operating Margin %						
SGA Expense						
Net Income						
Operating Cash Flow						
Capital Expenditure						
EBITDA						
Return on Assets %						
Return on Equity %						
Debt to Equity						

CONTACT INFORMATION:

Phone: 212-499-2000   Fax: 212-499-1750
Toll-Free:
Address: 155 Avenue of the Americas, 10/Fl, New York, NY 10013
United States

STOCK TICKER/OTHER:

Stock Ticker: Subsidiary   Exchange:
Employees: 450   Fiscal Year Ends: 12/31
Parent Company: Accenture plc

SALARIES/BONUSES:

Top Exec. Salary: $ Bonus: $
Second Exec. Salary: $ Bonus: $

OTHER THOUGHTS:

Estimated Female Officers or Directors: 1
Hot Spot for Advancement for Women/Minorities: Y

MyHeritage Ltd

www.myheritage.com

NAIC Code: 519130

TYPES OF BUSINESS:
Online Genealogy

BRANDS/DIVISIONS/AFFILIATES:
MyHeritage.com
Family Tree Builder

CONTACTS: *Note: Officers with more than one job title may be intentionally listed here more than once.*
Gilad Japhet, CEO
Russ Wilding, Chief Content Officer
Smadar Levi, CFO
Sagi Bashari, CTO
Uri Gonen, Sr. VP-Prod. Mgmt.
Russ Wilding, Chief Content Officer
Roger Bell, VP-Prod.
Noah Tutak, Gen. Mgr.-USA
Ran Peled, Chief Architect

GROWTH PLANS/SPECIAL FEATURES:
MyHeritage Ltd. owns and manages MyHeritage.com, a private social networking site which allows family members to connect with one another and upload and share family trees, events, videos and messages. The firm offers a series of tools and software which allow its 100 million members across 196 countries to update and maintain their family profiles. Family Tree Builder, a free windows software, provides tools for building geographical maps of family members' and ancestors' locations, photo albums, family charts, a report generator, tools for building family member profiles and making timelines, a digital scrapbook, a family statistic compiler and an automatic historical record search and match from WorldVitalRecords. Family Tree Builder is available in 42 languages and allows users to choose from Gregorian, Hebrew and French Revolutionary calendars. Users can upload files created in Family Tree Builder directly onto their MyHeritage.com profile for other family members to see. The genealogy tools offered by the firm allow users to cross compare their family trees with the other users on MyHeritage.com for matches using the firm's proprietary smart match technology. Users are able to confirm or reject matches pulled up by the matching technology and connect with possible family members through their MyHeritage.com accounts. The company comprises a global search engine that retrieves and delivers historical records of births, deaths, marriages, immigration, census and original documents. The search engine utilizes semantics analysis to find matches for family trees in newspapers, books and other free text documents. MyHeritage offers DNA testing through the maternal and paternal lines to find family matches using autosomal DNA.

FINANCIAL DATA: *Note: Data for latest year may not have been available at press time.*

In U.S. $	2018	2017	2016	2015	2014	2013
Revenue	165,000,000	133,000,000	60,000,000			
R&D Expense						
Operating Income						
Operating Margin %						
SGA Expense						
Net Income		18,100,000				
Operating Cash Flow						
Capital Expenditure						
EBITDA						
Return on Assets %						
Return on Equity %						
Debt to Equity						

CONTACT INFORMATION:
Phone: 972-3-6280000   Fax: 972-3-6280003
Toll-Free:
Address: 3 Ariel Sharon St., 4/Fl, Or Yehuda, 60250 Israel

STOCK TICKER/OTHER:
Stock Ticker: Private   Exchange:
Employees: 450   Fiscal Year Ends:
Parent Company:

SALARIES/BONUSES:
Top Exec. Salary: $ Bonus: $
Second Exec. Salary: $ Bonus: $

OTHER THOUGHTS:
Estimated Female Officers or Directors: 1
Hot Spot for Advancement for Women/Minorities:

Myspace LLC

NAIC Code: 519130

www.myspace.com

TYPES OF BUSINESS:

Social Networking
Online Content Distribution-Audio & Video

BRANDS/DIVISIONS/AFFILIATES:

Meredith Corporation

CONTACTS: *Note: Officers with more than one job title may be intentionally listed here more than once.*

Tim Vanderhook, CEO
Roger Mincheff, Pres.
Tim Vanderhook, CEO-Specific Media

GROWTH PLANS/SPECIAL FEATURES:

Myspace, LLC is an internet-based music social networking website with access to millions of songs, photos, personal profiles, blogs and videos. Its site enables users, such as individuals, bands, comedians and filmmakers, to create and customize content-rich internet profile pages, share user-generated video, participate in user groups and communicate with each other using various technologies, including instant messaging. In addition, Myspace provides a way for artists to connect with their fan base, and allows users to discover new music, films and other media. The website has approximately 50 million unique users. The Myspace mobile app features a tool for users to create and edit gif images and post them to their Myspace stream. It also allows users to stream available live streams of concerts. The app is available from the App Store and Google Play. Myspace app offers filters that can be added when a user has just taken a photo or just created a gif. The app allows users to play Myspace radio channels from the device. Myspace's niche no longer operates as a network of targeted video ads, but has expanded into an interactive media platform focused on brand marketing using integrated digital media messaging tools that engages users and produces loyalty. Myspace is owned by Meredith Corporation.

FINANCIAL DATA: *Note: Data for latest year may not have been available at press time.*

In U.S. $	2018	2017	2016	2015	2014	2013
Revenue						
R&D Expense						
Operating Income						
Operating Margin %						
SGA Expense						
Net Income						
Operating Cash Flow						
Capital Expenditure						
EBITDA						
Return on Assets %						
Return on Equity %						
Debt to Equity						

CONTACT INFORMATION:

Phone: 310-969-7400   Fax:
Toll-Free:
Address: 407 N. Maple Dr., Beverly Hills, CA 90210 United States

STOCK TICKER/OTHER:

Stock Ticker: Subsidiary   Exchange:
Employees: 150   Fiscal Year Ends: 12/31
Parent Company: Meredith Corporation

SALARIES/BONUSES:

Top Exec. Salary: $ Bonus: $
Second Exec. Salary: $ Bonus: $

OTHER THOUGHTS:

Estimated Female Officers or Directors:
Hot Spot for Advancement for Women/Minorities: Y

Namely Inc

www.namely.com

NAIC Code: 511210Q

TYPES OF BUSINESS:

Computer Software, Accounting, Banking & Financial
Human Resources Computer Software

GROWTH PLANS/SPECIAL FEATURES:

Namely, Inc. provides a cloud-based human resource platform for mid-market companies. The firm's software supplies support to human resources (HR) professionals with the technology and data needed to help employees thrive. The Namely platform handles all administration and compliance across HR, payroll, time, benefits, talent and managed services. Namely Analytics helps teams make strategic decisions. Namely HR Scholarship recognizes outstanding HR professionals and supports their career growth. Namely was established in 2012, and as of January 2019 processes over $12 billion in annual payroll, serving more than 1,000 mid-sized companies. The company has offices in New York, California, Texas and Georgia.

BRANDS/DIVISIONS/AFFILIATES:

Namely
Namely Analytics
Namely HR Scholarship

CONTACTS: Note: Officers with more than one job title may be intentionally listed here more than once.

Elisa Steele, CEO

FINANCIAL DATA: Note: Data for latest year may not have been available at press time.

In U.S. $	2018	2017	2016	2015	2014	2013
Revenue		35,000,000	30,000,000			
R&D Expense						
Operating Income						
Operating Margin %						
SGA Expense						
Net Income						
Operating Cash Flow						
Capital Expenditure						
EBITDA						
Return on Assets %						
Return on Equity %						
Debt to Equity						

CONTACT INFORMATION:

Phone: Fax:
Toll-Free: 855-626-3591
Address: 195 Broadway, 15/Fl, New York, NY 10007 United States

STOCK TICKER/OTHER:

Stock Ticker: Private   Exchange:
Employees: 350   Fiscal Year Ends:
Parent Company:

SALARIES/BONUSES:

Top Exec. Salary: $ Bonus: $
Second Exec. Salary: $ Bonus: $

OTHER THOUGHTS:

Estimated Female Officers or Directors:
Hot Spot for Advancement for Women/Minorities:

Naver Corporation

www.navercorp.com

NAIC Code: 519130

TYPES OF BUSINESS:

Online Portal
Online Game Portal
Online Advertising

BRANDS/DIVISIONS/AFFILIATES:

Naver.com
Naver Dictionary
LINE
SNOW
V LIVE
Papago
WHALE
Clova

CONTACTS: *Note: Officers with more than one job title may be intentionally listed here more than once.*

Seong-sook Han, CEO

GROWTH PLANS/SPECIAL FEATURES:

NAVER Corporation is a South Korea-based internet company that offers technology and services applicable to daily life. The firm developed the first domestic search engine in Korea, NAVER.com, as well as the NAVER Blog, NAVER Cafe and NAVER Post online platforms. It created diverse theme boards optimized for mobile devices, including news, sports, entertainment, shopping and video. NAVER Dictionary is offered in over 30 languages; and NAVER Encyclopedia is linked to the search engine and provides reliable search results built on a comprehensive database of knowledge. LINE is a global mobile platform that features messaging and connects with games, music, payment, deliver and call services in order to provide enhanced communication between people and businesses. SNOW is a mobile video messenger, offering photo and video sharing services. V LIVE lets celebrities broadcast live and explore new ways to engage viewers. Papago is a translation app that integrates artificial intelligence (AI) technologies including voice recognition, text-to-speech, machine translation and character recognition. WHALE seeks to liberate users from web surfing to omni-tasking split-screen features, quick search, automated translation, pop-up control and internal security systems. Clova is an AI platform that integrates speech/image recognition and artificial neural network translation to provide an interactive engine. WEBTOON is a mobile comics platform that reaches millions of monthly active users worldwide, and has expanded its IP business via publishing, movies and games. Last, GRAFOLIO is a content sharing platform on which creative artists can be discovered, shared and become more known for their art work. In addition, NAVER offers products and services for small businesses to grow them, including a smart online-to-offline (O2O) shopping window service, NAVER Pay, NAVER Booking, NAVER Store Form, NAVER Smart Place, NAVER Analytics, NAVER Cloud and more.

FINANCIAL DATA: *Note: Data for latest year may not have been available at press time.*

In U.S. $	2018	2017	2016	2015	2014	2013
Revenue		4,161,895,000	3,578,470,000	2,892,180,000	2,453,901,000	2,056,687,000
R&D Expense						
Operating Income		1,048,988,000	980,358,500	678,044,900	674,482,400	466,265,700
Operating Margin %		25.20%	27.39%	23.44%	27.48%	22.67%
SGA Expense		1,949,209,000	1,537,897,000	1,313,461,000	1,073,867,000	967,093,600
Net Income		687,541,900	666,570,900	461,469,000	404,278,400	1,687,953,000
Operating Cash Flow		836,193,700	1,035,498,000	761,797,100	693,419,400	558,616,900
Capital Expenditure		447,674,700	155,330,300	121,554,200	247,036,700	391,792,900
EBITDA		1,247,779,000	1,157,167,000	773,960,300	719,366,800	529,641,300
Return on Assets %		10.74%	13.93%	13.33%	14.91%	67.46%
Return on Equity %		18.49%	26.20%	26.46%	27.81%	112.68%
Debt to Equity		0.01	0.04	0.07	0.13	0.07

CONTACT INFORMATION:

Phone: 82-1588-3830   Fax: 82-31-784-1000
Toll-Free:
Address: 6, Buljeong-ro, Bundang-gu, Gyeonggi-do, Bundang-gu, Gyeonggi-do 463-867 South Korea

STOCK TICKER/OTHER:

Stock Ticker: NHNCF   Exchange: PINX
Employees: 2,501   Fiscal Year Ends: 12/31
Parent Company:

SALARIES/BONUSES:

Top Exec. Salary: $ Bonus: $
Second Exec. Salary: $ Bonus: $

OTHER THOUGHTS:

Estimated Female Officers or Directors:
Hot Spot for Advancement for Women/Minorities:

NaviSite Inc

www.navisite.com

NAIC Code: 519130

TYPES OF BUSINESS:

Web Site Hosting
Application Services Provider
Server & Application Management
Internet Application Solutions
e-Business Services
Electronic Software Distribution
Outsourcing Services

BRANDS/DIVISIONS/AFFILIATES:

Charter Communications Inc
Spectrum Enterprise

CONTACTS: Note: Officers with more than one job title may be intentionally listed here more than once.

Sumeet Sabharwal, Group VP
R. Brooks Borcherding, Pres.
Chris Patterson, VP-Prod. Mgmt.
Michael Poole, Sr. VP-Worldwide Delivery

GROWTH PLANS/SPECIAL FEATURES:

NaviSite, Inc. is an application services provider offering e-business-based internet outsourcing, cloud enabled hosting, server management, application management and internet application services. Its clients are primarily middle-market organizations, such as mid-sized companies, divisions of large multinational companies and government agencies. The firm's services allow its customers to outsource the hosting and management operations of their IT infrastructure and applications, such as commerce systems, enterprise software applications and e-mail. NaviSite's full suite of reliable and scalable managed services include application, cloud desktop, cloud infrastructure and hosting services for organizations looking to lower their capital and operational costs. NaviSite's solutions offer key benefits such as capital expenditure mitigation, faster time-to-value, enhanced client service and disaster recovery preparedness. The firm's support services are offered 24/7 every day of the year. NaviSite data centers are located in Massachusetts, California, Illinois and New York, in the U.S., as well as Redhill, Woking and Watford, in the U.K. NaviSite operates as a division of Spectrum Enterprise, which itself is a subsidiary of Charter Communications, Inc.

FINANCIAL DATA: Note: Data for latest year may not have been available at press time.

In U.S. $	2018	2017	2016	2015	2014	2013
Revenue						
R&D Expense						
Operating Income						
Operating Margin %						
SGA Expense						
Net Income						
Operating Cash Flow						
Capital Expenditure						
EBITDA						
Return on Assets %						
Return on Equity %						
Debt to Equity						

CONTACT INFORMATION:

Phone: 978-682-8300   Fax: 978-688-8100
Toll-Free: 888-298-8222
Address: 400 Minuteman Rd., Andover, MA 01810 United States

STOCK TICKER/OTHER:

Stock Ticker: Subsidiary   Exchange:
Employees: 300   Fiscal Year Ends: 07/31
Parent Company: Charter Communications Inc

SALARIES/BONUSES:

Top Exec. Salary: $ Bonus: $
Second Exec. Salary: $ Bonus: $

OTHER THOUGHTS:

Estimated Female Officers or Directors:
Hot Spot for Advancement for Women/Minorities:

Net2Phone Inc

NAIC Code: 517110

TYPES OF BUSINESS:

VoIP Service Providers
Outsourced Telecommunications Services
Calling Card Services
ISP Solutions

BRANDS/DIVISIONS/AFFILIATES:

IDT Corporation

CONTACTS: *Note: Officers with more than one job title may be intentionally listed here more than once.*

Liore Alroy, CEO
David Lando, COO

GROWTH PLANS/SPECIAL FEATURES:

Net2Phone, Inc. is a provider of retail voice over internet protocol (VoIP) cloud telephone products and services. The firm comprises the capacity for businesses to handle 450,000 simultaneous calls, but serves businesses of any size, whether small or large. Net2Phone's onboarding and implementation team sets up each customer's phone system as needed/required, and provides ongoing support services. The company offers two products: hosted PBX cloud phone systems and SIP trunking for business and call centers. Hosted business PBX (private branch exchange) is a phone system that is completed hosted, managed and maintained by Net2Phone. It features VoIP solutions for a fully-featured cloud PBX, and comprises a single platform that enables businesses to transfer calls, set up auto-attendant to answer and route calls, manage multiple offices and keep businesses connected even while on-the-go. The hosted PBX phone service includes unlimited calls, both domestic and international calls, for one low monthly price. SIP (session initiation protocol) trunking is a VoIP technology and streaming media service by which internet telephone service providers deliver telephone services and unified communications to customers equipped with SIP-based PBX facilities. This allows businesses and call centers to use their existing internet connection as a phone line, instead of physical leased line, providing cost-savings. Net2Phone's plans offer unlimited calling to/from 25 countries, a ported phone number, and more than 40 advanced features. Net2Phone is a subsidiary of IDT Corporation, a holding company with strong interest in telecommunications.

FINANCIAL DATA: *Note: Data for latest year may not have been available at press time.*

In U.S. $	2018	2017	2016	2015	2014	2013
Revenue						
R&D Expense						
Operating Income						
Operating Margin %						
SGA Expense						
Net Income						
Operating Cash Flow						
Capital Expenditure						
EBITDA						
Return on Assets %						
Return on Equity %						
Debt to Equity						

CONTACT INFORMATION:

Phone: 973-438-3111   Fax:
Toll-Free:
Address: 520 Broad St., Newark, NJ 07102 United States

STOCK TICKER/OTHER:

Stock Ticker: Subsidiary   Exchange:
Employees: 525   Fiscal Year Ends: 07/31
Parent Company: IDT Corporation

SALARIES/BONUSES:

Top Exec. Salary: $ Bonus: $
Second Exec. Salary: $ Bonus: $

OTHER THOUGHTS:

Estimated Female Officers or Directors:
Hot Spot for Advancement for Women/Minorities:

NetEase Inc

ir.netease.com

NAIC Code: 519130

TYPES OF BUSINESS:

Internet Portal
E-Mail
Instant Messaging
Chat Rooms
Online Games
e-Commerce Services
Search Engine
Wireless Services

BRANDS/DIVISIONS/AFFILIATES:

Westward Journey
Tianxia
Heroes of Tang Dynasty Zero
Ghost
World of Warcraft
StarCraft II
Diablo III
Youdao

CONTACTS: Note: Officers with more than one job title may be intentionally listed here more than once.

William Ding, CEO
Zhaoxuan Yang, CFO

GROWTH PLANS/SPECIAL FEATURES:

NetEase, Inc. operates a leading interactive online community in China and is a major provider of Chinese language content and services through its online games, internet portal and wireless value-added services businesses. The company offers online games services, an online services portal, advertising services and wireless value-added services. Its online gaming service focuses on offering massively multi-player online role-playing games (MMORPGs) to the Chinese market. These include the Westward Journey series, Tianxia, Heroes of Tang Dynasty Zero and Ghost. The firm also develops casual online games and licenses games from other publishers for release in Mainland China, including the popular World of Warcraft franchise. It operates other popular international online games, including Hearthstone: Heroes of Warcraft, StarCraft II and Diablo III: Reaper of Souls. The portal, a network of NetEase.com websites, provides users with Chinese language services among three core service categories: content, community and communication. NetEase content channels provide news, information and online entertainment to the Chinese public. Community and communication websites provide an array of free and fee-based community and communication services, including e-mail, blogging, photos, instant messaging, matchmaking, alumni directories, clubs, e-cards, chat rooms and community forums. Additionally, the company operates Youdao, a proprietary search engine; Youdao Dictionary; and Youdao Cloudnote, a cloud note-taking application. Advertising services include banner advertising, channel sponsorship, direct email, interactive media-rich sites, sponsored special events, games, contests and other activities. The firm's wireless services allow users to receive news and other information, download ringtones and logos and participate in matchmaking communities and interactive games through their mobile phones.

FINANCIAL DATA: Note: Data for latest year may not have been available at press time.

In U.S. $	2018	2017	2016	2015	2014	2013
Revenue		7,873,851,000	5,556,439,000	3,318,667,000	1,704,652,000	1,338,385,000
R&D Expense		636,205,000	443,448,500	314,198,300	192,618,100	134,129,600
Operating Income		1,768,830,000	1,837,968,000	1,058,364,000	693,502,500	633,464,400
Operating Margin %		22.46%	33.07%	31.89%	40.68%	47.33%
SGA Expense		1,366,223,000	871,471,700	578,164,200	343,855,700	210,074,700
Net Income		1,558,403,000	1,688,888,000	980,208,100	692,265,200	646,753,900
Operating Cash Flow		1,730,325,000	2,254,117,000	1,175,492,000	854,742,800	762,016,300
Capital Expenditure		367,368,300	165,916,200	149,999,100	89,992,000	31,994,300
EBITDA		1,885,523,000	1,885,634,000	1,084,917,000	718,893,200	656,512,100
Return on Assets %		16.59%	23.39%	18.83%	17.32%	20.28%
Return on Equity %		25.51%	34.41%	25.59%	21.80%	24.73%
Debt to Equity						

CONTACT INFORMATION:

Phone: 8610-8255-8163   Fax: 8610-8261-7823
Toll-Free:
Address: Bldg. 7, No. 10 Zibeiwang East Rd., Haidian Dist., Beijing, 100193 China

STOCK TICKER/OTHER:

Stock Ticker: NTES   Exchange: NAS
Employees: 15,948   Fiscal Year Ends: 12/31
Parent Company:

SALARIES/BONUSES:

Top Exec. Salary: $ Bonus: $
Second Exec. Salary: $ Bonus: $

OTHER THOUGHTS:

Estimated Female Officers or Directors:
Hot Spot for Advancement for Women/Minorities:

Netflix Inc

NAIC Code: 515210

TYPES OF BUSINESS:

Streaming Movies and TV Shows
DVD Rentals by Mail
Motion Picture Production

BRANDS/DIVISIONS/AFFILIATES:

CONTACTS: *Note: Officers with more than one job title may be intentionally listed here more than once.*

Reed Hastings, CEO
David Wells, CFO
Kelly Bennett, Chief Marketing Officer
David Hyman, General Counsel
Jonathan Friedland, Other Executive Officer
Jessica Neal, Other Executive Officer
Greg Peters, Other Executive Officer
Ted Sarandos, Other Executive Officer

GROWTH PLANS/SPECIAL FEATURES:

Netflix, Inc. is one of the largest online movie rental subscription services, providing access to a library of movie, television and other filmed entertainment titles to nearly 130 million subscribers in over 190 countries. The company has three operating segments: domestic streaming, international streaming and domestic DVD. The domestic and international streaming segments derive revenues from monthly membership fees for services consisting solely of streaming content. Domestic streaming membership plans are priced at $7.99 per month (basic), $10.99 per month (standard) of which can be watched on two screens at the same time, and $13.99 per month (premium) of which can be watched on up to four devices concurrently. International streaming membership is priced at the equivalent of USD $7 to $14 per month. The domestic DVD segment derives revenues from monthly membership fees for services consisting solely of DVD-by-mail. The price per plan for DVD-by-mail varies from $7.99 to $14.99 per month according to the plan chosen by the member. DVD-by-mail plans differ by the number of DVDs a member may have out at any given point and the type of DVD, either a standard DVD or an HD Blu-ray disc. Netflix's streaming service allows subscribers to view a growing library of movies and television episodes over the internet or on Netflix-ready devices such as Blu-ray players, internet-connected TVs, digital video players, smartphones and game consoles. The Netflix streaming content library includes media acquired through deals with corporations. Additionally, through its Netflix Studios division, the company produces original content available exclusively on Netflix.

FINANCIAL DATA: *Note: Data for latest year may not have been available at press time.*

In U.S. $	2018	2017	2016	2015	2014	2013
Revenue		11,692,710,000	8,830,669,000	6,779,511,000	5,504,656,000	4,374,562,000
R&D Expense		1,052,778,000	852,098,000	650,788,000	472,321,000	378,769,000
Operating Income		838,679,000	379,793,000	305,826,000	402,648,000	228,347,000
Operating Margin %		7.17%	4.30%	4.51%	7.31%	5.21%
SGA Expense		2,141,590,000	1,568,877,000	1,231,421,000	876,927,000	684,190,000
Net Income		558,929,000	186,678,000	122,641,000	266,799,000	112,403,000
Operating Cash Flow		-1,785,948,000	-1,473,984,000	-749,439,000	16,483,000	97,831,000
Capital Expenditure		173,302,000	107,653,000	91,248,000	69,726,000	54,143,000
EBITDA		795,436,000	468,149,000	336,884,000	453,616,000	248,590,000
Return on Assets %		3.42%	1.56%	1.42%	4.27%	2.39%
Return on Equity %		17.85%	7.61%	6.01%	16.72%	10.81%
Debt to Equity		1.81	1.25	1.06	0.48	0.37

CONTACT INFORMATION:

Phone: 408 540-3700   Fax: 408 540-3737
Toll-Free: 1-877-742-1480
Address: 100 Winchester Cir., Los Gatos, CA 95032 United States

STOCK TICKER/OTHER:

Stock Ticker: NFLX   Exchange: NAS
Employees: 4,700   Fiscal Year Ends: 12/31
Parent Company:

SALARIES/BONUSES:

Top Exec. Salary: $2,500,000   Bonus: $
Second Exec. Salary: Bonus: $
$1,761,538

OTHER THOUGHTS:

Estimated Female Officers or Directors: 3
Hot Spot for Advancement for Women/Minorities: Y

NetScout Systems Inc

www.netscout.com

NAIC Code: 511210B

TYPES OF BUSINESS:

Computer Software, Network Management, System Testing & Storage Application Management Solutions

BRANDS/DIVISIONS/AFFILIATES:

Adaptive Service Intelligence
nGeniusONE
InfiniStream

CONTACTS: Note: Officers with more than one job title may be intentionally listed here more than once.

Anil Singhal, CEO
Jean Bua, CFO
Michael Szabados, COO
John Downing, Executive VP, Divisional

GROWTH PLANS/SPECIAL FEATURES:

NetScout Systems, Inc. designs, develops, manufactures, markets, sells and supports a family of products that assures the performance and availability of critical business applications and services in complex, high-speed networks. Powered by NetScout's proprietary Adaptive Service Intelligence technology, its solutions are used to monitor customers' service delivery environment in order to identify performance issues and provide insight into network-based security threats. The firm markets its core service assurance and cybersecurity solutions into two primary markets: enterprise and service provider. Within the enterprise market, NetScout's nGeniusONE and InfiniStream technologies enable IT and government organizations to improve service issues and security threats before they become serious and affect large numbers of users. These products are based on real-time analytic information platforms that can be managed across both virtual and physical environments. The service provider market serves customers categorized into three groups: mobile operators, fixed-line and cable operators, and internet service providers. For mobile operators, NetScout products monitor radio access networks, and provide analytics that present insight into subscriber trends and their customer experiences. For fixed-line and cable operators, products and solutions enable them to monitor and manage their local area WiFi connectivity services as well as broadband and telephone services targeting small- and medium-sized businesses. These products and solutions provide comprehensive insight into IP services, service usage, service availability, application awareness, traffic load, network availability and network performance. Last, for internet service providers, products and solutions help protect their networks against distributed denial of service (DDos) attacks, and assist in rapidly locating and isolating advanced network threats.

FINANCIAL DATA: Note: Data for latest year may not have been available at press time.

In U.S. $	2018	2017	2016	2015	2014	2013
Revenue	986,787,000	1,162,112,000	955,419,000	453,669,000	396,647,000	350,550,000
R&D Expense	215,076,000	232,701,000	208,630,000	75,242,000	70,454,000	61,546,000
Operating Income	1,151,000	66,065,000	-25,082,000	96,773,000	78,014,000	65,594,000
Operating Margin %	0.11	5.68%	-2.62%	21.33%	19.66%	18.71%
SGA Expense	422,015,000	447,066,000	411,049,000	183,742,000	160,234,000	146,525,000
Net Income	79,812,000	33,291,000	-28,369,000	61,192,000	49,106,000	40,609,000
Operating Cash Flow	222,454,000	227,809,000	95,285,000	106,933,000	110,946,000	95,412,000
Capital Expenditure	16,594,000	32,148,000	30,370,000	12,982,000	14,152,000	11,948,000
EBITDA	147,477,000	222,232,000	113,961,000	115,447,000	96,884,000	82,491,000
Return on Assets %	2.29%	.92%	-1.33%	9.58%	8.46%	7.25%
Return on Equity %	3.54%	1.36%	-1.97%	14.48%	12.57%	11.37%
Debt to Equity	0.29	0.12	0.12			

CONTACT INFORMATION:

Phone: 978 614-4000   Fax: 978 614-4004
Toll-Free: 800-357-7666
Address: 310 Littleton Rd., Westford, MA 01886 United States

SALARIES/BONUSES:

Top Exec. Salary: $456,250   Bonus: $
Second Exec. Salary: $338,750   Bonus: $

STOCK TICKER/OTHER:

Stock Ticker: NTCT   Exchange: NAS
Employees: 3,113   Fiscal Year Ends: 03/31
Parent Company:

OTHER THOUGHTS:

Estimated Female Officers or Directors: 2
Hot Spot for Advancement for Women/Minorities:

Netskope Inc

NAIC Code: 511210E

www.netskope.com

TYPES OF BUSINESS:

Computer Software, Security & Anti-Virus
Cloud
Security

BRANDS/DIVISIONS/AFFILIATES:

Cloud XD
Netskope App Context Engine

CONTACTS: *Note: Officers with more than one job title may be intentionally listed here more than once.*

Sanjay Beri, CEO
Bobby Shoker, VP-Finance
Scott Hogrefe, VP-Mktg.
Chris Andrews, Sr. VP-Worldwide Sales

GROWTH PLANS/SPECIAL FEATURES:

Netskope, Inc. is a cloud access security broker. The firm provides a software-as-a-service (SaaS) platform that helps companies find, understand and use cloud applications relevant to them. Netskope's platform enables the discovery and monitoring of various known or unknown cloud applications running in their organizations, draw analytics from that data and provide policy enforcement, all in real-time. The company's patented Cloud XD technology eliminates blind spots by quickly targeting and controlling activities across thousands of cloud services and millions of websites. Once connected with Netskope, cloud app traffic is steered to its private cloud tenant via flexible deployment options. This enables Netskope users to perform the analysis and policy enforcement on the traffic, and therefore strengthening data security in the cloud. The company also offers an appliance that can be deployed on-premises. This ensures that all cloud traffic processing happens inside those data centers and the security metadata is physically constrained to the Netskope appliance. The Netskope App Context Engine lets users monitor and enforce cloud app policies in context, or for certain users or groups, on particular devices and browsers. For example, no sharing policies can be enforced from a mobile device for corporate insiders across cloud storage app when the recipient is outside the company. Netskope's solutions include malware and threat protection, cloud storage security, data loss prevention, encryption, vendor assurance, redundancy elimination and more. The firm is headquartered in California, USA, and holds 40 patent claims across four categories. Additional offices are located in Australia, the U.K. and Singapore.

FINANCIAL DATA: *Note: Data for latest year may not have been available at press time.*

In U.S. $	2018	2017	2016	2015	2014	2013
Revenue						
R&D Expense						
Operating Income						
Operating Margin %						
SGA Expense						
Net Income						
Operating Cash Flow						
Capital Expenditure						
EBITDA						
Return on Assets %						
Return on Equity %						
Debt to Equity						

CONTACT INFORMATION:

Phone: 650-397-5474   Fax:
Toll-Free: 800-979-6988
Address: 270 3rd St., Los Altos, CA 94022 United States

STOCK TICKER/OTHER:

Stock Ticker: Private   Exchange:
Employees: 610   Fiscal Year Ends:
Parent Company:

SALARIES/BONUSES:

Top Exec. Salary: $ Bonus: $
Second Exec. Salary: $ Bonus: $

OTHER THOUGHTS:

Estimated Female Officers or Directors:
Hot Spot for Advancement for Women/Minorities:

NeuLion Inc

NAIC Code: 519130

www.neulion.com

TYPES OF BUSINESS:

Internet Protocol Television
Television, web, sports media, mobile solutions and services.

BRANDS/DIVISIONS/AFFILIATES:

William Morris Endeavor Entertainment LLC
NeuLion Digital Platform
NeuLion CE SDK
MainConcept

CONTACTS: Note: Officers with more than one job title may be intentionally listed here more than once.

Charles Wang, Chmn.
Tim Alavathil, CFO
Michael Her, CTO
Roy Reichbach, Director
J. Wagner, Executive VP, Divisional
Ronald Nunn, Executive VP, Divisional
Horngwei Her, Executive VP, Divisional
Alexander Arato, General Counsel
Nancy Li, Vice Chairman of the Board

GROWTH PLANS/SPECIAL FEATURES:

NeuLion, Inc. is a technology product and service provider that specializes in the digital video broadcasting, distribution and monetization of live and on-demand content to internet-enabled devices. The firm's flagship solution, the NeuLion Digital Platform, is a complete end-to-end, cloud-based, fully integrated video solution that simplifies the digital video workflow and provides all the tools necessary for NeuLion's customers to monetize their digital video content. The NeuLion Digital Platform offers content owners and rights holders a highly configurable and scalable suite of digital technologies, together with services for back-end content preparation, management, marketing, monetization, secure delivery, real time analytics and end user application development, in an end-to-end solution that addresses the complexities associated with successfully streaming and marketing their content. Other solutions include the NeuLion consumer electronics (CE) software development kit (the CE SDK), which allows CE manufacturers to provide a secure, high quality video experience with premium screen resolution, up to Ultra HD/4K, across virtually all content formats, for a wide range of connected devices. Additionally, NeuLion offers a library of high quality video and audio compression-decompression programs, or codecs, that are licensed under the MainConcept brand. In May 2018, NeuLion was acquired by William Morris Endeavor Entertainment LLC, a privately-held holding company, for $250 million.

FINANCIAL DATA: Note: Data for latest year may not have been available at press time.

In U.S. $	2018	2017	2016	2015	2014	2013
Revenue		95,570,000	99,788,000	94,043,000	55,519,740	47,107,176
R&D Expense						
Operating Income						
Operating Margin %						
SGA Expense						
Net Income		-31,315,000	-1,753,000	25,916,000	3,567,230	-2,278,345
Operating Cash Flow						
Capital Expenditure						
EBITDA						
Return on Assets %						
Return on Equity %						
Debt to Equity						

CONTACT INFORMATION:

Phone: 516 622-830   Fax:
Toll-Free:
Address: 1600 Old Country Rd., Plainview, NY 11803 United States

STOCK TICKER/OTHER:

Stock Ticker: Subsidairy   Exchange: TSE
Employees: 767   Fiscal Year Ends: 12/31
Parent Company: William Morris Endeavor Entertainment LLC

SALARIES/BONUSES:

Top Exec. Salary: $ Bonus: $
Second Exec. Salary: $ Bonus: $

OTHER THOUGHTS:

Estimated Female Officers or Directors: 2
Hot Spot for Advancement for Women/Minorities: Y

NeuStar Inc

NAIC Code: 518210

www.home.neustar

TYPES OF BUSINESS:

Clearinghouse Services
Addressing Services
Domain Name Directories
Interoperability Services
Infrastructure

BRANDS/DIVISIONS/AFFILIATES:

Golden Gate Capital

CONTACTS: Note: Officers with more than one job title may be intentionally listed here more than once.

Lisa Hook, CEO
Paul Lalljie, CFO
Carolyn Ullerick, CFO
Shawn Donovan, CMO
Marjorie R. Bailey, Sr. VP-Human Resources
Leonard Kennedy, General Counsel
Brian Foster, Senior VP, Divisional
Venkat Achanta, Senior VP, Divisional
Steve Edwards, Senior VP, Divisional
Henry (Hank) Skorny, Senior VP, Divisional

GROWTH PLANS/SPECIAL FEATURES:

NeuStar, Inc., owned by private equity firm Golden Gate Capital, provides directory and policy management services to communications carriers and commercial businesses. The firm operates four divisions of services: marketing, security, data and NPAC (number portability administration center). Marketing services provides intelligence via cloud-based solutions that enable marketers to identify, verify and segment existing and potential customers for both marketing initiatives and fraud and risk mitigation; activation, enabling marketers to maximize the impact of online display ad targeting for specific prospect audiences and customers; and media intelligence, which provides a single, neutral media intelligence platform that uses a unified dashboard for measuring ad campaigns and conversion analytics. Security services provides domain name systems to protect clients' internet ecosystems and defend most standard transmission control protocol-based applications and domain name registries, operating the authoritative registries of internet domain names for the .biz, .us, .co, .au and .travel top-level domains as well as providing international registry gateways. Data services provides carrier provisioning via network services that enable carrier customers to exchange essential operating information with multiple carriers to provision and manage services for their subscribers; caller-name identification technology which provides authoritative current caller-name data and related information to telephony providers; and user authentication and rights management which supports the UltraViolet digital content locker that consumers use to access their entertainment content. NPAC services include the routing of calls and text messages among all the competing communications service providers in the U.S. and related connection services and system enhancements. In August 2017, Neustar announced the completion of the company's previously announced acquisition by a private investment group led by Golden Gate Capital.

FINANCIAL DATA: Note: Data for latest year may not have been available at press time.

In U.S. $	2018	2017	2016	2015	2014	2013
Revenue		1,270,339,392	1,209,847,040	1,049,958,016	963,587,968	902,041,024
R&D Expense						
Operating Income						
Operating Margin %						
SGA Expense						
Net Income			168,646,000	175,462,000	163,694,000	162,752,000
Operating Cash Flow						
Capital Expenditure						
EBITDA						
Return on Assets %						
Return on Equity %						
Debt to Equity						

CONTACT INFORMATION:

Phone: 571 434-5400   Fax: 571 434-5401
Toll-Free: 855-683-2677
Address: 21575 Ridgetop Cir., Sterling, VA 20166 United States

STOCK TICKER/OTHER:

Stock Ticker: Private   Exchange:
Employees: 1,988   Fiscal Year Ends: 12/31
Parent Company: Golden Gate Capital

SALARIES/BONUSES:

Top Exec. Salary: $ Bonus: $
Second Exec. Salary: $ Bonus: $

OTHER THOUGHTS:

Estimated Female Officers or Directors: 3
Hot Spot for Advancement for Women/Minorities: Y

New York Times Company (The)

NAIC Code: 511110

www.nytco.com

TYPES OF BUSINESS:

Newspaper Publishing
Newspaper Distribution
Newsprint & Paper Manufacturing
Online Publishing

BRANDS/DIVISIONS/AFFILIATES:

New York Times (The)
NYTimes.com
Times (The)
Wirecutter (The)
NYT Live
Madison Paper Industries

CONTACTS: Note: Officers with more than one job title may be intentionally listed here more than once.

Mark Thompson, CEO
Roland Caputo, CFO
Arthur Sulzberger, Chairman of the Board
R. Benten, Chief Accounting Officer
Meredith Kopit Levien, COO
A. Sulzberger, Director
Michael Golden, Director
Diane Brayton, Executive VP

GROWTH PLANS/SPECIAL FEATURES:

The New York Times Company (NYT) is a diversified media company with operations that include newspapers, digital media and paper mill investments. NYT's businesses consist of The New York Times; website NYTimes.com; mobile applications, including The Time's core news applications, as well as interest-specific apps such as NYT Cooking, Crossword and others; and related businesses such as The Times news services division, product review and recommendation website The Wirecutter, digital archive distribution, live events business NYT Live, as well as other products and services under The Times brand. The firm generates revenues principally from circulation and advertising, delivering breaking news and multimedia on local, national and world business and occurrences. The Times is currently printed at the company's production and distribution facility in New York, as well as under contract at 26 remote print sites throughout the U.S. The Time's award-winning content is available in print, web and mobile platforms. The Time's print edition is a daily newspaper in the U.S., with average circulation on a weekday being 540,000 and 1,066,000 for Sunday (as of December 2017). Internationally, average circulation for the international edition of the firm's newspaper is approximately 173,000, respectively. Additionally, NYT owns a 40% interest in a Maine paper mill, Madison Paper Industries. During 2017, NYT sold its 49% equity interest in Donohue Malbaie, Inc., and its 30% ownership in Women in the World Media, LLC.

The firm offers employees medical, dental and health insurance; a 401(k) plan; health and wellness programs; an employee stock purchase plan; tuition assistance; and a bonus plan.

FINANCIAL DATA: Note: Data for latest year may not have been available at press time.

In U.S. $	2018	2017	2016	2015	2014	2013
Revenue		1,675,639,000	1,555,342,000	1,579,215,000	1,588,528,000	1,577,230,000
R&D Expense						
Operating Income		122,456,000	116,408,000	136,585,000	94,498,000	156,087,000
Operating Margin %		7.30%	7.48%	8.64%	5.94%	9.89%
SGA Expense		875,906,000	749,107,000	763,221,000	770,580,000	715,753,000
Net Income		4,296,000	29,068,000	63,246,000	33,307,000	65,105,000
Operating Cash Flow		86,712,000	94,247,000	175,326,000	80,491,000	34,855,000
Capital Expenditure		84,753,000	30,095,000	26,965,000	35,350,000	16,942,000
EBITDA		202,775,000	136,074,000	204,740,000	165,681,000	239,864,000
Return on Assets %		.20%	1.26%	2.53%	1.29%	2.42%
Return on Equity %		.49%	3.47%	8.14%	4.24%	8.82%
Debt to Equity		0.27	0.29	0.29	0.58	0.81

CONTACT INFORMATION:

Phone: 212 556-1234   Fax:
Toll-Free:
Address: 620 Eighth Ave., New York, NY 10018 United States

STOCK TICKER/OTHER:

Stock Ticker: NYT
Employees: 3,710
Parent Company:

Exchange: NYS
Fiscal Year Ends: 12/31

SALARIES/BONUSES:

Top Exec. Salary: $1,107,904   Bonus: $
Second Exec. Salary: $1,019,231   Bonus: $

OTHER THOUGHTS:

Estimated Female Officers or Directors: 6
Hot Spot for Advancement for Women/Minorities: Y

Newegg Inc

NAIC Code: 454111

www.newegg.com

TYPES OF BUSINESS:

Online Retail-Computers & Electronics

BRANDS/DIVISIONS/AFFILIATES:

Newegg.com
community.newegg.com
NeweggBusiness.com
Rosewill Inc
Nutrend.com
GameCrate
Newegg Logistics

CONTACTS: *Note: Officers with more than one job title may be intentionally listed here more than once.*

Fred Chang, CEO
George Jiao, COO
Bob Bellack, CFO
Lee Cheng, General Counsel
Kunal Thakkar, VP-Oper.
Lee Cheng, Sr. VP-Corp. Dev.
Richard Quiroga, VP-Finance
Fred Chang, Chmn.
Fred Chang, Pres., China Oper.

GROWTH PLANS/SPECIAL FEATURES:

Newegg, Inc. is an online-only retailer of computers, computer hardware and accessories as well as other electronics. The firm's registered customer base of more than 35 million includes do-it-yourselfers, gamers, students, small-to-medium-sized businesses, IT professionals and resellers. Newegg stocks millions of items, including desktop computers, laptops, PDAs (personal digital assistants), cell phones, digital cameras, networking devices, gaming systems and accessories, software, home appliances and DVDs. In addition to the company's e-commerce site, Newegg.com, the company hosts community.newegg.com, a community of professionals and other knowledgeable persons offering advice and opinions, and NeweggBusiness.com, a business-to-business (B2B) website. Subsidiary Rosewill, Inc. offers private-label computer hardware and peripheral products on its Rosewill.com website. Nutrend.com offers automotive products. GameCrate.com provides game reviews, news and trailers. Newegg Logistics offers logistics solutions to help business-to-consumer and business-to-business eCommerce sellers and other organizations streamline order fulfillment, shipment and returns. The firm manages also newegg.com, newegg.ca and newegg.com.cn. Newegg, Inc. is a leading tech-focused eRetailer in North America, with a global reach into more than 50 countries in Europe, Asia Pacific, Latin America and the Middle East.

The company offers its employees benefits including disability, medical, dental and vision insurance; a 401(k) savings plan; an educational assistance program; paid time off and holidays; discounts to 24 Hour Fitness and Mattel Toy Stores; and tuition reimbursement.

FINANCIAL DATA: *Note: Data for latest year may not have been available at press time.*

In U.S. $	2018	2017	2016	2015	2014	2013
Revenue		2,810,000,000	2,650,000,000	2,610,000,000	2,600,000,000	2,800,000,000
R&D Expense						
Operating Income						
Operating Margin %						
SGA Expense						
Net Income						
Operating Cash Flow						
Capital Expenditure						
EBITDA						
Return on Assets %						
Return on Equity %						
Debt to Equity						

CONTACT INFORMATION:

Phone: 626-271-9700   Fax: 626-271-9403
Toll-Free: 800-390-1119
Address: 17560 Rowland St., City of Industry, CA 91748 United States

STOCK TICKER/OTHER:

Stock Ticker: Private
Employees: 2,600
Parent Company:

Exchange:
Fiscal Year Ends:

SALARIES/BONUSES:

Top Exec. Salary: $ Bonus: $
Second Exec. Salary: $ Bonus: $

OTHER THOUGHTS:

Estimated Female Officers or Directors:
Hot Spot for Advancement for Women/Minorities:

News Corporation

www.newscorp.com

NAIC Code: 511110

TYPES OF BUSINESS:

Newspaper Publishing
Magazine & Book Publishing
Advertising Services
Online Media
Sports Broadcasting
Business Information
Financial Information

BRANDS/DIVISIONS/AFFILIATES:

Wall Street Journal
News Corp Australia
News UK
New York Post (The)
New Foxtel
REA Group Limited
Move Inc
News IQ

CONTACTS: Note: Officers with more than one job title may be intentionally listed here more than once.

Robert Thomson, CEO
Susan Panuccio, CFO
Keith Murdoch, Chairman of the Board
Kevin Halpin, Chief Accounting Officer
Lachlan Murdoch, Co-Chairman
David Pitofsky, Executive VP

GROWTH PLANS/SPECIAL FEATURES:

News Corporation, doing business as News Corp, is a global media and entertainment company. The firm operates in five segments: news and information services, subscription video services, digital real estate services, book publishing and other. The news and information services segments consists of Dow Jones (which publishes The Wall Street Journal newspaper), News Corp Australia, News UK, The New York Post and News America Marketing. The subscription video services segment provides video sports, entertainment and news services to pay-TV subscribers and other commercial licensees. This happens primarily through cable, satellite and IP distribution. This segment includes New Foxtel, a video subscription service in Australia with over 200 channels, and Australian News Channel. The digital real estate services segment consists of the company's 61.6% interest in REA Group Limited, a digital advertising business specializing in real estate services. Operations in this segment include those of Move, Inc., which News Corp has an 80% interest in, providing online real estate services in the U.S. through realtor.com. The book publishing segment consists of HarperCollins Publishers, which publishes and distributes consumer books globally through print, digital and audio formats. The other segment includes general corporate overhead expenses; Strategy Group, which identifies new products and services to increase profitability; News IQ, New Corp's advertising platform; and costs related to U.K. Newspaper Matters. The company owns a 65% stake in New Foxtel, an Australian pay-TV provider. In March 2018, News Corp and Telstra, the other 35% stake holder in New Foxtel, signed an agreement to combine Foxtel and FOX SPORTS Australia. News Corp acquired Opcity, a real estate technology platform, in October 2018.

FINANCIAL DATA: Note: Data for latest year may not have been available at press time.

In U.S. $	2018	2017	2016	2015	2014	2013
Revenue	9,024,000,000	8,139,000,000	8,292,000,000	8,633,000,000	8,574,000,000	8,891,000,000
R&D Expense						
Operating Income	600,000,000	436,000,000	337,000,000	322,000,000	-529,000,000	140,000,000
Operating Margin %		5.35%	4.06%	3.72%	2.23%	1.57%
SGA Expense	3,049,000,000	2,725,000,000	2,722,000,000	2,756,000,000	2,665,000,000	2,783,000,000
Net Income	-1,514,000,000	-738,000,000	179,000,000	-147,000,000	239,000,000	506,000,000
Operating Cash Flow	757,000,000	494,000,000	952,000,000	831,000,000	854,000,000	501,000,000
Capital Expenditure	364,000,000	256,000,000	256,000,000	378,000,000	379,000,000	332,000,000
EBITDA	1,072,000,000	885,000,000	842,000,000	852,000,000	49,000,000	688,000,000
Return on Assets %		-4.92%	1.15%	-.94%	1.48%	3.52%
Return on Equity %		-6.62%	1.50%	-1.18%	1.85%	4.71%
Debt to Equity		0.02	0.03			

CONTACT INFORMATION:

Phone: 212 852-7000 Fax:
Toll-Free:
Address: 1211 Avenue of the Americas, New York, NY 10036 United States

STOCK TICKER/OTHER:

Stock Ticker: NWS Exchange: NAS
Employees: 26,000 Fiscal Year Ends: 06/30
Parent Company:

SALARIES/BONUSES:

Top Exec. Salary: $2,000,000 Bonus: $
Second Exec. Salary: $1,100,000 Bonus: $

OTHER THOUGHTS:

Estimated Female Officers or Directors: 6
Hot Spot for Advancement for Women/Minorities: Y

NewVoiceMedia

www.newvoicemedia.com

NAIC Code: 511210K

TYPES OF BUSINESS:

Computer Software, Sales & Customer Relationship Management Software

BRANDS/DIVISIONS/AFFILIATES:

Vonage Holdings Corporation

CONTACTS: *Note: Officers with more than one job title may be intentionally listed here more than once.*

Dennis Fois, CEO
Guy Sochovosky, CFO
Olivier Gachot, Chief Sales Officer
Artur Michalczyk, CTO

GROWTH PLANS/SPECIAL FEATURES:

NewVoiceMedia (NVM) provides a cloud-based solution for organizations to connect with their customers on a global basis. NVM's cloud communications contact center platform comprises 99.999% platform availability. The firm's customers benefit from enterprise-class communications and contact center functionality, with features and services such as communications managed via telephone and connected device, and ongoing support, upgrades and maintenance on a global scale. NVM offers easy add/removal of users, as well as quick-start options for small businesses. Company products cover sales, gamification, dialer, services, workforce management, PCI DSS (payment card industry data security standard) compliance and omni-channel strategies. Other solutions include mobile and home working, cloud contact centers, cloud adoption, disaster recovery, in-bound call center and global solutions. The company's products integrate with other formats such as Salesforce. NVM is headquartered in the U.K., with additional offices in the U.S., Australia, Poland and Germany. During 2018, NewVoiceMedia was acquired by Vonage Holdings Corporation.

FINANCIAL DATA: *Note: Data for latest year may not have been available at press time.*

In U.S. $	2018	2017	2016	2015	2014	2013
Revenue	61,133,100	40,377,500	33,395,600	21,422,300	15,702,700	9,268,750
R&D Expense						
Operating Income						
Operating Margin %						
SGA Expense						
Net Income	-21,518,000	-26,106,100	-27,366,800	-30,059,400	-18,326,400	-7,751,480
Operating Cash Flow						
Capital Expenditure						
EBITDA						
Return on Assets %						
Return on Equity %						
Debt to Equity						

CONTACT INFORMATION:

Phone: 44-207-785-8888   Fax:
Toll-Free:
Address: Jays Close, Basingstoke, Hampshire RG22 4BS United Kingdom

STOCK TICKER/OTHER:

Stock Ticker: Subsidiary   Exchange:
Employees: 388   Fiscal Year Ends: 01/31
Parent Company: Vonage Holdings Corporation

SALARIES/BONUSES:

Top Exec. Salary: $ Bonus: $
Second Exec. Salary: $ Bonus: $

OTHER THOUGHTS:

Estimated Female Officers or Directors:
Hot Spot for Advancement for Women/Minorities:

NIC Inc

NAIC Code: 519130

www.egov.com

TYPES OF BUSINESS:

E-Government Services
Internet Portal Services
Electronic Filing Software
Application Development
Online Campaign Expenditure Development

BRANDS/DIVISIONS/AFFILIATES:

CONTACTS: Note: Officers with more than one job title may be intentionally listed here more than once.

Harry Herington, CEO
Stephen Kovzan, CFO
Robert Knapp, COO
William Van Asselt, General Counsel
Jayne Holland, Other Executive Officer

GROWTH PLANS/SPECIAL FEATURES:

NIC, Inc. provides eGovernment software and services that help governments use technology to reduce internal costs, increase efficiencies and provide a higher level of service to businesses and citizens. It operates in two divisions: outsourced portal and software and services. The outsourced portal segment enters into long-term contracts with governments to design, build and operate web-based portals on their behalf. These portals consist of websites and applications that allow businesses and citizens to access government information online and complete transactions, including applying for permits, retrieving driver's license records or filing a government-mandated form or report. The self-funding business model allows the firm to generate revenues by sharing in the fees its collects from eGovernment transactions. NIC typically enters into multi-year contracts with government partners and manages operations for each contractual relationship through separate local subsidiaries. The software and services segment primarily includes NIC subsidiaries that provide software development and services, other than outsourced portal services, to state and local governments, as well as federal agencies.

The firm offers employees medical, dental, life, AD&D, prescription and disability coverage; an employee stock purchase program; and educational reimbursement.

FINANCIAL DATA: Note: Data for latest year may not have been available at press time.

In U.S. $	2018	2017	2016	2015	2014	2013
Revenue		336,508,000	317,914,700	292,376,300	272,096,600	249,278,700
R&D Expense						
Operating Income		78,337,000	77,857,990	67,294,580	63,014,070	52,610,050
Operating Margin %		23.27%	24.49%	23.01%	23.15%	21.10%
SGA Expense		50,780,000	47,062,870	43,098,320	38,936,540	40,924,640
Net Income		51,614,000	55,833,500	41,978,520	39,058,220	32,038,090
Operating Cash Flow		64,836,000	78,432,500	50,758,240	51,282,330	40,853,340
Capital Expenditure		4,771,000	5,646,404	4,453,495	5,380,800	6,717,034
EBITDA		85,266,000	84,607,120	75,679,990	72,191,090	60,943,140
Return on Assets %		19.05%	22.95%	20.07%	21.91%	19.50%
Return on Equity %		33.84%	44.32%	37.82%	39.46%	37.12%
Debt to Equity						

CONTACT INFORMATION:

Phone: 877 234-3468   Fax: 913 498-3472
Toll-Free: 877-234-3468
Address: 25501 W. Valley Parkway, Ste. 300, Olathe, KS 66061 United States

STOCK TICKER/OTHER:

Stock Ticker: EGOV   Exchange: NAS
Employees: 929   Fiscal Year Ends: 12/31
Parent Company:

SALARIES/BONUSES:

Top Exec. Salary: $500,000   Bonus: $
Second Exec. Salary: $325,000   Bonus: $

OTHER THOUGHTS:

Estimated Female Officers or Directors: 3
Hot Spot for Advancement for Women/Minorities: Y

NTT DOCOMO Inc

www.nttdocomo.com

NAIC Code: 517210

TYPES OF BUSINESS:

Mobile Telephone Service
Mobile Internet Services
Paging Service
GPS Tracking
Venture Capital

BRANDS/DIVISIONS/AFFILIATES:

docomo Wi-Fi
Nippon Telegraph and Telephone Corp (NTT)
NTT Group

CONTACTS: *Note: Officers with more than one job title may be intentionally listed here more than once.*

Kazuhiro Yoshizawa, CEO
Hiroshi Nakamura, CTO
Kaoru Kato, Pres.
Osamu Hirokado, CFO
Hiroyasu Asami, CIO
Seizo Onoe, CTO
Fumio Iwasaki, Sr. Exec. VP
Tsutomu Shindou, Exec. VP
Takashi Tanaka, Exec. VP
Kazuhiro Yoshizawa, Exec. VP

GROWTH PLANS/SPECIAL FEATURES:

NTT DOCOMO, Inc. is one of Japan's leading wireless communications service providers. The company has more than 76 million subscribers. It provides mobile telephone services over LTE and W-CDMA networks. The company operates both globally and domestically, and reports in two operating segments: mobile phone and all other operations. NTT DOCOMO offers standard cellular service through its Xi LTE and FOMA W-CDMA networks. In addition to standard services, the firm offers value-added services through its i-mode service. It also has a sp-mode ISP service for smart phones, which allows users to connect to the internet, access portals and DOCOMO markets, e-mail from a DOCOMO address, use content payment services and access public wireless LANs. Data communication services extend beyond smartphones and are also offered for PCs, tablets and other devices. The company sells USB-type, Express card-type and Wi-Fi routers, and its UIM card comes equipped in Sony's PlayStation Vita portable gaming console. The firm also has driver navigation, digital photo delivery and communication module services for corporate customers. Also for corporate customers, NTT offers vehicle management systems, a wireless credit card settlement system and telemetering systems. Public wireless LAN services operate under the brand docomo Wi-Fi. In cases of emergencies, in mountainous areas and aboard ships, the firm also provides satellite mobile communications services covering all of Japan and its surrounding waters. DOCOMO is a leading developer of a 5G network that it plans to deploy by 2020, as well as network function virtualization (NFV), NFC infrastructure and emerging Internet of Things (IoT). The parent company of the firm is Nippon Telegraph and Telephone Corp., the holding company of the NTT Group.

FINANCIAL DATA: *Note: Data for latest year may not have been available at press time.*

In U.S. $	2018	2017	2016	2015	2014	2013
Revenue	44,239,840,000	42,525,160,000	41,992,090,000	40,659,290,000	41,381,000,000	41,463,730,000
R&D Expense						
Operating Income	9,139,878,000	8,876,363,000	7,347,200,000	6,207,628,000	7,598,685,000	7,765,472,000
Operating Margin %		20.87%	17.49%	15.26%	18.36%	18.72%
SGA Expense	10,358,610,000	9,717,888,000	9,081,320,000	9,663,494,000	10,003,730,000	10,775,670,000
Net Income	6,906,185,000	6,052,779,000	5,086,617,000	3,803,920,000	4,310,710,000	4,597,367,000
Operating Cash Flow	14,020,670,000	12,173,660,000	11,215,600,000	8,932,334,000	9,281,704,000	8,648,755,000
Capital Expenditure	5,781,092,000	5,968,490,000	5,694,651,000	6,153,458,000	6,605,966,000	7,225,039,000
EBITDA	14,676,000,000	13,006,280,000	13,027,480,000	12,099,910,000	14,404,810,000	14,318,510,000
Return on Assets %		8.89%	7.63%	5.59%	6.30%	6.99%
Return on Equity %		12.04%	10.26%	7.44%	8.39%	9.44%
Debt to Equity		0.02	0.04	0.04	0.03	0.03

CONTACT INFORMATION:

Phone: 81 351561111   Fax: 81 351560271
Toll-Free:
Address: 2-11-1, Nagata-cho, Chiyoda-ku, Tokyo, 100-6150 Japan

STOCK TICKER/OTHER:

Stock Ticker: DCMYY   Exchange: PINX
Employees: 26,734   Fiscal Year Ends: 03/31
Parent Company: Nippon Telegraph and Telephone Corp (NTT)

SALARIES/BONUSES:

Top Exec. Salary: $ Bonus: $
Second Exec. Salary: $ Bonus: $

OTHER THOUGHTS:

Estimated Female Officers or Directors:
Hot Spot for Advancement for Women/Minorities:

Nutanix Inc

NAIC Code: 511210B

www.nutanix.com

TYPES OF BUSINESS:

Cloud-Based Data Storage

BRANDS/DIVISIONS/AFFILIATES:

Nutanix Acropolis
Nutanix Prism
Xi
Nutanix Calm
Nutanis Karbon
Minjar Inc
Netsil Inc

CONTACTS: Note: Officers with more than one job title may be intentionally listed here more than once.

Dheeraj Pandey, CEO
Duston Williams, CFO
Aaron Boynton, Controller
David Sangster, Executive VP, Divisional
Louis Attanasio, Other Executive Officer
Sunil Potti, Other Executive Officer
Tyler Wall, Other Executive Officer

GROWTH PLANS/SPECIAL FEATURES:

Nutanix, Inc. is software as a service (SaaS) company offering a virtualized data-center platform designed to replace older storage area network (SAN) and network attached storage (NAS) platforms. The Nutanix Enterprise Cloud OS software delivers invisible infrastructure for next-generation enterprise computing by natively converging infrastructure components into a turnkey hyperconverged solution. The firm's virtual computing platform is a scalable datacenter that can be executed in under 30 minutes. The platform's scalability comes from its modular design, which allows the program to accommodate growing data needs. Hardware platforms are branded under the NX-1000, 3000, 5000, 6000 or 8000 series. Additional product families include the Nutanix Acropolis, the Nutanix Prism and Xi. Acropolis converges compute, storage and virtualization resources in order to run any application at any scale. Prism is comprehensive management solution built with one-click technologies to radically simplify datacenter storage and virtualization operations. Xi cloud and platform services operate hybrid and multi-cloud environments, and include: Xi Beam, for optimizing the cloud spend and ensuring security compliance; Xi Epoch, for monitoring the health of multi-cloud applications and quickly troubleshooting issues; Xi Frame, for running secure, software-defined virtual desktop workspaces in any cloud environment; Xi IoT, for building and operation Internet of Things and Edge applications and infrastructure; and Xi Leap, for natively integrating cloud-based disaster recovery. In addition, Nutanix Calm adds native application orchestration and lifecycle management to the Nutanix Enterprise Cloud platform; and Nutanix Karbon makes it simple to deploy highly-available Kubernetes cluster and operate web-scale workloads. During 2018, Nutanix acquired: Minjar, Inc., a cloud technology solutions company; and Netsil, Inc., an observability and monitoring company for modern cloud applications and Kubernetes-native applications.

FINANCIAL DATA: Note: Data for latest year may not have been available at press time.

In U.S. $	2018	2017	2016	2015	2014	2013
Revenue	1,155,457,000	766,869,000	444,928,000	241,432,000	127,127,000	30,533,000
R&D Expense	313,777,000	288,619,000	116,400,000	73,510,000	38,037,000	16,496,000
Operating Income	-280,408,000	-426,951,000	-165,017,000	-118,765,000	-78,319,000	-44,600,000
Operating Margin %		-55.67%	-37.08%	-49.19%	-61.60%	-146.07%
SGA Expense	736,058,000	577,870,000	322,758,000	185,728,000	106,497,000	32,033,000
Net Income	-297,161,000	-458,011,000	-168,499,000	-126,127,000	-84,003,000	-44,734,000
Operating Cash Flow	92,555,000	13,822,000	3,636,000	-25,694,000	-45,707,000	-29,110,000
Capital Expenditure	62,372,000	50,181,000	42,294,000	23,308,000	19,032,000	9,339,000
EBITDA	-230,106,000	-388,552,000	-138,609,000	-102,198,000	-66,737,000	-41,974,000
Return on Assets %		-81.41%	-52.54%	-68.39%	-70.61%	
Return on Equity %						
Debt to Equity						

CONTACT INFORMATION:

Phone: 855-688-2649   Fax: 408-916-4039
Toll-Free:
Address: 1740 Technology Dr., Ste. 150, San Jose, CA 95110 United States

STOCK TICKER/OTHER:

Stock Ticker: NTNX   Exchange: NAS
Employees: 2,813   Fiscal Year Ends:
Parent Company:

SALARIES/BONUSES:

Top Exec. Salary: $578,314   Bonus: $
Second Exec. Salary: $350,000   Bonus: $

OTHER THOUGHTS:

Estimated Female Officers or Directors:
Hot Spot for Advancement for Women/Minorities:

Sales, profits and employees may be estimates. Financial information, benefits and other data can change quickly and may vary from those stated here.

Ocado Group plc

NAIC Code: 454111

TYPES OF BUSINESS:

Online Grocery Shopping

BRANDS/DIVISIONS/AFFILIATES:

Ocadolife
Ocado.com
Fetch

CONTACTS: *Note: Officers with more than one job title may be intentionally listed here more than once.*

Tim Steiner, CEO
Mark Richardson, COO
Duncan Tatton-Brown, CFO
Neill Abrams, Dir.-Legal & Bus. Affairs
Mark Richardson, Dir.-Oper.
Jason Gissing, Dir.-Commercial
Lord Rose, Chmn.

GROWTH PLANS/SPECIAL FEATURES:

Ocado Group plc operates a U.K.-based online shopping and fulfillment business, with more than 580,000 active shopping customers. Goods are selected via the company's website or mobile applications and can be delivered directly to the customer's homes. Ocado's inventory includes grocery; home and garden; pet products; baby and child products; beauty products; news products; and toys, games and sports products. Fresh products, such as meats, fruits and vegetables, are provided in part by Waitrose, another U.K.-based grocer. Shoppers can narrow down the lists by selecting only vegetarian, fair trade, kosher, fat-free, gluten-free, egg-free, milk-free, nut-free, organic, yeast-free and wheat-free products. The store also sells various wines, including whites, reds, fine wines, dessert wines, sparkling wines, rose, fortified, dry, medium-dry, low alcohol, pink champagne, fruit wines and wine in a box. Furthermore, the company's website features its Ocadolife section, which contains recipes and seasonal food suggestions. Delivery costs can either be paid by order or through flat monthly or annual fees. Ocado.com contains over 48,000 products including everyday items, its own brand, non-food and additional specialist items. Fetch is the company's specialist pet destination site that offers products such as pet food and medicinal products not typically found in supermarkets. Operations are based on three massive warehouses of about 350,000-square-feet each. Ocado is heavily focused on warehouse automation and efficient delivery. While the process of packing groceries for final delivery involves a great deal of human labor, it is nonetheless one of the world's leading companies in terms of the application of robotics for grocery retailing. In November 2018, Ocado, in partnership with The Kroger Co., announced that its first U.S. customer fulfillment center would be located in the Cincinnati, Ohio region, subject to state and local incentives. The site will serve customers throughout the country.

FINANCIAL DATA: *Note: Data for latest year may not have been available at press time.*

In U.S. $	2018	2017	2016	2015	2014	2013
Revenue	2,073,592,500	1,974,850,000	1,563,920,000	1,169,490,000	949,000,000	894,620,368
R&D Expense						
Operating Income						
Operating Margin %						
SGA Expense						
Net Income		1,349,120	14,765,500	12,670,000	7,000,000	-14,110,104
Operating Cash Flow						
Capital Expenditure						
EBITDA						
Return on Assets %						
Return on Equity %						
Debt to Equity						

CONTACT INFORMATION:

Phone: 44-1707-227800   Fax: 44-1707-227999
Toll-Free:
Address: Bldgs. 1&2 Trident Place, Hatfield Bus. Park, Mosquito Way, Hatfield, AL10 9UL United Kingdom

STOCK TICKER/OTHER:

Stock Ticker: OCDO
Employees: 12,233
Parent Company:

Exchange: London
Fiscal Year Ends: 11/30

SALARIES/BONUSES:

Top Exec. Salary: $ Bonus: $
Second Exec. Salary: $ Bonus: $

OTHER THOUGHTS:

Estimated Female Officers or Directors: 2
Hot Spot for Advancement for Women/Minorities:

Oclaro Inc

NAIC Code: 334210

www.oclaro.com

TYPES OF BUSINESS:

Fiber Optic Manufacturing
Lasers
System Integration
Modules
Subsystems
Phototonics Solutions
VCSELS

BRANDS/DIVISIONS/AFFILIATES:

CONTACTS: Note: Officers with more than one job title may be intentionally listed here more than once.

Gregory Dougherty, CEO
Pete Mangan, CFO
Mike Fernicola, Chief Accounting Officer
Craig Cocchi, COO
Marissa Peterson, Director
Lisa Paul, Executive VP, Divisional
David Teichmann, Executive VP
Yves LeMaitre, Other Executive Officer
Adam Carter, Other Executive Officer
Walter Jankovic, President, Divisional
Beck Mason, President, Divisional

GROWTH PLANS/SPECIAL FEATURES:

Oclaro, Inc. supplies core optical network technology to leading telecommunications and data communications equipment companies, as well as to datacenter and network operators worldwide. Communications equipment manufacturers integrate Oclaro's optical technology into the switching, routing and transport systems they offer to the global service and content providers that are building, upgrading and operating high-performance optical networks. The firm's products include: client-side transceivers, which support various link distances based on optical connectors and media types; line-side transceivers, which provide pluggable 100 gigabits per second (Gb/s) and 200 Gb/s solutions for metro and long-haul networks; tunable laser transmitters, which optimize performance and reduce the size of the product; lithium-niobate modulators, which are optical devices that manipulate the phase or the amplitude of an optical signal, and transfer information on an optical carrier by modulating the light; transponder modules, which provide both transmitter and receiver functions; and discrete lasers and receivers, which are used for metro and long-haul applications. Oclaro customers include ADVA Optical Networking; Amazon.com, Inc.; Ciena Corporation; Cisco Systems, Inc.; Coriant GmbH; Google, Inc.; Huawei Technologies Co., Ltd.; Juniper Networks, Inc.; Nocia/Alcatel-Lucent; and ZTE Corporation. In March 2018, Oclaro agreed to be acquired by Lumentum Holdings, Inc. for $1.8 billion. Lumentum is a provider of photonics products for optical networking and lasers for industrial and consumer markets.

FINANCIAL DATA: Note: Data for latest year may not have been available at press time.

In U.S. $	2018	2017	2016	2015	2014	2013
Revenue	543,169,984	600,968,000	407,913,984	341,276,000	390,871,008	586,028,032
R&D Expense						
Operating Income						
Operating Margin %						
SGA Expense						
Net Income	62,453,000	127,859,000	8,580,000	-56,692,000	17,819,000	-122,745,000
Operating Cash Flow						
Capital Expenditure						
EBITDA						
Return on Assets %						
Return on Equity %						
Debt to Equity						

CONTACT INFORMATION:

Phone: 408 383-1400   Fax: 408 919-6083
Toll-Free:
Address: 225 Charcot Ave., San Jose, CA 95131 United States

STOCK TICKER/OTHER:

Stock Ticker: OCLR   Exchange: NAS
Employees: 1,876   Fiscal Year Ends: 07/30
Parent Company:

SALARIES/BONUSES:

Top Exec. Salary: $ Bonus: $
Second Exec. Salary: $ Bonus: $

OTHER THOUGHTS:

Estimated Female Officers or Directors: 3
Hot Spot for Advancement for Women/Minorities: Y

OfferUp Inc

offerup.com

NAIC Code: 519130

TYPES OF BUSINESS:

Online Classified Ads Platform

BRANDS/DIVISIONS/AFFILIATES:

GROWTH PLANS/SPECIAL FEATURES:

OfferUp, Inc. operates an online and mobile eCommerce platform that allows individuals to sell items. Users can take a photo with their smartphone, upload it to the website/app and promote items for sale. In 2018, OfferUp had more than 42 million unique visitors based in the U.S. alone, with global ambitions on the horizon. Once the app is downloaded, people interested in purchasing items can browse the listings in order to find deals nearby. If interested, the potential buyer sends a chat message securely through the app without giving away personal information. Notifications are sent in real-time through the app when a buyer or seller sends a message. User profiles are also provided, describing buyers and sellers, along with ratings that are applied once transactions are complete. OfferUp is free to download. Identification verification is validated through the app as well.

CONTACTS: Note: Officers with more than one job title may be intentionally listed here more than once.

Nick Huzar, CEO
Bill Carr, COO
Rodrigo Brumana, CFO
Arean van Veelen, CTO

FINANCIAL DATA: Note: Data for latest year may not have been available at press time.

In U.S. $	2018	2017	2016	2015	2014	2013
Revenue						
R&D Expense						
Operating Income						
Operating Margin %						
SGA Expense						
Net Income						
Operating Cash Flow						
Capital Expenditure						
EBITDA						
Return on Assets %						
Return on Equity %						
Debt to Equity						

CONTACT INFORMATION:

Phone: 206-466-7710   Fax:
Toll-Free:
Address: 1425 Broadway, Ste. 422, Seattle, WA 98122 United States

STOCK TICKER/OTHER:

Stock Ticker: Private   Exchange:
Employees: 240   Fiscal Year Ends:
Parent Company:

SALARIES/BONUSES:

Top Exec. Salary: $ Bonus: $
Second Exec. Salary: $ Bonus: $

OTHER THOUGHTS:

Estimated Female Officers or Directors:
Hot Spot for Advancement for Women/Minorities:

OneSpan Inc

www.vasco.com

NAIC Code: 511210E

TYPES OF BUSINESS:

Computer Software, Security & Anti-Virus
Authentication Devices
Banking Transaction Support Products
Credit Card Verification Products
Remote Verification Products
Anti-Fraud Services

BRANDS/DIVISIONS/AFFILIATES:

DigiPass
Vacman
IndentiKey
OneSpan Sign
VASCO Data Security International Inc
Dealflo

CONTACTS: Note: Officers with more than one job title may be intentionally listed here more than once.

Mark Hoyt, CFO
T. Hunt, Chairman of the Board
Scott Clements, President

GROWTH PLANS/SPECIAL FEATURES:

OneSpan, Inc. (formerly VASCO Data Security International, Inc.) is a global provider of digital identity security, transaction security, customer onboarding and business productivity solutions. More than 10,000 customers, including over half of the top 100 global banks, rely on OneSpan solutions to protect their business processes. From digital onboarding to fraud mitigation to workflow management, OneSpan's unified, open platform reduces costs, accelerates customer acquisition and increases customer satisfaction. The company's solutions include eSignatures, compliance, mobile app security and omnichannel security. Its products include: DigiPass Authenticators, for mobile, apps, transaction data signing, card reading and public key infrastructure (PKI); DigiPass App Security, which includes behavioral authentication and runtime application self-protection (RASP) security; fraud management platforms, including the Vacman controller, the IdentiKey authentication server and the IdentiKey risk manager; and document eSignatures, which is provided under the OneSpan Sign brand name. OneSpan products can be purchased through OneSpan sales offices, as well as through a network of company partners. The firm's distributors and re-sellers can be found in over 60 countries worldwide. In May 2018, VASCO acquired Dealflo, and subsequently rebranded its corporate name to OneSpan, with a focus on its identity platform. OneSpan will trade on the Nasdaq under ticker symbol OSPN.

FINANCIAL DATA: Note: Data for latest year may not have been available at press time.

In U.S. $	2018	2017	2016	2015	2014	2013
Revenue		193,291,008	192,304,000	241,443,008	201,536,992	155,047,008
R&D Expense						
Operating Income						
Operating Margin %						
SGA Expense						
Net Income		-22,399,000	10,514,000	42,151,000	33,484,000	11,147,000
Operating Cash Flow						
Capital Expenditure						
EBITDA						
Return on Assets %						
Return on Equity %						
Debt to Equity						

CONTACT INFORMATION:

Phone: 312-766-4001   Fax:
Toll-Free:
Address: 121 West Wacker Dr., Ste. 2050, Chicago, IL 60601 United States

STOCK TICKER/OTHER:

Stock Ticker: VDSI   Exchange: NAS
Employees: 613   Fiscal Year Ends: 12/31
Parent Company:

SALARIES/BONUSES:

Top Exec. Salary: $ Bonus: $
Second Exec. Salary: $ Bonus: $

OTHER THOUGHTS:

Estimated Female Officers or Directors:
Hot Spot for Advancement for Women/Minorities:

OneWeb Ltd

www.oneweb.world

NAIC Code: 517410

TYPES OF BUSINESS:

Satellite Internet Access Services
Satellite Telephony and Communications

BRANDS/DIVISIONS/AFFILIATES:

OneWeb Satellites LLC

CONTACTS: *Note: Officers with more than one job title may be intentionally listed here more than once.*

Eric Beranger, CEO
David Tolley, CFO
Viviek Jhamb, Chief Commercial Officer
Heidi Dillard, Head-Human Resources & Facilities
Vikas Grover, CIO
Greg Wyler, Chmn.

GROWTH PLANS/SPECIAL FEATURES:

OneWeb Ltd. intends to be a major global provider of fast, inexpensive internet access and related telephone services. It has designed an advanced, low-Earth-orbit satellite constellation to provide global coverage, particularly to parts of the earth that currently lack reliable or affordable internet access. Its constellation will eventually consist of as many as 900 satellites. OneWeb's satellites are designed to orbit relatively close to the earth, allowing for better internet access speeds, while they interlock with each other electronically to create coverage over the entire planet. Small, low-cost user terminals will communicate with the satellite network and provide wireless internet access. These terminals will provide connectivity with no change in latency (speed) during satellite handovers in order to ensure continuous quality of voice, gaming and web surfing experience. Compared to traditional satellites, OneWeb units have fewer components, and are lighter in weight, easier to manufacture and cheaper to launch. The satellites contain on-board propulsion and state-of-the-art positioning GPS sensors that ground-track their placements within meters. The on-board propulsion systems are capable of performing maneuvers to steer clear of space debris. When an OneWeb satellite nears the end of its service life, it will de-orbit automatically. The initial phase of the constellation launch is slated to begin by early 2019. Investors in the firm include Qualcomm, Virgin Group, Airbus Group SE and Coca-Cola. Space launch rocket services have been contracted to Arianespace SA and Virgin Galactic. OneWeb broke ground on its $85 million high-volume satellite manufacturing plant in Exploration Park, Florida during 2017.

FINANCIAL DATA: *Note: Data for latest year may not have been available at press time.*

In U.S. $	2018	2017	2016	2015	2014	2013
Revenue						
R&D Expense						
Operating Income						
Operating Margin %						
SGA Expense						
Net Income						
Operating Cash Flow						
Capital Expenditure						
EBITDA						
Return on Assets %						
Return on Equity %						
Debt to Equity						

CONTACT INFORMATION:

Phone: 301-428-1868   Fax:
Toll-Free:
Address: 1400 Key Blvd, Arlington, VA 22209 United States

STOCK TICKER/OTHER:

Stock Ticker: Private   Exchange:
Employees: 90   Fiscal Year Ends:
Parent Company:

SALARIES/BONUSES:

Top Exec. Salary: $ Bonus: $
Second Exec. Salary: $ Bonus: $

OTHER THOUGHTS:

Estimated Female Officers or Directors:
Hot Spot for Advancement for Women/Minorities:

Sales, profits and employees may be estimates. Financial information, benefits and other data can change quickly and may vary from those stated here.

Onstream Media Corporation
www.onstreammedia.com

NAIC Code: 541810E

TYPES OF BUSINESS:
Online Video Management Services
Webcasting Services
Networking Services
Media Presentations
Systems Integration
Engineering Services

BRANDS/DIVISIONS/AFFILIATES:
MarketPlace365.com
Auction Video

CONTACTS: *Note: Officers with more than one job title may be intentionally listed here more than once.*
Randy Selman, CEO
Alan Saperstein, COO
Robert Tomlinson, CFO
Robert Tomlinson, CFO
David Glassman, CMO
Clifford Friedland, Sr. VP-Bus. Dev.
Clifford Friedland, Senior VP, Divisional

GROWTH PLANS/SPECIAL FEATURES:
Onstream Media Corporation is an online services provider of live and on-demand internet video, corporate audio and web communications and content management applications. Onstream's operations are organized into two groups: the digital media services group and the audio and web conferencing services group. The digital media services group consists of the webcasting division, the digital media services platform (DMSP) division, the user generated content (UGC) division, the smart encoding division and the MarketPlace365 service. The webcasting division provides corporate-oriented, web-based media services to the corporate market, including live audio and video webcasting and on-demand audio and video streaming. The DMSP division provides online, subscription-based services that include access to enabling technologies and features for clients to acquire, store, index, secure, manage, distribute and transform digital assets into saleable commodities. The UGC division, which also operates as Auction Video, provides a video ingestion and flash encoder that can be used on a stand-alone basis or in conjunction with the DMSP. The smart encoding division provides both automated and manual encoding and editorial services for processing, searching, retrieving and streaming digital media, which can include photos, videos, audio, engineering specs, architectural plans, web pages and other pieces of business collateral. MarketPlace365.com features online virtual tradeshows and communities in order to increase traffic for marketplace exhibitors. Onstream's audio and web conferencing services group, which generates more than half of its revenue, includes the infinite conferencing and onstream conferencing divisions, which provides reservationless and operator-assisted audio and web conferencing services; and the EDNet division, which provides connectivity within the entertainment and advertising industries. Headquartered in Florida, the firm has additional offices in New York, San Francisco and New Jersey.

FINANCIAL DATA: *Note: Data for latest year may not have been available at press time.*

In U.S. $	2018	2017	2016	2015	2014	2013
Revenue				16,143,310	16,933,190	17,218,000
R&D Expense						
Operating Income				-214,375	-180,228	-2,418,060
Operating Margin %				-1.32%	-1.06%	-14.04%
SGA Expense				11,216,500	11,435,170	13,332,510
Net Income				-8,597,009	-1,658,155	-7,169,502
Operating Cash Flow				343,322	457,492	504,271
Capital Expenditure				320,095	556,266	822,424
EBITDA				-6,027,243	1,388,251	-4,484,045
Return on Assets %				-85.32%	-12.08%	-47.01%
Return on Equity %				-5900.89%	-33.83%	-95.23%
Debt to Equity					0.61	0.23

CONTACT INFORMATION:
Phone: 954 917-6655   Fax: 954 917-6660
Toll-Free: 866-857-1960
Address: 1291 S.W. 29th Ave., Pompano Beach, FL 33069 United States

STOCK TICKER/OTHER:
Stock Ticker: ONSM
Employees: 82
Parent Company:

Exchange: PINX
Fiscal Year Ends: 09/30

SALARIES/BONUSES:
Top Exec. Salary: $271,751   Bonus: $
Second Exec. Salary: $247,047   Bonus: $

OTHER THOUGHTS:
Estimated Female Officers or Directors:
Hot Spot for Advancement for Women/Minorities:

Sales, profits and employees may be estimates. Financial information, benefits and other data can change quickly and may vary from those stated here.

Onvia Inc
NAIC Code: 541613

TYPES OF BUSINESS:
Government Contract Data by Online Subscription
Professional Services Marketing Support
Government Contract Marketing Support

BRANDS/DIVISIONS/AFFILIATES:
Deltek
GovWin

CONTACTS: *Note: Officers with more than one job title may be intentionally listed here more than once.*
Russ Mann, CEO
David Van Skilling, Chairman of the Board
Russell Mann, Director
Irvine Alpert, Executive VP
Christian Woerner, Senior VP, Divisional
Alberto Sutton, Senior VP, Divisional

GROWTH PLANS/SPECIAL FEATURES:
Onvia, Inc. is a Deltek company that operates as GovWin + Onvia. The firm provides enterprise, mid-market and small business customers with a comprehensive set of federal, state and local government contracting leads. The firm specializes in business-to-government (B2G) sales intelligence and acceleration. Clients grow their sales pipelines with access to bids, request for proposals and future spending data, along with agency contacts, competitor information and market analysis. These offerings are backed by GovWin + Onvia's smart search technology, customer relationship management (CRM) integration and support services. Industries served by the company include technology, telecommunications, professional business services, financial services, insurance, healthcare, architecture, engineering, construction, water, energy, operations, maintenance, transportation, education, environmental services and public safety. GovWin + Onvia offers market research services, including quarterly reports, special reports, surveys and indexes. After Onvia, Inc. was acquired by Deltek in late-2017, the parent firm merged its GovWin business with Onvia in 2018, creating a single platform called GovWin + Onvia.

FINANCIAL DATA: *Note: Data for latest year may not have been available at press time.*

In U.S. $	2018	2017	2016	2015	2014	2013
Revenue		25,000,000	24,567,000	23,588,266	22,624,728	22,019,772
R&D Expense						
Operating Income						
Operating Margin %						
SGA Expense						
Net Income			-813,000	-486,094	-727,279	-2,724,575
Operating Cash Flow						
Capital Expenditure						
EBITDA						
Return on Assets %						
Return on Equity %						
Debt to Equity						

CONTACT INFORMATION:
Phone: 206-282-5170   Fax: 206-373-8961
Toll-Free: 888-484-3374
Address: 509 Olive Way, Ste 400, Seattle, WA 98101 United States

STOCK TICKER/OTHER:
Stock Ticker: Subsidiary
Employees: 142
Parent Company: Deltek

Exchange:
Fiscal Year Ends: 12/31

SALARIES/BONUSES:
Top Exec. Salary: $ Bonus: $
Second Exec. Salary: $ Bonus: $

OTHER THOUGHTS:
Estimated Female Officers or Directors: 2
Hot Spot for Advancement for Women/Minorities:

Open Text Corporation

www.opentext.com

NAIC Code: 511210L

TYPES OF BUSINESS:

Enterprise Content Management
IT Hosting Services
Embedded Modules & Applications
Consulting Services

BRANDS/DIVISIONS/AFFILIATES:

EnCase
Liaison Technologies Inc
Hightail Inc

CONTACTS: Note: Officers with more than one job title may be intentionally listed here more than once.

Mark Barrenechea, CEO
Paul Duggan, Senior VP, Divisional
Madhu Ranganathan, CFO
Aditya Maheshwari, Chief Accounting Officer
David Jamieson, Chief Information Officer
Patricia Nagle, Chief Marketing Officer
P. Jenkins, Director
Muhi Majzoub, Executive VP, Divisional
Gordon Davies, Executive VP, Divisional
James McGourlay, Senior VP, Divisional
Simon Harrison, Senior VP, Divisional
Kasey Holman, Senior VP, Divisional
Prentiss Donohue, Senior VP, Divisional
Leslie Sarauer, Senior VP, Divisional

GROWTH PLANS/SPECIAL FEATURES:

Open Text Corporation is a provider of software products and services that assist organizations in finding, utilizing and sharing business information from any device. The company's technologies and business solutions address the growth of information volume and formats, allowing organizations to manage the information that flows into, out of and throughout the enterprise as part of daily operations. Open Text's products and services are designed to maximize the value of enterprise information while limiting its risks. Its solutions incorporate social and media technologies, and are delivered for on-premises deployment as well as through cloud and managed hosted services models. Customer experience management offerings include communications management, digital asset management, marketing optimization, experience analytics, web content management and workforce optimization. Enterprise content management offerings are facilitated with an integrated set of technologies that manage information throughout its lifecycle, improving business productivity, mitigating risks and controlling costs. Business network offerings include business-to-business integration, supply chain automation, fax solutions, identity and access management and business-to-business managed services. Digital process automation offerings include dynamic case management, cloud service brokerage, low-code development, active client management and media orchestration. Security offerings include the EnCase line of security products. Discovery solutions organize and visualize all relevant content, allowing businesses to make informed decisions. Open Text services include consulting, managed services, learning services, cloud managed services and optimize service programs. During 2018, Open Text acquired: Hightail, Inc., a cloud service for file sharing and creative collaboration; and Liaison Technologies, Inc., a provider of cloud-based information integration and data management solutions.

Open Text offers employees medical, dental and vision coverage; life insurance; educational assistance; and an employee assistance program.

FINANCIAL DATA: Note: Data for latest year may not have been available at press time.

In U.S. $	2018	2017	2016	2015	2014	2013
Revenue	2,815,241,000	2,291,057,000	1,824,228,000	1,851,917,000	1,624,699,000	1,363,336,000
R&D Expense	323,461,000	281,680,000	194,057,000	196,491,000	176,834,000	164,010,000
Operating Income	534,614,000	416,550,000	403,409,000	361,534,000	331,842,000	221,699,000
Operating Margin %		18.18%	22.11%	19.52%	20.42%	16.26%
SGA Expense	734,694,000	615,276,000	484,632,000	532,962,000	488,093,000	398,482,000
Net Income	242,224,000	1,025,659,000	284,477,000	234,327,000	218,125,000	148,520,000
Operating Cash Flow	709,885,000	439,253,000	525,722,000	523,031,000	417,127,000	318,502,000
Capital Expenditure	105,318,000	79,592,000	70,009,000	77,046,000	42,460,000	23,299,000
EBITDA	991,543,000	762,265,000	645,777,000	601,681,000	518,019,000	408,550,000
Return on Assets %		16.23%	5.96%	5.64%	6.63%	5.82%
Return on Equity %		37.22%	14.94%	13.50%	14.64%	11.80%
Debt to Equity		0.67	1.08	0.86	0.76	0.38

CONTACT INFORMATION:

Phone: 519 888-7111   Fax: 519 888-0677
Toll-Free: 800-499-6544
Address: 275 Frank Tompa Dr., Waterloo, ON N2L 0A1 Canada

STOCK TICKER/OTHER:

Stock Ticker: OTEX   Exchange: NAS
Employees: 10,900   Fiscal Year Ends: 06/30
Parent Company:

SALARIES/BONUSES:

Top Exec. Salary: $950,000   Bonus: $
Second Exec. Salary: Bonus: $
$498,175

OTHER THOUGHTS:

Estimated Female Officers or Directors: 4
Hot Spot for Advancement for Women/Minorities: Y

Sales, profits and employees may be estimates. Financial information, benefits and other data can change quickly and may vary from those stated here.

OpenTable Inc

NAIC Code: 519130

www.opentable.com

TYPES OF BUSINESS:

Restaurant Reservations Online

BRANDS/DIVISIONS/AFFILIATES:

Priceline Group Inc (The)
Table Maestro LLC
OpenTable.com
Guestcenter
opentable.com.au
opentable.co.uk
opentable.jp
opentable.com.mx

CONTACTS: *Note: Officers with more than one job title may be intentionally listed here more than once.*

Steve Hafner, CEO-KAYAK
Joseph Essas, CTO
Jocelyn Mangan, Sr. VP-Prod. Mgmt.
John Orta, General Counsel
Joel Brown, Sr. VP-Oper.
Douglas Boake, Sr. VP-Bus. Dev.
Michael Dodson, Sr. VP-Sales
Michael Xenakis, Managing Dir.-OpenTable Europe Ltd.
Elizabeth Casey, VP-Restaurant Prod.
Catherine Porter, VP-Intl. Dev.

GROWTH PLANS/SPECIAL FEATURES:

OpenTable, Inc., owned by Booking Holdings, Inc., offers online reservation and guest management solutions to restaurants and connected restaurant reservations to diners. The firm's solutions include its real-time restaurant reservation website for diners (OpenTable.com), its mobile app and its Electronic Reservation Book (ERB) for restaurant customers, known as Guestcenter. Guestcenter streamlines several business-critical functions and processes for restaurants, such as reservation management, table management, guest recognition, analytics, shift management and e-mail marketing. The OpenTable network includes more than 48,000 restaurant customers in all 50 states as well as internationally, with bookable restaurants in over 20 countries. International teams and offices include the U.K. (opentable.co.uk), Japan (opentable.jp), Mexico (opentable.com.mx) and Australia (opentable.com.au). The company finds restaurants for more than 27 million diners each month, and diners often submit restaurant reviews for information purposes. While OpenTable's service is free to diners, it collects the following fees from restaurants: installation fees for onsite installation and training, a fee for each restaurant guest seated through online reservations and a monthly subscription payment for the use of the company's software and hardware. The firm also operates through Table Maestro, LLC, a telephone reservation services provider. In June 2018, it was announced that OpenTable and KAYAK, a travel booking site under Booking Holdings LLC, would integrate teams for functionality with OpenTable reporting to KAYAK executives.

FINANCIAL DATA: *Note: Data for latest year may not have been available at press time.*

In U.S. $	2018	2017	2016	2015	2014	2013
Revenue	350,000,000	331,000,000	300,000,000	255,000,000	215,000,000	190,050,000
R&D Expense						
Operating Income						
Operating Margin %						
SGA Expense						
Net Income						
Operating Cash Flow						
Capital Expenditure						
EBITDA						
Return on Assets %						
Return on Equity %						
Debt to Equity						

CONTACT INFORMATION:

Phone: 415 344-4200   Fax:
Toll-Free: 800-6736-8225
Address: 1 Montgomery St. Ste 700, San Francisco, CA 94104 United States

STOCK TICKER/OTHER:

Stock Ticker: Subsidiary   Exchange:
Employees: 580   Fiscal Year Ends: 12/31
Parent Company: Booking Holdings Inc

SALARIES/BONUSES:

Top Exec. Salary: $ Bonus: $
Second Exec. Salary: $ Bonus: $

OTHER THOUGHTS:

Estimated Female Officers or Directors: 6
Hot Spot for Advancement for Women/Minorities: Y

Optimizely Inc

www.optimizely.com

NAIC Code: 511210G

TYPES OF BUSINESS:

Online Advertising Optimization Platform
Software

BRANDS/DIVISIONS/AFFILIATES:

Optimizely X

CONTACTS: *Note: Officers with more than one job title may be intentionally listed here more than once.*

Jay Larson, CEO
Dan Siroker, Chmn.

GROWTH PLANS/SPECIAL FEATURES:

Optimizely, Inc. provides an experimentation platform that enables businesses to deliver continuous experimentation and personalization across all connected devices. A strategic focus of the platform is to provide the ability to test one variation of a web page design against another variation, in order to determine which design drives the best results or the highest number of user responses. The Optimizely X platform allows customers to experiment into their technology stack, as well as across the entire customer experience and across the entire organization. Users can automatically add product, category and content recommendations to any website, leveraging machine learning to continuously improve the recommendations. Customers engage via mobile devices when experiments are run within apps. New features can be instantly rolled out through the apps, and over-the-top (OTT) TV experiences can be delivered by running experiments in any application built for tvOS or Android. Optimizely X is available in various languages, including Danish, French, German, Italian, Japanese, Portuguese, Spanish and Swedish. Customers of the firm include, but are not limited to, Weight Watchers, OpenTable, Microsoft, Zendesk, The New York Times, H&R Block and Charity:Water. Optimizely is based in California, with additional offices in the U.S., as well as in the Netherlands, the U.K., Germany and Australia. During 2018, Optimizely opened a U.S. office in Austin, Texas.

The company offers its employees medical coverage, public transit reimbursement, health programs, parental leave and other perks.

FINANCIAL DATA: *Note: Data for latest year may not have been available at press time.*

In U.S. $	2018	2017	2016	2015	2014	2013
Revenue						
R&D Expense						
Operating Income						
Operating Margin %						
SGA Expense						
Net Income						
Operating Cash Flow						
Capital Expenditure						
EBITDA						
Return on Assets %						
Return on Equity %						
Debt to Equity						

CONTACT INFORMATION:

Phone: 415-495-6546   Fax:
Toll-Free: 800-252-9480
Address: 631 Howard St., Ste. 100, San Francisco, CA 94105 United States

STOCK TICKER/OTHER:

Stock Ticker: Private   Exchange:
Employees: 400   Fiscal Year Ends:
Parent Company:

SALARIES/BONUSES:

Top Exec. Salary: $ Bonus: $
Second Exec. Salary: $ Bonus: $

OTHER THOUGHTS:

Estimated Female Officers or Directors:
Hot Spot for Advancement for Women/Minorities:

Sales, profits and employees may be estimates. Financial information, benefits and other data can change quickly and may vary from those stated here.

Oracle Corporation

www.oracle.com

NAIC Code: 511210J

TYPES OF BUSINESS:

Computer Software, Data Base & File Management
e-Business Applications Software
Internet-Based Software
Consulting Services
Human Resources Management Software
CRM Software
Middleware

BRANDS/DIVISIONS/AFFILIATES:

Zenedge
Aconex Limited
SparklineData
DataScience.com
goBalto
Talari Networks
Vocado
DataFox

CONTACTS: *Note: Officers with more than one job title may be intentionally listed here more than once.*

Lawrence Ellison, Chairman of the Board
William West, Chief Accounting Officer
Mark Hurd, Co-CEO
Safra Catz, Co-CEO
Jeffrey Henley, Director
Dorian Daley, Executive VP
Edward Screven, Executive VP

GROWTH PLANS/SPECIAL FEATURES:

Oracle Corporation is a leading enterprise software company, providing hardware products and services to over 430,000 customers throughout the world. The firm markets its integrated hardware and software systems directly to corporations. Oracle's products can be categorized into three broad business categories: cloud and license, hardware and services. The cloud and license business category represents 82% of total 2018 fiscal revenues, and includes Oracle cloud services, cloud license and on-premise license offerings, as well as license support services. The hardware business (10%) is comprised of hardware products and related hardware support services for on-premise IT environments. Its Oracle engineered systems are core to the firm's on-premise and cloud-based infrastructure offerings, and are pre-integrated products designed to integrate multiple Oracle technology components in order to work together to deliver enhanced performance, availability, security and operational efficiency relative to the customer's products. The services business (8%) offers consulting services, enhanced support services and education services. During 2018, Oracle acquired: Zenedge, a server, storage and networking solutions provider; Aconex Limited, a provider of cloud-based collaboration software for construction projects; SparklineData and DataScience.com, both of which offer middleware software; goBalto, a provider of health sciences solutions; Talari Networks, offering communications and media solutions; and Vocado, Iridize, Grapeshot and DataFox, each of which are cloud- or AI-based applications that provide a variety of solutions.

Oracle offers employees a 401(k) plan; employee assistance and employee stock purchase plans; and a Live and Work Well program.

FINANCIAL DATA: *Note: Data for latest year may not have been available at press time.*

In U.S. $	2018	2017	2016	2015	2014	2013
Revenue	39,831,000,000	37,728,000,000	37,047,000,000	38,226,000,000	38,275,000,000	37,180,000,000
R&D Expense	6,091,000,000	6,159,000,000	5,787,000,000	5,524,000,000	5,151,000,000	4,850,000,000
Operating Income	14,319,000,000	13,276,000,000	13,104,000,000	14,289,000,000	14,983,000,000	14,432,000,000
Operating Margin %	35.94	35.18%	35.37%	37.38%	39.14%	38.81%
SGA Expense	9,720,001,000	9,373,000,000	9,039,000,000	8,732,000,000	8,605,000,000	8,400,000,000
Net Income	3,825,000,000	9,335,000,000	8,901,000,000	9,938,000,000	10,955,000,000	10,925,000,000
Operating Cash Flow	15,386,000,000	14,126,000,000	13,561,000,000	14,336,000,000	14,921,000,000	14,224,000,000
Capital Expenditure	1,736,000,000	2,021,000,000	1,189,000,000	1,391,000,000	580,000,000	650,000,000
EBITDA	17,701,000,000	15,766,000,000	15,418,000,000	16,838,000,000	17,526,000,000	17,626,000,000
Return on Assets %	2.80%	7.55%	7.98%	9.87%	12.72%	13.64%
Return on Equity %	7.68%	18.45%	18.55%	20.80%	23.93%	24.73%
Debt to Equity	1.22	0.89	0.84	0.82	0.48	0.41

CONTACT INFORMATION:

Phone: 650 506-7000   Fax: 650 506-7200
Toll-Free: 800-392-2999
Address: 500 Oracle Pkwy., Redwood City, CA 94065 United States

STOCK TICKER/OTHER:

Stock Ticker: ORCL
Employees: 138,000
Parent Company:

Exchange: NYS
Fiscal Year Ends: 05/31

SALARIES/BONUSES:

Top Exec. Salary: $950,000   Bonus: $
Second Exec. Salary: Bonus: $
$950,000

OTHER THOUGHTS:

Estimated Female Officers or Directors: 6
Hot Spot for Advancement for Women/Minorities: Y

Oracle NetSuite

www.netsuite.com

NAIC Code: 511210H

TYPES OF BUSINESS:

Business Management Application Suites
Enterprise Resource Planning
Customer Relationship Management
E-Commerce Capabilities

BRANDS/DIVISIONS/AFFILIATES:

Oracle Corporation
NetSuite OneWorld
NetSuite CRM
SuiteCommerce

CONTACTS: Note: Officers with more than one job title may be intentionally listed here more than once.

Jim McGeever, Exec. VP-Oper.
Marc Huffman, Sr. VP-Sales
Douglas Solomon, General Counsel
Marc Huffman, President, Divisional

GROWTH PLANS/SPECIAL FEATURES:

Oracle NetSuite is a global business unit of Oracle Corporation and a leading vendor of cloud-based financials, enterprise resource planning (ERP) and omnichannel commerce software. The firm's solutions run the business of more than 40,000 companies, organizations and subsidiaries in over 100 countries. Oracle NetSuite's cloud ERP, customer relationship management (CRM) and eCommerce products enable customers to manage their back-office, front-office and web operations in a single application. From comprehensive financial management capabilities to inventory, supply chain and warehouse management solutions, Oracle NetSuite empowers businesses of all sizes, across all industries. NetSuite OneWorld delivers a real-time, unified global business management platform for enterprises that manages multi-national and multi-subsidiary operations at a fraction of the cost of traditional on-premise ERP solutions. NetSuite CRM software delivers a real-time, 360-degree view of a business' customers. It provides a seamless flow of information across the entire customer lifecycle, from lead to sales order, fulfillment, upsell, cross-sell and support. NetSuite's professional services automation solutions meet the needs of fledgling startups to growing enterprises. SuiteCommerce unifies every step of the multichannel, multi-location business, from e-commerce, point of sale and order management, to marketing, merchandising, inventory, financials and support. Oracle NetSuite products offer a variety of management and procurement solutions, including financial, order, production, supply chain, warehouse/fulfillment and human capital management. Industries served by the company include software/internet companies, wholesale distribution, advertising/digital marketing, media/publishing, financial services, healthcare, non-profit, retail, manufacturing, IT services, professional services, consulting, energy and education.

FINANCIAL DATA: Note: Data for latest year may not have been available at press time.

In U.S. $	2018	2017	2016	2015	2014	2013
Revenue		871,000,000	855,000,000	741,148,992	556,284,032	414,508,000
R&D Expense						
Operating Income						
Operating Margin %						
SGA Expense						
Net Income				-124,743,000	-100,037,000	-70,409,000
Operating Cash Flow						
Capital Expenditure						
EBITDA						
Return on Assets %						
Return on Equity %						
Debt to Equity						

CONTACT INFORMATION:

Phone: 650 627-1000   Fax: 650 627-1001
Toll-Free: 877-638-7848
Address: 2955 Campus Dr., Ste. 100, San Mateo, CA 94403-2511 United States

STOCK TICKER/OTHER:

Stock Ticker: Subsidiary   Exchange:
Employees: 3,357   Fiscal Year Ends: 12/31
Parent Company: Oracle Corporation

SALARIES/BONUSES:

Top Exec. Salary: $ Bonus: $
Second Exec. Salary: $ Bonus: $

OTHER THOUGHTS:

Estimated Female Officers or Directors: 3
Hot Spot for Advancement for Women/Minorities: Y

Orbitz Worldwide Inc

www.orbitz.com

NAIC Code: 561510

TYPES OF BUSINESS:
Online Reservation Systems
Discount Air Fares

BRANDS/DIVISIONS/AFFILIATES:
Expedia Inc

CONTACTS: *Note: Officers with more than one job title may be intentionally listed here more than once.*
Mark Okerstrom, CEO
Michael Randolfi, CFO
Scott Forbes, Director
James Rogers, General Counsel
Guillaume Cussac, Managing Director, Divisional
Chris Brown, Other Executive Officer
Samuel Fulton, Senior VP, Divisional
Barry Diller, Chmn.

GROWTH PLANS/SPECIAL FEATURES:
Orbitz Worldwide, Inc., a subsidiary of Expedia, Inc., is a global online travel company that uses technology to enable leisure and business travelers to search for, plan and book a broad range of travel products and services. Travel products include air travel, hotels, vacation packages, car rentals, cruises and travel insurance as well as destination services, such as ground transportation, event tickets and tours, through a portfolio of websites. For customers, the firm offers access to travel inventory from a broad base of suppliers. For suppliers, the company represents a distribution channel that reaches millions of potential customers. Orbitz offers more than 200 travel and booking sites in 75 countries; and more than 150 mobile websites in nearly 70 countries and 35 languages.

The company offers its employees medical, dental and vision coverage; travel discounts; a 401(k) plan; flexible spending accounts; short- and long-term disability coverage; tuition reimbursement; legal plan; fitness club discounts; and beverage services.

FINANCIAL DATA: *Note: Data for latest year may not have been available at press time.*

In U.S. $	2018	2017	2016	2015	2014	2013
Revenue		800,000,000	764,000,000	919,604,000	932,006,976	847,003,008
R&D Expense						
Operating Income						
Operating Margin %						
SGA Expense						
Net Income				50,400,000	17,280,000	165,084,992
Operating Cash Flow						
Capital Expenditure						
EBITDA						
Return on Assets %						
Return on Equity %						
Debt to Equity						

CONTACT INFORMATION:
Phone: 312 894-5000   Fax: 312 894-5001
Toll-Free: 888-656-4546
Address: 500 W. Madison St., Ste. 1000, Chicago, IL 60661 United States

STOCK TICKER/OTHER:
Stock Ticker: Subsidiary
Employees: 1,530
Parent Company: Expedia Inc

Exchange:
Fiscal Year Ends: 12/31

SALARIES/BONUSES:
Top Exec. Salary: $ Bonus: $
Second Exec. Salary: $ Bonus: $

OTHER THOUGHTS:
Estimated Female Officers or Directors: 3
Hot Spot for Advancement for Women/Minorities: Y

Overstock.com Inc

www.overstock.com

NAIC Code: 454111

TYPES OF BUSINESS:

Online Retail, General
Electronics
Media Products
Home & Bath Goods
Sporting Goods
Jewelry
Online Auctions

BRANDS/DIVISIONS/AFFILIATES:

Overstock.com
Club O
O.biz
Worldstock Fair Trade
Houserie

CONTACTS: *Note: Officers with more than one job title may be intentionally listed here more than once.*

Sam Noursalehi, CEO, Subsidiary
Patrick Byrne, CEO
Robert Hughes, CFO, Subsidiary
Gregory Iverson, CFO
Allison Abraham, Chairman of the Board
Ralph Daiuto, COO, Subsidiary
Jonathan Johnson, Director
Seth Moore, Other Executive Officer
Carter Lee, Senior VP, Divisional
John Knab, Senior VP, Divisional
Amit Goyal, Senior VP, Divisional
Vikram Raghavan, Senior VP, Divisional
Brian Popelka, Senior VP, Divisional

GROWTH PLANS/SPECIAL FEATURES:

Overstock.com, Inc. is an online closeout retailer, offering discount brand-name merchandise at clearance prices available for purchase every day via website or mobile app. Overstock.com is able to offer significant savings by purchasing overproduced products and cancelled orders from leading companies. Merchandise includes bed and bath goods, kitchenware, home and garden products, watches, jewelry, electronics, sporting goods, designer accessories and apparel. The company offers more than 2.8 million products under multiple shopping tabs on its main website. The company's warehouses generally ship between 2,000 and 5,000 orders per day and up to approximately 6,000 orders per day during peak periods. Overstock.com also maintains fulfillment partner relationships with roughly 4,100 third parties, allowing for merchandise of other retailers to be sold on the site. Additionally, Overstock.com offers live 24/7 customer service, low cost shipping and secure shopping. Club O is the company's loyalty program, where members pay an annual fee and receive a discount on certain items, free shipping and access to a special customer service hotline. The firm's O.biz website carries products in bulk and is primarily geared toward small and medium-sized businesses. Also, on its website, Overstock.com maintains Worldstock Fair Trade, an online marketplace through which artisans in the U.S. and around the world can sell their products and gain access to a broader market. The company serves international customers in over 100 countries. Overstock accepts digital currency Bitcoin as a payment choice, along with Visa, MasterCard and PayPal. In June 2018, Overstock launched Houserie, a newly-remodeled property management site that provides landlords and property managers a variety of services for managing single-home properties or multi-home complexes.

FINANCIAL DATA: *Note: Data for latest year may not have been available at press time.*

In U.S. $	2018	2017	2016	2015	2014	2013
Revenue		1,744,756,000	1,799,963,000	1,657,838,000	1,497,103,000	1,304,217,000
R&D Expense		115,878,000	106,760,000	98,533,000	86,258,000	
Operating Income		-46,634,000	-12,605,000	-534,000	11,563,000	16,094,000
Operating Margin %		-2.67%	-.70%	-.03%	.77%	1.23%
SGA Expense		271,307,000	237,194,000	206,655,000	181,238,000	231,566,000
Net Income		-109,878,000	12,522,000	2,446,000	8,854,000	88,509,000
Operating Cash Flow		-35,321,000	39,564,000	54,516,000	80,834,000	83,645,000
Capital Expenditure		23,586,000	72,281,000	59,738,000	41,481,000	18,080,000
EBITDA		-11,950,000	52,673,000	28,352,000	31,308,000	30,979,000
Return on Assets %		-23.31%	2.73%	.60%	2.54%	35.28%
Return on Equity %		-61.05%	7.68%	1.74%	7.02%	115.05%
Debt to Equity		0.31		0.09		

CONTACT INFORMATION:

Phone: 801 947-3100   Fax: 801 944-4629
Toll-Free: 800-989-0135
Address: 799 West Coliseum Way, Midvale, UT 84047 United States

STOCK TICKER/OTHER:

Stock Ticker: OSTK   Exchange: NAS
Employees: 1,800   Fiscal Year Ends: 12/31
Parent Company:

SALARIES/BONUSES:

Top Exec. Salary: $400,000   Bonus: $
Second Exec. Salary: $400,000   Bonus: $

OTHER THOUGHTS:

Estimated Female Officers or Directors: 2
Hot Spot for Advancement for Women/Minorities: Y

Ozon.ru
NAIC Code: 454111

TYPES OF BUSINESS:

Online Retail Store

BRANDS/DIVISIONS/AFFILIATES:

Ozon Delivery
Ozon Travel
Ozon Guide
Sapato.ru
LitRes.ru

CONTACTS: Note: Officers with more than one job title may be intentionally listed here more than once.

Alexander Shulgin, CEO
Peter Rozanski, Dir.-Mktg.
Svetlana Timofeeva, Dir.-HR
Anatoly Orlov, Dir.-IT

GROWTH PLANS/SPECIAL FEATURES:

Ozon.ru is sometimes referred to as the Amazon.com of Russia. It offers more than 5 million popular items in a wide variety of categories, including fitness trackers, smart watches, headphones, cookware, figurines, apparel, shoes, outerwear, toys, games, books, movies, jewelry, seasonal items, giftwrap and cards, food and beverages and much more. The site has approximately 15 million registered users, as well as over 1.5 million unique daily visitors. The company operates a large shipping company, Ozon Delivery, centrally located between Moscow and St. Petersburg. Ozon Delivery operates its own fleet of delivery trucks. In addition to receiving orders online, Ozon offers telephone ordering. Moreover, the firm operates Ozon Travel, a Russian travel booking site; Ozon Guide, an information website on various topics, including recipes, knitting, the best books to read, why coffees have different tastes, how to administer contacts onto one's eyes, music collections, how to choose a toothbrush, etc.; and LitRes.ru, a licensed e-book website, offering over 1 million e-books in Russian and foreign languages, with 5,000 new books every month and 1.5 million downloads every months. Subsidiary Sapato.ru is a Russian-based e-commerce platform offering various brands of shoes, bags, gloves and shoe care products. During 2018, Ozon established an innovative tech lab in Moscow to develop a tech platform, which is in addition to its robotics lab.

FINANCIAL DATA: Note: Data for latest year may not have been available at press time.

In U.S. $	2018	2017	2016	2015	2014	2013
Revenue		374,591,000	295,724,000	204,867,000		
R&D Expense						
Operating Income						
Operating Margin %						
SGA Expense						
Net Income						
Operating Cash Flow						
Capital Expenditure						
EBITDA						
Return on Assets %						
Return on Equity %						
Debt to Equity						

CONTACT INFORMATION:

Phone: 7-495-730-6767   Fax:
Toll-Free:
Address: 8 Marta St., Bldg. 14, Moscow, 127 083 Russia

STOCK TICKER/OTHER:

Stock Ticker: Private   Exchange:
Employees: Fiscal Year Ends:
Parent Company:

SALARIES/BONUSES:

Top Exec. Salary: $ Bonus: $
Second Exec. Salary: $ Bonus: $

OTHER THOUGHTS:

Estimated Female Officers or Directors: 1
Hot Spot for Advancement for Women/Minorities: Y

PagerDuty Inc

NAIC Code: 511210C

www.pagerduty.com

TYPES OF BUSINESS:

Computer Software, Telecom, Communications & VOIP

BRANDS/DIVISIONS/AFFILIATES:

CONTACTS: *Note: Officers with more than one job title may be intentionally listed here more than once.*

Jennifer Tejada, CEO
Howard Wilson, CFO
Jonathan Rende, Sr. VP-Product & Mktg.
Sophie Kitson, VP-People
Alex Solomon, CTO
Steven Chung, Sr. VP-Worldwide Sales & Srvcs.

GROWTH PLANS/SPECIAL FEATURES:

PagerDuty, Inc. provides an alarm aggregation and dispatching service for system administrators and support teams in the U.S. and internationally. This enterprise incident resolutions service integrates with IT operations and DevOps monitoring stacks in order to improve operational reliability and agility. Management process events are aggregated from the customer's monitoring systems and correlated into incidents, from which PagerDuty then streamlines by reducing alert noise and resolution times. This process enables customers to visualize the health of its applications, services and infrastructure while managing incident response workflows all in one place. It also allows them to customize the operations command console with powerful applications so that specific personnel only see what is relevant. This customization process ensures that the alert delivery is sending the right information to the right person or department every single time. Custom on-call schedules, rotations and escalations are configurable. Built-in integrations with ChatOps tools and helpdesk services enable real-time collaboration with the appropriate teams. System efficiency and employ productivity are analyzed by PagerDuty. Other features include enterprise-grade security and controls, service grouping, platform extensibility, live call routing, and always-on delivery. PagerDuty has more than 10,000 customers across 80 countries, including Evernote, Okta, DELL, Groupon, Google, AT&T, lululemon athletica and Concur, among others.

The company offers its employees medical coverage, paid time off, catered lunches and other perks.

FINANCIAL DATA: *Note: Data for latest year may not have been available at press time.*

In U.S. $	2018	2017	2016	2015	2014	2013
Revenue						
R&D Expense						
Operating Income						
Operating Margin %						
SGA Expense						
Net Income						
Operating Cash Flow						
Capital Expenditure						
EBITDA						
Return on Assets %						
Return on Equity %						
Debt to Equity						

CONTACT INFORMATION:

Phone: 650-989-2965   Fax:
Toll-Free: 866-935-1337
Address: 600 Townsend St., Ste. 200, San Francisco, CA 94103 United States

STOCK TICKER/OTHER:

Stock Ticker: Private   Exchange:
Employees: 500   Fiscal Year Ends:
Parent Company:

SALARIES/BONUSES:

Top Exec. Salary: $ Bonus: $
Second Exec. Salary: $ Bonus: $

OTHER THOUGHTS:

Estimated Female Officers or Directors:
Hot Spot for Advancement for Women/Minorities:

Pandora Media Inc

www.pandora.com

NAIC Code: 515111

TYPES OF BUSINESS:

Radio Networks, Traditional, Satellite and Online

BRANDS/DIVISIONS/AFFILIATES:

Sirius XM Holdings, Inc.
Pandora Plus
Pandora Premium
Pandor API

CONTACTS: *Note: Officers with more than one job title may be intentionally listed here more than once.*

Naveen Chopra, CFO
Karen Walker, Chief Accounting Officer
Aimee Lapic, Chief Marketing Officer
David Gerbitz, COO
Gregory Maffei, Director
Roger Lynch, Director
Stephen Bene, General Counsel
Kristen Robinson, Other Executive Officer
John Trimble, Other Executive Officer
Christopher Phillips, Other Executive Officer

GROWTH PLANS/SPECIAL FEATURES:

Pandora Media, Inc. is an internet-based music streaming service. Available in the U.S., Australia and New Zealand, and annually streams 21.96 billion hours of internet radio by 68.8 million active users. The company's website enables users to build unique virtual radio stations based on music preferences. The firm's technology is based in part on the Music Genome Project, which analyzes and catalogues thousands of songs from multiple genres to create a comprehensive database that breaks down songs by hundreds of individual musical attributes. Pandora's catalog contains over 1.5 million songs from more than 250,000 artists in 600 genres and sub-genres. The company offers free accounts, which are currently ad-supported but restrict the ability to skip songs; and premium subscriptions through Pandora Plus, which give listeners the ability to skip an unlimited amount of songs, has no limit on monthly listening hours, delivers higher quality audio and removes advertisements. The firm also operates Pandora Premium, its paid subscription service. Pandora Premium offers a unique, on-demand experience, providing users with the ability to search, play and collect songs and albums, build playlists on their own or with the tap of a button and automatically generate playlists based on the user's listening activity. The firm also offers mobile listening via smartphones and tablets. Pandora has established partnerships with consumer electronics manufacturers to integrate its Pandora API software into new devices, as well as automakers like Honda, Ford, Lexus and Mercedes. Pandora is now available on more than 1,000 partner integrations, including consumer electronic devices and various car models. In February 2019, Pandora was acquired by SiriusXM Holdings, Inc., the satellite radio service provider.

Pandora offers employees different insurance and savings plans.

FINANCIAL DATA: *Note: Data for latest year may not have been available at press time.*

In U.S. $	2018	2017	2016	2015	2014	2013
Revenue		1,466,812,032	1,384,825,984	1,164,043,008	920,801,984	600,233,024
R&D Expense						
Operating Income						
Operating Margin %						
SGA Expense						
Net Income		-518,395,008	-342,977,984	-169,660,992	-30,406,000	-27,017,000
Operating Cash Flow						
Capital Expenditure						
EBITDA						
Return on Assets %						
Return on Equity %						
Debt to Equity						

CONTACT INFORMATION:

Phone: 510 451-4100   Fax:
Toll-Free:
Address: 2101 Webster St., Ste. 1650, Oakland, CA 94612 United States

STOCK TICKER/OTHER:

Stock Ticker: Subsidiary   Exchange:
Employees: 2,488   Fiscal Year Ends: 12/31
Parent Company: Sirius XM Holdings, Inc.

SALARIES/BONUSES:

Top Exec. Salary: $ Bonus: $
Second Exec. Salary: $ Bonus: $

OTHER THOUGHTS:

Estimated Female Officers or Directors: 5
Hot Spot for Advancement for Women/Minorities: Y

PayPal Holdings Inc

www.paypal.com

NAIC Code: 522320

TYPES OF BUSINESS:

Payment Processing-Intermediary
Online Payment Systems
Web-Enabled Payments
Online Auction Technology
Credit Cards
Debit Cards
Account Management
Money Transfer

BRANDS/DIVISIONS/AFFILIATES:

eBay Inc
PayPal
PayPal Credit
Braintree
Venmo
Xoom
iZettle
Paydiant

CONTACTS: Note: Officers with more than one job title may be intentionally listed here more than once.

John Rainey, CFO
John Donahoe, Chairman of the Board
Aaron Karczmer, Chief Risk Officer
William Ready, COO
Louise Pentland, Executive VP
Jonathan Auerbach, Executive VP
Gary Marino, Executive VP
Daniel Schulman, President
Aaron Anderson, Vice President

GROWTH PLANS/SPECIAL FEATURES:

PayPal Holdings, Inc. is a leading technology platform and global online payment processing company. The firm's products allow businesses and consumers to cost-effectively send and receive payments within and between more than 200 markets and 100 currencies worldwide. The company has about 227 million active customer accounts worldwide. The PayPal system extends the existing financial infrastructure of bank accounts and credit cards, and can also be used to collect subscriptions, recurring payments and donations. Moreover, the firm is a leading payment processing provider for online auction services, with the bulk of the company's business coming from eBay. PayPal's combined payment solution capabilities are comprised of the PayPal, PayPal Credit, Braintree, Venmo, Xoom and Paydiant proprietary payments platform. These products make it safer and simpler for friends and family to transfer funds to each other, including cross border transfers. Merchants are provided an end-to-end payments solution that provides authorization and settlement capabilities, as well as instant access to funds. PayPal Credit provides the ability for consumers to receive a line of credit; Braintree specializes in mobile and web payment systems for eCommerce companies; Venmo is a mobile application which moves money between friends and family via mobile devices; Xoom enables consumers to send money, pay bills and send mobile phone reloads to family and friends around the world via mobile devices; and Paydiant provides cloud-based services for merchants, banks, and point-of-sale and ATM providers. During 2017, PayPal processed approximately 7.6 billion payment transactions, which translates to 33.6 payment transactions per active customer account. In June 2108, the firm announced it had agreed to acquire Simility, a fraud prevention and risk management platform, for $120 million. The following September, PayPal completed its acquisition of iZettle, a financial technology company, for $2.2 billion.

FINANCIAL DATA: Note: Data for latest year may not have been available at press time.

In U.S. $	2018	2017	2016	2015	2014	2013
Revenue		13,094,000,000	10,842,000,000	9,248,000,000	8,025,000,000	6,727,000,000
R&D Expense		953,000,000	834,000,000	947,000,000	890,000,000	727,000,000
Operating Income		2,259,000,000	1,586,000,000	1,509,000,000	1,268,000,000	1,091,000,000
Operating Margin %		17.25%	14.62%	16.31%	15.80%	16.21%
SGA Expense		9,077,000,000	7,698,000,000	6,184,000,000	5,351,000,000	4,456,000,000
Net Income		1,795,000,000	1,401,000,000	1,228,000,000	419,000,000	955,000,000
Operating Cash Flow		2,531,000,000	3,158,000,000	2,546,000,000	2,220,000,000	1,993,000,000
Capital Expenditure		667,000,000	669,000,000	722,000,000	492,000,000	391,000,000
EBITDA		3,064,000,000	2,310,000,000	2,117,000,000	1,784,000,000	1,544,000,000
Return on Assets %		4.85%	4.52%	4.83%	2.04%	4.98%
Return on Equity %		11.69%	9.84%	11.16%	5.35%	12.92%
Debt to Equity					0.04	0.06

CONTACT INFORMATION:

Phone: 408-967-1000   Fax: 650-864-8001
Toll-Free:
Address: 2211 N. First St., San Jose, CA 95131 United States

STOCK TICKER/OTHER:

Stock Ticker: PYPL   Exchange: NAS
Employees: 18,100   Fiscal Year Ends: 12/31
Parent Company:

SALARIES/BONUSES:

Top Exec. Salary: $1,000,000   Bonus: $
Second Exec. Salary: $650,000   Bonus: $

OTHER THOUGHTS:

Estimated Female Officers or Directors: 1
Hot Spot for Advancement for Women/Minorities: Y

Sales, profits and employees may be estimates. Financial information, benefits and other data can change quickly and may vary from those stated here.

Peapod LLC

NAIC Code: 454111

www.peapod.com

TYPES OF BUSINESS:

Groceries, Online Retail
Grocery Delivery Services
Media & Research Services

BRANDS/DIVISIONS/AFFILIATES:

Koninklijke Ahold Delhaize NV

CONTACTS: *Note: Officers with more than one job title may be intentionally listed here more than once.*

Selma Postma, Pres.
David Mchugh, VP-Operations
Thomas Parkinson, CTO
Norm Haberl, Sr. VP-Oper.
John Burchard, Chief Accounting Officer
Scott DeGraeve, Sr. VP-Supply Chain Dev.

GROWTH PLANS/SPECIAL FEATURES:

Peapod, LLC, a subsidiary of Koninklijke Ahold Delhaize NV, delivers groceries that consumers order over the internet via PC or mobile device. The company's grocery delivery service provides consumers with a virtual supermarket, personalized shopping, delivery and responsive telephone and email support. Peapod offers products in produce; meat and seafood; deli items; prepared foods; natural and organic foods; Kosher foods; office and school supplies; seasonal items; video products; pet items; health and beauty aids; and wine, beer and spirits. The firm has partnerships, offering their private label food products and using their facilities as secondary fulfillment spaces. Peapod also provides consumer goods companies with a forum for targeted interactive advertising, electronic coupons and extensive product research. The company operates through centralized distribution from its two warehouses in Chicago and Washington, D.C., which together total 150,000 square feet. It also owns 7,000-square-foot warerooms adjacent to its partner stores in Connecticut, Massachusetts, New York, New Jersey and Rhode Island. Peapod offers delivery to both homes and businesses and has over 200 pick-up locations. The firm's services are available in metro markets across New York, New Jersey, Connecticut, Chicago, Rhode Island, Massachusetts, New Hampshire, Wisconsin, Indiana, Pennsylvania, Maryland, District of Columbia and Virginia.

Employees receive medical, dental and prescription health benefits; a 401(k); short- and long-term disability coverage; life and accidental death and dismemberment insurance; and paid time off.

FINANCIAL DATA: *Note: Data for latest year may not have been available at press time.*

In U.S. $	2018	2017	2016	2015	2014	2013
Revenue	714,000,000	680,000,000	645,000,000	600,000,000	575,000,000	550,000,000
R&D Expense						
Operating Income						
Operating Margin %						
SGA Expense						
Net Income						
Operating Cash Flow						
Capital Expenditure						
EBITDA						
Return on Assets %						
Return on Equity %						
Debt to Equity						

CONTACT INFORMATION:

Phone: 847-583-9400   Fax: 847-583-9494
Toll-Free: 800-573-2763
Address: 300 S. Riverside Plaza, Chicago, IL 60606 United States

STOCK TICKER/OTHER:

Stock Ticker: Subsidiary   Exchange:
Employees: 4,600   Fiscal Year Ends: 12/31
Parent Company: Koninklijke Ahold Delhaize NV

SALARIES/BONUSES:

Top Exec. Salary: $ Bonus: $
Second Exec. Salary: $ Bonus: $

OTHER THOUGHTS:

Estimated Female Officers or Directors:
Hot Spot for Advancement for Women/Minorities:

Perficient Inc

www.perficient.com

NAIC Code: 541512

TYPES OF BUSINESS:

Consulting-On-Site Technical Services
Middleware
Web Services
Content Management Software
Enterprise Portal Services
IT Outsourcing

BRANDS/DIVISIONS/AFFILIATES:

Clarity Consulting

CONTACTS: *Note: Officers with more than one job title may be intentionally listed here more than once.*

Jeffrey Davis, CEO
Paul Martin, CFO
Thomas Hogan, COO

GROWTH PLANS/SPECIAL FEATURES:

Perficient, Inc. is an information technology (IT) consulting firm providing large enterprise companies with internet-based technology using third-party software products developed by its partners. Perficient's experience with platforms, including J2EE, .NET and Open-source, enables it to design, develop, implement and integrate custom application solutions that provide enterprise-specific functionality. The firm's technology solutions include business analytics; management consulting; business integration, including coherent architecture; customer relationship management (CRM); platform implementations, for a reliable Internet-based infrastructure; business process management (BPM); enterprise data and business intelligence; enterprise performance management (EPM); cloud services, helping clients leverage cloud technology; and platform implementations. Industries served include automotive, communications, healthcare, financial services, manufacturing, consumer markets, high tech, life sciences and energy. Perficient, headquartered in St, Louis, Missouri, serves its customers from a network of multiple markets throughout the U.S., Canada, the U.K., China and India. In 2018, Perficient acquired: Southport Services Group, LLC, a microstrategy consultant with expertise in analytics, business intelligence and data warehousing solutions; Stone Temple Consulting Corporation, a digital marketing agency; and Elixiter, Inc., a market consultant specializing in automation services.

The company offers employees flexible spending accounts; health, life, AD&D and disability insurance; referral bonuses; a 401(k); and a stock purchase plan.

FINANCIAL DATA: *Note: Data for latest year may not have been available at press time.*

In U.S. $	2018	2017	2016	2015	2014	2013
Revenue		485,261,000	486,982,000	473,621,000	456,692,000	373,325,000
R&D Expense						
Operating Income		30,339,000	33,457,000	36,487,000	42,409,000	34,262,000
Operating Margin %		6.25%	6.87%	7.70%	8.96%	9.17%
SGA Expense		108,192,000	101,264,000	99,963,000	90,202,000	77,601,000
Net Income		18,581,000	20,459,000	23,007,000	23,163,000	21,432,000
Operating Cash Flow		55,221,000	63,301,000	44,721,000	34,033,000	46,851,000
Capital Expenditure		4,322,000	6,051,000	4,391,000	7,148,000	7,978,000
EBITDA		48,728,000	50,383,000	53,235,000	57,145,000	45,498,000
Return on Assets %		3.88%	4.39%	5.11%	6.16%	7.22%
Return on Equity %		5.11%	5.77%	7.04%	8.21%	8.67%
Debt to Equity		0.15	0.08	0.16	0.17	0.07

CONTACT INFORMATION:

Phone: 314 930-2900   Fax: 512 531-6011
Toll-Free:
Address: 555 Maryville University Dr., Ste. 600, Saint Louis, MO 63141 United States

STOCK TICKER/OTHER:

Stock Ticker: PRFT   Exchange: NAS
Employees: 2,728   Fiscal Year Ends: 12/31
Parent Company:

SALARIES/BONUSES:

Top Exec. Salary: $596,587   Bonus: $300,000
Second Exec. Salary: $393,635   Bonus: $98,750

OTHER THOUGHTS:

Estimated Female Officers or Directors: 2
Hot Spot for Advancement for Women/Minorities:

Performics Inc

NAIC Code: 541810E

www.performics.com

TYPES OF BUSINESS:

Marketing Software
Search Engine Marketing
Affiliate Marketing Services
Data Feed Marketing
Online Lead Generation

BRANDS/DIVISIONS/AFFILIATES:

Publicis Groupe SA

CONTACTS: *Note: Officers with more than one job title may be intentionally listed here more than once.*

David Gould, Pres.
Craig Greenfield, COO
Jon Wegman, VP-Strategy & Planning
Lindsay Landsberg, Sr. VP-Bus. Dev.
Dona Ross, Sr. VP-Client Services
Luis Barreiro, Global Comm. Coordinator
Carrie Anger, Dir.-Acct.
Karishma Kiri, Sr. VP
Craig Greenfield, Exec. VP-Global Managing Dir.
Vidur Luthra, CEO-Resultrix
Frederic Joseph, CEO-EMEA

GROWTH PLANS/SPECIAL FEATURES:

Performics, Inc., a division of Publicis Groupe SA, provides performance-based marketing services and technologies for large, multi-channel retail companies. Performics utilizes its account managers, advanced market expertise and proprietary tracking and reporting technology platform to help clients acquire and retain online customers. Search engine marketing includes keyword management, paid listings, pay-per-click (PPC), paid inclusion and natural search optimization solutions. Performics collaborates with global brands, performing across paid, owned and earned media. The firm's services are divided into seven groups: performance media, performance content, planning and insights, analytics and technology, social media, local marketing and mobile marketing. Performance media includes media planning and optimization, buying, affiliate marketing, feeds, marketplace and digital co-operation. Performance content includes content strategy, creative development, content distribution, optimization and search engine optimization. Planning and insights include consumer insights, communications planning, competitive intelligence and strategic research. Analytics and technology includes business intelligence, data management personalization, cross-channel attribution modeling and predictive analysis. Social media balances media, content, insight and analytics to create measurable results via participant impressions and expressions. Local marketing is location-based targeting through search, content and data feeds. Last, mobile marketing measures the impact that mobile has on participant behavior, commerce, conversion and action. Performics is based in the U.S., with offices throughout the Americas, Europe, the Middle East, Africa and Asia Pacific.

The firm offers employees medical, disability and dental insurance; a 401(k) plan; flexible spending accounts; and tuition reimbursement.

FINANCIAL DATA: *Note: Data for latest year may not have been available at press time.*

In U.S. $	2018	2017	2016	2015	2014	2013
Revenue						
R&D Expense						
Operating Income						
Operating Margin %						
SGA Expense						
Net Income						
Operating Cash Flow						
Capital Expenditure						
EBITDA						
Return on Assets %						
Return on Equity %						
Debt to Equity						

CONTACT INFORMATION:

Phone: 312-739-0222   Fax: 312-739-0223
Toll-Free: 800-615-6126
Address: 111 E. Wacker, Ste. 1500, Chicago, IL 60601 United States

STOCK TICKER/OTHER:

Stock Ticker: Subsidiary   Exchange:
Employees: 3,400   Fiscal Year Ends: 12/31
Parent Company: Publicis Groupe SA

SALARIES/BONUSES:

Top Exec. Salary: $ Bonus: $
Second Exec. Salary: $ Bonus: $

OTHER THOUGHTS:

Estimated Female Officers or Directors: 6
Hot Spot for Advancement for Women/Minorities: Y

Photobucket Inc

www.photobucket.com

NAIC Code: 519130

TYPES OF BUSINESS:

Online Photo Sharing
Online Video Services

BRANDS/DIVISIONS/AFFILIATES:

Photobucket.com
Print Shop

CONTACTS: Note: Officers with more than one job title may be intentionally listed here more than once.

Ted Leonard, CEO
Tom Munro, Pres.
Jim Goss, VP-Oper.
Erin Robinson, VP-Finance
Darren Kelly, Chief Revenue Officer

GROWTH PLANS/SPECIAL FEATURES:

Photobucket, Inc. is a visual media company that hosts various formats of digital content online through the website Photobucket.com. Free accounts allow users to store photos, videos and GIFs, and share them via email or social sites, up to 2 gigabytes (GB) of storage. For those needing more storage, for an annual subscription of $11.48/month, the Expert plan offers 1TB of storage and allows watermark free image hosting, a lifetime storage promise, ad free browsing, ability to share on social media, ability to share private albums, editable captions and titles, unlimited photo albums, high speed cloud delivery network (CDN) and zero image upload compression; for $6.48/month, the Intermediate plan offers 250GB of storage, watermark free image hosting, a lifetime storage promise, ad free browsing, ability to share on social media, ability to share private albums, editable captions and titles and unlimited photo albums; and for $4.48/month, the Beginner plan offers 25GB of storage, watermark free image hosting, a lifetime storage promise, ad free browsing, ability to share on social media, ability to share private albums and editable captions and titles. The company's Print Shop and photo editor offers solutions for photo needs, as well as a variety of high-quality print products for purchase. Products include canvas prints, metal prints, traditional prints, home decorations, wall art, as well as photo books and gifts.

FINANCIAL DATA: Note: Data for latest year may not have been available at press time.

In U.S. $	2018	2017	2016	2015	2014	2013
Revenue						
R&D Expense						
Operating Income						
Operating Margin %						
SGA Expense						
Net Income						
Operating Cash Flow						
Capital Expenditure						
EBITDA						
Return on Assets %						
Return on Equity %						
Debt to Equity						

CONTACT INFORMATION:

Phone: 303-226-6800   Fax: 303-395-1165
Toll-Free:
Address: 2399 Black St., Ste. 160, Denver, CO 80201 United States

STOCK TICKER/OTHER:

Stock Ticker: Private   Exchange:
Employees: 126   Fiscal Year Ends: 12/31
Parent Company:

SALARIES/BONUSES:

Top Exec. Salary: $ Bonus: $
Second Exec. Salary: $ Bonus: $

OTHER THOUGHTS:

Estimated Female Officers or Directors: 1
Hot Spot for Advancement for Women/Minorities: Y

Piksel Inc

NAIC Code: 511210F

www.piksel.com

TYPES OF BUSINESS:

Computer Software, Multimedia, Graphics & Publishing

BRANDS/DIVISIONS/AFFILIATES:

Piksel Palette
Fuse Metadata
Fuse Publisher
Digital Showcase
Digital Enterprise

CONTACTS: *Note: Officers with more than one job title may be intentionally listed here more than once.*

Ralf Tillmann, Interim CEO
Mark Christie, CTO
Mark Portu, Chief Product Officer
Ralf Tillmann, Chief Strategy Officer
Kevin Joyce, Chief Commercial Officer

GROWTH PLANS/SPECIAL FEATURES:

Piksel, Inc. is a leading global provider of on-demand, internet Protocol (IP)-based video asset management systems. The company's software-as-a-service infrastructure allows customers to acquire, manage and distribute video streams to personal computers, mobile devices and IPTV-enabled television sets. Potential applications for this service range anywhere between on-demand commercial video distribution to internal corporate communications, human resources and training. The flagship service for the company is Piksel Palette, a cloud-based video asset management software system that enables media and entertainment, network operator and non-media enterprise clients to produce, manage and deliver live and on-demand, socially-enabled video experiences from any source to any screen. Piksel's Fuse Metadata offers consistency in how content is catalogued, presented and described. This product improves detail and accuracy of content information, and can augment content with entirely new, proprietary metadata unique to the customer's service. Fuse Publisher gives broadcasters and content owners the ability to automatically syndicate their content to a defined set of end points and distributors. Digital Showcase is a video solution for video over-the-top (OTT) television service. Its architecture allows easy ingestion and management of all types of video content for delivery in any format to any screen. When combining multichannel content management features with asset management, Digital Showcase becomes the high-performance engine for the multiscreen OTT strategy. Last, Digital Enterprise is an online video platform that enables organizations to distribute and manage their video content in one place. Piksel handles over 40,000 live events each year, monitored 24/7 from its state-of-the-art live streaming and monitoring center in Atlanta, U.S. Based in York, England, the firm has additional offices in Europe and the U.S.

FINANCIAL DATA: *Note: Data for latest year may not have been available at press time.*

In U.S. $	2018	2017	2016	2015	2014	2013
Revenue		60,727,400	52,735,800	64,028,500	68,240,700	48,909,800
R&D Expense						
Operating Income						
Operating Margin %						
SGA Expense						
Net Income			-2,379,250	-9,078,000	-8,771,770	-10,760,600
Operating Cash Flow						
Capital Expenditure						
EBITDA						
Return on Assets %						
Return on Equity %						
Debt to Equity						

CONTACT INFORMATION:

Phone: 440-8448-633600   Fax:
Toll-Free:
Address: 1 Innovation Close, York Science Park, York, YO10 5ZD United Kingdom

STOCK TICKER/OTHER:

Stock Ticker: Private
Employees: 800
Parent Company:

Exchange:
Fiscal Year Ends: 12/31

SALARIES/BONUSES:

Top Exec. Salary: $ Bonus: $
Second Exec. Salary: $ Bonus: $

OTHER THOUGHTS:

Estimated Female Officers or Directors:
Hot Spot for Advancement for Women/Minorities:

Ping An Healthcare and Technology Co Ltd   www.pahtg.com/en/

NAIC Code: 519130

TYPES OF BUSINESS:

Health Care Internet Portals
Healthcare Consultation

BRANDS/DIVISIONS/AFFILIATES:

CONTACTS: Note: Officers with more than one job title may be intentionally listed here more than once.

Tao Wang, CEO
Xue Bai, COO
Edwin Morris, CFO
Qi Wang, CTO
Tao Wang, Chmn.

GROWTH PLANS/SPECIAL FEATURES:

Ping An Healthcare and Technology Co., Ltd. operates an online and mobile healthcare platform, offering related consultations. The platform offers information about medical and wellness services such as family doctor services, consumer healthcare services, beauty care, medical insurance, pharmacies and health management. It connects consumers and patients with healthcare resources and enables them to retrieve information, obtain advice and book and manage appointments. Its nationwide network covers approximately 3,100 hospitals, 1,100 checkup centers, 500 dental clinics and 7,500 pharmacy outlets. As of December 31, 2017, there were nearly 193 million registered users, and the platform averages 370,000 daily online consultations. Consultation services include referrals, second opinions and appointment booking through the platform's AI-assisted in-house medical team and external doctors. Hospital partners may also provide consultation services through the system. In addition, Ping An Healthcare and Technology offers annual health membership programs to individuals and corporations in China. Health-related products can be purchased through the online or mobile platform, with more than 175,000 stock-keeping units to choose from. Ping An's mission is to build a global healthcare ecosystem that promotes healthy living via technology.

FINANCIAL DATA: Note: Data for latest year may not have been available at press time.

In U.S. $	2018	2017	2016	2015	2014	2013
Revenue		286,825,000	86,483,900	42,984,100		
R&D Expense						
Operating Income						
Operating Margin %						
SGA Expense						
Net Income		93,970,600	36,550,600	17,101,200		
Operating Cash Flow						
Capital Expenditure						
EBITDA						
Return on Assets %						
Return on Equity %						
Debt to Equity						

CONTACT INFORMATION:

Phone: Fax: 86 21 3863 3719
Toll-Free:
Address: 16-19/Fl, Block B, No. 166, Kaibin Rd., Ping An Bldg., Shanghai, Shanghai 201900 China

STOCK TICKER/OTHER:

Stock Ticker: 1833   Exchange: Hong Kong
Employees: Fiscal Year Ends: 12/31
Parent Company:

SALARIES/BONUSES:

Top Exec. Salary: $ Bonus: $
Second Exec. Salary: $ Bonus: $

OTHER THOUGHTS:

Estimated Female Officers or Directors:
Hot Spot for Advancement for Women/Minorities:

Pinterest Inc

www.pinterest.com

NAIC Code: 519130

TYPES OF BUSINESS:

Online Idea Sharing Site

BRANDS/DIVISIONS/AFFILIATES:

Pinterest.com
Pinterest Analytics

CONTACTS: *Note: Officers with more than one job title may be intentionally listed here more than once.*

Ben Silbermann, CEO
Evan Sharp, Chief Creative Officer
Joanne K. Bradford, Head-Partnerships

GROWTH PLANS/SPECIAL FEATURES:

Pinterest, Inc. is a San Francisco, California-based social media company founded in 2010 that operates an online pinboard-style social photo sharing website with more than 250 million monthly global users (as of December 2018). The company's website, Pinterest.com, offers a virtual Pinboard that allows its users to create, organize and manage various projects on the web through the posting of media content such as pictures and videos (referred to as pins). The site enables users to place digital pins in content they find on the web, such as recipes, craft ideas and articles, and keep them organized in one location for future reference. Users can classify their pins under the site's many categories, which include Design, DIY (Do It Yourself) & Crafts, Fitness, Food & Drink, Hair & Beauty, Home Decor, Humor, Kids, Women's Apparel, Outdoors, People, Pets, Travel & Places and Weddings & Events. The social networking aspect of Pinterest is that it allows users to view pinboards created by others, re-pin images from other users and share pins on additional social networking sites such as Facebook and Twitter, thus allowing those with shared interests to connect with each other. The website is currently available in over 30 different languages. The company also offers Pinterest Analytics, an analysis tool that enables website owners to see how pins originating from their websites are being used. Headquartered in San Francisco, California, Pinterest also has offices in New York, Chicago, Atlanta, Los Angeles, London, Paris, Berlin, Tokyo, Toronto and Sao Paulo. Historically, Pinterest did not generate revenues; however, it began selling promoted pins to advertisers as its first step towards advertising-fee generation.

Employees of Pinterest are given comprehensive medical benefits and equity in the company.

FINANCIAL DATA: *Note: Data for latest year may not have been available at press time.*

In U.S. $	2018	2017	2016	2015	2014	2013
Revenue	711,000,000	470,000,000	300,000,000	100,000,000	25,000,000	
R&D Expense						
Operating Income						
Operating Margin %						
SGA Expense						
Net Income						
Operating Cash Flow						
Capital Expenditure						
EBITDA						
Return on Assets %						
Return on Equity %						
Debt to Equity						

CONTACT INFORMATION:

Phone: 650-561-5407   Fax:
Toll-Free:
Address: 808 Brannan St., San Francisco, CA 94103 United States

STOCK TICKER/OTHER:

Stock Ticker: Private   Exchange:
Employees: 570   Fiscal Year Ends:
Parent Company:

SALARIES/BONUSES:

Top Exec. Salary: $ Bonus: $
Second Exec. Salary: $ Bonus: $

OTHER THOUGHTS:

Estimated Female Officers or Directors:
Hot Spot for Advancement for Women/Minorities: Y

Planet Labs Inc

www.planet.com

NAIC Code: 517410

TYPES OF BUSINESS:

Satellite Telecommunications Services
Satellite Manufacturing
Satellite Imagery
Mapping
Whole-Earth Imaging Datasets

BRANDS/DIVISIONS/AFFILIATES:

Terra Bella
Dove
SkySat
Planet
Planet Explorer

CONTACTS: Note: Officers with more than one job title may be intentionally listed here more than once.

Will Marshall, CEO
Hilary Salazar, VP-Mktg.
Nate Dickerman, Chief Commercial Officer
Robbie Schingler, Chief Strategy Officer
Brian Hernacki, Sr. VP-Software

GROWTH PLANS/SPECIAL FEATURES:

Planet Labs, Inc. builds small satellites for Earth observation. The firm has raised significant investor financing. By acquiring Google's satellite business unit, Terra Bella, in exchange for stock in Planet in early-2017, Planet has an excellent base of very high-resolution imaging satellites to complement the medium resolution satellites that had been its main focus. Planet offers customers a diverse selection of 3-meter (nearly 10 feet), 5-meter (more than 16 feet) and 80-centimeter (approximately 2.6 feet) data products under a single roof. Its platform downloads and processes more than 5 terabytes (TB) of data daily, enabling customers to build and run analytics at scale. Users can monitor areas of interest, validate information on the ground and discover trends relevant to one's industry. By September 2018, nearly 300 Dove-branded satellites had been launched in orbit, half of which were active. Through these satellites, the firm is able to image the entirety of Earth's landmass every day. The firm's SkySat constellation is equipped with traditional imaging, near-infrared, stereo and video capabilities. Its Planet platform delivers coverage of the Earth's open water and maritime areas, enabling users to identify vessels and objects, detect maritime movement, validate automatic identification system (AIS) feeds and uncover activity in uncharted areas. Planet Explorer is an easy-to-use tool for viewing imagery and obtaining analysis directly through a browser. Markets primarily served by the firm include agriculture, civil government, defense, intelligence, education, research, energy, infrastructure, emergency response, finance/business intelligence, forestry, insurance and mapping. Based in San Francisco, Planet Labs has office locations in California, Washington, and Washington DC, in the U.S., as well as in Germany and Canada. In December 2018, Planet Labs agreed to acquire geospatial software specialist, Boundless Spatial, Inc.

FINANCIAL DATA: Note: Data for latest year may not have been available at press time.

In U.S. $	2018	2017	2016	2015	2014	2013
Revenue						
R&D Expense						
Operating Income						
Operating Margin %						
SGA Expense						
Net Income						
Operating Cash Flow						
Capital Expenditure						
EBITDA						
Return on Assets %						
Return on Equity %						
Debt to Equity						

CONTACT INFORMATION:

Phone: 415-829-3313   Fax:
Toll-Free:
Address: 645 Harrison St., 4/Fl, San Francisco, CA 94107 United States

STOCK TICKER/OTHER:

Stock Ticker: Private   Exchange:
Employees: 460   Fiscal Year Ends:
Parent Company:

SALARIES/BONUSES:

Top Exec. Salary: $ Bonus: $
Second Exec. Salary: $ Bonus: $

OTHER THOUGHTS:

Estimated Female Officers or Directors:
Hot Spot for Advancement for Women/Minorities:

PointClickCare

NAIC Code: 511210D

www.pointclickcare.com

TYPES OF BUSINESS:

Computer Software, Healthcare & Biotechnology

BRANDS/DIVISIONS/AFFILIATES:

CONTACTS: *Note: Officers with more than one job title may be intentionally listed here more than once.*

Mike Wessinger, CEO
Dave Wessinger, COO
Paul Rybecky, CFO
Sarah Bettencourt, Exec. VP-Human Resources

GROWTH PLANS/SPECIAL FEATURES:

PointClickCare provides a cloud-based platform that supports a large network of senior care providers in the long-term and post-acute care (LTPAC) market. The company's technology connects providers across the LTPAC continuum, enabling person-centered care, with a deep emphasis on quality and outcomes. PointClickCare's software provides a coordinated, collaborative approach to senior care, and adheres to regulatory and compliance guidelines which helps providers with payer changes for faster reimbursement. Products offered by the firm include a core electronic health record (EHR) platform, care delivery management, quality and compliance, financial management, business intelligence, marketing, services and support, a pulse customer community, partner ecosystem and health data exchange. Industry solutions include skilled nursing, senior living, home care and continuing care retirement communities (CCRC). Solutions by role include administrator, clinical, business/office manager, owner/CEO, IT, wellness director and dietitian. Solutions for industry challenges include readmission management, reimbursement management, revenue cycle management, errors and omission tracking, occupancy rate management, quality and compliance management, interoperability and multi-dimensional scaling (MDS) analytics and management. PointClickCare is headquartered in Ontario, Canada, with an international office in Minnesota, USA.

FINANCIAL DATA: *Note: Data for latest year may not have been available at press time.*

In U.S. $	2018	2017	2016	2015	2014	2013
Revenue		159,319,000	141,000,000	125,382,000	102,210,000	82,133,000
R&D Expense						
Operating Income						
Operating Margin %						
SGA Expense						
Net Income				-3,072,000	-10,990,000	-3,286,000
Operating Cash Flow						
Capital Expenditure						
EBITDA						
Return on Assets %						
Return on Equity %						
Debt to Equity						

CONTACT INFORMATION:

Phone: 905-858-8885   Fax: 905-858-2248
Toll-Free: 800-277-5889
Address: 5570 Explorer Dr., Mississauga, ON L4W 0C4 Canada

STOCK TICKER/OTHER:

Stock Ticker: Private   Exchange:
Employees: 1,450   Fiscal Year Ends: 10/31
Parent Company:

SALARIES/BONUSES:

Top Exec. Salary: $ Bonus: $
Second Exec. Salary: $ Bonus: $

OTHER THOUGHTS:

Estimated Female Officers or Directors:
Hot Spot for Advancement for Women/Minorities:

Poshmark Inc

poshmark.com

NAIC Code: 454111

TYPES OF BUSINESS:

Electronic Shopping
Online Secondhand Clothing Store

BRANDS/DIVISIONS/AFFILIATES:

Posh Parties

CONTACTS: Note: Officers with more than one job title may be intentionally listed here more than once.

Manish Chandra, CEO
Gautam Golwala, CTO

GROWTH PLANS/SPECIAL FEATURES:

Poshmark, Inc. is an eCommerce fashion site where people buy, sell and/or share their personal style. The site has more than 2 million seller stylists, approximately 5,000 brands and millions of shoppers. Popular brands on the website or app include Nike, Michael Kors, Louis Vuitton, lululemon athletica, PINK Victoria's Secret, Coach and Chanel. Shopping categories include apparel for women/men/kids, handbags, shoes, jewelry, accessories, makeup and dresses. How Poshmark works: it connects people who like particular styles with the selling stylists, and enables them to browse and shop what they have for sale. For people who have items they'd like to sell, they take a picture of each item with a smartphone, fill in a description, set a price and list them on Poshmark. Items can be listed in less than 60 seconds. Posh Parties are virtual buying and selling events that happen in the Poshmark app, and are advertised via categories along with the times the selling events will take place. Users can browse, buy and list across a wide variety of themes and brands during Posh Parties. For sellers, when a sale is made, Poshmark provides a pre-paid, pre-addressed label ready to be put on a box/package and either placed at a USPS mailbox or have it picked up for free at the seller's home address. The seller's personal information and payment transaction is protected by Poshmark. Investors of Poshmark include Mayfield, Menlo, GGV Capital, Inventus Capital Partners, Uncork Capital, Union Grove Venture Partners, JF She Co. Inc., SV Angel, Ashton Kutcher, Guy Oseary and Rachel Zoe.

FINANCIAL DATA: Note: Data for latest year may not have been available at press time.

In U.S. $	2018	2017	2016	2015	2014	2013
Revenue						
R&D Expense						
Operating Income						
Operating Margin %						
SGA Expense						
Net Income						
Operating Cash Flow						
Capital Expenditure						
EBITDA						
Return on Assets %						
Return on Equity %						
Debt to Equity						

CONTACT INFORMATION:

Phone: 650-262-4771   Fax:
Toll-Free:
Address: 101 Redwood Shores Pkwy., 3/Fl, Redwood City, CA 94065 United States

STOCK TICKER/OTHER:

Stock Ticker: Private   Exchange:
Employees: Fiscal Year Ends:
Parent Company:

SALARIES/BONUSES:

Top Exec. Salary: $ Bonus: $
Second Exec. Salary: $ Bonus: $

OTHER THOUGHTS:

Estimated Female Officers or Directors:
Hot Spot for Advancement for Women/Minorities:

Procore Technologies Inc   www.procore.com

NAIC Code: 511210N

TYPES OF BUSINESS:

Computer Software, Product Lifecycle, Engineering, Design & CAD

BRANDS/DIVISIONS/AFFILIATES:

Procore
BIManywhere

CONTACTS: *Note: Officers with more than one job title may be intentionally listed here more than once.*

Tooey Courtemanche, CEO
Steve Zahm, Pres.
Rusty Reed, CFO
Dennis Lyandres, Exec. VP-Sales
Michelle Greer, VP-Human Resources
Sam Crigman, CTO

GROWTH PLANS/SPECIAL FEATURES:

Procore Technologies, Inc. provides cloud-based construction management software. Procore software is built on three fundamentals: listen to the problems customers have, develop easy-to-use solutions and ensure clients that they can use the software solutions immediately. The Procore software helps firms increase project efficiency and accountability by streamlining and mobilizing project communications and documentation. This real-time data minimizes risks and delays. The Procore suite of tools enable users worldwide to manage all types of construction projects, including plants, office buildings, apartment complexes, university facilities, retail centers and more. The Procore platform is divided into four categories: drawing and documents, field and quality, financial and technology. Drawing and docs include document management, drawing management, email tracking meeting minutes, photos, procure drive, RFIs, specifications, submittals and transmittals. Field and quality includes daily log, dashboard, directory, inspections, observations, punch list and scheduling. Financial includes accounting integrations, bidding, budgeting and forecasting, change management, contract management, cost management and timecard. Technology includes insights and connection. Industries served by the company include contractors, including global, regional, local and specialty; owners, including education, government, healthcare and multi-family; and professionals, including architects, engineers and construction managers. Solutions offered include connecting on the field and in the office, managing drawings and specs, collaborating anytime/anywhere and seamless integration/connection within all of the customer's technology. Procore is based in Carpinteria, California, with an international office in Sydney, Australia. During 2018, Procure acquired BIManywhere, a visual business information modeling (BIM) collaboration platform for construction and facilities management.

Procure offers its employees medical, dental and vision coverage; 401(k); and other programs.

FINANCIAL DATA: *Note: Data for latest year may not have been available at press time.*

In U.S. $	2018	2017	2016	2015	2014	2013
Revenue		60,000,000	55,000,000			
R&D Expense						
Operating Income						
Operating Margin %						
SGA Expense						
Net Income						
Operating Cash Flow						
Capital Expenditure						
EBITDA						
Return on Assets %						
Return on Equity %						
Debt to Equity						

CONTACT INFORMATION:

Phone: 866-477-6267   Fax: 866-281-2906
Toll-Free:
Address: 6309 Carpinteria Ave., Carpinteria, CA 93013 United States

STOCK TICKER/OTHER:

Stock Ticker: Private   Exchange:
Employees: 700   Fiscal Year Ends:
Parent Company:

SALARIES/BONUSES:

Top Exec. Salary: $ Bonus: $
Second Exec. Salary: $ Bonus: $

OTHER THOUGHTS:

Estimated Female Officers or Directors:
Hot Spot for Advancement for Women/Minorities:

Sales, profits and employees may be estimates. Financial information, benefits and other data can change quickly and may vary from those stated here.

Progress Software Corporation

web.progress.com

NAIC Code: 511210I

TYPES OF BUSINESS:

Software, Application Development & Integration
Consulting & Technical Support Services
Data Connectivity Products
Data Management Software

BRANDS/DIVISIONS/AFFILIATES:

Progress OpenEdge
Progress DataDirect Connect
Progress DataDirect Hybrid Data Pipeline
Modulus
Telerik Dev Tools
Telerik Dev Cloud
Telerik ALM

CONTACTS: Note: Officers with more than one job title may be intentionally listed here more than once.

Paul Jalbert, Chief Accounting Officer
Tony Murphy, Chief Information Officer
Loren Jarrett, Chief Marketing Officer
Dmitri Tcherevik, Chief Technology Officer
Michael Mark, Director Emeritus
John Egan, Director
Faris Sweis, General Manager, Divisional
Dimitre Taslakov, Other Executive Officer
Stephen Faberman, Other Executive Officer
Yogesh Gupta, President
Gary Quinn, Senior VP, Divisional
John Ainsworth, Senior VP, Divisional

GROWTH PLANS/SPECIAL FEATURES:

Progress Software Corporation develops, markets and distributes application infrastructure software for the development, deployment, integration and management of business applications software. The company's products provide enterprise integration, data interoperability and application development, including software-as-a-service (SaaS) enablement and delivery in the cloud. Solutions are used across a variety of industries. Products are generally sold as perpetual licenses, but certain products and business activities also use term or subscription licensing models. Over half of the company's worldwide license revenue originates from relationships with indirect channel partners, principally application partners and original equipment manufacturers (OEMs). The company offers several product lines. Progress OpenEdge is a complete development platform to build dynamic, business process-enabled applications for secure deployment across any platform, any mobile device and any cloud. Progress DataDirect Connect products provide data connectivity components that use industry-standard interfaces to connect applications running on various platforms. Progress DataDirect Hybrid Data Pipeline, a data access service that provides simple, secure access to organizations' cloud and on-premises data sources for hybrid cloud applications. This includes customer relations management, data management platforms or hosted analytics. Modulus is a control platform for running Node.js applications. Telerik Dev Tools is a cross-platform, user experience design, quality assurance, debugging and reporting suite for next generation web, mobile, desktop and HTML5 applications. Telerik Dev Cloud is a cloud-based application, design, deployment, hosting and testing suite featuring hybrid application development environment, backend as a service, analytics and mobile testing. Telerik ALM is an application lifecycle management suite for testing web, mobile and desktop applications that covers the process from idea to deployment. Progress Software Corporation has global headquarters in the U.S. and Europe.

FINANCIAL DATA: Note: Data for latest year may not have been available at press time.

In U.S. $	2018	2017	2016	2015	2014	2013
Revenue		397,572,000	405,341,000	377,554,000	332,533,000	333,996,000
R&D Expense		76,988,000	88,587,000	86,924,000	58,965,000	57,336,000
Operating Income		94,282,000	70,274,000	31,982,000	88,868,000	78,927,000
Operating Margin %		23.71%	17.33%	8.47%	26.72%	23.63%
SGA Expense		144,104,000	168,033,000	182,161,000	149,788,000	161,991,000
Net Income		37,417,000	-55,726,000	-8,801,000	49,458,000	74,907,000
Operating Cash Flow		105,686,000	102,845,000	104,540,000	107,694,000	4,580,000
Capital Expenditure		3,377,000	5,786,000	7,184,000	7,985,000	4,226,000
EBITDA		113,114,000	8,219,000	57,822,000	104,164,000	93,362,000
Return on Assets %		5.07%	-6.82%	-1.11%	7.14%	9.55%
Return on Equity %		9.56%	-11.99%	-1.65%	9.35%	13.00%
Debt to Equity		0.30	0.29	0.25		

CONTACT INFORMATION:

Phone: 781 280-4000   Fax: 781 280-4095
Toll-Free: 800-477-6473
Address: 14 Oak Park, Bedford, MA 01730 United States

SALARIES/BONUSES:

Top Exec. Salary: $575,000   Bonus: $
Second Exec. Salary: Bonus: $150,000
$283,462

STOCK TICKER/OTHER:

Stock Ticker: PRGS   Exchange: NAS
Employees: 1,912   Fiscal Year Ends: 11/30
Parent Company:

OTHER THOUGHTS:

Estimated Female Officers or Directors: 2
Hot Spot for Advancement for Women/Minorities: Y

ProQuest LLC

NAIC Code: 519130

www.proquest.com

TYPES OF BUSINESS:

Online Database of News and Information
Dissertation Publishing
Streaming Videos
eBook Platforms
Content Discovery Systems
Library Tools
Primary Research Collections
News Collections

BRANDS/DIVISIONS/AFFILIATES:

360 Link
iFound
OASIS
Ex Libris
PsycEXTRA
ProQuest Dialog
Alexander Street Press
Intota

CONTACTS: Note: Officers with more than one job title may be intentionally listed here more than once.

Matti Shem-Tov, CEO
Robert VanHees, CFO, Sr. VP
James Holmes, CMO
Kevin A. Norris, Chief People Officer
Roger Valade, CTO
Kevin A. Norris, General Counsel
Tim Wahlberg, Sr. VP
Simon Beale, Sr. VP
Kevin Sayar, Sr. VP
Rafael Sidi, Sr. VP
Andy Snyder, Chmn.

GROWTH PLANS/SPECIAL FEATURES:

ProQuest, LLC, a unit of Cambridge Information Group, is primarily a publisher of electronic research databases and related services, including deep archives of news and other types of information. The company's services are focused on subscriptions to ProQuest's vast databases, utilized by the world's top libraries, institutions of higher learning, research organizations and government agencies. Its management solutions include iFound integrated out-of-print and hard-to-find service that allows libraries to search and purchase second-hand books via the company's web-based search system, OASIS. Data services include the Bookwire App, which allows users to evaluate, order and purchase books via smartphones; and PsycEXTRA, a database of book reviews, bibliographic records and lay audience literature in relation to the field of psychology. Research tools such as ProQuest Research Companion, its flagship information literacy product, helps students research effectively and supports educators as they teach core information literacy principles of finding, evaluating and using information. The databases service includes access to scholarly journals, newspapers, reports, working papers and datasets, as well as digitized historical primary sources. Ebook platforms enable libraries and other clients to access hundreds of thousands of books online. News and newspapers provides access to approximately 5,000 journals, magazines and newspapers, as well as information by ProQuest Dialog and others for global news on trading. Primary sources offer access into The British Library and the U.S. Library of Congress for retrieval of historical documents. University student dissertation and theses dissemination and ordering services archive more than 90,000 new graduate works every year. The company also offers data on microfilm and provides online access to Safari, a collection of O'Reilly technical books.

FINANCIAL DATA: Note: Data for latest year may not have been available at press time.

In U.S. $	2018	2017	2016	2015	2014	2013
Revenue	590,000,000	572,000,000	560,000,000	550,000,000		
R&D Expense						
Operating Income						
Operating Margin %						
SGA Expense						
Net Income						
Operating Cash Flow						
Capital Expenditure						
EBITDA						
Return on Assets %						
Return on Equity %						
Debt to Equity						

CONTACT INFORMATION:

Phone: 734-761-4700   Fax:
Toll-Free: 800-521-0600
Address: 789 E. Eisenhower Pkwy, Ann Arbor, MI 48106-1346 United States

SALARIES/BONUSES:

Top Exec. Salary: $ Bonus: $
Second Exec. Salary: $ Bonus: $

STOCK TICKER/OTHER:

Stock Ticker: Private   Exchange:
Employees: 2,450   Fiscal Year Ends:
Parent Company: Cambridge Information Group Inc (CIG)

OTHER THOUGHTS:

Estimated Female Officers or Directors: 1
Hot Spot for Advancement for Women/Minorities:

PSI Capital Inc

www.psi-capital.com/#about

NAIC Code: 454111

TYPES OF BUSINESS:

Online Retail-Music Downloads
Music Portal
Music Merchandise
Digital Rights Digital Rights Management

BRANDS/DIVISIONS/AFFILIATES:

ARTISTdirect
ARTISTdirect Opportunity Fund
Ticket Fairy (The)
Venga
Rubicon Entertainment
Drama Club
World Armwrestling League

CONTACTS: Note: Officers with more than one job title may be intentionally listed here more than once.

James Graf, CEO
Augustine Wong, Pres.
Rene Rousselet, Principal Acct. Officer
Frederick W. Field, CEO-Artistdirect Records LLC
Laura Laytham, Sr. VP

GROWTH PLANS/SPECIAL FEATURES:

PSI Capital, Inc. owns and operates ARTISTdirect, an online platform for the music industry. The firm's ArtistDirect.com website offers multimedia music content, including news, artists and videos. News categories include the latest music, live show reviews and specific music by genre. Specific information about bands and artists are available, as well as music videos. Genres include, but are not limited to, pop, hip hop, R&B, soul, rock, country, hard rock, alternative rock, indie rock, electronica, punk, jazz, Latin, blues, new age and gospel. The Singer/Songwriter category highlights an ARTIST of the week, offers exclusive interviews and much more. ArtistDirectInterviews.com offers exclusive interviews with established and emerging artists from all over the world. ARTISTdirect offers free downloads as well as eCommerce options, and is available on web and mobile application across any device. ARTISTdirect serves as the catalyst for the $25 million ARTISTdirect Opportunity Fund, which was established to invest in high-growth ventures operating in compelling niches in the broader music industry ecosystem. Targeted sectors are engaged in new technology and include music rights, licensing and royalty payments, as well as fan-related big data, ticketing and related commerce and logistics capabilities. Current investments include The Ticket Fairy, Venga, Rubicon Entertainment, Drama Club and the World Armwrestling League.

FINANCIAL DATA: Note: Data for latest year may not have been available at press time.

In U.S. $	2018	2017	2016	2015	2014	2013
Revenue						
R&D Expense						
Operating Income						
Operating Margin %						
SGA Expense						
Net Income						
Operating Cash Flow						
Capital Expenditure						
EBITDA						
Return on Assets %						
Return on Equity %						
Debt to Equity						

CONTACT INFORMATION:

Phone: 323-569-8698   Fax:
Toll-Free:
Address: 1450 2nd St., Santa Monica, CA 90401 United States

STOCK TICKER/OTHER:

Stock Ticker: Private   Exchange:
Employees: 68   Fiscal Year Ends: 12/31
Parent Company:

SALARIES/BONUSES:

Top Exec. Salary: $ Bonus: $
Second Exec. Salary: $ Bonus: $

OTHER THOUGHTS:

Estimated Female Officers or Directors: 1
Hot Spot for Advancement for Women/Minorities:

Qualtrics LLC

NAIC Code: 511210J

www.qualtrics.com

TYPES OF BUSINESS:

Computer Software, Data Base & File Management

BRANDS/DIVISIONS/AFFILIATES:

XM
Qualtrics iQ

CONTACTS: *Note: Officers with more than one job title may be intentionally listed here more than once.*

Ryan Smith, CEO
Zig Serafin, COO
David Faugno, CFO

GROWTH PLANS/SPECIAL FEATURES:

Qualtrics, LLC is a private software-as-a-service and research software company. Its experience management (XM) platform is a software that pairs flexibility with stability so that businesses can listen to customers or employees, analyze behavior and feedback, engage in conversations with them and strategize experience gaps. Every experience can be managed in real-time. XM applications include customer experience, employee experience, product experience and brand experience, all of which are assessed individually as well as corporately, comprising the research core. Therefore, XM is a single platform with infinite use cases. Behavior can be tracked across diverse segments, companies can benchmark versus competitors, complex academic research can be conducted, advertisements and products can be tested and more. Conversations, surveys and research opportunities can be distributed through any channel, anytime to anyone, including email surveys, text messaging surveys, mobile sites, websites, social media sites, quick response (QR) codes, interactive voice responses (IVRs), receipt surveys and offline surveys. Qualtrics iQ is a predictive intelligence engine for the masses, and consists of a set of advanced intelligent features built directly into the XM platform. It is powered by machine learning and artificial intelligence (AI) to make predictive intelligence and statistical analysis accessible. It analyzes text responses of consumers and employees, predicts actions that will better drive business impact, uncovers data and trends and automatically identifies at-risk customers. Over 9,000 enterprises worldwide, including Fortune 100 companies and top business schools, rely on Qualtrics' technology. Industries served by the company include education, automotive, travel, hospitality, financial services, government, business-to-business (B2B), media, airlines and retail. The firm has offices in the U.S., Europe, Asia and Australia.

FINANCIAL DATA: *Note: Data for latest year may not have been available at press time.*

In U.S. $	2018	2017	2016	2015	2014	2013
Revenue		141,000,000	135,000,000	110,000,000	75,000,000	48,100,000
R&D Expense						
Operating Income						
Operating Margin %						
SGA Expense						
Net Income						
Operating Cash Flow						
Capital Expenditure						
EBITDA						
Return on Assets %						
Return on Equity %						
Debt to Equity						

CONTACT INFORMATION:

Phone: 385-340-9194   Fax:
Toll-Free: 800-340-9194
Address: 400 W. Qualtrics Dr., Ste. 100, Provo, UT 84604 United States

STOCK TICKER/OTHER:

Stock Ticker: Private   Exchange:
Employees: 1,243   Fiscal Year Ends:
Parent Company:

SALARIES/BONUSES:

Top Exec. Salary: $ Bonus: $
Second Exec. Salary: $ Bonus: $

OTHER THOUGHTS:

Estimated Female Officers or Directors:
Hot Spot for Advancement for Women/Minorities:

Quotient Technology Inc

www.quotient.com

NAIC Code: 541810E

TYPES OF BUSINESS:
Online Coupon Advertising & Distribution

BRANDS/DIVISIONS/AFFILIATES:
Coupons.com
Quotient Retailer iQ
Coupons for Change
Shopmium
Ahalogy
Elevaate

CONTACTS: Note: Officers with more than one job title may be intentionally listed here more than once.
Mir Aamir, CEO
Chad Summe, COO
Steven Boal, Chmn.
Ron Fior, CFO
Jason Young, CMO
Connie Chen, General Counsel
Mir Aamir, President

GROWTH PLANS/SPECIAL FEATURES:
Quotient Technology, Inc. provides digital promotions and media solutions that are driven by consumer-shopping insights. The company connects consumer packaged goods (CPG) brands and retailers with shoppers by delivering digital promotions and media to shoppers through mobile, web and social channels for nearly 2,000 brands. Brands, as well as retailers and publishers in the grocery, drug, dollar, club and mass merchandise channels, use Quotient's Quotient Retailer iQ platform to engage shoppers when they are choosing what products to buy and where to shop. The firm's promotions and media solutions reach millions of shoppers every day via its flagship site and mobile app, Coupons.com; the Shopmium mobile app in Europe; its publishing network of thousands of registered partner sites; and the web and mobile properties of Quotient's CPG and retail partners. Quotient also offers solutions for non-profits, including fundraising solutions and other initiatives. Quotient is based in Mountain View, California, and has offices in Marina Del Rey, California, Cincinnati, Ohio, New York, London, Paris and Bangalore. In June 2018, the firm acquired Ahalogy, a marketing firm that focuses on social media for CPGs and retailers. In October of that year, Elevaate, which runs an in-market technology platform that drives ecommerce sales through sponsored search and products ads.

Quotient offers its employees medical, dental and vision insurance; life and AD&D insurance; long- and short-term disability; an employee assistance program; and a 401(k) plan.

FINANCIAL DATA: Note: Data for latest year may not have been available at press time.

In U.S. $	2018	2017	2016	2015	2014	2013
Revenue		322,115,000	275,190,000	237,309,000	221,761,000	167,892,000
R&D Expense		50,009,000	50,503,000	48,367,000	49,583,000	40,102,000
Operating Income		-9,603,000	-26,183,000	-30,548,000	-26,265,000	-10,315,000
Operating Margin %		-2.98%	-9.51%	-12.87%	-11.84%	-6.14%
SGA Expense		140,957,000	136,000,000	127,287,000	112,257,000	86,025,000
Net Income		-15,077,000	-19,479,000	-26,730,000	-23,444,000	-11,249,000
Operating Cash Flow		48,457,000	21,815,000	9,231,000	11,458,000	-14,158,000
Capital Expenditure		6,475,000	6,387,000	13,806,000	9,691,000	14,485,000
EBITDA		3,650,000	3,532,000	-10,501,000	-5,859,000	-3,437,000
Return on Assets %		-3.04%	-5.69%	-8.18%	-10.06%	-8.45%
Return on Equity %		-4.24%	-6.74%	-9.85%	-13.59%	
Debt to Equity		0.36				

CONTACT INFORMATION:
Phone: 650-605-4600 Fax: 650-605-4700
Toll-Free:
Address: 400 Logue Ave., Mountain View, CA 94043 United States

STOCK TICKER/OTHER:
Stock Ticker: QUOT Exchange: NYS
Employees: 662 Fiscal Year Ends:
Parent Company:

SALARIES/BONUSES:
Top Exec. Salary: $494,548 Bonus: $
Second Exec. Salary: $465,987 Bonus: $

OTHER THOUGHTS:
Estimated Female Officers or Directors: 1
Hot Spot for Advancement for Women/Minorities:

Qurate Retail Inc

www.qurateretailgroup.com

NAIC Code: 454111

TYPES OF BUSINESS:

Online and Internet Businesses
e-Commerce

BRANDS/DIVISIONS/AFFILIATES:

QVC Inc
Zulily LLC
HSN Inc
HSN
Cornerstone
Liberty Interactive Corporation

CONTACTS: Note: Officers with more than one job title may be intentionally listed here more than once.

Michael George, CEO
Mark Carleton, CFO
Gregory Maffei, Chairman of the Board
Richard Baer, Other Executive Officer
Albert Rosenthaler, Other Executive Officer

GROWTH PLANS/SPECIAL FEATURES:

Qurate Retail, Inc. (formerly Liberty Interactive Corporation) is primarily engaged in selling consumer products through video and eCommerce channels throughout North America, Europe and Asia. The firm's wholly-owned subsidiaries include: QVC, Inc.; Zulily LLC; and HSN, Inc., along with its catalog retail business called Cornerstone. QVC serves 13 million customers in the U.S. alone, with 93% of sales deriving from repeat/reactivate customers. Existing customers usually order 25 items per year, on average. Internationally, its video commerce, eCommerce (website) and social commerce channels earned $8.8 billion in 2017 revenue, and reached 370 million homes worldwide, including the U.S., the U.K., Europe and Asia. QVC has 14 television networks, more than 220 active social pages, and more than 1 billion visit its websites annually. Zulily is an American eCommerce company based in Washington. Through its website and mobile app, consumers can shop new sales daily beginning at 6am Pacific Time, which feature prices of up to 70% off regular prices. How Zulily works is once sales have ended, the firm places one large order to the brands presented that day. The brands ship the items to Zulily in about 8-10 days, and then Zulily ships them individually from its warehouse to its consumers. This process keeps prices low and selections fresh. HSN stands for Home Shopping Network, and is an American broadcast, basic cable and satellite television network based in Florida. HSN broadcasts reach approximately 90 million households via live programming 364 days per year, as well as through its website HSN.com. Mobile apps are offered through iPad, iPhone and Android devices. In March 2018, Liberty Interactive Corporation reorganized its business, reattributing certain assets and liabilities to QVC and selling others, and subsequently changed its corporate name to Qurate Retail, Inc.

FINANCIAL DATA: Note: Data for latest year may not have been available at press time.

In U.S. $	2018	2017	2016	2015	2014	2013
Revenue		10,381,000,000	10,219,000,000	9,169,000,000	10,028,000,000	10,307,000,000
R&D Expense						
Operating Income		1,135,000,000	1,011,000,000	1,170,000,000	1,213,000,000	1,164,000,000
Operating Margin %		10.93%	9.89%	12.76%	12.09%	11.29%
SGA Expense		1,088,000,000	1,063,000,000	875,000,000	940,000,000	1,033,000,000
Net Income		1,208,000,000	473,000,000	640,000,000	520,000,000	438,000,000
Operating Cash Flow		1,222,000,000	1,273,000,000	981,000,000	1,204,000,000	972,000,000
Capital Expenditure		201,000,000	206,000,000	218,000,000	226,000,000	295,000,000
EBITDA		2,265,000,000	1,947,000,000	1,918,000,000	1,835,000,000	1,745,000,000
Return on Assets %		7.64%	3.20%	4.54%	3.73%	2.92%
Return on Equity %		20.68%	9.40%	13.50%	9.75%	6.54%
Debt to Equity		0.98	1.30	1.18	1.36	0.79

CONTACT INFORMATION:

Phone: 720 875-5300   Fax:
Toll-Free:
Address: 12300 Liberty Blvd, Englewood, CO 80112 United States

STOCK TICKER/OTHER:

Stock Ticker: QRTEA   Exchange: NAS
Employees: 21,080   Fiscal Year Ends: 12/31
Parent Company:

SALARIES/BONUSES:

Top Exec. Salary: $1,250,000   Bonus: $
Second Exec. Salary: Bonus: $
$1,059,227

OTHER THOUGHTS:

Estimated Female Officers or Directors: 1
Hot Spot for Advancement for Women/Minorities:

Rackspace Hosting Inc

www.rackspace.com

NAIC Code: 517110

TYPES OF BUSINESS:

Web Hosting Services
Data Centers
Cloud Computing Services
Server Farms

BRANDS/DIVISIONS/AFFILIATES:

Apollo Global Management LLC
RelationEdge

CONTACTS: *Note: Officers with more than one job title may be intentionally listed here more than once.*

Joseph Eazor, CEO
David Meredith, COO
Louis Alterman, CFO
Mark Bunting, CMO
Laura Sue D'Annunzio, Chief People Officer

GROWTH PLANS/SPECIAL FEATURES:

Rackspace Hosting, Inc. provides managed cloud services in the business information technology (IT) market worldwide. The firm actively offers six service categories: managed hosting, managed cloud, colocation, application services, professional services and security and compliance. It delivers advice and integrated managed services across public and private clouds, managed hosting and enterprise applications. The company partners with leading technology platform providers, including VMware, Alibaba Cloud, Amazon Web Services, Google Cloud Platform, Microsoft, OpenStack, Pivotal Cloud Foundry, Oracle and SAP. Rackspace's solutions include application management, business intelligence, database management, eCommerce hosting, email hosting, enterprise resource planning (ERP), productivity and collaboration, web content management, website hosting and exiting the data center. Industries served by the firm include automotive, business services, education, energy, financial services, government, healthcare, manufacturing and retail. Rackspace is owned by private equity firm, Apollo Global Management, LLC. Based in Texas, the company serves approximately 150,000 business customers, including most of the Fortune 100, from data centers on five continents. During 2018, Rackspace acquired RelationEdge, a full-service Salesforce platinum consulting partner and digital agency.

The firm offers employees medical, dental and vision insurance; a 401(k) plan; profit sharing; employee training; and an onsite fitness facility.

FINANCIAL DATA: *Note: Data for latest year may not have been available at press time.*

In U.S. $	2018	2017	2016	2015	2014	2013
Revenue		2,200,000,000	2,081,000,000	2,001,299,968	1,794,356,992	1,534,786,048
R&D Expense						
Operating Income						
Operating Margin %						
SGA Expense						
Net Income			135,200,000	126,200,000	110,553,000	86,737,000
Operating Cash Flow						
Capital Expenditure						
EBITDA						
Return on Assets %						
Return on Equity %						
Debt to Equity						

CONTACT INFORMATION:

Phone: 210 312-4000   Fax: 210 312-4300
Toll-Free: 800-961-2888
Address: 1 Fanatical Pl., City of Windcrest, San Antonio, TX 78218
United States

STOCK TICKER/OTHER:

Stock Ticker: Private   Exchange:
Employees: 6,200   Fiscal Year Ends: 12/31
Parent Company: Apollo Global Management LLC

SALARIES/BONUSES:

Top Exec. Salary: $ Bonus: $
Second Exec. Salary: $ Bonus: $

OTHER THOUGHTS:

Estimated Female Officers or Directors: 1
Hot Spot for Advancement for Women/Minorities:

Radware Ltd

NAIC Code: 511210B

www.radware.com

TYPES OF BUSINESS:

Computer Software, Network Management, System Testing & Storage
Internet Security Software
e-Commerce Software
Connectivity Software

BRANDS/DIVISIONS/AFFILIATES:

RAD Group
Application Delivery Controller
DefensePro
AppWall
DefenseFlow
Alteon D
LinkProof
FastView

CONTACTS: *Note: Officers with more than one job title may be intentionally listed here more than once.*

Roy Zisapel, CEO
Gabi Malka, COO
Doron Abramovitch, CFO
Anna Convery-Pelletier, CMO
David Aviv, CTO
Gadi Meroz, General Counsel
David Aviv, VP-Advanced Svcs.
Gilad Zlotkin, VP-Virtualization & Management
Terence Ying, VP-Asia Pacific
Yehuda Zisapel, Chmn.
Yoav Gazelle, VP-EMEA, Central & Latin America
Christina Aruza, VP-Corporate Mktg.

GROWTH PLANS/SPECIAL FEATURES:

Radware, Ltd. is a leader in integrated application delivery and cyber security products for virtual and cloud service providers. The company is one of several independent companies that operate under the RAD Group. Radware's solutions are categorized under two service offerings: application and network security, and application delivery. Its application network security solutions are designed to provide maximum threat coverage, accurate attack detection and shortest time to protection against numerous types of cyber-attacks that threaten the application infrastructure availability. It application delivery solutions are designed to ensure application service levels by improving the availability, performance and security of the application network infrastructure. This division's Application Delivery Controller (ADC) solutions include local and global server load balancing capabilities that integrate web performance optimization for application acceleration, application performance monitoring, multi-homing link load balancing and the web application firewall. This process enables payment card industry (PCI) compliance through mitigation of web application security threats and vulnerabilities, authentication gateway for single sign-on and user authentication, advanced denial of service protection (ADoS), bandwidth management and defense messaging signaling to Radware's attack mitigation solution. The company's solutions are available as fully-owned by the customer, or by subscription or by cloud-based services. Other key products include the DefensePro attack mitigation device, the AppWall web application firewall, the DefenseFlow cyber command and control application, the Alteon D line of next-gen application delivery controller/load balancer, the LinkProof next-gen multi-homing and enterprise gateway solution, and the FastView web performance optimization module, among others.

FINANCIAL DATA: *Note: Data for latest year may not have been available at press time.*

In U.S. $	2018	2017	2016	2015	2014	2013
Revenue		211,369,000	196,585,000	216,566,000	221,892,000	192,997,000
R&D Expense		59,003,000	51,732,000	49,987,000	44,081,000	40,983,000
Operating Income		-6,671,000	-12,749,000	17,999,000	25,079,000	17,569,000
Operating Margin %		-3.15%	-6.48%	8.31%	11.30%	9.10%
SGA Expense		126,321,000	121,907,000	110,380,000	113,000,000	97,710,000
Net Income		-7,493,000	-8,659,000	18,569,000	24,950,000	18,055,000
Operating Cash Flow		31,462,000	38,480,000	39,136,000	52,177,000	30,200,000
Capital Expenditure		7,210,000	9,404,000	13,774,000	10,857,000	8,712,000
EBITDA		4,561,000	3,480,000	35,847,000	33,181,000	30,430,000
Return on Assets %		-1.66%	-2.01%	4.24%	5.99%	4.83%
Return on Equity %		-2.43%	-2.79%	5.68%	7.94%	6.38%
Debt to Equity						

CONTACT INFORMATION:

Phone: 972 37668666   Fax: 972-3-7668982
Toll-Free:
Address: 22 Raoul Wallenberg St., Tel Aviv, 69710 Israel

STOCK TICKER/OTHER:

Stock Ticker: RDWR   Exchange: NAS
Employees: 979   Fiscal Year Ends: 12/31
Parent Company:

SALARIES/BONUSES:

Top Exec. Salary: $397,000   Bonus: $80,000
Second Exec. Salary: Bonus: $205,000
$263,000

OTHER THOUGHTS:

Estimated Female Officers or Directors: 3
Hot Spot for Advancement for Women/Minorities: Y

Sales, profits and employees may be estimates. Financial information, benefits and other data can change quickly and may vary from those stated here.

Rakuten Affiliate Network

www.linkshare.com

NAIC Code: 541810E

TYPES OF BUSINESS:

Affiliate Marketing Network
Market Research Services
Web Analytics Software
Commission Tracking Software

BRANDS/DIVISIONS/AFFILIATES:

Rakuten Inc
Rakuten Marketing

CONTACTS: *Note: Officers with more than one job title may be intentionally listed here more than once.*

Stuart Simms, CEO
Ken Dorward, CFO
Neal Richter, CTO
Reginald Rasch, General Counsel

GROWTH PLANS/SPECIAL FEATURES:

Rakuten Affiliate Network operates Rakuten Marketing, which offers integrated online marketing solutions that enable marketers to utilize digital marketing strategies. Integrated marketing strategies enhance performance across channels, and provide consumer journey and data insights in an effort to drive performance. Affiliate marketing strategies promote discovery and engage shoppers across the entire consumer journey. It connects advertisers with publishers to reach new audiences and influence repeat purchases. During 2018, Rakuten Marketing facilitated more than 110 million orders worldwide. The firm's data-driven display advertising strategies enable marketers to accurately identify consumers in the areas they spend their time and money, and does so across screens, social media and traditional publishers. Rakuten's team of experts engage in developing specific digital marketing strategies for its clients so they can receive incremental revenue. To Rakuten, as clients increase their customer footprint, sales will increase as well. Last, Rakuten's paid search advertising strategy reaches consumers across the funnel. Customers become engaged via product listing ads as they shop across platforms. Rakuten Marketing's advanced bidding algorithms and unique data optimize this marketing strategy and save costs. Headquartered in San Mateo, California, Rakuten Affiliate Network has offices throughout the U.S., as well as in Australia, Brazil, France, Germany, Japan, Singapore and the U.K. Rakuten Affiliate Network is a subsidiary of Rakuten, Inc.

The company offers employees medical, dental and vision coverage; flex health care accounts; short-term and long-term disability; tuition reimbursement; and a 401(k) plan. Benefits packages vary by location.

FINANCIAL DATA: *Note: Data for latest year may not have been available at press time.*

In U.S. $	2018	2017	2016	2015	2014	2013
Revenue						
R&D Expense						
Operating Income						
Operating Margin %						
SGA Expense						
Net Income						
Operating Cash Flow						
Capital Expenditure						
EBITDA						
Return on Assets %						
Return on Equity %						
Debt to Equity						

CONTACT INFORMATION:

Phone: 646-943-8200   Fax: 646-943-8204
Toll-Free: 800-875-5465
Address: 215 Park Ave. S., 2/Fl, New York, NY 10003 United States

STOCK TICKER/OTHER:

Stock Ticker: Subsidiary   Exchange:
Employees: 728   Fiscal Year Ends: 06/30
Parent Company: Rakuten Inc

SALARIES/BONUSES:

Top Exec. Salary: $ Bonus: $
Second Exec. Salary: $ Bonus: $

OTHER THOUGHTS:

Estimated Female Officers or Directors: 2
Hot Spot for Advancement for Women/Minorities:

Rakuten Commerce LLC

www.rakuten.com

NAIC Code: 454111

TYPES OF BUSINESS:

Consumer Electronics, Online Retail
Book, Game, DVD, VHS & Music Sales
Software & Accessories Sales
Music Downloads
Social Networking
Jewelry and Watches
Household Items

BRANDS/DIVISIONS/AFFILIATES:

Rakuten Inc
Rakuten.com
Rakuten Super Points

CONTACTS: *Note: Officers with more than one job title may be intentionally listed here more than once.*

Hiroshi Mikitani, CEO
Hiroshi Mikitani, Chmn. & CEO-Rakuten, Inc.
Fumio Kobayashi, Chief Marketplace Officer

GROWTH PLANS/SPECIAL FEATURES:

Rakuten Commerce, LLC does business as Rakuten.com, an online retailer. The firm offers over 18 million products, both directly and through third-party retailers that utilize the eCommerce marketplace. The wide variety of items sold include: computer hardware, accessories and software; electronics; jewelry and fragrances; wine; sporting goods; apparel; cellular products; books; bags; games and toys; and DVDs, CDs and music downloads. Rakuten's computer products include computers, printers, monitors, modems and peripherals as well as software from manufacturers including Microsoft, Norton and Adobe. The firm also offers hardback, paperback and audio book titles, enabling customers to read the first chapter of many books, submit book reviews and read professional/customer reviews. Rakuten's rewards program, Rakuten Super Points, enables users to earn points every time they purchase from its site. The points can be used to pay for a current purchase or be saved for future purchases. In addition to its U.S. site, Rakuten Commerce maintains eCommerce sites for Japan, France, Germany, the U.K. Austria, Brazil, Indonesia, Malaysia, Spain, Taiwan, Singapore and Thailand. Rakuten is a wholly-owned subsidiary of Rakuten, Inc. During 2018, Rakuten joined with Ebates to offer up to 40% cash back at more than 2,500 stores, including Macy's, Nike, Amazon and Walmart.

FINANCIAL DATA: *Note: Data for latest year may not have been available at press time.*

In U.S. $	2018	2017	2016	2015	2014	2013
Revenue						
R&D Expense						
Operating Income						
Operating Margin %						
SGA Expense						
Net Income						
Operating Cash Flow						
Capital Expenditure						
EBITDA						
Return on Assets %						
Return on Equity %						
Debt to Equity						

CONTACT INFORMATION:

Phone: 949-389-2000   Fax:
Toll-Free:
Address: 85 Enterprise, Ste. 100, Aliso Viejo, CA 92656 United States

STOCK TICKER/OTHER:

Stock Ticker: Subsidiary
Employees: 115
Parent Company: Rakuten Inc

Exchange:
Fiscal Year Ends: 12/31

SALARIES/BONUSES:

Top Exec. Salary: $ Bonus: $
Second Exec. Salary: $ Bonus: $

OTHER THOUGHTS:

Estimated Female Officers or Directors: 1
Hot Spot for Advancement for Women/Minorities:

Rakuten Inc

www.rakuten.co.jp

NAIC Code: 454111

TYPES OF BUSINESS:

E-Commerce
Internet Marketing
Credit Cards
Financing
Internet Portal
Online Travel Reservations
Online Securities Trading
Telecommunications

BRANDS/DIVISIONS/AFFILIATES:

Rakuten Books
Rakuten Ichiba
Rakuten Travel
Rakuten Mobile
Rakuten Insurance
Rakuten Bank
Rakuten TV
Rakuten Drone

CONTACTS: *Note: Officers with more than one job title may be intentionally listed here more than once.*

Hiroshi Mikitani, CEO
Kentaro Hyakuno, COO
Kenji Hirose, CFO
Naho Kono, CMO
Masatada Kobayashi, Chief People Officer
Yasufumi Hirai, CIO
Atsushi Kunishige, Exec. VP
Masatada Kobayashi, Sr. Exec. Officer
Hiroaki Yasutake, Sr. Exec. Officer
Kazunori Takeda, Sr. Exec. Officer
Hiroshi Mikitani, Chmn.

GROWTH PLANS/SPECIAL FEATURES:

Rakuten, Inc. is a diversified Japanese internet services company with more than 70 businesses. The firm's operations are divided into five segments: commerce, communications & energy, FinTech, media & sports and investment and incubation. The commerce segment provides shopping, leisure and lifestyle services via eCommerce channels, including internet shopping, online travel reservations and eBooks. Other brands within this division include, but are not limited to: Rakuten Books, Rakuten Ichiba, Rakuten Travel, Rakuten GORA, Rakuten Pay, Rakuten Delivery, Rakuten Beauty, Rakuten Super Logistics, and Rakuten Digital Commerce. The communications & energy segment provides communications services such as mobile telecommunications and energy solutions. This division's companies include: Rakuten Mobile, a mobile virtual operator service; Rakuten Communications, a telecommunications provider; and Rakuten Energy, offering electricity and energy-related services. Other brands include Rakuten Viber, and Rakuten Aquafadas. The FinTech segment provides computer programs and other technology used to support or enable banking/financial services, including credit card and other payment services, loyalty points programs, securities trading and insurance. Brands within this division include Rakuten Card, Rakuten Bank, Rakuten Securities, Rakuten Edy, Rakuten Life Insurance, Rakuten Insurance, Rakuten General Insurance Co. Ltd., Rakuten Point Card and Rakuten Card. The media & sports segment provides digital content, including video distribution and eBooks, online media, sports media and related marketing solutions. Brands within this division include Rakuten TV, Rakuten InfoSeek, Rakuten Recipe, Rakuten Min-Shu, Rakuten Data Marketing, Rakuten Linkshare, Rakuten Eagles, Vissel Kobe, among many others. Last, the investment & incubation segment manages the domestic and overseas corporate capital investment business and leads the development and provision of new services. This division's businesses include Rakuten Capital, Rakuten Ragri, Rakuten Drone, Rakuten AirMap, Rakuten Super English, ReDucate and Rakuten Cho-Mini Baito.

FINANCIAL DATA: *Note: Data for latest year may not have been available at press time.*

In U.S. $	2018	2017	2016	2015	2014	2013
Revenue		8,760,704,000	7,252,857,000	6,618,757,000	5,552,139,000	4,810,107,000
R&D Expense						
Operating Income		1,410,016,000	958,518,800	1,232,042,000	986,911,900	837,080,700
Operating Margin %		11.32%	13.40%	15.77%	17.92%	18.93%
SGA Expense		7,768,904,000	6,285,229,000	5,574,734,000	4,556,981,000	3,899,284,000
Net Income		1,025,759,000	352,432,100	412,177,200	654,997,800	397,929,700
Operating Cash Flow		1,503,191,000	284,765,500	725,781,100	1,037,585,000	13,774,490
Capital Expenditure		728,127,700	509,999,300	503,190,800	340,809,600	300,812,500
EBITDA		1,914,394,000	1,369,036,000	1,604,204,000	1,266,483,000	1,079,048,000
Return on Assets %		2.05%	.86%	1.11%	2.04%	1.61%
Return on Equity %		16.19%	5.71%	8.20%	19.57%	15.41%
Debt to Equity						

CONTACT INFORMATION:

Phone: 8150-5581-6910   Fax:
Toll-Free:
Address: 1-14-1 Tamagawa, Setagaya-ku, Tokyo, 158-0094 Japan

STOCK TICKER/OTHER:

Stock Ticker: RKUNF   Exchange: PINX
Employees: 14,845   Fiscal Year Ends: 12/31
Parent Company:

SALARIES/BONUSES:

Top Exec. Salary: $ Bonus: $
Second Exec. Salary: $ Bonus: $

OTHER THOUGHTS:

Estimated Female Officers or Directors:
Hot Spot for Advancement for Women/Minorities:

REA Group Ltd

www.rea-group.com

NAIC Code: 519130

TYPES OF BUSINESS:
Online Real Estate

BRANDS/DIVISIONS/AFFILIATES:
realestate.com.au
realcommercial.com.au
Flatmates.com.au
Spacely
iproperty.com.my
squarefoot.com.hk
Move Inc
PropTiger

GROWTH PLANS/SPECIAL FEATURES:
REA Group is a multinational digital advertising business specializing in property. The firm operates 20 brands across more than five countries and uses updated technology to deliver its products and services to both customers and consumers. REA Group's global footprint covers the continents of Australia, Asia and North America. In Australia, realestate.com.au is a residential property platform; realcommercial.com.au is a commercial property site; Flatmates.com.au is a share accommodation site; and Spacely is a short-term commercial and co-working property site. In Asia, iproperty.com.my is a property portal in Malaysia, rumah123.com in Indonesia, squarefoot.com.hk in Hong Kong, ThinkgOfLiving.com in Thailand, iproperty.com.sg in Singapore, and myfun.com in China. In the U.S., REA Group holds a significant share in Move, Inc., which operates realtor.com. In addition, REA Group holds a share in PropTiger in India, which operates housing.com and Makaan.

CONTACTS: Note: Officers with more than one job title may be intentionally listed here more than once.
Owen Wilson, CEO
Mary Lemonis, Chief People Officer
Hamish McLennan, Chmn.

FINANCIAL DATA: Note: Data for latest year may not have been available at press time.

In U.S. $	2018	2017	2016	2015	2014	2013
Revenue	607,704,100	470,262,800	441,254,800	366,370,100	306,494,100	235,731,800
R&D Expense						
Operating Income	290,625,000	236,242,600	207,070,700	177,091,700	139,956,600	99,152,250
Operating Margin %		50.23%	46.92%	48.33%	45.66%	42.06%
SGA Expense	220,660,700	186,909,600	184,893,200	153,426,000	132,781,500	110,590,600
Net Income	177,102,900	144,374,700	177,228,300	147,138,700	104,903,000	76,866,110
Operating Cash Flow						
Capital Expenditure	41,521,760	37,942,270	28,045,960	29,315,490	18,372,450	15,299,520
EBITDA	310,912,900	138,668,800	271,196,000	219,735,200	154,815,400	121,356,400
Return on Assets %		13.45%	23.49%	35.33%	32.78%	31.54%
Return on Equity %		27.12%	39.74%	43.50%	41.45%	38.85%
Debt to Equity		0.44	0.68			

CONTACT INFORMATION:
Phone: 61-3-9897-1121   Fax: 61-3-9897-1114
Toll-Free:
Address: 511 Church St., Richmond, VIC 3121 Australia

STOCK TICKER/OTHER:
Stock Ticker: RPGRY   Exchange: GREY
Employees: 1,423   Fiscal Year Ends: 06/30
Parent Company:

SALARIES/BONUSES:
Top Exec. Salary: $ Bonus: $
Second Exec. Salary: $ Bonus: $

OTHER THOUGHTS:
Estimated Female Officers or Directors:
Hot Spot for Advancement for Women/Minorities: Y

RealNetworks Inc

www.realnetworks.com

NAIC Code: 511210F

TYPES OF BUSINESS:

Computer Software, Multimedia, Graphics & Publishing
Computer Software-Streaming Audio & Video
Online Retail-Digital Media
Mobile Games
Mobile Music
Mobile Video

BRANDS/DIVISIONS/AFFILIATES:

RealPlayer
GameHouse
Zylom
Rhapsody International Inc
Napster

CONTACTS: Note: Officers with more than one job title may be intentionally listed here more than once.

Robert Glaser, CEO
Cary Baker, CFO
Michael Parham, General Counsel
Massimiliano Pellegrini, President

GROWTH PLANS/SPECIAL FEATURES:

RealNetworks, Inc. is a creator of digital media services and software. The company operates in three segments: consumer entertainment, mobile services and games. The consumer entertainment business consists of RealPlayer and related products and services. Nearly all this segments revenue is derived from legacy products and services related to the RealPlayer, and these revenues are primarily generated in the U.S. and Canada. The mobile services segment consists of digital media services to network service providers as software as a service (SaaS) offerings. Revenues from this segment are primarily in North America and Asia. Within the games business segment, the firm owns and operates a large casual game service, offering games via digital downloads, online subscription play, third-party portals, social networks and mobile devices. Casual games typically have simple graphics, rules and controls and are quick to learn; they include board, card, puzzle, word and hidden-object games. Games are primarily distributed in North America, Europe and Latin America through GameHouse and Zylom websites, as well as through websites owned or managed by third parties. This segment monetizes social and mobile games largely through sales of games licenses, advertising and microtransactions from mobile and social games. Additionally, the firm owns approximately 42% in Rhapsody International, Inc., which does business as Napster. Napster provides music products and services that enable consumers to have access to digital music content from a variety of devices.

FINANCIAL DATA: Note: Data for latest year may not have been available at press time.

In U.S. $	2018	2017	2016	2015	2014	2013
Revenue		78,718,000	120,468,000	125,296,000	156,212,000	206,196,000
R&D Expense		29,710,000	29,923,000	43,626,000	52,765,000	60,880,000
Operating Income		-18,105,000	-35,685,000	-63,908,000	-64,161,000	-53,518,000
Operating Margin %		-22.99%	-27.76%	-49.00%	-37.94%	-24.45%
SGA Expense		43,949,000	59,023,000	72,780,000	100,927,000	116,654,000
Net Income		-16,305,000	-36,550,000	-81,847,000	-71,815,000	-58,990,000
Operating Cash Flow		-21,350,000	-24,328,000	-68,982,000	-60,244,000	-49,879,000
Capital Expenditure		734,000	2,438,000	1,319,000	2,460,000	7,727,000
EBITDA		-15,169,000	-28,628,000	-53,498,000	-52,202,000	-34,770,000
Return on Assets %		-12.94%	-25.05%	-39.76%	-24.21%	-15.19%
Return on Equity %		-19.43%	-34.93%	-51.49%	-30.81%	-19.28%
Debt to Equity						

CONTACT INFORMATION:

Phone: 206 674-2700   Fax: 206 674-2699
Toll-Free:
Address: 1501 First Avenue South, Ste. 600, Seattle, WA 98134 United States

STOCK TICKER/OTHER:

Stock Ticker: RNWK   Exchange: NAS
Employees: 534   Fiscal Year Ends: 12/31
Parent Company:

SALARIES/BONUSES:

Top Exec. Salary: $450,000   Bonus: $
Second Exec. Salary: $400,000   Bonus: $

OTHER THOUGHTS:

Estimated Female Officers or Directors: 4
Hot Spot for Advancement for Women/Minorities: Y

Sales, profits and employees may be estimates. Financial information, benefits and other data can change quickly and may vary from those stated here.

RealPage Inc

www.realpage.com

NAIC Code: 511210H

TYPES OF BUSINESS:

Online Real Estate Management Services
Customer Service Centers

BRANDS/DIVISIONS/AFFILIATES:

ClickPay
RealPage Exchange

CONTACTS: *Note: Officers with more than one job title may be intentionally listed here more than once.*

Stephen Winn, CEO
William Hill, CFO
Ashley Chaffin Glover, Executive VP
William Chaney, Executive VP
Andrew Blount, Executive VP
David Monk, Executive VP

GROWTH PLANS/SPECIAL FEATURES:

RealPage, Inc. is a provider of on-demand software services for the rental housing industry. The company's products enable owners and managers of rental property to manage their marketing, pricing, screening, leasing, accounting, purchasing and other property operations. Its systems manage conventional, student, military, senior, commercial, mixed-use, vacation, urban and rural housing as well as tax credit-compliant housing. RealPage's products are cloud-based, with many available both online and for mobile devices. These products manage everything from marketing to pricing and other property operations, including property management, sales/marketing, applicant screening, revenue management, spend management, utility management, renters insurance, resident services and contact center. Supporting the firm's family of software-as-a-service (SaaS) products is its shared cloud services, including electronic payments, document management, decision support and learning. Platform-as-a-service (PaaS) is also offered through the RealPage Exchange, a toolkit of integration services for third-party application providers and infrastructure-as-a-service (IaaS), which reduces IT costs and improves integration performance and reliability to multi-family owners and operators. RealPage processes 600 billion transactions annually for nearly 12,500 property owners and managers. During 2018, RealPage acquired electronic payment platform, ClickPay, for $218 million; and agreed to acquire LeaseLabs as well as Rentlytics.

FINANCIAL DATA: *Note: Data for latest year may not have been available at press time.*

In U.S. $	2018	2017	2016	2015	2014	2013
Revenue		670,963,000	568,128,000	468,520,000	404,551,000	377,022,000
R&D Expense		89,452,000	60,800,000	54,935,000	50,871,000	47,594,000
Operating Income		30,010,000	31,994,000	9,186,000	-15,503,000	21,559,000
Operating Margin %		4.47%	5.63%	1.96%	-3.83%	5.71%
SGA Expense		271,711,000	206,365,000	183,910,000	172,230,000	142,083,000
Net Income		377,000	16,650,000	-9,218,000	-10,274,000	20,692,000
Operating Cash Flow		137,327,000	136,216,000	96,012,000	69,972,000	69,209,000
Capital Expenditure		49,752,000	75,241,000	33,384,000	37,322,000	33,879,000
EBITDA		98,399,000	86,828,000	55,077,000	25,803,000	53,304,000
Return on Assets %		.03%	2.35%	-1.54%	-1.91%	4.57%
Return on Equity %		.08%	4.68%	-2.81%	-3.19%	7.26%
Debt to Equity		1.26	0.30	0.12	0.06	

CONTACT INFORMATION:

Phone: 972 820-3000   Fax:
Toll-Free: 877-325-7243
Address: 2201 Lakeside Blvd., Richardson, TX 75082-4305 United States

STOCK TICKER/OTHER:

Stock Ticker: RP   Exchange: NAS
Employees: 4,400   Fiscal Year Ends: 12/31
Parent Company:

SALARIES/BONUSES:

Top Exec. Salary: $612,500   Bonus: $
Second Exec. Salary: Bonus: $
$420,833

OTHER THOUGHTS:

Estimated Female Officers or Directors: 6
Hot Spot for Advancement for Women/Minorities: Y

Red Hat Inc

www.redhat.com

NAIC Code: 511210I

TYPES OF BUSINESS:

Computer Software-Linux Operating Systems
Open-Source Software

BRANDS/DIVISIONS/AFFILIATES:

Red Hat Enterprise Linux
Red Hat JBoss Middleware
Red Hat Satellite
Red Hat Enterprise Linux
Red Hat Cloud
Red Had Mobile Application
Red Hat Storage

CONTACTS: Note: Officers with more than one job title may be intentionally listed here more than once.

James Whitehurst, CEO
Eric Shander, CFO
Narendra Gupta, Chairman of the Board
Michael Kelly, Chief Information Officer
Arun Oberoi, Executive VP, Divisional
Michael Cunningham, Executive VP
DeLisa Alexander, Executive VP
Paul Cormier, President, Divisional

GROWTH PLANS/SPECIAL FEATURES:

Red Hat, Inc. is a provider of open-source software solutions. The firm's solutions include its core enterprise operating system platform Red Hat Enterprise Linux, the enterprise middleware platform Red Hat JBoss Middleware Suite, virtual solutions, cloud storage and other Red Hat enterprise technologies. The company offers a choice of operating system platforms for servers, work stations and desktops that support multiple application areas, including the data center, edge-of-the-network applications, IT infrastructure, corporate desktop and technical/developer workstation. Red Hat JBoss Middleware delivers a suite of middleware products for service-oriented architectures, permitting web-enabled applications to run on open source and other platforms. The software provides an application infrastructure for building and deploying distributed applications that are accessible via the internet, corporate intranets, extranets and virtual private networks. Applications deployed on JBoss include online e-business, hotel and airline reservations, online banking, credit card processing, securities trading, healthcare systems, customer and partner portals, retail and point of sale systems (POS), telecommunications network infrastructure and grid-based systems. The integrated management service, Red Hat Satellite, permit Red Hat enterprise technologies to be updated and configured as well as the performance of these and other technologies to be monitored and managed in an automated fashion. Red Hat Cloud software enables customers to build and manage various cloud computing environments, including the Red Hat OpenStack platform, Red Hat Cloud infrastructure and more. The Red Hat Mobile Application platform enables customers to develop, integrate, deploy and manage mobile applications for the enterprise. Last, Red Hat Storage software enables firms to manage large, unstructured or semi-structured data at large scale via commodity hardware in hybrid cloud environments. In October 2018, Red Hat agreed to be acquired by IBM, a multinational information technology company, for $35 billion. The transaction is expected to close by then end of 2019.

FINANCIAL DATA: Note: Data for latest year may not have been available at press time.

In U.S. $	2018	2017	2016	2015	2014	2013
Revenue	2,920,461,000	2,411,803,000	2,052,230,000	1,789,489,000	1,534,615,000	1,328,817,000
R&D Expense	578,330,000	480,668,000	413,322,000	367,856,000	317,263,000	263,150,000
Operating Income	472,442,000	332,245,000	288,048,000	249,994,000	232,289,000	201,038,000
Operating Margin %	16.17	13.77%	14.03%	13.97%	15.13%	15.12%
SGA Expense	1,437,892,000	1,244,512,000	1,041,231,000	898,440,000	752,463,000	664,029,000
Net Income	258,803,000	253,703,000	199,365,000	180,201,000	178,292,000	150,204,000
Operating Cash Flow	923,138,000	783,717,000	716,092,000	622,795,000	540,580,000	465,297,000
Capital Expenditure	101,687,000	80,897,000	55,517,000	51,771,000	97,559,000	120,038,000
EBITDA	596,408,000	429,311,000	374,074,000	341,155,000	306,694,000	263,379,000
Return on Assets %	5.17%	5.83%	5.01%	5.21%	6.02%	5.66%
Return on Equity %	19.04%	19.65%	15.20%	12.69%	11.61%	10.29%
Debt to Equity	0.50	0.59	0.54	0.55		

CONTACT INFORMATION:

Phone: 919 754-3700   Fax: 919 754-3701
Toll-Free: 888-733-4281
Address: 100 East Davie St., Raleigh, NC 27601 United States

STOCK TICKER/OTHER:

Stock Ticker: RHT
Employees: 10,500
Parent Company:

Exchange: NYS
Fiscal Year Ends: 02/28

SALARIES/BONUSES:

Top Exec. Salary: $1,000,000   Bonus: $
Second Exec. Salary: Bonus: $
$700,000

OTHER THOUGHTS:

Estimated Female Officers or Directors: 3
Hot Spot for Advancement for Women/Minorities: Y

Reformation (The, LYMI Inc)

www.thereformation.com

NAIC Code: 454111

TYPES OF BUSINESS:

Electronic Shopping
Women's Clothing Stores

BRANDS/DIVISIONS/AFFILIATES:

Reformation (The)

CONTACTS: *Note: Officers with more than one job title may be intentionally listed here more than once.*

Yael Aflalo, CEO

GROWTH PLANS/SPECIAL FEATURES:

LYMI, Inc. does business as The Reformation and designs and manufactures clothes for women. The firm's fashion is designed and ready in about 30-to-40 days. Its main clothing range is fit on multiple women that are between 5'6" and 5'10", but The Reformation also has a petites collection for women under 5'2 as well as a collection for larger women, up to size 22. All pieces are made from sustainable materials, deadstock fabrics and repurposed vintage clothing. More than half of the company's garments are made with TENCEL, a semi-synthetic fiber manufactured from Eucalyptus trees; TENCEL X REFIBRA, combines 20% of recycled cotton waste with wood pulp; TENCEL Modal, a wood-based fiber; Viscose, man-made fiber from plant material; recycled materials, which use less resources than conventional cotton; and Alpaca. About 15% of its fabrics are vintage or deadstock, meaning they are given a second life. About 2%-5% of LYMI's products are made from vintage clothing. Apparel includes dresses, tops, wedding/party attire, jeans, bottoms, jumpsuits, outerwear, tees, pajamas and swimwear. The Reformation also offers accessories such as jewelry, bags, sunglasses, tights, socks, gloves, hats, scarves and more.

FINANCIAL DATA: *Note: Data for latest year may not have been available at press time.*

In U.S. $	2018	2017	2016	2015	2014	2013
Revenue		100,000,000	60,000,000	25,000,000		
R&D Expense						
Operating Income						
Operating Margin %						
SGA Expense						
Net Income						
Operating Cash Flow						
Capital Expenditure						
EBITDA						
Return on Assets %						
Return on Equity %						
Debt to Equity						

CONTACT INFORMATION:

Phone: 323-852-0005   Fax:
Toll-Free: 855-756-0560
Address: 8253 Melrose Ave., Los Angeles, CA 90046 United States

STOCK TICKER/OTHER:

Stock Ticker: Private   Exchange:
Employees: 550   Fiscal Year Ends:
Parent Company:

SALARIES/BONUSES:

Top Exec. Salary: $ Bonus: $
Second Exec. Salary: $ Bonus: $

OTHER THOUGHTS:

Estimated Female Officers or Directors:
Hot Spot for Advancement for Women/Minorities:

Sales, profits and employees may be estimates. Financial information, benefits and other data can change quickly and may vary from those stated here.

Register.com Inc

www.register.com

NAIC Code: 518210

TYPES OF BUSINESS:

Domain Name Registration Services
Trademark Search Services
Internet Site Support Services

BRANDS/DIVISIONS/AFFILIATES:

Web.com Group Inc

GROWTH PLANS/SPECIAL FEATURES:

Register.com, Inc., a subsidiary of Web.com Group, Inc., is a leading provider of global domain name registration and other internet services for small- and medium-sized businesses, large corporations and individual consumers. Register.com has over 2 million active domain names under management. The company also allows users to transfer their previously existing domain name to Register.com. Register.com's products are grouped into: domains, including .com, .org, .net, .info, .business, .guru, .company, .club, .nyc and more; websites, featuring do-it-myself, do-it-for-me, eCommerce and a call center option; hosting, including hosting packages, hosting help and security solutions; email, including web hosting packages and security solutions; and online marketing, including local business listings, premium services, search engine optimization, pay-per-click advertising, lead stream, take-a-payment and more.

CONTACTS: Note: Officers with more than one job title may be intentionally listed here more than once.

David Brown, Pres.
Alexander Ross, Sr. VP-Sales & Svcs.

FINANCIAL DATA: Note: Data for latest year may not have been available at press time.

In U.S. $	2018	2017	2016	2015	2014	2013
Revenue						
R&D Expense						
Operating Income						
Operating Margin %						
SGA Expense						
Net Income						
Operating Cash Flow						
Capital Expenditure						
EBITDA						
Return on Assets %						
Return on Equity %						
Debt to Equity						

CONTACT INFORMATION:

Phone: 212-798-9100   Fax:
Toll-Free: 866-455-1655
Address: 575 8th Ave., 11/Fl, New York, NY 10018 United States

STOCK TICKER/OTHER:

Stock Ticker: Subsidiary   Exchange:
Employees: 489   Fiscal Year Ends: 12/31
Parent Company: Web.com Group Inc

SALARIES/BONUSES:

Top Exec. Salary: $ Bonus: $
Second Exec. Salary: $ Bonus: $

OTHER THOUGHTS:

Estimated Female Officers or Directors:
Hot Spot for Advancement for Women/Minorities:

Renren Inc

NAIC Code: 519130

www.renren-inc.com/en

TYPES OF BUSINESS:

Social Networking
Online Games
Social Commerce
E-Commerce
Application Development

BRANDS/DIVISIONS/AFFILIATES:

Renren.com
Ping An Bank
Kaixin Auto Group

CONTACTS: *Note: Officers with more than one job title may be intentionally listed here more than once.*

Joseph Chen, CEO
James Jian Liu, COO
Thomas Jintao Ren, CFO
Rita Yi, VP-Human Resources
Jing Huang, VP-Renren.com
Ripley Hu, VP-Mktg.
Kitty Zhou, VP-56.com
Joseph Chen, Chmn.

GROWTH PLANS/SPECIAL FEATURES:

Renren, Inc. is a used automobile business and a software as a service (SaaS) business. The used automobile business provides car purchasers in China with access to a wide range of used vehicles. The firm focuses on premium car brands, like Audi, BMW, Mercedes-Benz, Land rover and Porsche. The firm also offers financing options through Ping An Bank and other partners, and offers value-added services including warranties, insurance and after-sale products, consisting of registration, detailing, maintenance and accessories. Renren owns 14 brick-and-mortar used car dealerships across China. The SaaS business includes Chime, an all-in-one real estate solution provider; and Geographic Farming, a real estate marketing and media services provider. The SaaS business operates primarily in the U.S. In November 2018, CM Seven Star Acquisition Corporation (CM7Star) acquired Kaxian Auto Group, a subsidiary of Renren in an all-stock exchange. The deal will see Kaixin's current shareholders and management will hold roughly 54% of issued and outstanding shares, and CM7Star will hold 46%. In that same month, Reren sold he firm's social networking service (SNS), Renren.com, to Beijing Infinities Interactive Media Co., Ltd. Renren.com enables users to connect and communicate with each other, share photos and access mobile live streaming. Renren.com and renren mobile application have a combined total of more than 257 million active users. The transaction is worth $20 million.

FINANCIAL DATA: *Note: Data for latest year may not have been available at press time.*

In U.S. $	2018	2017	2016	2015	2014	2013
Revenue		202,102,000	63,364,000	41,111,000	82,954,000	156,691,000
R&D Expense		23,678,000	20,750,000	32,392,000	50,675,000	80,530,000
Operating Income		-87,877,000	-73,013,000	-105,306,000	-105,462,000	-109,977,000
Operating Margin %		-43.48%	-115.22%	-350.41%	-127.13%	-72.40%
SGA Expense		81,903,000	63,860,000	77,305,000	89,769,000	117,442,000
Net Income		-110,427,000	-185,352,000	-220,128,000	60,460,000	63,733,000
Operating Cash Flow		-114,964,000	-11,005,000	-50,042,000	56,439,000	-73,035,000
Capital Expenditure		135,000	357,000	1,192,000	9,602,000	30,426,000
EBITDA		-161,050,000	-158,283,000	-203,609,000	-86,974,000	-90,789,000
Return on Assets %		-9.31%	-15.16%	-18.21%	4.77%	4.92%
Return on Equity %		-15.62%	-22.21%	-21.65%	5.09%	5.36%
Debt to Equity		0.07	0.12	0.13		

CONTACT INFORMATION:

Phone: 86 1084481818   Fax: 86 1051085666
Toll-Free:
Address: 18 Jiuxianqiao Middle Rd., N. Wing, 5/Fl, Chaoyang Dist., Beijing, 100016 China

STOCK TICKER/OTHER:

Stock Ticker: RENN
Employees: 988
Parent Company:

Exchange: NYS
Fiscal Year Ends: 12/31

SALARIES/BONUSES:

Top Exec. Salary: $ Bonus: $
Second Exec. Salary: $ Bonus: $

OTHER THOUGHTS:

Estimated Female Officers or Directors: 3
Hot Spot for Advancement for Women/Minorities: Y

Rent the Runway

www.renttherunway.com

NAIC Code: 454111

TYPES OF BUSINESS:

Online Rental of Luxury Apparel and Accessories

BRANDS/DIVISIONS/AFFILIATES:

CONTACTS: Note: Officers with more than one job title may be intentionally listed here more than once.

Jennifer Hyman, CEO
Beth Kaplan, COO
John Rucker, CFO
Laura Hollicay, CMO

GROWTH PLANS/SPECIAL FEATURES:

Rent the Runway is an online fashion service that provides designer dress and accessory rentals. Customers choose from thousands of items on the firm's site or app, as well as from a handful of brick-and-mortar stores. Online customers specify delivery dates, sizes, lengths, designer, trends and body type as well as the number of days they elect to rent. Dresses and accessories are rented for a fraction of their original costs. Members who rent for four or eight days under the Reserve renting option get a free backup size, as well as free returns and insurance. The Reserve plan starts at $30 per rental. Items are delivered via UPS or courier service at the client's home, office or hotel by 8pm on the delivery date. Returns are free, and customers are provided a pre-paid envelope to either be dropped off at a UPS store or scheduled for pick-up by 12pm on return date. Once returned, each dress and accessory is dry cleaned in an industrial-sized machine and steam-pressed, and then inspected by a seamstress. The Update plan is $89 per month, of which four pieces are shipped, free shipping and insurance and will be exchanged for new pieces each month. The Unlimited package is $159 a month, in which members receive an endless rotation of designer statement accessories including jewelry, handbags, outerwear and seasonal pieces. Three items are sent, and receivers can keep them for an unlimited amount of time, or return one, two or all three items in exchange for the same number of new items. The company's stores are located in Washington, D.C., Chicago, New York, San Francisco and Topanga

FINANCIAL DATA: Note: Data for latest year may not have been available at press time.

In U.S. $	2018	2017	2016	2015	2014	2013
Revenue	15,000,000	128,000,000	98,000,000	65,000,000	48,000,000	28,000,000
R&D Expense						
Operating Income						
Operating Margin %						
SGA Expense						
Net Income						
Operating Cash Flow						
Capital Expenditure						
EBITDA						
Return on Assets %						
Return on Equity %						
Debt to Equity						

CONTACT INFORMATION:

Phone: 646-832-3582   Fax:
Toll-Free: 800-509-0842
Address: 163 Varick St., Fl. 4, New York, NY 10013 United States

STOCK TICKER/OTHER:

Stock Ticker: Private   Exchange:
Employees: 375   Fiscal Year Ends:
Parent Company:

SALARIES/BONUSES:

Top Exec. Salary: $ Bonus: $
Second Exec. Salary: $ Bonus: $

OTHER THOUGHTS:

Estimated Female Officers or Directors:
Hot Spot for Advancement for Women/Minorities:

Return Path Inc

NAIC Code: 541810E

www.returnpath.com

TYPES OF BUSINESS:

Direct Marketing-E-Mail
Marketing-Opt-In E-Mail Lists
Technology Services

BRANDS/DIVISIONS/AFFILIATES:

Return Path Data Exchange
Return Path Help Center

CONTACTS: *Note: Officers with more than one job title may be intentionally listed here more than once.*

Matt Blumberg, CEO
George Bilbrey, Pres.
Jack Sinclair, CFO
Daniel Incandela, CMO
Cathy Hawley, Chief People Officer
Shawn Nussbaum, CTO
Dave Wilby, Sr. VP-Prod., Analytics & Professional Svcs
Ken Takahashi, VP-Emerging Markets
Joshua Baer, Chief Innovation Officer
Georges Smine, Gen. Mgr.-Mailbox Provider Svcs.
Matt Spielman, Chief Mktg. Officer
Matt Blumberg, Chmn.

GROWTH PLANS/SPECIAL FEATURES:

Return Path, Inc. provides email digital marketing services to Fortune 500 firms, online retailers, publishers, market researchers and catalogers. Through its Return Path Data Exchange, the firm unites a worldwide comprehensive source of data from the email ecosystem, partnering with more than 70 providers of mailbox and security solutions, covering 2.5 billion inboxes, approximately 70% of all inboxes. In addition, the company's consumer network of more than 2 million customers feed into the data platform, providing user behavior insights, brand affinity and consumer preferences. Return Path's solutions are divided into four groups: deliverability, optimization, client services and email fraud defense. Deliverability solutions cause emails to not be delivered as junk or spam mail, but to inboxes. These solutions help marketers understand their deliverability and take action to reach the right inbox and connect with the maximum number of customers. Optimization solutions help drive customer engagement and get marketers noticed by ensuring that their messages are the right messages, being relevant to customers. These solutions also help customers know when to send emails and when not to, enhancing the marketer's sending reputation instead of developing a poor one. Client services provides a variety of packages ranging from low-cost self-service solutions to full-service solutions with ongoing account management and consulting. Additionally, customers have access to the Return Path Help Center, which provides guided paths through key topics like deliverability, reputation, product best practices and more. Last, the company's email fraud defense solution is a cloud-based product that detects, blocks and responds to email threats that target employees and customers. This solution comprises real-time insights to help eliminate the impact of email fraud.

The firm offers employees comprehensive health benefits and employee assistance programs.

FINANCIAL DATA: *Note: Data for latest year may not have been available at press time.*

In U.S. $	2018	2017	2016	2015	2014	2013
Revenue		90,000,000	90,000,000	95,000,000	93,000,000	90,000,000
R&D Expense						
Operating Income						
Operating Margin %						
SGA Expense						
Net Income						
Operating Cash Flow						
Capital Expenditure						
EBITDA						
Return on Assets %						
Return on Equity %						
Debt to Equity						

CONTACT INFORMATION:

Phone: 212-905-5500   Fax: 212-905-5501
Toll-Free: 866-362-4577
Address: 3 Park Ave., 41/Fl, New York, NY 10016 United States

STOCK TICKER/OTHER:

Stock Ticker: Private   Exchange:
Employees: 562   Fiscal Year Ends: 12/31
Parent Company:

SALARIES/BONUSES:

Top Exec. Salary: $ Bonus: $
Second Exec. Salary: $ Bonus: $

OTHER THOUGHTS:

Estimated Female Officers or Directors: 2
Hot Spot for Advancement for Women/Minorities:

Revolve Group Inc

www.revolve.com

NAIC Code: 454111

TYPES OF BUSINESS:

Online Clothing Retailer
Online Fashion Retail
eCommerce

BRANDS/DIVISIONS/AFFILIATES:

CONTACTS: *Note: Officers with more than one job title may be intentionally listed here more than once.*

Michael Karanikolas, Co-CEO
David Pujades, COO
Jesse Timmermans, CFO
Lauren Yerkes, VP-Mktg. & Sales
David Staels, Chief Human Resources Officer
Raissa Gerona, Chief Brand Officer
Michael Mente, Co-CEO

GROWTH PLANS/SPECIAL FEATURES:

Revolve Group, Inc. is a next-generation fashion retailer that delivers an engaging customer experience through its online/mobile platform. The REVOLVE site offers more than 45,000 apparel, footwear, accessories and beauty style items, with over 500 emerging, established and owned brands. For more than 15 years, Revolve Group has invested in technology, data analytics and innovative marketing and merchandising strategies to build its next-generation platform and provide a 21st century fashion retail strategy for consumers and fashion brands alike. REVOLVE has more than 2.5 million website followers and receives 50 million page visits every month. Its top 20 designers include Amanda Uprichard, BB Dakota, Equipment, FAITHFUL THE BRAND, For Love & Lemons, Free People, Golden Goose, House of Harlow 1960, LEVI'S, Lovers + Friends, LoveShackFancy, Misa Los Angeles, MOTHER, NBD, Nike, Rag & Bone, RAYE, Tularosa, Wildfox Couture and Zimmermann. Revolve Group relies on third-party suppliers, manufacturers distributors and other vendors. The company receives and distributes merchandise at fulfillment centers in the U.S., none of which are operated by a third party.

FINANCIAL DATA: *Note: Data for latest year may not have been available at press time.*

In U.S. $	2018	2017	2016	2015	2014	2013
Revenue		399,597,000	312,082,000			
R&D Expense						
Operating Income						
Operating Margin %						
SGA Expense						
Net Income		5,000,000	2,198,000			
Operating Cash Flow						
Capital Expenditure						
EBITDA						
Return on Assets %						
Return on Equity %						
Debt to Equity						

CONTACT INFORMATION:

Phone: 562-677-9480   Fax:
Toll-Free:
Address: 16800 Edwards Rd., Cerritos, CA 90703 United States

STOCK TICKER/OTHER:

Stock Ticker: RVLV   Exchange: NYS
Employees: 742   Fiscal Year Ends: 12/31
Parent Company:

SALARIES/BONUSES:

Top Exec. Salary: $ Bonus: $
Second Exec. Salary: $ Bonus: $

OTHER THOUGHTS:

Estimated Female Officers or Directors:
Hot Spot for Advancement for Women/Minorities:

Rocket Internet SE

www.rocket-internet.de

NAIC Code: 519130

TYPES OF BUSINESS:

Internet Search Web Sites
eCommerce

BRANDS/DIVISIONS/AFFILIATES:

GROWTH PLANS/SPECIAL FEATURES:

Rocket Internet SE is a German internet and technology incubator and investment firm. A business incubator provides programs designed to support the development of entrepreneurial companies. Companies that successfully complete the incubation program will, statistically speaking, stay in business for the long term. Rocket has a tendency to stick with certain eCommerce and related technology business models, such as food/groceries, fashion, general merchandise and home & living, that have proven themselves successful. The firm, headquartered in Berlin, has a network of companies active in a large number of countries worldwide. Some of Rocket Internet's successful ventures have included dafiti, Hello Fresh, Global Fashion Group, Jumia, Home24, Delivery Hero, PrintVenue, CarMudi, LaModa, WestWing, Campsy, Expertlead, ZipJet and Zalora.

CONTACTS: Note: Officers with more than one job title may be intentionally listed here more than once.

Oliver Samwer, CEO
Mohamed Omaizat, Sr. VP-Corporate Finance
Ronny Rentner, CTO
Global CTO,
Jacob Bro, Global Chief Prod. Officer
Franziska Leonhardt, General Counsel
Patrick Fink, Global Head-Bus. Intelligence
Andreas Winiarski, Global Head-Public Rel.
Arnt Jeschke, Managing Dir.-Berlin
Eyad Alkassar, Managing Dir.-Middle East
Eduardo Goes, Managing Dir.-Latin America
Ian Marsh, Managing Dir.-U.K.
Don Phan, Managing Dir.-Vietnam

FINANCIAL DATA: Note: Data for latest year may not have been available at press time.

In U.S. $	2018	2017	2016	2015	2014	2013
Revenue		44,034,700	29,612,100	140,208,000	215,328,000	189,797,000
R&D Expense						
Operating Income						
Operating Margin %						
SGA Expense						
Net Income		-7,156,040	-888,185,000	-216,106,000	-55,745,400	239,804,000
Operating Cash Flow						
Capital Expenditure						
EBITDA						
Return on Assets %						
Return on Equity %						
Debt to Equity						

CONTACT INFORMATION:

Phone: 49-30-300131800   Fax:
Toll-Free:
Address: Charlottenstr 4, Berlin, 10969 Germany

STOCK TICKER/OTHER:

Stock Ticker: RKET
Employees: 171
Parent Company:

Exchange: Xetra
Fiscal Year Ends: 12/31

SALARIES/BONUSES:

Top Exec. Salary: $ Bonus: $
Second Exec. Salary: $ Bonus: $

OTHER THOUGHTS:

Estimated Female Officers or Directors: 2
Hot Spot for Advancement for Women/Minorities:

Rogers Communications Inc

NAIC Code: 517110

www.rogers.com

TYPES OF BUSINESS:

Cable TV Service
Internet Service Provider
Wireless Phone Service
Telephone Service
Television Broadcasting
Magazine Publishing
Radio Stations
Professional Sports Teams

BRANDS/DIVISIONS/AFFILIATES:

Rogers Unison
Rogers 4K TV
LTE-M
5G

CONTACTS: Note: Officers with more than one job title may be intentionally listed here more than once.

Alan Horn, CEO, Subsidiary
Deepak Khandelwal, Other Executive Officer
Joseph Natale, CEO
Anthony Staffieri, CFO
Edward Rogers, Chairman of the Board, Subsidiary
John Hill, Chief Information Officer
Jorge Fernandes, Chief Technology Officer
Philip Lind, Director
Melinda Rogers, Director
James Reid, Other Executive Officer
Frank Boulben, Other Executive Officer
Dale Hooper, Other Executive Officer
Lisa Durocher, Other Executive Officer
David Miller, Other Executive Officer
Dean Prevost, President, Divisional

GROWTH PLANS/SPECIAL FEATURES:

Rogers Communications, Inc. (RCI) is a Canadian company engaged in providing communications and media. The firm operates in four divisions: consumer services, media brands, business services and innovations. The consumer services division helps Canadians connect via communication channels, including wireless devices, home telephones, television, internet and home monitoring systems. This division is comprised of more than 10.1 million wireless subscribers, six customer service touch points, 6,058 cell towers, and 4.2 million homes utilizing RCI's cable services. The media brands division is comprised of 53 radio stations, 64 television networks, 9 magazine brands, four shop-at-home/digital services networks and three sports entertainment networks, providing a mix of television shows, sports, music, information and shopping across the entire country. The business services division delivers communications services and information technology solutions that help customers operate more efficiently, reduce costs and improve productivity and collaboration. These services and solutions include security, cloud and data centers, internet of Things, business collaboration via wireless-driven technology, and business network connectivity. This division's Rogers Unison offering enables Canadian businesses to offer their employees a way to communicate across multiple devices, via its fully-managed, truly mobile communications system. Last, the innovations division works to bring customers the fastest speeds and latest innovations. This division currently provides an LTE network, Rogers 4K TV and Gigabit internet. In April 2018, Rogers announced a partnership with Ericsson, a North American 5G developer, to bring 5G to Canada. Rogers announced a plan in October 2018 to launch a national LTE-M network to help businesses connect and track their assets in real time.

FINANCIAL DATA: Note: Data for latest year may not have been available at press time.

In U.S. $	2018	2017	2016	2015	2014	2013
Revenue		10,492,770,000	10,165,590,000	9,951,924,000	9,533,489,000	9,426,655,000
R&D Expense						
Operating Income		2,356,293,000	2,043,951,000	2,003,146,000	2,105,529,000	2,233,879,000
Operating Margin %		22.45%	20.10%	20.12%	22.08%	23.69%
SGA Expense						
Net Income		1,269,401,000	619,491,300	1,024,572,000	994,895,600	1,238,241,000
Operating Cash Flow		2,921,625,000	2,935,721,000	2,779,921,000	2,743,568,000	2,960,204,000
Capital Expenditure		1,770,187,000	1,855,506,000	1,943,793,000	1,813,218,000	1,797,638,000
EBITDA		3,921,714,000	3,156,809,000	3,675,401,000	3,575,986,000	3,663,531,000
Return on Assets %		5.98%	2.90%	4.95%	5.35%	7.72%
Return on Equity %		29.45%	15.16%	24.60%	26.42%	39.56%
Debt to Equity		1.99	2.90	2.76	2.52	2.60

CONTACT INFORMATION:

Phone: 416 935-2303   Fax: 416 935-3548
Toll-Free:
Address: 333 Bloor St. E., 10/Fl, Toronto, ON M4W 1G9 Canada

STOCK TICKER/OTHER:

Stock Ticker: RCI   Exchange: NYS
Employees: 24,500   Fiscal Year Ends: 12/31
Parent Company:

SALARIES/BONUSES:

Top Exec. Salary: $1,029,711   Bonus: $
Second Exec. Salary: $712,635   Bonus: $

OTHER THOUGHTS:

Estimated Female Officers or Directors: 6
Hot Spot for Advancement for Women/Minorities: Y

Rogue Wave Software Inc

www.roguewave.com

NAIC Code: 511210I

TYPES OF BUSINESS:

Software-Java-Based & C++
XML-Based Software
Terminal Emulation
GUI Application Development Software
Support Services
Application Consulting
Open Source Software

BRANDS/DIVISIONS/AFFILIATES:

Audax Group
Akana
HostAccess
CodeDynamics
Klocwork
SourcePro
Stingray
Zend

CONTACTS: *Note: Officers with more than one job title may be intentionally listed here more than once.*

Brian Pierce, CEO
Peter Bennfors, CFO
Christine Bottagaro, CMO
Rod Cope, CTO
Ted Smith, Sr.VP-Eng.
Jordan Welu, VP-Corp. Dev.
Scott Lasica, VP-Field Tech. Svcs

GROWTH PLANS/SPECIAL FEATURES:

Rogue Wave Software, Inc., a portfolio company of Audax Group, provides software applications that use object-oriented component technology, particularly C++ and Java. The company is based in Boulder, Colorado and has 2,000 customers around the world across several industries, including finance, telecommunications, energy, defense, aerospace and government. It offers software components for building distributed client-server, intranet and internet applications that scale to the enterprise, honor legacy investments and are highly customizable. Rogue Wave also provides customers with proven object-oriented development technology so that they can better apply the principles of the software to their own software development efforts. The company's products are marketed to professional programmers in all industrial segments through multiple distribution channels and are designed to enable customers to customize useful applications quickly. The products are also designed to support a broad range of development environments and methodologies. Products offered by the company include: Akana, a suite of application programming interface (API) management, API security and microservices solutions; HostAccess, a secure terminal emulation tool kit that supports over 30 different protocols; CodeDynamics, which looks at the complex C and C++ applications at execution time to help identify and correct bugs, memory issues and crashes; Klocwork, which supports continuous integration (CI) tools to perform analysis on incremental code changes; SourcePro, a complete enterprise C++ development platform; Stingray, for developing complex graphical user interface (GUI) applications that are easy to build, maintain and evolve with new technologies; and Zend, an open source framework that makes it easier for programmers to develop, debug, monitor and deploy modern web and mobile apps in PHP (hypertext preprocessor). In addition, the company offers consulting services for all matters pertinent to its software, such as porting, company-specific service-oriented architecture (SOA) design, platform and database migrations and performance enhancements.

FINANCIAL DATA: *Note: Data for latest year may not have been available at press time.*

In U.S. $	2018	2017	2016	2015	2014	2013
Revenue						
R&D Expense						
Operating Income						
Operating Margin %						
SGA Expense						
Net Income						
Operating Cash Flow						
Capital Expenditure						
EBITDA						
Return on Assets %						
Return on Equity %						
Debt to Equity						

CONTACT INFORMATION:

Phone: 303-473-9118   Fax: 303-473-9137
Toll-Free: 800-487-3217
Address: 1315 West Century Drive, Ste. 150, Louisville, CO 80027
United States

STOCK TICKER/OTHER:

Stock Ticker: Private   Exchange:
Employees: 400   Fiscal Year Ends: 12/31
Parent Company: Audax Group

SALARIES/BONUSES:

Top Exec. Salary: $ Bonus: $
Second Exec. Salary: $ Bonus: $

OTHER THOUGHTS:

Estimated Female Officers or Directors:
Hot Spot for Advancement for Women/Minorities:

Sales, profits and employees may be estimates. Financial information, benefits and other data can change quickly and may vary from those stated here.

Roofoods Limited (Deliveroo)

deliveroo.co.uk

NAIC Code: 519130

TYPES OF BUSINESS:

On Demand Food Delivery

BRANDS/DIVISIONS/AFFILIATES:

Deliveroo for Business

GROWTH PLANS/SPECIAL FEATURES:

Roofoods Limited, doing business as Deliveroo, is an on-demand food delivery service headquartered in London. Deliveroo operations in over 200 cities across 12 countries, including Australia, Belgium, France, Germany, Hong Kong, Italy, Ireland, Netherlands, Singapore, Spain, United Arab Emirates and the United Kingdom. The company delivers from more than 35,000 restaurants via more than 30,000 riders on scooters, motorbikes or bicycles. Deliveroo users download an app to their smartphones from which they order food. The firm's software contacts the desired restaurant to place the order, alerts a rider, bills the user and keeps him or her informed on delivery progress. Deliveroo for Business sets up accounts for businesses to enable their employees to order meals based on established allowance limits.

Roofoods employees enjoy social events such as game nights, yoga classes and weekly bake-offs as well as Friday lunches where dishes from associated restaurants are sampled.

CONTACTS:
Note: Officers with more than one job title may be intentionally listed here more than once.

Will Shu, CEO

FINANCIAL DATA:
Note: Data for latest year may not have been available at press time.

In U.S. $	2018	2017	2016	2015	2014	2013
Revenue	550,000,000	373,899,000	158,154,000	26,812,700		
R&D Expense						
Operating Income						
Operating Margin %						
SGA Expense						
Net Income		-247,601,000	-158,785,000	-44,658,700		
Operating Cash Flow						
Capital Expenditure						
EBITDA						
Return on Assets %						
Return on Equity %						
Debt to Equity						

CONTACT INFORMATION:

Phone: 203-322-3444   Fax:
Toll-Free:
Address: 22-24 Torrington Pl., London, WC1E 7HJ United Kingdom

STOCK TICKER/OTHER:

Stock Ticker: Private   Exchange:
Employees: 880   Fiscal Year Ends: 12/31
Parent Company:

SALARIES/BONUSES:

Top Exec. Salary: $ Bonus: $
Second Exec. Salary: $ Bonus: $

OTHER THOUGHTS:

Estimated Female Officers or Directors:
Hot Spot for Advancement for Women/Minorities:

Sabre Corporation

www.sabre-holdings.com

NAIC Code: 561510

TYPES OF BUSINESS:

Travel Reservations System for Airlines
Travel Marketing Solutions
Distribution & Technology Solutions
Consulting Services

BRANDS/DIVISIONS/AFFILIATES:

SabreSonic
Sabre AirVision Marketing & Planning
Sabre AirCentre Enterprise
SynXis
SynXis Property Manager Solutions

CONTACTS: *Note: Officers with more than one job title may be intentionally listed here more than once.*

Sean Menke, CEO
Douglas Barnett, CFO
Jami Kindle, Chief Accounting Officer
Lawrence Kellner, Director
Rachel Gonzalez, Executive VP
Kimberly Warmbier, Executive VP
Dave Shirk, Executive VP
Wade Jones, Executive VP
Clinton Anderson, Executive VP

GROWTH PLANS/SPECIAL FEATURES:

Sabre Corporation is a provider of travel products and services through two business segments: travel network and airline and hospitality solutions. The travel network segment comprises Sabre's global business-to-business travel marketplace, consisting primarily of its global distribution system (GDS), new distribution capability (NDC) and related solutions that add value for travel suppliers and travel buyers. GDS/NDC facilitates travel via inventory, prices and availability from its travel suppliers, including airlines, hotels, car rental brands, rail carriers, cruise lines and tour operators, with travel buyers, including online travel agencies, offline travel agencies, travel management companies and corporate travel departments. The airline and hospitality solutions business offers a broad portfolio of software technology products, through a software-as-a-service (Saas) and hosted delivery model, to airlines, hotel properties and other travel suppliers. The airline solutions division provide software that helps Sabre's airline customers better market, sell, serve and operate. Its SabreSonic suite provides capabilities and managing sales and customer service across an airline's touch points. Sabre AirVision Marketing & Planning is a suite of airline commercial planning solutions that focus on helping Sabre airline customers improve profitability and develop their brand. Sabre AirCentre Enterprise is a suite of solutions that drive operational effectiveness through holistic planning and management of airline, airport and customer operations. The hospitality solutions division provides software and solutions to hotel properties worldwide. Solutions include distribution through Sabre's SynXis central reservation system, property management through SynXis Property Manager Solutions, marketing services and consulting services that optimize distribution and marketing. In November 2018, Sabre Corporation agreed to acquire Farelogix, an innovator in the travel industry specializing in NDC technology solutions.

FINANCIAL DATA: *Note: Data for latest year may not have been available at press time.*

In U.S. $	2018	2017	2016	2015	2014	2013
Revenue		3,598,484,000	3,373,387,000	2,960,896,000	2,631,417,000	3,049,525,000
R&D Expense						
Operating Income		574,552,000	459,572,000	459,769,000	420,787,000	351,746,000
Operating Margin %		15.96%	13.62%	15.52%	15.99%	11.53%
SGA Expense		510,075,000	626,153,000	557,077,000	468,152,000	792,929,000
Net Income		242,531,000	242,562,000	545,482,000	69,223,000	-100,494,000
Operating Cash Flow		673,185,000	679,922,000	529,443,000	181,671,000	143,092,000
Capital Expenditure		316,436,000	327,647,000	286,697,000	227,227,000	226,026,000
EBITDA		932,409,000	900,272,000	878,685,000	625,659,000	477,800,000
Return on Assets %		4.26%	4.36%	10.78%	1.21%	-2.89%
Return on Equity %		36.84%	43.87%	192.59%		
Debt to Equity		4.90	5.25	6.56	36.54	

CONTACT INFORMATION:

Phone: 682-605-1000   Fax:
Toll-Free:
Address: 3150 Sabre Dr., Southlake, TX 76092 United States

STOCK TICKER/OTHER:

Stock Ticker: SABR   Exchange: NAS
Employees: 10,000   Fiscal Year Ends: 12/31
Parent Company:

SALARIES/BONUSES:

Top Exec. Salary: $844,231   Bonus: $
Second Exec. Salary: Bonus: $
$695,769

OTHER THOUGHTS:

Estimated Female Officers or Directors: 1
Hot Spot for Advancement for Women/Minorities:

Sabre Travel Network

www.sabretravelnetwork.com

NAIC Code: 561510

TYPES OF BUSINESS:

Airline Reservation Systems
Travel Application Service Provider
Online Reservation Systems
Business-to-Business Travel Services
Marketing Services

BRANDS/DIVISIONS/AFFILIATES:

Sabre Corporation
Sabre Global Distribution System
Sabre Red
TRAMS
GetThere
Sabre Labs

CONTACTS:
Note: Officers with more than one job title may be intentionally listed here more than once.

Wade Jones, Pres.
Jason Lovinger, VP-Global Sales
Jan Altemeier, Sr. VP-Global Oper.
Candi Clarke, VP-Acct. Mgmt. & Sales
Jay Jones, Sr. VP-The Americas
Hans Belle, VP
Rajiv Rajian, VP-Global Sales & Account Mgmt.
Harald Eisenacher, Sr. VP-EMEA
David Gross, Sr. VP-Travel Supplier Dist.

GROWTH PLANS/SPECIAL FEATURES:

Sabre Travel Network, a subsidiary of Sabre Corporation, distributes its travel agency customers' travel-related products and services through one of the world's largest distribution systems. The network provides travel agency subscribers with pricing information from airlines, hotels, car rental companies and cruise lines. With a presence in more than 160 countries, travel agencies subscribe to the Sabre Global Distribution System (GDS), enabling them to make reservations with over 400 airlines, 225,000 hotels, 40 car rental companies, 355 tour operators, 50 rail carriers and 20 cruise lines. The system allows users to check schedules, availability, pricing and policies. The Sabre GDS also provides information on currency, medical and visa requirements and weather. The Sabre Red platform features a portfolio of capabilities and applications through four benefit suites: Sabre Red Value Suite, providing access to accurate and best-priced travel options in the world; Sabre Red Service Suite, a personalized service for travel agencies; Sabre Red Revenue Suite, which helps lower costs and increase revenue; and Sabre Red Efficiency Suite, a workflow management solutions service. Other brands include TRAMS (Trams.com), which helps over 11,000 agency locations increase revenues, optimize customer management and streamline processes; and GetThere (GetThere.com), a leading web-based platform to book business travel and meetings, as well as the ability to integrate with expense systems for an end-to-end experience. Sabre's travel technology consists of an integrated open platform that powers co-creation by users and extensions by partners. Sabre Labs is continuously engaged in developing and supplying innovative technology products and solutions in the fields of automation, augmented reality, blockchain, artificial intelligence (AI)-powered chatbots and connected intelligence.

FINANCIAL DATA:
Note: Data for latest year may not have been available at press time.

In U.S. $	2018	2017	2016	2015	2014	2013
Revenue		2,550,470,000	2,374,849,000	2,102,792,000	1,854,785,000	1,821,498,000
R&D Expense						
Operating Income						
Operating Margin %						
SGA Expense						
Net Income		848,336,000	835,248,000	751,546,000	657,326,000	667,498,000
Operating Cash Flow						
Capital Expenditure						
EBITDA						
Return on Assets %						
Return on Equity %						
Debt to Equity						

CONTACT INFORMATION:

Phone: 682-605-1000   Fax:
Toll-Free:
Address: 3150 Sabre Dr., Southlake, TX 76092 United States

STOCK TICKER/OTHER:

Stock Ticker: Subsidiary   Exchange:
Employees: Fiscal Year Ends: 12/31
Parent Company: Sabre Corporation

SALARIES/BONUSES:

Top Exec. Salary: $ Bonus: $
Second Exec. Salary: $ Bonus: $

OTHER THOUGHTS:

Estimated Female Officers or Directors: 2
Hot Spot for Advancement for Women/Minorities:

Sage Intacct Inc

www.sageintacct.com

NAIC Code: 511210Q

TYPES OF BUSINESS:

Computer Software, Accounting, Banking & Financial
Software
Accounting

BRANDS/DIVISIONS/AFFILIATES:

Sage Group plc (The)

CONTACTS: *Note: Officers with more than one job title may be intentionally listed here more than once.*

Robert Reid, CEO
Haris Hadjiioannou, VP-Operations
Marc Linden, Sr. VP-Finance
Ian Howells, VP-Mktg.
Kathleen Lord, Sr. VP-Sales
Aaron Harris, CTO

GROWTH PLANS/SPECIAL FEATURES:

Sage Intacct, Inc. provides cloud-based enterprise resource planning (ERP) software for customers, from startups to public companies. The firm's cloud accounting software includes products that cover accounts payable, accounts receivable, cash management, collaboration, ledger, order management, purchasing, reporting and dashboards. Additional modules include contract and subscription billing, contract revenue management, fixed assets, inventory management, multi-entity and global consolidations, project accounting, sales and use tax, time and expense management and vendor payment services. Sage Intacct's integrated financial management system is designed to grow with its client's organization. This flexible solution can be utilized as the client's business evolves. It easily integrates with Salesforce and other solutions, and is configurable to exact requirements and needs. Custom applications can also be built on the Sage Intacct platform. Industries served by Sage Intacct include accounting firms, financial services, franchise, healthcare, hospitality, nonprofits, professional services, software, software-as-a-service (SaaS) and wholesale distribution. The company is based in California, USA, with international offices in India and Romania. It operates as a wholly-owned subsidiary of The Sage Group plc.

FINANCIAL DATA: *Note: Data for latest year may not have been available at press time.*

In U.S. $	2018	2017	2016	2015	2014	2013
Revenue		70,000,000	67,000,000			
R&D Expense						
Operating Income						
Operating Margin %						
SGA Expense						
Net Income						
Operating Cash Flow						
Capital Expenditure						
EBITDA						
Return on Assets %						
Return on Equity %						
Debt to Equity						

CONTACT INFORMATION:

Phone: 408-878-0900   Fax: 408-878-0910
Toll-Free: 877-968-0600
Address: 300 Park Ave., Ste,1400, San Jose, CA 95110 United States

STOCK TICKER/OTHER:

Stock Ticker: Subsidiary   Exchange:
Employees: 450   Fiscal Year Ends:
Parent Company: Sage Group plc (The)

SALARIES/BONUSES:

Top Exec. Salary: $ Bonus: $
Second Exec. Salary: $ Bonus: $

OTHER THOUGHTS:

Estimated Female Officers or Directors:
Hot Spot for Advancement for Women/Minorities:

Sales, profits and employees may be estimates. Financial information, benefits and other data can change quickly and may vary from those stated here.

SalesForce.com Inc

www.salesforce.com

NAIC Code: 511210K

TYPES OF BUSINESS:

Software, Sales & Marketing Automation
Customer Relationship Management Software
Software Subscription Services

BRANDS/DIVISIONS/AFFILIATES:

Sales Cloud
Service Cloud
Marketing Cloud
Community Cloud
Industries
IoT Cloud
Salesforce Quip
Salesforce Platform

CONTACTS: *Note: Officers with more than one job title may be intentionally listed here more than once.*

Mark Hawkins, CFO
Marc Benioff, Chairman of the Board
Joe Allanson, Chief Accounting Officer
Parker Harris, Chief Technology Officer
Keith Block, Co- President
Amy Weaver, General Counsel
Cynthia Robbins, Other Executive Officer
Alexandre Dayon, Other Executive Officer
Bret Taylor, Other Executive Officer
Maria Martinez, President, Divisional

GROWTH PLANS/SPECIAL FEATURES:

SalesForce.com, Inc. builds and delivers customer relationship management (CRM) applications through an on-demand web services platform. The firm's web-based services enable clients to track sales and marketing by delivering enterprise software as an online service, making software purchases similar to paying for a utility as opposed to a packaged product. The firm offers core cloud-based services such as sales force automation, customer service and support, marketing automation, community management, analytics, as well as a platform for building custom application. Products include Sales Cloud, Service Cloud, Marketing Cloud, Community Cloud, Industries, IoT (Internet of Things) Cloud, Commerce Cloud, Salesforce Quip and Salesforce Platform. Sales Cloud is a platform for sales force automation and solutions for partner relationship management; Service Cloud addresses customer service and support needs; Marketing Cloud is a digital marketing platform that manages customer interactions across email, mobile, social, web and connected products; Community Cloud creates trusted, branded destinations for customers, partners and employees to collaborate; Industries, offers cloud products that meet the specific needs of certain industries; IoT Cloud connects billions of events from devices, sensors, apps and more from the IoT to SalesForce, enabling companies to take action with the connected world; Commerce Cloud empowers brands to deliver a comprehensive digital commerce experience across web, mobile, social and store; Salesforce Quip is a next-generation productivity solution designed for teams with a mobile-first strategy; and Salesforce Platform is for building enterprise apps quickly via tools, frameworks and services. The Salesforce Platform also offers artificial intelligence, no-code, low-code and code development and integration services including Trailhead, Einstein, AI, Lightning, IoT, Heroku, analytics and the AppExchange.

SalesForce.com offers its employees paid time off, parental/family care, employee stock purchase plans, educational reimbursement, wellness allowances, volunteer time off and a 401(k) plan.

FINANCIAL DATA: *Note: Data for latest year may not have been available at press time.*

In U.S. $	2018	2017	2016	2015	2014	2013
Revenue	10,480,010,000	8,391,984,000	6,667,216,000	5,373,586,000	4,071,003,000	3,050,195,000
R&D Expense	1,553,073,000	1,208,127,000	946,300,000	792,917,000	623,798,000	429,479,000
Operating Income	235,768,000	64,228,000	114,923,000	-145,633,000	-286,074,000	-110,710,000
Operating Margin %	2.24	.76%	1.72%	-2.71%	-7.02%	-3.62%
SGA Expense	5,917,649,000	4,885,590,000	3,951,445,000	3,437,032,000	2,764,851,000	2,047,847,000
Net Income	127,478,000	179,632,000	-47,426,000	-262,688,000	-232,175,000	-270,445,000
Operating Cash Flow	2,737,965,000	2,162,198,000	1,612,585,000	1,173,714,000	875,469,000	736,897,000
Capital Expenditure	534,027,000	463,958,000	709,852,000	416,889,000	299,110,000	179,707,000
EBITDA	1,041,651,000	746,616,000	662,514,000	308,448,000	88,699,000	119,949,000
Return on Assets %	.66%	1.18%	- .40%	-2.64%	-3.16%	-5.58%
Return on Equity %	1.50%	2.87%	-1.05%	-7.49%	-8.66%	-13.85%
Debt to Equity	0.14	0.35	0.40	0.55	0.63	

CONTACT INFORMATION:

Phone: 415 901-7000   Fax: 415 901-7040
Toll-Free:
Address: Salesforce Tower, 415 Mission St., 3/Fl, San Francisco, CA 94105 United States

STOCK TICKER/OTHER:

Stock Ticker: CRM
Employees: 25,000
Parent Company:

Exchange: NYS
Fiscal Year Ends: 01/31

SALARIES/BONUSES:

Top Exec. Salary: $1,550,000   Bonus: $
Second Exec. Salary: $1,150,000   Bonus: $

OTHER THOUGHTS:

Estimated Female Officers or Directors: 4
Hot Spot for Advancement for Women/Minorities: Y

Salon Media Group Inc

www.salon.com

NAIC Code: 519130

TYPES OF BUSINESS:

Online News & Media
Online Communities

BRANDS/DIVISIONS/AFFILIATES:

Salon.com

GROWTH PLANS/SPECIAL FEATURES:

Salon Media Group, Inc. is a technology-based advertising media business that wholly-owns and operates Salon.com, a news website. Its writing style combines investigative journalism with personal essays, as well as quick-take commentary, articles, podcasts and original video. News topics include politics, culture, entertainment, race, religion, sustainability, innovation, technology and business. Salon targets educated, culturally-engaged audiences interested in original thoughts and reporting of the day's big stories. Advertising is the company's primary source of revenue, with internet advertising accounting for 78% of Salon's annual revenue; and revenue from referring users to third party websites accounting for the remaining 22%. Salon averages approximately 20 million unique viewers a month.

CONTACTS: Note: Officers with more than one job title may be intentionally listed here more than once.

Richard Gingras, CEO
Norman Blashka, CFO
John Warnock, Chairman of the Board
David Talbot, Founder
Joan Walsh, Other Corporate Officer
Benjamin Zagorski, Vice President, Divisional

FINANCIAL DATA: Note: Data for latest year may not have been available at press time.

In U.S. $	2018	2017	2016	2015	2014	2013
Revenue						
R&D Expense						
Operating Income						
Operating Margin %						
SGA Expense						
Net Income						
Operating Cash Flow						
Capital Expenditure						
EBITDA						
Return on Assets %						
Return on Equity %						
Debt to Equity						

CONTACT INFORMATION:

Phone: 415-870-7566   Fax: 415 645-9206
Toll-Free:
Address: 870 Market St., San Francisco, CA 94102 United States

STOCK TICKER/OTHER:

Stock Ticker: SLNM   Exchange: PINX
Employees: 44   Fiscal Year Ends: 03/31
Parent Company:

SALARIES/BONUSES:

Top Exec. Salary: $172,370   Bonus: $74,166
Second Exec. Salary: $194,925   Bonus: $46,875

OTHER THOUGHTS:

Estimated Female Officers or Directors: 3
Hot Spot for Advancement for Women/Minorities: Y

SAP SE

www.sap.com

NAIC Code: 511210H

TYPES OF BUSINESS:

Computer Software, Business Management & ERP
Consulting & Training Services
Hosting Services
Software Licensing
Software Development

BRANDS/DIVISIONS/AFFILIATES:

SAP HANA
Contextor SAS

CONTACTS: *Note: Officers with more than one job title may be intentionally listed here more than once.*

Bill McDermott, CEO
Christian Klein, COO
Luka Mucic, CFO
Stefan Ries, Chief Human Resources Officer
Luca Mucic, Head-Global Finance
Jim Hagemann Snabe, Co-CEO
Bernd Leukert, Head- Application Innovation

GROWTH PLANS/SPECIAL FEATURES:

SAP SE provides business-related software and cloud solutions so that enterprises can become digital businesses. The firm's products are categorized into eight divisions. The ERP (enterprise resource planning) and digital core division serves small, medium and large companies via the SAP HANA database management system software for data storage, analytics and insights, as well as ERP cloud solutions. The customer relationship/experience division offers software for understanding customers, predicting behavior and meeting their needs, and include the customer data cloud, marketing cloud, commerce cloud, sales cloud and services cloud. The network and spend management division's software helps to streamline procurement processes, reduce risk and gain visibility and control. Its solutions include supplier management, strategic sourcing, procurement, services procurement, selling/fulfillment and travel and expense. The digital supply division offers software for getting products to market faster and at less cost. Its technology solutions address supply chain, manufacturing, R&D, engineering and asset management. The human resources and people engagement division provides software for simplifying and integrating human capital management processes via on-premise and cloud HR software. Its solutions include core HR, payroll, learning and development, performance and compensation, recruiting and onboarding, time and attendance management, workforce planning, analytics and HR for small/medium companies. The digital platform division offers a software solution for managing data from any source, with the ability to develop, integrate and extend business applications. The analytics division offers software such as analytics cloud, business intelligence, enterprise planning and predictive analysis. Last, the intelligent technologies division offers software solutions in relation to the enterprise, Internet of Things (IoT), machine learning and blockchain. SAP SE serves more than 413,000 customers in over 180 countries. In November 2018, SAP acquired Contextor SAS.

SAP offers medical, dental, disability, life and vision insurance; and retirement stock and savings plans.

FINANCIAL DATA: *Note: Data for latest year may not have been available at press time.*

In U.S. $	2018	2017	2016	2015	2014	2013
Revenue		26,723,470,000	25,131,000,000	23,685,470,000	20,003,870,000	19,154,100,000
R&D Expense		3,818,289,000	3,467,444,000	3,240,762,000	2,655,260,000	2,599,444,000
Operating Income		5,763,885,000	5,880,074,000	5,552,011,000	5,427,849,000	5,182,941,000
Operating Margin %		21.56%	23.39%	23.44%	27.13%	27.05%
SGA Expense		9,111,724,000	8,281,314,000	7,346,106,000	5,918,804,000	5,692,122,000
Net Income		4,576,935,000	4,153,187,000	3,490,226,000	3,736,274,000	3,788,673,000
Operating Cash Flow		5,746,799,000	5,271,791,000	4,144,074,000	3,985,738,000	4,365,061,000
Capital Expenditure		1,452,362,000	1,140,247,000	724,472,600	839,522,500	644,735,000
EBITDA		7,490,773,000	7,289,151,000	6,294,710,000	6,284,458,000	6,296,988,000
Return on Assets %		9.26%	8.51%	7.66%	9.99%	12.33%
Return on Equity %		15.48%	14.68%	14.32%	18.45%	22.02%
Debt to Equity		0.19	0.24	0.37	0.45	0.22

CONTACT INFORMATION:

Phone: 49 6227747474   Fax: 49 6227757575
Toll-Free: 800-872-1727
Address: Dietmar-Hopp-Allee 16, Walldorf, 69190 Germany

STOCK TICKER/OTHER:

Stock Ticker: SAP
Employees: 95,000
Parent Company:

Exchange: NYS
Fiscal Year Ends: 12/31

SALARIES/BONUSES:

Top Exec. Salary: $1,309,974   Bonus: $
Second Exec. Salary: Bonus: $
$797,376

OTHER THOUGHTS:

Estimated Female Officers or Directors: 4
Hot Spot for Advancement for Women/Minorities: Y

Sapient Corporation

NAIC Code: 541512

publicis.sapient.com

TYPES OF BUSINESS:

IT Consulting
Internet Strategy Consulting
Interactive Marketing Software

BRANDS/DIVISIONS/AFFILIATES:

Publicis Groupe SA
Publicis.Sapient

CONTACTS: *Note: Officers with more than one job title may be intentionally listed here more than once.*

Alan Wexler, CEO
Alan Wexler, Executive VP
J. Moore, Founder
Joseph LaSala, General Counsel
Harry Register, Managing Director, Divisional
Christian Oversohl, Managing Director, Geographical
Laurie MacLaren, Senior VP, Divisional

GROWTH PLANS/SPECIAL FEATURES:

Sapient Corporation, a subsidiary of Publicis Groupe SA, is a business consulting and technology services firm focused on digital transformation and the dynamics of an always-on world. The firm's Publicis.Sapient platform is designed to help clients reimagine core business activities via transformation in order to drive growth and improve operating efficiency. The platform's digital transformation technology helps businesses in three key ways: creates business opportunities by rapidly reaching, meeting and/or changing customer expectations and behavior; creates new value via ongoing technological advances in marketing, sales, service, supply chain, IT and more; and stays ahead of competitors through smart/connected products and an enterprise-wide open ecosystem. According to Sapient, digital is at the core of transformation because the entire business eventually needs to be wired for the digital world, primarily change-sensitive technology architectures and rapid development methods. The Publicis.Sapient platform's data and analytics on customers provide strategy and direction to Sapient Corporation's business consulting services to its clients. Therefore, Sapient combines these technology capabilities with consulting expertise for the best outcomes for its business clients. Sapient Corporation serves financial services, retail, technology, communications, consumer packaged goods, travel/leisure, automotive, energy services, government, health and education sectors, among others. Based in the USA, the firm has operations worldwide, including the Americas, Europe and Asia-Pacific.

FINANCIAL DATA: *Note: Data for latest year may not have been available at press time.*

In U.S. $	2018	2017	2016	2015	2014	2013
Revenue		1,681,000,000	1,625,000,000	1,562,781,000	1,451,000,000	1,305,232,000
R&D Expense						
Operating Income						
Operating Margin %						
SGA Expense						
Net Income						
Operating Cash Flow						
Capital Expenditure						
EBITDA						
Return on Assets %						
Return on Equity %						
Debt to Equity						

CONTACT INFORMATION:

Phone: 617 621-0200   Fax: 617 621-1300
Toll-Free: 877-454-9860
Address: 131 Dartmouth St., Boston, MA 02116 United States

STOCK TICKER/OTHER:

Stock Ticker: Subsidiary   Exchange:
Employees: 11,900   Fiscal Year Ends: 12/31
Parent Company: Publicis Groupe SA

SALARIES/BONUSES:

Top Exec. Salary: $ Bonus: $
Second Exec. Salary: $ Bonus: $

OTHER THOUGHTS:

Estimated Female Officers or Directors: 2
Hot Spot for Advancement for Women/Minorities:

Sea Limited

NAIC Code: 511210M

TYPES OF BUSINESS:

Online Marketplace Tools
E-commerce

BRANDS/DIVISIONS/AFFILIATES:

Garena
Shopee
AirPay

CONTACTS: *Note: Officers with more than one job title may be intentionally listed here more than once.*

Forrest Li, CEO
Gang Ye, COO
Nicholas A. Nash, Pres.
Tony Tianyu Hou, CFO

GROWTH PLANS/SPECIAL FEATURES:

Sea Limited is an internet platform company engaged in digital entertainment, eCommerce and digital finance service businesses in Southeast Asia. Garena is the company's digital entertainment platform where users can access popular and engaging mobile and PC online games, curated and localized for seven markets. Garena operates each of the games, including League of Legends, FIFA Online, Point Blank, Blade & Soul and Arena of Valor. Garena is also an advocate and organizer of eSports events in Greater Southeast Asia. Shopee is a leading eCommerce platform in Southeast Asia, providing buyers and sellers with an easy, secure and fast online shopping experience via payment and logistical support. Product categories include consumer electronics, home furnishings and decor, health and beauty, baby items, toys, fashion, fitness equipment and more. Last, AirPay is the company's digital financial services platform, providing eWallet services to consumers through its AirPay app, and to small businesses through its partner-operated service counters. Via AirPay eWallet, consumers use either the AirPay app or one of the AirPay counters to make payments for everyday products and services such as food, entertainment, transportation, mobile communications and bill payments. AirPay counters act as a reverse ATM, putting cash into the network instead of taking it out. This process helps reach the large unbanked populations in the country.

FINANCIAL DATA: *Note: Data for latest year may not have been available at press time.*

In U.S. $	2018	2017	2016	2015	2014	2013
Revenue		414,190,000	345,670,000	292,124,000	160,756,000	
R&D Expense		29,323,000	20,809,000	17,732,000	11,053,000	
Operating Income		-502,356,000	-207,492,000	-83,060,000	-88,621,000	
Operating Margin %		-121.28%	-60.02%	-28.43%	-55.12%	
SGA Expense		563,842,000	299,755,000	176,217,000	113,751,000	
Net Income		-560,485,000	-222,867,000	-103,366,000	-88,383,000	
Operating Cash Flow		-334,230,000	-114,726,000	-25,097,000	2,458,000	
Capital Expenditure		79,746,000	24,539,000	76,668,000	41,593,000	
EBITDA		-481,086,000	-157,309,000	-58,165,000	-68,913,000	
Return on Assets %		-45.30%	-48.67%	-29.11%	-31.55%	
Return on Equity %		-326.47%	-510.49%			
Debt to Equity		1.54				

CONTACT INFORMATION:

Phone: 65-6270-8100   Fax:
Toll-Free:
Address: 1 Fusionopolis Pl., #17-10, Galaxis Bldg., Singapore, 138522 Singapore

STOCK TICKER/OTHER:

Stock Ticker: SE   Exchange: NYS
Employees: 5,400   Fiscal Year Ends:
Parent Company:

SALARIES/BONUSES:

Top Exec. Salary: $ Bonus: $
Second Exec. Salary: $ Bonus: $

OTHER THOUGHTS:

Estimated Female Officers or Directors:
Hot Spot for Advancement for Women/Minorities:

Seek Limited
NAIC Code: 519130

www.seek.com.au

TYPES OF BUSINESS:
Online Marketplace
Online Jobs Listings

BRANDS/DIVISIONS/AFFILIATES:

CONTACTS: *Note: Officers with more than one job title may be intentionally listed here more than once.*
Andrew Bassat, CEO
Isar Mazer, COO
Geoff Roberts, CFO
Kathleen McCudden, Group Human Resources Dir.

GROWTH PLANS/SPECIAL FEATURES:
SEEK Limited is a diverse group of companies engaged in job finding services for the employment, education and volunteer businesses, spanning more than 15 countries including Australia, New Zealand, China, India, Brazil, Mexico, Africa and Bangladesh. SEEK has exposure to approximately 3 billion people across its markets (as of November 2018). The company's technology solutions address the needs of jobseekers and hirers, and facilitate the matching between jobseekers and hirers across its online employment marketplaces. The company has relationships with over 190 million jobseekers and 900,000 hirers. SEEK provides voice-activated job search capability through Amazon's Alexa digital assistant device. In addition, SEEK's business section provides businesses that are for sale, including franchises. A link for finding a broker for business owners selling their assets is available on related www.seekbusiness.com websites. SEEK provides online education courses, consisting of more than 8,000 nationally-recognized courses across over 100 education institutions Australia-wide. Courses are categorized into the areas of healthcare, education, people, business building, technology and creative.

FINANCIAL DATA: *Note: Data for latest year may not have been available at press time.*

In U.S. $	2018	2017	2016	2015	2014	2013
Revenue	906,957,200	726,126,300	665,872,600	601,415,300	499,754,800	434,528,100
R&D Expense		58,992,500	50,374,840	38,744,480	29,553,000
Operating Income	223,008,500	178,869,200	-96,756,110	-49,674,210	-20,318,080	-18,090,100
Operating Margin %		24.63%	-14.53%	-8.25%	-4.06%	-4.16%
SGA Expense	517,550,700	439,501,200	627,969,000	540,180,800	432,985,400	370,634,800
Net Income	37,273,180	238,352,100	250,192,700	197,015,300	137,042,000	210,242,400
Operating Cash Flow						
Capital Expenditure	79,590,840	53,737,830	38,464,240	39,725,360	29,145,940	16,248,160
EBITDA	200,308,300	364,324,300	456,596,400	320,185,000	221,607,200	299,920,100
Return on Assets %		9.77%	10.85%	10.16%	8.81%	16.69%
Return on Equity %		23.99%	28.68%	27.61%	23.29%	51.01%
Debt to Equity		0.62	0.55	0.67	0.42	0.56

CONTACT INFORMATION:
Phone: 61 3 8517 4100   Fax: 61 3 9510 7244
Toll-Free:
Address: Level 6, 541 St Kilda Rd., Melbourne, VIC 3004 Australia

STOCK TICKER/OTHER:
Stock Ticker: SKLTY   Exchange: PINX
Employees: 1,005   Fiscal Year Ends: 06/30
Parent Company:

SALARIES/BONUSES:
Top Exec. Salary: $ Bonus: $
Second Exec. Salary: $ Bonus: $

OTHER THOUGHTS:
Estimated Female Officers or Directors:
Hot Spot for Advancement for Women/Minorities:

Segment.io Inc

segment.com

NAIC Code: 511210J

TYPES OF BUSINESS:
Computer Software, Data Base & File Management

BRANDS/DIVISIONS/AFFILIATES:

CONTACTS: Note: Officers with more than one job title may be intentionally listed here more than once.
Peter Reinhardt, CEO
Sandra Smith, CFO

GROWTH PLANS/SPECIAL FEATURES:
Segment.io, Inc. provides a platform for collecting and sending customer data. This platform utilizes a single application program interface (API) to capture the data across any marketing channel and device, and sends it anywhere. Channels and devices include mobile, web, server and cloud apps. The data is sent to hundreds of tools for analytics, marketing and data warehousing. Segment integrates with more than 180 models, through which business teams can use to create personalizing campaigns, analyze product usage, push notifications, email, chat live and more. Once Segment is integrated, business users have instant access to all the tools necessary for building relevant applications. Marketers can use the Segment dashboard to distribute the collected data to tools without having to file a task. Libraries batch and retry messages so data does not get lost. Integrations can be tested with Segment's live debugger for continuous assurance while building apps and sites. Open source software development kits (SDKs) provide visibility, from which users can see exactly how data is collected, translated and delivered. Segment offers three price ranges that scale with user growth: developer, which is free, and provides unlimited integrations, one source limit, one warehouse limit and one seat; team, which is a pay-as-you-go plan, provides unlimited integrations, unlimited sources, one warehouse limit and seven seats; and business, an annual contract, provides unlimited integrations, sources, warehouses and seats, as well as alerting features, data replay and premium support. Each plan provides access to Segment's core features of data collection and loading it into Segment; transforming and distributing data; sending data to tools and warehouses; building websites and apps; integrations; and cloud apps. In mid-2017, the firm raised $64 million in Series C funding let by Y Combinator Continuity Fund and GV (formerly Google Ventures).

FINANCIAL DATA: Note: Data for latest year may not have been available at press time.

In U.S. $	2018	2017	2016	2015	2014	2013
Revenue						
R&D Expense						
Operating Income						
Operating Margin %						
SGA Expense						
Net Income						
Operating Cash Flow						
Capital Expenditure						
EBITDA						
Return on Assets %						
Return on Equity %						
Debt to Equity						

CONTACT INFORMATION:
Phone: 415-649-6900   Fax:
Toll-Free:
Address: 101 15th St., San Francisco, CA 94103 United States

STOCK TICKER/OTHER:
Stock Ticker: Private   Exchange:
Employees: 100   Fiscal Year Ends:
Parent Company:

SALARIES/BONUSES:
Top Exec. Salary: $ Bonus: $
Second Exec. Salary: $ Bonus: $

OTHER THOUGHTS:
Estimated Female Officers or Directors:
Hot Spot for Advancement for Women/Minorities:

SendGrid Inc

NAIC Code: 511210F

TYPES OF BUSINESS:

Computer Software, Multimedia, Graphics & Publishing

BRANDS/DIVISIONS/AFFILIATES:

SendGrid API
SendGrid Marketing Campaigns

CONTACTS: *Note: Officers with more than one job title may be intentionally listed here more than once.*

Sameer Dholakia, CEO
Yancey Spruill, COO
Carrie Palin, CMO
Pattie Money, Chief People Officer

GROWTH PLANS/SPECIAL FEATURES:

SendGrid, Inc. provides a cloud-based platform that solves challenges of email delivery on behalf of growing companies. Many application emails do not get delivered, so SendGrid built an app for this kind of deliverability. The company is responsible for sending billions of emails for companies worldwide. The firm's SendGrid API (application program interface) email solution integrates with its customer's business application (whether content management system, framework, CRM or own code) and their email delivery begins via simple mail transfer protocol (SMTP) or API within five minutes or less. SendGrid secures email delivery with two-factor authentication, multi-user credentials, API key permissions, internet protocol (IP) access management and more. The firm's single platform can be shared with business' entire team for all its email sending needs. Marketers can easily send beautiful (templates are provided), well-targeted email marketing campaigns with the SendGrid Marketing Campaigns offering. This product provides 24/7 support and step-by-step resources, as well as the ability to design A/B tests with up to six subject lines or content variations. Campaign accounts are safeguarded with SendGrid's ISP (internet service provider) monitoring systems, and users can manage recipients, scheduling, content and testing all from one viewpoint. SendGrid Marketing Campaigns enables teams to define segments based on customer data and campaign engagement, add contacts to relative segments, and create static lists for groups of contacts to be managed manually. Key metrics such as track sends, delivery rates, bounces, spam reports, link clicks, opens and unsubscribes can be easily applied. In October 2018, the firm agreed to be acquired by Twilio, Inc. in an all-stock transaction valued at approximately $2 billion. The transaction is expected to close in the first half of 2019.

FINANCIAL DATA: *Note: Data for latest year may not have been available at press time.*

In U.S. $	2018	2017	2016	2015	2014	2013
Revenue		111,888,000	79,929,000	58,476,000	42,776,000	
R&D Expense						
Operating Income						
Operating Margin %						
SGA Expense						
Net Income		-6,253,000	-3,908,000	-5,854,000	-12,960,000	
Operating Cash Flow						
Capital Expenditure						
EBITDA						
Return on Assets %						
Return on Equity %						
Debt to Equity						

CONTACT INFORMATION:

Phone: Fax:
Toll-Free: 888-985-8363
Address: 1801 California St., Ste. 500, Denver, CO 80202 United States

STOCK TICKER/OTHER:

Stock Ticker: SEND Exchange:
Employees: 415 Fiscal Year Ends:
Parent Company:

SALARIES/BONUSES:

Top Exec. Salary: $ Bonus: $
Second Exec. Salary: $ Bonus: $

OTHER THOUGHTS:

Estimated Female Officers or Directors:
Hot Spot for Advancement for Women/Minorities:

ServiceMax Inc

www.servicemax.com

NAIC Code: 511210H

TYPES OF BUSINESS:
Computer Software, Business Management & ERP

BRANDS/DIVISIONS/AFFILIATES:
General Electric Company
GE Digital LLC

CONTACTS: *Note: Officers with more than one job title may be intentionally listed here more than once.*
Scott Berg, CEO
David Stippich, CFO
David Milam, CMO

GROWTH PLANS/SPECIAL FEATURES:

ServiceMax, Inc. provides cloud-based field service management solutions for technicians, managers and executives. The company's software solutions help companies to manage contracts, scheduling and parts. All in a single platform, ServiceMax products include cloud computing, mobile capabilities, service flow, offline synchronization, salesforce app cloud and collaboration. These products offer capabilities such as installed base management, work order management, mobile field service management, field service metrics/reporting/dashboards, warranty and contract management, field service scheduling and parts and returns management. Industries served by the company include life sciences and medical equipment, industrial manufacturing and equipment, retail and commercial services, building services, aerospace and defense, communications and media, energy and utilities and computer hardware. ServiceMax operates as a subsidiary of GE Digital, LLC, a unit of General Electric Company that connects streams of machine data to powerful analytics in order to provide industrial companies with insights. Based in California, USA, the firm has global offices in Europe, Asia, Australia and the Middle East. In December 2018, GE agreed to sell a majority stake in ServiceMax to Silver Lake, with GE retaining a 10% equity ownership.

The company offers its employees health benefits, base salary, performance-based bonus programs, stock options and career development opportunities.

FINANCIAL DATA: *Note: Data for latest year may not have been available at press time.*

In U.S. $	2018	2017	2016	2015	2014	2013
Revenue		70,000,000	60,000,000			
R&D Expense						
Operating Income						
Operating Margin %						
SGA Expense						
Net Income						
Operating Cash Flow						
Capital Expenditure						
EBITDA						
Return on Assets %						
Return on Equity %						
Debt to Equity						

CONTACT INFORMATION:
Phone: 925-965-7859   Fax: 925-391-3516
Toll-Free: 800-756-4960
Address: 2700 Camino Ramon, Ste. 450, San Ramon, CA 94583 United States

STOCK TICKER/OTHER:
Stock Ticker: Subsidiary   Exchange:
Employees: 430   Fiscal Year Ends:
Parent Company: General Electric Company

SALARIES/BONUSES:
Top Exec. Salary: $ Bonus: $
Second Exec. Salary: $ Bonus: $

OTHER THOUGHTS:
Estimated Female Officers or Directors:
Hot Spot for Advancement for Women/Minorities:

ServiceNow Inc

NAIC Code: 511210B

www.service-now.com

TYPES OF BUSINESS:

Cloud-Based Workflow Software

BRANDS/DIVISIONS/AFFILIATES:

Parlo

CONTACTS: *Note: Officers with more than one job title may be intentionally listed here more than once.*

Michael Scarpelli, CFO
Frederic Luddy, Director
John Donahoe, Director
David Schneider, Other Executive Officer
Patricia Wadors, Other Executive Officer
Chirantan Desai, Other Executive Officer

GROWTH PLANS/SPECIAL FEATURES:

ServiceNow, Inc. is a provider of cloud-based services that automate enterprise IT operations. The company's service includes a suite of applications built on its proprietary platform that automates workflow and provides integration between related business processes. The firm focuses on transforming enterprise IT by automating and standardizing business processes and consolidating IT across the global enterprise. Organizations deploy its service to create a single system of record for enterprise IT, lower operational costs and enhance efficiency. Additionally, customers use its extensible platform to build custom applications for automating activities unique to their business requirements. ServiceNow helps transform IT organizations from reactive, manual and task-oriented, to pro-active, automated and service-oriented organizations. The company's on-demand service enables organizations to define their IT strategy, design the systems and infrastructure that will support that strategy, and implement, manage and automate that infrastructure throughout its lifecycle while leveraging its self-service capability. The firm provides a broad set of integrated functionality that is highly configurable and extensible and can be efficiently implemented and upgraded. Its multi-instance architecture has proven scalability for global enterprises as well as having advantages in security, reliability and deployment location. The company offers its service under a Software-as-a-Service (SaaS) business model. Customers can rapidly deploy its service in a modular fashion, allowing them to solve immediate business needs and access, configure and build new applications as their requirements evolve. The firm's service, which is accessed through an intuitive web-based interface, can be easily configured to adapt to customer workflow and processes. ServiceNow serves more than 5,000 enterprise customers worldwide. During 2018, ServiceNow acquired: Parlo, an artificial intelligence (AT) workforce solution; and agreed to acquire the technology of FriendlyData, which makes it easy for non-technical users to ask quantitative questions and obtain fast answers directly or via data visualizations.

FINANCIAL DATA: *Note: Data for latest year may not have been available at press time.*

In U.S. $	2018	2017	2016	2015	2014	2013
Revenue		1,933,026,000	1,390,513,000	1,005,480,000	682,563,000	424,650,000
R&D Expense		377,518,000	285,239,000	217,389,000	148,258,000	78,678,000
Operating Income		-101,414,000	-152,808,000	-166,365,000	-151,835,000	-66,267,000
Operating Margin %		-5.24%	-30.40%	-16.54%	-22.24%	-15.60%
SGA Expense		1,157,150,000	859,400,000	625,043,000	437,364,000	256,980,000
Net Income		-149,130,000	-451,804,000	-198,426,000	-179,387,000	-73,708,000
Operating Cash Flow		642,825,000	159,921,000	315,091,000	138,900,000	81,746,000
Capital Expenditure		157,180,000	124,312,000	89,231,000	54,379,000	55,321,000
EBITDA		15,494,000	-335,476,000	-103,227,000	-105,980,000	-42,115,000
Return on Assets %		-5.49%	-23.52%	-12.27%	-13.83%	-8.95%
Return on Equity %		-30.71%	-94.74%	-39.86%	-43.59%	-23.11%
Debt to Equity		1.07	1.31			

CONTACT INFORMATION:

Phone: 408-501-8550　　Fax:
Toll-Free:
Address: 2225 Lawson Lane, Santa Clara, CA 95054 United States

STOCK TICKER/OTHER:

Stock Ticker: NOW　　　　　　　　Exchange: NYS
Employees: 4,801　　　　　　　　　Fiscal Year Ends: 12/31
Parent Company:

SALARIES/BONUSES:

Top Exec. Salary: $525,641　　Bonus: $
Second Exec. Salary:　　　　　Bonus: $
$450,000

OTHER THOUGHTS:

Estimated Female Officers or Directors:
Hot Spot for Advancement for Women/Minorities:

Shaw Communications Inc

www.shaw.ca

NAIC Code: 517110

TYPES OF BUSINESS:

Cable TV Service
Internet Service Provider
Satellite Services
Digital Phone Services
Internet Infrastructure Services
Video-On-Demand
Broadcast TV

BRANDS/DIVISIONS/AFFILIATES:

Freedom Mobile
Shaw Go WiFi
BlueSky TV
Shaw Direct

CONTACTS: Note: Officers with more than one job title may be intentionally listed here more than once.

Mcaleese Paul, CEO, Divisional
Jay Mehr, Pres.
Vito Culmone, CFO
J. Shaw, Chairman of the Board
Jim Little, Chief Marketing Officer
Zoran Stakic, Chief Technology Officer
Bradley Shaw, Director
Jim Shaw, Director
Janice Davis, Executive VP, Divisional
Trevor English, Executive VP
Peter Johnson, Executive VP
Chris Kucharski, President, Divisional
Ron McKenzie, Senior VP
Ron McKenzie, Senior VP, Divisional

GROWTH PLANS/SPECIAL FEATURES:

Shaw Communications, Inc. is a diversified Canadian communications company whose core business is providing broadband cable television, Internet, digital phone, telecommunications and satellite direct-to-home services. Shaw is organized into two business segments: Wireless and Wireline. The Wireless division, operated through Freedom Mobile, provides wireless voice and data services through an expanding and improving wireless network infrastructure. This segment now covers approximately 16 million people in some of Canada's largest urban centers, or almost half of the Canadian population. This segment currently operates in Ontario, Alberta and British Columbia, offering the leading alternative for mobile services to the three national wireless incumbent carriers. Through the Wireline segment, Shaw is one of the largest providers of residential communications services in Canada. The Wireline segment is divided into the Consumer and Business divisions. The Consumer connects consumers in their homes and on the go with broadband Internet, Shaw Go WiFi, video (including BlueSky TV) and traditional home phone services. Additionally, the Consumer division offer Satellite Services through Shaw Direct. Shaw Direct connects families across Canada with video and audio programming by satellite. Shaw Direct customers have access to over 550 digital video channels (including over 250 HD channels) and over 10,000 on-demand, pay-per-view and subscription movie and television titles. The Business division provides connectivity solutions to business customers of all sizes, from home offices to medium and large-scale enterprises. The range of services offered by Shaw Business includes: fiber internet, business internet, data connectivity, voice solutions, video and broadcast video.

FINANCIAL DATA: Note: Data for latest year may not have been available at press time.

In U.S. $	2018	2017	2016	2015	2014	2013
Revenue	3,886,845,000	3,621,984,000	3,623,468,000	4,071,579,000	3,888,328,000	3,814,880,000
R&D Expense						
Operating Income	468,142,600	741,163,900	841,321,200	1,062,409,000	1,067,602,000	1,013,443,000
Operating Margin %		20.46%	23.21%	26.09%	27.45%	26.56%
SGA Expense						
Net Income	44,514,350	631,361,900	905,125,100	635,071,400	635,813,200	553,461,800
Operating Cash Flow	1,002,315,000	1,114,343,000	1,233,789,000	1,142,535,000	1,290,916,000	1,015,669,000
Capital Expenditure	988,218,600	1,196,694,000	888,803,100	808,677,300	827,966,900	744,131,500
EBITDA	1,096,537,000	1,449,684,000	1,403,686,000	1,749,414,000	1,657,417,000	1,658,901,000
Return on Assets %		5.69%	8.09%	6.05%	6.48%	5.75%
Return on Equity %		13.54%	20.62%	16.65%	18.97%	18.47%
Debt to Equity		0.69	0.82	0.93	0.99	0.92

CONTACT INFORMATION:

Phone: 403 750-4500   Fax: 403 750-4501
Toll-Free: 888-472-2222
Address: 630 3rd Ave. SW, Ste. 900, Calgary, AB T2P 4L4 Canada

STOCK TICKER/OTHER:

Stock Ticker: SJR   Exchange: NYS
Employees: 14,000   Fiscal Year Ends: 08/31
Parent Company:

SALARIES/BONUSES:

Top Exec. Salary: $2,500,000   Bonus: $
Second Exec. Salary: Bonus: $
$1,750,000

OTHER THOUGHTS:

Estimated Female Officers or Directors: 3
Hot Spot for Advancement for Women/Minorities: Y

Shopify Inc

NAIC Code: 511210K

www.shopify.com

TYPES OF BUSINESS:

Computer Software, Sales & Customer Relations

BRANDS/DIVISIONS/AFFILIATES:

Shopify Plus
www.shopify.com/plus

CONTACTS: *Note: Officers with more than one job title may be intentionally listed here more than once.*

Russell Jones, CFO
Tobias Lutke, Chmn.
Harley Finkelstein, COO
Joseph Frasca, General Counsel
Craig Miller, Other Executive Officer
Toby Shannan, Senior VP, Divisional
Brittany Forsyth, Senior VP, Divisional
Jean-Michel Lemieux, Senior VP, Divisional
David Lennie, Senior VP, Divisional

GROWTH PLANS/SPECIAL FEATURES:

Shopify, Inc. is a cloud-based, multi-channel commerce platform designed for small- and medium-sized businesses. Merchants can use the Shopify software to design, set up and manage their stores across multiple sales channels, including web, mobile, social media, brick-and-mortar locations and pop-up shops. The platform also provides merchants with a back-office and single views of their business. Currently, the company serves over 600,000 businesses in approximately 175 countries, including Nestley, Kylie Cosmetics, Allbirds, MVMT, and many more. Shopify offers a free 14-day trial and provides its packages and rates in three groups: basic, Shopify and advanced Shopify. Basic is $29 per month, comes with a personal online store, and items can be sold via the online store, all Shopify points of sale (POS), Facebook and Pinterest. Shopify is $79 per month, is comprised of all of the Basic package but credit card purchase rates are cheaper, among other incentives. Advanced Shopify is $299 per month, with credit card purchase rates being cheaper than that of Pro, among other incentives. All packages allow an unlimited number of featured products, no transaction fees, discount codes and an unlimited amount of file storage. Shopify Plus is a cloud-based, fully-hosted enterprise eCommerce platform for high-volume merchants. Its website can be found at www.shopify.com/plus. In October 2018, the firm opened its first brick-and-mortar entrepreneur space in Los Angeles, California, which provides in-person help and support to merchants and aspiring entrepreneurs.

FINANCIAL DATA: *Note: Data for latest year may not have been available at press time.*

In U.S. $	2018	2017	2016	2015	2014	2013
Revenue		673,304,000	389,330,000	205,233,000	105,018,000	50,252,000
R&D Expense		135,997,000	74,336,000	39,722,000	25,915,000	13,682,000
Operating Income		-49,157,000	-37,165,000	-17,756,000	-21,615,000	-4,269,000
Operating Margin %		-7.30%	-9.54%	-8.65%	-20.58%	-8.49%
SGA Expense		293,413,000	172,324,000	89,105,000	57,495,000	27,326,000
Net Income		-39,995,000	-35,355,000	-18,790,000	-22,311,000	-4,837,000
Operating Cash Flow		7,901,000	14,017,000	15,756,000	-801,000	1,396,000
Capital Expenditure		24,262,000	26,236,000	21,036,000	22,700,000	4,504,000
EBITDA		-25,775,000	-23,198,000	-10,520,000	-16,943,000	-2,511,000
Return on Assets %		-4.98%	-9.62%	-11.08%	-23.36%	-5.04%
Return on Equity %		-5.66%	-11.67%	-21.35%		
Debt to Equity						

CONTACT INFORMATION:

Phone: 1-888-746-7439   Fax:
Toll-Free:
Address: 150 Elgin St., 8/Fl, Ottawa, ON K2P 1L4 Canada

STOCK TICKER/OTHER:

Stock Ticker: SHOP   Exchange: NYS
Employees: 632   Fiscal Year Ends:
Parent Company:

SALARIES/BONUSES:

Top Exec. Salary: $446,880   Bonus: $
Second Exec. Salary: Bonus: $
$335,160

OTHER THOUGHTS:

Estimated Female Officers or Directors:
Hot Spot for Advancement for Women/Minorities:

Shopping.com Ltd

www.shopping.com

NAIC Code: 454111

<table>
<tr><td colspan="2">

TYPES OF BUSINESS:
Online Comparison Shopping
Consumer Reviews

</td><td>

GROWTH PLANS/SPECIAL FEATURES:
Shopping.com Ltd., part of eBay, Inc.'s commerce network, provides an online comparison-shopping service to consumers and retailers. Shopping.com reaches hundreds of millions of shoppers each month through a single advertisement. The company also offers web-navigation tools as well as product reviews. Product categories include cars, clothing and accessories, computers, electronics, flowers and gifts, health and beauty, home and garden, jewelry and watches, kids and family, magazine and subscriptions, media, musical instruments and accessories, office, sports and outdoors and video games. Shopping.com provides retailers with highest high conversion to sales rate; its efficient presentation of product information via the internet enables quick consumer purchase decisions. Shopping.com partners with CNET, TheFind, Bing.com and many others. Features of the web site include the ability to shop for brands and listings of the most popular items on the site. The firm has operations in the U.S., U.K., Germany, France and Australia and is a leading eCommerce destination worldwide.

</td></tr>
</table>

BRANDS/DIVISIONS/AFFILIATES:
eBay Inc
Shopping.com

CONTACTS: Note: Officers with more than one job title may be intentionally listed here more than once.
Devin Wenig, CEO-eBay
Venky Natarajan, Global Head-Prod.
Bridget Davies, Managing Dir.-Global Bus.
Stephen Howard-Sarin, Sr. Dir.-North America Display Advertising

FINANCIAL DATA: Note: Data for latest year may not have been available at press time.

In U.S. $	2018	2017	2016	2015	2014	2013
Revenue						
R&D Expense						
Operating Income						
Operating Margin %						
SGA Expense						
Net Income						
Operating Cash Flow						
Capital Expenditure						
EBITDA						
Return on Assets %						
Return on Equity %						
Debt to Equity						

CONTACT INFORMATION:
Phone: 408-376-7400   Fax: 408-516-8811
Toll-Free:
Address: 2025 Hamilton Ave., San Jose, CA 95125 United States

STOCK TICKER/OTHER:
Stock Ticker: Subsidiary   Exchange:
Employees: 200   Fiscal Year Ends: 12/31
Parent Company: eBay Inc

SALARIES/BONUSES:
Top Exec. Salary: $ Bonus: $
Second Exec. Salary: $ Bonus: $

OTHER THOUGHTS:
Estimated Female Officers or Directors: 2
Hot Spot for Advancement for Women/Minorities:

Sales, profits and employees may be estimates. Financial information, benefits and other data can change quickly and may vary from those stated here.

Shutterfly Inc

www.shutterfly.com

NAIC Code: 519130

TYPES OF BUSINESS:

Online Photographic Service
Photo Printing
Gifts-Retail

BRANDS/DIVISIONS/AFFILIATES:

Shutterfly.com
Tiny Prints
Lifetouch
BorrowLenses
Groovebook
Lifetouch Inc

CONTACTS: Note: Officers with more than one job title may be intentionally listed here more than once.

Satish Menon, Chief Technology Officer
Dwayne Black, COO
William Lansing, Director
Ishantha Lokuge, Other Executive Officer
Tracy Layney, Other Executive Officer
Christopher North, President
Michele Anderson, Senior VP, Divisional
Scott Arnold, Senior VP, Divisional
Michael Pope, Senior VP
Lisa Blackwood-Kapral, Vice President

GROWTH PLANS/SPECIAL FEATURES:

Shutterfly, Inc. is a leading internet-based photograph publishing service, operating Shutterfly.com, Tiny Prints, Lifetouch, BorrowLenses and Groovebook. Through Shutterfly, consumers can upload, edit, share and print their photos. The company's revenue is primarily generated through the sale of personalized products such as professionally-bound photo books, calendars, high-quality prints, greeting cards and stationary. Customers may choose to print pictures in a range of sizes from wallet-sized prints to jumbo 20x30-inch enlargements as well as on a number of consumer goods, including mugs, mouse pads, tote bags, coasters, desk organizers, puzzles, playing cards, multi-media DVDs, magnets, keepsake boxes and ancillary products, such as frames, photo albums and scrap-booking accessories. The firm's Storytelling tool allows users to publish professional-looking photo books and digital scrapbooks. Additionally, the tool features photography and design tips, personal interviews and articles and the firm's favorite photo book style picks. Tiny Prints focuses on creating personalized birth announcements. Lifetouch is a professional photography business for schools and families. BorrowLenses is an online marketplace for photographic and video equipment rentals. Groovebook is a mobile photo book app subscription service that sends customers a keepsake book of their mobile photos on a periodic basis. The company maintains facilities in Redwood City, California; Santa Clara, California; Fort Mill, South Carolina; Shakopee, Minnesota; and Tempe, Arizona. During 2018, Shutterfly acquired Lifetouch, Inc.

The firm offers employees health and wellness benefits, performance rewards, employee discounts and more.

FINANCIAL DATA: Note: Data for latest year may not have been available at press time.

In U.S. $	2018	2017	2016	2015	2014	2013
Revenue		1,190,202,000	1,134,224,000	1,059,429,000	921,580,000	783,642,000
R&D Expense		168,383,000	166,909,000	155,318,000	133,623,000	108,995,000
Operating Income		86,664,000	49,110,000	18,265,000	6,245,000	22,058,000
Operating Margin %		7.28%	4.32%	1.72%	.67%	2.81%
SGA Expense		315,505,000	352,088,000	357,768,000	328,992,000	282,996,000
Net Income		30,085,000	15,906,000	-843,000	-7,860,000	9,285,000
Operating Cash Flow		239,524,000	193,423,000	165,037,000	166,488,000	147,268,000
Capital Expenditure		70,751,000	89,687,000	76,669,000	92,201,000	78,342,000
EBITDA		166,943,000	163,262,000	132,286,000	105,505,000	97,222,000
Return on Assets %		2.20%	1.32%	-.06%	-.60%	.87%
Return on Equity %		5.42%	2.73%	-.12%	-1.01%	1.25%
Debt to Equity		0.61	0.58	0.51	0.37	0.30

CONTACT INFORMATION:

Phone: 650 610-5200   Fax: 650 654-1299
Toll-Free: 888-225-7159
Address: 2800 Bridge Pkwy., Redwood City, CA 94065 United States

STOCK TICKER/OTHER:

Stock Ticker: SFLY
Employees: 2,084
Parent Company:

Exchange: NAS
Fiscal Year Ends: 12/31

SALARIES/BONUSES:

Top Exec. Salary: $700,000   Bonus: $
Second Exec. Salary: $415,000   Bonus: $

OTHER THOUGHTS:

Estimated Female Officers or Directors: 2
Hot Spot for Advancement for Women/Minorities:

SINA Corporation

NAIC Code: 519130

english.sina.com

TYPES OF BUSINESS:

Internet Portal-Chinese
E-Mail & Messaging Services
Search Engine
Online Games
Wireless Services
Online Auctions & Retail
Online News
Apps

BRANDS/DIVISIONS/AFFILIATES:

SINA.com Technology (China) Co Ltd
Starshining Mobile Technology (China) Ltd
Beijing New Media Information Technology Co Ltd
Beijing SINA Advertising Co Ltd
SINA (Shanghai) Management Co Ltd
Shanghai SINA Advertising Co Ltd
Weibo Internet Technology (China) Co Ltd
SINA.com

CONTACTS: Note: Officers with more than one job title may be intentionally listed here more than once.

Charles Chao, CEO
Hong Du, COO
Bonnie Yi Zhang, CFO
Gaofei Wang, Sr. VP
Tong Chen, Exec. VP
Charles Chao, Chmn.

GROWTH PLANS/SPECIAL FEATURES:

SINA Corporation is an online media company and mobile value-added services (MVAS) provider based in China. The company's business is maintained primarily through its wholly-owned subsidiaries SINA.com Technology (China) Co., Ltd.; Starshining Mobile Technology (China) Ltd.; Beijing New Media Information Technology Co., Ltd.; Beijing SINA Advertising Co., Ltd.; SINA (Shanghai) Management Co., Ltd.; Shanghai SINA Advertising Co., Ltd.; and Weibo Internet Technology (China) Co., Ltd. The firm provides services such as online portals, blogs, video and music streaming, online games, classified listings and e-commerce through SINA.com, SINA.cn and Weibo.com. SINA.com is an online brand advertising property in China, providing Chinese language online news and content as well as such advertising product offerings as banner, button and text-link advertisements that appear on pages within the SINA network. SINA.com has portals in mainland China, Taiwan, Hong Kong and North America and consists of various regional, interest-based channels such as SINA News, SINA Entertainment, SINA Technology, SINA Video, SINA Sports, SINA Auto and SINA Finance, among others. SINA.cn provides entertainment and information from the SINA portal for mobile users. Weibo.com offers microblogging and social networking services, allowing users to connect 24/7 via a third-party mobile platform. SINA generates the majority of its revenue from online advertising, mobile value-added services (MVAS) and fee-based offerings.

FINANCIAL DATA: Note: Data for latest year may not have been available at press time.

In U.S. $	2018	2017	2016	2015	2014	2013
Revenue		1,583,884,000	1,030,936,000	880,669,000	768,241,000	665,106,000
R&D Expense		267,392,000	216,228,000	209,771,000	192,322,000	146,332,000
Operating Income		388,576,000	113,470,000	12,222,000	-26,388,000	22,572,000
Operating Margin %		24.53%	11.00%	1.38%	-3.43%	3.39%
SGA Expense		513,779,000	346,542,000	323,296,000	311,966,000	225,138,000
Net Income		156,569,000	225,087,000	25,678,000	176,802,000	45,132,000
Operating Cash Flow		596,290,000	443,649,000	328,138,000	101,025,000	73,713,000
Capital Expenditure		44,907,000	37,688,000	45,466,000	102,853,000	97,685,000
EBITDA		421,778,000	141,938,000	49,004,000	18,882,000	57,609,000
Return on Assets %		3.10%	5.20%	.63%	5.35%	2.06%
Return on Equity %		5.66%	8.58%	1.09%	10.59%	3.87%
Debt to Equity		0.30	0.05		0.37	0.67

CONTACT INFORMATION:

Phone: 8610-8262-8881 Fax: 8610-8260-7166
Toll-Free:
Address: No. 8 SINA Plaza, Ctyd. 10, W. Xibeiwang E. Rd., Haidian Distr., Shanghai, Shanghai 100193 China

STOCK TICKER/OTHER:

Stock Ticker: SINA Exchange: NAS
Employees: 7,308 Fiscal Year Ends: 12/31
Parent Company:

SALARIES/BONUSES:

Top Exec. Salary: $ Bonus: $
Second Exec. Salary: $ Bonus: $

OTHER THOUGHTS:

Estimated Female Officers or Directors: 1
Hot Spot for Advancement for Women/Minorities:

Sales, profits and employees may be estimates. Financial information, benefits and other data can change quickly and may vary from those stated here.

Sisense Inc

www.sisense.com

NAIC Code: 511210H

TYPES OF BUSINESS:

Computer Software, Business Management & ERP

BRANDS/DIVISIONS/AFFILIATES:

CONTACTS: *Note: Officers with more than one job title may be intentionally listed here more than once.*

Amir Orad, CEO
Aviad Harell, COO
Todd Sloan, CFO
Saar Bitner, CMO
Nurit Shiber, VP-Human Resources
Guy Boyangu, CTO

GROWTH PLANS/SPECIAL FEATURES:

Sisense, Inc. is a developer and provider of the disruptive In-Chip data engine, which simplifies business analytics for complex data. The company's mission is to offer a complete solution for preparing, analyzing and visualizing big or disparate datasets. Sisense's products are agile, flexible and produce actionable results for companies within days (not months), and they enable business users and analysts to freely and simply explore their data. With Sisense, customers can create and manage complex data models from multiple sources in a simple drag-and-drop environment that anyone can understand. Its interactive web dashboards host visualization options from which all data can be explored from any angle, in order to obtain insights quickly. The firm's add-on products leverage the open Sisense platform, and are built using open Sisense application program interface (API) sets so that anyone can build one. By embedding Sisense into customer software, data can immediately become analyzed. The software platform is an end-to-end, single stack business intelligence (BI) solution that lets customers easily prepare, analyze and visualize complex data without any additional tools. The company's products are for businesses that need BI tools to measure their industry-specific metrics and key performance indicators, and provide on-time data analysis for BI professionals, department heads, executives and business users in order to make the best decisions possible. Industries served by the company include healthcare, finance, marketing, public sector, retail, travel/hospitality and embedded analytics. Sisense's investors include Bessemer Venture Partners, DFJ Growth, Battery Ventures, Genesis Partners, Insight Venture Partners and Opus Capital. Sisense is headquartered in New York, with an office in Scottsdale, Arizona, and international offices in the U.K. and Israel.

FINANCIAL DATA: *Note: Data for latest year may not have been available at press time.*

In U.S. $	2018	2017	2016	2015	2014	2013
Revenue						
R&D Expense						
Operating Income						
Operating Margin %						
SGA Expense						
Net Income						
Operating Cash Flow						
Capital Expenditure						
EBITDA						
Return on Assets %						
Return on Equity %						
Debt to Equity						

CONTACT INFORMATION:

Phone: 646-432-1507   Fax:
Toll-Free:
Address: 1359 Broadway, 4/Fl, New York, NY 10018 United States

STOCK TICKER/OTHER:

Stock Ticker: Private   Exchange:
Employees: 250   Fiscal Year Ends:
Parent Company:

SALARIES/BONUSES:

Top Exec. Salary: $ Bonus: $
Second Exec. Salary: $ Bonus: $

OTHER THOUGHTS:

Estimated Female Officers or Directors:
Hot Spot for Advancement for Women/Minorities:

SK Telecom Co Ltd

www.sktelecom.com

NAIC Code: 517210

TYPES OF BUSINESS:

Wireless Telecommunications Services
Multimedia Broadcasting
Online Shopping

BRANDS/DIVISIONS/AFFILIATES:

SK Broadband
SK Planet Co Ltd
SK Hynix
Keyco
Smart Toc Toc
IoT Blackbox
ADT Caps

CONTACTS: Note: Officers with more than one job title may be intentionally listed here more than once.

Park Jung-Ho, CEO
Dong Seob Jee, Head-Corp. Vision Dept.
Young Tae Kim, Exec. Dir.

GROWTH PLANS/SPECIAL FEATURES:

SK Telecom Co., Ltd. is one of Korea's leading wireless telecommunications services providers. Its core services and business segments include: cellular voice, fixed-line telecommunication, e-commerce and other. The cellular voice segment includes cellular voice service, wireless data service and wireless internet services. The fixed-line telecommunication segment includes telephone services, internet services and leased line services. The e-commerce segment includes online commerce services. The other segment includes SK Telecom's internet portal services and other immaterial operations. Subsidiaries of the firm include wholly-owned SK Broadband, an internet provider; SK Planet Co. Ltd., which operates the e-commerce business; and 20.1%-owned SK Hynix, a memory-chip maker. In 2017, the firm launched three devices based on the Internet of Things (IoT) technology: Keyco keychain, Smart Toc Toc vehicle alarm and the IoT Blackbox. SK Telecom plans to launch up to 50 IoT-based services and products by year's end.In May 2018, the firm announced that in partnership Macquarie they will take over Siren Holdings Korea, the company that holds 100% stake in ADT Caps.

FINANCIAL DATA: Note: Data for latest year may not have been available at press time.

In U.S. $	2018	2017	2016	2015	2014	2013
Revenue		15,585,540,000	15,204,620,000	15,244,580,000	15,268,650,000	14,768,930,000
R&D Expense		351,631,500	306,717,200	280,922,000	347,777,000	313,476,400
Operating Income		1,323,370,000	1,408,756,000	1,544,955,000	1,631,269,000	1,792,818,000
Operating Margin %		8.49%	9.26%	10.13%	10.68%	12.13%
SGA Expense		6,150,595,000	5,959,990,000	5,769,206,000	6,180,017,000	5,958,790,000
Net Income		2,312,769,000	1,490,915,000	1,350,927,000	1,602,301,000	1,457,997,000
Operating Cash Flow		3,430,079,000	3,774,658,000	3,360,966,000	3,271,346,000	3,165,650,000
Capital Expenditure		2,545,635,000	2,780,701,000	2,318,904,000	2,792,134,000	2,777,541,000
EBITDA		6,182,497,000	4,852,819,000	4,738,385,000	4,865,680,000	4,437,889,000
Return on Assets %		8.03%	5.54%	5.31%	6.54%	6.25%
Return on Equity %		15.37%	10.62%	10.09%	12.76%	12.88%
Debt to Equity		0.32	0.40	0.43	0.39	0.37

CONTACT INFORMATION:

Phone: 82-2-6100-2114   Fax: 82-2-6110-7830
Toll-Free:
Address: SK T-Tower, 65, Eulji-ro, Jung-gu, Seoul, 100-999 South Korea

STOCK TICKER/OTHER:

Stock Ticker: SKM
Employees: 25,844
Parent Company:

Exchange: NYS
Fiscal Year Ends: 12/31

SALARIES/BONUSES:

Top Exec. Salary: $ Bonus: $
Second Exec. Salary: $ Bonus: $

OTHER THOUGHTS:

Estimated Female Officers or Directors:
Hot Spot for Advancement for Women/Minorities:

Skype Technologies Sarl

NAIC Code: 511210C

www.skype.com

TYPES OF BUSINESS:

Computer Software, Telecom, Communications & VoIP

BRANDS/DIVISIONS/AFFILIATES:

Microsoft Corporation

GROWTH PLANS/SPECIAL FEATURES:

Skype Technologies Sarl, a subsidiary of Microsoft Corporation, offers software capabilities that enable users to make free voice and video calls over the internet. The firm's proprietary software and mobile applications help people stay connected not only through telephone calls, but also via instant messaging and photo- and file-sharing in real-time. Skype Technologies additional capabilities include purchasing tickets, surfing the internet for recipes and finding and dropping information into conversations. For businesses and friends who are not online, calling their mobile and landline numbers through Skype-to-Phone are offered at affordable rates. Calls can be made by phone, desktop, tablet, Xbox and even connected wearables. Skype numbers are available for purchase in 23 countries and regions, and can be used across devices. Those with Skype numbers pay a flat fee for unlimited incoming calls.

CONTACTS: Note: Officers with more than one job title may be intentionally listed here more than once.

Tony Bates, Pres.

FINANCIAL DATA: Note: Data for latest year may not have been available at press time.

In U.S. $	2018	2017	2016	2015	2014	2013
Revenue						
R&D Expense						
Operating Income						
Operating Margin %						
SGA Expense						
Net Income						
Operating Cash Flow						
Capital Expenditure						
EBITDA						
Return on Assets %						
Return on Equity %						
Debt to Equity						

CONTACT INFORMATION:

Phone: 352-26-20-15-82   Fax: 352-26-27-05-88
Toll-Free:
Address: 23-29 Rives de Clausen, Luxembourg, L-2165 Luxembourg

STOCK TICKER/OTHER:

Stock Ticker: Subsidiary
Employees: 1,400
Parent Company: Microsoft Corporation

Exchange:
Fiscal Year Ends: 12/31

SALARIES/BONUSES:

Top Exec. Salary: $ Bonus: $
Second Exec. Salary: $ Bonus: $

OTHER THOUGHTS:

Estimated Female Officers or Directors: 1
Hot Spot for Advancement for Women/Minorities: Y

Slack Technologies Inc

slack.com

NAIC Code: 511210C

TYPES OF BUSINESS:

Computer Software, Telecom, Communications & VOIP

BRANDS/DIVISIONS/AFFILIATES:

Slack

CONTACTS: Note: Officers with more than one job title may be intentionally listed here more than once.

Stewart Butterfield, CEO
Allen Shim, CFO

GROWTH PLANS/SPECIAL FEATURES:

Slack Technologies, Inc. is a computer software startup founded in 2009. It operates Slack, a platform that enables team communications in one place. The platform provides real-time messaging, archiving and searching services for various teams. Slack Technologies' products are divided into three groups: channels, direct messages and calls. Channels provides a way to organize team conversations in open channels. Direct messages reach colleagues directly, and are completely private and secure. Private groups is for sensitive information, with the ability to invite select team members that no one else can see or join. Prices range from free introductory access to a negotiable fee for enterprise companies. Free access includes search and browse of 10,000 most recent messages, 10 service integrations, free native apps for iOS/Android/Mac&Windows Desktop and 1:1 voice and video calls, 5GB file storage and two-factor identification. Standard access includes everything in Free, as well as searchable archive with unlimited messages, unlimited service integrations, custom retention policies, guest access, Google Authentication/Apps for Domains sign-on, configurable email ingestion and group voice/video calls, screen sharing, 10GB file storage and custom profiles. Plus access includes everything in Standard, as well as SAML-based single sign-on, compliance exports of all message history, support for external message and archival solutions, 99.99% guaranteed uptime SLA, user provisioning and deprovisioning, real-time active directory sync with OneLogic, Okta and Ping, and 20GB file storage. Enterprise will include everything in Plus, as well as federation across multiple teams with a unified team directory, unified security/data retention/compliance policies, organization-wide reporting, metrics and analytics, consolidated billing and administration across teams, 24/7 support with 2-hour response time, and 1TB storage per user.

FINANCIAL DATA: Note: Data for latest year may not have been available at press time.

In U.S. $	2018	2017	2016	2015	2014	2013
Revenue	240,000,000	160,000,000	88,000,000	18,500,000	10,000,000	4,500,000
R&D Expense						
Operating Income						
Operating Margin %						
SGA Expense						
Net Income						
Operating Cash Flow						
Capital Expenditure						
EBITDA						
Return on Assets %						
Return on Equity %						
Debt to Equity						

CONTACT INFORMATION:

Phone: 415-579-9122   Fax: 415-501-9196
Toll-Free:
Address: 155 5th St., 6/Fl., San Francisco, CA 94103 United States

SALARIES/BONUSES:

Top Exec. Salary: $ Bonus: $
Second Exec. Salary: $ Bonus: $

STOCK TICKER/OTHER:

Stock Ticker: Private   Exchange:
Employees: 650   Fiscal Year Ends:
Parent Company:

OTHER THOUGHTS:

Estimated Female Officers or Directors:
Hot Spot for Advancement for Women/Minorities:

Smartsheet Inc

NAIC Code: 511210H

TYPES OF BUSINESS:

Computer Software, Business Management & ERP

BRANDS/DIVISIONS/AFFILIATES:

Smartsheet.com Inc
Converse.AI
TernPro Inc
Slope

CONTACTS: *Note: Officers with more than one job title may be intentionally listed here more than once.*

Mark Mader, CEO
Jennifer Ceran, CFO
Jennifer Ceran, CFO
Kara Hamilton, Sr. VP-People Operations
Paul Porrini, General Counsel
Eugene Farrell, Senior VP, Divisional
Kara Hamilton, Senior VP, Divisional
Michael Arntz, Senior VP, Divisional
Andrew Lientz, Senior VP, Divisional
Geoffrey Barker, Chairman of the Board

GROWTH PLANS/SPECIAL FEATURES:

Smartsheet, Inc, formerly Smartsheet.com, Inc., provides a cloud-based software-as-a-service (SaaS) platform for managing and automating collaborative work. More than 77,000 brands and millions of information workers utilize Smartsheet to help them accelerate business execution and address the volume of collaborative work. The platform is easy to deploy and use, and its solutions include project management, IT, operations, sales, marketing, software development and human resources. Industries served by the company include retail, manufacturing, professional services, construction, education, technology, healthcare and government. The platform also offers accelerators, proven solutions that can be easily deployed. Accelerators include IT project management office (PMO), professional services, mergers and acquisitions, customer engagement and sales rep onboarding. Smartsheet's customers are in over 190 countries. Customers include Netflix, Hilton, Fortune Brands, Colliers International, Bayer, Cisco, Hewlett-Packard and many more. Smartsheet integrates with applications from Microsoft, Google, Salesforce, Dropbox, Workplace by Facebook and many others. Smartsheet.com is headquartered in Bellevue, Washington, with additional offices in Boston and Edinburgh, Scotland. In January 2018, the firm acquired Converse.AI, a U.K.-based pioneer in intelligent bots for business automation. In April of that year, Smartsheet began trading on the New York Stock Exchange. In January 2019, the firm acquired TernPro, Inc., the creator of Slope, a team creative management application.

FINANCIAL DATA: *Note: Data for latest year may not have been available at press time.*

In U.S. $	2018	2017	2016	2015	2014	2013
Revenue	111,253,000	66,964,000	40,751,000			
R&D Expense	37,590,000	19,640,000	12,900,000			
Operating Income	-48,978,000	-15,155,000	-14,349,000			
Operating Margin %	-44.02	-22.63%	-35.21%			
SGA Expense	100,959,000	48,346,000	33,603,000			
Net Income	-49,106,000	-15,184,000	-14,349,000			
Operating Cash Flow	-13,581,000	58,000	-4,660,000			
Capital Expenditure	9,481,000	1,820,000	1,084,000			
EBITDA	-44,902,000	-14,166,000	-13,782,000			
Return on Assets %	-62.09%	-26.99%				
Return on Equity %	-263.47%	-201.99%				
Debt to Equity	0.11	0.52				

CONTACT INFORMATION:

Phone:　　　　　　　　　Fax:
Toll-Free: 844-324-2360
Address: 10500 N.E. 8th St., Ste. 1300, Bellevue, WA 98004-4357
United States

STOCK TICKER/OTHER:

Stock Ticker: SMAR　　　　Exchange: NYS
Employees: 787　　　　　　Fiscal Year Ends:
Parent Company:

SALARIES/BONUSES:

Top Exec. Salary: $325,000　　Bonus: $
Second Exec. Salary: $230,000　　Bonus: $

OTHER THOUGHTS:

Estimated Female Officers or Directors:
Hot Spot for Advancement for Women/Minorities:

SMS Assist LLC

www.smsassist.com

NAIC Code: 511210H

TYPES OF BUSINESS:

Software Platform for Property Mangers
Contractor Referrals Software

BRANDS/DIVISIONS/AFFILIATES:

SMS Assist
ONE by SMS Assist
SMS University
Goldman Sachs Investment Partners
Insight Venture Partners
Pritzker Group Venture Capital
Huizenga Capital Management

CONTACTS: Note: Officers with more than one job title may be intentionally listed here more than once.

Taylor Rhodes, CEO
Marc Shiffman, Pres.
Jodi Navta, CMO
Becky Lowe, Chief Human Resources Officer
Jianqing Zhao, CTO
Michael Rothman, Chmn.

GROWTH PLANS/SPECIAL FEATURES:

SMS Assist, LLC provides a proprietary technology platform for the multi-site property management market. This platform is utilized by a network of more than 20,000 subcontractor affiliates and over 140,000 client locations. The SMS Assist technology allows transparency of all services performed. Its SMS Advantage solution is a fully-integrated multi-property management software that implements a complete business solution to seamlessly manage the entire maintenance operation from start to finish. ONE by SMS Assist integrates SMS clients, affiliates and employees on one proprietary technology platform. This results in: clients receiving real-time visibility, actionable big data analytics, transparency and savings; affiliates benefiting from improved communication, streamlined administration and increased sales growth; and SMS Assist having superior communication, visibility and management of all stakeholders in the value chain. The company provides referrals to contractors for services such as exterior maintenance, facilities maintenance, interior maintenance, property management services and residential property services. SMS University is the firm's training program, which provides training and a tool kit for all stakeholders to work in synergy with SMS Assist. Equity partners of the company include Goldman Sachs Investment Partners, Insight Venture Partners, Pritzker Group Venture Capital and Huizenga Capital Management.

SMS Assist offers its employees group benefits, continuing education, amenities, competitive salaries and advancement opportunities.

FINANCIAL DATA: Note: Data for latest year may not have been available at press time.

In U.S. $	2018	2017	2016	2015	2014	2013
Revenue						
R&D Expense						
Operating Income						
Operating Margin %						
SGA Expense						
Net Income						
Operating Cash Flow						
Capital Expenditure						
EBITDA						
Return on Assets %						
Return on Equity %						
Debt to Equity						

CONTACT INFORMATION:

Phone: 312-698-7000   Fax:
Toll-Free:
Address: 875 N. Michigan Ave., Ste. 2800, Chicago, IL 60611 United States

STOCK TICKER/OTHER:

Stock Ticker: Private   Exchange:
Employees: 700   Fiscal Year Ends:
Parent Company:

SALARIES/BONUSES:

Top Exec. Salary: $ Bonus: $
Second Exec. Salary: $ Bonus: $

OTHER THOUGHTS:

Estimated Female Officers or Directors:
Hot Spot for Advancement for Women/Minorities:

Snap Inc (Snapchat)

www.snapchat.com

NAIC Code: 519130

TYPES OF BUSINESS:

Social Media
Advertising Services

BRANDS/DIVISIONS/AFFILIATES:

Snapchat Stories
Snapcash
Discover
Lens Studio
Spectacles
Endless Summer
Class of Lies
Vivian

CONTACTS: Note: Officers with more than one job title may be intentionally listed here more than once.

Evan Spiegel, Co-Founder
Lara Sweet, Chief Accounting Officer
Lara Sweet, CAO
Robert Murphy, Co-Founder
Michael Lynton, Director
Michael OSullivan, General Counsel
Steve Horowitz, Vice President, Divisional

GROWTH PLANS/SPECIAL FEATURES:

Snap, Inc., founded in 2011, operates Snapchat, a social media picture messaging app for mobile devices. The application allows users to send each other photos and videos, called snaps, which disappear within one to 10 seconds of opening, depending on the sender's decision. Users can choose to replay snaps after they've expired and can alter their images with text or drawing. Users can send snaps between friends as well as strangers addressing it to Snapchat usernames. The app also offers Snapchat Stories, which allow users to create linked images that can be viewed an unlimited number of times in a 24-hour period before disappearing. Users can also create Bitojis, a cartoon version of the user, and send to other users to express mood. Additionally, the Snapcash service enables users to send money to their friends in the app, which is directly deposited into the recipient's bank account. Discover is a section of the Snapchat app in which users can watch videos or read stories from major media outlets. Snap also creates Spectacles, sunglasses that connect with Snapchat and capture video from a human perspective. Lens Studio is a free desktop app for Mac and Windows with easy-to-use guides and tools that students, creatives and developers can use to bring their creations to life. This means that the chats and stories from friends are on the left side of Snapchat, and the stories from publishers, creators and the community are on the right. Span generates revenue primarily through ads through sponsored Spectacles, Snap ads and promoted stories. In October 2018, Snap launched Snap originals, serialized shows and docuseries available through Snapchat. Shows include: Endless Summer, Class of Lies, Co-ed, Vivian, The Dead Girls Detective Agency, V/H/S and Good Luck America. Six additional series have been greenlit for production.

FINANCIAL DATA: Note: Data for latest year may not have been available at press time.

In U.S. $	2018	2017	2016	2015	2014	2013
Revenue		824,949,000	404,482,000	58,663,000		
R&D Expense		1,534,863,000	183,676,000	82,235,000		
Operating Income		-3,485,576,000	-520,385,000	-381,729,000		
Operating Margin %		-422.52%	-128.65%	-650.71%		
SGA Expense		2,058,200,000	289,531,000	175,816,000		
Net Income		-3,445,066,000	-514,643,000	-372,893,000		
Operating Cash Flow		-734,667,000	-611,245,000	-306,622,000		
Capital Expenditure		92,625,000	67,013,000	28,305,000		
EBITDA		-3,398,664,000	-491,184,000	-366,422,000		
Return on Assets %		-133.93%	-38.66%	-39.71%		
Return on Equity %		-159.64%	-49.29%	-48.79%		
Debt to Equity		0.01		0.01		

CONTACT INFORMATION:

Phone: 310-399-3339   Fax:
Toll-Free:
Address: 63 Market St., Venice, CA 90291 United States

STOCK TICKER/OTHER:

Stock Ticker: SNAP
Employees: 1,859
Parent Company:

Exchange: NYS
Fiscal Year Ends:

SALARIES/BONUSES:

Top Exec. Salary: $441,923   Bonus: $
Second Exec. Salary: $201,923   Bonus: $200,000

OTHER THOUGHTS:

Estimated Female Officers or Directors:
Hot Spot for Advancement for Women/Minorities:

Snapdeal

NAIC Code: 454111

www.snapdeal.com

TYPES OF BUSINESS:

Electronic Shopping

BRANDS/DIVISIONS/AFFILIATES:

Jasper Infotech Private Limited
DEN Snapdeal TV Shop

CONTACTS: Note: Officers with more than one job title may be intentionally listed here more than once.

Kunal Bahl, CEO

GROWTH PLANS/SPECIAL FEATURES:

Snapdeal is an online marketplace based in New Delhi, India, and owned by Jasper Infotech Private Limited. Snapdeal is one of the largest online marketplaces in the country. Its website offers an assortment of more than 35 million products across 800 categories. It is comprised of 300,000 sellers in more than 6,000 cities and towns throughout India. Manufacturers, wholesalers, distributors and retailers can register and sell authorized products on the site. Snapdeal services for sellers include receiving orders, servicing the orders received and the reception of payments. Sellers pay a small commission for what they sell. Seller subscriptions can be cancelled at any time. Gift cards are obtainable on the website. In its partnership with DEN Networks, Snapdeal's TV commerce channel, DEN Snapdeal TV Shop, serves Indian households and consumer segments that have limited or no internet access. Investment partners include SoftBank, BlackRock, Temasek, Foxconn, Alibaba, eBay Inc., Premji Invest, Intel Capital, Bessemer Venture Partners, Mr. Ratan Tata and many more.

FINANCIAL DATA: Note: Data for latest year may not have been available at press time.

In U.S. $	2018	2017	2016	2015	2014	2013
Revenue		198,956,000	222,957,000	148,855,000	26,828,900	
R&D Expense						
Operating Income						
Operating Margin %						
SGA Expense						
Net Income		-715,984,000	-503,772,000	-211,874,000	-42,218,500	
Operating Cash Flow						
Capital Expenditure						
EBITDA						
Return on Assets %						
Return on Equity %						
Debt to Equity						

CONTACT INFORMATION:

Phone: 91-9212692126   Fax:
Toll-Free:
Address: 246, 1/Fl, Okhla Industrial Area Phase III, New Delhi, 110020 India

STOCK TICKER/OTHER:

Stock Ticker: Private   Exchange:
Employees: 7,000   Fiscal Year Ends:
Parent Company: Jasper Infotech Private Limited

SALARIES/BONUSES:

Top Exec. Salary: $ Bonus: $
Second Exec. Salary: $ Bonus: $

OTHER THOUGHTS:

Estimated Female Officers or Directors:
Hot Spot for Advancement for Women/Minorities:

SoftBank Group Corp

NAIC Code: 517110

www.softbank.co.jp

TYPES OF BUSINESS:

Telecommunications Services
Broadband Infrastructure Services
E-Commerce Services
E-Finance Services
Media & Marketing Services
Technology Services
Cellular Telephone Service
Private Equity Investments

BRANDS/DIVISIONS/AFFILIATES:

Vision Fund
MONET Technologies Corporation

CONTACTS: *Note: Officers with more than one job title may be intentionally listed here more than once.*

Ken Miyauchi, CEO
Jun Shimba, Co-COO
Kazuhiko Fujihara, CFO
Yasuyuki Imai, Co-COO
Junichi Miyakawa, CTO
Ken Miyauchi, COO-SOFTBANK MOBILE Corp.
Ronald D. Fisher, Pres., SOFTBANK Holdings, Inc.
Masayoshi Son, Chmn.

GROWTH PLANS/SPECIAL FEATURES:

SoftBank Group Corp. is a Japanese holding company that operates in the information industry globally. The company has five operating segments: mobile, internet, energy, robot and business. The mobile segment offers smartphones, notebooks, smart watches, mobile connected healthcare devices, personal data communication devices, digital photo devices and mobile devices for children. Internet segment offers internet services, including wireless and optic fiber internet plans for the home. These services can be bundled with mobile phone packages in order to save on charges. The energy segment provides electric power service, as well as power via renewable energy. The robot segment consists of Pepper, the company's robot for the home, for the enterprise/business and/or for education environments. Last, the business segment provides: various business services via mobile and tablet devices, including fixed-mobile conversion solutions, device rental services, landline services, datacenter network services for addressing business challenges when needed; network services such as voice protocol, landline, wireless, data, internet and more; cloud services, which center around the categories of software-as-a-service (SaaS), infrastructure-as-a-service (IaaS), gateway and network; telephone service, including landline service; IBM Watson, a commercialized service for cognitive computing, for understanding humans via recognition, learning and experience technologies; Internet of Things (IoT), from building sensor networks to supplying network connectivity and related devices; digital marketing, which guides users to websites via ads; security services, providing secure access to protect the business from external threats; and datacenter services, connecting networks via mobile, cloud and hybrid formats. In addition, SoftBank manages investment funds and makes private equity and venture capital investments across a broad array of industries--often technology related. It has established the $98 billion Vision Fund in partnership with Saudi Arabia. In October 2018, SoftBank and Toyota Motor Corporation agreed to form a joint venture, MONET Technologies Corporation, to provide mobility services.

FINANCIAL DATA: *Note: Data for latest year may not have been available at press time.*

In U.S. $	2018	2017	2016	2015	2014	2013
Revenue	84,954,410,000	82,563,480,000	84,906,030,000	80,422,800,000	61,838,180,000	31,336,870,000
R&D Expense						
Operating Income	12,090,280,000	9,348,212,000	8,719,641,000	9,115,307,000	7,712,563,000	6,910,433,000
Operating Margin %	42.1	12.93%	11.79%	11.65%	16.28%	22.05%
SGA Expense	23,677,870,000	21,123,210,000	22,703,300,000	21,636,850,000	16,942,850,000	
Net Income	9,637,290,000	13,230,070,000	4,398,301,000	6,199,549,000	4,888,645,000	2,684,430,000
Operating Cash Flow	10,097,790,000	13,920,380,000	8,720,930,000	10,715,100,000	7,979,417,000	8,296,777,000
Capital Expenditure	9,877,143,000	8,566,173,000	12,623,920,000	12,966,160,000	12,720,760,000	5,088,694,000
EBITDA	23,065,400,000	24,603,980,000	26,415,820,000	25,657,480,000	19,513,850,000	10,129,480,000
Return on Assets %	3.72%	6.29%	2.27%	3.54%	4.54%	5.06%
Return on Equity %	23.69%	46.01%	17.36%	27.83%	29.90%	23.08%
Debt to Equity	2.66	3.39	3.54	3.43	4.10	1.02

CONTACT INFORMATION:

Phone: 81-3-6889-2000   Fax:
Toll-Free:
Address: 1-9-1 Higashi Shimbashi, Minato-ku, Tokyo, 105-7303 Japan

STOCK TICKER/OTHER:

Stock Ticker: SFTBF
Employees: 75,000
Parent Company:

Exchange: PINX
Fiscal Year Ends: 03/31

SALARIES/BONUSES:

Top Exec. Salary: $ Bonus: $
Second Exec. Salary: $ Bonus: $

OTHER THOUGHTS:

Estimated Female Officers or Directors:
Hot Spot for Advancement for Women/Minorities:

Sogou Inc

NAIC Code: 519130

www.sogou.com

TYPES OF BUSINESS:

Search Engine

BRANDS/DIVISIONS/AFFILIATES:

Sohu.com Inc
Tencent Holdings Ltd
Sogou Map
Typany Keyboard
Sogou (BV) Limited
Beijing Sogou Technology Development Co Ltd
Sogou Hong Kong Limited
Vast Creation Advertising Media Services Ltd

CONTACTS: *Note: Officers with more than one job title may be intentionally listed here more than once.*

Xiaochuan Wang, CEO

GROWTH PLANS/SPECIAL FEATURES:

Sogou, Inc., majority-owned by Sohu.com, Inc., operates the Chinese search engine Sogou.com. The firm's web and mobile app consists of its search engine features and classifieds online information. Sogou's research and development team continually seeks to enhance user experience through its proprietary search engine by making it as accessible and seamless as possible for everyone, anywhere. The company's voice recognition technology enables users to utilize the search engine via voice. Sougou also debuted a lip-reading program that can operate at up to 90% accuracy. Related products offered by the firm include: Sogou Map, Travel Translator and smartwatches. Nearly 90% of the site's traffic originates from China, with minor traffic from South Korea, Japan, the U.S. and Hong Kong. Sogou wholly-owns the Typany Keyboard app, which works with over 100 languages and comprises personalized prediction technology and comprehensive custom features using artificial intelligence (AI). Typany offers predictive text, autocorrect and the ability to search anything from its keyboard. Other wholly-owned subsidiaries include: Sogou (BVI) Limited; Beijing Sogou Technology Development Co., Ltd.; Sogou Hong Kong Limited; Vast Creation Advertising Media Services Limited; Beijing Sogou Network Technology Co., Ltd.; Sogou Technology Hong Kong Limited; Tianjin Sogou Network Technology Co., Ltd.; and Sogou (Shantou) Internet Microcredit Co., Ltd. Tencent Holdings Limited, Asia's largest internet company, owns an approximate 40% stake in Sogou.

FINANCIAL DATA: *Note: Data for latest year may not have been available at press time.*

In U.S. $	2018	2017	2016	2015	2014	2013
Revenue		908,357,000	660,408,000	591,803,000	386,382,000	
R&D Expense		172,829,000	138,364,000	131,072,000	123,339,000	
Operating Income		93,886,000	71,622,000	101,788,000	-31,925,000	
Operating Margin %		10.33%	10.84%	17.19%	-8.26%	
SGA Expense		184,241,000	147,686,000	110,664,000	129,318,000	
Net Income		82,200,000	56,112,000	99,499,000	-26,839,000	
Operating Cash Flow		182,188,000	149,664,000	205,991,000	91,869,000	
Capital Expenditure		64,155,000	86,895,000	61,538,000	12,584,000	
EBITDA		143,480,000	106,822,000	134,568,000	-2,449,000	
Return on Assets %		6.26%	5.96%	-2.50%	-27.81%	
Return on Equity %		13.92%				
Debt to Equity						

CONTACT INFORMATION:

Phone: 86 1062726666   Fax: 86 1062726588
Toll-Free:
Address: Level 15, No.1 Unit Zhongguancun, Haidian Distr., Beijing, 100084 China

STOCK TICKER/OTHER:

Stock Ticker: SOGO   Exchange: NYS
Employees: 2,217   Fiscal Year Ends:
Parent Company: Sohu.com Inc

SALARIES/BONUSES:

Top Exec. Salary: $382,602   Bonus: $607,485
Second Exec. Salary: $ Bonus: $

OTHER THOUGHTS:

Estimated Female Officers or Directors:
Hot Spot for Advancement for Women/Minorities:

Sales, profits and employees may be estimates. Financial information, benefits and other data can change quickly and may vary from those stated here.

Sohu.com Inc

NAIC Code: 519130

corp.sohu.com

TYPES OF BUSINESS:

Internet Portal-Chinese
Internet Service Provider
Online Gaming Portal
Real Estate Services
Wireless Media Content
Search Engine-Chinese
Apps

BRANDS/DIVISIONS/AFFILIATES:

Sohu Media Portal
sohu.com
Sohu Video
tv.sohu.com
focus.cn
Sogou Inc
Changyou
Tian Long Ba Bu

CONTACTS: Note: Officers with more than one job title may be intentionally listed here more than once.

Zhang Chaoyang, CEO
Belinda Wang, Co-Pres.
Lu Yangfeng, CFO
Zhang Xuemei, VP-Operations and Human Resources
Gang Fang, VP-Prod.
Xuemei (Sherry) Zhang, VP-Admin.
Lili Cui, VP-Brand Advertising Sales
Ye Deng, VP
Zhang Chaoyang, Chmn.

GROWTH PLANS/SPECIAL FEATURES:

Sohu.com, Inc. is Chinese online media, search and game service group which provides online products and services on computers and mobile devices in China. It operates through three subsidiaries: Sohu, Sogou Inc and Changyou. Sohu is a leading online media content provider offering various content, products and services across internet-enabled devices. Sohu runs Sohu Media Portal, an online news and information provider in China and provides content through sohu.com and the Sohu News mobile app; Sohu Video, an online video content provider in China through tv.sohu.com and the Sohu Video mobile app; and Focus, a real estate information and service provider in China through focus.cn. Sogou is a publicly traded internet search and search-related business. Sogou is China's second largest mobile search engine. Sogou Inc owns and operates the Sogou input method, China's largest input software. Changyou's business includes online games, platform channel and a cinema advertising business. The online game business offers computer and mobile games and are operated under the item-based revenue model, which allows players to play the games for free but can pay for in-game virtual items. Games include Tian Long Ba Bu, one of China's most popular client games, Dragon and various mobile games. Changyou's platform business consists of 17173.com, an information portal providing news, forums and videos on online games and players; RaidCall, which provides online music and entertainment services; and MoboTap, which provides software applications for computers and mobile devices through the dolphin Browser, and domestic online card and board games. The cinema advertising business which consists of the acquisition from operators of movie theaters and sales to advertisers of pre-film advertising slots.

FINANCIAL DATA: Note: Data for latest year may not have been available at press time.

In U.S. $	2018	2017	2016	2015	2014	2013
Revenue		1,860,962,000	1,650,431,000	1,937,091,000	1,673,077,000	1,400,274,000
R&D Expense		412,173,000	353,144,000	398,143,000	409,285,000	276,120,000
Operating Income		-120,130,000	-115,022,000	125,632,000	-149,063,000	188,440,000
Operating Margin %		-6.45%	-6.96%	6.33%	-9.12%	13.10%
SGA Expense		535,919,000	554,621,000	557,091,000	730,839,000	460,623,000
Net Income		-554,526,000	-224,021,000	-49,598,000	-166,657,000	-15,298,000
Operating Cash Flow		183,783,000	239,620,000	506,053,000	152,283,000	403,933,000
Capital Expenditure		145,317,000	288,854,000	243,288,000	210,186,000	211,848,000
EBITDA		31,228,000	112,086,000	362,998,000	59,398,000	319,129,000
Return on Assets %		-18.63%	-7.99%	-1.67%	-5.68%	-.60%
Return on Equity %		-63.58%	-20.05%	-4.06%	-13.18%	-1.26%
Debt to Equity		0.16			0.28	

CONTACT INFORMATION:

Phone: 011 861062726666   Fax:
Toll-Free:
Address: Level 18 Media Plaza, Block 3, No. 2 Kexueyuan S. Rd, Haidian District, Beijing, 100190 China

STOCK TICKER/OTHER:

Stock Ticker: SOHU
Employees: 10,000
Parent Company:

Exchange: NAS
Fiscal Year Ends: 12/31

SALARIES/BONUSES:

Top Exec. Salary: $602,664   Bonus: $
Second Exec. Salary: Bonus: $
$361,598

OTHER THOUGHTS:

Estimated Female Officers or Directors: 5
Hot Spot for Advancement for Women/Minorities: Y

Sopra Steria Group SA

www.soprasteria.com/en

NAIC Code: 541512

TYPES OF BUSINESS:

IT Consulting
Business Strategy Consulting
Business Process Outsourcing

BRANDS/DIVISIONS/AFFILIATES:

CIMPA PLM Services
BLUECARAT

CONTACTS: *Note: Officers with more than one job title may be intentionally listed here more than once.*

Vincent Paris, CEO
Christian Levi, Head-Sopra Consulting
Pierre Pasquier, Chmn.

GROWTH PLANS/SPECIAL FEATURES:

Sopra Steria Group SA was founded in 1968, and provides consulting and business process outsourcing services related to information technology (IT), systems integration and overall business strategy and management. The firm divides its business into eight categories. Consulting services range from management to technology consulting. Systems integration addresses the entire application life cycle from systems integration to application management services. Business software development provides software solutions for the financial services, human resources and real estate industries. Infrastructure management (IM) supports information technology infrastructure transformation through technologies integration and services operations around cloud, data centers and end-user environments. Business process services (BPS) designs solutions combining performance and profitability so that its customers can rely on the group to outsource finance, accounting, human resources and purchasing functions. Scientific, technical, industrial and embedded software engineering in order to both innovate and support large-scale industrial programs. Software testing and quality assurance in the areas of consulting, transformation and managed services. Last, CIMPA PLM Services, a subsidiary that specializes in product lifecycle management (PLM) services, operating across many industries. Sopra Steria's offerings include mobility, big data, cloud, cybersecurity, enhancing the value of assets, enterprise architecture, collaborative and information management, customer management, enterprise resource planning, banking solutions, human resources solutions and real estate software. The company provides its solutions and services to the aerospace, insurance, social, banking, defense, homeland security, public sector, healthcare, telecommunications, media, entertainment, transport, retail, energy utilities markets and many more. In May 2018, Sopra Steria acquired BLUECARAT, a German IT services company; and agreed to acquire it-economics, a German consulting firm specializing in digital transformation, agile development, and cloud services.

FINANCIAL DATA: *Note: Data for latest year may not have been available at press time.*

In U.S. $	2018	2017	2016	2015	2014	2013
Revenue		4,551,880,000	4,087,137,824	3,155,268,901	2,534,100,000	1,811,700,000
R&D Expense						
Operating Income						
Operating Margin %						
SGA Expense						
Net Income		205,314,000	164,145,000	97,891,600	109,100,000	95,900,000
Operating Cash Flow						
Capital Expenditure						
EBITDA						
Return on Assets %						
Return on Equity %						
Debt to Equity						

CONTACT INFORMATION:

Phone: 33-1-10-67-29-29   Fax: 33-1-40-67-29-30
Toll-Free:
Address: 9 bis, rue de Presbourg, Paris, 75116 France

STOCK TICKER/OTHER:

Stock Ticker: OR8   Exchange: Frankfurt
Employees: 41,661   Fiscal Year Ends: 12/31
Parent Company:

SALARIES/BONUSES:

Top Exec. Salary: $ Bonus: $
Second Exec. Salary: $ Bonus: $

OTHER THOUGHTS:

Estimated Female Officers or Directors: 1
Hot Spot for Advancement for Women/Minorities:

Sales, profits and employees may be estimates. Financial information, benefits and other data can change quickly and may vary from those stated here.

Spotify Technology SA

NAIC Code: 515111

www.spotify.com

TYPES OF BUSINESS:

Radio Networks, Traditional, Satellite and Online
Streaming Music Service
Internet Radio
Digital Music Sales

BRANDS/DIVISIONS/AFFILIATES:

Spotify Free
Spotify Premium
Spotify Platform
Mediachain
Niland

CONTACTS: *Note: Officers with more than one job title may be intentionally listed here more than once.*

Daniel Ek, CEO
Barry McCarthy, CFO
Seth Farbman, CMO
Katarina Berg, Chief Human Resources Officer
Gustav Soderstrom, Chief Research and Development Officer
Gustav Soderstrom, Chief Prod. Officer
Angela Watts, VP-Global Comm.
Ken Parks, Managing Dir.-USA
Stefan Zilch, Country Mgr.-Germany, Austria & Switzerland
Steve Savoca, Head-Content
Kate Vale, Managing Dir.-Australia & New Zealand
Jeff Levick, Chief Int'l Officer

GROWTH PLANS/SPECIAL FEATURES:

Spotify Technology S.A. is a web-based subscription music service offering podcast and streaming music to registered users in most of Europe and the Americas, Australia, New Zealand and parts of Asia, the Middle East and North Africa. Spotify has more than 170 million monthly active listeners, and over 83 million paying subscribers. The firm's library of music includes approximately 40 million tracks accessed via its proprietary Spotify streaming music player program. Users can download and install the music on a variety of platforms. They can create personalized playlists and also have the option to share these playlists with other Spotify users who can then edit the playlists and make their own updates. The firm's desktop platform is available for Mac, Windows and Linux-based systems. The company maintains licensing deals with major music labels. Spotify offers two main access tiers. Spotify Free allows free access to the online music library and is supported through advertisements, while the fee-based subscription service, Spotify Premium, offers a variety of upgraded features and is ad-free. Spotify Premium can access Spotify on a variety of mobile platforms, and select artists can make new album releases exclusively available on the service for a maximum of two weeks. A discounted Premium subscription tier is available for active college students in the U.S., as well as to more than 30 other countries. Moreover, Spotify connects users to a range of music sellers, providing links to online music stores where customers can purchase albums and individual songs for download. The Spotify Platform enables third-party developers to create music-based apps.

FINANCIAL DATA: *Note: Data for latest year may not have been available at press time.*

In U.S. $	2018	2017	2016	2015	2014	2013
Revenue		4,658,951,000	3,362,646,000	2,209,869,000		
R&D Expense		451,086,700	235,795,300	154,918,700		
Operating Income		-430,582,800	-397,548,600	-267,690,300		
Operating Margin %		-9.24%	-11.82%	-12.11%		
SGA Expense		946,598,600	618,535,600	370,210,000		
Net Income		-1,406,798,000	-613,979,100	-261,994,800		
Operating Cash Flow		203,900,300	115,049,900	-43,286,100		
Capital Expenditure		52,398,960	34,173,240	55,816,280		
EBITDA		-1,338,452,000	-560,441,000	-220,986,900		
Return on Assets %		-47.43%	-34.21%	-21.88%		
Return on Equity %		-262.20%		-100.43%		
Debt to Equity						

CONTACT INFORMATION:

Phone: 46-70-220-4607   Fax:
Toll-Free:
Address: 42-44, Ave. de la Gare, Luxembourg City, L-1610 Luxembourg

STOCK TICKER/OTHER:

Stock Ticker: SPOT
Employees: 2,960
Parent Company:

Exchange: NYS
Fiscal Year Ends: 12/31

SALARIES/BONUSES:

Top Exec. Salary: $ Bonus: $
Second Exec. Salary: $ Bonus: $

OTHER THOUGHTS:

Estimated Female Officers or Directors: 2
Hot Spot for Advancement for Women/Minorities:

Sprinklr Inc

NAIC Code: 511210F

www.sprinklr.com

TYPES OF BUSINESS:
Computer Software, Multimedia, Graphics & Publishing

BRANDS/DIVISIONS/AFFILIATES:

CONTACTS: Note: Officers with more than one job title may be intentionally listed here more than once.
Ragy Thomas, CEO
Carlos Dominguez, Pres.
Chris Lynch, CFO
Pavitar Singh, CTO
Vivek Kundra, COO

GROWTH PLANS/SPECIAL FEATURES:
Sprinklr, Inc. is the developer of enterprise software to help companies market, advertise, sell and research via social media content. Sprinklr clients deploy this proprietary integrated platform across the enterprise and then plug it into customer-facing systems like email, customer relations management and the website in order to have a unified system of engagement. This network strategy allows employees to collaborate in real-time across business units, markets and departmental silos to manage customer experience at scale, within a unified, integrated platform. Sprinklr's solutions include smart content planning and publishing, audience engagement and management, global governance and user management, measurable reporting, instant access from anywhere, social advertising, social listening, social data visualization, benchmarking and mobile applications for managing social activities. The company's products and services are utilized for customer engagement purposes in more than 150 countries, and for 1,000 brands, including Nike, McDonald's, Microsoft, P&G, Samsung and more. Its technology helps these brands market, advertise, care for customers, sell, research and commerce on Facebook, Twitter, LinkedIn and over 20 other channels globally, all from a single, integrated platform. Based in New York, the firm has offices throughout the U.S., as well as in the U.K., France, Germany, Japan, Brazil, United Arab Emirates, India, Singapore, China, Netherlands, Switzerland and Australia.

FINANCIAL DATA: Note: Data for latest year may not have been available at press time.

In U.S. $	2018	2017	2016	2015	2014	2013
Revenue		110,250,000	105,000,000	100,000,000		
R&D Expense						
Operating Income						
Operating Margin %						
SGA Expense						
Net Income						
Operating Cash Flow						
Capital Expenditure						
EBITDA						
Return on Assets %						
Return on Equity %						
Debt to Equity						

CONTACT INFORMATION:
Phone: 917-933-7800   Fax:
Toll-Free:
Address: 29 West 35th St., 7/Fl, New York, NY 10001 United States

STOCK TICKER/OTHER:
Stock Ticker: Private   Exchange:
Employees: 1,100   Fiscal Year Ends:
Parent Company:

SALARIES/BONUSES:
Top Exec. Salary: $ Bonus: $
Second Exec. Salary: $ Bonus: $

OTHER THOUGHTS:
Estimated Female Officers or Directors:
Hot Spot for Advancement for Women/Minorities:

Sprint Corporation

NAIC Code: 517210

TYPES OF BUSINESS:

Mobile Phone and Wireless Services
Internet Service Provider
Wireless Data Services
Long-Range Walkie-Talkie Service
Long-Distance Telephone Service
Network Services

BRANDS/DIVISIONS/AFFILIATES:

Softbank Group Corporation
Sprint
Virgin Mobile
Boost Mobile
Assurance Wireless

CONTACTS: *Note: Officers with more than one job title may be intentionally listed here more than once.*

Andrew Davies, CFO
Paul Schieber, Chief Accounting Officer
Kevin Crull, Chief Strategy Officer
John Saw, Chief Technology Officer
Nestor Cano, COO
Marcelo Claure, Director
Michel Combes, Director
Ronald Fisher, Director
Jorge Gracia, Other Executive Officer
Dow Draper, Other Executive Officer

GROWTH PLANS/SPECIAL FEATURES:

Sprint Corporation is a global communications company offering wireless and wireline communications products and services. The company operates through two business segments: wireless and wireline. The wireless segment provides wireless services on a postpaid and prepaid payment basis to retail subscribers, as well as on a wholesale basis, which includes the sale of wireless services that utilize the Sprint network but sold under the wholesaler's brand. The wireline segment provides a wide range of wireline services to other communications companies, as well as targeted business and consumer subscribers. Additionally, this division offers services to Sprint's wireless segment. Its services are provided through an all-digital global wireline network and a Tier 1 internet backbone. Wireline services include domestic and international data communications using various protocols such as multiprotocol label switching technologies, internet protocol, managed network services, voice over internet protocol (VoIP), session-initiated protocol and traditional voice services. Sprint's brands include Sprint, Virgin Mobile, Boost Mobile and Assurance Wireless on networks that utilize third generation and fourth generation (3G and 4G) code division multiple access (CDMA) or internet protocol technologies. The firm is 84%-owned by SoftBank Group Corporation. In mid-2018, Sprint and T-Mobile US, Inc. signed an agreement to merge, potentially creating a third giant wireless network operator to compete against AT&T, Inc. and Verizon Communications, Inc. The proposed transaction, still subject to approval by regulatory officials at the FCC and anti-trust officials at the U.S. Justice Department, is not expected to close until 2019.

Employee benefits include discounts on products; flexible spending accounts; medical, dental and vision coverage; various employee assistance programs; and a 401(k).

FINANCIAL DATA: *Note: Data for latest year may not have been available at press time.*

In U.S. $	2018	2017	2016	2015	2014	2013
Revenue	32,406,000,000	33,347,000,000	32,180,000,000	34,532,000,000	8,875,000,000	16,891,000,000
R&D Expense						
Operating Income	2,807,000,000	1,830,000,000	719,000,000	542,000,000	547,000,000	-661,000,000
Operating Margin %	8.66	5.48%	2.23%	1.56%		-3.91%
SGA Expense	8,087,000,000	7,994,000,000	8,479,000,000	9,563,000,000	2,371,000,000	4,841,000,000
Net Income	7,389,000,000	-1,206,000,000	-1,995,000,000	-3,345,000,000	-151,000,000	-1,860,000,000
Operating Cash Flow	10,062,000,000	4,168,000,000	3,897,000,000	2,450,000,000	522,000,000	-61,000,000
Capital Expenditure	10,895,000,000	3,958,000,000	7,070,000,000	6,167,000,000	1,640,000,000	3,993,000,000
EBITDA	11,248,000,000	9,874,000,000	7,416,000,000	3,481,000,000	1,718,000,000	2,037,000,000
Return on Assets %	8.66%	-1.46%	-2.46%	-4.02%		-2.70%
Return on Equity %	32.72%	-6.25%	-9.61%	-15.40%		-11.38%
Debt to Equity	1.42	1.90	1.47	1.49		1.25

CONTACT INFORMATION:

Phone: 800 829-0965   Fax: 913 624-3496
Toll-Free: 800-829-0965
Address: 6200 Sprint Pkwy., Overland Park, KS 66251 United States

SALARIES/BONUSES:

Top Exec. Salary: $349,315   Bonus: $1,298,630
Second Exec. Salary: $1,500,000   Bonus: $

STOCK TICKER/OTHER:

Stock Ticker: S   Exchange: NYS
Employees: 28,000   Fiscal Year Ends: 12/31
Parent Company: Softbank Group Corporation

OTHER THOUGHTS:

Estimated Female Officers or Directors: 2
Hot Spot for Advancement for Women/Minorities:

Squarespace Inc

www.squarespace.com

NAIC Code: 541511

TYPES OF BUSINESS:

Web (i.e., Internet) Page Design Services, Custom

BRANDS/DIVISIONS/AFFILIATES:

CONTACTS: *Note: Officers with more than one job title may be intentionally listed here more than once.*

Anthony Casalena, CEO
Nicole Anasenes, CFO

GROWTH PLANS/SPECIAL FEATURES:

Squarespace, Inc. operates an online web publishing platform that allows customers to create, update and manage websites. The company offers a range of templates for businesses, and also provides various mobile apps. Its mission is to provide an avenue from which users can create beautiful websites so that their creative ideas could succeed. The Squarespace platform has empowered millions of people, including local artists, individuals and entrepreneurs. Products include domains, websites, online stores, mobile apps and logos. Personal website fees are $12 per month if billed annually, or $16 per month if billed month-to-month. This offering includes unlimited bandwidth and storage, a mobile-optimized website, website metrics, a free custom domain (with annual purchase), SSL security, 24/7 customer support and allows two contributors. Business website fees are $18 per month if billed annually, or $26 on a month-to-month basis. This offering includes unlimited bandwidth, storage and contributors, among other features. Online store fees within the basic price plan is $26 per month if billed annually, or $30 on a month-to-month basis. This offering includes the ability to sell unlimited products, no transaction fees, a website with galleries and blogs, mobile-optimization and checkout, and more. Advanced online store fees are $40 per month if billed annually, or $46 for month-to-month. This plan offers everything in the basic online store price, but also includes abandoned checkout auto-recovery, as well as real-time carrier shipping features. Squarespace is primarily utilized by online stores, photographers, bloggers, artists, restaurants, musicians, wedding-related businesses and small businesses. Headquartered in New York, the firm has additional offices in Portland, Oregon, as well as Dublin, Ireland.

Squarespace offers its employees medical, dental and vision coverage; parental leave; and 401(k).

FINANCIAL DATA: *Note: Data for latest year may not have been available at press time.*

In U.S. $	2018	2017	2016	2015	2014	2013
Revenue		420,000,000	215,000,000	100,000,000		
R&D Expense						
Operating Income						
Operating Margin %						
SGA Expense						
Net Income						
Operating Cash Flow						
Capital Expenditure						
EBITDA						
Return on Assets %						
Return on Equity %						
Debt to Equity						

CONTACT INFORMATION:

Phone: 646-580-3456   Fax:
Toll-Free:
Address: 225 Varick St. 12/Fl, New York, NY 10014 United States

STOCK TICKER/OTHER:

Stock Ticker: Private   Exchange:
Employees: 563   Fiscal Year Ends:
Parent Company:

SALARIES/BONUSES:

Top Exec. Salary: $ Bonus: $
Second Exec. Salary: $ Bonus: $

OTHER THOUGHTS:

Estimated Female Officers or Directors:
Hot Spot for Advancement for Women/Minorities:

Stamps.com Inc

www.stamps.com

NAIC Code: 454111

TYPES OF BUSINESS:

Postage Stamps, Online Retail
Online Shipping Services
Postal Insurance

BRANDS/DIVISIONS/AFFILIATES:

Stamps.com
Endicia
NetStamps
PhotoStamps

CONTACTS: *Note: Officers with more than one job title may be intentionally listed here more than once.*

Ken McBride, CEO
Kyle Huebner, Pres.
Kenneth McBride, Chairman of the Board
Jeff Carberry, CFO
Sebastian Buerba, CMO
Jonathan Bourgoine, CTO
John Clem, Other Executive Officer
Steve Rifai, Other Executive Officer
Amine Khechfe, Other Executive Officer
Matthew Lipson, Other Executive Officer
Kyle Huebner, President
Ken McBride, Chmn.

GROWTH PLANS/SPECIAL FEATURES:

Stamps.com, Inc. offers internet-based postage solutions. The firm provides convenient and cost-effective web-based services for mailing and shipping letters, packages or parcels, which are marketed under the Stamps.com and Endicia brands for nearly 736,000 monthly subscribers. The company's software allows customers to go online and print U.S. postage stamps or shipping labels using an ordinary PC and laser or inkjet printer. Its postage service is designed to interact with word processing, contact and address management, accounting and corporate applications, invoices, statements, checks and other business documents. Stamps are offered at least 50% cheaper than a traditional postage meter. Additionally, the company offers easy tracking of postage expenditures. Stamps.com also offers NetStamps, a technology allowing customers to print or use postage without being online and which contains no destination addresses or expiration date. The PhotoStamps service allows customers to turn digital photographs into postage stamps. It offers branded insurance, so users may insure their mail or packages in an integrated online process; the insurance is offered alongside regular USPS insurance. Stamps.com is a membership-based service. Customers get their first month free and then pay $17.99 a month for Stamps.com's services. In addition to its partnership with the U.S. Postal Service, Stamps.com has PC Postage partnerships with several firms, including Microsoft Corp, Avery and Hewlett Packard. The company is also integrated with brand retail companies such as eBay, PayPal and Amazon.com so members can consolidate orders and print shipping labels with ease.

The firm offers employees medical, dental, vision and life insurance; identity theft protection; flexible spending accounts; a 401(k) plan; and an employee stock purchase plan.

FINANCIAL DATA: *Note: Data for latest year may not have been available at press time.*

In U.S. $	2018	2017	2016	2015	2014	2013
Revenue		468,709,000	364,305,000	213,957,000	147,269,000	127,819,000
R&D Expense		46,208,000	35,158,000	20,711,000	13,309,000	10,958,000
Operating Income		163,503,000	120,220,000	50,768,000	32,248,000	34,118,000
Operating Margin %		34.88%	32.99%	23.72%	21.89%	26.69%
SGA Expense		179,772,000	145,955,000	98,543,000	68,806,000	55,243,000
Net Income		150,603,000	75,229,000	-4,198,000	36,882,000	44,153,000
Operating Cash Flow		197,823,000	148,047,000	46,116,000	51,725,000	35,756,000
Capital Expenditure		6,813,000	7,750,000	2,291,000	2,858,000	5,282,000
EBITDA		185,361,000	139,678,000	2,528,000	37,081,000	36,656,000
Return on Assets %		23.36%	13.21%	-1.07%	16.69%	27.77%
Return on Equity %		34.60%	24.59%	-1.89%	19.57%	31.01%
Debt to Equity		0.12	0.37	0.65		

CONTACT INFORMATION:

Phone: 310 482-5800   Fax:
Toll-Free: 1-855-889-7867
Address: 1990 E. Grand Ave., El Segundo, CA 90245 United States

SALARIES/BONUSES:

Top Exec. Salary: $720,020   Bonus: $
Second Exec. Salary: Bonus: $400,000
$240,609

STOCK TICKER/OTHER:

Stock Ticker: STMP
Employees: 700
Parent Company:

Exchange: NAS
Fiscal Year Ends: 12/31

OTHER THOUGHTS:

Estimated Female Officers or Directors:
Hot Spot for Advancement for Women/Minorities:

Steel Connect Inc

www.moduslink.com

NAIC Code: 511210A

TYPES OF BUSINESS:

Computer Software, Supply Chain & Logistics
Web-Based Distribution & Fulfillment Services
Marketing Distribution Services
Consulting Services
Marketing Solutions

BRANDS/DIVISIONS/AFFILIATES:

ModusLink Corporation
ModusLink PTS Inc
IWCO Direct Inc
ModusLink Global Solutions Inc

CONTACTS: Note: Officers with more than one job title may be intentionally listed here more than once.

John Whitenack, CEO, Subsidiary
Warren Lichtenstein, CEO
Louis Belardi, CFO
Glen Kassan, Director

GROWTH PLANS/SPECIAL FEATURES:

Steel Connect, Inc. (formerly ModusLink Global Solutions, Inc.) is a leading provider of global supply chain business process outsourcing (BPO) to technology-based companies in the computing, software, consumer electronics, medical devices, retail and communications markets. The company provides these services through wholly-owned subsidiaries: ModusLink Corporation and ModusLink PTS, Inc. (together form ModusLink), and IWCO Direct Holdings, Inc. ModusLink provides supply chain business process management, serving clients in markets such as consumer electronics, communications, computing, medical devices, software and retail. ModusLink designs and executes elements in its clients' global supply chains to improve speed to market, product customization, flexibility, cost, quality and service. These benefits are delivered through a combination of industry expertise, innovative service solutions, integrated operations and technology. This division also produces and licenses an entitlement management solution powered by its enterprise-class Poetic software, which offers a solution for activation, provisioning, entitlement subscription and data collection from physical goods and digital products. ModusLink's integrated network consists of 20 sites operating in 21 languages in various countries throughout North America, Europe and Asia. IWCO Direct delivers highly-effective data-driven marketing solutions, including omnichannel marketing campaigns and direct mail strategies. Through its Mail-Gard division, IWCO Direct also offers business continuity and disaster recovery services to protect against unexpected business interruptions, along with providing print and mail outsourcing services. In early-2018, ModusLink Global Solutions, Inc. changed its corporate name to Steel Connect, as well as its Nasdaq ticker symbol to STCN, to encompass both its ModusLink and its IWCO Direct brands.

FINANCIAL DATA: Note: Data for latest year may not have been available at press time.

In U.S. $	2018	2017	2016	2015	2014	2013
Revenue	645,258,000	436,620,000	459,023,000	561,673,000	723,400,000	754,504,000
R&D Expense						
Operating Income	-20,727,000	-17,794,000	-32,846,000	-5,849,000	1,608,000	-13,735,000
Operating Margin %		-4.07%	-7.15%	-1.04%	.22%	-1.82%
SGA Expense	101,701,000	54,159,000	57,604,000	59,667,000	72,020,000	86,972,000
Net Income	36,715,000	-25,827,000	-61,281,000	-18,429,000	-16,282,000	-40,355,000
Operating Cash Flow	11,768,000	-24,445,000	-19,788,000	19,194,000	9,815,000	7,027,000
Capital Expenditure	18,423,000	4,730,000	7,936,000	8,518,000	4,489,000	7,296,000
EBITDA	31,672,000	-7,956,000	-37,584,000	3,599,000	7,739,000	-19,688,000
Return on Assets %		-8.19%	-15.40%	-4.10%	-4.09%	-11.48%
Return on Equity %		-34.68%	-53.16%	-11.65%	-9.91%	-25.06%
Debt to Equity		0.94	0.67	0.53	0.42	

CONTACT INFORMATION:

Phone: 781 663-5000   Fax:
Toll-Free: 888-996-6387
Address: 1601 Trapelo Rd., Ste. 170, Waltham, MA 02451 United States

STOCK TICKER/OTHER:

Stock Ticker: STCN
Employees: 1,990
Parent Company:

Exchange: NAS
Fiscal Year Ends: 07/31

SALARIES/BONUSES:

Top Exec. Salary: $600,000   Bonus: $
Second Exec. Salary: $325,000   Bonus: $

OTHER THOUGHTS:

Estimated Female Officers or Directors: 2
Hot Spot for Advancement for Women/Minorities:

Stitch Fix Inc

NAIC Code: 454111

TYPES OF BUSINESS:

Subscription-Based Apparel Selection
Personal Shopping Services Online
Men's Apparel
Women's Apparel

BRANDS/DIVISIONS/AFFILIATES:

CONTACTS: Note: Officers with more than one job title may be intentionally listed here more than once.

Katrina Lake, CEO
Paul Yee, CFO
Mike Smith, COO
Scott Darling, Other Executive Officer

GROWTH PLANS/SPECIAL FEATURES:

Stitch Fix, Inc. provides a subscription-based personal clothing and accessory platform and delivery service specifically tailored to individual customer's profiles. The company has created a suite of proprietary software tools and style-matching technology that guide apparel selections for each customer. Roughly 3,400 Stitch Fix stylists, mostly working from home, select clothing and accessories that will have a good chance of fitting each customer's tastes, lifestyle and body shape. The business model is based on convenience. Shoppers can avoid trips to physical stores, dressing rooms and parking. They can also save time and frustration, since the clothing shipped is more likely to fit well and is likely to be to the consumer's taste. Customers first provide general information online from which a style profile is created. Computer algorithms analyze the customer's profile and help guide the stylists in making choices for the customer's shipment. Once the consumer receives the box, she can try everything on, purchase what she likes and return the rest with free return shipping. The average price point for clothing is $55 to $60 per item in the normal package, but the company carries a wide variety of price points. A "Luxe Box" will feature more expensive items, from roughly $150 to $500 each. Those who choose to purchase all pieces within a shipment get a discount off the entire purchase. Apparel ranges from pants, skirts, shorts, dresses, sweaters, shirts, outerwear, scarves, jewelry, shoes and bags. Stitch Fix as founded with a focus on Women's apparel; however, more recently, it has extended into Petite, Maternity, Men's, Plus and Kids apparel. The company has warehouses spread across the U.S.

FINANCIAL DATA: Note: Data for latest year may not have been available at press time.

In U.S. $	2018	2017	2016	2015	2014	2013
Revenue	1,226,505,000	977,139,000	730,313,000			
R&D Expense						
Operating Income	43,024,000	31,640,000	64,228,000			
Operating Margin %		3.23%	8.79%			
SGA Expense	492,998,000	402,781,000	259,021,000			
Net Income	44,900,000	-594,000	33,181,000			
Operating Cash Flow	72,178,000	38,624,000	45,116,000			
Capital Expenditure	16,565,000	17,165,000	15,238,000			
EBITDA	53,566,000	39,295,000	67,772,000			
Return on Assets %		8.03%	17.31%			
Return on Equity %		32.26%	66.43%			
Debt to Equity						

CONTACT INFORMATION:

Phone: 415-882-7765   Fax:
Toll-Free:
Address: 1 Montgomery St., San Francisco, CA 94104 United States

STOCK TICKER/OTHER:

Stock Ticker: SFIX   Exchange: NAS
Employees: 5,800   Fiscal Year Ends: 07/31
Parent Company:

SALARIES/BONUSES:

Top Exec. Salary: $601,571   Bonus: $
Second Exec. Salary: Bonus: $
$511,288

OTHER THOUGHTS:

Estimated Female Officers or Directors:
Hot Spot for Advancement for Women/Minorities:

Stripe Inc

stripe.com

NAIC Code: 522320

TYPES OF BUSINESS:

Payment Processing -Intermediary

BRANDS/DIVISIONS/AFFILIATES:

Stripe Connect
Stripe Sigma
Stripe Radar
Stripe Issuing
Stripe Terminal

CONTACTS: Note: Officers with more than one job title may be intentionally listed here more than once.

Patrick Collison, CEO
John Collison, Pres.

GROWTH PLANS/SPECIAL FEATURES:

Stripe, Inc. is an online payment platform designed for private individuals and businesses, serving customers in over 120 countries. The firm offers a suite of application programming interfaces (APIs) that allow developers to easily integrate Stripe's payment platform into their web interface and mobile applications. Stripe's payments product accepts all major cards through its single, unified platform, and enables users to set up a marketplace and bill customers on a recurring basis. The company's billing platform enables businesses to design billing around customer experience, and features tools for building and scaling a recurring business model. Stripe's payments platforms for platforms is Stripe Connect, which is designed to accept money and pay out to third parties. It provides a complete set of building blocks to support virtually any business model, including on-demand businesses, eCommerce, crowdfunding and travel and events. Stripe Sigma enable business teams to run the company more efficiently, to provide analyze data and to manage production. Stripe Radar contains tools that make it easy for handling everything involved in establishing an internet business. Stripe Radar fights fraud through its detection features, even for businesses using machine learning. Stripe Issuing is an application program interface (API) for creating, distributing and managing physical and virtual payment cards. Last, Stripe Terminal is a programmable point of sale, extending the eCommerce presence into the physical world. It enables in-person payments for any business model via Stripe's pre-certified card readers, JavaScript and mobile SDKs, and cloud-based hardware management. Based in San Francisco, the firm has international offices in Dublin, London, Paris, Singapore, Tokyo and more.

FINANCIAL DATA: Note: Data for latest year may not have been available at press time.

In U.S. $	2018	2017	2016	2015	2014	2013
Revenue		1,500,000,000	1,000,000,000	400,000,000	150,000,000	45,000,000
R&D Expense						
Operating Income						
Operating Margin %						
SGA Expense						
Net Income						
Operating Cash Flow						
Capital Expenditure						
EBITDA						
Return on Assets %						
Return on Equity %						
Debt to Equity						

CONTACT INFORMATION:

Phone: 650-427-9276   Fax:
Toll-Free:
Address: 185 Berry St., Ste. 550, San Francisco, CA 94107 United States

STOCK TICKER/OTHER:

Stock Ticker: Private   Exchange:
Employees: 750   Fiscal Year Ends:
Parent Company:

SALARIES/BONUSES:

Top Exec. Salary: $ Bonus: $
Second Exec. Salary: $ Bonus: $

OTHER THOUGHTS:

Estimated Female Officers or Directors:
Hot Spot for Advancement for Women/Minorities:

Student Advantage LLC

www.shopandtravelusa.com/sa-mobile

NAIC Code: 541800

TYPES OF BUSINESS:

Marketing Services
Discount Service Company
Services for College Student Marketing

BRANDS/DIVISIONS/AFFILIATES:

CBORD Group Inc (The)
StudentAdvantage.com
Student Advantage Discount Card
Local Merchant
My Deals

CONTACTS: *Note: Officers with more than one job title may be intentionally listed here more than once.*

Jim Hoefflin, Pres.-CBORD Group
Sami Takieddine, Dir.-Oper., Atlanta
Shawn McCarthy, VP-Wide Area Commerce Solutions

GROWTH PLANS/SPECIAL FEATURES:

Student Advantage, LLC, a subsidiary of The CBORD Group, Inc., is a discount service company for the college market. Student Advantage works with universities, colleges and campus organizations, along with thousands of discount locations, to provide students with discounted purchases at their campuses, in stores throughout the country and online. The firm connects with students through its website, StudentAdvantage.com, and through the Student Advantage Discount Card, both of which provides students with discounts from the partnering discount locations. Student Advantage has partners across a vast number of industries, offering 350,000 discounts nationwide. There are three savings categories: travel savings, SA mobile discounts and traditional discounts. The travel category offers discounts on flights, car rentals and hotel reservations with more than 500,000 hotels and car rental locations. Members get $100 worth of travel credits that go toward a stay at over 400,000 nationwide hotels. SA mobile discounts work through the My Deals mobile app. This allows students to redeem deals directly from a mobile device, including categories like automotive, dining and food, entertainment and recreation, gold, health and beauty, home and garden, hotel, movies, services and shopping. Traditional discount provides university-specific ID cards, allowing students to save money and universities to generate extra income. Student Advantage's Local Merchant programs enable students to use their Discount Cards as a method of payment for off-campus dining, shopping and other purchase needs. Dedicated emails can be sent to Student Advantage cardholders from discount partners, offering information on upcoming deals. A one-year memberships costs $30.

FINANCIAL DATA: *Note: Data for latest year may not have been available at press time.*

In U.S. $	2018	2017	2016	2015	2014	2013
Revenue						
R&D Expense						
Operating Income						
Operating Margin %						
SGA Expense						
Net Income						
Operating Cash Flow						
Capital Expenditure						
EBITDA						
Return on Assets %						
Return on Equity %						
Debt to Equity						

CONTACT INFORMATION:

Phone: 844-462-2673   Fax:
Toll-Free: 800-333-2920
Address: 950 Danby Rd., Ste. 100C, Ithaca, NY 14850 United States

STOCK TICKER/OTHER:

Stock Ticker: Subsidiary   Exchange:
Employees: 448   Fiscal Year Ends: 12/31
Parent Company: CBORD Group Inc (The)

SALARIES/BONUSES:

Top Exec. Salary: $ Bonus: $
Second Exec. Salary: $ Bonus: $

OTHER THOUGHTS:

Estimated Female Officers or Directors:
Hot Spot for Advancement for Women/Minorities:

SugarCRM

NAIC Code: 511210K

www.sugarcrm.com

TYPES OF BUSINESS:

Customer Relationship Management Software

BRANDS/DIVISIONS/AFFILIATES:

CONTACTS: Note: Officers with more than one job title may be intentionally listed here more than once.

Larry Augustin, CEO
Karen Willem, CFO
Melissa Sargeant, CMO
Sherry Pulvers, VP-People & Places
Kirk Fjeldheim, CIO
Lila Tretikov, Chief Prod. Officer
Patricia Timm, General Counsel
S. Zachariah Sprackett, VP-Oper.
Majed Itani, VP-Dev.
Craig A. Lewis, Sr. VP-Global Svcs. & Channel Dev.
Glenn Cross, Exec. VP-Worldwide Field Oper.

GROWTH PLANS/SPECIAL FEATURES:

SugarCRM is a provider of open source customer relationship management (CRM) software. The firm's applications are deployed by over 2 million individual users in 120 countries and speaking 26 languages. The company helps companies build a unique customer experience via enhanced business relationships. The SugarCRM platform collects every bit of critical information across sales, service and marketing, and easily integrates with any application. It also offers personalized user experience that works seamlessly on all devices. Sugar's CRM solutions combine the adaptability of the Sugar platform, a rich ecosystem and customer relationship expertise to address critical business needs. Its relationship analytics solution allows organizations to leverage their collective relationships network asset by tapping into previously hidden insights, which are seamlessly integrated into the Sugar platform. It also captures and automates any relationship journey with rules-driven behavior regardless of size or complexity. Managing the journeys enable firms to follow their sales playbook, drive growth and increase retention. Sugar's CRM analytics, insights and solutions help clients better understand their customers and optimize each customer engagement to meet customer goals, which improves business goals in return. SugarCRM's current single investor is private equity firm, Accel-KKR.

FINANCIAL DATA: Note: Data for latest year may not have been available at press time.

In U.S. $	2018	2017	2016	2015	2014	2013
Revenue		300,000,000	290,000,000	285,000,000	247,000,000	175,000,000
R&D Expense						
Operating Income						
Operating Margin %						
SGA Expense						
Net Income						
Operating Cash Flow						
Capital Expenditure						
EBITDA						
Return on Assets %						
Return on Equity %						
Debt to Equity						

CONTACT INFORMATION:

Phone: 408-454-6900   Fax: 408-873-2872
Toll-Free: 877-842-7276
Address: 10050 N. Wolfe Rd., SW2-130, Cupertino, CA 95014 United States

STOCK TICKER/OTHER:

Stock Ticker: Private   Exchange:
Employees: 475   Fiscal Year Ends:
Parent Company:

SALARIES/BONUSES:

Top Exec. Salary: $ Bonus: $
Second Exec. Salary: $ Bonus: $

OTHER THOUGHTS:

Estimated Female Officers or Directors: 6
Hot Spot for Advancement for Women/Minorities: Y

Sumo Logic Inc

www.sumologic.com

NAIC Code: 511210J

TYPES OF BUSINESS:

Computer Software, Data Base & File Management

BRANDS/DIVISIONS/AFFILIATES:

CONTACTS: *Note: Officers with more than one job title may be intentionally listed here more than once.*

Ramin Sayar, CEO
Steve Fitz, Chief Revenue Officer
Sydney Carey, CFO
Suku Krishnaraj, CMO
Shea Kelly, VP-Human Resources
Christian Beedgen, CTO

GROWTH PLANS/SPECIAL FEATURES:

Sumo Logic, Inc. provides cloud-native data analytic software. The company's service analyzes more than 100 petabytes of data, more than 16 million searches and delivers millions of insights on a daily basis. Sumo Logic simplifies how businesses and organizations collect and analyze machine data in order to gain deep visibility across their full application and infrastructure stack. With Sumo Logic's service products, these entities can accelerate modern application delivery, monitor and troubleshoot in real-time and improve security and compliance. Sumo Logic's products collect and centralize data from any application, cloud, server, network device or sensor; searches and analyzes data in real-time across the full application stack; monitors and visualizes that data through real-time dashboards; implement custom alerts and notifications concerning data that deviates from calculated baselines or exceeds thresholds; and detects and predicts unwanted data and anomalies. Price plans include: free, for individuals and teams looking to try Sumo Logic for small projects, for an unlimited period of time; $90 per month for professionals, with 1 gigabyte (GB) per day for teams and businesses ready to make Sumo Logic the center of their monitoring and troubleshooting; and $150 per month for enterprises, with 1GB per day for larger teams and enterprises that need real-time, operational and security visibility and flexibility across multiple teams and regions. Sumo Logic is headquartered in Redwood City, California, with additional offices in New York and Colorado, USA, and internationally in the U.K., Poland, India, Australia and Japan.

FINANCIAL DATA: *Note: Data for latest year may not have been available at press time.*

In U.S. $	2018	2017	2016	2015	2014	2013
Revenue						
R&D Expense						
Operating Income						
Operating Margin %						
SGA Expense						
Net Income						
Operating Cash Flow						
Capital Expenditure						
EBITDA						
Return on Assets %						
Return on Equity %						
Debt to Equity						

CONTACT INFORMATION:

Phone: 650-810-8700   Fax: 650-961-1711
Toll-Free: 855-564-7866
Address: 305 Main St., Redwood City, CA 94063 United States

STOCK TICKER/OTHER:

Stock Ticker: Private   Exchange:
Employees: 290   Fiscal Year Ends:
Parent Company:

SALARIES/BONUSES:

Top Exec. Salary: $ Bonus: $
Second Exec. Salary: $ Bonus: $

OTHER THOUGHTS:

Estimated Female Officers or Directors:
Hot Spot for Advancement for Women/Minorities:

Suning.com Co Ltd

www.suning.com

NAIC Code: 454111

TYPES OF BUSINESS:

Electronic Shopping

BRANDS/DIVISIONS/AFFILIATES:

Suning Commerce Group Co Ltd
Yifuboa
Suning Payment
Alibaba

CONTACTS: Note: Officers with more than one job title may be intentionally listed here more than once.

En Long Hou, Pres.
Zhong Xiang Xiao, CFO
Jin Dong Zhang, Chmn.

GROWTH PLANS/SPECIAL FEATURES:

Suning.com Co., Ltd., formerly Suning Commerce Group Co., Ltd., is an online-to-offline China-based online smart retailer engaging primarily in household appliances, digital products and communication products. Suning engages in three business units: retail, finance and logistics. The retail business engages in the retail of mobile phones, cameras, TVs, portable electronics, refrigerators, office supplies, men and women's clothing, luggage, jewelry, clocks, shoes, watches, books, children's books, washing machine, kitchen and bathroom, computers, computer accessories, food and drink, toys, cleaning products, air conditioning units, car and motorcycles, car and motorcycle parts, exercise equipment, pet supplies, smart technology, makeup, home textiles, used cars, art supplies, medical supplies, health products, foreign products and more. The logistics segment provides logistics services throughout the entire supply chain process focusing on efficiency, customer experience, management and innovation. The segment has two warehouses focusing on the cloud and robotics and engages in the creation of unmanned vehicles and heavy trucks. The finance segment provides small and medium sized businesses with quality and comprehensive financial services. Services include payment, supply chain financing, consumer finance, investment and wealth management, crowd funding, insurance, investments and pre-paid cards. Customers must set up an account through Yifuboa, also known as Suning Payment, to pay for items on the site. In May 2018, the firm sold $1.5 billion of its shares in Alibaba, a Chinese conglomerate specializing in e-commerce, retail, internet, AI and technology.

FINANCIAL DATA: Note: Data for latest year may not have been available at press time.

In U.S. $	2018	2017	2016	2015	2014	2013
Revenue		28,855,700,000	21,381,400,000	20,883,100,000	17,701,300,000	17,221,600,000
R&D Expense						
Operating Income						
Operating Margin %						
SGA Expense						
Net Income		1,457,620,000	364,975,000	32,147,800	4,916,220	17,059,800
Operating Cash Flow						
Capital Expenditure						
EBITDA						
Return on Assets %						
Return on Equity %						
Debt to Equity						

CONTACT INFORMATION:

Phone: 86-25-6699-6699   Fax: 86-25-8441-8888
Toll-Free:
Address: 1 Suning St., Xuanwu Dist., Nanjing, 210042 China

SALARIES/BONUSES:

Top Exec. Salary: $ Bonus: $
Second Exec. Salary: $ Bonus: $

STOCK TICKER/OTHER:

Stock Ticker: 2024   Exchange: Shenzhen
Employees: 29,814   Fiscal Year Ends: 12/31
Parent Company:

OTHER THOUGHTS:

Estimated Female Officers or Directors:
Hot Spot for Advancement for Women/Minorities:

Support.com Inc

NAIC Code: 511210K

www.support.com

TYPES OF BUSINESS:

Software-Service & Support Automation
Real-Time Service Management Software

BRANDS/DIVISIONS/AFFILIATES:

Nexus

CONTACTS: *Note: Officers with more than one job title may be intentionally listed here more than once.*

Richard Bloom, CEO
Joshua Schechter, Director

GROWTH PLANS/SPECIAL FEATURES:

Support.com, Inc. is a leading provider of software and cloud-based services designed to assist small businesses and end-users in solving technology problems. Solutions include the cloud-based Nexus service platform, a scalable workforce of technology specialists, mobile and desktop applications for end-users and expertise in program design and execution. The company also makes available its Nexus platform on a software-as-a-service (SaaS) basis and licenses its end-user applications separately. The firm delivers its services via remote control and by telephone, leveraging the Nexus platform, with most technology specialists working from home. Service programs available for consumer markets include computer and mobile device set-up, security and support, virus and malware removal and wireless network set-up. Service programs available for small business markets include the consumer services plus managed services such as server and network monitoring and maintenance. Services can be purchased on a subscription basis, on a one-time incident basis, through small business plans or with prepaid service and gift cards. The company sells its products through direct sales to consumers and indirectly through channel partners such as brick-and-mortar and online retailers, anti-virus providers, PC/CE manufacturers and others. Support.com's sales and marketing efforts principally target North American consumers and small businesses. As technology is at the core of its business, the company maintains dedicated R&D teams in Sunnyvale, California and Eugene, Oregon.

The company offers employees life and AD&D insurance; a 401(k) plan; medical, dental and vision insurance; emergency travel assistance; an employee assistance program; and an educational reimbursement program.

FINANCIAL DATA: *Note: Data for latest year may not have been available at press time.*

In U.S. $	2018	2017	2016	2015	2014	2013
Revenue		60,121,000	61,660,000	77,333,000	82,991,000	88,163,000
R&D Expense		3,033,000	5,577,000	6,957,000	5,078,000	5,735,000
Operating Income		-1,437,000	-15,305,000	-14,224,000	-3,150,000	10,752,000
Operating Margin %		-2.39%	-24.82%	-18.39%	-3.79%	12.19%
SGA Expense		11,121,000	19,629,000	21,556,000	18,526,000	25,975,000
Net Income		-1,526,000	-15,956,000	-27,041,000	-3,483,000	10,383,000
Operating Cash Flow		-4,203,000	-11,450,000	-5,468,000	1,458,000	10,210,000
Capital Expenditure		63,000	561,000	1,896,000	231,000	221,000
EBITDA		-793,000	-13,557,000	-12,831,000	-1,784,000	12,486,000
Return on Assets %		-2.31%	-21.45%	-28.54%	-3.24%	10.64%
Return on Equity %		-2.68%	-24.80%	-32.37%	-3.64%	12.24%
Debt to Equity						

CONTACT INFORMATION:

Phone: 877 493-2778   Fax:
Toll-Free: 877-493-2778
Address: 1200 Crossman Ave., Ste. 210, Sunnyvale, CA 94089 United States

STOCK TICKER/OTHER:

Stock Ticker: SPRT
Employees: 1,525
Parent Company:

Exchange: NAS
Fiscal Year Ends: 12/31

SALARIES/BONUSES:

Top Exec. Salary: $480,000   Bonus: $
Second Exec. Salary: $160,019   Bonus: $

OTHER THOUGHTS:

Estimated Female Officers or Directors: 1
Hot Spot for Advancement for Women/Minorities:

SVMK Inc (SurveyMonkey)

www.surveymonkey.com

NAIC Code: 519130

TYPES OF BUSINESS:

Tools for Online Surveys
Survey Software

BRANDS/DIVISIONS/AFFILIATES:

Wufoo

CONTACTS: Note: Officers with more than one job title may be intentionally listed here more than once.

Timothy Maly, CFO
Leela Srinivasan, Chief Marketing Officer
Elizabeth Ducot, Chief Technology Officer
Alexander Lurie, Director
David Ebersman, Director
Lora Blum, General Counsel
Rebecca Cantieri, Other Executive Officer
John Schoenstein, Other Executive Officer
Jon Cohen, Other Executive Officer
Ross Moser, Other Executive Officer
Thomas Hale, President
Priyanka Carr, Senior VP, Divisional

GROWTH PLANS/SPECIAL FEATURES:

SVMK, Inc. operates a survey platform called SurveyMonkey. The platform offers software that enables companies to create, deploy and analyze online surveys, as well as other capabilities. With over 20 million questions answered daily through its surveys, the firm is a global leader in survey software. The platform enables companies, organizations and institutions to receive direct feedback from their customers, employees and students. Survey types include customer satisfaction, customer loyalty, event surveys, employee engagement, job satisfaction, human resources surveys, market research, opinion polls, concept testing and much more. SurveyMonkey offers both pre-configured survey templates and custom-designed surveys for more specific feedback requirements. SurveyMonkey provides four levels of subscription service. The free basic level includes 10 questions per survey and a maximum of 100 responses as well as real-time results and multi-channel data collection support. At the standard level, which costs $37 per month, services include unlimited surveys and questions per survey, 1,000 responses, custom survey design, data exports, 24/7 email support, unlimited filters, skip logic only and text analysis. The advantage level, at $32 per month/billed annually, adds advanced data exports, custom variables, analysis, audience panel credits and industry benchmarks. At the premier level, at $99 per month/billed annually, clients receive advanced branching and piping, block randomization, white label surveys and multi-lingual surveys. Discounted pricing is offered for students and educators, as well as for teams of three or more people. Enterprise plans offer compliance, advanced security and administration features. In addition to surveys, SurveyMonkey offers Wufoo, offering a platform for creating forms, invitations and online surveys, as well as for collecting data, registrations and payments. In September 2018, SVMK began trading on the Nasdaq under ticker symbol: SVMK.

FINANCIAL DATA: Note: Data for latest year may not have been available at press time.

In U.S. $	2018	2017	2016	2015	2014	2013
Revenue		218,773,000	207,295,000			
R&D Expense		53,660,000	37,985,000			
Operating Income		-19,017,000	-9,247,000			
Operating Margin %						
SGA Expense		121,451,000	110,802,000			
Net Income		-24,010,000	-76,350,000			
Operating Cash Flow		45,026,000	35,842,000			
Capital Expenditure		47,807,000	46,253,000			
EBITDA		28,227,000	-2,594,000			
Return on Assets %						
Return on Equity %						
Debt to Equity						

CONTACT INFORMATION:

Phone: 650-543-8400   Fax:
Toll-Free:
Address: One Curiosity Way, San Mateo, CA 94403 United States

STOCK TICKER/OTHER:

Stock Ticker: SVMK   Exchange: NAS
Employees: 266   Fiscal Year Ends: 12/31
Parent Company:

SALARIES/BONUSES:

Top Exec. Salary: $258,767   Bonus: $132,000
Second Exec. Salary: $350,000   Bonus: $

OTHER THOUGHTS:

Estimated Female Officers or Directors: 5
Hot Spot for Advancement for Women/Minorities: Y

Switch Inc

www.switch.com

NAIC Code: 518210

TYPES OF BUSINESS:

Data Processing, Hosting, and Related Services

BRANDS/DIVISIONS/AFFILIATES:

Switch COLO
Switch CONNECT
Switch CLOUD
Switch SAFE
Switch SUPERLOOP
Switch CITIES
Switch ON

CONTACTS: Note: Officers with more than one job title may be intentionally listed here more than once.

Rob Roy, CEO
Thomas Morton, Pres.
Gabe Nacht, CFO
Jessica Battaglia, VP-Human Resources
Missy Young, CIO
Rob Roy, Chmn.

GROWTH PLANS/SPECIAL FEATURES:

Switch, Inc. is a technology infrastructure ecosystem corporation that designs, constructs and operates advanced data centers. The firm's data center ecosystem offers clients a myriad of options for innovation, economies of scale, risk mitigation, sustainability and investment protection. Switch's primary solutions include Switch COLO, Switch CONNECT, Switch CLOUD, Switch SAFE, Switch SUPERLOOP, Switch CITIES and Switch ON. COLO provides colocation for a nation, which means a data center facility in which a business can rent space for servers and other computing hardware; CONNECT offers dynamic telecommunications purchasing at massive scale; CLOUD enables clients to directly access a mix of private, public and hybrid cloud environments; SAFE is an always-on, distributed denial of service (D/DoS) attack mitigation platform; SUPERLOOP is a geographically-redundant data center so that Switch clients can deploy mission-critical infrastructure and workloads in the world's largest active data center ecosystem; CITIES is Switch's community solutions division which utilizes the firm's internal teams and global technology partner ecosystem for the purpose of developing smart cities; and ON is the energy division that offers technology tools for the energy sector, using artificial intelligence (AI) combined with related hardware and connectivity to create green energy in relation to smart meters, solar arrays, battery storage, load balancing and phase alignment to mission critical energy grid systems. Current (as of January 2019) prime Switch locations include Las Vegas, Tahoe/Reno, Grand Rapids and Atlanta in the U.S., as well as Italy and Thailand.

FINANCIAL DATA: Note: Data for latest year may not have been available at press time.

In U.S. $	2018	2017	2016	2015	2014	2013
Revenue		378,275,000	318,352,000	265,870,000	207,306,000	166,835,000
R&D Expense						
Operating Income						
Operating Margin %						
SGA Expense						
Net Income		-15,208,000	31,368,000	73,472,000	56,509,000	39,914,000
Operating Cash Flow						
Capital Expenditure						
EBITDA						
Return on Assets %						
Return on Equity %						
Debt to Equity						

CONTACT INFORMATION:

Phone: 702-444-4111   Fax:
Toll-Free:
Address: 7135 S. Decatur Blvd., Las Vegas, NV 89118 United States

STOCK TICKER/OTHER:

Stock Ticker: SWCH
Employees: 689
Parent Company:

Exchange: NYS
Fiscal Year Ends: 12/31

SALARIES/BONUSES:

Top Exec. Salary: $ Bonus: $
Second Exec. Salary: $ Bonus: $

OTHER THOUGHTS:

Estimated Female Officers or Directors:
Hot Spot for Advancement for Women/Minorities:

Symantec Corporation

NAIC Code: 511210E

TYPES OF BUSINESS:

Computer Software, Security & Anti-Virus
Remote Management Products
Consulting-Cyber Security
Information Protection Products

BRANDS/DIVISIONS/AFFILIATES:

Norton
Javelin Networks
Appthority

CONTACTS: Note: Officers with more than one job title may be intentionally listed here more than once.

Gregory Clark, CEO
Daniel Schulman, Chairman of the Board
Nicholas Noviello, Chief Accounting Officer
Samir Kapuria, Executive VP, Divisional
Scott Taylor, Executive VP
Amy Cappellanti-Wolf, Senior VP

GROWTH PLANS/SPECIAL FEATURES:

Symantec Corporation provides a range of software, appliances and services designed to secure and manage information technology (IT) infrastructure. The company provides customers worldwide with software and services that protect, manage and control information risks related to security, data protection, storage, compliance and systems management. The firm has two operating segments: enterprise security and consumer security. The enterprise security segment protects organizations so they can securely conduct business while leveraging new platforms and data. This segment includes Symantec's threat protection products, information protection products, cyber security services, and website security offerings, previously named trust services. These products and services help secure information in transit and wherever it resides in the network path, from the user's device to the data's resting place. In addition, these products help to prevent the loss of confidential data by insiders, and help customers achieve and maintain compliance with laws and regulations. The consumer security focuses on making it simple for customers to be productive and protected at home and at work. The firm's Norton-branded services provide multi-layer security and identity protection on major desktop and mobile operating systems, to defend against increasingly complex online threats to individuals, families, and small businesses. Norton Security products help customers protect against increasingly complex threats and address the need for identity protection, while also managing the rapid increase in mobile and digital data, such as personal financial records, photos, music and videos. Symantec operates in over 40 countries. In November 2018, Symantec acquired Javelin Networks, which offers advanced software technology to defend enterprises against active director-based attacks; and acquired Appthority, which offers mobile application security analysis.

Symantec offers employees a 401(k) with company match, tuition reimbursement and adoption assistance.

FINANCIAL DATA: Note: Data for latest year may not have been available at press time.

In U.S. $	2018	2017	2016	2015	2014	2013
Revenue	4,834,000,000	4,019,000,000	3,600,000,000	6,508,000,000	6,676,000,000	6,906,000,000
R&D Expense	956,000,000	823,000,000	748,000,000	1,144,000,000	1,038,000,000	1,012,000,000
Operating Income	459,000,000	173,000,000	593,000,000	1,401,000,000	1,453,000,000	1,248,000,000
Operating Margin %		4.30%	16.47%	21.52%	21.76%	18.07%
SGA Expense	2,167,000,000	2,023,000,000	1,587,000,000	2,702,000,000	2,880,000,000	3,185,000,000
Net Income	1,138,000,000	-106,000,000	2,488,000,000	878,000,000	898,000,000	765,000,000
Operating Cash Flow	950,000,000	-220,000,000	796,000,000	1,312,000,000	1,281,000,000	1,593,000,000
Capital Expenditure	142,000,000	70,000,000	272,000,000	381,000,000	260,000,000	336,000,000
EBITDA	1,333,000,000	476,000,000	766,000,000	1,611,000,000	1,731,000,000	1,800,000,000
Return on Assets %		-.70%	19.90%	6.55%	6.43%	5.58%
Return on Equity %		-2.95%	51.77%	14.96%	16.00%	14.55%
Debt to Equity		1.97	0.60	0.29	0.36	0.38

CONTACT INFORMATION:

Phone: 650 527-8000   Fax:
Toll-Free:
Address: 350 Ellis St., Mountain View, CA 94043 United States

STOCK TICKER/OTHER:

Stock Ticker: SYMC   Exchange: NAS
Employees: 13,000   Fiscal Year Ends: 03/31
Parent Company:

SALARIES/BONUSES:

Top Exec. Salary: $1,000,000   Bonus: $
Second Exec. Salary: Bonus: $
$865,000

OTHER THOUGHTS:

Estimated Female Officers or Directors: 3
Hot Spot for Advancement for Women/Minorities: Y

Sales, profits and employees may be estimates. Financial information, benefits and other data can change quickly and may vary from those stated here.

Symphony Technology Group

www.stgpartners.com

NAIC Code: 511210H

TYPES OF BUSINESS:

Enterprise Management Software
Retail Industry Software
Analytic Services
Outsourcing

BRANDS/DIVISIONS/AFFILIATES:

Connexity
Dodge Data & Analytics
Jobrapido
Poplicus
Sigma3
Windshuttle Holdings LLC
System C Connected Care
Ventiv Technology

CONTACTS: *Note: Officers with more than one job title may be intentionally listed here more than once.*

William Chisholm, STG Managing Partner
Stephen Henkenmeier, CFO
Ravindar Chahal, Dir.-IT
Chris Langone, VP-Bus. Dev.
Mattias Derynck, VP-Investor Rel.
Stephen Combs, Chief Recruiting Officer
William Chisholm, Managing Dir.
Pallab Chatterjee, Managing Dir.
J.T.Treadwell, Managing Dir.
Romesh Wadhwani, Chmn.
Mahinder Mathrani, Managing Dir.-STG India

GROWTH PLANS/SPECIAL FEATURES:

Symphony Technology Group (STG) is a private equity firm based in Palo Alto that focuses its investments in the enterprise software and services markets. The company provides its portfolio of enterprises with the expertise and experience to deliver successful client service and become world-class businesses. STG's portfolio consists of 16 global companies that service a variety of industries, including AFS Technologies, Connexity, Dodge Data & Analytics, Erecuit, Extenda Retail, First Advantage, Fishbowl Inc., Jobrapido, Market Strategies and Morpace, Poplicus, Sigma3, Simmons, SPH Analytics, Symphony Talent, System C Connected Care, Ventiv Technology and Windshuttle Holdings, LLC. AFS Technologies is a provider of software solutions for consumer goods manufacturers and food distribution companies. Connexity is a technology-driven marketing solutions company which enables retailers and brands to understand their consumers better. Fishbowl Inc. is a customer engagement platform provider for the restaurant industry. Jobrapido is a leading job search engine operating in 58 countries with a strong presence in Europe. Symphony Talent is an omnichannel recruitment marketing and employer branding solution. System C Connected Care is a leading supplier of IT systems and services to the U.K. NHS and the wider health and social care sectors. Ventiv Technology provides technology that transforms how organizations manage risk. In May 2018, STG acquired Windshuttle Holdings, LLC, a SAP-centric robotic process automation and data management platform provider. In November of that same year, SPH Analytics and Morpace Health Division announced a potential merger, to be completed in early 2019.

FINANCIAL DATA: *Note: Data for latest year may not have been available at press time.*

In U.S. $	2018	2017	2016	2015	2014	2013
Revenue	2,900,000,000	2,800,000,000	2,750,000,000	2,725,000,000	2,700,000,000	2,600,000,000
R&D Expense						
Operating Income						
Operating Margin %						
SGA Expense						
Net Income						
Operating Cash Flow						
Capital Expenditure						
EBITDA						
Return on Assets %						
Return on Equity %						
Debt to Equity						

CONTACT INFORMATION:

Phone: 650-935-9500   Fax: 650-935-9501
Toll-Free:
Address: 2475 Hanover St., Palo Alto, CA 94304 United States

STOCK TICKER/OTHER:

Stock Ticker: Private   Exchange:
Employees: 15,250   Fiscal Year Ends: 12/31
Parent Company:

SALARIES/BONUSES:

Top Exec. Salary: $ Bonus: $
Second Exec. Salary: $ Bonus: $

OTHER THOUGHTS:

Estimated Female Officers or Directors:
Hot Spot for Advancement for Women/Minorities:

Talkdesk Inc

NAIC Code: 511210K

www.talkdesk.com

TYPES OF BUSINESS:

Computer Software, Sales & Customer Relationship Management

BRANDS/DIVISIONS/AFFILIATES:

CONTACTS: *Note: Officers with more than one job title may be intentionally listed here more than once.*

Tiago Paiva, CEO
Janice Rapp, Head-Product Mktg.
Peter Ekman, VP-People
Raoul Felix, CTO

GROWTH PLANS/SPECIAL FEATURES:

Talkdesk, Inc. provides cloud-based call center software solutions for businesses. The company's solutions enable users to optimize calls and know who is calling before answering the phone. The software also provides an overview of the customer with information from various departments within the business, including customer relations management, helpdesk, back office and social/networking sites. Talkdesk's products are grouped into two categories: platform and integrations. Platform products include agent productivity, application program interfaces (APIs), software developer kits (SKDs), artificial intelligence (AI), intelligent routing, mobile, omnichannel, outbound dialer, quality management, reporting, analytics, self-service, Talkdesk live, voice, voice analytics and workforce management. The integrations category includes Talkdesk for Salesforce, Talkdesk for Slack and Talkdesk for Zendesk, among others. This division's Callbar provides the flexibility to hand calls from anywhere on the desktop. Talkdesk automatically synchronizes customer data to display information the moment a call is received. And Talkdesk can be configured to automatically trigger events in connected applications to save representatives valuable time. Talkdesk solutions primarily serve businesses engaged in healthcare, eCommerce and business process outsourcing. Headquartered in California, USA, the firm has an additional offices in Brazil, Australia, the U.K. and Portugal.

FINANCIAL DATA: *Note: Data for latest year may not have been available at press time.*

In U.S. $	2018	2017	2016	2015	2014	2013
Revenue						
R&D Expense						
Operating Income						
Operating Margin %						
SGA Expense						
Net Income						
Operating Cash Flow						
Capital Expenditure						
EBITDA						
Return on Assets %						
Return on Equity %						
Debt to Equity						

CONTACT INFORMATION:

Phone: Fax:
Toll-Free: 888-743-3044
Address: 536 Mission St., 12/Fl, San Francisco, CA 94105 United States

STOCK TICKER/OTHER:

Stock Ticker: Private   Exchange:
Employees: 300   Fiscal Year Ends:
Parent Company:

SALARIES/BONUSES:

Top Exec. Salary: $ Bonus: $
Second Exec. Salary: $ Bonus: $

OTHER THOUGHTS:

Estimated Female Officers or Directors:
Hot Spot for Advancement for Women/Minorities:

Tata Consultancy Services Limited (TCS)   www.tcs.com
NAIC Code: 541512

TYPES OF BUSINESS:
IT Consulting
Software Engineering
Business Process Outsourcing
Research

BRANDS/DIVISIONS/AFFILIATES:
Tata Group
Tata America International Corporation
Tata Consultancy Services Asia Pacific Pte Ltd
Diligenta Limited
TCS e-Serve International Limited
TCS BaNCS

CONTACTS: *Note: Officers with more than one job title may be intentionally listed here more than once.*
Rajesh Gopinathan, CEO
N. Ganapathy Subramaniam, COO
N. Chandrasekaran, Chmn.

GROWTH PLANS/SPECIAL FEATURES:
Tata Consultancy Services Limited (TCS) is one of India's largest consulting companies and one of Asia's largest independent software and services organizations, with a presence in 46 countries. The firm is part of the Tata Group, an Asian conglomerate with interests in energy, telecommunications, financial services, chemicals, engineering and materials. TCS primarily provides IT consulting, services and business process outsourcing (BPO) for international businesses. TCS' services include application development and maintenance, business intelligence, enterprise solutions, assurance services, engineering and industrial services, infrastructure services, consulting, asset leveraged solutions and business process services. The company focuses on software engineering practices and standards as well as research and development in software engineering and technology. Its TCS BaNCS core banking software suite is used by retail banks, and includes functions for universal banking, core banking, payments, wealth management, foreign exchange, compliance and many more operations. The firm has formed alliances with leading technology companies, academic institutions and consulting firms to provide customers with expertise in technology fields in which it does not specialize. Development of new strategies and technologies occurs in the firm's global centers of excellence, located in several nations. TCS has offices throughout North America (with a regional headquarter in New York City), four of which are development centers and centers of excellence. A few of the company's 50 subsidiaries include Tata America International Corporation, Tata Consultancy Services Asia Pacific Pte Limited in Singapore, Diligenta Limited in the UK and TCS e-Serve International Limited in India.

FINANCIAL DATA: *Note: Data for latest year may not have been available at press time.*

In U.S. $	2018	2017	2016	2015	2014	2013
Revenue		18,094,166,016	16,664,653,824	14,517,606,400	12,548,294,656	9,661,615,104
R&D Expense						
Operating Income						
Operating Margin %						
SGA Expense						
Net Income		4,032,327,168	3,725,990,656	3,045,018,368	2,939,442,176	2,134,700,800
Operating Cash Flow						
Capital Expenditure						
EBITDA						
Return on Assets %						
Return on Equity %						
Debt to Equity						

CONTACT INFORMATION:
Phone: 91-22-6778-9999   Fax: 91-22-6778-9000
Toll-Free:
Address: Raveline St., 21 DS Marg, Mumbai, Maharasha 400021 India

STOCK TICKER/OTHER:
Stock Ticker: TTNQY   Exchange: PINX
Employees: 400,875   Fiscal Year Ends: 03/31
Parent Company: Tata Group

SALARIES/BONUSES:
Top Exec. Salary: $ Bonus: $
Second Exec. Salary: $ Bonus: $

OTHER THOUGHTS:
Estimated Female Officers or Directors:
Hot Spot for Advancement for Women/Minorities:

TD Ameritrade Holding Corporation

www.amtd.com

NAIC Code: 523120

TYPES OF BUSINESS:

Discount Stock Brokerage
Online Brokerage
Financial Planning
Clearing Services

BRANDS/DIVISIONS/AFFILIATES:

CONTACTS: *Note: Officers with more than one job title may be intentionally listed here more than once.*

Bharat Masrani, CEO, Subsidiary
Stephen Boyle, CFO
Joseph Moglia, Chairman of the Board
Timothy Hockey, Director
Thomas Nally, Executive VP, Divisional
Steven Quirk, Executive VP, Divisional
Peter deSilva, Executive VP, Divisional
Ellen Koplow, Executive VP

GROWTH PLANS/SPECIAL FEATURES:

TD Ameritrade Holding Corporation and its subsidiaries provide securities brokerage services and technology-based financial services to retail investors and business partners. With $1.2 trillion in total client assets (as of October 2018), the company provides its services through online, telephone, branch and mobile channels. Products and services include: support, with licensed representatives available by phone and email 24/7, as well as online and in-person for one-on-one support; trading tools and platforms, designed for active traders and long-term investors, offering tools to research stocks, place trades, identify potential market opportunities and manage portfolios; investment products, with access to equities, exchange-traded funds (ETFs), bonds, CDs, options, non-proprietary mutual funds, futures and foreign exchange trading; research, offering independent investment research access from third parties such as Morningstar, S&P Capital IQ, Jaywalk and TheStreet; clear pricing, which includes flat-rate commission on all online equity trades, a variety of commission-free investments, no platform fees, no share limits, no trade requirements to access advanced features and no opening deposit minimums; and free investor education resources. In October 2018, TD Ameritrade announced that it had made a strategic investment in ErisX, a regulated derivatives exchange and clearing organization that will include digital asset futures and spot contracts on a single platform. Earlier that year, TD Ameritrade completed the conversion of Scottrade brokerage accounts to TD Ameritrade, just a few months after closing the acquisition of Scottrade's brokerage business.

The firm offers its employees a 401(k) and profit-sharing plan.

FINANCIAL DATA: *Note: Data for latest year may not have been available at press time.*

In U.S. $	2018	2017	2016	2015	2014	2013
Revenue	5,342,000,000	3,605,000,000	3,274,000,000	3,211,000,000	3,108,000,000	2,796,000,000
R&D Expense						
Operating Income						
Operating Margin %						
SGA Expense	2,216,000,000	1,496,000,000	1,372,000,000	1,328,000,000	1,260,000,000	1,153,000,000
Net Income	1,473,000,000	872,000,000	842,000,000	813,000,000	787,000,000	675,000,000
Operating Cash Flow	1,908,000,000	687,000,000	1,468,000,000	746,000,000	1,025,000,000	739,000,000
Capital Expenditure	229,000,000	197,000,000	105,000,000	71,000,000	144,000,000	144,000,000
EBITDA						
Return on Assets %		2.58%	3.05%	3.23%	3.44%	3.26%
Return on Equity %		14.18%	16.91%	16.84%	16.70%	14.83%
Debt to Equity		0.35	0.35	0.36	0.26	0.22

CONTACT INFORMATION:

Phone: 402 331-7856   Fax:
Toll-Free: 800-237-8692
Address: 200 S. 108th Ave., Omaha, NE 68154 United States

STOCK TICKER/OTHER:

Stock Ticker: AMTD   Exchange: NAS
Employees: 6,010   Fiscal Year Ends: 09/30
Parent Company:

SALARIES/BONUSES:

Top Exec. Salary: $995,192   Bonus: $
Second Exec. Salary: $650,000   Bonus: $

OTHER THOUGHTS:

Estimated Female Officers or Directors: 4
Hot Spot for Advancement for Women/Minorities: Y

Teespring Inc

NAIC Code: 454111

teespring.com

TYPES OF BUSINESS:

Electronic Shopping

BRANDS/DIVISIONS/AFFILIATES:

teespring.com

CONTACTS: *Note: Officers with more than one job title may be intentionally listed here more than once.*

Walker Williams, CEO
Douglas Myers, VP-Global Oper.
Robert Chatwani, CMO

GROWTH PLANS/SPECIAL FEATURES:

Teespring, Inc. is an eCommerce platform established to enable anyone to design and sell products. The company was founded in 2011 by two Brown University students who developed a website in mere hours to sell commemorative shirts in lieu of the closing of their favorite local bar. The site was designed to accept prepaid orders before printing anything so as to bypass heavy upfront production costs. Obtaining hundreds of orders within hours, the concept and site was then launched, allowing anyone to create a crowdfunding campaign for custom apparel. The Teespring platform provides the tools to create unique designs, print them on the chosen merchandise and then sell them without the restrictions usually associated with starting an online store. The platform sells the items in campaigns (or limited edition runs) so they can be printed in bulk. Items include apparel, home decor, socks, iPhone cases, accessories, tote bags and beverage mugs. In addition, Teespring ships the merchandise from its Kentucky facility. Popular categories at the teespring.com site include age, family, hobbies and animals. Purchasing from Teespring supports the independent creators and the causes they care about. Teespring has offices in San Francisco, California; Providence, RI; Hebron, Kentucky; and London, England.

FINANCIAL DATA: *Note: Data for latest year may not have been available at press time.*

In U.S. $	2018	2017	2016	2015	2014	2013
Revenue		150,000,000	163,800,000	228,000,000	100,000,000	
R&D Expense						
Operating Income						
Operating Margin %						
SGA Expense						
Net Income			-7,800,000	-36,000,000		
Operating Cash Flow						
Capital Expenditure						
EBITDA						
Return on Assets %						
Return on Equity %						
Debt to Equity						

CONTACT INFORMATION:

Phone: 855-833-7774   Fax:
Toll-Free:
Address: 460 Bryant St., Ste. 200, San Francisco, CA 94107 United States

STOCK TICKER/OTHER:

Stock Ticker: Private   Exchange:
Employees: 312   Fiscal Year Ends:
Parent Company:

SALARIES/BONUSES:

Top Exec. Salary: $ Bonus: $
Second Exec. Salary: $ Bonus: $

OTHER THOUGHTS:

Estimated Female Officers or Directors:
Hot Spot for Advancement for Women/Minorities:

TEGNA Inc

NAIC Code: 515120

www.tegna.com

TYPES OF BUSINESS:
Television Broadcasting
Internet Broadcasting

BRANDS/DIVISIONS/AFFILIATES:
CareerBuilder
G/O Digital
Cars.com Inc

CONTACTS: *Note: Officers with more than one job title may be intentionally listed here more than once.*
David Lougee, CEO
Victoria Harker, CFO
Howard Elias, Chairman of the Board
Todd Mayman, Chief Administrative Officer
Lynn Beall, COO, Divisional

GROWTH PLANS/SPECIAL FEATURES:
TEGNA, Inc. is a media and digital media company that delivers content to consumers through broadcast television and digital media platforms. The firm's operations are divided by its four primary content delivery platforms: advertising and media services revenues, political advertising revenues, subscription revenues and other services. The advertising and media services revenues includes local and national non-political advertising, digital marketing services and advertising on stations' websites and tablet and mobile products. Advertising makes up the most significant portion of TEGNA's revenue. The segment includes 47 television stations in 39 markets. Through this segment, TEGNA is the largest independent station group of major network affiliates in the top 25 markets in the U.S., covering approximately one-third of all television households nationwide. The company's portfolio includes NBC, CBS, FOX and ABC stations operating on long-term affiliation agreements. Each of TEGNA's 47 television stations also has a digital presence across online, mobile and social media platforms. Political advertising revenues are driven by election cycles at the local and national level. These revenues are particularly prevalent in the second half of the year. The company's subscription revenues reflect fees paid by satellite, cable, OTT and telecommunications providers. Last, other services include the production of programming from third parties and production of advertising material. In June 2018, TEGNA announced the launch of DEALBOSS a commerce franchise for local stations and social platforms and in-air markets. In August of that year, TEGNA announced that it had acquired the leading television stations in Toledo, Ohio and Odessa-Midland, Texas.

FINANCIAL DATA: *Note: Data for latest year may not have been available at press time.*

In U.S. $	2018	2017	2016	2015	2014	2013
Revenue		1,903,026,000	3,341,198,000	3,050,945,000	6,008,174,000	5,161,362,000
R&D Expense						
Operating Income		550,331,000	1,004,204,000	854,301,000	1,154,395,000	797,483,000
Operating Margin %		28.91%	30.05%	28.00%	19.21%	15.45%
SGA Expense		342,339,000	1,093,837,000	1,068,221,000	1,539,476,000	1,291,858,000
Net Income		273,744,000	436,697,000	459,522,000	1,062,171,000	388,680,000
Operating Cash Flow		386,211,000	683,429,000	613,106,000	821,199,000	511,488,000
Capital Expenditure		76,886,000	94,796,000	118,767,000	150,354,000	110,407,000
EBITDA		657,507,000	1,148,955,000	1,158,809,000	1,895,028,000	924,749,000
Return on Assets %		4.05%	5.11%	4.65%	10.38%	4.97%
Return on Equity %		16.76%	19.56%	16.87%	35.71%	15.41%
Debt to Equity		3.02	1.77	1.91	1.37	1.37

CONTACT INFORMATION:
Phone: 703-873-6600   Fax:
Toll-Free:
Address: 7950 Jones Branch Dr., McLean, VA 22107-0150 United States

STOCK TICKER/OTHER:
Stock Ticker: TGNA
Employees: 10,121
Parent Company:

Exchange: NYS
Fiscal Year Ends: 12/31

SALARIES/BONUSES:
Top Exec. Salary: $908,333   Bonus: $1,000,000
Second Exec. Salary: $700,000   Bonus: $675,000

OTHER THOUGHTS:
Estimated Female Officers or Directors:
Hot Spot for Advancement for Women/Minorities:

Sales, profits and employees may be estimates. Financial information, benefits and other data can change quickly and may vary from those stated here.

Telecomunicaciones de Puerto Rico Inc

www.claropr.com

NAIC Code: 517110

TYPES OF BUSINESS:

Local Exchange Carrier
Telecommunications Equipment Rental, Sales & Billing
Wireless Internet Services
Cellular Service

BRANDS/DIVISIONS/AFFILIATES:

America Movil SAB de CV
Claro Puerto Rico
Claro

GROWTH PLANS/SPECIAL FEATURES:

Telecomunicaciones de Puerto Rico, Inc. (TELPRI), a subsidiary of America Movil SAB de CV and operating through Claro Puerto Rico, is the largest telecommunication services company in Puerto Rico. Offering wireline and fixed line services to both residential and enterprise customers, all marketed under the Claro name. Products and services for residential customers include mobile, internet, TV and fixed telephony. as well as bundled packages. To business customers, TELPRI provides mobile, internet, data, fixed telephony and cloud services. Data services features IBS trunking, virtual Ethernet link and IP-VPN (virtual private network) services. Finally, to the corporate client, which includes large-scale companies, the firm additionally offers data center services including collocation and virtual servers.

CONTACTS: Note: Officers with more than one job title may be intentionally listed here more than once.

Cristina Lambert, CEO
Aldo Figueroa, COO
Cristina Lambert, Pres.
Hector Houssay, CFO
Mariano Doble, CMO

FINANCIAL DATA: Note: Data for latest year may not have been available at press time.

In U.S. $	2018	2017	2016	2015	2014	2013
Revenue		800,000,000	1,020,000,000	1,100,000,000	1,200,000,000	
R&D Expense						
Operating Income						
Operating Margin %						
SGA Expense						
Net Income						
Operating Cash Flow						
Capital Expenditure						
EBITDA						
Return on Assets %						
Return on Equity %						
Debt to Equity						

CONTACT INFORMATION:

Phone: 787-792-6052   Fax: 787-282-0958
Toll-Free: 800-781-1314
Address: 1515 FD Roosevelt Ave., Guaynabo, 00968 Puerto Rico

STOCK TICKER/OTHER:

Stock Ticker: Subsidiary   Exchange:
Employees: 4,900   Fiscal Year Ends: 12/31
Parent Company: America Movil SAB de CV

SALARIES/BONUSES:

Top Exec. Salary: $ Bonus: $
Second Exec. Salary: $ Bonus: $

OTHER THOUGHTS:

Estimated Female Officers or Directors: 1
Hot Spot for Advancement for Women/Minorities:

Telenor ASA

www.telenor.com

NAIC Code: 517210

TYPES OF BUSINESS:

Mobile Telephone Services
Fixed-Line Telephone Services
Cable Services
Satellite Communications
Satellite Television Broadcasting

BRANDS/DIVISIONS/AFFILIATES:

VEON Ltd
Canal Digital Group
Telenor Satellite Broadcasting
Norkring
Telenor Digital
Telenor Digital Businesses

CONTACTS: *Note: Officers with more than one job title may be intentionally listed here more than once.*

Sigve Brekke, CEO
Jon Frederik Baksaas, Pres.
Jorgen C. Arentz Rostrup, CFO
Svien Henning Kirkeng, Exec. VP-Mktg. & Products
Cecilie Blydt Heuch, Chief People Officer
Ruza Sabanovic, Exec. VP-IT
Morten Karlsen Sorby, Head-Strategy & Regulatory Affairs
Rolv-Erik Spilling, Exec. VP
Hilde M. Tonne, Exec. VP
Berit Svendsen, Exec. VP
Bjorn Magnus Kopperud, Acting Head-Central & Eastern European Oper.
Gunn Waersted, Chmn.
Sigve Brekke, Head-Asia Oper.

GROWTH PLANS/SPECIAL FEATURES:

Telenor ASA, based in Norway, is a national telecommunications operator and an international provider of mobile services. Telenor's operations are focused in three major areas: mobile, fixed-line and broadcast. With 170 million subscribers, mobile services are the firm's chief basis for internationalization and growth, accounting for almost half its external revenue. The company has majority shareholdings in mobile operations in 13 markets, including Norway, Denmark, Sweden, Hungary, Serbia, Bulgaria, Montenegro, Thailand, Malaysia, Myanmar, Bangladesh and Pakistan. It also has interests in additional markets through its minority stake in VEON Ltd. Telenor provides fixed-line telecommunications services to residential and business markets through asymmetric digital subscriber line (ADSL) and fiber-optic lines as well as analogue (PSTN) and digital fixed-line (ISDN) telephony services. The company operates the national terrestrial broadcast network in Norway and is a leading provider of satellite broadcasting services in the Nordic region through its three geostationary satellites. Telenor's broadcast segment consists of the Canal Digital Group, which provides TV distribution services to nearly 1 million homes and businesses; transmission and encryption, which provides transmission services for broadcasters through subsidiaries Telenor Satellite Broadcasting and Norkring. Telenor Digital explores new ventures, creates and develops next-generation digital solutions for customers globally. Telenor Digital Businesses is a global unit that manages Telenor's investments in the digital business space, and combines new verticals with the company's existing core services. During 2017, Telenor sold 85% of Telenor Banka's capital, while retaining a 15% share; and reduced its ownership in VEON to 14.6%. In May 2018, Telenor sold subsidiary Telenor (India) Communications Private Limited to Bharti Airtel Limited.

FINANCIAL DATA: *Note: Data for latest year may not have been available at press time.*

In U.S. $	2018	2017	2016	2015	2014	2013
Revenue						
R&D Expense						
Operating Income						
Operating Margin %						
SGA Expense						
Net Income						
Operating Cash Flow						
Capital Expenditure						
EBITDA						
Return on Assets %						
Return on Equity %						
Debt to Equity						

CONTACT INFORMATION:

Phone: 47 81077000   Fax: 47 67890000
Toll-Free:
Address: Snaroyveien 30, Fornebu, N-1331 Norway

STOCK TICKER/OTHER:

Stock Ticker: TELNF   Exchange: PINX
Employees: 31,000   Fiscal Year Ends: 12/31
Parent Company:

SALARIES/BONUSES:

Top Exec. Salary: $ Bonus: $
Second Exec. Salary: $ Bonus: $

OTHER THOUGHTS:

Estimated Female Officers or Directors: 6
Hot Spot for Advancement for Women/Minorities: Y

Telephone and Data Systems Inc (TDS)

NAIC Code: 517110

www.tdsinc.com

TYPES OF BUSINESS:

Local Telephone Service
Cellular Telephone Services
Internet Access
Printing Services
Long-Distance Telephone Service
Data Networks
Broadband Service

BRANDS/DIVISIONS/AFFILIATES:

United States Cellular Corporation
TDS Telecommunications Corporation
OneNeck

CONTACTS: *Note: Officers with more than one job title may be intentionally listed here more than once.*

Kenneth Meyers, CEO, Subsidiary
Leroy Carlson, CEO
Douglas Shuma, CFO
Walter Carlson, Chairman of the Board
Kurt Thaus, Chief Information Officer
Douglas Chambers, Controller, Subsidiary
Jane McCahon, Secretary
Daniel DeWitt, Senior VP, Divisional
Scott Williamson, Senior VP, Divisional
Joseph Hanley, Senior VP, Divisional
Peter Sereda, Senior VP, Divisional

GROWTH PLANS/SPECIAL FEATURES:

Telephone and Data Systems, Inc. (TDS) is a diversified telecommunications service company with wireless telephone and wireline telephone operations. The firm operates primarily through two segments: United States Cellular Corporation (U.S. Cellular) and TDS Telecommunications Corporation (TDS Telecom). U.S. Cellular is one of the U.S.'s largest wireless telecommunications providers, providing services to customers via 5.1 million connections in 22 states. This segment focuses on retail consumers, government entities and small-to-mid-size business customers in industries such as construction, retail, agriculture, professional services and real estate. TDS Telecom provides broadband, video and voice services to approximately 1.2 million connections in 34 states through its wireline and cable divisions. The wireline division has operations located in a mix of rural, small town and suburban markets, with the largest concentrations of customers in the Upper Midwest and the Southeast. Wireline operates several incumbent local exchange carriers in 25 states and provides telecommunications services as a competitive local exchange carrier in the upper Midwest and the southeast. Wireline provide retail telecommunications services to both residential and commercial customers that reside within its respective service territories. The cable division operates cable systems in markets primarily in Colorado, New Mexico, Oregon, Texas and Utah. In addition, TDS offers hybrid IT solutions, including cloud and hosting solutions, managed services, enterprise application management, advanced IT services, hardware and local connectivity. These solutions are provided via data centers in Arizona, Colorado, Iowa, Minnesota, New Jersey, Oregon and Wisconsin under the OneNeck brand name.

TDS employees receive medical, dental and vision insurance; life insurance; a pension plan; a 401(k); disability coverage; domestic partner benefits; flexible spending accounts; stock purchase plans; an employee assistance plan; and product and entertainment discounts.

FINANCIAL DATA: *Note: Data for latest year may not have been available at press time.*

In U.S. $	2018	2017	2016	2015	2014	2013
Revenue		5,044,000,000	5,104,000,000	5,176,241,000	5,009,438,000	4,901,236,000
R&D Expense						
Operating Income		155,000,000	66,000,000	136,476,000	-204,370,000	-289,935,000
Operating Margin %		3.07%	1.29%	2.63%	-4.07%	-5.91%
SGA Expense		1,686,000,000	1,759,000,000	1,780,463,000	1,865,807,000	1,947,778,000
Net Income		153,000,000	43,000,000	219,037,000	-136,355,000	141,927,000
Operating Cash Flow		776,000,000	782,000,000	789,694,000	394,812,000	494,610,000
Capital Expenditure		685,000,000	636,000,000	800,628,000	799,496,000	883,797,000
EBITDA		892,000,000	1,112,000,000	1,420,682,000	795,705,000	1,409,752,000
Return on Assets %		1.63%	.45%	2.38%	-1.53%	1.61%
Return on Equity %		3.63%	1.04%	5.43%	-3.39%	3.49%
Debt to Equity		0.57	0.58	0.59	0.50	0.41

CONTACT INFORMATION:

Phone: 312-630-1900   Fax: 312-630-1908
Toll-Free:
Address: 30 N. LaSalle St., Ste. 4000, Chicago, IL 60602 United States

STOCK TICKER/OTHER:

Stock Ticker: TDS
Employees: 10,300
Parent Company:

Exchange: NYS
Fiscal Year Ends: 12/31

SALARIES/BONUSES:

Top Exec. Salary: $1,352,700   Bonus: $1,030,000
Second Exec. Salary: $996,000   Bonus: $1,066,100

OTHER THOUGHTS:

Estimated Female Officers or Directors: 5
Hot Spot for Advancement for Women/Minorities: Y

Tellabs Inc

NAIC Code: 334210

www.tellabs.com

TYPES OF BUSINESS:

Wireline & Wireless Products & Services
Consulting

BRANDS/DIVISIONS/AFFILIATES:

Marlin Equity Partners LLC

CONTACTS: *Note: Officers with more than one job title may be intentionally listed here more than once.*

Jim Norrod, CEO
Rich Schroder, COO
David Brown, CFO
Gerry Pagano, VP-Sales
James M. Sheehan, Chief Admin. Officer
James M. Sheehan, General Counsel
John M. Brots, Exec. VP-Global Oper.
Kenneth G. Craft, Exec. VP-Product Dev.

GROWTH PLANS/SPECIAL FEATURES:

Tellabs, Inc. provides products and services that enable customers to deliver wireline and wireless voice, data and video services to business and residential customers. It operates in two segments: enterprise and broadband. The enterprise segment offers a passive optical local area network (LAN) infrastructure, which is secure, scalable and sustainable. This division serves the business enterprise, federal government, hospitality, higher education, K-12 education and healthcare industries. The broadband segment offers solutions to service providers that deliver stability and scalability while increasing flexibility. These broadband solutions help telecommunications companies grow HSI (high-speed internet) subscribers, extend service area coverage and offer faster internet service speeds. They also enable Ethernet business services while continuing to support time-division multiplexing (TDM) and automated teller machine (ATM) services. Tellabs offers services such as technical support, professional network services and training. Tellabs is a subsidiary of Marlin Equity Partners, LLC.

The firm offers its employees medical, dental & vision insurance; company-paid life and AD&D insurance; short-and long-term disability; flexible spending accounts; health savings account; and a 401(k) retirement savings plan with company match.

FINANCIAL DATA: *Note: Data for latest year may not have been available at press time.*

In U.S. $	2018	2017	2016	2015	2014	2013
Revenue		1,391,000,000	1,372,000,000	1,375,000,000	1,325,000,000	1,100,000,000
R&D Expense						
Operating Income						
Operating Margin %						
SGA Expense						
Net Income						
Operating Cash Flow						
Capital Expenditure						
EBITDA						
Return on Assets %						
Return on Equity %						
Debt to Equity						

CONTACT INFORMATION:

Phone: 630-798-8800   Fax: 630-798-2000
Toll-Free:
Address: One Tellabs Center, 1415 W. Diehl Rd., Naperville, IL 60563 United States

STOCK TICKER/OTHER:

Stock Ticker: Private   Exchange:
Employees: 2,635   Fiscal Year Ends: 12/31
Parent Company: Marlin Equity Partners LLC

SALARIES/BONUSES:

Top Exec. Salary: $ Bonus: $
Second Exec. Salary: $ Bonus: $

OTHER THOUGHTS:

Estimated Female Officers or Directors: 1
Hot Spot for Advancement for Women/Minorities: Y

Tencent Holdings Ltd

www.tencent.com

NAIC Code: 519130

TYPES OF BUSINESS:

Websites and Services
Instant Messaging
Electronic Games
Value-added Services
Software
Advertising
Social Networking
Online Search Engine

BRANDS/DIVISIONS/AFFILIATES:

QQ
Weixin/WeChat
Tenpay
China Reading Limited (Tencent Literature)
QQ Mail
Tencent Open Platform
Tencent Cloud
Supercell Oy

CONTACTS: Note: Officers with more than one job title may be intentionally listed here more than once.

Huateng Ma, CEO
Chi Ping Lau, Pres.
John Lo, CFO
Yuxin Ren, COO
Chenye (Daniel) Xu, CIO
Zhidong Zhang, CTO
Shan Lu, Pres., Tech. & Eng. Group
James Mitchell, Chief Strategy Officer
Seng Yee Lau, Pres., Online Media Bus.
Taosang Tong, Pres., Social Network Group
Yuxin (Mark) Ren, Pres., Interactive Entertainment Bus.
Xiaoguang (Free) Wu, Sr. Exec. VP
Huateng Ma, Chmn.
David Wallerstein, Sr. Exec. VP-Intl Bus.

GROWTH PLANS/SPECIAL FEATURES:

Tencent Holdings, Ltd. is one of China's largest and most used internet service portal. The firm has seven primary lines of business: social networking, payment, entertainment, information, utilities, platform and artificial intelligence. The social networking services includes various messengers including QQ, an instant messaging (IM) platform for PC and mobile; Weixin/WeChat, a social community to connect, communicate and share information; and Qzone, a social networking platform that fulfills users' needs of self-expression, peer interaction and entertainment. Payment services include Tenpay, an online payment platform in China; Weixin/WeChat Pay, a payment solution for its users, enabling quick payment transactions on their mobile phones; and QQ Wallet, a mobile payment product incorporating multiple payment methods such as bank card payment, QR code payment and NFC payment. Entertainment services include Tencent Games, the largest online gaming community in China, China Reading Limited (Tencent Literature), an online reading platform; QQ Music, an online music platform; and Penguin e-Sports, an online streaming platform for watching games. Other services within this division include Interest Tribe, NOW Live, Tencent Comics and Tencent Pictures. Information services include Tencent News; Tencent Video, an online video interactive platform; and Tencent Microblog. Services offered within the utilities segment include the QQ Browser; Tencent Mobile Manager, mobile security and management software; Tencent Map; and QQ Mail, an email service. The platform services provided by Tencent include the Tencent Open Platform; allowing partners of Tencent to connect with QQ, Weixin and Ozone; and Tencent Cloud, a public cloud platform for corporate and individual users. In June 2016, Tencent acquired a controlling stake in game maker Supercell Oy. Artificial Intelligence services include Tencent AL Labs amd Tencent YouTu Lab. In December 2017, the firm invested $604 million in online retailer Vipshop Holdings Limited in exchange for a 7% stake in the firm.

FINANCIAL DATA: Note: Data for latest year may not have been available at press time.

In U.S. $	2018	2017	2016	2015	2014	2013
Revenue		34,602,900,000	22,112,620,000	14,970,380,000	11,487,540,000	8,795,826,000
R&D Expense						
Operating Income		10,252,650,000	7,377,276,000	5,326,076,000	3,834,612,000	2,519,975,000
Operating Margin %		29.62%	33.36%	35.57%	33.38%	28.64%
SGA Expense		7,379,168,000	5,034,856,000	3,611,940,000	3,194,831,000	2,282,459,000
Net Income		10,407,360,000	5,980,848,000	4,192,342,000	3,465,239,000	2,256,116,000
Operating Cash Flow		15,447,310,000	9,535,300,000	6,611,896,000	4,760,665,000	3,547,321,000
Capital Expenditure		4,657,769,000	2,729,403,000	1,907,264,000	966,220,900	885,011,100
EBITDA		16,720,180,000	9,685,203,000	6,461,848,000	5,049,701,000	3,388,250,000
Return on Assets %		15.04%	11.69%	12.05%	17.10%	16.98%
Return on Equity %		33.20%	27.89%	28.79%	34.51%	31.24%
Debt to Equity		0.43	0.53	0.41	0.38	0.21

CONTACT INFORMATION:

Phone: 86 75586013388   Fax: 86 75586013399
Toll-Free:
Address: Kejizhongyi Ave., Nanshan District, Shenzhen, Guangdong 518057 China

STOCK TICKER/OTHER:

Stock Ticker: TCEHY   Exchange: PINX
Employees: 46,000   Fiscal Year Ends: 12/31
Parent Company:

SALARIES/BONUSES:

Top Exec. Salary: $ Bonus: $
Second Exec. Salary: $ Bonus: $

OTHER THOUGHTS:

Estimated Female Officers or Directors:
Hot Spot for Advancement for Women/Minorities:

Sales, profits and employees may be estimates. Financial information, benefits and other data can change quickly and may vary from those stated here.

Tencent Music Entertainment Group

NAIC Code: 515111

www.qq.com

TYPES OF BUSINESS:
Radio Networks
Streaming Music Service
Internet Radio
Digital Music Sales

BRANDS/DIVISIONS/AFFILIATES:
Tencent Holdings Limited
Sony/ATV Music Publishing
QQ Music
Kugou
Kuwo

GROWTH PLANS/SPECIAL FEATURES:
Tencent Music Entertainment Group, founded in 2016, operates an online music entertainment platform that provides online music and music-centric social entertainment services in China. The firm's apps include QQ Music, Kugou and Kuwo, and have more than 700 million active users and 120 million paying subscribers. Parent Tencent Holdings Limited acquired China Music Corporation in 2016 to strengthen its music offerings, and subsequently changed China Music's name to Tencent Music Entertainment Group. In mid-2018, Sony/ATV Music Publishing acquired an equity stake in Tencent Music, and in October 2018, the firm filed for an initial public offering (IPO) of around $2 billion in the U.S. That December, Tencent Music announced that it intended to raise $1.15 billion in a U.S. IPO of American Depository Shares representing Class A ordinary shares.

CONTACTS:
Note: Officers with more than one job title may be intentionally listed here more than once.

Cussion Kar Shun Pang, CEO
Zhenyu Xie, Co-Pres.
Min Hu, CFO
Tony Cheuk Tung Yip, Chief Strategy Officer
Guomin Xie, Co-Pres.
Tong Tao Sang, Chmn.

FINANCIAL DATA:
Note: Data for latest year may not have been available at press time.

In U.S. $	2018	2017	2016	2015	2014	2013
Revenue		1,598,143,000	634,687,300			
R&D Expense						
Operating Income		204,334,100	13,534,950			
Operating Margin %						
SGA Expense		354,237,300	167,076,600			
Net Income		192,982,200	11,934,040			
Operating Cash Flow		363,842,800	127,053,900			
Capital Expenditure		11,206,360	5,967,022			
EBITDA		259,492,700	47,881,710			
Return on Assets %						
Return on Equity %						
Debt to Equity						

CONTACT INFORMATION:
Phone: 86-755-8601-3388   Fax:
Toll-Free:
Address: 17/Fl, Malata Bldg., Kejizhonegyi Rd., Midwest Dist. of Hi-tech Park, Nanshan Dist., Shenzhen, 518057 China

STOCK TICKER/OTHER:
Stock Ticker: TME
Employees: 2,459
Parent Company: Tencent Holdings Limited

Exchange: NYS
Fiscal Year Ends: 12/31

SALARIES/BONUSES:
Top Exec. Salary: $ Bonus: $
Second Exec. Salary: $ Bonus: $

OTHER THOUGHTS:
Estimated Female Officers or Directors:
Hot Spot for Advancement for Women/Minorities:

Teradata Corporation

www.teradata.com

NAIC Code: 511210J

TYPES OF BUSINESS:

Data Warehousing
Database & Data Mining Software
Consulting Services

BRANDS/DIVISIONS/AFFILIATES:

Teradata IntelliCloud
Teradata IntelliSphere
IntelliBase
IntelliFlex
Kylo
Presto
Covelant
GE Aviation

CONTACTS: *Note: Officers with more than one job title may be intentionally listed here more than once.*

Victor Lund, CEO
Mark Culhane, CFO
James Ringler, Chairman of the Board
Oliver Ratzesberger, COO
Daniel Harrington, Executive VP, Divisional
Eric Tom, Executive VP
Suzanne C, Executive VP
Laura Nyquist, Secretary

GROWTH PLANS/SPECIAL FEATURES:

Teradata Corporation provides analytics solutions and services that help companies achieve high-impact business outcomes through analytics at scale, enabled by Teradata's technology. The firm's products fall into six categories: software, cloud, ecosystem management, hardware, applications and open source. The software segment includes Teradata Vantage, a platform focused on persuasive data intelligence that can analyze all types of data at any time; and Teradata Database, the core of the Teradata SQL engine, allows complex analytics workloads to be broken down and distributed as efficiently as possible. The cloud segment features Teradata IntelliCloud, which comes as-a-service or do-it-yourself options. The ecosystem management product is Teradata IntelliSphere, a comprehensive software portfolio to enable a complete ability to control an analytical ecosystem. This product's features include an appcenter, a data lab, a query grid, a listener, a data stream and a data mover. The hardware segment includes a backup, archive and restore product; IntelliBase, a compact environment for data warehousing and low-cost data storage; and IntelliFlex, a purpose-built hardware platform for data analytics. The applications segment features a customer interaction manager, master data management, a real time marketing manager and Teradata analytics for enterprise solutions. The open source products include Kylo, Presto and Covelant. Teradata also offers consulting, including: business analytics consulting, helping businesses through solution-based selling that leverages analytics consulting; and ecosystem architecture consulting, which helps customers build analytical ecosystems using open source and commercial solutions. Industries served by the company include communications, media and entertainment, energy, natural resources, financial services, healthcare, life sciences, manufacturing, retail, travel and transportation. Teradata operates from more than 112 facilities located in 44 countries worldwide. In July 2018, the firm expanded its partnership with GE Aviation, allowing GE to become the exclusive provider of Teradata to commercial aviation markets.

FINANCIAL DATA: *Note: Data for latest year may not have been available at press time.*

In U.S. $	2018	2017	2016	2015	2014	2013
Revenue		2,156,000,000	2,322,000,000	2,530,000,000	2,732,000,000	2,692,000,000
R&D Expense		306,000,000	212,000,000	228,000,000	206,000,000	184,000,000
Operating Income		64,000,000	312,000,000	283,000,000	503,000,000	532,000,000
Operating Margin %		2.96%	13.43%	11.18%	18.41%	19.76%
SGA Expense		652,000,000	664,000,000	765,000,000	770,000,000	757,000,000
Net Income		-67,000,000	125,000,000	-214,000,000	367,000,000	377,000,000
Operating Cash Flow		324,000,000	446,000,000	401,000,000	680,000,000	510,000,000
Capital Expenditure		87,000,000	118,000,000	120,000,000	129,000,000	138,000,000
EBITDA		211,000,000	361,000,000	35,000,000	672,000,000	679,000,000
Return on Assets %		-2.69%	5.05%	-7.55%	11.78%	12.23%
Return on Equity %		-8.17%	13.73%	-16.74%	20.59%	20.73%
Debt to Equity		0.71	0.55	0.67	0.11	0.13

CONTACT INFORMATION:

Phone: 866 548-8348   Fax:
Toll-Free: 866-548-8348
Address: 10000 Innovation Dr., Dayton, OH 45342 United States

STOCK TICKER/OTHER:

Stock Ticker: TDC   Exchange: NYS
Employees: 10,093   Fiscal Year Ends: 12/31
Parent Company:

SALARIES/BONUSES:

Top Exec. Salary: $800,000   Bonus: $
Second Exec. Salary: Bonus: $
$515,346

OTHER THOUGHTS:

Estimated Female Officers or Directors: 2
Hot Spot for Advancement for Women/Minorities: Y

TheStreet Inc

NAIC Code: 519130

www.thestreet.com

TYPES OF BUSINESS:

Online Financial Information
Securities Research

BRANDS/DIVISIONS/AFFILIATES:

Deal LLC (The)
BoardEx
RateWatch
TheStreet.com
RealMoney
RealMoney Pro
Action Alerts PLUS

CONTACTS: *Note: Officers with more than one job title may be intentionally listed here more than once.*

Eric Lundberg, CFO
Lawrence Kramer, Chairman of the Board
James Cramer, Founder
Rachelle Zorn, President, Divisional
Margaret de Luna, President, Divisional
Jeffrey Davis, President, Divisional
David Callaway, President

GROWTH PLANS/SPECIAL FEATURES:

TheStreet, Inc. is a web-based provider of financial news, stock analysis, commentary and information. The company's business-to-business (B2B) and business-to-consumer (B2C) content and products provide individual and institutional investors, advisors and dealmakers with actionable information from the finance and business industries. TheStreet's B2B division provide news, data and analysis of mergers and acquisitions and changes in corporate control, relationship mapping services and competitive bank rate data. Subsidiary The Deal, LLC operates through a digital subscription business model, delivering coverage on changes in control, including mergers and acquisitions, private equity, corporate activism and restructuring. BoardEx is an institutional relationship capital management database and platform that currently holds in-depth profiles of approximately 1 million of the world's most important business leaders. Its proprietary software shows the relationships between and among these leaders and his/her contacts. RateWatch publishes bank rate market information, including competitive deposit, loan and fee rate data, primarily on a subscription basis, to financial institutions, government agencies, academic researchers, banks, credit unions and other commercial organizations. The Street's B2C division offers free content and houses the company's premium subscription products that target varying segments of the retail investing public. Its TheStreet.com website is a free, ad-supported digital platform that provides news and market analysis to individual investors. RealMoney and RealMoney Pro are the firm's premium subscription product line for consumers, offering investor commentary and analysis. Last, Action Alerts PLUS is a premium subscription offering that teaches consumers how to manage money for long-term growth. In December 2018, TheStreet agreed to sell its institutional business units, The Deal and BoardEx, to Euromoney Institutional Investor PLC for $87.3 million.

FINANCIAL DATA: *Note: Data for latest year may not have been available at press time.*

In U.S. $	2018	2017	2016	2015	2014	2013
Revenue		62,469,390	63,499,530	67,655,900	61,053,220	54,450,410
R&D Expense						
Operating Income		1,168,019	-6,476,846	-1,460,249	-3,403,709	-3,422,120
Operating Margin %		1.86%	-10.19%	-2.15%	-5.57%	-6.28%
SGA Expense		29,053,610	31,854,220	31,191,190	29,546,810	26,672,430
Net Income		2,626,837	-17,514,720	-1,543,003	-3,789,877	-3,785,701
Operating Cash Flow		5,889,108	-2,758,045	890,559	3,552,085	2,478,352
Capital Expenditure		2,505,816	3,676,051	3,365,509	1,931,173	1,118,679
EBITDA		6,300,278	-795,283	2,848,845	-224,332	346,416
Return on Assets %		33.89%	-19.31%	-1.79%	-3.78%	-3.43%
Return on Equity %		65.71%	-33.66%	-2.97%	-5.87%	-5.06%
Debt to Equity						

CONTACT INFORMATION:

Phone: 212 321-5000   Fax: 212 321-5016
Toll-Free: 866-321-8726
Address: 14 Wall St., 15/Fl, New York, NY 10005 United States

STOCK TICKER/OTHER:

Stock Ticker: TST
Employees: 650
Parent Company:

Exchange: NAS
Fiscal Year Ends: 12/31

SALARIES/BONUSES:

Top Exec. Salary: $507,500   Bonus: $
Second Exec. Salary: $329,875   Bonus: $

OTHER THOUGHTS:

Estimated Female Officers or Directors: 4
Hot Spot for Advancement for Women/Minorities: Y

ThinkGeek Inc

www.thinkgeek.com

NAIC Code: 454111

TYPES OF BUSINESS:

Online Retailing
Technology Oriented Web Sites
Forums

BRANDS/DIVISIONS/AFFILIATES:

GameStop Corp
Geeknet Inc
ThinkGeek.com
GeekPoints

GROWTH PLANS/SPECIAL FEATURES:

ThinkGeek, Inc. is an online and wholesale retailer that offers a variety of merchandise for the global geek community. The firm's products include clothing, accessories, bags, backpacks, home items, office items, toys and games, books, movies, collectibles, tools, outdoor items, electronics, gadgets and more. Gift cards are available on the ThinkGeek.com website. ThinkGeek also has more than 40 retail stores throughout the U.S. GeekPoints is the company's rewards program, allowing users to earn 10 points for every dollar spent in order to score free stuff. GeekPoints are available for use when orders are shipped. ThinkGeek operates as a subsidiary of Geeknet, Inc. which is owned by GameStop Corp.

CONTACTS: *Note: Officers with more than one job title may be intentionally listed here more than once.*

Shane Kim, CEO-GameStop
Kathryn McCarthy, Chairman of the Board
Jenny Gillespie, General Counsel

FINANCIAL DATA: *Note: Data for latest year may not have been available at press time.*

In U.S. $	2018	2017	2016	2015	2014	2013
Revenue		166,000,000	165,000,000	160,000,000	140,704,992	138,262,000
R&D Expense						
Operating Income						
Operating Margin %						
SGA Expense						
Net Income						-8,272,000	-234,000
Operating Cash Flow						
Capital Expenditure						
EBITDA						
Return on Assets %						
Return on Equity %						
Debt to Equity						

CONTACT INFORMATION:

Phone: 508-970-2002   Fax:
Toll-Free: 888-433-5788
Address: 11216 Waples Mill Rd., Ste. 100, Fairfax, VA 22030 United States

STOCK TICKER/OTHER:

Stock Ticker: Subsidiary   Exchange:
Employees: 120   Fiscal Year Ends: 12/31
Parent Company: GameStop Corp

SALARIES/BONUSES:

Top Exec. Salary: $ Bonus: $
Second Exec. Salary: $ Bonus: $

OTHER THOUGHTS:

Estimated Female Officers or Directors: 2
Hot Spot for Advancement for Women/Minorities:

Thomson Reuters Corporation

www.thomsonreuters.com

NAIC Code: 511120A

TYPES OF BUSINESS:

Information Services & Software
Legal & Regulatory Information Services
Financial Information & Technology
Health Care Information Tools
Scientific Data Tools

BRANDS/DIVISIONS/AFFILIATES:

CONTACTS: *Note: Officers with more than one job title may be intentionally listed here more than once.*

James Smith, CEO
Stephane Bello, CFO
David Thomson, Chairman of the Board
David Binet, Deputy Chairman
Rick King, Executive VP, Divisional
Neil Masterson, Executive VP
Brian Scanlon, Executive VP
Gustav Carlson, Executive VP
Mary-Alice Vuicic, Executive VP
Deirdre Stanley, General Counsel
Carla Jones, Other Executive Officer
Brian Peccarelli, President, Divisional
David Craig, President, Divisional
Susan Martin, President, Divisional
Gonzalo Lissarrague, President, Divisional

GROWTH PLANS/SPECIAL FEATURES:

Thomson Reuters provides specialized information in digital and print formats for professional markets, with operations in more than 100 countries for more than 100 years. Thomson Reuters offers corporations end-to-end solutions pertaining to regulatory, legal and compliance challenges. For government entities, the company offers information relating to operational and policy decision making. For legal firms, Thomson Reuters provides legal products and services that combine content, deep human expertise and intuitive technology for timely guidance and answers. For news and media sectors, the firm provides award-winning global multimedia content and real-time news coverage in a partnership manner. For accounting firms, corporations, financial institutions, governments and law firms, Thomson Reuters provides tax and accounting technology, guidance and expertise. In addition, Thomson Reuters Labs engage in exploring new business opportunities for Thomson Reuters, working with customers and partners to create quick, agile and collaborative experiments and proofs-of-concept. Its artificial intelligence (AI) center encompasses a team of scientists, engineers and designers with specialized skills in cognitive technologies. During 2018, the firm sold a 55% interest in its financial and risk business to Blackstone Group; and acquired Integration Point, an international player in global trade management operations.

FINANCIAL DATA: *Note: Data for latest year may not have been available at press time.*

In U.S. $	2018	2017	2016	2015	2014	2013
Revenue		11,333,000,000	11,166,000,000	12,209,000,000	12,607,000,000	12,702,000,000
R&D Expense						
Operating Income		1,755,000,000	1,390,000,000	1,734,000,000	2,545,000,000	1,516,000,000
Operating Margin %		15.48%	12.44%	14.20%	20.18%	11.93%
SGA Expense						
Net Income		1,395,000,000	3,098,000,000	1,255,000,000	1,909,000,000	137,000,000
Operating Cash Flow		2,029,000,000	2,984,000,000	2,838,000,000	2,366,000,000	2,103,000,000
Capital Expenditure		950,000,000	905,000,000	1,003,000,000	968,000,000	1,004,000,000
EBITDA		3,023,000,000	2,999,000,000	3,455,000,000	4,285,000,000	3,297,000,000
Return on Assets %		5.12%	10.87%	4.19%	6.04%	.41%
Return on Equity %		10.87%	24.60%	9.43%	12.70%	.81%
Debt to Equity		0.41	0.49	0.54	0.53	0.46

CONTACT INFORMATION:

Phone: 646 223-4000   Fax:
Toll-Free:
Address: 3 Times Square, New York, NY 10036 United States

STOCK TICKER/OTHER:

Stock Ticker: TRI   Exchange: NYS
Employees: 45,000   Fiscal Year Ends: 12/31
Parent Company:

SALARIES/BONUSES:

Top Exec. Salary: $1,591,530   Bonus: $
Second Exec. Salary: Bonus: $
$990,820

OTHER THOUGHTS:

Estimated Female Officers or Directors: 2
Hot Spot for Advancement for Women/Minorities: Y

Thumbtack Inc

www.thumbtack.com

NAIC Code: 519130

TYPES OF BUSINESS:

Internet Publishing and Broadcasting and Web Search Portals

BRANDS/DIVISIONS/AFFILIATES:

CONTACTS: *Note: Officers with more than one job title may be intentionally listed here more than once.*

Marco Zappacosta, CEO
Jonathan Swanson, Pres.
Sander Daniels, Dir.-Bus. Dev.

GROWTH PLANS/SPECIAL FEATURES:

Thumbtack, Inc. owns and operates an online marketplace for hiring workers in the U.S. The company enables customers to hire professionals from several categories, including home, events, lessons and wellness. For example, the home category includes hiring professions for house cleaning, lawn care, interior design, handyman services, electrical services and more; the events category includes disc jockey, wedding officiant, catering, makeup, photo booth rental, magician, hair styling, photography, face painting services and more; the lessons category includes singing, piano, martial arts training, reading/writing/math tutoring, art, acting, dance and more; and the wellness category includes personal training, massage therapy, life coach, yoga lessons, pilates training, personal chef services, physical therapy, relationship counseling and more. For customers, Thumbtack obtains answers about what one needs, shares those details with professionals who can complete the task and allows the customer to contact the professionals and hire if a price is agreed upon. Thumbtack keeps email and phone numbers private in order to avoid spam. For professionals, Thumbtack sends customer requests at no charge, and the professional then chooses to provide a quote only if the request looks like a fit.

FINANCIAL DATA: *Note: Data for latest year may not have been available at press time.*

In U.S. $	2018	2017	2016	2015	2014	2013
Revenue						
R&D Expense						
Operating Income						
Operating Margin %						
SGA Expense						
Net Income						
Operating Cash Flow						
Capital Expenditure						
EBITDA						
Return on Assets %						
Return on Equity %						
Debt to Equity						

CONTACT INFORMATION:

Phone: 855-846-2825   Fax:
Toll-Free: 800-343-1710
Address: 360 9th St., San Francisco, CA 94103 United States

STOCK TICKER/OTHER:

Stock Ticker: Private   Exchange:
Employees: 563   Fiscal Year Ends:
Parent Company:

SALARIES/BONUSES:

Top Exec. Salary: $ Bonus: $
Second Exec. Salary: $ Bonus: $

OTHER THOUGHTS:

Estimated Female Officers or Directors:
Hot Spot for Advancement for Women/Minorities:

TIBCO Software Inc

www.tibco.com

NAIC Code: 511210H

TYPES OF BUSINESS:

Computer Software, Business Process
Data Management Software
Consulting & Support Services

BRANDS/DIVISIONS/AFFILIATES:

TIBCO Cloud Live Apps
TIBCO Jaspersoft
TIBCO Cloud Integration
TIBCO Spotfire
TIBCO Mashery
TIBCO BusinessWorks
TIBCO ActiveMatrix BPM
Orchestra Networks

CONTACTS: Note: Officers with more than one job title may be intentionally listed here more than once.

Murray Rode, CEO
Matt Quinn, COO
Tom Berquist, CFO
Michele Haddad, Sr. VP-Global Human Resources
Sharon Mandell, CIO
Thomas Laffey, Executive VP, Divisional
Ram Menon, Executive VP
William Hughes, Executive VP
R. Bradley, President
John Ederer, Vice President, Divisional
Vivek Ranadive, Chmn.

GROWTH PLANS/SPECIAL FEATURES:

TIBCO Software, Inc. is a provider of infrastructure and business intelligence (BI) software worldwide. The company's products include: tibbr, an enterprise collaboration platform; TIBCO Cloud Live Apps, a low-code application platform that enables users to build smart apps in minutes; TIBCO Jaspersoft, a flexible BI architecture that enables choice of development options; TIBCO Cloud Integration, which helps users keep every part of their business seamlessly integrated; TIBCO Spotfire, which provides artificial intelligence (AI)-driven intuitive, scalable analytics for insight and decision-making purposes; TIBCO Business Works, a platform to streamline supply chain; TIBCO Data Science, a system to collaborate, operationalize and scale machine learning; TIBCO Mashery, a full lifecycle application programming interface (API) management software-as-a-service (SaaS) solution for internal APIs, B2B APIs and public API programs; TIBCO BusinessEvents, a rule-based event processing system; TIBCO BusinessWorks, which seamlessly connects all the applications and data sources that keeps a business running every day; TIBCO Active Spaces, an in-memory computing database; TIBCO Cloud Nimbus, a way to map business processes and operations; TIBCO Data Virtualization, an enterprise data virtualization solution; and TIBCO ActiveMatrix BPM, a business process management platform that facilitates business insights and actions by presenting the right data to the right person at the right time. TIBCO's solutions serve the banking, energy, insurance, manufacturing, retail, telecommunications and travel industries. In addition, the company offers education, support and consulting services to its customers. In June 2018, the firm acquired Scribe Software, a cloud-based integration service that connects software-as-a-service applications. In December of that same year, TIBCO acquired Orchestra Networks, a data management solutions firm.

TIBCO offers its employees medical, dental, vision, disability, life and AD&D insurance; a 401(k) program; credit union membership; an employee assistance program; a discount stock purchase plan; and tuition reimbursement.

FINANCIAL DATA: Note: Data for latest year may not have been available at press time.

In U.S. $	2018	2017	2016	2015	2014	2013
Revenue	1,225,000,000	1,100,000,000	1,000,000,000	1,000,000,000	1,022,400,000	1,069,950,016
R&D Expense						
Operating Income						
Operating Margin %						
SGA Expense						
Net Income						
Operating Cash Flow						
Capital Expenditure						
EBITDA						
Return on Assets %						
Return on Equity %						
Debt to Equity						

CONTACT INFORMATION:

Phone: 650 846-1000   Fax: 650 846-1218
Toll-Free: 800-420-8450
Address: 3307 Hillview Ave., Palo Alto, CA 94304 United States

STOCK TICKER/OTHER:

Stock Ticker: Private   Exchange:
Employees: 4,200   Fiscal Year Ends: 11/30
Parent Company: Vista Equity Partners

SALARIES/BONUSES:

Top Exec. Salary: $ Bonus: $
Second Exec. Salary: $ Bonus: $

OTHER THOUGHTS:

Estimated Female Officers or Directors: 2
Hot Spot for Advancement for Women/Minorities:

Sales, profits and employees may be estimates. Financial information, benefits and other data can change quickly and may vary from those stated here.

T-Mobile International AG

www.telekom.com/en

NAIC Code: 517210

TYPES OF BUSINESS:

Mobile Telecommunications Provider
Mobile Media Services

BRANDS/DIVISIONS/AFFILIATES:

Deutsche Telekom AG

CONTACTS: *Note: Officers with more than one job title may be intentionally listed here more than once.*

Timotheus Hottges, CEO
John J. Legere, Pres.
David A. Miller, Exec. VP-Gen Counsel
Peter A. Ewens, Exec. VP-Corp. Strat.
David R. Carey, Exec. VP-Corp. Svcs.
Alexander Andrew Kelton, Exec. VP-Bus. To Bus.
Thomas C. Keys, Exec. VP

GROWTH PLANS/SPECIAL FEATURES:

T-Mobile International AG, a wholly-owned subsidiary of Deutsche Telekom AG, is one of the world's leading companies in mobile communications. As one of Deutsche Telekom's business units, T-Mobile concentrates on markets in Europe and the U.S. The firm has approximately 170 million mobile customers, 28 million fixed-network lines and 19 million broadband lines worldwide. It owns network operations in the U.S., the Virgin Islands and Puerto Rico, as well as in over 12 European countries including Austria, Croatia, Czech Republic, Albania, Germany, Hungary, Macedonia, Montenegro, the Netherlands, Poland, Romania and Slovakia. T-Mobile was the first operator to launch a trans-Atlantic mobile network based on global system for mobile communications (GSM). The company offers its service through a fully integrated network of circuit switched data (CSD), and also provides general packet radio service (GPRS), third and fourth generation (3G/4G) service, universal mobile telecommunications system technologies (UMTS) and wireless local area network (WLAN) mobile access services. T-Mobile is currently (as of June 2018) laying the foundation for the rollout of 5G in Europe and the U.S. The firm offers various business solutions to small- and medium-sized businesses and individual customers through mobile access and mobile service portals. The company provides residential and business customers with mobile voice and data services on prepay or contractual basis. Additionally, T-Mobile offers international roaming services, sells mobile devices to customers in conjunction with its service offerings and operates HotSpot in select locations. In April 2018, the T-Mobile U.S, Inc. unit and Sprint Corporation agreed to merge in an all-stock transaction; the combined company will be named T-Mobile. It plans significant investment in 5G services in America..

Employee benefits include medical, dental and vision coverage; a wellness discount program; a 401(k); flexible spending accounts; life insurance; short- and long-term disability; employee assistance programs; and employee discounts.

FINANCIAL DATA: *Note: Data for latest year may not have been available at press time.*

In U.S. $	2018	2017	2016	2015	2014	2013
Revenue		35,500,000,000	34,000,000,000	32,053,000,192	29,564,000,256	24,419,999,744
R&D Expense						
Operating Income						
Operating Margin %						
SGA Expense						
Net Income				733,000,000	247,000,000	35,000,000
Operating Cash Flow						
Capital Expenditure						
EBITDA						
Return on Assets %						
Return on Equity %						
Debt to Equity						

CONTACT INFORMATION:

Phone: 49-228-936-15502   Fax: 49-228-936-15509
Toll-Free:
Address: Landgrabenweg 151, Bellevue, 98006-1350 Germany

STOCK TICKER/OTHER:

Stock Ticker: Subsidiary   Exchange:
Employees: 46,500   Fiscal Year Ends: 12/31
Parent Company: Deutsche Telekom AG

SALARIES/BONUSES:

Top Exec. Salary: $ Bonus: $
Second Exec. Salary: $ Bonus: $

OTHER THOUGHTS:

Estimated Female Officers or Directors:
Hot Spot for Advancement for Women/Minorities:

T-Mobile US Inc

www.t-mobile.com

NAIC Code: 517210

TYPES OF BUSINESS:

Mobile Phone and Wireless Services
Wireless Internet Services

BRANDS/DIVISIONS/AFFILIATES:

Deutsche Telekom AG
T-Mobile International AG
T-Mobile
MetroPCS

CONTACTS: *Note: Officers with more than one job title may be intentionally listed here more than once.*

J. Carter, CFO
Timotheus Hottges, Chairman of the Board
Neville Ray, Chief Technology Officer
G. Sievert, COO
John Legere, Director
Peter Ewens, Executive VP, Divisional
Elizabeth McAuliffe, Executive VP, Divisional
David Carey, Executive VP, Divisional
David Miller, Executive VP
Thomas Keys, President, Subsidiary
Peter Osvaldik, Senior VP, Divisional

GROWTH PLANS/SPECIAL FEATURES:

T-Mobile US, Inc. (T-Mobile) is a national provider of wireless voice, messaging and data services, and is one of the largest cellular companies in America. The firm offers wireless service under both the T-Mobile and MetroPCS brands. T-Mobile uses GSM (global system for mobile communications) technology and is a member of the North American GSM Alliance, a group of U.S. and Canadian digital wireless carriers that provide seamless GSM wireless communications for its members in North America and internationally. Along with GSM, the firm uses technology platforms based on HSPA+ (high speed packet access plus), CDMA (code division multiple access) and LTE (long-term evolution) to service over 72.6 million customers in the postpaid, prepaid and wholesale markets (as of early-2018). The company's products include internet and e-mail; games and applications for mobile devices; messaging; voicemail; mobile device wallpapers; music and sounds; and handset protection services in case of loss, theft, malfunction or accidental damage to the product. T-Mobile recently announced plans for full nationwide 5G coverage by 2020. The firm operates as a subsidiary of T-Mobile International AG, which itself is the mobile communications subsidiary of Deutsche Telekom AG. In mid-2018, Sprint Corporation and T-Mobile agreed to merge, potentially creating a third giant wireless network operator to compete against AT&T, Inc. and Verizon Communications, Inc. The proposed transaction, still subject to approval by regulatory officials at the FCC and anti-trust officials at the U.S. Justice Department, is not expected to close until 2019.

FINANCIAL DATA: *Note: Data for latest year may not have been available at press time.*

In U.S. $	2018	2017	2016	2015	2014	2013
Revenue		40,604,000,000	37,242,000,000	32,053,000,000	29,564,000,000	24,420,000,000
R&D Expense						
Operating Income		4,653,000,000	3,071,000,000	2,278,000,000	875,000,000	1,158,000,000
Operating Margin %		11.45%	7.96%	5.93%	1.94%	4.29%
SGA Expense		12,259,000,000	11,378,000,000	10,189,000,000	8,863,000,000	7,382,000,000
Net Income		4,536,000,000	1,460,000,000	733,000,000	247,000,000	35,000,000
Operating Cash Flow		7,962,000,000	6,135,000,000	5,414,000,000	4,146,000,000	3,545,000,000
Capital Expenditure		11,065,000,000	8,670,000,000	6,659,000,000	7,217,000,000	4,406,000,000
EBITDA		10,816,000,000	10,300,000,000	7,162,000,000	6,176,000,000	4,901,000,000
Return on Assets %		6.56%	2.18%	1.13%	.46%	.11%
Return on Equity %		21.96%	8.07%	4.20%	1.65%	.39%
Debt to Equity		0.53	1.19	1.23	1.19	1.18

CONTACT INFORMATION:

Phone: 425-378-4000   Fax: 425-378-4040
Toll-Free: 800-318-9270
Address: 12920 SE 38th St., Bellevue, WA 98006-1350 United States

SALARIES/BONUSES:

Top Exec. Salary: $1,618,590   Bonus: $
Second Exec. Salary: $944,231   Bonus: $

STOCK TICKER/OTHER:

Stock Ticker: TMUS   Exchange: NAS
Employees: 50,000   Fiscal Year Ends: 12/31
Parent Company: Deutsche Telekom AG

OTHER THOUGHTS:

Estimated Female Officers or Directors:
Hot Spot for Advancement for Women/Minorities:

Total System Services Inc (TSYS)

www.tsys.com

NAIC Code: 522320

TYPES OF BUSINESS:

Credit Card Processing
Risk Management Tools
Fraud Detection
Debt Collection Services
Printing Services
Customer Relationship Management
Business Process Management

BRANDS/DIVISIONS/AFFILIATES:

Netspend
iMobile3

CONTACTS: *Note: Officers with more than one job title may be intentionally listed here more than once.*

M. Woods, CEO
Paul Todd, CFO
Dorenda Weaver, Chief Accounting Officer
Patricia Watson, Chief Information Officer
G. Griffith, Secretary

GROWTH PLANS/SPECIAL FEATURES:

Total System Services, Inc. (TSYS) is a global payment solutions provider to financial and non-financial institutions. These solutions include payment processing services, merchant services and related payment services, as well as general purpose reloadable (GPR) pre-paid and payroll cards, demand deposit accounts and other financial service solutions to the underbanked and other consumers and businesses. TSYS offers seamless, secure and innovative solutions across the payments spectrum, from issuer processing and merchant acquiring to prepaid program management. TSYS' services are divided into three segments: merchant solutions, issuer solutions and Netspend. The merchant solutions segment offers payment processing solutions, as well as related equipment and security products. Payment processing covers credit/debit cards (including mobile, online and wireless processing), mobile point of sale, small business processing and telephone processing. These solutions are used by association, automotive, eCommerce, health, public services, mid-market corporate sales, petroleum/convenience store, restaurant and retail industries. The issuer solutions segment provides products and services that help people move money, supporting the entire lifecycle of an account. This division supports business-to-business (B2B) payment processes for business and governments, debit transactions, healthcare payments, loyalty solutions, pre-paid cards, disbursements and more. Last, Netspend provides Visa pre-paid debit cards and debit Mastercards. Netspend also offers programs for businesses to manage and simplify their spending and payroll, including incentives, disbursements and tips. Based in Georgia, USA, the firm has offices across 13 countries. During 2018, TSYS acquired iMobile3, a provider of products and value-added technology services to the payments industry.

The company offers U.S. employees life, AD&D, disability, medical, dental and vision insurance; flexible spending accounts; and adoption assistance.

FINANCIAL DATA: *Note: Data for latest year may not have been available at press time.*

In U.S. $	2018	2017	2016	2015	2014	2013
Revenue		4,927,965,000	4,170,077,000	2,779,541,000	2,446,877,000	2,132,353,000
R&D Expense						
Operating Income		734,044,000	573,382,000	534,107,000	434,857,000	400,467,000
Operating Margin %		14.89%	13.74%	19.21%	17.77%	18.78%
SGA Expense		616,601,000	603,633,000	390,253,000	343,128,000	295,555,000
Net Income		586,185,000	319,638,000	364,044,000	322,872,000	244,750,000
Operating Cash Flow		856,492,000	717,909,000	600,194,000	560,201,000	452,398,000
Capital Expenditure		126,220,000	96,726,000	144,588,000	147,052,000	137,833,000
EBITDA		1,141,689,000	950,123,000	795,853,000	682,875,000	605,818,000
Return on Assets %		9.21%	6.22%	9.44%	8.61%	8.51%
Return on Equity %		26.94%	16.21%	20.41%	19.52%	16.17%
Debt to Equity		1.17	1.57	0.75	0.83	0.90

CONTACT INFORMATION:

Phone: 706 649-2310   Fax: 706 649-2456
Toll-Free:
Address: One TSYS Way, Columbus, GA 31901-4222 United States

STOCK TICKER/OTHER:

Stock Ticker: TSS   Exchange: NYS
Employees: 11,500   Fiscal Year Ends: 12/31
Parent Company:

SALARIES/BONUSES:

Top Exec. Salary: $892,250   Bonus: $
Second Exec. Salary: $546,000   Bonus: $

OTHER THOUGHTS:

Estimated Female Officers or Directors: 3
Hot Spot for Advancement for Women/Minorities: Y

TradeStation Group Inc

NAIC Code: 523120

www.tradestation.com

TYPES OF BUSINESS:

Online Stock Brokerage
Financial Information
Stock Trading Software
Foreign Exchange Transactions
Futures Commission Merchant

BRANDS/DIVISIONS/AFFILIATES:

Monex Group Inc
TradeStation Securities inc
TradeStation
TradeStation Technologies Inc
TradingApp
IBFX Inc
TradeStation Europe Limited
Fully Paid Lending Program

CONTACTS: Note: Officers with more than one job title may be intentionally listed here more than once.

John Bartleman, Pres.
Greg Vance, CFO
Michael Fisch, Chief Technology Officer
Marc J. Stone, Chief Legal Officer
William P. Cahill, VP-Brokerage Oper.
Takashi Oyagi, Chief Strategic Officer
Edward Codispoti, VP-Finance

GROWTH PLANS/SPECIAL FEATURES:

TradeStation Group, Inc. is a is a leading online brokerage firm operating through its principal subsidiary, TradeStation Securities, Inc. TradeStation Securities is a licensed securities broker-dealer and a registered futures commission merchant. It offers the TradeStation analysis and trading platform to the active trader and certain institutional trader markets. The platform offers electronic order execution and enables clients to design, test, optimize, monitor and automate their own custom equities, options and futures trading strategies. TradeStation Securities is a member of the Boston Options Exchange, Chicago Board Options Exchange, Chicago Stock Exchange, International Securities Exchange and NASDAQ OMX. Its prime services division provides prime brokerage services, such as securities lending, to small- and mid-sized hedge funds and other firms. Subsidiary TradeStation Technologies, Inc. develops and offers strategy trading software tools and subscription services, and hosts the TradingApp store. IBFX, Inc. acts as TradeStation's broker, a self-clearing retail foreign exchange dealer. TradeStation Europe Limited is an FCA-authorized brokerage firm that introduces U.K. and other European accounts to TradeStation Securities, Inc. TradeStation Group itself operates as a wholly-owned subsidiary of Monex Group, Inc. In mid-2018, TradeStation launched its Fully Paid Lending Program, which allows qualified equities account holders the opportunity to earn interest income on lendable securities in their accounts.

TradeStation offers its employees a 401(k) and medical, dental and vision coverage.

FINANCIAL DATA: Note: Data for latest year may not have been available at press time.

In U.S. $	2018	2017	2016	2015	2014	2013
Revenue		155,000,000	135,000,000	124,338,000	111,422,000	102,326,000
R&D Expense						
Operating Income						
Operating Margin %						
SGA Expense						
Net Income				11,350,000	1,635,000	778,000
Operating Cash Flow						
Capital Expenditure						
EBITDA						
Return on Assets %						
Return on Equity %						
Debt to Equity						

CONTACT INFORMATION:

Phone: 954-652-7000   Fax: 954-652-7300
Toll-Free: 800-556-2022
Address: 8050 SW 10th St., Plantation, FL 33324 United States

STOCK TICKER/OTHER:

Stock Ticker: Subsidiary   Exchange:
Employees: 560   Fiscal Year Ends: 12/31
Parent Company: Monex Group Inc

SALARIES/BONUSES:

Top Exec. Salary: $ Bonus: $
Second Exec. Salary: $ Bonus: $

OTHER THOUGHTS:

Estimated Female Officers or Directors:
Hot Spot for Advancement for Women/Minorities:

Travelocity.com LP

www.travelocity.com

NAIC Code: 561510

TYPES OF BUSINESS:

Online Travel Services
Online Reservations
Retail Travel Service Kiosks
Corporate Travel Agency

BRANDS/DIVISIONS/AFFILIATES:

Expedia Inc
Travelscape LLC

GROWTH PLANS/SPECIAL FEATURES:

Travelocity.com, LP is a leading provider of online travel services for business and leisure travelers. The firm operates as a subsidiary of Travelscape, LLC, which itself is a wholly-owned subsidiary of Expedia, Inc. Travelocity provides access to vacation packages, domestic and international flights, hotel accommodations, rental car companies and cruises, as well as last-minute packages at discounted prices. More than 400 airlines and over 320,000 hotels worldwide can be searched through Travelocity's online and mobile platforms. Additionally, Travelocity has a customer care unit staffed by representatives able to answer questions, change travel arrangements and handle travel-related emergencies 24-hours-a-day.

CONTACTS:
Note: Officers with more than one job title may be intentionally listed here more than once.

Jonathan Perkel, Sr. VP
Carl Sparks, Pres.
Bradley E. Wilson, CMO
Scott Miskimens, CTO
Jonathan Perkel, General Counsel
Stephen Dumaine, Sr. VP-Global Strategy & Prod. Innovation
Yannis Karnis, Pres., Travelocity Business
Noreen Henry, Sr. VP-Global Partner Svcs.
Roshan Mendis, Pres., Travelocity North America & Zuji
Scott Quigley, VP-Sales & Customer Care

FINANCIAL DATA:
Note: Data for latest year may not have been available at press time.

In U.S. $	2018	2017	2016	2015	2014	2013
Revenue						
R&D Expense						
Operating Income						
Operating Margin %						
SGA Expense						
Net Income						
Operating Cash Flow						
Capital Expenditure						
EBITDA						
Return on Assets %						
Return on Equity %						
Debt to Equity						

CONTACT INFORMATION:

Phone: 682-605-1000   Fax: 972-582-2346
Toll-Free: 888-872-8356
Address: 5400 LBJ Fwy., Ste. 500, Dallas, TX 75240 United States

STOCK TICKER/OTHER:

Stock Ticker: Subsidiary   Exchange:
Employees: 1,554   Fiscal Year Ends: 12/31
Parent Company: Expedia Inc

SALARIES/BONUSES:

Top Exec. Salary: $ Bonus: $
Second Exec. Salary: $ Bonus: $

OTHER THOUGHTS:

Estimated Female Officers or Directors: 2
Hot Spot for Advancement for Women/Minorities:

Travelport Worldwide Limited

www.travelport.com

NAIC Code: 561510

TYPES OF BUSINESS:

Online Travel Reservation Systems
Travel Distribution Services & Solutions
Consumer Travel Reservation Sites

BRANDS/DIVISIONS/AFFILIATES:

Blackstone Group LP (The)
eNett International (Jersey) Limited
Elliott Associates LP

CONTACTS: Note: Officers with more than one job title may be intentionally listed here more than once.

Gordon Wilson, CEO
Douglas Steenland, Chmn.
Bernard Bot, CFO
Matthew Minetola, CIO
Terence Conley, Executive VP, Divisional
Philip Emery, Executive VP
Thomas Murphy, Executive VP
Matthew Minetola, Executive VP
Kurt Ekert, Executive VP
Gordon Wilson, President
Rochelle Boas, Secretary
Bryan Conway, Senior VP
Christopher Roberts, Vice President, Divisional
Kate Aldridge, Vice President, Divisional

GROWTH PLANS/SPECIAL FEATURES:

Travelport Worldwide Limited, one of the largest travel companies in the world, offers a variety of travel-related services to travel professionals and travel suppliers. Products and services include distribution technology, travel packaging, consultation and retail sales for both the business and consumer markets. The firm offers these services in more than 180 countries, with sales and support offices in 40 countries. Travelport facilitates travel commerce by connecting travel providers such as airlines and hotel chains with online and offline travel agencies and other travel buyers via its Travel Commerce Platform (TCP). In 2017, the TCP system processed more than 6 billion travel-related messages per day and approximately 18 billion application programming interface (API) calls every month. That same year it handled over 340 million segments sold by travel agencies and sold over 68 million hotel room nights and over 105 million car rental days. Travelport provides air distribution services to approximately 400 airlines globally, as well as hotel reservation services for approximately 310 hotel chains that represent approximately 145,000 hotel properties and serve over 38,000 rental car locations, 50 cruise-lines and tour operators and 14 major rail networks worldwide. Additionally, Travelport is a majority-owner and joint venture partner in eNett International (Jersey) Limited, a provider of payment solutions to the travel industry. Priceline, Orbitz Worldwide and Expedia are the company's largest OTA (online travel agency) customers, accounting for approximately 10% of net revenue. The company is owned by The Blackstone Group, among others. In March 2018, Elliott Associates LP acquired an 11.8% economic interest in Travelport.

FINANCIAL DATA: Note: Data for latest year may not have been available at press time.

In U.S. $	2018	2017	2016	2015	2014	2013
Revenue		2,447,279,000	2,351,356,000	2,221,000,000	2,148,000,000	2,076,000,000
R&D Expense						
Operating Income		285,889,000	200,613,000	191,000,000	161,000,000	208,000,000
Operating Margin %		11.68%	8.53%	8.59%	7.49%	10.01%
SGA Expense		448,070,000	510,688,000	456,000,000	430,000,000	396,000,000
Net Income		142,463,000	16,820,000	16,000,000	86,000,000	-206,000,000
Operating Cash Flow		317,662,000	299,019,000	262,000,000	58,000,000	100,000,000
Capital Expenditure		117,514,000	107,460,000	106,000,000	112,000,000	107,000,000
EBITDA		567,850,000	481,159,000	492,000,000	470,000,000	477,000,000
Return on Assets %		5.00%	.58%	.54%	2.87%	-6.59%
Return on Equity %						
Debt to Equity						

CONTACT INFORMATION:

Phone: 770-563-7400   Fax:
Toll-Free:
Address: Axis One, Axis Park 10 Hurricane Way Langley, Berkshire, SL3 8AG United Kingdom

STOCK TICKER/OTHER:

Stock Ticker: TVPT   Exchange: NYS
Employees: 5,000   Fiscal Year Ends: 12/31
Parent Company:

SALARIES/BONUSES:

Top Exec. Salary: $754,271   Bonus: $
Second Exec. Salary: $514,275   Bonus: $

OTHER THOUGHTS:

Estimated Female Officers or Directors:
Hot Spot for Advancement for Women/Minorities:

Travelzoo Inc

www.travelzoo.com

NAIC Code: 561510

TYPES OF BUSINESS:

Travel Services-Online

BRANDS/DIVISIONS/AFFILIATES:

Azzurro Capital Inc
Travelzoo Top 20
Travelzoo Network
Local Deals
Getaway

CONTACTS: *Note: Officers with more than one job title may be intentionally listed here more than once.*

Holger Bartel, CEO
Wayne Lee, CFO
Lisa Su, Chief Accounting Officer
Michael Peterson, Chief Technology Officer
Ralph Bartel, Director
Rachel Barnett, Director
Christian Smart, General Manager, Geographical

GROWTH PLANS/SPECIAL FEATURES:

Travelzoo, Inc. is a global internet media company that publishes travel and entertainment offers from travel and entertainment firms. Its publications and products, which serve 28 million subscribers, include the Travelzoo websites, Travelzoo e-mail newsletters, the Travelzoo smartphone app and Newsflash e-mail alert services. Travelzoo websites have a 24/7 publication schedule that reaches 9 million unique visitors each month. Travelzoo Top 20 is a weekly email newsletter. Newsflash is a regionally-targeted email alert service that provides a single, time-sensitive news offer within two hours of an offer being identified. Local Deals and Getaway are locally-targeted email alert systems with a twice-per-week publication schedule. Travelzoo Network is a network of third-party websites that list outstanding deals published by Travelzoo. Revenues are primarily from advertising fees, with Travelzoo's advertising base including more than 2,000 travel, entertainment and local businesses. Advertisers include airlines, hotels, cruise lines, vacation packagers, tour operators, destinations, car rental companies, travel agents, theater and performing arts groups, restaurants, spas and activity companies. Travelzoo operates in three geographical segments: Asia Pacific (Australia, China, Hong Kong, Japan, Taiwan and Southeast Asia), North America (U.S. and Canada) and Europe (France, Germany, Spain and the U.K.). The North American segment generates approximately 61% of the firm's 2017 revenue, with Europe generating 32% and Asia Pacific 7%. Azzurro Capital, Inc. holds a 57.8% stake in Travelzoo. During 2017, Travelzoo discontinued its SuperSearch and Fly.com operations to focus on its global Travelzoo brand.

FINANCIAL DATA: *Note: Data for latest year may not have been available at press time.*

In U.S. $	2018	2017	2016	2015	2014	2013
Revenue		106,524,000	128,552,000	141,716,000	142,076,000	158,234,000
R&D Expense		9,224,000	9,445,000	12,528,000		
Operating Income		4,545,000	11,068,000	7,146,000	13,467,000	24,278,000
Operating Margin %		4.26%	8.60%	5.04%	9.47%	15.34%
SGA Expense		79,846,000	93,726,000	103,218,000	110,703,000	116,554,000
Net Income		3,530,000	6,631,000	10,864,000	16,352,000	-5,011,000
Operating Cash Flow		2,076,000	8,722,000	4,192,000	1,530,000	16,852,000
Capital Expenditure		738,000	909,000	1,282,000	3,260,000	5,461,000
EBITDA		6,620,000	13,598,000	9,934,000	16,291,000	27,258,000
Return on Assets %		7.11%	10.86%	13.65%	15.93%	-4.71%
Return on Equity %		22.67%	33.61%	35.50%	45.96%	-13.42%
Debt to Equity						

CONTACT INFORMATION:

Phone: 212 484-4900   Fax: 212 521-4230
Toll-Free:
Address: 590 Madison Ave., 37/Fl., New York, NY 10022 United States

STOCK TICKER/OTHER:

Stock Ticker: TZOO   Exchange: NAS
Employees: 444   Fiscal Year Ends: 12/31
Parent Company: Azzurro Capital Inc

SALARIES/BONUSES:

Top Exec. Salary: $470,000   Bonus: $62,502
Second Exec. Salary: Bonus: $108,000
$320,000

OTHER THOUGHTS:

Estimated Female Officers or Directors: 2
Hot Spot for Advancement for Women/Minorities: Y

Trend Micro Inc

www.trendmicro.com

NAIC Code: 511210E

TYPES OF BUSINESS:

Computer Software, Security & Anti-Virus
Antivirus Software

BRANDS/DIVISIONS/AFFILIATES:

XGen
Moxa Inc

CONTACTS: Note: Officers with more than one job title may be intentionally listed here more than once.

Eva Chen, CEO
Kevin Simzer, COO
Mahendra Negi, CFO
Max Cheng, CIO
Raimund Genes, CTO
Steve Quane, Chief Product Officer
Felix Sterling, General Counsel
Wael Mohamed, Exec. VP-Corporate Strategy & Global Field Oper.
Jenny Chang, Chief Cultural Officer
Mitchel Chang, Sr. VP-Global Tech. Support
Oscar Chang, Chief Dev. Officer
Steve Chang, Chmn.
Oscar Chang, Exec. VP-Greater China Sales
Akihiko Omikawa, Gen. Manager-Japan Region & Consumer Business Unit

GROWTH PLANS/SPECIAL FEATURES:

Trend Micro, Inc. is a Japanese multinational cyber security and defense company. The firm's XGen security software addresses the full range of threats, both present and future threats. Instead of using separate, siloed security solutions, XGen security provides a cross-generational blend of threat defense techniques and a connected threat defense to protect organizations from unseen threats. XGen minimizes IT impact with solutions specifically designed for and integrated with leading customer platforms and applications on endpoints, networks, data centers and the cloud. It speeds response time via centralized visibility and control, and enables the automatic sharing of threat intelligence across security layers. Trend Micro's products and solutions are divided into three categories: hybrid cloud security, which addresses data center, virtualization, cloud security, container security, security for DevOps and solutions for security teams; network security, addressing intrusion prevention and advanced threat protection; and user protection, addressing endpoint security, email security, web security, endpoint and gateway suites, software-as-a-service application security and endpoint detection/response. The company's solutions are used for Ransomware, GDPR, compliance, cloud, health care, point of sale and end-of-support systems. Headquartered in Tokyo, Japan, the company has additional headquarters in the U.S. and Canada, as well as offices worldwide, including North America, Latin America, Australia, New Zealand, Asia-Pacific, Europe, the Middle East and Africa. In November 2018, Trend Micro signed a letter of intent with Moxa, Inc. to form a joint venture to tackle security needs in industrial Internet of Things (IoT) environments.

FINANCIAL DATA: Note: Data for latest year may not have been available at press time.

In U.S. $	2018	2017	2016	2015	2014	2013
Revenue						
R&D Expense						
Operating Income						
Operating Margin %						
SGA Expense						
Net Income						
Operating Cash Flow						
Capital Expenditure						
EBITDA						
Return on Assets %						
Return on Equity %						
Debt to Equity						

CONTACT INFORMATION:

Phone: 81-3-5334-3618   Fax: 81-3-5334-4008
Toll-Free: 800-228-5651
Address: Shinjuku Maynds Tower, 2-1-1 Yoyogi, Shibuya, Tokyo, 151-8583 Japan

STOCK TICKER/OTHER:

Stock Ticker: TMICY   Exchange: PINX
Employees: 5,970   Fiscal Year Ends: 12/31
Parent Company:

SALARIES/BONUSES:

Top Exec. Salary: $ Bonus: $
Second Exec. Salary: $ Bonus: $

OTHER THOUGHTS:

Estimated Female Officers or Directors: 3
Hot Spot for Advancement for Women/Minorities: Y

Sales, profits and employees may be estimates. Financial information, benefits and other data can change quickly and may vary from those stated here.

TripAdvisor Inc

www.tripadvisor.com

NAIC Code: 561510

TYPES OF BUSINESS:

Online Travel Information

BRANDS/DIVISIONS/AFFILIATES:

tripadvisor.com
TripAdvisor Business Advantage
TripAdvisor Premium for Restaurants
Bokun

CONTACTS: *Note: Officers with more than one job title may be intentionally listed here more than once.*

Stephen Kaufer, CEO
Gregory Maffei, Chmn.
Noel Watson, Chief Accounting Officer
Seth Kalvert, General Counsel
Dermot Halpin, President, Divisional
Ernst Teunisssen, Senior VP

GROWTH PLANS/SPECIAL FEATURES:

TripAdvisor, Inc. operates a major web-based travel network that offers traveling advice, reviews, flight searches and planning services such as TripAdvisor mobile. TripAdvisor's sites offer approximately 600 million reviews/opinions and receive 455 million unique monthly visitors. During 2017, more than half of TripAdvisor's average monthly unique visitor came from mobile phones, a channel that grew nearly 30% from the previous year. The firm's sites feature information across a broad base of global travel-related businesses, including 1.2 million hotels, inns, B&Bs and specialty lodging, 750,000 vacation rentals, 4.6 million restaurants and 915,000 activities and attractions worldwide. TripAdvisor-branded websites include tripadvisor.com in the U.S, as well as localized versions of the TripAdvisor website in 48 markets and 28 languages. The company's TripAdvisor Business Advantage and Premium for Restaurants is a business-to-business service designed to help its partners grow their businesses. For example, the service offers hoteliers and restauranteurs affordable marketing and business analytics tools to help attract customers and effectively manage their business pages on TripAdvisor. In April 2018, TripAdvisor acquired Bokun, a provider of business management technology for the tours, attractions and experiences industry. This purchase enables the firm to provide suppliers with technical solutions.

The firm offers employees benefits including medical, dental, discounted vision, life and disability insurance; flexible spending accounts; paid vacation; tuition assistance; fitness subsidies; sick and parental leave; adoption assistance; product discounts; free lunches, snacks and beverages; a 401(k); and a matching charitable gift program.

FINANCIAL DATA: *Note: Data for latest year may not have been available at press time.*

In U.S. $	2018	2017	2016	2015	2014	2013
Revenue		1,556,000,000	1,480,000,000	1,492,000,000	1,246,000,000	944,661,000
R&D Expense		243,000,000	243,000,000	207,000,000	171,000,000	130,673,000
Operating Income		124,000,000	166,000,000	232,000,000	340,000,000	294,574,000
Operating Margin %		7.96%	11.21%	15.54%	27.28%	31.18%
SGA Expense		1,006,000,000	899,000,000	902,000,000	630,000,000	466,474,000
Net Income		-19,000,000	120,000,000	198,000,000	226,000,000	205,443,000
Operating Cash Flow		238,000,000	321,000,000	382,000,000	387,000,000	349,523,000
Capital Expenditure		64,000,000	72,000,000	109,000,000	81,000,000	55,455,000
EBITDA		236,000,000	264,000,000	342,000,000	396,000,000	330,002,000
Return on Assets %		- .84%	5.49%	9.68%	13.17%	14.82%
Return on Equity %		-1.32%	8.23%	15.60%	22.71%	25.81%
Debt to Equity		0.23	0.11	0.20	0.29	0.35

CONTACT INFORMATION:

Phone: 781-800-5000   Fax:
Toll-Free:
Address: 400 1st Ave., Needham, MA 02494 United States

STOCK TICKER/OTHER:

Stock Ticker: TRIP
Employees: 1,614
Parent Company:

Exchange: NAS
Fiscal Year Ends: 12/31

SALARIES/BONUSES:

Top Exec. Salary: $700,000   Bonus: $350,000
Second Exec. Salary: $421,092   Bonus: $600,000

OTHER THOUGHTS:

Estimated Female Officers or Directors: 4
Hot Spot for Advancement for Women/Minorities: Y

trivago NV

NAIC Code: 561510

TYPES OF BUSINESS:

Online Reservation Systems

BRANDS/DIVISIONS/AFFILIATES:

trivago.com
TripHappy

CONTACTS: Note: Officers with more than one job title may be intentionally listed here more than once.

Rolf Schromgens, CEO

GROWTH PLANS/SPECIAL FEATURES:

Trivago NV operates trivago.com, a global online hotel search platform. The website allows travelers to make informed decisions by personalizing their hotel search and providing access to a deep supply of hotel information and prices. Approximately 4 billion annual users find a hotel through the company's platform, which spans 55 global regions and 33 different languages. Trivago focuses on machine learning and artificial intelligence in order to sustain its eCommerce network. Its fast and intuitive search engine compares 2 million hotels and alternative accommodations, featuring information, pictures, ratings, reviews, filters and other features. Travel agencies, hotel chains and independent hotels are provided a range of marketing tools and services to help their businesses grow. The network comprises online travel agents offering accommodation services in over 190 countries worldwide. More than half of trivago.com's traffic comes from branded sources. Headquartered in Dusseldorf, Germany, the firm has innovation centers in Spain, Germany and Netherlands. In August 2018, Trivago acquired TripHappy, a U.S. travel startup that leverages artificial intelligence (AI) to highlight relevant location and neighborhood information during the hotel search and discovery process.

FINANCIAL DATA: Note: Data for latest year may not have been available at press time.

In U.S. $	2018	2017	2016	2015	2014	2013
Revenue		1,179,413,000	859,079,800	561,674,700	352,362,500	
R&D Expense						
Operating Income		-23,070,350	-50,627,650	-54,529,090	-34,508,130	
Operating Margin %		-1.96%	-5.89%	-9.70%	-9.79%	
SGA Expense		1,192,191,000	889,055,400	578,640,600	351,025,200	
Net Income		-14,217,210	-57,731,120	-44,569,870	-26,308,830	
Operating Cash Flow		-11,773,820	35,479,790	-1,156,195	717,638	
Capital Expenditure		19,779,470	9,250,695	7,089,807	4,244,316	
EBITDA		-7,685,561	-29,211,280	-20,342,190	-346,289	
Return on Assets %		-1.19%	-5.73%	-5.17%	-3.07%	
Return on Equity %		-1.65%	-7.94%	-6.08%	-3.47%	
Debt to Equity						

CONTACT INFORMATION:

Phone: 49-211-54056110   Fax:
Toll-Free:
Address: Bennigsen-Platz 1, Dusseldorf, 40474 Germany

STOCK TICKER/OTHER:

Stock Ticker: TRVG
Employees: 1,230
Parent Company:

Exchange: NAS
Fiscal Year Ends:

SALARIES/BONUSES:

Top Exec. Salary: $240,000   Bonus: $72,000
Second Exec. Salary: Bonus: $72,000
$240,000

OTHER THOUGHTS:

Estimated Female Officers or Directors:
Hot Spot for Advancement for Women/Minorities:

TrueCar Inc

www.truecar.com

NAIC Code: 519130

TYPES OF BUSINESS:

Internet Publishing and Broadcasting and Web Search Portals

BRANDS/DIVISIONS/AFFILIATES:

TrueCar.com
TrueCar Certified Dealer
TrueTrade
TrueLoan
TrueLease

CONTACTS: Note: Officers with more than one job title may be intentionally listed here more than once.

Christopher Claus, Chairman of the Board
John Pierantoni, Chief Accounting Officer
Neeraj Gunsagar, Chief Marketing Officer
Victor Perry, Director
Brian Skutta, Executive VP, Divisional
Michael Darrow, Executive VP, Divisional
Jeff Swart, General Counsel

GROWTH PLANS/SPECIAL FEATURES:

TrueCar,Inc. provides comparative sales information for car makes and models in specific areas through its TrueCar.com web site. The online portal also provides information related to where vehicles are available, estimated prices for that make and model of car (referred to as upfront pricing information) all derived from the company's network of TrueCar Certified Dealers. The upfront pricing information generally includes guaranteed savings off MSRP which the consumer may then take to one of 15,000 TrueCar Certified Dealer in the form of a Guaranteed Savings Certificate that applies toward the purchase of the specified make and model of car. TrueCar benefits its network of TrueCar Certified Dealers by enabling them to attract these informed, in-market consumers in a cost-effective, accountable manner, which helps them to sell more cars. The network covers the entire U.S. and has accounted for millions of cars sold. Approximately 94% of the firm's revenue is derived from the fee that TrueCar Certified Dealers pay when a TrueCar.com user purchases a car from them. The remaining revenue comes from the sale of data and consulting services to the automotive and financial services industries. Current products under development include TrueTrade, which would provide users with an estimated daily market value for their existing cars and a guaranteed trade-in price; as well as both TrueLoan and TrueLease, which would provide users a convenient way to finance cars at TrueCar Certified Dealers.

FINANCIAL DATA: Note: Data for latest year may not have been available at press time.

In U.S. $	2018	2017	2016	2015	2014	2013
Revenue		323,149,000	277,507,000	259,838,000	206,649,000	133,958,000
R&D Expense		59,070,000	53,580,000	48,021,000	36,563,000	23,685,000
Operating Income		-33,663,000	-38,899,000	-63,982,000	-47,505,000	-22,628,000
Operating Margin %		-10.41%	-14.01%	-24.62%	-22.98%	-16.89%
SGA Expense		247,043,000	214,314,000	234,496,000	186,865,000	106,037,000
Net Income		-32,849,000	-41,708,000	-64,911,000	-48,429,000	-25,056,000
Operating Cash Flow		22,118,000	2,768,000	-11,369,000	3,104,000	-3,911,000
Capital Expenditure		19,809,000	16,639,000	29,836,000	15,896,000	8,404,000
EBITDA		-9,931,000	-15,178,000	-46,216,000	-34,196,000	-10,920,000
Return on Assets %		-9.67%	-13.97%	-21.66%	-20.53%	-15.66%
Return on Equity %		-12.21%	-18.24%	-26.94%	-26.80%	-23.82%
Debt to Equity		0.09	0.12	0.11	0.02	

CONTACT INFORMATION:

Phone: Fax:
Toll-Free: 800-200-2000
Address: 120 Broadway, Ste. 200, Santa Monica, CA 90401 United States

STOCK TICKER/OTHER:

Stock Ticker: TRUE   Exchange: NAS
Employees: 650   Fiscal Year Ends:
Parent Company:

SALARIES/BONUSES:

Top Exec. Salary: $800,000   Bonus: $195,488
Second Exec. Salary: Bonus: $134,699
$400,000

OTHER THOUGHTS:

Estimated Female Officers or Directors:
Hot Spot for Advancement for Women/Minorities:

Tucows Inc

www.tucowsinc.com

NAIC Code: 518210

TYPES OF BUSINESS:

Domain Name Registry Services
Digital Web Certificates
Software

BRANDS/DIVISIONS/AFFILIATES:

Ting
www.ting.com
Hover.com
eNom
Platypus

CONTACTS: Note: Officers with more than one job title may be intentionally listed here more than once.

Elliot Noss, CEO
Dave Singh, CFO
Hanno Liem, Chief Technology Officer
Allen Karp, Co-Chairman
Rawleigh Ralls, Co-Chairman
David Woroch, Executive VP, Divisional
Bret Fausett, Other Corporate Officer
Jason Silverstein, Vice President, Divisional
Jessica Johannson, Vice President, Divisional
Michael Goldstein, VP, Divisional
Ross Rader, VP, Divisional

GROWTH PLANS/SPECIAL FEATURES:

Tucows, Inc. is an internet services company focusing on domain name registration and related services. It operates two product and service-related groups: network access services and domain services. Network access cervices derives revenue from the firm's Ting brand of retail mobile phones and services. Ting serves individuals and small businesses nationally, and also offers fixed high-speed internet access in select cities and internet hosting and network consulting services to customers in Central Virginia. Ting provides customers with access to our provisioning and management tools via the www.ting.com website. The domain services group offers wholesale and retail domain name registration services, value added services and portfolio services. Revenues primarily comes from the registration fees charged to resellers in connection with new, renewed and transferred domain name registrations; the sale of retail internet domain name registration and email services to individuals and small businesses; and by making its portfolio of domain names available for sale. The segment's primary distribution channel is a global network of approximately 39,000 resellers in more than 150 countries who typically provide their customers, the end-users of the internet, with a critical component for establishing and maintaining an online presence. Within domain services is wholesale, or OpenSRS, which manages more than 28 million domain names and offers domain services, email services, a personal name service and secure socket layer (SSL) security certificate services. This division's retail internet domain name registration and email services is available on Tucows' Hover.com and eNom branded sites, which serve both individuals and small businesses. In addition, Tucows provides billing, provisioning and customer care software solutions to internet service providers (ISPs) through its Platypus brand of billing software.

FINANCIAL DATA: Note: Data for latest year may not have been available at press time.

In U.S. $	2018	2017	2016	2015	2014	2013
Revenue		329,420,700	189,818,900	172,939,500	147,667,100	129,934,900
R&D Expense		7,257,720	4,494,819	4,502,845	4,305,715	4,158,603
Operating Income		27,094,290	24,990,250	19,015,130	11,523,050	6,830,780
Operating Margin %		8.22%	13.16%	10.99%	7.80%	5.25%
SGA Expense		43,016,880	32,159,540	29,199,760	23,899,980	19,345,930
Net Income		22,326,590	16,067,150	11,373,730	6,374,096	4,180,464
Operating Cash Flow		31,896,640	21,649,700	13,346,010	8,877,344	8,704,107
Capital Expenditure		15,877,240	14,447,480	2,967,360	711,656	1,345,627
EBITDA		39,222,050	27,767,110	20,706,210	13,045,770	7,957,990
Return on Assets %		8.84%	11.33%	8.92%	5.15%	3.48%
Return on Equity %		45.55%	50.09%	36.70%	20.37%	15.63%
Debt to Equity		0.97	0.21			

CONTACT INFORMATION:

Phone: 416 535-0123   Fax: 416 531-5584
Toll-Free: 800-371-6992
Address: 96 Mowat Ave., Toronto, ON M6K 3M1 Canada

STOCK TICKER/OTHER:

Stock Ticker: TCX   Exchange: NAS
Employees: 375   Fiscal Year Ends: 12/31
Parent Company:

SALARIES/BONUSES:

Top Exec. Salary: $319,797   Bonus: $123,853
Second Exec. Salary: $208,677   Bonus: $106,549

OTHER THOUGHTS:

Estimated Female Officers or Directors: 1
Hot Spot for Advancement for Women/Minorities:

Sales, profits and employees may be estimates. Financial information, benefits and other data can change quickly and may vary from those stated here.

Tujia Online Information Technology (Beijing) Co Ltd

www.tujia.com
NAIC Code: 561510

TYPES OF BUSINESS:

Online Homestay Reservations
Room Rental Reservations

BRANDS/DIVISIONS/AFFILIATES:

CONTACTS: *Note: Officers with more than one job title may be intentionally listed here more than once.*

Justin Jun Luo, CEO
Melissa Yang, CIO

GROWTH PLANS/SPECIAL FEATURES:

Tujia Online Information Technology (Beijing) Co., Ltd operates Tujia, an online short-term rental platform in China Tujia covers 345 destinations in China and more than 1,000 destinations overseas. The platform has over 1 million online listings, including accommodation products and extension services such as homestays, apartments, villas and more Short-term rentals primarily serve the vacation traveler's accommodation needs, but are also used by business travelers, group travelers, holiday gatherings and more. Users can book via online or mobile channels, as well as WeChat and telephone. Tujia takes care of verifying that the listed properties are what and where they say they are, and provides tenants with an advanced payment guarantee fund. Tujia members also receive benefits of the local culture, as well as discounts at nearby coffee houses, attractions and more. The company welcomes landlords who have idle houses to rent/share, as well as new-home builders desiring to share a portion of their rooms for advertising/accommodation purposes. Owners and landlords publish their homes on Tujia's multiple website portals for free. The company also guides landlords through the process for a worry-free, seamless process. Tujia has signed contracts with more than 200 government agencies in China and has strategic partnership agreements with most of the Top 100 real estate development companies.

FINANCIAL DATA: *Note: Data for latest year may not have been available at press time.*

In U.S. $	2018	2017	2016	2015	2014	2013
Revenue						
R&D Expense						
Operating Income						
Operating Margin %						
SGA Expense						
Net Income						
Operating Cash Flow						
Capital Expenditure						
EBITDA						
Return on Assets %						
Return on Equity %						
Debt to Equity						

CONTACT INFORMATION:

Phone: 86-10-5975-6798   Fax: 86-10-5975-6717
Toll-Free:
Address: 10 Jiuxianqiao Rd., Chaoyang Dist., Beijing, Beijing 100015 China

STOCK TICKER/OTHER:

Stock Ticker: Private
Employees:
Parent Company:

Exchange:
Fiscal Year Ends:

SALARIES/BONUSES:

Top Exec. Salary: $ Bonus: $
Second Exec. Salary: $ Bonus: $

OTHER THOUGHTS:

Estimated Female Officers or Directors:
Hot Spot for Advancement for Women/Minorities:

Turbonomic Inc

turbonomic.com

NAIC Code: 511210M

TYPES OF BUSINESS:

Cloud Application Management Tools

BRANDS/DIVISIONS/AFFILIATES:

CONTACTS: *Note: Officers with more than one job title may be intentionally listed here more than once.*

Benjamin Nye, CEO
Shmuel Kliger, Pres.
Mo Garad, CFO
Tom Murphy, CMO
Mark Thurmond, COO
Charles Crouchman, CTO
Bill Veghte, Chmn.

GROWTH PLANS/SPECIAL FEATURES:

Turbonomic, Inc. provides an autonomic cloud platform that allows enterprises to accelerate their adoption of virtual, cloud and container deployments for mission-critical applications. The company claims the platform delivers faster application response time on less infrastructure. Its autonomic solution enables heterogeneous environments to self-manage in order to assure the performance of any application in any cloud. Turbonomic's patented decision engine analyzes application demand and allocates shared resources in real-time, maintaining a continuous state of application health. Solutions include private/public/hybrid cloud, DevOps, data center migration, virtual desktop infrastructure management, hyper-converged and more. Industries served by the firm include education, financial services, government, healthcare, service provider, retail, eCommerce and technology. Turbonomic has partnered with more than 2,000 enterprise customers and over 100 of the Fortune 500 to enable innovation. These customer partners include Fareportal, Georgetown University, Boston College, Aspirus, Houston Methodist, MedAmerica, EcoBank, PWC, SkyBet, Scentsy, DXC, Node4 and many more. Based in Boston, Massachusetts, Turbonomic has additional offices in New York, the U.K., Canada, Australia and Israel.

FINANCIAL DATA: *Note: Data for latest year may not have been available at press time.*

In U.S. $	2018	2017	2016	2015	2014	2013
Revenue						
R&D Expense						
Operating Income						
Operating Margin %						
SGA Expense						
Net Income						
Operating Cash Flow						
Capital Expenditure						
EBITDA						
Return on Assets %						
Return on Equity %						
Debt to Equity						

CONTACT INFORMATION:

Phone: 781-373-3540   Fax: 781-418-5210
Toll-Free: 844-438-8872
Address: 500 Boylston St., 7/Fl, Boston, MA 02116 United States

STOCK TICKER/OTHER:

Stock Ticker: Private   Exchange:
Employees: 400   Fiscal Year Ends:
Parent Company:

SALARIES/BONUSES:

Top Exec. Salary: $ Bonus: $
Second Exec. Salary: $ Bonus: $

OTHER THOUGHTS:

Estimated Female Officers or Directors:
Hot Spot for Advancement for Women/Minorities:

Sales, profits and employees may be estimates. Financial information, benefits and other data can change quickly and may vary from those stated here.

Twilio Inc

NAIC Code: 511210C

TYPES OF BUSINESS:

Computer Software, Telecom, Communications & VoIP
Cloud-Based Telephony Technology

BRANDS/DIVISIONS/AFFILIATES:

Twilio Connect
OpenVBX

CONTACTS: Note: Officers with more than one job title may be intentionally listed here more than once.

Jeff Lawson, CEO
Khozema Shipchandler, CFO
George Hu, COO
Karyn Smith, General Counsel

GROWTH PLANS/SPECIAL FEATURES:

Twilio, Inc. provides web-service infrastructure application programming interfaces (APIs) to build cloud communications applications. It offers APIs for enterprises to build communications applications for voice, VoIP and SMS (text messaging) in the cloud. The firm's technology allows app developers to integrate telephony services into their apps. When a voice call is initiated to a Twilio phone number, the company answers the call and then sends an HTTP request to the receiver's application (which could include a sales call center or tech support desk). The user's application then responds with an XML command that Twilio executes to the caller. A similar chain of events is enacted for SMS messages. Pricing for a Twilio account includes $1/month for a telephone number, less than 1 cent/minute for inbound calls, less than 1 cent for sent and received messages and 2 cents/minute for outbound calls (these refer to local connectivity). Toll-free numbers are $2 per month, and SIP interface, programmable call recording and conference calling (basic & global) are all priced less than 1 cent per minute. Using Twilio Connect, developers can add voice telephony and SMS messaging to their applications without the additional hassle of billing users for usage. For users that do not intend to build their own application, the firm also offers OpenVBX, a pre-built, open-source phone system application. The company serves a variety of industries, including health care, education, customer service, retail and manufacturing. Twilio is based in San Francisco, California with an additional office in London. More than 36,000 active users use Twilio's service. In October 2018, Twilio agreed to acquire SendGrid, Inc., a customer communication platform for transactional and marketing email, in an all-stock transaction valued at approximately $2 billion. The transaction is expected to close in the first half of 2019.

Employees of Twilio receive medical, dental and vision insurance; a 401(k) plan; and pre-tax commuter benefits..

FINANCIAL DATA: Note: Data for latest year may not have been available at press time.

In U.S. $	2018	2017	2016	2015	2014	2013
Revenue		399,020,000	277,335,000	166,919,000	88,846,000	49,920,000
R&D Expense		120,739,000	77,926,000	42,559,000	21,824,000	13,959,000
Operating Income		-66,074,000	-41,315,000	-35,393,000	-26,683,000	-26,850,000
Operating Margin %		-16.55%	-14.89%	-21.20%	-30.03%	-53.78%
SGA Expense		160,288,000	116,344,000	85,299,000	52,282,000	36,943,000
Net Income		-63,708,000	-41,324,000	-35,504,000	-26,758,000	-26,854,000
Operating Cash Flow		-3,260,000	10,091,000	-18,762,000	-17,360,000	-22,622,000
Capital Expenditure		26,818,000	26,486,000	10,618,000	5,170,000	3,452,000
EBITDA		-47,310,000	-33,000,000	-31,167,000	-24,927,000	-26,240,000
Return on Assets %		-14.77%	-14.49%	-36.60%	-48.67%	
Return on Equity %		-18.48%	-40.08%			
Debt to Equity						

CONTACT INFORMATION:

Phone: 650-270-2199   Fax:
Toll-Free: 877-889-4546
Address: 645 Harrison Street, 3/Fl, San Francisco, CA 94107 United States

STOCK TICKER/OTHER:

Stock Ticker: TWLO
Employees: 730
Parent Company:

Exchange: NYS
Fiscal Year Ends:

SALARIES/BONUSES:

Top Exec. Salary: $400,000   Bonus: $125,000
Second Exec. Salary: $502,308   Bonus: $

OTHER THOUGHTS:

Estimated Female Officers or Directors: 2
Hot Spot for Advancement for Women/Minorities:

Twitter Inc

www.twitter.com

NAIC Code: 519130

TYPES OF BUSINESS:

Real-Time Short Messaging
Advertising Services

BRANDS/DIVISIONS/AFFILIATES:

Twiter.com
Tweets
Twitterers
Periscope

CONTACTS: *Note: Officers with more than one job title may be intentionally listed here more than once.*

Ned Segal, CFO
Omid Kordestani, Chairman of the Board
Robert Kaiden, Chief Accounting Officer
Jack Dorsey, Director
Vijaya Gadde, Other Executive Officer

GROWTH PLANS/SPECIAL FEATURES:

Twitter, Inc. operates a social networking website, Twitter.com, which encourages users to post updates, or Tweets, to their profile page answering the question, What are you doing? Each message is limited to 280 characters (for all languages except Japanese, Korean and Chinese), the size of a doubled message service (SMS) text message. Users can send and receive Tweets via the Twitter website, text messages or external applications. Twitterers can make their profile page public or private and can include hash tags around certain words to make their public posts searchable. They can reTweet others' Tweets and post the Tweet on their profile and send direct messages to other Twitterers. In addition, users can attach poll questions to tweets, with polls being open for 24 hours and voters are not identifiable. Twitterers can elect to follow the Tweets of family, friends, co-workers, celebrities, news organizations and many others via Twitter's messaging service. Twitter makes the Twitter API (application programming interface) publicly available on its website, providing developers with all the tools necessary to create new Twittering applications for a variety of operating systems and platforms, including Windows, Mac OSX, Google Desktop, Android OS, iPhone and iPod Touch. Twitter and its products and services are available in multiple languages. In Addition to Twitter, the firm also operates Periscope, enabling anyone to broadcast and watch video live with others. As of mid-2018, Twitter had more than 335 million active users. Based in California, USA, the firm has 35+ offices worldwide.

Twitter employees receive benefits including paid parental leave, medical and dental coverage, wireless discounts, catered breakfast and lunch, a 401(k), Zipcar discounts, gym membership reimbursement and a commuter program.

FINANCIAL DATA: *Note: Data for latest year may not have been available at press time.*

In U.S. $	2018	2017	2016	2015	2014	2013
Revenue		2,443,299,000	2,529,619,000	2,218,032,000	1,403,002,000	664,890,000
R&D Expense		542,010,000	713,482,000	806,648,000	691,543,000	593,992,000
Operating Income		38,740,000	-367,208,000	-450,036,000	-538,866,000	-635,831,000
Operating Margin %		1.58%	-14.51%	-20.28%	-38.40%	-95.62%
SGA Expense		1,001,307,000	1,251,105,000	1,132,164,000	804,016,000	440,011,000
Net Income		-108,063,000	-456,873,000	-521,031,000	-577,820,000	-645,323,000
Operating Cash Flow		831,209,000	763,055,000	383,066,000	81,796,000	1,398,000
Capital Expenditure		160,742,000	218,657,000	347,280,000	201,630,000	75,744,000
EBITDA		405,686,000	61,306,000	-122,304,000	-330,701,000	-524,937,000
Return on Assets %		-1.51%	-6.86%	-8.66%	-12.91%	-30.74%
Return on Equity %		-2.23%	-10.18%	-13.03%	-17.57%	-47.76%
Debt to Equity		0.33	0.34	0.34	0.41	0.03

CONTACT INFORMATION:

Phone: 415-222-9670   Fax: 415-222-0922
Toll-Free:
Address: 1355 Market St., Ste. 900, San Francisco, CA 94103 United States

STOCK TICKER/OTHER:

Stock Ticker: TWTR
Employees: 3,583
Parent Company:

Exchange: NYS
Fiscal Year Ends: 12/31

SALARIES/BONUSES:

Top Exec. Salary: $500,000   Bonus: $
Second Exec. Salary: $500,000   Bonus: $

OTHER THOUGHTS:

Estimated Female Officers or Directors: 2
Hot Spot for Advancement for Women/Minorities: Y

Uber Inc

NAIC Code: 561599

TYPES OF BUSINESS:

Car Ride Dispatch Service, Mobile App-Based
Freight Truck Dispatch Service
Restaurant Meal Delivery Service
Transportation Marketplace Technologies
Self-Driving Truck Technologies
Self-Driving Car Technologies

BRANDS/DIVISIONS/AFFILIATES:

UberEATS
Uber Freight
JUMP Bikes
Uber for Business
Uber Air

CONTACTS: Note: Officers with more than one job title may be intentionally listed here more than once.

Dara Khosrowshahi, CEO
Nelson Chai, CFO
Rebecca Messina, CMO
Thuan Pham, CTO
Salle Yoo, General Counsel
Ryan Graves, Head-Global Oper.
Garrett Camp, Chmn.

GROWTH PLANS/SPECIAL FEATURES:

Uber, Inc. is a California-based creator of the Uber mobile app which connects drivers and ridesharing services with passengers. The application serves over 630 cities worldwide and is in cities in countries throughout the Americas, Europe, the Middle East, Africa and Asia Pacific. Upon receiving a ride request, Uber sends the closest drivers available to fulfill it. Riders can rate their experiences with drivers for other riders to view. The company retains a fee from each ride that it books and then passes the balance of the fare to the drivers. To begin their screening, drivers must upload their license, registration and proof of insurance, as well as other necessary information. Once approved, they can drive with Uber as an independent contractor and are provided everything needed to be a successful Uber driver. Uber has expanded very aggressively on a worldwide basis, although it merged its operations in China with local competitor Didi after incurring massive losses in China. This enabled the firm to concentrate expansion efforts and cash in on other markets, including the vast market in India. Uber has been purchasing cars in India, and leasing them out to local drivers who want to work with the firm. Uber is also expanding into delivery services of many types. Additional Uber divisions include: UberEATS, a restaurant-prepared meal delivery service available in dozens of cities worldwide; Uber Freight, connecting shippers with trucks; JUMP Bikes, featuring dockless bikes and e-assist; and Uber for Business, an all-in-one solution that simplifies how an organization gets around, whether it be a ride to the airport or a car for clients. As of late-2018 Uber was developing Uber Air, to enable shared, multimodal air transportation between suburbs, cities and ultimately within cities in 2023.

FINANCIAL DATA: Note: Data for latest year may not have been available at press time.

In U.S. $	2018	2017	2016	2015	2014	2013
Revenue	11,450,000,000	7,700,000,000	4,900,000,000	2,900,000,000	850,000,000	104,000,000
R&D Expense						
Operating Income						
Operating Margin %						
SGA Expense						
Net Income	-2,700,000,000	-4,500,000,000	-2,800,000,000	-2,200,000,000	-400,000,000	-56,000,000
Operating Cash Flow						
Capital Expenditure						
EBITDA						
Return on Assets %						
Return on Equity %						
Debt to Equity						

CONTACT INFORMATION:

Phone: 415-986-2715   Fax: 415-986-2104
Toll-Free:
Address: 1455 Market St., Ste. 400, San Francisco, CA 94103 United States

STOCK TICKER/OTHER:

Stock Ticker: Private
Employees: 18,000
Parent Company:

Exchange:
Fiscal Year Ends: 12/31

SALARIES/BONUSES:

Top Exec. Salary: $ Bonus: $
Second Exec. Salary: $ Bonus: $

OTHER THOUGHTS:

Estimated Female Officers or Directors: 1
Hot Spot for Advancement for Women/Minorities:

United Internet AG

NAIC Code: 517110

www.unitedinternet.de

TYPES OF BUSINESS:

Internet Service Provider
Online Advertising Services

BRANDS/DIVISIONS/AFFILIATES:

1&1
GMX
WEB.DE
Home.pl
Versatel
United Internet Media
united-domains
World4You

CONTACTS: *Note: Officers with more than one job title may be intentionally listed here more than once.*

Ralph Dommermuth, CEO
Frank Krause, CFO

GROWTH PLANS/SPECIAL FEATURES:

United Internet AG, a German company, is an international internet service provider (ISP). The firm has approximately 23 million fee-based customer contracts and over 36 million ad-financed free accounts in more than 10 countries. United Internet operates in two main segments: access and applications. The access business provides DSL broadband and mobile access products and related application to private and commercial customers. Access business brands include 1&1, GMX, STRATO and WEB.DE, which are broadband and mobile access producers; Home.pl, a market leader in the Polish webhosting market; mail.com, an international email service which offers home users supplier-neutral email addresses; and Versatel, which focuses on tailored telecommunication solutions. United Internet Media is an online marketer and online dialogue specialist for these brands. The application segment serves small companies, freelancers and private users with personal information management, web hosting, online advertising and new cloud applications. Application business brands include united-domains, Arsys, Fasthosts, InterNetX, Sedo and World4You. The company's primary customers are private individuals, home offices, small offices and small- to mid-sized companies. During 2018, United Internet acquired Austrian webhoster, World4You.

FINANCIAL DATA: *Note: Data for latest year may not have been available at press time.*

In U.S. $	2018	2017	2016	2015	2014	2013
Revenue						
R&D Expense						
Operating Income						
Operating Margin %						
SGA Expense						
Net Income						
Operating Cash Flow						
Capital Expenditure						
EBITDA						
Return on Assets %						
Return on Equity %						
Debt to Equity						

CONTACT INFORMATION:

Phone: 49 2602961631   Fax: 49 2602961013
Toll-Free:
Address: Elgendorfer Strasse 57, Montabaur, 56410 Germany

SALARIES/BONUSES:

Top Exec. Salary: $ Bonus: $
Second Exec. Salary: $ Bonus: $

STOCK TICKER/OTHER:

Stock Ticker: UDIRF   Exchange: PINX
Employees: 9,414   Fiscal Year Ends: 12/31
Parent Company:

OTHER THOUGHTS:

Estimated Female Officers or Directors:
Hot Spot for Advancement for Women/Minorities:

United Online Inc

www.untd.com

NAIC Code: 517110

TYPES OF BUSINESS:

Internet Service Provider

BRANDS/DIVISIONS/AFFILIATES:

B Riley Financial Inc
NetZero
Juno
NetZero Mobile Broadband
NetZero Home Wireless Broadband
NetZero Hotspot
Juno Turbo

CONTACTS: *Note: Officers with more than one job title may be intentionally listed here more than once.*

Edward Zinser, CFO
Howard Phanstiel, Director
Mark Harrington, Executive VP
Shahir Fakiri, General Manager, Divisional
Bryant Riley, Chmn.-B. Riley Financial, Inc.

GROWTH PLANS/SPECIAL FEATURES:

United Online, Inc., a subsidiary of B. Riley Financial, Inc., provides consumer products and internet and media services over the internet. These products feature value-priced internet access through the NetZero and Juno brands. Both brands offer a variety of plans, and customers can choose the option that best meets their connection needs. NetZero Wireless offers the NetZero Mobile Broadband and NetZero Home Wireless Broadband services. NetZero Mobile Broadband provides high-speed, affordable internet access to on-the-go consumers. There are four value-priced NetZero Mobile Broadband plans to choose from. Customers are not required to sign a contract, cannot incur overage charges and can upgrade their data plan at any time. New customers can try the service free for up to one year with the purchase of a NetZero Hotspot or NetZero Stick. NetZero Home Wireless Broadband is a secure, wireless internet access service designed for home or office use. NetZero and Juno each offer four types of nationwide dial-up service. The Free service provides 10 hours of access each month free of charge and includes NetZero email. The Basic service provides unlimited access along with email and spam protection. Customers who purchase the Accelerated Dial-Up service (either NetZero HiSpeed or Juno Turbo) can surf the web at up to 5 times the speed of standard dial-up. The Toll-free service allows customers who live in hard to serve areas to connect to the internet using a toll-free 800 access number. DSL service is available in select cities and includes Norton Antivirus online and MegaMail with built-in spam and email virus protection. Additionally, United Online provides advertising solutions to marketers with brand and direct response objectives through a full suite of display, search, email, and text-link opportunities across its internet properties.

FINANCIAL DATA: *Note: Data for latest year may not have been available at press time.*

In U.S. $	2018	2017	2016	2015	2014	2013
Revenue	193,000,000	191,000,000	184,400,000	151,118,000	217,244,992	233,614,000
R&D Expense						
Operating Income						
Operating Margin %						
SGA Expense						
Net Income			2,000,100	29,973,000	-5,429,000	-82,167,000
Operating Cash Flow						
Capital Expenditure						
EBITDA						
Return on Assets %						
Return on Equity %						
Debt to Equity						

CONTACT INFORMATION:

Phone: 818 287-3000   Fax: 818 287-3001
Toll-Free:
Address: 21255 Burbank Blvd, Ste 400, Woodland Hills, CA 91367 United States

STOCK TICKER/OTHER:

Stock Ticker: Subsidiary   Exchange:
Employees: 625   Fiscal Year Ends: 12/31
Parent Company: B Riley Financial Inc

SALARIES/BONUSES:

Top Exec. Salary: $ Bonus: $
Second Exec. Salary: $ Bonus: $

OTHER THOUGHTS:

Estimated Female Officers or Directors:
Hot Spot for Advancement for Women/Minorities:

US Interactive Inc

www.usinteractive.com

NAIC Code: 511210K

TYPES OF BUSINESS:

CRM Software

BRANDS/DIVISIONS/AFFILIATES:

USI Customer Management Platform
eViews
e2e Hub

CONTACTS: *Note: Officers with more than one job title may be intentionally listed here more than once.*

Sunil Mathur, CEO

GROWTH PLANS/SPECIAL FEATURES:

U.S. Interactive, Inc. (USI) is a software and services organization that develops and deploys internet-based customer management applications for communications and next generation service providers. The company has domestic and international offices, with locations California, USA; Mumbai, India; and Munich, Germany. The firm's USI Customer Management Platform is an integrated technology platform developed by the company and its affiliates. The platform is made up of three components: eViews, e2e Hub and connectors. eViews are the applications component of the U.S. Interactive platform for customer management services. These applications deliver a single, unified web-based view of the customer across order management, billing and customer service. e2e (enterprise-to-enterprise) Hub is the infrastructure that supports eViews. Connectors are the USI applications that integrate the commercial software of its affiliates. USI's customer base includes ISPs/ASPs (internet service providers/application service providers), CLECs (competitive local exchange carriers), broadband service and digital media providers and wireless carriers. The firm partners with companies that have quality products and services to provide technology options for its clients. Primary partners include BEA Systems, an e-business infrastructure software company; Portal, an integrated billing and e-CRM (electronic customer relationship management) solutions firm for communications and next-generation service providers; Commerce One, an e-marketplace company; IBM, an information technology company; Sun Microsystems, a technology sharing and marketing support company; and Vignette Corporation, which develops internet applications that enable businesses to use the web for publishing and commerce.

FINANCIAL DATA: *Note: Data for latest year may not have been available at press time.*

In U.S. $	2018	2017	2016	2015	2014	2013
Revenue						
R&D Expense						
Operating Income						
Operating Margin %						
SGA Expense						
Net Income						
Operating Cash Flow						
Capital Expenditure						
EBITDA						
Return on Assets %						
Return on Equity %						
Debt to Equity						

CONTACT INFORMATION:

Phone: 408-863-7500   Fax: 408-863-7501
Toll-Free:
Address: 2005 De La Cruz Blvd, Ste. 195, Santa Clara, CA 95050 United States

STOCK TICKER/OTHER:

Stock Ticker: Private   Exchange:
Employees: 700   Fiscal Year Ends: 12/31
Parent Company:

SALARIES/BONUSES:

Top Exec. Salary: $ Bonus: $
Second Exec. Salary: $ Bonus: $

OTHER THOUGHTS:

Estimated Female Officers or Directors:
Hot Spot for Advancement for Women/Minorities:

Ushahidi Inc

www.ushahidi.com

NAIC Code: 511210M

TYPES OF BUSINESS:

Visualization Software
Open Source Information Collection Software

BRANDS/DIVISIONS/AFFILIATES:

Ushahidi Platform
TenFour

CONTACTS: Note: Officers with more than one job title may be intentionally listed here more than once.

Nathaniel Manning, COO
Irene Wairimu, Dir-Finance
Steven Blumenfeld, Dir-Sales
Jon Shuler, R&D Manager
David Kobia, Dir.-Tech. Dev.
Sharon Rutto, Quality Assurance Engineer
Esther Ondigo, Admin. Assistant
Erik Hersman, Dir.-Oper.
Erik Hersman, Dir.-Strategy
Limo Taboi, Dir.-Finance
Nathaniel Manning, Dir.-Bus. Dev.
Linda Kamau, Developer
Emmanuel Kala, Developer
Angel Odour, Developer
Daudi Were, Project Dir.-Africa

GROWTH PLANS/SPECIAL FEATURES:

Ushahidi, Inc. is a nonprofit software company that develops open source software for data collection, visualization and interactive mapping. Ushahidi, meaning testimony in Swahili, is based on crowdsourcing concepts and seeks to make information regarding elections, crises and other geopolitical events more widely available and transparent. Ushahidi designs its products and initiatives with a global perspective. Combining eyewitness reports delivered by text message, email or over the web with media information and geographical mapping tools, the Ushahidi Platform facilitates the democratization of information. The platform was initially developed to respond to information challenges following reports of violence in the aftermath of presidential elections in Kenya in 2008. It has since been used to compile information on elections in India, Mexico, Lebanon and Afghanistan; protest movements in the Middle East; and post-natural disasters in Haiti, Chile, Japan, Russia and the U.S. TenFour was developed for emergency team check-ins via any device and channel. The core platform was created by volunteers and is managed by a team of developers based primarily in Africa, with additional developers located in the U.S., South America and Europe. Pricing plans are divided into two groups: self-service and enterprise. Self-service plans include: Ushahidi Demo, which is free for one month of unlimited use; and Ushahidi Basic, which is $499 per month. Enterprise plans include single deployments and multiple deployments (which can be integrated across an entire organization or project). Enterprise prices depend on what is needed, and include setup fees, remote training fees, software/hosting/maintenance fees and ongoing technical support fees.

FINANCIAL DATA: Note: Data for latest year may not have been available at press time.

In U.S. $	2018	2017	2016	2015	2014	2013
Revenue		3,520,014	3,136,112	4,582,441	3,031,186	2,618,308
R&D Expense						
Operating Income						
Operating Margin %						
SGA Expense						
Net Income		362,907	-449,817	58,921	-503,842	478,868
Operating Cash Flow						
Capital Expenditure						
EBITDA						
Return on Assets %						
Return on Equity %						
Debt to Equity						

CONTACT INFORMATION:

Phone: Fax:
Toll-Free:
Address: 12472 Lake Underhill Rd. #330, Orlando, FL 32828 United States

STOCK TICKER/OTHER:

Stock Ticker: Nonprofit
Employees: 31
Parent Company:

Exchange:
Fiscal Year Ends: 12/31

SALARIES/BONUSES:

Top Exec. Salary: $ Bonus: $
Second Exec. Salary: $ Bonus: $

OTHER THOUGHTS:

Estimated Female Officers or Directors: 6
Hot Spot for Advancement for Women/Minorities: Y

UTStarcom Inc

www.utstar.com

NAIC Code: 334210

TYPES OF BUSINESS:

Telecommunications Equipment
Broadband Equipment

BRANDS/DIVISIONS/AFFILIATES:

aioTV
UiTV

CONTACTS: *Note: Officers with more than one job title may be intentionally listed here more than once.*

Tim Ti, CEO
Zhaochen Huang, COO
Eric Lam, VP-Finance
Ellen Chen, VP-Human Resources
Steven Chen, Sr. VP-IT & Product
Jing Ou-Yang, Contact-Investor Rel.

GROWTH PLANS/SPECIAL FEATURES:

UTStarcom, Inc. provides media operational support services and broadband equipment products and services so that telecommunications carriers can power their customer's need for bandwidth. The company offers optical transport products that are based on multi-protocol label switch transport profile (MPLS-TP) and carrier Ethernet (CE) technologies. UTStarcom's fixed line and wireless broadband access solutions are coupled with a software-defined networking (SDN) platform to support network evolution. Access solutions include multi-services access network (MSAN), Ethernet access devices, fiber-to-the-X (FTTx) and Wi-Fi. In addition to the company's broadband business, UTStarcom invests in new media companies for the purpose of expanding its capabilities in the field of next generation video platforms and consumer entertainment technology, and include aioTV and UiTV. aioTV is an over-the top (OTT) middleware video platform for service provides and content owners worldwide, enabling them to aggregate multiple sources of live, on-demand and free video content into a single/unified TV experience, with a multi-screen user interface across connected devices. UiTV is an internet protocol television (IPTV) provider that partners with traditional telecommunications businesses to animate the infrastructure with rich, high-definition TV entertainment. UTStarcom has operations in Japan, the U.S., India and China.

FINANCIAL DATA: *Note: Data for latest year may not have been available at press time.*

In U.S. $	2018	2017	2016	2015	2014	2013
Revenue		120,000,000	120,000,000	117,103,000	129,420,000	164,439,008
R&D Expense						
Operating Income						
Operating Margin %						
SGA Expense						
Net Income				-20,657,000	-30,264,000	-22,721,000
Operating Cash Flow						
Capital Expenditure						
EBITDA						
Return on Assets %						
Return on Equity %						
Debt to Equity						

CONTACT INFORMATION:

Phone: 86-852-3951-9757   Fax: 86-852-3951-9898
Toll-Free:
Address: Level 6, 28 Hennessy Rd., Hong Kong,   Hong Kong

STOCK TICKER/OTHER:

Stock Ticker: UTSI
Employees: 562
Parent Company:

Exchange: NSA
Fiscal Year Ends: 12/31

SALARIES/BONUSES:

Top Exec. Salary: $ Bonus: $
Second Exec. Salary: $ Bonus: $

OTHER THOUGHTS:

Estimated Female Officers or Directors:
Hot Spot for Advancement for Women/Minorities:

VANCL

NAIC Code: 454111

www.vancl.com

TYPES OF BUSINESS:

Electronic Shopping

BRANDS/DIVISIONS/AFFILIATES:

GROWTH PLANS/SPECIAL FEATURES:

VANCL is a Chinese internet retailer of apparel, accessories, footwear and luggage. The firm began as an e-commerce specialty site for men's t-shirts but has since expanded its portfolio of products to become one of the more popular apparel brands in China. The online retailer now provides a full range of clothing options for not only men, but for women and children as well. In addition to clothing, the firm offers various footwear and accessories such as purses, wallets, backpacks and messenger bags. Its product designers come from around the globe, including Spain, Japan and Korea.

CONTACTS: *Note: Officers with more than one job title may be intentionally listed here more than once.*

Chen Nian, CEO

FINANCIAL DATA: *Note: Data for latest year may not have been available at press time.*

In U.S. $	2018	2017	2016	2015	2014	2013
Revenue						
R&D Expense						
Operating Income						
Operating Margin %						
SGA Expense						
Net Income						
Operating Cash Flow						
Capital Expenditure						
EBITDA						
Return on Assets %						
Return on Equity %						
Debt to Equity						

CONTACT INFORMATION:

Phone: 86-10-57695159   Fax: 86-10-59763401
Toll-Free:
Address: No. 20, Middle East 3rd Ring Rd., Bldg. A Landgent Center, 10/Fl, Beijing, 100022 China

STOCK TICKER/OTHER:

Stock Ticker: Private   Exchange:
Employees: 166   Fiscal Year Ends:
Parent Company:

SALARIES/BONUSES:

Top Exec. Salary: $ Bonus: $
Second Exec. Salary: $ Bonus: $

OTHER THOUGHTS:

Estimated Female Officers or Directors:
Hot Spot for Advancement for Women/Minorities:

Veeam Software Inc

www.veeam.com

NAIC Code: 511210B

TYPES OF BUSINESS:

Computer Software, Network Management, System Testing & Storage

BRANDS/DIVISIONS/AFFILIATES:

Veeam Availability Suite
Veeam Backup & Replication
Veeam ProPartner Program

CONTACTS: Note: Officers with more than one job title may be intentionally listed here more than once.

Andrei Baronov, CEO
William H. Largent, Exec. VP-Operations
Ratmir Timashev, Exec. VP-Sales & Mktg.

GROWTH PLANS/SPECIAL FEATURES:

Veeam Software offers software that delivers high-speed recovery, data loss avoidance, verified recoverability, leveraged data and complete visibility. The company's Veeam Availability Suite, which includes Veeam Backup & Replication, leverages virtualization, storage and cloud technologies that enable the modern data center in order to help organizations save time, mitigate risks and reduce capital and operational costs. Veeam's products address always-on enterprise challenges by enabling those customers to meet recovery time and point objectives of less than 15 minutes for all applications and data. Veeam offers software solutions for cloud and physical workloads, disaster recovery, backup, and monitoring and management. Its products are offered for a variety of business sectors and sizes, including vertical segment/government entities. The Veeam ProPartner Program is designed to help customers take advantage of opportunities presented by the needs of the always-on enterprise. Partners gain access to sales and marketing resources that drive both license and service business, close deals faster and gain a long-term competitive advantage. Veeam comprises nearly 60,000 partners and more than 320,000 customers worldwide, including 80% of the Fortune 500. Headquartered in Switzerland, the company has offices in more than 30 countries throughout the Americas, Europe, the Middle East, Africa and Asia-Pacific.

FINANCIAL DATA: Note: Data for latest year may not have been available at press time.

In U.S. $	2018	2017	2016	2015	2014	2013
Revenue						
R&D Expense						
Operating Income						
Operating Margin %						
SGA Expense						
Net Income						
Operating Cash Flow						
Capital Expenditure						
EBITDA						
Return on Assets %						
Return on Equity %						
Debt to Equity						

CONTACT INFORMATION:

Phone: 41-41-766-7131   Fax:
Toll-Free: 800-691-1991
Address: Linden Park, Lindenstr. 16, Baar, CH-6340 Switzerland

STOCK TICKER/OTHER:

Stock Ticker: Private   Exchange:
Employees: 2,225   Fiscal Year Ends:
Parent Company:

SALARIES/BONUSES:

Top Exec. Salary: $ Bonus: $
Second Exec. Salary: $ Bonus: $

OTHER THOUGHTS:

Estimated Female Officers or Directors:
Hot Spot for Advancement for Women/Minorities:

Vente-Privee

www.vente-privee.com

NAIC Code: 454111

TYPES OF BUSINESS:

Electronic Shopping

BRANDS/DIVISIONS/AFFILIATES:

GROWTH PLANS/SPECIAL FEATURES:

Vente-Privee is a members-only French online retailer offering designer brands for fashion, home, travel, jewelry and lifestyle products on a limited-time sales basis. Users sign up for free, and sales open daily at 6:00am. Merchandise can be held in the customer's cart basket for 15 minutes before it is released back into the eCommerce marketplace. The company's site was developed to host sales of designer brands with discounted prices from 50% to 70% off. Brands on the Vente-Privee site each have their own dedicated Boutique page featuring their products. The site has 30 million members across Europe and partners with more than 3,000 international brands. Brand names include Kooba, Effy, Mary Katrantzou, Wacoal, Godinger, Hush Puppies, Durance, Victor Mayer and Jacob & Co. Vente-Privee can be accessed via computer, laptop, smartphone or tablet.

CONTACTS: *Note: Officers with more than one job title may be intentionally listed here more than once.*

Jacques-Antoine Granjon, CEO
Timothy Quinn, VP-Finance
Katherine Wu Brady, CEO-Vente-Privee USA LLC

FINANCIAL DATA: *Note: Data for latest year may not have been available at press time.*

In U.S. $	2018	2017	2016	2015	2014	2013
Revenue		3,588,000,000	3,125,000,000	2,358,228,795	1,945,225,000	1,971,751,385
R&D Expense						
Operating Income						
Operating Margin %						
SGA Expense						
Net Income						
Operating Cash Flow						
Capital Expenditure						
EBITDA						
Return on Assets %						
Return on Equity %						
Debt to Equity						

CONTACT INFORMATION:

Phone: 0800 026 0687   Fax:
Toll-Free: 877-453-3909
Address: 249 avenue du President Wilson, La Plaine Saint Denis, Paris, 93210 France

STOCK TICKER/OTHER:

Stock Ticker: Private
Employees: 2,100
Parent Company:

Exchange:
Fiscal Year Ends: 12/31

SALARIES/BONUSES:

Top Exec. Salary: $ Bonus: $
Second Exec. Salary: $ Bonus: $

OTHER THOUGHTS:

Estimated Female Officers or Directors: 2
Hot Spot for Advancement for Women/Minorities:

Veon Ltd

veon.com

NAIC Code: 517210

TYPES OF BUSINESS:

Cell Phone Service
Wireless Internet Service
IPTV
Fixed-Line Telephony

GROWTH PLANS/SPECIAL FEATURES:

Veon Ltd. is a global provider of connectivity and internet services, serving more than 240 million customers. The company's services include voice, fixed broadband, data and digital, which are offered to customers in 12 countries. Veon operates in three business units: major markets, including Russia and Italy; emerging markets, including Pakistan, Algeria and Bangladesh; and Eurasia, including Ukraine, Uzbekistan, Kazakhstan, Kyrgyzstan, Tajikistan, Armenia and Georgia. The firm provides services under the Beeline, Kyivstar, banglalink, Jazz and Djezzy brands. In addition, Veon's joint venture VIP-CKH Luxembourg Sarl provides services under the WIND and 3 brand names, serving nearly 30 million customers in Italy.

BRANDS/DIVISIONS/AFFILIATES:

VIP-CKH Luxembourg Sarl
Beeline
Syivstar
banglalink
Jazz
Djezzy
WIND
3

CONTACTS: Note: Officers with more than one job title may be intentionally listed here more than once.

Kjell Morten Johnsen, COO
Trond Odegard Westlie, CFO
Jacky Simmonds, Dir.-Human Resources
Yogesh Malik, CTO
Jeffrey D. McGhie, General Counsel
Dmitry G. Kromsky, Head-CIS Bus. Unit
Anton Kudryashov, Head-Russia Bus. Unit
Ahmed Abou Doma, Head-Africa & Asia Bus. Unit
Romano Righetti, Group Chief Regulatory Officer
Ursula Burns, Chmn.
Maximo Ibarra, Head-Italy

FINANCIAL DATA: Note: Data for latest year may not have been available at press time.

In U.S. $	2018	2017	2016	2015	2014	2013
Revenue		9,474,000,000	8,885,000,000	9,625,000,000	19,627,000,000	22,546,000,000
R&D Expense						
Operating Income		1,596,000,000	1,296,000,000	808,000,000	3,652,000,000	3,419,000,000
Operating Margin %		16.84%	14.58%	8.39%	18.60%	15.16%
SGA Expense		3,529,000,000	3,424,000,000	4,336,000,000	6,725,000,000	8,373,000,000
Net Income		-483,000,000	2,328,000,000	-655,000,000	-647,000,000	-2,625,000,000
Operating Cash Flow		2,475,000,000	1,875,000,000	2,033,000,000	5,279,000,000	6,351,000,000
Capital Expenditure		2,037,000,000	1,651,000,000	2,207,000,000	4,489,000,000	3,955,000,000
EBITDA		2,902,000,000	3,113,000,000	2,301,000,000	6,163,000,000	4,967,000,000
Return on Assets %		-2.37%	8.45%	-1.74%	-1.42%	-4.99%
Return on Equity %		-9.36%	47.87%	-14.93%	-8.77%	-21.33%
Debt to Equity		2.38	1.35	2.15	4.78	2.75

CONTACT INFORMATION:

Phone: 31 207977200   Fax: 31 207977201
Toll-Free:
Address: Claude Debussylaan 88, Amsterdam, 1082 MD Netherlands

STOCK TICKER/OTHER:

Stock Ticker: VEON   Exchange: NAS
Employees: 41,994   Fiscal Year Ends: 12/31
Parent Company:

SALARIES/BONUSES:

Top Exec. Salary: $2,819,125   Bonus: $
Second Exec. Salary: Bonus: $
$1,268,606

OTHER THOUGHTS:

Estimated Female Officers or Directors: 1
Hot Spot for Advancement for Women/Minorities:

Veracode Inc

www.veracode.com

NAIC Code: 511210E

TYPES OF BUSINESS:
Computer Software, Security & Anti-Virus

BRANDS/DIVISIONS/AFFILIATES:
Thoma Bravo LLC

CONTACTS: *Note: Officers with more than one job title may be intentionally listed here more than once.*
Sam King, CEO
Mike McGuinness, Exec. VP-Sales
Chris Wysopal, CTO

GROWTH PLANS/SPECIAL FEATURES:
Veracode, Inc. provides cloud-based application security software solutions and services. The company's unified platform enables organizations to assess and improve the security of applications from inception through production. By doing so, these organizations can confidently innovate with the web and mobile applications they build, buy and assemble, as well as the components they integrate into their environments. Veracode is comprised of a powerful combination of automation, process and speed, and seamlessly integrates application security into software development. Without the need for additional staff or equipment, Veracode customers connect quickly, see results and prove value on day one, and consistently see improvement over time. The company's services and solutions include application security consulting, technical support, penetration testing, developer training, Veracode services packages, compliance, integrations, third-party security and more. Products by the firm include an application security platform, static analysis, software composition analysis, dynamic analysis, vendor application security testing and developer training. Veracode is headquartered in Massachusetts, USA, with an international office in the U.K. In December 2018, Veracode announced that Thoma Bravo, LLC, a leading private equity investment firm, had completed the acquisition of the firm from Broadcom, Inc. in an all-cash transaction valued at $950 million.

FINANCIAL DATA: *Note: Data for latest year may not have been available at press time.*

In U.S. $	2018	2017	2016	2015	2014	2013
Revenue						
R&D Expense						
Operating Income						
Operating Margin %						
SGA Expense						
Net Income						
Operating Cash Flow						
Capital Expenditure						
EBITDA						
Return on Assets %						
Return on Equity %						
Debt to Equity						

CONTACT INFORMATION:
Phone: 339-674-2500   Fax: 339-674-2502
Toll-Free:
Address: 65 Network Dr., Burlington, MA 01803 United States

STOCK TICKER/OTHER:
Stock Ticker: Private   Exchange:
Employees: 550   Fiscal Year Ends:
Parent Company: Thoma Bravo LLC

SALARIES/BONUSES:
Top Exec. Salary: $ Bonus: $
Second Exec. Salary: $ Bonus: $

OTHER THOUGHTS:
Estimated Female Officers or Directors:
Hot Spot for Advancement for Women/Minorities:

VeriFone Systems Inc (Verifone)

www.verifone.com

NAIC Code: 522320

TYPES OF BUSINESS:

Payment & Transaction Processing
Electronic Payment Devices
Wireless Payment Systems
Specialty Payment Services

BRANDS/DIVISIONS/AFFILIATES:

Francisco Partners
British Columbia Investment Management Corporation
VeriFone Inc
Verfone

CONTACTS: *Note: Officers with more than one job title may be intentionally listed here more than once.*

Paul Galant, CEO
Marc Rothman, CFO
Alex Hart, Director
Glen Robson, Executive VP, Divisional
Vin D'Agostino, Executive VP

GROWTH PLANS/SPECIAL FEATURES:

VeriFone Systems, Inc. (VeriFone), through its principle operating subsidiary VeriFone, Inc., designs and markets electronic payment technologies and services. The company focuses on point of sale (POS) payment systems for global financial institutions, payment processors, petroleum companies, large retailers, hospitality providers, taxis, government organizations and health care companies as well as independent sales organizations. VeriFone's payment solutions industry encompasses systems, software and services that enable the acceptance and processing of electronic payments for goods and services and provide other value-added functionality at the POS. The payment systems process a wide range of payment types, including signature and PIN-based debit cards, credit cards, radio frequency identification (RFID) cards and tokens, near field communication (NFC) enabled smartphones, smart cards, pre-paid gift and other stored-value cards, electronic bill payment, check authorization and conversion, signature capture and electronic benefits transfer. The firm's electronic payment systems are available in several distinctive modular configurations, including wireline, wireless, countertop, integrated and stand-alone payment terminal models. Customers are also offered support for installed systems, consulting and project management services for system deployment and customization of integrated software applications. The company's Verifone brand, with a lowercase f, represents its drive into the digital world where electronic payments, commerce and mobility converge. In August 2018, VeriFone announced that it has been acquired by an investor group led by Francisco Partners, a leading technology focused private equity firm, and including British Columbia Investment Management Corporation.

VeriFone offers its employees medical, dental and vision coverage; life and AD&D insurance; disability assistance; flexible spending accounts; an employee assistance program; tuition reimbursement; a 401(k) program; and access to a credit union.

FINANCIAL DATA: *Note: Data for latest year may not have been available at press time.*

In U.S. $	2018	2017	2016	2015	2014	2013
Revenue		1,870,976,000	1,992,148,992	2,000,456,960	1,868,873,984	1,702,221,056
R&D Expense						
Operating Income						
Operating Margin %						
SGA Expense						
Net Income		-173,828,992	-9,281,000	79,097,000	-38,130,000	-296,055,008
Operating Cash Flow						
Capital Expenditure						
EBITDA						
Return on Assets %						
Return on Equity %						
Debt to Equity						

CONTACT INFORMATION:

Phone: 408 232-7800   Fax: 408 232-7811
Toll-Free: 800-837-4366
Address: 88 W. Plumeria Dr., San Jose, CA 95134 United States

STOCK TICKER/OTHER:

Stock Ticker: Private   Exchange:
Employees: 5,900   Fiscal Year Ends: 10/31
Parent Company: Francisco Partners

SALARIES/BONUSES:

Top Exec. Salary: $ Bonus: $
Second Exec. Salary: $ Bonus: $

OTHER THOUGHTS:

Estimated Female Officers or Directors: 2
Hot Spot for Advancement for Women/Minorities: Y

Sales, profits and employees may be estimates. Financial information, benefits and other data can change quickly and may vary from those stated here.

Verio Inc

NAIC Code: 517210

www.verio.com

TYPES OF BUSINESS:

Internet Service Provider
Domain Name Registration
Web Site Hosting
Virtual Private Networks
e-Commerce Services

BRANDS/DIVISIONS/AFFILIATES:

Nippon Telegraph and Telephone Corporation (NTT)
NTT Communications

CONTACTS: *Note: Officers with more than one job title may be intentionally listed here more than once.*

Hideyuki Yamasawa, CEO
Hideyuki Yamasawa, Pres.
Fred Martin, Sr. VP-Oper.
Tomoyuki Sakae, VP-Corp. Svcs.
William Gunther, VP-Systems Dev. & Architecture
Fred Martin, Sr. VP-Customer Service
Fred White, VP-Product Mgmt.
Wataru Imajuku, VP-Global Service Dev. & Japanese Sales

GROWTH PLANS/SPECIAL FEATURES:

Verio, Inc. offers shared website hosting solutions, domain name registrations, virtual private server (VPS) hosting and other online services to individuals and small-to-medium-sized businesses. The company's hosting plans include free site-building software, as well as access to more than 200 other tools and services. Domain name registrations have hundreds of new domains available, as well as pre-registration services for soon-to-be-released domain extensions. Domain name Trademark capabilities are also available. Verio offers secure customer data and payments with SSL Certificates to enhance customer confidence from the business' website, to help boost Google rankings and utilizing encryption at lower costs. Email services through Microsoft Exchange offers businesses the latest in business-class email management and collaboration, including email, calendar, contact and task management from anywhere, any time. Verio's marketing services provide solutions for generating more traffic to the business' website, including design services, marketing services, G Suite by Google Cloud, PayPal credit card processing, email, search engine marketing and more. Marketing strategies include website, advertising and website traffic management and analytics. Verio operates as a wholly-owned subsidiary of NTT Communications, which itself is a subsidiary of Nippon Telegraph and Telephone Corporation.

FINANCIAL DATA: *Note: Data for latest year may not have been available at press time.*

In U.S. $	2018	2017	2016	2015	2014	2013
Revenue						
R&D Expense						
Operating Income						
Operating Margin %						
SGA Expense						
Net Income						
Operating Cash Flow						
Capital Expenditure						
EBITDA						
Return on Assets %						
Return on Equity %						
Debt to Equity						

CONTACT INFORMATION:

Phone: 561-912-2555   Fax:
Toll-Free: 800-438-8374
Address: 1203 N. Research Way, Orem, UT 84097 United States

STOCK TICKER/OTHER:

Stock Ticker: Subsidiary   Exchange:
Employees: 1,960   Fiscal Year Ends: 03/31
Parent Company: Nippon Telegraph and Telephone Corporation (NTT)

SALARIES/BONUSES:

Top Exec. Salary: $ Bonus: $
Second Exec. Salary: $ Bonus: $

OTHER THOUGHTS:

Estimated Female Officers or Directors:
Hot Spot for Advancement for Women/Minorities:

VeriSign Inc

NAIC Code: 511210E

www.verisigninc.com

TYPES OF BUSINESS:
Computer Software, Security & Anti-Virus
Domain Name Registration

BRANDS/DIVISIONS/AFFILIATES:
Registry Services
Security Services

CONTACTS: *Note: Officers with more than one job title may be intentionally listed here more than once.*
D. Bidzos, CEO
George Kilguss, CFO
Todd Strubbe, Executive VP
Thomas Indelicarto, Executive VP

GROWTH PLANS/SPECIAL FEATURES:
VeriSign, Inc. is a global provider of domain name registry services and internet security, enabling internet navigation for many of the world's most recognized domain names and providing protection for websites and enterprises around the world (Registry Services). VeriSign's Registry Services ensure the security, stability, and resiliency of key internet infrastructure and services, including the .com and .net domains, two of the internet's root servers and operation of the root-zone maintainer functions for the core of the internet's Domain Name System. Additionally, VeriSign's product suite also includes Security Services consisting of Distributed Denial of Service (DDoS) protection services and Managed Domain Name System (Managed DNS) Services. The sole reportable segment of the firm consists of Registry Services and Security Services.

Employees of VeriSign receive a flexible benefits package that includes health, dental, vision, disability and life insurance; flexible spending accounts; a 401(k); an employee assistance program; a group legal plan; domestic partner coverage; tuition assistance; adoption assistance; a college savings plan; and elder care referrals.

FINANCIAL DATA: *Note: Data for latest year may not have been available at press time.*

In U.S. $	2018	2017	2016	2015	2014	2013
Revenue		1,165,095,000	1,142,167,000	1,059,366,000	1,010,117,000	965,087,000
R&D Expense		52,342,000	59,100,000	63,718,000	67,777,000	70,297,000
Operating Income		707,722,000	686,572,000	605,946,000	564,427,000	528,232,000
Operating Margin %		60.74%	60.11%	57.19%	55.87%	54.73%
SGA Expense		211,705,000	198,253,000	196,914,000	189,488,000	179,545,000
Net Income		457,248,000	440,645,000	375,236,000	355,260,000	544,450,000
Operating Cash Flow		702,761,000	667,949,000	651,482,000	600,949,000	579,397,000
Capital Expenditure		49,499,000	169,574,000	40,656,000	39,327,000	65,594,000
EBITDA		785,226,000	754,904,000	656,772,000	632,995,000	592,187,000
Return on Assets %		17.33%	18.78%	16.63%	14.75%	23.05%
Return on Equity %						
Debt to Equity						

CONTACT INFORMATION:
Phone: 703 948-3200   Fax:
Toll-Free: 800-922-4917
Address: 12061 Bluemont Way, Reston, VA 20190 United States

SALARIES/BONUSES:
Top Exec. Salary: $842,308   Bonus: $
Second Exec. Salary: Bonus: $
$550,000

STOCK TICKER/OTHER:
Stock Ticker: VRSN   Exchange: NAS
Employees: 990   Fiscal Year Ends: 12/31
Parent Company:

OTHER THOUGHTS:
Estimated Female Officers or Directors:
Hot Spot for Advancement for Women/Minorities:

Verizon Communications Inc

www.verizon.com

NAIC Code: 517110

TYPES OF BUSINESS:

Mobile Phone and Wireless Services
Telecommunications Services
Wireless Services
Long-Distance Services
High-Speed Internet Access
Video-on-Demand Services
e-Commerce & Online Services

BRANDS/DIVISIONS/AFFILIATES:

Fios
Moment

CONTACTS: Note: Officers with more than one job title may be intentionally listed here more than once.

Hans Vestberg, CEO
Matthew Ellis, CFO
Lowell McAdam, Chairman of the Board
Anthony Skiadas, Chief Accounting Officer
Marc Reed, Chief Administrative Officer
Craig Silliman, Executive VP, Divisional
Rima Qureshi, Executive VP
Timothy Armstrong, Executive VP

GROWTH PLANS/SPECIAL FEATURES:

Verizon Communications, Inc. is one of the world's largest providers of communications services. Its primary network technology platforms are 3G CDMA (code division multiple access), based on spread-spectrum digital radio technology, and 4G LTE (long-term evolution), which provides higher throughput performance and more improved efficiencies than 3G. Verizon operates in two segments: wireless and wireline. Wireless products and services include wireless voice, data products and other value-added services and equipment sales across the U.S. Its network provides services to a customer base of 116.3 million. The wireline segment is comprised of four units: consumer markets, enterprise solutions, partner solutions and business markets. Consumer markets provides residential fixed connectivity solutions including internet, TV and voice services. These services are provided over Verizon's 100% fiber-optic network under the Fios brand, and over a copper-based network to customers not served by Fios. The enterprise solutions unit helps customers transform their businesses to compete in the digital economy, with solutions that adapt to increasingly dynamic needs for connectivity, security and collaboration. The partner solutions unit provides communications services such as data, voice, local dial tone and broadband to local, long distance and wireless carriers that use Verizon's facilities to provide services to their own customers. Last, the business markets unit offers tailored voice and networking products, Fios services, IP networking, advanced voice solutions, security and managed IT services to U.S.-based small/medium businesses, state/local governments and educational institutions. In April 2018, Verizon acquired Moment, a New York-based design and strategy firm.

Employee benefits include 401(k); corporate discounts; health and dependent care spending accounts; life and AD&D insurance; commuter spending accounts; medical, dental and vision coverage; disability; adoption reimbursement; and tuition assistance.

FINANCIAL DATA: Note: Data for latest year may not have been available at press time.

In U.S. $	2018	2017	2016	2015	2014	2013
Revenue		126,034,000,000	125,980,000,000	131,620,000,000	127,079,000,000	120,550,000,000
R&D Expense						
Operating Income		29,188,000,000	27,059,000,000	33,060,000,000	19,599,000,000	31,968,000,000
Operating Margin %		23.15%	21.47%	25.11%	15.42%	26.51%
SGA Expense		28,336,000,000	31,569,000,000	29,986,000,000	41,016,000,000	27,089,000,000
Net Income		30,101,000,000	13,127,000,000	17,879,000,000	9,625,000,000	11,497,000,000
Operating Cash Flow		25,305,000,000	22,715,000,000	38,930,000,000	30,631,000,000	38,818,000,000
Capital Expenditure		17,830,000,000	17,593,000,000	27,717,000,000	17,545,000,000	17,184,000,000
EBITDA		42,281,000,000	41,290,000,000	49,177,000,000	36,718,000,000	48,550,000,000
Return on Assets %		12.00%	5.37%	7.49%	3.79%	4.60%
Return on Equity %		91.74%	67.40%	124.47%	37.64%	31.93%
Debt to Equity		2.63	4.68	6.31	8.98	2.30

CONTACT INFORMATION:

Phone: 212 395-1000   Fax:
Toll-Free: 800-837-4966
Address: 1095 Avenue of the Americas, New York, NY 10036 United States

STOCK TICKER/OTHER:

Stock Ticker: VZ
Employees: 152,300
Parent Company:

Exchange: NYS
Fiscal Year Ends: 12/31

SALARIES/BONUSES:

Top Exec. Salary: $1,600,000   Bonus: $
Second Exec. Salary: $942,308   Bonus: $

OTHER THOUGHTS:

Estimated Female Officers or Directors: 5
Hot Spot for Advancement for Women/Minorities: Y

Verizon Media Group

NAIC Code: 519130

www.oath.com

TYPES OF BUSINESS:

Online Content Provider
Online Music Services
Online Communities
Entertainment & Information Offerings
Instant Messaging
E-Mail
Internet Service Provider

BRANDS/DIVISIONS/AFFILIATES:

Verizon Communications Inc
Yahoo!
TechCrunch
Oath: AdPlatforms
RYOT
Verizon
Aol
Oath Inc

GROWTH PLANS/SPECIAL FEATURES:

Verizon Media Group (formerly Oath, Inc.) is the digital content division of Verizon Communications, Inc. The firm comprises teams of creators and coders that develop content for consumers, as well as advertising solutions for brands and publishers worldwide. Brands the firm has built include Yahoo!, TechCrunch, Oath: AdPlatforms, Kanvas, Rivals, Autoblog, RYOT, Verizon, Aol. Verizon Media utilizes its expertise in media, scale and data to help advertisers build consumer connections. The company offers a publisher-driven solution that combines demand stream with insights and tools built for publishers by publishers. Its partnership strategy with clients makes full use of Verizon's media and technology assets in order to build lasting brands. In November 2018, Oath, Inc. announced a corporate-wide reorganization, with Oath being renamed as Verizon Media Group as of January 1, 2019. That same year, Oath divested Flickr, Moviefone and Polyvore, and discontinued go90.

CONTACTS: *Note: Officers with more than one job title may be intentionally listed here more than once.*

K. Guru Gowrappan, CEO
Julie Jacobs, Executive VP
Bob Lord, President
Susan Lyne, President, Subsidiary

FINANCIAL DATA: *Note: Data for latest year may not have been available at press time.*

In U.S. $	2018	2017	2016	2015	2014	2013
Revenue	2,100,000,000	2,050,000,000	2,000,000,000	2,225,100,000	2,527,200,000	2,319,899,904
R&D Expense						
Operating Income						
Operating Margin %						
SGA Expense						
Net Income						
Operating Cash Flow						
Capital Expenditure						
EBITDA						
Return on Assets %						
Return on Equity %						
Debt to Equity						

CONTACT INFORMATION:

Phone: 212 652-6400   Fax:
Toll-Free:
Address: 770 Broadway, New York, NY 10003 United States

STOCK TICKER/OTHER:

Stock Ticker: Subsidiary   Exchange:
Employees: 10,400   Fiscal Year Ends: 12/31
Parent Company: Verizon Communications Inc

SALARIES/BONUSES:

Top Exec. Salary: $ Bonus: $
Second Exec. Salary: $ Bonus: $

OTHER THOUGHTS:

Estimated Female Officers or Directors: 7
Hot Spot for Advancement for Women/Minorities: Y

VerticalResponse Inc

www.verticalresponse.com

NAIC Code: 541810E

TYPES OF BUSINESS:
Direct Marketing Software
E-Mail & Postcard Marketing
E-Mail Management
Design Services

BRANDS/DIVISIONS/AFFILIATES:
Deluxe Corporation

CONTACTS: *Note: Officers with more than one job title may be intentionally listed here more than once.*
Barry McCarthy, CEO-Deluxe Corp
Janine Popick, Pres.
David Williams, Sr. VP-Prod. & Mktg.
Joshua Feinberg, VP-Platform Mgmt.

GROWTH PLANS/SPECIAL FEATURES:
VerticalResponse, Inc. provides self-service email and social media marketing software solutions for reaching customers. The company's solutions enable users to create, send and track emails and social posts that look professional across every device. Customizable templates are provided, with easy drag-and-drop editor features. Text, images, brand colors, logos and social buttons can be added to create attractive emails. Website visitors can be turned into email subscribers through VerticalResponse tools such as adding a sign-up form to websites or sharing a link on social media. Other features include automated follow-up emails, advanced analytics reporting, landing page builder, A/B subject line testing, test kits for nearly 60 different devices, surveys and more. VerticalResponse offers a free, 60-day trial period at no cost and no commitment. Email marketing plans include Basic, for $11 a month; Pro at $16 per month; and Pro+ for $196 per month. These prices are subject to change based on a customer's email list size. Survey plans include a free plan that never expires and includes all basic features; Basic, for $19 a month that allows for unlimited asked questions and responses; and a coming soon Pro plan for $59 per month which includes more features than the Basic plan. VerticalResponse provides free articles and webinars on its website, offering businesses advice on marketing strategies through the firm's blog. Customers of the firm have included Habitat for Humanity, The YMCA, Pet Camp, Westway Studio, WorldBlu, Annies, Brix26 and more. The firm is a subsidiary of Deluxe Corporation.

FINANCIAL DATA: *Note: Data for latest year may not have been available at press time.*

In U.S. $	2018	2017	2016	2015	2014	2013
Revenue						
R&D Expense						
Operating Income						
Operating Margin %						
SGA Expense						
Net Income						
Operating Cash Flow						
Capital Expenditure						
EBITDA						
Return on Assets %						
Return on Equity %						
Debt to Equity						

CONTACT INFORMATION:
Phone: Fax:
Toll-Free: 866-683-7842
Address: 550 Kearny St., Ste. 710, San Francisco, CA 94108 United States

STOCK TICKER/OTHER:
Stock Ticker: Subsidiary
Employees: 120
Parent Company: Deluxe Corporation

Exchange:
Fiscal Year Ends: 12/31

SALARIES/BONUSES:
Top Exec. Salary: $ Bonus: $
Second Exec. Salary: $ Bonus: $

OTHER THOUGHTS:
Estimated Female Officers or Directors: 2
Hot Spot for Advancement for Women/Minorities: Y

Vibrant Media Inc

www.vibrantmedia.com

NAIC Code: 541810E

TYPES OF BUSINESS:

Online Advertising

BRANDS/DIVISIONS/AFFILIATES:

In-Image
In-Article
Vibrant Programmtic

CONTACTS: Note: Officers with more than one job title may be intentionally listed here more than once.

Doug Stevenson, CEO
James Piper, Sr. VP-Sales & Operations
Richard Brindley, CIO
Jeff Babka, Chief Admin. Officer
Julie R. Fenster, VP-Corp. Counsel
Brian White, Sr. VP-Publisher Solutions & Ad Oper.
Ariff Quli, Sr. VP-Sales Oper. & Global Accounts
Nicole Stein, Sr. VP-Sales, East Region
Will Kunkel, VP-Global Creative

GROWTH PLANS/SPECIAL FEATURES:

Vibrant Media, Inc. offers video and contextual advertising services. It's advertising products include In-Image, In-Article and Vibrant Programmatic. In-Image leverages editorial images for a company's brand and is optimized to fit any size of image needed. Vibrant In-Article is a contextual outstream video advertising solution. Vibrant Programmatic is a private, global exchange from which users can access Virbrant's contextual marketing solutions. The firm has strict content standards, refusing to offer services for sites containing, promoting or linking directly to gambling, violent content, drugs or pornography, for example. Its formats provide a polite experience, with the user never needing to leave editorial pages to view brand experiences. Its ultra-light Java Script keeps page weight down to adhere to IAB LEAN guidelines, and can be implemented via DFP. All of Vibrant's solutions are designed to deliver seamless experiences across all screens, and reach more than 450 million monthly unique users globally. Headquartered in New York, the firm has additional offices in San Francisco, Los Angeles, Chicago, London, Hamburg, Munchen and Dusseldorf.

Vibrant offers employees benefits including medical, dental, vision, life, disability and AD&D coverage; a 401(k); flexible spending accounts; paid vacation; and an employee assistance program.

FINANCIAL DATA: Note: Data for latest year may not have been available at press time.

In U.S. $	2018	2017	2016	2015	2014	2013
Revenue						
R&D Expense						
Operating Income						
Operating Margin %						
SGA Expense						
Net Income						
Operating Cash Flow						
Capital Expenditure						
EBITDA						
Return on Assets %						
Return on Equity %						
Debt to Equity						

CONTACT INFORMATION:

Phone: 646-312-6100   Fax:
Toll-Free:
Address: 524 Broadway, 9/Fl., New York, NY 10012 United States

STOCK TICKER/OTHER:

Stock Ticker: Private   Exchange:
Employees: 209   Fiscal Year Ends: 12/31
Parent Company:

SALARIES/BONUSES:

Top Exec. Salary: $ Bonus: $
Second Exec. Salary: $ Bonus: $

OTHER THOUGHTS:

Estimated Female Officers or Directors: 3
Hot Spot for Advancement for Women/Minorities: Y

Vimeo LLC

NAIC Code: 519130

www.vimeo.com

TYPES OF BUSINESS:

Online Video Sharing Services

BRANDS/DIVISIONS/AFFILIATES:

IAC/InterActiveCorp
Vimeo Video School

CONTACTS: *Note: Officers with more than one job title may be intentionally listed here more than once.*

Anjali Sud, CEO
Jessica Casano-Antonellis, Dir.-Communications
Blake Whitman, VP-Creative Dev.

GROWTH PLANS/SPECIAL FEATURES:

Vimeo, LLC, a subsidiary of IAC/InterActiveCorp, is an online video sharing community. Differing from other online video sites, Vimeo seeks uploads of user-created, noncommercial content only, with a focus on community interaction, high-definition video and creative video techniques. It features several different content channels, including art, activism & non-profit, animation & motion graphics, everyday life, experimental, films, science & technology and travel & events. Vimeo boasts 80 million creators worldwide. The site is free to users, but features paid subscription Plus for $84 a year, which enables users to upload up to 5 gigabytes (GB) of data per week (versus the 500 megabyte standard); Pro with up to 20GB of weekly storage for $240 a year; Business for companies, at $600 a year with 5 terabyte (TB) total storage; and Premium with 7 TB total storage at $900 per year. Other perks include priority uploading, unlimited HD uploads and individual pages with no banner ads. Additionally, the firm operates Vimeo Video School, an online video school, which offers users video shooting guides and tutorials created by Vimeo employees and other community members. Combining text, diagrams and videos, each lesson provides a step-by-step how-to for different video techniques.

Vimeo employees receive benefits including paid time off and holidays, a 401(k), flexible work schedules, an annual company outing, medical and dental coverage, tuition reimbursement and company match on charitable donations.

FINANCIAL DATA: *Note: Data for latest year may not have been available at press time.*

In U.S. $	2018	2017	2016	2015	2014	2013
Revenue		81,100,000	60,000,000	40,000,000		
R&D Expense						
Operating Income						
Operating Margin %						
SGA Expense						
Net Income						
Operating Cash Flow						
Capital Expenditure						
EBITDA						
Return on Assets %						
Return on Equity %						
Debt to Equity						

CONTACT INFORMATION:

Phone: 212-314-7300 Fax:
Toll-Free:
Address: 555 W. 18th St., New York, NY 10011 United States

STOCK TICKER/OTHER:

Stock Ticker: Subsidiary Exchange:
Employees: 301 Fiscal Year Ends:
Parent Company: IAC/InterActiveCorp

SALARIES/BONUSES:

Top Exec. Salary: $ Bonus: $
Second Exec. Salary: $ Bonus: $

OTHER THOUGHTS:

Estimated Female Officers or Directors: 1
Hot Spot for Advancement for Women/Minorities:

Vipshop Holdings Limited

ir.vipshop.com

NAIC Code: 454111

TYPES OF BUSINESS:

Electronic Shopping

BRANDS/DIVISIONS/AFFILIATES:

vipshop.com
vip.com
lefeng.com

GROWTH PLANS/SPECIAL FEATURES:

Vipshop Holdings Limited is a leading online discount retailer, with more than 310 million registered customers. Through its subsidiaries, the firm offers high quality and popular brand products to consumers throughout China, at a significant discount from retail prices. Most of Vipshop's revenue is derived from apparel sales, with shoes, purses, cosmetics, sportswear and sporting goods, home goods, toys and other goods accounting for the remaining sales revenue. Vipshop provides its branded merchandise through its vipshop.com, vip.com and lefeng.com websites, as well as through the Vipshop mobile app.

CONTACTS: Note: Officers with more than one job title may be intentionally listed here more than once.

Eric Ya Shen, CEO
Arthur Xiaobo Hong, COO
Donghao Yang, CFO
Bill Huang, CTO

FINANCIAL DATA: Note: Data for latest year may not have been available at press time.

In U.S. $	2018	2017	2016	2015	2014	2013
Revenue		10,611,450,000	8,236,134,000	5,851,059,000	3,406,782,000	1,496,448,000
R&D Expense		263,196,900	227,559,200	156,673,600	98,833,200	35,631,750
Operating Income		391,559,700	341,965,700	256,453,600	100,116,500	39,793,860
Operating Margin %		3.68%	4.15%	4.38%	2.93%	2.65%
SGA Expense		1,788,831,000	1,409,287,000	1,027,179,000	648,170,900	284,225,400
Net Income		283,747,200	296,432,400	231,355,200	123,915,500	46,127,950
Operating Cash Flow		142,808,400	412,075,600	278,716,100	456,500,100	385,501,700
Capital Expenditure		359,998,100	315,420,700	334,951,300	231,136,300	19,623,370
EBITDA		544,380,000	547,785,500	395,877,200	219,872,600	70,486,860
Return on Assets %		6.18%	9.02%	8.59%	7.26%	7.05%
Return on Equity %		19.47%	43.93%	52.21%	42.32%	31.85%
Debt to Equity		0.28	0.76	1.14	1.51	

CONTACT INFORMATION:

Phone: 8620-2233-0732   Fax:
Toll-Free:
Address: No. 20 Huahai St., Liwan Distr., Guangzhou, Guangdong 510370 China

STOCK TICKER/OTHER:

Stock Ticker: VIPS
Employees: 45,302
Parent Company:

Exchange: NYS
Fiscal Year Ends: 12/31

SALARIES/BONUSES:

Top Exec. Salary: $ Bonus: $
Second Exec. Salary: $ Bonus: $

OTHER THOUGHTS:

Estimated Female Officers or Directors:
Hot Spot for Advancement for Women/Minorities:

VitaCost.com Inc

www.vitacost.com

NAIC Code: 454111

TYPES OF BUSINESS:

Online Vitamin Sales

BRANDS/DIVISIONS/AFFILIATES:

Kroger Co (The)
ARO-Vitacost
Glonaturals
CSI Beauty
Tag Pet Health
Clean Collection (The)
Synergy
Root Sqaured

CONTACTS: *Note: Officers with more than one job title may be intentionally listed here more than once.*

W. Rodney McMullen, CEO-Kroger
Mary L. Marbach, General Counsel
Kathleen M. Reed, Dir.-Investor Rel.

GROWTH PLANS/SPECIAL FEATURES:

VitaCost.com, Inc., a subsidiary of The Kroger Co., is an online retailer and direct marketer of health and wellness products. The firm's products, which are priced up to 50% lower than manufacturers' suggested retail prices, include herbs, dietary supplements, organic body and personal care products, sports nutrition foods, vitamins, minerals, anti-oxidants and health foods. The company sells roughly 45,000 items from over 2,500 third-party brands, including New Chapter, Nature's Way, Twinlab, Source Naturals, Jarrow Formulas, Jason Desert Essence, Atkins, Bob's Red Mill, BSN, Optimum Nutrition, USP Labs and MuscleTech. Vitacost.com also sells items under its own brand names, which include ARO-Vitacost, Glonaturals, Synergy, CSI Beauty, Root Squared, Tag Pet Health and The Clean Collection. The company markets through its website and direct mail catalogs. The firm has over 2.1 million active customers, who typically make a purchase 2-3 times per year. VitaCost.com operates one brick-and-mortar store in Las Vegas.

FINANCIAL DATA: *Note: Data for latest year may not have been available at press time.*

In U.S. $	2018	2017	2016	2015	2014	2013
Revenue	445,000,000	432,000,000	430,000,000	425,000,000	418,116,000	382,744,000
R&D Expense						
Operating Income						
Operating Margin %						
SGA Expense						
Net Income						
Operating Cash Flow						
Capital Expenditure						
EBITDA						
Return on Assets %						
Return on Equity %						
Debt to Equity						

CONTACT INFORMATION:

Phone: 561 982-4180   Fax:
Toll-Free:
Address: 5400 Broken Sound Blvd. NW, Ste. 500, Boca Raton, FL 33487
United States

STOCK TICKER/OTHER:

Stock Ticker: Subsidiary   Exchange:
Employees: 800   Fiscal Year Ends: 12/31
Parent Company: Kroger Co (The)

SALARIES/BONUSES:

Top Exec. Salary: $ Bonus: $
Second Exec. Salary: $ Bonus: $

OTHER THOUGHTS:

Estimated Female Officers or Directors: 2
Hot Spot for Advancement for Women/Minorities: Y

Vodafone Group plc

NAIC Code: 517210

www.vodafone.com

TYPES OF BUSINESS:

Cell Phone Service
Paging & Messaging Services
Mobile Data Services
Internet Service
M2M Solutions
Enterprise Solutions & Managed Services

BRANDS/DIVISIONS/AFFILIATES:

Vodafone
Vodafone TV
Vodafone Idea Limited

CONTACTS: Note: Officers with more than one job title may be intentionally listed here more than once.

Hannes Ametsreiter, CEO
Gerhard Mack, Dir-Commercial Operations
Andreas Siemen, Dir-Finance
Manuel Cubero, CCO
Bettina Karsch, Dir.-Human Resources
Eric Kuisch, Dir.-IT
Rosemary Martin, General Counsel
Warren Finegold, Dir.-Strategy & Bus. Dev.
Matthew Kirk, Dir.-External Affairs
Morten Lundal, Chief Commercial Officer
Philipp Humm, CEO-Northern & Central Europe
Paulo Bertoluzzo, CEO-Southern Europe
Nick Jeffery, Dir-Group Enterprises
Gerard Kleisterlee, Chmn.
Nick Read, CEO-Asia-Pacific, Africa & Middle East Region

GROWTH PLANS/SPECIAL FEATURES:

Vodafone Group plc is one of the world's largest mobile telecommunications companies, providing a range of voice and data mobile telecommunications services in more than 25 countries and five continents. Through its subsidiaries, joint ventures and related undertakings, it has a significant presence in continental Europe, the U.K., the U.S., the Asia Pacific region and the Middle East and Africa. Its mobile subsidiaries operate under the Vodafone brand. Vodafone serves over 460 million customers. It operates 2G networks in all its mobile operating subsidiaries, principally through GSM networks, offering customers services such as voice, text messaging and basic data services, which include internet and e-mail access. The company's 3G networks provide customers with mobile broadband data access, allowing data download speeds of up to seven times faster than a dial-up modem. In Europe, Vodafone reaches more than 90% population coverage via 4G networks as well as 95% population coverage to emerging markets in India via 3G networks. The firm offers prepaid or contract plans for its customers. Prepaid customers pay in advance and are not bound by a contract, while contractual customers subscribe to a predetermined length of time and are invoiced for services, typically on a monthly basis. For its enterprise customers, Vodafone offers integrated fixed and mobile telephony, mobile e-mail and broadband, productivity services such as video conferencing, international roaming services and machine-to-machine (M2M) solutions. Leveraging its network infrastructure, the firm has introduced Vodafone TV in several of its markets. During 2017, Vodafone and Idea Cellular Ltd. agreed to merge their Indian operations, creating the country's largest carrier with roughly 35% of the market and 400 million subscribers. The merger was expected to close during 2018, and the combined company is to be named Vodafone Idea Limited.

FINANCIAL DATA: Note: Data for latest year may not have been available at press time.

In U.S. $	2018	2017	2016	2015	2014	2013
Revenue	53,049,390,000	54,256,840,000	59,182,430,000	65,774,240,000	52,864,430,000	60,067,640,000
R&D Expense						
Operating Income	4,964,232,000	4,189,639,000	2,575,410,000	3,161,999,000	3,321,087,000	7,410,301,000
Operating Margin %	9.35	7.72%	4.53%	5.07%	8.15%	12.33%
SGA Expense	10,998,090,000	11,879,750,000	12,537,610,000	14,331,800,000	10,033,570,000	11,429,680,000
Net Income	2,778,284,000	-7,172,962,000	-5,812,366,000	8,973,534,000	81,688,540,000	579,795,600
Operating Cash Flow	15,491,870,000	16,201,530,000	15,139,020,000	15,132,420,000	8,584,646,000	11,925,680,000
Capital Expenditure	9,298,536,000	10,093,630,000	17,122,210,000	13,836,470,000	9,268,440,000	10,428,210,000
EBITDA	17,715,400,000	17,948,920,000	15,413,460,000	19,345,820,000	5,331,110,000	15,553,120,000
Return on Assets %	1.62%	-3.88%	-3.02%	5.00%	45.27%	.30%
Return on Equity %	3.48%	-8.08%	-5.86%	8.94%	84.12%	.57%
Debt to Equity	0.48	0.30	0.44	0.33	0.30	0.40

CONTACT INFORMATION:

Phone: 44 163533251   Fax: 44 1635238080
Toll-Free:
Address: Vodafone House, The Connection, Newbury, Berkshire RG14 2FN United Kingdom

STOCK TICKER/OTHER:

Stock Ticker: VOD
Employees: 103,564
Parent Company:

Exchange: NAS
Fiscal Year Ends: 03/31

SALARIES/BONUSES:

Top Exec. Salary: $1,452,314   Bonus: $1,857,699
Second Exec. Salary: $911,800   Bonus: $1,170,691

OTHER THOUGHTS:

Estimated Female Officers or Directors: 2
Hot Spot for Advancement for Women/Minorities: Y

Sales, profits and employees may be estimates. Financial information, benefits and other data can change quickly and may vary from those stated here.

Vonage Holdings Corp

www.vonage.com

NAIC Code: 517110

TYPES OF BUSINESS:

VOIP Telecommunications

BRANDS/DIVISIONS/AFFILIATES:

Vonage Business
Nexmo

CONTACTS: *Note: Officers with more than one job title may be intentionally listed here more than once.*

David Pearson, CFO
Jeffrey Citron, Chairman of the Board
David Levi, Chief Accounting Officer
Sagi Dudai, Chief Technology Officer
Alan Masarek, Director
Lewis Black, General Manager, Divisional
Johan Hybinette, Other Executive Officer
Vinod Lala, Other Executive Officer
Omar Javaid, Other Executive Officer
Susan Quackenbush, Other Executive Officer
Randy Rutherford, Other Executive Officer
Kenneth Wyatt, Other Executive Officer
Valerie Kahn, Senior VP, Divisional
Jay Patel, Senior VP, Divisional
Kenneth Mcmahon, Senior VP, Divisional

GROWTH PLANS/SPECIAL FEATURES:

Vonage Holdings Corp. offers a cloud communications platform that enables businesses of all sizes to collaborate and to engage their customers efficiently, across any device. These business/enterprise customers can choose among two delivery models: purchase Vonage Business with a software-as-a-service (SaaS) model for a complete and configured unified communications solution; or purchase Nexmo, a Vonage application program interface (API) platform with a platform-as-a-service (PaaS) model, which comprises the firm's cloud communication in programmable modules, delivered via APIs. All of Vonage's cloud communications solutions are designed to allow businesses to be more productive by integrating communications with all their existing business productivity tools. The company's programmable solutions enable customers to engage with their customers via embedded voice, chat or messaging to create seamless and contextual communications that makes doing business easier for end customers. For consumer customers, Vonage enables users to access and utilize its services through a single identity, either a number or user name, regardless of how they are connected to the internet. This technology enables Vonage to offer individual customers attractively-priced voice and messaging services and other features worldwide, across a variety of devices. The company's consumer market primarily consists of those under-served within the North American region.

FINANCIAL DATA: *Note: Data for latest year may not have been available at press time.*

In U.S. $	2018	2017	2016	2015	2014	2013
Revenue		1,002,286,000	955,621,000	895,072,000	868,953,000	829,067,000
R&D Expense		29,630,000	29,759,000	27,220,000		
Operating Income		59,391,000	44,154,000	52,992,000	47,807,000	52,349,000
Operating Margin %		5.92%	4.62%	5.92%	5.50%	6.31%
SGA Expense		435,788,000	454,273,000	457,049,000	500,871,000	489,354,000
Net Income		-33,933,000	17,907,000	22,655,000	20,266,000	28,289,000
Operating Cash Flow		128,058,000	87,012,000	129,731,000	92,542,000	88,243,000
Capital Expenditure		33,289,000	37,734,000	34,006,000	24,255,000	22,180,000
EBITDA		133,184,000	116,172,000	114,263,000	99,437,000	88,618,000
Return on Assets %		-3.77%	2.07%	3.10%	3.07%	4.75%
Return on Equity %		-7.42%	4.31%	6.18%	5.93%	8.57%
Debt to Equity		0.45	0.68	0.51	0.41	0.32

CONTACT INFORMATION:

Phone: 732 528-2600   Fax: 732 287-9119
Toll-Free: 800-980-1455
Address: 23 Main St., Holmdel, NJ 07733 United States

STOCK TICKER/OTHER:

Stock Ticker: VG   Exchange: NYS
Employees: 1,883   Fiscal Year Ends: 12/31
Parent Company:

SALARIES/BONUSES:

Top Exec. Salary: $875,000   Bonus: $44,844
Second Exec. Salary: $530,500   Bonus: $21,179

OTHER THOUGHTS:

Estimated Female Officers or Directors: 1
Hot Spot for Advancement for Women/Minorities:

WalkMe Inc

www.walkme.com

NAIC Code: 511210K

TYPES OF BUSINESS:

Computer Software, Sales & Customer Relationship Management

BRANDS/DIVISIONS/AFFILIATES:

WalkMe Digital Adoption Platform
WalkMe Security
WalkMe AI
WalkMe Automation

CONTACTS: Note: Officers with more than one job title may be intentionally listed here more than once.

Dan Adika, CEO
Daniel Yelin, CFO

GROWTH PLANS/SPECIAL FEATURES:

WalkMe, Inc. is an eCommerce firm offering a web-based service that helps users navigate other web-based services. The company's WalkMe Digital Adoption Platform (DAP) adapts to the varying standards of every digital platform it engages with, shifting the burden of learning every new feature, new process and new platform from the user to the DAP. The WalkMe Security platform meets extensive compliance standards, utilizes Amazon's top-tier secure cloud services and complies with GDPR as a data processor in the provision of WalkMe's services to its customers, and can make the data processing addendum available for execution. WalkMe Security's platform and infrastructure undergoes routine pen-tests and are monitored continuously by WalkMe teams. The WalkMe AI platform leverages artificial intelligence (AI) to predict user intentions and proactively keep users engaged. It collects hundreds of data points from users in real-time, then segments them dynamically based on likelihood to churn, identifies the optimal time to engage with the user and automatically targets them with the right message at the right time. Last, the WalkMe Automation platform simplifies the user experience and boosts productivity by eliminating empty clicks and automating complex and redundant tasks. It is powered by user analytics and AI, with no coding, API or back-end integration required. Processes can be automated across multiple systems, including chat-bot interface or single-click automation. WalkMe's solutions span digital transformation, employee training, website navigation, employee productivity, customer success, software implementation, customer care, employee onboarding, customer onboarding and conversion rate optimization. Based in California, the firm has additional offices in New York and North Carolina in the U.S., as well as one in Sydney, Australia.

FINANCIAL DATA: Note: Data for latest year may not have been available at press time.

In U.S. $	2018	2017	2016	2015	2014	2013
Revenue						
R&D Expense						
Operating Income						
Operating Margin %						
SGA Expense						
Net Income						
Operating Cash Flow						
Capital Expenditure						
EBITDA						
Return on Assets %						
Return on Equity %						
Debt to Equity						

CONTACT INFORMATION:

Phone: Fax:
Toll-Free: 855-492-5563
Address: 525 Market St., 37/Fl, San Francisco, CA 94105 United States

STOCK TICKER/OTHER:

Stock Ticker: Private Exchange:
Employees: 300 Fiscal Year Ends:
Parent Company:

SALARIES/BONUSES:

Top Exec. Salary: $ Bonus: $
Second Exec. Salary: $ Bonus: $

OTHER THOUGHTS:

Estimated Female Officers or Directors:
Hot Spot for Advancement for Women/Minorities:

Walt Disney Company (The)

NAIC Code: 515210

corporate.disney.go.com

TYPES OF BUSINESS:

Cable TV Networks, Broadcasting & Entertainment
Filmed Entertainment
Merchandising
Television Networks
Music & Book Publishing
Online Entertainment Programs
Theme Parks, Resorts & Cruise Lines
Comic Book Publishing

BRANDS/DIVISIONS/AFFILIATES:

ESPN
Disney
Freeform
WABC
A+E
Viceland
Disneyland Resort
Marvel

CONTACTS: *Note: Officers with more than one job title may be intentionally listed here more than once.*

Robert Iger, CEO
Christine Mccarthy, CFO
Brent Woodford, Executive VP, Divisional
Alan Braverman, General Counsel
Mary Parker, Other Executive Officer
Zenia Mucha, Senior Executive VP, Divisional

GROWTH PLANS/SPECIAL FEATURES:

The Walt Disney Company (Disney) is an international entertainment company operating in four primary business segments: media networks, studio entertainment, consumer products and interactive media, and parks and resorts. The media networks segment is comprised of cable and broadcast television networks, television production and distribution operations, domestic television stations and radio networks and stations. It also has investments in entities that operate programming, distribution and content management services, including television networks. This division's primary cable networks include the ESPN, Disney and Freeform brands; broadcast stations include WABC, KABC, WLS, WPVI and others; and media business brands include A+E and Viceland. The studio entertainment segment produces and acquires live-action and animated motion pictures, direct-to-video content, musical recordings and live stage plays. This division distributes films primarily under the Walt Disney Pictures, Pixar, Marvel, Lucasfilm and Touchstone banners; and distributes Dreamworks Studios-produced live-action films that were released from 2010-2016. The consumer products and interactive media segment licenses the company's trade names, characters and visual and literary properties to various manufacturers, game developers, publishers and retailers worldwide. It also develops and publishes games, primarily for mobile platforms, and books, magazines and comic books. The parks and resorts segment provides family travel and leisure experiences through its cruise line, theme parks and resorts. Brands and companies within this division include Disneyland Resort, Walt Disney World, Disneyland Paris, Tokyo Disney Resort, Hong Kong Disneyland, Disney Cruise Line, Disney Vacation Club, Aulani Disney Resort & Spa, Adventures by Disney and Walt Disney Imagineering. In July 2018, Disney and Twenty-First Century Fox, Inc. (Fox) shareholders approved the $71.3 billion acquisition of Fox's Fox Entertainment Group, FX Networks, National Geographic Partners, Star TV and Hulu assets. Additionally, the U.S. Justice Department gave its approval contingent upon Fox's regional sports networks assets being sold to third parties.

FINANCIAL DATA: *Note: Data for latest year may not have been available at press time.*

In U.S. $	2018	2017	2016	2015	2014	2013
Revenue	59,434,000,000	55,137,000,000	55,632,000,000	52,465,000,000	48,813,000,000	45,041,000,000
R&D Expense						
Operating Income	14,837,000,000	13,873,000,000	14,358,000,000	13,224,000,000	11,540,000,000	9,450,000,000
Operating Margin %		25.16%	25.80%	25.20%	23.64%	20.98%
SGA Expense	8,860,000,000	8,176,000,000	8,754,000,000	8,523,000,000	8,565,000,000	
Net Income	12,598,000,000	8,980,000,000	9,391,000,000	8,382,000,000	7,501,000,000	6,136,000,000
Operating Cash Flow	14,295,000,000	12,343,000,000	13,213,000,000	10,909,000,000	9,780,000,000	9,452,000,000
Capital Expenditure	4,465,000,000	3,623,000,000	4,773,000,000	4,265,000,000	3,311,000,000	2,796,000,000
EBITDA	18,422,000,000	17,077,000,000	17,749,000,000	16,487,000,000	14,828,000,000	12,161,000,000
Return on Assets %		9.56%	10.42%	9.72%	9.06%	7.85%
Return on Equity %		21.23%	21.39%	18.73%	16.59%	14.40%
Debt to Equity		0.46	0.38	0.28	0.28	0.28

CONTACT INFORMATION:

Phone: 818 5601000   Fax:
Toll-Free:
Address: 500 S. Buena Vista St., Burbank, CA 91521 United States

STOCK TICKER/OTHER:

Stock Ticker: DIS   Exchange: NYS
Employees: 201,000   Fiscal Year Ends: 09/30
Parent Company:

SALARIES/BONUSES:

Top Exec. Salary: $2,500,000   Bonus: $
Second Exec. Salary: Bonus: $
$1,565,000

OTHER THOUGHTS:

Estimated Female Officers or Directors: 7
Hot Spot for Advancement for Women/Minorities: Y

Sales, profits and employees may be estimates. Financial information, benefits and other data can change quickly and may vary from those stated here.

Warby Parker

NAIC Code: 446130

www.warbyparker.com

TYPES OF BUSINESS:
Eyeglasses Sales Online and Retail

BRANDS/DIVISIONS/AFFILIATES:
Warby Parker
monocle

GROWTH PLANS/SPECIAL FEATURES:
Warby Parker offers Warby Parker branded prescription eyeglasses and sunglasses. The company sells its products online as well as through brick-and-mortar retail outlets and showrooms. Warby Parker's eyewear frames feature a vintage-inspired style, are designed in-house and sold directly to customers in order to avoid retail markups. A price of $95.00 is possible for a pair of Warby Parker glasses because of its in-house capabilities, which eliminates licensing fees. Customers can order online, with options of either acetate or metal materials, various colors, frame shapes and widths. Select eyewear styles offer home try-on, allowing customers to choose from five frames on the website, have them delivered to their homes and then try wearing them for five days free of charge. Warby Parker's signature offering is a monocle, available with a prescription lens. As of October 2018, the firm had approximately 85 retail outlets across the U.S., as well as two in Ontario, Canada.

CONTACTS: Note: Officers with more than one job title may be intentionally listed here more than once.
Neil Blumenthal, Co-CEO
David Gilboa, Co-CEO

FINANCIAL DATA: Note: Data for latest year may not have been available at press time.

In U.S. $	2018	2017	2016	2015	2014	2013
Revenue		315,000,000	250,000,000	62,500,000	40,000,000	35,000,000
R&D Expense						
Operating Income						
Operating Margin %						
SGA Expense						
Net Income						
Operating Cash Flow						
Capital Expenditure						
EBITDA						
Return on Assets %						
Return on Equity %						
Debt to Equity						

CONTACT INFORMATION:
Phone: 646-517-5223   Fax:
Toll-Free:
Address: 161 Ave. of the Americas, New York, NY 10013 United States

STOCK TICKER/OTHER:
Stock Ticker: Private   Exchange:
Employees: 559   Fiscal Year Ends:
Parent Company:

SALARIES/BONUSES:
Top Exec. Salary: $ Bonus: $
Second Exec. Salary: $ Bonus: $

OTHER THOUGHTS:
Estimated Female Officers or Directors:
Hot Spot for Advancement for Women/Minorities:

Sales, profits and employees may be estimates. Financial information, benefits and other data can change quickly and may vary from those stated here.

WatchGuard Technologies Inc

www.watchguard.com

NAIC Code: 511210E

TYPES OF BUSINESS:

Computer Software, Security & Anti-Virus
Firewall & VPN Appliances
Training & Technical Support
Online Services

BRANDS/DIVISIONS/AFFILIATES:

Gladiator Corporation
Percipient Networks

CONTACTS: *Note: Officers with more than one job title may be intentionally listed here more than once.*

Prakash Panjwani, CEO
Corey Nachreiner, Chief Technology Officer
Richard Barber, CFO
Michelle Welch, Sr. VP-Mktg.
Sean Price, Sr. VP-Sales
Wayson Vannatta, CIO
Sin-Yaw Wang, VP-Eng.
Dave R. Taylor, VP-Corp. Strategy
Jon Bickford, VP-Sales, U.S.
Shari McLaren, VP-Customer Svcs. & Support
Philippe Ortodoro, VP-Sales, EMEA
Corey Nachreiner, CTO
Scott Robertson, VP-Sales, Asia Pacific

GROWTH PLANS/SPECIAL FEATURES:

WatchGuard Technologies, Inc. develops and implements network security services designed to protect enterprises, small-to-medium-sized businesses and organizations that use the internet for eCommerce and secure communications. WatchGuard's solutions include: network security, including unified threat management, next-generation firewall, secure Wi-Fi, network visibility and managed security services; top security threat solutions, including advanced malware, unsecured wireless networks, network blind spots, data loss and ransomware; and regulatory compliance, including KCSiE (keeping children safe in education), GDPR (general data protection regulation), PCI DSS (payment card industry data security standard) and HIPAA (Health Insurance Portability and Accountability Act). These solutions primarily serve the education, retail and healthcare industries. WatchGuard's products and services are categorized into five groups: advanced security services, which includes advanced malware protection, data loss prevention, threat detection and response, access portal and wireless intrusion prevention; network security appliances, comprising a range of firewall appliances and solutions; management and visibility, which includes cloud and Wi-Fi network security visibility and management solutions, appliances and hardware; basic security services such as application control, gateway antivirus, intrusion prevention, reputation-based threat prevention, spam prevention, URL (uniform resource locator) filtering and network discovery; and wireless security hardware, including wireless access points, wireless intrusion prevention system (WIPS) sensors and tabletop wireless appliances. Based in Washington, USA, the firm has office locations throughout North America, Latin America, Europe, the Middle East, Africa and Asia Pacific. WatchGuard is privately-owned by Gladiator Corporation. In early-2018, WatchGuard acquired Percipient Networks, a developer of simple, affordable, automated security solutions for small/midsize organizations.

FINANCIAL DATA: *Note: Data for latest year may not have been available at press time.*

In U.S. $	2018	2017	2016	2015	2014	2013
Revenue						
R&D Expense						
Operating Income						
Operating Margin %						
SGA Expense						
Net Income						
Operating Cash Flow						
Capital Expenditure						
EBITDA						
Return on Assets %						
Return on Equity %						
Debt to Equity						

CONTACT INFORMATION:

Phone: 206-613-6600   Fax: 206-521-8342
Toll-Free: 800-734-9905
Address: 505 5th Ave. S., Ste. 500, Seattle, WA 98104 United States

STOCK TICKER/OTHER:

Stock Ticker: Private   Exchange:
Employees: 600   Fiscal Year Ends: 12/31
Parent Company: Gladiator Corporation

SALARIES/BONUSES:

Top Exec. Salary: $ Bonus: $
Second Exec. Salary: $ Bonus: $

OTHER THOUGHTS:

Estimated Female Officers or Directors: 1
Hot Spot for Advancement for Women/Minorities:

Wayfair LLC

NAIC Code: 454111

www.wayfair.com

TYPES OF BUSINESS:
Online Furniture Store

BRANDS/DIVISIONS/AFFILIATES:
CastleGate
Wayfair
Joss & Main
AllModern
Perigold
Birch Lane

CONTACTS: Note: Officers with more than one job title may be intentionally listed here more than once.
Niraj Shah, CEO
Michael Fleisher, CFO
Edmond Macri, Chief Marketing Officer
John Mulliken, Chief Technology Officer
Steven Conine, Co-Chairman
James Savarese, COO
Steve Oblak, Other Executive Officer

GROWTH PLANS/SPECIAL FEATURES:
Wayfair, LLC is an eCommerce home furnishings company. The firm offers more than 10 million products from over 10,000 suppliers. These products include furniture, decor, decorative accents, housewares, seasonal decor and other home goods. Wayfair is able to offer this vast selection of products because it holds minimal inventory. Products are shipped to customers directly from the suppliers, or from Wayfair's CastleGate fulfillment network. The company's CastleGate solution enables suppliers to forward-position their inventory, allowing faster delivery to the customer with lower rates of damage and lowering Wayfair's cost per order over time. Wayfair offers five distinct sites, including websites, mobile websites and mobile applications, with each site comprising a unique brand identity that offers a tailored shopping experience. Sites and Brands include: Wayfair, offering home furnishings; Joss & Main, offering furniture; AllModern, offering modern home design merchandise; Perigold, offering fine home decor and furnishings; and Birch Lane, a collection of classic furnishings and timeless home decor. Based in the U.S., the firm operates internationally in Canada, the U.K., Ireland, Germany and the British Virgin Islands.

FINANCIAL DATA: Note: Data for latest year may not have been available at press time.

In U.S. $	2018	2017	2016	2015	2014	2013
Revenue		4,720,895,000	3,380,360,000	2,249,885,000	1,318,951,000	915,843,000
R&D Expense						
Operating Income		-235,453,000	-196,217,000	-81,350,000	-147,784,000	-16,019,000
Operating Margin %		-4.98%	-5.80%	-3.49%	-11.24%	-1.74%
SGA Expense		1,354,276,000	1,004,028,000	621,183,000	457,902,000	239,721,000
Net Income		-244,614,000	-194,375,000	-77,443,000	-148,098,000	-15,526,000
Operating Cash Flow		33,634,000	62,814,000	135,121,000	4,125,000	34,413,000
Capital Expenditure		146,879,000	128,086,000	62,184,000	45,985,000	15,779,000
EBITDA		-148,433,000	-140,645,000	-48,904,000	-125,781,000	-2,928,000
Return on Assets %		-24.77%	-26.69%	-12.38%	-39.94%	-22.73%
Return on Equity %		-1575.35%	-120.75%	-28.25%	-261.84%	
Debt to Equity			0.36	0.11		

CONTACT INFORMATION:
Phone: 866-263-8325   Fax:
Toll-Free: 877-929-3247
Address: 4 Copley Pl., 7/Fl, Boston, MA 02116 United States

STOCK TICKER/OTHER:
Stock Ticker: W
Employees: 5,637
Parent Company:

Exchange: NYS
Fiscal Year Ends:

SALARIES/BONUSES:
Top Exec. Salary: $200,000   Bonus: $50,000
Second Exec. Salary: $200,000   Bonus: $50,000

OTHER THOUGHTS:
Estimated Female Officers or Directors: 5
Hot Spot for Advancement for Women/Minorities: Y

Web.com Group Inc

www.web.com

NAIC Code: 518210

TYPES OF BUSINESS:

Web Hosting Products & Services
Web Design Services

BRANDS/DIVISIONS/AFFILIATES:

1ShoppingCart.com
SolidCactus.com
Renovationexperts.com
Leads.com
Yodle Inc

CONTACTS: *Note: Officers with more than one job title may be intentionally listed here more than once.*

David Brown, CEO
Kevin Carney, CFO
Jennifer Lada, Chief Accounting Officer
Roseann Duran, Executive VP

GROWTH PLANS/SPECIAL FEATURES:

Web.com Group, Inc. is a provider of do-it-for-me (DIFM) and do-it-yourself (DIY) website building, internet marketing, lead generation and technology solutions that enable small- and mid-sized businesses to build and maintain an internet presence. The firm serves more than 3 million customers. Its primary service offerings include website design and publishing, internet marketing and advertising, search engine optimization, search engine submission, lead generation, logo design and web analytics. In addition to its primary service offerings, Web.com Group provides a variety of services to customers who desire more advanced capabilities, such as e-commerce solutions and other sophisticated internet marketing services and online lead generation. Web.com Group's DIFM services include custom website design services, with built-in marketing, analytics and hosting; local business listings, which enable websites to be promoted in the most frequently searched directories; Facebook business profile page including advertisings and postings; and eCommerce design setup and configuration, including the online store and shopping cart. The company also offers a variety of DIY website-building and marketing solutions for small- and mid sized businesses that are more technically savvy. Web.com's standardized, scalable managed hosting services place numerous customers on a single shared server. The firm's marketing activities include: 1ShoppingCart.com and SolidCactus.com, which offer a set of sales and marketing tools for businesses selling products and services online; Renovationexperts.com provides lead generation service specific to contractors, homebuilders and remodeling professionals; Leads.com offers leads in home services categories; and Yodle, Inc. provides cloud-based local marketing solutions to small businesses, including an online, mobile and social presence. In June 2018, Web.com agreed to be acquired by Siris Capital Group, LLC, for approximately $1.24 billion.

Employee benefits include medical, vision and dental coverage; life insurance; short- and long-term disability; an employee assistance program; tuition reimbursement; flexible spending accounts; and a 401(k) with company match.

FINANCIAL DATA: *Note: Data for latest year may not have been available at press time.*

In U.S. $	2018	2017	2016	2015	2014	2013
Revenue		749,260,992	710,505,024	543,460,992	543,937,024	492,315,008
R&D Expense						
Operating Income						
Operating Margin %						
SGA Expense						
Net Income		53,629,000	3,990,000	89,961,000	-12,458,000	-65,664,000
Operating Cash Flow						
Capital Expenditure						
EBITDA						
Return on Assets %						
Return on Equity %						
Debt to Equity						

CONTACT INFORMATION:

Phone: 904 680-6600   Fax: 904 880-0350
Toll-Free:
Address: 12808 Gran Bay Pkwy. W., Jacksonville, FL 32258 United States

STOCK TICKER/OTHER:

Stock Ticker: WEB   Exchange: NAS
Employees: 3,600   Fiscal Year Ends: 12/31
Parent Company:

SALARIES/BONUSES:

Top Exec. Salary: $ Bonus: $
Second Exec. Salary: $ Bonus: $

OTHER THOUGHTS:

Estimated Female Officers or Directors: 3
Hot Spot for Advancement for Women/Minorities: Y

Sales, profits and employees may be estimates. Financial information, benefits and other data can change quickly and may vary from those stated here.

WebEx Communications Inc

www.webex.com

NAIC Code: 517110

TYPES OF BUSINESS:

Videoconferencing Services
Online Conferencing Services & Software

BRANDS/DIVISIONS/AFFILIATES:

Cisco Systems Inc
Cisco WebEx
Cisco WebEx Cloud
Cisco WebEx Meetings
Cisco WebEx Teams
Cisco WebEx Calling

CONTACTS: Note: Officers with more than one job title may be intentionally listed here more than once.

Chuck Robbins, CEO-Cisco

GROWTH PLANS/SPECIAL FEATURES:

WebEx Communications, Inc., doing business as Cisco WebEx, provides on-demand collaboration, online meeting, web conferencing and video conferencing software applications. The company's services scale to business needs in order to reach and deliver anywhere in the world. More than 1.8 billion meeting minutes occur through Cisco WebEx each month through the 6.4 million registered users. Staff meetings, presentations and trainings do not have to be rescheduled or delayed, because they can be accessed anywhere in the world on any device, even mobile. WebEx products are designed to integrate with the rest of a business' IT investments. They are delivered over the Cisco WebEx Cloud, a highly available infrastructure for real-time web communications. Cisco WebEx Meetings is the audio and video calling software that easily allows for group meetings. Cisco WebEx Teams is an app for continuous teamwork through video meetings, group messaging, file sharing and white boarding. Cisco WebEx Calling is the phone system in the cloud, with all the benefits of a traditional office phones through Cisco IP phones. Cisco WebEx devices include cloud-enabled board, room and desk devices. The software can also be used for educational purposes. WebEx also provides events and trainings. Price plans include: Starter for $14.50 per month for up to 50 participants, 5 gigabytes (GB) of cloud storage and 9 host licenses; Plus for $19.95 per month for up to 100 people per meeting, 5 Gb of cloud storage and 50 host licenses; and Business for $29.95 per month for up to 200 people per meeting, 10 GB of cloud storage and 5-100 host licenses. Clients can save money when paying annually rather than monthly. Add-ons include Call Me Domestic for $4.00 per host per month and Call Me international $42.25 per host per month. WebEx operates as a subsidiary of Cisco Systems, Inc.

FINANCIAL DATA: Note: Data for latest year may not have been available at press time.

In U.S. $	2018	2017	2016	2015	2014	2013
Revenue						
R&D Expense						
Operating Income						
Operating Margin %						
SGA Expense						
Net Income						
Operating Cash Flow						
Capital Expenditure						
EBITDA						
Return on Assets %						
Return on Equity %						
Debt to Equity						

CONTACT INFORMATION:

Phone: 408-435-7048 Fax:
Toll-Free: 877-509-3239
Address: 855 East Tasman Drive, San Jose, CA 95035 United States

STOCK TICKER/OTHER:

Stock Ticker: Subsidiary Exchange:
Employees: 2,259 Fiscal Year Ends: 12/31
Parent Company: Cisco Systems Inc

SALARIES/BONUSES:

Top Exec. Salary: $ Bonus: $
Second Exec. Salary: $ Bonus: $

OTHER THOUGHTS:

Estimated Female Officers or Directors:
Hot Spot for Advancement for Women/Minorities:

WebMD Health Corp

NAIC Code: 519130

TYPES OF BUSINESS:
Health Care Internet Portals
Content Licensing

BRANDS/DIVISIONS/AFFILIATES:
KKR & Co Inc
Internet Brands Inc
WebMD Health Network
Medscape
MedicineNet.com
eMedicineHealth.com
RxList.com
WebMD.boots.com

CONTACTS: *Note: Officers with more than one job title may be intentionally listed here more than once.*
Steven L. Zatz, CEO
Martin Wygod, Chairman of the Board
Blake DeSimone, CFO
Kathleen Tourjee, VP-Human Resources
Michael Glick, Executive VP
Douglas Wamsley, Executive VP
Steven Zatz, President

GROWTH PLANS/SPECIAL FEATURES:
WebMD Health Corp. provides health information services to consumers, physicians, health care professionals, employers and health plan providers via the internet. Additionally, the company provides personalized telephonic, online or onsite health coaching and condition management services. The firm's public online service, WebMD Health Network, offers WebMD Health, its primary public portal; and Medscape from WebMD, a public portal for physicians and healthcare professionals. WebMD Health provides health and wellness articles and features decision-support services to help consumers make informed decisions about healthcare providers, health risks and treatment options. Available information and interactive tools include detailed data on specific diseases or conditions, physician location and individual healthcare data storage. Medscape from WebMD assists physicians and health care professionals in improving clinical knowledge with original content such as daily news, commentary, conference coverage and continuing medical education. Additional websites in the WebMD Health Network include MedicineNet.com, eMedicineHealth.com, RxList.com and WebMD.boots.com. The firm generates revenue from its public offerings primarily through advertising sales and sponsorships. Additionally, the company generates revenue through the sale of advertising in its WebMD Magazine consumer publication, distributed free of charge to physicians for use in their office waiting rooms; and is also available online through iOS app. Revenue is also generated from the private side through content and technology licensed to employers and health plans, either directly or through distributors. Private portals offered by WebMD enable employees and health plan members to learn about benefits, providers and treatment decisions, customized to a user's health insurance plan. During 2017, WebMD was acquired by KKR & Co., Inc.'s Internet Brands, Inc. subsidiary, and subsequently ceased from being publicly traded.

FINANCIAL DATA: *Note: Data for latest year may not have been available at press time.*

In U.S. $	2018	2017	2016	2015	2014	2013
Revenue		740,298,321	705,046,016	636,398,976	580,449,024	515,292,992
R&D Expense						
Operating Income						
Operating Margin %						
SGA Expense						
Net Income			91,304,000	64,024,000	42,063,000	15,116,000
Operating Cash Flow						
Capital Expenditure						
EBITDA						
Return on Assets %						
Return on Equity %						
Debt to Equity						

CONTACT INFORMATION:
Phone: 212-624-3700 Fax:
Toll-Free:
Address: 395 Hudson St., New York, NY 10011 United States

STOCK TICKER/OTHER:
Stock Ticker: Subsidiary Exchange:
Employees: 1,815 Fiscal Year Ends: 12/31
Parent Company: KKR & Co Inc

SALARIES/BONUSES:
Top Exec. Salary: $ Bonus: $
Second Exec. Salary: $ Bonus: $

OTHER THOUGHTS:
Estimated Female Officers or Directors: 1
Hot Spot for Advancement for Women/Minorities: Y

Westell Technologies Inc

www.westell.com

NAIC Code: 334210

TYPES OF BUSINESS:

Telecommunications Equipment-High-Speed Data Transmission
Broadband & DSL Solutions
Modems, Switches, Routers & Gateways
Home Networking Equipment
Data Conferencing Services

BRANDS/DIVISIONS/AFFILIATES:

CONTACTS: *Note: Officers with more than one job title may be intentionally listed here more than once.*

Thomas Minichiello, CFO
Kirk Brannock, Chairman of the Board
Alfred John, President
Jesse Swartwood, Senior VP, Divisional

GROWTH PLANS/SPECIAL FEATURES:

Westell Technologies, Inc. is a provider of in-building wireless, intelligent site management, cell site optimization and outside plant solutions focused on innovation and differentiation of telecommunication networks, where end users connect. The firm operates in three segments: in-building wireless (IBW), intelligent site management and services (ISMS) and communications network solutions (CNS). The IBW segment enable cellular coverage in stadiums, arenas, buildings, malls and other indoor areas not served well by the existing outdoor cellular network. Solutions include distributed antenna systems (DAS) conditioners, high-performance digital repeaters and bi-directional amplifiers (BDAs) and system components and antennas. ISMS includes a suite of remote monitoring and control devices which, when combined with the company's Optima management system, provides comprehensive machine-to-machine (M2M) communications that enable operators to remotely monitor, manage and control site infrastructure and support systems. The CNS segment consists of tower mounted amplifiers, which are small outdoor-hardened units mounted next to antennas on cell towers, enabling wireless service providers to improve the overall performance of a cell site; and outdoor network infrastructure consisting of a broad range of offerings, including cabinets, enclosures, mountings, synchronous optical networks/time division multiplexing (SONET/TDM) network interface units, power distribution units, copper and fiber connectivity panels, hardened Ethernet switches and systems integration services.

The company offers employees medical benefits, a 401(k) plan and credit union membership.

FINANCIAL DATA: *Note: Data for latest year may not have been available at press time.*

In U.S. $	2018	2017	2016	2015	2014	2013
Revenue	58,577,000	62,965,000	88,203,000	84,127,000	102,073,000	40,044,000
R&D Expense	7,375,000	12,367,000	19,317,000	17,348,000	11,339,000	7,326,000
Operating Income	-1,289,000	-11,717,000	-16,008,000	-24,000,000	-2,979,000	-11,243,000
Operating Margin %	-2.2	-18.60%	-18.14%	-28.52%	-2.91%	-28.07%
SGA Expense	14,892,000	18,335,000	25,653,000	27,085,000	28,690,000	17,349,000
Net Income	31,000	-15,941,000	-16,212,000	-58,007,000	5,367,000	-44,038,000
Operating Cash Flow	6,945,000	-7,011,000	-5,607,000	-9,287,000	1,597,000	-12,125,000
Capital Expenditure	408,000	596,000	1,932,000	2,137,000	443,000	379,000
EBITDA	3,668,000	-5,573,000	-8,910,000	-16,584,000	2,551,000	-9,862,000
Return on Assets %	.04%	-21.03%	-17.40%	-44.40%	3.50%	-25.70%
Return on Equity %	.05%	-26.82%	-21.63%	-52.06%	3.96%	-27.74%
Debt to Equity						

CONTACT INFORMATION:

Phone: 630 898-2500   Fax: 630 375-4931
Toll-Free:
Address: 750 N. Commons Dr., Aurora, IL 60504 United States

STOCK TICKER/OTHER:

Stock Ticker: WSTL   Exchange: NAS
Employees: 123   Fiscal Year Ends: 03/31
Parent Company:

SALARIES/BONUSES:

Top Exec. Salary: $300,000   Bonus: $
Second Exec. Salary: Bonus: $
$226,048

OTHER THOUGHTS:

Estimated Female Officers or Directors: 2
Hot Spot for Advancement for Women/Minorities:

WhatsApp Inc

www.whatsapp.com

NAIC Code: 511210C

TYPES OF BUSINESS:

Computer Software, Telecom, Communications & VoIP

BRANDS/DIVISIONS/AFFILIATES:

Facebook Inc
WhatsApp Web
WhatsApp Business

CONTACTS: *Note: Officers with more than one job title may be intentionally listed here more than once.*

Chris Daniels, CEO
Brian Acton, Co-Founder
Mark Zuckerberg, Chmn.

GROWTH PLANS/SPECIAL FEATURES:

WhatsApp, Inc., a subsidiary of Facebook, Inc., produces a cross-platform mobile messaging service for smartphone and web applications. Since WhatsApp uses a customized version of the open standard Extensible Messaging and Presence Protocol it is not only supported by the various smartphone platforms, it also allows the various platforms to communicate with each other via the use of the app's client-server system architecture. By using the app to message another app user, the client is able to exchange messages without having to pay the short message service fee that is usually applicable when sending a message over the phone. In addition to basic text messages, users are able to send video and audio messages, images, documents and their location, as well as voice and video calls using the apps integrated mapping features. The app offers group calls and video calls. The company's WhatsApp Web offering is a web client which can be used through a web browser by syncing with the user's mobile device connections. WhatsApp Business is a free Android app through which businesses can interact with customers. The app's tools can be used to automate, sort and quickly respond to messages. WhatsApp has over 1 billion active users in over 180 countries.

FINANCIAL DATA: *Note: Data for latest year may not have been available at press time.*

In U.S. $	2018	2017	2016	2015	2014	2013
Revenue						
R&D Expense						
Operating Income						
Operating Margin %						
SGA Expense						
Net Income						
Operating Cash Flow						
Capital Expenditure						
EBITDA						
Return on Assets %						
Return on Equity %						
Debt to Equity						

CONTACT INFORMATION:

Phone: Fax:
Toll-Free:
Address: 650 Castro St., Ste. 120-219, Mountain View, CA 94041 United States

STOCK TICKER/OTHER:

Stock Ticker: Subsidiary   Exchange:
Employees: 55   Fiscal Year Ends:
Parent Company: Facebook Inc

SALARIES/BONUSES:

Top Exec. Salary: $ Bonus: $
Second Exec. Salary: $ Bonus: $

OTHER THOUGHTS:

Estimated Female Officers or Directors:
Hot Spot for Advancement for Women/Minorities:

Whitepages Inc

www.whitepagesinc.com

NAIC Code: 519130

TYPES OF BUSINESS:

Online Directory
Local Business Services
Online Yellow & White Pages
Interactive Maps & Directions
Location-Based Searching
Search Engine

BRANDS/DIVISIONS/AFFILIATES:

Whitepages Pro
Whitepages Premium
411.com

CONTACTS: *Note: Officers with more than one job title may be intentionally listed here more than once.*

Rob Eleveld, CEO
Jason Eglit, CFO
Suki Hayre, VP-Admin.
Suki Hayre, VP-Finance
Craig Paris, Chief Revenue Officer
Alex Algard, Chmn.

GROWTH PLANS/SPECIAL FEATURES:

Whitepages, Inc. provides open search web properties to help verify identities worldwide. The company serves 35 million unique visitors per month. Its products include Whitepages Pro and Whitepages Premium. Pro offers businesses with global identity verification solutions via enterprise-scale application program interfaces (APIs) and web tools to help companies identify legitimate customers, prevent fraudulent transactions and smooth new customer account creation. Premium provides subscribers access to U.S. public records in order to verify contact details, phone numbers, bankruptcy history, criminal records and more. The company's proprietary fully-integrated Identity Graph database houses more than 5 billion global identity records which have been curated and corroborated from hundreds of different sources. Whitepages primarily serves the retail, travel and hospitality, banking, online lending, payments, marketing and lead generation and call centers industries. The firm returns identity data in over 100 countries to help global companies quickly validate and verify the good identities while spotting potential risk. Whitepages also runs 411.com, a people search using names, addresses, emails and business information.

The company offers employees medical, dental and vision insurance; short- and long-term disability coverage; life insurance; flexible spending accounts; a 401(k); incentive stock options; quarterly wellness reimbursement to support healthy lifestyle decisions; public transit discounts; and fitness club discounts.

FINANCIAL DATA: *Note: Data for latest year may not have been available at press time.*

In U.S. $	2018	2017	2016	2015	2014	2013
Revenue						
R&D Expense						
Operating Income						
Operating Margin %						
SGA Expense						
Net Income						
Operating Cash Flow						
Capital Expenditure						
EBITDA						
Return on Assets %						
Return on Equity %						
Debt to Equity						

CONTACT INFORMATION:

Phone: 206-973-5100   Fax: 206-621-1375
Toll-Free:
Address: 1301 Fifth Ave., Ste. 1600, Seattle, WA 98101 United States

STOCK TICKER/OTHER:

Stock Ticker: Private   Exchange:
Employees: 184   Fiscal Year Ends: 12/31
Parent Company:

SALARIES/BONUSES:

Top Exec. Salary: $ Bonus: $
Second Exec. Salary: $ Bonus: $

OTHER THOUGHTS:

Estimated Female Officers or Directors: 1
Hot Spot for Advancement for Women/Minorities:

Wikimedia Foundation

NAIC Code: 519130

www.wikimediafoundation.org

TYPES OF BUSINESS:

Online Dictionary
Online Encyclopedia
Online Educational Content

BRANDS/DIVISIONS/AFFILIATES:

Wikipedia
Wikiversity
Wikibooks
Wikisource
Wikiquote
Wikinews
MediaWiki
Wikidata

CONTACTS: *Note: Officers with more than one job title may be intentionally listed here more than once.*

Katherine Maher, Exec. Dir.
Jaime Villagomez, CFO
Victoria Coleman, CTO
Erik Moller, VP-Eng. & Prod. Dev.
Garfield Byrd, Chief Admin. Officer
Geoff Brigham, General Counsel
Frank Schulenburg, Sr. Dir.-Program Dev.
Lisa Seitz-Gruwell, Chief Revenue Officer
Anasuya Sengupta, Sr. Dir.-Grantmaking
Maria Sefidari, Chair of the Board of Trustees

GROWTH PLANS/SPECIAL FEATURES:

Wikimedia Foundation is a nonprofit charitable organization that operates Wikipedia, a free online encyclopedia that contains over 46 million articles and is offered in nearly 300 languages, with 1 billion unique devices a month. The foundation also administers a number of other resources, including: Wikiversity, a source for tutorials and learning development; Wikibooks, a source for free content textbooks; Wikisource, a collection of published texts; Wikiquote, a collection of quotations; Wikinews, a source for news entries written in the style of news stories; Wikispecies, a comprehensive catalog of species aimed at scientists; MediaWiki, a software application engine that manages Wiki content; Wiktionary, a dictionary and thesaurus; Wikivoyage, a free travel guide; Wikidata, a free knowledge base; and Wikimedia Commons, a collection of images and other media. Article contribution and editing of Wiki content is open to anyone, from anonymous volunteers to highly specialized professionals. The aim of the foundation is to foster the collection and development of educational content by people all over the world and to provide a free and public domain for the issuing of information. Because Wikipedia owns all of the servers that run each project, the sites feature no advertisements. Wikimedia is run by a staff with the help of numerous volunteers either contributing content, participating through committees or acting as interns. The foundation relies heavily on donations from individuals, but also receives money from grants and fundraising. Wikimedia has chapters in many different countries that support the aims of Wikimedia, but do not share control of Wikimedia sites

Wikimedia Foundation employees receive benefits including disability and life insurance; a 401(k); an annual professional development fund; a health and wellness program; pre-tax health care, child care, elder care, public transit and parking expenses savings; vacation time; and staff meals.

FINANCIAL DATA: *Note: Data for latest year may not have been available at press time.*

In U.S. $	2018	2017	2016	2015	2014	2013
Revenue		91,242,418	81,862,724	74,536,375	52,465,287	48,635,408
R&D Expense						
Operating Income						
Operating Margin %						
SGA Expense						
Net Income		22,105,660	15,915,259	21,939,593	6,564,542	12,930,612
Operating Cash Flow						
Capital Expenditure						
EBITDA						
Return on Assets %						
Return on Equity %						
Debt to Equity						

CONTACT INFORMATION:

Phone: 415-839-6885   Fax: 415-882-0495
Toll-Free:
Address: 1 New Montgomery St., Ste. 1600, San Francisco, CA 94104 United States

STOCK TICKER/OTHER:

Stock Ticker: Nonprofit   Exchange:
Employees: 208   Fiscal Year Ends: 06/30
Parent Company:

SALARIES/BONUSES:

Top Exec. Salary: $ Bonus: $
Second Exec. Salary: $ Bonus: $

OTHER THOUGHTS:

Estimated Female Officers or Directors: 4
Hot Spot for Advancement for Women/Minorities: Y

Windstream Holdings Inc

www.windstream.com

NAIC Code: 517110

TYPES OF BUSINESS:

Telephone Service--Local Exchange Carrier & Diversified
Network Access Services
High-Speed Internet Access
Enterprise Telecom & Data Services

BRANDS/DIVISIONS/AFFILIATES:

CONTACTS: *Note: Officers with more than one job title may be intentionally listed here more than once.*

Anthony Thomas, CEO
Robert Gunderman, CFO
John Eichler, Chief Accounting Officer
Alan Wells, Director
Kristi Moody, General Counsel
Jack Brooks, Other Executive Officer
Jeffery Small, President, Divisional
Layne Levine, President, Divisional

GROWTH PLANS/SPECIAL FEATURES:

Windstream Holdings, Inc. is a provider of advanced network communications and technology solutions for businesses throughout the U.S. The firm also offers broadband, entertainment and security solutions to consumers and small businesses primarily in rural areas within 18 states. Windstream also supplies core transport solutions on a local and long-haul fiber network spanning about 150,000 miles. The company operates through four segments: consumer and small business, enterprise, wholesale and competitive local exchange carrier consumer (CLEC consumer). The consumer and small business segment includes about 1.4 million residential and small business customers, offering high-speed internet access, related security products, telephone services, video services, online backup products, managed web design, fax-to-email services and related equipment. This division serves customers located in service areas in which Windstream is the incumbent local exchange carrier (ILEC). The enterprise segment provides advanced network communication and technology solutions to businesses across the U.S. This division targets mid- and large-size enterprise customers that consider their network and communications infrastructure as critical in operating their business. The wholesale segment leverages Windstream's nationwide network to provide 100 gigabytes per second (Gbps) bandwidth and transport services to wholesale customers, including telecom companies, content providers and cable and other network operators. Last, the CLEC consumer segment provides consumer internet services beyond Windstream's ILEC footprint. This division's services are grouped into two categories: access services, which include dial-up and high-speed internet access services; and value-added, which include revenues from ancillary services sold as add-on features to the firm's internet access services, such as security products, premium email, home networking and email storage.

FINANCIAL DATA: *Note: Data for latest year may not have been available at press time.*

In U.S. $	2018	2017	2016	2015	2014	2013
Revenue		5,852,900,000	5,387,000,000	5,765,300,000	5,829,500,000	5,988,100,000
R&D Expense						
Operating Income		427,700,000	549,500,000	625,100,000	583,400,000	1,047,800,000
Operating Margin %		7.30%	10.20%	10.84%	10.00%	17.49%
SGA Expense		896,800,000	797,700,000	866,500,000	983,800,000	923,400,000
Net Income		-2,116,600,000	-383,500,000	27,400,000	-39,500,000	241,000,000
Operating Cash Flow		950,700,000	924,400,000	1,026,600,000	1,467,300,000	1,519,400,000
Capital Expenditure		908,600,000	989,800,000	1,055,300,000	786,500,000	841,000,000
EBITDA		-179,300,000	1,600,600,000	2,223,100,000	1,893,600,000	2,309,500,000
Return on Assets %		-18.53%	-3.17%	.18%	-.30%	1.75%
Return on Equity %			-162.04%	8.99%	-7.41%	24.78%
Debt to Equity			56.94	33.17	35.29	10.26

CONTACT INFORMATION:

Phone: 501 748-7000   Fax:
Toll-Free: 866-445-5880
Address: 4001 Rodney Parham Rd., Little Rock, AR 72212 United States

STOCK TICKER/OTHER:

Stock Ticker: WIN
Employees: 1,259
Parent Company:

Exchange: NAS
Fiscal Year Ends: 12/31

SALARIES/BONUSES:

Top Exec. Salary: $187,500   Bonus: $1,010,000
Second Exec. Salary: $1,000,000   Bonus: $

OTHER THOUGHTS:

Estimated Female Officers or Directors: 3
Hot Spot for Advancement for Women/Minorities: Y

Wipro Limited

NAIC Code: 541512

www.wipro.com

TYPES OF BUSINESS:

IT Consulting
Computer Hardware & Software Design
Hydraulic Equipment
Medical Electronics
Lighting Equipment
Soaps & Toiletries

BRANDS/DIVISIONS/AFFILIATES:

Denim Group

CONTACTS: Note: Officers with more than one job title may be intentionally listed here more than once.

Abidali Z. Neemuchwala, CEO
Bhanumurthy B. M., Pres.
Jatin Dalal, CFO
Rishad Premji, Chief Strategy Officer
Saurabh Govil, Chief Human Resources Officer
Sangita Singh, Sr. VP- Health Care & Life Sciences
Anurag Behar, Chief Sustainability Officer
N.S. Bala, Sr. VP-Mfg. & High Tech.
Inderpreet Sawhney, Sr. VP
Rishad Premji, Chief Strategy Officer
Ayan Mukerji, Sr. VP-Media & Telecom
Vineet Agrawal, Pres., Wipro Consumer Care & Lighting
Anurag Behar, Chief Sustainability Officer
Alexis Samuel, Chief Process Officer
Rajat Mathur Rajat Mathur Rajat Mathur, Chief Sales & Oper. Officer-Growth Markets
Azim H. Premji, Chmn.
Ulrich Meister, Sr. VP-Continental Europe

GROWTH PLANS/SPECIAL FEATURES:

Wipro Limited is a leading global information technology (IT), consulting and business process services company. The firm's operations are divided into two segments: IT services and IT products. The IT services segment generates 95% of Wipro's annual revenue, and develops and integrates innovative solutions that enable Wipro clients to leverage IT in order to achieve business objectives at competitive costs. This division advises, designs and executes technology transformation products and solutions as well as support programs for its business and enterprise customers. The IT products segment provides a range of IT and IT-enables services such as digital strategy advisory, customer-centric design, technology consulting, IT consulting, custom applications design, development, re-engineering and maintenance, systems integration, package implementation, global infrastructure services, analytics services, business process services, research and development and hardware/software design to enterprises worldwide. Industries Wipro serves include aerospace and defense, communications, engineering and construction, new age, media, education, network equipment providers, platforms and software products, public sector, semiconductors, automotive, consumer electronics, healthcare, medical device, oil and gas, process and industrial manufacturing, retail, travel and transportation, banking, consumer packaged goods, insurance, natural resources, pharmaceutical and life sciences, professional services, securities and capital markets and utilities. In March 2018, Wipro acquired a minority stake in Denim Group, an application security solution provider. Wipro opened its Texas Technology Center in Plano, Texas. The Texas Technology Center focuses on developing niche capabilities in new and emerging technologies.

FINANCIAL DATA: Note: Data for latest year may not have been available at press time.

In U.S. $	2018	2017	2016	2015	2014	2013
Revenue	7,750,653,000	7,829,331,000	7,289,331,000	6,679,160,000	6,177,368,000	5,323,698,000
R&D Expense						
Operating Income	1,177,895,000	1,281,678,000	1,325,092,000	1,305,633,000	1,223,257,000	957,980,000
Operating Margin %	15.19	16.37%	18.17%	19.54%	19.80%	17.99%
SGA Expense	1,023,912,000	912,930,200	838,975,700	770,184,800	720,213,300	657,823,600
Net Income	1,139,132,000	1,207,610,000	1,264,893,000	1,230,839,000	1,109,061,000	943,940,200
Operating Cash Flow	1,198,193,000	1,319,673,000	1,121,949,000	1,113,257,000	965,817,900	1,001,735,000
Capital Expenditure	311,095,300	296,628,700	198,449,500	180,099,600	126,785,200	151,010,000
EBITDA	1,807,240,000	1,925,732,000	1,864,808,000	1,781,991,000	1,607,098,000	1,284,410,000
Return on Assets %	10.30%	11.18%	13.42%	15.69%	16.55%	15.15%
Return on Equity %	15.96%	17.21%	20.34%	23.02%	24.85%	23.31%
Debt to Equity	0.09	0.03	0.03	0.03	0.03	

CONTACT INFORMATION:

Phone: 91 8028440055   Fax: 91 8028440256
Toll-Free:
Address: Doddakannelli, Sarjapur Rd., Bangalore, Karnataka 560035 India

STOCK TICKER/OTHER:

Stock Ticker: WIT
Employees: 163,827
Parent Company:

Exchange: NYS
Fiscal Year Ends: 03/31

SALARIES/BONUSES:

Top Exec. Salary: $966,923   Bonus: $262,229
Second Exec. Salary: Bonus: $635,168
$225,549

OTHER THOUGHTS:

Estimated Female Officers or Directors: 3
Hot Spot for Advancement for Women/Minorities: Y

Wish.com

NAIC Code: 454111

www.wish.com

TYPES OF BUSINESS:

Electronic Shopping

BRANDS/DIVISIONS/AFFILIATES:

ContextLogic Inc

GROWTH PLANS/SPECIAL FEATURES:

Wish.com is a global eCommerce platform that lets users shop millions of products at deep discounts. The site has approximately 75 million active users worldwide, which in turn gives small business owners and entrepreneurs access to these consumers by providing affordable goods. Wish.com supports over 1 million merchant partners. More than 3 million products are sold every day. Expandly's multichannel management software integrates with Wish.com's platform, enabling eCommerce sellers all over the world to add another platform to their selling strategy. Wish.com operates as a subsidiary of ContextLogic, Inc., a provider of online services that include media sharing and communication tools, eCommerce platforms and personalized content.

Wish.com offers its employees medical, dental and vision insurance; a stocked office kitchen and daily-catered meals; paid time off; and team-building social excursions.

CONTACTS: Note: Officers with more than one job title may be intentionally listed here more than once.

Peter Szulczewski, CEO

FINANCIAL DATA: Note: Data for latest year may not have been available at press time.

In U.S. $	2018	2017	2016	2015	2014	2013
Revenue						
R&D Expense						
Operating Income						
Operating Margin %						
SGA Expense						
Net Income						
Operating Cash Flow						
Capital Expenditure						
EBITDA						
Return on Assets %						
Return on Equity %						
Debt to Equity						

CONTACT INFORMATION:

Phone: 415-503-3654   Fax:
Toll-Free: 800-266-0172
Address: 1 Sansome St., 40/Fl, San Francisco, CA 94104 United States

STOCK TICKER/OTHER:

Stock Ticker: Subsidiary   Exchange:
Employees: 103   Fiscal Year Ends:
Parent Company: ContextLogic Inc

SALARIES/BONUSES:

Top Exec. Salary: $ Bonus: $
Second Exec. Salary: $ Bonus: $

OTHER THOUGHTS:

Estimated Female Officers or Directors:
Hot Spot for Advancement for Women/Minorities:

Workday Inc

NAIC Code: 511210Q

www.workday.com

TYPES OF BUSINESS:

Human Resources Software
Enterprise Financial Planning Software

BRANDS/DIVISIONS/AFFILIATES:

Adaptive Insights

CONTACTS: *Note: Officers with more than one job title may be intentionally listed here more than once.*

Aneel Bhusri, CEO
Robynne Sisco, CFO
Diana McKenzie, Chief Information Officer
Christine Cefalo, Chief Marketing Officer
Joe Korngiebel, Chief Technology Officer
David Duffield, Co-Founder
George Still, Director
James Bozzini, Executive VP, Divisional
Chano Fernandez, Executive VP, Divisional
Mark Peek, Managing Director
Leighanne Levensaler, Managing Director
Petros Dermetzis, Other Executive Officer
Ashley Goldsmith, Other Executive Officer
James Shaughnessy, Senior VP
Philip Wilmington, Vice Chairman
Michael Stankey, Vice Chairman of the Board

GROWTH PLANS/SPECIAL FEATURES:

Workday, Inc. provides enterprise cloud applications for finance and human resources. The company delivers financial management, human capital management and analytics applications designed for the world's largest companies, educational institutions and government agencies. Its software covers human capital management (HCM), payroll, financial management, grants management, time tracking, procurement, employee expense management and insight applications. HCM software helps enterprises organize and manage a global workforce, with tools addressing workforce lifecycle management, compensation, absences, employee benefits administration and career and development planning. Payroll solutions are intended to streamline an organization's payroll functions across a global workforce. Financial management tools allow organizations to track and analyze core finance tasks, such as accounting, cash management, governance and compliance; revenue management, such as contracts, billing and revenue recognition; and business assets, including tangible and intangible assets, lifecycle depreciation and reclaiming business assets. Grants management tool allows educational and government organizations to follow grant activity access information for grant reporting. Time tracking services work with the firm's HCM, payroll and financial management software to collect, process and distribute workforce time data. Procurement allows customers to configure procurement business processes and efficiently work with and manage suppliers and purchase orders. Employee expense management automates configurable expense management business processes and leverages workers, roles, organizations and security policies from the firm's HCM program. Insight applications leverage advanced date science and machine learning methods to help customers make smarter financial and workforce decisions. The firm maintains data centers across the U.S. as well as internationally in Ireland, Amsterdam, the Netherlands and Canada. In August 2018, Workday acquired Adaptive Insights, a cloud-based company for modernizing business planning.

Employees receive health, vision and dental coverage; basic life and personal accident insurance; flexible spending accounts; disability coverage; and a 401(k).

FINANCIAL DATA: *Note: Data for latest year may not have been available at press time.*

In U.S. $	2018	2017	2016	2015	2014	2013
Revenue	2,143,050,000	1,569,407,000	1,162,346,000	787,860,000	468,938,000	273,657,000
R&D Expense	910,584,000	680,531,000	469,944,000	316,868,000	182,116,000	102,665,000
Operating Income	-303,223,000	-376,665,000	-264,659,000	-215,702,000	-153,282,000	-117,863,000
Operating Margin %	-14.14	-24.00%	-22.76%	-27.37%	-32.68%	-43.06%
SGA Expense	906,276,000	781,996,000	582,634,000	421,891,000	263,294,000	172,320,000
Net Income	-321,222,000	-408,278,000	-289,918,000	-247,982,000	-172,509,000	-119,190,000
Operating Cash Flow	465,727,000	348,655,000	258,637,000	102,003,000	46,263,000	11,214,000
Capital Expenditure	152,536,000	120,813,000	133,667,000	103,646,000	75,725,000	15,898,000
EBITDA	-133,263,000	-263,104,000	-171,030,000	-155,707,000	-116,518,000	-99,981,000
Return on Assets %	-7.91%	-13.84%	-11.39%	-10.93%	-11.00%	-20.09%
Return on Equity %	-23.41%	-35.51%	-25.63%	-21.44%	-19.38%	-57.48%
Debt to Equity	0.72	0.45	0.44	0.43	0.39	0.02

CONTACT INFORMATION:

Phone: 925-951-9000   Fax:
Toll-Free: 877-967-5329
Address: 6230 Stoneridge Mall Rd., Ste. 200, Pleasanton, CA 94588 United States

STOCK TICKER/OTHER:

Stock Ticker: WDAY   Exchange: NAS
Employees: 6,600   Fiscal Year Ends:
Parent Company:

SALARIES/BONUSES:

Top Exec. Salary: $401,539   Bonus: $475,000
Second Exec. Salary: $295,769   Bonus: $171,000

OTHER THOUGHTS:

Estimated Female Officers or Directors: 2
Hot Spot for Advancement for Women/Minorities:

Workfront Inc

www.workfront.com

NAIC Code: 511210H

TYPES OF BUSINESS:

Computer Software, Business Management & ERP
Software

BRANDS/DIVISIONS/AFFILIATES:

Workfront Fusion
Workfront DAM

CONTACTS: *Note: Officers with more than one job title may be intentionally listed here more than once.*

Alex Shootman, CEO
Jon Pexton, CFO
Heidi Melin, CMO
Laura Butler, Sr. VP-Human Resources
Steven ZoBell, Chief Product & Technology Officer

GROWTH PLANS/SPECIAL FEATURES:

Workfront, Inc. provides cloud-based enterprise work and project management software. Workfront can be customized to match business team's unique preferences and workflows. Its comprehensive work management solution encompasses the entire project lifecycle, from intake to planning to execution to fulfillment. It is also able to handle ad hoc requests. Every project's organization strategy, tracking, collaboration and requests happen in one place, providing a simple, but comprehensive view of what is happening and who is working on what. Communication with stakeholders and remote contributors is categorized contextually for the work/project at hand, reducing time wasted by sifting through email, IMs and voicemail. For teams with Agile aspirations, Workfront offers an integrated storyboard, backlog, burndown chart and more. Workfront Fusion is an integration platform that connects with other business-critical applications. Workfront DAM (digital asset management) streamlines the process of managing, sharing, publishing and tracking digital files and related content. Workfront consultants help build customized plans and processes within the software that supports the way teams operate, while also aligning with industry best practices to enable organizations to maximize value. Workfront is used by CEOs, CMOs, directors, managers, project managers, developers and creatives worldwide. The firm is headquartered in Utah, USA, with additional offices in the U.K., which serves Europe, the Middle East and Africa.

FINANCIAL DATA: *Note: Data for latest year may not have been available at press time.*

In U.S. $	2018	2017	2016	2015	2014	2013
Revenue						
R&D Expense						
Operating Income						
Operating Margin %						
SGA Expense						
Net Income						
Operating Cash Flow						
Capital Expenditure						
EBITDA						
Return on Assets %						
Return on Equity %						
Debt to Equity						

CONTACT INFORMATION:

Phone: 801-373-3266   Fax:
Toll-Free: 866-441-0001
Address: 3301 N. Thanksgiving Way, Ste. 100, Lehi, UT 84043 United States

STOCK TICKER/OTHER:

Stock Ticker: Private   Exchange:
Employees: 671   Fiscal Year Ends:
Parent Company:

SALARIES/BONUSES:

Top Exec. Salary: $ Bonus: $
Second Exec. Salary: $ Bonus: $

OTHER THOUGHTS:

Estimated Female Officers or Directors:
Hot Spot for Advancement for Women/Minorities:

Xaxis

www.xaxis.com

NAIC Code: 541810E

TYPES OF BUSINESS:

Internet Advertising
Web Design
Software
Direct Marketing
Promotions
Data Analysis

BRANDS/DIVISIONS/AFFILIATES:

WPP plc

GROWTH PLANS/SPECIAL FEATURES:

Xaxis is a global provider of outcome media solutions for the advertising industry. The firm combines brand-safe media access, programmatic expertise and 360-degree data with proprietary artificial intelligence (AI) to help global brands achieve the outcomes they seek from their digital media investments. Xaxis offers managed programmatic services in 47 markets across North America, Europe, Asia Pacific, Latin America, the Middle East and Africa. Xaxis operates as a subsidiary of WPP plc.

Xaxis offers its employees comprehensive health benefits, retirement options, paid vacation and sick days and more.

CONTACTS: *Note: Officers with more than one job title may be intentionally listed here more than once.*

Nicolas Bidon, CEO
Laura Probert, Global VP-Talent
Matt Haies, VP
Irene Bondar, Exec. VP-Global Client Oper.
Rob Schneider, Sr. VP-Corp. Strategy & Platform Dev.
Nicolle Pangis, Pres., Real Media Group
David J. Moore, Chmn.

FINANCIAL DATA: *Note: Data for latest year may not have been available at press time.*

In U.S. $	2018	2017	2016	2015	2014	2013
Revenue		860,000,000	850,000,000	825,000,000	800,000,000	
R&D Expense						
Operating Income						
Operating Margin %						
SGA Expense						
Net Income						
Operating Cash Flow						
Capital Expenditure						
EBITDA						
Return on Assets %						
Return on Equity %						
Debt to Equity						

CONTACT INFORMATION:

Phone: 646-259-4200   Fax:
Toll-Free:
Address: 175 Greenwich St., 30/Fl, New York, NY 10006 United States

STOCK TICKER/OTHER:

Stock Ticker: Subsidiary   Exchange:
Employees: 1,000   Fiscal Year Ends: 12/31
Parent Company: WPP plc

SALARIES/BONUSES:

Top Exec. Salary: $ Bonus: $
Second Exec. Salary: $ Bonus: $

OTHER THOUGHTS:

Estimated Female Officers or Directors: 3
Hot Spot for Advancement for Women/Minorities: Y

Sales, profits and employees may be estimates. Financial information, benefits and other data can change quickly and may vary from those stated here.

XO Communications LLC

www.xo.com

NAIC Code: 517110

TYPES OF BUSINESS:

Corporate Telecommunications-Broadband Networks
Web Site Hosting
Internet Services
Virtual Private Networks
Commercial Networking Services
Local & Long-Distance Voice Services
Wireless Services
VOIP Service

BRANDS/DIVISIONS/AFFILIATES:

Verizon Communications Inc

GROWTH PLANS/SPECIAL FEATURES:

XO Communications, LLC, a subsidiary of Verizon Communications, Inc., owns and operates a major internet protocol (IP) and Ethernet network which provides communications capabilities for its domestic and international customers. The firm provides secure private data networking, cloud connectivity, unified communications, voice, internet access and managed services solutions. Many of the most recognized companies and organizations trust XO Communications with their mission-critical communications. XO Communications serves several industries, including architecture, communications, construction, financial, food, healthcare, hospitality, insurance, manufacturing, media, entertainment, non-profit, professional services, real estate, retail, software, transportation and wholesale. During 2017, XO Holdings sold its fiber-optic network business, XO Communications, to Verizon Communications for approximately $1.8 billion.

CONTACTS: Note: Officers with more than one job title may be intentionally listed here more than once.

Christopher Ancell, CEO
Navid Haghighi, General Counsel
Steve Nocella, Exec. VP-Network Oper.
Ernie Ortega, Exec. VP-Sales & Mktg.
Michael Langan, Chief Bus. Intelligence Officer

FINANCIAL DATA: Note: Data for latest year may not have been available at press time.

In U.S. $	2018	2017	2016	2015	2014	2013
Revenue		1,600,000,000	1,570,000,000	1,550,000,000	1,520,000,000	1,433,600,000
R&D Expense						
Operating Income						
Operating Margin %						
SGA Expense						
Net Income						
Operating Cash Flow						
Capital Expenditure						
EBITDA						
Return on Assets %						
Return on Equity %						
Debt to Equity						

CONTACT INFORMATION:

Phone: 703-547-2000   Fax: 703-547-2881
Toll-Free: 866-349-0134
Address: 13865 Sunrise Valley Dr., Herndon, VA 20171 United States

STOCK TICKER/OTHER:

Stock Ticker: Subsidiary   Exchange:
Employees: 3,721   Fiscal Year Ends: 12/31
Parent Company: Verizon Communications Inc

SALARIES/BONUSES:

Top Exec. Salary: $ Bonus: $
Second Exec. Salary: $ Bonus: $

OTHER THOUGHTS:

Estimated Female Officers or Directors: 2
Hot Spot for Advancement for Women/Minorities: Y

XO Group Inc

NAIC Code: 519130

www.xogroupinc.com

TYPES OF BUSINESS:

Online Resource for Wedding Planning
Online Gift Registry
Wedding Books & Magazines
Online Community
Wedding Supplies

BRANDS/DIVISIONS/AFFILIATES:

Permira Holdings Limited
Spectrum Equity
theknot.com
WeddingWire.com
thebump.com
thenest.com
GigMasters
WeddingWire Inc

CONTACTS: *Note: Officers with more than one job title may be intentionally listed here more than once.*

Michael Steib, CEO
Gillian Munson, CFO
Dhanusha Sivajee, CMO
Michelle Dvorkin, Exec. VP-Human Resources
Nic Di Iorio, CTO
Michael Zeisser, Director
Paul Bascobert, Pres.

GROWTH PLANS/SPECIAL FEATURES:

XO Group, Inc. is one of the world's leading wedding media and services companies. The firm provides couples with planning information, interactive tools and a vast array of online resources. Its Knot wedding shop on theknot.com is one of the largest online wedding retailers in the world, offering supplies, favors and attendant gifts, among other items. WeddingWire.com offers free online wedding planning tools, including a checklist, guest list, seating chart, budget, vendor manager, a wedding website and more. Additional sites offered include: The Bump (thebump.com), a pregnancy and parenting brand, providing personalized information, content and tools for anyone at any stage of their journey, from fertility to pregnancy, as well as parenting through the toddler years; The Nest (thenest.com), which focuses exclusively on young nesters setting up homes and navigating new lives together; and GigMasters, an event marketplace to find and book entertainment, whether it is for the wedding day or baby's first birthday. In December 2018, XO Group was taken private by Permira Holdings Limited and Spectrum Equity, and was merged with WeddingWire, Inc. The combined entity announced that they will continue to offer The Knot and WeddingWire in the U.S., and other various sites outside the U.S.

FINANCIAL DATA: *Note: Data for latest year may not have been available at press time.*

In U.S. $	2018	2017	2016	2015	2014	2013
Revenue	170,000,000	160,556,000	152,116,000	141,644,000	143,664,000	133,814,000
R&D Expense						
Operating Income						
Operating Margin %						
SGA Expense						
Net Income		5,534,000	12,120,000	5,464,000	462,000	5,794,000
Operating Cash Flow						
Capital Expenditure						
EBITDA						
Return on Assets %						
Return on Equity %						
Debt to Equity						

CONTACT INFORMATION:

Phone: 212 219-8555   Fax: 212 219-1929
Toll-Free: 877-843-5668
Address: 195 Broadway, 25/Fl, New York, NY 10007 United States

STOCK TICKER/OTHER:

Stock Ticker: Private   Exchange:
Employees: 727   Fiscal Year Ends: 12/31
Parent Company:

SALARIES/BONUSES:

Top Exec. Salary: $ Bonus: $
Second Exec. Salary: $ Bonus: $

OTHER THOUGHTS:

Estimated Female Officers or Directors: 7
Hot Spot for Advancement for Women/Minorities: Y

Yandex NV

www.yandex.com

NAIC Code: 519130

TYPES OF BUSINESS:

Online Search Engine
Online Payment System
Investment Company
On Demand Transportation
Media Services
Ticketing

BRANDS/DIVISIONS/AFFILIATES:

yandex.ru
MatrixNet
Yandex.Market
Yandex.Taxi
Auto.ru
Yandex.Jobs
KinoPoisk
Yandex Zen

CONTACTS: Note: Officers with more than one job title may be intentionally listed here more than once.

Arkady Volozh, CEO
Gregory Abovsky, CFO
Elena Bunina, Dir.-Human Resources
Mikhail Parakhin, CTO
Dmitry Ivanov, Chief Product Officer
Anya Barski, VP-Eng.
Ekaterina Fadeeva, Chief Legal Officer
Mikhail Fadeev, Chief Systems Oper. Officer
Alexey Mazurov, Chief Dev. Officer
Dina Litvinova, Head-Press Svcs.
Katya Zhukova, Head-Investor Rel.
Dmitry Barsukov, Dir.-Corp. Finance
Elena Kolmanovskaya, Chief Editor
Anya Barski, CEO-Yandex Labs
Maxim Kiselev, Dir.-Bus. Dev.
Jane Zavalishina, CEO-Yandex.Money
John Boynton, Chmn.

GROWTH PLANS/SPECIAL FEATURES:

Yandex NV is an internet company that operates a popular search engine and website. The company's search engine, yandex.ru, is powered by the firm's proprietary MatrixNet technology, which generates more than half of all search traffic in Russia. This technology allows for a ranking formula that is longer and more complex than what previous technologies allowed for, thus producing search results that are more relevant. Yandex operates through five business segments: search and portal, e-commerce, taxi, classifies and experimental businesses. The search and portal segment includes Yandex's search engine and website services offered in Russia, Ukraine, Belarus, Turkey and Kazakhstan. The eCommerce segment includes the Yandex.Market service, which offers retailers an additional platform to reach customers seeking specific retailer, product or price information. Yandex.Market is priced on a cost-per-click basis, as well as a cost-per-action model. The taxi segment includes the Yandex.Taxi service, which provides on-demand transportation service in Russia and in Belarus. The classifieds segment includes Auto.ru, Yandex.Realty, Yandex.Jobs and Yandex.Travel. These sites allow users, both private and professional, to post listings in order to reach people interested in those related offerings. The experimental businesses segment comprises: media services and data factory. Media services includes KinoPoisk, a Russian language site dedicated to movies, television programs and celebrities; Yandex.Music, a media player service; Yandex.TV, a television streaming service; and Yandex.Afisha, from which users can select entertainment from a variety of options, and provides an opportunity to purchase tickets to cinemas, theaters and concerts online. The firm's discovery products include: Yandex Zen, which searches the web for fresh content and then presents it in an endless feed that informs, intrigues and inspires users via articles, news, videos, images and more; and Yandex Launcher, which allows users to fill their Android phones with content from the internet.

FINANCIAL DATA: Note: Data for latest year may not have been available at press time.

In U.S. $	2018	2017	2016	2015	2014	2013
Revenue		1,365,891,000	1,102,614,000	868,323,800	737,259,100	573,664,200
R&D Expense		272,454,900	229,918,800	194,905,200	128,407,100	84,622,070
Operating Income		189,314,100	186,569,400	147,678,400	222,526,900	186,424,200
Operating Margin %		13.86%	16.92%	17.00%	30.18%	32.49%
SGA Expense		393,281,400	259,733,300	168,474,500	113,013,400	94,932,980
Net Income		127,448,700	98,723,340	140,562,400	247,171,400	195,674,900
Operating Cash Flow		345,226,700	369,580,800	284,290,700	225,765,400	213,552,000
Capital Expenditure		179,918,100	139,778,200	189,444,800	140,562,400	71,682,610
EBITDA		383,420,700	316,661,200	274,865,600	299,423,000	240,433,000
Return on Assets %		7.17%	6.01%	9.36%	20.47%	23.31%
Return on Equity %		10.97%	9.23%	15.38%	33.26%	32.21%
Debt to Equity			0.24	0.39	0.47	0.35

CONTACT INFORMATION:

Phone: 7 495 739-22-22   Fax: 7 495 739-23-32
Toll-Free:
Address: Ulitsa Lva Tolstogo 16, Moscow, 119021 Russia

STOCK TICKER/OTHER:

Stock Ticker: YNDX   Exchange: NAS
Employees: 6,271   Fiscal Year Ends: 12/31
Parent Company:

SALARIES/BONUSES:

Top Exec. Salary: $ Bonus: $
Second Exec. Salary: $ Bonus: $

OTHER THOUGHTS:

Estimated Female Officers or Directors: 8
Hot Spot for Advancement for Women/Minorities: Y

Sales, profits and employees may be estimates. Financial information, benefits and other data can change quickly and may vary from those stated here.

Yardi Systems Inc

NAIC Code: 511210H

TYPES OF BUSINESS:

Computer Software, Business Management & ERP
Software
Real Estate

BRANDS/DIVISIONS/AFFILIATES:

Voyager
Yardi Breeze

CONTACTS: *Note: Officers with more than one job title may be intentionally listed here more than once.*

Anant Yardi, Pres.
Terri Dowen, Sr. VP-Sales

GROWTH PLANS/SPECIAL FEATURES:

Yardi Systems, Inc. provides software for the real estate industry. The company employs more than 6,000 professionals working in over 40 offices throughout North America, Europe, the Middle East, Asia and Australia. Yardi's web-based, fully integrated end-to-end Voyager platform offers mobile access for large portfolios to manage operations, execute leasing, run analytics and provide innovative resident, tenant and investor services. It is applicable for the following real estate environments: multi-family, office/industrial/retail, shared space, investment management, senior living, condo, co-op, home owner associations (HOA), single family homes, affordable housing, public housing, social housing, student housing, manufactured housing, military housing, airports, ports, parks/recreation, government services and self-storage. The Yardi Breeze platform is an online, software-as-a-service (SaaS) property management software for small-to-mid-size companies and owners of single-family homes, multi-family and commercial properties. It streamlines property management and accounting with rental property management software that features a single database and works with any browser. In short, Yardi Voyager is for real estate managers and investors with over 1,000 residential units or 1 million commercial square feet; and Yardi Breeze is for property owners and managers with less than Voyager's measures. Services offered by the firm include client services, training, SaaS and consulting.

FINANCIAL DATA: *Note: Data for latest year may not have been available at press time.*

In U.S. $	2018	2017	2016	2015	2014	2013
Revenue						
R&D Expense						
Operating Income						
Operating Margin %						
SGA Expense						
Net Income						
Operating Cash Flow						
Capital Expenditure						
EBITDA						
Return on Assets %						
Return on Equity %						
Debt to Equity						

CONTACT INFORMATION:

Phone: 805-699-2040   Fax: 805-699-2044
Toll-Free: 800-866-1124
Address: 430 S. Fairview Ave., Santa Barbara, CA 93117 United States

STOCK TICKER/OTHER:

Stock Ticker: Private   Exchange:
Employees: 5,014   Fiscal Year Ends:
Parent Company:

SALARIES/BONUSES:

Top Exec. Salary: $ Bonus: $
Second Exec. Salary: $ Bonus: $

OTHER THOUGHTS:

Estimated Female Officers or Directors:
Hot Spot for Advancement for Women/Minorities:

Yello Mobile Inc

yellomobile.com

NAIC Code: 511210C

TYPES OF BUSINESS:

Computer Software, Telecom, Communications & VOIP

BRANDS/DIVISIONS/AFFILIATES:

Coocha
Post Bay
BlueWeb
Pikicast
AdQUA
Healthcare O2O
Accommodation O2O
O2O Consulting

CONTACTS: Note: Officers with more than one job title may be intentionally listed here more than once.

Sang-Hyuk Lee, CEO

GROWTH PLANS/SPECIAL FEATURES:

Yello Mobile, Inc. is a mobile media company in South Korea. The firm is comprised of a group of companies that provide mobile applications which can be used 24-hours-a-day, seven days a week. Yello's portfolio of platforms and services are grouped into the following divisions: shopping media, media, travel, advertisement and offline-to-online (O2O). The shopping media portfolio includes: Coocha, an app for social commerce deals; Post Bay, an overseas direct purchase delivery service; Blueweb, a web hosting service provides; and Playauto, an online sales solutions provider. The media division offers media, entertainment and vertical apps such as: Pikicast, which delivers curated mobile content; Jihachul, providing real-time subway information; and AlarmMon, 1km, Poing and other apps designed to provide diverse user-centric content. The advertisement division comprises companies in digital marketing that provide creative digital marketing strategies, mobile ad network platforms and viral and SNS marketing platforms to make sure users reach their target audience. Its brands include AdQUA, Innobirds, e-motion, Yello Story, RecoBell, and FutureStream Networks. The travel division provides mobile apps that bring together top travel and leisure companies that offer various services, including travel reservations, flight information, hotel and guesthouse booking, and business management solutions for small/medium accommodation businesses. Last, the O2O division offers services businesses and individuals, such as marketing, IT, customer relations management (CRM), payment, MRO (maintenance, repair, operations) and consulting. For example, Healthcare O2O provides various services such as marketing, customer relations management (CRM) and business-to-business commerce infrastructure to offline healthcare clients; Accommodation O2O offers marketing, CRM and B2B infrastructure to offline accommodation businesses (hotel/motel); O2O Payment provides payment infrastructure to offline businesses; and O2O Consulting provides marketing, management and Internet of Things (IoT) consulting services to offline clients.

FINANCIAL DATA: Note: Data for latest year may not have been available at press time.

In U.S. $	2018	2017	2016	2015	2014	2013
Revenue		378,000,000	367,037,000	266,887,000	83,064,700	
R&D Expense						
Operating Income						
Operating Margin %						
SGA Expense						
Net Income			-23,209,200	-30,817,400	-7,369,380	
Operating Cash Flow						
Capital Expenditure						
EBITDA						
Return on Assets %						
Return on Equity %						
Debt to Equity						

CONTACT INFORMATION:

Phone: 82-02-591-6565   Fax: 82-02-512-1142
Toll-Free:
Address: 3/Fl. J-Twr., 139 Dosandaero, Seoul, 135-889 South Korea

STOCK TICKER/OTHER:

Stock Ticker: Private   Exchange:
Employees: Fiscal Year Ends:
Parent Company:

SALARIES/BONUSES:

Top Exec. Salary: $ Bonus: $
Second Exec. Salary: $ Bonus: $

OTHER THOUGHTS:

Estimated Female Officers or Directors:
Hot Spot for Advancement for Women/Minorities:

Yelp Inc

NAIC Code: 519130

www.yelp.com

TYPES OF BUSINESS:

Online Community-Business Reviews
Advertising Services
Users Ratings

BRANDS/DIVISIONS/AFFILIATES:

Yelp.com
Yelp Reservations

CONTACTS: *Note: Officers with more than one job title may be intentionally listed here more than once.*

Jeremy Stoppelman, CEO
Charles Baker, CFO
Diane Irvine, Chairman of the Board
Alan Ramsay, Chief Accounting Officer
Joseph Nachman, COO
Laurence Wilson, General Counsel

GROWTH PLANS/SPECIAL FEATURES:

Yelp, Inc. is a web-based company operating a number of online city guides, each consisting of user-generated review content covering the local area. The firm, through Yelp.com, offers extensive coverage for a number of major metropolitan areas throughout North America, including Atlanta, Los Angeles, Miami, Houston, New York, Portland, San Diego, Seattle and Washington, D.C. Yelp also offers its services in Canada, South America, Europe, Singapore and Australia. The company had approximately 75 million unique visitors per month via mobile web and 69 million unique visitors via desktop as of September 2018. In total, its visitors have written over 170 million reviews (as of January 2019). Yelp.com is a cross between a review service and a community-based site. To write reviews, users must register and create a profile page, which can include photos and personal information as well as links to all reviews written by a particular user. Reviews cover a wide variety of categories, including restaurants; shopping; nightlife; arts and entertainment; spas and salons; doctors and hospitals; auto mechanics; hotels; schools; banks; public services, such as buses and trains; real estate; and religious organizations, with users encouraged to create reviews for new categories. The site earns revenues through advertising, and local business owners are encouraged to create their own profiles, allowing them to track and respond to customer-generated reviews. Yelp can be accessed through applications available on iOS and Android phones. Yelp Reservations is an app for booking restaurant reservations.

FINANCIAL DATA: *Note: Data for latest year may not have been available at press time.*

In U.S. $	2018	2017	2016	2015	2014	2013
Revenue		846,813,000	713,069,000	549,711,000	377,536,000	232,988,000
R&D Expense						
Operating Income		14,994,000	-1,524,000	-21,324,000	11,059,000	-8,148,000
Operating Margin %		1.77%	-.21%	-3.87%	2.92%	-3.49%
SGA Expense		544,316,000	480,335,000	382,630,000	259,324,000	174,877,000
Net Income		152,858,000	-4,670,000	-32,900,000	36,473,000	-10,068,000
Operating Cash Flow		167,647,000	126,900,000	57,362,000	57,932,000	21,432,000
Capital Expenditure		30,245,000	37,364,000	43,508,000	42,127,000	21,099,000
EBITDA		56,192,000	33,822,000	8,280,000	28,649,000	3,307,000
Return on Assets %		14.54%	-.56%	-4.75%	6.36%	-2.86%
Return on Equity %		16.03%	-.62%	-5.13%	6.78%	-3.08%
Debt to Equity						

CONTACT INFORMATION:

Phone: 415 908-3801   Fax:
Toll-Free:
Address: 140 New Montgomery St., 9/Fl, San Francisco, CA 94105
United States

STOCK TICKER/OTHER:

Stock Ticker: YELP   Exchange: NYS
Employees: 4,256   Fiscal Year Ends: 12/31
Parent Company:

SALARIES/BONUSES:

Top Exec. Salary: $325,000   Bonus: $
Second Exec. Salary: Bonus: $
$325,000

OTHER THOUGHTS:

Estimated Female Officers or Directors: 5
Hot Spot for Advancement for Women/Minorities: Y

YesMail.com Inc

www.yesmarketing.com

NAIC Code: 541810E

TYPES OF BUSINESS:

Online Advertising & Marketing Services
E-Mail Marketing Services

BRANDS/DIVISIONS/AFFILIATES:

InfoGROUP Inc
Yes Marketing

CONTACTS: *Note: Officers with more than one job title may be intentionally listed here more than once.*

Michael Iaccarino, CEO-InfoGROUP
Jim Strum, Pres.
Michael Iaccarino, Chmn.-InfoGROUP
Ivy Shtereva, VP-Mktg.
David McRae, COO
Jonathan Quint, CIO
Sanjay Raghavaraju, VP-Client Services Eng.
Dana Hayman, VP-Strategy
Julie Anne Reda, VP-Product Mktg.
Sue Zabran, VP-Process & Efficiency
Ed Kuderna, VP-Client Experience
Linda Vetter, VP-Mktg.
Jason Warnock, VP-Market Intelligence & Deliverability
Matt Caldwell, VP-Creative
Marc Shull, Sr. Dir.-Customer Insights
Michael Iaccarino, Chmn.

GROWTH PLANS/SPECIAL FEATURES:

YesMail.com, Inc., a subsidiary of InfoGROUP, Inc. that does business as Yes Marketing, is a multichannel marketing and technology provider. The firm is organized into three segments: technology, services and data. The technology segment consists of database technologies, in which Yesmail designs, deploys and supports marketing databases on premises or through the cloud based upon the requirements of the customer; marketing applications, delivering solutions like cross-channel campaign planning, advanced segmentation, template creation and content management, analytics and integrated testing and reporting for channels like email or social media; and real-time application programming interfaces (API) with an average response time of 64.1 milliseconds. The firm's services include strategy, for planning multichannel strategies; analytics services, where analysts interpret data and give insights; creative services, for the design of emails, ads, social media, direct mail, landing pages and more; program management services, a program support model; campaign production services, which includes timeline management, audience targeting and segmentation, campaign testing and campaign automation; technology implementation; and custom engineering, to help customers make the most of technology. Data solutions include data assets, to personalize every consumer touchpoint; data acquisition, on existing customers and growing a larger audience; data hygiene, for clean data and campaigns; and data enhancement to find out more about individual consumers. YesMail.com is headquartered in Chicago with offices in Portland, New York City, Burlington, Dallas, Louisville, Omaha, San Francisco, London, Mississauga, Canada and Singapore.

YesMail offers employees medical, dental, vision and prescription coverage; flexible spending accounts; long- and short term disability; life and AD&D insurance; tuition reimbursement; employee assistance programs; paid holidays; paid time-off; and a 401(k) plan.

FINANCIAL DATA: *Note: Data for latest year may not have been available at press time.*

In U.S. $	2018	2017	2016	2015	2014	2013
Revenue						
R&D Expense						
Operating Income						
Operating Margin %						
SGA Expense						
Net Income						
Operating Cash Flow						
Capital Expenditure						
EBITDA						
Return on Assets %						
Return on Equity %						
Debt to Equity						

CONTACT INFORMATION:

Phone: Fax:
Toll-Free: 877-937-6245
Address: 200 W. Adams St., Ste. 1400, Chicago, IL 60606 United States

STOCK TICKER/OTHER:

Stock Ticker: Subsidiary   Exchange:
Employees: 266   Fiscal Year Ends: 12/31
Parent Company: INFOGROUP INC

SALARIES/BONUSES:

Top Exec. Salary: $ Bonus: $
Second Exec. Salary: $ Bonus: $

OTHER THOUGHTS:

Estimated Female Officers or Directors: 3
Hot Spot for Advancement for Women/Minorities: Y

YOOX Net-A-Porter Group SpA (YNAP)

www.ynap.com

NAIC Code: 454111

TYPES OF BUSINESS:

Online Apparel Sales

BRANDS/DIVISIONS/AFFILIATES:

Alberta Ferretti
Armani.com
Chloe
Karl Lagerfeld
Lanvin
Moncler
Stone Island
Valentino

CONTACTS: *Note: Officers with more than one job title may be intentionally listed here more than once.*

Federico Marchetti, CEO
Alberto Grignolo, COO
Enrico Cavatorta, CFO
Deborah Lee, Chief People Officer
Gabriele Tazzari, Dir.-R&D
Alex Alexander, CIO
Gabriele Tazzari, Dir.-Strategy, Governance & Innovation
Paolo Mascio, Dir.-Online Stores
Silvia Scagnelli, Mgr.-Investor Rel.
Alessandra Rossi, Dir.-Commercial
Alberto Grignolo, Gen. Mgr.
Davide di Dario, Dir.-Demand Planning
Luca Martines, Dir.-Asia Pacific

GROWTH PLANS/SPECIAL FEATURES:

YOOX Net-A-Porter Group SpA (YNAP) is an Italian internet mail order retailer of men's and women's multi-brand clothing and accessories. It was established via the 2015 merger between YOOX Group and The Net-A-Porter Group, both of which were premier online luxury fashion retailers. The company offers style-conscious customers around the world an unparalleled online retail experience through its net-a-porter.com, mrporter.com, yoox.com and theoutnet.com websites. Additionally, YNAP designs and manages online flagship stores for leading fashion and luxury brands looking to offer their latest collection on the internet. Among the 33 flagship stores are Alberta Ferretti, Armani.com, Chloe, Dunhill, Isabel Marant, Karl Lagerfeld, Lanvin, Moncler, Pomellato, Stone Island, Valentino and Y-3. Through a joint venture with the Kering Group, the company manages online flagship stores of several of the French firm's luxury brands, including Saint Laurent Paris, Bottega Veneta, Stella McCartney, Alexander McQueen, Balenciaga, Brioni and MCQ. YNAP has a client base of more than 3 million high-spending customers generating around 1 billion visits worldwide. The Group has offices and operations in the U.S., Europe, Middle East, Japan, China and Hong Kong, and delivers to more than 180 countries.

FINANCIAL DATA: *Note: Data for latest year may not have been available at press time.*

In U.S. $	2018	2017	2016	2015	2014	2013
Revenue						
R&D Expense						
Operating Income						
Operating Margin %						
SGA Expense						
Net Income						
Operating Cash Flow						
Capital Expenditure						
EBITDA						
Return on Assets %						
Return on Equity %						
Debt to Equity						

CONTACT INFORMATION:

Phone: 39028-311-2811   Fax: 39028-311-2821
Toll-Free:
Address: Via Morimondo 17, Milan, 20143 Italy

STOCK TICKER/OTHER:

Stock Ticker: YXOXF   Exchange: PINX
Employees: 4,703   Fiscal Year Ends: 12/31
Parent Company:

SALARIES/BONUSES:

Top Exec. Salary: $ Bonus: $
Second Exec. Salary: $ Bonus: $

OTHER THOUGHTS:

Estimated Female Officers or Directors: 4
Hot Spot for Advancement for Women/Minorities: Y

Youku Tudou Inc

NAIC Code: 519130

TYPES OF BUSINESS:

Online Video Service
Mobile Broadcasting
Video Production
Advertising Services

GROWTH PLANS/SPECIAL FEATURES:

Youku Tudou, Inc. is a multi-screen entertainment and media company in China. The firm is China's leading internet television platform, enabling users to search, view and share high-quality video content quickly and easily across multiple devices with 580 million monthly unique visitors. Its Youku and Tudou brands are among the most recognized online video brands in the country. Youku Tudou operates as a wholly-owned subsidiary of Alibaba Group Holding Ltd.

BRANDS/DIVISIONS/AFFILIATES:

Alibaba Group Holding Limited
Youku
Tudou

CONTACTS: Note: Officers with more than one job title may be intentionally listed here more than once.

Victor Wing Cheung Koo, CEO
Dele Liu, Pres.
Michael Ge Xu, CFO
Yawei Dong, CMO
Leo Jian Yao, CTO
Sunny Xiangyang Zhu, Chief Content Officer
Frank Ming Wei, Sr. VP
Weidong Yang, Sr. VP
Zhou Yu, Sr. VP
Victor Wing Cheung Koo, Chmn.

FINANCIAL DATA: Note: Data for latest year may not have been available at press time.

In U.S. $	2018	2017	2016	2015	2014	2013
Revenue	1,150,000,000	1,050,000,000	900,000,000	805,000,000	652,674,880	468,015,904
R&D Expense						
Operating Income						
Operating Margin %						
SGA Expense						
Net Income						
Operating Cash Flow						
Capital Expenditure						
EBITDA						
Return on Assets %						
Return on Equity %						
Debt to Equity						

CONTACT INFORMATION:

Phone: 86 10-5885-1881   Fax: 86-10-5970-8818
Toll-Free:
Address: Sinosteel Plz., 8 Haidian St., 11/Fl, Beijing, 100080 China

STOCK TICKER/OTHER:

Stock Ticker: Subsidiary   Exchange:
Employees: 2,797   Fiscal Year Ends: 12/31
Parent Company: Alibaba Group Holding Ltd

SALARIES/BONUSES:

Top Exec. Salary: $ Bonus: $
Second Exec. Salary: $ Bonus: $

OTHER THOUGHTS:

Estimated Female Officers or Directors:
Hot Spot for Advancement for Women/Minorities:

YouTube LLC

www.youtube.com

NAIC Code: 519130

TYPES OF BUSINESS:

Online Video Services
Video Subscriptions
Online Video Advertising Services

BRANDS/DIVISIONS/AFFILIATES:

Alphabet Inc
Google Corporation
YouTube Leanback
YouTube Partner
YouTube Insight
YouTubeToptics
YouTube Premium
YouTube Music

CONTACTS: *Note: Officers with more than one job title may be intentionally listed here more than once.*

Susan Wojcicki, CEO
Julie Supan, Dir.-Mktg.
Hunter Walk, Head-Product
Kevin Donahue, VP-Content
Julie Supan, Sr. Dir.-Mktg.

GROWTH PLANS/SPECIAL FEATURES:

YouTube, LLC, a subsidiary of Alphabet, Inc.'s Google, is a leading online video site, featuring significant amounts of user-generated content. It has partnered with major content providers such as WarnerMedia, ABC, CBS, Sony, National Geographic, EA and Activision. The website streams over 1 billion hours of video each day to 89 countries in 76 languages. YouTube derives most of its revenue through in-video advertising, sponsorships and brand channels. Advertisers have the option of purchasing promoted videos, which offer more visibility; 24-hour video banner ads on the website's homepage; the ability to hand-pick videos to advertise against; mobile advertisements; and the ability to advertise with content partners. The YouTube Partner program allows producers of original content that targets a wide audience to upload ad-supported videos, rentals, high quality content and live-streaming videos. Advertisers can track the impact of these advertisements with YouTube Insight, which counts page views, video popularity, demographics and audience attention. YouTube is also available through Apple TV and a variety of mobile devices. Other YouTube features and developments include: YouTube Topics search; a built-in video editor; comment searching; audience statistics; a caption editor; HTML5 video; music playlists; and low-latency pages. YouTube Premium is a monthly subscription that enables users to watch without seeing ads on most types of videos. However, YouTube channels paid for by sponsors, TV show rentals and movie rentals may still display ads. YouTube Premium also lets subscribers watch videos offline by saving them to a desktop or mobile devices for later viewing. YouTubeTV offers over 40 networks, a cloud DVR with no storage limits and six accounts per household for a monthly fee. YouTube Music was launched in 2018, a subscription music streaming service.

Alphabet offers its employees comprehensive health benefits, retirement plans and a variety of employee assistance programs.

FINANCIAL DATA: *Note: Data for latest year may not have been available at press time.*

In U.S. $	2018	2017	2016	2015	2014	2013
Revenue	6,600,000,000	6,250,000,000	5,000,000,000	4,354,000,000	4,000,000,000	3,125,000,000
R&D Expense						
Operating Income						
Operating Margin %						
SGA Expense						
Net Income						
Operating Cash Flow						
Capital Expenditure						
EBITDA						
Return on Assets %						
Return on Equity %						
Debt to Equity						

CONTACT INFORMATION:

Phone: 650-253-0000   Fax: 650-253-0001
Toll-Free:
Address: 901 Cherry Ave., San Bruno, CA 94066 United States

STOCK TICKER/OTHER:

Stock Ticker: Subsidiary   Exchange:
Employees: 850   Fiscal Year Ends: 12/31
Parent Company: Alphabet Inc

SALARIES/BONUSES:

Top Exec. Salary: $ Bonus: $
Second Exec. Salary: $ Bonus: $

OTHER THOUGHTS:

Estimated Female Officers or Directors: 2
Hot Spot for Advancement for Women/Minorities:

Sales, profits and employees may be estimates. Financial information, benefits and other data can change quickly and may vary from those stated here.

Zalando SE

NAIC Code: 454111

www.zalando.de

TYPES OF BUSINESS:

Electronic Shopping

BRANDS/DIVISIONS/AFFILIATES:

Zalando Lounge
zLabels
All About the Z
Zalon
Zalando Marketing Solutions
Zalando Partner Solutions
Offprice

CONTACTS: Note: Officers with more than one job title may be intentionally listed here more than once.

Robert Gentz, Co-CEO
David Schneider, Co-CEO
Rubin Ritter, Co-CEO

GROWTH PLANS/SPECIAL FEATURES:

Zalando SE is a private Berlin-based international e-commerce company specializing in men's, women's and children's clothing, accessories, footwear and home products. The firm works with international brands including Adidas, NIKE, Timberland, True Religion, Vero Moda, Alternative Apparel, Esprit Home, KAS and Desigual, as well as designer labels such as Apepazza and Latitude Femme. The Zalando web site allows shoppers to browse by brand, product or sale-priced merchandise and includes its Inspire Me page, enabling users to browse products by new arrivals, trending brands, must-have items or popular styles. Zalando's web sites and stores reach consumers in European 17 countries. The firm works together with apparel and accessory manufacturers that supply 300,000 different items of merchandise across approximately 2,000 brands. Its off-price business sells pre-season items; and the Zalando Lounge exclusively offers registered members sales promotions at discounted prices. In addition, outlet stores are located in Berlin, Cologne and Frankfurt, Germany. zLabels includes the firm's own brands, offering products such as shoes, clothing and accessories. Zalando's digital magazine, All About the Z, allows for a behind-the-scene look at projects and ideas the firm is working on. Zalon is a place where customers can be directly-advised by selected stylists when making their purchases. Zalando Marketing Solutions offers personalized marketing services to brand partners. Zalando Partner Solutions helps others in the industry succeed digitally, whether by linking stocks to multiple retailers, digitizing processes in wholesale or integrating offline stores into the Zalando platform. The firm's Offprice business sells previous season's assortments at discount prices. Zalando makes its own logistics capabilities available to external partners.

FINANCIAL DATA: Note: Data for latest year may not have been available at press time.

In U.S. $	2018	2017	2016	2015	2014	2013
Revenue		4,000,000,000	3,890,936,893	3,371,528,400	2,523,517,200	1,933,376,350
R&D Expense						
Operating Income						
Operating Margin %						
SGA Expense						
Net Income				220,835,724	89,955,900	-131,600,000
Operating Cash Flow						
Capital Expenditure						
EBITDA						
Return on Assets %						
Return on Equity %						
Debt to Equity						

CONTACT INFORMATION:

Phone: 49-030-209681038   Fax:
Toll-Free:
Address: Tamara-Danz-Str. 1, Berlin, 10243 Germany

STOCK TICKER/OTHER:

Stock Ticker: Private
Employees: 11,998
Parent Company:

Exchange:
Fiscal Year Ends: 12/31

SALARIES/BONUSES:

Top Exec. Salary: $ Bonus: $
Second Exec. Salary: $ Bonus: $

OTHER THOUGHTS:

Estimated Female Officers or Directors:
Hot Spot for Advancement for Women/Minorities:

Zappos.com Inc

NAIC Code: 454111

www.zappos.com

TYPES OF BUSINESS:

Online Shoe Retail
Outlet Sales
Shoes
Housewares
Clothing
Bags & Handbags
Watches

BRANDS/DIVISIONS/AFFILIATES:

Amazon.com Inc
Zappos IP Inc
Zappos Retail Inc
Zappos.com
Zappos Gift Cards Inc
Zappos Insights Inc
6pm.com LLC
Zappos Merchandising Inc

CONTACTS: Note: Officers with more than one job title may be intentionally listed here more than once.

Tony Hsieh, CEO
Arun Rajan, COO
Hollie Delaney, Chief Human Resources Officer
John Bunvh, Technical Advisor to Zappos CEO

GROWTH PLANS/SPECIAL FEATURES:

Zappos.com, Inc., a subsidiary of Amazon.com, Inc., is an online retailer of shoes, handbags and other accessories, offering millions of products from over 1,200 footwear and apparel brands. Its inventory includes shoes, bags and handbags, clothing, beauty products, eyewear, sporting goods, housewares and watches. Due to massive growth, the firm was restructured into seven separate companies under the Zappos family umbrella. Zappos.com, Inc., the management company for the group, provides finance, treasury, accounting, help desk, human resources, information technology, legal and training services to the Zappos family of companies. Zappos Gift Cards, Inc. sells gift cards and gift certificates for use on the company's websites. Zappos Insights, Inc. provides business consulting and corporate culture advisory services to third-party companies and individuals. The Pipeline team provides a four-week training class on Zappos and teaches classes in management, Microsoft Office and more. Zappos IP, Inc. provides website software development, project management, marketing and content services and creative services to the Zappos family of companies and follows customer experience trends. Zappos Merchandising, Inc. focuses on product purchasing, brand acquisition and vendor relationship management. Zappos Retail, Inc., doing business as ZRetail, oversees the actual sale of products on Zappos.com. Finally, 6pm.com LLC operates e-commerce site 6pm.com, which sells discount branded shoes, clothing, bags and accessories for men, women and children.

Employee benefits include medical, dental and vision coverage; life insurance; flexible spending accounts; an employee assistance program; fitness classes; a 401(k); local business discounts; and onsite wellness services. Zappos has implemented an employee organization and management practice known as Holacracy, in which employees do not have job titles and are expected, to a large extent, to manage themselves.

FINANCIAL DATA: Note: Data for latest year may not have been available at press time.

In U.S. $	2018	2017	2016	2015	2014	2013
Revenue	2,950,500,000	2,810,000,000	2,512,000,000	2,400,000,000	2,200,000,000	2,100,000,000
R&D Expense						
Operating Income						
Operating Margin %						
SGA Expense						
Net Income				97,000,000	54,500,000	
Operating Cash Flow						
Capital Expenditure						
EBITDA						
Return on Assets %						
Return on Equity %						
Debt to Equity						

CONTACT INFORMATION:

Phone: 702-943-7777   Fax: 702-943-7778
Toll-Free: 800-927-7671
Address: 400 E. Stewart Ave., Las Vegas, NV 89101 United States

STOCK TICKER/OTHER:

Stock Ticker: Subsidiary   Exchange:
Employees: 1,441   Fiscal Year Ends: 12/31
Parent Company: Amazon.com Inc

SALARIES/BONUSES:

Top Exec. Salary: $ Bonus: $
Second Exec. Salary: $ Bonus: $

OTHER THOUGHTS:

Estimated Female Officers or Directors:
Hot Spot for Advancement for Women/Minorities:

Zillow Inc

NAIC Code: 519130

TYPES OF BUSINESS:

Online Real Estate Information

BRANDS/DIVISIONS/AFFILIATES:

Zillow
Trulia
StreetEasy
HotPads
Naked Apartments
Zestimates
Mortech
dotloop

CONTACTS: *Note: Officers with more than one job title may be intentionally listed here more than once.*

Spencer Rascoff, CEO
Allen Parker, CFO
Richard Barton, Chairman of the Board
Jennifer Rock, Chief Accounting Officer
Aimee Johnson, Chief Marketing Officer
David Beitel, Chief Technology Officer
Amy Bohutinsky, COO
Lloyd Frink, Director
Errol Samuelson, Other Executive Officer
Kathleen Philips, Other Executive Officer
Greg Schwartz, Other Executive Officer
Stanley Humphries, Other Executive Officer
Jeremy Wacksman, President, Divisional

GROWTH PLANS/SPECIAL FEATURES:

Zillow, Inc. operates a real estate information marketplace dedicated to providing information about homes, real estate listings and mortgages and enabling homeowners, buyers, sellers and renters to connect with real estate and mortgage professionals. The company maintains a database of over 110 million homes in the U.S. that are either for sale, for rent or not currently on the market. Individuals and businesses that use Zillow have updated information on more than 68 million homes and added millions of home photos, creating exclusive home profiles that are available nowhere else. These profiles include detailed information about homes, such as property descriptions, listing information and purchase and sale histories. Zillow's real estate and rental marketplaces comprise consumer brands such as Zillow, Trulia, StreetEasy, HotPads, Naked Apartments, RealEstate.com and OutEast.com. In conjunction with the database, the firm offers users its proprietary automated valuation models, Zestimates and Rent Zestimates, on more than 100 million homes. Zillow also owns and operates a number of brands for real estate and mortgage professionals, including Mortech, dotloop, Bridge Interactive and New Home Feed.

FINANCIAL DATA: *Note: Data for latest year may not have been available at press time.*

In U.S. $	2018	2017	2016	2015	2014	2013
Revenue		1,076,794,000	846,589,000	644,677,000	325,893,000	197,545,000
R&D Expense		319,985,000	273,066,000	198,565,000	86,406,000	48,498,000
Operating Income		12,589,000	-192,682,000	-93,036,000	-23,202,000	-16,949,000
Operating Margin %		1.16%	-22.75%	-14.43%	-7.11%	-8.57%
SGA Expense		659,017,000	694,614,000	477,534,000	233,228,000	147,186,000
Net Income		-94,420,000	-220,438,000	-148,874,000	-43,610,000	-12,453,000
Operating Cash Flow		258,191,000	8,645,000	22,659,000	45,519,000	31,298,000
Capital Expenditure		78,635,000	71,722,000	68,108,000	44,242,000	25,972,000
EBITDA		-46,334,000	-112,310,000	-72,644,000	12,422,000	6,305,000
Return on Assets %		-2.95%	-7.01%	-7.86%	-6.93%	-2.73%
Return on Equity %		-3.63%	-8.45%	-9.11%	-7.54%	-2.93%
Debt to Equity		0.14	0.14	0.08		

CONTACT INFORMATION:

Phone: 206 470-7000   Fax:
Toll-Free:
Address: 1301 Second Ave., Fl. 31, Seattle, WA 98101 United States

STOCK TICKER/OTHER:

Stock Ticker: Z   Exchange: NAS
Employees: 2,776   Fiscal Year Ends: 12/31
Parent Company:

SALARIES/BONUSES:

Top Exec. Salary: $717,286   Bonus: $
Second Exec. Salary: Bonus: $50,000
$484,380

OTHER THOUGHTS:

Estimated Female Officers or Directors: 2
Hot Spot for Advancement for Women/Minorities: Y

ZipRecruiter Inc

www.ziprecruiter.com

NAIC Code: 519130

TYPES OF BUSINESS:

Online Jobs Site

BRANDS/DIVISIONS/AFFILIATES:

ZipSearch
ZipAlerts
ZipPost

CONTACTS: *Note: Officers with more than one job title may be intentionally listed here more than once.*

Ian Siegel, CEO
Jeff Zwelling, COO
Dave Travers, CFO
Eyal Gutentag, CMO
Amy Klimek, Sr. VP-Human Resources
Craig Ogg, CTO

GROWTH PLANS/SPECIAL FEATURES:

ZipRecruiter, Inc. operates a web-based job recruitment platform and marketplace. The platform enables employers to post and manage job-related information, and for candidates to search job openings. More than 7 million active job seekers utilize the site each month, and over 40 million job alert emails are sent to subscribers via web and mobile app. More than 1 million employers have used ZipRecruiter to hire, and over 10,000 new companies subscribe every month. For job seekers, ZipRecruiter offers free accounts and features for searching and browsing available jobs, as well as testimonials. For employers, the site offers the ability to post jobs, distribute openings across various job boards, access resumes and read testimonials. Price plans for employers range from free to fee-based subscriptions. ZipRecruiter's publisher program is a partnership that enables partners to connect their audiences with the ZipRecruiter job marketplace. The firm's proprietary matching algorithm displays only the most relevant jobs in order to maximize partner earning potential. ZipAlerts are email notifications sent to job-/skill-specific seekers, and display the job opening as well as the employer's brand. Partners have the ability to block the jobs they no longer want sent. ZipPost is a referral program in which partners provide business owner referrals to ZipRecruiter, and ZipRecruiter will pay the partner for them.

ZipRecruiter offers its employees 100% health benefits, a 401(k), a bonus plan, flexible hours and time off, as well as other perks.

FINANCIAL DATA: *Note: Data for latest year may not have been available at press time.*

In U.S. $	2018	2017	2016	2015	2014	2013
Revenue						
R&D Expense						
Operating Income						
Operating Margin %						
SGA Expense						
Net Income						
Operating Cash Flow						
Capital Expenditure						
EBITDA						
Return on Assets %						
Return on Equity %						
Debt to Equity						

CONTACT INFORMATION:

Phone: Fax:
Toll-Free: 877-252-1062
Address: 401 Wilshire Blvd., Fl. 11, Santa Monica, CA 90401 United States

STOCK TICKER/OTHER:

Stock Ticker: Private   Exchange:
Employees: 400   Fiscal Year Ends:
Parent Company:

SALARIES/BONUSES:

Top Exec. Salary: $ Bonus: $
Second Exec. Salary: $ Bonus: $

OTHER THOUGHTS:

Estimated Female Officers or Directors:
Hot Spot for Advancement for Women/Minorities:

Zoho Corporation Private Limited

www.zoho.com

NAIC Code: 511210H

TYPES OF BUSINESS:

Enterprise Management Software
CRM Tools
Ecommerce Tools

BRANDS/DIVISIONS/AFFILIATES:

Zoho One
Zoho Expense
Zoho G Suite
PageSense
Zoho Flow

CONTACTS: Note: Officers with more than one job title may be intentionally listed here more than once.

Raj P. Sabhlok, Pres.

GROWTH PLANS/SPECIAL FEATURES:

Zoho Corporation Private Limited provides cloud-based enterprise information technology (IT) management software. The company's single platform, Zoho One, enables users to run a business completely from the cloud. Zoho's mobile apps are engineered for ease, speed and enhanced functionality to manage businesses from anywhere, anytime. Users can customize apps with Zoho's creator tool; manage the entire recruitment process through the app; create online reports via intelligent analytics; manage email campaigns; offer live chat to increase sales; improve customer service; manage invoices, track payments and upload expense receipts; invoice; and access and update expenses as well as inventory. The firm's apps cover sales and marketing, email and collaboration, business process, finance, IT, help desk, customer relations management and human resources solutions. Access to all the Zoho apps and Office 365 can occur at the same time by connecting Zoho to Office 365. The Zoho Expense app for Apple Watch offers mileage tracking, which can be followed and recorded directly from the watch. Mileage is automatically calculated through the global positioning system in the phone and recorded in Zoho Expense. Zoho's G Suite for work is a cloud-based business solution with over 70 integrations across more than 25 products. PageSense is a website optimization tool that includes heatmaps, funnel analysis and forecasting. Zoho Flow is a drag-and-drop integration platform that allows users to create workflows between cloud applications. Flow enables users to build workflows without having to know any line of code. Based in India, the firm has offices in the U.S., China, Japan, Singapore, Dubai and the Netherlands.

FINANCIAL DATA: Note: Data for latest year may not have been available at press time.

In U.S. $	2018	2017	2016	2015	2014	2013
Revenue		270,678,000	299,011,000	248,410,000		
R&D Expense						
Operating Income						
Operating Margin %						
SGA Expense						
Net Income		43,968,200	80,599,000			
Operating Cash Flow						
Capital Expenditure						
EBITDA						
Return on Assets %						
Return on Equity %						
Debt to Equity						

CONTACT INFORMATION:

Phone: 044-67447070   Fax: 044-67447172
Toll-Free:
Address: Estancia IT Park, Plot #140 & 151, GST Rd., Vallancherry Village, Kanchipuram District 603 202 India

STOCK TICKER/OTHER:

Stock Ticker: Private   Exchange:
Employees: 5,200   Fiscal Year Ends: 03/31
Parent Company:

SALARIES/BONUSES:

Top Exec. Salary: $ Bonus: $
Second Exec. Salary: $ Bonus: $

OTHER THOUGHTS:

Estimated Female Officers or Directors:
Hot Spot for Advancement for Women/Minorities:

Zoom Video Communications Inc

NAIC Code: 511210C

TYPES OF BUSINESS:

Computer Software, Telecom, Communications & VOIP

BRANDS/DIVISIONS/AFFILIATES:

CONTACTS: *Note: Officers with more than one job title may be intentionally listed here more than once.*

Eric S. Yuan, CEO
Kelly Steckelberg, CFO
Marta Paul, Head-Human Resources
Harry D. Moseley, CIO

GROWTH PLANS/SPECIAL FEATURES:

Zoom Video Communications, Inc. designs and develops cloud-based video and web conferencing software. Zoom's software unifies cloud video conferencing, online meetings, group messaging and conference room solutions into one simple-to-use platform. The company's solutions work across multiple room systems. Zoom's software conferencing application program interface (API) runs within a business conference room or workspace. Cloud video conferencing features include HD video and voice, full-screen with gallery views, dual stream/dual screen, feature-rich mobile apps, and various ways to join the conferences (Zoom Room, view-only, voice only and more). Zoom products are secure, with secure socket layer encryption, AES 256-bits encryption, HTTPS access, role-based access control features and administration control features. The firm also offers a hybrid cloud service with 24/7 online monitoring and instant global service backup. Partner integrations provide content sharing, scheduling/starting meetings, unified log-in, marketing/process automation and room collaboration. Pricing plans range from free to $100 per month, among other options. Zoom is headquartered in San Jose, California, with additional U.S. offices in California, Colorado and Kansas, as well as international offices in Sydney, London, Paris and Amsterdam.

FINANCIAL DATA: *Note: Data for latest year may not have been available at press time.*

In U.S. $	2018	2017	2016	2015	2014	2013
Revenue						
R&D Expense						
Operating Income						
Operating Margin %						
SGA Expense						
Net Income						
Operating Cash Flow						
Capital Expenditure						
EBITDA						
Return on Assets %						
Return on Equity %						
Debt to Equity						

CONTACT INFORMATION:

Phone: 650-397-6096   Fax:
Toll-Free: 888-799-9666
Address: 55 Almaden Blvd., Fl. 6, San Jose, CA 95113 United States

STOCK TICKER/OTHER:

Stock Ticker: Private   Exchange:
Employees: 390   Fiscal Year Ends:
Parent Company:

SALARIES/BONUSES:

Top Exec. Salary: $ Bonus: $
Second Exec. Salary: $ Bonus: $

OTHER THOUGHTS:

Estimated Female Officers or Directors:
Hot Spot for Advancement for Women/Minorities:

Zscaler Inc

www.zscaler.com

NAIC Code: 511210E

TYPES OF BUSINESS:
Computer Software, Security & Anti-Virus

BRANDS/DIVISIONS/AFFILIATES:
Zscaler Internet Access
Zscaler Private Access
Zscaler App

CONTACTS:
Note: Officers with more than one job title may be intentionally listed here more than once.

Jagtar Chaudhry, CEO
Remo Canessa, CFO
Amit Sinha, Chief Technology Officer
Manoj Apte, Other Executive Officer
Robert Schlossman, Other Executive Officer

GROWTH PLANS/SPECIAL FEATURES:
Zscaler, Inc. operates a cloud-based internet security platform. Its flagship services, Zscaler Internet Access and Zscaler Private Access, create fast, secure connections between users and applications, regardless of device, location or network. The firm's services are 100% cloud delivered and offer simple, enhanced security and optimal user experience. Zscaler is used in more than 192 countries via its global cloud security platform that protects thousands of enterprises and government agencies from cyberattacks and data loss. Its proprietary, multi-tenant cloud architecture is distributed across more than 100 data centers on six continents. The firm's security-as-a-service enables full secure sockets layer (SSL) inspection. In addition, the Zscaler App works with Zscaler Internet Access to deliver the full security stack from the cloud, providing mobile users in-depth, always-on protection. The app also works with Zscaler Private Access to enable remote access to Asure, Amazon Web Services and data center apps without the use of a virtual private network (VPN). The company is headquartered in California, USA, with additional offices in New York and Virginia, and internationally in the U.K., the Netherlands, Germany, France, India, Australia and Singapore. In August 2018, Zscaler acquired the artificial intelligence (AI) Team and AI Technology of TrustPath, an internet security startup.

FINANCIAL DATA:
Note: Data for latest year may not have been available at press time.

In U.S. $	2018	2017	2016	2015	2014	2013
Revenue	190,174,000	125,717,000	80,325,000	53,707,000		
R&D Expense	39,379,000	33,561,000	20,940,000	15,034,000		
Operating Income	-34,624,000	-35,073,000	-26,843,000	-12,418,000		
Operating Margin %		-27.89%	-33.41%	-23.12%		
SGA Expense	147,544,000	99,757,000	66,101,000	36,660,000		
Net Income	-33,646,000	-35,460,000	-27,438,000	-12,832,000		
Operating Cash Flow	17,307,000	-6,019,000	-11,916,000	-3,279,000		
Capital Expenditure	15,170,000	8,174,000	6,247,000	6,705,000		
EBITDA	-26,636,000	-28,233,000	-21,971,000	-9,564,000		
Return on Assets %		-21.08%	-23.50%			
Return on Equity %						
Debt to Equity						

CONTACT INFORMATION:
Phone: 408-533-0288   Fax:
Toll-Free:
Address: 110 Rose Orchard Way, San Jose, CA 95134 United States

STOCK TICKER/OTHER:
Stock Ticker: ZS   Exchange: NAS
Employees: 950   Fiscal Year Ends: 07/31
Parent Company:

SALARIES/BONUSES:
Top Exec. Salary: $300,000   Bonus: $
Second Exec. Salary: Bonus: $
$300,000

OTHER THOUGHTS:
Estimated Female Officers or Directors:
Hot Spot for Advancement for Women/Minorities:

Zulily LLC

www.zulily.com

NAIC Code: 454111

TYPES OF BUSINESS:

Apparel
Online Women's and Children's Clothing

BRANDS/DIVISIONS/AFFILIATES:

Qurate Retail Group
QVC Inc

GROWTH PLANS/SPECIAL FEATURES:

Zulily, LLC is an online provider of discount children's and infants' clothing, accessories, toys, shoes and books; women's and maternity clothing, shoes and accessories; and home items, including flower order discounts, picture frames and kitchenware. The site offers 50-60 new sales events daily with discounts of up to 90% off. Sales, called events, last 72 hours before the offers end and are replaced with another brand's products. The site's users receive email newsletters alerting them of new offers and, from their mobile devices, can mark brands as their favorites and can choose to be notified if a discontinued offer becomes available again. Zulily ships internationally to over 100 countries. Zulily recently (late-2017) launched its first private label credit card in partnership with Synchrony, which will allow cardholders to utilize Smart-pay, a flexible payment option. The firm operates as a subsidiary of QVC, Inc., which itself is owned by Qurate Retail Group.

CONTACTS: Note: Officers with more than one job title may be intentionally listed here more than once.

Jeff Yurcisin, Pres.
Luke T. Friang, CIO
Deirdre Runnette, General Counsel
Lori Twomey, Other Executive Officer
Darrell Cavens, President
David Atchison, Senior VP, Divisional
Brian Swartz, Senior VP
Tad Larsen, Vice President, Divisional

FINANCIAL DATA: Note: Data for latest year may not have been available at press time.

In U.S. $	2018	2017	2016	2015	2014	2013
Revenue	1,565,000,000	1,500,000,000	1,400,000,000	1,030,177,000	1,200,078,976	695,708,992
R&D Expense						
Operating Income						
Operating Margin %						
SGA Expense						
Net Income						
Operating Cash Flow						
Capital Expenditure						
EBITDA						
Return on Assets %						
Return on Equity %						
Debt to Equity						

CONTACT INFORMATION:

Phone: 877-779-5615   Fax: 206-724-0534
Toll-Free: 877-779-5614
Address: 2601 Elliott Ave., Ste. 200, Seattle, WA 98121 United States

STOCK TICKER/OTHER:

Stock Ticker: Subsidiary   Exchange:
Employees: 2,907   Fiscal Year Ends:
Parent Company: Qurate Retail Group

SALARIES/BONUSES:

Top Exec. Salary: $ Bonus: $
Second Exec. Salary: $ Bonus: $

OTHER THOUGHTS:

Estimated Female Officers or Directors: 3
Hot Spot for Advancement for Women/Minorities: Y

Zuora Inc

www.zuora.com

NAIC Code: 522320

TYPES OF BUSINESS:

Recurring Billing Software Tools
Subscription Management Tools
Online Billing and Subscription Tools
Games and Apps Subscription Tools

BRANDS/DIVISIONS/AFFILIATES:

Zuora Central

CONTACTS: Note: Officers with more than one job title may be intentionally listed here more than once.

Tien Tzuo, CEO
Marc Diouane, Pres.
Tyler Sloat, CFO
David Gee, CMO
Brent Cromley, Sr. VP-IT
Guillaume Vives, Sr. VP-Prod. Mgmt.
Marc Aronson, Sr. VP-Eng.
Marc Diouane, Exec. VP-Field Oper.
Stuart Laidlaw, VP-Bus. Dev.
Richard Terry-Lloyd, VP-Emerging Markets
Todd Pearson, Sr. VP-Customer Success
Keith Costello, Sr. VP-Global Svcs.

GROWTH PLANS/SPECIAL FEATURES:

Zuora, Inc. is a cloud-based enterprise software developer offering an online platform for businesses to build, operate and maintain subscription and recurring revenue activities. The firm helps companies across numerous industries to develop and monetize subscription-based business models, whether on a periodic subscription or per-usage basis. Industries served by Zuora include cloud application, cloud infrastructure, communication, media, education, healthcare, Internet of Things and business-to-consumer. Its Zuora Central platform covers all aspects of a subscription process, from pricing, launch and quoting to ordering, billing, payments and renewals. Zuora offers a number of software tools and products to support the growing market for subscription-based services in the following areas: subscription management, multi-channel commerce, subscription quoting, recurring billing, global payments, recurring revenue, analytics and technology. The company has also developed specific comprehensive systems for several market sectors, including providers of cloud-based services, telecom service providers and media publishers such as newspapers. Zuora is headquartered in California, with satellite offices throughout North America, Europe, China, Japan and Australia.

FINANCIAL DATA: Note: Data for latest year may not have been available at press time.

In U.S. $	2018	2017	2016	2015	2014	2013
Revenue		115,000,000	110,000,000	100,000,000		
R&D Expense						
Operating Income						
Operating Margin %						
SGA Expense						
Net Income						
Operating Cash Flow						
Capital Expenditure						
EBITDA						
Return on Assets %						
Return on Equity %						
Debt to Equity						

CONTACT INFORMATION:

Phone: 650-241-4508   Fax:
Toll-Free: 800-425-1281
Address: 3050 S. Delaware St., Ste. 301, San Mateo, CA 94403 United States

STOCK TICKER/OTHER:

Stock Ticker: Private
Employees: 630
Parent Company:

Exchange:
Fiscal Year Ends: 01/21

SALARIES/BONUSES:

Top Exec. Salary: $ Bonus: $
Second Exec. Salary: $ Bonus: $

OTHER THOUGHTS:

Estimated Female Officers or Directors:
Hot Spot for Advancement for Women/Minorities:

Zynga Inc

NAIC Code: 511210G

TYPES OF BUSINESS:

Computer Software, Electronic Games, Apps & Entertainment
Social Media Gaming
Apps

BRANDS/DIVISIONS/AFFILIATES:

FarmVille
Words with Friends
Zynga Poker
Games for Good at Zynga

CONTACTS: *Note: Officers with more than one job title may be intentionally listed here more than once.*

Gerard Griffin, CFO
Mark Pincus, Chairman of the Board
Jeffrey Buckley, Chief Accounting Officer
Matthew Bromberg, COO
Frank Gibeau, Director
Phuong Phillips, Other Executive Officer
Jeffrey Ryan, Other Executive Officer
Bernard Kim, President, Divisional

GROWTH PLANS/SPECIAL FEATURES:

Zynga, Inc. is a leading developer of online social games for social media sites, online networks and mobile devices. The company's games are hosted on a variety of social networks including Facebook. Its products include casino games, word games, board games, role playing games and party games. Zynga's most successful games include FarmVille, FarmVille 2, Words with Friends and Zynga Poker. The company also administers Games for Good at Zynga, which donates money and educational goods to international nonprofits. The firm has received funding from Kleiner Perkins Caufield & Beyers, Foundry Group, Union Square Ventures, Institutional Venture Partners, Avalon Ventures, SoftBank and The Pilot Group. More than 64 million consumers play Zynga's games each month.In December 2017, the firm acquired the mobile card game studio of Peak Games, a leading global mobile gaming company.

FINANCIAL DATA: *Note: Data for latest year may not have been available at press time.*

In U.S. $	2018	2017	2016	2015	2014	2013
Revenue		861,390,000	741,420,000	764,717,000	690,410,000	873,266,000
R&D Expense		256,012,000	320,300,000	361,931,000	396,553,000	413,001,000
Operating Income		25,724,000	-93,572,000	-146,056,000	-244,741,000	-55,414,000
Operating Margin %		2.98%	-12.62%	-19.09%	-35.44%	-6.34%
SGA Expense		320,683,000	276,146,000	312,857,000	325,028,000	267,321,000
Net Income		26,639,000	-108,173,000	-121,510,000	-225,900,000	-36,982,000
Operating Cash Flow		94,577,000	60,016,000	-44,447,000	-4,511,000	28,674,000
Capital Expenditure		9,971,000	10,313,000	7,832,000	9,201,000	7,813,000
EBITDA		56,018,000	-51,802,000	-91,741,000	-161,847,000	73,633,000
Return on Assets %		1.37%	-5.36%	-5.43%	-9.76%	-1.52%
Return on Equity %		1.65%	-6.42%	-6.59%	-11.97%	-1.99%
Debt to Equity						

CONTACT INFORMATION:

Phone: 800 762-2530   Fax:
Toll-Free:
Address: 699 8th St., San Francisco, CA 94103 United States

STOCK TICKER/OTHER:

Stock Ticker: ZNGA   Exchange: NAS
Employees: 1,681   Fiscal Year Ends: 12/31
Parent Company:

SALARIES/BONUSES:

Top Exec. Salary: $1,000,000   Bonus: $
Second Exec. Salary: Bonus: $
$500,000

OTHER THOUGHTS:

Estimated Female Officers or Directors: 2
Hot Spot for Advancement for Women/Minorities:

ADDITIONAL INDEXES

CONTENTS:

INDEX OF FIRMS NOTED AS HOT SPOTS FOR ADVANCEMENT FOR WOMEN & MINORITIES

NeuStar Inc
New York Times Company (The)
News Corporation
NIC Inc
Oclaro Inc
Open Text Corporation
OpenTable Inc
Oracle Corporation
Oracle NetSuite
Orbitz Worldwide Inc
Overstock.com Inc
Ozon.ru
Pandora Media Inc
PayPal Holdings Inc
Performics Inc
Photobucket Inc
Pinterest Inc
Progress Software Corporation
Radware Ltd
REA Group Ltd
RealNetworks Inc
RealPage Inc
Red Hat Inc
Renren Inc
Rogers Communications Inc
SalesForce.com Inc
Salon Media Group Inc
SAP SE
Shaw Communications Inc
Skype Technologies Sarl
Sohu.com Inc
SugarCRM
SVMK Inc (SurveyMonkey)
Symantec Corporation
TD Ameritrade Holding Corporation
Telenor ASA
Telephone and Data Systems Inc (TDS)
Tellabs Inc
Teradata Corporation
TheStreet Inc
Thomson Reuters Corporation
Total System Services Inc (TSYS)
Travelzoo Inc
Trend Micro Inc
TripAdvisor Inc
Twitter Inc
Ushahidi Inc
VeriFone Systems Inc (Verifone)
Verizon Communications Inc
Verizon Media Group
VerticalResponse Inc
Vibrant Media Inc
VitaCost.com Inc
Vodafone Group plc
Walt Disney Company (The)
Wayfair LLC
Web.com Group Inc
WebMD Health Corp

Wikimedia Foundation
Windstream Holdings Inc
Wipro Limited
Xaxis
XO Communications LLC
XO Group Inc
Yandex NV
Yelp Inc
YesMail.com Inc
YOOX Net-A-Porter Group SpA (YNAP)
Zillow Inc
Zulily LLC

INDEX OF SUBSIDIARIES, BRAND NAMES AND AFFILIATIONS

INDEX OF SUBSIDIARIES, BRAND NAMES AND AFFILIATIONS, CONT.

Altice Business; **Altice USA Inc**
Altice Media Solutions; **Altice USA Inc**
Altice NV; **Altice USA Inc**
Always On; **Crackle Inc (dba SonyCrackle)**
AM Holding Inc; **Alibris Inc**
Amadeus Altea Suite; **Amadeus IT Group SA**
Amadeus IT Holding SA; **Amadeus IT Group SA**
Amadeus.net; **Amadeus IT Group SA**
Amazon EC2; **Amazon Web Services Inc (AWS)**
Amazon Go; **Amazon.com Inc**
Amazon Marketplace; **Amazon.com Inc**
Amazon Prime; **Amazon.com Inc**
Amazon Web Services (AWS); **Amazon.com Inc**
Amazon.com Inc; **AbeBooks Inc**
Amazon.com Inc; **Amazon Web Services Inc (AWS)**
Amazon.com Inc; **Audible Inc**
Amazon.com Inc; **Zappos.com Inc**
Amblin Partners; **Comcast Corporation**
America Movil SAB de CV; **Telecomunicaciones de Puerto Rico Inc**
American Greetings Corporation LLC; **AG Interactive Inc**
American Natural Gas; **HC2 Holdings Inc**
Americanas.com; **B2W-Companhia Global Do Varejo**
AmericanGreetings.com; **AG Interactive Inc**
AmericanGreetings.com; **American Greetings Corporation LLC**
AncestryDNA; **Ancestry.com LLC**
AncestryProGenealogists; **Ancestry.com LLC**
Android; **Alphabet Inc (Google)**
ANGI Homeservices Inc; **IAC/InterActiveCorp**
Angie's List; **ANGI Homeservices Inc**
Angie's List; **IAC/InterActiveCorp**
Answers Corporation; **ForeSee Results Inc**
Anycast; **Cloudflare Inc**
Anypoint Design Center; **MuleSoft LLC**
Anypoint Management Center; **MuleSoft LLC**
Anypoint Platform; **MuleSoft LLC**
Aol; **Verizon Media Group**
AOL Inc; **MapQuest.com Inc**
Apalon; **IAC/InterActiveCorp**
Apartments.com; **CoStar Group Inc**
Aperture LLC; **E*Trade Financial Corporation**
Apollo Global Management LLC; **Rackspace Hosting Inc**
Apollo Global Management LLC; **CareerBuilder Inc**
Apollo OPT; **ECI Telecom Ltd**
App Annie Connect; **App Annie Limited**
App iQ; **AppDynamics Inc**
AppBilling; **AppDirect Inc**
AppDevices; **AppDirect Inc**
AppDistribution; **AppDirect Inc**
AppDynamics Inc; **Cisco Systems Inc**
AppGate Insight; **Cyxtera Technologies Inc**
AppGate SDP; **Cyxtera Technologies Inc**
AppHelp; **AppDirect Inc**
AppInsights; **AppDirect Inc**
Apple TV; **Apple Inc**

Apple Watch; **Apple Inc**
Application Delivery Controller; **Radware Ltd**
AppMarket; **AppDirect Inc**
AppNexus Publisher; **AppNexus Inc**
AppReserller; **AppDirect Inc**
Appthority; **Symantec Corporation**
AppWall; **Radware Ltd**
AppWise; **AppDirect Inc**
Aptrinsic; **Gainsight Inc**
Apttus Omni; **Apttus Corporation**
Aquiire; **Coupa Software Inc**
Archives.com; **Ancestry.com LLC**
Argo Smart Routing; **Cloudflare Inc**
Ariba Network; **Ariba Inc**
Arista cEOS; **Arista Networks Inc**
Armani.com; **YOOX Net-A-Porter Group SpA (YNAP)**
ARO-Vitacost; **VitaCost.com Inc**
ARTISTdirect; **PSI Capital Inc**
ARTISTdirect Opportunity Fund; **PSI Capital Inc**
Ashmore Group plc; **ECI Telecom Ltd**
ASOS Black; **ASOS plc**
ASOS Curve; **ASOS plc**
ASOS Maternity; **ASOS plc**
ASOS Swim; **ASOS plc**
ASOS Tall; **ASOS plc**
ASOS White; **ASOS plc**
Assurance Wireless; **Sprint Corporation**
At Bat; **Major League Baseball Advanced Media LP (MLBAM)**
AT&T; **Hulu LLC**
AT&T Inc; **AppNexus Inc**
AT&T Inc; **DirecTV LLC (DIRECTV)**
AT&T Inc; **AlienVault Inc**
Athenahealth Inc; **Epocrates Inc**
Atos; **Atos SE**
Atos Worldgrid; **Atos SE**
au; **KDDI Corporation**
au HIKARI; **KDDI Corporation**
au Smart Pass; **KDDI Corporation**
au Smart Value; **KDDI Corporation**
au Smart Value; **KDDI Corporation**
Auction Video; **Onstream Media Corporation**
Audax Group; **Rogue Wave Software Inc**
Audible.com; **Audible Inc**
AudibleListener; **Audible Inc**
Authorize.net Payment Gateway; **Authorize.Net Holdings Inc**
Auto.com; **Cars.com Inc**
Auto.ru; **Yandex NV**
Autobytel Inc; **AutoWeb Inc**
Autobytel.com; **AutoWeb Inc**
Autohome Mall; **Autohome Inc**
autohome.com.cn; **Autohome Inc**
Autotrader; **Cox Automotive Inc**
AWG-WIFI; **Boingo Wireless Inc**
AWS Free Tier; **Amazon Web Services Inc (AWS)**

INDEX OF SUBSIDIARIES, BRAND NAMES AND AFFILIATIONS, CONT.

INDEX OF SUBSIDIARIES, BRAND NAMES AND AFFILIATIONS, CONT.

INDEX OF SUBSIDIARIES, BRAND NAMES AND AFFILIATIONS, CONT.

INDEX OF SUBSIDIARIES, BRAND NAMES AND AFFILIATIONS, CONT.

INDEX OF SUBSIDIARIES, BRAND NAMES AND AFFILIATIONS, CONT.

INDEX OF SUBSIDIARIES, BRAND NAMES AND AFFILIATIONS, CONT.

Hightail Inc; **Open Text Corporation**
Hikari Tsushin Inc; **E-machitown Co Ltd**
Hiperos; **Coupa Software Inc**
Home Box Office Inc (HBO); **AT&T Inc**
Home.pl; **United Internet AG**
HomeAdvisor; **ANGI Homeservices Inc**
HomeAway Inc; **Expedia Inc**
HomeAway.co.uk; **HomeAway Inc**
HomeAway.com; **HomeAway Inc**
HomeAway.de; **HomeAway Inc**
HomeAway.es; **HomeAway Inc**
HomePod; **Apple Inc**
HomeStars; **ANGI Homeservices Inc**
Honest Beauty; **Honest Company Inc (The)**
honestbeauty.com; **Honest Company Inc (The)**
Hoover's Handbooks; **Hoover's Inc**
HostAccess; **Rogue Wave Software Inc**
Hotels.com Rewards; **Hotels.com LP**
Hotelscan; **lastminute.com NV (lm holding)**
HotPads; **Zillow Inc**
Hotwire.com; **Expedia Inc**
Hotwire.com; **Hotwire Inc**
Houserie; **Overstock.com Inc**
Houzz Shop; **Houzz Inc**
Houzz.com; **Houzz Inc**
Hover.com; **Tucows Inc**
HSN; **Qurate Retail Inc**
HSN Inc; **Qurate Retail Inc**
Huaewi Matebook; **Huawei Technologies Co Ltd**
Huawei Marine Networks; **Huawei Technologies Co Ltd**
Huawei TalkBand; **Huawei Technologies Co Ltd**
Huawei Watch; **Huawei Technologies Co Ltd**
Huizenga Capital Management; **SMS Assist LLC**
Hulu with Live TV; **Hulu LLC**
Hunza Inc; **mixi Inc**
IAC Films; **IAC/InterActiveCorp**
IAC/InterActiveCorp; **ANGI Homeservices Inc**
IAC/InterActiveCorp; **Dotdash**
IAC/InterActiveCorp; **Match Group Inc**
IAC/InterActiveCorp; **Vimeo LLC**
iApps; **F5 Networks Inc**
IberLibros.com; **AbeBooks Inc**
IBFX Inc; **TradeStation Group Inc**
Ibibo Group Holdings (Singapore) Pte Ltd; **MakeMyTrip Limited**
Ibibo Group Private Limited; **MakeMyTrip Limited**
IBM POWER9; **IBM Technology Services & Cloud Platforms**
IBM Research; **IBM Technology Services & Cloud Platforms**
iCall; **F5 Networks Inc**
iCIMS Connect; **iCIMS Inc**
iCIMS Offer; **iCIMS Inc**
iCIMS Onboard; **iCIMS Inc**
iCIMS Recruit; **iCIMS Inc**

iCIMS UNIFi; **iCIMS Inc**
iControl; **AutoWeb Inc**
iControl; **F5 Networks Inc**
ID Analytics Inc; **LifeLock Inc**
IdentityLink; **LiveRamp Holdings Inc**
Idera Inc; **Embarcadero Technologies Inc**
IDT Corporation; **Net2Phone Inc**
iFound; **ProQuest LLC**
IGTV; **Instagram**
IIJ ISDN/F; **Internet Initiative Japan Inc**
IIJ Line Management/F; **Internet Initiative Japan Inc**
Illumio Adaptive Security Platform; **Illumio**
i-mercury Capital Inc; **mixi Inc**
Immunity Inc; **Cyxtera Technologies Inc**
iMobile3; **Total System Services Inc (TSYS)**
INAP; **Internap Corporation**
In-Article; **Vibrant Media Inc**
InDemand; **Indiegogo Inc**
IndentiKey; **OneSpan Inc**
Industries; **SalesForce.com Inc**
InfiniStream; **NetScout Systems Inc**
InfoGROUP Inc; **YesMail.com Inc**
Infomart Dallas; **Equinix Inc**
Infor CloudSuite; **Infor**
Infor Coleman; **Infor**
Infor UpgradeX; **Infor**
In-Image; **Vibrant Media Inc**
InMobi Advertising Cloud; **InMobi Pte Ltd**
InMobi Marketing Cloud; **InMobi Pte Ltd**
Inovalon Holdings Inc; **ABILITY Network Inc**
Insight Venture Partners; **SMS Assist LLC**
Instagram; **Facebook Inc**
Instagram Stories; **Instagram**
Instapro; **ANGI Homeservices Inc**
Intel Corporation; **McAfee LLC**
IntelliBase; **Teradata Corporation**
IntelliFlex; **Teradata Corporation**
Interactive Data Managed Solutions; **FactSet Research Systems Inc**
InterBase; **Embarcadero Technologies Inc**
Interflora; **FTD Companies Inc**
International Business Machines Corporation (IBM); **IBM Global Services**
International Business Machines Corporation (IBM); **IBM Technology Services & Cloud Platforms**
Internet Brands Inc; **WebMD Health Corp**
Intota; **ProQuest LLC**
Intralinks VIA Elite; **Intralinks Inc**
Intralinks VIA Pro; **Intralinks Inc**
Intralinks Virtual Data Room; **Intralinks Inc**
Intuit Tax Freedom Project; **Intuit Inc**
iOS; **Apple Inc**
IoT Blackbox; **SK Telecom Co Ltd**
IoT Cloud; **SalesForce.com Inc**
iPad; **Apple Inc**

INDEX OF SUBSIDIARIES, BRAND NAMES AND AFFILIATIONS, CONT.

INDEX OF SUBSIDIARIES, BRAND NAMES AND AFFILIATIONS, CONT.

Longreads; **Automattic Inc**
LookSmart Network; **LookSmart Group Inc**
LookSmart Publisher Solutions; **LookSmart Group Inc**
LoopNet; **CoStar Group Inc**
LoveScout24; **Match Group Inc**
LTE-M; **Rogers Communications Inc**
Luxury Tours & Travel Pte Ltd; **MakeMyTrip Limited**
Luxury Tours (Malaysia) Sdn Bhd; **MakeMyTrip Limited**
Madison Paper Industries; **New York Times Company (The)**
MailChimp; **MailChimp (The Rocket Science Group LLC)**
MainConcept; **NeuLion Inc**
MajesticAthletic.com; **Fanatics Inc**
MakeMyTrip (India) Private Limited; **MakeMyTrip Limited**
MakeMyTrip Inc; **MakeMyTrip Limited**
Managed IP PBX; **Cox Communications Inc**
Mansion Global; **MarketWatch Inc**
Map iQ; **AppDynamics Inc**
Maplebear Inc; **Instacart**
MapQuest Developers Network; **MapQuest.com Inc**
MapQuest Enterprise Solutions; **MapQuest.com Inc**
MapQuest Gas Prices; **MapQuest.com Inc**
MapQuest Mobile; **MapQuest.com Inc**
MapQuest Route Planner; **MapQuest.com Inc**
MapR Data Platform; **MapR Technologies Inc**
MapR-DB; **MapR Technologies Inc**
MapR-Edge; **MapR Technologies Inc**
MapR-ES; **MapR Technologies Inc**
MapR-XD; **MapR Technologies Inc**
Maps; **Alphabet Inc (Google)**
Marchex Audience Targeting; **Marchex Inc**
Marchex Call Analytics; **Marchex Inc**
Marchex Call Marketplace; **Marchex Inc**
Marchex Innovation Development Lab; **Marchex Inc**
Marchex Omnichannel Analytics Cloud; **Marchex Inc**
Market Data Intelligence; **App Annie Limited**
Marketing Cloud; **Digitas**
Marketing Cloud; **SalesForce.com Inc**
Marketo Inc; **Adobe Systems Inc**
MarketPlace365.com; **Onstream Media Corporation**
MarketWatch; **Dow Jones & Company Inc**
MarketWatch Weekend; **MarketWatch Inc**
MarketWatch.com Radio Network; **MarketWatch Inc**
Marktplaats; **eBay Inc**
Marlin Equity Partners LLC; **Tellabs Inc**
Marvel; **Walt Disney Company (The)**
Mary & Martha; **Hallmark Cards Inc**
Mass Effect; **Electronic Arts Inc (EA)**
Match; **Match Group Inc**
Match Group Inc; **IAC/InterActiveCorp**
MatrixNet; **Yandex NV**
Maven; **LivePerson Inc**
Max; **Apttus Corporation**

Medallia Experience Cloud; **Medallia Inc**
Mediachain; **Spotify Technology SA**
MediaWiki; **Wikimedia Foundation**
Medicare.com; **EHealth Inc**
MedicineNet.com; **WebMD Health Corp**
Medicity; **Health Catalyst**
Medscape; **Internet Brands Inc**
Medscape; **WebMD Health Corp**
Meituan.com; **Meituan Dianping**
MenuPages; **GrubHub Inc**
MercadoCredito; **MercadoLibre Inc**
MercadoEnvios; **MercadoLibre Inc**
MercadoLibre Classifieds Service; **MercadoLibre Inc**
MercadoLibre Marketplace; **MercadoLibre Inc**
MercadoPago; **MercadoLibre Inc**
MercadoShops; **MercadoLibre Inc**
Mercury NFV; **ECI Telecom Ltd**
Meredith Corporation; **Myspace LLC**
MessageBroker; **BluJay Solutions Ltd**
Messenger; **Facebook Inc**
Metronode; **Equinix Inc**
MetroPCS; **T-Mobile US Inc**
mHelpDesk; **ANGI Homeservices Inc**
Microsoft Corporation; **GitHub Inc**
Microsoft Corporation; **LinkedIn Corporation**
Microsoft Corporation; **Skype Technologies Sarl**
MindMeld; **Cisco Systems Inc**
Minjar Inc; **Nutanix Inc**
Mint; **Intuit Inc**
mixi America Inc; **mixi Inc**
mixi recruitment Inc; **mixi Inc**
Mobage; **DeNA Co Ltd**
Mobaoku; **DeNA Co Ltd**
Mobike; **Meituan Dianping**
Mobile Learning; **Blackboard Inc**
Mobile TeleSystems LLC; **Mobile TeleSystems PJSC**
Mobile.de; **eBay Inc**
MobileSTAR; **BluJay Solutions Ltd**
Modulus; **Progress Software Corporation**
ModusLink Corporation; **Steel Connect Inc**
ModusLink Global Solutions Inc; **Steel Connect Inc**
ModusLink PTS Inc; **Steel Connect Inc**
Moment; **Verizon Communications Inc**
Moncler; **YOOX Net-A-Porter Group SpA (YNAP)**
MONET Technologies Corporation; **SoftBank Group Corp**
Monex Group Inc; **TradeStation Group Inc**
Moneyish; **MarketWatch Inc**
MongoDB Atlas; **MongoDB Inc**
MongoDB Charts; **MongoDB Inc**
MongoDB Compass; **MongoDB Inc**
MongoDB Connector for Apache Spark; **MongoDB Inc**
MongoDB Enterprise Advanced; **MongoDB Inc**
MongoDB Mobile; **MongoDB Inc**
MongoDB Ops Manager; **MongoDB Inc**

INDEX OF SUBSIDIARIES, BRAND NAMES AND AFFILIATIONS, CONT.

INDEX OF SUBSIDIARIES, BRAND NAMES AND AFFILIATIONS, CONT.

INDEX OF SUBSIDIARIES, BRAND NAMES AND AFFILIATIONS, CONT.

INDEX OF SUBSIDIARIES, BRAND NAMES AND AFFILIATIONS, CONT.

INDEX OF SUBSIDIARIES, BRAND NAMES AND AFFILIATIONS, CONT.

INDEX OF SUBSIDIARIES, BRAND NAMES AND AFFILIATIONS, CONT.

Titanfall; **Electronic Arts Inc (EA)**
Tmall.com; **Alibaba Group Holding Limited**
T-Mobile; **T-Mobile US Inc**
T-Mobile International AG; **T-Mobile US Inc**
Top Producer; **Move Inc (Realtor.com)**
TPC Capital; **Avaya Holdings Corp**
TradeStation; **TradeStation Group Inc**
TradeStation Europe Limited; **TradeStation Group Inc**
TradeStation Securities inc; **TradeStation Group Inc**
TradeStation Technologies Inc; **TradeStation Group Inc**
TradingApp; **TradeStation Group Inc**
TRAMS; **Sabre Travel Network**
Translation Workspace; **Lionbridge Technologies Inc**
Travelocity; **Expedia Inc**
Travelscape LLC; **Travelocity.com LP**
Travelzoo Network; **Travelzoo Inc**
Travelzoo Top 20; **Travelzoo Inc**
Trip Huddle; **KAYAK**
Trip Savvy; **Dotdash**
Trip Watcher; **Hotwire Inc**
TripAdvisor Business Advantage; **TripAdvisor Inc**
TripAdvisor Premium for Restaurants; **TripAdvisor Inc**
tripadvisor.com; **TripAdvisor Inc**
TripHappy; **trivago NV**
TriPlay Communications Ltd; **eMusic.com Inc**
TripStarter; **Hotwire Inc**
trivago GmbH; **Expedia Inc**
trivago.com; **trivago NV**
TrueCar Certified Dealer; **TrueCar Inc**
TrueCar.com; **TrueCar Inc**
TrueLease; **TrueCar Inc**
TrueLoan; **TrueCar Inc**
TrueTrade; **TrueCar Inc**
Trulia; **Zillow Inc**
Trust Networks Inc; **Internet Initiative Japan Inc**
TSG Consumer Partners LLC; **BackCountry.com**
Tudou; **Youku Tudou Inc**
Turbo; **Intuit Inc**
Turbo Tax; **Intuit Inc**
Turner Broadcasting System Inc; **AT&T Inc**
tv.sohu.com; **Sohu.com Inc**
Tweets; **Twitter Inc**
Twilio Connect; **Twilio Inc**
Twiter.com; **Twitter Inc**
Twitterers; **Twitter Inc**
Two Of You Together (The); **eHarmony Inc**
Twoo; **Match Group Inc**
Typany Keyboard; **Sogou Inc**
Uber Air; **Uber Inc**
Uber for Business; **Uber Inc**
Uber Freight; **Uber Inc**
UberEATS; **Uber Inc**
UiTV; **UTStarcom Inc**
Unata; **Instacart**
Unified Security Management; **AlienVault Inc**

Unified Spend Suite; **Coupa Software Inc**
Unify; **Atos SE**
United Internet Media; **United Internet AG**
United States Cellular Corporation; **Telephone and Data Systems Inc (TDS)**
united-domains; **United Internet AG**
Unitymedia; **Liberty Global plc**
UPC; **Liberty Global plc**
US Bancorp; **Elavon Inc**
Ushahidi Platform; **Ushahidi Inc**
USI Customer Management Platform; **US Interactive Inc**
USM Anywhere; **AlienVault Inc**
V LIVE; **Naver Corporation**
Vacman; **OneSpan Inc**
Valentino; **YOOX Net-A-Porter Group SpA (YNAP)**
Vantage; **Frontier Communications Corporation**
VASCO Data Security International Inc; **OneSpan Inc**
Vast Creation Advertising Media Services Ltd; **Sogou Inc**
VaultPress; **Automattic Inc**
Veeam Availability Suite; **Veeam Software Inc**
Veeam Backup & Replication; **Veeam Software Inc**
Veeam ProPartner Program; **Veeam Software Inc**
Venga; **PSI Capital Inc**
Venmo; **PayPal Holdings Inc**
Ventiv Technology; **Symphony Technology Group**
VEON Ltd; **Telenor ASA**
Verfone; **VeriFone Systems Inc (Verifone)**
VeriFone Inc; **VeriFone Systems Inc (Verifone)**
Verizon; **Verizon Media Group**
Verizon Communications Inc; **Verizon Media Group**
Verizon Communications Inc; **XO Communications LLC**
Versatel; **United Internet AG**
Very Well; **Dotdash**
Vibrant Programmtic; **Vibrant Media Inc**
Viceland; **Walt Disney Company (The)**
Video Business Intelligence; **MediaPlatform Inc**
Vimeo; **IAC/InterActiveCorp**
Vimeo Video School; **Vimeo LLC**
VinSolutions; **Cox Automotive Inc**
vip.com; **Vipshop Holdings Limited**
VIP-CKH Luxembourg Sarl; **Veon Ltd**
VIPRION; **F5 Networks Inc**
vipshop.com; **Vipshop Holdings Limited**
Virgin Media; **Liberty Global plc**
Virgin Mobile; **Sprint Corporation**
VirtuStream; **Dell Technologies Inc**
Visa Inc; **Authorize.Net Holdings Inc**
Visa Inc; **CyberSource Corporation**
Visual Studio; **Microsoft Corporation**
Vivian; **Snap Inc (Snapchat)**
Vivonet; **Infor**

INDEX OF SUBSIDIARIES, BRAND NAMES AND AFFILIATIONS, CONT.

INDEX OF SUBSIDIARIES, BRAND NAMES AND AFFILIATIONS, CONT.

INDEX OF SUBSIDIARIES, BRAND NAMES AND AFFILIATIONS, CONT.

A Short E-Commerce & Internet Business Glossary

3G Cellular: Short for third-generation, this term refers to high speed enhancements to mobile telephone service. 3G enables wireless e-mail, Internet browsing and data transfer. 3G will be largely replaced by advanced 4G and 5G technologies.

3GPP: Third Generation Partnership Project. It is an organization set up to create and monitor advanced 3G wireless standards.

3PF: See "Third-Party Fulfillment (3PF)."

3PL: See "Third-Party Logistics (3PL)."

4G Cellular: An advancement in speed and capabilities over 3G wireless networks. 4G not only features high data transfer speeds, it also has an enhanced ability to support interactive multimedia, internet access, mobile video and other vital tasks. It will eventually be surpassed by 5G and higher networks, with 5G beginning to rollout on a major basis in the 2020s.

4PL: See "Fourth-Party Logistics (4PL)."

5G Cellular: A wireless technology that is expected to produce blinding download speeds of one gigabyte per second (Gbps), and perhaps as high as 10 Gbps. The first specifications for 5G were agreed to by the global wireless industry from 2017 to 2019. Significant rollout was expected to begin in the early 2020s. While certain 5G features can be used to boost speeds of earlier 4G networks, a true rollout requires major investment in new cellular infrastructure and systems.

802.11: See "Wi-Fi".

802.11n (MIMO): Multiple Input Multiple Output. MIMO is a standard in the series of 802.11 Wi-Fi specifications for wireless networks. It can provide very high speed network access. 802.11n also boasts better operating distances than many networks. MIMO uses spectrum more efficiently without any loss of reliability. The technology is based on several different antennas all tuned to the same channel, each transmitting a different signal. Advancements include MU-MIMO (Multi-User MIMO) and OFDMA (Orthogonal Frequency-Division Multiple Access), each of which improves network throughput.

802.15: See "Ultrawideband (UWB)." For 802.15.1, see "Bluetooth."

802.16: See "WiMAX."

Active Server Page (ASP): A web page that includes one or more embedded programs, usually written in Java or Visual Basic code. See "Java."

Active X: A set of technologies developed by Microsoft Corporation for sharing information across different applications.

ADM: The application, development and maintenance of software.

ADN: See "Advanced Digital Network (ADN)."

Advanced Digital Network (ADN): See "Integrated Digital Network (IDN)."

AI: See "Artificial Intelligence (AI)."

Ajax: Asynchronous JavaScript and XML. It is a technology that enables web page data to update within a browser on a continuous basis, thus updating the page on the fly. This means that applications that reside on the Internet, such as instant messaging, can appear to run so quickly that they seem like programs that are local to a user's computer. An example is Google Inc.'s Google Maps, launched in 2005. During that year, Microsoft also announced services that will run via Ajax.

Ambient Backscatter: Ambient Backscatter converts wireless signals into both a source of power and a communication medium. It enables battery-free devices to communicate by backscattering existing wireless signals. Backscatter communication is vastly more power-efficient than traditional radio communication. Since it leverages the ambient RF signals that are already around us, it does not require a dedicated power source.

Analog: A form of transmitting information characterized by continuously variable quantities. Digital transmission, in contrast, is characterized by discrete bits of information in numerical steps. An analog signal responds to changes in light, sound, heat and pressure.

Analytics: With regard to software, the programs that analyze data for noteworthy trends. For example, retailers use analytics to track sales and inventory for positive or negative trends over time. This enables them to better predict the future need for inventory and to establish the most effective pricing and marketing of individual items.

ANSI: American National Standards Institute. Founded in 1918, ANSI is a private, non-profit organization that administers and coordinates the U.S. voluntary standardization and conformity assessment system. Its mission is to enhance both the global competitiveness of U.S. business and the quality of U.S. life by promoting and facilitating voluntary consensus standards and conformity assessment systems, and safeguarding their integrity. See www.ansi.org.

APAC: Asia Pacific Advisory Committee. A multi-country committee representing the Asia and Pacific region.

Applets: Small, object-based applications written in Java that net browsers can download from the Internet on an as-needed basis. These may be software, accessories (such as spell checkers or calculators), information-packed databases or other items. See "Object Technology."

Application Program Interface (API): A set of protocols, routines and tools used by computer programmers as a way of setting common definitions regarding how one piece of software communicates with another.

Application Service Provider (ASP): A web site that enables utilization of software and databases that reside permanently on a service company's remote web server, rather than having to be downloaded to the user's computer. Advantages include the ability for multiple remote users to access the same tools over the Internet and the fact that the ASP provider is responsible for developing and maintaining the software. (ASP is also an acronym for "active server page," which is not related.) For the latest developments in ASP, see "Software as a Service (SaaS)."

Applications: Computer programs and systems that allow users to interface with a computer and that collect, manipulate, summarize and report data and information. Also, see "Apps."

Applied Research: The application of compounds, processes, materials or other items discovered during basic research to practical uses. The goal is to move discoveries along to the final development phase.

Apps: Short for applications, apps are small software programs designed to run primarily on mobile devices such as smartphones and tablets. Also known as "mobile apps."

Archie: This software tool can be used to find files stored on anonymous FTP sites, as long as the user knows the file name or a sub-string of the file name that is being searched for. See "File Transfer Protocol (FTP)."

ARPANet: Advanced Research Projects Agency Network. The forefather of the Internet, ARPANet was developed during the latter part of the 1960s by the United States Department of Defense.

ARPU: See "Average Revenue Per User (ARPU)."

Artificial Intelligence (AI): The use of computer technology to perform functions somewhat like those normally associated with human intelligence, such as reasoning, learning and self-improvement.

ASCII: American Standard Code for Information Exchange. There are 128 standard ASCII codes that represent all Latin letters, numbers and punctuation. Each ASCII code is represented by a seven-digit binary number, such as 0000000 or 0000111. This code is accepted as a standard throughout the world.

ASP: See "Application Service Provider (ASP)."

Asymmetrical Digital Subscriber Line (ADSL): High-speed technology that enables the transfer of data over existing copper phone lines, allowing more bandwidth downstream than upstream.

Asynchronous Communications: A stream of data routed through a network as generated instead of in organized message blocks. Most personal computers use this format to send data.

Asynchronous Transfer Mode (ATM): A digital switching and transmission technology based on high speed. ATM allows voice, video and data signals to be sent over a single telephone line at speeds from 25 million to 1 billion bits per second (bps). This digital ATM speed is much faster than traditional analog phone lines, which allow no more than 2 million bps. See "Broadband."

Augmented Reality: Any technology designed to enhance a user's experience by adding to the environment with computer-generated means. For example, MARA (Mobile Augmented Reality Applications) is a method of enabling detailed information about a specific geographic location to appear on a cell phone's screen, pioneered by Nokia. It relies on special tools within the cell phone, including a camera, GPS, a compass and Internet access. A MARA-equipped phone might display details about a restaurant's offerings, downloaded from the Internet, when the phone's digital camera is aimed at a restaurant's front entry. Or, the screen might display information from a service like Google Maps as an overlay on the digital camera image.

Average Revenue Per User (ARPU): A measure of the average monthly billing revenue of a wireless company on a per user basis.

Baby Boomer: Generally refers to people born from 1946 to 1964. In the U.S., the initial number of Baby Boomers totaled about 78 million. The term evolved to describe the children of soldiers and war industry workers who were involved in World War II and who began forming families after the war's end. In 2011, the oldest Baby Boomers began reaching the traditional retirement age of 65.

Backbone: Traditionally the part of a communications network that carries the heaviest traffic; the high-speed line or series of connections that forms a large pathway within a network or within a region. The combined networks of AT&T, MCI and other large telecommunications companies make up the backbone of the Internet.

Back-Office: Generally considered to include such areas as accounting, human resources, call centers, financial transaction processing. A back-office application is a software program designed to handle back-office tasks. Also, see "Business Process Outsourcing (BPO)."

Bandwidth: The data transmission capacity of a network, measured in the amount of data (in bits and bauds) it can transport in one second. A full page of text is about 15,000 to 20,000 bits. Full-motion, full-screen video requires about 10 million bits per second, depending on compression.

Basic Research: Attempts to discover compounds, materials, processes or other items that may be largely or entirely new and/or unique. Basic research may start with a theoretical concept that has yet to be proven. The goal is to create discoveries that can be moved along to applied research. Basic research is sometimes referred to as "blue sky" research.

Baud: Refers to how many times the carrier signal in a modem switches value per second or how many bits a modem can send and receive in a second.

Beam: The coverage and geographic service area offered by a satellite transponder. A global beam effectively covers one-third of the earth's surface. A spot beam provides a very specific high-powered downlink pattern that is limited to a particular geographical area to which it may be steered or pointed.

Behavioral Targeting: An advertising method that attempts to target ads to individual consumers based on their history of activities or purchases.

Big Data: The massive sets of data that are generated and captured to a growing extent by a wide variety of enterprises. For example, the digitization of health care records is creating big data sets. Likewise, consumer activities on an extremely popular website like Facebook create big data sets. A growing trend will be the generation of big data sets by remote wireless sensors. The challenges created by big data include the steps of data capture, storage, visualization and analysis. The opportunities include targeted online advertising; greater efficiency in health care, energy, business and industry, as well as intelligent transportation systems and better outcomes in health care.

Binhex: A means of changing non-ASCII (or non-text) files into text/ASCII files so that they can be used, for example, as e-mail.

Bit: A single digit number, either a one or a zero, which is the smallest unit of computerized data.

Bits Per Second (Bps): An indicator of the speed of data movement.

Blog (Web Log): A web site consisting of a personal journal, news coverage, special-interest content or other data that is posted on the Internet, frequently updated and intended for public viewing by anyone who might be interested in the author's thoughts. Short for "web log," blog content is frequently distributed via RSS (Real Simple Syndication). Blog content has evolved to include video files (VLOGs) and audio files (Podcasting) as well as text. Also, see "Real Simple Syndication (RSS)," "Video Blog (VLOG)," "Moblog"; "Podcasting," and "User Generated Content (UGC)."

Bluetooth: An industry standard for a technology that enables wireless, short-distance infrared connections between devices such as cell phone headsets, Palm Pilots or PDAs, laptops, printers and Internet appliances.

BPL: See "Broadband Over Power Lines (BPL)."

BPO: See "Business Process Outsourcing (BPO)."

Bps: See "Bits Per Second (Bps)."

Brand: A marketing strategy that places a focus on the brand name of a product, service or firm in order to increase the brand's market share, increase sales, establish credibility, improve satisfaction, raise the profile of the firm and increase profits. Also, see "Brand."

Branding: A marketing strategy that places a focus on the brand name of a product, service or firm in order to increase the brand's market share, increase sales, establish credibility, improve satisfaction, raise the profile of the firm and increase profits. Also, see "Brand."

Broadband: The high-speed transmission range for telecommunications and computer data. Broadband generally refers to any transmission at 2 million bps (bits per second) or higher (much higher than analog speed). A broadband network can carry voice, video and data all at the same time. Internet users enjoying broadband access typically connect to the Internet via DSL line, cable modem or T1 line. Several wireless methods offer broadband as well.

Broadband Over Power Lines (BPL): Refers to the use of standard electric power lines to provide fast Internet service. Internet data is converted into radio frequency signals, which are not affected by electricity. Subscribers utilize special modems.

Browser: A program that allows a user to read Internet text or graphics and to navigate from one page to another. The most popular browsers are Microsoft Internet Explorer and Netscape Navigator. Firefox is an open source browser introduced in 2005 that is rapidly gaining popularity.

B-to-B, or B2B: See "Business-to-Business."

B-to-C, or B2C: See "Business-to-Consumer."

B-to-E, or B2E: See "Business-to-Employee."

B-to-G, or B2G: See "Business-to-Government."

Buffer: A location for temporarily storing data being sent or received. It is usually located between two devices that have different data transmission rates.

Business Process Outsourcing (BPO): The process of hiring another company to handle business activities. BPO is one of the fastest-growing segments in the offshoring sector. Services include human resources management, billing and purchasing and call centers, as well as many types of customer service or marketing activities, depending on the industry involved. Also, see "Knowledge Process Outsourcing (KPO)" and Business Transformation Outsourcing (BTO)."

Business Transformation Outsourcing (BTO): A segment within outsourcing in which the client company revamps its business processes with the goal of transforming its business by following a collaborative approach with its outsourced services provider.

Business-to-Business: An organization focused on selling products, services or data to commercial customers rather than individual consumers. Also known as B2B.

Business-to-Consumer: An organization focused on selling products, services or data to individual consumers rather than commercial customers. Also known as B2C.

Business-to-Employee: A corporate communications system, such as an intranet, aimed at conveying information from a company to its employees. Also known as B2E.

Business-to-Government: An organization focused on selling products, services or data to government units rather than commercial businesses or consumers. Also known as B2G.

Byte: A set of eight bits that represent a single character.

Cable Modem: An interface between a cable television system and a computer or router. Most cable modems are external devices that connect to the PC through a standard 10Base-T Ethernet card and twisted-pair wiring. External Universal Serial Bus (USB) modems and internal PCI modem cards are also available.

Caching: A method of storing data in a temporary location closer to the user so that it can be retrieved quickly when requested.

CAFTA-DR: See "Central American-Dominican Republic Free Trade Agreement (CAFTA-DR)."

Capability Maturity Model (CMM): A global process management standard for software development established by the Software Engineering Institute at Carnegie Mellon University.

Captive Offshoring: Used to describe a company-owned offshore operation. For example, Microsoft owns and operates significant captive offshore research and development centers in China and elsewhere that are offshore from Microsoft's U.S. home base. Also see "Offshoring."

Carrier: In communications, the basic radio, television or telephony center of transmit signal. The carrier in an analog signal is modulated by varying volume or shifting frequency up or down in relation to the incoming signal. Satellite carriers operating in the analog mode are usually frequency-modulated.

CATV: Cable television.

CDMA: See "Code Division Multiple Access (CDMA)."

Central American-Dominican Republic Free Trade Agreement (CAFTA-DR): A trade agreement signed into law in 2005 that aimed to open up the Central American and Dominican Republic markets to American goods. Member nations include Guatemala, Nicaragua, Costa Rica, El Salvador, Honduras and the Dominican Republic. Before the law was signed, products from those countries could enter the U.S.

almost tariff-free, while American goods heading into those countries faced stiff tariffs. The goal of this agreement was to create U.S. jobs while at the same time offering the non-U.S. member citizens a chance for a better quality of life through access to U.S.-made goods.

Central Processing Unit (CPU): The part of a computer that interprets and executes instructions. It is composed of an arithmetic logic unit, a control unit and a small amount of memory.

CGI: See "Common Gateway Interface (CGI)."

CGI-BIN: The frequently used name of a directory on a web server where CGI programs exist.

Channel Definition Format (CDF): Used in Internet-based broadcasting. With this format, a channel serves as a web site that also sends an information file about that specific site. Users subscribe to a channel by downloading the file.

Click Through: In advertising on the Internet, click through refers to how often viewers respond to an ad by clicking on it. Also known as click rate.

Client/Server: In networking, a way of running a large computer setup. The server is the host computer that acts as the central holding ground for files, databases and application software. The clients are all of the PCs connected to the network that share data with the server. This represents a vast change from past networks, which were connected to expensive, complicated "mainframe" computers.

Cloud: Refers to the use of outsourced servers to store and access data, as opposed to computers owned or managed by one organization. Firms that offer cloud services for a fee run clusters of servers networked together, often based on open standards. Such cloud networks can consist of hundreds or even thousands of computers. Cloud services enable a client company to immediately increase computing capability without any investment in physical infrastructure. (The word "cloud" is also broadly used to describe any data or application that runs via the Internet.) The concept of cloud is also increasingly linked with software as a service.

Code Division Multiple Access (CDMA): A cellular telephone multiple-access scheme whereby stations use spread-spectrum modulations and orthogonal codes to avoid interfering with one another. IS-95 (also known as CDMAOne) is the 2G CDMA standard. CDMA2000 is the 3G standard. CDMA in the 1xEV-DO standard offers data transfer speeds up to 2.4 Mbps. CDMA 1xRTT is a slower standard offering speeds of 144 kbps.

Codec: Hardware or software that converts analog to digital and digital to analog (in both audio and video formats). Codecs can be found in digital telephones, set-top boxes, computers and videoconferencing equipment. The term is also used to refer to the compression of digital information into a smaller format.

Co-Location: Refers to the hosting of computer servers at locations operated by service organizations. Co-location is offered by firms that operate specially designed co-location centers with high levels of security, extremely high-speed telecommunication lines for Internet connectivity and reliable backup electrical power systems in case of power failure, as well as a temperature-controlled environment for optimum operation of computer systems.

Commerce Chain Management (CCM): Refers to Internet-based tools to facilitate sales, distribution, inventory management and content personalization in the e-commerce industry. Also see "Supply Chain."

Common Gateway Interface (CGI): A set of guidelines that determines the manner in which a web server receives and sends information to and from software on the same machine.

Competitive Local Exchange Carrier (CLEC): A newer company providing local telephone service that competes against larger, traditional firms known as ILECs (incumbent local exchange carriers).

Compression: A technology in which a communications signal is squeezed so that it uses less bandwidth (or capacity) than it normally would. This saves storage space and shortens transfer time. The original data is decompressed when read back into memory.

Computer-Assisted Software Engineering (CASE): The application of computer technology to systems development activities, techniques and methodologies. Sometimes referred to as "computer-aided systems engineering."

Consumer Valuation: See "Buying Power Score."

Contract Manufacturing: A business arrangement whereby a company manufactures products that will be sold under the brand names of its client companies. For example, a large number of consumer electronics, such as laptop computers, are manufactured by contract manufacturers for leading brand-name computer companies such as Dell and Apple. Many other types of products, such as shoes and apparel, are made under contract manufacturing. Also see "Original Equipment Manufacturer (OEM)" and "Original Design Manufacturer (ODM)."

Cookie: A piece of information sent to a web browser from a web server that the browser software saves and then sends back to the server upon request. Cookies are used by web site operators to track the actions of users returning to the site.

Cost Per Click (CPC): Online advertising that is billed on a response basis. An advertiser sells a banner ad and is paid by the number of users who click on the ad.

Cost Per Thousand (CPM): A charge for advertising calculated on a fixed amount multiplied by the number of users who view an ad, computed in thousands.

CPC: See "Cost Per Click (CPC)."

CPM: See "Cost Per Thousand (CPM)."

CRM: See "Customer Relationship Management (CRM)."

Crowdsourcing: A method of gathering data that capitalizes on users of a web site or database to find and post the data. Wikipedia is a well known example.

Customer Relationship Management (CRM): Refers to the automation, via sophisticated software, of business processes involving existing and prospective customers. CRM may cover aspects such as sales (contact management and contact history), marketing (campaign management and telemarketing) and customer service (call center history and field service history). Well known providers of CRM software include Salesforce, which delivers via a Software as a Service model (see "Software as a Service (Saas)"), Microsoft and Oracle.

Cyberspace: Refers to the entire realm of information available through computer networks and the Internet.

Data Base Management System (DBMS): A software system used to store, retrieve and manipulate data in an organized fashion. Usually consists of dictionary, manipulation, security and access components.

Data Over Cable Service Interface Specification (DOCSIS): A set of standards for transferring data over cable television. DOCSIS 3.0 will enable very high-speed Internet access that may eventually reach 160 Mbps.

Datanets: Private networks of land-based telephone lines, satellites or wireless networks that allow corporate users to send data at high speeds to remote locations while bypassing the speed and cost constraints of traditional telephone lines.

DBMS: See "Data Base Management System (DBMS)."

Dedicated Internet Access (DIA): A high speed Internet service with dedicated access from the carrier to the customer.

Demographics: The breakdown of the population into statistical categories such as age, income, education and sex.

Dial-Up Access: The connection of a computer or other device to a network through a modem and a public telephone network. The only difference between dial-up access and a telephone connection is that computers are at each end of the connection rather than people. Dial-up access is slower than DSL, cable modem and other advanced connections.

Digital: The transmission of a signal by reducing all of its information to ones and zeros and then regrouping them at the reception end. Digital transmission vastly improves the carrying capacity of the spectrum while reducing noise and distortion of the transmission.

Digital Local Telephone Switch: A computer that interprets signals (dialed numbers) from a telephone caller and routes calls to their proper destinations. A digital switch also provides a variety of calling features not available in older analog switches, such as call waiting.

Digital Millennium Copyright Act: A U.S. law created in 1998. It was written in response to the rapid growth of content on the Internet. The act contains a "safe harbor" provision that enables Internet site publishers to promptly eliminate most faults or penalties of infringement if they promptly remove online content when notified by the proper owners of that content's copyright.

Digital Rights Management (DRM): Restrictions placed on the use of digital content by copyright holders and hardware manufacturers. DRM for Apple, Inc.'s iTunes, for example, allows downloaded music to be played only on Apple's iPod player and iPhones, per agreement with music production companies Universal Music Group, SonyBMG, Warner Music and EMI.

Digital Subscriber Line (DSL): A broadband (high-speed) Internet connection provided via telecommunications systems. These lines are a cost-effective means of providing homes and small businesses with relatively fast Internet access. Common variations include ADSL and SDSL. DSL competes with cable modem access and wireless access.

Direct Broadcast Satellite (DBS): A high-powered satellite authorized to broadcast television programming directly to homes. Home subscribers use a dish and a converter to receive and translate the TV signal. An example is the DirecTV service. DBS operates in the 11.70- to 12.40-GHz range.

Direct Marketing: A form of non-store retailing in which customers are exposed to merchandise through catalogs, direct-mail brochures, telemarketing or television. Direct marketing may be used to generate direct-response purchases, store traffic, sales leads or a combination thereof.

Disaster Recovery: A set of rules and procedures that allow a computer site to be put back in operation after a disaster has occurred. Moving backups off-site constitutes the minimum basic precaution for disaster recovery. The remote copy is used to recover data if the local storage is inaccessible after a disaster.

Discount Broker: A broker or brokerage firm that executes buy and sell transactions at commission rates lower than a full-service broker or brokerage.

Disintermediate: A business or distribution model that bypasses the middleman in marketing or retailing. For example, a web site that enables end-consumers to purchase apparel direct from a designer or manufacturer, bypassing retail stores and traditional catalogs, is attempting to disintermediate the supply chain.

Disk Mirroring: A data redundancy technique in which data is recorded identically on multiple separate disk drives at the same time. When the primary disk is off-line, the alternate takes over, providing continuous access to data. Disk mirroring is sometimes referred to as RAID.

Disruptive: A new technology or business model that unexpectedly threatens to displace existing products or services. For example, the manner in which email has disrupted standard postal service. By some estimates, in order to be disruptive, a new model must provide at least 80% of the value of existing methods, at no more than 20% of traditional costs.

Distributed Internet applications Architecture (DNA): A current Microsoft project, also known as Windows DNA, that is dependent on Active Directory and is designed to provide secure delivery of software components over the Internet and intranets.

Domain: A name that has server records associated with it. See "Domain Name."

Domain (Top-Level): Either an ISO country code or a common domain name such as .com, .org or .net.

Domain Name: A unique web site name registered to a company, organization or individual (e.g., plunkettresearch.com).

Domain Name System Security Extensions (DNSSEC): A suite of specifications for securing data provided by the Domain Name System (DNS) as used on Internet Protocol (IP) networks. Based on specifications by the Internet Engineering Task Force (IETF), it provides origin authentication of DNS data and data integrity.

DS-1: A digital transmission format that transmits and receives information at a rate of 1,544,000 bits per second.

DSL: See "Digital Subscriber Line (DSL)."

Duplicate Host: A single host name that maps to duplicate IP addresses.

Dynamic HTML: Web content that changes with each individual viewing. For example, the same site could appear differently depending on geographic location of the reader, time of day, previous pages viewed or the user's profile.

Echo Boomers: See "Generation Y."

E-Commerce: The use of online, internet-based sales methods. The phrase is used to describe both business-to-consumer and business-to-business sales.

EDI: See "Electronic Data Interchange (EDI)."

EFT: See "Electronic Funds Transfer (EFT)."

Electronic Data Interchange (EDI): An accepted standard format for the exchange of data between various companies' networks. EDI allows for the transfer of e-mail as well as orders, invoices and other files from one company to another.

Electronic Funds Transfer (EFT): Moving money from one account to another via electronic means.

E-Mail (eMail): The use of software that allows the posting of messages (text, audio or video) over a network. E-mail can be used on a LAN, a WAN or the Internet, as well as via online services or wireless devices that are Internet enabled. It can be used to send a message to a single recipient or may be broadcast to a large group of people at once.

EMEA: The region comprised of Europe, the Middle East and Africa.

Enterprise Application: A major software tool intended to manage data over an extremely large corporate or government user base (e.g., SAP, Oracle).

Enterprise Resource Planning (ERP): An integrated information system that helps manage all aspects of a business, including accounting, ordering and human resources, typically across all locations of a major corporation or organization. ERP is considered to be a critical tool for management of large organizations. Suppliers of ERP tools include SAP and Oracle.

ERP: See "Enterprise Resource Planning (ERP)."

E-Score: See "Buying Power Score."

Ethernet: The standard format on which local area network equipment works. Abiding by Ethernet standards allows equipment from various manufacturers to work together.

EU: See "European Union (EU)."

EU Competence: The jurisdiction in which the European Union (EU) can take legal action.

European Community (EC): See "European Union (EU)."

European Union (EU): A consolidation of European countries (member states) functioning as one body to facilitate trade. Previously known as the European Community (EC). The EU has a unified currency, the Euro. See europa.eu.int.

EV-DO (CDMA 2000 1xEV-DO): A 3G (third generation) cellular telephone service standard that is an improved version of 1xRTT. The EV-DO (Evolution-Data Optimized) standard introduced in 2004 allows data download speeds of as much as 2.4 Mbps. A version introduced in 2006 allows up to 14.7 Mbps data download speeds. EV-DO is also known as CDMA 2000 1xEV-DO. EV-DO's capabilities are used by the entertainment industry to enable video via cell phone.

Exabyte: A measure of data equal to 1,024 petabytes, or 10 bytes to the 18th power (one billion billion, or one quintillion). Generally used to describe total volume of Internet traffic worldwide. Analysts estimate that all the world's printed material would fill five exabytes.

Expert Systems: A practical development of AI that requires creation of a knowledge base of facts and rules furnished by human experts and uses a defined set of rules to access this information in order to suggest solutions to problems. See "Artificial Intelligence (AI)."

Extensible Markup Language (XML): A programming language that enables designers to add extra functionality to documents that could not otherwise be utilized with standard HTML coding. XML was developed by the World Wide Web Consortium. It can communicate to various software programs the actual meanings contained in HTML documents. For example, it can enable the gathering and use of information from a large number of databases at once and place that information into one web site window. XML is an important protocol to web services. See "Web Services."

Extranet: A computer network that is accessible in part to authorized outside persons, as opposed to an intranet, which uses a firewall to limit accessibility.

FAQ: See "Frequently Asked Questions (FAQ)."

FASB: See "Financial Accounting Standards Board (FASB)."

FCC: See "Federal Communications Commission (FCC)."

FDDI: See "Fiber Distributed Data Interface (FDDI)."

Federal Communications Commission (FCC): The U.S. Government agency that regulates broadcast television and radio, as well as satellite transmission, telephony and all uses of radio spectrum.

Fiber Distributed Data Interface (FDDI): A token ring passing scheme that operates at 100 Mbps over fiber-optic lines with a built-in geographic limitation of 100 kilometers. This type of connection is faster than both Ethernet and T-3 connections. See "Token Ring."

Fiber to the Home (FTTH): Refers to the extension of a fiber-optic system through the last mile so that it touches the home or office where it will be used. This can provide high speed Internet access at speeds of 15 to 100 Mbps, much faster than typical T1 or DSL line. FTTH is now commonly installed in new communities where telecom infrastructure is being built for the first time. Another phrase used to describe such installations is FTTP, or Fiber to the Premises.

Fiber to the Node (FTTN): Refers to the extension of a fiber-optic system through the last mile so that it touches a central neighborhood junction close to the home or office where it will be used. The remaining distance is covered by existing copper phone line that uses DSL (digital subscriber line) technology to speed data transfer.

File Server: A computer that is modified to store and transfer large amounts of data to other computers. File servers often receive data from mainframes and store it for transfer to other, smaller computers, or from small computers to mainframes.

File Transfer Protocol (FTP): A widely used method of transferring data and files between two Internet sites.

Financial Accounting Standards Board (FASB): An independent organization that establishes the Generally Accepted Accounting Principles (GAAP).

Firewall: Hardware or software that keeps unauthorized users from accessing a server or network. Firewalls are designed to prevent data theft and unauthorized web site manipulation by "hackers."

Fixed Wireless: Refers to the use of Wi-Fi, WiMAX or other wireless receivers that remain fixed in a stationary place, to provide Internet service.

Flash Sale: Online sales events, generally advertised to by email to people who have asked to be notified. Flash sales are very limited in time. They tend to offer apparel, accessories and travel.

Folksonomy: A user-created taxonomy of Internet site content based on key words or concepts. This is a collaborative effort in a wiki-like environment that enables participants to organize data, such as photos, into categories. A widely known example is #hashtag system used on Twitter.

Fourth-Party Logistics (4PL): A service that integrates a company's third-party logistics providers into a single entity for ease of use. Often formed by a telecommunications company, a 4PL is also called a lead logistics provider. A 4PL service provider provides a top layer of business processes, generally technology-driven, to the client's supply chain. Also see "Third-Party Logistics (3PL)."

Frame Relay: An accepted standard for sending large amounts of data over phone lines and private datanets. The term refers to the way data is broken down into standard-size "frames" prior to transmission.

Freemium: A business model in which a product or service (usually a digital game, software or web service) is offered at no charge to the user, but advanced features and services are promoted for purchase.

Frequency: The number of times that an alternating current goes through its complete cycle in one second. One cycle per second is referred to as one hertz; 1,000 cycles per second, one kilohertz; 1 million cycles per second, one megahertz; and 1 billion cycles per second, one gigahertz.

Frequency Band: A term for designating a range of frequencies in the electromagnetic spectrum.

Frequently Asked Questions (FAQ): Answers inquiries about a given topic. Generally, FAQs come in the form of a help file or a hypertext document.

Front-Office Application: A computer program tailored to the needs of the customer relations portions of a business, such as sales and marketing.

FTP: See "File Transfer Protocol (FTP)."

FTTC: Fiber to the curb. See "Fiber to the Home (FTTH)."

FTTP: Fiber to the premises. See "Fiber to the Home (FTTH)."

Fuzzy Logic: Recognizes that some statements are not just "true" or "false," but also "more or less certain" or "very unlikely." Fuzzy logic is used in artificial intelligence. See "Artificial Intelligence (AI)."

GAAP: See "Generally Accepted Accounting Principles (GAAP)."

Gamification: The use of game design and practices to enhance non-game content in order to attract users and increase engagement. For example, the use of games in online advertising and marketing, or the use of games in online education.

Gateway: A device connecting two or more networks that may use different protocols and media. Gateways translate between the different networks and can connect locally or over wide area networks.

GDP: See "Gross Domestic Product (GDP)."

Generally Accepted Accounting Principles (GAAP): A set of accounting standards administered by the Financial Accounting Standards Board (FASB) and enforced by the U.S. Security and Exchange

Commission (SEC). GAAP is primarily used in the U.S.

Generation C: Creative consumers who are active in unpaid, consumer-generated content, such as Wikipedia, blogging, YouTube and consumer-generated advertising.

Generation M: A very loosely defined term that is sometimes used to refer to young people who have grown up in the digital age. "M" may refer to any or all of media-saturated, mobile or multi-tasking. The term was most notably used in a Kaiser Family Foundation report published in 2005, "Generation M: Media in the Lives of 8-18 year olds." Also, see "Generation Y" and "Generation Z."

Generation X: A loosely-defined and variously-used term that describes people born between approximately 1965 and 1980, but other time frames are recited. Generation X is often referred to as a group influential in defining tastes in consumer goods, entertainment and/or political and social matters.

Generation Y: Refers to people born between approximately 1982 and 2002. In the U.S., they number more than 90 million, making them the largest generation segment in the nation's history. They are also known as Echo Boomers, Millenials or the Millenial Generation. These are children of the Baby Boom generation who will be filling the work force as Baby Boomers retire.

Generation Z: Some people refer to Generation Z as people born after 1991. Others use the beginning date of 2001, or refer to the era of 1994 to 2004. Members of Generation Z are considered to be natural and rapid adopters of the latest technologies.

Geofencing: The practice of setting virtual boundaries around a physical location and targeting mobile device users within those areas for a variety of purposes including search and rescue, advertising and social interaction.

Gigabyte: 1,024 megabytes.

Gigahertz (GHz): One billion cycles per second. See "Frequency."

Global System for Mobile Communications (GSM): The standard cellular format used throughout Europe, making one type of cellular phone usable in every nation on the continent and in the U.K. In the U.S., Cingular and T-Mobile also run GSM networks. The original GSM, introduced in 1991, has transfer speeds of only 9.6 kbps. GSM EDGE offers 2.75G data transfer speeds of up to 473.6 kbps. GSM GPRS offers slower 2.5G theoretical speeds of 144 kbps.

Graphic Interchange Format (GIF): A widely used format for image files.

Gross Domestic Product (GDP): The total value of a nation's output, income and expenditures produced with a nation's physical borders.

Gross National Product (GNP): A country's total output of goods and services from all forms of economic activity measured at market prices for one calendar year. It differs from Gross Domestic Product (GDP) in that GNP includes income from investments made in foreign nations.

Groupware: A type of software that enables various people on a network to contribute to one document at the same time, sharing ideas, molding the final product and monitoring its progress along the way. Groupware is a new way of group "thinking" without physical meetings. Lotus Notes pioneered this market.

GSM: See "Global System for Mobile Communications (GSM)."

Handheld Devices Markup Language (HDML): A text-based markup language designed for display on a smaller screen (e.g., a cellular phone, PDA or pager). Enables the mobile user to send, receive and redirect e-mail as well as access the Internet (HDML-enabled web sites only).

HDML: See "Handheld Devices Markup Language (HDML)."

HDSL: See "High-Data-Rate Digital Subscriber Line (HDSL)."

Helper Applications: Applications that allow the user to view or play downloadable files.

HFC: Hybrid Fiber Coaxial. A type of cable system.

High-Data-Rate Digital Subscriber Line (HDSL): High-data-rate DSL, delivering up to T1 or E1 speeds.

Hosting: Maintaining a computer application for a third party. Hosting may include databases, web sites and proprietary applications.

Hot Spot: A location where access to the Internet is available via Wi-Fi.

HTML: See "Hypertext Markup Language (HTML)."

HTML5: A specification for Internet development that represents the fifth major revision of the Hypertext Markup Language, or HTML. HTML5 is designed to better handle the types of Internet content that are rapidly growing in popularity, such as online video, audio and interactive documents and pages. For example, HTML5 enables the designer to embed images, audio and video directly into a web-based document.

HTTP: See "Hypertext Transfer Protocol (HTTP)."

Hyperlink: On the Internet, an element in a web page that links to another page or to another place in the same document. Generally, the user clicks on the hyperlink in order to follow it.

Hypertext Markup Language (HTML): A language for coding text for viewing on the World Wide Web. HTML is unique because it enables the use of hyperlinks from one site to another, creating a web.

Hypertext Transfer Protocol (HTTP): The protocol used most frequently on the World Wide Web to move hypertext files between clients and servers on the Internet.

IAAS: Infrastructure as a Service. See "Cloud Computing."

ICANN: The Internet Corporation for Assigned Names and Numbers. ICANN acts as the central coordinator for the Internet's technical operations.

ICT: See "Information and Communication Technologies (ICT)."

Idea Management: Software designed to enable employees, investors, management, customers and vendors to share ideas and opportunities for innovation in a secure environment. The goal is to foster faster development of new products and services. Idea management may be an adjunct to crowdsourcing. See "Crowdsourcing."

IDN: See "Integrated Digital Network (IDN)."

IEEE: See "Institute of Electrical and Electronic Engineers (IEEE)."

IFRS: See "International Financials Reporting Standards (IFRS)."

ILEC: See "Incumbent Local Exchange Carrier (ILEC)."

IM: See "Instant Messaging (IM)."

Impressions: In Internet advertising, the total number of times an ad is displayed on a web page. Impressions are not the same as "hits," which count the number of times each page or element in a page is retrieved. Since a single complicated page on a web site could consist of five or more individual elements, including graphics and text, one viewer calling up that page would register multiple hits but just a single impression.

Incumbent Local Exchange Carrier (ILEC): A traditional telephone company that was providing local service prior to the establishment of the Telecommunications Act of 1996, when upstart companies (CLECs, or competitive local exchange carriers) were enabled to compete against the ILECS and were granted access to their system wiring.

Industry Code: A descriptive code assigned to any company in order to group it with firms that operate in similar businesses. Common industry codes include the NAICS (North American Industrial Classification System) and the SIC (Standard Industrial Classification), both of which are standards widely used in America, as well as the International Standard Industrial Classification of all Economic Activities (ISIC), the Standard International Trade Classification established by the United Nations (SITC) and the General Industrial Classification of Economic Activities within the European Communities (NACE).

Information and Communication Technologies (ICT): A term used to describe the relationship between the myriad types of goods, services and networks that make up the global information and communications system. Sectors involved in ICT include landlines, data networks, the Internet, wireless communications, (including cellular and remote wireless sensors) and satellites.

Information Technology (IT): The systems, including hardware and software, that move and store voice, video and data via computers and telecommunications.

Infrastructure (Telecommunications): The entity made up of all the cable and equipment installed in the worldwide telecommunications market. Most of today's telecommunications infrastructure is connected by copper and fiber-optic cable, which represents a huge capital investment that telephone companies would like to continue to utilize in as many ways as possible.

Initial Public Offering (IPO): A company's first effort to sell its stock to investors (the public). Investors in an up-trending market eagerly seek stocks offered in many IPOs because the stocks of newly public companies that seem to have great promise may appreciate very rapidly in price, reaping great profits for those who were able to get the stock at the first offering. In the United States, IPOs are regulated by the SEC (U.S. Securities Exchange Commission) and by the state-level regulatory agencies of the states in which the IPO shares are offered.

Insourcing: A unique and increasingly popular business method. It is similar to "outsourcing," in that it is a continuing business service or process provided to a company by an outside organization. The intent is to enable the client company to focus on its core strengths, while hiring outside firms to provide other needs such as warehouse, call center or human resources management. However, with insourcing, the services provider moves into or near the client company's facility and sets up shop. For example, ARAMARK has a business unit that will set up and manage an employee cafeteria within a client company's facility. (Occasionally, the term "insourcing" has also been used to describe the creation of jobs in America by foreign firms.) Also see "Third-Party Logistics (3PL)."

Instant Messaging (IM): A type of e-mail that is viewed and then deleted. IM is used between opt-in networks of people for leisure or business purposes.

Institute of Electrical and Electronic Engineers (IEEE): An organization that sets global technical standards and acts as an authority in technical areas including computer engineering, biomedical technology, telecommunications, electric power, aerospace and consumer electronics, among others. www.ieee.org.

Integrated Digital Network (IDN): A network that uses both digital transmission and digital switching.

Integrated Services Digital Networks (ISDN): Internet connection services offered at higher speeds than standard "dial-up" service. While ISDN was considered to be an advanced service at one time, it has been eclipsed by much faster DSL, cable modem and T1 line service.

Intellectual Property (IP): The exclusive ownership of original concepts, ideas, designs, engineering plans or other assets that are protected by law. Examples include items covered by trademarks, copyrights and patents. Items such as software, engineering plans, fashion designs and architectural designs, as well as games, books, songs and other entertainment items are among the many things that may be considered to be intellectual property. (Also, see "Patent.")

Interactive: In entertainment, advertising and communications, interactive refers to systems that enable the viewer or user to interact via a response or two-way communication. For example, interactive television advertising may enable the viewer to respond via a set-top box, immediately purchasing the item being advertised.

Interactive TV (ITV): Allows two-way data flow between a viewer and the cable TV system. A user can exchange information with the cable system—for example, by ordering a product related to a show he/she is watching or by voting in an interactive survey.

Interexchange Carrier (IXC or IEC): Any company providing long-distance phone service between LECs and LATAs. See "Local Exchange Carrier (LEC)" and "Local Access and Transport Area (LATA)."

Interface: Refers to (1) a common boundary between two or more items of equipment or between a terminal and a communication channel, (2) the electronic device that interconnects two or more devices or items of equipment having similar or dissimilar characteristics or (3) the electronic device placed between a terminal and a communication channel to protect the network from the hazard of excess voltage levels.

International Financials Reporting Standards (IFRS): A set of accounting standards established by the International Accounting Standards Board (IASB) for the preparation of public financial statements. IFRS has been adopted by much of the world, including the European Union, Russia and Singapore.

International Telecommunications Union (ITU): The international body responsible for telephone and computer communications standards describing interface techniques and practices. These standards include those that define how a nation's telephone and data systems connect to the worldwide communications network.

Internet: A global computer network that provides an easily accessible way for hundreds of millions of users to send and receive data electronically when appropriately connected via computers or wireless devices. Access is generally through HTML-enabled sites on the World Wide Web. Also known as the Net.

Internet Appliance: A non-PC device that connects users to the Internet for specific or general purposes. A good example is an electronic game machine with a screen and Internet capabilities.

Internet of Things (IoT): A concept whereby individual objects, such as kitchen appliances, automobiles, manufacturing equipment, environmental sensors or air conditioners, are connected to the Internet. The objects must be able to identify themselves to other devices or to databases. The ultimate goals may include the collection and processing of data, the control of instruments and machinery, and eventually, a new level of synergies, artificial intelligence and operating efficiencies among the objects. The Internet of Things is often referred to as IoT. Related technologies and topics include RFID, remote wireless sensors, telecommunications and nanotechnology.

Internet Protocol (IP): A set of tools and/or systems used to communicate across the World Wide Web.

Internet Service Provider (ISP): A company that sells access to the Internet to individual subscribers. Leading examples are MSN and AOL.

Internet Telephony: See "Voice Over Internet Protocol (VOIP)."

Internet2: An advanced networking consortium led by the U.S. research and education community that develops and deploys cutting edge network applications.

Intranet: A network protected by a firewall for sharing data and e-mail within an organization or company. Usually, intranets are used by organizations for internal communication.

IoT: See "Internet of Things (IoT)."

IP: See "Intellectual Property (IP)."

IP Number/IP Address: A number or address with four parts that are separated by dots. Each machine on the Internet has its own IP (Internet protocol) number, which serves as an identifier.

IPL: International Private Line.

ISDN: See "Integrated Services Digital Networks (ISDN)."

ISO 9000, 9001, 9002, 9003: Standards set by the International Organization for Standardization. ISO 9000, 9001, 9002 and 9003 are the highest quality certifications awarded to organizations that meet exacting standards in their operating practices and procedures.

IT: See "Information Technology (IT)."

IT-Enabled Services (ITES): The portion of the Information Technology industry focused on providing business services, such as call centers, insurance claims processing and medical records transcription, by utilizing the power of IT, especially the Internet. Most ITES functions are considered to be back-office procedures. Also, see "Business Process Outsourcing (BPO)."

ITES: See "IT-Enabled Services (ITES)."

ITU: See "International Telecommunications Union (ITU)."

ITV: See "Interactive TV (ITV)."

Java: A programming language developed by Sun Microsystems that allows web pages to display interactive graphics. Any type of computer or operating systems can read Java.

Joint Photographic Experts Group (JPEG): A widely used format for digital image files.

Just-in-Time (JIT) Delivery: Refers to a supply chain practice whereby manufacturers receive components on or just before the time that they are needed on the assembly line, rather than bearing the cost of maintaining several days' or weeks' supply in a warehouse. This adds greatly to the cost-effectiveness of a manufacturing plant and puts the burden of warehousing and timely delivery on the supplier of the components.

Kilobyte: One thousand (or 1,024) bytes.

Kilohertz (kHz): A measure of frequency equal to 1,000 Hertz.

Knowledge Management (KM): Includes techniques and technologies that help users find their way through existing information. Also defined as capturing and growing knowledge as employees in an organization interact with customers, partners and products.

Knowledge Process Outsourcing (KPO): The use of outsourced and/or offshore workers to perform business tasks that require judgment and analysis. Examples include such professional tasks as patent research, legal research, architecture, design, engineering, market research, scientific research, accounting and tax return preparation. Also, see "Business Process Outsourcing (BPO)."

LAC: An acronym for Latin America and the Caribbean.

Large-Scale Integration (LSI): The placement of thousands of electronic gates on a single chip. This makes the manufacture of powerful computers possible.

LATA: See "Local Access and Transport Area (LATA)."

LDCs: See "Least Developed Countries (LDCs)."

Leased Line: A phone line that is rented for use in continuous, long-term data connections.

Least Developed Countries (LDCs): Nations determined by the U.N. Economic and Social Council to be the poorest and weakest members of the international community. There are currently 50 LDCs, of which 34 are in Africa, 15 are in Asia Pacific and the remaining one (Haiti) is in Latin America. The top 10 on the LDC list, in descending order from top to 10th, are Afghanistan, Angola, Bangladesh, Benin, Bhutan, Burkina Faso, Burundi, Cambodia, Cape Verde and the Central African Republic. Sixteen of the LDCs are also Landlocked Least Developed Countries (LLDCs) which present them with additional difficulties often due to the high cost of transporting trade goods. Eleven of the LDCs are Small Island Developing States (SIDS), which are often at risk of extreme weather phenomenon (hurricanes, typhoons, Tsunami); have fragile ecosystems; are often dependent on foreign energy sources; can have high disease rates for HIV/AIDS and malaria; and can have poor market access and trade terms.

LEC: See "Local Exchange Carrier (LEC)."

Li-Fi: Optical wireless systems that operate somewhat like Wi-Fi, but they utilize light to transfer data.

LINUX: An open, free operating system that is shared readily with millions of users worldwide. These users continuously improve and add to the software's code. It can be used to operate computer networks and Internet appliances as well as servers and PCs.

LMDS: Local Multipoint Distribution Service. A fixed, wireless, point-to-multipoint technology designed to distribute television signals.

Local Access and Transport Area (LATA): An operational service area established after the breakup of AT&T to distinguish local telephone service from long-distance service. The U.S. is divided into over 160 LATAs.

Local Area Network (LAN): A computer network that is generally within one office or one building. A LAN can be very inexpensive and efficient to set up when small numbers of computers are involved. It may require a network administrator and a serious investment if hundreds of computers are hooked up to the LAN. A LAN enables all computers within the office to share files and printers, to access common databases and to send e-mail to others on the network.

Local Exchange Carrier (LEC): Any local telephone company, i.e., a carrier, that provides ordinary phone service under regulation within a service area. Also see "Incumbent Local Exchange Carrier (ILEC)" and "Competitive Local Exchange Carrier (CLEC)."

Location Based Advertising (LBA): The ability for advertisers and information providers to push information to mobile consumers based on their locations. For example, GPS equipped cell phones have the potential to alert consumers on the go to nearby restaurants, entertainment attractions, and special sale events at retailers.

LOHAS: Lifestyles of Health and Sustainability. A marketing term that refers to consumers who choose to purchase and/or live with items that are natural, organic, less polluting, etc. Such consumers may also prefer products powered by alternative energy, such as hybrid cars.

LSI: See "Large-Scale Integration (LSI)."

M2M: See "Machine-to-Machine (M2M)."

M2M2P: Machine-to-machine-to-people. Also, see "Machine-to-Machine (M2M)."

Machine-to-Machine (M2M): Refers to the transmission of data from one device to another, typically through wireless means such as Wi-Fi or cellular. For example, a Wi-Fi network might be employed to control several machines in a household from a central computer. Such machines might include air conditioning and entertainment systems. Wireless sensor networks (WSNs) will be a major growth factor in M2M communications, in everything from factory automation to agriculture and transportation. In logistics and retailing, M2M can refer to the use of RFID tags to transmit information. See "Radio Frequency Identification (RFID)."

Mainframe Computer: One of the largest types of computer, usually capable of serving many users simultaneously, with exceptional processing speed.

MAN: See "Metropolitan Area Network (MAN)."

Managed Service Provider (MSP): An outsourcer that deploys, manages and maintains the back-end software and hardware infrastructure for Internet businesses.

Market Segmentation: The division of a consumer market into specific groups of buyers based on demographic factors.

Marketing: Includes all planning and management activities and expenses associated with the promotion of a product or service. Marketing can encompass advertising, customer surveys, public relations and many other disciplines. Marketing is distinct from selling, which is the process of sell-through to the end user.

Mashup: A web page that takes data from two or more web sites and joins them together to create a new point of view. For example, weather forecasts from weather.com, a beach camera from Miami, Miami restaurant reviews from Zagat.com and sports news from ESPN.com might be overlaid on a mashup to create a new site that would provide data for people who were traveling to a Super Bowl in Miami.

Massively Multiplayer Online Role Playing Games (MMORPG): A genre of games in which users from anywhere in the world can connect to a central server, which hosts a virtual game environment. Players can then interact with one another in cooperative or adversarial game settings. Users often pay monthly subscription fees to access the content.

MAU: Monthly Average Users.

Mbps (Megabits per second): One million bits transmitted per second.

M-Commerce: Mobile e-commerce over wireless devices.

Megabytes: One million bytes, or 1,024 kilobytes.

Megahertz (MHz): A measure of frequency equal to 1 million Hertz.

Merchant Services: Credit card transaction processing services, typically provided by a retail bank. Merchant services include the processing and clearing of credit card transactions and the forwarding of the funds received to the client's bank account.

Mesh Network: A network that uses multiple Wi-Fi repeaters or "nodes" to deploy a wireless Internet access network. Typically, a mesh network is operated by the users themselves. Each user installs a node at his or her locale, and plugs the node into his/her local

Internet access, whether DSL, cable or satellite. Other users within the mesh can access all other nodes as needed, or as they travel about. A mesh network can provide access to an apartment complex, an office building, a campus or an entire city. Meraki is a leading node brand in this sector.

Metasearch: Online search platforms that search several third-party travel sites at once. They then display the combined search results in a consolidated page. Metasearch sites may also sell advertising. This type of search platform is particularly common in the travel industry.

Metropolitan Area Network (MAN): A data and communications network that operates over metropolitan areas and recently has been expanded to nationwide and even worldwide connectivity of high-speed data networks. A MAN can carry video and data.

Microprocessor: A computer on a digital semiconductor chip. It performs math and logic operations and executes instructions from memory. (Also known as a central processing unit or CPU.)

Middleware: Software that interprets requests between applications. Also used to describe software that helps an application communicate with an underlying operating system. Generally, middleware integrates various types of systems by acting as a conversion or translation layer.

Millenials: See "Generation Y."

Millions of Instructions per Second (MIPS): A unit used to compare relative computing power, measured in millions. For example, 25 MIPS is 25 million machine instructions per second.

MIME: See "Multipurpose Internet Mail Extensions (MIME)."

MIMO: See "802.11n (MIMO)."

MMS: See "Multimedia Messaging System (MMS)."

Mobile Apps: See "Apps."

Moblog: Mobile blog. This is a blog created by cell phone or other mobile device. It often consists largely of photos taken by a cell phone's built-in camera. Also, see "Blog (Web Log)."

Modem: A device that allows a computer to be connected to a phone line, which in turn enables the computer to receive and exchange data with other machines via the Internet.

Modulator: A device that modulates a carrier. Modulators are found in broadcasting transmitters and satellite transponders. The devices are also used by cable TV companies to place a baseband video television signal onto a desired VHF or UHF channel. Home video tape recorders also have built-in modulators that enable the recorded video information to be played back using a television receiver tuned to VHF channel 3 or 4.

MOOC: Massive open online course. An online educational course designed to be open to the public with the potential to attract an extremely large, global audience.

Moppers: Mobile shoppers.

MP3: A subsystem of MPEG used to compress sound into digital files. It is the most commonly used format for downloading music and audio books. MP3 compresses music significantly while retaining CD-like quality. MP3 players are personal, portable devices used for listening to music and audio book files. See "MPEG."

MPEG, MPEG-1, MPEG-2, MPEG-3, MPEG-4: Moving Picture Experts Group. It is a digital standard for the compression of motion or still video for transmission or storage. MPEGs are used in digital cameras and for Internet-based viewing.

MSP: See "Managed Service Provider (MSP)."

Multicasting: Sending data, audio or video simultaneously to a number of clients. Also known as broadcasting.

Multimedia: Refers to a presentation using several different media at once. For example, an encyclopedia in CD-ROM format is generally multimedia because it features written text, video and sound in one package.

Multimedia Messaging System (MMS): See "Text Messaging."

Multi-Protocol Label Switching (MPLS): A technology that enables network operators to route

Internet traffic around network failures and bottlenecks.

Multipurpose Internet Mail Extensions (MIME): A widely used method for attaching non-text files to e-mails.

MU-MIMO: Mulit-User, Mutiple-Inut, Multiple-Output. See "802.11n (MIMO)."

NAICS: North American Industrial Classification System. See "Industry Code."

Nanosecond (NS): A billionth of a second. A common unit of measure of computer operating speed.

National Telecommunications and Information Administration (NTIA): A unit of the Department of Commerce that addresses U.S. government telecommunications policy, standards setting and radio spectrum allocation. www.ntia.doc.gov.

Network: In computing, a network is created when two or more computers are connected. Computers may be connected by wireless methods, using such technologies as 802.11b, or by a system of cables, switches and routers.

Network Effect: A phenomenon whereby each additional user added to a system brings disproportionately greater utility to the existing user base. Excellent examples include the telephone, fax machine and social media. This is a business effect that can rapidly and exponentially grow a user base.

Network Effects: A phenomenon where each additional user added brings disproportionately greater utility to the existing user base.

Network Information Center (NIC): Any organization responsible for supplying information about a network.

Network Numbers: The first portion of an IP address, which identifies the network to which hosts in the rest of the address are connected.

Neural Networks: Computer architecture that enables redundancy and self-repair of communications paths and supports high traffic loads through routing decisions.

New Media: A wide array of digital communication technologies, including Internet development tools and services, desktop and portable personal computers, workstations, servers, audio/video compression and editing equipment, graphics hardware and software, high-density storage services and video conferencing systems.

Node: Any single computer connected to a network or a junction of communications paths in a network.

Non-Store Retailing: A form of retailing that is not store-based. Non-store retailing can be conducted through vending machines, direct-selling, direct-marketing, party-based selling, catalogs, television programming, telemarketing and Internet-based selling.

NS: See "Nanosecond (NS)."

NTIA: See "National Telecommunications and Information Administration (NTIA)."

Object Technology: By merging data and software into "objects," a programming system becomes object-oriented. For example, an object called "weekly inventory sold" would have the data and programming needed to construct a flow chart. Some new programming systems–including Java–contain this feature. Object technology is also featured in many Microsoft products. See "Java."

OC3, up to OC768: Very high-speed data lines that run at speeds from 155 to 39,813.12 Mbps.

ODM: See "Original Design Manufacturer (ODM)."

OECD: See "Organisation for Economic Co-operation and Development (OECD)."

OEM: See "Original Equipment Manufacturer (OEM)."

OFDMA: Orthogonal Frequency-Division Multiple Access. See "802.11n (MIMO)."

Offshoring: The rapidly growing tendency among U.S., Japanese and Western European firms to send knowledge-based and manufacturing work overseas. The intent is to take advantage of lower wages and operating costs in such nations as China, India, Hungary and Russia. The choice of a nation for offshore work may be influenced by such factors as language and education of the local workforce, transportation systems or natural resources. For example, China and India are graduating high numbers of skilled engineers and scientists from their universities. Also, some nations are noted for large numbers of workers skilled in the English language, such as the Philippines and India. Also see "Captive Offshoring" and "Outsourcing."

Onshoring: The opposite of "offshoring." Providing or maintaining manufacturing or services within or nearby a company's domestic location. Sometimes referred to as reshoring.

Open Source (Open Standards): A software program for which the source code is openly available for modification and enhancement as various users and developers see fit. Open software is typically developed as a public collaboration and grows in usefulness over time. See "LINUX."

Operating System (OS): The software that allows applications like word processors or web browsers to run on a computer. For example, Microsoft Windows and Apple iOS are operating systems.

Organisation for Economic Co-operation and Development (OECD): A group of more than 30 nations that are strongly committed to the market economy and democracy. Some of the OECD members include Japan, the U.S., Spain, Germany, Australia, Korea, the U.K., Canada and Mexico. Although not members, Estonia, Israel and Russia are invited to member talks; and Brazil, China, India, Indonesia and South Africa have enhanced engagement policies with the OECD. The Organisation provides statistics, as well as social and economic data; and researches social changes, including patterns in evolving fiscal policy, agriculture, technology, trade, the environment and other areas. It publishes over 250 titles annually; publishes a corporate magazine, the OECD Observer; has radio and TV studios; and has centers in Tokyo, Washington, D.C., Berlin and Mexico City that distributed the Organisation's work and organizes events.

Original Design Manufacturer (ODM): A contract manufacturer that offers complete, end-to-end design, engineering and manufacturing services. ODMs design and build products, such as consumer electronics, that client companies can then brand and sell as their own. For example, a large percentage of

laptop computers, cell phones and PDAs are made by ODMs. Also see "Original Equipment Manufacturer (OEM)" and "Contract Manufacturing."

Original Equipment Manufacturer (OEM): 1) A company that manufactures a component (or a completed product) for sale to a customer that will integrate the component into a final product. The OEM's customer will put its own brand name on the end product and distribute or resell it to end users. 2) A firm that buys a component and then incorporates it into a final product, or buys a completed product and then resells it under the firm's own brand name. This usage is most often found in the computer industry, where OEM is sometimes used as a verb. Also see "Original Design Manufacturer (ODM)" and "Contract Manufacturing."

OS: See "Operating System (OS)."

Outsourcing: The hiring of an outside company to perform a task otherwise performed internally by the company, generally with the goal of lowering costs and/or streamlining work flow. Outsourcing contracts are generally several years in length. Companies that hire outsourced services providers often prefer to focus on their core strengths while sending more routine tasks outside for others to perform. Typical outsourced services include the running of human resources departments, telephone call centers and computer departments. When outsourcing is performed overseas, it may be referred to as offshoring. Also see "Offshoring."

OWL: See "Web Ontology Language (OWL)."

P2P: See "Peer-to-Peer (P2P)."

Packet Switching: A higher-speed way to move data through a network, in which files are broken down into smaller "packets" that are reassembled electronically after transmission.

Participatory Sensing: The use of cell phones to gather information from a wide variety of users who transmit photos or comments about local conditions to a central repository. The information is then processed and analyzed by a database. For example, whatsinvasive.com is an effort to gather user generated data that documents invasive plants in America's national parks.

Passive Optical Network (PON): A telecommunications network that brings high speed fiber optic cable all the way (or most of the way) to the end user. Also, see "Fiber to the Home (FTTH)."

Passive Wi-Fi: An 802.11 wireless technology that requires dramatically less electric power than traditional Wi-Fi requires. This makes passive Wi-Fi ideal for widespread use in remote wireless sensor networks and other high-volume applications. Also see "Ambient Backscatter".

Patent: An intellectual property right granted by a national government to an inventor to exclude others from making, using, offering for sale, or selling the invention throughout that nation or importing the invention into the nation for a limited time in exchange for public disclosure of the invention when the patent is granted. In addition to national patenting agencies, such as the United States Patent and Trademark Office, and regional organizations such as the European Patent Office, there is a cooperative international patent organization, the World Intellectual Property Organization, or WIPO, established by the United Nations.

Paywall: A system that restricts access to a web site to only those with paid subscriptions to the sites.

PC: See "Personal Computer (PC)."

PCMCIA: Personal Computer Memory Card International Association.

PDA: See "Personal Digital Assistant (PDA)."

Peer-to-Peer (P2P): Refers to a connection between computers that creates equal status between the computers. P2P can be used in an office or home to create a simple computer network. However, P2P more commonly refers to networks of computers that share information online. For example, peer-to-peer music sharing networks enable one member to search the hard drives of other members to locate music files and then download those files. These systems can be used for legal purposes. Nonetheless, they became notorious as systems that enable members to collect music and videos for free, circumventing copyright and other legal restrictions. At one time Napster was widely known as a P2P music system that enabled users to circumvent copyright.

Personal Communication Service (PCS): A type of cellular mobile telephone service.

Personal Computer (PC): An affordable, efficient computer meant to be used by one person. The device may be a desktop computer or a laptop. Frequently, the PC is connected to a local area network (LAN), or uses wireless methods such as Wi-Fi to access the Internet. PCs are used both in the home and in the office. There is no firm agreement on whether tablets should be regarded as PCs.

Personal Digital Assistant (PDA): A handheld or pocket-size device containing address and calendar information, as well as e-mail, games and other features. A Blackberry is a PDA.

Personal Television (PTV): Television programming that has been manipulated to a viewer's personal taste. For example, the TiVo service allows viewers to eliminate commercials, watch programming stored in memory or watch selected real-time moments in slow motion.

Petabyte: 1,024 terabytes, or about 1 million gigabytes.

PLM: See "Product Lifecyle Management (PLM)."

Plug-In: Any small piece of software that adds extra functions to a larger piece of software.

Podcasting: The creation of audio files as webcasts. The name comes from the ability of these files to be used on iPods and portable MP3 players. They can also be listened to on personal computers. Podcasts can be anything from unique radio-like programming to sales pitches to audio press releases. Audio RSS (Real Simple Syndication) enables the broadcast of these audio files to appropriate parties. Also see "Real Simple Syndication (RSS)," "Video Blog (VLOG)" and "Blog (Web Log)."

Point-to-Point Protocol (PPP): A protocol that enables a computer to use the combination of a standard telephone line and a modem to make TCP/IP connections.

PON: See "Passive Optical Networking (PON)."

POP: An acronym for both "Point of Presence" and "Post Office Protocol." Point of presence refers to a location that a network can be connected to (generally used to count the potential subscriber base of a cellular phone system). Post office protocol refers to the way in which e-mail software obtains mail from a mail server.

Port: An interface (or connector) between the computer and the outside world. The number of ports on a communications controller or front-end processor determines the number of communications channels that can be connected to it. The number of ports on a computer determines the number of peripheral devices that can be attached to it.

Portal: A comprehensive web site that is designed to be the first site seen when a computer logs on to the web. Portal sites are aimed at broad audiences with common interests and often have links to e-mail usage, a search engine and other features. Yahoo! and msn.com are portals.

Positioning: The design and implementation of a merchandising mix, price structure and style of selling to create an image of the retailer, relative to its competitors, in the customer's mind.

Predictive Analytics: See "Analytics."

Pre-N: A wireless technology introduced in 2004 before the higher-speed 802.11n standard was completed. See "802.11n (MIMO)."

Product Lifecycle (Product Life Cycle): The prediction of the life of a product or brand. Stages are described as Introduction, Growth, Maturity and finally Sales Decline. These stages track a product from its initial introduction to the market through to the end of its usefulness as a commercially viable product. The goal of Product Lifecycle Management is to maximize production efficiency, consumer acceptance and profits. Consequently, critical processes around the product need to be adjusted during its lifecycle, including pricing, advertising, promotion, distribution and packaging.

Product Lifecycle Management (PLM): See "Product Lifecycle (Product Life Cycle)."

Programmatic Buying: An automated method of placing advertising that enables advertisers to closely define the amount of money they want to spend along with the type of audience and behavior of the audience in which they are willing to invest. While programmitic buying was initially used in online advertising, it has since migrated to TV and other types of ads.

Protocol: A set of rules for communicating between computers. The use of standard protocols allows products from different vendors to communicate on a common network.

PTV: See "Personal Television (PTV)."

Public Switched Telephone Network (PSTN): A term that refers to the traditional telephone system.

Quantified Self: An evolving concept that refers to the use of electronic devices and electronic communications to gather, record and transmit personal information. An extreme practice of quantified self would be a person who uses a wearable, digital camera to record his surroundings 24/7, and who blogs, tweets or posts to social media his daily activities on a continuous basis. The most practical application of quantified self will most likely be in mobile health, (the personal health Internet). Examples include the wearing of wireless heart monitors, sleep monitors or pedometers that record daily health and exercise data in order to manage health problems or improve fitness.

R&D: Research and development. Also see "Applied Research" and "Basic Research."

Radio Frequency Identification (RFID): A technology that applies a special microchip-enabled tag to an individual item or piece of merchandise or inventory. RFID technology enables wireless, computerized tracking of that inventory item as it moves through the supply chain from factory to transport to warehouse to retail store or end user. Also known as radio tags.

RAM: See "Random Access Memory (RAM)."

Random Access Memory (RAM): Computer memory used to hold programs and data temporarily.

RDF: See "Resource Description Framework (RDF)."

Real Audio: A helper software application that enables the user to hear real-time audio via the Internet.

Real Simple Syndication (RSS): Uses XML programming language to let web logs and other data be broadcast to appropriate web sites and users. Formerly referred to as RDF Site Summary or Rich Site Summary, RSS also enables the publisher to create a description of the content and its location in the form of an RSS document. Also useful for distributing audio files. See "Podcasting."

Real Time: A system or software product specially designed to acquire, process, store and display large amounts of rapidly changing information almost instantaneously, with microsecond responses as changes occur.

Real-Time Bidding (RTB): RTB is a function on advanced exchanges that buy and sell online ads. This RTB technology enables an advertiser to automatically place a bid, in real time, based on various attributes of a web page and its visitors. (Also see "Programmatic Buying.")

Reshoring: See "Onshoring."

Resource Description Framework (RDF): A software concept that integrates many different software applications using XML as a syntax for the exchange of data. It is a core concept for development of the Semantic Web, an enhanced World Wide Web envisioned by W3C, the global organization that oversees development of the web. RDF may be useful for the syndication of news or the aggregation of all types of data for specific uses.

Responsive Web Design: Also known as RWD, responsive web design eliminates the need for separate web sites for viewing by desktop computers and the smaller screens found on various types of wireless devices. RWD automatically presents the correct web page based on the type of device that is accessing the site. RWD utilizes CSS3 media queries. Older browsers may not be able to view responsive web pages correctly. Consequently, the best design practice is to include a specific file that is able to handle and convert the CSS3 queries into pages that are viewable in older browsers.

Router: An electronic device that enables networks to communicate with each other. For example, the local area network (LAN) in an office connects to a router to give the LAN access to an Internet connection such as a T1 or DSL. Routers can be bundled with several added features, such as firewalls.

RSS: See "Real Simple Syndication (RSS)."

Ruby: An open source programming language first released in Japan in 1995. It is an object-oriented scripting language. "Ruby on Rails" is a framework that enables very rapid web site development. See www.rubyonrails.org.

SaaS: See "Software as a Service (SaaS)."

Satellite Broadcasting: The use of Earth-orbiting satellites to transmit, over a wide area, TV, radio, telephony, video and other data in digitized format.

Scalable: Refers to a network that can grow and adapt as customer needs increase and change. Scalable networks can easily manage increasing numbers of workstations, servers, user workloads and added functionality.

S-Commerce: The sale of goods and services through social media such as Facebook.

SCSI: See "Small Computer System Interface (SCSI)."

SDSL: See "Digital Subscriber Line (DSL)."

Search Engine Optimization (SEO): The process of improving a website's positioning in search engines such as Google, Yahoo, and Bing. SEO is used to drive more traffic to a website.

Semantic Web: An initiative started by the World Wide Web Consortium (W3C) that is focused on improving the way users access databases and online content by adding semantic metadata to content that will clearly define the relationships between data. Users will get much better search results, and web site developers will be able to create pages that update results and content based on related data on-the-fly. Data will automatically be shared across applications and across organizations.

Semiconductor: A generic term for a device that controls electrical signals. It specifically refers to a material (such as silicon, germanium or gallium arsenide) that can be altered either to conduct electrical current or to block its passage. Carbon nanotubes may eventually be used as semiconductors. Semiconductors are partly responsible for the miniaturization of modern electronic devices, as they are vital components in computer memory and processor chips. The manufacture of semiconductors is carried out by small firms, and by industry giants such as Intel and Advanced Micro Devices.

SEO: See "Search Engine Optimization (SEO).

Serial Line Internet Protocol (SLIP): The connection of a traditional telephone line, or serial line, and modem to connect a computer to an Internet site.

Server: A computer that performs and manages specific duties for a central network such as a LAN. It may include storage devices and other peripherals. Competition within the server manufacturing industry is intense among leaders Dell, IBM, HP and others.

Service Level Agreement (SLA): A detail in a contract between a service provider and the client. The agreement specifies the level of service that is expected during the service contract term. For example, computer or Internet service contracts generally stipulate a maximum amount of time that a system may be unusable.

Servicemark (Service Mark): Similar to a trademark, except that it identifies and distinguishes the source of a service rather than a product. The servicemark may include a logo or other identifying word or mark meant to distinguish a service from others and indicate the provider of the service. An "SM" indicates that a servicemark has been applied for (or that the owner intends to protect the servicemark) but is still pending, while ® indicates it has been processed and is legally upheld. Servicemarks must be renewed on a regular basis with the appropriate regulatory authorities. In America, trademarks are registered with the U.S. Patent and Trademark Office. There are also cooperative, international servicemark and trademark agreements and agencies. (Also, see "Trademark, (Trade Mark).")

Set-Top Box: Sits on top of a TV set and provides enhancement to cable TV or other television reception. Typically a cable modem, this box may enable interactive enhancements to television viewing. For example, a cable modem is a set-top box that enables Internet access via TV cable. See "Cable Modem."

Shareware: Software that is available for users to download for free from the Internet, usually with the expectation that they will register or pay for the

software if they continue to use it. Many shareware programs are set to expire after a period of time.

Shockwave: An authoring tool that allows multimedia presentations to appear on the Internet. Shockwave enables interactive graphics, sound and animation to be viewed on the web.

SIC: Standard Industrial Classification. See "Industry Code."

Simple Mail Transfer Protocol (SMTP): The primary form of protocol used in the transference of e-mail.

Simple Network Management Protocol (SNMP): A set of communication standards for use between computers connected to TCP/IP networks.

Simple Object Access Protocol (SOAP): A method for applications to communicate with each other using HTTP web protocols. SOAP is an important protocol in web services.

SLIP: See "Serial Line Internet Protocol (SLIP)."

Slugs: Small graphical icons that are frequently used in order to establish a visual language. They often function as buttons, such as sound slugs, which inform the user of the size of a sound file and, when clicked, download the file.

Small Computer System Interface (SCSI): A dominant, international standard interface used by UNIX servers and many desktop computers to connect to storage devices; a physical connection between devices.

Small to Medium Enterprise (SME): A term used to refer to smaller businesses. For example, in the European Union, SME businesses are officially considered to have fewer than 250 employees and less that 50 million Euros in annual sales. SMEs make up the vast majority of all businesses and provide the vast majority of all employment.

Smart Dust: The use of vast quantities of self-powered, remote wireless sensors to gather local data and transmit it to a central database for predictive analytics purposes, and for monitoring of environmental, structural stress and other local conditions.

SMDS: See "Switched Multimegabit Data Service (SMDS)."

SME: See "Small to Medium Enterprise (SME)."

SNMP: See "Simple Network Management Protocol (SNMP)."

Social Graph: An analysis of relationships between individuals, generally within the realm of the Internet. Social graphs track different kids of relationships such as coworkers, users of specific web sites or enthusiasts of a particular hobby. Advertise hope to devise technologies that exploit social graphs in order to reach targeted customers.

Social Media (Social Networks): Sites on the Internet that feature user generated content (UGC). Such media include wikis, blogs and specialty web sites such as MySpace.com, Facebook, YouTube, Yelp and Friendster.com. Social media are seen as powerful online tools because all or most of the content is user-generated.

Social, Mobile, Analytics and Cloud (SMAC): Refers to the four fastest growing trends in computing and data.

Software as a Service (SaaS): Refers to the practice of providing users with software applications that are hosted on remote servers and accessed via the Internet. Excellent examples include the CRM (Customer Relationship Management) software provided in SaaS format by Salesforce. An earlier technology that operated in a similar, but less sophisticated, manner was called ASP or Application Service Provider.

SONET: See "Synchronous Optical Network Technology (SONET)."

Spam: A term used to refer to generally unwanted, solicitous, bulk-sent e-mail. In recent years, significant amounts of government legislation have been passed in an attempt to limit the use of spam. Also, many types of software filters have been introduced in an effort to block spam on the receiving end. In addition to use for general advertising purposes, spam may be used in an effort to spread computer viruses or to commit financial or commercial fraud.

SRDF: See "Symmetrix Remote Data Facility (SRDF)."

Storage Area Network (SAN): Links host computers to advanced data storage systems.

Streaming Media: One-way audio and/or video that is compressed and transmitted over a data network. The media is viewed or heard almost as soon as data is fed to the receiver; there is usually a buffer period of a few seconds.

Structured Query Language (SQL): A language set that defines a way of organizing and calling data in a computer database. SQL is becoming the standard for use in client/server databases.

Subsidiary, Wholly-Owned: A company that is wholly controlled by another company through stock ownership.

Supply Chain: The complete set of suppliers of goods and services required for a company to operate its business. For example, a manufacturer's supply chain may include providers of raw materials, components, custom-made parts and packaging materials.

Switch: A network device that directs packets of data between multiple ports, often filtering the data so that it travels more quickly.

Switched Multimegabit Data Service (SMDS): A method of extremely high-speed transference of data.

Symmetrix Remote Data Facility (SRDF): A high-performance, host-independent business solution that enables users to maintain a duplicate copy of all or some of their data at a remote site.

Synchronous Optical Network Technology (SONET): A mode of high-speed transmission meant to take full advantage of the wide bandwidth in fiber-optic cables.

T1: A standard for broadband digital transmission over phone lines. Generally, it can transmit at least 24 voice channels at once over copper wires, at a high speed of 1.5 Mbps. Higher speed versions include T3 and OC3 lines.

T3: Transmission over phone lines that supports data rates of 45 Mbps. T3 lines consist of 672 channels, and such lines are generally used by Internet service providers. They are also referred to as DS3 lines.

Tagging: A method of describing web sites with simple words so that links can be grouped by categories and easily found again in the future for access. Also, groups of tagged links can be shared for viewing by others. See http: //del.icio.us.

TCP/IP: Transmission Control Protocol/Internet Protocol. The combination of a network and transport protocol developed by ARPANet for internetworking IP-based networks.

Telecommunications: Systems and networks of hardware and software used to carry voice, video and/or data within buildings and between locations around the world. This includes telephone wires, satellite signals, wireless networks, fiber networks, Internet networks and related devices.

Telepresence: The use of highly sophisticated digital video cameras, microphones and high speed Internet connections to create a video conference for remote participants that is nearly life-like. Conference participants may consult with each other from specially-equipped rooms that can be almost anywhere in the world. With the most advanced equipment, such as that produced by Cisco, the images on screens can be near life-size and the results can be of almost face-to-face quality.

Telnet: A terminal emulation program for TCP/IP networks like the Internet, which runs on a computer and connects to a particular network. Directions entered on a computer that is connected using Telnet will be read and followed just as if they had been entered on the server itself. Through Telnet, users are able to control a server and communicate with other servers on the same network at the same time. Telnet is commonly used to control web servers remotely.

Terabyte: A measure of data equal to 1,024 gigabytes, or about 1 trillion bytes of data.

Text Messaging: The transmission of very short, text messages in a format similar to e-mail. Generally, text messaging is used as an additional service on cell phones. The format has typically been SMS (Short Messaging System), but a newer standard is evolving: MMS (Multimedia Messaging System). MMS can transmit pictures, sound and video as well as text.

Third-Party Fulfillment (3PF): A 3PL company that focuses on warehousing, order processing and shipping, especially for retail and online sellers. See "Third-Party Logistics (3PL)" and "Insourcing."

Third-Party Logistics (3PL): A specialist firm in logistics, which may provide a variety of transportation, warehousing and logistics-related services to buyers or sellers. These tasks were previously performed in-house by the customer. When 3PL services are provided within the client's own facilities, it can also be referred to as insourcing. Also see "Fourth-Party Logistics (4PL)."

Token Ring: A local area network architecture in which a token, or continuously repeating frame, is passed sequentially from station to station. Only the station possessing the token can communicate on the network.

Trademark (Trade Mark): A name or phrase that has been registered by a company or organization for its exclusive use. A "TM" indicates that a trademark has been applied for (or that the owner intends to protect the trademark) but is still pending, while ® indicates it has been processed and is legally upheld. A trademark may or may not include an accompanying, distinctive design or font for the word or phrase. Trademarks must be renewed on a regular basis with the appropriate regulatory authorities. In America, trademarks are registered with the U.S. Patent and Trademark Office. There are also cooperative, international trademark agreements and agencies.

Transaction Authority Markup Language (XAML): A computer programming code (developer language) created by Microsoft as part of its effort to launch the operating system code named Longhorn to facilitate the processing of online transactions.

U-Commerce (U Commerce): Ubiquitous Commerce, Universal Commerce or Ultimate Commerce (ubiquitous meaning ever-present), depending on whom you ask. It describes the concept that buyers and sellers have the potential to interact anywhere, anytime thanks to the use of wireless devices, such as cell phones, by buyers to connect with sellers via the Internet where orders can be placed online and payments can be made via credit card or PayPal. The Association for Information Systems states that the qualities of U-Commerce include ubiquity, uniqueness, universality and unison.

UDDI: See "Universal Description, Discovery and Integration (UDDI)."

UGC: See "User Generated Content (UGC)."

UI: User interface: The software and hardware that enable humans to interact with machines; typically a great user interface is a key differentiator for companies. For example, Windows is a user interface that enables users to access computers.

Unified Communications: The use of advanced technology to replace traditional telecommunications infrastructure such as PBX, fax and even the desktop telephone. Special software operating on a local or remote server enables each office worker to have access, via the desktop PC, to communications tools that include VOIP phone service, email, voice mail, fax, instant messaging (IM), collaborative calendars and schedules, contact information such as address books, audio conferencing and video conferencing.

Uniform Resource Locator (URL): The address that allows an Internet browser to locate a homepage or web site.

Universal Description, Discovery and Integration (UDDI): A vital protocol used in web services. UDDI enables businesses to create a standard description of their activities so that they can be searched for appropriately by automatic software tools.

UNIX: A multi-user, multitasking operating system that runs on a wide variety of computer systems, from PCs to mainframes.

URL: See "Uniform Resource Locator (URL)."

User Generated Content (UGC): Data contributed by users of interactive web sites. Such sites can include wikis, blogs, entertainment sites, shopping sites or social networks such as Facebook. UGC data can also include such things as product reviews, photos, videos, comments on forums, and how-to advice. Also see "Social Media (Social Networks)."

UX: User experience: overall interaction that a user has with a product or service; the human-device interaction is a key point of differentiation for most tech companies.

Value Added Tax (VAT): A tax that imposes a levy on businesses at every stage of manufacturing based on the value it adds to a product. Each business in the supply chain pays its own VAT and is subsequently repaid by the next link down the chain; hence, a VAT is ultimately paid by the consumer, being the last link in the supply chain, making it comparable to a sales tax. Generally, VAT only applies to goods bought for consumption within a given country; export goods are exempt from VAT, and purchasers from other countries taking goods back home may apply for a VAT refund.

VDSL: Very high-data-rate digital subscriber line, operating at data rates from 55 to 100 Mbps.

Vendor Relationship Mangement (VRM): A process whereby consumers can use online tools and other means to manage their relationships with the firms ("vendors") that they buy from. An example is the ability of a consumer to set personal preferences in an online account. Some observers expect VRM to rapidly evolve into sophisticated technology that enables the consumer to be in control of the buyer-seller cycle while enjoying maximum-possible choices and lowest-possible prices.

Vertical Integration: A business model in which one company owns many (or all) of the means of production of the many goods that comprise its product line. For example, founder Henry Ford designed Ford Motor Company's early River Rogue plant so that coal, iron ore and other needed raw materials arrived at one end of the plant and were processed into steel, which was then converted on-site into finished components. At the final stage of the plant, completed automobiles were assembled.

Video Blog (VLOG): The creation of video files as webcasts. VLOGs can be viewed on personal computers and wireless devices that are Internet-enabled. They can include anything from unique TV-like programming to sales pitches to music videos, news coverage or audio press releases. Online video is one of the fastest-growing segments in Internet usage. Leading e-commerce companies such as Microsoft, through its MSN service, Google and Yahoo!, as well as mainstream media firms such as Reuters, are making significant investments in online video services. Real Simple Syndication (RSS) enables the broadcasting of these files to appropriate parties. Also see "Real Simple Syndication (RSS)," "Podcasting" and "Blog (Web Log)."

Virtual Private Network (VPN): Cordons off part of a public network to create a private LAN.

Virtual Reality: A life-like scene, representation or world that has been generated by computers. The website secondlife.com is a well known example.

Virtual Storage Access Method (VSAM): A data storage and retrieval mechanism designed to maintain large quantities of data on external disks or drums on computers designed for virtual storage systems.

VLOG: See "Video Blog (VLOG)."

Voice Over Internet Protocol (VOIP): The ability to make telephone calls and send faxes over IP-based data networks, i.e., real-time voice between computers via the Internet. Leading providers of VOIP service include independent firms Skype and Vonage. However, all major telecom companies, such as SBC are planning or offering VOIP service. VOIP can offer greatly reduced telephone bills to users, since toll charges, certain taxes and other fees can be bypassed. Long-distance calls can pass to anywhere in the world using VOIP. Over the mid-term, many telephone handsets, including cellular phones, will have the ability to detect wireless networks offering VOIP connections and will switch seamlessly between landline and VOIP or cellular and VOIP as needed.

VOIP: See "Voice Over Internet Protocol (VOIP)."

VPN: See "Virtual Private Network (VPN)."

VRM: See "Vendor Relationship Management (VRM)."

WAN: See "Wide Area Network (WAN)."

WAP: See "Wireless Access Protocol (WAP)."

Web 2.0: Generally refers to the evolving system of advanced services available via the Internet. These services include collaborative sites that enable multiple users to create content such as wikis, sites such as photo-sharing services that share data among large or small groups and sites such as Friendster and MySpace that enable consumers to form groups of people with similar interests. Common features of Web 2.0 are tagging, social networks and folksonomies.

Web 3.0: See "Semantic Web."

Web of Things: See "Internet of Things (IoT)."

Web Ontology Language (OWL): A markup language that is related to RDF. See "Resource Description Framework (RDF)" and "Semantic Web."

Web Services: Self-contained modular applications that can be described, published, located and invoked over the World Wide Web or another network. Web services architecture evolved from object-oriented design and is geared toward e-business solutions. Microsoft Corporation is focusing on web services with its .NET initiative. Also see "Extensible Markup Language (XML)."

Web Services Description Language (WSDL): An important protocol to web services that describes the web service being offered.

Weblog: See "Blog (Web Log)."

Webmaster: Any individual who runs a web site. Webmasters generally perform maintenance and upkeep.

Website Meta-Language (WML): A free HTML generation toolkit for the Unix operating system.

Wide Area Network (WAN): A regional or global network that provides links between all local area networks within a company. For example, Ford Motor Company might use a WAN to enable its factory in Detroit to talk to its sales offices in New York and Chicago, its plants in England and its buying offices in Taiwan. Also see "Local Area Network (LAN)."

Widget: A small software application that can be embedded into a web page. These applications can be designed to contain games, cartoons, entertainment, helpful data or just about anything that might engage the user's attention.

WiFi: See "Wi-Fi."

Wi-Fi: Wireless Fidelity. Refers to 802.11 wireless network specifications. The 802.XX standards are set by the IEEE (Institute of Electrical and Electronics Engineers). Wi-Fi enables very high speed local networks in homes, businesses, factories, industrial and transportation infrastructure, public spaces and vehicles. Wi-Fi networks enable computing devices of all types to connect to each other and to the internet, including smartphones, laptops, desktops and tablet computers. In addition, Wi-Fi enables machine-to-machine (M2M) communication between devices, providing a backbone for the Internet of Things. These networks can be made reasonably secure when strong passwords are required and additional cybersecurity measures are in place. (Also, see 'Internet of Things".)

Wiki: A web site that enables large or small groups of users to create and co-edit data. The best known example is Wikipedia, a high traffic web site that presents a public encyclopedia that is continuously written and edited by a vast number of volunteer contributors and editors who include both experts and enthusiasts in various subjects. Also, see "User Generated Content (UGC)."

WiMAX: An advanced wireless standard with significant speed and distance capabilities, WiMAX is officially known as the 802.16 standard. Using microwave technologies, it has the theoretical potential to broadcast at distances up to 30 miles and speeds of up to 70 Mbps. The 802.XX standards are set by the IEEE (Institute of Electrical and Electronics Engineers).

Wireless: Transmission of voice, video or data by a cellular telephone or other wireless device, as opposed to landline, fiber or cable. It includes Bluetooth, Cellular, Wi-Fi, WiMAX and other local or long-distance wireless methods.

Wireless Access Protocol (WAP): A technology that enables the delivery of internet pages in a smaller format readable by screens on smartphones.

Wireless Cable: A pay television service that delivers multiple programming services to subscribers equipped with special antennae and tuners. It is an alternative to traditional, wired cable TV systems.

Wireless LAN (WLAN): A wireless local area network. WLANs frequently operate on 802.11-enabled equipment (Wi-Fi).

Wireless Sensor Network (WSN): Consists of a grouping of remote sensors that transmit data wirelessly to a receiver that is collecting data into a database. Special controls may alert the network's manager to changes in the environment, traffic or hazardous conditions. Long-term collection of data from remote sensors can be used to establish patterns and make predictions. The use of WSNs is growing

rapidly, in such applications as environmental monitoring, agriculture, military intelligence, surveillance, factory automation, home automation and traffic control. (Also, see "Internet of Things".)

WLAN: See "Wireless LAN (WLAN)."

WML: See "Website Meta-Language (WML)."

Workstation: A high-powered desktop computer, usually used by engineers.

World Trade Organization (WTO): One of the only globally active international organizations dealing with the trade rules between nations. Its goal is to assist the free flow of trade goods, ensuring a smooth, predictable supply of goods to help raise the quality of life of member citizens. Members form consensus decisions that are then ratified by their respective parliaments. The WTO's conflict resolution process generally emphasizes interpreting existing commitments and agreements, and discovers how to ensure trade policies to conform to those agreements, with the ultimate aim of avoiding military or political conflict.

World Wide Web: A computer system that provides enhanced access to various sites on the Internet through the use of hyperlinks. Clicking on a link displayed in one document takes you to a related document. The World Wide Web is governed by the World Wide Web Consortium, located at www.w3.org. Also known as the web.

WoT: Web of Things. See "Internet of Things."

WPA: Wireless Protected Access. A basic security standard for wireless networking, including Wi-Fi.

WSDL: See "Web Services Description Language (WSDL)."

WTO: See "World Trade Organization (WTO)."

YouTube: A web site that allows any user to post video content to be shared with others. Other users can then rate or comment on the video to share their views. Most YouTube videos can be embedded in outside web sites for others to view without having to visit YouTube. The site offers videos ranging from news to entertainment to training and education. The YouTube firm is owned by Google.